IVOR HORTON'S BEGINNING JAVA®

IVOR HORTON'S BEGINNING

Java®

IVOR HORTON'S BEGINNING

Java®

Java 7 Edition

Ivor Horton

WILEY

John Wiley & Sons, Inc.

Ivor Horton's Beginning Java®, Java 7 Edition

Published by
John Wiley & Sons, Inc.
10475 Crosspoint Boulevard
Indianapolis, IN 46256
www.wiley.com

Published simultaneously in Canada

ISBN: 978-0-470-40414-0
ISBN: 978-1-118-17342-8 (ebk)
ISBN: 978-1-118-17341-1 (ebk)
ISBN: 978-1-118-17340-4 (ebk)

Manufactured in the United States of America

10 9 8 7 6 5 4 3 2 1

For general information on our other products and services please contact our Customer Care Department within the United States at (877) 762-2974, outside the United States at (317) 572-3993 or fax (317) 572-4002.

Wiley also publishes its books in a variety of electronic formats and by print-on-demand. Not all content that is available in standard print versions of this book may appear or be packaged in all book formats. If you have purchased a version of this book that did not include media that is referenced by or accompanies a standard print version, you may request this media by visiting http://booksupport.wiley.com. For more information about Wiley products, visit us at www.wiley.com.

Library of Congress Control Number: 2011934635

This is for Charlie Williams and his irrepressible smile.

CREDITS

ABOUT THE AUTHOR

IVOR HORTON started out as a mathematician, but shortly after graduating, he was lured into messing about with computers by a well-known manufacturer. He has spent many happy years programming occasionally useful applications in a variety of languages as well as teaching mainly scientists and engineers to do likewise. He has extensive experience in applying computers to problems in engineering design and to manufacturing operations in a wide range of industries. He is the author of a number of tutorial books on programming in C, C++, and Java. When not writing programming books or providing advice to others, he leads a life of leisure.

ABOUT THE TECHNICAL EDITORS

MARC GREGOIRE is a software engineer from Belgium. He graduated from the Catholic University of Leuven, Belgium, with a degree in "Burgerlijk ingenieur in de computer wetenschappen" (equivalent to master of science in engineering in computer science). The year after, he received the cum laude degree of master in artificial intelligence at the same university. After his studies, Marc started working for a big software consultancy company called Ordina Belgium. As a consultant, he worked for Siemens and Nokia Siemens Networks on critical 2G and 3G software running on Solaris for big telecom operators. This required working in international teams stretching from South America and USA to EMEA and Asia. Now, Marc is working for Nikon Metrology on 3D scanning software.

His main expertise is C/C++, and specifically Microsoft VC++ and the MFC framework. Next to C/C++, Marc also likes C# and uses PHP for creating web pages. In addition to his main interest for Windows development, he also has experience in developing C++ programs running 24x7 on Linux platforms; for example, EIB home automation controlling and monitoring software. Since April 2007, he's received the yearly Microsoft MVP (Most Valuable Professional) award for his Visual C++ expertise.

Marc is an active member on the CodeGuru forum (as Marc G) and wrote some articles and FAQ entries for CodeGuru. He also creates freeware and shareware programs that are distributed through his website at www.nuonsoft.com, and maintains a blog on www.nuonsoft.com/blog/.

AL SCHERER is a Development Manager of eCommerce Technologies at Follett Higher Education Group. He has seven years of experience designing and coding applications as a Software Architect in addition to 10 years of development experience. Al has built applications using Assembler, C, C++ and a number of other programming languages and has worked extensively in Java since Version 1.1. He holds Sun Java certifications as a Programmer, Business Components Developer and Web Components Developer. In his spare time, Al applies his passion for technology via technical writing and editing, working on nine software books over the last few years. He holds a BS in Engineering from University of Illinois at Urbana-Champaign and an MBA from Northwestern University.

ACKNOWLEDGMENTS

OF COURSE THIS BOOK is not all my own work. The John Wiley & Sons, and Wrox Press editorial and production team transformed my draft into the finished book. I'm especially indebted to Project Editor Maureen Spears, who has been there from way back at the beginning and has been incredibly helpful throughout. Charlotte Kughen has done a great job of untangling my grammar and identifying my sometimes obscure references. I'd like to thank the Technical Editors for their thorough review of the text and checking out all the examples in the book; their many constructive comments undoubtedly helped make the book much better that it would otherwise have been.

As always, the love and support of my wife Eve has been essential for me to finish this book. She remains patient and cheerful, even when I am not necessarily the same.

CONTENTS

WELCOME

WELCOME TO *Ivor Horton's Beginning Java, Java 7 Edition*, a comprehensive and easy-to-use tutorial guide to learning the Java language and the Java platform application program interface (API). This book provides you with the essential know-how for developing programs using the Java Development Kit 7 (JDK 7) or later.

In this book, as well as teaching you Java, I introduce you to a wide variety of topics that will be relevant to you as a Java programmer. I have structured the book so that you learn Java programming in a carefully designed and logical way so that at each stage you build on what you have learned at the previous stage.

WHO IS THIS BOOK FOR?

Java programming is a vast, well-established area that is still expanding as the capabilities of the language and associated libraries increase. Since its release, the growth of Java as the object-oriented language of choice for Internet programming, cross-platform applications, and teaching has been phenomenal. In my view this is due to three things: the system-independent nature of Java, the simplicity and power of the language, and the extraordinary range of programming tasks for which Java is an effective and easy-to-use tool. Java is the language of choice of many programmers for major application development, offering advantages in ease of development and maintenance compared to other languages, as well as built-in capability to run on a variety of computers and operating systems without code changes. With Java you can do a lot more, more quickly, and more easily.

In this book I aim to provide you with a comprehensive understanding of the language, plus experience of programming in a range of Java application contexts to give you a solid base in each of these core areas. Every aspect of Java that is covered in the book is illustrated by fully working program examples that you can and should create and run for yourself. There are also exercises at the end of each chapter to give you the opportunity to try out what you've learned. With an understanding of the topics in this book, you can start to write fully featured and effective Java programs.

The word *Beginning* in the title refers more to the style of the book's teaching than to your skill level. It could equally well be called *Straight into Java*, because I designed the tutorial structure so that, whether you're a seasoned programmer from another language or a newcomer to programming in general, the book will accommodate your knowledge level.

I have assumed as a minimum that you know something about programming, in that you understand at least the fundamental concepts of how programs work. However, you don't need to have significant prior programming experience to use the book successfully. The pace of the book is fairly rapid, but without stinting on any of the necessary explanations of how Java works.

WHAT'S COVERED IN THIS BOOK

The book aims to teach you Java programming following a logical format:

- ➤ First, it covers some of the main terms and concepts that underpin programming in Java. This will give you a perspective and reference frame for the detail that follows.

- ➤ Second, it provides you with a clear explanation of all the features of the Java language—the basic data types, the control structures that manipulate data, the object-oriented features of the language, the way runtime errors are handled, and how threads are used. It also provides a solid introduction to generic types in Java and how you can apply them in your own programs. The book doesn't just explain what the language elements do, but also how you can apply them in practice.

➤ Third, it gives you an extensive introduction to the key packages in the Java class library—among others, the `java.math`, `java.io`, `java.nio.file`, `java.util`, `java.awt`, `java.awt.event`, `java.applet`, `javax.swing`, and `javax.xml` packages are all covered and illustrated with full working examples. These packages cover file handling, printing, collection classes, helper objects, graphical user interfaces, applets, and XML.

➤ Fourth, it guides you through the process of building a substantial application, Sketcher, in which you apply the Java language capabilities and the Java class library in a realistic context. The sketching application has menus, toolbars, and a status panel to give you a grounding in putting together a basic application user interface. You also implement the capability to draw and manipulate a number of elements, handle text, print sketches on your local printer, and save sketches to disk. Assembling an application with this range of functions gives you a much better understanding of how you apply Java in practical projects of your own, something that's hard to appreciate from any number of more trivial examples.

➤ Lastly, it introduces the fundamentals of XML and then shows how you can use the XML and XSLT capability that comes with the JDK to work with XML and to read and write XML files.

As you progress through each of these topics, I introduce you to the theory and then illustrate it with an appropriate example and a clear explanation. You can learn quickly on a first read and look back over things to brush up on all the essential elements when you need to. The short examples in each chapter are designed mainly to illustrate a class and its methods or some new piece of theory in action. They focus specifically on showing you how the particular language features or methods work.

To get the most from the chapters, I strongly recommend that you try out the examples as you read. Type them in yourself, even if you have downloaded the example source code. It really does make a difference. The examples also provide a good base for experimentation and hopefully inspire you to create programs of your own. It's important to try things out—you learn as much (if not more) from your mistakes as you learn from the things that work the first time. And I guarantee that you *will* make mistakes!

The source code for all of the example programs in the book is available at www.wrox.com.

WHAT YOU NEED TO USE THIS BOOK

This book has been tested against the JDK 7 release code. The examples use the latest language features introduced in JDK 7 so you should be using JDK 7 or later for all the examples to compile. Other requirements for most of the chapters are fairly minimal: a copy of a program text editor and a command-line window from which to run the Java tools. Details of the requirements for making the best use of the book and how to acquire and install what you need are provided in Chapter 1.

CONVENTIONS

To help you get the most from the text and keep track of what's happening, I've used a number of conventions throughout the book.

For example, when discussing code, I have two conventions:

 Italic notes are used to hold asides on what I have just explained in the text or on program code.

and

 These boxes hold important, not-to-be-forgotten information that is directly relevant to the surrounding text.

When I introduce important words, I italicize them. I show keyboard strokes as Ctrl+A.

Console output to the command-line is shown as:

```
C:\> java ShowStyle
When the command line and terminal output are shown, it's in this style.
```

Code that appears in the text and filenames are identified with a different font, such as aVariable and MyFile.java.

Code fragments that show a particular mechanism or technique are shown like this:

```
if(life == aimless) {
  DoSomethingElse();
}
```

Where a previous code fragment has been changed in some way, the changes are shown bolded:

```
if(life==aimless) {
  DoSomethingNew();
}
```

If code is available for download you will see the following icon before the code:

Available for download on Wrox.com

I present code for complete working examples in a Try It Out section, which is used to split the code up where that's helpful, to highlight the component parts, and to show the progression of the application. When it's important, which is most of the time, I follow the code with a How It Works section to explain any salient points of the code in relation to previous theory. The following gives an example of a Try It Out and How It Works.

TRY IT OUT

New code for complete examples in a Try It Out section is shown bolded:

```
public class Motto {
  public static void main(String[] args) {
    System.out.println("He who fights and runs away");
    System.out.println("Lives to run away another day.");
  }
}
```

Complete code examples that are modifications of an earlier example show the new code as bolded:

```
public class Saying {
  public static void main(String[] args) {
    System.out.println("I used to think I was indecisive");
    System.out.println("but now I'm not so sure.");
  }
}
```

Some of the code for a complete example can appear in the sections preceding a Try It Out section. This is particularly the case from Chapter 17 onward, when you work with the Sketcher example that you develop over several chapters, ending up with quite a large program with more than 2000 lines of code. Some of the enhancements you add to the program involve quite a lot of code. When extending the functionality involves adding or modifying 30 or 40 or more lines of code, I don't put this in the book as a single large chunk because it would look a bit daunting and would not be easy to take in. I present and explain such units of code incrementally, in smaller more digestible units. This is to make it easier for you to follow and understand what is going on. Code in the text that is part of a complete example is generally identified as such, and the new or modified lines of code are always shown bolded.

How It Works

Finally, code fragments in a How It Works section as part of the explanation that are from the complete example are shown unbolded, like this:

```
System.out.println("I used to think I was indecisive");
System.out.println("but now I'm not so sure.");
```

SOURCE CODE

As you work through the examples in this book, you may choose either to type in all the code manually or to use the source code files that accompany the book. All of the source code used in this book is available for download at www.wrox.com. When you're at the site, simply locate the book's title (either by using the Search box or by using one of the title lists) and click the Download Code link on the book's detail page to obtain all the source code for the book.

 Because many books have similar titles, you may find it easiest to search by ISBN; for this book, the ISBN is 978-0-0470-40414-0.

After you download the code, just decompress it with your favorite compression tool. Alternatively, you can go to the main Wrox code download page at www.wrox.com/dynamic/books/download.aspx to see the code available for this book and all other Wrox books.

ERRATA

We make every effort to ensure that there are no errors in the text or in the code. However, no one is perfect, and mistakes do occur. If you find an error in one of our books, such as a spelling mistake or a faulty piece of code, we would be very grateful for your feedback. By sending in errata you may save another reader hours of frustration, and at the same time you are helping us provide even higher quality information.

To find the errata page for this book, go to www.wrox.com and locate the title using the Search box or one of the title lists. Then, on the book details page, click the Book Errata link. On this page you can view all errata that has been submitted for this book and posted by Wrox editors. A complete book list, including links to each book's errata, is also available at www.wrox.com/misc-pages/booklist.shtml.

If you don't spot "your" error on the Book Errata page, go to www.wrox.com/contact/techsupport.shtml and complete the form to send us the error you have found. We'll check the information and, if appropriate, post a message to the book's errata page and fix the problem in subsequent editions of the book.

P2P.WROX.COM

For author and peer discussion, join the P2P forums at p2p.wrox.com. The forums are a web-based system for you to post messages relating to Wrox books and related technologies and interact with other readers and technology users. The forums offer a subscription feature to e-mail you topics of interest of your choosing when new posts are made to the forums. Wrox authors, editors, other industry experts, and your fellow readers are present on these forums.

At http://p2p.wrox.com you can find a number of different forums that help you not only as you read this book, but also as you develop your own applications. To join the forums, just follow these steps:

1. Go to p2p.wrox.com and click the Register link.
2. Read the terms of use and click Agree.
3. Complete the required information to join as well as any optional information you want to provide and then click Submit.
4. You receive an e-mail with information describing how to verify your account and complete the joining process.

 You can read messages in the forums without joining P2P, but in order to post your own messages, you must join.

After you join, you can post new messages and respond to messages other users post. You can read messages at any time on the Web. If you would like to have new messages from a particular forum e-mailed to you, click the Subscribe to This Forum icon by the forum name in the forum listing.

For more information about how to use the Wrox P2P, be sure to read the P2P FAQs for answers to questions about how the forum software works as well as many common questions specific to P2P and Wrox books. To read the FAQs, click the FAQ link on any P2P page.

1

Introducing Java

WHAT YOU WILL LEARN IN THIS CHAPTER:

- ➤ The basic characteristics of the Java language
- ➤ How Java programs work on your computer
- ➤ Why Java programs are portable between different computers
- ➤ The basic ideas behind object-oriented programming
- ➤ How a simple Java program looks and how you can run it using the Java Development Kit
- ➤ What HTML is and how to use it to include a Java program in a web page

This chapter should give you an appreciation of what the Java language is all about. Understanding the details of what I discuss in this chapter is not important at this stage; you see all of the topics again in greater depth in later chapters of the book. The intent of this chapter is to introduce you to the general ideas that underpin what I cover through the rest of the book, as well as the major contexts in which Java programs can be used and the kind of program that is applicable in each context.

WHAT IS JAVA ALL ABOUT?

Java is an innovative programming language that has become the language of choice for programs that need to run on a variety of different computer systems. First of all, Java enables you to write small programs called *applets*. These are programs that you can embed in web pages to provide some intelligence. Being able to embed executable code in a web page introduces a vast range of exciting possibilities. Instead of being a passive presentation of text and graphics, a web page can be interactive in any way that you want. You can include animations, games, interactive transaction processing—the possibilities are almost unlimited.

Of course, embedding program code in a web page creates special security requirements. As an Internet user accessing a page with embedded Java code, you need to be confident that it won't do anything that might interfere with the operation of your computer or damage the data you have on your system. This implies that execution of the embedded code must be controlled in such a way that it prevents accidental damage to your computer environment, as well as ensure that any Java code that was created with malicious intent is effectively inhibited. Java implicitly incorporates measures to minimize the possibility of such occurrences arising with a Java applet.

Java's support for the Internet and network-based applications generally doesn't end with applets. For example, Java Server Pages (JSP) provides a powerful means of building a server application that can dynamically create and download HTML pages to a client that are precisely customized for the specific request that is received. Of course, the pages that are generated by JSP can themselves contain Java applets.

Java also enables you to write large-scale application programs that you can run unchanged on any computer with an operating system environment in which Java is supported. This applies to the majority of computers in use today. The slogan that was coined to illustrate the cross-platform capability of Java, "write once, run anywhere," has been amply demonstrated to be the case. You can develop code on a PC and it will run on a Java-enabled cell phone. You can even write programs that work both as ordinary applications and as applets.

Java has matured immensely in recent years. The breadth of function provided by the standard core Java has grown incredibly. Java provides you with comprehensive facilities for building applications with an interactive graphical user interface (GUI), extensive image processing and graphics programming facilities, as well as support for XML, accessing relational databases and communicating with remote computers over a network. Just about any kind of application can now be programmed effectively in Java, with the implicit plus of complete portability.

Of course, Java is still developing and growing. The latest Java Development Kit, JDK 7, adds many new facilities that include new language features as well as significant additions to the supporting libraries. You learn about all of these in this book.

FEATURES OF THE JAVA LANGUAGE

The most important characteristic of Java is that it was designed from the outset to be machine independent. You can run Java programs unchanged on any machine and operating system combination that supports Java. Of course, there is still the slim possibility of the odd glitch, as you are ultimately dependent on the implementation of Java on any particular machine, but Java programs are intrinsically more portable than programs written in other languages. An application written in Java only requires a single set of source code statements, regardless of the number of different computer platforms on which it is run. In any other programming language, the application frequently requires the source code to be tailored to accommodate different computer environments, particularly if an extensive graphical user interface is involved. Java offers substantial savings in time and resources in developing, supporting, and maintaining major applications on several different hardware platforms and operating systems.

Possibly the next most important characteristic of Java is that it is *object-oriented*. The object-oriented approach to programming is an implicit feature of all Java programs, so you find out what this means later in this chapter. Object-oriented programs are easier to understand and less time-consuming to maintain and extend than programs that have been written without the benefit of using objects.

Not only is Java object-oriented, but it also manages to avoid many of the difficulties and complications that are inherent in some object-oriented languages, making it easy to learn and very straightforward to use. By and large, it lacks the traps and "gotchas" that arise in some other programming languages. This makes the learning cycle shorter, and you need less real-world coding experience to gain competence and confidence. It also makes Java code easier to test.

Java has a built-in ability to support national character sets. You can write Java programs as easily for use in Greece or Japan as you can for English-speaking countries, assuming you are familiar with the national languages involved, of course. You can even build programs from the outset to support several different national languages with automatic adaptation to the environment in which the code executes.

LEARNING JAVA

Java is not difficult to learn, but there is a great deal to it. Although the Java language is very powerful, it is fairly compact, so acquiring an understanding of the Java language should take less time than you think. However, there's much more to Java than just the language. To be able to program effectively in Java, you need to understand the libraries that go with the language, and these are very extensive. It is also important to become familiar with open source projects, especially those developed by the Apache folks.

In this book, the sequence in which you learn how the language works and how you apply it has been carefully structured so that you gain expertise and confidence with programming in Java through a relatively easy and painless process. As far as possible, each chapter avoids the use of things that you haven't learned about already. A consequence, though, is that you won't be writing Java applications with application windows and a Graphical User Interface (GUI) right away. Although it may be an appealing idea, this would be a bit like learning to swim by jumping in the pool at the deep end. Generally speaking, there is good evidence that by starting in the shallow end of the pool and learning how to float before you try to swim, you minimize the chance of drowning, and there is a high expectation that you can end up being a competent swimmer.

Java Programs

As I have already noted, there are two basic kinds of programs you can write in Java. Programs that are to be embedded in a web page are called Java applets, and normal standalone programs are called Java applications. You can further subdivide Java applications into console applications, which only support character output to your computer screen (console output typically goes to the command line on a PC under Microsoft Windows, for example), and windowed applications, which can create and manage multiple windows. The latter use the typical GUI mechanisms of window-based programs—menus, toolbars, dialogs, and so on.

While you are learning the Java language basics, you use console applications as examples to understand how things work. These are applications that use simple command-line input and output. With this approach you can concentrate on understanding the specifics of the language without worrying about any of the complexity involved in creating and managing windows. After you are comfortable with using all the features of the Java language, you move on to window-based applications and applet examples.

Learning Java—the Road Ahead

Before starting out on any journey, it is always helpful to have an idea of where you're heading and what route you should take, so let's take a look at a brief road map of where you're going with Java. There are seven broad stages you progress through in learning Java using this book:

1. The first stage is this chapter. It sets out some fundamental ideas about the structure of Java programs and how they work. This includes such things as what object-oriented programming is all about and how an executable program is created from a Java source file. Getting these concepts straight at the outset makes learning to write Java programs that much easier for you.

2. Next, in Chapters 2 to 4, I explain how statements are put together, what facilities you have for storing basic data in a program, how you perform calculations, and how you make decisions based on the results of them. These are the nuts and bolts you need for the next stages.

3. In the third stage, in Chapters 5 and 6, you learn about *classes*—how you define them and how you can use them. Classes are blueprints for objects, so this is where you learn the object-oriented characteristics of Java. By the time you are through this stage, you should have learned all the basics of how the Java language works so you are ready to progress further into how you can apply it.

4. In the fourth stage, in Chapters 7 through 12, you learn how you deal with errors and how you read and write files. Of course, file input/output is an essential capability in the majority of applications.

5. The fifth stage is covered by Chapters 13 to 15. These chapters explain how you define generic class types, which are blueprints for creating sets of similar classes. You also learn about a range of utility classes and capabilities from the support libraries that you can apply in many different program contexts.

6. In the sixth stage, in Chapters 16 to 21, you learn in detail how you implement applications or applets with a graphical user interface, and how you handle interactions with the user in this context. This amounts to applying the GUI capabilities provided by the Java class libraries. You also learn how you manage concurrent threads of execution within a Java program, which is fundamental to effective GUI programming. When you finish this stage, you should be equipped to write your own fully fledged applications and applets in Java.

7. In the last stage you learn about the Extensible Markup Language, XML, which is a powerful tool for representing data that is to be transferred from one computer to another. You apply the Java support classes for XML in a practical context, writing and reading XML files.

At the end of the book, you should be a knowledgeable Java programmer. The rest is down to experience.

Throughout this book I use complete examples to explore how Java works. You should create and run all of the examples, even the simplest, preferably by typing them in yourself. Don't be afraid to experiment with them. If there is anything you are not quite clear on, try changing an example around to see what happens, or better still—write an example of your own. If you're uncertain how some aspect of Java that you have already covered works, don't look it up right away—try out a few things and see if you can figure it out. Making mistakes is a very effective way to learn.

THE JAVA ENVIRONMENT

You can execute Java programs on a variety of computers using a range of operating systems. Your Java programs run just as well on a PC running any supported version of Microsoft Windows as it does on Linux or a Sun Solaris workstation. This is possible because a Java program does not execute directly on your computer. It runs on a standardized environment called the *Java 2 Platform* that has been implemented as software in the form of the *Java Runtime Environment (JRE)* on a wide variety of computers and operating systems. The Java Platform consists of two elements—a software implementation of a hypothetical computer called the *Java Virtual Machine (JVM)* and the *Java Application Programming Interface (Java API)*, which is a set of software components that provides the facilities you need to write a fully fledged interactive application in Java.

A *Java compiler* converts the Java source code that you write into a binary program consisting of *bytecodes*. Bytecodes are machine instructions for the JVM. When you execute a Java program, a program called the *Java interpreter* inspects and deciphers the bytecodes for it, checks it out to ensure that it has not been tampered with and is safe to execute, and then executes the actions that the bytecodes specify within the JVM. A Java interpreter can run standalone, or it can be part of a web browser such as Google Chrome, Mozilla Firefox, or Microsoft Internet Explorer where it can be invoked automatically to run applets in a web page.

Because your Java program consists of bytecodes rather than native machine instructions, it is completely insulated from the particular hardware on which it is run. Any computer that has the Java environment implemented handles your program as well as any other, and because the Java interpreter sits between your program and the physical machine, it can prevent unauthorized actions in the program from being executed.

In the past, there has been a penalty for all this flexibility and protection in the speed of execution of your Java programs. An interpreted Java program would typically run at only one-tenth of the speed of an equivalent program using native machine instructions. With present Java machine implementations, much of the performance penalty has been eliminated, and in programs that are not computation intensive—you really wouldn't notice this anyway. With the JVM that is supplied with the current Java 2 Development Kit (JDK) available from the Oracle website, there are very few circumstances where you notice any appreciable degradation in performance compared to a program compiled to native machine code.

Java Program Development

For this book you need the Java 2 Platform, Standard Edition (J2SE) version 7 or later. The JDK is available from www.oracle.com/technetwork/java/javase/downloads/index.html. You can choose from versions of the JDK for Solaris, Linux, and Microsoft Windows, and there are versions supporting either 32-bit or 64-bit operating system environments.

Using a Program Code Editor

To create the Java program source files that you use with the JDK, you need some kind of code editor. There are several excellent professional Java program development tools available that provide friendly environments for creating and editing your Java source code and compiling and debugging your programs. These are powerful tools for the experienced programmer that improve productivity and provide extensive debugging capabilities. However, for learning Java using this book, I recommend that you resist the temptation to use any of these for the time being.

So why am I suggesting that you are better off *not* using a tool that makes programming easier and faster? There are several reasons. Firstly, the professional development systems tend to hide a lot of things you need to get to a grip on if you are to get a full understanding of how Java works. Secondly, the professional development environments are geared to managing complex applications with a large amount of code, which introduces complexity that you really are better off without while you are learning. Virtually all commercial Java development systems provide prebuilt facilities of their own to speed development. Although this is helpful for production program development, it really does get in the way when you are trying to learn Java. A further consideration is that productivity features supported by a commercial Java development are sometimes tied to a specific version of the Java 2 Platform. This means that some features of the latest version of Java might not work. The professional Java development tools that provide an Interactive Development Environment (IDE) are intended primarily for knowledgeable and experienced programmers, so start with one when you get to the end of the book.

So what *am* I recommending? Stick to using JDK 7 from Oracle with a simple program text editor or development environment for creating and managing your source code. Quite a number of shareware and freeware code editors around are suitable, some of which are specific to Java, and you should have no trouble locating one. I can make two specific suggestions.

➤ I find that the JCreator editor from www.jcreator.com is particularly good and is easy to install. There's a free version, JCreator LE, and a paid version with more functionality. The free version is perfectly adequate for learning but you may want to upgrade to the paid version when you have reached the end of the book.

➤ Notepad++ is a free source code editor running in the Microsoft Windows environment that you can download from http://notepad-plus-plus.org. It supports syntax highlighting for Java. It is also handy as a simple editor for XML files.

➤ I recommend the NetBeans IDE that you can download from http://netbeans.org , which is also free. This is a sophisticated professional interactive development environment that supports not only Java, but also many other programming languages. Nonetheless, it is easy to use and there is extensive online documentation. If you have plans to progress into programming using other languages, there's a good chance that you will find the NetBeans IDE supports them.

Whichever code editor you choose to use, I recommend that you only use the simplest project creation options. In particular you should avoid using any of the program project types that provide prebuilt skeleton program code while you are working your way through this book. By coding everything yourself you will maximizes your learning experience. Of course, after you have assimilated everything in the book, you are ready to enhance your Java program development capability with the full capabilities of a pro development tool.

A good place to start looking if you want to investigate what other editors are available is the www.download.com website.

Installing the JDK

Detailed instructions on how to install the JDK for your particular operating system are available from the JDK download website at www.oracle.com/technetwork/java/javase/downloads/index.html, so I won't go into all the variations for different systems here. However, you should watch out for a few things that may not leap out from the pages of the installation documentation.

First of all, the JDK and the documentation are separate, and you install them separately. If you are pushed for disk space, you don't have to install the documentation because you can access it online. The current location for the online documentation for the JDK is http://download.java.net/jdk7/docs/api but this could conceivably change. The documentation download for the JDK consists of a ZIP archive containing a large number of HTML files structured in a hierarchy. You should install the JDK before you unzip the documentation archive. If you install the JDK to drive C: under Windows, the directory structure shown in Figure 1-1 is created.

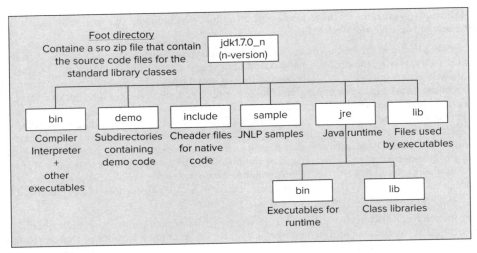

FIGURE 1-1

This structure appears in your `C:\Program Files\Java` directory (or `C:\Program Files (X86)\Java` if you install the 32-bit version of the JDK with a 64-bit version of Windows 7). The `jdk1.7.0` directory in Figure 1-1 is sometimes referred to as the root directory for Java. In some contexts it is also referred to as the Java home directory. The actual root directory name may have the release version number appended, in which case the actual directory name is of the form `jdk1.7.0_01`, for example. Figure 1-1 shows the fundamental subdirectories to the root directory.

The `sample` directory contains sample applications that use JNLP, which is the Java Network Launching Protocol that is used for executing applications or applets from a network server without the need for a browser or the need to download and install the code.

You don't need to worry about the contents of most of these directories, at least not when you get started. The installation process should add the path for the `jdk1.7.0_n\bin` directory to the paths defined in your `PATH` environment variable, which enables you to run the compiler and the interpreter from anywhere without having to specify the path to it. If you installed the JDK to your C: drive, then the path is `C:\Program Files\Java\jdk1.7.0_n\bin`.

A word of warning—if you have previously installed a commercial Java development product check that it has not modified your `PATH` environment variable to include the path to its own Java executables. If it has and the path precedes the path to JDK 7, when you try to run the Java compiler or interpreter, you will get the versions supplied with the commercial product rather that those that came with JDK 7. One way to fix this is to remove the path or paths that cause the problem. If you don't want to remove the paths that were inserted for the commercial product, you have to use the full path specification when you want to run the compiler or interpreter from the JDK.

The `jre` directory contains the Java Runtime Environment facilities that are used when you execute a Java program. The classes in the Java libraries are stored in the `jre\lib directory`. They don't appear individually though. They are all packaged up in the archive, `rt.jar`. Leave this alone. The JRE takes care of retrieving what it needs from the archive when your program executes.

The `CLASSPATH` environment variable is a frequent source of problems and confusion to newcomers to Java. The current JDK does not require `CLASSPATH` to be defined, and if it has been defined by some other Java version or system, it may cause problems. Check to see whether `CLASSPATH` has been defined on your system. If you have to keep the `CLASSPATH` environment variable—maybe because you want to keep the system that defined it or you share the machine with someone who needs it—you have to use a command-line option to define `CLASSPATH` temporarily whenever you compile or execute your Java code. You see how to do this a little later in this chapter.

If you want the JDK documentation installed in the hierarchy shown in Figure 1-1, then you should extract the documentation from the archive to the jdk1.7.0_n directory. This creates a new subdirectory, docs (or possibly docs_www), to the root directory, and installs the documentation files in that. To look at the documentation, you just open the index.html file that is in the docs subdirectory.

Extracting the Source Code for the Class Libraries

The source code for the class libraries is included in the archive src.zip that you find in the jdk1.7.0 root directory. Many Java IDEs can access the contents of this zip directly without unpacking it. After you have learned the basics of the Java language, browsing this source is very educational, and it can also be helpful when you are more experienced with Java in giving a better understanding of how things work—or when they don't, why they don't.

You can extract the source files from the src.zip archive using the Winzip utility, the WinRAR utility, the JAR utility that comes with the JDK, or any other utility that unpacks .zip archives—but be warned—there's a lot of it, and it takes a while!

Extracting the contents of src.zip to the root directory \jdk1.7.0 creates a new subdirectory, src, and installs the source code in subdirectories to this. To look at the source code for a particular class, just open the .java file that you are interested in using with your Java program editor or any plain text editor.

Compiling a Java Program

Java source code is always stored in files with the extension .java. After you have created the source code for a program and saved it in a .java file, you need to process the source using a Java compiler. Using the compiler that comes with the JDK, you make the directory that contains your Java source file the current directory, and then enter the following command:

```
javac MyProgram.java
```

Here, javac is the name of the Java compiler, and MyProgram.java is the name of the program source file. This command assumes that the current directory contains your source file. If it doesn't, the compiler isn't able to find your source file. It also assumes that the source file corresponds to the Java language as defined in the current version of the JDK. There is a command-line option, -source, that you can use to specify the Java language version, so for JDK 7, the preceding command to execute the compiler is equivalent to the following:

```
javac -source 1.7 MyProgram.java
```

In practice you can ignore the -source command-line option unless you are compiling a Java program that was written using an older version of the JDK. You get the current source version compiled by default. To compile code written for JDK 6 you would write:

```
javac -source 1.6 oldSourceCode.java
```

Here's a simple program that you use to can try out the compiler:

Available for download on Wrox.com

```java
public class MyProgram {
  public static void main(String[] args) {
    System.out.println("Rome wasn't burned in a day!");
  }
}
```

MyProgram.java

This just outputs a line of text to the command line when it executes. As this is just to try out the compiler, I'm not explaining how the program works at this point. Of course, you must type the code in exactly as shown and save it in a file with the name MyProgram.java. The file name without the extension is always the same as the class name in the code. If you have made any mistakes the compiler issues error messages.

If you need to override an existing definition of the CLASSPATH environment variable—perhaps because it has been set by a Java development system you have installed—the command would be the following:

```
javac -classpath . MyProgram.java
```

The value of CLASSPATH follows the -classpath option specification and here it is just a period. A period defines the path to the current directory, whatever that happens to be. This means that the compiler looks for your source file or files in the current directory. If you forget to include the period, the compiler is not able to find your source files in the current directory. If you include the -classpath . command-line option in any event it does no harm. If you need to add more paths to the CLASSPATH specification, they must be separated by semicolons. If a path contains spaces, it must be delimited by double quotes.

Note that you should avoid storing your source files within the directory structure that was created for the JDK, as this can cause problems. Set up separate directories of your own to hold the source code for your programs and keep the code for each program in its own directory.

Assuming your program contains no errors, the compiler generates a bytecode program that is the equivalent of your source code. The compiler stores the bytecode program in a file with the same name as the source file, but with the extension .class. Java executable modules are always stored in a file with the extension .class. By default, the .class file is stored in the same directory as the source file.

The command-line options I have introduced here are by no means all the options you have available for the compiler. You are able to compile all of the examples in the book just knowing about the options I have discussed. There is a comprehensive description of all the options within the documentation for the JDK. You can also specify the -help command-line option to get a summary of the standard options you can use. To get a summary of the Java compiler options, enter the following on the command line:

```
javac -help
```

To get usage information for the java application launcher, enter the following command:

```
java -help
```

If you are using some other product to develop your Java programs, you are probably using a much more user-friendly, graphical interface for compiling your programs that doesn't involve entering commands such as those shown in this section. However, the file name extensions for your source file and the object file that results from it are just the same.

Executing a Java Application

To execute the bytecode program in the .class file with the Java interpreter in the JDK, you make the directory containing the .class file current and enter the command:

```
java MyProgram
```

Note that you use just the name MyProgram to identify the program, not the name of the file that the compiler generates, MyProgram.class. It is a common beginner's mistake to use the latter by analogy with the compile operation. If you put a .class file extension on MyProgram, your program won't execute, and you get an error message:

```
Exception in thread "main" java.lang.NoClassDefFoundError: MyProgram/class
```

Although the javac compiler expects to find the name of a *file* that contains your source code, the java interpreter expects the name of a *class* (and that class must contain a main() method, as I explain later in this chapter). The class name is MyProgram in this case. The MyProgram.class file contains the compiled MyProgram class. I explain what a class is shortly.

The -enableassertions option is necessary for programs that use *assertions*, and because you use assertions after you have learned about them it's a good idea to get into the habit of always using this option. You can abbreviate the -enableassertions option to -ea if you want. The previous command with assertions enabled is:

```
java -enableassertions MyProgram
```

If you want to override an existing CLASSPATH definition, the option is the same as with the compiler. You can also abbreviate --classpath to -cp with the compiler or the Java interpreter. Here's how the command looks using that abbreviation:

```
java -ea -cp . MyProgram
```

To execute your program, the Java interpreter analyzes and then executes the bytecode instructions. The JVM behaves identically in all computer environments that support Java, so you can be sure your program is completely portable. As I already said, your program runs just as well on a Linux Java implementation as it runs on an implementation for Microsoft Windows, Solaris, or any other operating system that supports Java. (Beware of variations in the level of Java supported, though. Some environments lag a little, so implementations supporting the current JDK version might be available later than under Windows or Solaris.)

Executing an Applet

The Java compiler in the JDK compiles both applications and applets. However, an applet is not executed in the same way as an application. You must embed an applet in a web page before it can be run. You can then execute it either within a Java-enabled web browser, or by using the appletviewer, a bare-bones browser provided as part of the JDK. It is a good idea to use the appletviewer to run applets while you are learning. This ensures that if your applet doesn't work, it is almost certainly your code that is the problem, rather than some problem of Java integration with the browser.

If you have compiled an applet and included it in a web page stored as MyApplet.html in the current directory that contains the .class file, you can execute it by entering the following command:

```
appletviewer MyApplet.html
```

So how do you put an applet in a web page?

The Hypertext Markup Language

The *Hypertext Markup Language*, or *HTML* as it is commonly known, is used to define a web page. When you define a web page as an HTML document, it is stored in a file with the extension .html. An HTML document consists of a number of elements, and each element is identified by *tags*. The document begins with <html> and ends with </html>. These delimiters, <html> and </html>, are tags, and each element in an HTML document should be enclosed between a similar pair of tags between angle brackets. All element tags are case-insensitive, so you can use uppercase or lowercase, or even a mixture of the two. Here is an example of an HTML document consisting of a title and some other text:

```
<html>
  <head>
    <title>This is the title of the document</title>
  </head>
  <body>
    You can put whatever text you like here. The body of a document can contain
    all kinds of other HTML elements, including <B>Java applets</B>.
    Note how each element always begins with a start tag identifying the
    element, and ends with an end tag that is the same as the start tag but
    with a slash added. The pair of tags around 'Java applets' in the previous
    sentence will display the text as bold.
  </body>
</html>
```

There are two elements that can appear directly within the <html> element, a <head> element and a <body> element, as in the example. The <head> element provides information about the document, and is not strictly part of it. The text enclosed by the `<title>` element tags that appears here within the `<head>` element are displayed as the window title when the page is viewed.

Other element tags can appear within the `<body>` element, and they include tags for headings, lists, tables, links to other pages, and Java applets. There are some elements that do not require an end tag because they are considered to be empty. An example of this kind of element tag is `<hr>`, which specifies a horizontal rule, a line across the full width of the page. You can use the `<hr>` tag to divide a page and separate one type of element from another. Another is `<center>`, which centers the output from the applet.

Adding an Applet to an HTML Document

For many element tag pairs, you can specify an *element attribute* in the starting tag that defines additional or qualifying data about the element. This is how a Java applet is identified in an `<applet>` tag. Here is an example of how you might include a Java applet in an HTML document:

```html
<html>
  <head>
    <title> A Simple Program </title>
  </head>
  <body>
    <hr>
    <applet code = "MyFirstApplet.class"  width = 350  height = 200 >
    </applet>
    <hr/>
  </body>
</html>
```

Directory "MyFirstApplet"

The two bolded lines between tags for horizontal lines specify that the bytecodes for the applet are contained in the file `MyFirstApplet.class`. The name of the file containing the bytecodes for the applet is specified as the value for the `code` attribute in the `<applet>` tag. The other two attributes, `width` and `height`, define the width and height of the region on the screen that is used by the applet when it executes. These always have to be specified to run an applet. Here is the Java source code for a simple applet:

```java
import javax.swing.JApplet;
import java.awt.Graphics;

public class MyFirstApplet extends JApplet {

  public void paint(Graphics g) {
    g.drawString("To climb a ladder, start at the bottom rung.", 20, 90);

  }
}
```

Directory "MyFirstApplet"

You might get the following warning message when you compile this program:

```
warning: [serial] serializable class MyFirstApplet has no definition
  of serialVersionUID
```

You can safely ignore this. You learn about serializable classes in Chapter 12.

CONFER PROGRAMMER TO PROGRAMMER ABOUT THIS TOPIC.

→ Visit p2p.wrox.com ←

Note that Java is case-sensitive. You can't enter `public` with a capital `P`—if you do, the program won't compile. This applet just displays a message when you run it. The mechanics of how the message gets displayed are irrelevant here—the example is just to illustrate how an applet goes into an HTML page. If you compile this code and save the previous HTML page specification in the file `MyFirstApplet.html` in the same directory as the Java applet `.class` file, you can run the applet using `appletviewer` from the JDK with the command:

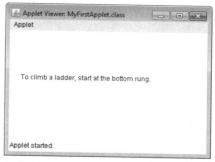

FIGURE 1-2

```
appletviewer MyFirstApplet.html
```

This displays the window shown in Figure 1-2:

Because the height and width of the window for the applet are specified in pixels, the physical dimensions of the `appletviewer` window depend on the resolution and size of your monitor.

OBJECT-ORIENTED PROGRAMMING IN JAVA

As I said at the beginning of this chapter, Java is an object-oriented language. When you use a programming language that is not object-oriented, you must express the solution to every problem essentially in terms of numbers and characters—the basic kinds of data that you can manipulate in the language. In an object-oriented language like Java, things are different. Of course, you still have numbers and characters to work with—these are referred to as the *primitive data types*—but you can define other kinds of entities that are relevant to your particular problem. You solve your problem in terms of the entities or objects that occur in the context of the problem. This not only affects how a program is structured, but also the terms in which the solution to your problem is expressed.

If your problem concerns baseball players, your Java program is likely to have `BaseballPlayer` objects in it; if you are producing a program dealing with fruit production in California, it may well have objects that are `Oranges` in it. Apart from seeming to be an inherently sensible approach to constructing programs, object-oriented programs are usually easier to understand.

In Java almost everything is an object. If you haven't delved into object-oriented programming before, or maybe because you have, you may feel this is a bit daunting. But fear not. Objects in Java are particularly easy. So easy, in fact, that you are going to start out by understanding some of the ideas behind Java objects right now. In that way you can be on the right track from the outset.

This doesn't mean you are going to jump in with all the precise nitty-gritty of Java that you need for describing and using objects. You are just going to get the concepts straight at this point. You do this by taking a stroll through the basics using the odd bit of Java code where it helps the ideas along. All the code that you use here is fully explained in later chapters. Concentrate on understanding the notion of objects first. Then you can ease into the specific practical details as you go along.

So What Are Objects?

Anything can be thought of as an object. Objects are all around you. You can consider `Tree` to be a particular class of objects: trees in general. The notion of a `Tree` in general is a rather abstract concept—although any tree fits the description, it is more useful to think of more specific types of tree. Hence, the Oak tree in my yard which I call `myOak`, the Ash tree in your yard which you call `thatDarnedTree`, and a `generalSherman`, the well-known redwood, are actual instances of specific types of tree, subclasses of `Tree` that in this case happen to be `Oak`, `Ash`, and `Redwood`. Note how we drop into the jargon here—*class* is a term that describes a specification for a collection of objects with common properties. Figure 1-3 shows some classes of trees and how you might relate them.

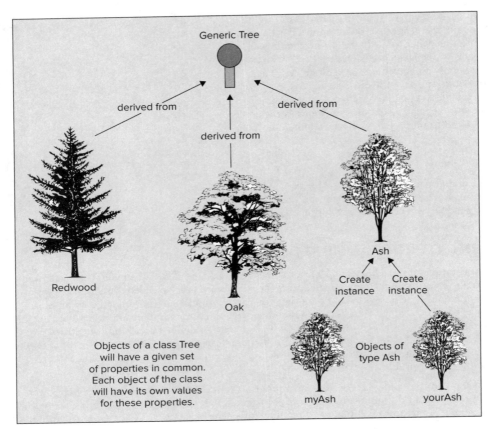

FIGURE 1-3

A class is a specification, or blueprint—expressed as a piece of program code—that defines what goes to make up a particular sort of object. A subclass is a class that inherits all the properties of the parent class, but that also includes extra specialization. Particular classes of `Tree`, such as `Oak` or `Ash`, have all the characteristics of the most general type, `Tree`; otherwise, they could not be considered to be such. However, each subclass of `Tree`, such as `Oak`, has its own characteristics that differentiate `Oak` objects from other types of `Tree`.

Of course, you define a class specification to fit what you want to do in your application context. There are no absolutes here. For my trivial problem, the specification of a `Tree` class might just consist of its species name and its height. If you are an arboriculturalist, then your problem with trees may require a much more complex class, or more likely a set of classes, that involves a mass of arboreal characteristics.

Every object that your program uses must have a corresponding class definition somewhere for objects of that type. This is true in Java as well as in other object-oriented languages. The basic idea of a class in programming parallels that of classifying things in the real world. It is a convenient and well-defined way to group things together.

An *instance* of a class is a technical term for an existing object of that class. `Ash` is a specification for a type of object, and `yourAsh` representing a particular tree is an object constructed to that specification. `yourAsh` is an instance of the class `Ash`. After you have a class defined you can create objects, or instances, of that class. This raises the question of what differentiates an object of a given class from an object of another class, an `Ash` class object, say, from a `Redwood` object. In other words, what sort of information defines a class?

What Defines a Class of Objects?

You may have already guessed the answer. A class definition identifies all the parameters that define an object of that particular class type, at least, so far as your needs go. Someone else might define the class differently, with a larger or smaller set of parameters to define the same sort of object—it all depends on what you want to do with the class. You decide what aspects of the objects you include to define that particular class of object, and you choose them depending on the kinds of problems that you want to address using the objects of the class. Let's think about a specific class of objects.

If you were defining a class `Hat`, for example, you might use just two parameters in the definition. You could include the type of hat as a string of characters such as `"Fedora"` or `"Baseball cap"` and its size as a numeric value. The parameters that define an object of a class are referred to as *instance variables* or *attributes* of a class, or class *fields*. The instance variables can be basic types of data such as numbers, but they can also be other class objects. For example, the name of a `Hat` object could be of type `String`—the class `String` defines objects that are strings of characters.

Of course there are lots of other things you could include to define a `Hat` if you wanted to, `color`, for example, which might be another string of characters such as `"Blue."` To specify a class you just decide what set of attributes meet your requirements, and those are what you use. This is called *data abstraction* in the parlance of the object-oriented aficionado because you just abstract the attributes you want to use from the myriad possibilities for a typical object.

In Java the definition of the class `Hat` would look something like this:

```
class Hat {
   // Stuff defining the class in detail goes here.
   // This could specify the name of the hat, the size,
   // maybe the color, and whatever else you felt was necessary.
}
```

 WARNING *Because the word* `class` *has this special role in Java it is called a* keyword, *and it is reserved for use only in this context. There are lots of other keywords in Java that you pick up as we go along. You need to remember that you must not use any of keywords for any other purposes. If you want to know what they all are, the complete set is in Appendix A.*

The name of the class follows the word `class`, and the details of the definition appear between the curly braces.

I'm not going into the detail of how the class `Hat` is defined because you don't need it at this point. The lines appearing between the braces are not code; they are actually *program comments* because they begin with two successive forward slashes. The compiler ignores anything on a line that follows two successive forward slashes, so you can use this to add explanations to your programs. Generally, the more useful comments you can add to your programs, the better. You see in Chapter 2 that there are other ways you can write comments in Java.

Each object of your class has a particular set of values defined that characterize that particular object. You could have an object of type `CowboyHat`, which might be defined by values such as `"Stetson"` for the type of the hat, `"White"` for the color, and the size as `6`. This is illustrated in Figure 1-4.

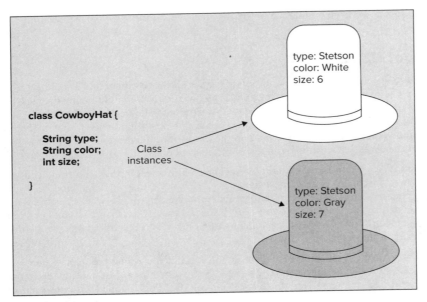

FIGURE 1-4

Although Figure 1-4 shows CowboyHat objects defined by a set of three values that you would not normally expect to change for a given instance, in general the parameter values that define an object are not necessarily fixed. You would expect the type and size attributes for a particular CowboyHat object to stay fixed because hats don't usually change their size—at least, not unless it's raining—but you could have other attributes, as illustrated in Figure 1-5.

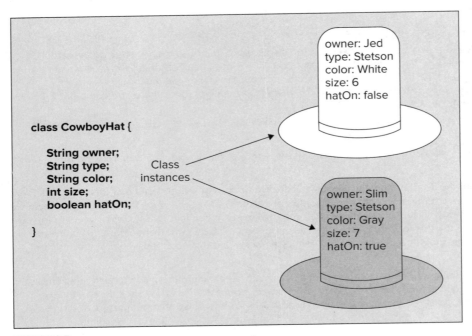

FIGURE 1-5

You might have a parameter `owner`, which would record the owner's name, so the value stored as the attribute `owner` could be changed when the hat was sold or otherwise transferred to someone else. You might also have a parameter `hatOn`, for example, which would indicate whether the hat was on or off the owner's head; the value `true` would indicate that the owner was indeed wearing the hat, whereas the value `false` would mean that the hat had been removed and was just lying about somewhere.

Operating on Objects

In spite of what you might think from looking at Figure 1-5, a class object is not just a collection of various items of data. In addition to the parameters that characterize an object, a class specifies what you can do with an object—that is, it defines the operations that are possible on objects of the class. Clearly, for objects to be of any use in a program, you need to decide what you can do with them. The operations that you specify for objects of a given type depend on what sort of objects you are talking about, the attributes they contain, and how you intend to use them.

For the `CowboyHat` class in Figure 1-5, you may want to have operations that you could refer to as `putHatOn` and `takeHatOff`, which would have meanings that are fairly obvious from their names, and do make sense for `CowboyHat` objects. These operations on a particular `CowboyHat` object would set the value of `hatOn` for the object. To determine whether your `CowboyHat` was on or off, you would just need to look at this value. Conceivably, you might also have an operation `changeOwner` by which you could set the instance variable recording the current owner's name to a new value. Figure 1-6 shows two operations applied in succession to a `CowboyHat` object.

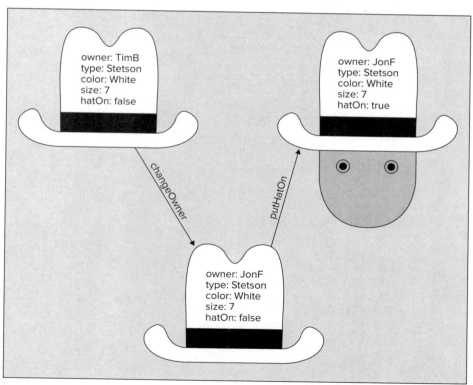

FIGURE 1-6

Of course, for each type of object you can have any operation that makes sense for you. If you want to have a `shootHoleIn` operation for `Hat` objects, that's no problem. You just have to define what that operation does to an object.

You are probably wondering at this point how an operation for a class is defined. As you see in detail a bit later, it boils down to a self-contained block of program code called a *method* that is identified by the name you give to it. You can pass data items—which can be integers, floating-point numbers, character strings, or class objects—to a method, and these are processed by the code in the method. A method may also return a data item as a result. Performing an operation on an object amounts to *executing* the method that defines that operation for the object.

 WARNING *Of course, the only operations you can perform on an instance of a particular class are those defined within the class, so the usefulness and flexibility of a class is going to depend on the thought that you give to its definition. We look into these considerations more in Chapter 5.*

Just so you can recognize one when you see it, let's take a look at an example of a complete class definition. The code for the class `CowboyHat` we have been talking about might be as illustrated in Figure 1-7.

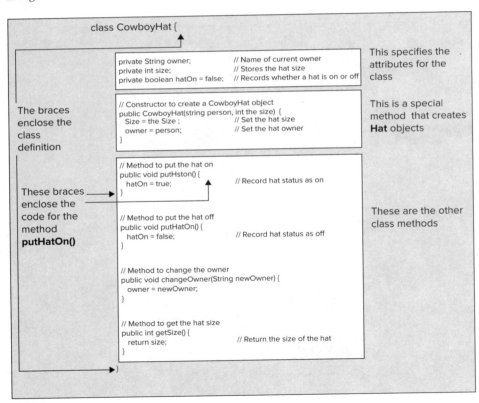

FIGURE 1-7

This code would be saved in a file with the name `CowboyHat.java`. The name of a file that contains the definition of a class is always the same as the class name, and the extension is `.java` to identify that the file contains Java source code.

The code that defines the class appears between the braces that follow the identification for the class, as shown in Figure 1-7. The code for each of the methods in the class also appears between braces. The class has three instance variables, `owner`, `size`, and `hatOn`, and this last variable is always initialized as `false`. Each object that is created according to this class specification has its own independent copy of each of these variables, so each object has its own unique values for the owner, the hat size, and whether the hat is on or off.

The `private` keyword, which has been applied to each instance variable, ensures that only code within the methods of the class can access or change the values of these directly. The `CowboyHat` class methods are `public` so they are accessible generally from outside the class. Methods of a class can also be specified as `private`, which means they can only be invoked from methods inside the class.

Being able to prevent access to some members of a class from outside is an important facility. It protects the internals of the class from being changed or used incorrectly. Someone using your class in another program can get access only to the bits to which you want them to have access. This means that you can change how the class works internally without affecting other programs that may use it. You can change any of the things inside the class that you have designated as `private`, and you can even change the code inside any of the public methods, as long as the method name and the number and types of values passed to it or returned from it remain the same.

Our `CowboyHat` class also has five methods, so you can do five different things with a `CowboyHat` object. One of these is a special method called a *constructor*, which creates a `CowboyHat` object—this is the method with the name, `CowboyHat`, that is the same as the class name. Constructors always have the same name as the class. The items between the parentheses that follow the name of the constructor specify data that is to be passed to the method when it is executed—that is, when a `CowboyHat` object is created.

 WARNING *In practice you might need to define a few other methods for the class to be useful; you might want to compare* CowboyHat *objects for example, to see if one was larger than another. However, at the moment you just need to get an idea of how the code looks. The details are of no importance here, as you return to all this in Chapter 5.*

Java Program Statements

As you saw in the `CowboyHat` class example, the code for each method in the class appears between braces, and it consists of *program statements*. A semicolon terminates each program statement. A statement in Java can spread over several lines if necessary because the end of each statement is determined by the semicolon, not by the end of a line. Here is a Java program statement:

```
hatOn = false;
```

If you wanted to, you could also write this as

```
hatOn =
        false;
```

You can generally include spaces and tabs, and spread your statements over multiple lines to enhance readability if it is a particularly long statement, but sensible constraints apply. You can't put a space in the middle of a name, for instance. If you write `hat On`, for example, the compiler reads this as two words.

Encapsulation

At this point we can introduce another bit of jargon you can use to impress or bore your friends—*encapsulation.* Encapsulation refers to the hiding of items of data and methods within an object. This is achieved by specifying them as `private` in the definition of the class. In the `CowboyHat` class, the instance variables `owner`, `type`, `size`, and `hatOn` were encapsulated. They were accessible only through the methods defined for the class. Therefore, the only way to alter the values they contain is to call a method that does that. Being able to encapsulate members of a class in this way is important for the security and integrity of class objects. You may have a class with data members that can take on only particular values or values within a particular range. The age of a person, for example, is generally greater than zero and less than 150, at least until medical science extends the range. By hiding the data members and forcing the use of a method to set or change the values, you can ensure that only legal values are set.

I mentioned earlier another major advantage of encapsulation—the ability to hide the implementation of a class. By allowing only limited access to the members of a class, you have the freedom to change the internals of the class without necessitating changes to programs that use the class. As long as the external characteristics of the methods that can be called from outside the class remain unchanged, the internal code can be changed in any way that you, the programmer, want.

A particular object, an instance of `CowboyHat`, incorporates, or encapsulates, the `owner`, the `size` of the object, and the status of the hat in the instance variable `hatOn`. Only the constructor, and the `putHatOn()`, `takeHatOff()`, `changeOwner()`, and `getSize()` methods can be accessed externally.

> **NOTE** *Whenever I am referring to a method in the text, I add a pair of parentheses after the method name to distinguish it from other things that have names. Some examples of this appear in the preceding paragraph. A method always has parentheses in its definition and in its use in a program, as you'll see, so it makes sense to represent it in this way in the text.*

Classes and Data Types

Programming is concerned with specifying how data of various kinds is to be processed, massaged, manipulated, or transformed. Classes define the types of objects that a program works with so you can consider defining a class to be the same as defining a data type. Thus, `Hat` is a type of data, as is `Tree`, and any other class you care to define. Java also contains a library of standard classes that provide you with a whole range of programming tools and facilities. For the most part then, your Java program processes, massages, manipulates, or transforms class objects.

There are some basic types of data in Java that are not classes, and these are called *primitive types.* I go into these in detail in the next chapter, but they are essentially data types for numeric values such as 99 or 3.75, for single characters such as *A* or *?*, and for logical values that can be `true` or `false`. Java also has classes that correspond to each of the primitive data types for reasons that you see later. There is an `Integer` class that defines objects that encapsulate integers, for example. Every entity in your Java program that is not of a primitive data type is an object of a class—either a class that you define yourself, a class supplied as part of the Java environment, or a class that you obtain from somewhere else, such as from a specialized support package.

Classes and Subclasses

Many sets of objects that you might define in a class can be subdivided into more specialized subsets that can also be represented by different classes, and Java provides you with the capability to define one class as a more specialized version of another. This reflects the nature of reality. There are always lots of ways of dividing a cake—or a forest. `Conifer`, for example, could be a subclass of the class `Tree`. The `Conifer` class would have all the instance variables and methods of the `Tree` class, plus some additional instance variables and/or methods that make it a `Conifer` in particular. You refer to the `Conifer` class as a *subclass* of the class `Tree`, and the class `Tree` as a *superclass* of the class `Conifer`.

When you define a class such as `Conifer` using another class such as `Tree` as a starting point, the class `Conifer` is said to be *derived* from the class `Tree`, and the class `Conifer` *inherits* all the attributes of the class `Tree`.

Advantages of Using Objects

As I said at the outset, object-oriented programs are written using objects that are specific to the problem being solved. Your pinball machine simulator may well define and use objects of type `Table`, `Ball`, `Flipper`, and `Bumper`. This has tremendous advantages, not only in terms of easing the development process and making the program code easier to understand, but also in any future expansion of such a program. Java provides a whole range of standard classes to help you in the development of your program, and you can develop your own generic classes to provide a basis for developing programs that are of particular interest to you.

Because an object includes the methods that can operate on it as well as the data that defines it, programming using objects is much less prone to error. Your object-oriented Java programs should be more robust than the equivalent in a procedural programming language. Object-oriented programs take a little longer to design than programs that do not use objects because you must take care in the design of the classes that you need, but the time required to write and test the code is sometimes substantially less than that for procedural programs. Object-oriented programs are also much easier to maintain and extend.

Annotations

A Java source file can contain *annotations*. An annotation is not a Java language statement, but a special statement that changes the way program statements are treated by the compiler or the libraries. You can define your own annotations but most Java programmers never need to do so, so I'm not going into the how. The reason for mentioning annotations is that you make use of a couple of annotations with some of the examples in the book.

To clarify the sort of thing an annotation does, I'm introducing you to one now. Earlier in this chapter you compiled `MyFirstApplet` and got a warning message from the compiler. This warning had no value in the context of this program, and you could have suppressed it by adding the following annotation immediately preceding the `MyFirstApplet` class definition:

```
@SuppressWarnings("serial")
```

This annotation tells the compiler not to issue `serial` warning messages, where `serial` is the message type. You could use this annotation to suppress any type of warning message, but obviously it is sensible to only suppress warnings that really are irrelevant in a particular context.

Generic Classes

I have already mentioned generic classes so I had better explain a bit more about them. It often occurs that you want to define classes for objects that store collections of things, people maybe, or temperatures, or names perhaps. A class that stores a collection of people is likely to be very much the same as another class that stores a collection of temperatures. The principle difference is the type of thing that is stored. This is where a generic class type comes in. A generic class is a recipe for creating classes of a similar nature. You can specify a generic class representing a collection of things that you can use to create a class that can store a collection of things of a particular type. I explain generic classes in detail in Chapter 13 and you learn about classes for storing collections of things in Chapter 14.

JAVA PROGRAM STRUCTURE

Let's summarize how a Java program is structured:

➤ A Java program always consists of one or more classes.

➤ You put the program code for each class in a separate file, and you must give each file the same name as that of the class that is defined within it.

➤ A Java source file name must have the extension `.java`.

Thus your file containing the class `Hat` is called `Hat.java`, and your file containing the class `BaseballPlayer` must have the file name `BaseballPlayer.java`.

NOTE *You see in Chapter 5 that a class definition can be nested inside another class. This means that a `.java` file can contain the definitions for more than one class type. The file name in such cases is the same as the name of the outer class.*

A typical program consists of several files, as Figure 1-8 illustrates.

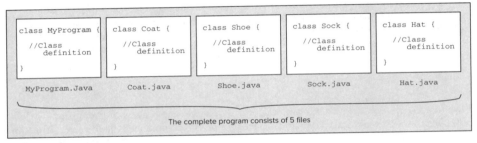

```
class MyProgram {

    //Class
      definition

}
```
MyProgram.Java

```
class Coat {

    //Class
      definition

}
```
Coat.java

```
class Shoe {

    //Class
      definition

}
```
Shoe.java

```
class Sock {

    //Class
      definition

}
```
Sock.java

```
class Hat {

    //Class
      definition

}
```
Hat.java

The complete program consists of 5 files

FIGURE 1-8

The program in Figure 1-8 clearly majors on apparel, with four of the five classes representing clothing. Each source file contains a class definition, and all of the files that go to make up the program are stored in the same directory. The source files for your program contain all the code that you wrote, but this is not everything that is ultimately included in the program. There is also code from the *Java standard class library*, so let's take a peek at what that can do.

Java's Class Library

A library in Java is a collection of classes—usually providing related facilities—that you can use in your programs. The Java class library provides you with a whole range of goodies, some of which are essential for your programs to work at all, and some of which make writing your Java programs easier. To say that the standard class library covers a lot of ground would be something of an understatement, so I won't be going into it in detail here, and this book certainly does not cover it all—you would probably risk a hernia lifting a book that did. However, you learn how to apply many of the most commonly used facilities the Java libraries provide throughout the book.

The class library is a set of classes so it is stored in sets of files where each file contains a class definition. Related classes are grouped together into a set called a *package*, and each package is stored in a separate directory on disk. A class in a package can access any of the other classes in the package. A class in another package may or may not be accessible. You learn more about this in Chapter 5.

A package name is based on the path to the directory in which the classes belonging to the package are stored. Classes in the package `java.lang`, for example, are stored in the directory path `java\lang` (or `java/lang` under UNIX). This path is relative to a particular directory that is automatically known by the Java runtime environment that executes your code. You can also create your own packages that contain classes of your own that you want to reuse in different contexts and that are related in some way.

The JDK includes a growing number of standard packages—well over 200 the last time I counted. To give you some idea of the scale, one package, `java.awt`, contains more than 100 classes. Some of the packages you run into most frequently are listed in Table 1-1.

TABLE 1-1: Frequently Used Standard Packages

PACKAGE NAME	DESCRIPTION
`java.lang`	Classes that support the basic language features and the handling of arrays and strings. Classes in this package are always available directly in your programs by default because this package is always automatically loaded with your program.
`java.io`	Classes for stream input and output operations.
`java.nio.file`	Classes for file input and output.
`java.util`	Utility classes of various kinds, including classes for managing data within collections or groups of data items.
`javax.swing`	These classes provide easy-to-use and flexible components for building graphical user interfaces (GUIs). The components in this package are referred to as *Swing components*.
`java.awt`	Classes in this package provide the original GUI components (JDK 1.1) as well as some basic support necessary for Swing components.
`java.awt.geom`	These classes define two-dimensional geometric shapes.
`java.awt.event`	The classes in this package are used in the implementation of windowed applications to handle events in your program. Events are things such as moving the mouse, pressing the left mouse button, or clicking on a menu item.

You can use any of the classes from the `java.lang` package in your programs by default. To use classes from the other packages, you typically use `import` statements to identify the names of the classes that you need from each package. This enables you to reference the classes by the simple class name. Without an `import` statement you would need to specify the fully qualified name of each class from a package each time you refer to it. As you see in a moment, the fully qualified name for a class includes the package name as well as the basic class name. Using fully qualified class names generally would make your program code rather cumbersome, and certainly less readable. It would also make it a lot more tedious to type in.

You can use an `import` statement to import the name of a single class from a package into your program, or all the class names. The two `import` statements at the beginning of the code for the applet you saw earlier in this chapter are examples of importing a single class name. The first was:

```
import javax.swing.JApplet;
```

This statement imports the `JApplet` class name that is defined in the `javax.swing` package. Formally, the name of the `JApplet` class is not really `JApplet`—it is the fully qualified name `javax.swing.JApplet`. You can use the unqualified name only when you import the class or the complete package containing it into your program. You can still reference a class from a package even if you don't import it, though—you just need to use the full class name, `javax.swing.JApplet`. You could try this out with the applet you saw earlier if you like. Just delete the two import statements from the file and use the full class names in the program. Then recompile it. It should work the same as before. Thus, the fully qualified name for a class is the name of the package in which it is defined, followed by a period, followed by the name given to the class in its definition.

You could import the names of all the classes in the `javax.swing` package with the statement:

```
import javax.swing.*;
```

The asterisk specifies that all the class names in the package are to be imported. Importing just the class names that your source code uses makes compilation more efficient, but when you are using a lot of classes from a package you find it more convenient to import all the names. This saves typing reams of import statements for one thing. I use the * notation to import all the names in a package in many of the working examples in the book to keep the number of lines to a reasonable level. However, there is a downside associated with importing all the names in a package.

If you import just the class names that you need from library packages, you minimize the risk of name collisions. A name collision occurs when a class name that you have imported from a package is identical to a name you have given to one of your own classes. This obviously creates some confusion when you compile your code because the compiler is not able to deduce which class you are referencing when you use the class name. By default, an unadorned class name is taken to be the class in your program. Using the * in an `import` statement to import all the names in a package greatly increases the likelihood of name collisions.

Sometimes name collisions are unavoidable. For example, the name `Action` is used in two different packages for different types. When a name collision occurs, you can use the fully qualified name for either or both of the names that collide to enable the compiler to understand what you are referencing.

 NOTE You read more on how to use `import` statements in Chapter 5, as well as more about how packages are created and used, and you explore the use of classes from the standard packages in considerable depth throughout the book.

The standard classes do not appear directly in files and directories on your hard disk. They are contained in a single compressed file, `rt.jar`, that is stored in the `jre/lib` directory. This directory is created when you install the JDK on your computer. A .jar file is a Java archive—a compressed archive of Java classes. The name `rt` stands for run time because `rt.jar` contains all the classes that comprise Java's core API. The standard classes that your executable program requires are loaded automatically from `rt.jar`, so you don't have to be concerned with it directly at all.

Java Applications

Every Java application contains a class that defines a method called `main()`. The name of the class that contains `main()` is the name that you use as the argument to the Java interpreter when you run an application. You can call the class whatever you want, but the method that is executed first in an application is always called `main()`. When you run your Java application, execution starts with the `main()` method. The `main()` method typically causes methods belonging to other classes to be executed, but the simplest possible Java application program consists of one class containing just the `main()` method. As you see below, the `main()` method has a particular fixed form, and if it is not of the required form, it is not recognized by the Java interpreter as the method where execution starts.

You can see how this works by taking a look at just such a Java program. You need to enter the program code using your favorite Java editor. When you have entered the code, save the file with the same name as that used for the class and with the extension `.java`. For this example the file name is `OurFirstProgram.java`. The code for the program is shown in Figure 1-9.

CONFER PROGRAMMER TO PROGRAMMER ABOUT THIS TOPIC.
Visit p2p.wrox.com

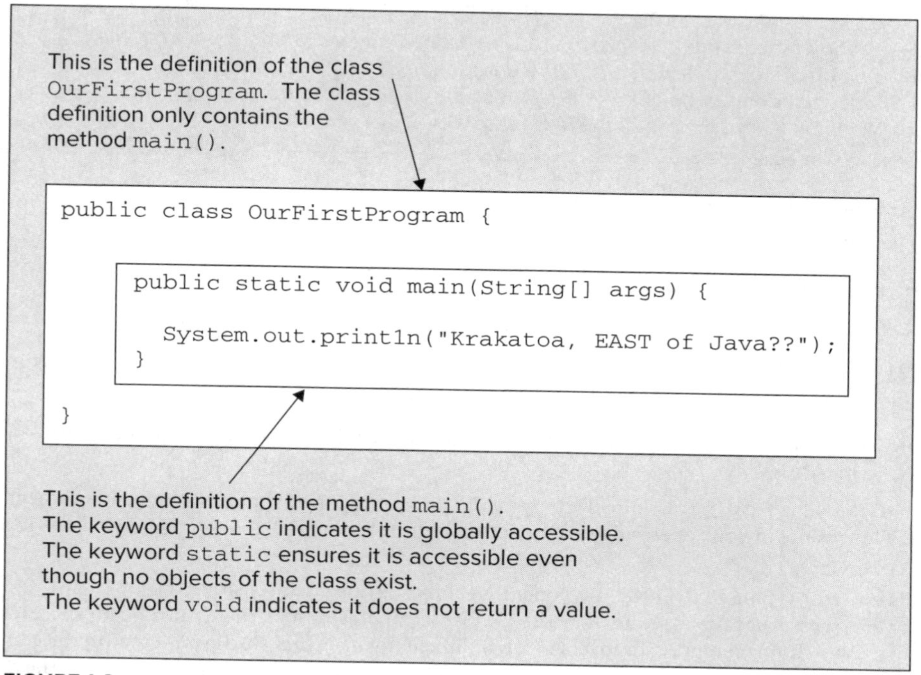

This is the definition of the class
`OurFirstProgram`. The class
definition only contains the
method `main()`.

```java
public class OurFirstProgram {

    public static void main(String[] args) {

        System.out.println("Krakatoa, EAST of Java??");
    }

}
```

This is the definition of the method `main()`.
The keyword `public` indicates it is globally accessible.
The keyword `static` ensures it is accessible even
though no objects of the class exist.
The keyword `void` indicates it does not return a value.

FIGURE 1-9

The program consists of a definition for a class I have called `OurFirstProgram`. The class definition contains only one method, the method `main()`. The first line of the definition for the method `main()` is always of the form:

```java
public static void main(String[] args)
```

The code for the method appears between the pair of curly braces. This version of the method has only one executable statement:

```java
System.out.println("Krakatoa, EAST of Java??");
```

So what does this statement do? Let's work through it from left to right:

➤ `System` is the name of a standard class that contains objects that encapsulate the standard I/O devices for your system—the keyboard for command-line input and command-line output to the display. It is contained in the package `java.lang`, so it is always accessible just by using the simple class name `System`.

➤ The object `out` represents the standard output stream—the command line on your display screen—and is a data member of the class `System`. The member, `out`, is a special kind of member of the `System` class. Like the method `main()` in our `OurFirstProgram` class, it is static. This means that `out` exists even though there are no objects of type `System` (more on this in forthcoming chapters). Using the class name, `System`, separated from the member name `out` by a period—`System.out`—references the `out` member of the class.

➤ The bit at the rightmost end of the statement, `println("Krakatoa, EAST of Java??")`, calls the `println()` method that belongs to the object `out`. It outputs the text string that appears between the parentheses to the command line. This demonstrates one way in which you can call a class method—by using the object name followed by the method name, with a period separating them. The stuff between the parentheses following the name of a method is information that is passed to the method when it is executed. As I said, for `println()` it is the text you want to output to the command line.

> **NOTE** For completeness, the keywords `public`, `static`, and `void` that appear in the method definition are explained briefly in the annotations to the program code in Figure 1-9, but you need not be concerned if these seem a bit obscure at this point. I come back to them in much more detail in Chapter 5.

You can compile this program with the command

```
javac -source 1.7 OurFirstProgram.java
```

or with the `-classpath` option specified:

```
javac -classpath . OurFirstProgram.java
```

or you can just write the following:

```
javac OurFirstProgram.java
```

If it didn't compile, there's something wrong somewhere. Here's a checklist of possible sources of the problem:

➤ The path to the `jdk1.7.0_n\bin` directory is not defined in the string for your `PATH` environment variable. This results in your operating system not being able to find the `javac` compiler that is in that directory.

➤ You made an error typing in the program code. Remember Java is case-sensitive, so `OurfirstProgram` is not the same as `OurFirstProgram`, and of course, there must be no spaces in the class name. If the compiler discovers an error, it usually identifies the line number in the code where the error is found. In general, watch out for confusing zero, 0, with a small letter o, or the digit one, 1, with the small letter l. All characters such as periods, commas, and semicolons in the code are essential and must be in the right place. Parentheses, (), curly braces, {}, and square brackets, [], always come in matching pairs and are not interchangeable.

➤ The source file name must match the class name exactly. The slightest difference results in an error. The file must have the extension `.java`.

After you have compiled the program successfully, you can execute it with the following command:

```
java -ea OurFirstProgram
```

The `-ea` option is not strictly necessary because this program does not use assertions, but if you get used to putting it in, you won't forget it when it is necessary. If you need the `-classpath` option specified, use the following:

```
java -ea -classpath . OurFirstProgram
```

Assuming the source file compiled correctly, and the `jdk1.7.0_n\bin` directory is defined in your path, the most common reason for the program failing to execute is a typographical error in the class name, `OurFirstProgram`. The second most common reason is writing the file name with its extension, `OurFirstProgram.class`, in the command. It should be just the class name, `OurFirstProgram`.

When you run the program, it displays the text

```
Krakatoa, EAST of Java??
```

JAVA AND UNICODE

Programming to support languages that use anything other than the Latin character set has been a major problem historically. There are a variety of 8-bit character sets defined for many national languages, but if you want to combine the Latin character set and Cyrillic in the same context, for example, things can get difficult. If you want to handle Japanese as well, it becomes impossible with an 8-bit character set because with 8 bits you have only 256 different codes, so there just aren't enough character codes to go round.

Unicode is a standard character set that was developed to allow the characters necessary for almost all languages to be encoded. It uses a 16-bit code to represent a character (so each character occupies 2 bytes), and with 16 bits up to 65,535 non-zero character codes can be distinguished. With so many character codes available, there is enough to allocate each major national character set its own set of codes, including character sets such as Kanji, which is used for Japanese and requires thousands of character codes. It doesn't end there though. Unicode supports three encoding forms that allow up to a million additional characters to be represented.

As you see in Chapter 2, Java source code is in Unicode characters. Comments, identifiers (names in other words—see Chapter 2), and character and string literals can all use any characters in the Unicode set that represent letters. Java also supports Unicode internally to represent characters and strings, so the framework is there for a comprehensive international language capability in a program. The normal ASCII set that you are probably familiar with corresponds to the first 128 characters of the Unicode set. Apart from being aware that each character usually occupies 2 bytes, you can ignore the fact that you are handling Unicode characters in the main, unless of course you are building an application that supports multiple languages from the outset.

I say each Unicode character usually occupies 2 bytes because Java supports Unicode 4.0, which allows 32-bit characters called *surrogates*. You might think the set of 64K characters that you can represent with 16 bits would be sufficient, but it isn't. Eastern languages such as Japanese, Korean, and Chinese alone involve more than 70,000 ideographs (an ideograph is a graphical symbol, sometimes called an ideogram). Surrogates are used to represent characters that are not contained within the basic multilingual set that is defined by 16-bit characters.

SUMMARY

In this chapter you've looked at the basic characteristics of Java, and how portability between different computers is achieved. I have also introduced you to the elements of object-oriented programming. There are bound to be some aspects of what I've discussed that you don't feel are completely clear to you. Don't worry about it. Everything I have discussed here I revisit again in more detail later in the book.

CONFER PROGRAMMER TO PROGRAMMER ABOUT THIS TOPIC.
⟹ Visit p2p.wrox.com ⟸

▶ WHAT YOU LEARNED IN THIS CHAPTER

TOPIC	CONCEPT
Applets and Applications	Java applets are programs that are designed to be embedded in an HTML document. Java applications are standalone programs. Java applications can be console programs that only support text output to the command line, or they can be window-based applications with a GUI.
Object-Oriented Programs	Java programs are intrinsically object-oriented. Object-oriented programs are implemented in terms of problem-specific types of data rather that primitive types such as characters and numerical values.
Classes	A class is a definition of a particular type of object. A class contains specifications for the type of data needed to define an object of the type and defines the operations that you can carry out on objects.
Class Methods	A class method is a block of code within a class definition that specifies an operation for an object of the class type.
Constructors	A constructor is a special kind of method within a class definition that can create objects of the class type.
Java Source Files	Java source code is stored in files with the extension `.java`.
Compiled Java Code	Java programs are compiled to bytecodes, which are instructions for the .JVM. The JVM is the same on all the computers on which it is implemented, thus ensuring the portability of Java programs.
Java Object Code Files	Java object code is stored in files with the extension `.class`.
Java Program Execution	Java programs are executed by the Java interpreter, which analyzes the bytecodes and carries out the operations they specify.
Unicode	Unicode is a 16-bit character encoding that enables multiple national language character sets to be supported. Java source programs are represented internally as Unicode and Java supports programming applications with multilingual capability.

RESOURCES

You can download the source code for the examples in this book from www.wrox.com.

The source code download includes ancillary files, such as .gif files containing icons, for example, where they are used in the examples. I also include the solutions to the exercises that appear at the end of most chapters.

YOU CAN DOWNLOAD THE CODE FOUND IN THIS BOOK. VISIT WROX.COM AND SEARCH FOR ISBN 9780470404140.

2

Programs, Data, Variables, and Calculation

WHAT YOU WILL LEARN IN THIS CHAPTER:

➤ How to declare and define variables of the basic integer and floating-point types

➤ How to write an assignment statement

➤ How integer and floating-point expressions are evaluated

➤ How to output data from a console program

➤ How mixed integer and floating-point expressions are evaluated

➤ What casting is and when you must use it

➤ What boolean variables are

➤ What determines the sequence in which operators in an expression are executed

➤ How to include comments in your programs

In this chapter you look at the entities in Java that are not objects—numbers and characters. This gives you all the elements of the language you need to perform numerical calculations, and you apply these in a few working examples.

DATA AND VARIABLES

A *variable* is a named piece of memory that you use to store information in your Java program—an item of data of some description. Each named piece of memory that you define can only store data of one particular type. If you define a variable to store integers, for example, you can't use it to store a value that is a decimal fraction, such as 0.75. If you've defined a variable that you use to refer to a Hat object, you can only use it to reference an object of type Hat (or any of its subclasses, as you will see in Chapter 6). Because the type of data that each variable can store is fixed, the compiler can verify that each variable you define in your program is not used in a manner or a context that is inappropriate to its type. If a method in your program is supposed to process integers, the compiler is able to detect when you inadvertently try to use the method with some other kind of data, for example, a string or a numerical value that is not integral.

Explicit data values that appear in your program are called *literals*. Each literal is also of a particular type: 25, for example, is an integer literal of type int. I will go into the characteristics of the various types of literals that you can use as I discuss each variable type.

Before you can use a variable you must specify its name and type in a declaration statement. First consider what flexibility you have in choosing a name for a variable.

Naming Your Variables

The name that you choose for a variable, or indeed the name that you choose for anything in Java, is called an *identifier*. An identifier can be any length, but it must start with a letter, an underscore (_), or a dollar sign ($). The rest of an identifier can include any characters except those used as operators in Java (such as +, -, or *), but you are generally better off if you stick to letters, digits, and the underscore character.

Java is case sensitive, so the names `republican` and `Republican` are not the same. You must not include blanks or tabs in the middle of a name, so `Betty May` is out, but you could have `BettyMay` or even `Betty_May`. Note that you can't have `6Pack` as a name because you cannot start a name with a numeric digit. Of course, you could use `sixPack` as an alternative.

Subject to the restrictions I have mentioned, you can name a variable almost anything you like, except for two additional restraints: you can't use a *keyword* as a name for something, and a name can't be anything that could be interpreted as a constant value—as a literal in other words. Keywords are words that are part of the Java language. You saw some keywords in the previous chapter, and you will learn a few more in this chapter. If you'd like to know what they all are now, see the complete list in Appendix A. The restriction on constant values is there because, although it is obvious why a name can't be 1234 or 37.5, constants can also be alphabetic, such as `true` and `false`, which are literals of the type `boolean`. Of course, the basic reason for these rules is that the compiler has to be able to distinguish between your variables and other things that can appear in a program. If you try to use a name for a variable that makes this impossible, then it's not a legal name.

Clearly, it makes sense to choose names for your variables that give a good indication of the sort of data they hold. If you want to record the size of a hat, for example, `hatSize` is a good choice for the variable name whereas `qqq` would be a bad choice. It is a common convention in Java to start variable names with a lowercase letter and, where you have a name that combines several words, to capitalize the first letter of each word, as in `hatSize` or `moneyWellSpent`. You are in no way obliged to follow this convention, but because almost all the Java world does, it helps to do so.

> **NOTE** *If you feel you need more guidance in naming conventions (and coding conventions in general) take a look at* `www.oracle.com/technetwork/java/codeconv-138413.html`.

Variable Names and Unicode

Even though you may be entering your Java programs in an environment that stores ASCII characters, all Java source code is in Unicode. Although the original source code that you create may be ASCII, it is converted to Unicode characters internally, before it is compiled. Although you can write any Java language statement using ASCII, the fact that Java supports Unicode provides you with immense flexibility. It means that the identifiers that you use in your source program can use any national language character set that is defined within the Unicode character set, so your programs can use French, Greek, or Russian variable names, for example, or even names in several different languages, as long as you have the means to enter them in the first place. The same applies to character data that your program defines.

> **NOTE** *The Java compiler assumes that your source code is in the default character encoding for the environment in which you are working. If it is not, you must specify the* -encoding *option to tell the compiler about the character encoding for you source code. For example, if you have created the source file* Test.java *in Unicode, you can compile it with the following command:*
>
> ```
> javac.exe -encoding unicode JavaTest.java
> ```

Variables and Types

As I mentioned earlier, each variable that you declare can store values only of a type consistent with the data type of that variable. You specify the type of a particular variable by using a type name in the variable declaration. For instance, here's a statement that declares a variable that can store integers:

```
int numberOfCats;
```

The data type in this case is `int` and the variable name is `numberOfCats`. The semicolon marks the end of the statement. The variable, `numberOfCats`, can only store values of type `int`. Of course, `int` is a keyword.

Many of your variables will be used to reference objects, but let's leave those on one side for the moment as they have some special properties. The only things in Java that are not objects are variables that correspond to one of eight basic data types, defined within the language. These fundamental types are referred to as *primitive types*, and they enable you to define variables for storing data that fall into one of three categories:

➤ Numeric values, which can be either integer or floating-point

➤ A single Unicode character

➤ Logical values that can be `true` or `false`

All of the type names for the basic variable types are keywords in Java so you must not use them for other purposes. Let's take a closer look at each of the primitive data types and get a feel for how you can use them.

INTEGER DATA TYPES

There are four types of variables that you can use to store integer data. All of these are signed—that is, they can store both negative and positive values. The four integer types differ in the range of values they can store, so the choice of type for a variable depends on the range of data values you are likely to need.

The four integer types in Java are shown in Table 2-1:

TABLE 2-1: Java Integer Types

DATA TYPE	DESCRIPTION
byte	Variables of this type can have values from −128 to +127 and occupy 1 byte (8 bits) in memory
short	Variables of this type can have values from −32768 to 32767 and occupy 2 bytes (16 bits) in memory
int	Variables of this type can have values from −2147483648 to 2147483647 and occupy 4 bytes (32 bits) in memory
long	Variables of this type can have values from −9223372036854775808 to 9223372036854775807 and occupy 8 bytes (64 bits) in memory

Although I said that the choice of type depends on the range of values that you want to be able to store, in practice you'll be using variables of type `int` or type `long` to store integers most of the time, for reasons that I explain a little later. Let's take a look at declarations for variables of each of these types:

```
byte   smallerValue;
short  pageCount;
int    wordCount;
long   bigValue;
```

Each of these statements declares a variable of the type specified.

The range of values that can be stored by each integer type in Java is shown in the preceding table and this is always the same, regardless of what kind of computer you are using. This is also true of the other primitive types that you will see later in this chapter. This has the rather useful effect that your program executes in the same way on computers that might be quite different. This is not necessarily the case with other programming languages.

Of course, although I have expressed the range of possible values for each type as decimal values, integers are stored internally as binary numbers, and it is the number of bits available to store each type that determines the maximum and minimum values, as shown in Figure 2-1.

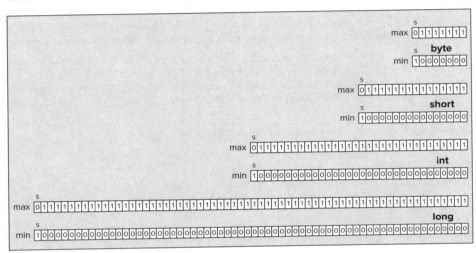

FIGURE 2-1

For each of the binary numbers shown in Figure 2-1, the leftmost bit is the sign bit, marked with an *s*. When the sign bit is 0 the number is positive, and when it is 1 the number is negative. Negative binary numbers are represented in what is called *2's complement form*. If you are not familiar with this, you can find an explanation of how it works in Appendix B.

Integer Literals

Before you use integer variables you need to understand how you write integer values of various types. As I said earlier, a value of any kind in Java is referred to as a literal. So 1, 10.5, and "This is text" are all examples of literals.

Integer literals can be of type int or type long. Any integer literal that you specify as a sequence of decimal digits is of type int by default. Thus 1, −9999, and 123456789 are all literals of type int. If you want to define an integer literal of type long, you need to append an L to the value. The values 1L, −9999L, and 123456789L are all of type long. You could use a lowercase letter *l*, but don't—it is too easily confused with the digit *1*.

Very large integer literals with lots of digits can be difficult to read; you can make such literals more readable by separating groups of digits using the underline character in the way you use a comma to separate groups of digits when writing numbers outside of programming. For example, you can write the value 1,234,567,890 as the literal 1234567899L or as the literal 1_234_567_890L. You could also use multiple underscores in sequence if you feel it is necessary: 1__234__567__890L. Underscores can only appear interior to a literal, so each set of one or more underlines in a literal must be bounded by digits both sides; putting them anywhere else results in a compiler error message. As you will see later in this chapter, you can use underscores in other kinds of numeric literals too.

You are perhaps wondering how you specify literals of type byte or short. You can't. Because of the way integer arithmetic works in Java, they just aren't necessary in the main. You see a couple of instances where an integer literal may be interpreted by the compiler as type byte or short later in this chapter, but these situations are the exception.

You can write integer literals in four different ways:

- ➤ As decimal values that are numbers to base 10
- ➤ As hexadecimal values that are numbers to base 16
- ➤ As binary values that are numbers to base 2
- ➤ As octal values that are numbers to base 8

You have seen how to write decimal integer literals. Let's look at the others.

Hexadecimal Literals

Hexadecimal literals in Java have *0x* or *0X* in front of them and follow the usual convention of using the letters *A* to *F* (or *a* to *f*) to represent digits with values 10 to 15, respectively. In case you are a little rusty on hexadecimal values, here are some examples:

0x100 is $(1 \times 16^2) + (0 \times 16^1) + (0 \times 16^0)$ which is 256 in decimal.

0x1234 is $(1 \times 16^3) + (2 \times 16^2) + (3 \times 16^1) + (4 \times 16^0)$ which is 4660 in decimal.

0xDEAF is $(13 \times 16^3) + (14 \times 16^2) + (10 \times 16^1) + (15 \times 16^0)$ which is 57007 in decimal.

0xCAB is $(12 \times 16^2) + (10 \times 16^1) + (11 \times 16^0)$ which is 3243 in decimal.

If you are not familiar with hexadecimal numbers, you can find an explanation of how these work in Appendix B. All the hexadecimal literals in the preceding table are of type `int`. If you want to specify a hexadecimal literal of type `long`, you must append *L* to the literal just as with decimal literals. For example, 0xFL is a hexadecimal literal that is equivalent to the decimal value 15. Of course, you can write a literal such as 0xAABBCCD9L as 0xAABB_CCD9L. The underscore character here separates the hexadecimal digits into groups of four. Each group of four hexadecimal digits corresponds to 2 bytes in memory. As with decimal integer literals, underscores can only appear between digits in hexadecimal literals so 0x_3ABC and 0x3ABC_ are both errors.

Binary Literals

It is sometimes convenient to specify an integer literal as a binary value. Placing `0b` or `0B` in front of a literal identifies it as a binary number. In this case the digits can only be 0 or 1. For example, 0b110010101011 or 0B110010101011 is the same value as 0xCAB or the decimal value 3243. You can use the underline character in binary literals too, so you could also write the value as 0b1100_1010_1011, which is much easier to read. Each group of four binary digits corresponds to one hexadecimal digit. Of course, binary literals can also be of type `long`; you just append an L to the number. 0b_1000 and 0b1000_ are both errors because underscores can only appear between digits.

Octal Literals

You write literals that are octal numbers with a leading zero so 035 and 067 are examples of octal numbers of type `int` and 0777777L is an octal literal of type `long`. The latter could also be written 0777_777L. Octal numbers can only use the digits 0 to 7 and each octal digit defines 3 bits. Octal numbers were used frequently in the days when machines used words of lengths that were a multiple of 3 bits to store a number.

You will rarely find it necessary to use octal numbers these days, but you should take care not to use them by accident. If you put a leading zero at the start of an integer literal, the Java compiler thinks you are specifying an octal value. Unless one of the digits is greater than 7, which results in the compiler flagging it as an error, you won't know that you have done this and the value will not be what you think it is.

Declaring Integer Variables

As you saw earlier, you can declare a variable of type `long` with the statement:

```
long bigOne;
```

This statement is a declaration for the variable `bigOne`. This specifies that the variable `bigOne` stores a value of type `long`. When this statement is compiled, 8 bytes of memory are allocated for the variable `bigOne`. Java does not automatically initialize a variable such as this. If you want your variables to have an initial value rather than a junk value left over from when the memory was last used, you must specify your own value in the declaration. To declare and initialize the variable `bigOne` to 2,999,999,999, you just write:

```
long bigOne = 2_999_999_999L;
```

The variable is set to the value following the equal sign. It is good practice to always initialize your variables when you declare them. I inserted underlines to make the literal easier to read. Note that if you try to use a variable in a calculation that has not had a value assigned to it, your program does not compile. There are also circumstances where the compiler cannot determine whether or not a variable has been initialized before it is used if you don't initialize it when you declare it, even though it may be obvious to you that it has been. This is also flagged as an error, but if you get into the habit of always initializing variables when you declare them, you can avoid all of these problems.

You can declare a variable just about anywhere in your program, but you must declare each variable before you use it in a calculation. The placement of the declaration has an effect on whether a particular variable is accessible at a given point in a program, and we look deeper into the significance of this in the next chapter. Broadly, you should group related variable declarations together, immediately before the code that uses them.

You can declare and define multiple variables in a single statement. For example:

```
long bigOne = 999_999_999L, largeOne = 100_000_000L;
```

Here I have declared two variables of type `long`. A comma separates each variable from the next. You can declare as many variables as you like in a single statement, although it is usually better to stick to declaring one variable in each statement as it helps to make your programs easier to read. A possible exception occurs with variables that are closely related—an (x,y) coordinate pair representing a point, for example, which you might reasonably declare as the following:

```
int xCoord = 0, yCoord = 0;       // Point coordinates
```

On the same line as the declaration of these two variables, I have a comment following the double slash, explaining what the variables are about. The compiler ignores everything from the double slash (//) until the end of the line. Explaining the purpose of your variables in comments is a good habit to get into, as it can be quite surprising how something that was as clear as crystal when you wrote it transmogrifies into something as clear as mud a few weeks later. You can add comments to your programs in other ways that you see a little later in this chapter.

You can also spread a single declaration over several lines if you want. This also can help to make your program more readable. For example:

```
int miles    = 0,       // One mile is 8 furlongs
    furlongs = 0,       // One furlong is 220 yards
    yards    = 0,       // One yard is 3 feet
    feet     = 0;
```

This defines four variables of type `int` in a single statement with the names `miles`, `furlongs`, `yards`, and `feet`. Each variable has 0 as its initial value. Naturally, you must be sure that an initializing value for a variable is within the range of the type concerned; otherwise, the compiler complains. Your compiler is intelligent enough to recognize that you can't get a quart into a pint pot or, alternatively, a very large `long` constant into a variable of type `int`, `short`, or `byte`. Because the statement is spread over four lines, I am able to add a comment on each of the first three lines to explain something about the variable that appears on it.

To complete the set of variables that store integers, you can declare and initialize a variable of type `byte` and one of type `short` with the following two statements:

```
byte luckyNumber = 7;
short smallNumber = 1234;
```

Here the compiler can deduce that the integer literals are to be of type `byte` and `short`, respectively, and can convert the literals to the appropriate type. It is your responsibility to make sure the initial value fits within the range of the variable that you are initializing. If it doesn't, the compiler rejects the statement and outputs an error message.

Most of the time you will find that variables of type `int` will cover your needs for dealing with integers, with type `long` being necessary now and again when you have some really big integer values to deal with. Variables of type `byte` and `short` do save a little memory, but unless you have a lot of values of these types to store, that is, values with a very limited range, they won't save enough to be worth worrying about. They also introduce complications when you use them in calculations, as you will see shortly, so generally you should not use them unless it is absolutely necessary. Of course, when you are reading data from some external source, a disk file for instance, you need to make the type of variable for each data value correspond to what was written originally.

FLOATING-POINT DATA TYPES

Numeric values that are not integral are stored as *floating-point* numbers. A floating-point number has a fixed number of digits of accuracy but a very wide range of values. You get a wide range of values, even though the number of digits is fixed, because the decimal point can "float." For example the values 0.000005, 500.0, and 5,000,000,000,000.0 can be written as 5×10^{-6}, 5×10^{2}, and 5×10^{12} respectively—you have just one significant digit 5, but you get three different numbers by moving the decimal point around.

There are two primitive binary floating-point types in Java: type `float` and type double, described in Table 2-2. These give you a choice in the number of digits available to represent your data values, and in the range of values that can be accommodated.

TABLE 2-2: Java Primitive Binary Floating-Point Types

DATA TYPE	DESCRIPTION
float	Variables of this type can have values from −3.4E38 (-3.4×10^{38}) to +3.4E38 ($+3.4 \times 10^{38}$) and occupy 4 bytes in memory. Values are represented with approximately 7 decimal digits accuracy. The smallest non-zero `float` value that you can have is approximately 1.4×10^{-45}.
double	Variables of this type can have values from −1.7E308 (-1.7×10^{308}) to +1.7E308 ($+1.7 \times 10^{308}$) and occupy 8 bytes in memory. Values are represented with approximately 17 decimal digits accuracy. The smallest non-zero `double` value that you can have is approximately 4.9×10^{-324}.

The number of digits in representing a floating-point value is called its *precision*.

NOTE *All floating-point operations and the definitions for values of type* `float` *and type* `double` *conform to the IEEE 754 standard.*

As with integer calculations, floating-point calculations in Java produce the same results on any computer.

Floating-Point Literals

Floating-point literals are of type `double` by default, so 1.0 and 345.678 are both of type `double`. When you want to specify a value of type `float`, you just append an *f*, or an *F*, to the value, so 1.0f and 345.678F are both literals of type `float`. A literal of type `double` can have *d* or *D* appended to it, but this is rarely used in practice. You can use underlines to make floating point literals clearer so you can write 12345678.75 as 12_345_678.75. You can also use underlines to the right of the decimal point if you think it helps, so you can write 7.123456789 as 7.123_456_789. However, 1_.234 and 1._234 are errors.

When you need to write very large or very small floating-point values, you usually want to write them with an exponent—that is, as a decimal value multiplied by a power of 10. You can do this in Java by writing the number as a decimal value followed by an *E*, or an *e*, preceding the power of 10 that you require. For example, the distance from Earth to the sun is approximately 149,600,000 kilometers, more conveniently written as 1.496E8. Because the *E* (or *e*) indicates that what follows is the exponent, this is equivalent to 1.496×10^8. At the opposite end of the scale, the mass of an electron is around 0.00000000000000000000000000009 grams. This is much more convenient, not to say more readable, when it is written as 9.0E−28 grams.

Declaring Floating-Point Variables

You declare floating-point variables in a similar way to what you've already used for integers. You can declare and initialize a variable of type `double` with the following statement:

```
double sunDistance = 1.496E8;
```

This declares the variable with the name `sunDistance` and initializes it with the appropriate value.

Declaring a variable of type `float` is much the same. For example:

```
float electronMass = 9E-28F;
```

This defines and initializes the variable `electronMass`.

You can, of course, declare more than one variable of a given type in a single statement:

```
float hisWeight = 185.2F, herWeight = 108.5F;
```

Remember that you must put the *F* or *f* at the end of literals of type `float`. If you leave it out, the literal is of type `double`, and the compiler won't automatically convert it to type `float`.

FIXING THE VALUE OF A VARIABLE

Sometimes you declare and initialize a variable with a value that should never change, for example:

```
int feet_per_yard = 3;
double mm_per_inch = 25.4;
```

Both these values should be fixed. There are always 3 feet to a yard, and an inch is always 25.4 millimeters. Although they are fixed values for which you could use a literal in calculations, it is very convenient to store them in a variable because using suitable names makes it clear in your program what they mean. If you use the value 3 in your program code it could mean anything—but the name `feet_per_yard` leaves no doubt as to what it is.

Generally you want to prevent the values of these variables from being modified. Accidental changes to the number of feet in a yard could make the results of your program suspect, to say the least. Java provides you with a way to fix the value of any variable by using the `final` keyword when you declare it, for example:

```
final int FEET_PER_YARD = 3;      // Constant values
final double MM_PER_INCH = 25.4;  // that cannot be changed
```

The `final` keyword specifies that the value of a variable is final and must not be changed. The compiler checks your code for any violations of this and flags them as errors. I've used uppercase letters for the names of the variables here because it is a convention in Java to write constants in this way. This makes it easy to see which variables are defined as constant values. Obviously, any variable you declare as final must have an initial value assigned as you can't specify it later.

Now that you know how to declare and initialize variables of the basic types, you are nearly ready to write a program. You just need to look at how you express the calculations you want carried out, and how you store the results.

ARITHMETIC CALCULATIONS

You store the result of a calculation in a variable by using an *assignment statement*. An assignment statement consists of three elements: the name of the variable where you want the result stored; the assignment operator, =, that indicates that this is indeed an assignment operation; and an arithmetic expression that defines the calculation you want to perform to produce the result. The whole thing is terminated by a semicolon that marks the end of the assignment statement. Here's a simple example of an assignment statement:

```
numFruit = numApples + numOranges;      // Calculate the total fruit
```

When this statement executes, the value of the expression to the right of the assignment operator, =, is calculated, and the result is stored in the variable that appears to the left of the = sign. In this case, the values stored in the variables numApples and numOranges are added together, and the result is stored in the variable numFruit. Of course, you have to declare and initialize all three variables before using this assignment statement.

Incrementing a variable by a given amount is a common requirement in programming. Look at the following assignment statement:

```
numApples = numApples + 1;
```

The result of evaluating the expression on the right of the = is one more than the value of numApples. This result is stored back in the variable numApples, so the overall effect of executing the statement is to increment the value in numApples by 1. You will see an alternative, more concise, way of producing the same effect shortly.

You can write multiple assignments in a single statement. Suppose you have three variables a, b, and c that you have defined to be of type int, and you want to set all three to 777. You can do this with the following statement:

```
a = b = c = 777;
```

Note that an assignment is different from initializing a variable in a declaration. Initialization causes a variable to have the value of the constant that you specify when it is created. An assignment involves copying data from one place in memory to another. For the preceding assignment statement, the compiler allocates some memory (4 bytes) to store the constant 777 as type int. This value is then copied to the variable c. The value in c is extracted and copied to b. Finally the value in b is copied to a. (However, strictly speaking, the compiler may optimize these assignments when it compiles the code to reduce the inefficiency of performing successive assignments of the same value in the way I have described.)

With simple assignments of a constant value to a variable of type short or byte, the constant is stored as the type of the variable on the left of the =, rather than type int. For example:

```
short value = 0;
value = 10;
```

Here you have a declaration statement for the variable value, followed by an assignment statement. When the declaration executes, it allocates space for the variable value and arranges for its initial value to be 0. The assignment statement that follows the declaration statement needs to have 10 available as an integer literal of type short, occupying 2 bytes, because value is of type short. The compiler converts the literal value 10, which is of type int, to type short. The value 10 is then copied to the variable value.

Now let's look in more detail at how you perform calculations with integers.

Integer Calculations

The basic operators you use in calculations involving integers are +, −, *, and /, and these have the usual meanings—add, subtract, multiply, and divide, respectively. (The % operator is also a basic operator and I'll discuss that later in this chapter.) Each of these is a *binary* operator; that is, they combine two operands to produce a result. 2 + 3, for example, results in 5. An *operand* is just the term for a value to which an operator is applied. The priority or precedence that applies when an expression using these operators is evaluated is the same as you learned at school, so multiplication and division operations are executed before any addition or subtraction. Evaluating the expression

```
20 - 3 * 3 - 9 / 3
```

produces the value 8 because it is equivalent to 20 − 9 − 3.

As you also have learned in school, you can use parentheses in arithmetic calculations to change the sequence of operations. Expressions within parentheses are always evaluated first, starting with the innermost set of parentheses when they are nested. You use parentheses to override the default sequence of operations. Therefore the expression

```
(20 − 3) × (3 − 9) / 3
```

is equivalent to 17 * (−6) / 3, which results in −34.

Of course, you use these operators with variables that store integer values as well as integer literals. You could calculate a value to be stored in a variable, `area`, of type `int` from values stored in the variables `length` and `width`, also of type `int`, by writing the following:

```
area = length * width;
```

As I said earlier, these arithmetic operators are binary operators, so called because they require two operands. There are also *unary* versions of the + and – operators that apply to a single operand to the right of the operator. Note that the unary – operator is not just a sign, as in a literal such as -345; it is an operator that has an effect. When applied to a variable, it results in a value that has the opposite sign to that of the value stored in the variable. For example, if the variable `count` has the value -10, the expression `-count` has the value +10. Of course, applying the unary + operator to the value of a variable results in the same value.

Let's try out some simple arithmetic in a working application.

TRY IT OUT Apples and Oranges

Key in the code for this example and save it in a file with the name `Fruit.java`. Remember from the previous chapter that each source file contains a class definition, and that the name of the file is the same as that of the class with the extension `.java`. Store the file in a directory that is separate from the hierarchy containing the JDK. You can give the directory any name that you want, even the name `Fruit` if that helps to identify the program that it contains.

Available for download on Wrox.com

```
public class Fruit {
  public static void main(String[] args) {
    // Declare and initialize three variables
    int numOranges = 5;                          // Count of oranges
    int numApples = 10;                          // Count of apples
    int numFruit = 0;                            // Count of fruit

    numFruit = numOranges + numApples;           // Calculate the total fruit count

    // Display the result
    System.out.println("A totally fruity program");
    System.out.println("Total fruit is " + numFruit);
  }
}
```

code snippet Fruit.java

In some Java development environments, the output may not be displayed long enough for you to see it when you run the program. If this is the case, you can add a few lines of code to get the program to wait until you press Enter before it ends. The additional lines to do this are shown bolded in the following listing:

Available for download on Wrox.com

```
import java.io.IOException;  // For code that delays ending the program
public class FruitWait {
  public static void main(String[] args) {
    // Declare and initialize three variables
    int numOranges = 5;                  // Count of oranges
    int numApples = 10;                  // Count of apples
    int numFruit = 0;                    // Count of fruit

    numFruit = numOranges + numApples;   // Calculate the total fruit count
    // Display the result
    System.out.println("A totally fruity program");
```

```
      System.out.println("Total fruit is " + numFruit);
      // Code to delay ending the program
      System.out.println("(press Enter to exit)");
      try {
        System.in.read();              // Read some input from the keyboard
      } catch (IOException e) {         // Catch the input exception
        return;                         // and just return
      }
    }
  }
```

code snippet FruitWait.java

I have changed the class name from `Fruit` to `FruitWait` to distinguish it from the previous version of the program. The file `FruitWait.java` is in the code download for the book. I won't go into this extra code here. If you need to, just put it in for the moment. You will learn exactly how it works later in the book.

How It Works

The stuff between the parentheses following `main`—that is `String[] args`—provides a means of accessing data that passed to the program from the command line when you run it. I go into this in detail later in the book so you can just ignore it for now, though you must always include it in the first line of `main()`. If you don't, the program compiles but doesn't execute.

All that additional code in the body of the `main()` method in the `FruitWait.java` version just waits until you press Enter before ending the program. If necessary, you can include this in all of your console programs at each point in the code where the program terminates to make sure they don't disappear before you can read the output. It won't make any difference to how the rest of the program works. I will defer discussing in detail what is happening in the bit of code that I have added until I get to explaining exceptions in Chapter 7.

If you run the `FruitWait.java` version of this program, the output is the following:

```
A totally fruity program
Total fruit is 15
(press Enter to exit)
```

The original version does not output the third line.

The basic elements of the code in the original version of the program are shown in Figure 2-2:

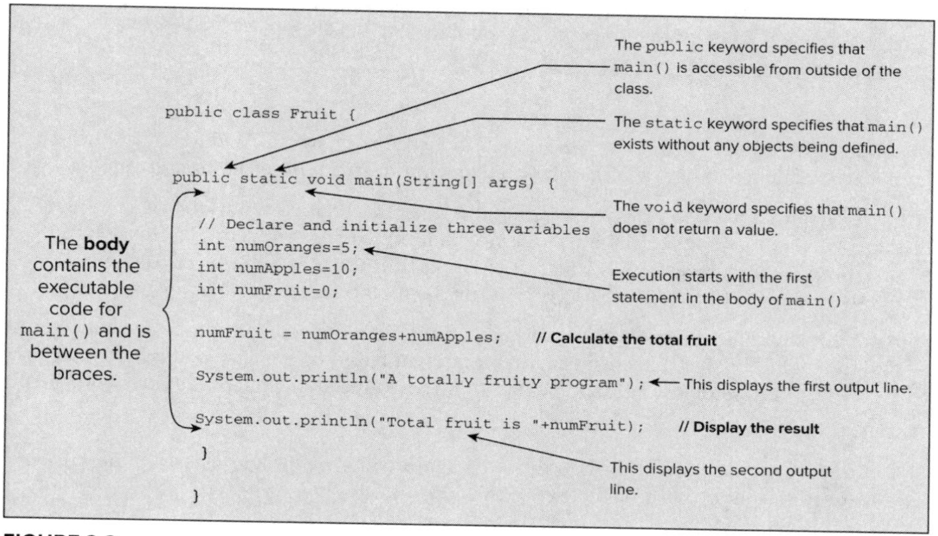

FIGURE 2-2

The original version of the program consists of just one class, `Fruit`, and just one method, `main()`. Execution of an application always starts at the first executable statement in the method `main()`. There are no objects of the class `Fruit` defined, but the method `main()` can still be executed because I have specified it as `static`. The method `main()` is always specified as `public` and `static` and with the return type `void`. The effects of these three keywords on the method are as follows:

`public`	Specifies that the method is accessible from outside the `Fruit` class.
`static`	Specifies that the method is a class method that is to be executable, even though no class objects have been created. (Methods that are not static can be executed only for a particular object of the class, as you will see in Chapter 5.)
`void`	Specifies that the method does not return a value.

Don't worry if these are not completely clear to you at this point—you see them all again later.

The first three statements in `main()` declare the variables `numOranges`, `numApples`, and `numFruit` to be of type `int` and initialize them to the values 5, 10, and 0 respectively. The next statement adds the values stored in `numOranges` and `numApples`, and stores the result, 15, in the variable `numFruit`. We then generate some output from the program.

Producing Output

The next two statements use the `println()` method, which displays text output. The statement looks a bit complicated, but it breaks down quite simply, as Figure 2-3 shows.

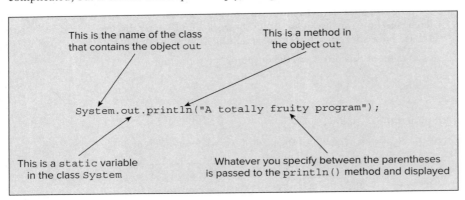

FIGURE 2-3

The text between double quotes, `"A totally fruity program"`, is a character string. Whenever you need a string constant, you just put the sequence of characters that you want in the string between double quotes.

You can see from the annotations in Figure 2-3 how you execute methods that belong to an object. Here you execute the method `println()`, which belongs to the object `out`, which, in turn, is a variable that is a static member of the class `System`. Because the object `out` is static, it exists even if there are no objects of type `System` in existence. This is analogous to the use of the keyword `static` for the method `main()`.

Most objects in a program are not static members of a class though, so calling a method for an object typically just involves the object name and the method name. For instance, if you guessed based on the last example that to call the `putHatOn()` method for an object `cowboyHat` of the type `Hat` that I introduced in Chapter 1, you would write

```
cowboyHat.putHatOn();
```

you would be right. Don't worry if you didn't though. I go into this again when we look at classes in detail. For the moment, any time you want to output something as text to the console, you just write

```
System.out.println( whateverYouWantToDisplay );
```

with whatever character string you want to display plugged in between the parentheses.

Thus, the second statement in the example

```
System.out.println("Total fruit is " + numFruit);
```

outputs the character string "Total fruit is" followed by the value of `numFruit` converted to a character string, that is "15". So what's the + doing here—it's obviously not arithmetic we are doing, is it? The addition operator has a special effect when used with operands that are character strings—it joins them together to produce a single string. But `numFruit` is not a string, is it? No, but the left operand, `"Total fruit is "` is, and this causes the compiler to decide that the whole thing is an expression working on character strings. Therefore, the compiler inserts code that converts the value of the right operand, `numFruit`, to a character string to be compatible with the left operand. The effect of the + operation is to tack the string representation of the value of `numFruit` on to the end of the string `"Total fruit is "`. The composite string is then passed to the `println()` method to display it on your screen. Dashed clever, these compilers.

If you want to output the value of `numOranges` as well, you could write the following:

```
System.out.println("Total fruit is " + numFruit + " and oranges = " + numOranges);
```

Try it out by adding it to the program if you like. You should get this output:

```
Total fruit is 15 and oranges = 5
```

Integer Division and Remainders

When you divide one integer by another and the result is not exact, any remainder is discarded, so the final result is always an integer. The division 3 / 2, for example, produces the result 1, and 11 / 3 produces the result 3. This makes it easy to divide a given quantity equally among a given number of recipients. To divide `numFruit` equally between four children, you could write:

```
int numFruitEach = 0;        // Number of fruit for each child
numFruitEach = numFruit/4;
```

The result of division when the operands are positive is fairly obvious. It's the result of dividing the right operand, called the *divisor*, into the left operand, referred to as the *dividend*, a whole number of times. The situation when either or both operands are negative deserves a little more exploration.

If you divide 7 by −3, the result is −2. Similarly, if you divide −10 by 4 the result is −2. If you divide −5 by −3 the result is +1. The magnitude of the result of dividing a value *a* by a value *b* is the same, regardless of the sign of the operands, but the sign of the result depends on the sign of the operands. The sign of the result is positive when the operands both have the same sign and negative when the operands are of different signs and the divisor is not greater than the dividend (in which case the result is zero). There is one peculiar exception to this. When the divisor is a negative integer of the largest possible magnitude and the divisor is −1, the result is the same as the dividend, which is negative and therefore violates the rule. You can see why this is so by considering specifics.

The value −2_147_483_648 is the negative value of type int that has the largest magnitude. Dividing this by −1 should result in the value +2_147_483_648, but the largest positive integer you can have as type int is 2_147_483_647, so this result cannot be represented as type int. Therefore, the result is arbitrarily the original dividend, −2_147_483_648.

Dividing by zero is something you should avoid. If you accidentally cause this to be attempted, your program terminates because an exception of type `ArithmeticException` is thrown. You will learn what exceptions are and what you can do about them in Chapter 7.

Of course, there are circumstances where you may want to obtain the remainder after a division, and on these occasions you can calculate the remainder using the modulus operator, %. If you wanted to know how many fruit were left after dividing the total by 4, you could write the following:

```
int remainder = 0;
remainder = numFruit%4;        // Calculate the remainder after division by 4
```

When either or both operands to the remainder operator are negative, the result may not seem to be obvious. Keep in mind, though, that it is related to the divide operation, so if you can work out what the result of a division is, you can deduce the result of the remainder operation. You can get a clear idea of what happens by considering a few examples.

The result of the operation 8 % (−3) is +2. This is evident if you recall that from the earlier discussion of division you know that the result of 8 / (−3) is −2. If you multiply the result of the division by the divisor, (−2) * (−3), the result is +6, so a remainder of +2 makes sense. The expression (−8) % 3 produces −2, which again, you can deduce from the result of (−8) / 3 being −2. You have to add −2 to the result of (−2) * 3 to get the original value, −8. Lastly (−8) % (−3) results in −2, which is also consistent with the divide operation applied to the same operands.

The modulus operator has the same precedence as multiplication and division and therefore executes before any add or subtract operations in the same expression. You could add these statements to the program, too, if you want to see the modulus operator in action. The following statement outputs the following results:

```
System.out.println("The number of fruit each is " + numFruitEach
                  + " and there are " + remainder + " left over.");
```

The Increment and Decrement Operators

If you want to increment an integer variable by one, you can use the increment operator instead of using an assignment. You write the increment operator as two successive plus signs, ++. For example, if you have an integer variable count that you've declared as

```
int count = 10;
```

you can then write the statement

```
++count;              // Add 1 to count
```

This statement increases the value of count to 11. To decrease the value of count by 1, you can use the decrement operator, −−:

```
--count;              // Subtract 1 from count
```

At first sight, apart from reducing the typing a little, this doesn't seem to have much of an advantage over writing the following:

```
count = count - 1;    // Subtract 1 from count
```

However, a big advantage of the increment and decrement operators is that you can use them in an expression. Try changing the arithmetic statement calculating the sum of numApples and numOranges in the previous example:

```
public class Fruit {
  public static void main(String[] args)    {
    // Declare and initialize three variables
    int numOranges = 5;
    int numApples = 10;
    int numFruit = 0;

    // Increment oranges and calculate the total fruit
    numFruit = ++numOranges + numApples;
    System.out.println("A totally fruity program");
    // Display the result
    System.out.println("Value of oranges is " + numOranges);
    System.out.println("Total fruit is " + numFruit);
  }
}
```

I bolded the lines that have been altered or added. In addition to the change to the numFruit calculation, I added an extra statement to output the final value of numOranges. The value of numOranges is increased to 6 before the value of numApples is added, so the value of numFruit is 16. Thus, the statement changes the value stored in numOranges as well as the value stored in numFruit. You could try the decrement operation in the example as well.

A further property of the increment and decrement operators is that they work differently in an expression depending on whether you put the operator in front of the variable to which it applies or following it. When you put the operator in front of a variable, as in the example you have just seen, it's called the *prefix form*. The converse case, with the operator following the variable, is called the *postfix form*. If you change the statement in the example to

```
numFruit = numOranges++ + numApples;
```

and run it again, you find that numOranges still ends up with the value 6, but the total stored in numFruit has remained 15. This is because the effect of the postfix increment operator is to change the value of numOranges to 6 after the original value, 5, has been used in the expression to supply the value of numFruit. The postfix decrement operator works similarly, and both operators can be applied to any type of integer variable.

As you see, no parentheses are necessary in the expression numOranges++ + numApples. You could even write it as numOranges+++numApples and it still means the same thing, but it is certainly a lot less obvious that this is the case. Someone who doesn't have all the rules for evaluating Java expressions at his fingertips might guess, wrongly, that the expression executes as numOranges+(++numApples). Such potential confusion is really the programmer's fault. You can write it as

```
(numOranges++) + numApples
```

to make it absolutely clear where the ++ operator belongs. It is a good idea to always add parentheses to clarify things when there is some possibility of misinterpretation.

Computation with Shorter Integer Types

I have deliberately used variables of type int in all the previous examples. Computations with variables of the shorter integer types introduce some complications. This is because all binary integer operations in Java work only with both operands of type int or both operands of type long. With arithmetic expressions using variables of type byte or short, the values of the variables are first converted to type int, and the calculation is carried out using 32-bit arithmetic. The result is therefore type int—a 32-bit integer. This has an interesting effect that you can see in the context of the previous example. Try changing the types of the variables numOranges, numApples, and numFruit in the original version of the program to type short. For example:

```
short numOranges = 5;
short numApples = 10;
short numFruit = 0;
```

You will find that the program no longer compiles. The problem is with this statement:

```
numFruit = numOranges + numApples;
```

Because the expression numOranges + numApples produces a 32-bit result, the compiler cannot store this value in numFruit, as the variable numFruit is only 16 bits long. To make the code acceptable to the compiler, you must modify the assignment statement so that the 32-bit result of the addition is converted back to a 16-bit number. You do this by changing the statement to:

```
numFruit = (short)(numOranges + numApples);
```

The statement now calculates the sum of numOranges and numApples and then converts, or *casts*, the 32-bit result to type short before storing it in numFruit. This is called an *explicit cast*, and the conversion process is referred to as *casting*. The cast to type short is the expression (short), and the cast applies to whatever is immediately to the right of (short), so the parentheses around the expression numOranges + numApples are necessary. Without them the cast applies only to the variable numOranges, which is type short anyway, and the code still does not compile.

If the variables here were of type byte, you would need to cast the result of the addition to type byte. You would write such a cast as (byte). This is a strong clue to how you write casts to other types. In general, you write a cast to any given type, typename, as the typename between parentheses—thus (typename).

The effect of the cast to type `short` in the example is just to take the least significant 16 bits of the result, discarding the most significant 16 bits. The least significant bits are those at the right-hand end of the number because the bits in a binary number in Java increase in value from right to left. Thus, the most significant bits are those at the left-hand end. For the cast to type `byte` only the least significant 8 bits are kept. This means that if the magnitude of the result of the addition is such that more than 16 bits are necessary to represent it (or 8 bits in the case of a cast to `byte`), your answer will be wrong. You get no indication from the compiler that this has occurred because it was you, after all, that expressly specified the cast, and the compiler assumes that you know what you are doing. To minimize the possibility for such hidden and mystifying errors, you should avoid explicit casts in your programs unless they are absolutely essential.

An integer arithmetic operation involving a value of type `long` is always carried out using 64-bit values. If the other number in such an operation is not of type `long`, the compiler arranges for it to be cast to type `long` before the operation is executed. For example:

```
long result = 0;
long factor = 10L;
int number = 5;
result = factor*number;
```

To execute the last statement, the multiplication is carried out using `long` values because the variable `factor` is of type `long`. The value stored in `number` is converted to type a, and that is multiplied by the value of `factor`.

All other integer arithmetic operations involving types other than `long` are carried out with 32-bit values. Thus, you really need to consider only two kinds of integer literals:

➤ Type `long` for operations with 64-bit values where the value has an *L* appended

➤ Type `int` for operations with 32-bit values for all other cases where there is no *L* at the end of the number

Errors in Integer Arithmetic

As I mentioned earlier, if you divide an integer value by zero, no sensible result can be produced so an exception is thrown. An exception is the way of signaling errors in Java that I will discuss in detail in Chapter 7. Using the `%` operator with a variable or expression for the right-hand operand that has a zero value also causes an exception to be thrown.

If an integer expression results in a value that is outside the range of the type of the result, the result is truncated to the number of bits for the type you are using and therefore is incorrect, but this is not indicated in any way. It is up to you to make sure that the integer types that you are using in your program are always able to accommodate any value that might be produced by your calculations.

Problems can arise with intermediate results in some situations. Even when the ultimate result of an expression is within the legal range, the result of any intermediate calculation that is outside the range is truncated, thus causing an incorrect result to be produced. To take a trivial example—if you multiply 1000000 by 2000000 and divide by 500000 using type `int`, you do not obtain the correct result if the multiplication is executed first. This is because the result of the multiplication exceeds the maximum that can be stored as type `int`. Obviously where you know this sort of problem can occur, you may be able to circumvent it by using parentheses to make sure the division takes place first—but you need to remember that integer division produces an integer result, so a different sequence of execution can produce a different answer.

Floating-Point Calculations

The four basic arithmetic operators (+, -, *, /) are also available for use in floating-point expressions, as is `%`, which I will come to shortly. You can try some of these out in another version of the `Fruit` program, which I'm calling `AverageFruit`.

TRY IT OUT Average Fruit

Make the following changes to the `Fruit.java` file and save this as `AverageFruit.java`. If necessary, you can add the code you used earlier to make the program wait for the Enter key to be pressed before finishing.

Available for
download on
Wrox.com

```java
public class AverageFruit {
  public static void main(String[] args) {
    // Declare and initialize three variables
    double numOranges = 50.0E-1;      // Initial value is 5.0
    double numApples = 1.0E1;         // Initial value is 10.0
    double averageFruit = 0.0;
    averageFruit = (numOranges + numApples)/2.0;
    System.out.println("A totally fruity program");
    System.out.println("Average fruit is " + averageFruit);
  }
}
```

code snippet AverageFruit.java

This produces the following output:

```
A totally fruity program
Average fruit is 7.5
```

How It Works

The program just computes the average number of fruits of different kinds by dividing the total by 2.0.

As you can see, I have used various representations for the initializing values for the variables in the program, which are now of type `double`. It's not the ideal way to write 5.0, but at least it demonstrates that you can write a negative exponent value.

Other Floating-Point Arithmetic Operators

You can use `++` and `--` operators with floating point variables, and they have the same effect as with integer variables, incrementing or decrementing the floating-point variable to which they are applied by 1.0. You can use them in prefix or postfix form, and their operation in each case is the same as with integer variables.

You can apply the modulus operator, `%`, to floating-point values, too. For an operation of the form:

```
floatOperand1 % floatOperand2
```

The result is the floating-point remainder after dividing `floatOperand2` into `floatOperand1` an integral number of times. For example, the expression `12.6 % 5.1` gives the result 2.4 (actually 2.4000006 because decimal values that are not integral do not always have an exact representation as binary floating-point values). In general, the sign of the result of applying the modulus operator to floating-point values is the sign of the dividend. The magnitude of the result of a floating-point remainder operation is the largest integral value such that the magnitude of the result of multiplying the divisor by the result of the remainder operation does not exceed the dividend.

Error Conditions in Floating-Point Arithmetic

There are two error conditions that can occur with floating-point operations that are signaled by a special result value being generated. One occurs when a calculation produces a value that is outside the range that can be represented by the floating-point type you are using, and the other arises when the result is mathematically indeterminate, such as when your calculation is effectively dividing zero by zero.

To illustrate the first kind of error you could use a variable to specify the number of types of fruit. You could define the variable

```
double fruitTypes = 2.0;
```

and then rewrite the calculation as

```
averageFruit = (numOranges + numApples)/fruitTypes;
```

This in itself is not particularly interesting, but if you happened to set `fruitTypes` to 0.0, the output from the program would be the following:

```
A totally fruity program
Average fruit is Infinity
```

The value `Infinity` indicates a positive but effectively infinite result, in that it represents a value that is greater than the largest number that can be stored as type `double`. An effectively infinite result that was negative would be output as `-Infinity`. You don't actually need to divide by zero to produce this effect; any calculation that generates a value that exceeds the maximum value that can be represented as type `double` has the same effect. For example, repeatedly dividing by a very small number, such as 1.0E-300, yields an out-of-range result.

If you want to see what an indeterminate result looks like, you can replace the statement to calculate `averageFruit` with the following:

```
averageFruit = (numOranges - 5.0)/(numApples - 10.0);
```

This statement doesn't make much sense, but it produces an indeterminate result. The value of `averageFruit` is output as `NaN`. This value is referred to as *Not-a-Number*, indicating an indeterminate value. A variable with an indeterminate value contaminates any subsequent expression in which it is used, so any operation involving an operand value of `NaN` produces the same result of `NaN`.

A value that is `Infinity` or `-Infinity` is unchanged when you add, subtract, or multiply by finite values, but if you divide any finite value by `Infinity` or `-Infinity` the result is zero.

 NOTE *If a floating-point operation results in a negative value that is so small it cannot be represented, the result is −0.0. Although −0.0 is considered to be numerically identical to 0.0, dividing a positive value by −0.0 produces* `-Infinity` *whereas dividing a positive value by 0.0 produces* `Infinity`.

Mixed Arithmetic Expressions

You have probably guessed from earlier discussions that you can mix values of the basic types together in a single expression. The way mixed expressions are treated is governed by some simple rules that apply to each operator in such an expression. The rules, in the sequence in which they are checked, follow:

1. If either operand is of type `double`, the other is converted to `double` before the operation is carried out.
2. If either operand is of type `float`, the other is converted to `float` before the operation is carried out.
3. If either operand is of type `long`, the other is converted to `long` before the operation is carried out.

The first rule in the sequence that applies to a given operation is the one that is carried out. If neither operand is `double`, `float`, or `long`, they must be `int`, `short`, or `byte`, so they are converted to type `int` where necessary and use 32-bit arithmetic to produce the result, as you saw earlier in the chapter.

Explicit Casting

It may well be that the default treatment of mixed expressions listed in the preceding section is not what you want. For example, suppose you have defined a `double` variable `result`, and two variables, `three` and `two`, of type `int` with the values 3 and 2 respectively. If you compute the value of `result` with the statement

```
result = 1.5 + three/two;
```

the value stored is 2.5, because `three/two` is executed as an integer operation and produces the result 1. You may have wanted the term `three/two` to produce the value 1.5 so the overall result would be 3.0. You could do this using an explicit cast:

```
result = 1.5 + (double)three/two;
```

This causes the value stored in `three` to be converted to type `double` before the divide operation takes place. Then rule 1 applies for the divide operation, and the operand `two` is also converted to type `double` before the divide operation is executed. Hence, the value of `result` in this case is 3.0.

> **NOTE** You can cast a value from any primitive type to any other, but you need to take care that you don't unintentionally lose information when you do so. Obviously casting from one integer type to another with a more limited range has the potential for losing information, as does casting any floating-point value to an integer. Casting from type `double` to type `float` can also produce an effective infinity when the original value is greater than the maximum value for a value of type `float`.

Automatic Type Conversions in Assignments

When the type of the result of an arithmetic expression on the right of an assignment operator differs from the type of the variable on the left, an automatic cast is applied to the result as long as there is no possibility of losing information. If you think of the basic types that you have seen so far as being in the sequence

`byte→ short→ int→ long→ float→ double`

then an automatic conversion is made as long as it is upward through the sequence of types—that is, from left to right. If you want to go in the opposite direction, from type `double` to type `float` or `long`, for example, then you must insert an explicit cast into your code for the result of the expression on the right of the assignment operator.

THE OP= OPERATORS

The `op=` operators are used in statements of the form

```
lhs op= rhs;
```

where `op` can be any of the arithmetic operators (+, -, *, /, %). It also works with some other operators you haven't seen yet. The preceding statement is basically a shorthand representation of this statement:

```
lhs = lhs op (rhs);
```

The right-hand side (`rhs`) is in brackets because it is worked out first—then the result is combined with the left-hand side (`lhs`) using the operation `op`. Let's look at a few examples of this to make sure it's clear. To increment an `int` variable `count` by 5 you can write:

```
count += 5;
```

This has the same effect as the following statement:

```
count = count + 5;
```

Of course, the expression to the right of the `op=` operator can be anything that is legal in the context, so the statement

```
result /= a % b/(a + b);
```

is equivalent to

```
result = result/(a % b/(a + b));
```

What I have said so far about op= operations is not quite the whole story. If the type of the result of the rhs expression is different from the type of lhs, the compiler automatically inserts a cast to convert the rhs value to the same type as lhs. This would happen with the last example if result was of type int and a and b were of type double, for example. This is quite different from the way the normal assignment operation is treated. A statement using the op= operator is really equivalent to:

```
lhs = (type_of_lhs)(lhs op (rhs));
```

The automatic conversion is inserted by the compiler regardless of what the types of lhs and rhs are. Of course, this can result in information being lost due to the cast, and you get no indication that it has occurred. This is different from ordinary assignment statements where an automatic cast is allowed only when the range of values for the type of lhs is greater that the range for the type of rhs.

The complete set of op= operators are the following:

+=	-=	*=	/=	%=	
<<=	>>=	>>>=	&=	|=	^=

You will learn about the operators on the second row later in the book.

MATHEMATICAL FUNCTIONS AND CONSTANTS

Sooner or later you are likely to need mathematical functions in your programs, even if it's only to obtain an absolute value or calculate a square root. Java provides a range of methods that support such functions as part of the standard library that is stored in the package java.lang, and all these are available in your program automatically.

The methods that support various additional mathematical functions are implemented in the Math class as static methods, so to reference a particular function you can just write Math and the name of the method you want to use separated by a period. For example, the sqrt() method calculates the square root of whatever you place between the parentheses. To use the sqrt() method to produce the square root of the floating-point value that you've stored in a variable, aNumber, you write Math.sqrt(aNumber).

The class Math includes a range of methods for standard trigonometric functions. The most commonly used are shown in Table 2-3:

TABLE 2-3: Class Math Trigonometric Functions

METHOD	FUNCTION	ARGUMENT TYPE	RESULT TYPE
sin(arg)	sine of the argument	double in radians	double
cos(arg)	cosine of the argument	double in radians	double
tan(arg)	tangent of the argument	double in radians	double
asin(arg)	$\sin^{-1}$ (arc sine) of the argument	double	double in radians with values from $-\pi/2$ to $\pi/2$
acos(arg)	$\cos^{-1}$ (arc cosine) of the argument	double	double in radians, with values from 0.0 to π
atan(arg)	$\tan^{-1}$ (arc tangent) of the argument	double	double in radians with values from $-\pi/2$ to $\pi/2$
atan2(arg1,arg2)	$\tan^{-1}$ (arc tangent) of arg1/arg2	Both double	double in radians with values from $-\pi$ to π

As with all methods, the arguments that you put between the parentheses following the method name can be any expression that produces a value of the required type. The toRadians() method in the Math class converts a double argument that is an angular measurement in degrees to radians. There is a complementary method, `toDegrees()`, to convert in the opposite direction. The `Math` class also defines `double` values for e and π, which you can access as `Math.E` and `Math.PI` respectively. If you are not familiar with these trigonometric operations you can safely ignore them.

You also have a range of numerical functions implemented as static methods in the `Math` class and at least some of these are useful to you. These are shown in Table 2-4:

TABLE 2-4: Math Class Numerical Functions

METHOD	FUNCTION	ARGUMENT TYPE	RESULT TYPE
`abs(arg)`	Calculates the absolute value of the argument	`int`, `long`, `float`, or `double`	The same type as the argument
`max (arg1,arg2)`	Returns the larger of the two arguments, both of the same type	`int`, `long`, `float`, or `double`	The same type as the arguments
`min (arg1,arg2)`	Returns the smaller of the two arguments, both of the same type	`int`, `long`, `float`, or `double`	The same type as the arguments
`ceil(arg)`	Returns the smallest integer that is greater than or equal to the argument	`double`	`double`
`floor(arg)`	Returns the largest integer that is less than or equal to the argument	`double`	`double`
`round(arg)`	Calculates the nearest integer to the argument value	`float` or `double`	Of type `int` for a `float` argument, of type `long` for a `double` argument
`rint(arg)`	Calculates the nearest integer to the argument value	`double`	`double`

Where more than one type of argument is noted in the table, there are actually several methods, one for each type of argument, but all have the same name. You will see how this is possible in Java implementing class methods, covered in Chapter 5.

Several methods implement mathematical functions in the `Math` class. You'll probably be surprised at how often you find uses for some of these. The mathematical methods you have available are shown in Table 2-5:

TABLE 2-5: Math Class Mathematical Functions

METHOD	FUNCTION	ARGUMENT TYPE	RESULT TYPE
`sqrt(arg)`	Calculates the square root of the argument	`double`	`double`
`cbrt(arg)`	Calculates the cube root of the argument	`double`	`double`
`pow(arg1,arg2)`	Calculates the first argument raised to the power of the second argument, $arg1^{arg2}$	Both `double`	`double`
`hypot( arg1,arg2)`	Calculates the square root of $(arg1^2 + arg2^2)$	Both `double`	`double`
`exp(arg)`	Calculates e raised to the power of the argument, e^{arg}	`double`	`double`
`expm1(arg)`	Calculates e raised to the power of the argument minus 1, $e^{arg} - 1$	`double`	`double`
`log(arg)`	Calculates the natural logarithm (base e) of the argument	`double`	`double`
`log1p(arg)`	Calculates the natural logarithm (base e) of arg + 1	`double`	`double`

continues

TABLE 2-5 *(continued)*

METHOD	FUNCTION	ARGUMENT TYPE	RESULT TYPE
log10(arg)	Calculates the base 10 logarithm of the argument	double	double
random()	Returns a pseudo-random number greater than or equal to 0.0 and less than 1.0	None	double

I have not discussed all the methods in the Math class here, just the most commonly used ones. You may want to explore the JDK documentation to get a feeling for the rest.

You can try out a sample of the contents of the Math class in an example to make sure you know how they are used.

TRY IT OUT The Math Class

You are planning a new circular pond in which you want to keep fish. Your local aquatics supplier tells you that they can stock the pond with fish at the rate of 2 inches of fish length per square foot of pond surface area. Your problem is to calculate the radius of the pond that will accommodate 20 fish averaging 10 inches in length. The solution, of course, is to write a Java program—what else? The following program calculates the radius of a pond in feet and inches that can provide a home for the number of fish you would like to keep:

```java
public class PondRadius {
  public static void main(String[] args) {
    // Calculate the radius of a pond
    // which can hold 20 fish averaging 10 inches long
    int fishCount = 20;            // Number of fish in pond
    int fishLength = 10;           // Average fish length
    int inchesPerFoot = 12;        // Number of inches in one foot
    int lengthPerSqFt = 2;         // Fish length per square foot of surface
    double radius = 0.0;           // Pond radius in feet

    int feet = 0;                  // Pond radius - whole feet
    int inches = 0;                //              - and whole inches

    double pondArea = (double)(fishCount*fishLength)/lengthPerSqFt;
    radius = Math.sqrt(pondArea/Math.PI);

    // Get the whole feet and nothing but the feet
    feet = (int)Math.floor(radius);
    inches = (int)Math.round(inchesPerFoot*(radius - feet));  // Get the inches

    System.out.println(
              "To hold " + fishCount + " fish averaging " + fishLength +
              " inches long you need a pond with an area of \n" +
              pondArea + " square feet.");
    System.out.println("The radius of a pond with area " + pondArea +
                  " square feet is " +
                  feet + " feet " + inches + " inches.");
  }
}
```

Save the program source file as PondRadius.java. When you compile and run it, you should get the following output:

```
To hold 20 fish averaging 10 inches long you need a pond with an area of
100.0 square feet.
The radius of a pond with area 100.0 square feet is 5 feet 8 inches.
```

How It Works

You first define the variables that specify initial data followed by the variables feet and inches that you will use to store the result. You then calculate the pond surface area in feet with this statement:

```java
double pondArea = (double)(fishCount*fishLength)/lengthPerSqFt;
```

You cast the total length of fish to be in the pond, `fishCount*fishLength`, to type `double` to force the division by the number of inches per square foot of pond surface to be done using floating-point values rather than integers.

The next calculation uses the `sqrt()` method to calculate the radius. Because the area of a circle with radius r is given by the formula πr^2, the radius must be $\sqrt{(area/\pi)}$, so you specify the argument to the `sqrt()` method as the expression `pondArea/Math.PI`, where `Math.PI` references the value of π that is defined in the `Math` class:

```
radius = Math.sqrt(pondArea/Math.PI);
```

The result is in feet as a value of type `double`.

To get the number of whole feet you use the `floor()` method:

```
feet = (int)Math.floor(radius);   // Get the whole feet and nothing but the feet
```

Note that the cast to type `int` of the value that is produced by the `floor()` method is essential in this statement; otherwise, you get an error message from the compiler. The value returned from the `floor()` method is type `double`, and the compiler will not cast this to type `int` automatically because the process potentially loses information.

Finally, you get the number of inches by subtracting the value for whole feet from the original radius, multiplying the fraction of a foot by 12 to get the equivalent inches, and then rounding the result to the nearest integer using the `round()` method:

```
inches = (int)Math.round(inchesPerFoot*(radius - feet));   // Get the inches
```

To output the result, you specify a combination (or concatenation) of strings and variables as an argument to the two `println()` method calls:

```
System.out.println(
          "To hold " + fishCount + " fish averaging " + fishLength +
          " inches long you need a pond with an area of \n" +
          pondArea + " square feet.");
System.out.println("The radius of a pond with area " + pondArea +
              " square feet is " +
              feet + " feet " + inches + " inches.");
```

Each statement is spread over three lines for convenience here. The `\n` that appears in the first output statement specifies a newline character, so the output is on two lines. Any time you want the next bit of output to begin a new line, just add `\n` to the output string. You can't enter a newline character just by pressing Enter because when you do that the cursor just moves to the next line. That's why it's specified as `\n`. There are other characters like this that you cannot enter directly that are covered a little later in this chapter.

Importing the Math Class Methods

It would be a lot more convenient if you were able to avoid having to qualify the name of every method in the `Math` class that you use with the class name. The code would be a lot less cluttered if you could write `floor(radius)` instead of `Math.floor(radius)`, for example. Well, you can. All you need to do is put the following statement at the beginning of the source file:

```
import static java.lang.Math.*;        // Import static class members
```

This statement makes the names of all the static members of the `Math` class available for use in your program code without having to qualify them with the class name. This includes constants such as `PI` as well as static methods. You can try this statement in the `PondRadius` example. With this statement at the beginning of the source file, you are able to remove the qualification by the class name `Math` from all the members of this class that the program uses.

The `*` in the statement indicates that all static names are to be imported. If you want to import just the names from the `Math` class that the `PondRadius` program uses, you write the following:

```
import static java.lang.Math.floor;    // Import floor
import static java.lang.Math.sqrt;     // Import sqrt
import static java.lang.Math.round;    // Import round
import static java.lang.Math.PI;       // Import PI
```

These statements import individually the four names from the Math class that the program references. You could use these four statements at the beginning of the program in place of the previous import statement that imports all the static names. I will discuss this form of the import statement further in Chapter 5.

STORING CHARACTERS

Variables of type char store a single character code. They each occupy 16 bits (2 bytes) in memory because all characters in Java are stored as Unicode. To declare and initialize a character variable myCharacter you could use the following statement:

```
char myCharacter = 'X';
```

This initializes the variable with the Unicode character representation of the letter X. You must always put single quotes as delimiters for a character literal in a statement as in this example, 'X'. This is necessary to enable the compiler to distinguish between the character 'X' and a variable with the name X. Note that you can't use double quotes as delimiters here because they are used to delimit a character string. A character string such as "X" is quite different from the literal of type char, 'X'.

Character Escape Sequences

In general, the characters that you are able to enter directly from your keyboard are a function of the keys you have available and the set of character codes they map to according to your operating system. Whatever that is, it is a small subset of the characters defined by the Unicode encoding. To enable you to enter any Unicode character as part of your program source code you can define Unicode characters by specifying the hexadecimal representation of the character codes in an *escape sequence*. An escape sequence is simply an alternative means of specifying a character that is often, but not exclusively, by its code. A backslash indicates the start of an escape sequence, so you have already met the escape sequence for a newline character, \n.

You create an escape sequence for a Unicode character by preceding the four hexadecimal digits of the character code by \u. Because the Unicode coding for the letter X is the hexadecimal value 0x0058 (the low order byte is the same as the ASCII code), you could also declare and define myCharacter with this statement:

```
char myCharacter = '\u0058';
```

You place the escape sequence between single quotes to define the character literal. The result is the same as the previous statement where you used 'X' as the initial value for myCharacter. You can enter any Unicode character in this way, as long as you know its code of course.

 NOTE *You can get more information on the full Unicode character set on the Internet by visiting* www.unicode.org/.

Because the backslash indicates the beginning of an escape sequence, you must always use the escape sequence, \\, to specify a backslash character as a character literal or in a text string.

As you have seen, you write a character string (a String literal as shown in Chapter 4) enclosed between double quotes and a character literal between single quotes. For this reason you also need the escape sequences \' and \" to specify these characters. For example, to produce the output

```
"It's freezing in here", he said coldly.
```

you could write

```
System.out.println("\"It\'s freezing in here\", he said coldly.");
```

In fact, it's not strictly necessary to use an escape sequence to specify a single quote within a string, but obviously it is when you want to specify a single quote as a character literal. Of course, it is always necessary to specify a double quote within a string using an escape sequence, otherwise it would be interpreted as the end of the string.

There are other escape sequences that you use to define control characters (shown in Table 2-6).

TABLE 2-6: Escape Sequences

CHARACTER	DESCRIPTION
\b	Backspace
\f	Form feed
\n	New line
\r	Carriage return
\t	Tab

Character Arithmetic

You can perform arithmetic on char variables. With myCharacter containing the character 'X', the statement

```
myCharacter += 1;     // Increment to next character
```

results in the value of myCharacter being changed to 'Y'. This is because the Unicode code for 'Y' is one more than the code for 'X'. You could use the increment operator ++ to increase the code stored in myCharacter by just writing the following:

```
++myCharacter;        // Increment to next character
```

When you use variables of type char in an arithmetic expression, their values are converted to type int to carry out the calculation. It doesn't necessarily make a whole lot of sense, but you could write the following statements that calculate with values of type char:

```
char aChar = 0;
char bChar = '\u0028';
aChar = (char)(2*bChar + 8);
```

These statements leave the aChar variable holding the code for the letter X—which is 0x0058.

TRY IT OUT   **Arithmetic with Character Codes**

This example demonstrates arithmetic operations with values of type char:

```
public class CharCodeCalcs {
  public static void main(String[] args){
    char letter1 = 'A';             // letter1 is 'A'
    char letter2 = (char)(letter1+1);  // letter2 is 'B'
    char letter3 = letter2;            // letter3 is also 'B'
    System.out.println("Here\'s a sequence of letters: "+ letter1 + letter2 +
                                               (++letter3));
    // letter3 is now 'C'
    System.out.println("Here are the decimal codes for the letters:\n"+
                     letter1 + ": " + (int)letter1 +
              "  " + letter2 + ": " + (int)letter2 +
              "  " + letter3 + ": " + (int)letter3);
  }
}
```

This example produces the output:

```
Here's a sequence of letters: ABC
Here are the decimal codes for the letters:
A: 65  B: 66  C: 67
```

How It Works

The first three statements in `main()` define three variables of type `char`:

```
char letter1 = 'A';                    // letter1 is 'A'
char letter2 = (char)(letter1+1);      // letter2 is 'B'
char letter3 = letter2;                // letter3 is also 'B'
```

The cast to type `char` of the initial value for `letter2` is essential. Without it, the code does not compile. The expression `letter1+2` produces a result of type `int`, and the compiler does not insert an automatic cast to allow the value to be used as the initial value for `letter2`.

The next statement outputs three characters:

```
System.out.println("Here\'s a sequence of letters: "+ letter1 + letter2 +
                                                            (++letter3));
```

The first two characters displayed are those stored in `letter1` and `letter2`. The third character is the value stored in `letter3` after the variable has been incremented by 1.

By default the `println()` method treats a variable of type `char` as a character for output. You can still output the value stored in a `char` variable as a numerical value simply by casting it to type `int`. The next statement demonstrates this:

```
System.out.println("Here are the decimal codes for the letters:\n"+
                   letter1 + ": " + (int)letter1 +
              "  " + letter2 + ": " + (int)letter2 +
              "  " + letter3 + ": " + (int)letter3);
```

This statement outputs the value of each of the three variables as a character followed by its decimal value.

Of course, you may prefer to see the character codes as hexadecimal values. You can display any value of type `int` as a hexadecimal string by enlisting the help of a static method that is defined in the `Integer` class in the standard library. Add an extra output statement to the example as the last statement in `main()`:

```
System.out.println("Here are the hexadecimal codes for the letters:\n"+
                   letter1 + ": " + Integer.toHexString(letter1) +
              "  " + letter2 + ": " + Integer.toHexString(letter2) +
              "  " + letter3 + ": " + Integer.toHexString(letter3));
```

This statement outputs the character codes as hexadecimal values so you see this additional output:

```
Here are the hexadecimal codes for the letters:
A: 41  B: 42  C: 43
```

The `toHexString()` method generates a string representation of the argument you supply. Here you just have the name of a variable of type `char` as the argument in each of the three uses of the method, but you could put in any expression that results in a value of type `int`. Because the method requires an argument of type `int`, the compiler inserts a cast to type `int` for each of the arguments `letter1`, `letter2`, and `letter3`.

The `Integer` class is related to the primitive type `int` in that an object of type `Integer` "wraps" a value of type `int`. You will understand the significance of this better when you investigate classes in Chapter 5. There are also classes of type `Byte`, `Short`, and `Long` that relate to values of the corresponding primitive types. The `Long` class also defines a static method `toHexString()` that you use to obtain a string that is a hexadecimal representation of a value of type `long`. These classes also contain other useful utility methods that I introduce later when a suitable context arises.

Of course, you can use the static import statement that I introduced in the context of the `Math` class to import the names of static members of other classes such as `Integer` and `Long`. For example, the following statement at the beginning of a source file enables you to use the `toHexString()` method without having to qualify it with the `Integer` class name:

```
import static java.lang.Integer.toHexString;
```

BITWISE OPERATIONS

As you already know, all these integer variables I have been talking about are represented internally as binary numbers. A value of type int consists of 32 binary digits, known to us computer fans as bits. You can operate on the bits that make up integer values using the bitwise operators, of which there are four available, as shown in Table 2-7:

TABLE 2-7: Bitwise Operators

BIT	OPERATOR
&	AND
|	OR
^	Exclusive OR
~	Complement

Each of these operators operates on the individual bits in its operands as follows:

➤ The bitwise AND operator, &, combines corresponding bits in its two operands such that if both bits are 1, the result is 1 — otherwise the result is 0.

➤ The bitwise OR operator, |, combines corresponding bits such that if either or both bits are 1, then the result is 1. Only if both bits are 0 is the result 0.

➤ The bitwise exclusive OR (XOR) operator, ^, combines corresponding bits such that if both bits are the same the result is 0; otherwise, the result is 1.

➤ The complement operator, ~, takes a single operand in which it inverts all the bits, so that each 1 bit becomes 0, and each 0 bit becomes 1.

Table 2-8 shows examples of the effect of each of these operators:

TABLE 2-8: Operator Examples

OPERATOR	EXAMPLE
a	0b0110_0110_1100_1101
b	0b0000_0000_0000_1111
a & b	0b0000_0000_0000_1101
a | b	0b0110_0110_1100_1111
a ^ b	0b0110_0110_1100_0010
~a	0b1001_1001_0011_0010

This shows the binary digits that make up the operands a and b and the results of four bitwise operations. The three binary bitwise operations produces the result by applying the operation to each corresponding pair of bits from its operands in turn. The complement operator just flips the state of each bit in its operand so that 0 changes to 1 and 1 changes to 0 in the value that results.

Because you are concerned with individual bits when using bitwise operations, writing a constant as a normal decimal value is not going to be particularly convenient, and a binary literal is the obvious choice. If you are comfortable working with hexadecimal literals and can convert from binary to hexadecimal and vice versa very quickly, these provide a more compact way of representing bit patterns. There's more on working with binary and hexadecimal values in Appendix B.

Using the AND and OR Operators

If you think of the variable b in the previous section as a mask that is applied to the value of a, you can view the & operator as keeping bits unchanged where the mask is 1 and setting the other bits to 0. *Mask* is a term used to refer to a particular configuration of bits designed to operate on specific bits when it is combined with a variable using a bitwise operator. So, if you want to select a particular bit out of an integer variable, to determine whether it is 1 or 0 for example, just AND it with a mask that has that bit set to 1 and all the others as 0.

You can also envisage what the & operator does from another perspective. The operation forces a bit to 0 if the corresponding mask bit is 0 and leaves a bit unchanged if the mask bit is 1. Thus the & operator provides you with a way to switch off specific bits in a word leaving the rest as they were. Just create a mask with 0 bits in the positions that you want to make 0 and with 1 bits everywhere else.

The | operator forces a bit to be 1 in a variable when the corresponding mask bit is 1, and each mask bit that is 0 leaves the corresponding bit unchanged. Thus you can use the | operator to set particular bits in a variable to 1.

The & and | operators are the most frequently used of the bitwise operators, mainly for dealing with variables where the individual bits are used as state indicators of some kind—for things that can be either true or false, or on or off. You could use a single bit as a state indicator determining whether something should be displayed, with the bit as 1, or not displayed, with the bit as 0. To take a simple example, to select the third bit from the right in the int variable indicators, you can write the following:

```
thirdBit = indicators & 0b0100;    // Select the 3rd bit, 0x4 in hexadecimal
```

The third bit of the variable thirdBit is the same as the third bit in indicators and all the other bits is zero. I can illustrate how this works by assuming the variable indicators contains the binary value 0b1111_1111_0000_1111, which you could also write as the hexadecimal value 0xFF07:

indicators	0b1111_1111_0000_1111
mask	0b0000_0000_0000_0100
indicators & mask	0b0000_0000_0000_0100

All these values should have 32 bits, and I am only showing 16 bits here, but you see all you need to know how it works. The mask value sets all the bits in the result to zero except for the third bit, which is set to that of the indicators variable. Here, the result of the expression is non-zero because the third bit in indicators is 1.

On the other hand, if the variable indicators contained the value 0xFF09 the result is different:

indicators	0b1111_1111_0000_1001
mask	0b0000_0000_0000_0100
indicators & mask	0b0000_0000_0000_0000

The result of the expression is now zero because the third bit of indicators is zero.

As I said, you can use the | operator to set a particular bit on. For example, to set the third bit in indicators on, you can write the following:

```
indicators = indicators | mask;   // Set the 3rd bit on
```

You can see how this applies to the last value you had for indicators:

indicators	0b1111_1111_0000_1001
mask	0b0000_0000_0000_0100
indicators | mask	0b1111_1111_0000_1101

As you can see, the effect is just to switch the third bit of `indicators` on, leaving all the other bits unchanged. Of course, if the third bit was already on, it would stay on.

You can also use the bitwise operators in the `op=` form. Setting the third bit in the variable `indicators` is usually written as:

```
indicators |= mask;
```

Although there is nothing wrong with the original statement, the preceding one is just a bit more concise.

To set a bit off you need to use the `&` operator again, with a mask that has 0 for the bit you want as 0, and 1 for all the others. To set the third bit of `indicators` off you could write:

```
indicators &= ~mask;                    // Set the 3rd bit off, mask value 0x4
```

The `~` operator provides a useful way of specifying a value with all bits 1 apart from one. The mask variable contains a value with the third bit as 1 and the other bits as 0. Applying the `~` operator to this flips each bit, so that the 0 bits are 1 and the 1 bit is zero. With `indicators` having the value `0xFF07`, this would work as follows:

`indicators`	`0b1111_1111_0000_0111`
`mask`	`0b0000_0000_0000_0100`
`~mask`	`0b1111_1111_1111_0100`
`indicators & ~mask`	`0b1111_1111_0000_0011`

Let's see some of these bitwise operations in action.

TRY IT OUT   Bitwise AND and OR Operations

This example exercises some of the operations that you saw in the previous section:

```
import static java.lang.Integer.toBinaryString;

public class BitwiseOps {
  public static void main(String[] args) {
    int indicators = 0b1111_1111_0000_0111;  // Same as 0xFF07
    int selectBit3 = 0b0000_0000_0000_0100;  // Mask to select the 3rd bit, 0x4

    // Try the bitwise AND to select the third bit in indicators
    System.out.println("indicators             = " +
                                          toBinaryString(indicators));
    System.out.println("selectBit3             = " +
                                          toBinaryString(selectBit3));
    indicators &= selectBit3;
    System.out.println("indicators & selectBit3 = " +
                                          toBinaryString(indicators));

    // Try the bitwise OR to switch the third bit on
    indicators = 0b1111_1111_0000_1001;       // Same as 0xFF09
    System.out.println("\nindicators           = "+
                                          toBinaryString(indicators));
    System.out.println("selectBit3           = "+
                                          toBinaryString(selectBit3));
    indicators |= selectBit3;
    System.out.println("indicators | selectBit3 = " +
                                          toBinaryString(indicators));

    // Now switch the third bit off again
    indicators &= ~selectBit3;
```

```
        System.out.println("\nThe third bit in the previous value of indicators" +
                                                " has been switched off");

        System.out.println("indicators & ~selectBit3 = " +
                                                toBinaryString(indicators));

    }
}
```

This example produces the following output:

```
indicators                = 1111111100000111
selectBit3                = 100
indicators & selectBit3   = 100

indicators                = 1111111100001001
selectBit3                = 100
indicators | selectBit3   = 1111111100001101

The third bit in the previous value of indicators has been switched off
indicators & ~selectBit3 = 1111111100001001
```

How It Works

The example uses the code fragments that I discussed in the previous section so you can see from the output that they work as described. One new capability introduced here is the use of the static toBinaryString() method that is defined in the Integer class. There's a static import statement for the name of this method, so its use is not qualified by the class name in the example. The toBinaryString() method produces a string containing a binary representation of the value of type int that is passed as the argument to the method. You can see from the output for the value of selectBit3 that the string does not include leading zeros. Obviously, the output would be better with leading zeros displayed but you need to know more about handling strings to be able to fix this. By the end of Chapter 4, you will be in a position to do so.

Using the Exclusive OR Operator

The ^ operator has the slightly surprising ability to interchange two values without moving either value somewhere else. The need for this turns up most frequently in tricky examination questions. Suppose you execute the following three statements with integer variables a and b:

```
a ^= b;
b ^= a;
a ^= b;
```

The effect of these statements is to interchange the values of a and b, but remember this works only for integers. You can try this out with a couple of arbitrary values for a and b, 0b1101_0000_0000_1111 and 0b1010_1011_1010_1101, respectively—again, I am just showing 16 bits for each variable. The first statement changes a to a new value:

a	0b1101_0000_0000_1111
b	0b1010_1011_1010_1101
a from a^b	0b0111_1011_1010_0010

The next statement calculates a new value of b using the new value of a:

a	0b0111_1011_1010_0010
b	0b1010_1011_1010_1101
b from b^a	0b1101_0000_0000_1111

So b now has a value that looks remarkably like the value that a started out with. Let's look at the last step, which calculates a new value for a using the new value of b:

a	0b0111_1011_1010_0010
b	0b1101_0000_0000_1111
a from a^b	0b1010_1011_1010_1101

Lo and behold, the value of a is now the original value of b. When you get to do some graphics programming later in the book, you see that this application of the exclusive OR operator is quite useful.

Don't forget—all of these bitwise operators can be applied only to integers. They don't work with any other type of value. As with the arithmetic expressions, the bitwise operations are carried out with 32 bits for integers of type short and of type byte, so a cast to the appropriate type is necessary for the result of the expression on the right of the assignment operator.

One note of caution—special care is needed when initializing variables of type byte and type short with hexadecimal values to avoid being caught out. For example, you might be tempted to initialize a variable of type byte to 1111 1111 with the statement:

```
byte allBitsOne = 0xFF;    // Wrong!!
```

In fact, this results in a compiler error message, and it doesn't help to use 0b1111_1111 as the value. The literal 0xFF is 1111 1111, so what's the beef here? The beef is that neither 0xFF nor 0b1111_1111 are 1111 1111 at all. These literals are type int, so they are the binary value 0000 0000 0000 0000 0000 0000 1111 1111. This happens to be equivalent to the decimal value 255, which is outside the range of type byte. The byte value you are looking for, 1111 1111, is equivalent to the decimal value −1, so the correct way to initialize allBitsOne to 1s is to write:

```
byte allBitsOne = 0xFFFFFFFF;    // Correct - well done!!
```

Now the compiler happily chops off the high order bits to produce the result you are looking for.

Shift Operations

Another mechanism that you have for working with integer variables at the bit level is *shifting*. You can shift the bits in an integer to the right or the left. You can also envisage the process of shifting binary digits right or left as dividing or multiplying by powers of two, respectively. Shifting the binary value of 3, which is 0011, to the left one bit multiplies it by 2. It becomes binary 0110, which is decimal 6. Shifting it to the right by 1 bit divides it by 2. It becomes binary 0001, which is 1.

Java has three shift operators:

<<	Shift left, filling with zeros from the right
>>	Shift right, propagating the sign bit from the left
>>>	Shift right, filling with zeros from the left

The effect of each of the shift operators is shown in Figure 2-4.

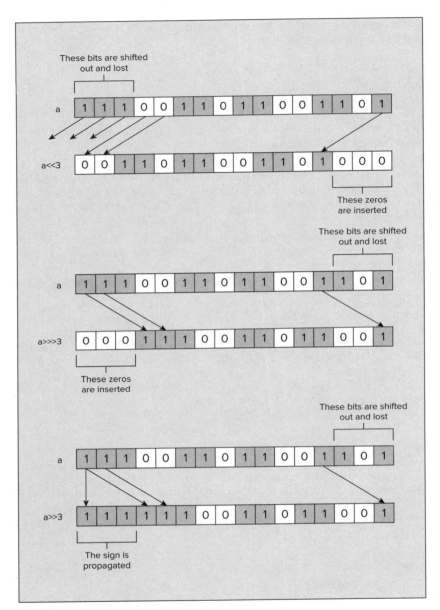

FIGURE 2-4

Of course, if the high order bit in the >> operation in Figure 2-4 were zero, there would be three zeros at the leftmost end of the result.

Shift operations are often used in combination with the other bitwise operators I have discussed to extract parts of an integer value. In many operating systems a single 32-bit value is sometimes used to store multiple values. For example, you could store two 16-bit screen coordinates in a single 32-bit word. This is illustrated in Figure 2-5.

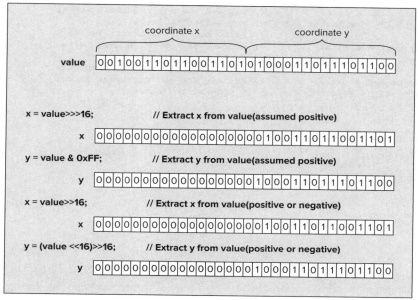

FIGURE 2-5

Figure 2-5 shows how you can use the shift operations to extract either the left or the right 16 bits from the variable `value`. You can see here why you have an extra shift right operation that propagates the leftmost bit. It is related to the notion of a shift as multiplying or dividing by a power of 2, and the implications of that in the context of negative integers that are represented in 2's complement form (see Appendix B). When the sign bit is not propagated, the shift right operation does not have a numerical interpretation for negative values because the sign bit is treated the same as any other bit, and zeros are inserted from the right. When the sign bit is propagated, the effect for negative values is the same as for positive values—namely that each bit position shifted is a division by 2.

TRY IT OUT Using Shift Operations

This example uses the shift operators with the bitwise operators to pack four values of type `char` into a variable of type `long`. Here's the code:

```
import static java.lang.Long.toHexString;

public class PackingCharacters {
  public static void main(String[] args) {
    char letterA = 'A';
    char letterB = 'B';
    char letterC = 'C';
    char letterD = 'D';
    long packed = 0L;
    packed = letterD;                    // Store D
    packed = (packed << 16) | letterC;   // Shift and add the next letter - C
    packed = (packed << 16) | letterB;   // Shift and add the next letter - B
    packed = (packed << 16) | letterA;   // Shift and add the next letter - A
    System.out.println("packed now contains 0x" + toHexString(packed));

    // Now unpack the letters and output them
    long mask = 0xFFFF;                   // Rightmost 16 bits as 1
    char letter = (char)(packed & mask);  // Extract the rightmost letter
    System.out.println("From right to left the letters in packed are:");
    System.out.println("  " + letter + "  0x" + toHexString(letter));
    packed >>= 16;                        // Shift out the rightmost letter
```

```
        letter = (char)(packed & mask);        // Extract the new rightmost letter
        System.out.println("   " + letter + "  0x" + toHexString(letter));
        packed >>= 16;                          // Shift out the rightmost letter
        letter = (char)(packed & mask);        // Extract the new rightmost letter
        System.out.println("   " + letter + "  0x" + toHexString(letter));
        packed >>= 16;                          // Shift out the rightmost letter
        letter = (char)(packed & mask);        // Extract the new rightmost letter
        System.out.println("   " + letter + "  0x" + toHexString(letter));
    }
}
```

The output from this example is the following:

```
packed now contains 0x44004300420041
```

From right to left the letters in packed are:

```
A   0x41
B   0x42
C   0x43
D   0x44
```

How It Works

The first four statements in main() define variables initialized with the letters to be packed into the variable, packed, of type long that is defined in the fifth statement in main(). The packing process begins by storing the first character in packed:

```
packed = letterD;                     // Store D
```

The rightmost 16 bits in packed now contain the character code D. This eventually ends up in the leftmost 16 bits of packed. The next statement inserts the next letter, C, into packed:

```
packed = (packed << 16) | letterC;    // Shift and add the next letter - C
```

The letter is inserted by first shifting the contents of packed left by 16 bits, and then ORing the value of letterC with the result. At this point, the leftmost 32 bits of packed are zero and the rightmost 32 bits contain D followed by C.

The next two statements repeat the same process to insert B and then A:

```
packed = (packed << 16) | letterB;    // Shift and add the next letter - B
packed = (packed << 16) | letterA;    // Shift and add the next letter - A
```

Now the variable packed holds the codes for all four characters in the sequence D, C, B, and A.

The output produced by the next statement confirms this:

```
System.out.println("packed now contains 0x" + toHexString(packed));
```

This statement uses the toHexString() method defined in the Long class to generate a string containing a hexadecimal representation of the value of packed. Because you have a static import statement for the name of this method, you don't need to qualify it with the class name. You can see from the output that this consists of the character code values 0x44, 0x43, 0x42, and 0x41, which are the codes for the letters D through A.

The program then demonstrates how you can use the shift operators combined with the bitwise AND to extract the four char values from packed. The first step is to define a mask to select the rightmost 16 bits in a value of type long:

```
long mask = 0xFFFF;                   // Rightmost 16 bits as 1
```

The next statement uses mask to pick out the rightmost character code in packed:

```
char letter = (char)(packed & mask);  // Extract the rightmost letter
```

The cast to type char of the value that results from ANDing mask with packed is necessary because the compiler does not insert an automatic cast from type long to type char.

The next two statements output a heading followed by the first letter as a letter and its code:

```
System.out.println("From right to left the letters in packed are:");
System.out.println("  " + letter + "  0x" + toHexString(letter));
```

To get at the next character, you can shift out the character just extracted and AND the result with `mask` once again:

```
packed >>= 16;                          // Shift out the rightmost letter
letter = (char)(packed & mask);         // Extract the new rightmost letter
```

The result of the shift right operation is stored in `packed`, so ANDing `mask` with `packed` extracts the next letter. Extraction of the next two letters is achieved by repeating exactly the same process of shifting and then ANDing with `mask`. From the output you can see that it all works as it should.

Methods for Bitwise Operations

In addition to the basic Java language facilities for operations on integers at the bit level, you also have some methods available in library classes that provide you with a few extra capabilities. I won't go into great detail on these as they're rather specialized, but I'll outline the methods and explain what they do so you are aware of them.

The methods that implement bitwise operations are defined in the `Integer` and `Long` classes in the `java.lang` package. The methods in the `Integer` class apply to values of type `int`, and the methods in the `Long` class apply to values of type `long`. Both classes define the static methods for bitwise operations, shown in Table 2-9:

TABLE 2-9: Static Methods for Bitwise Operations

METHOD	DESCRIPTION
bitCount(arg)	Returns the number of 1 bits in the binary integer that you supply as arg. The count is returned as a value of type int.
highestOneBit(arg)	Returns an integer with a single 1 bit in the position corresponding to the leftmost 1 bit in arg. The value is returned as the same type as arg.
lowestOneBit(arg)	Returns an integer with a single 1 bit in the position corresponding to the rightmost 1 bit in arg. The value is returned as the same type as arg.
numberOfLeadingZeros(arg)	Returns the number of 0 bits preceding the leftmost 1 bit in arg. The value is returned as type int. If arg is zero then the method returns the total number of bits in arg, which is 32 for type int and 64 for type long.
numberOfTrailingZeros(arg)	Returns the number of 0 bits following the rightmost 1 bit in arg. The value is returned as type int. If arg is zero then the method returns the total number of bits in arg, which is 32 for type int and 64 for type long.
reverse(arg)	Returns the value that is obtained by reversing the order of bits in arg. The value is returned as the same type as arg.
rotateLeft(arg, distance)	Returns the value obtained by rotating the bits in arg left by distance bits positions, where distance is a value of type int. Rotating left means that bits shifted out on the left are shifted into vacated bit positions on the right. The value is returned as the same type as arg.
rotateRight(arg, distance)	Returns the value obtained by rotating the bits in arg right by distance bits positions, where distance is a value of type int. Rotating right means that bits shifted out on the right are shifted into vacated bit positions on the left. The value is returned as the same type as arg.

The return value is of the same type as the argument in each case where the result is a transformed version of the argument. Where it is simply a count, the value returned is of type `int`.

If you think about what you would need to do yourself to implement what these methods do, you'll realize they can save a lot of effort. To count how many 1 bits there are in an integer, you would need to work through each of the bits in a loop checking for a 1 bit in each case. With the `bitCount()` method, you get the result with a single operation. It may well be faster than you could implement it for yourself, too. Let's consider some examples of how you use these methods.

First, suppose you define an integer variable as follows:

```
int data = 0x0F00;          // data is:  0b0000_0000_0000_0000_0000_1111_0000_0000
```

You can now apply the `bitCount()` method to this. You must use the method in the `Integer` class because `data` is of type `int`:

```
int bits = Integer.bitCount(data);      // Result is 4
```

The variable `bits` is set to 4 because `data` contains four 1 bits.

Here's a definition of another integer variable, this time of type `long`:

```
long number = 0xF000_0000_0000_000FL;
```

The bit pattern in `number` has the first byte as 1111 0000 and the last byte as 0000 1111; all the other bytes are zero. Note that the `L` on the end of the literal is essential here. Without it you are specifying a literal of type `int`, and type `int` only has 32 bits so you get an error message from the compiler.

You could rotate the bits in `number` left by two with the following statement:

```
long result = Long.rotateLeft(number, 2);
```

The variable `result` are set to a value where the first byte is 0xC0, the last byte is 0x3F, and all the other bits are zero. The bits in `number` are shifted left by two bit positions, and the two 1 bits that are shifted out on the left are shifted in on the right as this is a rotation operation on the bits.

Let's see some of these methods working for real.

TRY IT OUT Methods for Operations on Bits

You can see the effects of some of the methods I have discussed by just outputting the results of some of the operations. The example also makes use of another static method that is defined in both the `Integer` and `Long` classes that you've seen in an earlier example—the `toBinaryString()` method that creates a string representation of a binary integer. Here's the code:

```
import static java.lang.Long.*;

public class TryBitMethods {
  public static void main(String[] args) {
    long number = 0xF000_0000_0000_000FL;
    System.out.println("number:\n" + toBinaryString(number));
    long result = rotateLeft(number,2);
    System.out.println(
                "number rotated left 2 bits:\n" + toBinaryString(result));
    result = rotateRight(number, 3);
    System.out.println(
                "number rotated right 3 bits:\n" + toBinaryString(result));
    result = reverse(result);
    System.out.println("Previous result reversed:\n" + toBinaryString(result));
    System.out.println("Bit count in number:" + bitCount(number));
  }
}
```

This program produces the following output:

```
number:
1111000000000000000000000000000000000000000000000000000000001111
number rotated left 2 bits:
1100000000000000000000000000000000000000000000000000000000111111
number rotated right 3 bits:
```

```
11111110000000000000000000000000000000000000000000000000000001
Previous result reversed:
10000000000000000000000000000000000000000000000000000001111111
Bit count in number: 8
```

I inserted \n characters in the output to put the binary value on the line following its description because it would not fit within the page width in the book. You might find it more convenient to remove the newlines but insert spaces to make the binary values align vertically. They are easier to compare that way.

How It Works

The program applies a variety of the methods for bit operation in the Long class to the value in number. The toBinaryString() method in the Long class creates a string representation of the binary value that is passed to the method, and you output that using the println() method. By comparing the bit patterns produced by each method with the original, you can clearly see what the methods do. You might like to try the same thing with the methods in the Integer class. Because there is an import statement for all the static members of the Long class, none of the methods from the Long class that the program uses need to be qualified with the class name.

VARIABLES WITH A FIXED SET OF INTEGER VALUES

You often need variables that can have values only from a predefined fixed set. For example, suppose you want to define an integer variable with the name weekday, which stores an integer value representing a day of the week. The variable ideally needs to be limited to seven possible values, one for each of Monday through Sunday. This is a situation where a facility called an *enumerated type*, or simply an *enumeration*, is a natural choice. You could define an enumeration for this situation with the following declaration statement:

```
enum Day {Monday, Tuesday, Wednesday, Thursday, Friday, Saturday, Sunday }
```

This defines a new type, Day, for variables that can store only one or other of the values specified between the braces. The names Monday, Tuesday, and so on through to Sunday are called *enumeration constants*, and they identify the only values that are allowed for variables of type Day. In fact these names correspond to integer values, starting from 0 in this case, but they are not the same as integer variables because they exist only within the context of the enumeration, Day.

Note the absence of a semicolon at the end of the definition of the Day enumeration. Because you are defining a type here, no semicolon is required after the closing brace. I used a capital D at the beginning of the type name, Day, because by convention types that you define begin with a capital letter. The names for the enumeration constants would usually be written beginning with a small letter, but in this case I used a capital letter at the beginning because that's how the days of the week are usually written. You could just as well write the enumeration constants with a small letter.

With this new type, you can now define the variable weekday like this:

```
Day weekday = Day.Tuesday;
```

This declares the variable weekday to be of type Day and initializes it with the value, Tuesday. Note that the enumeration constant that provides the initial value for weekday must be qualified with the name of the enumeration type here. If you leave the qualifier out, the compiler does not recognize the constant. There is a way to get around this, but you have to wait until Chapter 5 to find out about it. A variable of a given enumeration type can only be set to one or other of the enumeration constants that you defined for the type.

An enumeration can contain as many or as few enumeration constants as you need. Here's an enumeration type for the months in the year:

```
enum Month { January, February, March   , April  , May     , June,
          July   , August  , September, October, November, December }
```

You could define a variable of this type like this:

```
Month current = Month.September;      // Initialize to September
```

If you later want to change the value stored in the variable, you can set it to a different enumeration constant:

```
current = Month.October;
```

The `current` variable now contains the enumeration constant, `October`.

Let's see an enumeration in action in an example.

TRY IT OUT   **Using an Enumeration**

Here's a program that defines the `Day` enumeration and some variables of that type.

```
public class TryEnumeration {
   // Define an enumeration type for days of the week
   enum Day {Monday, Tuesday, Wednesday, Thursday, Friday, Saturday, Sunday}

   public static void main(String[] args) {
     // Define three variables of type Day
     Day yesterday = Day.Thursday;
     Day today = Day.Friday;
     Day tomorrow = Day.Saturday;

     // Output the values of the Day variables
     System.out.println("Today is " + today);
     System.out.println("Tomorrow will be " + tomorrow);
     System.out.println("Yesterday was " + yesterday);
   }
}
```

This produces the output:

```
Today is Friday
Tomorrow will be Saturday
Yesterday was Thursday
```

How It Works

The code itself is essentially what you saw in the previous section. There is the declaration of the enumerated type, `Day`, with definitions of three variables of that type in `main()`. You then have output statements for the values of the three variables. Note that `enum` types cannot be local to a method. If you put the definition for the `Day` type within `main()`, the example does not compile. Here the `Day` type is local to the class `TryEnumeration` that contains the `main()` method. You could put the definition for `Day` outside the `TryEnumeration` class, in which case it is global.

The output is very interesting. It doesn't display the numerical values of the variables of type `Day` but their names. This is the default way in which a value of an enumeration type is represented as a string because the names are more important than the values in most enumeration types. After all, the values that they have serve only to differentiate one enumeration constant from another.

This is just a small fraction of the capabilities of enumerations. I introduced the concept at this point because enumeration constants—the values that a variable of an enumeration type may have—are always integers. You will find out more about how you can use them as you progress through subsequent chapters, but you have to wait until Chapter 6 for the full story.

BOOLEAN VARIABLES

Variables of type `boolean` can have only one of two values, `true` or `false`. The values `true` and `false` are `boolean` literals. The `boolean` type is named after the mathematician, George Boole, who invented Boolean algebra, and variables of this type are described as `boolean` variables. You can define a variable of type `boolean` called `state` with the following statement:

```
boolean state = true;
```

This statement also initializes the variable `state` with the value `true`.

You can also set the value of a `boolean` variable in an assignment statement. For example, the statement

```
state = false;
```

sets the value of the variable `state` to `false`.

At this point you can't do much with a `boolean` variable, other than to set its value to `true` or `false`, but as you see in the next chapter, `boolean` variables become much more useful in the context of decision making in a program, particularly when you can use expressions that produce a result of type `boolean`.

Several operators combine `boolean` values, including operators for `boolean` AND, `boolean` OR, and `boolean` negation (these are `&&`, `||`, and `!`, respectively), as well as comparison operators that produce a `boolean` result. Rather than go into these here in the abstract, I defer discussion until the next chapter where I also go into how you can apply them in practice to alter the sequence of execution in a program.

 NOTE Note that variables of type `boolean` differ from the other primitive data types in that they cannot be cast to any other basic type, and the other primitive types cannot be cast to type `boolean`.

OPERATOR PRECEDENCE

I have already introduced the idea of a pecking order for operators that determines the sequence in which they are executed in a statement. A simple arithmetic expression such as 3 + 4 * 5 results in the value 23 because the multiply operation is executed first—it takes precedence over the addition operation. I can now formalize the position by classifying all the operators present in Java according to their precedence. Each operator in Java has a set priority or precedence in relation to the others, as shown in the following table. Operators with a higher precedence are executed before those of a lower precedence. Precedence is highest for operators in the top line in the table, down through to the operators in the bottom line, which have the lowest precedence. Operators that appear on the same line of the table have the same precedence (see Table 2-10):

TABLE 2-10: The Associativity of Operator Precedence Groups

OPERATOR PRECEDENCE GROUP	ASSOCIATIVITY
(), [], postfix ++, postfix --	left
unary +, unary -, prefix ++, prefix --, ~, !	right
(type), new	left
*, /, %	left
+, -	left
<<, >>, >>>	left
< ,<= , >, >=, instanceof	left
==, !=	left
&	left
^	left
|	left
&&	left
||	left
?:	left
=, +=, -=, *=, /=, %=, <<=, >>=, >>>=, &=, |=, ^=	right

Most of the operators that appear in the table you have not seen yet, but you will learn about them all in this book eventually, and it is handy to have them all gathered together in a single precedence table that you can refer to when necessary.

By definition, the postfix ++ operator changes the value of its operand after the other operators in the expression in which it appears have been executed, despite its high precedence. In this case, precedence determines what it applies to; in other words, the postfix ++ acts only on the variable that appears immediately before it. For this reason the expression numOranges+++numApples that we saw earlier in the chapter is evaluated as (numOranges++) + numApples rather than numOranges + (++numApples).

The sequence of execution of operators with equal precedence in a statement is determined by a property called associativity. The operators that appear on the same line in Table 2-10 form a group of operators that are either *left-associative* or *right-associative*. A left-associative operator attaches to its immediate left operand. This results in an expression involving several left-associative operators with the same precedence in the same expression being executed in sequence starting with the leftmost and ending with the rightmost. Right-associative operators of equal precedence in an expression bind to their right operand and consequently are executed from right to left. For example, if you write the following statement

```
a = b + c + 10;
```

the left associativity of the group to which the + operator belongs implies that this is effectively

```
a = (b + c) + 10;
```

On the other hand, = and op= are right-associative, so if you have int variables a, b, c, and d each initialized to 1, the statement

```
a += b = c += d = 10;
```

sets a to 12, b and c to 11, and d to 10. The statement is equivalent to:

```
a += (b = (c += (d = 10)));
```

 NOTE *Note that these statements are intended to illustrate how associativity works and are not a recommended approach to coding.*

You will probably find that you will learn the precedence and associativity of the operators in Java by just using them in your programs, so don't spend time trying to memorize them. You may need to refer to the table from time to time, but as you gain experience you will gain a feel for where the operators sit and eventually you will automatically know when you need parentheses and when not.

PROGRAM COMMENTS

I have been adding comments in all the examples so far, so you already know that everything following // in a line is ignored by the compiler (except when the // appears in a character string between double quotes of course). Another use for // is to change lines of codes into comments so that they aren't executed — to "comment them out" in other words. If you want to remove some code from a program temporarily, you just add // at the beginning of each line that you want to eliminate. Removing the // later restores the line of code.

It is often convenient to include multiple lines of comment in a program — for example, at the beginning of a method to explain what it does. An alternative to using // at the beginning of each line in a block of comments is to put /* at the beginning of the first comment line and */ at the end of the last comment line. Everything between the /* and the */ is ignored. By this means you can annotate your programs, like this for example:

```
/****************************************
 * This is a long explanation of        *
 * some particularly important          *
 * aspect of program operation.         *
 ***************************************/
```

Here I have used asterisks to highlight the comment. Of course, you can frame blocks like this in any way that you like, or even not at all, just so long as there is /* at the beginning and */ at the end.

Documentation Comments

You can also include comments in a program that are intended to produce separate documentation for the program. These are called *documentation comments*. A program called `javadoc` processes the documentation comments in the source code for a program to generate separate documentation for the code. All the documentation that you get with the SDK is produced in this way.

The documentation that is generated by `javadoc` is in the form of HTML web pages that can be viewed using a browser such as Firefox or Internet Explorer. A full discussion of documentation comments is outside the scope of this book—not because they are difficult; they aren't. However, it would need a lot of pages to cover them properly, and there are already a lot of pages in the book. Here I just describe them sufficiently so that you will recognize documentation comments when you see them.

A documentation comment begins with `/**` and ends with `*/`. An example of a simple documentation comment is the following:

```
/**
 *    This is a documentation comment.
 */
```

Any asterisks at the beginning of each line in a documentation comment are ignored, as are any spaces preceding the first asterisk.

A documentation comment can also include HTML tags, as well as special tags beginning with @ that are used to document methods and classes in a standard form. The @ character is followed by a keyword that defines the purpose of the tag. Table 2-11 shows some of the keywords that you can use:

TABLE 2-11: HTML Tag Keywords

KEYWORD	DESCRIPTION

`@author`	Used to define the author of the code. For example, I could specify that I am the author by adding the tag:
	
	`/**`
	`* @author Ivor Horton`
	`*/`

`@deprecated`	Used in the documentation of library classes and methods to indicate that they have been superseded and generally should not be used in new applications. This is primarily used within the class libraries to identify obsolete methods.

`@exception`	Used to document exceptions that the code can throw and the circumstance that can cause this to occur. For example, you might add the following documentation comment preceding your definition of a method to indicate the type of exception that the method may throw:
	
	`/**`
	`* @exception IOException  When an I/O error occurs.`
	`*/`

`{@link}`	Generates a link to another part of the documentation within the documentation that is produced. You can use this tag to embed a link to another class or method within descriptive text for your code. The curly brackets are used to separate the link from the rest of the in-line text.
`@param`	Used to describe the parameters for a method.

continues

TABLE 2-11 *(continued)*

KEYWORD	DESCRIPTION
`@return`	Used to document the value returned from a method.

`@see`	Used to specify cross-references to some other part of the code such as another class or a method. For example:
	
	`/**`
	`* @see Object#clone()`
	`*/`
	
	It can also just specify a string that represents an external reference not identifiable by a URL. For example:
	
	`/**`
	`* @see "Beginning Java 7"`
	`*/`
	
	It can also reference a URL.

`@throws`	A synonym for `@exception`.
`@version`	Used to describe the current version of the code.

You can use any HTML tags within a documentation comment except for header tags. The HTML tags you insert are used to structure and format the documentation appropriately when it is viewed, and `javadoc` adds HTML tags to format the comments that include the special @ tags that I mentioned in the preceding table.

The outline here really only gives you a hint as to what documentation comments are and doesn't do justice to the power and scope of `javadoc`. For that you need to look into it in detail. If you want to see real examples of `javadoc` comments, take a look at one or other of the source code files for the library classes. The SDK comes with the `javadoc` program and its documentation. `javadoc` also has its own home page on the Javasoft website at `www.oracle.com/technetwork/java/javase/documentation/javadoc-137458.html`.

SUMMARY

In this chapter you have seen all of the basic types of variables that are available in Java. All other types that you define for yourself are ultimately defined in terms of these primitive types. The discussion of `boolean` variables will be more meaningful in the context of the next chapter because their primary use is in decision making and modifying the execution sequence in a program.

EXERCISES

1. Write a console program to define and initialize a variable of type `byte` to 1, and then successively multiply it by 2 and display its value 8 times. Explain the reason for the last result.

2. Write a console program to declare and initialize a `double` variable with some value such as 1234.5678. Retrieve the integral part of the value and store it in a variable of type `long`, and retrieve the first four digits of the fractional part and store them in an integer of type `short`. Display the value of the `double` variable by outputting the two values stored as integers.

3. Write a program that defines a floating-point variable initialized with a dollar value for your income and a second floating-point variable initialized with a value corresponding to a tax rate of 35 percent. Calculate and output the amount of tax you must pay with the dollars and cents stored as separate integer values (use two variables of type `int` to hold the tax, perhaps `taxDollars` and `taxCents`).

4.   The diameter of the sun is approximately 865,000 miles. The diameter of Earth is approximately 7600 miles. Use the methods in the class `Math` to calculate the following:

> ➤   The volume of Earth in cubic miles
>
> ➤   The volume of the sun in cubic miles
>
> ➤   The ratio of the volume of the sun to the volume of Earth

▶ WHAT YOU LEARNED IN THIS CHAPTER

TOPIC	CONCEPT
Primitive types	Primitive types are types that are built in to the Java language. Variables of the primitive types store numerical values that are integers or floating-point values, `boolean` values, or Unicode characters.
Integer types	The integer types are `byte`, `short`, `int`, and `long`, and variables of these types occupy 1, 2, 4, and 8 bytes, respectively.
Storing characters	Variables of type `char` occupy 2 bytes and can store a single Unicode character code.
Storing logical values	Variables of type `boolean` can have only the value `true` or the value `false`.
Floating-point types	The floating-point types are `float` and `double`, occupying 4 and 8 bytes respectively.
Integer calculations	Integer expressions are evaluated using 64-bit operations for variables of type `long` and using 32-bit operations for all other integer types. You must, therefore, add a cast for all assignment operations storing a result of type `byte`, type `short`, or type `char`.
Floating-point calculations	A floating-point operation can produce a result that is outside the range of the type of the result. Values that are outside the range of a floating-point type are represented by a special value that is displayed as either `Infinity` or `-Infinity`. The result of a floating-point operation can also be indeterminate, which is displayed as NaN.
Casting	You can convert a value of one type to another by using an explicit cast. A cast is automatically supplied where necessary for `op=` assignment operations. You cannot cast to or from values of type `boolean`.
Order of operations	The order of execution of operators in an expression is determined by their precedence. Where operators are of equal precedence, the order of execution is determined by their associativity.
Enumeration types	You use an enumeration type to define variables that can only be assigned values from a fixed set that you specified as part of the enumeration. An enumeration type cannot be defined within a method.

3

Loops and Logic

WHAT YOU WILL LEARN IN THIS CHAPTER:

➤ How you compare data values

➤ How you can define logical expressions

➤ How you can use logical expressions to alter the sequence in which program statements are executed

➤ How you can select different expressions depending on the value of a logical expression

➤ How to choose between options in a fixed set of alternatives

➤ How long your variables last

➤ How you can repeat a block of code a given number of times

➤ How you can repeat a block of code as long as a given logical expression is true

➤ How you can break out of loops and statement blocks

➤ What assertions are and how you use them

In this chapter you look at how you make decisions and choices in your Java programs. You also learn how to make your programs repeat a set of actions until a specific condition is met.

All your programs of any consequence will use at least some, and often most, of the language capabilities and programming techniques I cover in this chapter, so make sure you have a good grasp of them.

But first, how do you make decisions in code and so affect the way the program runs?

MAKING DECISIONS

Making choices will be a fundamental element in all your programs. You need to be able to make decisions such as, "If the user wants to enter more data, then read another value from the keyboard," or, "If the bank balance is large, buy the car with the go-faster stripes, else renew the monthly bus ticket." Whatever decision you want to make, in programming terms it requires the ability to make comparisons between variables, constants, and the values of expressions and then execute one group of statements or another, depending on the result of a given comparison. Thus, the first step to understanding how you make decisions in a program is to look at how you make comparisons.

Making Comparisons

Java provides you with six relational operators (see Table 3-1) for comparing two data values. The data values you are comparing can be variables, constants, or expressions with values drawn from Java's primitive data types—`byte`, `short`, `int`, `long`, `char`, `float`, or `double`.

TABLE 3-1: Java Relational Operators

RELATIONAL OPERATORS	DESCRIPTION
>	Produces the value `true` if the left operand is greater than the right operand, and `false` otherwise.
>=	Produces the value `true` if the left operand is greater than or equal to the right operand, and `false` otherwise.
==	Produces the value `true` if the left operand is equal to the right operand, and `false` otherwise.
!=	Produces the value `true` if the left operand is not equal to the right operand, and `false` otherwise.
<=	Produces the value `true` if the left operand is less than or equal to the right operand, and `false` otherwise.
<	Produces the value `true` if the left operand is less than the right operand, and `false` otherwise.

As you see, each operator produces either the value `true` or the value `false`, and so is eminently suited to the business of making decisions. This also implies that you can use a `boolean` variable to store the result of a comparison. You saw how to declare variables of type `boolean` in the previous chapter. For example, you could define a `boolean` variable `state` and set its value to be the result of an expression using a comparison as follows:

```
boolean state = false;    // Define and initialize the variable
state = x - y < a + b;    // Store the result of comparing x-y with a+b
```

The value of the variable `state` is set to `true` in the assignment statement if `x - y` is less than `a + b`, and to `false` otherwise.

To understand how the preceding expression is evaluated, refer to the precedence table for operators that I introduced in the last chapter. You can see that the comparison operators are all of lower precedence than the arithmetic operators, so arithmetic operations are always completed before any comparisons are made, unless of course there are parentheses dictating otherwise. The expression:

```
x - y == a + b
```

produces the result `true` if `x - y` is equal to `a + b` because these arithmetic sub-expressions are evaluated first, and the values that result are the operands for the `==` operator. Of course, it is helpful to put the parentheses in, even though they are not strictly necessary. It leaves no doubt as to what is happening if you write:

```
(x - y) == (a + b)
```

Note that if the left and right operands of a relational operator are of differing types, values are promoted in the same way as you saw in the previous chapter for mixed arithmetic expressions. So if `aDouble` is of type `double` and `number` is of type `int` in the following expression

```
aDouble < number + 1
```

the result of the expression `number + 1` is calculated as type `int`, and this value is promoted to type `double` before comparing it with the value of `aDouble`.

The if Statement

The first statement you look at that can make use of the result of a comparison is the `if` statement. The `if` statement, in its simplest configuration, is of the form

```
if(expression)
   statement;
```

where `expression` can be any expression that produces a value `true` or `false`. You can see a graphical representation of this logic in Figure 3-1.

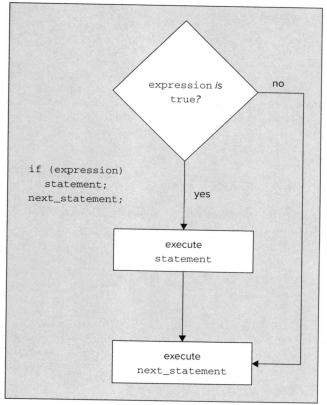

FIGURE 3-1

If the value of `expression` is `true`, the statement that follows the `if` is executed; otherwise, it isn't. A practical example of this is as follows:

```
if(number%2 != 0)        // Test if number is odd
   ++number;             // If so make it even
```

The `if` condition between the parentheses tests whether the value of `number` is odd by comparing the remainder that results from dividing it by 2 with 0. If the remainder isn't equal to 0, the value of `number` is odd, so you add 1 to make it even. If the value of number is even, the statement incrementing `number` is not executed.

 NOTE Notice how the statement on the second line is indented. This is to show that it is subject to the `if` condition. You should always indent statements in your Java programs as cues to the program structure. You will learn more guidelines on the use of statement indenting as you work with more complicated examples.

You may sometimes see a simple `if` written on a single line. The previous example could have been written:

```
if(number%2 != 0) ++number;   // If number is odd, make it even
```

This is perfectly legal. The compiler ignores excess spaces and newline characters. The semicolon acts as the delimiter for a statement. Writing an `if` in this way saves a little space, and occasionally it can be an aid to clarity, when you have a succession of such comparisons, for example, but generally it is better to write the action statement on a separate line from the condition being tested.

Statement Blocks

In general, wherever you can have one executable statement in Java, you can also have a block of statements enclosed between braces, `{}`. This applies to the statements within a statement block, so you can always nest a statement block between braces inside another statement block, and you can do this to any depth. The ability to use a block wherever you can have a statement means that you can use a statement block within the basic `if` statement that you just saw. Therefore, the `if` statement can equally well be of the following form:

```
if(expression) {
  statement 1;
  statement 2;
  ...
  statement n;
}
```

Now if the value of `expression` is `true`, all the statements enclosed in the following block are executed; if `expression` is `false`, the statements in the block are not executed. Of course, without the braces to enclose the block, the code no longer has a statement block:

```
if(expression)
  statement 1;
  statement 2;
  ...
  statement n;
```

Here, only the first statement, `statement 1`, is omitted when the `if` expression is `false`; the remaining statements are always executed regardless of the value of `expression`. You can see from this that indenting is just a visual cue to the logic. It has no effect on how the program code executes. This looks as though the sequence of statements belongs to the `if`, but only the first statement does because there are no braces. The indenting is incorrect and misleading here and the code should be written as:

```
if(expression)
  statement 1;
statement 2;
  ...
statement n;
```

> **NOTE** In this book, I have adopted the convention of having the opening brace on the same line as the `if` condition. The closing brace is then aligned with the first character, i, in the keyword `if`. I indent all the statements within the block from the braces so that they are easily identified as belonging to the block. This is consistent with the pattern I have been using with a block defining a class and a block belonging to a method. There are other conventions that you can use if you prefer. In another common convention, the braces bounding a block appear on their own line and are aligned. The most important consideration is that you are consistent in whatever convention you adopt.

As a practical example of an `if` statement that includes a statement block, you could write the following:

```
if(number%2 != 0) {                           // Test if number is odd
  // If so make it even and output a message
  ++number;
```

```
        System.out.println("Number was forced to be even and is now " + number);
    }
```

Now both statements between the braces are executed if the `if` expression is `true`, and neither of them is executed if the `if` expression is `false`.

> **NOTE** It is good practice to always put opening and closing braces around the code dependent on an `if` condition, even when there is only a single action statement. This helps to make the code easier to follow and minimizes the possibility of the program logic being confused.

Statement blocks are more than just a convenient way of grouping statements together—they affect the life and accessibility of variables. You will learn more about statement blocks when I discuss variable scope later in this chapter. In the meantime, let's look a little deeper into what you can do with the `if` statement.

The else Clause

You can extend the basic `if` statement by adding an `else` clause. This provides an alternative choice of statement, or statement block, that is executed when the `expression` in the `if` statement is `false`. You can see the syntax of this statement, and how the program's control flow works, in Figure 3-2.

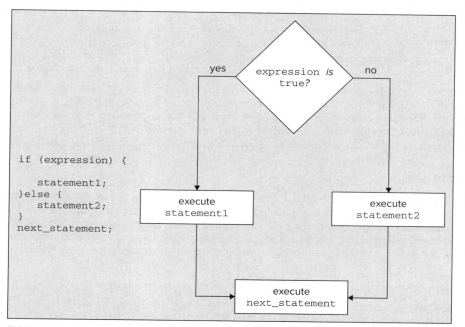

FIGURE 3-2

This provides an explicit choice between two courses of action—one for when the `if` expression is `true` and another for when it is `false`.

You can apply this in a console program and try out the `random()` method from the `Math` class at the same time.

TRY IT OUT if-else

When you have entered the program text, save it in a file called `NumberCheck.java`. Compile it and then run it a few times to see what results you get.

Available for
download on
Wrox.com

```java
public class NumberCheck {
  public static void main(String[] args) {
    int number = 0;
    number = 1+(int)(100*Math.random());// Get a random integer between 1 & 100
    if(number%2 == 0) {                  // Test if it is even
      System.out.println("You have got an even number, " + number);// It's even

    } else {
      System.out.println("You have got an odd number, " + number); // It's odd
    }
  }
}
```

NumberCheck.java

How It Works

You saw the `random()` method that is defined in the standard `Math` class in the previous chapter. It returns a random value of type `double` between 0.0 and 1.0, but the result is always less than 1.0, so the largest number you can get is 0.9999. . . (with the number of recurring digits being limited to the maximum number that the type `double` allows, of course). Consequently, when you multiply the value returned by 100.0 and convert this value to type `int` with the explicit cast, you discard any fractional part of the number and produce a random integer between 0 and 99. Adding 1 to this results in a random integer between 1 and 100, which you store in the variable `number`. You then generate the program output in the `if` statement. If the value of `number` is even, the first `println()` call is executed; otherwise, the second `println()` call in the `else` clause is executed.

Note the use of indentation here. It is evident that `main()` is within the class definition because indentation relative to the first line of the class definition provides you with a cue to that. The code for `main()` is clearly distinguished because it is indented relative to the first line of the method. You can also see immediately which statement is executed when the `if` expression is `true` and which applies when it is `false`.

Nested if Statements

The statement that is executed when an `if` expression is `true` can be another `if`, as can the statement in an `else` clause. This enables you to express such convoluted logic as "if my bank balance is healthy, then I will buy the car if I have my check book with me, else I will buy the car if I can get a loan from the bank." An `if` statement that is nested inside another can also itself contain a nested `if`. You can continue nesting `if`s one inside the other like this for as long as you still know what you are doing—or even beyond if you enjoy confusion.

To illustrate the nested `if` statement, I can modify the `if` from the previous example:

```java
if(number%2 == 0) {                  // Test if it is even
  if(number < 50) {                  // Output a message if number is < 50
    System.out.println("You have got an even number < 50, " + number);
  }

} else {
  System.out.println("You have got an odd number, " + number); // It is odd
}
```

Now the message for an even value is displayed only if the value of `number` is also less than 50. There are three possible outcomes from this code fragment: If `number` is even and less than 50, you see a message to that effect; if number is even and is not less than 50, there is no output; and finally; if number is odd, a message is displayed.

The braces around the nested if are necessary here because of the else clause. The braces constrain the nested if in the sense that if it had an else clause, it would have to appear between the braces enclosing the nested if. If the braces were not there, the program would still compile and run but the logic would be different. Let's see how.

With nested ifs, the question of which if statement a particular else clause belongs to often arises. If you remove the braces from the preceding code, you have:

```
if(number%2 == 0)                   // Test if it is even
  if(number < 50 )                  // Output a message if number is < 50
    System.out.println("You have got an even number < 50, " + number);
  else
    System.out.println("You have got an odd number, " + number); // It is odd
```

This has substantially changed the logic from the previous version, in spite of the fact that the indentation implies otherwise. The else clause now belongs to the nested if that tests whether number is less than 50, so the second println() call is executed only for *even* numbers that are greater than or equal to 50. This is clearly not what was intended because it makes nonsense of the output in this case, but it does illustrate the rule for connecting elses to ifs, which is:

> An else *always belongs to the nearest preceding* if *in the same block that is not already spoken for by another* else.

You need to take care that the indenting of statements with nested ifs is correct. It is easy to convince yourself that the logic is as indicated by the indentation, even when this is completely wrong.

Let's try the if-else combination in another program.

TRY IT OUT   Deciphering Characters the Hard Way

Create the class LetterCheck, and code its main() method as follows:

```
public class LetterCheck {
  public static void main(String[] args) {
    char symbol = 'A';
    symbol = (char)(128.0*Math.random());       // Generate a random character

    if(symbol >= 'A') {                          // Is it A or greater?
      if(symbol <= 'Z') {                        // yes, and is it Z or less?
        // Then it is a capital letter
        System.out.println("You have the capital letter " + symbol);

      } else {                                   // It is not Z or less
        if(symbol >= 'a') {                      // So is it a or greater?
          if(symbol <= 'z') {                    // Yes, so is it z or less?
            // Then it is a small letter
            System.out.println("You have the small letter " + symbol);

          } else {                               // It is not less than z
            System.out.println(
            "The code is greater than a but it's not a letter");
          }

        } else {
          System.out.println(
                  "The code is less than a and it's not a letter");
        }
      }

    } else {
```

```
            System.out.println("The code is less than A so it's not a letter");
        }
    }
}
```

How It Works

This program figures out whether the character stored in the variable `symbol` is an uppercase letter, a lowercase letter, or some other character. The program first generates a random character with a numeric code between 0 and 127, which corresponds to the characters in the basic 7-bit ASCII (ISO 646) character set. The Unicode coding for the ASCII characters is numerically the same as the ASCII code values. Within this character set, the letters A to Z are represented by a contiguous group of ASCII codes with decimal values from 65 to 90. The lowercase letters are represented by another contiguous group with ASCII code values that have decimal values from 97 to 122. So to convert any capital letter to a lowercase letter, you just need to add 32 to the character code.

The `if` statements are a bit convoluted, so let's look at the diagram of the logic in Figure 3-3.

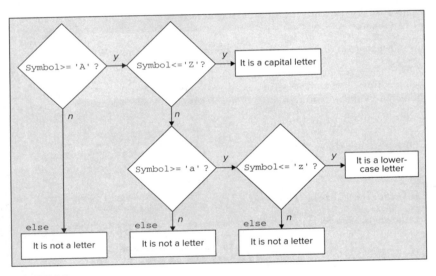

FIGURE 3-3

You have four `if` statements altogether. The first `if` tests whether `symbol` is `'A'` or greater. If it is, it could be a capital letter, a small letter, or possibly something else. But if it isn't, it is not a letter at all, so the `else` for this `if` statement (toward the end of the program) produces a message to that effect.

The nested `if` statement, which is executed if `symbol` is `'A'` or greater, tests whether it is `'Z'` or less. If it is, then `symbol` definitely contains a capital letter, and the appropriate message is displayed. If it isn't then it may be a small letter, so another `if` statement is nested within the `else` clause of the first nested `if` to test for this possibility.

The `if` statement in the `else` clause tests for `symbol` being greater than `'a'`. If it isn't, you know that `symbol` is not a letter, and a message is displayed. If it is, another `if` checks whether `symbol` is `'z'` or less. If it is you have a small letter, and if not you don't have a letter at all.

You have to run the example a few times to get all the possible messages to come up. They all will—eventually.

After having carefully crafted our convoluted and cumbersome condition checking, I can now reveal that there is a much easier way to achieve the same result. You'll see that in the section "Logical Operators" that follows immediately after a brief word on working with enumeration values.

Comparing Enumeration Values

You can't compare variables of an enumeration type using the comparison operators but you can compare them using a method that every enumeration object provides. Suppose you define an enumeration type as:

```
enum Season { spring, summer, fall, winter }
```

You can now define and initialize a variable of type `Season` with the following statement:

```
Season season = Season.summer;
```

If you later want to check what the `season` variable currently holds, you could write:

```
if(season.equals(Season.spring)) {
  System.out.println("Spring has sprung, the grass is riz.");
} else {
  System.out.println("It isn\'t Spring!");
}
```

This calls the `equals()` method for the enumeration referred to by `season`. This method compares the value in `season` with the value between the parentheses and results in `true` if they are equal or `false` if they are unequal. You could use the `equals()` method to compare `season` with another variable of type `Season`, for example:

```
Season best = Season.winter;           // A new variable initialized to winter
if(season.equals(best)) {
  System.out.println("season is the same as best, and is equal to "+ best);
} else {
  System.out.println(" season has the value "+season +
                          " and best has the value " + best);
}
```

After defining the variable, `best`, you test whether the value of `season` is the same value as `best`. If it is, the first output statement is executed. If `best` and `season` are not equal, the output statement in the `else` block is executed.

LOGICAL OPERATORS

The tests you have put in the `if` expressions have been relatively simple so far. Real life is typically more complicated. You often want to combine a number of conditions so that you execute a particular course—for example, if they are all `true` simultaneously. You can ride the roller coaster if you are older than 12 years old, taller than 4 feet tall, and shorter than 6 feet. Failure on any count and it's no-go. Sometimes, though, you may need to test for any one of a number of conditions being `true`—for example, you get a lower price entry ticket if you are under 16, or over 65.

You can deal with both of these cases, and more, using *logical operators* to combine several expressions that have a value `true` or `false`. Because they operate on `boolean` values, they are also referred to as *boolean operators*. There are six logical operators that operate on `boolean` values as shown in Table 3-2.

TABLE 3-2: Logical Operators

SYMBOL	LONG NAME
&	logical AND
&&	conditional AND
|	logical OR
||	conditional OR
^	exclusive OR (XOR)
!	logical negation (NOT)

The AND and OR operators are very simple; the only point of potential confusion is the fact that you have the choice of two operators for each of AND and OR. The extra operators are the bitwise & and | from the previous chapter that you can also apply to `boolean` values where they have an effect that is subtly different from && and ||. Let's first consider what each of these is used for in general terms and then look at how you can use some of them in an example.

Logical AND Operations

You can use either of the AND operators, && or &, where you have two logical expressions that must both be `true` for the result to be `true`—that is, you only want to be rich and healthy. Either AND operator produces the same result from the logical expression. I come back to how they differ in a moment. First, let's explore how they are used. All of the following discussion applies equally well to & as well as to &&.

Let's see how logical operators can simplify the last example. You could use the && operator if you test a variable of type `char` to determine whether it contains an uppercase letter or not. The value being tested must be both greater than or equal to 'A' AND less than or equal to 'Z'. Both conditions must be `true` for the value to be a capital letter. Taking the example from our previous program, with a value stored in a `char` variable `symbol`, you could implement the test for an uppercase letter in a single `if` by using the && operator:

```
if(symbol >= 'A' && symbol <= 'Z')
    System.out.println("You have the capital letter " + symbol);
```

If you look at the precedence table in Chapter 2, you see that the relational operators are executed before the && operator, so no parentheses are necessary. Here, the output statement is executed only if both of the conditions combined by the operator && are `true`. However, as I have said before, it is a good idea to add parentheses if they make the code easier to read. It also helps to avoid mistakes.

In fact, the result of an && operation is very simple. It is `true` only if both operands are `true`; otherwise, the result is `false`.

You can now rewrite the set of `if`s from the last example.

TRY IT OUT   Deciphering Characters the Easy Way

You can replace the outer `if-else` loop and its contents in `LetterCheck.java` as shown in the following code:

Available for download on Wrox.com

```
public class LetterCheck2 {
  public static void main(String[] args) {
    char symbol = 'A';
    symbol = (char)(128.0*Math.random());      // Generate a random character
    if(symbol >= 'A' && symbol <= 'Z') {       // Is it a capital letter
      System.out.println("You have the capital letter " + symbol);
    } else {
      if(symbol >= 'a' && symbol <= 'z') {     // or is it a small letter?
        System.out.println("You have the small letter " + symbol);
      } else {                                 // It is not less than z
        System.out.println("The code is not a letter");
      }
    }
  }
}
```

LetterCheck2.java

The output should be the same as the previous version of the code.

How It Works

Using the && operator has condensed the example down quite a bit. You now can do the job with two `if`s, and it's certainly easier to follow what's happening.

You might want to note that when the statement in an else clause is another if, the if is sometimes written on the same line as the else, as in the following:

```
if(symbol >= 'A' && symbol <= 'Z') {          // Is it a capital letter
   System.out.println("You have the capital letter " + symbol);
} else if(symbol >= 'a' && symbol <= 'z') {   // or is it a small letter?
   System.out.println("You have the small letter " + symbol);

} else {                                       // It is not less than z
   System.out.println("The code is not a letter");
}
```

I think the original is clearer in this particular case, but writing else if can sometimes make the code easier to follow.

&& versus &

So what distinguishes && from &? The difference is that the conditional && does not bother to evaluate the right-hand operand if the left-hand operand is false because the result is already determined in this case to be false. This can make the code a bit faster when the left-hand operand is false.

For example, consider the following statements:

```
int number = 50;
if(number<40 && (3*number - 27)>100) {
   System.out.println("number = " + number);
}
```

Here the expression (3*number - 27)>100 is never executed because the expression number<40 is always false. On the other hand, if you write the statements as

```
int number = 50;
if(number<40 & (3*number - 27)>100) {
   System.out.println("number = " + number);
}
```

the effect is different. The whole logical expression is always evaluated, so even though the left-hand operand of the & operator is false and the result is a foregone conclusion after that is known, the right-hand operand (3*number - 27)>100 is still evaluated.

So, you can just use && all the time to make your programs a bit faster and forget about &, right? Wrong—it all depends on what you are doing. Most of the time you can use &&, but there are occasions when you want to be sure that the right-hand operand is evaluated. Equally, in some instances, you want to be certain the right-hand operand won't be evaluated if the left operand is false.

For example, the first situation can arise when the right-hand expression involves modifying a variable—and you want the variable to be modified in any event. An example of a statement like this is:

```
if(++value%2 == 0 & ++count < limit) {
   // Do something
}
```

Here, the variable count is incremented in any event. If you use && instead of &, count is incremented only if the left operand of the AND operator is true. You get a different result depending on which operator is used.

I can illustrate the second situation with the following statement:

```
if(count > 0 && total/count > 5) {
   // Do something...
}
```

In this case, the right operand for the && operation is executed only if the left operand is true—that is, when count is positive. Clearly, if you were to use & here, and count happened to be zero, you would be attempting to divide the value of total by 0, which in the absence of code to prevent it would terminate the program.

Logical OR Operations

The OR operators, | and ||, apply when you want a true result if either or both of the operands are true. The logical OR, ||, works in a similar way to the && operator in that it omits the evaluation of the right-hand operand when the left-hand operand is true. Obviously if the left operand for the || operator is true, the result is true regardless of whether the right operand is true or false.

Let's take an example. A reduced entry ticket price is issued to under 16-year-olds and to those aged 65 or older; this could be tested using the following if:

```
if(age < 16 || age >= 65) {
   ticketPrice *= 0.9;        // Reduce ticket price by 10%
}
```

The effect here is to reduce ticketPrice by 10 percent if either condition is true. Clearly in this case, both conditions cannot be true.

With an | or an || operation, you get a false result only if both operands are false. If either or both operands are true, the result is true.

Exclusive OR Operations

The exclusive OR results in true when its operands are different, so when one operand has the value true and the other has the value false, the result is true. When both operands have the same value, either both true or both false, the result is false. Thus the exclusive OR operator is useful on those rare occasions when you want to establish whether or not two boolean values are different.

Boolean NOT Operations

The third type of logical operator, !, applies to one boolean operand, and the result is the inverse of the operand value. So if the value of a boolean variable, state, is true then the expression !state has the value false, and if it is false, then !state evaluates to true. To see how the operator is used with an expression, you could rewrite the code fragment you used to provide discounted ticket price as the following:

```
if(!(age >= 16 && age < 65)) {
   ticketPrice *= 0.9;        // Reduce ticket price by 10%
}
```

The expression (age >= 16 && age < 65) is true if age is from 16 to 64. People of this age do not qualify for the discount, so the discount should be applied only when this expression is false. Applying the ! operator to the result of the expression does what you want.

You could also apply the ! operator in an expression that was a favorite of Charles Dickens:

```
!(Income > Expenditure)
```

If this expression is true, the result is misery, at least as soon as the bank starts bouncing your checks.

Of course, you can use any of the logical operators in combination when necessary. If the theme park decides to give a discount on the price of entry to anyone who is younger than 12 years old and shorter than 48 inches tall, or to someone who is older than 65 and taller than 72 inches tall, you could apply the discount with this test:

```
if((age < 12 && height < 48) || (age > 65 && height > 72)) {
   ticketPrice *= 0.8;           // 20% discount on the ticket price
}
```

The parentheses are not strictly necessary here, as && has a higher precedence than ||, but adding the parentheses makes it clearer how the comparisons combine and makes the code a little more readable.

WARNING Don't confuse the bitwise operators &, |, ^, and ! with the logical operators that look the same. Which type of operator you are using in any particular instance is determined by the type of operand with which you use it. The bitwise operators apply to integer types and produce an integer result. The logical operators apply to operands that have boolean values and produce a result of type boolean — true or false. You can use both bitwise and logical operators in an expression when it is convenient to do so.

Character Testing Using Standard Library Methods

Although testing characters using logical operators is a useful way of demonstrating how these operators work, in practice there is an easier way. The standard Java packages provide a range of standard methods to do the sort of testing for particular sets of characters such as letters or digits that you have been doing with if statements. They are all available within the Character class, which is automatically available in your programs. For example, you could have written the if statement in the LetterCheck2 program as shown in the following example.

TRY IT OUT Deciphering Characters Trivially

In the following example, the if expressions in main() that were in the LetterCheck2 class have been replaced by expressions that call methods in the Character class to do the testing:

Available for download on Wrox.com

```java
import static java.lang.Character.isLowerCase;
import static java.lang.Character.isUpperCase;

public class LetterCheck3 {
  public static void main(String[] args) {
    char symbol = 'A';
    symbol = (char)(128.0*Math.random());       // Generate a random character

    if(isUpperCase(symbol)) {
      System.out.println("You have the capital letter " + symbol);
    } else {
      if(isLowerCase(symbol)) {
        System.out.println("You have the small letter " + symbol);
      } else {
        System.out.println("The code is not a letter");
      }
    }
  }
}
```

LetterCheck3.java

How It Works

Because you have the import statements for the isUpperCase and isLowerCase method names at the beginning of the source file, you can call these methods without using the Character class name as qualifier. The isUpperCase() method returns true if the char value that you pass to it is uppercase, and false if it is not. Similarly, the isLowerCase() method returns true if the char value you pass to it is lowercase.

Table 3-3 shows some of the other methods included in the Character class that you may find useful for testing characters. In each case, you put the argument of type char that is to be tested between the parentheses following the method name.

TABLE 3-3: Methods Useful for Testing Characters

METHOD	DESCRIPTION
isDigit()	Returns the value `true` if the argument is a digit (0 to 9), and `false` otherwise.
isLetter()	Returns the value `true` if the argument is a letter, and `false` otherwise.
isLetterOrDigit()	Returns the value `true` if the argument is a letter or a digit, and `false` otherwise.

isWhitespace()	Returns the value `true` if the argument is whitespace, which is any one of the following characters:
	    space (' ')
	    tab ('\t')
	    newline ('\n')
	    carriage return ('\r')
	    form feed ('\f')
	The method returns `false` otherwise.

You can find information on other methods in the `Character` class in the JDK documentation for the class.

THE CONDITIONAL OPERATOR

The *conditional operator* is sometimes called a *ternary operator* because it involves three operands. It is best understood by looking at an example. Suppose you have two variables of type int with the names yourAge and myAge, and you want to assign the greater of the values stored in yourAge and myAge to a third variable, older, which is also of type int. You can do this with the following statement:

```
older = yourAge > myAge ? yourAge : myAge;
```

The conditional operator has a logical expression as the first of its three operands—in this case, it is the expression yourAge>myAge. If this expression is `true`, the operand that follows the ? symbol—in this case, yourAge—is evaluated to produce the value resulting from the operation. If the expression yourAge>myAge is `false`, the third operand that comes after the colon—in this case, myAge—is evaluated to produce the value from the operation. Thus, the result of this conditional expression is yourAge, if yourAge is greater than myAge, and myAge otherwise. This value is then stored in the variable older. The use of the conditional operator in this assignment statement is equivalent to the `if` statement:

```
if(yourAge > myAge) {
  older = yourAge;

} else {
  older = myAge;
}
```

Remember, though, the conditional operator is an operator and not a statement, so you can use it in a more complex expression involving other operators.

The conditional operator can be written generally as:

```
logical_expression ? expression1 : expression2
```

If the logical_expression evaluates as `true`, the result of the operation is the value of expression1, and if logical_expression evaluates to `false`, the result is the value of expression2. Note that if expression1 is evaluated because logical_expression is `true`, then expression2 is not, and vice versa.

You can use the conditional operator in lots of circumstances, and one common application of it is to control output, depending on the result of an expression or the value of a variable. You can vary a message by selecting one text string or another depending on the condition specified.

Conditional Plurals

Type in the following code, which adds the correct ending to 'hat' depending on how many hats you have:

```
public class ConditionalOp {
  public static void main(String[] args) {
    int nHats = 1;                      // Number of hats
    System.out.println("I have " + nHats + " hat" + (nHats == 1 ? "." : "s."));

    nHats++;                            // Increment number of hats
    System.out.println("I have " + nHats + " hat" + (nHats == 1 ? "." : "s."));
  }
}
```

ConditionalOp.java

The output from this program is the following:

```
I have 1 hat.
I have 2 hats.
```

How It Works

The result of executing the conditional operator in the program is a string containing just a period when the value of nHats is 1, and a string containing an s followed by a period in all other cases. The effect of this is to cause the output statement to automatically adjust the output between singular and plural. You can use the same technique in other situations, such as where you need to choose "he" or "she" for example, as long as you are able to specify a logical expression to differentiate the situation in which you should use one rather than the other. A more challenging application you could try is to append "st," "nd," "rd," or "th" to a date value, such as in "3rd November" or "4th July."

THE SWITCH STATEMENT

You use the switch statement to select from multiple choices that are identified by a set of fixed values for a given expression. The expression that selects a choice must produce a result of an integer type other than long, or a value of an enumeration type, or a string. Thus, the expression that controls a switch statement can result in a value of type char, byte, short, or int, an enumeration constant, or a String object.

In normal use the switch statement operates rather like a rotary switch in that you can select one of a fixed number of choices. For example, on some makes of washing machine you choose between the various machine settings in this way, with positions for cotton, wool, synthetic fiber, and so on, which you select by turning the knob to point to the option that you want.

Here's a switch statement reflecting this logic for a washing machine:

```
switch(wash) {
  case 1:                           // wash is 1 for Cotton
    System.out.println("Cotton selected");
    // Set conditions for cotton...
    break;
  case 2:                           // wash is 2 for Linen
    System.out.println("Linen selected");
    // Set conditions for linen...
    break;
  case 3:                           // wash is 3 for Wool
    System.out.println("Wool selected");
    // Set conditions for wool...
    break;
  default:                          // Not a valid value for wash
    System.out.println("Selection error");
    break;
}
```

The selection in the `switch` statement is determined by the value of the expression that you place between the parentheses after the keyword `switch`. In this case it's simply the integer variable `wash` that would need to be previously declared as of type `char`, `byte`, `short`, or `int`. You define the possible `switch` options by one or more *case values*, also called *case labels*, which you define using the keyword `case`. In general, a case label consists of the `case` keyword followed by a constant value that is the value that selects the case, followed by a colon. The statements to be executed when the case is selected follow the case label. You place all the case labels and their associated statements between the braces for the `switch` statement. You have three case values in the example, plus a special case with the label `default`, which is another keyword. A particular case value is selected if the value of the `switch` expression is the same as that of the particular case value. The `default` case is selected when the value of the `switch` expression does not correspond to any of the values for the other cases. Although I've written the cases in the preceding `switch` sequenced by their case values, they can be in any order.

When a particular case is selected, the statements that follow that case label are executed. So if `wash` has the value 2, the statements that follow

```
case 2:                    // wash is 2 for Linen
```

are executed. In this case, these are:

```
System.out.println("Linen selected");
// Set conditions for linen...
break;
```

When a `break` statement is executed here, it causes execution to continue with the statement following the closing brace for the `switch`. The `break` is not mandatory as the last statement for each case, but if you don't put a `break` statement at the end of the statements for a case, the statements for the next case in sequence are executed as well, through to whenever another `break` is found or the end of the `switch` block is reached. This is not usually what you want. The `break` after the `default` statements in the example is not strictly necessary, but it does protect against the situation when you might add another case label at the end of the `switch` statement block and overlook the need for the `break` at the end of the last case.

You need a case label for each choice to be handled in the `switch`, and the case values must all be different. The `default` case you have in the preceding example is, in general, optional. As I said, it is selected when the value of the expression for the `switch` does not correspond with any of the case values that you have defined. If you don't specify a `default` case and the value of the `switch` expression does not match any of the case labels, none of the statements in the `switch` are executed, and execution continues at the statement following the closing brace of the `switch` statement.

You could rewrite the previous `switch` statement to use a variable of an enumeration type as the expression controlling the `switch`. Suppose you have defined the `WashChoice` enumeration type like this:

```
enum WashChoice { cotton, linen, wool }       // Define enumeration type
```

You can now code the switch statement like this:

```
WashChoice wash = WashChoice.linen;            // Initial definition of variable
// Some more code that might change the value of wash...

switch(wash) {
  case cotton:
    System.out.println("Cotton selected");
    // Set conditions for cotton...
    break;
  case linen:
    // Set conditions for linen...
    System.out.println("Linen selected");
    break;
  case wool:
    System.out.println("Wool selected");
    // Set conditions for wool...
    break;
}
```

The `switch` is controlled by the value of the `wash` variable. Note how you use the enumeration constants as case values. You must write them *without* the enumeration type name as a qualifier in this context; otherwise, the code does not compile. Using enumeration constants as the case values makes the `switch` much more self-explanatory. It is perfectly clear what each case applies to. Because you cannot assign a value to a variable of an enumeration type that is not a defined enumeration constant, it is not necessary to include a default case here.

Here's how you could write the `switch` statement to use an expression that results in a string:

```
switch(wash.toLowerCase()) {
  case "cotton":
    System.out.println("Cotton selected");
    // Set conditions for cotton...
    break;
  case "linen":
    System.out.println("Linen selected");
    // Set conditions for linen...
    break;
  case "wool":
    System.out.println("Wool selected");
    // Set conditions for wool...
    break;
  default:                              // Not a valid value for wash
    System.out.println("Selection error");
    break;
}
```

The `wash` variable here must be of type `String`—you will learn about the `String` class in Chapter 4. The `toLowerCase()` method from the `String` class converts the string stored in `wash` to lowercase so the `switch` works regardless of whether upper- or lowercase letters are used to specify the choice of wash.

The General Case of the switch Statement

The flowchart shown in Figure 3-4 shows the logic of the general `switch` statement.

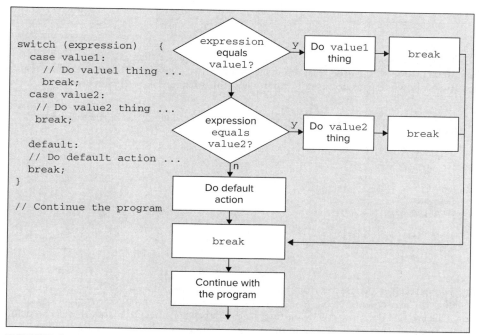

FIGURE 3-4

NOTE *While Figure 3-4 show the logic of the* switch *statement, the compiler may implement the process differently, often using a lookup table for case values.*

Each case value is notionally compared with the value of an expression. If one matches then the code for that case is executed, and the break branches to the first statement after the switch. As I said earlier, if you don't include the break statements, the logic is quite different, as shown in Figure 3-5.

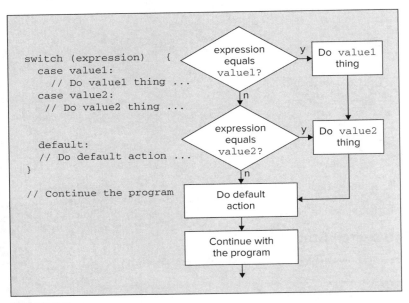

FIGURE 3-5

Now when a case label value is equal to the switch expression, the code for that case is executed and followed by the statements for all the other cases that succeed the case that was selected, including that for the default case if that follows. This is not usually what you want, so make sure you don't forget the break statements.

You can arrange to execute the same statements for several different case labels, as in the following switch statement:

```
char yesNo = 'N';
// more program logic…

switch(yesNo) {
  case 'n': case 'N':
      System.out.println("No selected");
      break;
  case 'y': case 'Y':
      System.out.println("Yes selected");
      break;
}
```

Here the variable yesNo receives a character from the keyboard somehow. You want a different action depending on whether the user enters "Y" or "N", but you want to be able to accept either uppercase or lowercase entries. This switch does just this by putting the case labels together. Note that there is no default case here. If yesNo contains a character other than those identified in the case statements, the switch statement has no effect. In practice, you might add a default case in this kind of situation to output a message indicating when the value in yesNo is not valid.

Of course, you could also implement this logic using if statements:

```
if(yesNo=='n' || yesNo=='N') {
  System.out.println("No selected");
  } else {
  if(yesNo=='y' || yesNo=='Y') {
    System.out.println("Yes selected");
  }
}
```

I prefer the switch statement as I think it's easier to follow, but you decide for yourself. Let's try an example.

TRY IT OUT   Making the switch

This example uses a switch controlled by an integer type and a switch controlled by a variable of an enumeration type:

Available for download on Wrox.com

```
public class TrySwitch {
  enum WashChoice {cotton, linen, wool, synthetic}        // Define enumeration type

  public static void main(String[] args) {
    // Variable to define the choice of wash
    WashChoice wash = WashChoice.cotton;

    // The clothes variable specifies the clothes to be washed by an integer
    // 1:shirts    2:sweaters  3:socks  4:sheets  5:pants
    int clothes = 3;

    switch(clothes) {
      case 1:
        System.out.println("Washing shirts.");
        wash = WashChoice.cotton;
        break;
      case 2:
        System.out.println("Washing sweaters.");
        wash = WashChoice.wool;
        break;
      case 3:
        System.out.println("Washing socks.");
        wash = WashChoice.wool;
        break;
      case 4:
        System.out.println("Washing sheets.");
        wash = WashChoice.linen;
        break;
      case 5:
        System.out.println("Washing pants.");
        wash = WashChoice.synthetic;
        break;
      default:
        System.out.println("Unknown washing - default synthetic.");
        wash = WashChoice.synthetic;
        break;
    }
    System.out.println("Wash is "+ wash);

    // Now select the wash temperature
    switch(wash) {
      case wool:
        System.out.println("Temperature is 120.");
```

```
        break;
      case cotton:
        System.out.println("Temperature is 170.");
        break;
      case synthetic:
        System.out.println("Temperature is 130.");
        break;
      case linen:
        System.out.println("Temperature is 180.");
        break;
    }
  }
}
```

TrySwitch.java

You should get the following output from this example:

```
Washing socks.
Wash is wool
Temperature is 120.
```

How It Works

This looks like a lot of code, but it's because of the number of cases in the two `switch` statements. Obviously you don't really need to use two switch statements here, but I used two to show integers and enumeration constants as case values.

You first define an enumeration type, `WashChoice`. You then define a variable of this type in the `main()` method with the following statement:

```
WashChoice wash = WashChoice.cotton;    // Variable to define the choice of wash
```

The initial value for `wash` here is arbitrary. You could have chosen any of the possible enumeration constants for the `WashChoice` type.

Next, you define and initialize a variable identifying the type of clothes to be washed:

```
int clothes = 3;
```

The initial value for `clothes` corresponds to socks and in a more practical example would be arrived at by means other than just assigning the value. You use the `clothes` variable to control the next `switch` statement. For each case in the `switch`, you output what is to be washed and set the value for the `wash` variable to the appropriate enumeration constant. You would usually put a default case in this sort of `switch` statement because its control expression is numeric, and if the value was derived by some computation or other, there is always the possibility of an invalid value being produced. If there is no default case and the `switch` expression results in a value that does not correspond to any of the cases, execution just continues with the statement following the `switch` block.

After the first `switch`, you output the wash type:

```
System.out.println("Wash is "+ wash);
```

You saw in the previous chapter that the string representation of a value that is an enumeration constant is the name of the value as it appears in the type definition.

Lastly, you use the `wash` variable as the expression selecting a case in the next `switch`. Because a variable of an enumeration type must have an enumeration constant as a value, and all possible values are represented by cases in the `switch`, you don't need a default case here.

Note that you could have defined the values for the various types of clothes as constant values:

```
final int SHIRTS = 1;
final int SWEATERS = 2;
final int SOCKS = 3;
```

```
final int SHEETS = 4;
final int PANTS = 5;
```

The value set for the `clothes` variable would then have been much more obvious:

```
int clothes = SOCKS;
```

Of course, you could also have used an enumeration for the `clothes` type, too, but I'll leave you to work out what that would look like.

VARIABLE SCOPE

The *scope* of a variable is the part of the program over which the variable name can be referenced—in other words, where you can use the variable in the program. Every variable that I have declared so far in program examples has been defined within the context of a method, the method `main()`. Variables that are declared within a method are called *local variables*, as they are only accessible within the confines of the method in which they are declared. However, they are not necessarily accessible everywhere in the code for the method in which they are declared. Look at the next code fragment, which shows variables defined within nested blocks:

```
{
  int n = 1;                                    // Declare and define n

  // Reference to n is OK here
  // Reference to m here is an error because m does not exist yet

  {
    // Reference to n here is OK too
    // Reference to m here is still an error

    int m = 2;                                  // Declare and define m

    // Reference to m and n are OK here - they both exist
  }        // m dies at this point

  // Reference to m here is now an error
  // Reference to n is still OK though
}          // n dies at this point so you can't refer to it in following statements
```

A variable does not exist before its declaration; you can refer to it only after it has been declared. It continues to exist until the end of the block in which it is defined, and that includes any blocks nested within the block containing its declaration. The variable n is created as the first statement in the outer block. It continues to exist within the inner block too. The variable m exists only within the inner block because that's where its declaration appears. After the brace at the end of the inner block, m no longer exists so you can't refer to it. The variable n is still around, though, and it survives until the closing brace of the outer block.

So, the rule that determines the accessibility of local variables is simple. Local variables are accessible only from the point in the program where they are declared to the end of the block that contains the declaration. At the end of the block in which they are declared, they cease to exist. I can demonstrate this with an example.

TRY IT OUT Scoping

Here's a version of the `main()` method that demonstrates how variable scope works:

```
public class Scope {
  public static void main(String[] args) {
    int outer = 1;                              // Exists throughout the method

    {
      // You cannot refer to a variable before its declaration
      // Uncomment the following statement for an error
```

```
        // System.out.println("inner = " + inner);

        int inner = 2;
        System.out.println("inner = " + inner);      // Now it is OK
        System.out.println("outer = " + outer);      // and outer is still here

        // All variables defined in the enclosing outer block still exist,
        // so you cannot redefine them here
        // Uncomment the following statement for an error
        // int outer = 5;
    }

    // Any variables declared in the previous inner block no longer exist
    // so you cannot refer to them
    // Uncomment the following statement for an error
    // System.out.println("inner = " + inner);

    // The previous variable, inner, does not exist so you can define a new one
    int inner = 3;
    System.out.println("inner = " + inner);          // ... and output its value
    System.out.println("outer = " + outer);          // outer is still around
  }
}
```

Scope.java

As it stands, this program produces the following output:

```
inner = 2
outer = 1
inner = 3
outer = 1
```

If you uncomment the three statements as suggested, it won't compile and each statement results in an error message from the compiler.

How It Works

The main() method in this program has one block nested inside the block that contains the code for the method. The variable outer is defined right at the start, so you can refer to this anywhere within the method main(), including inside the nested block. You are not allowed to re-declare a variable, so the commented statement that re-declares outer within the inner block causes a compiler error if you remove the double slash at the beginning of the line.

The variable inner is defined inside the nested block with the initial value 2, and you can refer to it anywhere from its declaration to the end of the inner block. After the closing brace of the inner block, the variable inner no longer exists, so the commented output statement that refers to inner is illegal. However, because the variable inner has expired, you can declare another one with the same name and with the initial value 3.

Note that all this is just to demonstrate the lifetime of local variables. It is not good practice to redefine variables that have expired, because of the obvious potential for confusion. Also, although I have only used variables of type int in the preceding example, scoping rules apply to variables of any type.

 NOTE *There are other variables called class variables that have much longer lifetimes when they are declared in a particular way. The variables PI and E in the standard library class Math are examples of these. They hang around as long as your program is executing. There are also variables that form part of a class object called instance variables. You will learn more about these in Chapter 5.*

LOOPS

A *loop* enables you to execute a statement or block of statements repeatedly. The need to repeat a block of code arises in almost every program. If you did the first exercise at the end of the last chapter, based on what you had learned up to that point, you would have come up with a program along the lines of the following:

```java
public class TryExample1_1 {
  public static void main(String[] args) {
    byte value = 1;
    value *= 2;
    System.out.println("Value is now "+value);
    value *= 2;
    System.out.println("Value is now "+value);
    value *= 2;
    System.out.println("Value is now "+value);
    value *= 2;
    System.out.println("Value is now "+value);
    value *= 2;
    System.out.println("Value is now "+value);
    value *= 2;
    System.out.println("Value is now "+value);
    value *= 2;
    System.out.println("Value is now "+value);
    value *= 2;
    System.out.println("Value is now "+value);
  }
}
```

The same pair of statements has been entered eight times. This is a rather tedious way of doing things. If the program for the company payroll had to include separate statements to do the calculation for each employee, it would never get written. A loop removes this sort of difficulty. You can write the method `main()` to do the same as the preceding code like so:

```java
public static void main(String[] args) {
  byte value = 1;
  for(int i = 0 ; i < 8 ; ++i) {
    value *= 2;
    System.out.println("Value is now " + value);
  }
}
```

This uses one particular kind of loop—called a `for` loop. The `for` loop statement on the third line causes the statements in the following block to be repeated eight times. The number of times it is to be repeated is determined by the stuff between parentheses following the keyword `for`—you will see how in a moment. The point is that you could, in theory, repeat the same block of statements as many times as you want—a thousand or a million or a billion—it is just as easy and it doesn't require any more lines of code. The primary purpose of the `for` loop is to execute a block of statements a given number of times.

In general, a loop has two parts to it: it has a *loop body*, which is the code that is to be repeated and can be a single statement or a block of statements, and it has a *loop control mechanism* that determines how many times the loop body should execute.

Varieties of Loop

There are four kinds of loop statements you can use. I introduce these in outline first to give an overview of all the possibilities.

1. The Numerical for Loop

```java
for (initialization_expression ; loop_condition ; increment_expression) {
  // statements
}
```

I have described this loop as the *numerical* for loop as a rough indication of how it is used and to distinguish it from another variety of for loop that I describe in a moment. The numerical for loop is usually just referred to as a for loop. The loop body for this loop is the block of statements between the braces. The braces are optional when the loop body is just a single statement. The code to control the for loop appears in parentheses following the keyword for.

As you can see, the loop control mechanism has three parts separated by semicolons. The first part, the initialization_expression, executes once before the loop starts. You typically use this expression to initialize a counter for the number of loop iterations—for example, i = 0. With a loop controlled by a counter, which can be an integer or a floating-point variable, you typically count up or down by whatever increment or decrement you choose until the variable reaches some defined limit.

Execution of this loop continues as long as the condition you specify in the second part of the control mechanism, the loop_condition, is true. This expression is checked at the beginning of each loop iteration, and as long as it is true, the loop body executes. When loop_condition is false, the loop ends and execution continues with the statement following the loop block. For example, if you use i<10 as the loop_condition expression, the loop continues as long as the variable i has a value less than 10. The third part of the control information between the parentheses, the increment_expression, is usually used to increment the loop counter. This is executed at the end of each loop iteration. This could be ++i, which would increment the loop counter, i, by one. Of course, you might want to increment the loop counter in steps other than 1. For example, you might write i += 2 as the increment_expression to go in steps of 2, or even something more complicated such as i = 2*i+1.

2. The Collection-Based For Loop

```
for (type identifier : iterable_expression) {
   // statements
}
```

You can't fully appreciate the capabilities of this loop until you have learned about arrays in Chapter 4 and Collection classes in Chapter 14, so I just give you a brief indication here of what you can do with it so you know about all the loop statements you have available. This for loop has two control elements separated by a colon that appear between the parentheses following the for keyword. The first element is an identifier of the type that you specify, and the second is an expression specifying a collection of objects or values of the specified type. The loop executes once for each item of the specified type that appears in the collection, and you can refer to the current item in the loop body using the identifier that you specified as the first control element.

3. The While Loop

```
while (expression) {
   // statements
}
```

This loop executes as long as the logical expression between the parentheses is true. When expression is false, the loop ends and execution continues with the statement following the loop block. The expression is tested at the beginning of the loop, so if it is initially false, the loop body is not executed at all. An example of a while loop condition might be yesNo=='y' || yesNo=='y'. This expression is true if the variable yesNo contains 'y' or 'y,' so yesNo might hold a character entered from the keyboard in this instance.

4. The Do-While Loop

```
do {
   // statements
} while (expression);
```

This loop is similar to the while loop, except that the expression controlling the loop is tested at the end of the loop block. This means that the loop body always executes at least once, even if the expression is always false.

The basic logic of each of the four kinds of loop is shown in Figure 3-6.

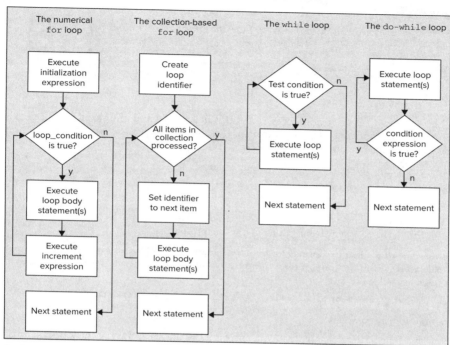

FIGURE 3-6

The two versions of the for loop have quite different mechanisms controlling the number of iterations. You can also see quite clearly that the primary difference between the while loop and the do-while loop is where the test is carried out.

Let's explore each of these loops in turn and see how they work in a practical context.

TRY IT OUT   The Numerical for Loop

Let's start with a very simple example. Suppose you want to calculate the sum of the integers from 1 to a given value. You can do this using the for loop as shown in the following example:

```java
public class ForLoop {
  public static void main(String[] args) {
    int limit = 20;                  // Sum from 1 to this value
    int sum = 0;                     // Accumulate sum in this variable

    // Loop from 1 to the value of limit, adding 1 each cycle
    for(int i = 1; i <= limit; ++i) {
      sum += i;                      // Add the current value of i to sum
    }
    System.out.println("sum = " + sum);
  }
}
```

ForLoop.java

This program produces the output

```
sum = 210
```

but you can try it out with different values for limit.

 NOTE *The more mathematically minded will realize that the sum of the integers from 1 to n is given by the formula $\frac{1}{2}n(n+1)$. However, using that would not demonstrate how a loop works.*

How It Works

All the work is done in the for loop. The loop counter is i, and this is declared and initialized within the for loop statement. The three elements that control the operation of the for loop appear between the parentheses that follow the keyword for. In sequence, their purpose is to:

➤ Set the initial conditions for the loop, particularly the loop counter

➤ Specify the condition for the loop to continue

➤ Increment the loop counter

The control elements in a for loop are always separated by semicolons, but as you see later, any or all of the control elements can be omitted; the two semicolons must always be present.

The first control element is executed when the loop is first entered. Here you declare and initialize the loop counter i. Because it is declared within the loop, it does not exist outside it. If you try to output the value of i after the loop with a statement such as

```
System.out.println("Final value of i = " + i);  // Will not work outside the loop
```

you find that the program no longer compiles.

Where the loop body consists of just a single statement, you can omit the braces and write the loop like this:

```
for (int i = 1; i <= limit; ++i)
    sum += i;                           // Add the current value of i to sum
```

In general, it's better practice to keep the braces in as it makes it clearer where the loop body ends.

If you need to initialize and/or declare other variables for the loop, you can do it here by separating the declarations by commas. For example, you could write the following:

```
for (int i = 1, j = 0; i <= limit; ++i) {
    sum += i * j++;                     // Add the current value of i*j to sum
}
```

In this fragment, I initialize an additional variable j, and, to make the loop vaguely sensible, I have modified the value to add the sum to i*j++, which is the equivalent of i*(i-1) in this case. Note that j is incremented after the product i*j has been calculated. You could declare other variables here, but note that it would not make sense to declare sum at this point. If you can't figure out why, delete or comment out the original declaration of sum in the example and put it in the for loop instead to see what happens. The program won't compile—right? After the loop ends, the variable sum no longer exists, so you can't reference it. This is because all variables that you declare within the loop control expressions are logically within the block that is the body of the loop; they cease to exist after the end of the block.

The second control element in a for loop is a logical expression that is checked at the beginning of each iteration through the loop. If the expression is true, the loop continues, the loop body executes, and as soon as it is false, the loop is finished. In our program, the loop ends when i is greater than the value of limit.

The third control element in a for loop typically increments the loop variable, as you have seen in the example. You can put multiple expressions here, too, so you could rewrite the previous code fragment that added j to the loop as:

```
for (int i = 1, j = 0; i <= limit; ++i, ++j) {
    sum += i*j;                         // Add the current value of i*j to sum
}
```

Again, there can be several expressions here, and they do not need to relate directly to the control of the loop. You could even rewrite the original loop for summing integers so that the summation occurs in the loop control element:

```
for (int i = 1; i <= limit; sum += i, ++i) {
  ;
}
```

Now the loop statement is empty—you just have the semicolon to terminate it. The semicolon is optional, but putting in shows that you meant the block to be empty. This version of the code doesn't really improve things, though, as it's certainly not so easy to see what is happening and there are hazards in writing the loop this way. If you were to reverse the sequence of adding to sum and incrementing i as follows

```
for (int i = 1; i <= limit; ++i, sum += i) {  // Wrong!!!
  ;
}
```

you would generate the wrong answer. This is because the expression ++i would be executed before sum += i, so the wrong value of i is used.

You can omit any or all of the elements that control the for loop, but you must include the semicolons. It is up to you to make sure that the loop does what you want. I could rewrite the loop in the program as:

```
for (int i = 1; i <= limit; ) {
  sum += i++;                          // Add the current value of i to sum
}
```

I have simply transferred the operation of incrementing i from the for loop control expression to the loop body. The for loop works just as before. However, this is not a good way to write the loop, as it makes it much less obvious how the loop counter is incremented.

TRY IT OUT The Collection-Based for Loop

You can't do a whole lot with the collection-based for loop yet. This will come into its own later in the book, especially after Chapter 14, and you will learn more about what you can do with it in the next chapter. One thing that it does apply to and that you have learned something about is an enumeration. Here's how you could apply the collection-based for loop to iterate through all the possible values in an enumeration:

Available for
download on
Wrox.com

```
public class CollectionForLoop {
  enum Season { spring, summer, fall, winter }    // Enumeration type definition

  public static void main(String[] args) {
    for(Season season : Season.values()) {        // Vary over all values
      System.out.println(" The season is now " + season);
    }
  }
}
```

CollectionForLoop.java

This generates the following output:

```
The season is now spring
The season is now summer
The season is now fall
The season is now winter
```

How It Works

The season variable of type Season that appears in the first control expression between the parentheses for the for loop is assigned a different enumeration constant value in each iteration of the loop. The second control expression, following the colon, identifies the collection that is the source of values for the variable declared in the first control expression. In this case it is an enumeration, but, in general, there are other collections you can use, as you see in Chapter 14. In the next chapter you will learn about arrays where both forms of the `for` loop can be used.

In this example, the enumeration defines four values, `spring`, `summer`, `fall`, and `winter`, so the variable `season` is assigned each of these values in turn, as the output shows.

TRY IT OUT The while Loop

You can write the program for summing integers again using the `while` loop, which shows you how the loop mechanism differs from the `for` loop:

Available for download on Wrox.com

```java
public class WhileLoop {
  public static void main(String[] args) {
    int limit = 20;                // Sum from 1 to this value
    int sum = 0;                   // Accumulate sum in this variable
    int i = 1;                     // Loop counter

    // Loop from 1 to the value of limit, adding 1 each cycle
    while(i <= limit) {
      sum += i++;                  // Add the current value of i to sum
    }
    System.out.println("sum = " + sum);
  }
}
```

WhileLoop.java

You should get the following result:

```
sum = 210
```

How It Works

The `while` loop is controlled wholly by the logical expression that appears between the parentheses that follow the keyword `while`. The loop continues as long as this expression has the value `true`, and how it ever manages to arrive at the value `false` to end the loop is up to you. You need to be sure that the statements within the loop eventually result in this expression being `false`. Otherwise, you have a loop that continues indefinitely.

How the loop ends in the example is clear. You have a simple count as before, and you increment i in the loop statement that accumulates the sum of the integers. Sooner or later i will exceed the value of `limit`, and the `while` loop will end.

You don't always need to use the testing of a count limit as the loop condition. You can use any logical condition you want.

TRY IT OUT The do-while Loop

And last, but not least, you have the `do-while` loop.

As I said at the beginning of this topic, the `do-while` loop is much the same as the `while` loop, except for the fact that the continuation condition is checked at the end of the loop. You can write an integer-summing program with this kind of loop too:

Available for download on Wrox.com

```java
public class DoWhileLoop {
  public static void main(String[] args) {
    int limit = 20;                // Sum from 1 to this value
    int sum = 0;                   // Accumulate sum in this variable
    int i = 1;                     // Loop counter

    // Loop from 1 to the value of limit, adding 1 each cycle
```

```
 7! is 5040
 8! is 40320
 9! is 362880
10! is 3628800
11! is 39916800
12! is 479001600
13! is 6227020800
14! is 87178291200
15! is 1307674368000
16! is 20922789888000
17! is 355687428096000
18! is 6402373705728000
19! is 121645100408832000
20! is 2432902008176640000
```

How It Works

All the variables used in this example are of type `long`. Factorial values grow very rapidly so by using type `long` you allow much larger factorials to be calculated than if you used type `int`. You still could have declared `factor` and `i` as type `int` without limiting the size of the factorial value that the program can produce, but the compiler would then need to insert casts to make the `int` values type `long` whenever they were involved in an operation with a value of type `long`.

The outer loop, controlled by `i`, walks through all the integers from 1 to the value of `limit`. In each iteration of the outer loop, the variable `factorial` is initialized to 1, and the nested loop calculates the factorial of the current value of `i` using `factor` as the control counter that runs from 2 to the current value of `i`. The resulting value of `factorial` is then displayed before going to the next iteration of the outer loop.

Although you have nested a `for` loop inside another `for` loop here, as I said at the outset, you can nest any kind of loop inside any other. You could have written the nested loop as the following:

```
for (long i = 1L; i <= limit; ++i) {
  factorial = 1L;                 // Initialize factorial
  long factor = 2L;
  while (factor <= i) {
    factorial *= factor++;
  }
  System.out.println(i + "! is " + factorial);
}
```

Now you have a `while` loop nested in a `for` loop. It works just as well, but it is rather more naturally coded as two nested `for` loops because they are both controlled by a counter.

 NOTE *If you have been concentrating, you may well have noticed that you don't really need nested loops to display the factorial of successive integers. You can do it with a single loop that multiplies the current factorial value by the loop counter. However, this would be a very poor demonstration of a nested loop.*

The continue Statement

There are situations where you may want to skip all or part of a loop iteration. Suppose you want to sum the values of the integers from 1 to some limit, except that you don't want to include integers that are multiples of three. You can do this using an `if` and a `continue` statement:

```
for(int i = 1; i <= limit; ++i) {
  if(i % 3 == 0) {
    continue;                     // Skip the rest of this iteration
  }
  sum += i;                       // Add the current value of i to sum
}
```

The continue statement is executed in this example when i is an exact multiple of 3, causing the rest of the current loop iteration to be skipped. Program execution continues with the next iteration if there is one, and if not, with the statement following the end of the loop block. The continue statement can appear anywhere within a block of loop statements. You may even have more than one continue in a loop.

The Labeled continue Statement

Where you have nested loops, there is a special form of the continue statement that enables you to stop executing the inner loop—not just the current iteration of the inner loop—and continue at the beginning of the next iteration of the outer loop that immediately encloses the current loop. This is called the labeled continue statement.

To use the labeled continue statement, you need to identify the loop statement for the enclosing outer loop with a *statement label*. A statement label is simply an identifier that is used to reference a particular statement. When you need to reference a particular statement, you write the statement label at the beginning of the statement in question, separated from the statement by a colon. Let's look at an example.

TRY IT OUT   Labeled continue

You could add a labeled continue statement to omit the calculation of factorials of odd numbers greater than 10. This is not the best way to do this, but it does demonstrate how the labeled continue statement works:

Available for download on Wrox.com

```java
public class Factorial2 {
  public static void main(String[] args) {
    long limit = 20L;     // to calculate factorial of integers up to this value
    long factorial = 1L; // factorial will be calculated in this variable

    // Loop from 1 to the value of limit
    OuterLoop:
    for(long i = 1L; i <= limit; ++i) {
      factorial = 1;               // Initialize factorial
      for(long j = 2L; j <= i; ++j) {
        if(i > 10L && i % 2L == 1L) {
          continue OuterLoop;          // Transfer to the outer loop
        }
        factorial *= j;
      }
      System.out.println(i + "! is " + factorial);
    }
  }
}
```

Factorial2.java

If you run this it produces the following output:

```
1! is 1
2! is 2
3! is 6
4! is 24
5! is 120
6! is 720
7! is 5040
8! is 40320
9! is 362880
10! is 3628800
12! is 479001600
14! is 87178291200
16! is 20922789888000
18! is 6402373705728000
20! is 2432902008176640000
```

How It Works

The outer loop has the label `OuterLoop`. In the inner loop, when the condition in the `if` statement is `true`, the labeled `continue` is executed causing an immediate transfer to the beginning of the next iteration of the outer loop. The condition in the `if` statements causes the calculation of the factorial to be skipped for odd values greater than 10.

In general, you can use the labeled `continue` to exit from an inner loop to any enclosing outer loop, not just the one immediately enclosing the loop containing the labeled `continue` statement.

Using the break Statement in a Loop

You have seen how to use the `break` statement in a `switch` block. Its effect is to exit the `switch` block and continue execution with the first statement after the `switch`. You can also use the `break` statement to break out from a loop. When `break` is executed within a loop, the loop ends immediately, and execution continues with the first statement following the loop. To demonstrate this, you write a program to find prime numbers. In case you have forgotten, a prime number is an integer that is only exactly divisible by itself and 1.

TRY IT OUT   Calculating Primes I

There's a little more code to this than the previous example. This program finds all the primes from 2 to 50:

```java
public class Primes {
  public static void main(String[] args) {
    int nValues = 50;                        // The maximum value to be checked
    boolean isPrime = true;                  // Is true if we find a prime

    // Check all values from 2 to nValues
    for(int i = 2; i <= nValues; ++i) {
      isPrime=true;                          // Assume the current i is prime

      // Try dividing by all integers from 2 to i-1
      for(int j = 2; j < i; ++j) {
        if(i % j == 0) {                     // This is true if j divides exactly
          isPrime = false;                   // If we got here, it was an exact division
          break;                             // so exit the loop
        }
      }
      // We can get here through the break, or through completing the loop
      if(isPrime)                            // So is it prime?
        System.out.println(i);               // Yes, so output the value
    }
  }
}
```

Primes.java

You should get the following output:

```
2
3
5
7
11
13
17
19
23
29
31
```

```
37
41
43
47
```

How It Works

There are much more efficient ways to calculate primes, but this program demonstrates the `break` statement in action. The first step in `main()` is to declare two variables:

```
int nValues = 50;             // The maximum value to be checked
boolean isPrime = true;       // Is true if we find a prime
```

The first variable is the upper limit for integers to be checked to see if they are prime. The `isPrime` variable is used to record whether a particular value is prime or not.

The basic idea of the program is to go through the integers from 2 to the value of `nValues` and check each one to see if it has an integer divisor less than itself. The nested loops do this:

```
for(int i = 2; i <= nValues; ++i) {
  isPrime=true;                 // Assume the current i is prime

  // Try dividing by all integers from 2 to i-1
  for(int j = 2; j < i; ++j) {
    if(i % j == 0) {            // This is true if j divides exactly
      isPrime = false;          // If we got here, it was an exact division
      break;                    // so exit the loop
    }
  }
  // We can get here through the break, or through completing the loop
  if(isPrime)                   // So is it prime?
    System.out.println(i);      // Yes, so output the value
}
```

The outer loop is indexed by `i` and steps through the possible values that need to be checked for primeness. The inner loop is indexed by `j`, the value of `j` being a trial divisor. This determines whether any integer less than the value being tested for primality is an exact divisor.

The checking is done in the `if` statement in the inner loop. If `j` divides `i` exactly, `i%j` is 0, so `isPrime` is set to `false`. In this case the `break` executes to exit the inner loop—there is no point in continuing as you now know that the value being tested is not prime. The next statement to be executed is the `if` statement after the closing brace of the inner loop block. You can also reach this point by a normal exit from the loop that occurs when the value is prime so you need a way to determine whether the current value of `i` was found to be prime or not. The `isPrime` variable solves this problem. You just check the value of `isPrime` and if it has the value `true`, you have a prime to display so you execute the `println()` call.

You could simplify this example if you used the labeled `continue` statement instead of the `break` statement as in the next Try It Out.

TRY IT OUT   Calculating Primes II

Try the following changes to the code in the `Primes` class:

Available for download on Wrox.com

```
public class Primes2 {
  public static void main(String[] args) {
    int nValues = 50;                      // The maximum value to be checked

    // Check all values from 2 to nValues
    OuterLoop:
    for(int i = 2; i <= nValues; ++i) {
      // Try dividing by all integers from 2 to i-1
```

```
        for(int j = 2; j < i; ++j) {
          if(i%j == 0) {                         // This is true if j divides exactly
             continue OuterLoop;                 // so exit the loop
          }
        }
        // We only get here if we have a prime
        System.out.println(i);                   // so output the value
      }
    }
  }
```

If you've keyed it in correctly, you get the same output as the previous example.

How It Works

You no longer need the `isPrime` variable to indicate whether you have a prime or not, as the output statement can be reached only through a normal exit from the inner loop. When this occurs it means you have found a prime. If you get an exact divisor in the inner loop, it implies that the current value of `i` is not prime, so the labeled `continue` statement transfers immediately to the next iteration of the outer loop.

Breaking Indefinite Loops

You will find that sometimes you need to use a loop where you don't know in advance how many iterations will be required. This can arise when you are processing external data items that you might be reading in from the keyboard, for example, and you cannot know in advance how many there will be. You can often use a `while` loop in these circumstances, with the loop condition determining when the loop should end, but sometimes it can be convenient to use an indefinite loop instead and use a `break` statement in the loop body to end the loop. An indefinite loop is a loop where the control condition is such that the loop apparently continues to execute indefinitely. In this case, the mechanism to end the loop must be in the body of the loop.

TRY IT OUT   Calculating Primes III

Suppose you want the `Primes` program to generate a given number of primes, rather than check up to a given integer value. In this case, you don't know how many numbers you need to check to generate the required number of primes. This is a case where an indefinite loop is useful. You can code this as follows:

```
public class Primes3 {
  public static void main(String[] args) {
    int nPrimes = 50;                       // The maximum number of primes required

    OuterLoop:
    for(int i = 2 ; ; ++i) {                // This loop runs forever
      // Try dividing by all integers from 2 to i-1
      for(int j = 2; j < i; ++j) {
        if(i % j == 0) {                    // This is true if j divides exactly
          continue OuterLoop;               // so exit the loop
        }
      }
      // We only get here if we have a prime
      System.out.println(i);                // so output the value
      if(--nPrimes == 0) {                  // Decrement the prime count
        break;                              // It is zero so we have them all
      }
    }
  }
}
```

This program outputs the first 50 primes.

How It Works

This program is very similar to the previous version. The principal differences are that nPrimes contains the number of primes required, so the program produces the first 50 primes, instead of finding the primes between 2 and 50, and the for outer loop, controlled by i, has the loop condition omitted, so the loop has no direct mechanism for ending it. The loop must be terminated by the code within the loop; otherwise, it continues to execute indefinitely.

Here the termination of the outer loop is controlled by the if statement following the output statement. As you find each prime, the value is displayed, after which the value of nPrimes is decremented in the if statement:

```
if(--nPrimes == 0) {        // Decrement the prime count
  break;                    // It is zero so we have them all
}
```

The break statement is executed when nPrimes has been decremented to zero, and this exits the outer loop.

The Labeled break Statement

Java also has a labeled break statement. This enables you to jump immediately to the statement following the end of any enclosing statement block or loop that is identified by the label in the labeled break statement. The label precedes the opening brace of the block that it identifies. Figure 3-7 illustrates how the labeled break statement works.

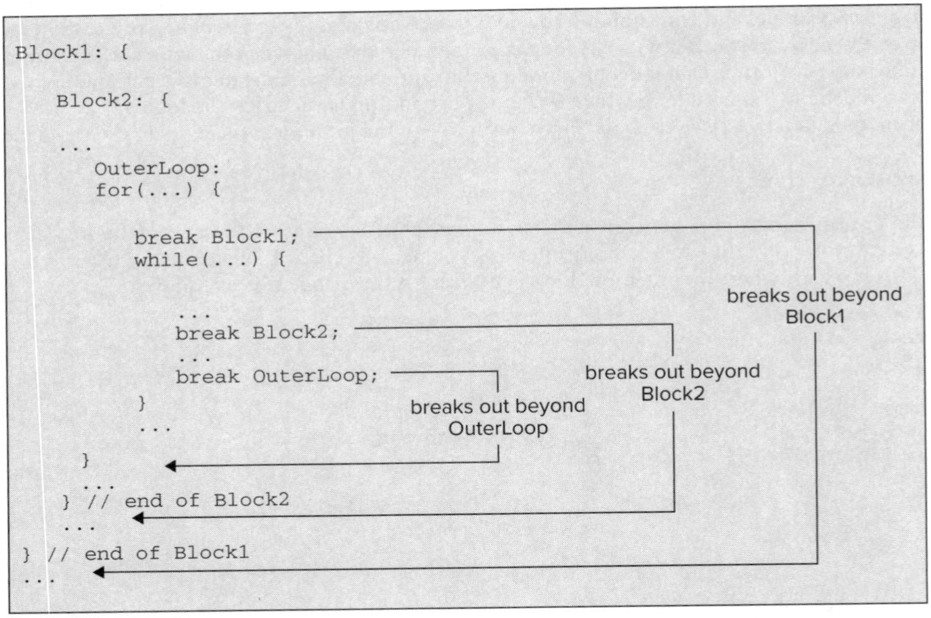

```
Block1: {

   Block2: {

   ...
      OuterLoop:
      for(...) {

         break Block1;
         while(...) {
                                                    breaks out beyond
                                                         Block1
            ...
            break Block2;
            ...
            break OuterLoop;           breaks out beyond
         }                                  Block2
         ...             breaks out beyond
      }                     OuterLoop
      ...
   } // end of Block2
   ...
} // end of Block1
...
```

FIGURE 3-7

The labeled break enables you to break out to the statement following an enclosing block or loop that has an identifying label, regardless of how many levels of nested blocks there are. You might have several loops nested one within the other, for example, where you could use the labeled break to exit from the innermost loop (or indeed any of them) to the statement following the outermost loop. You just need to add a label to the beginning of the relevant block or loop that you want to break out of, and use that label in the break statement.

Just to see it working you can alter the previous example to use a labeled break statement:

```
public class Primes4 {
  public static void main(String[] args) {
    int nPrimes = 50;                    // The maximum number of primes required

    // Check all values from 2 to nValues
    OuterLoop:
    for(int i = 2 ; ; ++i) {             // This loop runs forever
      // Try dividing by all integers from 2 to i-1
      for(int j = 2; j < i; ++j) {
        if(i % j == 0) {                 // This is true if j divides exactly
          continue OuterLoop;            // so exit the loop
        }
      }
      // We only get here if we have a prime
      System.out.println(i);            // so output the value
      if(--nPrimes == 0) {              // Decrement the prime count
        break OuterLoop;                // It is zero so we have them all
      }
    }
    // break OuterLoop goes to here
  }
}
```

The program works in exactly the same way as before. The labeled break ends the loop operation beginning with the label OuterLoop, and so effectively branches to the point indicated by the comment.

Of course, in this instance its effect is no different from that of an unlabeled break. However, in general this would work wherever the labeled break statement was within OuterLoop. For example, it could be nested inside another inner loop, and its effect would be just the same—control would be transferred to the statement following the end of OuterLoop. The following code fragment illustrates this sort of situation. The label this time is Outside:

```
Outside:
for(int i = 0 ; i<count1 ; ++i) {
  ...
  for(int j = 0 ; j<count2 ; ++j) {
    ...
    for(int k = 0 ; k<count3 ; ++k) {
      ...
      break Outside;
      ...
    }
  }
}
// The labeled break transfers to here...
```

The labeled break is not needed very often, but when you need to break out of a deeply nested set of loops, it can be invaluable because it makes it a simple operation.

ASSERTIONS

Every so often you will find that the logic in your code leads to some logical condition that should always be true. If you test an integer and establish that it is odd, it is certainly true that it cannot be even, for example. You may also find yourself writing a statement or statements that, although they could be executed in theory, in practice they never really should be. I don't mean by this the usual sorts of errors that occur, such as some incorrect data being entered somehow, which should be handled ordinarily by the normal code. I mean circumstances where if the statements were to be executed, it would imply that something was very seriously wrong with the program or its environment. These are precisely the circumstances to which *assertions* apply.

NOTE *For assertions to have an effect when you run your program, you must specify the* -enableassertions *option. For example:*

```
java -enableassertions MyProg
```

You can also use its abbreviated form -ea:

```
java -ea MyProg
```

If you don't specify this option when you run the program, assertions are ignored.

A simple assertion is a statement of the form:

```
assert logical_expression;
```

Here, assert is a keyword, and logical_expression is any expression that results in a value of true or false. When this statement executes, if logical_expression evaluates to true, then the program continues normally. If logical_expression evaluates to false, the program is terminated with an error message starting with:

```
java.lang.AssertionError
```

This is followed by more information about where the error occurred in the code. When this occurs, the program is said to *assert*.

Let's consider an example. Suppose you have a variable of type int that stores the number of days in the current month. You might use it like this:

```
if(daysInMonth == 30) {
    System.out.println("Month is April, June, September, or November");

} else if(daysInMonth == 31) {
    System.out.println(
            "Month is January, March, May, July, August, October, or December.");
} else {
    assert daysInMonth == 28 || daysInMonth == 29;
    System.out.println("Month is February.");
}
```

You are presuming that daysInMonth is valid—that is, it has one of the values 28, 29, 30, or 31. Maybe it came from a file that is supposed to be accurate so you should not need to check it, but if it turns out not to be valid, the assertion detects it and ends the program.

You could have written this slightly differently:

```
if(daysInMonth == 30) {
    System.out.println("Month is April, June, September, or November");

} else if(daysInMonth == 31) {
    System.out.println(
            "Month is January, March, May, July, August, October, or December.");

} else if(daysInMonth == 28 || daysInMonth == 29) {
    System.out.println("Month is February.");

} else {
    assert false;
}
```

Here, if daysInMonth is valid, the program should never execute the last else clause. An assertion with the logical expression as false always asserts and terminates the program.

More Complex Assertions

There is a slightly more complex form of assertions that have this form:

```
assert logical_expression : string_expression;
```

Here, `logical_expression` must evaluate to a `boolean` value, either `true` or `false`. If `logical_expression` is `false` then the program terminates with an error message including the string that results from `string_expression`.

For example, you could have written the assertion in the last code fragment as:

```
assert false : "daysInMonth has the value " + daysInMonth;
```

Now if the program asserts, the output includes information about the value of `daysInMonth`.

Let's see how it works in practice.

TRY IT OUT A Working Assertion

Here's some code that is guaranteed to assert—if you compile and execute it correctly:

Available for download on Wrox.com

```java
public class TryAssertions {
  public static void main(String args[]) {
    int daysInMonth = 32;
    if(daysInMonth == 30) {
      System.out.println("Month is April, June, September, or November");

    } else if(daysInMonth == 31) {
      System.out.println(
          "Month is January, March, May, July, August, October, or December.");

    } else if(daysInMonth == 28 || daysInMonth == 29) {
      System.out.println("Month is February.");

    } else {
      assert false;
    }
  }
}
```

TryAssertions.java

Don't forget that, after you have compiled the program, you must execute it with assertions enabled, like this:

```
java -enableassertions TryAssertions
```

You should then get the following output:

```
Exception in thread "main" java.lang.AssertionError
        at TryAssertions.main(TryAssertions.java:15)
```

How It Works

Because you have set `daysInMonth` to an invalid value, the assertion statement is executed, and that results in the error message. You could try out the other form of the assertion in the example:

```
assert false : "daysInMonth has the value " + daysInMonth;
```

Now you should see that the output includes the string resulting from the second expression in the assertion statement:

```
Exception in thread "main" java.lang.AssertionError: daysInMonth has the value 32
        at TryAssertions.main(TryAssertions.java:16)
```

I will use assertions from time to time in the examples in subsequent chapters.

SUMMARY

In this chapter you have learned about all of the essential mechanisms for making decisions in Java. You have also learned all of the looping facilities that you have available when programming in Java. You will use all of these capabilities in examples throughout the rest of the book.

EXERCISES

You can download the source code for the examples in the book and the solutions to the following exercises from www.wrox.com.

1. Write a program to display a random choice from a set of six choices for breakfast (you could use any set—for example, scrambled eggs, waffles, fruit, cereal, toast, or yogurt).

2. When testing whether an integer is a prime, it is sufficient to try to divide by integers up to and including the square root of the number being tested. Rewrite the program example from this chapter to use this approach.

3. A lottery requires that you select six different numbers from the integers 1 to 49. Write a program to do this for you and generate five sets of entries.

4. Write a program to generate a random sequence of capital letters that does not include vowels.

▶ **WHAT YOU LEARNED IN THIS CHAPTER**

TOPIC	CONCEPT
Relational Operators	You can use relational operators to compare values, and such comparisons result in values of either `true` or `false`. The relational operators are: `>   >=   ==   !=   <=   <`
Logical Operators	You can combine basic comparisons and logical variables in more complex logical expressions by using logical operators. The logical operators are: `&   &&   |   ||   ^   !`
The `if` Statement	The `if` statement is a basic decision-making tool in Java. It enables you to choose to execute a block of statements if a given logical expression has the value `true`. You can optionally execute another block of statements if the logical expression is `false` by using the `else` keyword.
The Conditional Operator	You can use the conditional operator to choose between two expressions depending on the value of a logical expression.
The `switch` Statement	You can use the `switch` statement to choose from a fixed number of alternatives.
Variable Scope	The variables in a method come into existence at the point at which you declare them and cease to exist after the end of the block that immediately encloses their declaration. The program extent where the variable is accessible is the scope of the variable.
Loops	You have four ways of repeating a block of statements: a numerical `for` loop, a collection-based `for` loop, a `while` loop, or a `do-while` loop.
`continue` Statements	The `continue` statement enables you to skip to the next iteration in the loop containing the `continue` statement. The labeled `continue` statement enables you to skip to the next iteration in an outer loop enclosing the labeled `continue` that is identified by the label. The labeled loop need not be the loop immediately enclosing the labeled `continue`.
`break` Statements	The `break` statement enables you to break out of a loop or switch statement. The labeled `break` statement enables you to break out of a loop or a switch and continue execution at the point in the code identified by the label. This is not necessarily the block that encloses it directly.
Assertions	You use an assertion statement to verify logical conditions that should always be `true`, or as code in parts of a program that should not be reached, but theoretically can be.

Arrays and Strings

WHAT YOU WILL LEARN IN THIS CHAPTER

➤ What arrays are and how you declare and initialize them
➤ How you access individual elements of an array
➤ How you can use individual elements of an array
➤ How to declare arrays of arrays
➤ How you can create arrays of arrays with different lengths
➤ How to create String objects
➤ How to create and use arrays of String objects
➤ What operations are available for String objects
➤ What StringBuffer objects are and how they relate to operations on String objects
➤ What operations are available for StringBuffer objects

In this chapter you start to use Java objects. You are first introduced to arrays, which enable you to deal with a number of variables of the same type through a single variable name, and then you look at how to handle character strings. Some of what I discuss in this chapter relates to objects, and as I have not yet covered in detail how you define a class (which is an object type definition), I have to skate over some aspects of how objects work, but all is revealed in Chapter 5.

ARRAYS

With the basic built-in Java data types that you've seen in the previous chapters, each identifier corresponds to a single variable. But when you want to handle sets of values of the same type—the first 1,000 primes, for example—you really don't want to have to name them individually. What you need is an *array*.

You should first have a rough idea of what an array is and how it works. An array is an object that is a named set of variables of the same type. Each variable in the array is called an *array element*. To reference a particular element in an array, you use the array name combined with an integer value of type int, called an *index*. You put the index between square brackets following the array name; for example, data[99] refers to the element in the data array corresponding to the index value 99. The index for an array element is the offset of that particular element from the beginning of the array. The first element has an index of 0, the second has an index of 1, the third an index of 2, and so on. Thus, data[99] refers to the hundredth element in the `data` array. The index value does not need to be an integer literal. It can be any expression that results in a value of type `int` that is equal to or greater than zero. Obviously a `for` loop is going to be very useful for processing array elements—which is one reason why you had to wait until now to hear about arrays.

Array Variables

An array variable and the array it refers to are separate entities. The memory that is allocated for an array variable stores a *reference* to an array object, not the array itself. The array object itself is a distinct entity that is elsewhere in memory. All variables that refer to objects store references that record the memory locations of the objects they refer to.

You are not obliged to create an array when you declare an array variable. You can first create the array variable and later use it to store a reference to a particular array.

You could declare the integer array variable `primes` with the following statement:

```
int[] primes;              // Declare an integer array variable
```

The variable `primes` is now a placeholder for an integer array that you have yet to define. No memory has been allocated to hold an array itself at this point. The `primes` variable is simply a location in memory that can store a reference to an array. You see in a moment that to create the array itself you must specify its type and how many elements it is to contain. The square brackets following the type in the previous statement indicates that the variable is for referencing an array of `int` values, and not for storing a single value of type `int`. The type of the array variable is `int[]`.

You may come across an alternative notation for declaring an array variable:

```
int primes[];              // Declare an integer array variable
```

Here the square brackets appear after the variable name, rather than after the type name. This is exactly equivalent to the previous statement so you can use either notation. Many programmers prefer the original notation, as `int[]` tends to indicate more clearly that the type is an array of values of type `int`.

Defining an Array

After you have declared an array variable, you can define an array that it references:

```
primes = new int[10];      // Define an array of 10 integers
```

This statement creates an array that stores 10 values of type `int` and stores a *reference* to the array in the variable `primes`. The reference is simply where the array is in memory. You could also declare the array variable and define the array of type `int` to hold 10 prime numbers with a single statement, as shown in Figure 4-1.

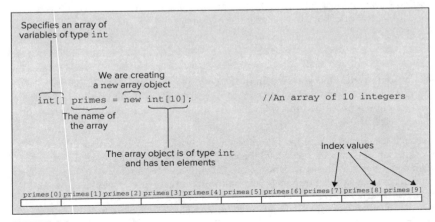

FIGURE 4-1

The first part of the definition specifies the type of the array. The element type name, int in this case, is followed by an empty pair of square brackets to indicate you are declaring an array rather than a single variable of type int. The part of the statement that follows the equal sign defines the array. The keyword new indicates that you are allocating new memory for the array, and int[10] specifies you want capacity for 10 variables of type int in the array. Because each element in the primes array is a variable of type int that requires 4 bytes, the whole array occupies 40 bytes, plus 4 bytes for the primes variable to store the reference to the array. When an array is created like this, all the array elements are initialized to a default value automatically. The initial value is zero in the case of an array of numerical values, is false for boolean arrays, is '\u0000' for arrays storing type char, and is null for an array of objects of a class type.

Consider the following statement:

```
double[] myArray = new double[100];
```

This statement is a declaration of the array variable myArray. The statement also defines the array because the array size is specified. The variable myArray refers to an array of 100 values of type double, and each element has the value 0.0 assigned by default. Because there are 100 elements in this array, the legal index values range from 0 to 99.

The Length of an Array

You can refer to the length of the array—the number of elements it contains—using length, a data member of the array object. For example, for the array myArray that you defined in the previous section, you can refer to its length as myArray.length, which has the value 100. You can use the length member of an array to control a numerical for loop that iterates over the elements of an array.

Accessing Array Elements

As I said earlier, you refer to an element of an array by using the array name followed by the element's index value enclosed between square brackets. You can specify an index value by any expression that produces a zero or positive result of type int. If you use a value of type long as an index, you get an error message from the compiler; if your calculation of an index uses long variables and the result is of type long, you need to cast it to type int. You no doubt recall from Chapter 2 that arithmetic expressions involving values of type short and type byte produce a result of type int, so you can use those in an index expression.

You refer to the first element of the primes array as primes[0], and you reference the fifth element in the array as primes[4]. The maximum index value for an array is one less than the number of elements in the array. Java checks that the index values you use are valid. If you use an index value that is less than 0, or greater than the index value for the last element in the array, an *exception* is thrown—throwing an exception is just the way errors at execution time are signaled, and there are different types of exceptions for signaling various kinds of errors. The exception type in this case is an ArrayIndexOutOfBoundsException. When such an exception is thrown, your program is terminated unless there is some provision in your code for dealing with it. You look at exceptions in detail in Chapter 7, including how you can deal with exceptions and prevent termination of your program.

The primes array is an example of what is sometimes referred to as a *one-dimensional array*, because each of its elements is referenced using one index—running from 0 to 9 in this case. You see later that arrays can also have two or more dimensions, the number of dimensions being the same as the number of indexes required to access an element of the array.

Reusing Array Variables

As I explained at the beginning of this chapter, an array variable is separate from the array that it references. Rather like the way an ordinary variable can store different values at different times, you can use an array variable to store a reference to different arrays at different points in your program. Suppose you have declared and defined the variable primes as before, like this:

```
int[] primes = new int[10];    // Allocate an array of 10 integer elements
```

This produces an array of 10 elements of type int. Perhaps a bit later in your program you want to use the array variable `primes` to refer to a larger array, with 50 elements, say. You could simply write the following:

```
primes = new int[50];          // Allocate an array of 50 integer elements
```

Now the `primes` variable refers to a new array of values of type int that is entirely separate from the original. When this statement is executed, the previous array of 10 elements is discarded, along with all the data values you may have stored in it. The variable `primes` can now be used to reference only elements of the new array. This is illustrated in Figure 4-2.

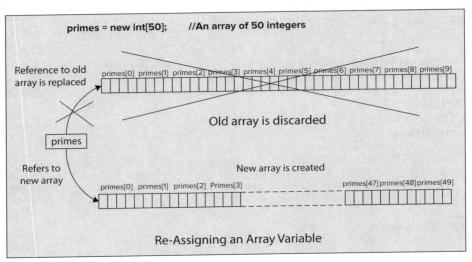

FIGURE 4-2

After executing the statement shown in Figure 4-2, the array variable `primes` now points to a new integer array of 50 elements with index values running from 0 to 49. Although you can change the array that an array variable references, you can't alter the type of value that an element stores. All the arrays referenced by a given variable must correspond to the original type that you specified when you declared the array variable. The variable `primes`, for example, can only reference arrays of type `int[]`. You have used an array of elements of type int in the illustration, but the same thing applies equally well when you are working with arrays of elements of type `long` or `double` or of any other type. Of course, you are not restricted to working with arrays of elements of primitive types. You can create arrays of elements to store references to any type of object, including objects of the classes that you define yourself in Chapter 5.

Initializing Arrays

You can initialize the elements in an array with your own values when you declare it, and at the same time determine how many elements it has. To do this, you simply add an equal sign followed by the list of element values enclosed between braces following the specification of the array variable. For example, you can define and initialize an array with the following statement:

```
int[] primes = {2, 3, 5, 7, 11, 13, 17};    // An array of 7 elements
```

This creates the `primes` array with sufficient elements to store all of the initializing values that appear between the braces—seven in this case. The array size is determined by the number of initial values so no other information is necessary to define the array. The values are assigned to the array elements in sequence, so in this example `primes[0]` has the initial value 2, `primes[1]` has the initial value 3, `primes[2]` has the initial value 5, and so on through the rest of the elements in the array.

If you want to set only some of the array elements to specific values explicitly, you can create the array with the number of elements you want and then use an assignment statement for each element for which you supply a value. For example:

```
int[] primes = new int[100];
primes[0] = 2;
primes[1] = 3;
```

The first statement declares and defines an integer array of 100 elements, all of which are initialized to zero by default. The two assignment statements then set values for the first two array elements.

You can also initialize the elements in an array using a for loop to iterate over all the elements and set the value for each:

```
double[] data = new double[50];          // An array of 50 values of type double
for(int i = 0 ; i < data.length ; ++i) { // i from 0 to data.length-1
  data[i] = 1.0;
}
```

For an array with length elements, the index values for the elements run from 0 to length-1. The for loop control statement is written so that the loop variable i starts at 0 and is incremented by 1 on each iteration up to data.length-1. When i is incremented to data.length, the loop ends. Thus, this loop sets each element of the array to 1. Using a for loop in this way is one standard idiom for iterating over the elements in an array. You see later that you can use the collection-based for loop for iterating over and *accessing* the values of the array elements. Here you are *setting* the values so the collection-based for loop cannot be applied.

Using a Utility Method to Initialize an Array

You can also use a method that is defined in the Arrays class in the java.util package to initialize an array. For example, to initialize the data array defined as in the previous fragment, you could use the following statement:

```
Arrays.fill(data, 1.0);                    // Fill all elements of data with 1.0
```

The first argument to the fill() method is the name of the array to be filled. The second argument is the value to be used to set the elements. This method works for arrays of any primitive type. Of course, for this statement to compile correctly you need an import statement at the beginning of the source file:

```
import java.util.Arrays;
```

This statement imports the Arrays class name into the source file so you can use it as you have in the preceding code line. Without the import statement, you can still access the Arrays class using the fully qualified name. In this case the statement to initialize the array is:

```
java.util.Arrays.fill(data, 1.0);          // Fill all elements of data with 1.0
```

This is just as good as the previous version of the statement.

Of course, because fill() is a static method in the Arrays class, you could import the method name into your source file:

```
import static java.util.Arrays.fill;
```

Now you can call the method with the name unadorned with the class name:

```
fill(data, 1.0);                           // Fill all elements of data with 1.0
```

You can also set part of an array to a particular value with another version of the fill() method:

```
double[] data = new double[100];
fill(data, 5, 11, 1.5);
```

This specifies that a range of elements in the array are to be set to a given value. You supply four arguments to this version of the fill() method. The first argument is the name of the array, data. The second argument is the index of the first element to be set. The third argument is 1 beyond the index of the last element to be set. The fourth argument is the value for the elements. This sets all the elements from data[5] to data[10] inclusive to 1.5.

There are versions of the fill() method for each of the primitive element types so you can use it to set values for any array of elements of a primitive type.

Initializing an Array Variable

You can initialize an array variable with a reference to an existing array of the same type. For example, you could declare the following array variables:

```
long[] even = {2L, 4L, 6L, 8L, 10L};
long[] value = even;
```

Here the array reference stored in even is used to initialize the array value in its declaration. This has the effect shown in Figure 4-3.

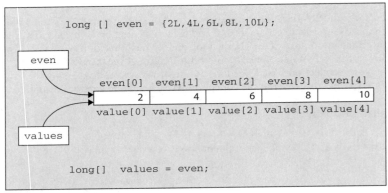

FIGURE 4-3

You have created two array variables, but you have only one array. Both arrays refer to the same set of elements, and you can access the elements of the array through either variable name—for example, even[2] refers to the same variable as value[2]. One use for this is when you want to switch the arrays referenced by two variables. If you were sorting an array by repeatedly transferring elements from one array to another, by flipping the array you were copying from with the array you were copying to, you could use the same code. For example, if you declared array variables as

```
double[] inputArray = new double[100];    // Array to be sorted
double[] outputArray = new double[100];   // Reordered array
double[] temp;                            // Temporary array reference
```

when you want to switch the array referenced by outputArray to be the new input array, you could write the following:

```
temp = inputArray;             // Save reference to inputArray in temp
inputArray = outputArray;      // Set inputArray to refer to outputArray
outputArray = temp;            // Set outputArray to refer to what was inputArray
```

None of the array elements are moved here. Just the addresses of where the arrays are located in memory are swapped, so this is a very fast process. Of course, if you want to replicate an array, you have to create a new array of the same size and type, and then copy the value of each element of the old array to your new array.

 NOTE *I'm sure that you realize that you can copy the contents of an array to a new array using a loop. In Chapter 15 you learn about methods in the Arrays class that can do this more efficiently.*

Using Arrays

You can use array elements in expressions in exactly the same way as you might use a single variable of the same data type. For example, if you declare an array `samples`, you can fill it with random values between 0.0 and 100.0 with the following code:

```
double[] samples = new double[50];      // An array of 50 double values
for(int i = 0; i < samples.length; ++i) {
   samples[i] = 100.0*Math.random();    // Generate random values
}
```

This shows how the numerical `for` loop is ideal when you want to iterate through the elements in an array to set their values. Of course, this is not an accident. A major reason for the existence of the `for` loop is precisely for iterating over the elements in an array.

To show that array elements can be used in exactly the same way as ordinary variables, I could write the following statement:

```
double result = (samples[10]*samples[0] - Math.sqrt(samples[49]))/samples[29];
```

This is a totally arbitrary calculation, of course. More sensibly, to compute the average of the values stored in the `samples` array, you could write

```
double average = 0.0;                   // Variable to hold the average

for(int i = 0; i < samples.length; ++i) {
   average += samples[i];               // Sum all the elements
}
average /= samples.length;              // Divide by the total number of elements
```

Within the loop, you accumulate the sum of all the elements of the array `samples` in the variable `average`. You then divide this sum by the number of elements.

Notice how you use the length of the array, `samples.length`, all over the place. It appears in the `for` loop and in floating-point form as a divisor to calculate the average. When you use arrays, you often find that references to the length of the array are strewn all through your code. As long as you use the `length` member of the array, the code is independent of the number of array elements. If you change the number of elements in the array, the code automatically deals with that. You should always use the `length` member when you need to refer to the length of an array—never use explicit values.

Using the Collection-Based for Loop with an Array

You can use a collection-based `for` loop as an alternative to the numerical `for` loop when you want to process the values of all the elements in an array. For example, you could rewrite the code fragment from the previous section that calculated the average of the values in the `samples` array like this:

```
double average = 0.0;                   // Variable to hold the average
for(double value : samples) {
   average += value;                    // Sum all the elements
}
average /= samples.length;              // Divide by the total number of elements
```

The `for` loop iterates through the values of all elements of type `double` in the `samples` array in sequence. The `value` variable is assigned the value of each element of the `samples` array in turn. Thus, the loop achieves the same result as the numerical `for` loop that you used earlier—the sum of all the elements is accumulated in `average`. When you are processing all the elements in an array, you should use the collection-based `for` loop because it is easier to read and less error-prone than the numerical `for` loop. Of course, when you want to process only data from part of the array, you still must use the numerical `for` loop with the loop counter ranging over the indexes for the elements you want to access.

It's important to remember that the collection-based `for` loop iterates over the *values* stored in an array. It does not provide access to the elements for the purpose of setting their values. Therefore, you use it only when you are accessing all the values stored in an array to use them in some way. If you want to recalculate the values in the array, use the numerical `for` loop.

Let's try out an array in an improved program to calculate prime numbers:

TRY IT OUT   Even More Primes

Try out the following code, derived, in part, from the code you used in Chapter 3:

Available for
download on
Wrox.com

```java
import static java.lang.Math.ceil;
import static java.lang.Math.sqrt;

public class MorePrimes {
    public static void main(String[] args) {
        long[] primes = new long[20];        // Array to store primes
        primes[0] = 2L;                      // Seed the first prime
        primes[1] = 3L;                      // and the second
        int count = 2;                       // Count of primes found Ð up to now,
                                             // which is also the array index

        long number = 5L;                    // Next integer to be tested

        outer:
        for( ; count < primes.length; number += 2L) {
            // The maximum divisor we need to try is square root of number
            long limit = (long)ceil(sqrt((double)number));

            // Divide by all the primes we have up to limit
            for(int i = 1; i < count && primes[i] <= limit; ++i) {
                if(number%primes[i] == 0L) {     // Is it an exact divisor?
                    continue outer;              // Yes, so try the next number
                }
            }
            primes[count++] = number;        // We got one!
        }

        for(long n : primes) {
            System.out.println(n);           // Output all the primes
        }
    }
}
```

MorePrimes.java

This program computes as many prime numbers as the capacity of the `primes` array allows.

How It Works

Any number that is not a prime must be a product of prime factors, so you only need to divide a prime number candidate by prime numbers that are less than or equal to the square root of the candidate to test for whether it is prime. This is fairly obvious if you think about it. For every factor a number has that is greater than the square root of the number, the result of division by this factor is another factor that is less than the square root. You perhaps can see this more easily with a specific example. The number 24 has a square root that is a bit less than 5. You can factorize it as 2 * 12, 3 * 8, 4 * 6; then you come to cases where the first factor is greater than the square root so the second is less, 6 * 4, 8 * 3, and so on, and so you are repeating the pairs of factors you already have.

You first declare the array `primes` to be of type `long` and define it as having 20 elements. You set the first two elements of the `primes` array to 2 and 3, respectively, to start the process off, as you use the primes you have in the array as divisors when testing a new candidate.

The variable `count` is the total number of primes you have found, so this starts out as 2 because you have already stored 2 and 3 in the first two elements of the primes array. Note that because you use `count` as the `for` loop control variable, you omit the first expression between parentheses in the loop statement, as the initial value of `count` has already been set.

You store the candidate to be tested in `number`, with the first value set as 5. The `for` loop statement labeled `outer` is slightly unusual. First of all, the variable `count` that determines when the loop ends is not incremented in the `for` loop statement, but in the body of the loop. You use the third control expression between the `for` loop parentheses to increment `number` in steps of two because you don't want to check even numbers. The `for` loop ends when `count` is equal to the length of the array. You test the value in `number` in the inner `for` loop by dividing `number` by all of the prime numbers you have in the `primes` array that are less than, or equal to, the square root of the candidate. If you get an exact division, the value in `number` is not prime, so you go immediately to the next iteration of the `outer` loop via the `continue` statement.

You calculate the limit for divisors you need to try with the following statement:

```
long limit = (long)ceil(sqrt((double)number));
```

The `sqrt()` method from the `Math` class produces the square root of `number` as a `double` value, so if `number` has the value 7, for example, a value of about 2.64575 is returned. This is passed to the `ceil()` method, which is also a member of the `Math` class. The `ceil()` method returns a value of type `double` that is the minimum whole number that is not less than the value passed to it. With `number` as 7, this returns 3.0, the smallest integral value not less than the square root of 7. You want to use this number as the limit for your integer divisors, so you cast it to type `long` and store the result in `limit`. You are able to call the `sqrt()` and `ceil()` methods without qualifying their names with the class to which they belong because you have imported their names into the source file.

The cast of `number` to type `double` is not strictly necessary. You could write the statement as:

```
long limit = (long)ceil(sqrt(number));
```

The compiler will insert the cast for you. However, by putting the explicit cast in, you indicate that it was your intention.

If you don't get an exact division, you exit normally from the inner loop and execute the statement:

```
primes[count++] = number;                // We got one!
```

Because `count` is the number of values you have stored, it also corresponds to the index for the next free element in the `primes` array. Thus, you use `count` as the index to the array element in which you want to store the value of `number` and then increment `count`.

When you have filled the `primes` array, the `outer` loop ends and you output all the values in the array in the loop:

```
for(long n : primes) {
  System.out.println(n);                 // Output all the primes
}
```

This loop iterates through all the elements of type `long` in the `primes` array in sequence. On each iteration n contains the value of the current element, so that is written out by the `println()` method.

You can express the logical process of this program as the following sequence of steps:

1. Take the **number** in question and determine its square root.
2. Set the **limit** for divisors to be the smallest integer that is greater than this square root value.
3. Test to see if the **number** can be divided exactly (without remainder) by any of the **primes** already in the primes **array** that are less than the **limit** for divisors.
4. If any of the existing primes divide into the current **number**, discard the current **number** and start a new iteration of the loop with the next candidate **number**.
5. If none of the divisors divide into **number** without a remainder, it is a prime, so enter the existing **number** in the first available empty slot in the array and then move to the next iteration for a new candidate **number**.
6. When the **array** of primes is full, stop looking for new primes and output all the prime number values from the array.

Arrays of Arrays

You have worked only with one-dimensional arrays up to now, that is, arrays that use a single index. Why would you ever need the complications of using more indexes to access the elements of an array?

Consider a specific example. Suppose that you have a fanatical interest in the weather, and you are intent on recording the temperature each day at 10 separate geographical locations throughout the year. After you have sorted out the logistics of actually collecting this information, you can use an array of 10 elements corresponding to the number of locations, where each of these elements is an array of 365 elements to store the temperature values. You declare this array with the statement:

```
float[][] temperature = new float[10][365];
```

This is called a *two-dimensional array* because it has two dimensions—one with index values running from 0 to 9, and the other with index values from 0 to 364. The first index relates to a geographical location, and the second index corresponds to the day of the year. That's much handier than a one-dimensional array with 3650 elements, isn't it?

Figure 4-4 shows the organization of the two-dimensional array.

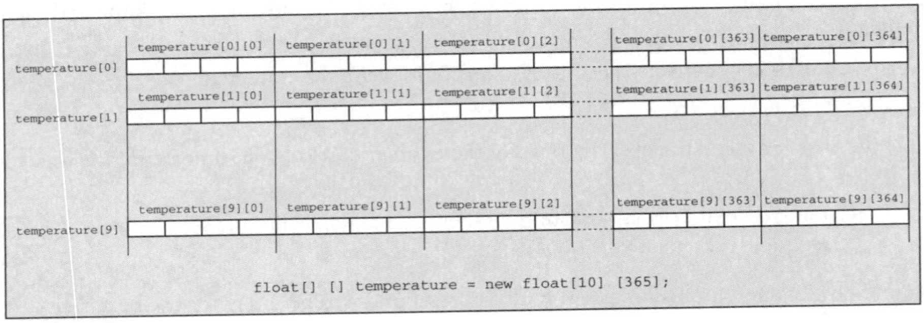

FIGURE 4-4

There are 10 one-dimensional arrays that make up the two-dimensional array, and they each have 365 elements. In referring to an element, the first pair of square brackets encloses the index for a particular array and the second pair of square brackets encloses the index value for an element within that array. So to refer to the temperature for day 100 for the sixth location, you use `temperature[5][99]`. Because each `float` variable occupies 4 bytes, the total space required to store the elements in this two-dimensional array is $10 \times 365 \times 4$ bytes, which is a total of 14,600 bytes.

For a fixed value for the second index in a two-dimensional array, varying the first index value is often referred to as accessing a *column* of the array. Similarly, fixing the first index value and varying the second, you access a *row* of the array. The reason for this terminology should be apparent from Figure 4-4.

You could equally well have used two statements to create the last array, one to declare the array variable and the other to define the array:

```
float [][] temperature;              // Declare the array variable
temperature = new float[10][365];    // Create the array
```

The first statement declares the array variable `temperature` for two-dimensional arrays of type `float`. The second statement creates the array with ten elements, each of which is an array of 365 elements of type `float`.

Let's exercise this two-dimensional array in a program to calculate the average annual temperature for each location.

The Weather Fanatic

To save you having to wander around 10 different locations armed with a thermometer, you'll generate the temperatures as random values between −10 degrees and 35 degrees. This assumes you are recording temperatures in degrees Celsius. If you prefer Fahrenheit, you could generate values from 14 degrees to 95 degrees to cover the same range.

```java
public class WeatherFan {
  public static void main(String[] args) {
    float[][] temperature = new float[10][365];        // Temperature array

    // Generate random temperatures
    for(int i = 0; i < temperature.length; ++i) {
      for(int j = 0; j < temperature[i].length; ++j) {
        temperature[i][j] = (float)(45.0*Math.random() Ð 10.0);
      }
    }

    // Calculate the average per location
    for(int i = 0; i < temperature.length; ++i) {
      float average = 0.0f;        // Place to store the average

      for(int j = 0; j < temperature[i].length; ++j) {
        average += temperature[i][j];
      }

      // Output the average temperature for the current location
      System.out.println("Average temperature at location "
                + (i+1) + " = " + average/(float)temperature[i].length);
    }
  }
}
```

WeatherFan.java

When I ran the program, I got the following output:

```
Average temperature at location 1 = 12.2733345
Average temperature at location 2 = 12.012519
Average temperature at location 3 = 11.54522
Average temperature at location 4 = 12.490543
Average temperature at location 5 = 12.574791
Average temperature at location 6 = 11.950315
Average temperature at location 7 = 11.492908
Average temperature at location 8 = 13.176439
Average temperature at location 9 = 12.565457
Average temperature at location 10 = 12.981103
```

You should get different results.

How It Works

After declaring the array `temperature` you fill it with random values using nested `for` loops. Note how `temperature.length` used in the outer loop refers to the length of the first dimension, 10 in this case. In the inner loop you use `temperature[i].length` to refer to the length of the second dimension, 365. You could use any index value here; `temperature[0].length` would have been just as good for all the elements because the lengths of the rows of the array are all the same in this case. In the next section you will learn how you create arrays with rows of varying length.

The `Math.random()` method generates a value of type `double` from 0.0 up to, but excluding, 1.0. This value is multiplied by 45.0 in the expression for the temperature, which results in values between 0.0 and 45.0. Subtracting 10.0 from this value gives you the range you require, − 10.0 to 35.0.

You then use another pair of nested `for` loops, controlled in the same way as the first, to calculate the averages of the stored temperatures. The outer loop iterates over the locations and the inner loop sums all the temperature values for a given location. Before the execution of the inner loop, the variable `average` is declared and initialized, and this is used to accumulate the sum of the temperatures for a location in the inner loop. After the inner loop has been executed, you output the average temperature for each location, identifying the locations by numbers 1 to 10, one more than the index value for each location. Note that the parentheses around `(i+1)` here are essential. To get the average, you divide the variable `average` by the number of samples, which is `temperature[i].length`, the length of the array holding temperatures for the current location. Again, you could use any index value here because, as you have seen, they all return the same value, 365.

You can write the nested loop to calculate the average temperatures as nested collection-based `for` loops, like this:

```
int location = 0;                             // Location number
for(float[] temperatures : temperature) {
   float average = 0.0f;        // Place to store the average

   for(float t : temperatures) {
      average += t;
   }

   // Output the average temperature for the current location
   System.out.println("Average temperature at location "
           + (++location) + " = " + average/(float)temperatures.length);
}
```

The outer loop iterates over the elements in the array of arrays, so the loop variable `temperatures` reference each of the one-dimensional arrays in `temperature` in turn. The type of the `temperatures` variable is `float[]` because it stores a reference to a one-dimensional array from the array of one-dimensional arrays, `temperature`. As in the earlier example, the explicit cast for `temperatures.length` to type `float` is not strictly necessary.

The inner `for` loop iterates over the elements in the array that is currently referenced by `temperatures`, and the loop variable `t` is assigned the value of each element from the `temperatures` in turn. You have to define an extra variable, `location`, to record the location number as this was previously provided by the loop variable `i`, which is not present in this version. You increment the value of `location` in the output statement using the prefix form of the increment operator so the location values are 1, 2, 3, and so on.

Arrays of Arrays of Varying Length

When you create an array of arrays, the arrays in the array do not need to be all the same length. You could declare an array variable, `samples`, with the statement:

```
float[][] samples;                    // Declare an array of arrays
```

This declares the array object `samples` to be of type `float[][]`. You can then define the number of elements in the first dimension with the statement:

```
samples = new float[6][];             // Define 6 elements, each is an array
```

The `samples` variable now references an array with six elements, each of which can hold a reference to a one-dimensional array. You can define these arrays individually if you want:

```
samples[2] = new float[6];            // The 3rd array has 6 elements
samples[5] = new float[101];          // The 6th array has 101 elements
```

This defines two of the six possible one-dimensional arrays that can be referenced through elements of the `samples` array. The third element in the `samples` array now references an array of 6 elements of type `float`, and the sixth element of the `samples` array references an array of 101 elements of type `float`. Obviously, you cannot use an array until it has been defined, but you could conceivably use these two and define the others later—not a likely approach, though!

If you want the array `samples` to have a triangular shape, with one element in the first row, two elements in the second row, three in the third row, and so on, you can define the arrays in a loop:

```
for(int i = 0; i < samples.length; ++i) {
   samples[i] = new float[i+1];       // Allocate each array
}
```

The effect of this is to produce the array layout that is shown in Figure 4-5.

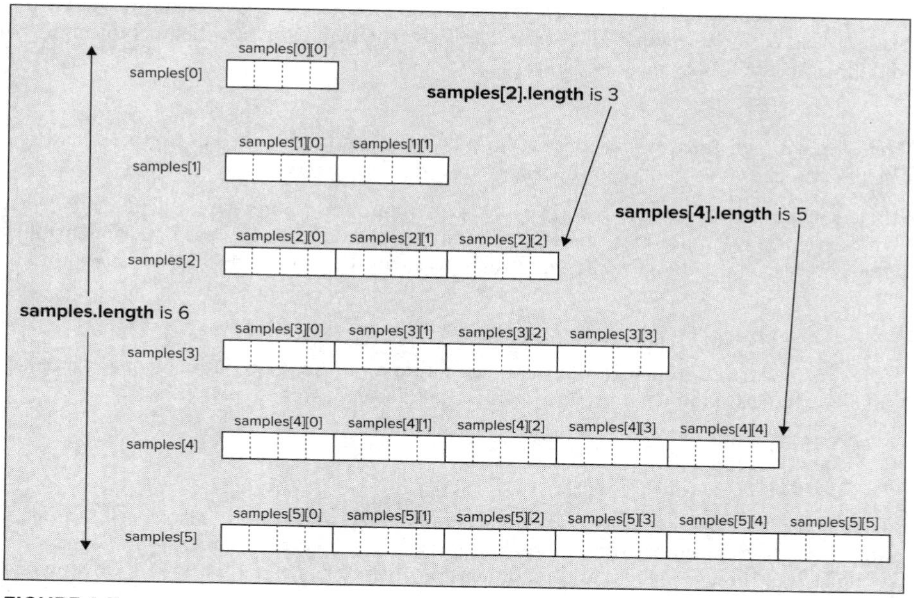

FIGURE 4-5

The 21 elements in the array occupy 84 bytes. When you need a two-dimensional array with rows of varying length, allocating them to fit the requirement can save a considerable amount of memory compared to just using rectangular arrays where the row lengths are all the same.

To check out that the array is as shown in Figure 4-5, you can define it in a program using the code fragments you have just seen and include statements to display the `length` member for each of the one-dimensional arrays.

You could use a numerical `for` loop to initialize the elements in the `samples` array, even though the rows may differ in length:

```
for(int i = 0; i < samples.length; ++i) {
  for(int j = 0 ; j < samples[i].length ; ++j) {
    samples[i][j] = 99.0f;              // Initialize each element to 99
  }
}
```

Of course, for the loops to execute properly the arrays must already have been created. The upper limit for the control variable in the inner loop is `samples[i].length`. The expression `samples[i]` references the current row in the two-dimensional array so `samples[i].length` is the number of elements in the current row. The outer loop iterates over the rows in the `samples` array, and the inner loop iterates over all the elements in a row.

You can also achieve the same result with slightly less code using the `fill()` method from the `Arrays` class that you saw earlier:

```
for(int i = 0; i < samples.length; ++i) {
  java.util.Arrays.fill(samples[i], 99.0f); // Initialize elements in a row to 99
}
```

Because the `fill()` method fills all the elements in a row, you need only one loop that iterates over the rows of the array.

Multidimensional Arrays

You are not limited to two-dimensional arrays either. If you are an international java bean grower with multiple farms across several countries, you could arrange to store the results of your bean counting in the array declared and defined in the following statement:

```
long[][][] beans = new long[5][10][30];
```

The array, beans, has three dimensions. It provides for holding bean counts for each of up to 30 fields per farm, with 10 farms per country in each of 5 countries.

You can envisage this as just a three-dimensional array, but remember that beans is really an array of five elements, each of which holds a reference to a two-dimensional array, and each of these two-dimensional arrays can be different. For example, if you really want to go to town, you can declare the array beans with the statement:

```
long[][][] beans = new long[3][][];          // Three two-dimensional arrays
```

Each of the three elements in the first dimension of beans can hold a different two-dimensional array, so you could specify the first dimension of each explicitly with the following statements:

```
beans[0] = new long[4][];
beans[1] = new long[2][];
beans[2] = new long[5][];
```

These three arrays have elements that each hold a one-dimensional array, and you can also specify the sizes of these independently. Note how the empty square brackets indicate there is still a dimension undefined. You could give the arrays in each of these elements random dimensions between 1 and 7 with the following code:

```
for(int i = 0; i < beans.length; ++i)        // Vary over 1st dimension
  for(int j = 0; j < beans[i].length; ++j)   // Vary over 2nd dimension
    beans[i][j] = new long[(int)(1.0 + 6.0*Math.random())];
```

If you can find a sensible reason for doing so, or if you are just a glutton for punishment, you can extend this to four or more dimensions.

Arrays of Characters

All the arrays you have defined have contained elements storing numerical values so far. You can also have arrays of characters. For example, you can declare an array variable of type char[] to hold 50 characters with the following statement:

```
char[] message = new char[50];
```

Keep in mind that characters are stored as Unicode UTF-16 in Java so each element occupies 2 bytes.

If you want to initialize every element of this array to a space character, you can either use a for loop to iterate over the elements of the array, or just use the fill() method in the Arrays class, like this:

```
java.util.Arrays.fill(message, ' ');         // Store a space in every element
```

Of course, you can use the fill() method to initialize the elements with any character you want. If you put '\n' as the second argument to the fill() method, the array elements all contain a newline character.

You can also define the size of an array of type char[] by the characters it holds initially:

```
char[] vowels = { 'a', 'e', 'i', 'o', 'u'};
```

This defines an array of five elements, initialized with the characters appearing between the braces. This is fine for things such as vowels, but what about proper messages?

Using an array of type char[], you can write statements such as:

```
char[] sign = {'F', 'l', 'u', 'e', 'n', 't', ' ',
               'G', 'i', 'b', 'b', 'e', 'r', 'i', 's', 'h', ' ',
               's', 'p', 'o', 'k', 'e', 'n', ' ',
               'h', 'e', 'r', 'e'};
```

Well, you get the message—just—but it's not a very friendly way to deal with it. It looks like a collection of characters, which is what it is. What you really need is something a bit more integrated—something that looks like a message but still gives you the ability to get at the individual characters if you want. What you need is a `String`.

STRINGS

You will need to use character strings in most of your programs—headings, names, addresses, product descriptions, messages—the list is endless. In Java, ordinary strings are objects of the class `String`. The `String` class is a standard class that comes with Java, and it is specifically designed for creating and processing strings. The definition of the `String` class is in the `java.lang` package so it is accessible in all your programs by default. Character in strings are stored as Unicode UTF-16.

String Literals

You have already made extensive use of string literals for output. Just about every time the `println()` method was used in an example, you used a string literal as the argument. A *string literal* is a sequence of characters between double quotes:

```
"This is a string literal!"
```

This is actually a `String` literal with a capital `S`—in other words, a constant object of the class `String` that the compiler creates for use in your program.

As I mentioned in Chapter 2, some characters can't be entered explicitly from the keyboard so you can't include them directly in a string literal. You can't include a newline character by pressing the Enter key because doing so moves the cursor to a new line. You also can't include a double quote character as it is in a string literal because this is used to indicate where a string literal begins and ends. You can specify all of these characters in a string in the same way as you did for `char` constants in Chapter 2—you use an escape sequence. All the escape sequences you saw when you looked at `char` constants apply to strings. The statement

```
System.out.println("This is \na string constant!");
```

produces the output

```
This is
a string constant!
```

because \n is interpreted as a newline character. Like values of type `char`, strings are stored internally as Unicode characters. You can also include Unicode character codes in a string as escape sequences of the form \unnnn where nnnn are the four hexadecimal digits of the Unicode coding for a particular character. The Greek letter π, for example, is `\u03C0`.

> **WARNING** *When you want to display Unicode characters, the environment in which they are to appear must support displaying Unicode. If you try to write Unicode characters such as that for π to the command line under MS Windows, for example, they will not display correctly.*

You recall from my preliminary discussion of classes and objects in Chapter 1 that a class usually contains data members and methods, and naturally, this is true of the `String` class. The sequence of characters in the string is stored in a data member of the `String` object and the methods for the `String` object enable you to process the data in a variety of ways. I will go into the detail of how a class is defined in Chapter 5, so in this chapter I concentrate on how you can create and use objects of the class `String` without explaining the mechanics of why things work the way that they do. You already know how to define a `String` literal. The next step is to learn how you declare a `String` variable and how you create `String` objects.

Creating String Objects

Just to make sure there is no confusion in your mind, a String variable is simply a variable that stores a reference to an object of the class String. You declare a String variable in much the same way as you define a variable of one of the basic types. You can also initialize it in the declaration, which is generally a good idea:

```
String myString = "My inaugural string";
```

This declares the variable myString as type String and initializes it with a reference to a String object encapsulating the string "My inaugural string". You can store a reference to another string in a String variable, after you have declared it, by using an assignment. For example, you can change the value of the String variable myString to the following statement:

```
myString = "Strings can be knotty";
```

The effect of this is illustrated in Figure 4-6.

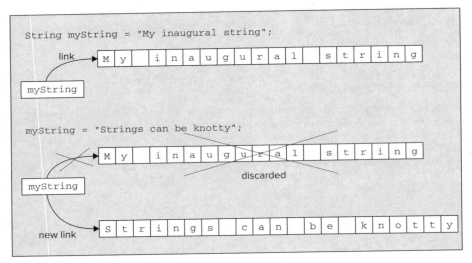

FIGURE 4-6

The String object itself is distinct from the variable you use to refer to it. In the same way as you saw with array objects, the variable myString stores a reference to a String object, not the object itself, so in other words, a String variable records where the String object is in memory. When you declare and initialize myString, it references the object corresponding to the initializing string literal. When you execute the assignment statement, the original reference is overwritten by the reference to the new string and the old string is discarded. The variable myString then contains a reference to the new string.

String objects are said to be *immutable*—which just means that they cannot be changed. This means that you cannot extend or otherwise modify the string that an object of type String represents. When you execute a statement that combines existing String objects, you are *always* creating a new String object as a result. When you change the string referenced by a String variable, you throw away the reference to the old string and replace it with a reference to a new one. The distinction between a String variable and the string it references is not apparent most of the time, but you see situations later in this chapter where it is important to understand this, so keep it in mind.

You should also keep in mind that characters in a string are Unicode characters, so each one typically occupies 2 bytes, with the possibility that they can be 4 bytes if you are using characters represented as surrogates. This is also not something you need worry about most of the time, but there are occasions where you need to be conscious of that, too.

Of course, you can declare a variable of type `String` without initializing it:

```
String anyString;            // Uninitialized String variable
```

The `anyString` variable that you have declared here does not refer to anything. However, if you try to compile a program that attempts to use `anyString` before it has been initialized by some means, you get an error. If you don't want a `String` variable to refer to anything at the outset—for example, if you may or may not assign a `String` object to it before you use the variable—then you must initialize it to a special `null` value:

```
String anyString = null;     // String variable that doesn't reference a string
```

The literal `null` is an object reference value that does not refer to anything. Because an array is essentially an object, you can also use `null` as the value for an array variable that does not reference anything.

You can test whether a `String` variable refers to anything or not by a statement such as:

```
if(anyString == null) {
    System.out.println("anyString does not refer to anything!");
}
```

The variable `anyString` continues to be `null` until you use an assignment to make it reference a particular string. Attempting to use a variable that has not been initialized is an error. When you declare a `String` variable, or any other type of variable in a block of code without initializing it, the compiler can detect any attempts to use the variable before it has a value assigned and flags it as an error. As a rule, you should always initialize variables as you declare them.

You can use the literal `null` when you want to discard a `String` object that is currently referenced by a variable. Suppose you define a `String` variable like this:

```
String message = "Only the mediocre are always at their best";
```

A little later in the program, you want to discard the string that `message` references. You can just write this statement:

```
message = null;
```

The value `null` replaces the original reference stored so `message` now does not refer to anything.

Arrays of Strings

You can create arrays of strings. You declare an array of `String` objects with the same mechanism that you used to declare arrays of elements for the basic types. You just use the type `String` in the declaration. For example, to declare an array of five `String` objects, you could use the statement:

```
String[] names = new String[5];
```

It should now be apparent that the argument to the method `main()` is an array of `String` objects because the definition of the method always looks like this:

```
public static void main(String[] args) {
    // Code for method...
}
```

You can also declare an array of `String` objects where the initial values determine the size of the array:

```
String[] colors = {"red", "orange", "yellow", "green",
                                     "blue", "indigo", "violet"};
```

This array has seven elements because there are seven initializing string literals between the braces.

Of course, as with arrays storing elements of primitive types, you can create arrays of strings with any number of dimensions.

You can try out arrays of strings with a small example.

Available for
download on
Wrox.com

TRY IT OUT Twinkle, Twinkle, Lucky Star

Let's create a console program to generate your lucky star for the day:

```
public class LuckyStars {
  public static void main(String[] args) {
    String[] stars = {
                        "Robert Redford"  , "Marilyn Monroe",
                        "Boris Karloff"   , "Lassie",
                        "Hopalong Cassidy", "Trigger"
                     };
    System.out.println("Your lucky star for today is "
                        + stars[(int)(stars.length*Math.random())]);
  }
}
```

LuckyStars.java

When you compile and run this program, it outputs your lucky star. For example, I was fortunate enough to get the following result:

```
Your lucky star for today is Marilyn Monroe
```

How It Works

This program creates the array `stars` of type `String[]`. The array length is set to however many initializing values appear between the braces in the declaration statement, which is 6 in this case.

You select a random element from the array by creating a random index value within the output statement with the expression `(int)(stars.length*Math.random())`. Multiplying the random number produced by the method `Math.random()` by the length of the array, you get a value between 0.0 and 6.0 because the value returned by `random()` is between 0.0 and 1.0. The result won't ever be exactly 6.0 because the value returned by the `random()` method is strictly less than 1.0, which is just as well because this would be an illegal index value. The result is then cast to type `int` and results in a value from 0 to 5, making it a valid index value for the `stars` array.

Thus the program selects a random string from the array and displays it, so you should see different output if you execute the program repeatedly.

OPERATIONS ON STRINGS

There are many kinds of operations that can be performed on strings, but let's start with one you have used already, joining two or more strings to form a new, combined string. This is often called *string concatenation*.

Joining Strings

To join two `String` objects to form a new, single string you use the + operator, just as you have been doing with the argument to the `println()` method in the program examples thus far. The simplest use of this is to join two strings together:

```
myString = "The quick brown fox" + " jumps over the lazy dog";
```

This joins the two strings on the right of the assignment and stores the result in the `String` variable `myString`. The + operation generates a completely new `String` object that is separate from the two original `String` objects that are the operands, and a reference to this new object is stored in `myString`. Of course, you also use the + operator for arithmetic addition, but if either of the operands for the + operator is a `String` object or literal, then the compiler interprets the operation as string concatenation and converts the operand that is not a `String` object to a string.

Here's an example of concatenating strings referenced by `String` variables:

```
String date = "31st ";
String month = "December";
String lastDay = date + month;          // Result is "31st December"
```

If a `String` variable that you use as one of the operands to + contains `null`, then this is automatically converted to the string `"null"`. So if the `month` variable were to contain `null` instead of a reference to the string `"December"`, the result of the concatenation with `date` would be the string `"31st null"`.

Note that you can also use the += operator to concatenate strings. For example:

```
String phrase = "Too many";
phrase += " cooks spoil the broth";
```

After executing these statements, the variable `phrase` refers to the string `"Too many cooks spoil the broth"`. Of course, this does not modify the string `"Too many"`. The string that is referenced by `phrase` after this statement has been executed is a completely new `String` object. This is illustrated in Figure 4-7.

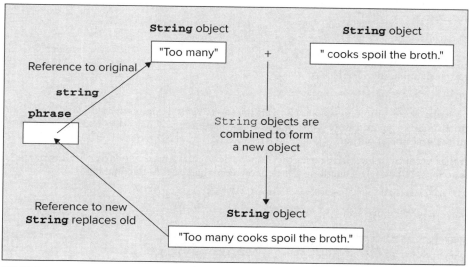

FIGURE 4-7

Let's see how some variations on the use of the + operator with `String` objects work in an example.

TRY IT OUT String Concatenation

Enter the following code for the class `JoinStrings`:

Available for
download on
Wrox.com

```
public class JoinStrings {
    public static void main(String[] args) {

        String firstString = "Many ";
        String secondString = "hands ";
        String thirdString = "make light work";

        String myString;                    // Variable to store results

        // Join three strings and store the result
        myString = firstString + secondString + thirdString;
        System.out.println(myString);

        // Convert an integer to String and join with two other strings
        int numHands = 99;
        myString = numHands + " " + secondString + thirdString;
        System.out.println(myString);

        // Combining a string and integers
```

```
myString = "fifty-five is " + 5 + 5;
System.out.println(myString);

// Combining integers and a string
myString = 5 + 5 + " is ten";
System.out.println(myString);
}
```

JoinStrings.java

If you run this example, it produces some interesting results:

```
Many hands make light work
99 hands make light work
fifty-five is 55
10 is ten
```

How It Works

The first statement after defining the variables is:

```
myString = firstString + secondString + thirdString;
```

This joins the three string values stored in the `String` variables—`firstString`, `secondString`, and `thirdString`—into a single string and stores this in the variable `myString`. This is then used in the next statement to present the first line of output.

The next statement that produces a new string uses the + operator you have used regularly with the `println()` method to combine strings, but clearly something a little more complicated is happening here:

```
myString = numHands + " " + secondString + thirdString;
```

This operation is illustrated in Figure 4-8.

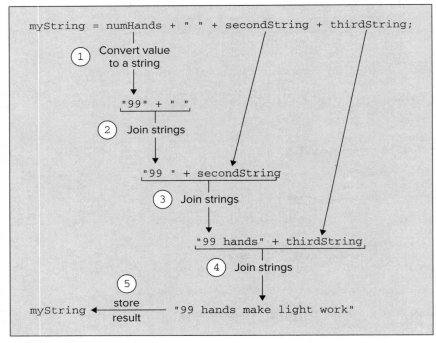

FIGURE 4-8

Behind the scenes, the value of the variable numHands is being converted to a string that represents this value as a decimal digit character. This is prompted by the fact that it is combined with the string literal, " ", using the + operator. Dissimilar types in a binary operation cannot be operated on, so one operand must be converted to the type of the other if the operation is to be possible. Here the compiler arranges that the numerical value stored in numHands is converted to type String to match the type of the right operand of the + operator. If you look back at the table of operator precedence, you'll see that the associativity of the + operator is from left to right, so the strings are combined in pairs starting from the left, as shown in Figure 4-8.

The left-to-right associativity of the + operator is important in understanding how the next two lines of output are generated. The two statements involved in creating these strings look very similar. Why does 5 + 5 result in 55 in one statement and 10 in the other? The reason is illustrated in Figure 4-9.

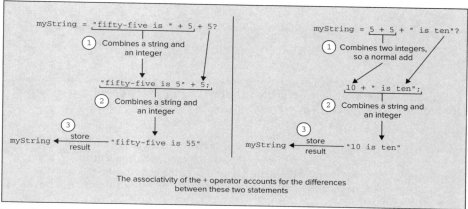

FIGURE 4-9

The essential difference between the two is that the first statement always has at least one operand of type String, so the operation is one of string concatenation, whereas in the second statement the first operation is an arithmetic addition because both operands are integers. In the first statement, each of the integers is converted to type String individually. In the second, the numerical values are added, and the result, 10, is converted to a string representation to allow the literal "is ten" to be concatenated.

You don't need to know about this at this point, but in case you were wondering, the conversion of values of the basic types to type String is actually accomplished by using a static method, toString(), of a standard class that corresponds to the basic type. Each of the primitive types has an equivalent class defined, so for the primitive types I have already discussed there are the *wrapper classes* shown in Table 4-1.

TABLE 4-1: Wrapper Classes

BASIC TYPE	WRAPPER CLASS
byte	Byte
short	Short
int	Integer
long	Long
float	Float
double	Double
boolean	Boolean
char	Character

The classes in the table are called wrapper classes because objects of each of these class types *wrap* a value of the corresponding primitive type. Whenever a value of one of the basic types appears as an operand to + and the other operand is a `String` object, the compiler arranges to pass the value of the basic type as the argument to the `toString()` method that is defined in the corresponding wrapper class. The `toString()` method returns the `String` equivalent of the value. All of this happens automatically when you are concatenating strings using the `+` operator. As you see later, these are not the only classes that have a `toString()` method—all classes do. I won't go into the significance of these classes now, as I cover these in more detail in Chapter 5.

The `String` class also defines a method, `valueOf()`, that creates a `String` object from a value of any type. You just pass the value you want converted to a string as the argument to the method. For example

```
String doubleString = String.valueOf(3.14159);
```

You call the `valueOf()` method using the name of the class `String`, as shown in the preceding line. This is because the method is a `static` member of the `String` class. You learn what `static` means in this context in Chapter 5.

Comparing Strings

Here's where the difference between the `String` variable and the string it references becomes apparent. To compare values stored in variables of the primitive types for equality, you use the `==` operator. This does *not* apply to `String` objects (or any other objects). The expression

```
string1 == string2
```

checks whether the two `String` variables refer to the same string. If they reference separate strings, this expression has the value `false`, regardless of whether or not the strings happen to be identical. In other words, the preceding expression does not compare the strings themselves; it compares the references to the strings, so the result is `true` only if `string1` and `string2` both refer to one and the same string. You can demonstrate this with a little example.

TRY IT OUT Two Strings, Identical but Not the Same

In the following code, you test to see whether `string1` and `string3` refer to the same string:

Available for
download on
Wrox.com

```java
public class MatchStrings {
  public static void main(String[] args) {

    String string1 = "Too many ";
    String string2 = "cooks";
    String string3 = "Too many cooks";

    // Make string1 and string3 refer to separate strings that are identical
    string1 += string2;

    // Display the contents of the strings
    System.out.println("Test 1");
    System.out.println("string3 is now: " + string3);
    System.out.println("string1 is now: " + string1);

    if(string1 == string3) {               // Now test for identity
      System.out.println("string1 == string3 is true." +
                         " string1 and string3 point to the same string");
    } else {
      System.out.println("string1 == string3 is false." +
                        " string1 and string3 do not point to the same string");
    }

    // Now make string1 and string3 refer to the same string
    string3 = string1;
    // Display the contents of the strings
    System.out.println("\n\nTest 2");
```

```
System.out.println("string3 is now: " + string3);
System.out.println("string1 is now: " + string1);

if(string1 == string3) {              // Now test for identity
  System.out.println("string1 == string3 is true." +
                     " string1 and string3 point to the same string");
} else {
  System.out.println("string1 == string3 is false." +
                     " string1 and string3 do not point to the same string");
}
}
```

MatchStrings.java

You have created two scenarios in this example. In the first, the variables string1 and string3 refer to separate String objects that happen to encapsulate identical strings. In the second, they both reference the same String object. The program produces the following output:

```
Test 1
string3 is now: Too many cooks
string1 is now: Too many cooks
string1 == string3 is false. string1 and string3 do not point to the same string

Test 2
string3 is now: Too many cooks
string1 is now: Too many cooks
string1 == string3 is true. string1 and string3 point to the same string
```

How It Works

The three variables string1, string2, and string3 are initialized with the string literals you see. After executing the assignment statement, the string referenced by string1 is identical to that referenced by string3, but as you see from the output, the comparison for equality in the if statement returns false because the variables refer to two separate strings. Note that if you were to just initialize string1 and string3 with the same string literal, "Too many cooks", only one String object would be created, which both variables would reference. This would result in both comparisons being true.

Next you change the value of string3 so that it refers to the same string as string1. The output demonstrates that the if expression has the value true, and that the string1 and string3 objects do indeed refer to the same string. This clearly shows that the comparison is *not* between the strings themselves, but between the references to the strings. So how do you compare the strings?

Comparing Strings for Equality

To compare two String variables, that is, to decide whether the strings they reference are equal or not, you must use the equals() method, which is defined for objects of type String . For example, to compare the String objects referenced by the variables string1 and string3 you could write the following statement:

```
if(string1.equals(string3)) {
    System.out.println("string1.equals(string3) is true." +
                       " so strings are equal.");
}
```

This calls the equals() method for the String object referenced by string1 and passes string3 as the argument. The equals() method does a case-sensitive comparison of corresponding characters in the strings and returns true if the strings are equal and false otherwise. Two strings are equal if they are the same length, that is, have the same number of characters, and each character in one string is identical to the corresponding character in the other.

Of course, you could also use the `equals()` method for the string referenced by `string3` to do the comparison:

```
if(string3.equals(string1)) {
    System.out.println("string3.equals(string1) is true." +
                               " so strings are equal.");
}
```

This is just as effective as the previous version.

To check for equality between two strings ignoring the case of the string characters, you use the method `equalsIgnoreCase()`. Let's put these methods in the context of an example to see them working.

TRY IT OUT   String Identity

Make the following changes to the `MatchStrings.java` file of the previous example:

Available for
download on
Wrox.com

```
public class MatchStrings2 {
  public static void main(String[] args) {

    String string1 = "Too many ";
    String string2 = "cooks";
    String string3 = "Too many cooks";

    // Make string1 and string3 refer to separate strings that are identical
    string1 += string2;

    // Display the contents of the strings
    System.out.println("Test 1");
    System.out.println("string3 is now: " + string3);
    System.out.println("string1 is now: " + string1);

    if(string1.equals(string3)) {                     // Now test for equality
      System.out.println("string1.equals(string3) is true." +
                                " so strings are equal.");
    } else {
      System.out.println("string1.equals(string3) is false." +
                                " so strings are not equal.");
    }

    // Now make string1 and string3 refer to strings differing in case
    string3 = "TOO many cooks";
    // Display the contents of the strings
    System.out.println("\nTest 2");
    System.out.println("string3 is now: " + string3);
    System.out.println("string1 is now: " + string1);

    if(string1.equals(string3)) {                     // Compare for equality
      System.out.println("string1.equals(string3) is true " +
                                " so strings are equal.");
    } else {
      System.out.println("string1.equals(string3) is false" +
                                " so strings are not equal.");
    }

    if(string1.equalsIgnoreCase(string3)) {        // Compare, ignoring case
      System.out.println("string1.equalsIgnoreCase(string3) is true" +
                                " so strings are equal ignoring case.");
    } else {
      System.out.println("string1.equalsIgnoreCase(string3) is false" +
                                " so strings are different.");
    }
  }
}
```

MatchStrings2.java

Of course, if you don't want to create another source file, leave the class name as it was before, as MatchStrings. If you run this example, you should get the following output:

```
Test 1
string3 is now: Too many cooks
string1 is now: Too many cooks
string1.equals(string3) is true. so strings are equal.

Test 2
string3 is now: TOO many cooks
string1 is now: Too many cooks
string1.equals(string3) is false so strings are not equal.
string1.equalsIgnoreCase(string3) is true so strings are equal ignoring case.
```

How It Works

In the if expression, you've called the equals() method for the object string1 to test for equality with string3. This is the syntax you've been using to call the method println() in the object out. In general, to call a method belonging to an object, you write the object name, then a period, and then the name of the method. The parentheses following the method name enclose the information to be passed to the method, which is string3 in this case. The general form for calling a method for an object is shown in Figure 4-10.

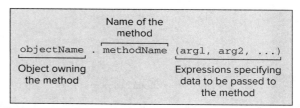

FIGURE 4-10

NOTE *You learn more about this in Chapter 5, when you look at how to define your own classes. For the moment, just note that you don't necessarily need to pass any arguments to a method because some methods don't require any arguments. On the other hand, several arguments can be required. It all depends on how the method was defined in the class.*

The equals() method requires one argument that you put between the parentheses. This must be the String object that is to be compared with the original object. As you saw earlier, the method returns true if the string passed to it (string3 in the example) is identical to the string pointed to by the String object that owns the method; in this case, string1. As you also saw in the previous section, you could just as well call the equals() method for the object string3, and pass string1 as the argument to compare the two strings. In this case, the expression to call the method would be

```
string3.equals(string1)
```

and you would get exactly the same result.

The statements in the program code after outputting the values of string3 and string1 are:

```
if(string1.equals(string3)) {                 // Now test for equality
   System.out.println("string1.equals(string3) is true." +
                      " so strings are equal.");
} else {
   System.out.println("string1.equals(string3) is false." +
                   " so strings are not equal.");
}
```

The output from this shows that calling the equals() method for string1 with string3 as the argument returns true. After the if statement you make string3 reference a new string. You then compare the values of string1 and string3 once more, and, of course, the result of the comparison is now false.

Finally, you compare `string1` with `string3` using the `equalsIgnoreCase()` method. Here the result is `true` because the strings differ only in the case of the first three characters.

String Interning

Having convinced you of the necessity for using the `equals` method for comparing strings, I can now reveal that there is a way to make comparing strings with the `==` operator effective. The mechanism to make this possible is called *string interning*. String interning ensures that no two `String` objects encapsulate the same string, so all `String` objects encapsulate unique strings. This means that if two `String` variables reference strings that are identical, the references must be identical, too. To put it another way, if two `String` variables contain references that are not equal, they must refer to strings that are different. So how do you arrange that all `String` objects encapsulate unique strings? You just call the `intern()` method for every new `String` object that you create. To show how this works, I can amend a bit of an earlier example:

```
String string1 = "Too many ";
String string2 = "cooks";
String string3 = "Too many cooks";

// Make string1 and string3 refer to separate strings that are identical
string1 += string2;
string1 = string1.intern();              // Intern string1
```

The `intern()` method checks the string referenced by `string1` against all the `String` objects currently in existence. If it already exists, the current object is discarded, and `string1` contains a reference to the existing object encapsulating the same string. As a result, the expression `string1 == string3` evaluates to `true`, whereas without the call to `intern()` it evaluated to `false`.

All string constants and constant `String` expressions are automatically interned. That's why `string1` and `string3` would reference the same object if you were to use the same initializing string literal. Suppose you add another variable to the previous code fragment:

```
String string4 = "Too " + "many ";
```

The reference stored in `string4` is automatically the same as the reference stored in `string1`. Only `String` expressions involving variables need to be interned explicitly by calling `intern()`. You could have written the statement that created the combined string to be stored in `string1` with this statement:

```
string1 = (string1 + string2).intern();
```

This now interns the result of the expression `(string1 + string2)`, ensuring that the reference stored in `string1` is unique.

String interning has two benefits. First, it reduces the amount of memory required for storing `String` objects in your program. If your program generates a lot of duplicate strings then this is significant. Second, it allows the use of `==` instead of the `equals()` method when you want to compare strings for equality. Because the `==` operator just compares two references, it is much faster than the `equals()` method, which involves a sequence of character-by-character comparisons. This implies that you may make your program run much faster, but only in certain cases. Keep in mind that the `intern()` method has to use the `equals()` method to determine whether a string already exists. More than that, it compares the current string against a succession of, and possibly all, existing strings in order to determine whether the current string is unique. Realistically, you should stick to using the `equals()` method in the majority of situations and use interning only when you are sure that the benefits outweigh the cost.

 WARNING *If you use string interning, you must remember to ALWAYS intern your strings. Otherwise the == operator will not work properly.*

Checking the Start and End of a String

It can be useful to be able to check just part of a string. You can test whether a string starts with a particular character sequence by using the `startsWith()` method for the `String` object. The argument to the method is the string that you want to look for at the beginning of the string. The argument string can be of any length, but if it's longer than the original string you are testing, it will always return `false`. If `string1` has been defined as `"Too many cooks"`, the expression `string1.startsWith("Too")` has the value `true`. So would the expression `string1.startsWith("Too man")`. Here's an example of using this method:

```
String string1 = "Too many cooks";
if(string1.startsWith("Too")) {
   System.out.println("The string does start with \"Too\" too!");
}
```

The comparison is case-sensitive so the expression `string1.startsWith("tOO")` results in the value `false`.

A complementary method `endsWith()` checks for what appears at the end of a string, so the expression `string1.endsWith("cooks")` has the value `true`. The test is case-sensitive here, too.

Sequencing Strings

You'll often want to place strings in order—for example, when you have a collection of names. Testing for equality doesn't help because to sort strings you need to be able to determine whether one string is greater than or less than another. What you need is the `compareTo()` method in the `String` class. This method compares the `String` object for which it is called with the `String` argument you pass to it and returns an integer that is negative if the `String` object is less than the argument that you passed, zero if the `String` object is equal to the argument, and positive if the `String` object is greater than the argument. Of course, sorting strings requires a clear definition of what the terms *less than*, *equal to*, and *greater than* mean when applied to strings, so I explain that first.

The `compareTo()` method compares two strings by comparing successive corresponding characters, starting with the first character in each string. The process continues until either corresponding characters are found to be different, or the last character in one or both strings is reached. Characters are compared by comparing their Unicode representations—so two characters are equal if the numeric values of their Unicode representations are equal. One character is greater than another if the numerical value of its Unicode representation is greater than that of the other. A character is less than another if its Unicode code is less than that of the other.

One string is greater than another if the first character that differs from the corresponding character in the other string is greater than the corresponding character in the other string. So if `string1` has the value `"mad dog"`, and `string2` has the value `"mad cat"`, then the expression

```
string1.compareTo(string2)
```

returns a positive value as a result of comparing the fifth characters in the strings: the `'d'` in `string1` with the `'c'` in `string2`.

What if the corresponding characters in both strings are equal up to the end of the shorter string, but the other string has more characters? In this case the longer string is greater than the shorter string, so `"catamaran"` is greater than `"cat"`.

One string is less than another string if it has a character less than the corresponding character in the other string, and all the preceding characters are equal. Thus, the following expression returns a negative value:

```
string2.compareTo(string1)
```

Two strings are equal if they contain the same number of characters and corresponding characters are identical. In this case the `compareTo()` method returns 0.

You can exercise the `compareTo()` method in a simple example.

TRY IT OUT | Ordering Strings

In this example you create three strings that you can compare using the `compareTo()` method. Enter the following code:

Available for
download on
Wrox.com

```java
public class SequenceStrings {
  public static void main(String[] args) {

    // Strings to be compared
    String string1 = "A";
    String string2 = "To";
    String string3 = "Z";

    // Strings for use in output
    String string1Out = "\"" + string1 + "\"";      // string1 with quotes
    String string2Out = "\"" + string2 + "\"";      // string2 with quotes
    String string3Out = "\"" + string3 + "\"";      // string3 with quotes

    // Compare string1 with string3
    int result = string1.compareTo(string3);
    if(result < 0) {
      System.out.println(string1Out + " is less than " + string3Out);
    } else if(result > 0) {
      System.out.println(string1Out + " is greater than " + string3Out);
    } else {
      System.out.println(string1Out + " is equal to " + string3Out);
    }

    // Compare string2 with string1
    result = string2.compareTo(string1);
    if(result < 0) {
      System.out.println(string2Out + " is less than " + string1Out);

    } else if(result > 0) {
      System.out.println(string2Out + " is greater than " + string1Out);
    } else {
      System.out.println(string2Out + " is equal to " + string1Out);
    }
  }
}
```

SequenceStrings.java

The example produces the following output:

```
"A" is less than "Z"
"To" is greater than "A"
```

How It Works

You should have no trouble with this example. It declares and initializes three `String` variables: `string1`, `string2`, and `string3`. You then create three further `String` variables that correspond to the first three strings with double quote characters at the beginning and the end. This is just to simplify the output statements.

You have an assignment statement that stores the result of comparing `string1` with `string3`:

```java
int result = string1.compareTo(string3);
```

You can now use the value of `result` to determine how the strings are ordered:

```java
if(result < 0) {
  System.out.println(string1Out + " is less than " + string3Out);
} else if(result > 0) {
```

```
        System.out.println(string1Out + " is greater than " + string3Out);
    } else {
        System.out.println(string1Out + " is equal to " + string3Out);
    }
```

The first `if` statement determines whether `string1` is less than `string3`. If it is, then a message is displayed. If `string1` is not less than `string3`, then either they are equal or `string1` is greater than `string3`. The `else if` statement determines which is the case and outputs a message accordingly.

You compare `string2` with `string1` in the same way.

As with the `equals()` method, the argument to the `compareTo()` method can be any expression that results in a `String` object.

Accessing String Characters

When you are processing strings, sooner or later you need to access individual characters in a `String` object. To refer to a character at a particular position in a string you use an index of type `int` that is the offset of the character position from the beginning of the string.

This is exactly the same principle you used for referencing an array element. The first character in a string is at position 0, the second is at position 1, the third is at position 2, and so on. However, although the principle is the same, the practice is not. You can't use square brackets to access characters in a string—you must use a method.

Extracting String Characters

You extract a character from a `String` object by using the `charAt()` method. This accepts an integer argument that is the offset of the character position from the beginning of the string—in other words, an index. If you attempt to use an index that is less than 0 or greater than the index for the last position in the string, you cause an exception to be thrown, which causes your program to be terminated. I discuss exactly what exceptions are, and how you should deal with them, in Chapter 7. For the moment, just note that the specific type of exception thrown in this case is called `IndexOutOfBoundsException`. Its name is rather a mouthful, but quite explanatory.

To avoid unnecessary errors of this kind, you obviously need to be able to determine the length of a `String` object. To obtain the length of a string, you just need to call its `length()` method. Note the difference between this and the way you got the length of an array. Here you are calling a method, `length()`, for a `String` object, whereas with an array you were accessing a data member, `length`. You can explore the use of the `charAt()` and `length()` methods in the `String` class with another example.

TRY IT OUT   Getting at Characters in a String

In the following code, the soliloquy is analyzed character-by-character to determine the vowels, spaces, and letters that appear in it:

Available for
download on
Wrox.com

```
public class StringCharacters {
  public static void main(String[] args) {
    // Text string to be analyzed
    String text = "To be or not to be, that is the question;"
                 +"Whether 'tis nobler in the mind to suffer"
                 +" the slings and arrows of outrageous fortune,"
                 +" or to take arms against a sea of troubles,"
                 +" and by opposing end them?";
    int spaces  = 0,                       // Count of spaces
        vowels  = 0,                       // Count of vowels
        letters = 0;                       // Count of letters

    // Analyze all the characters in the string
```

```
        int textLength = text.length();                    // Get string length

      for(int i = 0; i < textLength; ++i) {
        // Check for vowels
        char ch = Character.toLowerCase(text.charAt(i));
        if(ch == 'a' || ch == 'e' || ch == 'i' || ch == 'o' || ch == 'u') {
          vowels++;
        }

        //Check for letters
        if(Character.isLetter(ch)) {
          letters++;
        }

        // Check for spaces
        if(Character.isWhitespace(ch)) {
          spaces++;
        }
      }

      System.out.println("The text contained vowels:    " + vowels + "\n" +
                         "                     consonants: " + (letters-vowels) + "\n"+
                         "                     spaces:    " + spaces);

    }
```

StringCharacters.java

Running the example, you see the following output:

```
The text contained vowels:    60
                   consonants: 93
                   spaces:     37
```

How It Works

The `String` variable `text` is initialized with the quotation you see. All the counting of letter characters is done in the `for` loop, which is controlled by the index `i`. The loop continues as long as `i` is less than the length of the string, which is returned by the method `text.length()` and which you saved in the variable `textLength`.

Starting with the first character, which has the index value 0, you retrieve each character from the string by calling its `charAt()` method. You use the loop index `i` as the index to the character position string. The method returns the character at index position `i` as a value of type `char`, and you convert this to lowercase, where necessary, by calling the static method `toLowerCase()` in the class `Character`. The character to be converted is passed as an argument, and the method returns either the original character or, if it is uppercase, the lowercase equivalent. This enables you to deal with all the characters in the string as if they were lowercase.

There is an alternative to using the `toLowerCase()` method in the `Character` class. The `String` class also contains a `toLowerCase()` method that converts a whole string to lowercase and returns a reference to the converted string. You could convert the string `text` to lowercase with the following statement:

```
    text = text.toLowerCase();           // Convert string to lower case
```

This statement replaces the original string with the lowercase equivalent. If you want to retain the original, you can store the reference to the lowercase string in another variable of type `String`. The `String` class also defines the `toUpperCase()` method for converting a string to uppercase, which you use in the same way as the `toLowerCase()` method.

The `if` expression checks for any of the vowels by ORing the comparisons with the five vowels together. If the expression is `true`, you increment the `vowels` count. To check for a letter of any kind you use the `isLetter()` method in the `Character` class, and accumulate the total letter count in the variable `letters`. This enables you to calculate the number of consonants by subtracting the number of vowels from the total number of letters.

Finally, the loop code checks for a space by using the isWhitespace() method in the class Character. This method returns true if the character passed as an argument is a Unicode whitespace character. As well as spaces, whitespace in Unicode also includes horizontal and vertical tab, newline, carriage return, and form-feed characters. If you just wanted to count the spaces in the text, you could explicitly compare for a space character. After the for loop ends, you just output the results.

Searching Strings for Characters

There are two methods available to you in the String class that search a string: indexOf() and lastIndexOf(). Each of these comes in four different flavors to provide a range of search possibilities. The basic choice is whether you want to search for a single character or for a substring, so let's look first at the options for searching a string for a given character.

To search a string text for a single character, 'a' for example, you could write:

```
int index = 0;                      // Position of character in the string
index = text.indexOf('a');          // Find first index position containing 'a'
```

The method indexOf() searches the contents of the string text forward from the beginning and return the index position of the first occurrence of 'a'. If 'a' is not found, the method returns the value –1.

> **NOTE** *This is characteristic of both search methods in the class* String. *They always return either the index position of what is sought or –1 if the search objective is not found. It is important that you check the index value returned for –1 before you use it to index a string; otherwise, you get an error when you don't find what you are looking for.*

If you wanted to find the last occurrence of 'a' in the String variable text, you just use the method lastIndexOf():

```
index = text.lastIndexOf('a');          // Find last index position containing 'a'
```

The method searches the string backward, starting with the last character in the string. The variable index therefore contains the index position of the last occurrence of 'a', or –1 if it is not found.

You can now find the first and last occurrences of a character in a string, but what about the ones in the middle? Well, there's a variation of each of the preceding methods that has a second argument to specify a "from position" from which to start the search. To search forward from a given position, startIndex, you would write:

```
index = text.indexOf('a', startIndex);
```

This version of the method indexOf() searches the string for the character specified by the first argument starting with the position specified by the second argument. You could use this to find the first 'b' that comes after the first 'a' in a string with the following statements:

```
int aIndex = -1;                        // Position of 1st 'a'
int bIndex = -1;                        // Position of 1st 'b' after 'a'
aIndex = text.indexOf('a');             // Find first 'a'
if(aIndex >= 0) {                       // Make sure you found 'a'
   bIndex = text.indexOf('b', aIndex+1); // Find 1st 'b' after 1st 'a'
}
```

After you have the index value from the initial search for 'a', you need to check that 'a' was really found by verifying that aIndex is not negative. You can then search for 'b' from the position following 'a'. As you can see, the second argument of this version of the method indexOf() is separated from the first argument by a comma. Because the second argument is the index position from which the search is to start, and aIndex is the position at which `'a'` was found, you should increment `aIndex` to the position following `'a'` before using it in the search for `'b'` to avoid checking for `'b'` in the position you already know contains `'a'`.

If `'a'` happened to be the last character in the string, it wouldn't matter because the `indexOf()` method just returns –1 if the index value is beyond the last character in the string. If you somehow supplied a negative index value to the method, it simply searches the whole string from the beginning.

Of course, you could use the `indexOf()` method to count how many times a particular character occurred in a string:

```
int aIndex = -1;                          // Search start position
int count = 0;                            // Count of 'a' occurrences
while((aIndex = text.indexOf('a', ++aIndex)) > -1) {
  ++count;
}
```

The `while` loop condition expression calls the `indexOf()` method for the `String` object referenced by `text` and stores the result in the variable `aIndex`. If the value stored is greater than –1, it means that `'a'` was found, so the loop body executes and `count` is incremented. Because `aIndex` has –1 as its initial value, the search starts from index position 0 in the string, which is precisely what you want. When a search reaches the end of the string without finding `'a'`, –1 is returned by the `indexOf()` method and the loop ends.

Searching for Substrings

The `indexOf()` and `lastIndexOf()` methods also come in versions that accept a string as the first argument, which searches for this string rather than a single character. In all other respects they work in the same way as the character searching methods you have just seen. I summarize the complete set of `indexOf()` methods in Table 4-2.

TABLE 4-2: IndexOf () Methods

METHOD	DESCRIPTION
`indexOf(int ch)`	Returns the index position of the first occurrence of the character `ch` in the `String` for which the method is called. If the character `ch` does not occur, –1 is returned.
`indexOf(int ch, int index)`	Same as the preceding method, but with the search starting at position `index` in the string. If the value of `index` is less than or equal to 0, the entire string is searched. If `index` is greater than or equal to the length of the string, –1 is returned.
`indexOf(String str)`	Returns the index position of the first occurrence of the substring `str` in the `String` object for which the method is called. If the substring `str` does not occur, –1 is returned.
`indexOf(String str, int index)`	Same as the preceding method, but with the search starting at position `index` in the string. If the value of `index` is less than or equal to 0, the entire string is searched. If `index` is greater than or equal to the length of the string, –1 is returned.

The four flavors of the `lastIndexOf()` method have the same parameters as the four versions of the `indexOf()` method. The last occurrence of the character or substring that is sought is returned by the `lastIndexOf()` method. Also because the search is from the end of the string, if `index` is less than 0, –1 is returned, and if `index` is greater than or equal to the length of the string, the entire string is searched.

The `startsWith()` method that I mentioned earlier in the chapter also comes in a version that accepts an additional argument that is an offset from the beginning of the string being checked. The check for the matching character sequence then begins at that offset position. If you have defined a string as

```
String string1 = "The Ides of March";
```

then the expression `string1.startsWith("Ides", 4)` has the value `true`.

I can show the `indexOf()` and `lastIndexOf()` methods at work with substrings in an example.

Exciting Concordance Entries

You'll use the indexOf() method to search the quotation you used in the last "Try It Out" example for "and" and the lastIndexOf() method to search for "the".

```java
public class FindCharacters {
  public static void main(String[] args) {
    // Text string to be analyzed
    String text = "To be or not to be, that is the question;"
                + " Whether 'tis nobler in the mind to suffer"
                + " the slings and arrows of outrageous fortune,"
                + " or to take arms against a sea of troubles,"
                + " and by opposing end them?";

    int andCount = 0;              // Number of and's
    int theCount = 0;              // Number of the's

    int index = -1;                // Current index position

    String andStr = "and";         // Search substring
    String theStr = "the";         // Search substring

    // Search forwards for "and"
    index = text.indexOf(andStr);  // Find first 'and'
    while(index >= 0) {
      ++andCount;
      index += andStr.length();    // Step to position after last 'and'
      index = text.indexOf(andStr, index);
    }

    // Search backwards for "the"
    index = text.lastIndexOf(theStr); // Find last 'the'
    while(index >= 0) {
      ++theCount;
      index -= theStr.length();       // Step to position before last 'the'
      index = text.lastIndexOf(theStr, index);
    }
    System.out.println("The text contains " + andCount + " ands\n"
                     + "The text contains " + theCount + " thes");
  }
}
```

FindCharacters.java

The program produces the following output:

```
The text contains 2 ands
The text contains 5 thes
```

 NOTE *If you were expecting the* "the" *count to be 3, note that there is one instance in* "whether" *and another in* "them". *If you want to find three, you need to refine your program to eliminate such pseudo-occurrences by checking the characters on either side of the* "the" *substring.*

How It Works

You define the String variable, text, as before, and set up two counters, andCount and theCount, for the two words. The variable index keeps track of the current position in the string. You then have String variables andStr and theStr holding the substrings you will be searching for.

To find the instances of `"and"`, you first find the index position of the first occurrence of `"and"` in the string `text`. If this index is negative, `text` does not contain `"and"`, and the `while` loop does not execute, as the condition is `false` on the first iteration. Assuming there is at least one `"and"`, the `while` loop block executes and `andCount` is incremented for the instance of `"and"` you have just found. The `indexOf()` method returns the index position of the first character of the substring, so you have to move the index forward to the character following the last character of the substring you have just found. This is done by adding the length of the substring, as shown in Figure 4-11.

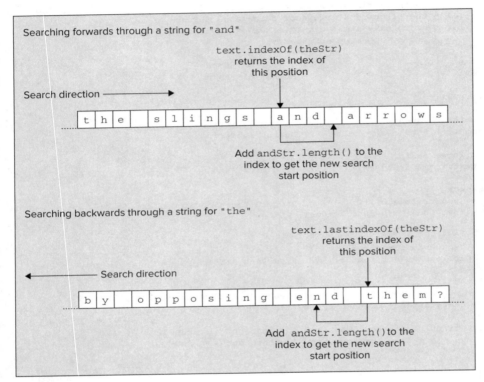

Searching forwards through a string for `"and"`

`text.indexOf(theStr)` returns the index of this position

Search direction ⟶

| t | h | e | | s | l | i | n | g | s | | a | n | d | | a | r | r | o | w | s |

Add `andStr.length()` to the index to get the new search start position

Searching backwards through a string for `"the"`

`text.lastindexOf(theStr)` returns the index of this position

⟵ Search direction

| b | y | | o | p | p | o | s | i | n | g | | e | n | d | | t | h | e | m | ? |

Add `andStr.length()` to the index to get the new search start position

FIGURE 4-11

You are then able to search for the next occurrence of the substring by passing the new value of `index` to the `indexOf()` method. The loop continues as long as the index value returned is not –1.

To count the occurrences of the substring `"the"` the program searches the string `text` backward by using the method `lastIndexOf()` instead of `indexOf()`. This works in much the same way, the only significant difference being that you decrement the value of `index`, instead of incrementing it. This is because the next occurrence of the substring has to be at least that many characters back from the first character of the substring you have just found. If the string `"the"` happens to occur at the beginning of the string you are searching, the `lastIndexOf()` method is called with a negative value for `index`. This does not cause any problem—it just results in –1 being returned in any event.

Extracting Substrings

The `String` class includes the `substring()` method, which extracts a substring from a string. There are two versions of this method. The first version extracts a substring consisting of all the characters from a given index position up to the end of the string. This works as illustrated in the following code fragment:

```
String place = "Palm Springs";
String lastWord = place.substring(5);
```

After executing these statements, lastWord contains the string "Springs", which corresponds to the substring starting at index position 5 in place through to the end of the string. The method copies the substring from the original to form a new String object. This version of the method is useful when a string has basically two constituent substrings, but a more common requirement is to be able to extract several substrings from a string in which each substring is separated from the next by a particular delimiter character such as a comma, a slash, or even just a space. The second version of substring() helps with this.

The second version of the substring() method enables you to extract a substring from a string by specifying the index positions of the first character in the substring and one beyond the last character of the substring as arguments to the method. With the variable place being defined as before, the following statement results in the variable segment being set to the string "ring":

```
String segment = place.substring(7, 11);
```

NOTE With either version of the substring() method, an exception is thrown if you specify an index that is outside the bounds of the string. As with the charAt() method, the substring() method throws IndexOutOfBoundsException if the index value is not valid.

You can see how substring() works with a more substantial example.

TRY IT OUT   Word for Word

You can use the indexOf() method in combination with the substring() method to extract a sequence of substrings that are separated by spaces in a single string:

```
public class ExtractSubstrings {
  public static void main(String[] args) {
    String text = "To be or not to be";      // String to be segmented
    int count = 0;                           // Number of substrings
    char separator = ' ';                    // Substring separator

    // Determine the number of substrings
    int index = 0;
    do {
      ++count;                               // Increment substrings count
      ++index;                               // Move past last position
      index = text.indexOf(separator, index);
    } while (index != -1);

    // Extract the substring into an array
    String[] subStr = new String[count];     // Allocate for substrings
    index = 0;                               // Substring start index
    int endIndex = 0;                        // Substring end index
    for(int i = 0; i < count; ++i) {
      endIndex = text.indexOf(separator,index); // Find next separator

      if(endIndex == -1) {                   // If it is not found
        subStr[i] = text.substring(index);   // extract to the end
      } else {                                         // otherwise
        subStr[i] = text.substring(index, endIndex);  // to end index
      }

      index = endIndex + 1;                  // Set start for next cycle
```

```
    }

    // Display the substrings
    for(String s : subStr) {                    // For each string in subStr
      System.out.println(s);                    //  display it
    }
  }
```

ExtractSubstrings.java

When you run this example, you should get the following output:

```
To
be
or
not
to
be
```

How It Works

After setting up the string `text` to be segmented into substrings, a `count` variable to hold the number of substrings, and the separator character, `separator`, the program has three distinct phases:

1. The first phase counts the number of substrings by using the `indexOf()` method to find separators. The number of separators is always one less than the number of substrings. By using the `do-while` loop, you ensure that the value of `count` is one more than the number of separators because there is always one loop iteration for when the separator is not found.

2. The second phase extracts the substrings in sequence from the beginning of the string and stores them in an array of `String` variables that has `count` elements. A separator follows each substring from the first to the penultimate so you use the version of the `substring()` method that accepts two index arguments for these. The last substring is signaled by a failure to find the separator character when `endIndex` is −1. In this case you use the `substring()` method with a single argument to extract the substring through to the end of the string `text`.

3. The third phase simply outputs the contents of the array by displaying each element in turn, using a collection-based `for` loop. The `String` variable, `s`, defined in the loop references each string in the array in turn. You display each string by passing `s` as the argument to the `println()` method.

What you have been doing here is breaking a string up into *tokens*—substrings in other words—that are separated by *delimiters*—characters that separate one token from the next. This is such a sufficiently frequent requirement that Java provides you with an easier way to do this—using the `split()` method in the `String` class.

Tokenizing a String

The `split()` method in the `String` class is specifically for splitting a string into tokens. It does this in a single step, returning all the tokens from a string as an array of `String` objects. To do this it makes use of a facility called *regular expressions*, which I discuss in detail in Chapter 15. However, you can still make use of the `split()` method without knowing about how regular expressions work, so I ignore this aspect here. Just keep the `split()` method in mind when you get to Chapter 15.

The `split()` method expects two arguments. The first is a `String` object that specifies a *pattern* for a delimiter. Any delimiter that matches the pattern is assumed to be a separator for a token. Here I talk only about patterns that are simply a set of possible delimiter characters in the string. You see in Chapter 15 that the pattern can be much more sophisticated than this. The second argument to the `split()` method is an integer value that is a count of the maximum number of times the pattern can be applied to find tokens and, therefore, affects the maximum number of tokens that can be found. If you specify the second argument as zero, the pattern is applied as many times as possible and any trailing empty tokens discarded. This can arise if several delimiters at the end of the string are being analyzed. If you specify the limit as a negative integer, the pattern is also applied as many times as possible, but trailing empty tokens are retained and returned. As I said earlier, the tokens found by the method are returned in an array of type `String[]`.

The key to tokenizing a string is providing the appropriate pattern defining the set of possible delimiters. At its simplest, a pattern can be a string containing a sequence of characters, each of which is a delimiter. You must specify the set of delimiters in the string between square brackets. This is necessary to distinguish a simple set of delimiter characters from more complex patterns. Examples are the string `"[abc]"` defining `'a'`, `'b'`, and `'c'` as delimiters, or `"[, .:;]"` specifying a comma, a period, a space, a colon, or a semicolon as delimiters. There are many more powerful ways of defining a pattern, but I defer discussing that until Chapter 15.

To see how the `split()` method works, consider the following code fragment:

```
String text = "to be or not to be, that is the question.";
String[] words = text.split("[, .]", 0);  // Delimiters are comma, space, or period
```

The first statement defines the string to be analyzed and split into tokens. The second statement calls the `split()` method for the `text` object to tokenize the string. The first argument to the method specifies a comma, a space, or a period as possible delimiters. The second argument specifies the limit on the number of applications of the delimiter pattern as zero, so it is applied as many times as necessary to tokenize the entire string. The `split()` method returns a reference to an array of strings that are stored in the `words` variable. In case you hadn't noticed, these two lines of code do the same thing as most of the code in `main()` in the previous working example!

Another version of the `split()` method requires a single argument of type `String` specifying the pattern. This is equivalent to using the version with two arguments, where the second argument is zero, so you could write the second statement in the previous code fragment as:

```
String[] words = text.split("[, .]");  // Delimiters are comma, space, or period
```

This produces exactly the same result as when you specify the second argument as 0. Now, it's time to explore the behavior of the `split()` method in an example.

TRY IT OUT   Using a Tokenizer

Here you split a string completely into tokens with alternative explicit values for the second argument to the `split()` method to show the effect:

```
public class StringTokenizing {
  public static void main(String[] args) {
    String text = "To be or not to be, that is the question."; // String to segment
    String delimiters = "[, .]";        // Delimiters are comma, space, and period
    int[] limits = {0, -1};             // Limit values to try

    // Analyze the string
    for(int limit : limits) {
      System.out.println("\nAnalysis with limit = " + limit);
      String[] tokens = text.split(delimiters, limit);
      System.out.println("Number of tokens: " + tokens.length);
      for(String token : tokens) {
        System.out.println(token);
      }
    }
  }
}
```

StringTokenizing.java

The program generates two blocks of output. The first block of output corresponding to a limit value of 0 is:

```
Analysis with limit = 0
Number of tokens: 11
To
be
```

```
or
not
to
be

that
is
the
question
```

The second block of output corresponding to a limit value of –1 is:

```
Analysis with limit = -1
Number of tokens: 12
To
be
or
not
to
be

that
is
the
question
```

In this second case, you have an extra empty line at the end.

How It Works

The string identifying the possible delimiters for tokens in the text is defined by the statement:

```
String delimiters = "[, .]";          // Delimiters are comma, space, and period
```

The characters between the square brackets are the delimiters, so here you have specified that comma, space, and period are delimiters. If you want to include other characters as delimiters, just add them between the square brackets. For example, the string `"[, .:;!?]"` adds a colon, a semicolon, an exclamation point, and a question mark to the original set.

You also have an array of values for the second argument to the `split()` method call:

```
int[] limits = {0, -1};               // Limit values to try
```

I included only two initial values for array elements to keep the amount of output in the book at a minimum, but you should try a few extra values.

The outer collection-based `for` loop iterates over the limit values in the `limits` array. The `limit` variable is assigned the value of each element in the `limits` array in turn. The same string is split into tokens on each iteration, with the current limit value as the second argument to the `split()` method. You display the number of tokens produced by the `split()` method by outputting the length of the array that it returns. You then output the contents of the array that the `split()` method returns in the nested collection-based `for` loop. The loop variable, `token`, references each string in the `tokens` array in turn.

If you look at the first block of output, you see that an array of 11 tokens was returned by the `split()` method. The text being analyzed contains 10 words, and the extra token arises because there are two successive delimiters, a comma followed by a space, in the middle of the string, which causes an empty token to be produced. It is possible to make the `split()` method recognize a comma followed (or preceded) by one or more spaces as a single delimiter, but you will have to wait until Chapter 15 to find out how it's done.

The second block of output has 12 tokens. This is because there is an extra empty token at the end of the list of tokens that is eliminated when the second argument to the `split()` method is 0. The extra token is there because the end of the string is always a delimiter, so the period followed by the end of the string identifies an empty token.

Modified Versions of String Objects

You can use a couple of methods to create a new `String` object that is a modified version of an existing `String` object. These methods don't change the original string, of course—as I said, `String` objects are immutable.

To replace one specific character with another throughout a string, you can use the `replace()` method. For example, to replace each space in the string `text` with a slash, you can write:

```
String newText = text.replace(' ', '/');      // Modify the string text
```

The first argument of the `replace()` method specifies the character to be replaced, and the second argument specifies the character that is to be substituted in its place. I have stored the result in a new variable `newText` here, but you can save it back in the original `String` variable, `text`, if you want to effectively replace the original string with the new modified version.

To remove whitespace from the beginning and end of a string (but not the interior) you can use the `trim()` method. You can apply this to a string as follows:

```
String sample = "   This is a string   ";
String result = sample.trim();
```

After these statements execute, the `String` variable `result` contains the string `"This is a string"`. This can be useful when you are segmenting a string into substrings and the substrings may contain leading or trailing blanks. For example, this might arise if you were analyzing an input string that contained values separated by one or more spaces.

Creating Character Arrays from String Objects

You can create an array of variables of type `char` from a `String` object by using the `toCharArray()` method that is defined in the `String` class. Because this method creates an array of type `char[]` and returns a reference to it, you only need to declare the array variable of type `char[]` to hold the array reference—you don't need to allocate the array. For example:

```
String text = "To be or not to be";
char[] textArray = text.toCharArray();      // Create the array from the string
```

The `toCharArray()` method returns an array containing the characters of the `String` variable `text`, one per element, so `textArray[0]` contain `'T'`, `textArray[1]` contains `'o'`, `textArray[2]` contain `' '`, and so on.

You can also extract a substring as an array of characters using the method `getChars()`, but in this case you do need to create an array that is large enough to hold the characters and pass it as an argument to the method. Of course, you can reuse a single array to store characters when you want to extract and process a succession of substrings one at a time and thus avoid having to repeatedly create new arrays. Of necessity, the array you are using must be large enough to accommodate the longest substring. The method `getChars()` expects four arguments. In sequence, these are:

➤ The index position of the first character to be extracted from the string (type `int`)
➤ The index position following the last character to be extracted from the string (type `int`)
➤ The name of the array to hold the characters extracted (type `char[]`)
➤ The index of the array element to hold the first character (type `int`)

You could copy a substring from `text` into an array with the following statements:

```
String text = "To be or not to be";
char[] textArray = new char[3];
text.getChars(9, 12, textArray, 0);
```

This copies characters from `text` at index positions 9 to 11 inclusive, so `textArray[0]` is `'n'`, `textArray[1]` is `'o'`, and `textArray[2]` is `'t'`.

Using the Collection-Based for Loop with a String

You can't use a `String` object directly as the source of values for a collection-based `for` loop, but you have seen already that you can use an array. The `toCharArray()` method therefore provides you with a way to iterate over the characters in a string using a collection-based `for` loop. Here's an example:

```
String phrase = "The quick brown fox jumped over the lazy dog.";
int vowels = 0;
for(char ch : phrase.toCharArray()) {
  ch = Character.toLowerCase(ch);
  if(ch == 'a' || ch == 'e' || ch == 'i' || ch == 'o' || ch == 'u') {
    ++vowels;
  }
}
System.out.println("The phrase contains " + vowels + " vowels.");
```

This fragment calculates the number of vowels in the `String` `phrase` by iterating over the array of type `char[]` that the `toCharArray()` method for the string returns. The result of passing the value of the loop variable `ch` to the static `toLowerCase()` method in the `Character` class is stored back in `ch`. Of course, you could also use a numerical `for` loop to iterate over the element's characters in the string directly using the `charAt()` method.

Obtaining the Characters in a String as an Array of Bytes

You can extract characters from a string into a `byte[]` array using the `getBytes()` method in the class `String`. This converts the original string characters into the character encoding used by the underlying operating system—which is usually ASCII. For example:

```
String text = "To be or not to be";    // Define a string
byte[] textArray = text.getBytes();     // Get equivalent byte array
```

The byte array `textArray` contains the same characters as in the `String` object, but stored as 8-bit characters. The conversion of characters from Unicode to 8-bit bytes is in accordance with the default encoding for your system. This typically means that the upper byte of the Unicode character is discarded, resulting in the ASCII equivalent. Of course, it is quite possible that a string may contain Unicode characters that cannot be represented in the character encoding in effect on the local machine. In this case, the effect of the `getBytes()` method is unspecified.

Creating String Objects from Character Arrays

The `String` class also has a static method, `copyValueOf()`, to create a `String` object from an array of type `char[]`. Recall that you can use a static method of a class even if no objects of the class exist.

Suppose you have an array defined as follows:

```
char[] textArray = {'T', 'o', ' ', 'b', 'e', ' ', 'o', 'r', ' ',
                    'n', 'o', 't', ' ', 't', 'o', ' ', 'b', 'e' };
```

You can create a `String` object encapsulating these characters as a string with the following statement:

```
String text = String.copyValueOf(textArray);
```

This results in the object `text` referencing the string `"To be or not to be"`.

You can achieve the same result like this:

```
String text = new String(textArray);
```

This calls a constructor for the `String` class, which creates a new object of type `String` that encapsulates a string containing the characters from the array. The `String` class defines several constructors for defining `String` objects from various types of arrays. You learn more about constructors in Chapter 5.

Another version of the `copyValueOf()` method can create a string from a subset of the array elements. It requires two additional arguments to specify the index of the first character in the array to be extracted and the count of the number of characters to be extracted. With the array defined as previously, the statement

```
String text = String.copyValueOf(textArray, 9, 3);
```

extracts three characters starting with `textArray[9]`, so text contains the string `"not"` after this operation.

There's a class constructor that does the same thing:

```
String text = new String(textArray, 9, 3);
```

The arguments are the same here as for the `copyValueOf()` method, and the result is the same.

MUTABLE STRINGS

`String` objects cannot be changed, but you have been creating strings that are combinations and modifications of existing `String` objects, so how is this done? Java has two other standard classes that encapsulate strings, the `StringBuffer` class and the `StringBuilder` class, and both `StringBuffer` and `StringBuilder` objects can be altered directly. Strings that can be changed are referred to as *mutable strings*, in contrast to `String` objects that are *immutable strings*. Java uses objects of the `StringBuffer` class type internally to perform many of the operations that involve combining `String` objects. After the required string has been formed as a `StringBuffer` object, it is then converted to an object of type `String`.

You have the choice of using either a `StringBuffer` object or a `StringBuilder` object whenever you need a string that you can change directly, so what's the difference? In terms of the operations these two classes provide, there is no difference, but `StringBuffer` objects are safe for use by multiple threads, whereas `StringBuilder` objects are not. You learn about threads in Chapter 16, but in case you're not familiar with the term, *threads* are just independent execution processes within a program that can execute concurrently. For example, an application that involves acquiring data from several remote sites could implement the data transfer from each remote site as a separate thread. This would allow these relatively slow operations to execute in parallel, sharing processor time in a manner determined by the operating system. This usually means that the elapsed time for acquiring all the data from the remote sites is much less than if the operations were executed sequentially in a single thread of execution.

Of course, if concurrent threads of execution access the same object, there is potential for problems. Complications can arise when one thread might be accessing an object while another is in the process of modifying it. When this sort of thing is possible in your application, you must use the `StringBuffer` class to define mutable strings if you want to avoid trouble. The `StringBuffer` class operations have been coded to prevent errors arising from concurrent access by two or more threads. If you are sure that your mutable strings will be accessed only by a single thread of execution, then you should use `StringBuilder` objects because operations on these will be faster than with `StringBuffer` objects.

So when should you use mutable `String` objects rather than immutable `String` objects? `StringBuffer` and `StringBuilder` objects come into their own when you are transforming strings frequently—adding, deleting, or replacing substrings in a string. Operations are faster and easier using mutable objects. If you have mainly static strings that you occasionally need to concatenate in your application, then `String` objects are the best choice. Of course, if you want to, you can mix the use of both mutable and immutable in the same program.

As I said, the `StringBuilder` class provides the same set of operations as the `StringBuffer` class. I describe mutable string operations in terms of the `StringBuffer` class for the rest of this chapter because this is always a safe choice, but don't forget that all the operations that I discuss in the context of `StringBuffer` are available with the `StringBuilder` class, which is faster but not thread-safe.

Creating StringBuffer Objects

You can create a `StringBuffer` object that contains a given string with the following statement:

```
StringBuffer aString = new StringBuffer("A stitch in time");
```

This declares a `StringBuffer` object, `aString`, and initializes it with the string `"A stitch in time"`. When you are initializing a `StringBuffer` object, you must use this syntax, with the keyword `new`, the `StringBuffer` class name, and the initializing value between parentheses. You cannot just use the string as the initializing value as you did with `String` objects. This is because there is rather more to a `StringBuffer` object than just the string that it contains initially, and of course, a string literal is a `String` object by definition.

You can also create a `StringBuffer` object using a reference stored in a variable of type `String`:

```
String phrase = "Experience is what you get when you're expecting something else.";
StringBuffer buffer = new StringBuffer(phrase);
```

The `StringBuffer` object, `buffer`, contains a string that is the same as that encapsulated by the `String` object, `phrase`.

You can just create the `StringBuffer` variable, in much the same way as you created a `String` variable:

```
StringBuffer myString = null;
```

This variable does not refer to anything until you initialize it with a defined `StringBuffer` object. For example, you could write:

```
myString = new StringBuffer("Many a mickle makes a muckle");
```

This statement creates a new `StringBuffer` object encapsulating the string `"Many a mickle makes a muckle"` and stores the reference to this object in `myString`. You can also initialize a `StringBuffer` variable with an existing `StringBuffer` object:

```
StringBuffer aString = myString;
```

Both `myString` and `aString` now refer to a single `StringBuffer` object.

The Capacity of a StringBuffer Object

The `String` objects that you have been using each contain a fixed string, and when you create a `String` object, memory is allocated to accommodate however many Unicode characters are in the string it encapsulates. Everything is fixed so memory usage is not a problem. A `StringBuffer` object is a little different. It contains a block of memory called a *buffer*, which may or may not contain a string, and if it does, the string need not occupy the entire buffer. Thus, the length of a string in a `StringBuffer` object can be different from the length of the buffer that the object contains. The length of the buffer is referred to as the *capacity* of the `StringBuffer` object.

After you have created a `StringBuffer` object, you can find the length of the string it contains, by using the `length()` method for the object:

```
StringBuffer aString = new StringBuffer("A stitch in time");
int theLength = aString.length();
```

If the object `aString` were defined as in the preceding declaration, the variable `theLength` would have the value 16. However, the capacity of the object is larger, as illustrated in Figure 4-12.

CONFER PROGRAMMER TO PROGRAMMER ABOUT THIS TOPIC.

→ **Visit p2p.wrox.com** ←

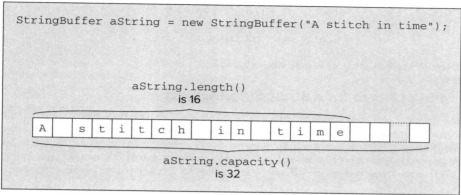

```
StringBuffer aString = new StringBuffer("A stitch in time");
```

aString.length()
is 16

| A | | s | t | i | t | c | h | | i | n | | t | i | m | e | | | | |

aString.capacity()
is 32

FIGURE 4-12

When you create a `StringBuffer` object from an existing string, the capacity is the length of the string plus 16. Both the capacity and the length are in units of Unicode characters, so twice as many bytes are occupied in memory.

The capacity of a `StringBuffer` object is not fixed, though. It grows automatically as you add to the string to accommodate a string of any length. You can also specify the initial capacity when you create a `StringBuffer` object. For example, the following statement creates a `StringBuffer` object with a specific value for the capacity:

```
StringBuffer newString = new StringBuffer(50);
```

This creates an object, `newString`, with the capacity to store 50 characters. If you omit the capacity value in this declaration, the object has a default capacity of 16 characters. Thus, the `StringBuffer` object that you create here has a buffer with a capacity of 50 characters that is initially empty—no string is stored in it.

A `String` object is always a fixed string, so capacity is irrelevant—it is always just enough to hold the characters in the string. A `StringBuffer` object, on the other hand, is a container in which you can store a string of any length, and it has a capacity at any given instant for storing a string up to a given size. Although you can set the capacity, it is unimportant in the sense that it is just a measure of how much memory is available to store Unicode characters at this particular point in time. You can get by without worrying about the capacity of a `StringBuffer` object at all because the capacity required to cope with what your program is doing is always provided automatically. It just gets increased as necessary.

So why have I mentioned the capacity of a `StringBuffer` object at all? While it's true you can use `StringBuffer` objects ignoring their capacity, the capacity of a `StringBuffer` object is important in the sense that it affects the amount of overhead involved in storing and modifying a string. If the initial capacity is small, and you store a string that is long, or you add to an existing string significantly, you need to allocate extra memory. Allocating additional memory takes time, and if it occurs frequently, it can add a substantial overhead to the processor time your program needs to complete the task. It is more efficient to make the capacity of a `StringBuffer` sufficient for the needs of your program.

To find out what the capacity of a `StringBuffer` object is at any given time, you use the `capacity()` method for the object:

```
int theCapacity = aString.capacity();
```

This method returns the number of Unicode characters the object can currently hold. For `aString` defined as shown, this is 32. When you create a `StringBuffer` object containing a string, its capacity is 16 characters greater than the minimum necessary to hold the string.

The `ensureCapacity()` method enables you to change the default capacity of a `StringBuffer` object. You specify the minimum capacity you need as the argument to the method. For example:

```
aString.ensureCapacity(40);
```

If the current capacity of the aString object is less than 40, this increases the capacity of aString by allocating a new larger buffer, but not necessarily with a capacity of 40. The capacity is the larger of either the value that you specify, 40 in this case, or twice the current capacity plus 2, which is 66, given that aString is defined as before. You might want to do this sort of thing when you are reusing an existing StringBuffer object in a new context where the strings are longer.

Changing the String Length for a StringBuffer Object

You can change the length of the string contained in a StringBuffer object with the method setLength(). Note that the length is a property of the string the object holds, as opposed to the capacity, which is a property of the string buffer. When you increase the length for a StringBuffer object, you are adding characters to the existing string and the extra characters contain '\u0000'. A more common use of this method is to decrease the length, in which case the string is truncated. If aString contains "A stitch in time", the statement

```
aString.setLength(8);
```

results in aString containing the string "A stitch", and the value returned by the length() method is 8. The characters that were cut from the end of the string by this operation are lost.

To increase the length to what it was before, you could write:

```
aString.setLength(16);
```

Now aString contains the string:

```
"A stitch\u0000\u0000\u0000\u0000\u0000\u0000\u0000\u0000"
```

The setLength() method does not affect the capacity of the object unless you set the length to be greater than the capacity. In this case the capacity is increased to accommodate the new string length to a value that is twice the original capacity plus two if the length you set is less than this value. If you specify a length that is greater than twice the original capacity plus two, the new capacity is the same as the length you set. If the capacity of aString is 66, executing the statement

```
aString.setLength(100);
```

sets the capacity of the object, aString, to 134. If you supplied a value for the length of 150, then the new capacity would be 150. You must not specify a negative length here. If you do, IndexOutOfBoundsException is thrown.

Adding to a StringBuffer Object

The append() method enables you to add a string to the end of the existing string stored in a StringBuffer object. This method comes in quite a few flavors, but perhaps the simplest adds the string contained within a String or a StringBuffer object to a StringBuffer object. This works with string literals too.

Suppose you define a StringBuffer object with the following statement:

```
StringBuffer aString = new StringBuffer("A stitch in time");
```

You can add to it with the statement:

```
aString.append(" saves nine");
```

After this aString contains "A stitch in time saves nine". The length of the string contained in the StringBuffer object is increased by the length of the string that you add. You don't need to worry about running out of space though. The capacity is always increased automatically whenever necessary to accommodate the longer string.

The append() method returns a reference to the extended StringBuffer object, so you could also assign it to another StringBuffer object. Instead of the previous statement, you could have written:

```
StringBuffer bString = aString.append(" saves nine");
```

Now both `aString` and `bString` point to the same `StringBuffer` object.

If you take a look at the operator precedence table in Chapter 2, you see that the ' . ' operator (sometimes called the member selection operator) that you use to execute a particular method for an object has left-to-right associativity. You can therefore write multiple append operations in a single statement:

```
StringBuffer proverb = new StringBuffer();              // Capacity is 16
proverb.append("Many").append(" hands").append(" make").
                    append(" light").append(" work.");
```

The second statement is executed from left to right, so that the string contained in the object `proverb` is progressively extended until it contains the complete string. The reference that each call to `append()` returns is used to call `append()` again for the same object, `proverb`.

Appending a Substring

Another version of the `append()` method adds part of a `String` or a `StringBuffer` object to a `StringBuffer` object. This version of `append()` requires three arguments: a reference to the `String` or `StringBuffer` object from which the substring to be appended is obtained, the index position of the first character in the object for the substring that is to be appended, and the index position of one past the last character to be appended. If you supply `null` as the first argument, the substring from will be extracted from the string `"null"`.

To illustrate the workings of this, suppose you create a `StringBuffer` object and a `String` object with the following statements:

```
StringBuffer buf = new StringBuffer("Hard ");
String aString = "Waxworks";
```

You can then append part of the `aString` object to the `buf` object with this statement:

```
buf.append(aString, 3, 7);
```

This operation is shown in Figure 4-13.

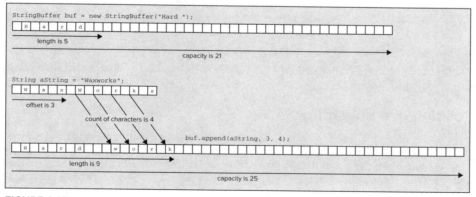

FIGURE 4-13

This operation appends the substring of `aString` that starts at index position 3 and ends at index position 6, inclusive, to the `StringBuffer` object `buf`. The object `buf` then contains the string `"Hard work"`. The capacity of `buf` would be automatically increased if the resultant's length exceeds the capacity.

Appending Basic Types

You have a set of versions of the `append()` method that enable you to `append()` the string equivalent of values of any of the primitive types to a `StringBuffer` object. These versions of `append()` accept arguments of any of the following types: `boolean`, `char`, `byte`, `short`, `int`, `long`, `float`, or `double`. In each case, the value is converted to a string equivalent of the value, which is appended to the object, so a `boolean` variable is appended as either `"true"` or `"false,"` and for numeric types the string is a decimal representation of the value. For example

```
StringBuffer buf = new StringBuffer("The number is ");
long number = 99L;
buf.append(number);
```

results in `buf` containing the string `"The number is 99"`.

There is nothing to prevent you from appending constants to a `StringBuffer` object. For example, if you now execute the statement

```
buf.append(12.34);
```

the object `buf` contains `"The number is 9912.34"`.

There is also a version of the `append()` method that accepts an array of type `char[]` as an argument. The contents of the array are appended to the `StringBuffer` object as a string. A further variation on this enables you to append a subset of the elements from an array of type `char[]` by using two additional arguments: one to specify the index of the first element to be appended, and another to specify the total number of elements to be appended. An example of how you might use this is as follows:

```
char[] text = { 'i', 's', ' ', 'e', 'x', 'a', 'c', 't', 'l', 'y'};
buf.append(text, 2, 8);
```

This appends the string `" exactly"` to `buf`, so after executing this statement `buf` contains `"The number is 9912.34 exactly"`.

You may be somewhat bemused by the plethora of `append()` method options, so let's collect all the possibilities together. You can append any of the following types to a `StringBuffer` object:

boolean	char	String	Object
int	long	float	double
byte	short	char[]	

In each case the `String` equivalent of the argument is appended to the string in the `StringBuffer` object.

I haven't discussed type `Object` yet—I included it in the table here for the sake of completeness. You learn about this type of object in Chapter 6.

Finding the Position of a Substring

You can search the buffer of a `StringBuffer` object for a given substring by calling the `indexOf()` method or the `lastIndexOf()` method. The simpler of the two versions of this method requires just one argument, which is the string you are looking for, and the method returns the index position of the last occurrence of the string you are searching for as a value of type `int`. The method returns −1 if the substring is not found. For example:

```
StringBuffer phrase = new StringBuffer("one two three four");
int position = phrase.lastIndexOf("three");
```

The value returned is the index position of the first character of the last occurrence of `"three"` in phrase, which is 8. Remember, the first character is at index position 0. Of course, if the argument to the `lastIndexOf()` method was `"t"`, the result would be the same because the method finds the last occurrence of the substring in the buffer.

The second version of the `lastIndexOf()` method requires an additional argument that specifies the index position in the buffer where the search is to start. For example:

```
position = phrase.lastIndexOf("three", 8);
```

This statement searches backward through the string for the first character of the substring starting at index position 8 in `phrase`, so the last nine characters (index values 9 to 17) in the buffer are not examined. Even through `"three"` extends beyond index position 8, it will be found by this statement and 8 will be returned. The index constraint is on the search for the first character, not the whole string.

Replacing a Substring in the Buffer

You use the `replace()` method for a `StringBuffer` object to replace a contiguous sequence of characters with a given string. The string that you specify as the replacement can contain more characters than the substring being replaced, in which case the string is extended as necessary. The `replace()` method requires three arguments. The first two are of type `int` and specify the start index in the buffer and one beyond the end index of the substring to be replaced. The third argument is of type `String` and is the string to be inserted. Here's an example of how you might use the `replace()` method:

```
StringBuffer phrase = new StringBuffer("one two three four");
String substring = "two";
String replacement = "twenty";

// Find start of last occurrence of "two"
int position = phrase.lastIndexOf(substring);
phrase.replace(position, position+substring.length(), replacement);
```

The first three statements define the original `StringBuffer` object, the `substring` to be replaced, and the string to replace the `substring`. The next statement uses the `lastIndexOf()` method to find the position of the first character of the last occurrence of `substring` in `phrase`. The last statement uses the `replace()` method to substitute `replacement` in place of `substring`. To get the index value for one beyond the last character of `substring`, you just add the length of `substring` to its position index. Because `replacement` is a string containing more characters than `substring`, the length of the string in `phrase` is increased, and the new contents are `"one twenty three four"`.

I have not bothered to insert code to check for the possibility of –1 being returned in the preceding code fragment, but naturally in a real-world context it is essential to do this to avoid the program being terminated when the `substring` is not present.

Inserting Strings

To insert a string into a `StringBuffer` object, you use the `insert()` method of the object. The first argument specifies the index of the position in the object where the first character is to be inserted. For example, if `buf` contains the string `"Many hands make light work"`, the statement

```
buf.insert(4, " old");
```

inserts the string `" old"` starting at index position 4, so `buf` contains the string `"Many old hands make light work"` after executing this statement.

Many versions of the `insert()` method accept a second argument of any of the same range of types that apply to the `append()` method, so you can use any of the following with the `insert()` method:

boolean	char	String	Object
int	long	float	double
byte	short	char[]	StringBuffer

In each case the string equivalent of the second argument is inserted starting at the index position specified by the first argument.

If you need to insert a subset of an array of type `char[]` into a `StringBuffer` object, you can call the version of `insert()` that accepts four arguments, shown below:

```
insert(int index, char[] str, int offset, int length)
```

This method inserts a substring into the `StringBuffer` object starting at position `index`. The substring is the `String` representation of `length` characters from the `str[]` array, starting at position `offset`.

If the value of `index` is outside the range of the string in the `StringBuffer` object, or the `offset` or `length` values result in illegal indexes for the array `str`, then an exception of type `StringIndexOutOfBounds` `Exception` is thrown.

There's another version of `insert()` that you can use to insert a substring of a `String` or `StringBuffer` object into a `StringBuffer` object. The first argument is the offset index for the insertion; the second is the reference to the source of the substring; the third argument is the index for the first character of the substring; and the last argument is the index of one beyond the last character in the substring.

 NOTE *If you look in the JDK documentation for* `StringBuffer`, *you see parameters for* `insert()` *and other methods of type* `CharSequence`. *This type allows a* `String` *or* `StringBuffer` *reference to be supplied (as well as some other types). I avoid discussing* `CharSequence` *further at this point because it is different from a class type and it needs an in-depth explanation. I explain this in Chapter 6.*

Extracting Characters from a Mutable String

The `StringBuffer` class includes the `charAt()` and `getChars()` methods, both of which work in the same way as the methods of the same name in the `String` class which you've already seen. The `charAt()` method extracts the character at a given index position, and the `getChars()` method extracts a range of characters and stores them in an array of type `char[]` starting at a specified index position.

You should note that there is no equivalent to the `getBytes()` method for `StringBuffer` objects. However you can obtain a `String` object from a `CharBuffer` object by calling its `toString()` method, then you can call `getBytes()` for the `String` object to obtain the `byte[]` array corresponding to the `StringBuffer` object.

Other Mutable String Operations

You can change a single character in a `StringBuffer` object by using the `setCharAt()` method. The first argument indicates the index position of the character to be changed, and the second argument specifies the replacement character. For example, the statement

```
buf.setCharAt(3, 'Z');
```

sets the fourth character in the string to `'Z'`.

You use the `deleteCharAt()` method to remove a single character from a `StringBuffer` object at the index position specified by the argument. For example:

```
StringBuffer phrase = new StringBuffer("When the boats come in");
phrase.deleteCharAt(10);
```

After these statements have executed, `phrase` contains the string `"When the bats come in"`.

If you want to remove several characters from a `StringBuffer` object you use the `delete()` method. This method requires two arguments: The first is the index of the first character to be deleted, and the second is the index position following the last character to be deleted. For example:

```
phrase.delete(5, 9);
```

This statement deletes the substring `"the "` from `phrase`, so it then contains the string `"When bats come in"`.

You can completely reverse the sequence of characters in a `StringBuffer` object with the `reverse()` method. For example, if you define the object with the declaration

```
StringBuffer palindrome = new StringBuffer("so many dynamos");
```

you can then transform it with the statement:

```
palindrome.reverse();
```

which results in `palindrome` containing the useful phrase `"somanyd ynam os"`.

Creating a String Object from a StringBuffer Object

You can produce a `String` object from a `StringBuffer` object by using the `toString()` method of the `StringBuffer` class. This method creates a new `String` object and initializes it with the string contained in the `StringBuffer` object. For example, to produce a `String` object containing the proverb that you created in the previous section, you could write:

```
String saying = proverb.toString();
```

The object `saying` contains `"Many hands make light work"`.

The `toString()` method is used extensively by the compiler together with the `append()` method to implement the concatenation of `String` objects.

Suppose you have the following strings defined:

```
String str1 = "Many", str2=" hands", str3=" make", str4=" light", str5=" work.";
```

When you write a statement such as

```
String saying = str1 + str2 + str3 + str4 + str5;
```

the compiler implements this as:

```
String saying = new StringBuffer().append(str1).append(str2).
                                   append(str3).append(str4).
                                   append(str5).toString();
```

The expression to the right of the = sign is executed from left to right, so the segments of the string encapsulated by the objects are appended to the `StringBuffer` object that is created until finally the `toString()` method is invoked to convert it to a `String` object. `String` objects can't be modified, so any alteration or extension of a `String` object involves the use of a `StringBuffer` object, which can be changed.

It's time to see a `StringBuffer` object in action.

TRY IT OUT   Using a StringBuffer Object to Assemble a String

This example just exercises some of the `StringBuffer` operations you have seen by assembling a string from an array of words and then inserting some additional characters into the string:

```java
public class UseStringBuffer {
  public static void main(String[] args) {
    StringBuffer sentence = new StringBuffer(20);
    System.out.println("\nStringBuffer object capacity is " +
                                    sentence.capacity() +
                          " and string length is "+sentence.length());

    // Append all the words to the StringBuffer object
    String[] words = {"Too"  , "many", "cooks", "spoil", "the" , "broth"};
    sentence.append(words[0]);
    for(int i = 1 ; i < words.length ; ++i) {
      sentence.append(' ').append(words[i]);
    }

    // Show the result
    System.out.println("\nString in StringBuffer object is:\n" +
                                            sentence.toString());
```

```
System.out.println("StringBuffer object capacity is now " +
                                 sentence.capacity()+
                     " and string length is "+sentence.length());


// Now modify the string by inserting characters
sentence.insert(sentence.lastIndexOf("cooks")+4,"ie");
sentence.insert(sentence.lastIndexOf("broth")+5, "er");
System.out.println("\nString in StringBuffer object is:\n" + sentence);
System.out.println("StringBuffer object capacity is now " +
                                  sentence.capacity() +
                      " and string length is "+sentence.length());


    }
}
```

UseStringBuffer.java

The output from this example is:

```
StringBuffer object capacity is 20 and string length is 0

String in StringBuffer object is:
Too many cooks spoil the broth
StringBuffer object capacity is now 42 and string length is 30

String in StringBuffer object is:
Too many cookies spoil the brother
StringBuffer object capacity is now 42 and string length is 34
```

How It Works

You first create a `StringBuffer` object with a buffer capacity of 20 characters with the following statement:

```
StringBuffer sentence = new StringBuffer(20);
```

The output statement that follows just displays the buffer capacity and the initial string length. You obtain these by calling the `capacity()` and `length()` methods, respectively, for the `sentence` object. The string length is zero because you have not specified any buffer contents.

The next four statements create an array of words and append those words to `sentence`:

```
String[] words = {"Too"    , "many", "cooks", "spoil", "the"  , "broth"};
sentence.append(words[0]);
for(int i = 1 ; i < words.length ; ++i) {
   sentence.append(' ').append(words[i]);
```

To start the process of building the string, you append the first word from the `words` array to `sentence`. You then append all the subsequent words in the `for` loop, preceding each word with a space character.

The next output statement displays the buffer contents as a string by calling the `toString()` method for `sentence` to create a `String` object. You then output the buffer capacity and string length for `sentence` once more. The output shows that the capacity has been automatically increased to 42 and the length of the string is 30.

In the last phase of the program you insert the string `"ie"` after the substring `"cook"` with the statement:

```
sentence.insert(sentence.lastIndexOf("cooks")+4,"ie");
```

The `lastIndexOf()` method returns the index position of the last occurrence of `"cooks"` in sentence, so you add 4 to this to specify the insertion position after the last letter of `"cook"`. You use the same mechanism to insert the string `"er"` following `"broth"` in the buffer.

Finally, you output the string and the capacity and string length with the last two statements in `main()`:

```
System.out.println("\nString in StringBuffer object is:\n" + sentence);
System.out.println("StringBuffer object capacity is now "+ sentence.capacity() +
                   " and string length is "+sentence.length());
```

Note that the first output statement does not call the `toString()` method explicitly. The compiler inserts the call for you to convert the `StringBuffer` object to a `String` object. This is necessary to make it compatible with the + operator for `String` objects.

SUMMARY

You should now be thoroughly familiar with how to create and use arrays. Most people have little trouble dealing with one-dimensional arrays, but arrays of arrays are a bit trickier so try to practice using these.

You have also acquired a good knowledge of what you can do with `String` objects, as well as `StringBuffer` and `StringBuilder` objects. Most operations with these objects are very straightforward and easy to understand. Being able to decide which methods you should apply to the solution of specific problems is a skill that comes with a bit of practice.

EXERCISES

You can download the source code for the examples in the book and the solutions to the following exercises from www.wrox.com.

1. Create an array of `String` variables and initialize the array with the names of the months from January to December. Create an array containing 12 random decimal values between 0.0 and 100.0. Display the names of each month along with the corresponding decimal value. Calculate and display the average of the 12 decimal values.

2. Write a program to create a rectangular array containing a multiplication table from 1*1 up to 12*12. Output the table as 13 columns with the numeric values right-aligned in the columns. (The first line of output is the column headings, the first column with no heading, then the numbers 1 to 12 for the remaining columns. The first item in each of the succeeding lines is the row heading, which ranges from 1 to 12.)

3. Write a program that sets up a `String` variable containing a paragraph of text of your choice. Extract the words from the text and sort them into alphabetical order. Display the sorted list of words. You could use a simple sorting method called the bubble sort. To sort an array into ascending order the process is as follows:

    a. Starting with the first element in the array, compare successive elements (0 and 1, 1 and 2, 2 and 3, and so on).

    b. If the first element of any pair is greater than the second, interchange the two elements.

    c. Repeat the process for the whole array until no interchanges are necessary. The array elements are now in ascending order.

4. Define an array of ten `String` elements each containing an arbitrary string of the form `"month/day/year"`; for example,`"10/29/99"` or `"12/5/01"`. Analyze each element in the array and output the date represented in the form 29th October 1999.

5. Write a program that reverses the sequence of letters in each word of your chosen paragraph from Exercise 3. For instance, `"To be or not to be."` becomes `"oT eb ro ton ot eb."`

CONFER PROGRAMMER TO PROGRAMMER ABOUT THIS TOPIC.
Visit p2p.wrox.com

▶ **WHAT YOU LEARNED IN THIS CHAPTER**

TOPIC	CONCEPT
Using an Array	You use an array to hold multiple values of the same type, identified through a single variable name.
Accessing Array Elements	You reference an individual element of an array by using an index value of type `int`. The index value for an array element is the offset of that element from the first element in the array, so the index of the first element is 0.
Using Array Elements	An array element can be used in the same way as a single variable of the same type.
The Number of Array Elements	You can obtain the number of elements in an array by using the `length` member of the array object.
Arrays of Arrays	An array element can also contain an array, so you can define arrays of arrays, or arrays of arrays of arrays, and so on.
`String` Objects	A `String` object stores a fixed character string that cannot be changed. However, you can assign a given `String` variable to a different `String` object.
String Length	You can obtain the number of characters stored in a `String` object by using the `length()` method for the object.
`String` Class Methods	The `String` class provides methods for joining, searching, and modifying strings—the modifications being achieved by creating a new `String` object.
Mutable Strings	`StringBuffer` and `StringBuilder` objects can store a string of characters that you can modify.
`StringBuffer` and `StringBuilder` Objects	`StringBuffer` and `StringBuilder` objects support the same set of operations. `StringBuffer` objects are safe when accessed by multiple threads of execution whereas `StringBuilder` object are not.
Length and Capacity of a `StringBuffer` object	You can get the number of characters stored in a `StringBuffer` object by calling its `length()` method, and you can find out the current maximum number of characters it can store by using its `capacity()` method. You can change both the length and the capacity for a `StringBuffer` object.
Creating a `String` Object from a `StringBuffer` object	You can create a `String` object from a `StringBuffer` object by using the `toString()` method of the `StringBuffer` object.

5

Defining Classes

WHAT YOU WILL LEARN IN THIS CHAPTER

➤ What a class is, and how you define a class

➤ How to implement class constructors

➤ How to define class methods

➤ What method overloading is

➤ What a recursive method is and how it works

➤ How to create objects of a class type

➤ What packages are and how you can create and use them

➤ What access attributes are and how you should use them in your class definitions

➤ What nested classes are and how you use them

In this chapter you explore the heart of the Java language: classes. Classes specify the objects you use in object-oriented programming. These form the basic building blocks of any Java program, as you saw in Chapter 1. Every program in Java involves classes because the code for a program can appear only within a class definition.

You explore the details of how a class definition is put together, how to create your own classes, and how to use classes to solve your own computing problems. And in the next chapter, you build on this to look at how object-oriented programming helps you work with sets of related classes.

WHAT IS A CLASS?

As you saw in Chapter 1, a class is a prescription for a particular kind of object—it defines a new *type*. You use the definition of a class to create objects of that class type—that is, to create objects that incorporate all the components specified as belonging to that class.

 NOTE *In case that's too abstract, look back to the previous chapter where you used the* String *class. The* String *class is a comprehensive definition for a* String *object, with all the operations you are likely to need specified. Whenever you create a new* String *object, you are creating an object with all the characteristics and operations specified by the class definition. Every* String *object has all the methods that the* String *class defines built in. This makes* String ***objects indispensable and string handling within a program easy.***

The String class lies toward one end of a spectrum in terms of complexity in a class. The String class is intended to be usable in any program. It includes facilities and capabilities for operating on String objects to cover virtually all circumstances in which you are likely to use strings. In most cases your own classes won't need to be this elaborate. You will typically be defining a class to suit your particular application, and you will make it as simple or complex as necessary. Some classes, such as a Plane or a Person, for example, may well represent objects that can potentially be very complicated, but the application requirements may be very limited. A Person object might just contain a name, address, and phone number, for example, if you are just implementing an address book. In another context, such as in a payroll program, you might need to represent a Person with a whole host of properties, such as age, marital status, length of service, job code, pay rate, and so on. How you define a class depends on what you intend to do with objects of your class.

In essence, a class definition is very simple. There are just two kinds of things that you can include in a class definition:

➤ **Fields:** These are variables that store data items that typically differentiate one object of the class from another. They are also referred to as *data members* of a class.

➤ **Methods:** These define the operations you can perform for the class—so they determine what you can do to, or with, objects of the class. Methods typically operate on the fields—the data members of the class.

The fields in a class definition can be of any of the primitive types, or they can be references to objects of any class type, including the one that you are defining.

The methods in a class definition are named, self-contained blocks of code that typically operate on the fields that appear in the class definition. Note, though, that this doesn't necessarily have to be the case, as you might have guessed from the main() methods you have written in all the examples up to now.

Fields in a Class Definition

An object of a class is also referred to as an *instance* of that class. When you create an object, the object contains all the fields that were included in the class definition. However, the fields in a class definition are not all the same—there are two kinds.

One kind of field is associated with the class and is shared by all objects of the class. There is only one copy of each of these kinds of fields no matter how many class objects are created, and they exist even if no objects of the class have been created. This kind of variable is referred to as a *class variable* because the field belongs to the class and not to any particular object, although as I've said, all objects of the class share it. These fields are also referred to as *static fields* because you use the static keyword when you declare them.

The other kind of field in a class is associated with each object uniquely—each instance of the class has its own copy of each of these fields, each with its own value assigned. These fields differentiate one object from another, giving an object its individuality—the particular name, address, and telephone number in a given Person object, for example. These are referred to as *non-static fields* or *instance variables* because you specify them without using the static keyword, and each instance of a class type has its own independent set.

Because this is extremely important to understand, let's summarize the two kinds of fields that you can include in your classes:

➤ **Non-static fields, also called instance variables:** Each object of the class has its own copy of each of the non-static fields or instance variables that appear in the class definition. Each object has its own values for each instance variable. The name instance variable originates from the fact that an object is an *instance* or an occurrence of a class, and the values stored in the instance variables for the object differentiate the object from others of the same class type. You declare an instance variable within the class definition in the usual way, with a type name and a variable name, and it can have an initial value specified.

➤ **Static fields, also called class variables:** A given class has only one copy of each of its static fields or class variables, and these are shared between and among all the objects of the class. Each class variable exists even if no objects of the class have been created. Class variables belong to the class, and they can be referenced by any object or class method, not just methods belonging to instances of that class. If the value of a static field is changed, the new value is available equally in all the objects of the class. This is quite different from non-static fields, where changing a value for one object does not affect the values in other objects. A static field must be declared using the keyword `static` preceding the type name.

Look at Figure 5-1, which illustrates the difference between class variables and instance variables.

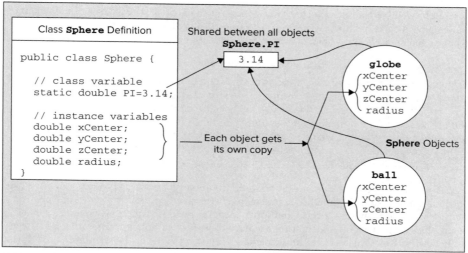

FIGURE 5-1

Figure 5-1 shows a schematic of a class, `Sphere`, that has one class variable, `PI`, and four instance variables, `radius`, `xCenter`, `yCenter`, and `zCenter`. Each of the objects, `globe` and `ball`, has its own set of variables with the names `radius`, `xCenter`, `yCenter`, and `zCenter`, but both share a single copy of the class variable `PI`.

Why would you need two kinds of variables in a class definition? The instance variables are clearly necessary because they store the values that distinguish one particular object from another. The radius and the coordinates of the center of the sphere are fundamental to determining how big a particular `Sphere` object is, and where it is in space. However, although the variable `PI` is a fundamental parameter for every sphere—to calculate the volume, for example—it would be wasteful to store a value for `PI` in every `Sphere` object because it is always the same. As you know, it is also available from the standard class `Math` so it is somewhat superfluous in this case, but you get the general idea. So, one use for class variables is to hold constant values such as π that are common to all objects of the class.

Another use for class variables is to track data values that are common to all objects of a class and that need to be available even when no objects have been defined. For example, if you want to keep a count of how many objects of a class have been created in your program, you could define a variable to store the count of the number of objects as a class variable. It would be essential to use a class variable, because you would still want to be able to use your `count` variable even when no objects have been declared.

Methods in a Class Definition

The methods that you define for a class provide the actions that can be carried out using the variables specified in the class definition. Analogous to the variables in a class definition, there are two varieties of methods—*instance methods* and *class methods*. You can execute class methods even when no objects of a class exist, whereas instance methods can be executed only in relation to a particular object, so if no objects exist, you have no way to execute any of the instance methods defined in the class. Again, like class variables, class methods are declared using the keyword `static`, so they are sometimes referred to as *static methods*. You saw in the previous chapter that the `valueOf()` method is a static member of the `String` class.

Because static methods can be executed when there are no objects in existence, they cannot refer to instance variables. This is quite sensible if you think about it—trying to operate with variables that might not exist is bound to cause trouble. In fact the Java compiler won't let you try. If you reference an instance variable in the code for a static method, it doesn't compile—you just get an error message. The `main()` method, where execution of a Java application starts, must always be declared as static, as you have seen. The reason for this should be apparent by now. Before an application starts execution, no objects exist, so to start execution, you need a method that is executable even though there are no objects around—a static method therefore.

The `Sphere` class might well have an instance method `volume()` to calculate the volume of a particular object. It might also have a class method `objectCount()` to return the current count of how many objects of type `Sphere` have been created. If no objects exist, you could still call this method and get the count 0.

> **NOTE** Note that although instance methods are specific to objects of a class, there is only ever one copy of each instance method in memory that is shared by all objects of the class, as it would be extremely expensive to replicate all the instance methods for each object. A special mechanism ensures that each time you call a method the code executes in a manner that is specific to an object, but I'll defer explaining how this is possible until a little later in this chapter.

Apart from the `main()` method, perhaps the most common use for static methods is when you use a class just as a container for a bunch of utility methods, rather than as a specification for a set of objects. All executable code in Java has to be within a class, but lots of general-purpose functions you need don't necessarily have an object association—calculating a square root, for example, or generating a random number. The mathematical functions that are implemented as class methods in the standard `Math` class are good examples. These methods don't relate to class objects at all—they operate on values of the primitive types. You don't need objects of type `Math`; you just want to use the methods from time to time, and you can do this as you saw in Chapter 2. The `Math` class also contains some class variables containing useful mathematical constants such as e and π.

Accessing Variables and Methods

You may want to access fields and methods that are defined within a class from outside it. It is considered bad practice to make the fields available directly but there can be exceptions to this—you'll find some in the standard libraries. You'll see later that it is possible to declare class members with restrictions on accessing them from outside, but let's cover the principles that apply where the members are accessible. I'll consider accessing static members—that is, static fields and methods—and instance members separately.

You can access a static member of a class using the class name, followed by a period, followed by the member name. With a class method you also need to supply the parentheses enclosing any arguments to the method after the method name. The period here is called the dot operator. So, if you want to calculate the square root of π you can access the class method `sqrt()` and the class variable `PI` that are defined in the `Math` class as follows:

```
double rootPi = Math.sqrt(Math.PI);
```

This shows how you call a static method—you just prefix it with the class name and put the dot operator between them. You also reference the static data member, `PI`, in the same way—as `Math.PI`. If you have a reference to an object of a class type available then you can also use that to access a static member of the class because every object always has access to the static members of its class. You just use the variable name, followed by the dot operator, followed by the member name.

Of course, as you've seen in previous chapters, you can import the names of the static members of the class by using an `import` statement. You can then refer to the names of the static members you have imported into your source file without qualifying their names at all.

Instance variables and methods can be called only using an object reference, because by definition they relate to a particular object. The syntax is exactly the same as I have outlined for static members. You put the name of the variable referencing the object followed by a period, followed by the member name. To use a method `volume()` that has been declared as an instance method in the `Sphere` class, you might write:

```
double ballVolume = ball.volume();
```

Here the variable `ball` is of type `Sphere` and it contains a reference to an object of this type. You call its `volume()` method, which calculates the volume of the `ball` object, and the result that is returned is stored in the variable `ballVolume`.

Final Fields

You can declare a field in a class to be `final`, which means that the field cannot be modified by the methods in the class. You can provide an initial value for a final field when you declare it. For example:

```
final double PI = 3.14;
```

If you don't provide an initial value for a final field when you declare it, you must initialize it in a *constructor*, which you learn about a little later in this chapter.

DEFINING CLASSES

To define a class you use the keyword `class` followed by the name of the class followed by a pair of braces enclosing the details of the definition. Let's consider a concrete example to see how this works in practice. The definition of the `Sphere` class that I mentioned earlier could be:

```
class Sphere {
  static final double PI = 3.14;    // Class variable that has a fixed value
  static int count = 0;             // Class variable to count objects

  // Instance variables
  double radius;                    // Radius of a sphere

  double xCenter;                   // 3D coordinates
  double yCenter;                   // of the center
  double zCenter;                   // of a sphere

  // Plus the rest of the class definition...
}
```

You name a class using an identifier of the same sort you've been using for variables. By convention, though, class names in Java begin with a capital letter, so the class name is `Sphere` with a capital S. If you adopt this approach, you will be consistent with most of the code you come across. You could enter this source code and save it as the file `Sphere.java`. You add to this class definition and use it in a working example a little later in this chapter.

You may have noticed that in the examples in previous chapters the keyword `public` in this context preceded the keyword `class` in the first line of the class definition. The effect of the keyword `public` is bound up with the notion of a *package* containing classes, but I'll defer discussing this until a little later in this chapter when you have a better idea of what makes up a class definition.

The keyword `static` in the first line of the `Sphere` class definition specifies the variable `PI` as a class variable rather than an instance variable. The variable `PI` is also initialized with the value 3.14. The keyword `final` tells the compiler that you do not want the value of this variable to be changed, so the compiler checks that this variable is not modified anywhere in your program. Obviously, this is a very poor value for π. You would normally use `Math.PI`—which is defined to 20 decimal places, close enough for most purposes.

NOTE *Whenever you want to make sure that a variable will not be modified, you just need to declare the variable with the keyword* final. *By convention, variables that are constants have names in capital letters.*

You have also declared the next variable, count, using the keyword static. All objects of the Sphere class have access to and share the one copy of count and the one copy of PI that exist. You have initialized the variable count to 0, but because you have not declared it using the keyword final, you can change its value.

The next four variables in the class definition are instance variables, as they don't have the keyword static applied to them. Each object of the class has its own separate set of these variables, storing the radius and the coordinates of the center of the sphere. Although you haven't put initial values for these variables here, you can do so if you want. If you don't specify an initial value, a default value is assigned automatically when the object is created. Fields of numeric types are initialized with zero, fields of type char are initialized with '\u0000,' and fields that store class references or references to arrays are initialized with null.

There has to be something missing from the definition of the Sphere class—there is no way to set the value of radius and the other instance variables after a particular Sphere object is created. There is nothing to update the value of count either. Adding these things to the class definition involves using methods, so the next step is to understand how a method is put together.

DEFINING METHODS

You have been producing versions of the main() method since Chapter 1, so you already have an idea of how a method is constructed. Nonetheless, I'll go through how you define methods from the beginning to make sure everything is clear.

Let's start with the fundamental concepts. A *method* is a self-contained block of code that has a name and has the property that it is reusable—the same method can be executed from as many different points in a program as you require. Methods also serve to break up large and complex calculations that might involve many lines of code into more manageable chunks. You execute a method by *calling* it using its name, and the method may or may not return a value when its execution finishes. Methods that do not return a value are always called in a statement that just specifies the call. Methods that do return a value are usually called from within an expression, and the value that is returned by such a method is used in the evaluation of the expression. If a method that returns a value is called by itself in a statement—in other words, not in an expression—then the value it returns is discarded.

The basic structure of a method is shown in Figure 5-2.

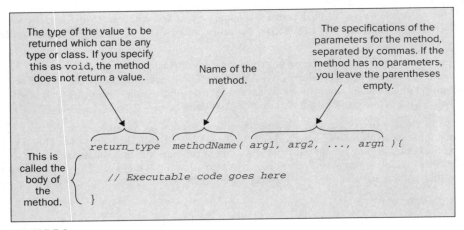

FIGURE 5-2

When you specify the return type for a method, you are defining the type for the value that is returned by the method when you execute it. The method must always return a value of this type. To define a method that does not return a value, you specify the return type as void. Something called an *access attribute* can optionally precede the return type in a method definition, but I'll defer looking into this until later in this chapter.

The *parameters* to a method appear in its definition between the parentheses following the method name. These specify what information is to be passed to the method when you execute it, and the values that you supply for the parameters when you call a method are described as *arguments*. The parameter names are used in the body of the method to refer to the corresponding argument values that you supply when you call the method. Your methods do not have to have parameters specified. A method that does not require any information to be passed to it when it is executed has an empty pair of parentheses after the name.

Returning from a Method

To return a value from a method when its execution is complete you use a return statement. For example

```
return return_value;                    // Return a value from a method
```

After executing the return statement in a method, the program continues from the point where the method was called. The value return_value that is returned by the method can be any expression that produces a value of the type specified for the return value in the declaration of the method. Methods that return a value—that is, methods declared with a return type other than void—must always finish by executing a return statement that returns a value of the appropriate type. Note, though, that you can put several return statements within a method if the logic requires this. If a method does not return a value, you can just use the keyword return by itself to end execution of the method:

```
return;                                  // Return from a method
```

For methods that do not return a value, falling through the closing brace enclosing the body of the method is equivalent to executing a return statement.

The Parameter List

The *parameter list* appears between the parentheses following the method name. This specifies the type of each value that can be passed as an argument to the method, and the variable name that is used in the body of the method to refer to each argument value passed to the method when it is called. The difference between a *parameter* and an *argument* is sometimes confusing because people often, incorrectly, use them interchangeably. I try to differentiate them consistently, as follows:

➤   A *parameter* has a name and a type and appears in the parameter list in the definition of a method. A parameter defines the type of value that can be passed to the method when it is called.

➤   An *argument* is a value that is passed to a method when it is executed, and the value of the argument is referenced by the parameter name during execution of the method. Of course, the type of the argument value must be consistent with the type specified for the corresponding parameter in the definition of the method.

This is illustrated in Figure 5-3.

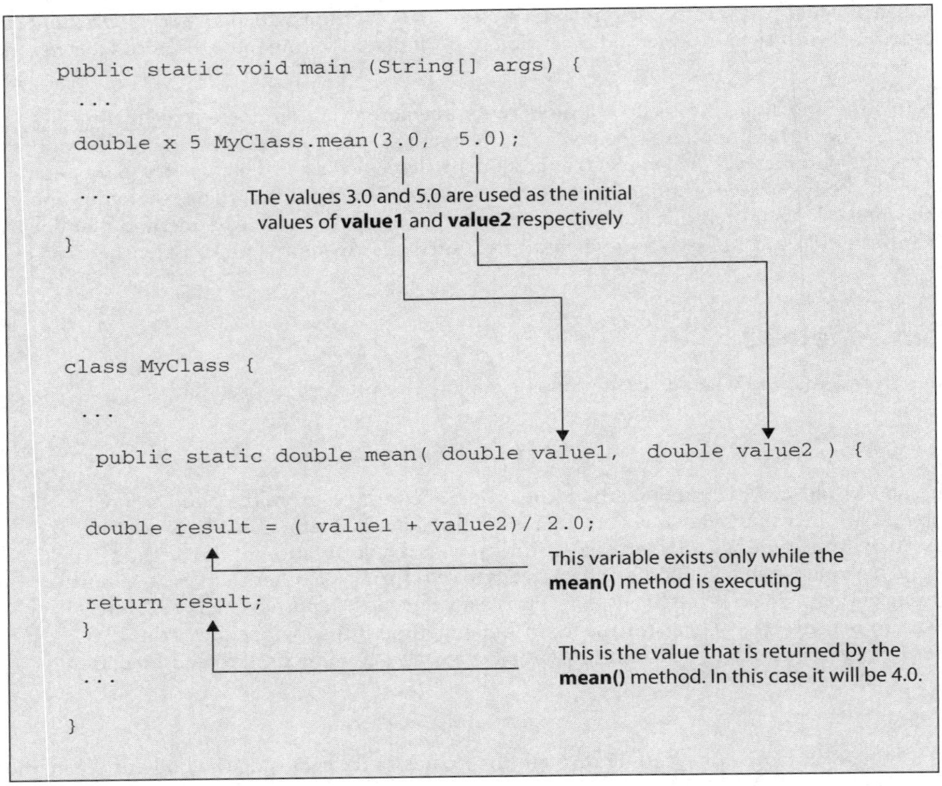

```
public static void main (String[] args) {
  ...
  double x 5 MyClass.mean(3.0,  5.0);
```
               The values 3.0 and 5.0 are used as the initial
               values of **value1** and **value2** respectively
```
  ...
}


class MyClass {

  ...

   public static double mean( double value1,  double value2 ) {

   double result = ( value1 + value2)/ 2.0;
```
                          This variable exists only while the
                          mean() method is executing
```
   return result;
   }
```
                          This is the value that is returned by the
                          mean() method. In this case it will be 4.0.
```
   ...

}
```

FIGURE 5-3

In Figure 5-3 you have the definition of a method mean(). The definition of this method appears within the definition of the class MyClass. You can see that the method has two parameters, value1 and value2, both of which are of type double. The parameter names are used to refer to the arguments 3.0 and 5.0, respectively, within the body of the method when it is called by the statement shown. Because this method has been defined as static, you can call it only using the class name.

When you call the mean() method from another method (from main() in this case, but it could be from some other method), the values of the arguments that you pass are the initial values assigned to the corresponding parameters before execution of the body of the method begins. You can use any expression you like for an argument when you call a method, as long as the value it produces is of the same type as the corresponding parameter in the definition of the method. With the method mean(), both parameters are of type double, so both argument values must always be of type double.

The method mean() defines the variable result, which exists only within the body of the method. This variable is newly created each time you execute the method and is destroyed when execution of the method ends. All the variables that you declare within the body of a method are local to the method, and are only around while the method is being executed. Variables declared within a method are called *local variables* because they are local to the method. The scope of a local variable is as I discussed in Chapter 2, from the point at which you declare it to the closing brace of the immediately enclosing block, and local variables are not initialized automatically. If you want your local variables to have initial values, you must supply the initial value when you declare them.

How Argument Values Are Passed to a Method

You need to be clear about how the argument values are passed to a method; otherwise, you may run into problems. In Java, all argument values are transferred to a method using what is called the *pass-by-value* mechanism. Figure 5-4 illustrates how this works.

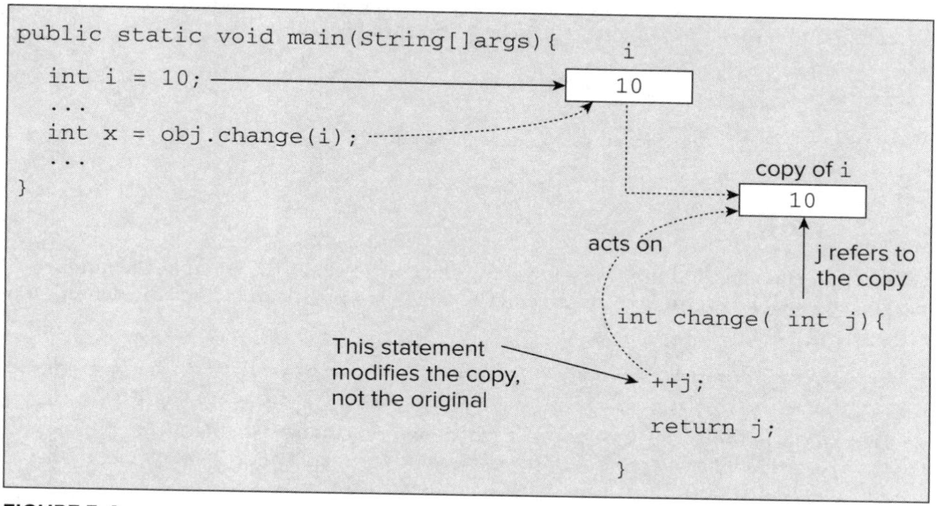

```
public static void main(String[]args){          i
    int i = 10;                              ┌─────────┐
    ...                                      │   10    │
    int x = obj.change(i);                   └─────────┘
    ...
}
```

copy of i

```
┌─────────┐
│   10    │
└─────────┘
```

acts on   j refers to the copy

```
int change( int j){

    ++j;

    return j;

}
```

This statement modifies the copy, not the original

FIGURE 5-4

Pass-by-value just means that for each argument value that you pass to a method, a copy of the value is made, and it is the copy that is passed to the method and referenced through the parameter name, not the original variable. This implies that if you use a variable of any of the primitive types as an argument, the method cannot modify the value of this variable in the calling program. In the example shown in Figure 5-4, the change() method modifies the copy of i that is created automatically and referenced using the parameter name j. Thus, the value of j that is returned is 11, and this is stored in the variable x when the return from the method executes. However, the original value of i remains at 10.

 NOTE *Although the pass-by-value mechanism applies to all types of arguments, the effect for objects is different from that for variables of the primitive types. A method can change an object that is passed as an argument. This is because a variable of a class type contains a reference to an object, not the object itself. Thus, when you use a variable of a class type as an argument to a method, a copy of a reference to the object is passed to the method, not a copy of the object itself. Because a copy of a reference still refers to the same object, the parameter name used in the body of a method refers to the original object that was passed as the argument.*

Final Parameters

You can specify any of the parameters for a method as `final`. This has the effect of preventing modification of any argument value that is substituted for the parameter when you call the method. The compiler checks that your code in the body of the method does not attempt to change any final parameters. Because the pass-by-value mechanism makes copies of values of the basic types, `final` really makes sense only when it is applied to parameters that are references to class objects, as you see later on. Specifying a parameter of a method as `final` prevents accidental modification of the object reference that is passed to the method, but it does not prevent modification of the object itself.

Another important use for the `final` keyword is for declaring classes or methods as final, and you learn more about this in Chapter 6.

Defining Class Methods

You define a class method by adding the keyword `static` to its definition. For example, the class `Sphere` could have a class method to return the value stored in the static variable `count`:

```
class Sphere {
  // Class definition as before...

  // Static method to report the number of objects created
  static int getCount() {
    return count;                         // Return current object count
  }
}
```

This method needs to be a class method because you want to be able to get at the count of the number of objects that exist even when it is zero. You can amend the `Sphere.java` file to include the definition of `getCount()`.

> **NOTE** Remember that you cannot directly refer to any of the instance variables in the class within a static method. This is because a static method can be executed when no objects of the class have been created, and therefore no instance variables exist.

Accessing Class Data Members in a Method

An instance method can access any of the data members of the class, just by using the appropriate name. Let's extend the class `Sphere` a little further by adding a method to calculate the volume of a `Sphere` object:

```
class Sphere {
  static final double PI = 3.14;      // Class variable that has a fixed value
  static int count = 0;               // Class variable to count objects

  // Instance variables
  double radius;                      // Radius of a sphere

  double xCenter;                     // 3D coordinates
  double yCenter;                     // of the center
  double zCenter;                     // of a sphere

  // Static method to report the number of objects created
  static int getCount(){
    return count;                     // Return current object count
  }

  // Instance method to calculate volume
  double volume() {
    return 4.0/3.0*PI*radius*radius*radius;
  }

  // Plus the rest of the class definition...
}
```

You can see that the `volume()` method is an instance method because it is not declared as static. It has no parameters, but it does return a value of type `double`—the calculated volume. The method uses the class variable `PI` and the instance variable `radius` in the volume calculation—this is the expression `4.0/3.0*PI*radius*radius*radius` (corresponding to the formula $(4/3)\pi r^3$ for the volume of a sphere) in the `return` statement. The value that results from this expression is returned to the point where the method is called for a `Sphere` object.

You know that each object of the class has its own separate set of instance variables, so how is an instance variable for a particular object selected in a method? How does the `volume()` method pick up the value of a radius variable for a particular `Sphere` object?

The Variable this

Every instance method has a variable with the name `this` that refers to the current object for which the method is being called. The compiler uses `this` implicitly when your method refers to an instance variable of the class. For example, when the method `volume()` refers to the instance variable `radius`, the compiler inserts the `this` object reference so that the reference is equivalent to `this.radius`. The return statement in the definition of the `volume()` method is actually the following:

```
return 4.0/3.0*PI*this.radius*this.radius*this.radius;
```

The statement actually refers to the `radius` field for the object referenced by the variable `this`. In general, every reference to an instance variable is in reality prefixed with `this`. You could put it in yourself, but there's no need, the compiler does it for you. In fact, it is not good practice to clutter up your code with `this` unnecessarily. However, there are occasions where you have to include it, as you will see.

When you execute a statement such as

```
double ballVolume = ball.volume();
```

where `ball` is an object of the class `Sphere`, the variable `this` in the method `volume()` refers to the object `ball`, so the instance variable `radius` for the `ball` object is used in the calculation.

NOTE *I mentioned earlier that only one copy of each instance method for a class exists in memory, even though there may be many different objects. You can see that the variable* `this` *allows the same instance method to work for different class objects. Each time an instance method is called, the* `this` *variable is set to reference the particular class object to which it is being applied. The code in the method then relates to the specific members of the object referred to by* `this`.

You have seen that there are four different potential sources of data available to you when you write the code for a method:

➤ Arguments passed to the method, which you refer to by using the parameter names

➤ Data members, both instance variables and class variables, which you refer to by their names

➤ Local variables that you declare in the body of the method

➤ Values that are returned by other methods that are called from within the method

The names of variables that are declared within a method are local to the method. You can use a name for a local variable or a parameter in a method that is the same as that of an instance variable. If you find it necessary or convenient to do this then you must use the name `this` when you refer to the data member of the class from within the method. The variable name by itself always refers to the variable that is local to the method, not the instance variable.

For example, suppose you want to add a method to change the radius of a `Sphere` object to a new radius value that is passed as an argument. You could code this as:

```
void changeRadius(double radius) {
  // Change the instance variable to the argument value
  this.radius = radius;
}
```

In the body of the `changeRadius()` method, `this.radius` refers to the instance variable, and `radius` by itself refers to the parameter. No confusion in the duplication of names exists here. It is clear that you are receiving a radius value as a parameter with the name `radius` and storing it in the `radius` variable for the class object.

Initializing Data Members

You have seen how you were able to supply an initial value for the static members PI and count in the Sphere class with the following declaration:

```
class Sphere {
  static final double PI = 3.14;      // Class variable that has a fixed value
  static int count = 0;               // Class variable to count objects

  // Rest of the class...
}
```

You can also initialize ordinary non-static data members in the same way. For example:

```
class Sphere {
  static final double PI = 3.14;      // Class variable that has a fixed value
  static int count = 0;               // Class variable to count objects

  // Instance variables
  double radius = 5.0;                // Radius of a sphere

  double xCenter = 10.0;              // 3D coordinates
  double yCenter = 10.0;              // of the center
  double zCenter = 10.0;              // of a sphere

  // Rest of the class...
}
```

Now every object of type Sphere starts out with a radius of 5.0 and has the center at the point (10.0, 10.0, 10.0).

Some things can't be initialized with a single expression. For example, if you have a large array as a data member that you want to initialize, with a range of values that required some kind of calculation, this could be a job for an *initialization block*.

Using Initialization Blocks

An initialization block is a block of code between braces that is executed before an object of the class is created. There are two kinds of initialization blocks:

➤ A *static initialization block* is a block defined using the keyword static and is executed once when the class is loaded. A static initialization block can initialize only static data members of the class.

➤ A *non-static initialization block* is executed for each object that is created and thus can initialize instance variables in a class.

This is easiest to understand by considering a working example.

TRY IT OUT Using an Initialization Block

Let's define a simple class with a static initialization block first of all:

Available for
download on
Wrox.com

```
class TryInitialization {
  static int[] values = new int[10];           // Static array  member

  // Initialization block
  static {
    System.out.println("Running initialization block.");
    for(int i = 0 ; i < values.length ; ++i) {
      values[i] = (int)(100.0*Math.random());
    }
  }

  // List values in the array for an object
  void listValues() {
    System.out.println();                       // Start a new line
    for(int value : values) {
```

```
      System.out.print(" " + value);            // Display values
    }
    System.out.println();                        // Start a new line
  }

  public static void main(String[] args) {
    TryInitialization example = new TryInitialization();
    System.out.println("\nFirst object:");
    example.listValues();

    example = new TryInitialization();
    System.out.println("\nSecond object:");
    example.listValues();
  }
```

TyInitialization.java

When you compile and run this, you get identical sets of values for the two objects—as might be expected because the values array is static:

```
Running initialization block.

First object:

 40 97 88 63 58 48 84 5 32 67

Second object:

 40 97 88 63 58 48 84 5 32 67
```

How It Works

The TryInitialization class has a static member, values, that is an array of 10 integers. The static initialization block is the code

```
static {
  System.out.println("Running initialization block.");
  for(int i = 0 ; i < values.length ; ++i) {
    values[i] = (int)(100.0*Math.random());
  }
}
```

This initializes the values array with pseudo-random integer values generated in the for loop. The output statement in the block is there just to record when the initialization block executes. Because this initialization block is static, it is only ever executed once during program execution, when the class is loaded.

The listValues() method provides you with a means of outputting the values in the array. The print() method you are using in the listValues() method works just like println(), but without starting a new line after displaying the output, so you get all the values on the same line.

In main(), you generate an object of type TryInitialization and then call its listValues() method. You then create a second object and call the listValues() method for that. The output demonstrates that the initialization block only executes once, and that the values reported for both objects are the same.

Because the values array is a static member of the class, you could list the element's values through a static method that would not require any objects to have been created. Try temporarily adding the keyword static to the declaration of the listValues() method in the class:

```
static void listValues() {
  System.out.println();                          // Start a new line
  for(int value : values) {
    System.out.print(" " + value);               // Display values
  }
  System.out.println();                          // Start a new line
}
```

You can now call the method using the class name, so add two extra statements at the beginning of main():

```
System.out.println("\nNo object:");
TryInitialization.listValues();
```

If you compile and execute the program with these changes, you get an additional record of the values in the values array. You still get the output from calling listValues() using the two object references. Every object has access to the static members of its class. Of course, the values in the output are different from the previous execution because they are pseudo-random values.

If you restore the program to its original state, and then delete the static modifier before the initialization block and recompile and run the program again, you get the output along the lines of the following:

```
Running initialization block.

First object:

 66 17 98 59 99 18 40 96 40 21

Running initialization block.

Second object:

 57 86 79 31 75 99 51 5 31 44
```

Now you have a non-static initialization block. You can see from the output that the values are different for the second object because the non-static initialization block is executed each time an object is created. In fact, the values array is static, so the array is shared between all objects of the class. You could demonstrate this by amending main() to store each object separately and calling listValues() for the first object after the second object has been created. Amend the main() method in the program to read as follows:

```
public static void main(String[] args) {
    TryInitialization example = new TryInitialization();
    System.out.println("\nFirst object:");
    example.listValues();
    TryInitialization nextexample = new TryInitialization();
    System.out.println("\nSecond object:");
    nextexample.listValues();

    example.listValues();
}
```

While you have demonstrated that this is possible, you do not normally want to initialize static variables with a non-static initialization block.

As I said at the outset, a non-static initialization block can initialize instance variables, too. If you want to demonstrate this, you just need to remove the static modifier from the declaration of values and compile and run the program once more.

You can have multiple initialization blocks in a class, in which case they execute in the sequence in which they appear. The static blocks execute when the class is loaded, and the non-static blocks execute when each object is created. Initialization blocks are useful, but you need more than that to create objects properly.

CONSTRUCTORS

When you create an object of a class, a special kind of method called a *constructor* is always invoked. If you don't define any constructors for your class, the compiler supplies a *default constructor* in the class, which does nothing. The default constructor is also described as the *no-arg constructor* because it requires no arguments to be specified when it is called. The primary purpose of a constructor is to provide you with the means of initializing the instance variables uniquely for the object that is being created. If you are creating a `Person` object with the name John Doe, then you want to be able to initialize the member holding the person's name to `"John Doe"`. This is precisely what a constructor can do. Any initialization blocks that you have defined in a class are always executed before a constructor.

A constructor has two special characteristics that differentiate it from other class methods:

➤ A constructor never returns a value, and you must not specify a return type—not even of type `void`.

➤ A constructor always has the same name as the class.

To see a practical example you could add a constructor to the `Sphere` class definition:

```
class Sphere {
  static final double PI = 3.14;          // Class variable that has a fixed value
  static int count = 0;                    // Class variable to count objects

  // Instance variables
  double radius;                           // Radius of a sphere

  double xCenter;                          // 3D coordinates
  double yCenter;                          // of the center
  double zCenter;                          // of a sphere

  // Class constructor
  Sphere(double theRadius, double x, double y, double z) {
    radius = theRadius;                    // Set the radius

    // Set the coordinates of the center
    xCenter = x;
    yCenter = y;
    zCenter = z;
    ++count;                               // Update object count
  }

  // Static method to report the number of objects created
  static int getCount() {
    return count;                          // Return current object count
  }

  // Instance method to calculate volume
  double volume() {
    return 4.0/3.0*PI*radius*radius*radius;
  }
}
```

The definition of the constructor is in boldface type in the preceding code. As you can see, the constructor has the same name as the class and has no return type specified. A constructor can have any number of parameters, including none. The default constructor has no parameters, as is indicated by its alternative description—the no-arg constructor. In this case the `Sphere` class constructor has four parameters, and each of the instance variables is initialized with the value of the appropriate parameter. Here's a situation where you might have used the name `radius` for the parameter, in which case you would need to use the keyword `this` to refer to the instance variable of the same name. The last action of the constructor is to increment the class variable `count` by 1, so that `count` accumulates the total number of objects created.

The Default Constructor

As I said, if you don't define any constructors for a class, the compiler supplies a default constructor that has no parameters and does nothing. Before you defined a constructor for the `Sphere` class, the compiler would have supplied one, defined like this:

```
Sphere() {
}
```

It has no parameters and no statements in its body so it does nothing—except enable you to create an object of type Sphere, of course. The object created by the default constructor has fields with their default values set. If you have defined any non-static initialization blocks within a class, they are executed each time any constructor executes, immediately before the execution of the code in the body of the constructor. Whenever you create an object, a constructor is called. When you have not defined any constructors for a class, the default constructor is called each time you create an object of that class type.

Note that if you define a constructor of any kind for a class, the compiler does not supply a default constructor. If you still need a no-arg constructor—and you will find many occasions when you do—you must define it explicitly in addition to the other constructors in the class.

Creating Objects of a Class

When you declare a variable of type Sphere with the following statement

```
Sphere ball;                          // Declare a variable
```

no constructor is called because no object is created. All you have created at this point is the variable ball, which can store a reference to an object of type Sphere, if and when you create one. Figure 5-5 shows this.

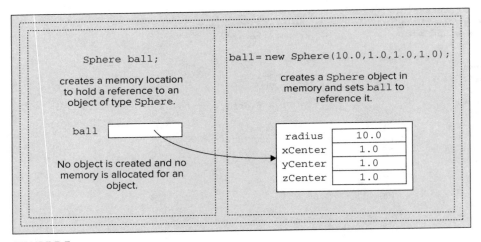

FIGURE 5-5

Recall from the discussion of String objects and arrays that the variable and the object it references are distinct entities. To create an object of a class you must use the keyword new followed by a call to a constructor. To initialize ball with a reference to an object, you could write:

```
ball = new Sphere(10.0, 1.0, 1.0, 1.0);          // Create a sphere
```

Now you have a Sphere object with a radius of 10.0 located at the coordinates (1.0, 1.0, 1.0). The object is created in memory and occupies a sufficient number of bytes to accommodate all the data necessary to define the object. The variable ball records where in memory the object is—it acts as a reference to the object. This is illustrated in Figure 5-5.

Of course, you can do the whole thing in one step with the following statement:

```
Sphere ball = new Sphere(10.0, 1.0, 1.0, 1.0);    // Create a sphere
```

This declares the variable ball and defines the Sphere object to which it refers.

You can create another variable that refers to the same object as ball:

```
Sphere myBall = ball;
```

Now the variable `myBall` refers to the same object as `ball`. You still have only one object, but you have two different variables that reference it. You could have as many variables as you like referring to the same object.

As I mentioned earlier, the separation of the variable and the object has an important effect on how objects are passed to a method, so let's look at that in more detail.

Passing Objects to a Method

When you pass an object as an argument to a method, the mechanism that applies is called *pass-by-reference*, because a copy of the reference contained in the variable is transferred to the method, not a copy of the object itself. The effect of this is shown in Figure 5-6.

Figure 5-6 presumes that you have defined a method, `changeRadius()`, in the class `Sphere`, that alters the radius value for an object, and that you have a method `change()` in some other class that calls `changeRadius()`. When the variable `ball` is used as an argument to the method `change()`, the pass-by-reference mechanism causes a copy of the contents of `ball` to be made and stored in `s`. The variable `ball` just stores a reference to the `Sphere` object, and the copy contains that same reference and therefore refers to the same object. No copying of the actual object occurs. This is a major plus in terms of efficiency when passing arguments to a method. Objects can be very complex, involving a lot of instance variables. If objects themselves were always copied when passed as arguments, it could be very time-consuming and make the code very slow.

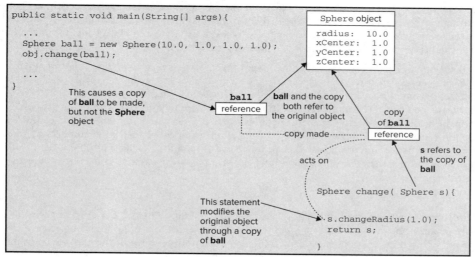

FIGURE 5-6

Because the copy of the reference from `ball` refers to the same object as the original, when the `changeRadius()` method is called, the original object is changed. You need to keep this in mind when writing methods that have objects as parameters because this is not always what you want.

In the example shown, the method `change()` returns the modified object. In practice, you probably want this to be a distinct object, in which case you need to create a new object from `s`. You see how you can write a constructor to do this a little later in this chapter.

 NOTE *Remember that this only applies to objects. If you pass a variable of a primitive type, such as* int *or* double *to a method for example, a copy of the value is passed. You can modify the value passed as much as you want in the method, but it doesn't affect the original value.*

The Lifetime of an Object

The lifetime of an object is determined by the variable that holds the reference to it—assuming there is only one. If you have the declaration

```
Sphere ball = new Sphere(10.0, 1.0, 1.0, 1.0);   // Create a sphere
```

then the `Sphere` object that the variable `ball` refers to dies when the variable `ball` goes out of scope, which is at the end of the block containing this declaration. Where an instance variable is the only one referencing an object, the object survives as long as the instance variable owning the object survives.

 NOTE *A slight complication can arise with objects, though. As you have seen, several variables can reference a single object. In this case, the object survives as long as a variable still exists somewhere that references the object.*

As you have seen before, you can reset a variable to refer to nothing by setting its value to `null`. If you write the statement

```
ball = null;
```

the variable `ball` no longer refers to an object, and assuming there is no other variable referencing it, the `Sphere` object that it originally referenced is destroyed. Note that while the object has been discarded, the variable `ball` still continues to exist and you can use it to store a reference to another `Sphere` object. The lifetime of an object is determined by whether any variable anywhere in the program still references it.

The process of disposing of dead objects is called *garbage collection*. Garbage collection is automatic in Java, but this doesn't necessarily mean that objects disappear from memory straight away. It can be some time after the object becomes inaccessible to your program. This won't affect your program directly in any way. It just means you can't rely on memory occupied by an object that is done with being available immediately. For the most part it doesn't matter; the only circumstances where it might be is if your objects were very large, millions of bytes, say, or you were creating and getting rid of very large numbers of objects. In this case, if you are experiencing problems you can try to call the static `gc()` method that is defined in the `System` class to encourage the Java Virtual Machine (JVM) to do some garbage collecting and recover the memory that the objects occupy:

```
System.gc();
```

This is a best efforts deal on the part of the JVM. When the `gc()` method returns, the JVM has tried to reclaim the space occupied by discarded objects, but there's no guarantee that it has all been recovered. There's also the possibility that calling the `gc()` method may make things worse. If the garbage collector is executing some preparations for recovering memory, your call undoes that and in this way slows things up.

DEFINING AND USING A CLASS

To put what you know about classes to use, you can use the `Sphere` class in an example.

You will be creating two source files. In a moment you will create the file `CreateSpheres.java`, which contains the definition of the `CreateSpheres` class that has the method `main()` defined as a static method. As usual, this is where execution of the program starts. The other file is the `Sphere.java` file, which contains the definition of the `Sphere` class that you have been assembling. The `Sphere` class definition should look like this:

```
class Sphere {
   static final double PI = 3.14;      // Class variable that has a fixed value
   static int count = 0;               // Class variable to count objects

   // Instance variables
```

```
      double radius;                              // Radius of a sphere

      double xCenter;                             // 3D coordinates
      double yCenter;                             // of the center
      double zCenter;                             // of a sphere
      // Class constructor
      Sphere(double theRadius, double x, double y, double z) {
        radius = theRadius;                       // Set the radius

        // Set the coordinates of the center
        xCenter = x;
        yCenter = y;
        zCenter = z;
        ++count;                                  // Update object count
      }

      // Static method to report the number of objects created
      static int getCount() {
        return count;                             // Return current object count
      }

      // Instance method to calculate volume
      double volume() {
        return 4.0/3.0*PI*radius*radius*radius;
      }
    }
```

Directory "CreateSpheres"

Both files need to be in the same directory or folder—I suggest you name the directory Create Spheres. Then copy or move the latest version of Sphere.java to this directory.

TRY IT OUT   Using the Sphere Class

Enter the following code for the file CreateSpheres.java and place it in the Create Spheres directory:

```
class CreateSpheres {
  public static void main(String[] args) {
    System.out.println("Number of objects = " + Sphere.getCount());

    Sphere ball = new Sphere(4.0, 0.0, 0.0, 0.0);        // Create a sphere
    System.out.println("Number of objects = " + ball.getCount());

    Sphere globe = new Sphere(12.0, 1.0, 1.0, 1.0);      // Create a sphere
    System.out.println("Number of objects = " + Sphere.getCount());

    // Output the volume of each sphere
    System.out.println("ball volume = " + ball.volume());
    System.out.println("globe volume = " + globe.volume());
  }
```

Directory "Create Spheres"

This file should be in the same directory as the file containing the Sphere class definition. Compile the source files and then run CreateSpheres, and you should get the following output:

```
Number of objects = 0
Number of objects = 1
Number of objects = 2
ball volume = 267.94666666666666
globe volume = 7234.559999999999
```

This is the first time you have run a program involving two source files. If you are using the JDK compiler, then compile `CreateSpheres.java` with the current directory as `Create Spheres` using the command

```
javac CreateSpheres.java
```

The compiler finds and compiles the `Sphere.java` source file automatically. If all the source files for a program are in the current directory then compiling the file containing a definition of `main()` compiles all the source files for the program.

Note that by default the `.class` files generated by the compiler are stored in the current directory — that is, the directory containing your source code. If you want the `.class` files stored in a different directory then you can use the `-d` option with the Java compiler to specify where they should go. For example, to store the class files in a directory called `C:\classes`, you type:

```
javac -d C:/classes CreateSpheres.java
```

How It Works

The `Sphere` class definition includes a constructor that creates objects, and the method `volume()` to calculate the volume of a particular sphere. It also contains the `static` method `getCount()` you saw earlier, which returns the current value of the class variable `count`. You need to define this method as `static` because you want to be able to call it regardless of how many objects have been created, including the situation when there are none.

The method `main()` in the `CreateSpheres` class puts the `Sphere` class through its paces. When the program is compiled, the compiler looks for a file with the name `Sphere.class`. If it does not find the `.class` file, it looks for `Sphere.java` to provide the definition of the class `Sphere`. As long as this file is in the current directory, the compiler is able to find it and compile it.

The first thing the program does is call the `static` method `getCount()`. Because no objects exist, you must use the class name to call it at this point. You then create the object `ball`, which is a `Sphere` object, with a radius of 4.0 and its center at the origin point (0.0, 0.0, 0.0). You call the `getCount()` method again, this time using the object name. This demonstrates that you can call a `static` method through an object. You create another `Sphere` object, `globe`, with a radius of 12.0. You call the `getCount()` method again, this time using the class name. Static methods like this are usually called using the class name. After all, the reason for calling this particular method is to find out how many objects exist, so presumably you cannot be sure that any objects exist at that point. A further reason to use the class name rather than a reference to an object when calling a static method is that it makes it quite clear in the source code that it *is* a static method that is being called. You can't call a non-static method using the class name.

The program finally outputs the volume of both objects by calling the `volume()` method for each, from within the expressions, specifying the arguments to the `println()` method calls.

METHOD OVERLOADING

Java enables you to define several methods in a class with the same name, as long as each method has a unique set of parameters. Defining two or more methods with the same name in a class is called *method overloading*.

The name of a method together with the types and sequence of the parameters form the *signature* of the method; the signature of each method in a class must be distinct to allow the compiler to determine exactly which method you are calling at any particular point. The return type has no effect on the signature of a method. You cannot differentiate between two methods just by the return type. This is because the return type is not necessarily apparent when you call a method. For example, suppose you write a statement such as:

```
Math.round(value);
```

Although the preceding statement is pointless because it discards the value that the round() method produces, it does illustrate why the return type cannot be part of the signature for a method. The compiler has no way to know from this statement what the return type of the method round() is supposed to be. Thus, if there were several different versions of the method round(), and the return type were the only distinguishing aspect of the method signature, the compiler would be unable to determine which version of round() you wanted to use.

You will find many circumstances where it is convenient to use method overloading. You have already seen that the Math class contains two versions of the method round(), one that accepts an argument of type float and the other that accepts an argument of type double. You can see now that method overloading makes this possible. It would be rather tedious to have to use a different name for each version of round() when they both do essentially the same thing. The valueOf() method in the String class is another example. There is a version of this method for each of the basic types. One context in which you regularly need to use overloading is when you write constructors for your classes, which will I explain now.

Multiple Constructors

Constructors are methods that can be overloaded, just like any other method in a class. In most situations, you want to generate objects of a class from different sets of initial defining data. If you just consider the Sphere class, you could conceive of a need to define a Sphere object in a variety of ways. You might well want a constructor that accepted just the (x, y, z) coordinates of a point, and have a Sphere object created with a default radius of 1.0. Another possibility is that you may want to create a default Sphere with a radius of 1.0 positioned at the origin, so no arguments would be specified at all. This requires two constructors in addition to the one you have already written. Let's try it.

TRY IT OUT   Multiple Constructors for the Sphere Class

I suggest you put the files for this example in the Create Spheres 2 directory. The code for the extra constructors is as follows:

Available for download on Wrox.com

```
class Sphere {
   // First Constructor and variable declarations
   ...
   // Construct a unit sphere at a point
   Sphere(double x, double y, double z) {
     xCenter = x;
     yCenter = y;
     zCenter = z;
     radius = 1.0;
     ++count;                           // Update object count
   }

   // Construct a unit sphere at the origin
   Sphere() {
     xCenter = 0.0;
     yCenter = 0.0;
     zCenter = 0.0;
     radius = 1.0;
     ++count;                           // Update object count
   }

   // The rest of the class as before...
}
```

Directory "Create Spheres 2"

The statements in the default constructor that set three fields to zero are not really necessary, as the fields are set to zero by default. They are there just to emphasize that the primary purpose of a constructor is to enable you to set initial values for the fields.

If you add the following statements to the `CreateSpheres` class, you can test out the new constructors:

```java
public class CreateSpheres {
    public static void main(String[] args) {
        System.out.println("Number of objects = " + Sphere.getCount());

        Sphere ball = new Sphere(4.0, 0.0, 0.0, 0.0);          // Create a sphere
        System.out.println("Number of objects = " + ball.getCount());

        Sphere globe = new Sphere(12.0, 1.0, 1.0, 1.0);        // Create a sphere
        System.out.println("Number of objects = " + Sphere.getCount());

        Sphere eightBall = new Sphere(10.0, 10.0, 0.0);
        Sphere oddBall = new Sphere();
        System.out.println("Number of objects = " + Sphere.getCount());

        // Output the volume of each sphere
        System.out.println("ball volume = " + ball.volume());
        System.out.println("globe volume = " + globe.volume());
        System.out.println("eightBall volume = " + eightBall.volume());
        System.out.println("oddBall volume = " + oddBall.volume());
    }
}
```

Directory "Create Spheres 2"

Now the program should produce the following output:

```
Number of objects = 0
Number of objects = 1
Number of objects = 2
Number of objects = 4
ball volume = 267.94666666666666
globe volume = 7234.559999999999
eightBall volume = 4.1866666666666665
oddBall volume = 4.1866666666666665
```

How It Works

When you create a `Sphere` object, the compiler selects the constructor to use based on the types of the arguments you have specified. So, the first of the new constructors is applied in the first statement that you added to `main()`, as its signature fits with the argument types used. The second statement that you added clearly selects the last constructor, as no arguments are specified. The other additional statements are there just to generate some output corresponding to the new objects. You can see from the volumes of `eightBall` and `oddBall` that they both are of radius 1—in both instances the result is the value of $4\pi/3$.

It is the number and types of the parameters that affect the signature of a method, not the parameter names. If you want a constructor that defines a `Sphere` object at a point, by specifying the diameter rather than the radius, you have a problem. You might try to write it as:

```java
// Illegal constructor!!!
// This WON'T WORK because it has the same signature as the original!!!
Sphere(double diameter, double x, double y, double z) {
    xCenter = x;
    yCenter = y;
    zCenter = z;
    radius = diameter/2.0;
    ++count;
}
```

If you add this method to the `Sphere` class and recompile, you get a compile-time error. This constructor has four arguments of type `double`, so its signature is identical to the first constructor that you wrote for the class. This is not permitted—hence the compile-time error. When the number of parameters is the same in two overloaded methods, at least one pair of corresponding parameters must be of different types.

Calling a Constructor from a Constructor

One class constructor can call another constructor in the same class in its first executable statement. This can often save duplicating a lot of code. To refer to another constructor in the same class, you use `this` as the method name, followed by the appropriate arguments between parentheses. In the `Sphere` class, you could have defined the constructors as:

```
class Sphere {
  // Construct a unit sphere at the origin
  Sphere() {
    radius = 1.0;
    // Other data members will be zero by default
    ++count;                          // Update object count
  }

  // Construct a unit sphere at a point
  Sphere(double x, double y, double z)
  {
    this();                          // Call the constructor with no arguments
    xCenter = x;
    yCenter = y;
    zCenter = z;
  }

  Sphere(double theRadius, double x, double y, double z) {
    this(x, y, z);                   // Call the 3 argument constructor
    radius = theRadius;              // Set the radius
  }
  // The rest of the class as before...
}
```

In the constructor that accepts the point coordinates as arguments, you call the default constructor to set the radius and increment the count of the number of objects. In the constructor that sets the radius, as well as the coordinates, you call the constructor with three arguments to set the coordinates, which in turn call the constructor that requires no arguments.

Duplicating Objects Using a Constructor

When you were looking at how objects were passed to a method, you came across a requirement for duplicating an object. The need to produce an identical copy of an object occurs surprisingly often.

Suppose you declare a `Sphere` object with the following statement:

```
Sphere eightBall = new Sphere(10.0, 10.0, 0.0);
```

Later in your program you want to create a new object `newBall`, which is identical to the object `eightBall`. If you write

```
Sphere newBall = eightBall;
```

this compiles okay, but it won't do what you want. You might remember from my earlier discussion that the variable `newBall` references the same object as `eightBall`. You don't have a distinct object. The variable `newBall`, of type `Sphere`, is created but no constructor is called, so no new object is created.

Of course, you could create `newBall` by specifying the same arguments to the constructor as you used to create `eightBall`. In general, however, it may be that `eightBall` has been modified in some way during execution of the program, so you don't know that its instance variables have the same values—for example, the position might have changed. This presumes that you have some other class methods that alter the instance variables. You could provide the capability for duplicating an existing object by adding a constructor to the class that accepts an existing `Sphere` object as an argument:

```
// Create a sphere from an existing object
Sphere(final Sphere oldSphere) {
  radius = oldSphere.radius;
  xCenter = oldSphere.xCenter;
  yCenter = oldSphere.yCenter;
  zCenter = oldSphere.yCenter;
  ++count;                                     // Increment the object count
}
```

This works by copying the values of the instance variables of the `Sphere` object that is passed as the argument to the corresponding instance variables of the new object. Thus the new object that this constructor creates is identical to the `Sphere` object that is passed as the argument.

Now you can create `newBall` as a distinct object by writing:

```
Sphere newBall = new Sphere(eightBall);      // Create a copy of eightBall
```

The next section recaps what you have learned about methods and constructors with another example.

USING OBJECTS

You will create a program to do some simple 2D geometry. This gives you an opportunity to use more than one class. You will define two classes, a class that represents point objects and a class that represents line objects; you will then use these to find the point at which two lines intersect. You can put the files for the example in a directory or folder with the name `Try Geometry`. Quite a few lines of code are involved, so you will put it together piecemeal and get an understanding of how each piece works as you go.

TRY IT OUT   The Point Class

You first define a basic class for point objects:

```
import static java.lang.Math.sqrt;

class Point {
  // Coordinates of the point
  double x;
  double y;

  // Create a point from coordinates
  Point(double xVal, double yVal) {
    x = xVal;
    y = yVal;
  }

  // Create a point from another Point object
  Point(final Point oldPoint) {
    x = oldPoint.x;                 // Copy x coordinate
    y = oldPoint.y;                 // Copy y coordinate
  }

  // Move a point
  void move(double xDelta, double yDelta) {
    // Parameter values are increments to the current coordinates
    x += xDelta;
    y += yDelta;
  }

  // Calculate the distance to another point
```

```
double distance(final Point aPoint) {
    return sqrt((x - aPoint.x)*(x - aPoint.x) + (y - aPoint.y)*(y - aPoint.y));
}

// Convert a point to a string
public String toString() {
    return Double.toString(x) + ", " + y;     // As "x, y"
}
```

Directory "Try Geometry"

You should save this as `Point.java` in the directory `Try Geometry`.

How It Works

This is a simple class that has just two instance variables, x and y, which are the coordinates of the `Point` object. At the moment you have two constructors. One creates a `Point` object from a coordinate pair passed as arguments of type `double`, and the other creates a new `Point` object from an existing one.

Three methods are included in the class. You have the `move()` method, which moves a `Point` to another position by adding an increment to each of the coordinates. You also have the `distance()` method, which calculates the distance from the current `Point` object to the `Point` object passed as the argument. This uses the Pythagorean theorem to compute the distance, as shown in Figure 5-7.

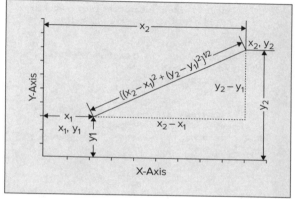

FIGURE 5-7

Finally, you have a `toString()` method, which returns a string representation of the coordinates of the current point. If a class defines the `toString()` method and an object of that class is used as an operand of the string concatenation operator +, the method is called to represent the object as a string. The compiler automatically inserts a call to `toString()` when necessary. For example, suppose `thePoint` is an object of type `Point`, and you write the statement:

```
System.out.println("The point is at " + thePoint);
```

The `toString()` method is automatically invoked to convert the object referenced by the variable `thePoint` to a `String`, and the resultant string is appended to the `String` literal. You have specified the `toString()` method as `public`, as this is essential here for the class to compile. I will defer explanations as to why this is necessary until a little later in this chapter.

Note how you use the static `toString()` method defined in the `Double` class to convert the x value to a `String`. The compiler inserts a call to the same method automatically for the y value, as the left operand of the + operation is a `String` object. Note that you could equally well have used the `valueOf()` method in the `String` class. In this case the statement would be written like this:

```
return String.valueOf(x) + ", " + y;      // As "x, y"
```

TRY IT OUT The Line Class

You can use `Point` objects in the definition of the class `Line`:

```
class Line {
  Point start;                                        // Start point of line
  Point end;                                          // End point of line

  // Create a line from two points
  Line(final Point start, final Point end) {
    this.start = new Point(start);
    this.end = new Point(end);
  }

  // Create a line from two coordinate pairs
  Line(double xStart, double yStart, double xEnd, double yEnd) {
    start = new Point(xStart, yStart);     // Create the start point
    end = new Point(xEnd, yEnd);           // Create the end point
  }

  // Calculate the length of a line
  double length() {
    return start.distance(end);            // Use the method from the Point class
  }

  // Convert a line to a string
  public String toString() {
    return "(" + start+ "):(" + end + ")";   // As "(start):(end)"
  }                                       // that is, "(x1, y1):(x2, y2)"
}
```

Directory "Try Geometry"

You should save this as the file `Line.java` in the `Try Geometry` directory.

How It Works

You shouldn't have any difficulty with this class definition, as it is very straightforward. The `Line` class stores two `Point` objects as instance variables. There are two constructors for `Line` objects—one accepting two `Point` objects as arguments and the other accepting the (*x*, *y*) coordinates of the start and end points. You can see how you use the variable `this` to differentiate the class instance variables, `start` and `end`, from the parameter names in the constructor.

Note how the constructor that accepts `Point` objects works:

```
// Create a line from two points
Line(final Point start, final Point end) {
  this.start = new Point(start);
  this.end = new Point(end);
}
```

With this implementation of the constructor, two new `Point` objects are created that are identical to, but independent of, the objects passed to the constructor. If you don't think about what happens, you might be tempted to write it as:

```
// Create a line from two points - a poor implementation!
Line(final Point start, final Point end) {
  this.start = start;                  // Dependent on external object!!!
  this.end = end;                      // Dependent on external object!!!
}
```

The important thing to note here is that the way the constructor is implemented could cause problems that might be hard to track down. In this version of the constructor no new points are created. The `start` and `end` members of the object refer to the `Point` objects that are passed as arguments. The `Line` object is implicitly dependent on the `Point` objects that are used to define it. If these were changed outside the `Line` class, by using the `move()` method, for example, this would "silently" modify the `Line` object. You might consciously decide that this is what you want, so the `Line` object continues to be dependent on its associated `Point` objects. The rationale for this in a drawing package, for example, might be that this would allow a point to be moved, and all lines based on the point would also be moved accordingly. However, this is different from allowing such interdependencies by accident. In general, you should take care to avoid creating implicit dependencies between objects unless they are what you intended.

In the `toString()` method for the `Line` class, you are able to use the `Point` objects directly in the formation of the `String` representation of a `Line` object. This works because the `Point` class also defines a `toString()` method.

You've now defined two classes. In these class definitions, you've included the basic data that defines an object of each class type. You've also defined some useful methods for operating on objects, and added constructors for a variety of input parameters. Note how the `Point` class is used in the definition of the `Line` class. It is quite natural to define a line in terms of two `Point` objects, and the `Line` class is much simpler and more understandable than if it were defined entirely in terms of the individual *x* and *y* coordinates. To further demonstrate how classes can interact, and how you can solve problems directly, in terms of the objects involved, let's devise a method to calculate the intersection of two `Line` objects.

Creating a Point from Two Lines

You can add the method to determine the point of intersection between two lines to the `Line` class. Figure 5-8 illustrates how the mathematics works out.

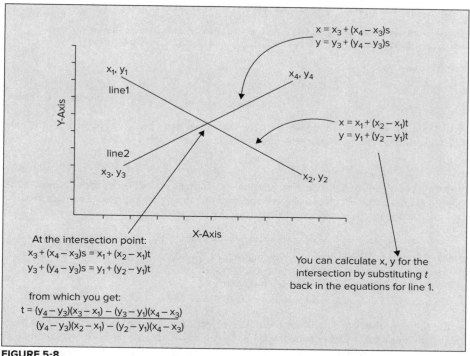

FIGURE 5-8

You can ignore the mathematics if you want to, as it is not the most important aspect of the example. If you are willing to take the code in the new method on trust, then skip to the next "Try It Out" section. On the other hand, you shouldn't find it too difficult if you can still remember what you did in high school math.

One way to get the intersection of two lines is to use equations such as those shown in Figure 5-8. These are called parametric equations because they use a parameter value (s or t) as the variable for determining points on each line. The parameters s and t vary between 0 and 1 to give points on the lines between the defined start and end points. When a parameter s or t is 0 the equations give the coordinates of the start point of a line, and when the parameter value is 1 you get the end point of the line.

Where two lines intersect, the equations for the lines must produce the same (x, y) values, so, at this point, the right-hand sides of the equations for x for the two lines must be equal, and the same goes for the equations for y. This gives you two equations in s and t, and with a bit of algebraic juggling you can eliminate s to get the equation shown for t. You can then replace t in the equations, defining line 1 to get x and y for the intersection point.

TRY IT OUT   Calculating the Intersection of Two Lines

You can use these results to write the additional method you need in the `Line` class. Add the following code to the class definition in `Line.java`:

Available for
download on
Wrox.com

```
// Return a point as the intersection of two lines
Point intersects(final Line line1) {
    Point localPoint = new Point(0, 0);

    double num = (end.y - start.y)*(start.x - line1.start.x) -
                 (end.x - start.x)*(start.y - line1.start.y);

    double denom = (end.y - start.y)*(line1.end.x - line1.start.x) -
                   (end.x - start.x)*(line1.end.y - line1.start.y);

    localPoint.x = line1.start.x + (line1.end.x - line1.start.x)*num/denom;
    localPoint.y = line1.start.y + (line1.end.y - line1.start.y)*num/denom;

    return localPoint;
}
```

Directory "Try Geometry"

Because the `Line` class definition refers to the `Point` class, the `Line` class can't be compiled without the other being available. When you compile the `Line` class, the compiler compiles the other class, too.

How It Works

The `intersects()` method is called for one `Line` object and takes another `Line` object as the argument. In the code, the local variables `num` and `denom` are the numerator and denominator in the expression for t in Figure 5-8. You then use these values to calculate the x and y coordinates for the intersection point.

WARNING *If the lines are parallel, the denominator in the equation for t is zero, something you should really check for in the code. For the moment you ignore it and end up with coordinates that are* `Infinity` *if it occurs.*

Note how you get at the values of the coordinates for the `Point` objects defining the lines. The dot notation for referring to a member of an object is just repeated when you want to reference a member of a member. For example, for the object `line1`, the expression `line1.start` refers to the `Point` object at the beginning of the line. Therefore, `line1.start.x` refers to its x coordinate, and `line1.start.y` accesses its y coordinate.

Now you have a Line class defined that you can use to calculate the intersection point of two Line objects. You need a program to test the code out.

TRY IT OUT   The TryGeometry Class

You can exercise the two classes you have defined with the following code in the method main():

```
public class TryGeometry {
  public static void main(String[] args) {
    // Create two points and display them
    Point start = new Point(0.0, 1.0);
    Point end = new Point(5.0, 6.0);
    System.out.println("Points created are " + start + " and " + end);


    // Create two lines and display them
    Line line1 = new Line(start, end);
    Line line2 = new Line(0.0, 3.0, 3.0, 0.0);
    System.out.println("Lines created are " + line1 + " and " + line2);

    // Display the intersection
    System.out.println("Intersection is " + line2.intersects(line1));

    // Now move the end point of line1 and show the new intersection
    end.move(1.0, -5.0);
    System.out.println("Intersection is " + line1.intersects(line2));
  }
```

Directory "Try Geometry"

Save the TryGeometry.java file in the Try Geometry directory along with the other two class files, Point. java and Line.java. The program produces the following output:

```
Points created are 0.0, 1.0 and 5.0, 6.0
Lines created are (0.0, 1.0):(5.0, 6.0) and (0.0, 3.0):(3.0, 0.0)
Intersection is 1.0, 2.0
Intersection is 1.0, 2.0
```

How It Works

You first create two Point objects, which you use later in the program to create the object line1. You then display the points using the println() method. The toString() method that you defined in the Point class is used automatically to generate the String representation for each Point object.

After creating line1 from the two points, you use the other constructor in the Line class to create line2 from two pairs of coordinates. You then display the two lines. The toString() member of the Line class is invoked here to create the String representation of each Line object, and this in turn calls the toString() method in the Point class.

The next statement calls the intersects() method from the line2 object and returns the Point object at the intersection of the two lines, line1 and line2, as part of the argument to the println() method that outputs the point. As you see, you are not obliged to save an object when you create it. Here you just use it to create the string to be displayed. After the output statement has executed, the intersection point object is discarded.

You use the move() method in the class Point to modify the coordinates of the object end that you used to create line1. You then get the intersection of the two lines again, this time calling the intersects() method from line1. The output demonstrates that line1 is independent of the object end, as moving the point has made no difference to the intersection.

If you change the constructor in the Line class to the earlier version that does not create new Point objects to define the line, you can run the example again to see the effect. The output is:

```
Points created are 0.0, 1.0 and 5.0, 6.0
Lines created are (0.0, 1.0):(5.0, 6.0) and (0.0, 3.0):(3.0, 0.0)
Intersection is 1.0, 2.0
Intersection is 2.0, 1.0
```

Changing the end object now alters the line, so you get a different intersection point for the two lines after you move the end point. This is because the Line object, line1, contains references to the Point objects defined in main(), not references to independent Point objects.

RECURSION

The methods you have seen so far have been called from within other methods, but a method can also call itself. A method that calls itself is described as a *recursive method*, and the process is referred to as *recursion*. You can also have indirect recursion where a method A calls another method B, which in turn calls the method A. Clearly you must include some logic in a recursive method so that it eventually stops calling itself if the process is not to continue indefinitely. You can see how this might be done with a simple example.

You can write a method that calculates integer powers of a variable—in other words, evaluate x^n, or $x*x...*x$ where x is multiplied by itself *n* times. You can use the fact that you can obtain x^n by multiplying x^{n-1} by x. To put this in terms of a specific example, you can calculate 2^4 as 2^3 multiplied by 2, and you can get 2^3 by multiplying 2^2 by 2, and 2^2 is produced by multiplying 2^1 by 2.

TRY IT OUT   **Calculating Powers**

Here is the complete program, including the recursive method power():

```java
public class PowerCalc {
  public static void main(String[] args) {
    double x = 5.0;
    System.out.println(x + " to the power 4 is " + power(x,4));
    System.out.println("7.5 to the power 5 is " + power(7.5,5));
    System.out.println("7.5 to the power 0 is " + power(7.5,0));
    System.out.println("10 to the power -2 is " + power(10,-2));
  }

  // Raise x to the power n
  static double power(double x, int n) {
    if(n > 1)
      return x*power(x, n-1);        // Recursive call
    else if(n < 0)
      return 1.0/power(x, -n);       // Negative power of x
    else
      return n == 0 ? 1.0 : x;       // When n is 0 return 1, otherwise x
  }
}
```

PowerCalc.java

This program produces the following output:

```
5.0 to the power 4 is 625.0
7.5 to the power 5 is 23730.46875
7.5 to the power 0 is 1.0
10 to the power -2 is 0.01
```

How It Works

The power() method has two parameters, the value x and the power n. The method performs four different actions, depending on the value of n:

$n > 1$	A recursive call to `power()` is made with n reduced by 1, and the value that is returned is multiplied by x. This is effectively calculating x^n as x times x^{n-1}.
$n < 0$	x^{-n} is equivalent to $1/x^n$ so this is the expression for the return value. This involves a recursive call to `power()` with the sign of n reversed.
$n = 0$	x^0 is defined as 1, so this is the value returned.
$n = 1$	x^1 is x, so x is returned.

As a rule, you should use recursion only where there are evident advantages in the approach, as recursive method calls have quite of lot of overhead. This particular example could be more easily programmed as a loop, and it would execute much more efficiently. You could also use the `Math.pow()` method to produce the result. One example of where recursion can be applied very effectively is in the handling of data structures such as trees. Unfortunately these don't make convenient illustrations of how recursion works at this stage of the learning curve because of their complexity.

Before you can dig deeper into classes, you need to take an apparent detour to understand what a package is in Java.

UNDERSTANDING PACKAGES

Packages are implicit in the organization of the standard classes as well as your own programs, and they influence the names you can use for classes and the variables and methods they contain. Essentially, a *package* is a uniquely named collection of classes. The primary reason for grouping classes in packages is to avoid possible name clashes with your own classes when you are using prewritten classes in an application. The names used for classes in one package do not interfere with the names of classes in another package or your program because the class names in a package are all qualified by the package name. Thus, the `String` class you have been using is in the `java.lang` package, so the full name of the class is `java.lang.String`. You have been able to use the unqualified name because all the classes in the `java.lang` package are always available in your program code; there's an implicit `import` statement in effect for all the names in the `java.lang` package. If you happened to have defined a class of your own with the name `String`, using the name `String` would refer to your class, but you could still use the library class that has the same name by using its full name in your code, `java.lang.String`.

Every class in Java is contained in a package, including all those you have defined in the examples. You haven't seen many references to package names so far because you have been implicitly using the *default package* to hold your classes, and this doesn't have a name.

All of the standard classes in Java are contained within a set of packages, and each package contains classes that are related in some way. The package that contains most of the standard classes that you have used so far is called `java.lang`, so called because the classes in this package provide Java language–related support. You haven't seen any explicit reference to `java.lang` in your code either, because this package is automatically available to your programs. Things are arranged this way because some of the classes in `java.lang`, such as `String`, are used in every program. If you use a class from the other packages containing standard classes, you need either to use the fully qualified name of the class or to explicitly import the full class name into your program.

Packaging Up Your Classes

Putting one of your classes in a named package is very simple. You just add a package statement as the first statement in the source file containing the class definition. Note that it must always be the *first* statement. Only comments or blank lines are allowed to precede the package statement. A *package statement* consists of the keyword `package` followed by the package name and is terminated by a semicolon. If you want the classes in a package to be accessible outside the package, you must declare the class using the keyword `public` in the first line of your class definition. Class definitions that aren't preceded by the keywordo `public` are accessible only from methods in classes that belong to the same package.

For example, to include the `Line` class in a package called `Geometry`, the contents of the file `Line.java` needs to be:

```
package Geometry;

public class Line {
  // Details of the class definition
}
```

Each class that you want to include in the package `Geometry` must contain the same package statement at the beginning, and you must save all the files for the classes in the package in a directory with the same name as the package, that is, `Geometry`. Note the use of the `public` keyword in the definition of the `Line` class. This makes the class accessible generally. If you omit the `public` keyword from the class definition, the class is accessible only from methods in classes that are in the `Geometry` package.

Note that you also need to declare the constructors and methods in the class as `public` if you want them to be accessible from outside of the package. I return to this in more detail a little later in this chapter.

Packages and the Directory Structure

Packages are actually a little more complicated than they appear at first sight, because a package is intimately related to the directory structure in which it is stored. You already know that the definition of a class with the name `ClassName` must be stored in a file with the name `ClassName.java`, and that all the files for classes within a package `PackageName` must be included in a directory with the name `PackageName`. You can compile the source for a class within a package and have the `.class` file that is generated stored in a different directory, but the directory name must still be the same as the package name.

As you are aware from the existence of the `java.lang` package that contains the `String` class, a package can have a composite name that is a combination of two or more simple names. You can specify a package name as any sequence of names separated by periods. For example, you might have developed several collections of classes dealing with geometry, perhaps one that works with 2D shapes and another with 3D shapes. In this case you might include the class `Sphere` in a package with the statement

```
package Geometry.Shapes3D;
```

and the class for circles in a package using the statement

```
package Geometry.Shapes2D;
```

In this situation, the files containing the classes in the `Geometry.Shapes3D` packages are expected to be in the directory `Shapes3D` and the files containing the classes in the `Geometry.Shapes2D` packages are expected to be in the directory `Shapes2D`. Both of these directories must be subdirectories of a directory with the name `Geometry`. In general, you can have as many names as you like separated by periods to identify a package, but the package name must reflect the directory structure in which the package is stored.

Compiling a Package

Compiling the classes in a package can be a bit tricky unless you are clear on how you go about it. I'll describe what you need to do assuming you are using the JDK under Microsoft Windows. The path to the package directory must be explicitly made known to the compiler in the value that is set for CLASSPATH, even when the current directory is the one containing the package. The easiest way to specify CLASSPATH is by using the -classpath option when you invoke the compiler.

The path to the package directory is the path to the directory that *contains* the package directory, and therefore does not include the package directory itself. For example, if you have stored the source files for classes that are in the `Geometry` package in the directory with the path `C:\Beg Java Stuff\Geometry` then the path to the `Geometry` directory is `C:\Beg Java Stuff`. Many beginners mistakenly specify the path as `C:\Beg Java Stuff\Geometry`, in which case the package is not found.

As I said, you can tell the compiler about the path to your package by using the -classpath option on the command line. Assuming that the Geometry directory is a subdirectory of C:\Beg Java Stuff, you could compile the Line.java source file with the command:

```
javac -classpath "C:\Beg Java Stuff" Line.java
```

The command must be executed with Geometry as the current directory. This results in both the Line.java and Point.java files being compiled because Line.java refers to the other class. Because the directory in the path contains spaces, you have to enclose the path string between double quotes.

If the Point and Line classes were not interrelated, you could still compile the two source files or, indeed, any number of source files, in the Geometry package with the following command:

```
javac -classpath "C:\Beg Java Stuff" *.java
```

Accessing a Package

How you access a package when you are compiling a program that uses the package depends on where you have put it. There are a couple of options here. The first, but not the best, is to leave the .class files for the classes in the package in the directory with the package name.

Let's look at that before going on to the second possibility.

With the .class files in the original package directory, either the path to your package must appear in the string that has been set for the CLASSPATH environment variable, or you must use the -classpath option on the command line when you invoke the compiler or the interpreter. This overrides the CLASSPATH environment variable if it happens to be set. Note that it is up to you to make sure that the classes in your package are in the right directory. Java does not prevent you from saving a file in a directory that is quite different from that appearing in the package statement. Of the two options here, using the -classpath option on the command line is preferable, because it sets the classpath transiently each time and can't interfere with anything you do subsequently. In any event, you can explore both possibilities.

If you elect to use the CLASSPATH environment variable, it needs to contain only the paths to your packages. The standard packages that are supplied with Java do not need to be considered, as the compiler and the interpreter can always find them.

Of course, you can have as many paths as you want defined in CLASSPATH. They just need to be separated by semicolons under Windows. If you are using Windows 7 then you can create and set environment variables through the Advanced system settings option in the dialog that you can access by selecting System in Control Panel.

Under Linux, the mechanism to set CLASSPATH depends on the shell you are using, so check the documentation for it.

If you are using the JDK, you can always specify where your packages can be found by using the -classpath option when you execute the Java compiler or the interpreter. This has the advantage that it applies only for the current compilation or execution, so you can easily set it to suit each run. The command to compile MyProgram.java defining the classpath to include C:\MySource and C:\MyPackages would be:

```
javac -classpath "C:\MySource;C:\MyPackages" MyProgram.java
```

The compiler will find files in the current directory without specifying a period in the classpath as long as the files are not in a package. The directory containing the package directory must appear in the classpath. If you don't set the classpath, or you set it incorrectly, Java is not able to find the classes in any new packages you might create. If you omit the period from the -classpath string when executing your program, you get a message to the effect that main() cannot be found and your program does not run.

Another way to make your packages available after you have compiled them is by making them *extensions* to the set of standard packages.

Using Extensions

Extensions are .jar files stored within the ext directory that is created when you install the JDK. The default directory structure that is created is shown in Figure 5-9.

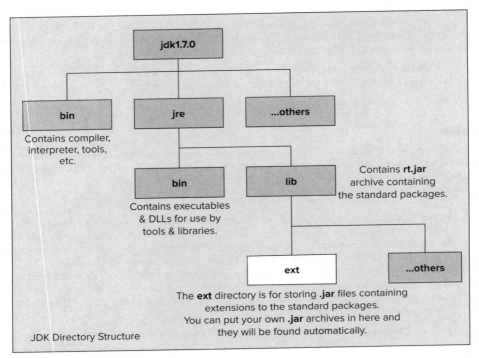

FIGURE 5-9

The classes and packages in the .jar archives that you place in the ext directory are automatically accessible when you compile or run your Java programs without the need to set the CLASSPATH environment variable or use the -classpath command-line option. When you create a .jar file for a package, you need to make sure that you add the .class files with the directory structure corresponding to the package name—you can't just add the .class files to the archive. For example, suppose you want to store the Geometry package in an archive. Assuming you have already compiled the package and the current directory contains the package directory, you can use the following command to create the archive:

```
C:\Beg Java Stuff>jar cvf Geometry.jar Geometry\*.class
```

This creates the archive Geometry.jar and adds all the .class files that are in the Geometry directory to it. All you now need to do to make the package available to any program that needs it is to copy it to the ext directory in the JDK directory hierarchy shown in Figure 5-9.

The jar utility does a lot more than I have described here. If you want to know more about what it can do, look into the "Tools and Utilities" section of the JDK documentation.

Adding Classes from a Package to Your Program

You used the import statement frequently in examples but nonetheless I'm describing it here from the ground up. Assuming they have been defined with the public keyword, you can add all or any of the classes in a named package to the code in your program by using an import *statement*. You can then reference the classes that you make available to your program through the import statement just by using the class names. For example, to make available all the classes in the package `Geometry.Shapes3D` to a source file, you just need to add the following `import` statement to the beginning of the file:

```
import Geometry.Shapes3D.*;   // Include all classes from this package
```

The keyword `import` is followed by the specification of what you want to import. The wildcard *, following the period after the package name, selects all the classes in the package, rather like selecting all the files in a directory. Now you can refer to any public class in the package just by using the class name. Again, the names of other classes in your program must be different from the names of the classes in the package. Importing all the names in a package is not an approach you should adopt generally as it defeats the primary objective of putting classes in packages. It's usually better to import just the names from a package that your code references.

If you want to add a particular class rather than an entire package, you specify its name explicitly in the `import` statement:

```
import Geometry.Shapes3D.Sphere;   // Include the class Sphere
```

This includes only the `Sphere` class in the source file. By using a separate `import` statement for each individual class from the package, you ensure that your source file includes only the classes that you need. This reduces the likelihood of name conflicts with your own classes, particularly if you are not fully familiar with the contents of the package and it contains a large number of classes.

 NOTE *The * can be used only to select all the classes in a package. You can't use `Geometry.*` to select all the packages in the `Geometry` directory.*

Packages and Names in Your Programs

A package creates a self-contained environment for naming your classes. As I've said, this is the primary reason for having packages in Java. You can specify the names for classes in one package without worrying about whether the same names have been used elsewhere. Java makes this possible by treating the package name as part of the class name—actually as a prefix. This means that the class `Sphere` in the package `Geometry.Shapes3D` has the full name `Geometry.Shapes3D.Sphere`. If you don't use an `import` statement to incorporate the class in your program, you can still make use of the class by referring to it using its full class name. If you needed to do this with the class `Sphere`, you might declare a variable with the statement:

```
Geometry.Shapes3D.Sphere ball = new Geometry.Shapes3D.Sphere(10.0, 1.0, 1.0, 1.0);
```

Although this is rather verbose and certainly doesn't help the readability of the program, it does ensure you have no conflict between this class and any other `Sphere` class that might be part of your program. You can usually contrive that your class names do not conflict with those in the commonly used standard Java packages, but in cases where you can't manage this, you can always fall back on using fully qualified class names. Indeed, on some occasions, you have to do this. This is necessary when you are using two different classes from different packages that share the same basic class name.

Importing Static Class Members

As you have seen in some of the examples, you can import the names of static members of a class from a named package into your program. This enables you to reference such static members by their simple unqualified names. In the `Sphere` class that you developed earlier in this chapter, you could have used the constant `PI` that is defined in the `Math` class by using its fully qualified name, `Math.PI`, in the definition of the volume method:

```
double volume() {
  return 4.0/3.0*Math.PI*radius*radius*radius;
}
```

This obviates the need for the static member of the `Sphere` class with the name `PI` and would provide a much more accurate definition of the value of π.

However, the `Math` prefix to the name `PI` doesn't really add to the clarity of the code, and it would be better without it. You can remove the need for prefixing `PI` with the `Math` class name by importing the `PI` member name from the `Math` class:

```
import static java.lang.Math.PI;

class Sphere {
  // Class details as before…
  double volume() {
    return 4.0/3.0*PI*radius*radius*radius;
  }
}
```

It is clear what `PI` means here and the code is not cluttered up with the class name prefix.

You can also import all the static members of a class using `*` notation. For example:

```
import static java.lang.Math.*;      // Import all static members of the Math class
```

With this statement at the beginning of a source file, you can refer to any of the static members of the `Math` class without qualifying them with the class name. Thus you can use methods such as `sqrt()`, `abs()`, `random()`, and so on, without the need for the `Math` prefix to the method names. Of course, using the `*` notation to import all the static names in a class does increase the risk of clashes between the names you are importing and the names you define in your code.

Note that the `import` statement, and that includes its use for importing static members of a class, applies only to classes that are defined in a named package. This is particularly relevant in the context of static import. If you want to import the names of a static member of a class that you define then you *must* put the definition of a class in a named package. You cannot import the names of static members of a class that is defined in the default package that has no name. The class name in a static `import` statement must always be qualified with its package name.

Standard Packages

All of the standard classes that are provided with Java are stored in standard packages. There is a substantial and growing list of standard packages but some of the ones you may hear about most frequently are found in Table 5-1.

TABLE 5-1: Java Standard Packages

PACKAGE	DESCRIPTION
`java.lang`	Contains classes that are fundamental to Java (e.g., the `Math` class) and all of these are available in your programs automatically. You do not need an import statement to include them.
`java.nio.file`	Contains classes supporting file I/O in conjunction with the classes in the `java.io` package. This package is new in JDK 7.
`java.awt`	Contains classes that support Java's graphical user interface (GUI). Although you can use these classes for GUI programming, it is almost always easier and better to use the alternative Swing classes.
`javax.swing`	Provides classes supporting the "Swing" GUI components. These are not only more flexible and easier to use than the `java.awt` equivalents, but they are also implemented largely in Java with minimal dependency on native code.
`java.awt.event`	Contains classes that support event handling.
`java.awt.geom`	Contains classes for drawing and operating with 2D geometric entities.

PACKAGE	DESCRIPTION
`javax.swing.border`	Classes to support generating borders around Swing components.
`javax.swing.event`	Classes supporting event handling for Swing components.
`java.applet`	Contains classes that enable you to write applets—programs that are embedded in a web page.
`java.util`	Contains classes that support a range of standard operations for managing collections of data, accessing date and time information, and analyzing strings.

The standard packages and the classes they contain cover an enormous amount of ground, so even in a book of this size it is impossible to cover them all exhaustively. There are now many more classes in the standard packages than there are pages in this book. However, you will apply some classes from all of the packages in the preceding table, plus one or two others besides, in later chapters of the book.

Standard Classes Encapsulating the Primitive Data Types

You saw in the previous chapter that you have classes available that enable you to define objects that encapsulate values of each of the primitive data types in Java. These classes are:

Boolean	Character	Byte
Short	Integer	Long
Float	Double	

These are all contained in the package `java.lang` along with quite a few other classes, such as the `String` and `StringBuffer` classes that you saw in Chapter 4. Each of these classes encapsulates a value of the corresponding primitive type and includes methods for manipulating and interrogating objects of the class, as well as a number of very useful static methods that provide utility functions for the underlying primitive types.

Converting between Primitive Type Values and Strings

Each class provides a static `toString()` method to convert a value of the corresponding primitive type to a `String` object, as you saw in the last chapter. There is also a non-static `toString()` method in each class that returns a `String` representation of a class object.

Conversely, there are methods to convert from a `String` object to a primitive type. For example, the static `parseInt()` member in the `Integer` class accepts a `String` representation of an integer as an argument and returns the equivalent value as type `int`. An alternative version of this method accepts a second argument of type `int` that specifies the radix to be used when interpreting the string. This enables you to parse strings that are hexadecimal or octal values, for example. If the `String` object cannot be parsed for any reason, if it contains invalid characters, for example, the method throws an exception of type `NumberFormatException`. All the standard classes encapsulating numerical primitive types and the `Boolean` class define static methods to parse strings and return a value of the corresponding primitive type. You have the methods `parseShort()`, `parseByte()`, `parseInt()`, and `parseLong()` in the classes for integer types, `parseFloat()` and `parseDouble()` for floating-point classes, and `parseBoolean()` for `Boolean`.

The classes for primitive numerical types and the `Boolean` class defines a static method `valueOf()` that converts a string to an object of the class type containing the value represented by the string. If the string does not represent a valid value, `NumberFormatException` is thrown. The method for the `Boolean` class returns a `Boolean` object with the value `true` if the string is equal to `true` ignoring case. Any other string results in `false` being returned.

WARNING *At the time of writing, the methods, such as* `parseInt()`, *for converting strings to numerical values throw an exception of type* `NumberFormatException` *if the string to be parsed contains underline characters, even though underlines are legal in numerical literals. This is regarded as a bug so it may well be fixed by the time you are reading this. If not, you can always write a method to remove underlines from any string that is to be converted to a numerical value.*

Converting Objects to Values

Each class encapsulating a primitive data value also defines a `xxxValue()` method (where xxx is the corresponding primitive type name) that returns the value that is encapsulated by an object as a value of the corresponding primitive type. For example, if you have created an object `number` of type `Double` that encapsulates the value 1.14159, then the expression `number.doubleValue()` results in the value 1.14159 as type `double`.

Primitive Class Constants

The classes that wrap numerical primitive types each contain the `static final` constants `MAX_VALUE` and `MIN_VALUE` that define the maximum and minimum values that can be represented. The floating-point classes also define the constants `POSITIVE_INFINITY`, `NEGATIVE_INFINITY`, and `NaN` (it stands for **Not a Number**, as it is the result of 0/0), so you can use these in comparisons to test whether such values have arisen during calculations. Alternatively, you can test floating-point values with the static methods `isInfinite()` and `isNaN()` — you pass your variable as an argument, and the methods return `true` for an infinite value or the `NaN` value, respectively. There are also non-static versions for use with an object of the class type. Remember that an infinite value can arise without necessarily dividing by zero. Any computation that results in an exponent that is too large to be represented produces either `POSITIVE_INFINITY` or `NEGATIVE_INFINITY`.

Many other operations are supported by these classes, so it is well worth browsing the JDK documentation for them. In particular, the `Character` class defines a large number of static methods for testing and classifying characters.

Autoboxing Values of Primitive Types

Circumstances can arise surprisingly often where you want to pass values of a primitive type to a method that requires the argument to be a reference to an object. The compiler supplies automatic conversions of primitive values to the corresponding class type when circumstances permit this. This can arise when you pass a value of type `int` to a method where the parameter type is type `Integer`, for example. Conversions from a primitive type to the corresponding class type are called *boxing conversions*, and automatic conversions of this kind are described as *autoboxing*.

The compiler also inserts unboxing conversions when necessary to convert a reference to an object of a wrapper class for a primitive type such as `double` to the value that it encapsulates. The compiler does this by inserting a call to the `xxxValue()` method for the object. You can see this in action in the following little example.

TRY IT OUT   **Autoboxing in Action**

This program is contrived to force boxing and unboxing conversions to occur:

Available for download on Wrox.com

```
public class AutoboxingInAction {
  public static void main(String[] args) {
    int[] values = { 3, 97, 55, 22, 12345 };

    // Array to store Integer objects
    Integer[] objs = new Integer[values.length];

    // Call method to cause boxing conversions
    for(int i = 0 ; i < values.length ; ++i) {
```

```
      objs[i] = boxInteger(values[i]);
    }

    // Use method to cause unboxing conversions
    for(Integer intObject : objs) {
      unboxInteger(intObject);
    }
  }

  // Method to cause boxing conversion
  public static Integer boxInteger(Integer obj) {
    return obj;
  }

  // Method to cause unboxing conversion
  public static void unboxInteger(int n) {
    System.out.println("value = " + n);
  }
```

AutoboxingInAction.java

This example produces the following output:

```
value = 3
value = 97
value = 55
value = 22
value = 12345
```

How It Works

You have defined the `boxInteger()` method with a parameter type of type `Integer`. When you call this method in the first `for` loop in `main()`, you pass values of type `int` to it from the `values` array. Because the `boxInteger()` method requires the argument to be a reference to an object of type `Integer`, the compiler arranges for autoboxing to occur by inserting a boxing conversion to convert the integer value to an object of type `Integer`. The method returns a reference to the object that results, and you store this in the `Integer[]` array `objs`.

The second `for` loop in `main()` passes each reference to an `Integer` object from the `objs` array to the `unboxInteger()` method. Because you have specified the method parameter type as type `int`, the method cannot accept a reference to an object of type `Integer` as the argument directly. The compiler inserts an unboxing conversion to obtain the value of type `int` that the object encapsulates. This value is then passed to the method, and you output it.

Autoboxing is particularly useful when you need to insert values of primitive types into a collection—you learn about the collection classes that are available in the class libraries in Chapter 14, but you see more on boxing and unboxing conversions in Chapter 13.

CONTROLLING ACCESS TO CLASS MEMBERS

I have not yet discussed in any detail how you control the accessibility of class members from outside the class—from a method in another class in other words. You know that you can refer to any of the static members of the same class in the code for a static class method, and a non-static method can refer to any member of the same class. The degree to which variables and methods within one class are accessible from other classes is a bit more complicated. It depends on what *access attributes* you have specified for the members of a class, whether the classes are in the same package, and whether you have declared the class as public. This is why you had to understand packages first.

Using Access Attributes

Let's start by considering classes that are in the same package. Within a given package, any class has direct access to any other class name in the same package—for declaring variables or specifying method parameter types, for example—but the variables and methods that are members of that other class are not necessarily accessible. The accessibility of these is controlled by *access attributes*. The name of a class in one package can be accessed from a class in another package only if the class to be accessed is declared as `public`. Classes not declared as `public` can be accessed only by classes within the same package.

You have four possibilities when specifying an access attribute for a class member, and each possibility has a different effect overall. The options you have for specifying the accessibility of a variable or a method in a class are found in Table 5-2.

TABLE 5-2: Access Attributes for a Class Member

ATTRIBUTE	PERMITTED ACCESS
No access attribute	From methods in any class in the same package.
`public`	From methods in any class anywhere as long as the class has been declared as `public`.
`private`	Accessible only from methods inside the class. No access from outside the class at all.
`protected`	From methods in any class in the same package and from any subclass anywhere.

The table shows you how the access attributes you set for a class member determine the parts of the Java environment from which you can access it. I will discuss subclasses in the next chapter, so don't worry about these for the moment. I will describe how and when you use the `protected` attribute then. Note that `public`, `private`, and `protected` are all keywords. Specifying a member as `public` makes it completely accessible, and at the other extreme, making it `private` restricts access to members of the same class.

This may sound more complicated than it actually is. Figure 5-10 shows the access allowed between classes within the same package.

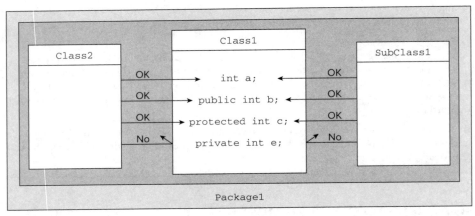

FIGURE 5-10

Within a package such as `package1` in Figure 5-11, only the `private` members of the class `Class1` can't be directly accessed by methods in other classes in the same package. If you declare a class member to be `private`, it can be accessed only by methods in the same class.

As I said earlier, a class definition must have an access attribute of `public` if it is to be accessible from outside the package that contains it. Figure 5-11 shows the situation where the classes seeking access to the members of a public class are in different packages.

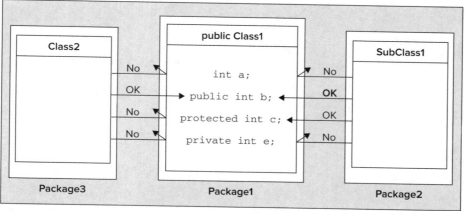

FIGURE 5-11

Here access is more restricted. The only members of `Class1` that can be accessed from an ordinary class, `Class2`, in another package, are those specified as `public`. Keep in mind that the class `Class1` must also have been defined with the attribute `public` for this to be the case. A class that is not defined as `public` cannot be accessed at all from a class in another package.

From a subclass of `Class1` that is in another package, the members of `Class1` without an access attribute cannot be reached, and neither can the `private` members—these can never be accessed externally under any circumstances.

Specifying Access Attributes

As you probably gathered from the diagrams in the previous section, to specify an access attribute for a class member, you just add the appropriate keyword to the beginning of the declaration. Here is the `Point` class you saw earlier, but now with access attributes defined for its members:

TRY IT OUT Accessing the Point Class

Make the following changes to your `Point` class. If you save it in a new directory, do make sure `Line.java` is copied there as well. It is useful later if they are in a directory with the name `Geometry`.

```java
import static java.lang.Math.sqrt;

public class Point {
  // Create a point from its coordinates
  public Point(double xVal, double yVal) {
    x = xVal;
    y = yVal;
  }

  // Create a Point from an existing Point object
  public Point(final Point aPoint) {
    x = aPoint.x;
    y = aPoint.y;
  }

  // Move a point
  public void move(double xDelta, double yDelta) {
    // Parameter values are increments to the current coordinates
    x += xDelta;
```

```
      y += yDelta;
    }

    // Calculate the distance to another point
    public double distance(final Point aPoint) {
      return sqrt((x - aPoint.x)*(x - aPoint.x)+(y - aPoint.y)*(y - aPoint.y));
    }

    // Convert a point to a string
    public String toString() {
      return Double.toString(x) + ", " + y;     // As "x, y"
    }

    // Coordinates of the point
    private double x;
    private double y;
  }
```

Directory "Geometry"

The members have been resequenced within the class, with the `private` members appearing last. You should maintain a consistent ordering of class members according to their access attributes, as it makes the code easier to follow. The ordering adopted most frequently is for the most accessible members to appear first and the least accessible last, but a consistent order is more important than the particular order you choose.

How It Works

Now the instance variables x and y cannot be accessed or modified from outside the class, as they are private. The only way these can be set or modified is through methods within the class, either with constructors or the `move()` method. If it is necessary to obtain the values of x and y from outside the class, as it might well be in this case, a simple function does the trick. For example

```
    public double getX() {
      return x;
    }
```

Couldn't be easier really, could it? This makes x freely available, but prevents modification of its value from outside the class. In general, such methods are referred to as *accessor* methods and usually have the form `getXXX()`. Methods that allow a private data member to be changed are called *mutator* methods and are typically of the form `setXXX()`, where a new value is passed as an argument. For example:

```
    public void setX(double inputX) {
      x = inputX;
    }
```

It may seem odd to use a method to alter the value of a `private` data member when you could just make it `public`. The main advantage of using a method in this way is that you can apply validity checks on the new value that is to be set and prevent inappropriate values from being assigned. Of course, if you really don't want to allow the value of a private member to be changed, you don't include a mutator method for the class.

Choosing Access Attributes

As you can see from the table of access attributes, all the classes you have defined so far have had members that are freely accessible within the same package. This applies both to the methods and the variables that were defined in the classes. This is not good object-oriented programming practice. As I said in Chapter 1, one of the ideas behind objects is to keep the data members encapsulated so they cannot be modified by all and sundry, even from other classes within the same package. On the other hand, the methods in your classes that provide the operations you want to allow with objects of the class type generally need to be accessible. They provide the outside interface to the class and define the set of operations that are possible with objects of the class. Therefore, in the majority of situations with simple classes (i.e., no subclasses), you should be explicitly specifying your class members as either public or private, rather than omitting the access attributes.

Broadly, unless you have good reasons for declaring them otherwise, the variables in a public class should be private and the methods that are called from outside the class should be public. Even where access to the values of the variables from outside a class is necessary, you don't need to make them public or leave them without an access attribute. As you've just seen, you can provide access quite easily by adding a simple public method to return the value of a data member.

Of course, there are always exceptions:

➤ For classes in a package that are not public, and therefore not accessible outside the package, it may sometimes be convenient to allow other classes in the package direct access to the data members.

➤ If you have data members that have been specified as final so that their values are fixed and they are likely to be useful outside the class, you might as well declare them to be public.

➤ You may well have methods in a class that are intended to be used only internally by other methods in the same class. In this case you should specify these as private.

➤ In a class like the standard class Math, which is just a convenient container for utility functions and standard data values, you should make everything public.

All of this applies to simple classes. You see in the next chapter, when you look at subclasses, that there are some further aspects of class structure that you must take into account.

Using Package and Access Attributes

Let's put together an example that uses a package that you create. You could put the Point and Line classes that you defined earlier in package with the name Geometry. You can then write a program that imports these classes and tests them. You should already have the Geometry directory set up if you followed my suggestion with the previous example.

TRY IT OUT   Packaging Up the Line and Point Classes

The source and .class files for each class in the package must be in a directory with the name Geometry. Remember that you need to ensure the path to the directory (or directories if you are storing .class files separately) Geometry appears in the CLASSPATH environment variable setting before you try to compile or use either of these two classes. You can best do this by specifying the -classpath option when you run the compiler or the interpreter.

To include the class Point in the package, the code in Point.java is changed to:

Available for
download on
Wrox.com

```java
package Geometry;

import static java.lang.Math.sqrt;
public class Point {

  // Create a point from its coordinates
  public Point(double xVal, double yVal) {
    x = xVal;
    y = yVal;
  }

  // Create a Point from an existing Point object
  public Point(final Point aPoint) {
    x = aPoint.x;
    y = aPoint.y;
  }

    // Move a point
```

```
public void move(double xDelta, double yDelta) {
  // Parameter values are increments to the current coordinates
  x += xDelta;
  y += yDelta;
}

// Calculate the distance to another point
public double distance(final Point aPoint) {
  return sqrt((x - aPoint.x)*(x - aPoint.x)+(y - aPoint.y)*(y - aPoint.y));
}

// Convert a point to a string
public String toString() {
  return Double.toString(x) + ", " + y;     // As "x, y"
}

// Retrieve the x coordinate
public double getX() {
  return x;
}

// Retrieve the y coordinate
public double getY() {
  return y;
}

// Set the x coordinate
public void setX(double inputX) {
  x = inputX;
}

// Set the y coordinate
public void setY(double inputY) {
  y = inputY;
}

// Coordinates of the point
private double x;
private double y;
}
```

Directory "Geometry"

Note that you have added the getX(), getY(), setX(), and setY() methods to the class to make the private data members accessible.

The Line class also needs to be amended to make the methods public and to declare the class as public. You have to change its intersects() method so that it can access the private data members of Point objects using the set...() and get...() methods in the Point class. The code in Line.java, with changes highlighted, is:

```
package Geometry;

public class Line {

  // Create a line from two points
  public Line(final Point start, final Point end) {
    this.start = new Point(start);
    this.end = new Point(end);
```

```
      }

      // Create a line from two coordinate pairs
      public Line(double xStart, double yStart, double xEnd, double yEnd) {
        start = new Point(xStart, yStart);    // Create the start point
        end = new Point(xEnd, yEnd);          // Create the end point
      }

      // Calculate the length of a line
      public double length() {
        return start.distance(end);           // Use the method from the Point class
      }

      // Return a point as the intersection of two lines -- called from a Line object
      public Point intersects(final Line line1) {

        Point localPoint = new Point(0, 0);

        double num = (end.getY() - start.getY()) * (start.getX()-line1.start.getX())
                   - (end.getX() - start.getX()) * (start.getY() - line1.start.getY());

        double denom = (end.getY() - start.getY()) * (line1.end.getX() - line1.start.getX())
                     - (end.getX() - start.getX()) * (line1.end.getY() - line1.start.getY());

        localPoint.setX(line1.start.getX() + (line1.end.getX() -
                                        line1.start.getX())*num/denom);
        localPoint.setY(line1.start.getY() + (line1.end.getY() -
                                        line1.start.getY())*num/denom);

        return localPoint;
      }

      // Convert a line to a string
      public String toString() {
        return "(" + start+ "):(" + end + ")";  // As "(start):(end)"
      }                                          // that is, "(x1, y1):(x2, y2)"

      // Data members
      Point start;                              // Start point of line
      Point end;                                // End point of line
    }
```

Directory "Geometry"

Here you have left the data members of the class without an access attribute so they are accessible from the Point class, but not from classes outside the Geometry package.

How It Works

The package statement at the beginning of each source file defines the package to which the class belongs. Remember, you still have to save it in the correct directory, Geometry. Without the public attribute, the classes are not available to classes outside the Geometry package.

Because you have declared the data members in the class Point as private, they are not accessible directly. You have added the methods getX(), getY(), setX(), and setY() to the Point class to make the values accessible to any class that needs them.

The static import statement that you added earlier for the sqrt() method in the Math class enables the distance() method to access the sqrt() method without using the Math qualifier.

The Line class hasn't been updated since the earlier example, so you first have to sort out the access attributes. The two instance variables are declared as before, without any access attribute, so they can be accessed from within the package but not from classes outside the package. This is an occasion where exposing the data members within the package is very convenient, and you can do it without exposing the data members to any classes using the package. And you have updated the intersects() method to reflect the changes in accessibility made to the members of the Point class.

You can now write the program that is going to import and use the package that you have just created.

TRY IT OUT   Testing the Geometry Package

You can create a succession of points and create a line joining each pair of successive points in the sequence. You can then calculate the total line length.

Available for
download on
Wrox.com

```java
import Geometry.*;     // Import the Point and Line classes

public class TryPackage {
  public static void main(String[] args) {
    double[][] coords = { {1.0, 0.0}, {6.0, 0.0}, {6.0, 10.0},
                          {10.0,10.0}, {10.0, -14.0}, {8.0, -14.0}};
    // Create an array of points and fill it with Point objects
    Point[] points = new Point[coords.length];
    for(int i = 0; i < coords.length; i++)
      points[i] = new Point(coords[i][0],coords[i][1]);

    // Create an array of lines and fill it using Point pairs
    Line[] lines = new Line[points.length - 1];
    double totalLength = 0.0;                     // Store total line length here
    for(int i = 0; i < points.length - 1; i++) {
      lines[i] = new Line(points[i], points[i+1]); // Create a Line
      totalLength += lines[i].length();            // Add its length
      System.out.println("Line " + (i+1) + ' ' + lines[i] +
                          " Length is " + lines[i].length());

    }
    // Output the total length
    System.out.println("\nTotal line length = " + totalLength);
  }
}
```

Directory "TryPackage"

You should save this as TryPackage.java in the directory TryPackage. If the path to your Geometry directory on a PC running Windows is C:\Packages\Geometry, you can compile this with the following command:

```
javac -classpath "C:\Packages" TryPackage.java
```

This assumes the current directory is the one containing the TryPackage.java file, which is the TryPackage directory if you followed my suggestion. The -classpath option specifies the directory containing your Geometry package. Without this the compiler is not able to find the classes in the Geometry package, and the compilation fails.

After you have a successful compilation, you can execute the program with the following command:

```
java -classpath ".;C:\Packages" TryPackage
```

Here -classpath includes a period for the current directory. Without it, the program will not execute because TryPackage will not be found. When the program executes, you should see the following output:

```
Line 1 (1.0, 0.0):(6.0, 0.0)   Length is 5.0
Line 2 (6.0, 0.0):(6.0, 10.0)   Length is 10.0
Line 3 (6.0, 10.0):(10.0, 10.0)   Length is 4.0
```

```
Line 4 (10.0, 10.0):(10.0, -14.0)    Length is 24.0
Line 5 (10.0, -14.0):(8.0, -14.0)    Length is 2.0

Total line length = 45.0
```

How It Works

This example is a handy review of how you can define arrays and also shows that you can declare an array of objects in the same way as you declare an array of one of the basic types. The dimensions of the array of arrays, coords, are determined by the initial values that you specified between the braces. The number of values within the outer braces determines the first dimension. Each of the elements in the array is itself an array of length two, with each pair of element values enclosed within their own braces.

Because there are six sets of these, you have an array of six elements, each of which is itself an array of two elements. Each of these elements corresponds to the (*x,y*) coordinates of a point.

 NOTE *You can see from this that you could create an array of arrays with each row having a different number of elements. The number of initializing values that appear between each inner pair of braces determines the length of each row, so the rows could all be of different lengths in the most general case.*

You declare an array of Point objects with the same length as the number of (*x,y*) pairs in the coords array. This array is filled with Point objects in the for loop, which you create using the pairs of coordinate values from the coords array.

Because each pair of Point objects defines a Line object, you need one less element in the lines array than you have in the points array. You create the elements of the lines array in the second for loop using successive Point objects and accumulate the total length of all the line segments by adding the length of each Line object to totalLength as it is created. On each iteration of the for loop, you output the details of the current line. Finally, you output the value of totalLength, which in this case is 45.

Note that the import statement in TryPackage.java adds the classes from the Geometry package to your program. These classes can be added to any application using the same import statement. You might like to try putting the classes in the Geometry package in a .jar file and try it out as an extension. Let's look at one other aspect of generating your own packages—compiling just the classes in the package without any program that makes use of them. You can try this out on the Geometry package if you delete the Line.class and Point.class files from the package directory.

You can compile just the classes in the Geometry package with the following command:

```
javac -classpath "C:\Packages" Geometry/*.java
```

This compiles both the Line and Point classes so you should see the .class files restored in the Geometry directory. The files to be compiled are specified relative to the current directory as Geometry/*.java. Under Microsoft Windows this could equally well be Geometry*.java. This specifies all files in the Geometry subdirectory to the current directory. Unless the current directory is the one containing the classes in the package, the classpath must contain the path to the package directory; otherwise, the compiler is not able to find the package.

NESTED CLASSES

All the classes you have defined so far have been separate from each other—each stored away in its own source file. Not all classes have to be defined like this. You can put the definition of one class inside the definition of another class. The inside class is called a *nested class*. A nested class can itself have another class nested inside it, if need be.

When you define a nested class, it is a member of the enclosing class in much the same way as the other class members. A nested class can have an access attribute just like other class members, and the accessibility from outside the enclosing class is determined by the attributes in the same way:

```
public class Outside {

  // Nested class
  public class Inside {
    // Details of Inside class...
  }

  // More members of Outside class...
}
```

Here the class `Inside` is nested inside the class `Outside`. The `Inside` class is declared as a public member of `Outside`, so it is accessible from outside `Outside`. Obviously, a nested class should have some specific association with the enclosing class. Arbitrarily nesting one class inside another would not be sensible. The enclosing class here is referred to as a *top-level class*. A top-level class is a class that contains a nested class but is not itself a nested class.

The nested class here has meaning only in the context of an object of type `Outside`. This is because the `Inside` class is not declared as a static member of the class `Outside`. Until an object of type `Outside` has been created, you can't create any `Inside` objects. However, when you declare an object of a class containing a nested class, no objects of the nested class are necessarily created—unless of course the enclosing class's constructor creates them. For example, suppose you create an object with the following statement:

```
Outside outer = new Outside();
```

No objects of the nested class, `Inside`, are created. If you now want to create an object of the type of the nested class, you must refer to the nested class type using the name of the enclosing class as a qualifier. For instance, having declared an object of type `Outside`, you can create an object of type `Inside` as follows:

```
Outside.Inside inner = outer.new Inside();     // Define a nested class object
```

Here you have created an object of the nested class type that is associated with the object `outer` that you created earlier. You are creating an object of type `Inside` in the context of the object `outer`. Within non-static methods that are members of `Outside`, you can use the class name `Inside` without any qualification, as it is automatically qualified by the compiler with the `this` variable. So you could create a new `Inside` object from within a method of the object `Outside`:

```
Inside inner = new Inside();                   // Define a nested class object
```

This statement is equivalent to:

```
this.Inside inner = this.new Inside();         // Define a nested class object
```

All this implies that a static method cannot create objects of a non-static nested class type. Because the `Inside` class is not a static member of the `Outside` class, such a member could refer to an object that does not exist—which would be an error if there are no `Inside` objects extant in the context of an `Outside` object. Because `Inside` is not a static member of the `Outside` class, if a static method in the `Outside` class tried to create an object of type `Inside` directly, without first invoking an object of type `Outside`, it would be trying to create an object outside of that object's legitimate scope—an illegal maneuver.

Further, because the `Inside` class is not a static member of the `Outside` class, it cannot in turn contain any static data members itself. Because `Inside` is not static, it cannot act as a freestanding class with static members—this would be a logical contradiction.

You typically use nested classes to define objects that at least have a strong association with objects of the enclosing class type, and often there is a tight coupling between the two. A further use for nested classes is for grouping a set of related classes under the umbrella of an enclosing class. You use this approach in examples later on in the book.

Static Nested Classes

To make objects of a nested class type independent of objects of the enclosing class type, you can declare the nested class as `static`:

```
public class Outside {
  public static class Skinside {
    // Details of Skinside
  }

  // Nested class
  public class Inside {
    // Details of Inside class...
  }
  // More members of Outside class...
}
```

Now with `Skinside` inside `Outside` declared as `static`, you can declare objects of this nested class type independent from any objects of type `Outside`, and regardless of whether you have created any `Outside` objects or not. For example:

```
Outside.Skinside example = new Outside.Skinside();
```

This is significantly different from what you needed to do for a non-static nested class. Now you must use the nested class name qualified by the enclosing class name as the type for creating the object. Thus, the name of a static nested class exists within the context of the outer class and therefore the nested class name is qualified by the enclosing class name. Note that a static nested class can have static members, whereas a non-static nested class cannot. A class containing both a static and a non-static nested class is illustrated in Figure 5-12.

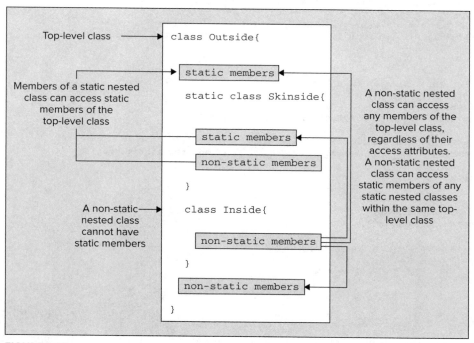

FIGURE 5-12

If the preceding discussion seems a bit confusing in the abstract, you can get a better idea of how a nested class works in practice with a simple example. You create a class `MagicHat` that defines an object containing a variable number of `Rabbit` objects. You put the definition for the class `Rabbit` inside the definition of the class `MagicHat`, so `Rabbit` is an example of a nested class. The basic structure of `MagicHat.java` is:

```
public class MagicHat {
  // Definition of the MagicHat class...

  // Nested class to define a rabbit
  static class Rabbit {
    // Definition of the Rabbit class...
  }
}
```

Here the nested class is defined as `static` because you want to be able to have static members of this class. You will see a little later in the chapter how it might work with a non-static nested class.

TRY IT OUT   Rabbits out of Hats

Let's add the details of the `MagicHat` class definition:

```
import java.util.Random;                        // Import Random class

public class MagicHat {
  static int maxRabbits = 5;                     // Maximum rabbits in a hat
  static Random select = new Random();           // Random number generator

  // Constructor for a hat
  public MagicHat(String hatName) {
    this.hatName = hatName;                       // Store the hat name
    rabbits = new Rabbit[1+select.nextInt(maxRabbits)]; // Random rabbits

    for(int i = 0 ; i < rabbits.length ; ++i) {
      rabbits[i] = new Rabbit();                  // Create the rabbits
    }
  }

  // String representation of a hat
  public String toString() {
    // Hat name first...
    String hatString = "\n" + hatName + " contains:\n";

    for(Rabbit rabbit : rabbits) {
      hatString += "    " + rabbit;               // Add the rabbits strings
    }
    return hatString;
  }

  private String hatName;                         // Name of the hat
  private Rabbit rabbits[];                        // Rabbits in the hat

  // Nested class to define a rabbit
  static class Rabbit {
    // Definition of the Rabbit class...
  }
}
```

Directory "TryNestedClass"

You can save the source file in a new directory, `TryNestedClass`. Instead of the old `Math.random()` method that you have been using up to now to generate pseudo-random values, you are using an object of the class `Random` that is defined in the `java.util` package. An object of type `Random` has a variety of methods to generate pseudo-random values of different types, and with different ranges. The method `nextInt()` that you are using here returns an integer that is zero or greater, but less than the integer value you pass as an argument. Thus, if you pass the length of an array to it, it generates a random index value that is always legal for the array size.

You can now add the definition of the `Rabbit` class. When you create a `Rabbit` object, you want it to have a unique name so you can distinguish one `Rabbit` from another. You can generate unique names by selecting one of a limited set of fixed names and then appending an integer that is different each time the base name is used. Here's what you need to add for the `Rabbit` class definition:

```
public class MagicHat {

    // Definition of the MagicHat class - as before...

    // Nested class to define a rabbit
    static class Rabbit {
        // A name is a rabbit name from rabbitNames followed by an integer
        static private String[] rabbitNames = {"Floppsy", "Moppsy",
                                                "Gnasher", "Thumper"};
        static private int[] rabbitNamesCount = new int[rabbitNames.length];
        private String name;                        // Name of the rabbit

        // Constructor for a rabbit
        public Rabbit() {
            int index = select.nextInt(rabbitNames.length);  // Get random name index
            name = rabbitNames[index] + (++rabbitNamesCount[index]);
        }

        // String representation of a rabbit
        public String toString() {
            return name;
        }
    }
}
```

Directory "TryNestedClass"

Note that the constructor in the `Rabbit` class can access the `select` member of the enclosing class, `MagicHat`, without qualification. This is possible only with static members of the enclosing class—you can't refer to non-static members of the enclosing class here because there is no object of type `MagicHat` associated with it.

You can use the following application class to try out the nested class:

```
public class TryNestedClass {
    static public void main(String[] args) {
        // Create three magic hats and output them
        System.out.println(new MagicHat("Gray Topper"));
        System.out.println(new MagicHat("Black Topper"));
        System.out.println(new MagicHat("Baseball Cap"));
    }
}
```

Directory "TryNestedClass"

You should save this source file in the same directory as `MagicHat.java`. When I ran the program, I got the following output:

```
Gray Topper contains:
    Floppsy1    Moppsy1    Gnasher1    Floppsy2    Thumper1

Black Topper contains:
    Moppsy2    Gnasher2    Floppsy3    Floppsy4

Baseball Cap contains:
    Moppsy3
```

You are likely to get something different.

How It Works

Each `MagicHat` object contains a random number of `Rabbit` objects. The constructor for a `MagicHat` object stores the name of the hat in its private member `hatName` and generates a `Rabbit` array with at least one, and up to `maxRabbits`, elements. This is done with the expression `1+select.nextInt(maxRabbits)`. Calling `nextInt()` with the argument `maxRabbits` returns a value that is from 0 to `maxRabbits-1`, inclusive. Adding 1 to this results in a value from 1 to `maxRabbits`, inclusive. The array so created is then filled with `Rabbit` objects.

The `MagicHat` class also has a `toString()` method that returns a `String` object containing the name of the hat and the names of all the rabbits in the hat. This assumes that the `Rabbit` class also has a `toString()` method defined. You are able to use the `toString()` implicitly in an output statement when you create and display `MagicHat` class objects.

The base names that you use to generate rabbit names are defined in the `static` array `rabbitNames[]` in the `Rabbit` class. The count for each base name, which you append to the base name to produce a unique name for a rabbit, is stored in the `static` array `rabbitNamesCount[]`. This has the same number of elements as the `rabbitNames` array, and each element stores a value to be appended to the corresponding name in the `rabbitNames` array. The `Rabbit` class has the data member `name` to store a name that is initialized in the constructor. A random base name is selected from the `rabbitNames[]` array using an index value from 0 up to one less than the length of this array. You then append the current count for the name incremented by 1, so successive uses of any base name, such as `Gnasher`, for example, produce names `Gnasher1`, `Gnasher2`, and so on. The `toString()` method for the class returns the name for the `Rabbit` object.

The `main()` method in `TryNestedClass` creates three `MagicHat` objects and outputs the string representation of each of them. Putting the object as an argument to the `println()` method calls the `toString()` method for the object automatically, and the `String` object that is returned is output to the screen.

If you look at the `.class` files that are produced by the compiler, the `Rabbit` class has its own file with the name `MagicHat$Rabbit.class`. Thus the name of the nested `Rabbit` class is qualified with the name of the class that contains it, `MagicHat`.

Using a Non-Static Nested Class

In the previous example, you could make the `Rabbit` class non-static by deleting the keyword `static` from its definition. However, if you try that, the program no longer compiles and runs. The problem is the static data members `rabbitNames` and `rabbitNamesCount` in the `Rabbit` class. You saw earlier that a non-static nested class cannot have static members, so you must find an alternative way of dealing with names if you want to make `Rabbit` a non-static nested class.

You could consider making these arrays non-static. This has several disadvantages. First, each `Rabbit` object would have its own copy of these arrays—an unnecessary duplication of data. A more serious problem is that the naming process would not work. Because each object has its own copy of the `rabbitNamesCount` array, the names that are generated are not going to be unique.

The answer is to keep `rabbitNames` and `rabbitNamesCount` as static, but put them in the `MagicHat` class instead. Let's see that working.

TRY IT OUT   Accessing the Top-Level Class Members

You need to modify the class definition to the following:

```
public class MagicHat {
    static int maxRabbits = 5;                 // Maximuum rabbits in a hat
    static Random select = new Random();       // Random number generator
    static private String[] rabbitNames = {"Floppsy", "Moppsy",
                                            "Gnasher", "Thumper"};
```

```
   static private int[] rabbitNamesCount = new int[rabbitNames.length];

   // Constructor for a hat
   public MagicHat(final String hatName) {
     this.hatName = hatName;                          // Store the hat name
     rabbits = new Rabbit[1+select.nextInt(maxRabbits)]; // Random rabbits

     for(int i = 0 ; i < rabbits.length ; ++i) {
       rabbits[i] = new Rabbit();                     // Create the rabbits
     }
   }

   // String representation of a hat
   public String toString() {
     // Hat name first...
     String hatString = "\n" + hatName + " contains:\n";

     for(Rabbit rabbit : rabbits) {
       hatString += "    " + rabbit;                  // Add the rabbits strings
     }
     return hatString;
   }
   private String hatName;                            // Name of the hat
   private Rabbit rabbits[];                          // Rabbits in the hat

   // Nested class to define a rabbit
   class Rabbit {
     private String name;                             // Name of the rabbit

     // Constructor for a rabbit
     public Rabbit() {
       int index = select.nextInt(rabbitNames.length);  // Get random name index
       name = rabbitNames[index] + (++rabbitNamesCount[index]);
     }

     // String representation of a rabbit
     public String toString() {
       return name;
     }
   }
 }
```

Directory "TryNestedClass2"

I put this version in the new folder `TryNestedClass2`. The only changes are the deletion of the `static` keyword in the definition of the `Rabbit` class and the movement of data members relating to rabbit names to the `MagicHat` class. You can run this with the same version of `TryNestedClass`, and it should produce output much the same as before.

How It Works

Although the output is much the same, what is happening is distinctly different. The `Rabbit` objects that are created in the `MagicHat` constructor are now associated with the current `MagicHat` object that is being constructed. The `Rabbit()` constructor call is actually `this.Rabbit()`.

Using a Nested Class Outside the Top-Level Class

You can create objects of an inner class outside the top-level class containing the inner class. As I discussed, how you do this depends on whether the nested class is a static member of the enclosing class. With the first version of the `MagicHat` class, with a static `Rabbit` class, you could create an independent rabbit by adding the following statement to the end of `main()`:

```
System.out.println("An independent rabbit: " + new MagicHat.Rabbit());
```

This `Rabbit` object is completely free—there is no `MagicHat` object to contain and restrain it. In the case of a non-static `Rabbit` class, things are different. Let's try this using a modified version of the previous program.

TRY IT OUT   Free-Range Rabbits (Almost)

You can see how this works by modifying the `main()` method in `TryNestedClass` to create another `MagicHat` object, and then create a `Rabbit` object for it:

Available for
download on
Wrox.com

```
static public void main(String[] args) {
    // Create three magic hats and output them
    System.out.println(new MagicHat("Gray Topper"));
    System.out.println(new MagicHat("Black Topper"));
    System.out.println(new MagicHat("Baseball Cap"));
    MagicHat oldHat = new MagicHat("Old hat");           // New hat object
    MagicHat.Rabbit rabbit = oldHat.new Rabbit();        // Create rabbit object
    System.out.println(oldHat);                          // Show the hat
    System.out.println("\nNew rabbit is: " + rabbit);    // Display the rabbit
}
```

Directory "TryNestedClass3"

I put this in the `TryNestedClass3` folder. The output that I got was as follows:

```
Gray Topper contains:
 Thumper1

Black Topper contains:
 Moppsy1 Thumper2 Thumper3

Baseball Cap contains:
 Floppsy1 Floppsy2 Thumper4

Old hat contains:
 Floppsy3 Thumper5 Thumper6 Thumper7 Thumper8

New rabbit is: Thumper9
```

How It Works

The new code first creates a `MagicHat` object, `oldHat`, which has its own rabbits. You then use this object to create an object of the class `MagicHat.Rabbit`. This is how a nested class type is referenced—with the top-level class name as a qualifier. You can only call the constructor for the nested class in this case by qualifying it with a `MagicHat` object name. This is because a non-static nested class can refer to members of the top-level class—including instance members. Therefore, an instance of the top-level class must exist for this to be possible.

Note how the top-level object is used in the constructor call. The object name qualifier goes before the keyword `new`, which precedes the constructor call for the inner class. This creates an object, `rabbit`, in the context of the object `oldHat`. This doesn't mean `oldHat` has `rabbit` as a member. It means that if top-level members are used in the inner class, they are the members for `oldHat`. You can see from the example that the name of the new rabbit is not part of the `oldHat` object, although it is associated with `oldHat`. You could demonstrate this by modifying the `toString()` method in the `Rabbit` class to:

```
public String toString() {
    return name + " parent: "+hatName;
}
```

If you run the program again, you see that when each `Rabbit` object is displayed, it also shows its parent hat.

Local Nested Classes

You can define a class inside a method—where it is called a *local nested class*. It is also referred to as a *local inner class* because a non-static nested class is often referred to as an *inner class*. You can create objects of a local inner class only locally—that is, within the method in which the class definition appears. This is useful when the computation in a method requires the use of a specialized class that is not required or used elsewhere. A good example is listeners for events that arise as a result of user interaction with an application. You learn about listeners in Chapter 18.

A local inner class can refer to variables declared in the method in which the definition appears, but only if they are `final`.

SUMMARY

In this chapter you learned the essentials of defining your own classes. You can now create your own class types to fit the context of the problems you are dealing with. You will build on this in the next chapter to enable you to add more flexibility to the operations on your class objects by learning how to realize inheritance.

EXERCISES

You can download the source code for the examples in the book and the solutions to the following exercises from www.wrox.com.

1. Define a class for rectangle objects defined by two points: the top-left and bottom-right corners of the rectangle. Include a constructor to copy a rectangle, a method to return a rectangle object that encloses the current object and the rectangle passed as an argument, and a method to display the defining points of a rectangle. Test the class by creating four rectangles and combining these cumulatively to end up with a rectangle enclosing them all. Output the defining points of all the rectangles you create.

2. Define a class, `mcmLength`, to represent a length measured in meters, centimeters, and millimeters, each stored as integers. Include methods to add and subtract objects, to multiply and divide an object by an integer value, to calculate an area resulting from the product of two objects, and to compare objects. Include constructors that accept three arguments—meters, centimeters, and millimeters; one integer argument in millimeters; one `double` argument in centimeters; and no arguments, which creates an object with the length set to zero. Check the class by creating some objects and testing the class operations.

3. Define a class, `tkgWeight`, to represent a weight in tons, kilograms, and grams, and include a similar range of methods and constructors as the previous example. Demonstrate this class by creating and combining some class objects.

4. Put both the previous classes in a package called `Measures`. Import this package into a program that calculates and displays the total weight of the following: 200 carpets—size: 4 meters by 2 meters 9 centimeters, that weigh 1.25 kilograms per square meter; and 60 carpets—size: 3 meters 57 centimeters by 5 meters, that weigh 1.05 kilograms per square meter.

CONFER PROGRAMMER TO PROGRAMMER ABOUT THIS TOPIC.

Visit p2p.wrox.com

▶ WHAT YOU LEARNED IN THIS CHAPTER

TOPIC	CONCEPT
Class Definitions	A class definition specifies the variables and methods that are members of the class.
Class Files	Each class must be saved in a file with the same name as the class, and with the extension `.java`.
Class Variables	Class variables are declared using the keyword `static`, and one instance of each class variable is shared among all objects of a class.
Instance Variables	Each object of a class has its own instance variables—these are variables declared in the class without using the keyword `static`.
Static Methods	Methods that are specified as `static` can be called even if no class objects exist, but a `static` method cannot refer to instance variables.
Non-Static Methods	Methods that are not specified as `static` can access any of the variables in the class directly.
Recursive Methods	Recursive methods are methods that call themselves.
Class Member Access	Access to members of a class is determined by the access attributes that are specified for each of them. These can be `public`, `private`, `protected`, or nothing at all.
Packages	Classes can be grouped into a package. If a class in a package is to be accessible from outside the package, the class must be declared using the keyword `public`.
Package Members	To designate that a class is a member of a package, you use a `package` statement at the beginning of the file containing the class definition.
Using a Package Member	To add classes from a package to a file, you use an `import` statement immediately following any package statement in the file.
Nested Classes	A nested class is a class that is defined within the definition of another class. Objects of a nested class type can be created only in the context of an object of the outer class type.
Creating Static Nested Class Objects	Objects of a static nested class type can be created independently, but the static nested class name must be qualified by the outer class name.

Extending Classes and Inheritance

➤ How to reuse classes by defining a new class based on an existing class

➤ What polymorphism is and how to define your classes to take advantage of it

➤ What an abstract method is

➤ What an abstract class is

➤ What an interface is and how you can define your own interfaces

➤ How to use interfaces in your classes

➤ How interfaces can help you implement polymorphic classes

A very important part of object-oriented programming enables you to create a new class based on a class that has already been defined. The class that you use as the base for your new class can be one that you have defined, a standard class in Java, or a class defined by someone else—perhaps from a package supporting a specialized application area.

This chapter focuses on how you can reuse existing classes by creating new classes based on the ones you have and explores the ramifications of using this facility, and the additional capabilities it provides. You also delve into an important related topic—*interfaces*—and how you can use them.

USING EXISTING CLASSES

Let's start by understanding the jargon. Defining a new class based on an existing class is called *derivation*. The new class, or *derived class*, is referred to as a *direct subclass* of the class from which it is derived. The original class is called a *base class* because it forms the base for the definition of the derived class. The original class is also referred to as a *superclass* of the derived class. You can also derive a new class from a derived class, which in turn was derived from some other derived class, and so on. This is illustrated in Figure 6-1.

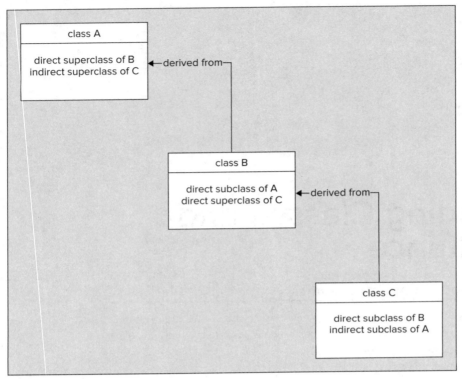

FIGURE 6-1

This shows just three classes in a hierarchy, but there can be as many as you like.

Let's consider a more concrete example. You could define a class Dog that could represent a dog of any kind:

```
class Dog {
  // Members of the Dog class...
}
```

This might contain a data member identifying the name of a particular dog, such as *Lassie* or *Poochy*, and another data member to identify the breed, such as *Border Collie* or *Pyrenean Mountain Dog*. From the Dog class, you could derive a Spaniel class that represented dogs that were spaniels:

```
class Spaniel extends Dog {
  // Members of the Spaniel class...
}
```

The extends keyword that you use here identifies that Dog is a base class for Spaniel, so an object of type Spaniel has members that are inherited from the Dog class, in addition to the members of the Spaniel class that appear in its definition. The breed is *Spaniel* for all instances of the class Spaniel, although in general the name for each spaniel may be different. The Spaniel class might have some additional data members that characterize the specifics of what it means to be a spaniel. You see in a moment how you can arrange for the base class data members to be set appropriately.

A Spaniel object is a specialized instance of a Dog object. This reflects real life. A spaniel is obviously a dog and has all the properties of a basic dog, but it has some unique characteristics of its own that distinguish it from all the dogs that are not spaniels. The inheritance mechanism that adds all the properties of the base class—Dog in this instance—to those in the derived class is a good model for the real world. The members of the derived class define the properties that differentiate it from the base type, so when you derive one class from another, you can think of your derived class as a specification for objects that are specializations of the base class object. Another way of thinking about this is that the base class defines a set of objects and a derived class defines a specific subset of those that have particular defining characteristics.

CLASS INHERITANCE

In summary, when you derive a new class from a base class, the process is additive in terms of what makes up a class definition. The additional members that you define in the new class establish what makes a derived class object different from a base class object. Any members that you define in the new class are in addition to those that are already members of the base class. For your `Spaniel` class that you derived from `Dog`, the data members to hold the name and the breed that are defined for the class `Dog` are automatically in the class `Spaniel`. A `Spaniel` object always has a complete `Dog` object inside it—with all its data members and methods. This does not mean that all the members defined in the `Dog` class are available to methods that are specific to the `Spaniel` class. Some are and some aren't. The inclusion of members of a base class in a derived class so that they are accessible in that derived class is called *class inheritance*. An *inherited member* of a base class is one that is *accessible* within the derived class. If a base class member is not accessible in a derived class, then it is not an inherited member of the derived class, but base class members that are not inherited still form part of a derived class object.

An inherited member of a derived class is a full member of that class and is freely accessible to any method in the class. Objects of the derived class type contain all the inherited members of the base class—both fields and methods, as well as the members that are specific to the derived class. Remember that a derived class object always contains a complete base class object within it, including all the fields and methods that are not inherited. The next step is to take a closer look at how inheritance works and how the access attribute of a base class member affects its visibility in a derived class.

You need to consider several aspects of defining and using a derived class. First of all, you need to know which members of the base class are inherited in the derived class. I explain what this implies for data members and methods separately—there are some subtleties here you need to be quite clear on. I also look at what happens when you create an object of the derived class. There are some wrinkles in this context that require closer consideration. Let's start by looking at the data members that are inherited from a base class.

Inheriting Data Members

Figure 6-2 shows which access attributes permit a class member to be inherited in a subclass. It shows what happens when the subclass is defined in either the same package or a different package from that containing the base class. Remember that inheritance implies accessibility of the member in a derived class, not just presence.

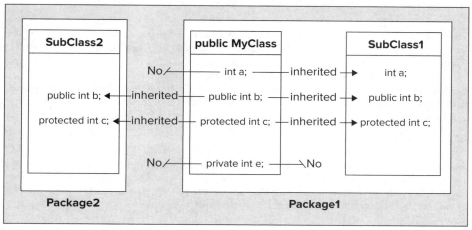

FIGURE 6-2

NOTE *Remember that a class itself can be specified as* public. *This makes the class accessible from any package anywhere. A class that is not declared as* public *can be accessed only from classes within the same package. This means, for example, that you cannot define objects of a non-*public *class type within classes in other packages. It also means that to derive a new class from a class in a different package, the base class must be declared as* public. *If the base class is not declared as* public, *it cannot be reached directly from outside the package.*

As you can see from Figure 6-2, a subclass that you define in the same package as its base class inherits everything except for private data members of the base. If you define a subclass outside the package containing the base class, the private data members are not inherited, and neither are any data members in the base class that you have declared without access attributes. Members defined as private in the base class are never inherited under any circumstances. The base class, MyClass, must be declared as public in Package1, otherwise it would not be accessible from Package2 as the base class for SubClass2.

You should also be able to see where the explicit access specifiers now sit in relation to one another. The public specifier is the least restrictive on class members because a public member is available everywhere, protected comes next, and prevents access from classes outside of a package, but does not limit inheritance—provided the class itself is public. Putting no access specifier on a class member limits access to classes within the same package and prevents inheritance in subclasses that are defined in a different package. Because of this, class members without an access specifier are often referred to as *package-private*. The most restrictive is private because access is constrained to the same class.

The inheritance rules apply to members of a class that you have declared as static—as well as non-static members. Recall that only one occurrence of each static variable in a class exists and is shared by all objects of the class, whereas each object has its own set of instance variables. So, for example, a variable that you declare as private and static in the base class is not inherited in a derived class, whereas a variable that you declare as protected and static are inherited and are shared between all objects of a derived class type, as well as objects of the base class type.

Hidden Data Members

You can define a data member in a derived class with the same name as a data member in the base class. This is not a recommended approach to class design generally, but it's possible that it can arise unintentionally. When it occurs, the base class data member may still be inherited, but are hidden by the derived class member with the same name. The hiding mechanism applies regardless of whether the respective types or access attributes are the same or not—the base class member is hidden in the derived class if the names are the same.

Any use of the derived class member name always refers to the member defined as part of the derived class. To refer to the inherited base class member, you must qualify it with the keyword super to indicate it is the member of the superclass that you want. Suppose you have a data member value as a member of the base class, and a data member with the same name in the derived class. In the derived class, the name value references the derived class member, and the name super.value refers to the member inherited from the base class. Note that you cannot use super.super.something to refer to a member name hidden in the base class of a base class.

In most situations you won't need to refer to inherited data members in this way, as you would not deliberately set out to use duplicate names. The situation can commonly arise if you are using a class as a base that is subsequently modified by adding data members—it could be a Java library class, for example, or some other class in a package designed and maintained by someone else. Because your code does not presume the existence of the base class member with the same name as your derived class data member, hiding the inherited member is precisely what you want. It enables the base class to be altered without breaking your code.

Inherited Methods

Ordinary methods in a base class, by which I mean methods that are not constructors, are inherited in a derived class in the same way as the data members of the base class. Those methods declared as `private` in a base class are not inherited, and those that you declare without an access attribute are inherited only if you define the derived class in the same package as the base class. The rest are all inherited.

Constructors are different from ordinary methods. Constructors in the base class are never inherited, regardless of their attributes. You can look into the intricacies of constructors in a class hierarchy by considering how derived class objects are created.

Objects of a Derived Class

I said at the beginning of this chapter that a derived class extends a base class. This is not just jargon—it really does do this. As I have said several times, inheritance is about what members of the base class are *accessible* in a derived class, not what members of the base class *exist* in a derived class object. An object of a subclass contains *all* the members of the original base class, plus any new members that you have defined in the derived class. This is illustrated in Figure 6-3.

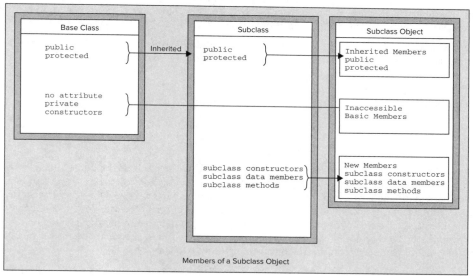

FIGURE 6-3

The base members are all there in a derived class object—you just can't access some of them in the methods that you have defined for the derived class. The fact that you can't access some of the base class members does not mean that they are just excess baggage—they are essential members of your derived class objects. A `Spaniel` object needs all the `Dog` attributes that make it a `Dog` object, even though some of these may not be accessible to the `Spaniel` methods. Of course, the base class methods that are inherited in a derived class can access all the base class members, including those that are not inherited.

Though the base class constructors are not inherited in your derived class, you can still call them to initialize the base class members. More than that, if you don't call a base class constructor from your derived class constructor, the compiler tries to arrange to do it for you. The reasoning behind this is that because a derived class object has a base class object inside it, a good way to initialize the base part of a derived class object is using a base class constructor.

To understand this better, let's take a look at how it works in practice.

Deriving a Class

Let's take a simple example. Suppose you have defined a class to represent an animal as follows:

```
public class Animal {
  public Animal(String aType) {
    type = new String(aType);
  }

  public String toString() {
    return "This is a " + type;
  }

  private String type;
}
```

Directory "TestDerived"

This has a member, `type`, to identify the type of animal, and its value is set by the constructor. It is `private` and is therefore not inherited in a class derived from `Animal`. You also have a `toString()` method for the class to generate a string representation of an object of the class.

You can now define another class, based on the class `Animal`, to define dogs. You can do this immediately, without affecting the definition of the class `Animal`. You could write the basic definition of the class `Dog` as:

```
public class Dog extends Animal {
  // constructors for a Dog object

  protected String name;              // Name of a Dog
  protected String breed;             // Dog breed
}
```

You use the keyword `extends` in the definition of a subclass to identify the name of the direct superclass. The class `Dog` inherits only the method `toString()` from the class `Animal`, because the `private` data member and the constructor cannot be inherited. Of course, a `Dog` object has a `type` data member that needs to be set to `"Dog"`; it just can't be accessed by methods that you define in the `Dog` class. You have added two new instance variables in the derived class. The `name` member holds the name of the particular dog, and the `breed` member records the kind of dog it is. These are both `protected` and therefore are accessible in any class derived from `Dog`. All you need to add is the means of creating `Dog` class objects.

Derived Class Constructors

You can define two constructors for the subclass `Dog`, one that just accepts an argument for the name of a dog and another that accepts both a name and the breed of the `Dog` object. For any derived class object, you need to make sure that the `private` base class member, `type`, is properly initialized. You do this by calling a base class constructor from the derived class constructor:

```
public class Dog extends Animal {
  public Dog(String aName) {
    super("Dog");                     // Call the base constructor
    name = aName;                     // Supplied name
    breed = "Unknown";                // Default breed value
  }

  public Dog(String aName, String aBreed) {
    super("Dog");                     // Call the base constructor
    name = aName;                     // Supplied name
```

```
      breed = aBreed;                            // Supplied breed
   }

   protected String name;                        // Name of a Dog
   protected String breed;                       // Dog breed
 }
```

Directory "TestDerived"

The statement in the derived class constructors that calls the base class constructor is

```
super("Dog");                                    // Call the base constructor
```

The use of the `super` keyword here as the method name calls the constructor in the superclass—the direct base class of the class `Dog`, which is the class `Animal`. This initializes the `private` member `type` to `"Dog"` because this is the argument passed to the base constructor. The superclass constructor is always called in this way in the subclass, using the name `super` rather than the base class constructor name `Animal`. The `super` keyword has other uses in a derived class. You have already seen that you can access a hidden member of the base class by qualifying the member name with `super`.

Calling the Base Class Constructor

You should always call an appropriate base class constructor from the constructors in your derived class. The base class constructor call must be the first statement in the body of the derived class constructor. If the first statement in a derived class constructor is not a call to a base class constructor, the compiler inserts a call to the default no-arg base class constructor for you:

```
super();                                 // Call the default base constructor
```

Unfortunately, this can result in a compiler error, even though the offending statement was inserted automatically. How does this come about?

When you define your own constructor in a class, as is the case for the `Animal` class, no default constructor is created by the compiler. It assumes you are taking care of all the details of object construction, including any requirement for a default constructor. If you have not defined your own default constructor in a base class—that is, a constructor that has no parameters—when the compiler inserts a call to the default constructor from your derived class constructor, you get a message saying that the constructor is not there.

TRY IT OUT   Testing a Derived Class

You can try out the `Dog` class with the following code:

Available for download on Wrox.com

```
public class TestDerived {
   public static void main(String[] args) {
      Dog aDog = new Dog("Fido", "Chihuahua");    // Create a dog
      Dog starDog = new Dog("Lassie");            // Create a Hollywood dog
      System.out.println(aDog);                   // Let's hear about it
      System.out.println(starDog);                // and the star
   }
}
```

Directory "TestDerived"

Of course, the files containing the `Dog` and `Animal` class definitions must be in the same directory as `TestDerived.java`. I put them all in a folder with the name `TestDerived`. The example produces the following rather uninformative output:

```
This is a Dog
This is a Dog
```

How It Works

Here you create two Dog objects and then output information about them using the println() method. This implicitly calls the toString() method for each. You could try commenting out the call to super() in the constructors of the derived class to see the effect of the compiler's efforts to call the default base class constructor.

You have called the inherited method toString() successfully, but this knows only about the base class data members. At least you know that the private member, type, is being set up properly. What you really need though is a version of toString() for the derived class.

Overriding a Base Class Method

You can define a method in a derived class that has the same signature as a method in the base class. Having the same signature means that the method names must be the same and the parameter lists must contain the same number of parameters with identical types. The access attribute for the method in the derived class can be the same as that in the base class or it can be less restrictive, but it cannot be more restrictive. This means that if you declare a method as public in the base class, for example, any derived class definition of the method must also be declared as public. You cannot omit the access attribute in the derived class in this case, or specify it as private or protected.

When you define a new version of a base class method in this way, the derived class method is called for a derived class object, not the method inherited from the base class. The method in the derived class *overrides* the method in the base class. The base class method is still there though, and it is still possible to call it in a derived class. Let's see an overriding method in a derived class in action.

TRY IT OUT   Overriding a Base Class Method

You can add the definition of a new version of toString() to the definition of the derived class, Dog:

```
// Present a dog's details as a string
public String toString() {
  return "It's " + name + " the " + breed;
}
```

With this change to the example, the output is now:

```
It's Fido the Chihuahua
It's Lassie the Unknown
```

How It Works

The toString() method in the Dog class overrides the base class method because it has the same signature. Recall from Chapter 5 that the signature of a method is determined by its name and the parameter list. So, now whenever you use the toString() method for a Dog object either explicitly or implicitly, this method is called—not the base class method.

 NOTE *You are obliged to declare the* toString() *method as* public. *When you override a base class method, you cannot change the access attributes of the new version of the method to be more stringent than that of the base class method that it overrides. Because* public *is the least stringent access attribute, you have no other choice.*

Of course, ideally you would like to output the member, type, of the base class, but you can't reference this in the derived class because it is not inherited. However, you can still call the base class version of toString(). It's another job for the super keyword.

TRY IT OUT Calling a Base Class Method from a Derived Class

You can rewrite the derived class version of `toString()` to call the base method:

```
// Present a dog's details as a string
public String toString() {
  return super.toString() + "\nIt's " + name + " the " + breed;
}
```

Directory "TestDerived"

Running the example again produces the following output:

```
This is a Dog
It's Fido the Chihuahua
This is a Dog
It's Lassie the Unknown
```

How It Works

You use the `super` keyword to identify the base class version of `toString()` that is hidden by the derived class version. You used the same notation to refer to superclass data members that were hidden by derived class data members with the same name. Calling the base class version of `toString()` returns the `String` object for the base part of the object. You then append extra information to this about the derived part of the object to produce a `String` object specific to the derived class.

THE @Override ANNOTATION

When you define a method in a derived class that is intended to override a superclass method, it is easy to make a mistake in the signature for the derived class method. If the name and parameter list of your derived class method are not identical to that of the superclass method, you are defining an *overload* for the base class method, not an *override*.

The `@Override` annotation is intended to protect you from this kind of error. Here's how you could use the `@Override` annotation in the `Dog` class:

```
public class Dog extends Animal {
  public Dog(String aName) {
    super("Dog");                         // Call the base constructor
    name = aName;                         // Supplied name
    breed = "Unknown";                    // Default breed value
  }

  public Dog(String aName, String aBreed) {
    super("Dog");                         // Call the base constructor
    name = aName;                         // Supplied name
    breed = aBreed;                       // Supplied breed
  }

  // Present a dog's details as a string
  @Override
  public String toString() {
    return super.toString() + "\nIt's " + name + " the " + breed;
  }

  protected String name;                  // Name of a Dog
  protected String breed;                 // Dog breed
}
```

Obviously you are unlikely to make an error in the parameter list for the `toString()` method that is inherited from the `Object` class. However, you might spell the name as `ToString()`, in which case you do not have an override for `toString()`; you have just added a new method.

Any method you mark with the `@Override` annotation causes the compiler to verify that the signature of the method is the same as a method with the same name in a superclass. If it is not, you get an error message. It is therefore a good idea to use the `@Override` annotation for all your methods that override an inherited method.

CHOOSING BASE CLASS ACCESS ATTRIBUTES

You now know the options available to you in defining the access attributes for classes you expect to use to define subclasses. You know what effect the attributes have on class inheritance, but how do you decide which you should use?

There are no hard and fast rules—what you choose depends on what you want to do with your classes in the future, but there are some guidelines you should consider. They follow from basic object-oriented principles:

➤ You should declare the methods that make up the external interface to a class as `public`. As long as there are no overriding methods defined in a derived class, public base class methods are inherited and fully available as part of the external interface to the derived class. You should not normally make data members public unless they are constants intended for general use.

➤ If you expect other people will use your classes as base classes, your classes will be more secure if you keep data members `private`, and provide `public` methods for accessing and manipulating them when necessary. In this way you control how a derived class object can affect the base class data members.

➤ Making base class members `protected` allows them to be accessed from other classes in the same package, but prevents direct access from a class in another package. Base class members that are `protected` are inherited in a subclass and can, therefore, be used in the implementation of a derived class. You can use the `protected` option when you have a package of classes in which you want uninhibited access to the data members of any class within the same package—because they operate in a closely coupled way, for instance—but you want free access to be limited to subclasses in other packages.

➤ Omitting the access attribute for a class member makes it directly available to other classes in the same package while preventing it from being inherited in a subclass that is not in the same package—it is effectively `private` when viewed from another package.

POLYMORPHISM

Class inheritance is not just about reusing classes that you have already defined as a basis for defining a new class. It also adds enormous flexibility to the way in which you can program your applications, with a mechanism called *polymorphism*. So what is polymorphism?

The word *polymorphism* generally means the ability to assume several different forms or shapes. In programming terms it means the ability of a single variable of a given type to be used to reference objects of different types and to automatically call the method that is specific to the type of object the variable references. This enables a single method call to behave differently, depending on the type of the object to which the call applies. This is illustrated in Figure 6-4.

CONFER PROGRAMMER TO PROGRAMMER ABOUT THIS TOPIC.

Visit p2p.wrox.com

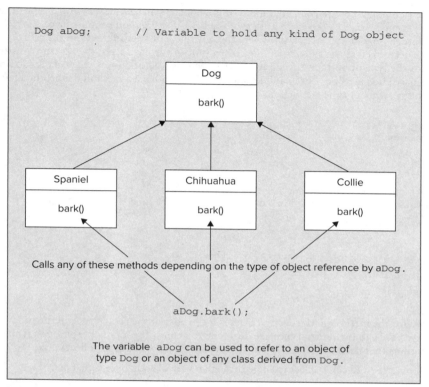

FIGURE 6-4

A few requirements must be fulfilled to get polymorphic behavior, so let's step through them.

First of all, polymorphism works with derived class objects. It also depends on a new capability that is possible within a class hierarchy that you haven't met before. Up to now you have always been using a variable of a given type to reference objects of the same type. Derived classes introduce some new flexibility in this. Of course, you can store a reference to a derived class object in a variable of the derived class type, but you can also store it in a variable of any direct or indirect base class type. More than that, a reference to a derived class object *must* be stored in a variable of a direct or indirect class type for polymorphism to work. For example, Figure 6-4 illustrates how a variable of type Dog can be used to store a reference to an object of any type derived from Dog. If the Dog class were derived from the Animal class here, a variable of type Animal could also be used to reference Spaniel, Chihuahua, or Collie objects.

Polymorphism means that the actual type of the object involved in a method call determines which method is called, rather than the type of the variable being used to store the reference to the object. In Figure 6-4, if aDog contains a reference to a Spaniel object, the bark() method for that object is called. If it contains a reference to a Collie object, the bark() method in the Collie class is called. To get polymorphic operation when calling a method, the method must be declared as a member of the base class—the class type of the variable you are using—as well as being declared as a member of the class type of the object involved. So in the example, the Dog class must contain a bark() method, as must each of the derived classes. You cannot call a method for a derived class object using a variable of a base class type if the method is not a member of the base class. Any definition of the method in a derived class must have the same signature as in the base class and must have an access specifier that is no more restrictive.

Methods that have the same signature have the same name, and have parameter lists with the same number of parameters and corresponding parameters are of the same type. You have a bit more flexibility with the return type when you are defining a polymorphic method. For polymorphic behavior, the return type of the method in the derived class must either be the same as that of the base class method or must be of a type that is a subclass of the return type in the base class. Where the return types are different but the return type of the method in the derived class is a subclass of the return type in the base class, the return types are said to be *covariant*. Thus the type of object returned by the derived class method is just a specialization of the type returned by the base class method. For example, suppose that you have a method defined in a base class `Animal` that has a return type of type `Animal`:

```
public class Animal {
  Animal createCreature() {
    // Code to create an Animal object and return a reference to it...
  }

  // Rest of the class definition ...
}
```

You can redefine the `createCreature()` method in a derived class `Dog` like this:

```
public class Dog extends Animal {
  @Override
  Dog createCreature() {
    // Code to create a Dog object and return a reference to it...
  }

  // Rest of the class definition...
}
```

As long as the return type for the method in the derived class is a subclass of the return type in the base class, as you have here, even though the return types are different you can still get polymorphic behavior. I can summarize the conditions that need to be met if you want to use polymorphism as follows:

➤ The method call for a derived class object must be through a variable of a base class type.

➤ The method called must be defined in the derived class.

➤ The method called must also be declared as a member of the base class.

➤ The method signatures for the method in the base and derived classes must be the same.

➤ Either the method return type must be the same in the base and derived classes or the return types must be covariant.

➤ The method access specifier must be no more restrictive in the derived class than in the base.

When you call a method using a variable of a base class type, polymorphism results in the method that is called being selected based on the type of the object stored, not the type of the variable. Because a variable of a base type can store a reference to an object of any derived type, the kind of object stored is not known until the program executes. Thus the choice of which method to execute has to be made dynamically when the program is running—it cannot be determined when the program is compiled. The `bark()` method that is called through the variable of type `Dog` in the earlier illustration may do different things depending on what kind of object the variable references. As you later see, this introduces a whole new level of capability in programming using objects. It implies that your programs can adapt at run time to accommodate and process different kinds of data quite automatically.

Note that polymorphism applies only to methods. It does not apply to data members. When you access a data member of a class object, the variable type always determines the class to which the data member belongs. This implies that a variable of type `Dog` can only be used to access data members of the `Dog` class. Even when it references an object of a derived type, `Spaniel`, for example, you can only use it to access data members of the `Dog` part of a `Spaniel` object.

Using Polymorphism

As you have seen, polymorphism relies on the fact that you can assign an object of a subclass type to a variable that you have declared as being of a superclass type. Suppose you declare the variable:

```
Animal theAnimal = null;              // Declare a variable of type Animal
```

You can quite happily make `theAnimal` refer to an object of any of the subclasses of the class `Animal`. For example, you could use it to reference an object of type `Dog`:

```
theAnimal = new Dog("Rover");
```

As you might expect, you could also initialize the variable `theAnimal` to reference an object when you declare it:

```
Animal theAnimal = new Dog("Rover");
```

This principle applies quite generally. You can use a variable of a base class type to store a reference to an object of any class type that you have derived, directly or indirectly, from the base. You can see what magic can be wrought with this in practice by extending the previous example. You can add a new method to the class `Dog` that displays the sound a `Dog` makes. You can add a couple of new subclasses that represent some other kinds of animals.

TRY IT OUT   Listening to the Animals

This example provides animals with a voice via a `sound()` method. I put the source files in a folder with the name `AnimalVoices`. You need to make one change to the class `Animal`. To select the method `sound()` dynamically for derived class objects, it needs to be a member of the base class. Add a content-free version of a method `sound()` to the `Animal` class:

Available for
download on
Wrox.com

```
class Animal {
   // Rest of the class as before...

   // Dummy method to be implemented in the derived classes
   public void sound(){}
}
```

Directory "AnimalVoices"

Only a particular `Animal` object makes a specific sound, so the `sound()` method in this class does nothing.

First of all, you enhance the class `Dog` by adding a method to display the sound that a dog makes:

Available for
download on
Wrox.com

```
public class Dog extends Animal {
   // A barking method
   @Override
   public void sound() {
     System.out.println("Woof     Woof");
   }

   // Rest of the class as before...
}
```

Directory "AnimalVoices"

You can also derive a class `Cat` from the class `Animal`:

Available for
download on
Wrox.com

```
public class Cat extends Animal {
  public Cat(String aName) {
    super("Cat");                    // Call the base constructor
    name = aName;                    // Supplied name
    breed = "Unknown";               // Default breed value
  }

  public Cat(String aName, String aBreed) {
    super("Cat");                    // Call the base constructor
    name = aName;                    // Supplied name
    breed = aBreed;                  // Supplied breed
  }

  // Return a String full of a cat's details
```

```
@Override public String toString() {
  return super.toString() + "\nIt's " + name + " the " + breed;
}

// A miaowing method
@Override
public void sound() {
  System.out.println("Miiaooww");
}

protected String name;                  // Name of a cat
protected String breed;                 // Cat breed
}
```

Just to make it a crowd, you can derive another class—of ducks:

```
public class Duck extends Animal {
  public Duck(String aName) {
    super("Duck");                      // Call the base constructor
    name = aName;                       // Supplied name
    breed = "Unknown";                  // Default breed value
  }

  public Duck(String aName, String aBreed) {
    super("Duck");                      // Call the base constructor
    name = aName;                       // Supplied name
    breed = aBreed;                     // Supplied breed
  }

  // Return a String full of a duck's details
  @Override
  public String toString() {
    return super.toString() + "\nIt's " + name + " the " + breed;
  }

  // A quacking method
  @Override
  public void sound() {
    System.out.println("Quack quackquack");
  }

  protected String name;                // Duck name
  protected String breed;               // Duck breed
}
```

The data members of both classes are protected, so they are accessible in any derived class, but not from any class that is not in the same package.

You can fill the whole farmyard, if you need the practice, but three kinds of animal are sufficient to show you how polymorphism works.

You need a program that uses these classes. To give the classes a workout, you can create an array of type `Animal` and populate its elements with different subclass objects. You can then select an object randomly from the array, so that there is no possibility that the type of the object selected is known ahead of time. Here's the code to do that:

```
import java.util.Random;

public class TryPolymorphism {
  public static void main(String[] args) {
    // Create an array of three different animals
    Animal[] theAnimals = {
```

```
                        new Dog("Rover", "Poodle"),
                        new Cat("Max", "Abyssinian"),
                        new Duck("Daffy","Aylesbury")
                     };

      Animal petChoice;                    // Choice of pet

      Random select = new Random();        // Random number generator
      // Make five random choices of pet
      for(int i = 0; i < 5; ++i) {
        // Choose a random animal as a pet
        petChoice = theAnimals[select.nextInt(theAnimals.length)];

        System.out.println("\nYour choice:\n" + petChoice);
        petChoice.sound();                 // Get the pet's reaction
      }
    }
  }
```

Directory "AnimalVoices"

When I ran this I got the following output:

```
Your choice:
This is a Duck
It's Daffy the Aylesbury
Quack quackquack
Your choice:
This is a Cat
It's Max the Abyssinian
Miiaooww

Your choice:
This is a Duck
It's Daffy the Aylesbury
Quack quackquack
Your choice:
This is a Duck
It's Daffy the Aylesbury
Quack quackquack

Your choice:
This is a Cat
It's Max the Abyssinian
Miiaooww
```

The chances are good that you will get a different set than this, and a different set again when you rerun the example. The output from the example clearly shows that the methods are being selected at run time, depending on which object happens to get stored in the variable petChoice.

How It Works

The definition of the sound() method in the Animal class has no statements in the body, so it does nothing if it is executed. You see a little later in this chapter how you can avoid including the empty definition for the method but still get polymorphic behavior in the derived classes.

You need the import statement because you use a Random class object in the example to produce pseudo-random index values in the way you have seen before. The array theAnimals of type Animal contains a Dog object, a Cat object, and a Duck object. You select objects randomly from this array in the for loop using the Random object select, and store the selection in petChoice. You then call the toString() and sound() methods using the object reference stored. The effect is that the appropriate method is selected automatically to suit the object stored, so the program operates differently depending on what type of object is referenced by petChoice.

Of course, you call the `toString()` method implicitly in the argument to `println()`. The compiler inserts a call to this method to produce a `String` representation of the object referenced by `petChoice`. The particular `toString()` method is automatically selected to correspond with the type of object referenced by `petChoice`. This would still work even if you had not included the `toString()` method in the base class. You see a little later in this chapter that there is a `toString()` method in every class that you define, regardless of whether you define one or not.

Polymorphism is a fundamental part of object-oriented programming. You make extensive use of polymorphism in many of the examples you develop later in the book, and you will find that you use it often in your own applications and applets. But this is not all there is to polymorphism in Java, and I will come back to it again later in this chapter.

MULTIPLE LEVELS OF INHERITANCE

As I indicated at the beginning of the chapter, there is nothing to prevent a derived class from being used as a base class. For example, you could derive a class `Spaniel` from the class `Dog` without any problem:

TRY IT OUT **A Spaniel Class**

Start the `Spaniel` class off with this minimal code:

Available for download on Wrox.com

```
class Spaniel extends Dog {
    public Spaniel(String aName) {
        super(aName, "Spaniel");
    }
}
```

Directory "AnimalVoices"

To try this out you can add a `Spaniel` object to the array `theAnimals` in the previous example, by changing the statement to the following:

Available for download on Wrox.com

```
Animal[] theAnimals = {
                        new Dog("Rover", "Poodle"),
                        new Cat("Max", "Abyssinian"),
                        new Duck("Daffy","Aylesbury"),
                        new Spaniel("Fido")
                      };
```

Directory "AnimalVoices"

Don't forget to add in the comma after the `Duck` object. Try running the example again a few times.

How It Works

The class `Spaniel` inherits members from the class `Dog`, including the members of `Dog` that are inherited from the class `Animal`. The class `Dog` is a direct superclass, and the class `Animal` is an indirect superclass of the class `Spaniel`. The only additional member of `Spaniel` is the constructor. This calls the `Dog` class constructor using the keyword `super` and passes the value of `aName` and the `String` object `"Spaniel"` to it.

If you run the `TryPolymorphism` class a few times, you should get a choice of the `Spaniel` object from time to time. Thus, the class `Spaniel` is also participating in the polymorphic selection of the methods `toString()` and `sound()`, which in this case are inherited from the parent class, `Dog`. The inherited `toString()` method works perfectly well with the `Spaniel` object, but if you wanted to provide a unique version, you could add it to the `Spaniel` class definition. This would then be automatically selected for a `Spaniel` object rather than the method inherited from the `Dog` class.

ABSTRACT CLASSES

In the `Animal` class, you introduced a version of the `sound()` method that did nothing because you wanted to call the `sound()` method in the subclass objects dynamically. The method `sound()` has no meaning in the context of the generic class `Animal`, so implementing it does not make much sense. This situation often arises in object-oriented programming. You will often find yourself creating a superclass from which you will derive a number of subclasses, just to take advantage of polymorphism.

To cater to this, Java has *abstract classes*. An abstract class is a class in which one or more methods are declared, but not defined. The bodies of these methods are omitted, because, as in the case of the method `sound()` in the `Animal` class, implementing the methods does not make sense. Because they have no definition and cannot be executed, they are called *abstract methods*. The declaration for an abstract method ends with a semicolon and you specify the method with the keyword `abstract` to identify it as such. To declare that a class is abstract you just use the keyword `abstract` in front of the `class` keyword in the first line of the class definition.

You could have defined the class `Animal` as an abstract class by amending it as follows:

```
public abstract class Animal {
  public abstract void sound();    // Abstract method

  public Animal(String aType) {
    type = new String(aType);
  }

  public String toString() {
    return "This is a " + type;
  }

  private String type;
}
```

The previous program works just as well with these changes. It doesn't matter whether you prefix the class name with `public abstract` or `abstract public`; they are equivalent, but you should be consistent in your usage. The sequence `public abstract` is typically preferred. The same goes for the declaration of an abstract method, but both `public` and `abstract` must precede the return type specification, which is `void` in this case.

An abstract method cannot be `private` because a `private` method cannot be inherited and therefore cannot be redefined in a subclass.

You cannot instantiate an object of an abstract class, but you can declare a variable of an abstract class type. With the new abstract version of the class `Animal`, you can still write:

```
Animal thePet = null;                  // Declare a variable of type Animal
```

just as you did in the `TryPolymorphism` class. You can then use this variable to store objects of the subclasses, `Dog`, `Spaniel`, `Duck`, and `Cat`.

When you derive a class from an abstract base class, you don't have to define all the abstract methods in the subclass. In this case the subclass is also abstract and you aren't able to instantiate any objects of the subclass either. If a class is abstract, you must use the `abstract` keyword when you define it, even if it only inherits an abstract method from its superclass. Sooner or later you must have a subclass that contains no abstract methods. You can then create objects of this class type.

THE UNIVERSAL SUPERCLASS

I must now reveal something I have been keeping from you. *All* the classes that you define are subclasses by default—whether you like it or not. All your classes have a standard class, `Object`, as a base, so `Object` is a superclass of every class. You never need to specify the class `Object` as a base in the definition of your classes—it happens automatically.

There are some interesting consequences of having `Object` as a universal superclass. For one thing, a variable of type `Object` can store a reference to an object of any class type. This is useful when you want to write a method that needs to handle objects of unknown type. You can define a parameter to the method of type `Object`, in which case a reference to any type of object can be passed to the method. When necessary you can include code in the method to figure out what kind of object it actually is (you see some of the tools that enable you to do this a little later in this chapter).

Of course, your classes inherit members from the class `Object`. These all happen to be methods, of which seven are `public`, and two are `protected`. The seven `public` methods are shown in Table 6-1.

TABLE 6-1: Object Class Methods

METHOD	PURPOSE
`toString()`	This method returns a `String` object that describes the current object. In the inherited version of the method, this is the name of the class, followed by `'@'` and the hexadecimal representation for the object. This method is called automatically when you concatenate objects with `String` variables using +. You can override this method in your classes to create your own string for an object of your class.
`equals()`	This compares the reference to the object passed as an argument with the reference to the current object and returns `true` if they are equal. Thus `true` is returned if the current object and the argument are the same object (not just equal—they must be one and the same object). It returns `false` if they are different objects, even if the objects have identical values for their data members.
`getClass()`	This method returns an object of type `Class` that identifies the class of the current object. You learn a little more about this later in this chapter.
`hashCode()`	This method calculates a hashcode value for an object and returns it as type `int`. Hashcode values are used in classes defined in the package `java.util` for storing objects in hash tables. You see more about this in Chapter 14.
`notify()`	This is used to wake up a thread associated with the current object. I discuss how threads work in Chapter 16.
`notifyAll()`	This is used to wake up all threads associated with the current object. I also discuss this in Chapter 16.
`wait()`	This method causes a thread to wait for a change in the current object. I discuss this method in Chapter 16, too.

Note that `getClass()`, `notify()`, `notifyAll()`, and `wait()` cannot be overridden in your own class definitions—they are *fixed* with the keyword `final` in the class definition for `Object` (see the section on the `final` modifier later in this chapter).

It should be clear now why you could get polymorphic behavior with `toString()` in your derived classes when your base class did not define the method. There is always a `toString()` method in all your classes that is inherited from `Object`. This means that, ideally, we should have used the `@Override` annotation with this method in the `Animal` class, or indeed any class that implements `toString()`.

The two `protected` methods that your classes inherit from `Object` are shown in Table 6-2.

TABLE 6-2: Protected Object Class Methods

METHOD	PURPOSE
`clone()`	This method creates an object that is a copy of the current object regardless of type. It can be of any type, as an `Object` variable can refer to an object of any class. Note that `clone()` does not work with all class objects and does not always do precisely what you want, as you see later in this section.
`finalize()`	This method may be called to clean up when an object is destroyed. There is rarely any reason to override this method.

Because all your classes inherit the methods defined in the `Object` class I explain the most important ones in a little more detail.

The toString() Method

You have already made extensive use of the `toString()` method, and you know that it is used by the compiler to obtain a `String` representation of an object when necessary. It is obvious now why you must always declare the `toString()` method as `public` in a class. It is declared as such in the `Object` class and you can't declare it as anything else.

You can see what the `toString()` method that is inherited from the `Object` class outputs for an object of one of your classes by commenting out the `toString()` method in `Animal` class in the previous example. A typical sample of the output for an object is:

```
Your choice:
Spaniel@b75778b2
It's Fido the Spaniel
Woof    Woof
```

The second line here is generated by the `toString()` method implemented in the `Object` class. This is inherited in the `Animal` class, and it is called because you no longer override it. The hexadecimal digits following the @ in the output are the hashcode of the object, which is produced by the `hashcode()` method that is inherited from `Object`.

Obviously, knowing that `toString()` is inherited from `Object` in the `Animal` class, it would have been appropriate to use the `@Override` annotation for the method in the `Animal` class.

Determining the Type of an Object

The `getClass()` method that all your classes inherit from `Object` returns an object of type `Class` that identifies the class of an object. Suppose you have a variable `pet` of type `Animal` that might contain a reference to an object of type `Dog`, `Cat`, `Duck`, or even `Spaniel`. To figure out what sort of thing it really refers to, you could write the following statements:

```
Class objectType = pet.getClass();              // Get the class type
System.out.println(objectType.getName());       // Output the class name
```

The method `getName()` is a member of the `Class` class, and it returns the fully qualified name of the actual class of the object for which it is called as a `String` object. Thus, the second statement outputs the name of the class for the `pet` object. If `pet` referred to a `Duck` object, this would output:

```
Duck
```

This is the fully qualified name in this case, as the class is in the default package, which has no name. For a class defined in a named package, the class name would be prefixed with the package name. If you just wanted to output the class identity, you need not explicitly store the `Class` object. You can combine both statements into one:

```
System.out.println(pet.getClass().getName());   // Output the class name
```

This will produce the same output as before.

Remember that the `Class` object returns the actual class of an object. Suppose you define a `String` object like this:

```
String saying = "A stitch in time saves nine.";
```

You could store a reference to this `String` object as type `Object`:

```
Object str = saying;
```

The following statement displays the type of `str`:

```
System.out.println(str.getClass().getName());
```

This statement outputs the type name as `java.lang.String`. The fact that the reference is stored in a variable of type `Object` does not affect the underlying type of the object itself.

When your program is executing, there are instances of the `Class` class in existence that represent each of the classes and interfaces in your program (I explain what an interface type is a little later in this chapter). There is also a `Class` object for each array type in your program as well as every primitive type. The Java Virtual Machine (JVM) generates these when your program is loaded. Because `Class` is primarily intended for use by the JVM, it has no public constructors, so you can't create objects of type `Class` yourself.

Although you can use the `getClass()` method to get the `Class` object corresponding to a particular class or interface type, there is a more direct way. If you append `.class` to the name of any class, interface, or primitive type, you have a reference to the `Class` object for that class.

For example, `java.lang.String.class` references the `Class` object for the `String` class and `Duck.class` references the `Class` object for the `Duck` class. Similarly, `int.class` is the class object for the primitive type, `int`, and `double.class` is the one corresponding to type `double`. This may not seem particularly relevant at this point, but keep it in mind. Since there is only one `Class` object for each class or interface type, you can test for the class of an object programmatically. Given a variable `pet` of type `Animal`, you could check whether the object referenced was of type `Duck` with the following statement:

```
if(pet.getClass() == Duck.class) {
   System.out.println("By George - it is a duck!");
}
```

This tests whether the object referenced by `pet` is of type `Duck`. Because each `Class` object is unique, this is a precise test. If `pet` contained a reference to an object that was a subclass of `Duck`, the result of the comparison in the `if` would be `false`. You see a little later in this chapter that you have an operator in Java, `instanceof`, that does almost the same thing—but not quite.

Note that the `Class` class is not an ordinary class. It is an example of a *generic type*. I discuss generic types in detail in Chapter 13, but for now, be aware that `Class` really defines a set of classes. Each class, interface, array type, and primitive type that you use in your program is represented by an object of a unique class from the set defined by the `Class` generic type.

Duplicating Objects

As you saw in the summary at the beginning of this section, the `protected` method `clone()` that is inherited from the `Object` class creates a new object that is a copy of the current object. It does this only if the class of the object to be cloned indicates that cloning is acceptable. This is the case if the class implements the `Cloneable` interface. Don't worry about what an interface is at this point—you learn about this a little later in this chapter.

The `clone()` method that is inherited from `Object` clones an object by creating a new object of the same type as the current object and setting each of the fields in the new object to the same value as the corresponding fields in the current object. When the data members of the original object refer to class objects, the objects referred to are not duplicated when the clone is created—only the references are copied from the fields in the old object to the fields in the cloned object. This isn't typically what you want to happen—both the old and the new class objects can now be modifying a single shared mutable object that is referenced through their corresponding data members, not recognizing that this is occurring.

Using the `clone()` method to duplicate objects can be complicated and cumbersome. If you need to clone objects of your class types, the simplest approach is to ignore the `clone()` method and implement a *copy constructor* in your class. A copy constructor is just a constructor that duplicates an object that is passed as an argument to it. Let's look at an example to see how duplicating objects using a copy constructor works.

TRY IT OUT Duplicating Objects

Let's suppose you define a class `Flea` like this:

```java
public class Flea extends Animal {
  // Constructor
  public Flea(String aName, String aSpecies) {
    super("Flea");                    // Pass the type to the base
    name = aName;                     // Supplied name
    species = aSpecies;               // Supplied species
  }

  // Copy Constructor
  public Flea(Flea flea) {
    super(flea);              // Call the base class copy constructor
    name = flea.name;
    species = flea.species;
  }

  // Change the flea's name
  public void setName(String aName) {
    name = aName;                     // Change to the new name
  }

  // Return the flea's name
  public String getName() {
    return name;
  }

  // Return the species
  public String getSpecies() {
    return species;
  }

  @Override
  public void sound() {
    System.out.println("Psst");
  }

  // Present a flea's details as a String
  @Override
  public String toString() {
    return super.toString() + "\nIt's " + name + " the " + species;
  }

  protected String name;              // Name of flea!
  protected String species;           // Flea species
}
```

Directory "DuplicateObjects"

The class has a copy constructor that creates a duplicate of the `Flea` object that is passed to it. It calls the base class copy constructor to set the `type`. You have defined accessor methods for the name and the species of flea. This is a common technique for providing access to private or protected data members of a class when this is necessary. You also have a public method `setName()` that enables you to change the name from outside of the class.

The base class needs a copy constructor too, so add the following definition to the `Animal` class:

```java
public Animal(Animal animal) {
  type = animal.type;
}
```

Directory "DuplicateObjects"

This sets the `type` member to the type for the object that is passed as the argument.

The `Dog` class needs a copy constructor too, and it is useful to provide methods to access the data members:

```java
public class Dog extends Animal {
  public Dog(String aName) {
    super("Dog");                          // Call the base constructor
    name = aName;                          // Supplied name
    breed = "Unknown";                     // Default breed value
  }

  public Dog(String aName, String aBreed) {
    super("Dog");                          // Call the base constructor
    name = aName;                          // Supplied name
    breed = aBreed;                        // Supplied breed
  }

  // Copy constructor
  public Dog(Dog dog) {
    super(dog);                                        // Call base copy constructor
    name = dog.name;
    breed = dog.breed;
  }

  // Rename the dog
  public void setName(String name) {
    this.name = name;
  }

  // Return the dog's name
  public String getName() {
    return name;
  }

  // Return the breed
  public String getBreed() {
    return breed;
  }

  // Present a dog's details as a string
  @Override
  public String toString() {
    return super.toString() + "\nIt's " + name + " the " + breed;
  }

  // A barking method
  @Override
  public void sound() {
    System.out.println("Woof    Woof");
  }

  protected String name;                   // Name of a Dog
  protected String breed;                  // Dog breed
}
```

Directory "DuplicateObjects"

You can now derive a class `PetDog` from `Dog` that contains a `Flea` object as a member:

```java
public class PetDog extends Dog {
  // Constructor
  public PetDog(String name, String breed, String fleaName, String fleaSpecies) {
    super(name, breed);
    petFlea = new Flea("Max","circus flea");       // Initialize petFlea
```

```
    }

    // Copy constructor
    public PetDog(PetDog pet) {
      super(pet);                             // Call base copy constructor
      petFlea = new Flea(pet.petFlea);        // Duplicate the flea
    }

    // Return the flea
    public Flea getFlea() {
      return petFlea;
    }

    @Override
    public void sound() {
      System.out.println("Woof");
    }

    // Return a String for the pet dog
    @Override
    public String toString() {
      return super.toString() + " - a pet dog.\nIt has a flea:\n" + petFlea;
    }

    protected Flea petFlea;                          // The pet flea
}
```

Directory "DuplicateObjects"

This class defines a specialized type of Dog object that has a flea. To make it possible to clone a PetDog object, you implemented a copy constructor. Note how the copy constructor passes the PetDog object to the Dog class copy constructor. This is legal because the Dog class copy constructor has a parameter of type Dog and a PetDog object is a specialized type of Dog. In general you can pass an object of any type that is a subclass of the parameter type to a method.

You can try out creating and duplicating a PetDog object with the following code:

Available for download on Wrox.com

```
public class DuplicateObjects {
    public static void main(String[] args) {
      PetDog myPet = new PetDog("Fang", "Chihuahua", "Max", "Circus flea");
      System.out.println("\nMy pet details:\n"+ myPet);
      PetDog yourPet = new PetDog(myPet);
      System.out.println("\nYour pet details:\n"+yourPet);
      yourPet.setName("Gnasher");                 // Change your dog's name
      yourPet.getFlea().setName("Atlas");         // Change your dog's flea's name
      System.out.println("\nYour pet details:\n"+yourPet);
      System.out.println("\nMy pet details:\n"+ myPet);
    }
}
```

Directory "DuplicateObjects"

I put the files in a DuplicateObjects folder. You need to add the files containing the new versions of the Dog and Animal classes.

This produces the following output:

```
My pet details:
This is a Dog
It's Fang the Chihuahua - a pet dog.
It has a flea:
This is a Flea
It's Max the circus flea

Your pet details:
```

```
This is a Dog
It's Fang the Chihuahua - a pet dog.
It has a flea:
This is a Flea
It's Max the circus flea

Your pet details:
This is a Dog
It's Gnasher the Chihuahua - a pet dog.
It has a flea:
This is a Flea
It's Atlas the circus flea

My pet details:
This is a Dog
It's Fang the Chihuahua - a pet dog.
It has a flea:
This is a Flea
It's Max the circus flea
```

How It Works

The first block of output shows the details of the original pet. The next block shows that the duplicate pet has exactly the same characteristics as the original. The third block shows the details of the duplicate after the dog's name and its flea's name have been changed. The last block of output shows that the original pet is unaffected by the change to the duplicate, thus demonstrating that the objects are completely independent of one another.

It is important to ensure that all mutable data members are duplicated in a copy constructor operation. If you simply copy the references for such data members, changes to one object affect the copy because they share the same objects as members. The copy constructor in the `PetDog` class creates a new `Flea` object for the new `PetDog` object by calling the copy constructor for the `Flea` class. The members inherited from `Dog` are both `String` objects. These are immutable, so you don't need to worry about creating duplicates of them.

METHODS ACCEPTING A VARIABLE NUMBER OF ARGUMENTS

You can write a method so that it accepts an arbitrary number of arguments when it is called, and the arguments that are passed do not need to be of the same type. Such methods are called *Varargs* methods. The reason I have waited until now to mention this is that understanding how this works depends on having an understanding of the role of the `Object` class. You indicate that a method accepts a variable number of arguments by specifying the last parameter as follows:

```
Object ... args
```

The method can have zero or more parameters preceding this, but this must be last for obvious reasons. The ellipsis (three periods) between the type name `Object` and the parameter name `args` enables the compiler to determine that the argument list is variable. The parameter name `args` represents an array of type `Object[]`, and the argument values are available in the elements of the array as type `Object`. Within the body of the method, the length of the `args` array tells you how many arguments were supplied.

Let's consider a very simple example to demonstrate the mechanism. Suppose you want to implement a static method that accepts any number of arguments and outputs the arguments to the command line—whatever they are. You could code it like this:

```java
public static void printAll(Object ... args) {
  for(Object arg : args) {
    System.out.print("  " + arg);
  }
  System.out.println();
}
```

The arguments can be anything. Values of primitive types are autoboxed because the method expects reference arguments. The loop outputs the string representation of each of the arguments on a single line, the string being produced by invoking the `toString()` method for whatever the argument is. Let's see it working.

TRY IT OUT Displaying Arguments of any Type

Here's a program that exercises the `printAll()` method:

Available for download on Wrox.com

```java
public class TryVariableArgumentList {
  public static void main(String[] args) {
    printAll( 2, "two", 4, "four", 4.5, "four point five");    // Six arguments
    printAll();                                                // No arguments
    printAll(25, "Anything goes", true, 4E4, false);           // Five arguments
  }

  public static void printAll(Object ... args) {
    for(Object arg : args) {
      System.out.print("  " + arg);
    }
    System.out.println();
  }
}
```

TryVariableArgumentList.java

This program produces the following output:

```
2   two   4   four   4.5   four point five

25   Anything goes   true   40000.0   false
```

How It Works

You can see from the output that the `printAll()` method works as advertised and accepts an arbitrary number of arguments. The first call of the `printAll()` method mixes arguments of type `int`, type `String`, and type `double`. Each numerical value is converted to an object of the corresponding wrapper class type by a boxing conversion that the compiler inserts. The output strings are then produced by calls to the `toString()` method for the objects, also expedited by the compiler. The second call to the method results in an empty line. The last line of output shows that autoboxing works with `boolean` values as well as values of the other primitive types.

The standard class libraries use the variable argument list capability to define the `printf()` method in the `java.io.PrintStream` class. This method produces formatted output for an arbitrary sequence of values of various types, where the formatting is specified by the first argument. `System.out` happens to be of type `PrintStream` so you can use `printf()` to produce formatted output to the command line. I discuss how you use the `printf()` method to produce output with more precise control over the format in which it is displayed in Chapter 8 in the context of streams.

Limiting the Types in a Variable Argument List

You don't have to specify the type of the variable argument list as type `Object`; you can specify it as any class or interface type. The arguments must be of the type that you specify, or any subtype of that type. Specifying the type of the variable argument list as `Object` maximizes flexibility because any types of argument can be supplied, but there may be occasions where you want to restrict the types of the arguments that can be supplied. For example, if you want to define a method that computes the average of an arbitrary number of values that are to be supplied as individual arguments then you really want to be sure that the arguments can only be numerical values. Here's how you could do this:

```java
public static double average(Double ... args) {
  if(args.length == 0) {
```

```
       return 0.0;
    }
    double ave = 0.0;
    for(double value : args) {
      ave += value;
      }
    return ave/args.length;
}
```

In this case the arguments must be of type `Double` or of a type derived from `Double`, or—because of autoboxing conversion supplied by the compiler—of type `double`.

CASTING OBJECTS

You can cast an object to another class type, but only if the current object type and the new class type are in the same hierarchy of derived classes, and one is a superclass of the other. For example, earlier in this chapter you defined the classes `Animal`, `Dog`, `Spaniel`, `PetDog`, `Cat`, and `Duck`, and these are related in the hierarchy shown in Figure 6-5.

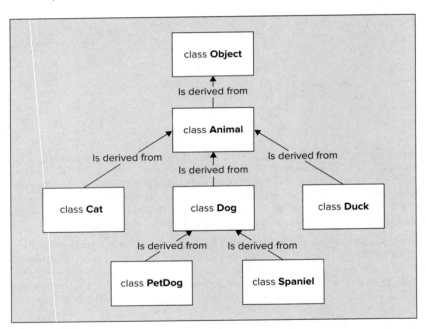

FIGURE 6-5

You can cast a reference to an object of a given class type upwards through its direct and indirect superclasses. For example, you could cast a reference to an object of type `Spaniel` directly to type `Dog`, type `Animal`, or type `Object`. You could write:

```
Spaniel aPet = new Spaniel("Fang");
Animal theAnimal = (Animal)aPet;        // Cast the Spaniel to Animal
```

When you are assigning an object reference to a variable of a superclass type, you do not have to include the cast. You could write the assignment as:

```
Animal theAnimal = aPet;                // Cast the Spaniel to Animal
```

This would work just as well. The compiler is always prepared to insert a cast to a superclass type when necessary.

When you cast an object reference to a superclass type, Java retains full knowledge of the actual class to which the object belongs. If this were not the case, polymorphism would not be possible. Because information about the original type of an object is retained, you can cast down a hierarchy as well. However, you must always write the cast explicitly because the compiler is not prepared to insert it. For the cast to work, the object must be a legitimate instance of the class you are casting to—that is, the class you are casting to must be the original class of the object, or must be a superclass of the object. For example, you could cast a reference stored in the variable theAnimal shown in the preceding example to type Dog or type Spaniel because the object was originally a Spaniel, but you could not cast it to Cat or Duck because an object of type Spaniel does not have Cat or Duck as a superclass. To cast theAnimal to type Dog, you would write the following:

```
Dog aDog = (Dog)theAnimal;              // Cast from Animal to Dog
```

Now the variable aDog refers to an object of type Spaniel that also happens to be a Dog. Remember, you can only use the variable aDog to call the polymorphic methods from the class Spaniel that override methods that exist in Dog. You can't call methods that are not defined in the Dog class. If you want to call a method that is in the class Spaniel and not in the class Dog, you must first cast aDog to type Spaniel.

Although you cannot cast between unrelated objects, from Spaniel to Duck for example, you can achieve a conversion by writing a suitable constructor, but obviously only where it makes sense to do so. You just write a constructor in the class to which you want to convert and make it accept an object of the class you are converting from as an argument. If you really thought Spaniel to Duck was a reasonable conversion, you could add the constructor to the Duck class:

```
public Duck(Spaniel aSpaniel) {
    // Back legs off, and staple on a beak of your choice...
    super("Duck");             // Call the base constructor
    name = aSpaniel.getName();
    breed = "Barking Coot";  // Set the duck breed for a converted Spaniel
}
```

This uses the getName() method in the Dog class that is inherited in the class Spaniel, and which returns the value of name for an object. This constructor accepts a Spaniel and turns out a Duck. This is quite different from a cast though. This creates a completely new object that is separate from the original, whereas a cast presents the same object as a different type.

When to Cast Objects

You will have cause to cast objects in both directions through a class hierarchy. For example, whenever you execute methods polymorphically, you are storing objects in a variable of a base class type and calling methods in a derived class. This generally involves casting the derived class objects to the base class. Another reason you might want to cast up through a hierarchy is to pass an object of several possible subclasses to a method. By specifying a parameter as a base class type, you have the flexibility to pass an object of any derived class to it. You could pass a Dog, Duck, or Cat object to a method as an argument for a parameter of type Animal, for example.

The reason you might want to cast down through a class hierarchy is to execute a method unique to a particular class. If the Duck class has a method layEgg(), for example, you can't call this using a variable of type Animal, even though it references a Duck object. As I said, casting downward through a class hierarchy always requires an explicit cast.

TRY IT OUT   Casting Down to Lay an Egg

Let's amend the Duck class and use it along with the Animal class in an example. Add layEgg() to the Duck class as:

```
public class Duck extends Animal {
  public void layEgg() {
    System.out.println("Egg laid");
  }
    // Rest of the class as before...
  }
```

Directory "Lay Eggs"

If you now try to use this with the code:

```
public class LayEggs {
  public static void main(String[] args) {
    Duck aDuck = new Duck("Donald", "Eider");
    Animal aPet = aDuck;                      // Cast the Duck to Animal
    aPet.layEgg();                            // This won't compile!
  }
}
```

Directory "Lay Eggs"

you get a compiler message to the effect that `layEgg()` is not found in the class `Animal`.

Because you know this object is really a `Duck`, you can make it work by writing the call to `layEgg()` in the preceding code as:

```
((Duck)aPet).layEgg();                       // This works fine
```

The object pointed to by `aPet` is first cast to type `Duck`. The result of the cast is then used to call the method `layEgg()`. If the object were not of type `Duck`, the cast would cause an exception to be thrown.

 WARNING *In general, you should avoid explicitly casting objects as much as possible because it increases the potential for an invalid cast and can therefore make your programs unreliable. Most of the time, you should find that if you design your classes carefully, you won't need explicit casts very often.*

Identifying Objects

There are circumstances when you may not know exactly what sort of object you are dealing with. This can arise if a derived class object is passed to a method as an argument for a parameter of a base class type for example, in the way that I discussed in the previous section. A parameter of type `Animal` could have a `Duck`, a `Dog`, or a `Flea` object passed as the argument. In some situations you may need to cast the object to its actual class type, perhaps to call a class-specific method. If you try to make the cast and it turns out to be illegal, an exception is thrown, and your program ends unless you have made provision for catching the exception. One way to obviate this situation is to verify that the object is of the type you expect before you make the cast.

You saw earlier in this chapter how you could use the `getClass()` method to obtain the `Class` object corresponding to the class type, and how you could compare it to a `Class` instance for the class you are looking for. You can also do this using the `instanceof` operator. For example, suppose you have a variable `pet` of type `Animal`, and you want to cast it to type `Duck`. You could code this as:

```
if(pet instanceof Duck) {
  Duck aDuck = (Duck)pet;          // It is a duck so the cast is OK
  aDuck.layEgg();                  // and You can have an egg for tea
}
```

If `pet` does not refer to a `Duck` object, an attempt to cast the object referenced by `pet` to `Duck` causes an exception to be thrown. This code fragment executes the cast and lay an egg only if `pet` does point to a `Duck` object. The preceding code fragment could have been written much more concisely as:

```
if(pet instanceof Duck) {
  ((Duck)pet).layEgg();            // It is a duck so You can have an egg for tea
}
```

So what is the difference between this and using `getClass()`? Well, it's quite subtle. The `instanceof` operator checks whether a cast of the object referenced by the left operand to the type specified by the right operand is legal. The result is `true` if the object is the same type as the right operand, *or of any subclass type*. You can illustrate the difference by choosing a slightly different example.

Suppose `pet` stores a reference to an object of type `Spaniel`. You want to call a method defined in the `Dog` class, so you need to check that `pet` does really reference a `Dog` object. You can check whether you have a `Dog` object or not with the following statements:

```
if(pet instanceof Dog) {
  System.out.println("You have a dog!");
} else {
  System.out.println("It's definitely not a dog!");
}
```

You get confirmation that you have a `Dog` object here, even though it is actually a `Spaniel` object. This is fine, though, for casting purposes. As long as the `Dog` class is in the class hierarchy for the object, the cast works okay, so the operator is telling you what you need to know. However, suppose you write:

```
if(pet.getClass() == Dog.class) {
  System.out.println("You have a dog!");
}
else {
  System.out.println("It's definitely not a dog!");
}
```

Here the `if` expression is `false` because the class type of the object is `Spaniel`, so its `Class` object is different from that of `Dog.class`—you would have to write `Spaniel.class` instead of `Dog.class` to get the value `true` from the `if` expression.

You can conclude from this that for casting purposes you should always use the `instanceof` operator to check the type of a reference. You only need to resort to checking the `Class` object corresponding to a reference when you need to confirm the exact type of the reference.

MORE ON ENUMERATIONS

When I introduced enumerations in Chapter 2, I said that there was more to enumerations than simply a type with a limited range of integer values. In fact, an enumeration type is a special form of class. When you define an enumeration type in your code, the enumeration constants that you specify are created as instances of a class that has the `Enum` class, which is defined in the `java.lang` package, as a superclass. The object that corresponds to each enumeration constant stores the name of the constant in a field, and the enumeration class type inherits the `toString()` method from the `Enum` class. The `toString()` method in the `Enum` class returns the original name of the enumeration constant, so that's why you get the name you gave to an enumeration constant displayed when you output it using the `println()` method.

You have seen that you can put the definition of an enumeration type in the definition of a class. You can also put the definition in a separate source file. In this case you specify the name of the file containing the enumeration type definition in the same way as for any other class type. An enumeration that you define in its own source file can be accessed by any other source file in exactly the same way as any other class definition.

An object representing an enumeration constant also stores an integer field. By default, each constant in an enumeration is assigned an integer value that is different from all the others. The values are assigned to the enumeration constants in the sequence in which you specify them, starting with zero for the first constant, one for the second, and so on. You can retrieve the value for a constant by calling its `ordinal()` method, but you should not need to do this in general.

You have already seen in Chapter 3 that you can compare values of an enumeration type for equality using the `equals()` method. For example, assuming that you have defined an enumeration type, `Season`, with enumeration constants `spring`, `summer`, `fall`, and `winter`, you could write the following:

```
Season now = Season.winter;
if(now.equals(Season.winter))
   System.out.println("It is definitely winter!");
```

The `equals()` method is inherited from the `Enum` class in your enumeration class type. Your enumeration class type also inherits the `compareTo()` method that compares instances of the enumeration based on their ordinal values. It returns a negative integer if the value for the instance for which the method is called is less than the instance that you pass as the argument, 0 if they are equal, and a positive integer if the value of the current instance is greater than the value for the argument. Thus, the sequence in which you specify the enumeration constants when you define them determines the order that the `compareTo()` method implements. You might use it like this:

```
if(now.compareTo(Season.summer) > 0)
   System.out.println("It is definitely getting colder!");
```

The `values()` method for an enumeration that I introduced in Chapter 3 is a static member of your enumeration class type. This method returns a collection object containing all the enumeration constants that you can use in a collection-based `for` loop. You learn about collection classes in Chapter 14.

Adding Members to an Enumeration Class

Because an enumeration is a class, you have the possibility to add your own methods and fields when you define the enumeration type. You can also add your own constructors to initialize any additional fields you introduce. Let's take an example. Suppose you want to define an enumeration for clothing sizes—jackets, say. Your initial definition might be like this:

```
public enum JacketSize { small, medium, large, extra_large, extra_extra_large }
```

You then realize that you would really like to record the average chest size applicable to each jacket size. You could amend the definition of the enumeration like this:

Available for
download on
Wrox.com

```
public enum JacketSize {
   small(36), medium(40), large(42), extra_large(46), extra_extra_large(48);

   // Constructor
   JacketSize(int chestSize) {
     this.chestSize = chestSize;
   }
   // Method to return the chest size for the current jacket size
   public int chestSize() {
     return chestSize;
   }

   private int chestSize;                    // Field to record chest size
}
```

Directory "TryJackets"

Note how the list of enumeration constants now ends with a semicolon. Each constant in the list has the corresponding chest size between parentheses, and this value is passed to the constructor that you have added to the class. In the previous definition of `JacketSize`, the appearance of each enumeration constant results in a call to the default constructor for the class. In fact, you could put an empty pair of parentheses after the name of each constant, and it would still compile. However, this would not improve the clarity of the code. Because you have defined a constructor, no default constructor is defined for the enumeration class, so you cannot write enumeration constants just as names. You must put the parentheses enclosing a value for the chest size following each enumeration constant. Of course, if you want to have the option of omitting the chest size for some of the constants in the enumeration, you can define your own default constructor and assign a default value for the `chestSize` field.

Even though you have added your own constructor, the fields inherited from the base class, `Enum`, that store the name of the constant and its ordinal value are still set appropriately. The ordering of the constants that `compareTo()` implements are still determined by the sequence in which the constants appear in the definition. Note that you must not declare a constructor in an enumeration class as `public`. If you do, the enum class definition does not compile. The only modifier that you are allowed to apply to a constructor in a class defining an enumeration is `private`, which results in the constructor being callable only from inside the class.

The chest size is recorded in a private data member so there is also a `chestSize()` method to allow the value of `chestSize` to be retrieved.

Let's see it working.

TRY IT OUT   **Embroidering an Enumeration**

First, create a new directory, `TryJackets`, for the example and save the `JacketSize.java` file containing the definition of the enumeration from the previous section in it. Now create another file containing the following definition:

```java
public enum JacketColor { red, orange, yellow, blue, green }
```

Directory "TryJackets"

This should be in a file with the name `JacketColor.java`.

Now you can define a class that represents a jacket:

```java
public class Jacket {
  public Jacket(JacketSize size, JacketColor color) {
    this.size = size;
    this.color = color;
  }

  @Override
  public String toString() {
    StringBuffer str = new StringBuffer("Jacket ");
    return str.append(size).append(" in ").append(color).toString();
  }

  private JacketSize size;
  private JacketColor color;
}
```

Directory "TryJackets"

Finally, you need a file containing code to try out some jackets:

```java
public class TryJackets {
  public static void main(String[] args) {

    // Define some jackets
    Jacket[] jackets = {new Jacket(JacketSize.medium, JacketColor.red),
                        new Jacket(JacketSize.extra_large, JacketColor.yellow),
                        new Jacket(JacketSize.small, JacketColor.green),
                        new Jacket(JacketSize.extra_extra_large, JacketColor.blue)
                          };

    // Output colors available
    System.out.println("Jackets colors available are:\n");
    for(JacketColor color: JacketColor.values()) {
      System.out.print("   " + color);
    }

    // Output sizes available
    System.out.println("\n\nJackets sizes available are:\n");
    for(JacketSize size: JacketSize.values()) {
      System.out.print("   " + size);
```

```
      }

      System.out.println("\n\nJackets in stock are:");
      for(Jacket jacket: jackets) {
        System.out.println(jacket);
      }
    }
  }
```

Directory "TryJackets"

When you compile and execute this program you get the following output:

```
Jackets colors available are:

  red   orange   yellow   blue   green

Jackets sizes available are:

  small   medium   large   extra_large   extra_extra_large

Jackets in stock are:
Jacket medium in red
Jacket extra_large in yellow
Jacket small in green
Jacket extra_extra_large in blue
```

How It Works

The `main()` method in the `TryJackets` class defines an array of `Jacket` objects. It then lists the sizes and colors available for a jacket simply by using the collection-based `for` loop to list the constants in each enumeration. Because the enumeration constants are objects, the compiler inserts a call to the `toString()` method for the objects to produce the output. You use the same kind of `for` loop to list the contents of the array of `Jacket` objects. This also involves an implicit call to the `toString()` method for each `Jacket` object.

Because you have defined the `JacketSize` and `JacketColor` enumerations in separate classes, they are accessible from any source file in the same directory. To make them even more widely available, you could put them in a package.

The `Jacket` class uses the enumeration types to define private fields recording the size and color of a jacket. Note how the `toString()` method in the `Jacket` class is able to use the size and color members as though they were strings. The compiler inserts a call to the `toString()` method for the enumeration type that applies. You can override the `toString()` method for an enumeration type. For example, you might decide you prefer to define the `toString()` method in the `JacketSize` enumeration like this:

```
@Override
public String toString() {
  switch(this) {
    case small:
      return "S";
    case medium:
      return "M";
    case large:
      return "L";
    case extra_large:
      return "XL";
    default:
      return "XXL";
  }
}
```

Note how you can use `this` as the control expression for the `switch` statement. This is because `this` references the current instance, which is an enumeration constant. Because the expression is an enumeration constant, the case labels are the constant names. They do not need to be qualified by the name of the enumeration. With this implementation of `toString()` in the `JacketSize` enumeration, the output is:

```
Jackets colors available are:

  red  orange  yellow  blue  green

Jackets sizes available are:

  S  M  L  XL  XXL

Jackets in stock are:
Jacket M in red
Jacket XL in yellow
Jacket S in green
Jacket XXL in blue
```

Thus, you can see from this example that you can treat an enumeration type just like any other class type.

DESIGNING CLASSES

A basic problem in object-oriented programming is deciding how the classes in your program should relate to one another. One possibility is to create a hierarchy of classes by deriving classes from a base class that you have defined and adding methods and data members to specialize the subclasses. The `Animal` class and the subclasses derived from it are an example of this. Another possibility is to define a set of classes that are not hierarchical, but that have data members that are themselves class objects. A `Zoo` class might well have objects of types derived from `Animal` as members, for example. You can have class hierarchies that contain data members that are class objects—you already have this with the classes derived from `Animal` because they have members of type `String`. The examples so far have been relatively clear-cut as to which approach to choose, but it is not always so evident. Quite often you have a choice between defining your classes as a hierarchy and defining classes that have members that are class objects. Which is the best approach to take?

Like almost all questions of this kind, there are no clear-cut answers. If object-oriented programming were a process that you could specify by a fixed set of rules that you could just follow blindly, you could get the computer to do it. There are some guidelines though, and some contexts in which the answer may be more obvious.

Aside from the desirability of reflecting real-world relationships between types of objects, the need to use polymorphism is a primary reason for using subclasses (or interfaces, as you see shortly). This is the essence of object-oriented programming. Having a range of related objects that can be treated equivalently can greatly simplify your programs. You have seen how having various kinds of animals specified by classes derived from a common base class, `Animal`, enables us to act on different types of animals as though they are the same, producing different results depending on what kind of animal is being dealt with, and all this automatically.

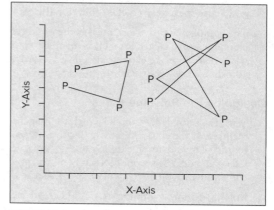

A Classy Example

Many situations involve making judgments about the design of your classes. The way to go may well boil down to a question of personal preference. Let's try to see how the options look in practice by considering a simple example. Suppose you want to define a class `PolyLine` to represent geometric entities that consist of a number of connected line segments, as illustrated in Figure 6-6.

FIGURE 6-6

Figure 6-6 shows two polylines, one defined by four points, the other defined by six points.

It seems reasonable to represent points as objects of a class `Point`. Points are well-defined objects that occur in the context of all kinds of geometric entities. You have seen a class for points earlier, which you put in the `Geometry` package. Rather than repeat the whole class, let's just define the bare bones of what you need in this context:

Available for
download on
Wrox.com

```
public class Point {
    // Create a point from its coordinates
    public Point(double xVal, double yVal) {
        x = xVal;
        y = yVal;
    }

    // Create a point from another point
    public Point(Point point) {
        x = point.x;
        y = point.y;
    }

    // Convert a point to a string
    @Override
    public String toString() {
        return x+","+y;
    }

    // Coordinates of the point
    protected double x;
    protected double y;
}
```

Directory "TryPolyLine"

Save the source file containing this code in a new directory, `TryPolyLine`. You add all the files for the example to this directory. Both data members of `Point` are inherited in any subclass because they are specified as `protected`. They are also insulated from interference from outside the package containing the class. The `toString()` method enables `Point` objects to be concatenated to a `String` object for automatic conversion—in an argument passed to the `println()` method, for example.

The next question you might ask is, "Should I derive the class `PolyLine` from the class `Point`?" This has a fairly obvious answer. A polyline is clearly not a kind of point, so it is not logical to derive the class `PolyLine` from the `Point` class. This is an elementary demonstration of what is often referred to as the *is a* test. If you can say that one kind of object *is a* specialized form of another kind of object, you may have a good case for a derived class (but not always—there may be other reasons not to!). If not, you don't.

The complement to the *is a* test is the *has a* test. If one object *has a* component that is an object of another class, you have a case for a class member. A `House` object *has a* door, so a variable of type `Door` is likely to be a member of the class `House`. The `PolyLine` class contains several points, which looks promising, but you should look a little more closely at how you might store them, as there are some options.

Designing the PolyLine Class

With the knowledge you have of Java, an array of `Point` objects looks like a good candidate to be a member of the class. There are disadvantages, though. A common requirement with polylines is to be able to add segments to an existing object. With an array storing the points you need to create a new array each time you add a segment, then copy all the points from the old array to the new one. This could be time-consuming if you have a `PolyLine` object with a lot of segments.

You have another option. You could create a *linked list* of points. In its simplest form, a linked list of objects is an arrangement where each object in the list has a reference to the next object as a data member. As long as you have a variable containing a reference to the first `Point` object, you can access all the points in the list, as shown in Figure 6-7.

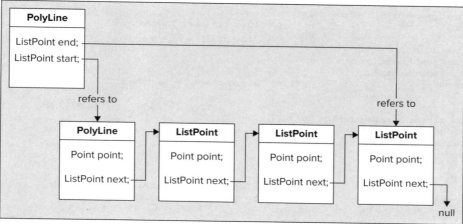

FIGURE 6-7

Figure 6-7 illustrates the basic structure you might have for a linked list of points stored as a `PolyLine`. The points are stored as members of `ListPoint` objects. In addition to constructors, the `PolyLine` class needs a method to add points, but before you look into that, let's consider the `ListPoint` class in more detail.

You could take one of at least three approaches to define the `ListPoint` class, and you could make arguments in favor of all three.

➤ You could define the `ListPoint` class with the *x* and *y* coordinates stored explicitly. The main argument against this would be that you have already encapsulated the properties of a point in the `Point` class, so why not use it?

➤ You could regard a `ListPoint` object as something that contains a reference to a `Point` object, plus members that refer to following `ListPoint` objects in the list. This is not an unreasonable approach. It is easy to implement and not inconsistent with an intuitive idea of a `ListPoint`.

➤ You could view a `ListPoint` object as a specialized kind of `Point`, so you would derive the `ListPoint` class from `Point`. Whether or not this is reasonable depends on whether you see this as valid. To my mind, this is stretching the usual notion of a point somewhat—I would not use this.

The best option looks to me to be the second approach. You could implement the `ListPoint` class with a data member of type `Point`, which defines a basic point with its coordinates. A `ListPoint` object would have an extra data member, `next`, of type `ListPoint` that is intended to contain a reference to the next object in the list. With this arrangement, you can find all the points in a `PolyLine` object by starting with its `start` member, which stores a reference to its first `ListPoint` object. This contains a reference to the next `ListPoint` object in its `next` member, which in turn contains a reference to the next, and so on through to the last `ListPoint` object. You know it is the last one because its `next` member, which usually points to the next `ListPoint` object, is `null`. Let's try it.

TRY IT OUT   The ListPoint Class

You can define the `ListPoint` class using the `Point` class with the following code:

Available for
download on
Wrox.com

```
public class ListPoint {
    // Constructor
    public ListPoint(Point point) {
        this.point = point;                    // Store point reference
```

```
      next = null;                        // Set next ListPoint as null
    }

    // Set the pointer to the next ListPoint
    public void setNext(ListPoint next) {
      this.next = next;                    // Store the next ListPoint
    }

    // Get the next point in the list
    public ListPoint getNext() {
      return next;                         // Return the next ListPoint
    }

    // Return String representation
    @Override
    public String toString() {
      return "(" + point + ")";
    }

      private ListPoint next;              // Refers to next ListPoint in the list
      private Point point;                 // The point for this list point
    }
```

Directory "TryPolyLine"

Save this file in the same directory as the `Point` class, `TryPolyLine`.

How It Works

A `ListPoint` object is a means of creating a list of `Point` objects that originate elsewhere so you don't need to worry about duplicating `Point` objects stored in the list. You can just store the reference to the `Point` object passed to the constructor in the data member, `point`. The data member, `next`, should contain a reference to the next `ListPoint` in the list, and because that is not defined here, you set `next` to `null`.

The `setNext()` method enables the `next` data member to be set for the existing last point in the list when a new point is added to the list. A reference to the new `ListPoint` object is passed as an argument to the method. The `getNext()` method enables the next point in the list to be determined, so this method is the means by which you can iterate through the entire list.

By implementing the `toString()` method for the class, you enable the automatic creation of a `String` representation for a `ListPoint` object when required. Here you differentiate the `String` representation of the `ListPoint` object by enclosing the `String` representation of `point` between parentheses.

You could now have a first stab at implementing the `PolyLine` class.

> **TRY IT OUT**   **The PolyLine Class**

You can define the `PolyLine` class to use the `ListPoint` class as follows:

Available for
download on
Wrox.com

```
public class PolyLine {
    // Construct a polyline from an array of points
    public PolyLine(Point[] points) {
        if(points != null) {                  // Make sure there is an array
            for(Point p : points) {
                addPoint(p);
            }
        }
    }

    // Add a Point object to the list
    public void addPoint(Point point) {
```

```
        ListPoint newEnd = new ListPoint(point);       // Create a new ListPoint
        if(start == null) {
          start = newEnd;                               // Start is same as end
        } else {
          end.setNext(newEnd);               // Set next variable for old end as new end
        }
        end = newEnd;                                   // Store new point as end
      }

      // String representation of a polyline
      @Override
      public String toString() {
        StringBuffer str = new StringBuffer("Polyline:");
        ListPoint nextPoint = start;                    // Set the 1st point as start
        while(nextPoint != null) {
          str.append(" "+ nextPoint);                   // Output the current point
          nextPoint = nextPoint.getNext();              // Make the next point current
        }
        return str.toString();
      }

      private ListPoint start;                          // First ListPoint in the list
      private ListPoint end;                            // Last ListPoint in the list
    }
```

Directory "TryPolyLine"

This source file also goes in the `TryPolyLine` directory.

You might want to be able to add a point to the list by specifying a coordinate pair. You could overload the `addPoint()` method to do this:

Available for
download on
Wrox.com

```
// Add a point defined by a coordinate pair to the list
public void addPoint(double x, double y) {
  addPoint(new Point(x, y));
}
```

Directory "TryPolyLine"

You just created a new `Point` object in the expression that is the argument to the other version of `addPoint()`.

You might also want to create a `PolyLine` object from an array of coordinates. The constructor to do this would be:

Available for
download on
Wrox.com

```
// Construct a polyline from an array of coordinates
public PolyLine(double[][] coords) {
  if(coords != null) {
    for(int i = 0; i < coords.length ; ++i) {
      addPoint(coords[i][0], coords[i][1]);
    }
  }
}
```

Directory "TryPolyLine"

How It Works

The `PolyLine` class has the data members `start` and `end` that you saw in Figure 6-7. These reference the first and last points of the list, or `null` if the list is empty. Storing the end point in the list is not essential because you can always find it by going through the list starting with `start`. However, having a reference to the last point saves a lot of time when you want to add a point to the list. The constructor accepts an array of `Point` objects and uses the `addPoint()` method to add all the points in the array to the list.

Adding a point to the list is deceptively simple. All the `addPoint()` method does is create a `ListPoint` object from the `Point` object passed as an argument, sets the `next` member of the old end point in the list to refer to the new point, and finally stores a reference to the new end point in the member `end`.

The `toString()` method returns a string representing the `PolyLine` object as a list of point coordinates. Note how the `next` member of the `ListPoint` objects controls the loop that runs through the list. When the last `ListPoint` object is reached, the `next` member will be returned as `null` and the `while` loop ends. You can now give the `PolyLine` class a whirl.

TRY IT OUT   Using PolyLine Objects

You can create a simple example to illustrate the use of the `PolyLine` class:

```java
public class TryPolyLine {
  public static void main(String[] args) {
    // Create an array of coordinate pairs
    double[][] coords = { {1, 1}, {1, 2}, { 2, 3},
                          {-3, 5}, {-5, 1}, {0, 0} };

    // Create a polyline from the coordinates and display it
    PolyLine polygon = new PolyLine(coords);
    System.out.println(polygon);
    // Add a point and display the polyline again
    polygon.addPoint(10, 10);
    System.out.println(polygon);

    // Create Point objects from the coordinate array
    Point[] points = new Point[coords.length];
    for(int i = 0; i < points.length; ++i)
    points[i] = new Point(coords[i][0],coords[i][1]);

    // Use the points to create a new polyline and display it
    PolyLine newPoly = new PolyLine(points);
    System.out.println(newPoly);
  }
}
```

Directory "TryPolyLine"

Remember that all three classes, `Point`, `ListPoint`, and `PolyLine`, need to be together in the same folder as this class, which is the `TryPolyLine` directory if you followed my initial suggestion. If you have keyed everything in correctly, the program outputs three `PolyLine` objects:

```
Polyline: (1.0,1.0) (1.0,2.0) (2.0,3.0) (-3.0,5.0) (-5.0,1.0) (0.0,0.0)
Polyline: (1.0,1.0) (1.0,2.0) (2.0,3.0) (-3.0,5.0) (-5.0,1.0) (0.0,0.0) (10.0,10.0)
Polyline: (1.0,1.0) (1.0,2.0) (2.0,3.0) (-3.0,5.0) (-5.0,1.0) (0.0,0.0)
```

The first and the third lines of output are the same, with the coordinates from the `coords` array. The second has the extra point (10, 10) at the end.

The `PolyLine` class works well enough but it doesn't seem very satisfactory. Adding all the code to create and manage a list for what is essentially a geometric entity is not very object-oriented is it? Come to think of it, why are you making a list of points? Apart from the type of the data members of the `ListPoint` class, there's very little to do with `Point` objects in its definition; it's all to do with the linking mechanism. You might also have lots of other requirements for lists. If you were implementing an address book for instance, you would want a list of names. A cookery program would need a list of recipes. You might need lists for all kinds of things—maybe even a list of lists! Let's see if there's a better approach.

A General-Purpose Linked List

Let's put together a more general-purpose linked list and then use it to store polylines as before. You should save the source files for this in a new directory, as you implement them as a whole new example. I put the source files in a directory with the name `TryLinkedList` in the code download for the book.

The key to implementing a simple, general-purpose linked list is the `Object` class discussed earlier in this chapter. Because the `Object` class is a superclass of every class, you can use a variable of type `Object` to store any kind of object. You could re-implement the `ListPoint` class in the form of a `ListItem` class. This represents an element in a linked list that can reference any type of object:

Available for
download on
Wrox.com

```
class ListItem {
  // Constructor
  public ListItem(Object item) {
    this.item = item;            // Store the item
    next = null;                 // Set next as end point
  }

  // Return class name & object
  @Override
  public String toString() {
    return "ListItem " + item ;
  }

  ListItem next;                 // Refers to next item in the list
  Object item;                   // The item for this ListItem
}
```

Directory "TryPolyLine2"

It's basically similar to the `ListPoint` class except that you have omitted the methods to set and retrieve the next member reference. You see why these are not necessary in a moment. The `toString()` method assumes that the object referenced by `item` implements a `toString()` method. You won't use the `toString()` method here when you come to exercise the general linked list class you're implementing, but it is a good idea to implement the `toString()` method for your classes anyway. If you do, meaningful representations of class objects can always be output using the `println()` method, which is very handy for debugging.

You can now use objects of this class in a definition of a class that represents a linked list.

Defining a Linked List Class

The mechanics of creating and handling the linked list is similar to what you had in the `PolyLine` class, but externally you need to deal in the objects that are stored in the list, not in terms of `ListItem` objects. In fact, you don't need to have the `ListItem` class separate from the `LinkedList` class. You can make it an inner class:

Available for
download on
Wrox.com

```
public class LinkedList {
  // Default constructor - creates an empty list
  public LinkedList() {}

  // Constructor to create a list containing one object
  public LinkedList(Object item) {
    if(item != null) {
      current = end = start = new ListItem(item); // item is the start and end
    }
  }

  // Construct a linked list from an array of objects
  public LinkedList(Object[] items) {
    if(items != null) {
      // Add the items to the list
      for(Object item : items) {
        addItem(item);
```

```
        }
      current = start;
    }
  }

  // Add an item object to the list
  public void addItem(Object item) {
    ListItem newEnd = new ListItem(item);    // Create a new ListItem
    if(start == null) {                      // Is the list empty?
      start = end = newEnd;           // Yes, so new element is start and end
    } else {                                 // No, so append new element
      end.next = newEnd;                     // Set next variable for old end
      end = newEnd;                          // Store new item as end
    }
  }

  // Get the first object in the list
  public Object getFirst() {
    current = start;
    return start == null ? null : start.item;
  }

  // Get the next object in the list
  public Object getNext() {
    if(current != null) {
      current = current.next;                // Get the reference to the next item
    }
    return current == null ? null : current.item;
  }

  private ListItem start = null;             // First ListItem in the list
  private ListItem end = null;               // Last ListItem in the list
  private ListItem current = null;           // The current item for iterating

  // ListItem as a nested class
  private class ListItem {
    // ListItem class definition as before...
  }
}
```

Directory "TryPolyLine2"

Save this source file in the new directory for the example. You can use this class to create a linked list containing any types of objects. The class has data members to track the first and last items in the list, plus the member current, which is used to iterate through the list. You have three class constructors. The default constructor creates an empty list. You have a constructor to create a list with a single object, and another to create a list from an array of objects. Any list can also be extended by means of the addItem() method. Each of the constructors, apart from the default, sets the current member to the first item in the list, so if the list is not empty, this refers to a valid first item.

You can see that because the ListItem class is a member of the LinkedList class, you can refer to its data members directly within methods in the LinkedList class. This obviates the need for any methods in the ListItem class to get or set its fields. Because it is private it is not accessible outside the LinkedList class so there is no risk associated with this—as long as you code the LinkedList class correctly, of course.

The addItem() method works in much the same way as the addPoint() method did in the PolyLine class. It creates a new ListItem object and updates the next member of the previous last item to refer to the new one. The complication is the possibility that the list might be empty. The check in the if takes care of this. You take special steps if start holds a null reference.

The getFirst() and getNext() methods are intended to be used together to access all the objects stored in the list. The getFirst() method returns the object stored in the first ListItem object in the list and sets the current data member to refer to the first ListItem object. After calling the getFirst() method, successive calls to the getNext() method return subsequent objects stored in the list. The method updates current to refer to the next ListItem object, each time it is called. When the end of the list is reached, getNext() returns null.

TRY IT OUT   Using the General Linked List

You can now define the PolyLine class so that it uses a LinkedList object. All you need to do is put a LinkedList variable as a class member that you initialize in the class constructors, and implement all the other methods you had in the previous version of the class to use the LinkedList object:

Available for
download on
Wrox.com

```java
public class PolyLine {
  // Construct a polyline from an array of coordinate pairs
  public PolyLine(double[][] coords) {
    Point[] points = new Point[coords.length];    // Array to hold points

    // Create points from the coordinates
    for(int i = 0; i < coords.length ; ++i) {
      points[i] = new Point(coords[i][0], coords[i][1]);
    }

    // Create the polyline from the array of points
    polyline = new LinkedList(points);
  }

  // Construct a polyline from an array of points
  public PolyLine(Point[] points) {
    polyline = new LinkedList(points);          // Create the polyline
  }

  // Add a Point object to the list
  public void addPoint(Point point) {
    polyline.addItem(point);                    // Add the point to the list
  }

  // Add a point from a coordinate pair to the list
  public void addPoint(double x, double y) {
    polyline.addItem(new Point(x, y));          // Add the point to the list
  }

  // String representation of a polyline
  @Override
  public String toString() {
    StringBuffer str = new StringBuffer("Polyline:");
    Point point = (Point) polyline.getFirst();
                                                // Set the 1st point as start
    while(point != null) {
      str.append(" ("+ point+ ")");             // Append the current point
      point = (Point)polyline.getNext();        // Make the next point current
    }
    return str.toString();
  }

  private LinkedList polyline;                   // The linked list of points
}
```

Directory "TryPolyLine2"

You can exercise this using the same code as last time—in the TryPolyLine.java file. Copy this file to the directory for this example. Don't forget to copy Point.java, too. I changed the name of the file from TryPolyLine.java to TryPolyLine2.java and the class name of course.

How It Works

The `PolyLine` class implements all the methods that you had in the class before, so the `main()` method in the `TryPolyLine` class works just the same. Under the covers, the methods in the `PolyLine` class work a little differently. The work of creating the linked list is now in the constructor for the `LinkedList` class. The `PolyLine` class constructors just assemble a point array if necessary and call the `LinkedList` constructor. Similarly, the `addPoint()` method creates a `Point` object from the coordinate pair it receives and passes it to the `addItem()` method for the `LinkedList` object, `polyline`.

Note that the cast from `Point` to `Object` when the `addItem()` method is called is automatic. A cast from any class type to type `Object` is always automatic because the class is up the class hierarchy—remember that all classes have `Object` as a base. In the `toString()` method, you must insert an explicit cast to store the object returned by the `getFirst()` or the `getNext()` method. This cast is down the hierarchy so you must specify the cast explicitly.

You could use a variable of type `Object` to store the objects returned from `getFirst()` and `getNext()`, but this would not be a good idea. You would not need to insert the explicit cast, but you would lose a valuable check on the integrity of the program. You put objects of type `Point` into the list, so you would expect objects of type `Point` to be returned. An error in the program somewhere could result in an object of another type being inserted. If the object is not of type `Point`—due to the said program error, for example—the cast to type `Point` fails and you get an exception. A variable of type `Object` can store anything. If you use this, and something other than a `Point` object is returned, it does not register at all.

Now that you have gone to the trouble of writing your own general linked list class, you may be wondering why someone hasn't done it already. Well, they have! The `java.util` package defines a `LinkedList` class that is much better than this one. Still, putting your own together was a good experience, and I hope you found it educational, if not interesting. The way you have implemented the `LinkedList` class here is not the best approach. In Chapter 13 you learn about *generic types*, which enable you to define a linked list class that is type-safe. You look at the standard class in the `java.util` package that implements a linked list using the generic types capability in Chapter 14.

USING THE FINAL MODIFIER

You have already used the `final` keyword to fix the value of a static data member of a class. You can also apply this keyword to the definition of a method, and to the definition of a class.

It may be that you want to prevent a subclass from overriding a method in your class. When this is the case, simply declare that method as `final`. Any attempt to override a `final` method in a subclass results in the compiler flagging the new method as an error. For example, you could declare the method `addPoint()` as `final` within the class `PolyLine` by writing its definition in the class as:

```
public final void addPoint(Point point) {
  polyline.addItem(point);                    // Add the point to the list
}
```

Any class derived from `PolyLine` is not able to redefine this method. Obviously, an `abstract` method cannot be declared as `final`—because it must be defined in a subclass somewhere.

If you declare a class as `final`, you prevent any subclasses from being derived from it. To declare the class `PolyLine` as `final`, you define it as:

```
public final class PolyLine {
  // Definition as before...
}
```

If you now attempt to define a class based on `PolyLine`, you get an error message from the compiler. An abstract class cannot be declared as `final` because this prevents the abstract methods in the class from ever being defined. Declaring a class as `final` is a drastic step that prevents the functionality of the class being extended by derivation, so you should be very sure that you want to do this.

INTERFACES

In the classes that you derived from the class `Animal`, you had a common method, `sound()`, that was implemented individually in each of the subclasses. The method signature was the same in each class, and the method could be called polymorphically. The main point to defining the class `Animal` first and then subsequently defining the classes `Dog`, `Cat`, and so on, from it was to be able to get polymorphic behavior. When all you want is a set of one or more methods to be implemented in a number of different classes so that you can call them polymorphically, you can dispense with the base class altogether.

You can achieve the same result much easier by using a Java facility called an *interface*. The name indicates its primary use—specifying a set of methods that represent a particular class interface, which can then be implemented appropriately in a number of different classes. All of the classes then share this common interface, and the methods in it can be called polymorphically through a variable of the interface type. This is just one aspect of what you can do using an interface. I start by examining what an interface is from the ground up and then look at what you can do with it.

An *interface* is essentially a collection of related constants and/or abstract methods, and in most cases it contains just methods. An interface doesn't define what a method does. It just defines its form—its name, its parameters, and its return type, so by definition the methods in an interface are abstract.

To make use of an interface, you *implement* the interface in a class—that is, you declare that the class implements the interface using the `implements` keyword and you write the code for each of the methods that the interface declares as part of the class definition. When a class implements an interface, any constants that were defined in the interface definition are available directly in the class, just as though they were inherited from a base class. An interface can contain either constants, or abstract methods, or both.

The methods in an interface are always `public` and `abstract`, so you do not need to specify them as such; it is considered bad programming practice to specify any attributes for them, and you definitely cannot add any attributes other than the defaults, `public` and `abstract`. This implies that methods declared in an interface can never be `static`, so an interface always declares instance methods. The constants in an interface are always `public`, `static`, and `final`, so you do not need to specify the attributes for these either.

An interface is defined just like a class, but using the keyword `interface` rather than the keyword `class`. You store an interface definition in a `.java` file with the same name as the interface. The name that you give to an interface must be different from that of any other interface or class in the same package. Just as for classes, the members of the interface—the constants and/or method declarations—appear between a pair of braces that delimit the body of the interface definition.

Encapsulating Constants in a Program

You will often find that a program makes use of a set of constant values that you really want to define only once. You might have values representing standard colors that your program uses or perhaps constants that are used in calculations such as conversion factors from one set of units to another. In Java versions prior to 5.0, a common approach was to define a set of related constants in an interface and then implement the interface in any class that used any of the constants. This approach has largely been made obsolete by the static import capability.

The capability to import static members of a class that was introduced in Java 5 provides an excellent way of dealing with constants in a program. However, the use of an interface for such purposes was very widespread prior to Java 5, so I first explain briefly how that works to equip you for when you run into it. I then explain how you use static import to access constants that you have defined in a class, which is a much cleaner and better way of making a set of constants available wherever they are needed.

Constants in an Interface

Suppose you are writing a program that converts measurements between metric and imperial units. Here's how the constants that such a program might use could be defined in an interface:

```
public interface ConversionFactors {
    double INCH_TO_MM = 25.4;
    double OUNCE_TO_GRAM = 28.349523125;
    double POUND_TO_GRAM = 453.5924;
    double HP_TO_WATT = 745.7;
    double WATT_TO_HP = 1.0/HP_TO_WATT;
}
```

The ConversionFactors interface defines five constants for conversions of various kinds. Constants defined in an interface are automatically public, static, and final. You have no choice about this—constants defined in an interface always have these attributes. Because the constants are static and final, you must always supply initializing values for constants defined in an interface. The names given to these in the ConversionFactors interface use capital letters to indicate that they are final and cannot be altered—this is a common convention in Java. You can define the value of one constant in terms of a preceding constant, as in the definition of WATT_TO_HP. If you try to use a constant that is defined later in the interface—if, for example, the definition for WATT_TO_HP appeared first—your code does not compile.

Because you have declared the interface as public, the constants are also available outside the package containing the ConversionFactors interface. You can access constants defined in an interface in the same way as for public and static fields in a class—by just qualifying the name with the name of the interface. For example, you could write:

```
public class MyClass {
    // This class can access any of the constants defined in ConversionFactors
    // by qualifying their names...
    public static double poundsToGrams(double pounds) {
        return pounds*ConversionFactors.POUND_TO_GRAM;
    }

    // Plus the rest of the class definition...
}
```

Because the ConversionFactors interface includes only constants, a class can gain access to them using their unqualified names by declaring that it implements the interface. This has been the technique employed in the past. For example, here's a class that implements the ConversionFactors interface:

```
public class MyOtherClass implements ConversionFactors {
    // This class can access any of the constants defined in ConversionFactors
    // using their unqualified names, and so can any subclasses of this class...
    public static double poundsToGrams(double pounds) {
        return pounds*POUND_TO_GRAM;
    }

    // Plus the rest of the class definition...
}
```

The constants defined in the ConversionFactors interface are now members of MyOtherClass and therefore are inherited in any derived classes.

Although this technique of using an interface as a container for constants works and has been widely used in the past, using a class to contain the constants as static fields and then importing the names of the fields as required provides a simpler more effective approach. This is now the recommended technique for handling sets of constants in a program. Let's see how it works.

Constants Defined in a Class

You could define a class to hold the same set of constants that you saw defined in an interface in the previous section, like this:

```
package conversions;                            // Package for conversions

public class ConversionFactors {
  public static final double INCH_TO_MM = 25.4;
  public static final double OUNCE_TO_GRAM = 28.349523125;
  public static final double POUND_TO_GRAM = 453.5924;
  public static final double HP_TO_WATT = 745.7;
  public static final double WATT_TO_HP = 1.0/HP_TO_WATT;
}
```

Directory "TryConversions/conversions"

Of course, you can access the members of the `ConversionsFactors` class from outside by using the qualified names of the data members—`ConversionFactor.HP_TO_WATT`, for example. An alternative and possibly more convenient approach is to import the static members of the class into any class that needs to use any of the constants. This allows the constants to be referred to by their unqualified names. In this case, the class must be in a named package, because the `import` statement cannot be applied to the unnamed package.

Here's how you might use it:

```
import static conversions.ConversionFactors.*;   // Import static members

public class MyOtherClass {
  // This class can access any of the constants defined in ConversionFactors

  public static double poundsToGrams(double pounds) {
    return pounds*POUND_TO_GRAM;
  }

  // Plus the rest of the class definition...
}
```

Now you can access any of the static members of the `ConversionFactors` class using their unqualified names from any source file. All that is necessary is the `import` statement for the static members of the class. Alternatively, you could just import the static members you want to use. For example, you could use the following `import` statement if you just want to use the constant with the name `POUND_TO_GRAM`:

```
import static conversions.ConversionFactors.POUND_TO_GRAM;
```

Let's see it working in an example.

TRY IT OUT   Importing Constants into a Program

Save the `ConversionFactors` class definition `ConversionFactors.java` in a directory with the name `conversions`. Here's a simple class that uses the constants defined in the utility class `ConversionFactors`:

```
import static conversions.ConversionFactors.*;   // Import static members

public class TryConversions {
  public static double poundsToGrams(double pounds) {
    return pounds*POUND_TO_GRAM;
  }

  public static double inchesToMillimeters(double inches) {
    return inches*INCH_TO_MM;
  }

  public static void main(String args[]) {
    int myWeightInPounds = 180;
    int myHeightInInches = 75;
    System.out.println("My weight in pounds: " +myWeightInPounds +
                       " \t-in grams: "+ (int)poundsToGrams(myWeightInPounds));
```

```
System.out.println("My height in inches: " +myHeightInInches +
            " \t-in millimeters: "+ (int)inchesToMillimeters(myHeightInInches));
    }
}
```

Directory "TryConversions"

Save the `TryConversions.java` file in the `TryConversions` directory. Don't forget that you must include the path to your conversions package when you compile this program. If the `conversions` directory is a subdirectory of `C:\MyPackages`, the command to compile the program with `TryConversions` as the current directory is:

```
javac -classpath "C:\MyPackages" TryConversions.java
```

When you compile and execute this example, you should see the following output:

```
My weight in pounds: 180     -in grams: 81646
My height in inches: 75      -in millimeters: 1905
```

How It Works

The fact that you have used only static methods to access the constants from the utility class is unimportant—it's just to keep the example simple. They are equally accessible from instance methods in a class.

The two conversion methods use the conversion factors defined in the `ConversionFactors` class. Because you have imported the static fields from the `ConversionFactors` class in the `conversions` package into the `TryConversions.java` source file, you can use the unqualified names to refer to the constants.

Interfaces Declaring Methods

The primary use for an interface is to define the external form of a set of methods that represent a particular functionality. Let's consider an example. Suppose that you want to specify a set of methods to be used for conversions between metric and imperial measurements. You could define such an interface like this:

Available for download on Wrox.com

```
public interface Conversions {
    double inchesToMillimeters (double inches);
    double ouncesToGrams(double ounces);
    double poundsToGrams(double pounds);
    double hpToWatts(double hp);
    double wattsToHP(double watts);
}
```

Directory "TryConversions2"

This interface declares five methods to perform conversions. Every method that is declared in the interface must have a definition within a class that implements the interface if you are going to create objects of the class type. A class that implements this interface would look like this:

```
public class MyClass implements Conversions {
    // Implementations for the methods in the Conversions interface
    // Definitions for the other class members...
}
```

Because the methods in an interface are, by definition, public, you must use the `public` keyword when you define them in your class—otherwise, your code does not compile. The implementation of an interface method in a class must not have an access specifier that is more restrictive than that implicit in the abstract method declaration, and you can't get less restrictive than `public`.

A class can implement more than one interface. In this case, you write the names of all the interfaces that the class implements separated by commas following the `implements` keyword. Here's an example:

```
public class MyClass implements Conversions, Definitions, Detections {
  // Definition of the class including implementation of interface methods
}
```

This class implements three interfaces with the names `Conversions`, `Definitions`, and `Detections`. The class body contains definitions for the methods declared in all three interfaces.

TRY IT OUT   Implementing an Interface

You can use the `Conversions` interface in a modified version of the previous example. Redefine the `TryConversions` class in the `TryConversions.java` source file as follows:

Available for download on Wrox.com

```
import static conversions.ConversionFactors.*;   // Import static members

public class TryConversions implements Conversions {
  public double wattsToHP (double watts) {
    return watts*WATT_TO_HP;
  }
  public double hpToWatts (double hp) {
    return hp*HP_TO_WATT;
  }

  public double ouncesToGrams(double ounces) {
    return ounces*OUNCE_TO_GRAM;
  }

  public double poundsToGrams(double pounds) {
    return pounds*POUND_TO_GRAM;
  }

  public double inchesToMillimeters(double inches) {
    return inches*INCH_TO_MM;
  }

  public static void main(String args[]) {
    int myWeightInPounds = 180;
    int myHeightInInches = 75;

    TryConversions converter = new TryConversions();
    System.out.println("My weight in pounds: " +myWeightInPounds +
      " \t-in grams: "+ (int)converter.poundsToGrams(myWeightInPounds));
    System.out.println("My height in inches: " + myHeightInInches
                       + " \t-in millimeters: "
                       + (int)converter.inchesToMillimeters(myHeightInInches));
  }
}
```

Directory "TryConversions2"

Save the file in a new directory, `TryConversions2`, and add a source file containing the definition for the `Conversions` interface to the same directory. You name a file containing an interface definition in a similar way to that of a class—the file name should be the same as the interface name, with the extension `.java`. Thus, the source file containing the `Conversions` interface definition is `Conversions.java`.

How It Works

The methods you were using in the original definition of the class are now not declared as `static`. Because interface methods are by definition instance methods, you cannot declare them as static in the class that implements the interface. As the methods are now instance methods, you have to create a `TryConversions` object, `converter`, to call them.

Of course, in this instance, statically importing the constants that are used by the interface method implementations is a clumsy way of doing things. Because the constants are clearly related to the methods, it would probably be better to define all the constants in the `Conversions` interface in addition to the method declarations.

Of course, you don't *have to* implement every method in the interface, but there are some consequences if you don't.

A Partial Interface Implementation

You can omit the implementation of one or more of the methods from an interface in a class that implements the interface, but in this case the class inherits some abstract methods from the interface so you would need to declare the class itself as `abstract`:

```
import static conversions.ConversionFactors.INCH_TO_MM;
import static conversions.ConversionFactors.OUNCE_TO_GRAM;

public abstract class MyClass implements Conversions {
  // Implementation of two of the methods in the interface
  @Override public double inchesToMillimeters(double inches) {
    return inches*INCH_TO_MM;
  }

  @Override public double ouncesToGrams(double ounces) {
    return ounces*OUNCE_TO_GRAM;
  }

  // Definition of the rest of the class...
}
```

You cannot create objects of type `MyClass`. To arrive at a useful class, you must define a subclass of `MyClass` that implements the remaining methods in the interface. The declaration of the class as `abstract` is mandatory when you don't implement all of the methods that are declared in an interface. The compiler complains if you forget to do this.

Note the use of the `@Override` annotation. For a class that implements an interface and is not abstract, there is no need to use the `@Override` annotation because the compiler always generates an error message if you fail to implement any interface method with the correct signature. However, if you want to use the annotation in this case, you are free to do so. When you declare a class as `abstract`, no error message is produced for an incorrect signature for an interface method because the compiler has no way to know what you intended. The `@Override` annotation on interface method implementations ensure such errors are flagged in an abstract class.

Extending Interfaces

You can define one interface based on another by using the keyword `extends` to identify the base interface name. This is essentially the same form as you use to derive one class from another. The interface doing the extending acquires all the methods and constants from the interface it extends. For example, the interface `Conversions` would perhaps be more useful if it contained the constants that the original interface `ConversionFactors` contained. This would obviate the need for a separate class containing the constants, so there would be no need for the static import statement.

You could do this by defining the interface `Conversions` as follows:

```
public interface Conversions extends ConversionFactors {
  double inchesToMillimeters(double inches);
  double ouncesToGrams(double ounces);
  double poundsToGrams(double pounds);
  double hpToWatts(double hp);
  double wattsToHP(double watts);
}
```

Now the interface `Conversions` also contains the members of the interface `ConversionFactors`. Any class implementing the `Conversions` interface has the constants from `ConversionFactors` available to implement the methods. Analogous to the idea of a superclass, the interface `ConversionFactors` is referred to as a *super-interface* of the interface `Conversions`.

Of course, because the constants and the methods involved in conversion operations are closely related, it would have been much better to put them all in a single interface definition. But then it wouldn't demonstrate one interface extending another.

Interfaces and Multiple Inheritance

Unlike a class, which can extend only one other class, an interface can extend any number of other interfaces. To define an interface that inherits the members of several other interfaces, you specify the names of the interfaces separated by commas following the keyword `extends`. For example:

```
public interface MyInterface extends HisInterface, HerInterface {
  // Interface members - constants and abstract methods...
}
```

Now `MyInterface` inherits all the methods and constants that are members of `HisInterface` and `HerInterface`. This is described as *multiple inheritance*. In Java, classes do not support multiple inheritance, only interfaces do.

Some care is necessary when you use this capability. If two or more super-interfaces declare a method with the same signature—that is, with identical names and parameters—the method must have the same return type in all the interfaces that declare it. If they don't, the compiler reports an error. This is because it would be impossible for a class to implement both methods, as they have the same signature. If the method is declared identically in all the interfaces that declare it, then a single definition in the class satisfies all the interfaces. As I said in the previous chapter, every method in a class must have a unique signature, and the return type is not part of it.

Using Interfaces

What you have seen up to now has primarily illustrated the mechanics of creating an interface and incorporating it into a class. The really interesting question is—what should you use interfaces for?

An interface that declares methods defines a standard set of operations. Different classes can add such a standard interface by implementing it. Thus, objects of a number of different class types can share a common set of operations. Of course, a given operation in one class may be implemented quite differently from how it is implemented in another class. But the way in which you invoke the operation is the same for objects of all class types that implement the interface. For this reason it is often said that an interface defines a *contract* for a set of operations.

I hinted at the third and perhaps most important use of interfaces at the beginning of this discussion. An interface defines a type, so you can expedite polymorphism across a set of classes that implement the same interface. This is an extremely useful and powerful facility. Let's have a look at how this works.

Interfaces and Polymorphism

You can't create objects of an interface type, but you can create a variable of an interface type. For example:

```
Conversions converter = null;       // Variable of the Conversions interface type
```

If you can't create objects of type `Conversions`, what good is it? Well, you use it to store a reference to an object of any class type that implements `Conversions`. This means that you can use this variable to call the methods declared in the `Conversions` interface polymorphically. The `Conversions` interface is not a good example to show how this works. Let's consider a real-world parallel that I can use to better demonstrate this idea, that of home audio/visual equipment and a remote control. I'm grateful to John Ganter who suggested this idea to me after reading a previous edition of this book.

You have a TV, possibly an audio receiver, and almost certainly a DVD player around your home, and each of them has its own remote control. All the remote controls probably have some common subset of buttons—power on/off, volume up, volume down, mute, and so on. After you have more than four or so remotes cluttering the place up, you might consider one of those fancy universal remote control devices to replace them—sort of a single definition of a remote control, to suit all equipment.

A universal remote has a lot of similarities to an interface. By itself a universal remote does nothing. It defines a set of buttons for standard operations, but the operation of each button must be programmed specifically to suit each kind of device that you want to control. You can represent the TV, VCR, DVD, and so on by classes, each of which makes use of the same remote control interface—the set of buttons, if you like—but each in a different way. Even though it uses the same button on the remote, Power On for the TV, for example, is quite different from Power On for the VCR. Let's see how that might look in a concrete example.

TRY IT OUT   Defining Interfaces

Here's how you might define an interface to model a simple universal remote:

Available for download on Wrox.com

```java
public interface RemoteControl {
    boolean powerOnOff();          // Returns new state, on = true
    int volumeUp(int increment);   // Returns new volume level
    int volumeDown(int decrement); // Returns new volume level
    void mute();                   // Mutes sound output
    int setChannel(int channel);   // Set the channel number and return it
    int channelUp();               // Returns new channel number
    int channelDown();             // Returns new channel number
}
```

Directory "TryRemoteControl"

The methods declared here in the `RemoteControl` interface should be self-explanatory. I have included just a few of the many possible remote operations here to conserve space in the book. You could add more if you want. You could have separate power on and power off methods, for example, tone controls, and so on. There is no definition for any of these methods here. Methods declared in an interface are always `abstract`—by definition. Nor is there an access attribute for any of them. Methods declared in an interface are always `public` by default.

Now any class that requires the use of the functionality provided by a `RemoteControl` just has to declare that it implements the interface and include the definitions for each of the methods in the interface. For example, here's the TV:

Available for download on Wrox.com

```java
import static java.lang.Math.max;
import static java.lang.Math.min;

public class TV implements RemoteControl {
    public TV(String make, int screensize) {
        this.make = make;
        this.screensize = screensize;
        // In practice you would probably have more
        // arguments to set the max and min channel
        // and volume here plus other characteristics for a particular TV.
    }

    public boolean powerOnOff() {
        power = !power;
        System.out.println(make + " "+ screensize + " inch TV power "
                    + (power ? "on.":"off."));
        return power;
    }

    public int volumeUp(int increment) {
```

```
    if(!power) {                         // If the power is off
      return 0;                          // Nothing works
    }

    // Set volume - must not be greater than the maximum
    volume += increment;
    volume = min(volume, MAX_VOLUME);
    System.out.println(make + " "+ screensize + " inch TV volume level: "
                   + volume);
    return volume;
  }

  public int volumeDown(int decrement) {
    if(!power) {                         // If the power is off
      return 0;                          // Nothing works
    }

    // Set volume - must not be less than the minimum
    volume -= decrement;
    volume = max(volume, MIN_VOLUME);
    System.out.println(make + " "+ screensize + " inch TV volume level: "
                   + volume);
    return volume;
  }

  public void mute() {
    if(!power) {                         // If the power is off
      return;                            // Nothing works
    }

    volume = MIN_VOLUME;
    System.out.println(make + " "+ screensize + " inch TV volume level: "
                   + volume);
  }

  public int setChannel(int newChannel) {
    if(!power) {                         // If the power is off
      return 0;                          // Nothing works
    }

    // Channel must be from MIN_CHANNEL to MAX_CHANNEL
    if(newChannel>=MIN_CHANNEL && newChannel<=MAX_CHANNEL)
      channel = newChannel;
    System.out.println(make + " "+ screensize + " inch TV tuned to channel: "
                   + channel);
    return channel;
  }

  public int channelUp() {
    if(!power) {                         // If the power is off
      return 0;                          // Nothing works
    }

    // Wrap channel up to MIN_CHANNEL when MAX_CHANNEL is reached
    channel = channel<MAX_CHANNEL ? ++channel : MIN_CHANNEL;
    System.out.println(make + " "+ screensize + " inch TV tuned to channel: "
                   + channel);
    return channel;
  }

  public int channelDown() {
    if(!power)  {                        // If the power is off
```

```
      return 0;                                 // Nothing works
    }

    // Wrap channel down to MAX_CHANNEL when MIN_CHANNEL is reached
    channel = channel>MIN_CHANNEL ? --channel : MAX_CHANNEL;
    System.out.println(make + " "+ screensize + " inch TV tuned to channel: "
                       + channel);
    return channel;
  }

  private String make = null;
  private int screensize = 0;
  private boolean power = false;

  private final int MIN_VOLUME = 0;
  private final int MAX_VOLUME = 100;
  private int volume = MIN_VOLUME;

  private final int MIN_CHANNEL = 0;
  private final int MAX_CHANNEL = 999;
  private int channel = MIN_CHANNEL;
}
```

Directory "TryRemoteControl"

This class implements all the methods declared in the RemoteControl interface, and each method outputs
a message to the command line so you know when it is called. Of course, if you omitted any of the interface
method definitions in the class, the class would be abstract and you would have to declare it as such.

A DVDPlayer class defining a DVD player/recorder might also implement RemoteControl:

Available for
download on
Wrox.com

```
import static java.lang.Math.max;
import static java.lang.Math.min;

public class DVDPlayer implements RemoteControl {
  public DVDPlayer(String make) {
    this.make = make;
  }

  public boolean powerOnOff() {
    power = !power;
    System.out.println(make + " DVD Player power "+ (power ? "on.":"off."));
    return power;
  }

  public int volumeUp(int increment) {
    if(!power) {                              // If the power is off
      return 0;                               // Nothing works
    }

    // Set volume - must not be greater than the maximum
    volume += increment;
    volume = min(volume, MAX_VOLUME);
    System.out.println(make + " DVD Player volume level: " + volume);
    return volume;
  }

  public int volumeDown(int decrement) {
    if(!power) {                              // If the power is off
      return 0;                               // Nothing works
    }

    // Set volume - must not be less than the minimum
```

```
      volume -= decrement;
      volume = max(volume, MIN_VOLUME);
      System.out.println(make + " DVD Player volume level: " + volume);
      return volume;
   }

   public void mute() {
      if(!power) {                            // If the power is off
         return;                              // Nothing works
      }

      volume = MIN_VOLUME;
      System.out.println(make + " DVD Player volume level: " + volume);
   }

   public int setChannel(int newChannel) {
      if(!power) {                            // If the power is off
         return 0;                            // Nothing works
      }

      // Channel must be from MIN_CHANNEL to MAX_CHANNEL
      if(newChannel>=MIN_CHANNEL && newChannel<=MAX_CHANNEL) {
         channel = newChannel;
      }
      System.out.println(make + " DVD Player tuned to channel: " + channel);
      return channel;
   }

   public int channelUp() {
      if(!power) {                            // If the power is off
         return 0;                            // Nothing works
      }

      // Wrap channel round to MIN_CHANNEL when MAX_CHANNEL is reached
      channel = channel<MAX_CHANNEL ? ++channel : MIN_CHANNEL;
      System.out.println(make + " DVD Player tuned to channel: " + channel);
      return channel;
   }

   public int channelDown() {
      if(!power) {                            // If the power is off
         return 0;                            // Nothing works
      }

      // Wrap channel round to MAX_CHANNEL when MIN_CHANNEL is reached
      channel = channel>MIN_CHANNEL ? --channel : MAX_CHANNEL;
      System.out.println(make + " DVD Player tuned to channel: " + channel);
      return channel;
   }

   private String make = null;
   private boolean power = false;

   private final int MIN_VOLUME = 0;
   private final int MAX_VOLUME = 100;
   private int volume = MIN_VOLUME;

   private final int MIN_CHANNEL = 0;
   private final int MAX_CHANNEL = 99;
   private int channel = MIN_CHANNEL;
}
```

Directory "TryRemoteControl"

Of course, you could continue to define classes for other kinds of devices that use the remote, but these two are sufficient to demonstrate the principle.

Let's see how you can use the RemoteControl interface and these two classes in a working example.

TRY IT OUT   Polymorphism Using an Interface Type

You want to demonstrate polymorphic behavior with these classes. By introducing a bit of "randomness" into the example, you can avoid having any prior knowledge of the objects involved. Here's the class to operate both TV and DVD player objects via a variable of type RemoteControl:

```java
import static java.lang.Math.random;

public class TryRemoteControl {
    public static void main(String args[]) {
        RemoteControl remote = null;

        // You will create five objects to operate using our remote
        for(int i = 0 ; i<5 ; ++i) {
            // Now create either a TV or a DVD Player/Recorder at random
            if(random()<0.5)
                // Random choice of TV make and screen size
                remote = new TV(random()<0.5 ? "Sony" : "Hitachi",
                                random()<0.5 ? 46 : 40);
            else // Random choice of DVD Player/Recorder
                remote = new DVDPlayer(random()<0.5 ? "Panasonic": "JVC");

            // Now operate it, whatever it is
            remote.powerOnOff();                    // Switch it on
            remote.channelUp();                     // Set the next channel up
            remote.volumeUp(10);                    // Turn up the sound
        }
    }
}
```

Directory "TryRemoteControl"

This should be in the same directory as the source files for the two classes and the interface defined earlier. When you compile and run this, you should see output recording a random selection of five TV and DVD player objects operated by the RemoteControl variable. I got the following:

```
JVC DVD Player power on.
JVC DVD Player tuned to channel: 1
JVC DVD Player volume level: 10
Panasonic DVD Player power on.
Panasonic DVD Player tuned to channel: 1
Panasonic DVD Player volume level: 10
Sony 46 inch TV power on.
Sony 46 inch TV tuned to channel: 1
Sony 46 inch TV volume level: 10
Sony 40 inch TV power on.
Sony 40 inch TV tuned to channel: 1
Sony 40 inch TV volume level: 10
Panasonic DVD Player power on.
Panasonic DVD Player tuned to channel: 1
Panasonic DVD Player volume level: 10
```

How It Works

The variable remote is of type RemoteControl so you can use it to store a reference to any class object that implements the RemoteControl interface. Within the for loop, you create either a TV or a DVDPlayer object at random. The TV or DVDPlayer object is of a randomly chosen make, and any TV object is either 46 inches or

40 inches—again chosen at random. The object that is created is then operated through remote by calling its `powerOnOff()`, `channelUp()`, and `volumeUp()` methods. Because the type of the object is determined at run time, and at random, the output demonstrates you are clearly seeing polymorphism in action here through a variable of an interface type.

Using Multiple Interfaces

Of course, a `RemoteControl` object in the previous example can be used to call only the methods that are declared in the interface. If a class implements some other interface besides `RemoteControl`, then to call the methods declared in the second interface you need either to use a variable of that interface type to store the object reference or to cast the object reference to its actual class type. Suppose you have a class defined as the following:

```
public MyClass implements RemoteControl, AbsoluteControl {
    // Class definition including methods from both interfaces...
}
```

Because this class implements `RemoteControl` and `AbsoluteControl`, you can store an object of type `MyClass` in a variable of either interface type. For example:

```
AbsoluteControl ac = new MyClass();
```

Now you can use the variable `ac` to call methods declared in the `AbsoluteControl` interface. However, you cannot call the methods declared in the `RemoteControl` interface using `ac`, even though the object reference that it holds has these methods. One possibility is to cast the reference to the original class type, like this:

```
((MyClass)ac).powerOnOff();
```

Because you cast the reference to type `MyClass`, you can call any of the methods defined in that class. You can't get polymorphic behavior like this though. The compiler determines the method that is called when the code is compiled. To call the methods in the `RemoteControl` interface polymorphically, you have to have the reference stored as that type. Provided you know that the object is of a class type that implements the `RemoteControl` interface, you can get a reference of type `RemoteControl` from the reference stored in the variable `ac`. Like this, for example:

```
if(ac instanceof RemoteControl)
    ((RemoteControl)ac).mute();
```

Even though the interfaces `RemoteControl` and `AbsoluteControl` are unrelated, you can cast the reference in `ac` to type `RemoteControl`. This is possible because the object that is referenced by `ac` is actually of type `MyClass`, which happens to implement both interfaces and therefore incorporates both interface types.

If you got a bit lost in this last section don't worry about it. You won't need this level of knowledge about interfaces very often.

Interface Types as Method Parameters

Of course, you can specify that a parameter to a method is of an interface type. This has a special significance in that a reference to an object of any type can be passed as an argument as long as the object type implements the interface. By specifying a parameter as an interface type you are implying that the method is interested only in the interface methods. As long as an object is of a type that implements those methods, it is acceptable as an argument.

Methods within the standard class libraries often have parameters of interface types. The `String`, `StringBuilder`, and `StringBuffer` classes (plus the `CharBuffer` class that you see later in the book) implement the `CharSequence` interface. You'll see lots of class methods that have a parameter of type `CharSequence`, in which case such methods will accept references to any of the class types I've mentioned as arguments. For example, the `StringBuilder` and `StringBuffer` classes both have constructors with a parameter of type `CharSequence`. You can therefore create new objects of these two class types from an object of any class that implement the interface.

Nesting Classes in an Interface Definition

You can put the definition of a class inside the definition of an interface. The class is an inner class to the interface. An inner class to an interface is `static` and `public` by default. The code structure would be like this:

```
interface Port {
  // Methods & Constants declared in the interface...

  class Info {
    // Definition of the class...
  }
}
```

This declares the interface `Port` with an inner class `Info`. Objects of the inner class are of type `Port.Info`. You might create one with a statement like this:

```
Port.Info info = new Port.Info();
```

The standard class library includes a number of interfaces with inner classes, including one with the name `Port` (in the `javax.sound.sampled` package) that has an inner class with the name `Info`, although the `Info` class does not have the default constructor that I have used in the illustration here. The circumstances where you might define a class as an inner class to an interface would be when objects of the inner class type have a strong logical association with the interface.

A class that implements the interface would have no direct connection with the inner class to the interface — it would just need to implement the methods declared by the interface, but it is highly likely it would make use of objects of the inner class type.

Interfaces and the Real World

An interface type is sometimes used to reference an object that encapsulates something that exists outside of Java, such as a particular physical device. This is done when the external device does not require methods implemented in Java code because all the function is provided externally. The interface method declarations just identify the mechanism for operating on the external object.

The example of the `Port` interface in the library is exactly that. A reference of type `Port` refers to an object that is a physical port on a sound card, such as that for the speaker or the microphone. The inner class, `Port.Info`, defines objects that encapsulate data to define a particular port. You can't create a `Port` object directly because there is no class of type `Port`. Indeed, it doesn't necessarily make sense to do so because your system may not have any ports. Assuming your PC has sound ports, you obtain a reference of type `Port` to an object that encapsulates a real port, such as the microphone, by calling a static method defined in another class. The argument to the method is a reference to an object of type `Port.Info` specifying the kind of port that you want. All the methods defined in the `Port` interface correspond to methods written in native machine code that operate on the port. To call them you just use the `Port` reference that you have obtained.

ANONYMOUS CLASSES

There are occasions where you need to define a class for which you will only ever want to define one object in your program, and the only use for the object is to pass it directly as an argument to a method. In this case, as long as your class extends an existing class, or implements an interface, you have the option of defining the class as an *anonymous class*. The definition for an anonymous class appears in the new expression, in the statement where you create and use the object of the class, so that there is no necessity to provide a name for the class.

I illustrate how this is done using an example. Suppose you want to define an object of a class that implements the interface `ActionListener` for one-time use. You could do this as follows:

```
pickButton.addActionListener(new ActionListener() {
                                // Code to define the class
                                // that implements the ActionListener interface
                             }
                          );
```

The class definition appears in the `new` expression that creates the argument to the `addActionListener()` method. This method requires a reference of type `ActionListener`—in other words, a reference to a class that implements the `ActionListener` interface. The parentheses following the name of the interface indicate you are creating an object reference of this type, and the details of the class definition appear between the braces. The anonymous class can include data members as well as methods, but obviously not constructors because the class has no name. Here, all the methods declared in the `ActionListener` interface would need to be defined. You use this approach in practice when you are implementing window-based applications later in the book.

If the anonymous class extends an existing class, the syntax is much the same. In this case, you are calling a constructor for the base class, and if this is not a default constructor, you can pass arguments to it by specifying them between the parentheses following the base class name. The definition of the anonymous class must appear between braces, just as in the previous example.

An anonymous class can be convenient when the class definition is short and simple. You shouldn't use the approach to define classes of any complexity as it makes the code very difficult to understand.

SUMMARY

You should now understand polymorphism and how to apply it. You will find that this technique can be utilized to considerable advantage in the majority of your Java programs. It certainly appears in many of the examples in the remaining chapters.

EXERCISES

You can download the source code for the examples in the book and the solutions to the following exercises from www.wrox.com.

1. Define an abstract base class `Shape` that includes `protected` data members for the (x, y) position of a shape, a `public` method to move a shape, and a `public abstract` method `show()` to output a shape. Derive subclasses for lines, circles, and rectangles. Also, define the class `PolyLine` that you saw in this chapter with `Shape` as its base class. You can represent a line as two points, a circle as a center and a radius, and a rectangle as two points on diagonally opposite corners. Implement the `toString()` method for each class. Test the classes by selecting ten random objects of the derived classes, and then invoking the `show()` method for each. Use the `toString()` methods in the implementation of `show()` in the derived classes.

2. Define a class, `ShapeList`, that can store an arbitrary collection of any objects of subclasses of the `Shape` class.

3. Implement the classes for shapes using an interface for the common methods, rather than inheritance from the superclass, while still keeping `Shape` as a base class.

4. Extend the `LinkedList` class that you defined in this chapter so that it supports traversing the list backward as well as forward.

5. Add methods to the class `LinkedList` to insert and delete elements at the current position.

6. Implement a method in the `LinkedList` class to insert an object following an object passed as an argument. Assume the objects stored in the list implement an `equals()` method that compares the `this` object with an object passed as an argument and returns `true` if they are equal.

▶ WHAT YOU LEARNED IN THIS CHAPTER

TOPIC	CONCEPT
Abstract Methods	An abstract method is a method that has no body defined for it and is declared using the keyword `abstract`.
Abstract Classes	An abstract class is a class that contains one or more abstract methods. It must be defined with the attribute `abstract`.
Derived Classes	You can define one class based on another. This is called class derivation or inheritance. The base class is called a superclass, and the derived class is called a subclass. A superclass can also be a subclass of another superclass.
The Universal Superclass	Every class has the `Object` class as a base so every class inherits members from the `Object` class. The `toString()` method is inherited from the `Object` class.
Abstract Derived Classes	A subclass of an abstract class must also be declared as `abstract` if it does not provide definitions for all of the abstract methods inherited from its superclass.
Class Inheritance	A subclass inherits certain members of its superclass. An inherited member of a class can be referenced and used as though it were declared as a normal member of the class.
Constructors under Inheritance	A subclass does not inherit the superclass constructors.
Private and Package-Private Class Members	The `private` members of a superclass are not inherited in a subclass. If the subclass is not in the same package as the superclass, then members of the superclass that do not have an access attribute are not inherited.
Implementing Derived Class Constructors	The first statement in the body of a constructor for a subclass should call a constructor for the superclass. If it does not, the compiler inserts a call for the default constructor for the superclass.
Polymorphism	A subclass can override a method inherited from its superclass by re-implementing it in the subclass. If two or more subclasses, with a common base class, override a common set of methods, these methods can be selected for execution dynamically at run time. This behavior is termed *polymorphism.*
Polymorphic Behavior	The subclass method selected by a polymorphic call is determined by the type of the object that is used to call the method.
Using Variables of a Superclass Type	A variable of a superclass type can point to an object of any of its subclasses. Such a variable can then be used to execute the subclass methods inherited from the superclass polymorphically.
`@Override`	You should use the `@Override` annotation for derived class methods that can be called polymorphically to guard against errors arising from an incorrect method signature in the derived class.
Static Import	You can import the static members of a class that is defined in a named package into a class to allow the imported static members to be referenced by their unqualified names.
Enumeration Class Types	An enumeration type is a specialized form of class, and the enumeration constants that you define are instances of the enumeration class type.
Nested Classes	A class defined inside another class is called a *nested* class or *inner* class. An inner class may itself contain inner classes.
Interfaces	An interface can contain constants, abstract methods, and inner classes.
Implementing Interfaces in a Class	A class can implement one or more interfaces by declaring them in the class definition and including the code to implement each of the interface methods.
Partial Interface Implementation	A class that does not define all the methods for an interface it implements must be declared as `abstract`.
Interface Types and Polymorphism	If several classes implement a common interface, the methods declared as members of the interface can be executed polymorphically by using a variable of the interface type to store references to objects of the class types.

7

Exceptions

WHAT YOU WILL LEARN IN THIS CHAPTER

➤   What an exception is

➤   How you handle exceptions in your programs

➤   The standard exceptions in Java

➤   How to guarantee that a particular block of code in a method will always be executed

➤   How to define and use your own types of exceptions

➤   How to throw exceptions in your programs

Java uses exceptions as a way of signaling problems when you execute a program. Exceptions act as a control mechanism through which a program may be able to recover from an exceptional event. They provide important debug information (through stack traces) that help you figure what went wrong. Problems signaled by exceptions can be, but aren't always, serious (as I describe later in this chapter). The standard classes use them extensively. Because they arise in your Java programs when things go wrong—and if something can go wrong in your code, sooner or later it will—they are a very basic consideration when you are designing and writing your programs.

The reason I've been sidestepping the question of exceptions for the past six chapters is that you first needed to understand classes and inheritance before you could understand what an exception is and appreciate what happens when an exception occurs. Now that you have a good grasp of these topics I can delve into how to use and deal with exceptions in a program.

THE IDEA BEHIND EXCEPTIONS

An exception usually signals an error and is so called because errors in your Java programs are bound to be the exception rather than the rule—by definition! An exception doesn't always indicate an error though—it can also signal some particularly unusual event in your program that deserves special attention.

If you try to deal with the myriad and often highly unusual and often unexpected error conditions that might arise in your application code, your program structure soon becomes very complicated and difficult to understand. One major benefit of having an error signaled by an exception is that it separates the code that deals with errors from the code that is executed when things are moving along smoothly. Another positive aspect of exceptions is that they provide a way of enforcing a response to particular errors. With many kinds of exceptions, you must include code in your program to deal with them; otherwise, your code does not compile. These exceptions are referred to as *checked exceptions. Unchecked exceptions* are exceptions where you have the option of dealing with them or not.

One important idea to grasp is that not all errors in your programs need to be signaled by exceptions. Exceptions should be reserved for the unusual or catastrophic situations that can arise. A user entering incorrect input to your program, for instance, is a normal event and should be handled without resorting to exceptions. The reason for this is that dealing with exceptions involves quite a lot of processing overhead, so if your program is handling exceptions a lot of the time it runs a lot slower than it needs to.

An exception in Java is an object that's created when an abnormal situation arises in your program. Exceptions can be created by the JVM, by standard library class methods, or by your application code. This exception object has fields that store information about the nature of the problem. The exception is said to be *thrown*—that is, the object identifying the exceptional circumstance is tossed as an argument to a specific piece of program code that has been written specifically to deal with that kind of problem. The code receiving the exception object as a parameter is said to *catch* it.

The situations that cause exceptions are quite diverse, but they fall into four broad categories, as shown in Table 7-1.

TABLE 7-1: Exceptions in Java

EXCEPTION	DESCRIPTION
Code or data errors	For example, if you attempt an invalid cast of an object, you try to use an array index that's outside the limits for the array, or an integer arithmetic expression has a zero divisor.
Standard method exceptions	For example, if you use the `substring()` method in the `String` class, it can throw a `StringIndexOutOfBoundsException` exception.
Throwing your own exceptions	You see later in this chapter how you can throw a few of your own when you need to.
Java errors	These can be due to errors in executing the Java Virtual Machine, which runs your compiled program, but usually arise as a consequence of an error in your program.

Before you look at how you make provision in your programs for dealing with exceptions, you should understand what specific classes of exceptions could arise.

TYPES OF EXCEPTIONS

An exception is always an object of some subclass of the standard class `Throwable`. This is true for exceptions that you define and throw yourself, as well as the standard exceptions that are defined in Java's standard packages. It's also true for exceptions that are thrown by methods in one or another of the standard packages.

Two direct subclasses of `Throwable`—`Error` and `Exception`—are the parent of all the standard exceptions. Both these classes have subclasses that identify specific exception conditions. Figure 7-1 shows the `Throwable` class hierarchy.

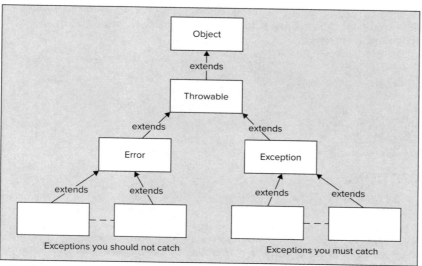

Exceptions you should not catch

Exceptions you must catch

FIGURE 7-1

Exceptions of Type Error

The exceptions that are defined by the `Error` class and its subclasses all represent conditions that you aren't expected to do anything about, so you aren't expected to catch them. `Error` has several direct subclasses including `ThreadDeath`, `LinkageError`, and `VirtualMachineError`. These are unchecked exceptions. You can do little or nothing to recover from these types of errors during the execution of the program. All you can hope to do (if you're lucky) is read the error message that is generated by the exception being thrown and then, particularly in the case of a `LinkageError` exception, try to figure out what might be wrong with your code to cause the problem.

Exceptions of Type RuntimeException

Almost all the exceptions that are represented by subclasses of `Exception` are checked exceptions so you must include code in your programs to deal with them if your code may cause them to be thrown. In methods whose code has the potential to throw a checked exception, you must either handle the checked exception within the method or register that your method may throw such an exception. If you don't, your program does not compile. You see in a moment how to handle exceptions and how to specify that a method can throw an exception.

Exceptions of type `RuntimeException` are exempt from the requirement to catch them, even though `RuntimeException` is derived from `Exception`. The reason that the compiler allows you to ignore `RuntimeException` exceptions is that they generally arise because of serious errors in your code. In most cases you can do little to recover the situation. However, in a few instances, it may be useful to include code to recognize them.

You need to know when these various types of exception can be thrown and how you can handle them. You try out some of the `RuntimeException` exceptions later in the chapter, as some of them are very easy to generate, but let's see what other sorts of exception classes have `Exception` as a base.

Other Subclasses of Exception

All the other classes derived from the class `Exception` are checked exceptions so the compiler verifies that you either have provided code to handle the exception in a method where the exception may be thrown or that you've indicated that the method can throw such an exception. If you do neither, your code doesn't compile. You look more at how you ensure that the code does compile in the next two sections.

Apart from those that are subclasses of RuntimeException, all exceptions thrown by methods in the Java class library are checked. In Chapter 8 you look at input and output where the code is liberally sprinkled with provisions for exceptions being thrown.

 NOTE *You see later in this chapter that when you want to define your own exceptions, you do this by subclassing the Exception class. Wherever your exception can be thrown by a method, the compiler verifies either that it is caught in the method or that the method definition indicates that it can be thrown by the method, just as it does for the built-in exceptions.*

DEALING WITH EXCEPTIONS

As I discussed in the previous sections, if your code can throw exceptions other than those of type Error or type RuntimeException (you can assume that I generally include the subclasses when I talk about Error and RuntimeException exceptions), you must do something about it. Whenever you write code that can throw a checked exception, you have a choice. You can supply code within the method to deal with any exception that is thrown, or you can essentially ignore it by enabling the method containing the exception-throwing code to pass it on to the code that invoked the method.

Let's first see how you can pass an exception on.

Specifying the Exceptions a Method Can Throw

Suppose you have a method that can throw an exception that is neither a subclass of RuntimeException nor of Error. This could be an exception of type IOException, for example, which can be thrown if your method involves some file input or output operations. If the exception isn't caught and disposed of in the method, you must at least declare that the exception can be thrown. But how do you do that?

You do it simply by adding a throws clause in the method signature. Suppose you write a method that uses the methods from classes that support input/output that are defined in the package java.io. You see in the chapters devoted to I/O operations that some of these can throw exceptions represented by objects of classes IOException and FileNotFoundException. Neither of these is a subclass of RuntimeException or Error, so the possibility of an exception being thrown needs to be declared. Because the method can't handle any exceptions it might throw, if only for the simple reason that you don't know how to do it yet, it must be defined as:

```
double myMethod() throws IOException, FileNotFoundException {
  // Detail of the method code...
}
```

As the preceding fragment illustrates, to declare that your method can throw exceptions you just put the throws keyword after the parameter list for the method. Then add the list of classes for the exceptions that might be thrown, separated by commas. This propagates—if another method calls this method, it too must take account of the exceptions this method can throw. The calling method definition must either deal with the exceptions or declare that it can throw these exceptions as well. It's a simple choice. You either pass the buck or decide that the buck stops here. The compiler checks for this and your code does not compile if you don't do one or the other. The reasons for this become obvious when you look at the way a Java program behaves when it encounters an exception.

Handling Exceptions

If you want to deal with checked exceptions where they occur, you can include three kinds of code blocks in a method to handle them—try, catch, and finally blocks:

> A try block encloses code that may give rise to one or more exceptions. Code that can throw an exception that you want to catch must be in a try block.

➤ A `catch` block encloses code that is intended to handle exceptions of a particular type that may be thrown in the associated `try` block. I get to how a `catch` block is associated with a `try` block later in this chapter.

➤ The code in a `finally` block is always executed before the method ends, regardless of whether any exceptions are thrown in the `try` block.

Let's dig into the detail of `try` and `catch` blocks first and then come back to the application of a `finally` block a little later.

The try Block

You can do something about many of the exceptions that are thrown. In the last two chapters you'll be working with XML documents where exceptions are thrown to indicate errors in the XML. You will usually want to catch these and report the location of an error in the document. When you want to catch an exception, the code in the method that might cause the exception to be thrown must be enclosed in a `try` block. Code that can cause exceptions need not be in a `try` block, but in this case, the method containing the code won't be able to catch any exceptions that are thrown and the method must declare that it can throw the types of exceptions that are not caught.

A `try` block is simply the keyword `try`, followed by braces enclosing the code that can throw the exception:

```
try {
  // Code that can throw one or more exceptions
}
```

Although I am discussing primarily exceptions that you must deal with here, a `try` block is also necessary if you want to catch exceptions of type `Error` or `RuntimeException`. When you come to a working example in a moment, you use an exception type that you don't have to catch, simply because exceptions of this type are easy to generate.

The catch Block

You enclose the code to handle an exception of a given type in a `catch` block. The `catch` block must immediately follow the `try` block that contains the code that may throw that particular exception. A `catch` block consists of the keyword `catch` followed by a single parameter between parentheses. The parameter identifies the type of exception that the block is to deal with. This is followed by the code to handle the exception enclosed between braces:

```
try {
  // Code that can throw one or more exceptions

} catch(IOException e) {
  // Code to handle the exception
}
```

This `catch` block handles exceptions of type `IOException` or of any subclass of `IOException`. If other checked exceptions can be thrown that are not declared in the method signature, this won't compile. I'll come back to handling multiple exception types in a moment.

TRY IT OUT Using a try and a catch Block

This example throws an unchecked exception. I chose to do this rather that an example throwing checked exceptions because the condition for an `ArithmeticException` to be thrown is very easy to generate. The following code is really just an exhaustive log of the program's execution:

```
public class TestTryCatch {
  public static void main(String[] args) {
    int i = 1;
    int j = 0;

    try {
```

```
        System.out.println("Try block entered " + "i = "+ i + " j = "+j);
        System.out.println(i/j);                    // Divide by 0 - exception thrown
        System.out.println("Ending try block");

    } catch(ArithmeticException e) {                // Catch the exception
        System.out.println("Arithmetic exception caught");
    }

    System.out.println("After try block");
  }
}
```

TestTryCatch.java

If you run the example, you should get the following output:

```
Try block entered i = 1 j = 0
Arithmetic exception caught
After try block
```

How It Works

The variable j is initialized to 0, so that the divide operation in the try block causes an ArithmeticException exception to be thrown by the Java Virtual Machine. The first line in the try block enables you to track when the try block is entered, and the second line throws an exception. The third line can be executed only if the exception isn't thrown—which can't occur in this example.

The output shows that when the exception is thrown, control transfers immediately to the first statement in the catch block. It's the evaluation of the expression that is the argument to the println() method that throws the exception, so the println() method never gets called. After the catch block has been executed, execution then continues with the statement following the catch block. The statements in the try block following the point where the exception occurred aren't executed. You could try running the example again after changing the value of j to 1 so that no exception is thrown. The output in this case is:

```
Try block entered i = 1 j = 1
1
Ending try block
After try block
```

From this you can see that the entire try block is executed. Execution then continues with the statement after the catch block. Because no arithmetic exception was thrown, the code in the catch block isn't executed.

 WARNING *You need to take care when adding try blocks to existing code. A try block is no different to any other block between braces when it comes to variable scope. Variables declared in a try block are available only until the closing brace for the block. It's easy to enclose the declaration of a variable in a try block, and, in doing so, inadvertently limit the scope of the variable and cause compiler errors.*

The catch block itself is a separate scope from the try block. If you want the catch block to output information about objects or values that are set in the try block, make sure the variables are declared in an outer scope.

try catch Bonding

The try and catch blocks are bonded together. You must not separate them by putting statements between the two blocks, or even by putting braces around the try keyword and the try block itself. If you have a loop block that is also a try block, the catch block that follows is also part of the loop. You can see this with a variation of the previous example.

TRY IT OUT   A Loop Block That Is a try Block

You can make j a loop control variable and count down so that eventually you get a zero divisor in the loop:

```java
public class TestLoopTryCatch {
  public static void main(String[] args) {
    int i = 12;

    for(int j=3 ; j > =-1 ; --j) {
      try {
        System.out.println("Try block entered  i = " + i + " j = " + j);
        System.out.println(i/j);                    // Divide by 0 - exception thrown
        System.out.println("Ending try block");

      } catch(ArithmeticException e) {            // Catch the exception
        System.out.println("Arithmetic exception caught: " + e);
      }
    }

    System.out.println("After try block");
  }
}
```

TestLoopTryCatch.java

This produces the following output:

```
Try block entered  i = 12 j = 3
4
Ending try block
Try block entered  i = 12 j = 2
6
Ending try block
Try block entered  i = 12 j = 1
12
Ending try block
Try block entered  i = 12 j = 0
Arithmetic exception caught: java.lang.ArithmeticException: / by zero
Try block entered  i = 12 j = -1
-12
Ending try block
After try block
```

How It Works

The try and catch blocks are all part of the loop because the catch is inextricably bound to the try. You can see this from the output. On the fourth iteration, you get an exception thrown because j is 0. However, after the catch block is executed, you still get one more iteration with j having the value –1.

Even though the try and catch blocks are both within the for loop, they have separate scopes. Variables declared within the try block cease to exist when an exception is thrown. You can demonstrate that this is so by declaring an arbitrary variable—k, say—in the try block, and then adding a statement to output k in the catch block. Your code does not compile in this case.

Suppose you wanted the loop to end when an exception was thrown. You can easily arrange for this. Just put the whole loop in a try block, thus:

```java
public static void main(String[] args) {
  int i = 12;
  try {
    System.out.println("Try block entered.");
```

```
    for(int j=3 ; j > =-1 ; --j) {
      System.out.println("Try block entered   i = " + i + " j = " + j);
      System.out.println(i/j);           // Divide by 0 - exception thrown
    }
    System.out.println("Ending try block");

  } catch(ArithmeticException e) {      // Catch the exception
      System.out.println("Arithmetic exception caught: " + e);
  }

  System.out.println("After try block");
}
```

TestLoopTryCatch2.java

With this version of main(), the program produces the following output:

```
Try block entered.
Try block entered   i = 12 j = 3
4
Try block entered   i = 12 j = 2
6
Try block entered   i = 12 j = 1
12
Try block entered   i = 12 j = 0
Arithmetic exception caught: java.lang.ArithmeticException: / by zero
After try block
```

Now, you no longer get the output for the last iteration because control passes to the catch block when the exception is thrown, and that is now outside the loop.

Multiple catch Blocks

If a try block can throw several different kinds of exception, you can put several catch blocks after the try block to handle them:

```
try {
  // Code that may throw exceptions

} catch(ArithmeticException e) {
    // Code for handling ArithmeticException exceptions
} catch(IndexOutOfBoundsException e) {
    // Code for handling IndexOutOfBoundsException exceptions
}
// Execution continues here...
```

Exceptions of type ArithmeticException are caught by the first catch block, and exceptions of type IndexOutOfBoundsException are caught by the second. Of course, if an ArithmeticException is thrown, only the code in that catch block is executed. When it is complete, execution continues with the statement following the last catch block.

When you need to catch exceptions of several different types that may be thrown in a try block, the order of the catch blocks can be important. When an exception is thrown, it is caught by the first catch block that has a parameter type that is the same as that of the exception, or a type that is a superclass of the type of the exception. An extreme case would be if you specified the catch block parameter as type Exception. This would catch any exception that is of type Exception, or of a class type that is derived from Exception. This includes virtually all the exceptions you are likely to meet in the normal course of events.

This has implications for multiple `catch` blocks relating to exception class types in a hierarchy. The `catch` blocks must be in sequence with the most derived type first and the most basic type last. Otherwise, your code does not compile. The simple reason for this is that if a `catch` block for a given class type precedes a `catch` block for a type that is derived from the first, the second `catch` block can never be executed, and the compiler detects that this is the case.

Suppose you have a `catch` block for exceptions of type `ArithmeticException` and another for exceptions of type `Exception` as a catch-all. If you write them in the following sequence, exceptions of type `ArithmeticException` could never reach the second `catch` block because they are always caught by the first:

```
// Invalid catch block sequence - won't compile!
try {
  // try block code

} catch(Exception e) {
  // Generic handling of exceptions
} catch(ArithmeticException e) {
  // Specialized handling for these exceptions
}
```

Of course, this wouldn't get past the compiler—it would be flagged as an error.

In principle, if you're only interested in generic exceptions, all the error handling code can be localized in one `catch` block for exceptions of the superclass type. However, in general it is more useful and better practice to have a `catch` block for each of the specific types of exceptions that a `try` block can throw. That enables you to indentify and deal with each type of exception individually.

Catching Multiple Exception Types in a Block

You can catch an exception that may be any of two or more different types in a single `catch` block. You specify the possible types for the `catch` block parameter separated by `|`. Here's a fragment showing how you do this:

```
try {
  // Code that can throw exceptions
  // of type ArithmeticException and ArrayStoreException...
} catch(ArithmeticException|ArrayStoreException e) {
  // Code to handle exception of either type...
}
```

The `catch` block is executed if an exception of either type `ArithmeticException` or type `ArrayStoreException` is thrown in the `try` block. This is particularly useful when you want to handle exceptions of two or more different types in the same way because it avoids having to write multiple `catch` blocks containing the same code. This can arise quite easily when you call several methods in a single block, each of which may throw an exception of a different type. When you want to handle more than one type of exception in the same way, you can use the multiple types form for the `catch` block parameter.

Of course, you can still have multiple `catch` blocks, each of which may respond to one or more exception types.

The finally Block

The immediate nature of an exception being thrown means that execution of the `try` block code breaks off, regardless of the importance of the code that follows the point at which the exception was thrown. This introduces the possibility that the exception leaves things in an unsatisfactory state. You might have opened a file, for example, and because an exception was thrown, the code to close the file is not executed.

The `finally` block provides the means for you to clean up at the end of executing a `try` block. You use a `finally` block when you need to be sure that some particular code is run before a method returns, no matter what exceptions are thrown within the associated `try` block. A `finally` block is always executed, regardless of whether or not exceptions are thrown during the execution of the associated `try` block. If a file needs to be closed, or a critical resource released, you can guarantee that it is done if the code to do it is put in a `finally` block.

The `finally` block has a very simple structure:

```
finally {
    // Clean-up code to be executed last
}
```

Just like a `catch` block, a `finally` block is associated with a particular `try` block, and it must be located immediately following any `catch` blocks for the `try` block. If there are no `catch` blocks then you position the `finally` block immediately after the `try` block. If you don't do this, your program does not compile.

> **NOTE** The primary purpose for the `try` block is to identify code that may result in an exception being thrown. However, you can use it to contain code that doesn't throw exceptions for the convenience of using a `finally` block. This can be useful when the code in the `try` block has several possible exit points—`break` or `return` statements, for example—but you always want to have a specific set of statements executed after the `try` block has been executed to make sure things are tidied up, such as closing any open files. You can put these in a `finally` block. Note that if a value is returned within a `finally` block, this return overrides any return statement executed in the `try` block.

Structuring a Method

You've looked at the blocks you can include in the body of a method, but it may not always be obvious how they are combined. The first thing to get straight is that a `try` block plus any corresponding `catch` blocks and the `finally` block all bunch together in that order:

```
try {
    // Code that may throw exceptions...

} catch(ExceptionType1 e) {
    // Code to handle exceptions of type ExceptionType1 or subclass
} catch(ExceptionType2 e) {
    // Code to handle exceptions of type ExceptionType2 or subclass
... // more catch blocks if necessary
} finally {
    // Code always to be executed after try block code
}
```

You can't have just a `try` block by itself. Each `try` block must always be followed by at least one block that is either a `catch` block or a `finally` block.

You must not include other code between a `try` block and its `catch` blocks, or between the `catch` blocks and the `finally` block. You can have other code that doesn't throw exceptions after the `finally` block, and you can have multiple `try` blocks in a method. In this case, your method might be structured as shown in Figure 7-2.

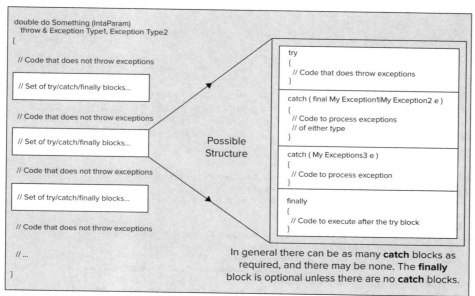

In general there can be as many **catch** blocks as required, and there may be none. The **finally** block is optional unless there are no **catch** blocks.

FIGURE 7-2

The doSomething() method in Figure 7-2 deals with exceptions of either type MyException1 or MyException2 in the first catch block. The second catch block is executed for exceptions of type MyException3. The method can also throw two other types of exceptions that are not caught within the method, and these are identified in the throws clause that follows the parameter list for the method. The code in the finally block always gets executed, regardless of whether an exception is thrown or not.

In many cases, a method needs only a single try block followed by all the catch blocks for the exceptions that need to be processed in the method, perhaps followed by a finally block. Java, however, gives you the flexibility to have as many try blocks as you want. This makes it possible for you to separate various operations in a method by putting each of them in their own try block—an exception thrown as a result of a problem with one operation does not prevent subsequent operations from being executed.

Execution Sequence

You saw how the sequence of execution proceeds with the simple case of a try block and a single catch block. Let's explore the sequence in which code executes when you have the try-catch-finally combinations of blocks, when different exceptions are thrown. This is easiest to comprehend by considering an example. You can use the following code to create a range of exceptions and conditions.

TRY IT OUT   Execution Sequence of a try Block

It is convenient, in this example, to use an input statement to pause the program. The method you use can throw an exception of a type defined in the java.io package. You start by importing the java.io.IOException class name into the source file. Give the class that contains main() the name TryBlockTest. You define another method, divide(), in this class that is called in main(). The overall structure of the TryBlockTest class source file is:

Available for download on Wrox.com

```java
import java.io.IOException;
public class TryBlockTest {
  public static void main(String[] args) {
    // Code for main()..
  }

  // Divide method
```

```
  public static int divide(int[] array, int index) {
    // Code for divide()...
  }
}
```

TryBlockTest.java

The idea behind the `divide()` method is to pass it an array and an index as arguments. By choosing the values in the array and the index value judiciously, you are able to cause exceptions of type `ArithmeticException` and `ArrayIndexOutOfBoundsException` to be thrown. You use a `try` block plus two `catch` blocks for the exceptions, and you throw in a `finally` block for good measure. Here's the code for `divide()`:

Available for
download on
Wrox.com

```
  public static int divide(int[] array, int index) {
    try {
      System.out.println("\nFirst try block in divide() entered");
      array[index + 2] = array[index]/array[index + 1];
      System.out.println("Code at end of first try block in divide()");
      return array[index + 2];
    } catch(ArithmeticException e) {
      System.out.println("Arithmetic exception caught in divide()");
      System.out.println("index = " + index +
        " Expression: " + "array[" + index + "]/array["+ (index+1) +"] is " +
                              array[index] + "//" + array[index+1]);
    } catch(ArrayIndexOutOfBoundsException e) {
      System.out.println("Index-out-of-bounds exception caught in divide()");
      System.out.println("array length = " + array.length +
                                          " index = " + index);
    } finally {
      System.out.println("finally block in divide()");
    }

    System.out.println("Executing code after try block in divide()");
    return array[index + 2];
  }
```

TryBlockTest.java

You can define the `main()` method with the following code:

Available for
download on
Wrox.com

```
  public static void main(String[] args) {
    int[] x = {10, 5, 0};                    // Array of three integers

    // This block only throws an exception if the divide() method does
    try {
      System.out.println("First try block in main() entered");
      System.out.println("result = " + divide(x,0));  // No error
      x[1] = 0;                                  // Will cause a divide by zero
      System.out.println("result = " + divide(x,0));  // Arithmetic error
      x[1] = 1;                                  // Reset to prevent divide by zero
      System.out.println("result = " + divide(x,1));  // Index error
    } catch(ArithmeticException e) {
      System.out.println("Arithmetic exception caught in main()");
    } catch(ArrayIndexOutOfBoundsException e) {
      System.out.println("Index-out-of-bounds exception caught in main()");
    }

    System.out.println("Outside first try block in main()");
    System.out.println("\nPress Enter to exit");

    // This try block is just to pause the program before returning
    try {
      System.out.println("In second try block in main()");
      System.in.read();                          // Pauses waiting for input...
      return;
    } catch(IOException e) {               // The read() method can throw exceptions
```

```
        System.out.println("I/O exception caught in main()");
      } finally {                            // This will always be executed
        System.out.println("finally block for second try block in main()");
      }

      System.out.println("Code after second try block in main()");
    }
```

TryBlockTest.java

Because the read() method for the object in (this object represents the standard input stream and complements the out object, which is the standard output stream) can throw an I/O exception, it must be called in a try block and have an associated catch block, unless you choose to add a throws clause to the header line of main().

If you run the example, it produces the following output:

```
First try block in main() entered

First try block in divide() entered
Code at end of first try block in divide()
finally block in divide()
result = 2

First try block in divide() entered
Arithmetic exception caught in divide()
index = 0  Expression: array[0]/array[1] is 10/0
finally block in divide()
Executing code after try block in divide()
result = 2

First try block in divide() entered
Index-out-of-bounds exception caught in divide()
array length = 3  index = 1
finally block in divide()
Executing code after try block in divide()
Index-out-of-bounds exception caught in main()
Outside first try block in main()

Press Enter to exit
In second try block in main()

finally block for second try block in main()
```

How It Works

All the try, catch, and finally blocks in the example have output statements so you can trace the sequence of execution. Note that the finally block is executed, whatever happens in the divide() method, even when the normal return is executed in the try block in divide().

Within the divide() method, the code in the try block can throw an ArithmeticException if the element array[index+1] of the array passed to it is 0. It can also throw an ArrayIndexOutOfBoundsException in the try block if the index value passed to it is negative, or it results in index+2 being beyond the array limits. Both these exceptions are caught by one or other of the catch blocks, so they are not apparent in the calling method main().

Note, however, that the last statement in divide() can also throw an ArrayIndexOutOfBoundsException:

```
    return array[index+2];
```

This statement is outside the try block, so the exception is not caught. The exception is therefore thrown by the method when it is called in main(). However, you aren't obliged to declare that the divide() method throws this exception because the ArrayIndexOutOfBoundsException class is a subclass of RuntimeException and is therefore exempted from the obligation to deal with it.

The main() method has two try blocks. The first try block encloses three calls to the divide() method. The first call executes without error; the second call causes an arithmetic exception in the method; and the third call causes an index-out-of-bounds exception. There are two `catch` blocks for the first `try` block in `main()` to deal with these two potential exceptions.

The `read()` method in the second `try` block in `main()` can cause an I/O exception to be thrown. Because this is one of the exceptions that the compiler checks for, you must either put the statement that calls the `read()` method in a `try` block and have a `catch` block to deal with the exception or declare that `main()` throws the `IOException` exception. If you don't do one or the other, the program does not compile.

Using the `read()` method in this way has the effect of pausing the program until the Enter key is pressed. You look at `read()`, and other methods for I/O operations in the next four chapters. The `IOException` class is in the package `java.io`, so you need the `import` statement for this class because you refer to it in the `catch` block using its unqualified name. Of course, if you referred to it as `java.io.IOException`, you would not need to import the class name. Remember that only classes defined in `java.lang` are included in your program automatically.

Normal Execution of a Method

The first line of output from the `TryBlockTest` example indicates that execution of the `try` block in `main()` has begun. The next block of output from the example is the result of a straightforward execution of the `divide()` method:

```
First try block in divide() entered
Code at end of first try block in divide()
finally block in divide()
result = 2
```

No exceptions occur in `divide()`, so no `catch` blocks are executed.

The code at the end of the `divide()` method, following the `catch` blocks, isn't executed because the `return` statement in the `try` block ends the execution of the method. However, the `finally` block in `divide()` is executed before the return to the calling method occurs. If you comment out the `return` statement at the end of the `divide()` method's `try` block and run the example again, the code that follows the `finally` block is executed.

The sequence of execution when no exceptions occur is shown in Figure 7-3.

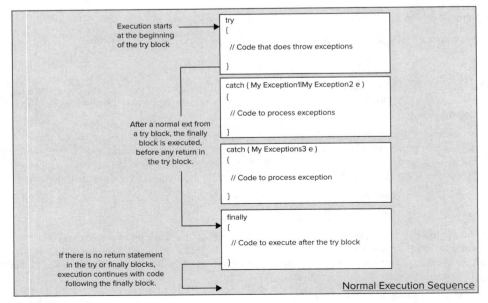

FIGURE 7-3

Figure 7-3 illustrates the normal sequence of execution in an arbitrary `try-catch-finally` set of blocks. If there's a return statement in the `try` block, this is executed immediately after the `finally` block completes execution—so this prevents the execution of any code following the `finally` block. A return statement in a `finally` block causes an immediate return to the calling point, and the code following the `finally` block isn't executed in this case.

Execution When an Exception Is Thrown

The next block of output corresponds to an `ArithmeticException` being thrown and caught in the `divide()` method:

```
First try block in divide() entered
Arithmetic exception caught in divide()
index = 0  Expression: array[0]/array[1] is 10/0
finally block in divide()
Executing code after try block in divide()
result = 2
```

The exception is thrown because the value of the second element in the array x is zero. When the exception occurs, execution of the code in the `try` block is stopped, and you can see that the code that follows the `catch` block for the exception in the `divide()` method is then executed. The `finally` block executes next, followed by the code after the `finally` block. The value in the last element of the array isn't changed from its previous value, because the exception occurs during the computation of the new value, before the result is stored.

The general sequence of execution in a `try-catch-finally` set of blocks when an exception occurs is shown in Figure 7-4.

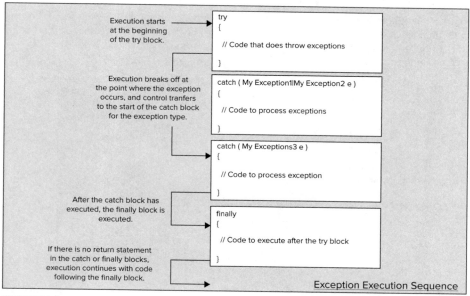

FIGURE 7-4

Execution of the `try` block stops at the point where the exception occurs, and the code in the `catch` block for the exception is executed immediately. If there is a `return` statement in the `catch` block, this isn't executed until after the `finally` block has been executed. As I discussed earlier, if a `return` statement that returns a value is executed within a `finally` block, that value is returned, not the value from any previous `return` statement.

If an exception is thrown in a `finally` block, this will terminate the execution of the code in the `finally` block and the method. You can see the effect if you add the following statement to the `finally` block in `divide()`:

```
int result = array[index]/array[index+1];
```

When `ArithmeticException` is thrown in the `try` block, the same exception is thrown in the `finally` block as a result of this statement. You will see from the output that the `divide()` method terminates and the exception is caught in `main()`. Try moving the statement to the catch block for `ArithmeticException`. You'll see that the `finally` block still executes even though an exception is thrown in the `catch` block.

Execution When an Exception Is Not Caught

The next block of output is a consequence of the third call to the `divide()` method:

```
First try block in divide() entered
Index-out-of-bounds exception caught in divide()
array length = 3  index = 1
finally block in divide()
Executing code after try block in divide()
Index-out-of-bounds exception caught in main()
Outside first try block in main()
```

This causes an `ArrayIndexOutOfBoundsException` to be thrown in the `try` block, which is then caught. However, the code at the end of the method, which is executed after the `finally` block, throws another exception of this type. This can't be caught in the `divide()` method because the statement throwing it isn't in a `try` block. Because this exception isn't caught in the `divide()` method, the method terminates immediately at the point where the `divide()` method was called. This causes the code in the relevant `catch` block in `main()` to be executed as a consequence of the uncaught exception.

An exception that isn't caught in a method is always propagated upward to the calling method. It continues to propagate up through each level of calling method until either it is caught or the `main()` method is reached. If it isn't caught in `main()`, the program terminates and a suitable message is displayed. This situation is illustrated in Figure 7-5.

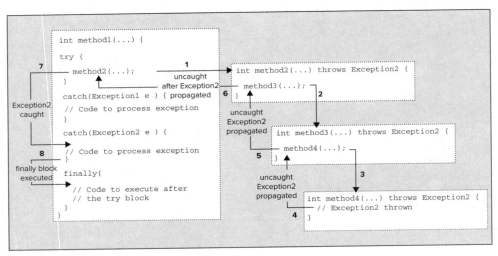

FIGURE 7-5

The sequence of events in Figure 7-5 is shown by the numbers on the arrows. It shows `method1()` calling `method2()`, which calls `method3()`, which calls `method4()`, in which an exception of type `Exception2` is thrown. This exception isn't caught in `method4()`, so execution of `method4()` ceases, and the exception is thrown to `method3()`. It isn't caught and continues to be thrown until it reaches `method1()` where there's a `catch` block to handle it.

In our `TryBlockTest` example, execution continues in `main()` with the output statements outside the first `try` block. The `read()` method pauses the program until you press the Enter key. No exception is thrown, and execution ends after the code in the `finally` block is executed. The `finally` block is tied to the `try` block that immediately precedes it and is executed even though there's a return statement in the `try` block.

Nested try Blocks

I don't go into these in detail, but you should note that you can have nested `try` blocks, as Figure 7-6 illustrates.

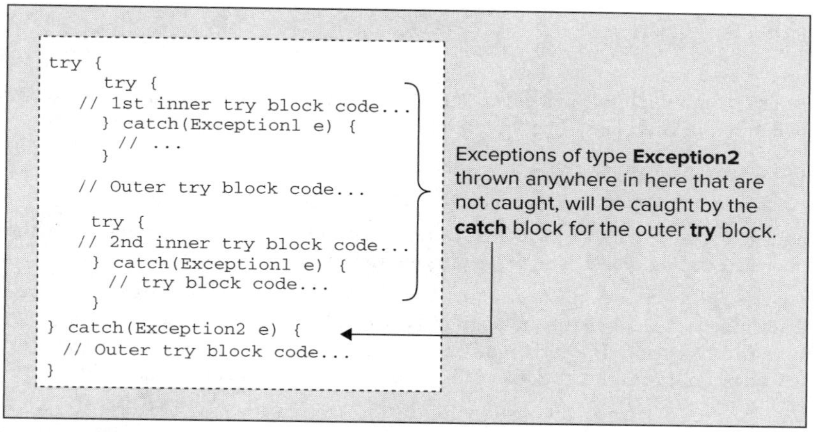

```
try {
    try {
    // 1st inner try block code...
    } catch(Exception1 e) {
    // ...
    }

    // Outer try block code...

    try {
    // 2nd inner try block code...
    } catch(Exception1 e) {
    // try block code...
    }
} catch(Exception2 e) {
    // Outer try block code...
}
```

Exceptions of type **Exception2** thrown anywhere in here that are not caught, will be caught by the **catch** block for the outer **try** block.

FIGURE 7-6

The `catch` blocks for the outer `try` block can catch any exceptions that are thrown, but not caught, by any code within the block, including code within inner `try-catch` blocks. In the example shown in Figure 7-6, the `catch` block for the outer `try` block catches any exception of type `Exception2`. Such exceptions could originate anywhere within the outer `try` block. The illustration shows two levels of nesting, but you can specify more if you know what you're doing.

Rethrowing Exceptions

Even though you may need to recognize that an exception has occurred in a method by implementing a `catch` clause for it, this is not necessarily the end of the matter. In many situations, the calling program may need to know about it—perhaps because it affects the continued operation of the program or because the calling program may be able to compensate for the problem.

If you need to pass an exception that you have caught on to the calling program, you can rethrow it from within the `catch` block using a `throw` statement. For example:

```
try {
    // Code that originates an arithmetic exception

} catch(ArithmeticException e) {
    // Deal with the exception here
    throw e;                      // Rethrow the exception to the calling program
}
```

The `throw` statement is the keyword `throw` followed by the exception object to be thrown. When you look at how to define your own exceptions later in this chapter, you use exactly the same mechanism to throw them.

EXCEPTION OBJECTS

Well, you now understand how to put `try` blocks together with `catch` blocks and `finally` blocks in your methods. You may be thinking at this point that it seems a lot of trouble to go to just to display a message when an exception is thrown. You may be right, but whether you can do so very much more depends on the nature and context of the problem. In many situations a message may be the best you can do, although you can produce messages that are a bit more informative than those you've used so far in our examples. For one thing, I have totally ignored the exception object that is passed to the `catch` block.

The exception object that is passed to a `catch` block can provide additional information about the nature of the problem that originated it. To understand more about this, let's first look at the members of the base class for exceptions `Throwable` because these are inherited by all exception classes and are therefore contained in every exception object that is thrown.

The Throwable Class

The `Throwable` class is the class from which all Java exception classes are derived — that is, every exception object contains the methods defined in this class. The `Throwable` class has five constructors:

➤   `Throwable()` creates an object with no detail message.

➤   `Throwable(String message)` create an object containing `message` as the message.

➤   `Throwable(String message, Throwable cause)` creates an object containing `message` as the message and a second `Throwable` object, `cause`, specifying the cause of the exception.

➤   `Throwable(String message, Throwable cause, boolean suppress, boolean stackTrace)` creates an object containing `message` as the message and a second `Throwable` object, `cause`, specifying the cause of the exception. If `suppress` is `true`, it allows exception to be suppressed in order to deliver this exception. If `stackTrace` is `true`, recording of the stack trace is enabled.

➤   `Throwable(Throwable cause)` creates an object with the message `cause.toString()` if cause is not `null`, and `cause` as the cause of the exception.

The constructors with `Throwable` parameters provide the basis for storing a reference to one exception inside another. The `cause` reference can be obtained by calling `getCause()` for a `Throwable` object. This allows exceptions to be chained, so when one exception has been thrown, you can create another exception that provides more information about the problem and record within it a reference to the original exception that caused the new exception to be thrown. This ensures that information available from the original exception is not lost. You'll see that you can define you own exception classes to allow exception chaining.

Objects of type `Throwable` can contain the following information:

➤   A message, which I have just referred to as being initialized by a constructor.

➤   A `Throwable` object identifying the cause of the exception.

➤   A record of the **execution stack** at the time the object was created.

➤   A record of exceptions suppressed in order to deliver this exception.

The *execution stack* keeps track of all the methods that are in execution at any given instant. It provides the means whereby executing a return gets back to the calling point for a method. The record of the execution stack that is stored in the exception object consists of the line number in the source code where the exception originates followed by a trace of the method calls that immediately precede the point at which the exception occurs. This is made up of the fully qualified name for each of the methods called, plus the line number in the source file where each method call occurs. The method calls are in sequence with the most recent method call appearing first. This helps you to understand how this point in the program was reached.

The `Throwable` class has the following public methods that enable you to access the message, the cause, and the stack trace as shown in Table 7-2.

TABLE 7-2: Throwable Class Public Methods

METHOD	DESCRIPTION
getMessage()	This returns the contents of the message, describing the current exception. This is typically the fully qualified name of the exception class (it is a subclass of Throwable) and a brief description of the exception.
getCause()	Returns the Throwable that records the cause for this exception. This will typically be the exception that caused this exception to be thrown.
printStackTrace()	This outputs the message and the stack trace to the standard error output stream—which is the screen in the case of a console program.
printStackTrace (PrintStream s)	This is the same as the previous method except that you specify the output stream as an argument. Calling the previous method for an exception object e is equivalent to e.printStackTrace(System.err);

You can get the stack trace as an array of StackTraceElement references by calling getStackTrace() for a Throwable object. Each StackTraceElement object records information about the execution point in a method when the exception was thrown. There will be a StackTraceElement array element for each method in the call stack when the exception was thrown. The following StackTraceElement methods provide you with details of a stack trace entry:

➤ getClassName() returns the fully qualified name of the class containing the execution point for this stack trace entry.

➤ getFileName() returns the name of the source file containing the execution point.

➤ getLineNumber() returns the line number for the execution point in the source file.

➤ getMethodName() returns the name of the method containing the execution point.

Another Throwable method, fillInStackTrace(), updates the stack trace to the point at which this method is called. For example, if you put a call to this method in the catch block

e.fillInStackTrace();

the line number recorded in the stack record for the method in which the exception occurs is the line where fillInStackTrace() is called. The main use of this is when you want to rethrow an exception (so it is caught by the calling method) and record the point at which it is rethrown. For example:

```
e.fillInStackTrace();                    // Record the throw point
throw e;                                  // Rethrow the exception
```

In practice, it's often more useful to throw an exception of your own that encapsulates the exception that caused your exception to be thrown. This is referred to as *exception chaining*. You see how to define your own exceptions in the next section and use chained exceptions, but first, let's exercise some of the methods defined in the Throwable class and see the results.

TRY IT OUT   Dishing the Dirt on Exceptions

The easiest way to try out some of the methods I've just discussed is to make some changes to the catch blocks in the divide() method you have in the TryBlockTest class example. I make the class for this example TryBlockTest2. The main() method is the same as for TryBlockTest. Here's the modified version of divide():

Available for download on Wrox.com

```
public static int divide(int[] array, int index) {
    try {
        System.out.println("\nFirst try block in divide() entered");
        array[index + 2] = array[index]/array[index + 1];
        System.out.println("Code at end of first try block in divide()");
        return array[index + 2];

    } catch(ArithmeticException e) {
```

```
        System.err.println("Arithmetic exception caught in divide()\n" +
                         "\nMessage in exception object:\n\t" +
                          e.getMessage());
        System.err.println("\nStack trace output:\n");
        e.printStackTrace();
        System.err.println("\nEnd of stack trace output\n");
      } catch(ArrayIndexOutOfBoundsException e) {
        System.err.println("Index-out-of-bounds exception caught in divide()\n" +
                         "\nMessage in exception object:\n\t" + e.getMessage());
        System.err.println("\nStack trace output:\n");
        e.printStackTrace();
        System.out.println("\nEnd of stack trace output\n");
      } finally {
        System.err.println("finally clause in divide()");
      }
      System.out.println("Executing code after try block in divide()");
      return array[index + 2];
    }
```

TryBlockTest2.java

If you recompile the program and run it again, it produces all the output as before but with extra information when exceptions are thrown in the `divide()` method. The output generated for the `ArithmeticException` is:

```
Message in exception object:
Arithmetic exception caught in divide()

Message in exception object:
      / by zero

Stack trace output:

java.lang.ArithmeticException: / by zero
      at TryBlockTest2.divide(TryBlockTest2.java:44)
      at TryBlockTest2.main(TryBlockTest2.java:12)

End of stack trace output
```

The output generated for the `ArrayIndexOutOfBoundsException` is:

```
Index-out-of-bounds exception caught in divide()

Message in exception object:
      3

Stack trace output:

java.lang.ArrayIndexOutOfBoundsException: 3
     at TryBlockTest2.divide(TryBlockTest2.java:44)
     at TryBlockTest2.main(TryBlockTest2.java:14)

End of stack trace output
```

How It Works

The code in each of the `catch` blocks in the `divide()` method output the message associated with the exception object e by calling its `getMessage()` method. You could have just put e here, which would invoke the `toString()` method for e, and in this case, the class name for e would precede the message. The message for the arithmetic exception identifies it as being caused by a divide by zero. The message for the index out of bounds exception is just the invalid index value.

There are a couple of extra `println()` calls around the call to `printStackTrace()` to make it easier to find the stack trace in the output.

The first stack trace, for the arithmetic exception, indicates that the error originated at line 44 in the source file `TryBlockText.java` and the last method call was at line 14 in the same source file. The second stack trace provides similar information about the index-out-of-bounds exception, including the offending index value. As you can see, with the stack trace output, it's very easy to see where the error occurs and how this point in the program is reached.

Standard Exceptions

The majority of predefined exception classes in Java don't provide detailed information about the conditions that created the exception. The type alone serves to differentiate one exception from another in most cases. This general lack of detailed information is because it can often be gleaned only by prior knowledge of the computation that is being carried out.

This should spark the glimmer of an idea. If you need more information about the circumstances surrounding an exception, *you* are going to have to obtain it and, equally important, communicate it to the appropriate point in your program. This leads to the notion of defining your own exceptions.

DEFINING YOUR OWN EXCEPTIONS

There are three basic reasons for defining your own exception classes:

➤ You want to add information when a standard exception occurs, and you can do this by rethrowing an object of your own exception class.

➤ You may have error conditions that arise in your code that warrant the distinction of a special exception class.

➤ To consolidate exceptions into a smaller, more manageable set (making it easier on calling methods).

However, you should bear in mind that there's a lot of overhead in throwing exceptions, so it is not a valid substitute for "normal" recovery code that you would expect to be executed frequently. If you have recovery code that is executed often, then it doesn't belong in a `catch` block, but rather in something like an `if-else` statement.

Let's see how you create your own exceptions.

Defining an Exception Class

Your exception classes must always have `Throwable` as a superclass; otherwise, they do not define an exception. Although you can derive them from any of the standard exception classes, your best policy is to derive them from the `Exception` class or from a subclass of `Exception`. This allows the compiler to keep track of where such exceptions are thrown in your program and checks that they are either caught or declared as thrown in a method. If you use `RuntimeException` or one of its subclasses, the compiler checking for `catch` blocks of your exception class are suppressed.

Let's go through an example of how you define an exception class:

```
public class DreadfulProblemException extends Exception {
  // Constructors
  public DreadfulProblemException(){ }          // Default constructor

  public DreadfulProblemException(String s) {
    super(s);                                    // Call the base class constructor
  }
}
```

This is the minimum you should supply in your exception class definition. By convention, your exception class should include a default constructor and a constructor that accepts a `String` object as an argument. The message stored in the superclass `Exception` (in fact, in `Throwable`, which is the superclass of `Exception`) is automatically initialized with the name of your class, whichever constructor for your class objects is used.

The String passed to the second constructor is appended to the name of the class to form the message stored in the exception object. Of course, you can subclass any of the classes derived from Exception.

You can add other constructors in your exception class. In general, you want to do so, particularly when you're rethrowing your own exception after a standard exception has been thrown because you are likely to want additional parameters for passing information relating to your exceptions. In addition, you typically want to add instance variables to the exception class that store additional information about the problem, plus methods that enable the code in a catch block to get at the data. Because your exception class is ultimately derived from Throwable, the stack trace information is automatically available for your exceptions along with the capability for creating chained exceptions. If you plan to use exception chaining, you will want to define at least one constructor with a Throwable parameter so that a reference to a previous exception in a chain can be passed. In this case the class constructors could be:

```java
public class DreadfulProblemException extends Exception {
  // Constructors
  public DreadfulProblemException(){ }         // Default constructor

  public DreadfulProblemException(String s) {
    super(s);                                  // Call the base class constructor
  }

  // Constructor providing for chained exceptions
  public DreadfulProblemException(String s, Throwable cause) {
    super(s, cause);                           // Call the base class constructor
  }
}
```

The exception chaining capability is built into the base class because it is defined in Throwable. Therefore you can just pass the Throwable argument that is passed to your constructor to the base class constructor.

Even when you have not provided a constructor in your exception class that accepts a Throwable reference, you can still chain your exception object to the exception that caused your exception to be thrown. Your exception class inherits the initCause() method from Throwable that accepts an argument of type Throwable. Calling this method chains your exception to the previous exception. Note that you can only call this method for an exception once, and you must not call it at all if you created your exception object with a Throwable cause argument. The initCause() method will throw IllegalStateException if either is the case. It will also throw IllegalArgumentException if you pass a reference to your exception object as the argument; an exception cannot be its own cause.

Throwing Your Own Exception

As you saw earlier, you throw an exception with a statement that consists of the throw keyword, followed by an exception object. This means you can throw your own exception in a method with the following statements:

```java
DreadfulProblemException e = new DreadfulProblemException();
throw e;
```

The method ceases execution at this point—unless the preceding code snippet is in a try block with a catch block that catches this exception. The exception will be thrown to the calling program if it is not caught. The message in the exception object consists only of the qualified name of the exception class.

If you want to add a specific message to the exception, you could define it as:

```java
DreadfulProblemException e = new DreadfulProblemException("Uh-Oh, trouble.");
```

You're using a different constructor here. In this case the message stored in the superclass is a string that consists of the class name with the string passed to the constructor appended to it. The getMessage() method inherited from Throwable, therefore, returns a String object containing the following string:

```java
"DreadfulProblemException: Uh-Oh, trouble."
```

You can also create an exception object and throw it in a single statement. For example:

```
throw new DreadfulProblemException("Terrible difficulties");
```

In all the examples of throwing your own exception, the stack trace record inherited from the superclass `Throwable` is set up automatically.

If you plan to use your exception type in a `catch` block to provide further information about an exception that has been thrown, you can make provision for recording the original exception:

```
try {
  // Code that may throw SomeException...
} catch SomeException e) {
  // Analyze the cause...
  throw new DreadfulProblemException("Disaster strikes!", e);
}
```

This fragment throws an object of your exception class that you create with a constructor that accepts a second argument of type `Throwable` to record the previous exception object. This will enable the code that catches your exception to access the `SomeException` object that caused your exception to be thrown and extract information from that.

An Exception Handling Strategy

You should think through what you want to achieve with the exception handling code in your program. There are no hard-and-fast rules. In some situations you may be able to correct a problem and enable your program to continue as though nothing happened. In other situations, outputting the stack trace and a fast exit is the best approach—a fast exit being achieved by calling the `exit()` method in the `System` class. Here you take a look at some of the things you need to weigh when deciding how to handle exceptions.

Consider the last example where you handled arithmetic and index-out-of-bounds exceptions in the `divide()` method. Although this was a reasonable demonstration of the way the various blocks worked, it wasn't a satisfactory way of dealing with the exceptions in the program for at least two reasons.

➤ First, it does not make sense to catch the arithmetic exceptions in the `divide()` method without passing them on to the calling method. After all, it is the calling method that set the data up, and only the calling program has the potential to recover the situation.

➤ Second, by handling the exceptions completely in the `divide()` method, you allow the calling program to continue execution without any knowledge of the problem that arose. In a real situation this would undoubtedly create chaos, as further calculations would proceed with erroneous data.

You could have simply ignored the exceptions in the `divide()` method by having no `try-catch` combination for the exception. This might not be a bad approach in this particular situation, but the first problem the calling program would have is determining the source of the exception. After all, such exceptions might also arise in the calling program itself. A second consideration could arise if the `divide()` method were more complicated. There could be several places where such exceptions might be thrown, and the calling method would have a hard time distinguishing them.

An Example of an Exception Class

Another possibility is to catch the exceptions in the method where they originate and then pass them on to the calling program. You can pass them on by throwing new exceptions that provide more granularity in identifying the problem (by having more than one exception type or by providing additional data within the new exception type). For example, you could define more than one exception class of your own that represents an `ArithmeticException`, where each reflected the specifics of a particular situation. This situation is illustrated in Figure 7-7. The numbers on the arrows indicate the sequence.

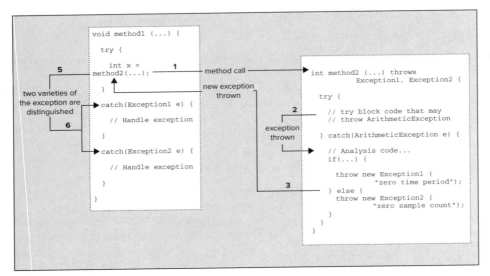

FIGURE 7-7

Figure 7-7 shows how two different circumstances causing an `ArithmeticException` in `method2()` are differentiated in the calling method, `method1()`. The `method2()` method can throw an exception either of type `Exception1` or of type `Exception2`, depending on the analysis that is made in the `catch` block for the `ArithmeticException` type. The calling method has a separate `catch` block for each of the exceptions that may be thrown.

You could also define a new exception class that had instance variables to identify the problem more precisely. Let's suppose that in the last example you wanted to provide more information to the calling program about the error that caused each exception in the `divide()` method. The primary exception can be either an `ArithmeticException` or an `ArrayIndexOutOfBoundsException`, but because you're dealing with a specific context for these errors, you could give the calling program more information by throwing your own exceptions.

It would also make sense to make your exceptions chained exceptions that also recorded the originating exception. Let's take the `ArithmeticException` case as a model and define an exception class to use in the program to help identify the reason for the error more precisely. This is just for illustration purposes and is not intended to imply that you need to catch exceptions of type `ArithmeticException`.

TRY IT OUT   **Chaining Exceptions**

This is the first step in creating a new variation on the `TryBlockTest` example called `TryChainedExceptions`. You can define a new exception class that you will use when an `ArithmeticException` is thrown in the `divide()` method:

```
public class ZeroDivideException extends Exception {
   private int index = -1;                   // Index of array element causing error

   // Default Constructor
   public ZeroDivideException(){ }

   // Constructor that can be chained
   public ZeroDivideException(String s, Throwable cause) {
     super(s, cause);                         // Call the base constructor
   }

   // Contructor recording an index value & can be chained
```

```
public ZeroDivideException(int index, Throwable cause) {
  super(cause);                              // Call the base constructor
  this.index = index;                        // Set the index value
}

// Get the array index value for the error
public int getIndex() {
  return index;                              // Return the index value
}
}
```

Directory "TryChainedExceptions"

How It Works

You might think that because this exception type is a form of arithmetic exception, it would be advantageous to derive the class from ArithmeticException. Of course, if you did this, the new exception type would have RuntimeException as an indirect base class, and therefore such exceptions would not need to be caught. Because you have derived the ZeroDivideException class from the Exception class, the compiler checks that the exceptions thrown are either caught or identified as thrown in a method.

Your class inherits all the members of the class Throwable via the Exception class, so you get the stack trace record, the message for the exception, and the ability to record the originating exception for free. It also inherits the toString() method, which is satisfactory in this context, but you could override this if desired. The Exception class has five constructors with the same parameters as the Throwable class constructors. You can therefore to pass a Throwable reference to record the originating exception to the base class constructor, so the ArithmeticException that was originally thrown is still available from your exception object.

You've added a data member, index, to store the index value of the zero divisor in the array passed to divide(). This gives the calling program a chance to fix this value if appropriate in the catch block for the exception. This might arise in an application with data that might be logged automatically in a manufacturing plant for example, where because of the conditions, some erroneous data is to be expected. In this case, the catch block needs to include code that enables the divide() method to be called again with the corrected array to reprocess the data. There may be circumstances where the index cannot be supplied. In this case the default value that is an invalid index value will allow code that catches the exception to determine when this is the case.

Let's now put it to work in the TryChainedExceptions example.

TRY IT OUT   Using Chained Exceptions

The computations in this example are completely arbitrary and have been contrived so that exceptions will be thrown. The TryChainedExceptions class defines two static methods, main() and divide(). You'll use the new exception class in two contexts—in the divide() method when you catch a standard ArithmeticException and in the calling method main() to catch the new exception. Let's define the divide() method first:

```
public static int divide(int[] array, int index) throws ZeroDivideException {
  try {
    System.out.println("\nFirst try block in divide() entered");
    array[index] = array[index+2]/array[index + 1];
    System.out.println("Code at end of first try block in divide()");
    return array[index + 2];

  } catch(ArithmeticException e) {
    System.out.println("Arithmetic exception caught in divide()");
    ZeroDivideException zde = new ZeroDivideException(index + 1, e);
    System.out.println("Throwing ZeroDivideException");
```

```
          throw zde;                              // Throw the new exception
        } catch(ArrayIndexOutOfBoundsException e) {
          System.out.println(
                    "Index-out-of-bounds index exception caught in divide()");
        }
        System.out.println("Executing code after try block in divide()");
        return array[index];
      }
    }
```

Directory "TryChainedExceptions"

Note the `throws` clause in the method definition. Without this you will get an error message from the compiler. The statements in the `catch` block for `ArithmeticException` creates and throws a new exception.

This new exception needs to be caught in the calling method `main()`:

```
public static void main(String[] args) {
  int[] x = {10, 5, 0, 3, 12, 0, 6};           // Array of  integers
  System.out.print("Values: ");
  for(int xValue : x) {
    System.out.print("   " + xValue);
  }
  System.out.println();

  for(int i = 0 ; i < x.length ; ++i) {
    // This block only throws an exception if method divide() does
    try {
      System.out.println("First try block in main()entered");
      System.out.println("result = " + divide(x,i));
    } catch(ZeroDivideException e) {
      System.out.println("\nZeroDivideException caught in main()");
      int index = e.getIndex();    // Get the index for the error
      if(index > 0) {              // Verify it is valid and now fix the array
        x[index] = 1;                    // ...set the divisor to 1...
        x[index + 1] = x[index - 1];  // ...and set the result
        e.printStackTrace();
        System.err.println("Zero divisor at x[" + index + "] corrected to " +
                                                           x[index]);
      }
    } catch(ArithmeticException e) {
      System.out.println("Arithmetic exception caught in main()");
    } catch(ArrayIndexOutOfBoundsException e) {
      System.out.println("Index-out-of-bounds exception caught in main()");
    }
    System.out.println("Outside first try block in main()");
  }
  System.out.print("Values: ");
  for(int xValue : x) {
    System.out.print("   " + xValue);
  }
  System.out.println();
}
```

Directory "TryChainedExceptions"

You should put the `TryChainedExceptions` class file and the file for the `ZeroDivideException` class together in the same directory.

The output from this example includes:

```
Values:   10  5  0  3  12  0  6
First try block in main()entered
```

```
... more output
First try block in divide() entered
Arithmetic exception caught in divide()
Throwing ZeroDivideException

ZeroDivideException caught in main()
ZeroDivideException: java.lang.ArithmeticException: / by zero
        at TryChainedExceptions.divide(TryChainedExceptions.java:49)
        at TryChainedExceptions.main(TryChainedExceptions.java:16)
Caused by: java.lang.ArithmeticException: / by zero
        at TryChainedExceptions.divide(TryChainedExceptions.java:43)
        ... 1 more
Zero divisor at x[2] corrected to 1
Outside first try block in main()
... more output

First try block in divide() entered
Index-out-of-bounds index exception caught in divide()
Executing code after try block in divide()
result = 1
Outside first try block in main()
First try block in main()entered
... more output

Outside first try block in main()
Values:   0  5  2  0  12  1  12
```

How It Works

The main() method creates an array of integers and iterates over the elements in the for loop. The divide() method is called in a try block, so any exceptions throw by divide() can be caught in main(). The divide() methods sets the value of the array element corresponding to the index value that is passed. The value is the ratio of elements at index+2 and index+1. When the divisor is zero, an ArithmeticException is thrown and caught by the catch block in divide().

The catch block for ArithmeticException creates an instance of the new exception class ZeroDivideException and passes the index for the element with the zero value and the reference to the ArithmeticException to the constructor. The new exception is thrown to notify the calling program, main().

The main() method catches the ZeroDivideException and corrects the element in error by setting its value to 1. This allows the process to continue. You can see from the output that the ZeroDivideException object has the complete stack trace available, including that relating to the ArithmeticException and the ArithmeticException message is also there. This is because the ZeroDivideException chains to the ArithmeticException.

The loop in main() iterates over all the index values for the array. Because divide() references elements at index+1 and index+2, ArrayIndexOutOfBoundsException is inevitably thrown in the try block in divide(). This exception is not rethrown in the catch block and so can never be caught in main().

 WARNING *The example has a try-catch block combination inside the loop to enable you to see several exceptions being thrown and caught, but this is not a good idea in practice. Setting up try-catches are resource-intensive, so repeatedly doing that inside a loop could result in a lot of overhead.*

Chains with Multiple Links

The previous example shows two exceptions in a chain, but there are no limitations on this. Where the method call stack goes through several levels, you can chain as many exceptions together as necessary. You can access the previous exception to the last exception thrown by calling its getCause() method. You can then call getCause() for the Throwable reference you have obtained to get the next exception in the chain. You can repeat this process until getCause() returns null, which signals that you have reach the end of a chain of exceptions.

SUMMARY

In this chapter you learned what exceptions are and how to deal with them in your programs. You should make sure that you consider exception handling as an integral part of developing your Java programs. The robustness of your program code depends on how effectively you deal with the exceptions that can be thrown within it. Having said that, you should keep in mind that exceptions involve considerable overhead and should be reserved for very unusual situations. Problems that arise in the normal course of events should be handled without recourse to throwing exceptions.

EXERCISES

You can download the source code for the examples in the book and the solutions to the following exercises from www.wrox.com.

1. Write a program that generates exceptions of type NullPointerException, NegativeArraySizeException, and IndexOutOfBoundsException. Record the catching of each exception by displaying the message stored in the exception object and the stack trace record.

2. Add an exception class to the last example that differentiates between the index-out-of-bounds error possibilities, rethrows an appropriate object of this exception class in divide(), and handles the exception in main().

3. Write a program that calls a method that throws an exception of type ArithmeticException at a random iteration in a for loop. Catch the exception in the method and pass the iteration count when the exception occurred to the calling method by using an object of an exception class you define.

4. Add a finally block to the method in the previous example to output the iteration count when the method exits.

▶ WHAT YOU LEARNED IN THIS CHAPTER

TOPIC	CONCEPT
Exceptions	Exceptions identify abnormal errors that arise in your program. Exceptions are objects of subclasses of the `Throwable` class.
Standard Exceptions	Java includes a set of standard exceptions that may be thrown automatically, as a result of errors in your code, or may be thrown by methods in the standard classes in Java.
Uncaught Exceptions	If a method throws exceptions that aren't caught, and aren't represented by subclasses of the `Error` class or the `RuntimeException` class, then you must identify the exception classes in a `throws` clause in the method definition.
Catching Exceptions	If you want to handle an exception in a method, you must place the code that may generate the exception in a `try` block. A method may have several `try` blocks.
`catch` Blocks	Exception handling code is placed in a `catch` block that immediately follows the `try` block that contains the code that can throw the exception. A `try` block can have multiple `catch` blocks that each deals with a different type of exception.
`finally` Blocks	A `finally` block is used to contain code that must be executed after the execution of a `try` block, regardless of how the `try` block execution ends. A `finally` block is always executed before execution of the method ends.
Throwing Exceptions	You can throw an exception by using a `throw` statement. You can throw an exception anywhere in a method. You can also rethrow an existing exception in a `catch` block to pass it to the calling method.
Defining Exceptions	You can define your own exception classes. In general, your exceptions classes should be derived from the `Exception` class to ensure that they are checked exceptions. The compiler ensures that all checked exceptions are dealt with in the code where such exceptions may be thrown.
Chained Exceptions	When you throw a new exception in a `catch` block, you can record the previous exception by creating your exception object to store a reference to the previous exception or by calling `initCause()` for your new exception object.

Understanding Streams

WHAT YOU WILL LEARN IN THIS CHAPTER

➤ What a stream is and what the main classes that Java provides to support stream operations are

➤ What stream readers and writers are and what they are used for

➤ How to read data from the keyboard

➤ How to format data that you write to the command line

This is the first of five chapters devoted to input and output. This chapter introduces *streams*, and deals with keyboard input and output to the command line. In subsequent chapters you learn how to work with files.

STREAMS AND INPUT/OUTPUT OPERATIONS

Streams are fundamental to input and output in your programs in the most instances. The package that supports stream input/output primarily is java.io but other packages such as java.nio.file define stream classes, too. The java.io defines a large number of classes and interfaces, many of which have a significant number of methods. It is quite impractical to go into them all in detail in this book so my strategy in this and in the following chapters discussing file I/O is to take a practical approach. I provide an overall grounding in the concepts and equip you with enough detailed knowledge of the classes involved to enable you to do a number of specific, useful, and practical things in your programs. These are:

➤ To be able to read data from the keyboard

➤ To be able to write formatted output to a stream, such as System.out

➤ To be able to read and write files containing strings and basic types of data

➤ To be able to read and write files containing objects

To achieve this, I first give you an overview of the important stream classes in this chapter and how they interrelate. I'll go into the detail selectively, just exploring the classes and methods that you need to accomplish the specific things I noted.

Two areas where you must use the facilities provided by the stream classes are reading from the keyboard and writing to the command line or the console window of an IDE. I cover both of these in this chapter along with some general aspects of the stream classes and the relationships between them. You learn about how you use streams to read and write binary and character data files in Chapters 10 and 11. You look into how you read from and write objects to a file in Chapter 12.

UNDERSTANDING STREAMS

A *stream* is an abstract representation of an input or output device that is a source of, or destination for, data. The stream concept enables you to transfer data to and from diverse physical devices such as disk files, communications links, or just your keyboard, in essentially the same way.

In general you can write data to a stream or read data from a stream. You can visualize a stream as a sequence of bytes that flows into or out of your program. Figure 8-1 illustrates how physical devices map to streams.

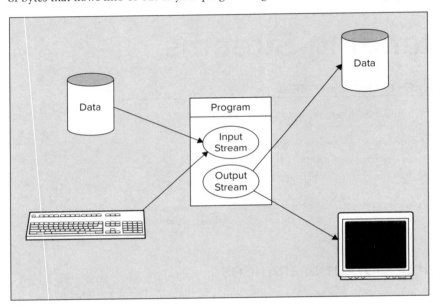

FIGURE 8-1

Input and Output Streams

A stream to which you can write data is called an *output stream*. The output stream can go to any device to which a sequence of bytes can be transferred, such as a file on a hard disk, or a network connection. An output stream can also go to your display screen, but only at the expense of limiting it to a fraction of its true capability. Stream output to your display is output to the command line. When you write to your display screen using a stream, it can display characters only, not graphical output. Graphical output requires more specialized support that I discuss from Chapter 17 onward.

> **NOTE** Note that although a printer can be considered notionally as a stream, printing in Java does not work this way. A printer in Java is treated as a graphical device, so sending output to the printer is very similar to displaying graphical output on your display screen. You learn how printing works in Java in Chapter 21.

You read data from an *input stream*. In principle, this can be any source of serial data, but is typically a disk file, the keyboard, or a connection to a remote computer.

Under normal circumstances, file input and output for the machine on which your program is executing is available only to Java *applications*. It's not available to Java applets except to a strictly limited extent. If this were not so, a malicious Java applet embedded in a web page could trash your hard disk. An IOException is normally thrown by any attempted operation on disk files on the local machine in a Java applet. The directory containing the class file for the applet and its subdirectories are freely accessible to the applet. Also, the security features in Java can be used to control what an applet (and an application running under a Security Manager) can access so that an applet can access only files or other resources *for which it has explicit permission*.

The main reason for using a stream as the basis for input and output operations is to make your program code for these operations independent of the device involved. This has two advantages. First, you don't have to worry about the detailed mechanics of each device, which are taken care of behind the scenes. Second, your program works for a variety of input/output devices without any changes to the code.

Stream input and output methods generally permit very small amounts of data, such as a single character or byte, to be written or read in a single operation. Transferring data to or from a stream like this may be extremely inefficient, so a stream is often equipped with a *buffer* in memory, in which case it is called a *buffered stream*. A buffer is simply a block of memory that is used to batch up the data that is transferred to or from an external device. Reading or writing a stream in reasonably large chunks reduces the number of input/output operations necessary and thus makes the process more efficient.

When you write to a buffered output stream, the data is sent to the buffer and not to the external device. The amount of data in the buffer is tracked automatically, and the data is usually sent to the device when the buffer is full. However, you will sometimes want the data in the buffer to be sent to the device before the buffer is full, and methods are provided to do this. This operation is usually termed *flushing* the buffer.

Buffered input streams work in a similar way. Any read operation on a buffered input stream reads data from the buffer. A read operation for the device that is the source of data for the stream is read only when the buffer is empty and the program has requested data. When this occurs, a complete buffer-full of data is read into the buffer automatically from the device, or less if insufficient data is available.

Binary and Character Streams

The java.io package supports two types of streams—*binary streams*, which contain binary data, and *character streams*, which contain character data. Binary streams are sometimes referred to as *byte streams*. These two kinds of streams behave in different ways when you read and write data.

When you write data to a binary stream, the data is written to the stream as a series of bytes, exactly as it appears in memory. No transformation of the data takes place. Binary numerical values are just written as a series of bytes, 4 bytes for each value of type int, 8 bytes for each value of type long, 8 bytes for each value of type double, and so on. As you saw in Chapter 2, Java stores its characters internally as Unicode characters, which are 16-bit characters, so each Unicode character is written to a binary stream as 2 bytes, the high byte being written first. Supplementary Unicode characters that are surrogates consist of two successive 16-bit characters, in which case the two sets of 2 bytes are written in sequence to the binary stream with the high byte written first in each case.

Character streams are used for storing and retrieving text. You may also use character streams to read text files not written by a Java program. All binary numeric data has to be converted to a textual representation before being written to a character stream. This involves generating a character representation of the original binary data value. Reading numeric data from a stream that contains text involves much more work than reading binary data. When you read a value of type int from a binary stream, you know that it consists of 4 bytes. When you read an integer from a character stream, you have to determine how many characters from the stream make up the value. For each numerical value you read from a character stream, you have to be able to recognize where the value begins and ends and then convert the *token*—the sequence of characters that represents the value—to its binary form. Figure 8-2 illustrates this.

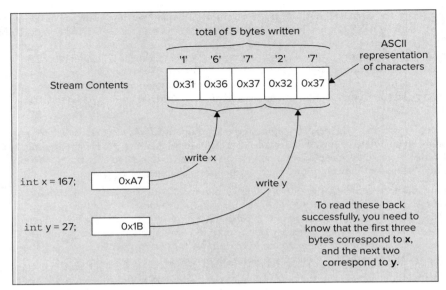

FIGURE 8-2

When you write strings to a stream as character data, by default the Unicode characters are automatically converted to the local representation of the characters in the host machine, and these are then written to the stream. When you read a string, the default mechanism converts the data from the stream back to Unicode characters from the local machine representation. With character streams, your program reads and writes Unicode characters, but the stream contains characters in the equivalent character encoding used by the local computer.

You don't have to accept the default conversion process for character streams. Java allows named mappings between Unicode characters and sets of bytes to be defined, called *charsets*, and you can select an available charset that is to apply when data is transferred to, or from, a particular character stream. This is important when the data is being transferred to or from another computer where the data representation is different from your PC. Without the correct mapping, your PC will not interpret data from the destination machine correctly, and vice versa. I don't go into charsets in detail, but you can find more information on defining and using charsets in the JDK documentation for the `Charset` class.

THE CLASSES FOR INPUT AND OUTPUT

There are quite a number of stream classes but, as you will see later, they form a reasonably logical structure. After you see how they are related, you shouldn't have much trouble using them. I work through the class hierarchy from the top down, so you can see how the classes hang together and how you can combine them in different ways to suit different situations.

The package `java.io` contains two classes that provide the foundation for Java's support for stream I/O, shown in Table 8-1.

TABLE 8-1: Package java.io Classes

CLASS	DESCRIPTION
InputStream	The base class for byte stream input operations
OutputStream	The base class for byte stream output operations

`InputStream` and `OutputStream` are both *abstract* classes. As you are well aware by now, you cannot create instances of an abstract class—these classes serve only as a base from which to derive classes with more concrete input or output capabilities. However, both of the classes declare methods that define a basic set of operations for the streams they represent, so the fundamental characteristics of how a stream is accessed are set by these classes. Generally, the `InputStream` and `OutputStream` subclasses represent byte streams and provide the means of reading and writing binary data as a series of bytes.

Both classes implement the `Closeable` interface. This interface declares just one method, `close()`, which closes the stream and releases any resources that the stream object is holding. The `Closeable` interface extends the `AutoCloseable` interface that also declares the `close()` method so classes that implement `Closeable` also implement `AutoCloseable`. Classes that implement the `AutoCloseable` interface can have their `close()` method called automatically when the class object is created within a special `try` block. I discuss this in Chapter 9.

Basic Input Stream Operations

As you saw in the previous section, the `InputStream` class is abstract, so you cannot create objects of this class type. Nonetheless, input stream objects are often accessible via a reference of this type, so the methods identified in this class are what you get. The `InputStream` class includes three methods for reading data from a stream, shown in Table 8-2.

TABLE 8-2: InputStream Class Methods

METHOD	DESCRIPTION
`read()`	This method is abstract, so it has to be defined in a subclass. The method returns the next byte available from the stream as type `int`. If the end of the stream is reached, the method returns the value –1. An exception of type `IOException` is thrown if an I/O error occurs.
`read(byte[] array)`	This method reads bytes from the stream into successive elements of `array`. The maximum of `array.length` bytes is read. The method does not return until the input data is read or the end of the stream is detected. The method returns the number of bytes read or –1 if no bytes were read because the end of the stream was reached. If an I/O error occurs, an exception of type `IOException` is thrown. If the argument to the method is `null` then a `NullPointerException` is thrown. An input/output method that does not return until the operation is completed is referred to as a *blocking* method, and you say that the methods *blocks* until the operation is complete.
`read(byte[] array, int offset, int length)`	This works in essentially the same way as the previous method, except that up to `length` bytes are read into `array` starting with the element `array[offset]`. The method returns the number of bytes read or –1 if no bytes were read because the end of the stream was reached.

These methods read data from the stream simply as bytes. No conversion is applied. If any conversion is required—for a stream containing bytes in the local character encoding, for example—you must provide a way to handle this. You see how this might be done in a moment.

You can skip over bytes in an `InputStream` by calling its `skip()` method. You specify the number of bytes to be skipped as an argument of type `long`, and the actual number of bytes skipped is returned, also a value of type `long`. This method can throw an `IOException` if an error occurs.

You can close an `InputStream` by calling its `close()` method. After you have closed an input stream, subsequent attempts to access or read from the stream cause an `IOException` to be thrown because the `close()` operation has released the resources held by the stream object, including the source of the data, such as a file. I discuss closing a stream in more detail in Chapter 9.

Buffered Input Streams

The `BufferedInputStream` class defines an input stream that is buffered in memory and thus makes read operations on the stream more efficient. The `BufferedInputStream` is derived from the `FilterInputStream` class, which has `InputStream` as a base.

You create a `BufferedInputStream` object from another input stream, and the constructor accepts a reference of type `InputStream` as an argument. The `BufferedInputStream` class overrides the methods inherited from `InputStream` so that operations are via a buffer; it implements the abstract `read()` method. Here's an example of how you create a buffered input stream:

```
BufferedInputStream keyboard = new BufferedInputStream(System.in);
```

The argument `System.in` is an `InputStream` object that is a static member of the `System` class and encapsulates input from the keyboard. You look into how you can read input from the keyboard a little later in this chapter.

The effect of wrapping a stream in a `BufferedInputStream` object is to buffer the underlying stream in memory so that data can be read from the stream in large chunks—up to the size of the buffer that is provided. The data is then made available to the `read()` methods directly from the buffer in memory and the buffer is replenished automatically. A real read operation from the underlying stream is executed only when the buffer is empty.

With a suitable choice of buffer size, the number of input operations from the underlying stream that are needed is substantially reduced, and the process is a whole lot more efficient. This is because for many input streams, each read operation carries quite a bit of overhead, beyond the time required to actually transfer the data. The buffer size that you get by default when you call the `BufferedInputStream` constructor as in the previous code fragment is 8192 bytes. This is adequate for most situations where modest amounts of data are involved. The `BufferedInputStream` class also defines a constructor that accepts a second argument of type `int` that enables you to specify the size in bytes of the buffer to be used.

Basic Output Stream Operations

The `OutputStream` class contains three `write()` methods for writing binary data to the stream. As can be expected, these mirror the `read()` methods of the `InputStream` class. This class is also abstract, so only subclasses can be instantiated. The principal direct subclasses of `OutputStream` are shown in Figure 8-3.

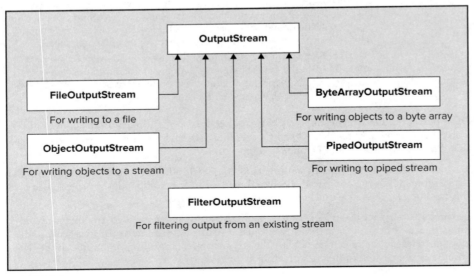

FIGURE 8-3

You investigate the methods belonging to the `ObjectOutputStream` class in Chapter 12, when you learn how to write objects to a file.

> **NOTE** Note that this is not the complete set of output stream classes. The `FilterOutputStream` class has a further eight subclasses, including the `BufferedOutputStream` class, which does for output streams what the `BufferedInputStream` class does for input streams. There is also the `PrintStream` class, which you look at a little later in this chapter, because output to the command line is via a stream object of this type.

Stream Readers and Writers

Stream readers and *writers* are objects that can read and write byte streams as character streams. So a character stream is essentially a byte stream fronted by a reader or a writer. The base classes for stream readers and writers are shown in Table 8-3.

TABLE 8-3: Base Class for Stream Readers and Writers

CLASS	DESCRIPTION
Reader	The base class for reading a character stream
Writer	The base class for writing a character stream

`Reader` and `Writer` are both abstract classes. Both classes implement the `AutoCloseable` interface, which declares the `close()` method. The `Reader` class also implements the `Readable` interface, which declares the `read()` method for reading characters into a `CharBuffer` object that is passed as the argument to the method. The `Reader` class defines two further `read()` methods. One of these requires no arguments and reads and returns a single character from the stream and returns it as type `int`. The other expects an array of type `char[]` as the argument and reads characters into the array that is passed to the method. The method returns the number of characters that were read or −1 if the end of the stream is reached. The reader has an abstract `read()` method as a member, which is declared like this:

```
public abstract int read(char[] buf, int offset, int length) throws IOException;
```

This method is the reason the `Reader` class is abstract and has to be implemented in any concrete subclass. The method reads `length` characters into the `buf` array starting at position `buf[offset]`. The method also returns the number of characters that were read or −1 if the end of the stream was reached.

Another `read()` method reads characters into a buffer:

```
public int read(CharBuffer buffer) throws IOException;
```

This reads characters into the `CharBuffer` buffer specified by the argument. No manipulation of the buffer is performed. The method returns the number of characters transferred to `buffer` or −1 if the source of characters is exhausted.

All four `read()` methods can throw an exception of type `IOException`, and the `read()` method declared in `Readable` can also throw an exception of `NullPointerException` if the argument is `null`.

The `Writer` class implements the `Appendable` interface. This declares three versions of the `append()` method; one takes an argument of type `char` and appends the character that is passed to it to whatever stream the `Writer` encapsulates, another accepts an argument of type `CharSequence` and appends that to the underlying stream, and the third appends a subsequence of a character sequence to the stream. Recall from Chapter 6 that a `CharSequence` reference can refer to an object of type `String`, an object of type `StringBuilder`, an object of type `StringBuffer`, or an object of type `CharBuffer`, so the `append()`

method handles any of these. The `Writer` class has five `write()` methods (shown in Table 8-4), all of which have a `void` return type and throw an `IOException` if an I/O error occurs.

TABLE 8-4: Writer Class write () Methods

METHOD	DESCRIPTION
`write(int ch)`	Writes the character corresponding to the low-order 2 bytes of the integer argument, `ch`.
`write(char[] buf)`	Writes the array of characters `buf`.
`write(char[] buf, int offset, int length)`	This is an abstract method that writes `length` characters from `buf` starting at `buf[offset]`.
`write(String str)`	Writes the string `str`.
`write(String str, int offset, int length)`	Writes `length` characters from `str` starting with the character at index position `offset` in the string.

The `Reader` and `Writer` classes and their subclasses are not really streams themselves, but provide the methods you can use for reading and writing an underlying stream as a character stream. Thus, you typically create a `Reader` or `Writer` object using an underlying `InputStream` or `OutputStream` object that encapsulates the connection to the external device that is the ultimate source or destination of the data.

Using Readers

The `Reader` class has the direct subclasses shown in Figure 8-4.

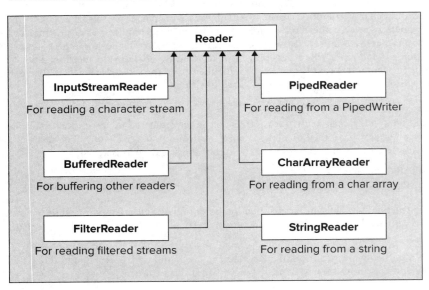

FIGURE 8-4

You can read an input stream as a character stream using an `InputStreamReader` object that you could create like this:

```
InputStreamReader keyboard = new InputStreamReader(System.in);
```

The parameter to the `InputStreamReader` constructor is of type `InputStream`, so you can pass an object of any class derived from `InputStream` to it. The preceding example creates an `InputStreamReader` object, `keyboard`, from the object `System.in`, the keyboard input stream.

The `InputStreamReader` class defines the abstract `read()` method that it inherits from `Reader` and redefines the `read()` method without parameters. These methods read bytes from the underlying stream and return them as Unicode characters using the default conversion from the local character encoding. In addition to the preceding example, there are also three further constructors for `InputStreamReader` objects (shown in Table 8-5).

TABLE 8-5: InputStreamReader Object Constructors

METHOD	DESCRIPTION

`InputStreamReader(`
    `InputStream in,`
    `Charset s)`
	Constructs an object with `in` as the underlying stream. The object uses `s` to convert bytes to Unicode characters.

`InputStreamReader(`
    `InputStream in,`
    `CharsetDecoder dec)`
	Constructs an object that uses the charset decoder `dec` to transform bytes that are read from the stream `in` to a sequence of Unicode characters.

`InputStreamReader(`
    `InputStream in,`
    `String charsetName)`
	Constructs an object that uses the charset identified in the name `charsetName` to convert bytes that are read from the stream `in` to a sequence of Unicode characters.

A `java.nio.charset.Charset` object defines a mapping between Unicode characters and bytes. A `Charset` can be identified by a name that is a string that conforms to the IANA conventions for `Charset` registration. A `java.nio.charset.CharsetDecoder` object converts a sequence of bytes in a given charset to bytes. Consult the class documentation in the JDK for the `Charset` and `CharsetDecoder` classes for more information.

Of course, the operations with a reader are much more efficient if you buffer it with a `BufferedReader` object like this:

```
BufferedReader keyboard = new BufferedReader(new InputStreamReader(System.in));
```

Here, you wrap an `InputStreamReader` object around `System.in` and then buffer it using a `BufferedReader` object. This makes the input operations much more efficient. Your read operations are from the buffer belonging to the `BufferedReader` object, and this object takes care of filling the buffer from `System.in` when necessary via the underlying `InputStreamReader` object.

A `CharArrayReader` object is created from an array and enables you to read data from the array as though it were from a character input stream. A `StringReader` object class does essentially the same thing, but obtains the data from a `String` object.

Using Writers

The main subclasses of the `Writer` class are as shown in Figure 8-5.

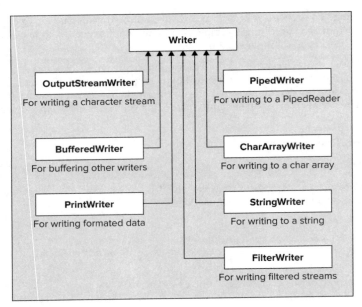

FIGURE 8-5

Let's discuss just a few details of the most commonly used of these classes.

The OutputStreamWriter class writes characters to an underlying binary stream. It also has a subclass, FileWriter, that writes characters to a stream encapsulating a file. Both of these are largely superseded by the new I/O facilities.

Note that the PrintWriter class has no particular relevance to printing, in spite of its name. The PrintWriter class defines methods for formatting binary data as characters and writing it to a character stream. It defines overloaded print() and println() methods that accept an argument of each of the primitive types, of type char[], of type String, and of type Object. The data that is written is a character representation of the argument. Numerical values and objects are converted to a string representation using the static valueOf() method in the String class. Overloaded versions of this method exist for all the primitive types plus type Object. In the case of an argument that is an Object reference, the valueOf() method just calls the toString() method for the object to produce the string to be written to the stream. The print() methods just write the string representation of the argument, whereas the println() method appends \n to the output. You can create a PrintWriter object from a stream or from another Writer object.

An important point note when using a PrintWriter object is that its methods do not throw I/O exceptions. To determine whether any I/O errors have occurred, you have to call the checkError() method for the PrintWriter object. This method returns true if an error occurred and false otherwise.

The StringWriter and CharArrayWriter classes are for writing character data to a StringBuffer object, or an array of type char[]. You typically use these to perform data conversions so that the results are available to you from the underlying array or string. For example, you could combine the capabilities of a PrintWriter with a StringWriter to obtain a String object containing binary data converted to characters:

```
StringWriter strWriter = new StringWriter();
PrintWriter writer = new PrintWriter(strWriter);
```

Now you can use the methods for the writer object to write to the StringBuffer object underlying the StringWriter object:

```
double value = 2.71828;
writer.println(value);
```

You can get the result back as a `StringBuffer` object from the original `StringWriter` object:

```
StringBuffer str = strWriter.getBuffer();
```

Of course, the formatting done by a `PrintWriter` object does not help make the output line up in neat columns. If you want that to happen, you have to do it yourself. You see how you might do this for command-line output a little later in this chapter.

Let's now turn to keyboard input and command-line output.

THE STANDARD STREAMS

Your operating system typically defines three standard streams that are accessible through members of the `System` class in Java:

➤ A *standard input stream* that usually corresponds to the keyboard by default. This is encapsulated by the `in` member of the `System` class and is of type `InputStream`.

➤ A *standard output stream* that corresponds to output on the command line or in the console window of an IDE. This is encapsulated by the `out` member of the `System` class and is of type `PrintStream`.

➤ A *standard error output stream* for error messages that usually maps to the command-line output by default. This is encapsulated by the `err` member of the `System` class and is also of type `PrintStream`.

You can reassign any of these to another stream within a Java application. The `System` class provides the static methods `setIn()`, `setOut()`, and `setErr()` for this purpose. The `setIn()` method requires an argument of type `InputStream` that specifies the new source of standard input. The other two methods expect an argument of type `PrintStream`.

Because the standard input stream is of type `InputStream`, you are not exactly overwhelmed by the capabilities for reading data from the keyboard in Java. Basically, you can read a byte or an array of bytes using a `read()` method as standard, and that's it. If you want more than that, reading integers, or decimal values, or strings as keyboard input, you're on your own. Let's see what you can do to remedy that.

Getting Data from the Keyboard

To get sensible input from the keyboard, you have to be able to scan the stream of characters and recognize what they are. When you read a numerical value from the stream, you have to look for the digits and possibly the sign and decimal point, figure out where the number starts and ends in the stream, and finally convert it to the appropriate value. To write the code to do this from scratch would take quite a lot of work. Fortunately, you can get a lot of help from the class libraries. One possibility is to use the `java.util.Scanner` class, but I defer discussion of that until Chapter 15 because you need to understand another topic before you can use `Scanner` objects effectively. The `StreamTokenizer` class in the `java.io` package is another possibility, so let's look further into that.

The term *token* refers to a data item such as a number or a string that, in general, consists of several consecutive characters of a particular kind from the stream. For example, a number is usually a sequence of characters that consists of digits, maybe a decimal point, and sometimes a sign in front. The class has the name `StreamTokenizer` because it can read characters from a stream and parse it into a series of tokens that it recognizes.

You create a `StreamTokenizer` object from a stream reader object that reads data from the underlying input stream. To read the standard input stream `System.in` you can use an `InputStreamReader` object that converts the raw bytes that are read from the stream from the local character encoding to Unicode characters before the `StreamTokenizer` object sees them. In the interest of efficiency it would be a good idea to buffer the data from the `InputStreamReader` through a `BufferedReader` object that buffers the data in memory. With this in mind, you could create a `StreamTokenizer` object like this:

```
StreamTokenizer tokenizer = new StreamTokenizer(
                    new BufferedReader(
                        new InputStreamReader(System.in)));
```

The argument to the `StreamTokenizer` object is the original standard input stream `System.in` inside an `InputStreamReader` object that converts the bytes to Unicode inside a `BufferedReader` object that supplies the stream of Unicode characters via a buffer in memory.

Before you can make use of the `StreamTokenizer` object for keyboard input, you need to understand a bit more about how it works.

Tokenizing a Stream

The `StreamTokenizer` class defines objects that can read an input stream and parse it into tokens. The input stream is read and treated as a series of separate bytes, and each byte is regarded as a Unicode character in the range `'u\0000'` to `'u\00FF'`. A `StreamTokenizer` object in its default state can recognize the following kinds of tokens (shown in Table 8-6):

TABLE 8-6: StreamTokenizer Object Tokens

TOKEN	DESCRIPTION
Numbers	A sequence consisting of the digits 0 to 9, plus possibly a decimal point, and a + or − sign.
Strings	Any sequence of characters between a pair of single quotes or a pair of double quotes.
Words	Any sequence of letters or digits 0 to 9 beginning with a letter. A letter is defined as any of A to Z and a to z or \u00A0 to \u00FF. A word follows a whitespace character and is terminated by another whitespace character, or any character other than a letter or a digit.
Comments	Any sequence of characters beginning with a forward slash, /, and ending with the end-of-line character. Comments are ignored and not returned by the tokenizer.
Whitespace	All byte values from '\u0000' to '\u0020', which includes space, backspace, horizontal tab, vertical tab, line feed, form feed, and carriage return. Whitespace acts as a delimiter between tokens and is ignored (except within a quoted string).

To retrieve a token from the stream, you call the `nextToken()` method for the `StreamTokenizer` object:

```
int tokenType = 0;
try {
  while((tokenType = tokenizer.nextToken()) != tokenizer.TT_EOF) {
      // Do something with the token...
  }

} catch (IOException e) {
  e.printStackTrace(System.err);
  System.exit(1);
}
```

The `nextToken()` method can throw an exception of type `IOException`, so we put the call in a `try` block. The value returned depends on the token recognized, indicating its type, and from this value you can determine where to find the token itself. In the preceding fragment, you store the value returned in `tokenType` and compare its value with the constant `TT_EOF`. This constant is a static field of type `int` in the `StreamTokenizer` class that is returned by the `nextToken()` method when the end of the stream has been read. Thus the `while` loop continues until the end of the stream is reached. The token that was read from the stream is itself stored in one of two instance variables of the `StreamTokenizer` object. If the data item is a number, it is stored in a public data member `nval`, which is of type `double`. If the data item is a quoted string or a word, a reference to a `String` object that encapsulates the data item is stored in the public data member `sval`, which is of type `String`, of course. The analysis that segments the stream into tokens is fairly simple, and the way in which an arbitrary stream is broken into tokens is illustrated in Figure 8-6.

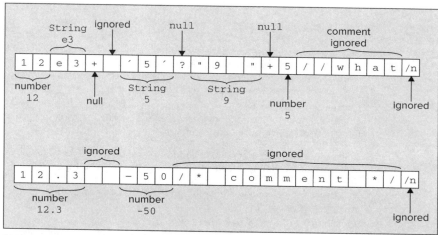

FIGURE 8-6

As I've said, the `int` value that is returned by the `nextToken()` method indicates what kind of data item was read. It can be any of the constant static variables shown in Table 8-7 defined in the `StreamTokenizer` class:

TABLE 8-7: Constant Static Variables

TOKEN VALUE	DESCRIPTION
TT_NUMBER	The token is a number that has been stored in the public field `nval` of type `double` in the tokenizer object.
TT_WORD	The token is a word that has been stored in the public field `sval` of type `String` in the tokenizer object.
TT_EOF	The end of the stream has been reached.
TT_EOL	An end-of-line character has been read. This is set only if the `eolIsSignificant()` method has been called with the argument, `true`. Otherwise, end-of-line characters are treated as whitespace and ignored.

If a quoted string is read from the stream, the value that is returned by `nextToken()` is the quote character used for the string as type `int` — either a single quote or a double quote. In this case, you retrieve the reference to the string that was read from the `sval` member of the tokenizer object. The value indicating what kind of token was read last is also available from a public data member `ttype`, of the `StreamTokenizer` object, which is of type `int`.

Customizing a Stream Tokenizer

You can modify default tokenizing mode by calling one or other of the methods found in Table 8-8.

TABLE 8-8: Methods that Modify Tokenizing Modes

METHOD	DESCRIPTION
resetSyntax()	Resets the state of the tokenizer object so no characters have any special significance. This has the effect that all characters are regarded as ordinary and are read from the stream as single characters so no tokens are identified. The value of each character is stored in the `ttype` field.

continues

TABLE 8-8 *(continued)*

METHOD	DESCRIPTION
ordinaryChar(int ch)	Sets the character ch as an ordinary character. An ordinary character is a character that has no special significance. It is read as a single character whose value is stored in the ttype field. Calling this method does not alter the state of characters other than the argument value.
ordinaryChars(int low, int hi)	Causes all characters from low to hi inclusive to be treated as ordinary characters. Calling this method does not alter the state of characters other than those specified by the argument values.
whitespaceChars(int low, int hi)	Causes all characters from low to hi inclusive to be treated as whitespace characters. Unless they appear in a string, whitespace characters are treated as delimiters between tokens. Calling this method does not alter the state of characters other than those specified by the argument values.
wordChars(int low, int hi)	Specifies that the characters from low to hi inclusive are word characters. A word is at least one of these characters. Calling this method does not alter the state of characters other than those specified by the argument values.
commentChar(int ch)	Specifies that ch is a character that indicates the start of a comment. All characters to the end of the line following the character ch are ignored. Calling this method does not alter the state of characters other than the argument value.
quoteChar(int ch)	Specifies that matching pairs of the character ch enclose a string. Calling this method does not alter the state of characters other than the argument value.
slashStarComments(boolean flag)	If the argument is false, this switches off recognizing comments between /* and */. A true argument switches it on again.
slashSlashComments(boolean flag)	If the argument is false, this switches off recognizing comments starting with a double slash. A true argument switches it on again.
lowerCaseMode(boolean flag)	An argument of true causes strings to be converted to lowercase before being stored in sval. An argument of false switches off lowercase mode.
pushback()	Calling this method causes the next call of the nextToken() method to return the ttype value that was set by the previous nextToken() call and to leave sval and nval unchanged.

If you want to alter a tokenizer, it is usually better to reset it by calling the resetSyntax() method and then calling the other methods to set up the tokenizer the way that you want. If you adopt this approach, any special significance attached to particular characters is apparent from your code. The resetSyntax() method makes all characters, including whitespace and ordinary characters, so that no character has any special significance. In some situations you may need to set a tokenizer up dynamically to suit retrieving each specific kind of data that you want to extract from the stream. When you want to read the next character as a character, even if it would otherwise be part of a token, you just need to call resetSyntax() before calling nextToken(). The character is returned by nextToken() and stored in the ttype field. To read tokens subsequently, you have to set the tokenizer up appropriately.

Let's see how you can use this class to read data items from the keyboard.

TRY IT OUT Creating a Formatted Input Class

One way of reading formatted input is to define your own class that uses a `StreamTokenizer` object to read from standard input. You can define a class, `FormattedInput`, that defines methods to return various types of data items entered via the keyboard:

```java
import java.io.StreamTokenizer;
import java.io.BufferedReader;
import java.io.InputStreamReader;
import java.io.IOException;

public class FormattedInput {

  // Method to read an int value...

  // Method to read a double value...

  // Plus methods to read various other data types...

  // Helper method to read the next token
  private int readToken() {
    try {
      ttype = tokenizer.nextToken();
      return ttype;

    } catch (IOException e) {   // Error reading in nextToken()
      e.printStackTrace();
      System.exit(1);          // End the program
    }
    return 0;
  }

  // Object to tokenize input from the standard input stream
  private StreamTokenizer tokenizer = new StreamTokenizer(
                              new BufferedReader(
                                new InputStreamReader(System.in)));
  private int ttype;                    // Stores the token type code
}
```

Directory "TestFormattedInput"

The default constructor is quite satisfactory for this class, because the instance variable `tokenizer` is already initialized. The `readToken()` method is there for use in the methods that read values of various types. It makes the `ttype` value returned by `nextToken()` available directly, and saves having to repeat the `try` and `catch` blocks in all the other methods.

All you need to add are the methods to read the data values that you want. Here is one way to read a value of type `int`:

```java
  // Method to read an int value
  public int readInt() {
    for (int i = 0; i < 5; ++i) {

      if (readToken() == StreamTokenizer.TT_NUMBER) {
        return (int) tokenizer.nval;   // Value is numeric, so return as int
      } else {
        System.out.println("Incorrect input: " + tokenizer.sval
                           + " Re-enter an integer");
        continue;                      // Retry the read operation
      }

    }
```

```
            System.out.println("Five failures reading an int value"
                               + " - program terminated");
            System.exit(1);                        // End the program
            return 0;
        }
```

Directory "TestFormattedInput"

This method gives the user five chances to enter a valid input value before terminating the program. Terminating the program is likely to be inconvenient to say the least in many circumstances. If you instead make the method throw an exception in the case of failure here, and let the calling method decide what to do, this would be a much better way of signaling that the right kind of data could not be found.

You can define your own exception class for this. Let's define it as the type `InvalidUserInputException`:

```
public class InvalidUserInputException extends Exception {
    public InvalidUserInputException() {}

    public InvalidUserInputException(String message) {
        super(message);
    }
    private static final long serialVersionUID = 90001L;
}
```

Directory "TestFormattedInput"

You haven't had to add much to the base class capability. You just need the ability to pass your own message to the class. The significant things you have added are your own exception type name and a member `serialVersionUID`, which is a version identifier for a serializable class type. This is there because the base class is serializable and your class inherits this capability. Serialization is the process of writing an object to a file; you learn more about this in Chapter 12.

Now you can change the code for the `readInt()` method so it works like this:

```
public int readInt() throws InvalidUserInputException {
    if (readToken() != StreamTokenizer.TT_NUMBER) {
        throw new InvalidUserInputException("readInt() failed."
                                + "Input data not numeric");
    }
    return (int) tokenizer.nval;
}
```

Directory "TestFormattedInput"

If you need a method to read an integer value and return it as one of the other integer types, `byte`, `short`, or `long`, you could implement it in the same way, but just cast the value in `nval` to the appropriate type. You might want to add checks that the original value was an integer, and maybe that it was not out of range for the shorter integer types. For example, to do this for type `int`, you could code it as the following:

```
public int readInt() throws InvalidUserInputException {
    if (readToken() != StreamTokenizer.TT_NUMBER) {
        throw new InvalidUserInputException("readInt() failed."
                                + "Input data not numeric");
    }

    if (tokenizer.nval > (double) Integer.MAX_VALUE
            || tokenizer.nval < (double) Integer.MIN_VALUE) {
        throw new InvalidUserInputException("readInt() failed."
                                + "Input outside range of type int");
    }

    if (tokenizer.nval != (double) (int) tokenizer.nval) {
```

```
        throw new InvalidUserInputException("readInt() failed."
                                     + "Input not an integer");
      }
      return (int) tokenizer.nval;
    }
```

Directory "TestFormattedInput"

The `Integer` class makes the maximum and minimum values of type `int` available in the public members `MAX_VALUE` and `MIN_VALUE`. Other classes corresponding to the basic numeric types provide similar fields. To determine whether the value in `nval` is really a whole number, you cast it to an integer and then cast it back to `double` and see whether it is the same value.

The code to implement `readDouble()` is very simple. You don't need the cast for the value in `nval` because it is type `double` anyway:

Available for
download on
Wrox.com

```
    public double readDouble() throws InvalidUserInputException {
      if (readToken() != StreamTokenizer.TT_NUMBER) {
        throw new InvalidUserInputException("readDouble() failed."
                                     + "Input data not numeric");
      }
      return tokenizer.nval;
    }
```

Directory "TestFormattedInput"

A `readFloat()` method would just need to cast `nval` to type `float`.

Reading a string is slightly more involved. You could allow input strings to be quoted or unquoted as long as they were alphanumeric and did not contain whitespace characters. Here's how the method might be coded to allow that:

Available for
download on
Wrox.com

```
    public String readString() throws InvalidUserInputException {
      if (readToken() == StreamTokenizer.TT_WORD || ttype == '\"'
             || ttype == '\"') {
        return tokenizer.sval;
      } else {
        throw new InvalidUserInputException("readString() failed."
                                     + "Input data is not a string");
      }
    }
```

Directory "TestFormattedInput"

If either a word or a string is recognized, the token is stored as type `String` in the `sval` field of the `StreamTokenizer` object.

Let's see if it works.

TRY IT OUT   Formatted Keyboard Input

You can try out the `FormattedInput` class in a simple program that iterates round a loop a few times to give you the opportunity to try out correct and incorrect input:

Available for
download on
Wrox.com

```
    public class TestFormattedInput {
      public static void main(String[] args) {
        FormattedInput kb = new FormattedInput();
        for (int i = 0; i < 5; ++i) {
          try {
            System.out.print("Enter an integer:");
```

```
            System.out.println("Integer read:" + kb.readInt());
            System.out.print("Enter a double value:");
            System.out.println("Double value read:" + kb.readDouble());
            System.out.print("Enter a string:");
            System.out.println("String read:" + kb.readString());
          } catch (InvalidUserInputException e) {
            System.out.println("InvalidUserInputException thrown.\n"
                                + e.getMessage());
          }
        }
      }
    }
  }
```

Directory "TestFormattedInput"

It is best to run this example from the command line. Some Java development environments are not terrific when it comes to keyboard input. If you try a few wrong values, you should see your exception being thrown.

How It Works

This just repeats requests for input of each of the three types of value you have provided methods for, over five iterations. Of course, after an exception of type `InvalidUserInputException` is thrown, the loop goes straight to the start of the next iteration—if there is one.

This code isn't foolproof. Bits of an incorrect entry can be left in the stream to confuse subsequent input and you can't enter floating-point values with exponents. However, it does work after a fashion and it's best not to look a gift horse in the mouth.

Writing to the Command Line

Up to now, you have made extensive use of the `println()` method from the `PrintStream` class in your examples to output formatted information to the screen. The `out` object in the expression `System.out.println()` is of type `PrintStream`. This class outputs data of any of the basic types as a string. For example, an `int` value of `12345` becomes the string `"12345"` as generated by the `valueOf()` method from the `String` class. However, you also have the `PrintWriter` class that I discussed earlier in the chapter to do the same thing because this class has all the methods that `PrintStream` provides.

The principle difference between the two classes is that with the `PrintWriter` class you can control whether or not the stream buffer is flushed when the `println()` method is called, whereas with the `PrintStream` class you cannot. The `PrintWriter` class flushes the stream buffer only when one of the `println()` methods is called, if automatic flushing is enabled. A `PrintStream` object flushes the stream buffer whenever a newline character is written to the stream, regardless of whether it was written by a `print()` or a `println()` method.

Both the `PrintWriter` and `PrintStream` classes format basic data as characters. In addition to the `print()` and `println()` methods that do this, they also define the `printf()` method mentioned in Chapter 6. This method gives you a great deal more control over the format of the output and also accepts an arbitrary number of arguments to be formatted and displayed.

The printf() Method

The `printf()` method that is defined in the `PrintStream` and `PrintWriter` classes produces formatted output for an arbitrary sequence of values of various types, where the formatting is specified by the first argument to the method. `System.out` happens to be of type `PrintStream`, so you can use `printf()` to produce formatted output to the command line. The `PrintStream` and `PrintWriter` classes define two versions of the `printf()` method, shown in Table 8-9.

TABLE 8-9: printf() Method Versions

VERSION	DESCRIPTION
`printf(String format,` `       Object ... args)`	Outputs the values of the elements in `args` according to format specifications in `format`. An exception of type `NullPointerException` is thrown if `format` is `null`.

`printf(Locale loc,`
`       String format,`
`       Object ... args)`
	This version works as the preceding version does except that the output is tailored to the locale specified by the first argument. I explain how you define objects of the `java.util.Locale` class type a little later in this chapter.

The `format` parameter is a string that should contain at least one format specification for each of the argument values that follow the format argument. The format specification for an argument value just defines how the data is to be presented and is of the following general form:

```
%[argument_index$][flags][width][.precision]conversion
```

The square brackets around components of the format specification indicate that they are optional, so the minimum format specification if you omit all of the optional parts is `%conversion`.

The options that you have for the various components of the format specification for a value are shown in Table 8-10.

TABLE 8-10: Format Specification Options

OPTION	DESCRIPTION
`conversion`	This is a single character specifying how the argument is to be presented. The commonly used values are the following: `'d'`, `'o'`, and `'x'` apply to integer values and specify that the output representation of the value should be decimal, octal, or hexadecimal, respectively. `'f'`, `'g'`, and `'a'` apply to floating-point values and specify that the output representation should be decimal notation, scientific notation (with an exponent), or hexadecimal with an exponent, respectively. `'c'` specifies that the argument value is a character and should be displayed as such. `'s'` specifies that the argument is a string. `'b'` specifies that the argument is a boolean value, so it is output as `"true"` or `"false"`. `'h'` specifies that the hashcode of the argument is to be output in hexadecimal form. `'n'` specifies the platform line separator so `"%n"` has the same effect as `"\n"`.
`argument_index`	This is a decimal integer that identifies one of the arguments that follow the format string by its sequence number, where `"1$"` refers to the first argument, `"2$"` refers to the second argument, and so on. You can also use `'<'` in place of a sequence number followed by $ to indicate that the argument should be the same as that of the previous format specification in the format string. Thus `"<"` specifies that the format specification applies to the argument specified by the preceding format specification in the format string.

continues

TABLE 8-10 *(continued)*

OPTION	DESCRIPTION
flags	This is a set of flag characters that modify the output format. The flag characters that are valid depend on the conversion that is specified. The most used ones are the following: '-' and '^' apply to anything and specify that the output should be left-justified and uppercase, respectively. '+' forces a sign to be output for numerical values. '0' forces numerical values to be zero-padded.
width	Specifies the field width for outputting the argument and represents the minimum number of characters to be written to the output.
precision	This is used to restrict the output in some way depending on the conversion. Its primary use is to specify the number of digits of precision when outputting floating-point values.

The best way to explain how you use this is through examples. I start with the simplest and work up from there.

Formatting Numerical Data

I suggest that you set up a program source file with an empty version of main() into which you can plug a succession of code fragments to try them out. You'll find TryFormattedOutput.java in the download with the code fragments that are bold in the text commented out in main(). You can just comment out the one you want to try but as always, it's better to type them in yourself.

The minimal format specification is a percent sign followed by a conversion specifier for the type of value you want displayed. For example:

```
int a = 5, b = 15, c = 255;
double x = 27.5, y = 33.75;
System.out.printf("x = %f y = %g", x, y);
System.out.printf(" a = %d b = %x c = %o", a, b, c);
```

TryFormattedOutput.java

Executing this fragment produces the following output:

```
x = 27.500000 y = 33.750000 a = 5 b = f c = 377
```

There is no specification of the argument to which each format specifier applies, so the default action is to match the format specifiers to the arguments in the sequence in which they appear. You can see from the output that you get six decimal places after the decimal point for floating-point values, and the field width is set to be sufficient to accommodate the number of characters in each output value. Although there are two output statements, all the output appears on a single line, so you can deduce that printf() works like the print() method in that it just transfers output to the command line starting at the current cursor position.

The integer values also have a default output field width that is sufficient for the number of characters in the output. Here you have output values in normal decimal form, in hexadecimal form, and in octal representation. Note that there must be at least as many arguments as there are format specifiers. If you remove c from the argument list in the last printf() call, you get an exception of type MissingFormatArgumentException thrown. If you have more arguments than there are format specifiers in the format string, on the other hand, the excess arguments are simply ignored.

By introducing the argument index into the specification in the previous code fragment, you can demonstrate how that works:

```
int a = 5, b = 15, c = 255;
double x = 27.5, y = 33.75;
System.out.printf("x = %2$f y = %1$g", x, y);
System.out.printf(" a = %3$d b = %1$x c = %2$o", a, b, c);
```

TryFormattedOutput.java

This produces the following output:

```
x = 33.750000 y = 27.500000 a = 255 b = 5 c = 17
```

Here you have reversed the sequence of the floating-point arguments in the output by using the argument index specification to select the argument for the format specifier explicitly. The integer values are also output in a different sequence from the sequence in which the arguments appear so the names that are output do not correspond with the variables.

To try out the use of "<" as the argument index specification, you could add the following statement to the preceding fragment:

```
System.out.printf("%na = %3$d b = %<x c = %<o", a, b, c);
```

TryFormattedOutput.java

This produces the following output on a new line:

```
a = 255 b = ff c = 377
```

You could equally well use "\n" in place of "%n" in the format string. The second and third format specifiers use "<" as the argument index, so all three apply only to the value of the first argument. The arguments b and c are ignored.

Note that if the format conversion is not consistent with the type of the argument to which you apply it, an exception of type IllegalFormatConversion is thrown. This would occur if you attempted to output any of the variables a, b, and c, which are of type int, with a specifier such as "%f", which applies only to floating-point values.

Specifying the Width and Precision

You can specify the field width for any output value. Here's an example of that:

```
int a = 5, b = 15, c = 255;
double x = 27.5, y = 33.75;
System.out.printf("x = %15f y = %8g", x, y);
System.out.printf("a = %1$5d b = %2$5x c = %3$2o", a, b, c);
```

TryFormattedOutput.java

Executing this results in the following output:

```
x =        27.500000 y = 33.750000 a =     5 b =      f c = 377
```

You can see from the output that you get the width that you specify only if it is sufficient to accommodate all the characters in the output value. The second floating-point value, y, occupies a field width of 9, not the 8 that is specified. When you want your output to line up in columns, you must be sure to specify a field width that is sufficient to accommodate every output value.

Where the specified width exceeds the number of characters for the value, the field is padded on the left with spaces so the value appears right-justified in the field. If you want the output left-justified in the field, you just use the '-' flag character. For example:

```
System.out.printf("%na = %1$-5d b = %2$-5x c = %3$-5o", a, b, c);
```

This statement produces output left-justified in the fields, thus:

```
a = 5      b = f      c = 377
```

You can add a precision specification for floating-point output:

```
double x = 27.5, y = 33.75;
System.out.printf("x = %15.2f y = %14.3f", x, y);
```

Here the precision for the first value is two decimal places, and the precision for the second value is 3 decimal places. Therefore, you get the following output:

```
x =            27.50 y =            33.750
```

Formatting Characters and Strings

The following code fragment outputs characters and their code values:

Available for
download on
Wrox.com

```
int count = 0;
for(int ch = 'a' ; ch<= 'z' ; ch++) {
  System.out.printf("      %1$4c%1$4x", ch);
  if(++count%6 == 0) {
    System.out.printf("%n");
  }
}
```

TryFormattedOutput.java

Executing this produces the following output:

```
a   61      b   62      c   63      d   64      e   65      f   66
g   67      h   68      i   69      j   6a      k   6b      l   6c
m   6d      n   6e      o   6f      p   70      q   71      r   72
s   73      t   74      u   75      v   76      w   77      x   78
y   79      z   7a
```

First the format specification %1$4c is applied to the first and only argument following the format string. This outputs the value of ch as a character because of the 'c' conversion specification and in a field width of 4. The second specification is %1$4x, which outputs the same argument—because of the 1$—as hexadecimal because the conversion is 'x' and in a field width of 4.

You could write the output statement in the loop as:

```
System.out.printf("      %1$4c%<4x", ch);
```

The second format specifier is %<4x, which outputs the same argument as the preceding format specifier because of the '<' following the % sign.

Because a % sign always indicates the start of a format specifier, you must use "%%" in the format string when you want to output a % character. For example:

```
int percentage = 75;
System.out.printf("\n%1$d%%", percentage);
```

The format specifier %1$d outputs the value of percentage as a decimal value. The %% that follows in the format string displays a percent sign, so the output is:

```
75%
```

You use the %s specifier to output a string. Here's an example that outputs the same string twice:

Available for
download on
Wrox.com

```
String str = "The quick brown fox.";
    System.out.printf("%nThe string is:%n%s%n%1$25s", str);
```

TryFormattedOutput.java

This produces the following output:

```
The string is:
The quick brown fox.
    The quick brown fox.
```

The first instance of `str` in the output is produced by the `"%s"` specification that follows the first `"%n"`, and the second instance is produced by the `"%1$25s"` specification. The `"%1$25s"` specification has a field width that is greater than the length of the string so the string appears right-justified in the output field. You could apply the `'-'` flag to obtain the string left-justified in the field.

You have many more options and possibilities for formatted output. Try experimenting with them yourself, and if you want details of more specifier options, read the JDK documentation for the `printf()` method in the `PrintStream` class.

The Locale Class

You can pass an object of type `java.util.Locale` as the first argument to the `printf()` method, preceding the format string and the variable number of arguments that you want displayed. The `Locale` object specifies a language or a country + language context that affects the way various kinds of data, such as dates or monetary amounts, is presented.

You have three constructors available for creating `Locale` objects that accept one, two, or three arguments of type `String`. The first argument specifies a language as a string of two lowercase letters representing a Language Code defined by the standard ISO-639. Examples of language codes are `"fr"` for French, `"en"` for English, and `"be"` for Belarusian. The second argument specifies a country as a string of two uppercase letters representing a country code defined by the ISO-3166 standard. Examples of country codes are `"US"` for the USA, `"GB"` for the United Kingdom, and `"CA"` for Canada. The third argument is a vendor or browser-specific code such as `"WIN"` for Windows or `"MAC"` for Macintosh.

However, rather than using a class constructor, more often than not you use one of the `Locale` class constant static data members that provide predefined `Locale` objects for common national contexts. For example, you have members JAPAN, ITALY, and GERMANY for countries and JAPANESE, ITALIAN, and GERMAN for the corresponding languages. Consult the JDK documentation for the `Locale` class for a complete list of these.

Formatting Data into a String

The `printf()` method produces the string that is output by using an object of type `java.util.Formatter`, and it is the `Formatter` object that is producing the output string from the format string and the argument values. A `Formatter` object is also used by a static method `format()` that is defined in the `String` class, and you can use this method to format data into a string that you can use wherever you like—for displaying data in a component in a windowed application, for example. The static `format()` method in the `String` class comes in two versions, and the parameter lists for these are the same as for the two versions of the `printf()` method in the `PrintStream` class just discussed, one with the first parameter as a `Locale` object followed by the format string parameter and the variable parameter list and the other without the `Locale` parameter. Thus, all the discussion of the format specification and the way it interacts with the arguments you supply applies equally well to the `String.format()` method, and the result is returned as type `String`.

For example, you could write the following to output floating-point values:

```
double x = 27.5, y = 33.75;
String outString = String.format("x = %15.2f y = %14.3f", x, y);
```

`outString` contains the data formatted according to the first argument to the `format()` method. You could pass `outString` to the `print()` method to output it to the command line:

```
System.out.print(outString);
```

You get the following output:

```
x =           27.50 y =         33.750
```

This is exactly the same output as you got earlier using the `printf()` method, but obviously `outString` is available for use anywhere.

You can use a `java.util.Formatter` object directly to format data. You first create the `Formatter` object like this:

```
StringBuffer buf = new StringBuffer();
java.util.Formatter formatter = new java.util.Formatter(buf);
```

The `Formatter` object generates the formatted string in the `StringBuffer` object `buf`—you could also use a `StringBuilder` object for this purpose, of course. You now use the `format()` method for the `formatter` object to format your data into `buf` like this:

```
double x = 27.5, y = 33.75;
formatter.format("x = %15.2f y = %14.3f", x, y);
```

If you want to write the result to the command line, the following statement does it:

```
System.out.print(buf);
```

The result of executing this sequence of statements is exactly the same as from the previous fragment.

A `Formatter` object can format data and transfer it to destinations other than `StringBuilder` and `StringBuffer` objects, but I defer discussion of this until I introduce file output in Chapter 10.

SUMMARY

In this chapter, I have introduced the facilities for inputting and outputting basic types of data to a stream. You learned how to read data from the keyboard and how to format output to the command line. Of course, you can apply these mechanisms to any character stream. You work with streams again when you learn about reading and writing files.

EXERCISES

You can download the source code for the examples in the book and the solutions to the following exercises from www.wrox.com.

1. Use a `StreamTokenizer` object to parse a string entered from the keyboard containing a series of data items separated by commas and output each of the items on a separate line.

2. Create a class defining an object that parses each line of input from the keyboard that contains items separated by an arbitrary delimiter (for example, a colon, or a comma, or a forward slash, and so on) and return the items as an array of type `String[]`. For example, the input might be:

   ```
   1/one/2/two
   ```

   The output would be returned as an array of type `String[]` containing `"1"`, `"one"`, `"2"`, `"two"`.

3. Write a program to generate 20 random values of type `double` between −50 and +50 and use the `printf()` method for `System.out` to display them with two decimal places in the following form:

   ```
    1) +35.93    2) -46.94    3) +42.27    4) +32.09    5) +29.21
    6) +13.87    7) -47.87    8) +30.67    9) -25.20   10) +29.67
   11) +48.62   12)  +6.70   13) +28.97   14) -41.64   15) +16.67
   16) +17.01   17)  +9.62   18) -15.21   19)  +7.46   20)  +4.09
   ```

4. Use a `Formatter` object to format 20 random values of type `double` between −50 and +50 and output the entire set of 20 in a single call of `System.out.print()` or `System.out.println()`.

▶ WHAT YOU LEARNED IN THIS CHAPTER

TOPIC	CONCEPT
Streams	A stream is an abstract representation of a source of serial input or a destination for serial output.
Stream Classes	The classes supporting stream operations are contained in the package `java.io`.
Stream Operations	Two kinds of stream operations are supported. Binary stream operations result in streams that contain bytes, and character stream operations are for streams that contain characters in the local machine character encoding.
Byte Streams	No conversion occurs when characters are written to, or read from, a byte stream. Characters are converted from Unicode to the local machine representation of characters when a character stream is written.
Byte Stream Classes	Byte streams are represented by subclasses of the classes `InputStream` and `OutputStream`.
Character Stream Classes	Character stream operations are provided by subclasses of the `Reader` and `Writer` classes.
Formatted Output to a Stream	The `printf()` method that is defined in the `PrintStream` and `PrintWriter` classes formats an arbitrary number of argument values according to a format string that you supply. You can use this method for the `System.out` object to produce formatted output to the command line.
Formatting Using a `String` Class Method	The static `format()` method that is defined in the `String` class formats an arbitrary number of argument values according to a format string that you supply and returns the result as a `String` object. This method works in essentially the same way as the `printf()` method in the `PrintStream` class.
The `Formatter` Class	An object of the `Formatter` class that is defined in the `java.util` package can format data into a `StringBuilder` or `StringBuffer` object, as well as other destinations.

Accessing Files and Directories

WHAT YOU WILL LEARN IN THIS CHAPTER

➤ How you can access the file system on your computer
➤ How you can inspect files and directories
➤ How to create new files and directories
➤ How to move and copy files and directories
➤ How you can move and copy a directory and its contents
➤ How you can examine the contents of a directory tree

In this chapter, you explore how you identify, access, and manipulate files and directories (sometimes referred to as folders) on your hard drive. This includes the ability to create, copy, move, and delete files and directories.

You learn how you read and write files starting in the next chapter. Java has more than one way to work with files and directories. The original capability came with JDK 1.0. This was augmented in JDK 1.4 with NIO (New I/O). I only discuss the latest and greatest facility for file operations referred to as NIO2 that was introduced in JDK 7.

ACCESSING THE FILE SYSTEM

The starting point for working with files and directories is a `java.nio.file.FileSystem` object. A `FileSystem` object encapsulates the file storage system on your computer. What this storage system consists of and how it is organized depends on the operating system you are using. The `FileSystem` class has no public constructors so you need another way to create such an object.

The `java.nio.file.FileSystems` class defines static factory methods for file systems. You can obtain the `FileSystem` object that encapsulates the storage system on your machine by calling the `getDefault()` method that is defined in the `FileSystems` class, like this:

```
FileSystem fileSystem = FileSystems.getDefault();
```

The `fileSystem` object encapsulates the default file system on your computer. You can use this object to access the files and directories within the file system.

After you have a `FileSystem` object representing the file system on your machine, you can identify the devices and partitions within it as `java.nio.FileStore` objects. To obtain the file stores on your computer, you call `getFileStores()` for the `FileSystem` object:

```
Iterable<FileStore> stores = fileSystem.getFileStores();
```

The result is returned as an object of type `Iterable<FileStore>`. This is a generic type that you learn about in Chapter 13; for now just take it for granted. The `Iterable<>` type is defined in the `java.lang` package as an `Iterable<FileStore>` object represents a collection of `FileStore` objects that you can iterate over using the collection-based `for` loop that you read about in Chapter 3. A `FileStore` object has methods that provide information about the storage that it represents. The more interesting ones are presented in Table 9-1.

TABLE 9-1: FileStore Methods

METHOD	DESCRIPTION
`name()`	Returns the name of the file store as type `String`.
`type()`	Returns the type of the file store as type `String`.
`getTotalSpace()`	Returns the total capacity of the file store in bytes as a value of type `long`. Throws an exception of type `IOException` if an error occurs.
`getUnallocatedSpace()`	Returns the unallocated space available in the file store in bytes as a value of type `long`.

The last two methods in the table can throw an exception of type `IOException` if an I/O error occurs. Let's try these in an example.

TRY IT OUT Getting Information about File Stores

This program lists details of the file stores on a system:

Available for download on Wrox.com

```java
import java.nio.file.FileStore;
import java.nio.file.FileSystems;
import java.nio.file.FileSystem;
import java.io.IOException;

public class GetFileStores {

    public static void main(String[] args) {
        FileSystem fileSystem = FileSystems.getDefault();
        Iterable<FileStore> stores = fileSystem.getFileStores();
        long gigabyte = 1_073_741_824L;
        for(FileStore store:stores){
            try {
            System.out.format(
                "\nStore: %-20s %-5s      Capacity: %5dgb        Unallocated: %6dgb",
                store.name(),
                store.type(),
                store.getTotalSpace()/gigabyte,
                store.getUnallocatedSpace()/gigabyte);
            } catch(IOException e) {
              e.printStackTrace();
            }
        }
    }
}
```

GetFileStores.java

On my system I get the following output:

```
Store: Windows7          NTFS     Capacity:   231gb     Unallocated:   139gb
Store: New Volume        NTFS     Capacity:   931gb     Unallocated:   897gb
Store: share             NTFS     Capacity:   917gb     Unallocated:   822gb
```

How It Works

The `getDefault()` method in the `FileSystems` class returns the default file system as an object of type `FileSystem`. Calling the `getFileStores()` method for `filesystem` returns the `Iterable<FileStore>` collection of `FileStore` objects within the file system. The collection-based `for` loop iterates over each of the `FileStore` objects in the collection and outputs the details. The capacity and available storage values are divided by `gigabyte` to express the results in gigabytes. Because some of the `FileStore` class methods can throw exceptions, the output statement is in a try block.

WORKING WITH PATH OBJECTS

A `java.nio.file.Path` object encapsulates a system-dependent file path to a file or directory. `Path` is an interface type so you cannot create `Path` objects directly. You call the `getPath()` method for a `FileSystem` object to obtain a `Path` object encapsulating a given file or directory path:

```
Path path = fileSystem.getPath(
                "C:/Program Files (x86)/Java/jdk1.7.0/src/java/nio/file");
```

The argument is a string specifying the path. On my system, this happens to be the path to the directory file, which contains the source files for classes in the `java.nio.file` package. The `getPath()` method throws an exception of type `java.nio.file.InvalidPathException` if the path string is not a valid path for your storage system. This is an unchecked exception so you are not obliged to catch it.

You can also specify the path as a series of strings:

```
Path path = fileSystem.getPath("C:/Program Files (x86)",
                                "Java","jdk1.7.0/src/java/nio/file");
```

The three arguments here are joined to form the path string that is the same as the code fragment above. Note that a path separator is inserted between strings when you specify more than one argument. In general you can use as many strings as you like to specify the path.

The path that a `Path` object encapsulates may or may not reference a real file or directory on your computer. A `Path` object is fundamental to creating, reading, and writing data files.

You can use a `Path` object in four basic ways:

➤ You can analyze or compare `Path` objects without involving your physical file system; you are simply comparing or analyzing the path specifications in abstract.

➤ You can access the physical file system to determine whether a file or directory exists.

➤ You can access the physical file system to create a physical file or directory.

➤ You can access a file in the physical file system to read it or write it.

I discuss the first three possibilities in this chapter. You find out about reading and writing files in subsequent chapters. Let's look at how you create a `Path` object corresponding to a given path.

You can also create a `Path` object using the static `get()` method that is defined in the `java.nio.file.Paths` class. The `Paths` class is a helper class that defines two versions of the `get()` method. One creates a `Path` object from a string that you supply as the argument specifying the path; the other creates a `Path` object from a `java.net.URI` object. The `URI` class encapsulates a *uniform resource identifier*, commonly known as a *URI*. A URI is used to reference a resource on the World Wide Web and the most common form of URI is a *URL*—a *uniform resource locator*.

Here's how you might create a `Path` object from a `String` object:

```
Path myPath = Paths.get(
                  "C:/Program Files (x86)/Java/jdk1.7.0/src/java/nio/file");
```

This creates a `Path` object encapsulating the same path as you created with the `getPath()` method. The `get()` method is the equivalent of calling the `getPath()` method for the default `FileSystem` object. As with the `getPath()` method, the `Paths.get()` method accepts a series of string arguments specifying the path.

To specify a path to a physical file, you just need to make sure that the string refers to a file and not a directory. For example:

```
Path myFile = Paths.get(
            "C:/Program Files (x86)/Java/jdk1.7.0/src/java/nio/file/Path.java");
```

This statement sets the object `myFile` to the path that corresponds to the source file that contains the definition of the `Path` interface.

 NOTE A `Path` object only encapsulates the path to a file, not the file itself. You see later in this chapter how you use a path object to access a physical file.

The other `get()` method in the `Paths` class enables you to define a `Path` object from an object of type `URI`. The `URI` class provides several constructors for creating URI objects, but getting into the detail of these is too much of a diversion from our present topic.

Absolute and Relative Paths

In general, the pathname that you use to create a `Path` object has two parts: an optional prefix or root element followed by a series of names separated by the system default separator character for pathnames. Under MS Windows the prefix for a path on a local drive is a string defining the drive, such as `"C:\\"` or `"C:/"`. Under UNIX the prefix is a forward slash, `"/"`. A path that includes a prefix is an *absolute path* and a path without a prefix is a *relative path*. The last name in a path can be a directory name or a file name. All other names must be directory names.

The pathnames I have used in the preceding code fragments have all been absolute paths, because I included the drive letter in the path for Windows; a forward slash identifies a root directory in a UNIX system. You can check whether a path object is an absolute path by calling its `isAbsolute()` method:

```
Path path = FileSystems.getDefault().getPath(
                  "C:/Program Files (x86)/Java/jdk1.7.0/src/java/nio/file");
if(path.isAbsolute())
   System.out.println("Path is absolute.");
```

This fragment outputs the message confirming that `path` is absolute.

If you omit the root element in a path specification, you have a relative path and the pathname string is interpreted as a path *relative* to the current directory. This implies that you can reference a file that is in the same directory as your program by just the file name.

For example:

```
Path myFile = Paths.get("output.txt");
```

This statement creates a `Path` object encapsulating a pathname string that is just the name `"output.txt"`. This is interpreted as being the name of a file in the current directory when the `Path` object is used. Unless it has been changed programmatically, the current directory is the directory that was current when program execution was initiated. You see in a moment how you can obtain the absolute path from a `Path` object, regardless of how the `Path` object was created.

You could also refer to a file in a subdirectory of the current directory using a relative path:

```
Path myFile = Paths.get("dir", "output.txt");
```

If the current directory is `C:\Projects\Test`, the `myFile` object references the path to the file `C:\Projects\Test\dir\output.txt`. Thus, you can use a relative path specification to reference files in the current directory, or in any subdirectory of the current directory.

Symbolic Links

Some operating systems support the use of symbolic links in a file or directory path. A *symbolic link* is a special kind of file that contains a relative or absolute path to another file. The path in a symbolic link is usually just a string specifying the path, and a `Path` element is identified as a symbolic link by an attribute to the element. A symbolic link appears as the last element in a path and acts as a transparent redirection mechanism for accessing a file or directory.

Microsoft Windows supports symbolic links. You can use the `MKLINK` function from the command line under Microsoft Windows to create a symbolic link if you have administrator privileges. I discuss file attributes a little later in this chapter and I mention symbolic links again in that context.

 TIP *To create a symbolic link in Windows 7 from the command line you must open a command-line window with administrator privileges. To do this, select the Start button and enter* **Command** *in the search box. Right-click Command Prompt in the list of results and select Run as Administrator from the pop-up. You then have a command window in which you can execute the* `MKLINK` *command.*

Accessing System Properties

In some circumstances you might want to specify a path that is specific to the current environment. In this case, accessing one of the *system properties* can help. A system property specifies values for parameters related to the system environment in which your program is executing. Each system property is identified by a unique name and has a value associated with the name that is defined as a string. A set of standard system properties is always available, and you can access the values of any of these by passing the name of the property that you are interested in to the static `getProperty()` method that is defined in the `java.lang.System` class. The value of the property is returned as type `String`.

For example, the directory that is currently the default base for relative paths is defined by the property that has the name `"user.dir"`, so you can access the path to this directory with the following statement:

```
String currentDir = System.getProperty("user.dir");
```

The `"file.separator"` property identifies the character used as an element separator in a path on the current system. You can retrieve this with the statement:

```
String separator = System.getProperty("file.separator");
```

You could then use the results of the previous two fragments to specify explicitly where the file with the name `"output.txt"` is located:

```
Path dataFile = Paths.get(currentDir + separator + "output.txt");
```

Of course, this is equivalent to just specifying the file name as the relative path, so you have not achieved anything new, other than using the separator specific to the current system. Of course, you could use multiple string arguments to the `get()` method and have the separator characters inserted for you.

Another system property with the name `"user.home"` has a value that defines a path to the user's home directory. You could therefore specify that the `"output.txt"` file is to be in this directory as follows:

```
Path dataFile = Paths.get(System.getProperty("user.home"), "output.txt");
```

The location of the user's home directory is system dependent, but wherever it is you can access it in this way without building system dependencies into your code.

Naturally, you could specify the second argument to the constructor here to include directories that are to be subdirectories of the home directory. For instance:

```
Path dataFile = Paths.get(
                    System.getProperty("user.home"), "dir", "output.txt");
```

On my system this defines the following path:

```
C:\Users\Ivor\dir\output.txt
```

Of course, this in no way guarantees that the `dir` subdirectory exists. To be sure, you need to check that it does. You see how to do this, and how to create files and directories, a little later in this chapter.

If you would like to see what the full set of standard system properties are, you can find the complete list in the JDK documentation for the static `getProperties()` method in the `System` class. You can also retrieve the current set of properties on your system and their values by calling the `getProperties()` method, so let's put a little program together to do that.

TRY IT OUT   Getting the Default System Properties

Here's the program to list the keys and values for the current set of system properties on your computer:

Available for download on Wrox.com

```
public class TryProperties {
  public static void main(String[] args) {
    java.util.Properties properties = System.getProperties();
    properties.list(System.out);
  }
}
```

TryProperties.java

This outputs all the system properties.

How It Works

The `getProperties()` method returns the set of system properties encapsulated in an object of type `Properties`. The `Properties` class is defined in the `java.util` package, and I chose to use the fully qualified class name rather than an import statement for it. You call the `list()` method for the `Properties` object to output the properties to the stream that is passed as the argument, in this case `System.out`, which corresponds to your display screen.

Setting System Properties

As I discussed in the previous section, after you know the key for a system property you can obtain its value, which is a `String` object, by calling the static `getProperty()` method in the `System` class with the key for the property you are interested in as the argument. You can also change the value for a system property by calling the static `setProperty()` method in the `System` class. The `setProperty()` method expects two arguments; the first is a `String` object identifying the property to be changed, and the second is a `String` object that is the new property value.

You also have the possibility to remove the current value that is set for a property by using the static `clearProperty()` method in the `System` class. You just pass a string specifying the property key as the argument. It is possible that the Java security manager may not permit this operation to be carried out, in which case an exception of type `SecurityException` is thrown. The `clearProperty()` method throws an exception of type `NullPointerException` if the argument is `null`, or an exception of type `IllegalArgumentException` if you pass an empty string as the argument.

For a specific example of where you might want to set a system property, suppose that you want to change the specification for the system property that specifies the current working directory. That property has the key `"user.dir"`, so you could use the following statement:

```
System.setProperty("user.dir", "C:/MyProjects");
```

Executing this statement changes the current working directory to `"C:/MyProjects"`. Now when you are using a relative path, it is relative to this directory. You can change the system property that defines the current directory as often as you like in your program, so you can always adjust the current directory to be the one containing the file you are working with if that is convenient. Of course, when you do this, you need to be sure that the directory does exist, so it is wise to verify that the directory is there before executing the call to the `setProperty()` method. That sort of verification is the next topic of this chapter.

Testing and Checking Path Objects

First of all, you can get information about a `Path` object by using the methods for the object shown in Table 9-2.

TABLE 9-2: Methods That Retrieve Information about a Path Object

METHOD	DESCRIPTION
`getName(int n)`	Returns the nth name element in this path as a `Path` object. Path elements are indexed from 0 starting with the root element or element that is closest to the root in a relative path. The method throws an `IllegalArgumentException` if n is not valid for the path.
`getFileName()`	Returns the name of the file or directory referenced by this path as a `Path` object. This is the name element furthest from the root element.
`getNameCount()`	Returns the number of elements in the path as a value of type `int`.
`isAbsolute()`	Returns `true` if the `Path` object refers to an absolute pathname and `false` otherwise.
`subpath(` `int beginIndex,` `int endIndex)`	Returns a relative path that is formed by the sequence of path elements from `beginIndex` to `endIndex-1`. The method throws an exception of type `IllegalArgumentException` if either argument is not a valid index for the path.
`startsWith(` `Path path)`	Returns `true` if the current path starts with the path specified by the argument and `false` otherwise. An overload of this method accepts a `String` argument.
`endsWith(` `Path path)`	Returns `true` if the current path ends with the path specified by the argument and `false` otherwise. An overload of this method accepts a `String` argument.
`getParent()`	Returns a `Path` object containing the path for the parent directory of the file or directory represented by the current `Path` object. This is the original path without the last name. The method returns `null` if there is no parent specified.
`getRoot()`	Returns the root element of the current `Path` object as a `Path` object, or `null` if this `Path` object does not have a parent.

All of the preceding operations involve just the information encapsulated by the `Path` object. The file or directory itself is not queried and may or may not exist.

You can compare a given `Path` object `path1` for equality with another `Path` object, `path2`, using the `equals()` method:

```
if(path1.equals(path2) {
    // Paths are equal...
}
```

Equality is system dependent and comparisons may or may not be case sensitive. The `equals()` method for a `Path` object simply compares the paths without checking whether the path's reference a real file or directory.

To convert a relative path to an absolute path you call its `toAbsolutePath()` method:

```
Path absolutePath = path.toAbsolutePath();
```

If the `Path` object is already an absolute path, the method returns a reference to the same object.

Querying Files and Directories

The `java.nio.file.Files` class defines static methods that provide a wide range of operations with paths, files and directories. Let's look at a few of the most interesting methods. You can use the `Files` class methods in Table 9-3 to examine the file or directory that is identified by a `Path` object.

TABLE 9-3: File Class Methods that Examine Files and Directories

METHOD	DESCRIPTION
`exists(` `   Path path)`	Returns `true` if the file or directory referred to by `path` exists and `false` otherwise. You can specify a second argument that is a value from the `java.nio.file.LinkOption` type to specify how symbolic links are to be handled. The default is `NOFOLLOW_LINKS` so links are not followed.
`notExists(` `   Path path)`	Returns `true` if the file or directory referred to by `path` does not exist and `false` otherwise. There is an optional second argument that is the same as with the `exists()` method.
`isHidden(` `   Path path)`	Returns `true` if `path` refers to a file that is hidden and `false` otherwise. How a file is hidden is system dependent. Under UNIX a hidden file has a name that begins with a period. Under Windows a file is hidden if it is marked as such within the file system.

`isSameFile(`
`   Path path1,`
`   Path path2)`
	Returns `true` if `path1` references the same file as `path2`. If `path1` and `path2` are equal `Path` objects, this method does not check whether the file exists. The method can throw an `IOException` if an I/O error occurs.

> **NOTE** *All operations that access the file system on the local machine can throw an exception of type* `SecurityException` *if access is not authorized—in an applet, for example. This is the case with all of the methods here. However, for an exception of type* `SecurityException` *to be thrown, a security manager must exist on the local machine, but by default a Java application has no security manager. An applet, on the other hand, always has a security manager by default. A detailed discussion of Java security is beyond the scope of this book.*

Obtaining File Attributes

To determine whether a `Path` object references a file or a directory, you can use the static `isDirectory()` and `isRegularFile()` methods in the `Files` class. With both methods the first argument is the `Path` object you are interested in. You can specify `NOFOLLOW_LINKS` as the optional second argument if you do not want links to be followed.

You can also query the attributes of a file by calling the static `readAttributes()` method that is defined in the `Files` class with the Path object specifying the file:

```
try{
   BasicFileAttributes attr = Files.readAttributes(path, BasicFileAttributes.class);
}catch(IOException e) {
   System.err.println(e);
}
```

The second argument to the method is the class type for the attributes you require. Here, the attributes are returned as a reference to an object of type `BasicFileAttributes` that contains attributes common to most file systems. You also have the possibility of being more specific by specifying `PosixFilesAttributes` `.class` or `DosFileAttributes.class`. All these are interface types defined in the `java.nio.file` `.attribute` package. You can optionally specify `NOFOLLOW_LINKS` as the third argument if you do not want symbolic links to be followed. The method throws an `UnsupportedOperationException` if the attributes type is not supported and an `IOException` if an I/O error occurs.

The `BasicFilesAttributes` interface defines the methods shown in Table 9-4 that you can use to get information about a directory or file path:

TABLE 9-4: BasicFilesAttributes Methods that Retrieve Directory or Path Information

METHODS	DESCRIPTION
`isDirectory()`	Returns `true` if the `path` references a directory.
`isRegularFile()`	Returns `true` if the `path` references a regular file.
`isSymbolicLink()`	Returns `true` if the `path` references a symbolic link.
`isOther()`	Returns `true` if the `path` references something other than a regular file, a directory, or a symbolic link.
`creationTime()`	Returns a `FileTime` object specifying the time the file was created.
`lastAccessTime()`	Returns a `FileTime` object specifying the time the file was last accessed.
`lastModifiedTime()`	Returns a `FileTime` object specifying the time the file was last modified.
`size()`	Returns the size of the file in bytes as a value of type `long`.
`fileKey()`	Returns a reference of type `Object` to a key that uniquely identifies the file or `null` if a key is not available.

A `java.nio.file.attribute.FileTime` object is a timestamp value for a file. You can use its `toString()` method to get a string representation of its value.

To see how some of these methods go together, you can try a simple example.

TRY IT OUT Testing a Path for a File or Directory

Try the following source code:

Available for download on Wrox.com

```java
import java.nio.file.Path;
import java.nio.file.Paths;
import java.nio.file.FileSystem;
import java.nio.file.FileSystems;
import java.nio.file.Files;
import java.nio.file.attribute.BasicFileAttributes;
import java.io.IOException;

public class TryPath {
  public static void main(String[] args) {
    FileSystem fileSystem = FileSystems.getDefault();

    Path path = fileSystem.getPath("garbage.java");
    checkPath(path);

    path = Paths.get(System.getProperty("user.dir"));
    checkPath(path);

    // Amend the following path to your environment
    path = fileSystem.getPath("D:", "Beginning Java SE 7", "Projects",
                                       "TryPath", "src", "TryPath.java");
    checkPath(path);
    return;
  }

  // Check the attributes of a path
  static void checkPath(Path path) {
```

```
      System.out.println("\n" + path + " has " + path.getNameCount() +
                                                " elements.");

   if(path.isAbsolute()) {
     System.out.println(path + " is an absolute path.");
     System.out.println("The parent path is " + path.getParent());
     System.out.println("The root is " + path.getRoot());
   }
   else{
     System.out.println(path + " is a relative path.");
     path = path.toAbsolutePath();
   }

   if(Files.notExists(path)) {
     System.out.println(path + " does not exist.");
       return;
   }

   try {
     BasicFileAttributes attr = Files.readAttributes(
                                 path, BasicFileAttributes.class);

     if(attr.isDirectory())
       System.out.println(path.getFileName() + " is a directory.");
     else if(attr.isRegularFile()) {
       System.out.println(path.getFileName() + " is a file containing " +
                                          attr.size() + " bytes.");

     }
     System.out.println(path + " was created "+ attr.creationTime());
     System.out.println(path + " was last accessed "+ attr.lastAccessTime());
     System.out.println(path + " was last modified "+
                                          attr.lastModifiedTime());

     System.out.println(path + " is "+ attr.size() + " bytes.");
   } catch(IOException e) {
     System.err.println(e);
   }
 }
}
```

TryPath.java

On my machine, the example produces the following output:

```
garbage.java has 1 elements.
garbage.java is a relative path.
D:\Beginning Java SE 7\Projects\TryPath\classes\garbage.java does not exist.

D:\Beginning Java SE 7\Projects\TryPath\classes has 4 elements.
D:\Beginning Java SE 7\Projects\TryPath\classes is an absolute path.
The parent path is D:\Beginning Java SE 7\Projects\TryPath
The root is D:\
classes is a directory.
D:\Beginning Java SE 7\Projects\TryPath\classes
                                was created 2011-03-23T18:33:22.217037Z
D:\Beginning Java SE 7\Projects\TryPath\classes was last accessed
                                        2011-03-23T18:59:28.113457Z
D:\Beginning Java SE 7\Projects\TryPath\classes was last modified
                                        2011-03-23T18:59:28.113457Z
D:\Beginning Java SE 7\Projects\TryPath\classes is 0 bytes.

D:\Beginning Java SE 7\Projects\TryPath\src\TryPath.java has 5 elements.
D:\Beginning Java SE 7\Projects\TryPath\src\TryPath.java is an absolute path.
The parent path is D:\Beginning Java SE 7\Projects\TryPath\src
The root is D:\
```

```
TryPath.java is a file containing 2121 bytes.
D:\Beginning Java SE 7\Projects\TryPath\src\TryPath.java was created
                                   2011-03-23T18:33:22.315038Z
D:\Beginning Java SE 7\Projects\TryPath\src\TryPath.java was last accessed
                                   2011-05-08T10:48:55.974509Z
D:\Beginning Java SE 7\Projects\TryPath\src\TryPath.java was last modified
                                   2011-05-08T10:48:55.976509Z
D:\Beginning Java SE 7\Projects\TryPath\src\TryPath.java is 2121 bytes.
```

How It Works

The analysis of a path is carried out in the static `checkPath()` method so I'm explaining that first. The first statement in this method calls the `getNameCount()` for the `Path` object that is passed as the argument to obtain the number of elements in the path. The `if` statement that follows calls `isAbsolute()` for the `Path` object to determine if the object contains an absolute or a relative path. Up to this point there has been no interaction with the file system. All operations just involve the `Path` object.

If the path is not absolute, the `toAbsolutePath()` method for the `Path` object is called to convert it. This does access the file system and has the potential to throw a `SecurityException` if you are not permitted to access the file.

Next the static `notExists()` method in the `Files` class is called to see whether `path` references something real. This obviously involves accessing the file system. If the `path` does not reference a file or directory that exists, the `checkPath()` method returns after outputting the fact.

Having established that `path` refers to a real file or directory, the static `readAttributes()` method in the `Files` class is called with `path` as the first argument to obtain the attributes for whatever `Path` references. The method then calls the `isDirectory()` method for the `BasicFileAttributes` object to determine if `path` references a directory. The second argument determines that the basic file attributes are retrieved. You use the `BasicFileAttributes` object to decide whether `path` references a file or a directory and to obtain various properties of the file or directory.

The `main()` method calls `checkPath()` for three different paths, with the results that you see. You should supply your own path specifications in this example to suit your particular environment.

Other Path Operations

The `resolve()` method for a `Path` object reference resolves the current path, which should be a directory, against the `Path` object that is supplied as the argument and returns the resultant `Path` object. Typically the current path is an absolute path and the argument is a relative path, and the result is the path that is produced by joining the argument path to the current path. For example, if the current path is `C:\Temp` and the argument path is `output.txt`, the result is the path `C:\Temp\output.txt`. If the argument is an absolute path, the argument path is returned, and if the argument is `null`, the current `Path` object is returned. You use this method later in this chapter when you get to copy files.

A second version of the `resolve()` method accepts a `String` argument. This converts the argument to a `Path` object and then works in the same way as the version previously mentioned.

The `relativize()` method is the inverse of the `resolve()` method. It returns a `Path` object that, when resolved against the current path, results in the `Path` argument. Thus if the current path is `C:\Junk` and the argument path is `C:\Junk\Temp1\Temp2` then the path `\Temp1\Temp2` is returned.

The `resolveSibling()` method resolves the path supplied as the argument against the parent of the path for which you call the method. So if you call this method for a `Path` object representing `"C:\junk\file"` with the argument `Path` object representing `"newFile"`, the method returns a `Path` object representing `"C:\junk\newFile"`. An overload of the method accepts an argument of type `String` to specify the path. This is useful when we get to renaming files later in this chapter.

CREATING AND DELETING DIRECTORIES AND FILES

When you need to write a new file, you obviously have to be able to create the file initially, and in many cases, you create a new directory that is to contain the file. I discuss creating directories first and then move on to file creation.

 NOTE *All the directories and files that the examples create in this and subsequent chapters are on the D: drive or partition. I have coded them like this to avoid adding them to my C: drive, which is my system drive. If you do not have a drive or partition D: you need to change the paths in the examples to suit your environment. Take extra care to avoid typos in paths if they reference your system drive.*

Creating Directories

You create a directory by calling the static `createDirectory()` method in the `Files` class with a `Path` object that specifies the directory to be created as the argument. This can be an absolute or a relative path. The new directory is appended to the current directory if the `Path` object is a relative path. Here's how you could create a new directory in the current directory:

```
Path path =Paths.get("newDir");
try {
   Files.createDirectory(path);
} catch(IOException e) {
   e.printStackTrace(System.err);
}
```

This creates the directory `newDir` in the current directory. The `createDirectory()` method throws an exception of type `java.nio.FileAlreadyExistsException` if a file or directory exists in the directory in which you are creating the new directory with the same name as the directory you are trying to create. With the example, the new directory will be created in the current directory because the path is relative. You see this exception thrown if you execute the code fragment twice. It can throw a `NoSuchFileException` if any of the parents for the required directory do not exist. The `createDirectory()` method also throws an exception of type `java.io.IOException` if an I/O error occurs. These exceptions are checked exceptions so you should call the method from within a `try` block and provide for catching at least the `IOException` exception; this catches the other exception because it is a subclass of `IOException`.

If the `Path` object refers to an absolute path, the parent path for the new directory must already exist if the creation is to succeed with the `createDirectory()` method. When you have the possibility that some elements in the path for a directory that you want to create may not exist, you can call the static `createDirectories()` method that is defined in the `Files` class with the `Path` object as the argument. This creates all the required directories. Here's an example:

```
Path path = Paths.get("D:/Garbage/dir/dir1/dir2");
try {
   Files.createDirectories(path);
} catch(IOException e) {
   e.printStackTrace(System.err);
}
```

If any of the subdirectories of the final directory `dir2` do not exist, they are created. When you are creating a new directory that you specify by an absolute path, using the `createDirectories()` method obviates the need to verify that the parent exists. As well as the `IOException`, this method can throw an exception of type `FileAlreadyExistsException` if a file already exists with the same path. If the directory already exists, this exception is not thrown. If the `createDirectories()` method fails for some reason, some of the parent directories may be created before the failure occurs.

Let's try creating some directories in an example.

TRY IT OUT Creating Directories

Here's an example that uses both methods for creating directories:

```java
import java.nio.file.*;
import java.io.IOException;

public class CreatingDirectories {
  public static void main(String[] args) {
    Path relPath = Paths.get("junkDir");
    createSingleDirectory(relPath);       // Create directory in current
    createSingleDirectory(relPath);       // then try it again...

    Path absPath = Paths.get("D:/Garbage/dir1/dir2/dir3");
    createSingleDirectory(absPath);       // Try creating as single directory
    createMultipleDirectories(absPath); // Now do it right
    createMultipleDirectories(absPath); // then try it again...
  }

  static void createSingleDirectory(Path path) {
    try {
      Files.createDirectory(path);
      path = path.toAbsolutePath();
      System.out.println("\n" + path + " directory created.");
    } catch(NoSuchFileException e) {
      System.err.println("\nDirectory creation failed:\n" + e);
    } catch(FileAlreadyExistsException e) {
      System.err.println("\nDirectory creation failed:\n" + e);
    } catch(IOException e) {
      System.err.println("\nDirectory creation failed:\n" + e);
    }
  }

  static void createMultipleDirectories(Path path) {
    try {
      Files.createDirectories(path);
      path = path.toAbsolutePath();
      System.out.println("\n" + path + " directory created.");
    } catch(IOException e) {
      System.err.println("\nDirectory creation failed:\n" + e);
    }
  }
}
```

CreatingDirectories.java

You should get the following output as long as the directories created in the example do not exist before the program executes:

```
junkDir directory created.
D:\Beginning Java SE 7\Projects\CreatingDirectories\classes\junkDir
                                                        directory created.

Directory creation failed:
java.nio.file.FileAlreadyExistsException: junkDir

Directory creation failed:
java.nio.file.NoSuchFileException: D:\Garbage\dir1\dir2\dir3

D:\Garbage\dir1\dir2\dir3 directory created.

D:\Garbage\dir1\dir2\dir3 directory created.
```

Don't forget to delete the directories that were created after you have run the example.

How It Works

The `createSingleDirectory()` method uses the `createDirectory()` method from the `Files` class with the `Path` object that is passed to it as the argument to create the new directory. Any of the three possible I/O exceptions that may be thrown are caught individually. Note that the catch clause for `IOException` must be last, because the other two exception types are derived from `IOException`. The output shows that when this method is called for the relative path, `relPath`, the first time around the directory is created and the second time `FileAlreadyExistsException` is thrown, as you would expect. Calling the method for the absolute path, `absPath`, causes `NoSuchFileException` to be thrown because the parent path does not exist. Since the actions are the same for both, you catch either of them as type `IOException` in a single catch block.

The `createMultipleDirectories()` method calls the static `createDirectories()` method in the `Files` class. The `createDirectories()` method creates all the directories required for the path and therefore the directory specified by `absPath` is created when `createMultipleDirectories()` is called. The second time the method is called, no exception is thrown. If the directory that is specified by the `Path` object that is passed to `createDirectories()` already exists, the method does nothing. `FileAlreadyExistsException` is thrown only when there is a file or symbolic link with the same name as the requested directory already in existence.

Creating Files

To create a new empty file you can call the static `createFile()` method in the `Files` class with the `Path` object that specifies the file path as the argument. If the file already exists, the `FileAlreadyExistsException` exception is thrown by the method. The method also throws an exception of type `IOException` if an I/O error occurs. Note that the parent directory for the new file must exist before you create the file. The `createFile()` method throws an exception of type `java.nio.file.NoSuchFileException` if the parent directory does not exist. Here's an example:

```
Path path = Paths.get("D:/Garbage/dir/dir1/dir2/junk.txt");
try {
  Files.createFile(path);
} catch(NoSuchFileException e) {
  System.err.println("File not created.\n" + e);
} catch(FileAlreadyExistsException e) {
  System.err.println("File not created.\n" + e);
} catch(IOException e) {
  System.err.println(e);
}
```

The fragment above creates the file with the name `junk.txt` in the `dir2` directory. If the parent directory for the file does not exist, the exception of type `NoSuchFileException` is thrown and caught in this case. Of course, you could always ensure that the parent directory exists, like this:

```
Path path = Paths.get("D:/Garbage/dir/dir1/dir2/junk.txt");
try {
  Files.createDirectories(path.getParent());      // Create parent
  Files.createFile(path);
} catch(FileAlreadyExistsException e) {
  System.err.println("File not created.\n" + e);
} catch(IOException e) {
  System.err.println(e);
}
```

Now the parent directory is always created before attempting to create the file. If the parent already exists, then the `createDirectories()` method does nothing. The `NoSuchFileException` exception now is not thrown, but it is still possible that the `createFile()` method throws an exception of type `FileAlreadyExistsException`. You can see this happen if you execute the preceding fragment twice.

Deleting Files and Directories

The `Files` class defines a `delete()` method that deletes a file or a directory. A directory has to be empty before it can be deleted. Attempting to delete a directory that is not empty results in the `delete()` method throwing an exception of type `java.nio.file.DirectoryNotEmptyException`. For example, after executing the fragment in the previous section that creates `junk.txt`, the following code throws the `DirectoryNotEmptyException` exception:

```
Path path = Paths.get("D:/Garbage/dir/dir1/dir2/junk.txt");
try {
  Files.delete(path.getParent());             // Delete parent directory
} catch(DirectoryNotEmptyException e) {
  System.err.println("Directory not deleted.\n"+ e);
} catch(IOException e) {
    System.err.println(e);
}
```

However, if you first delete the file, you are able to delete the directory:

```
Path path = Paths.get("D:/Garbage/dir/dir1/dir2/junk.txt");
try {
  Files.delete(path);                         // Delete file
  Files.delete(path.getParent());             // Delete parent directory
} catch(DirectoryNotEmptyException e) {
  System.err.println("Directory not deleted.\n"+ e);
} catch(IOException e) {
    System.err.println(e);
}
```

This fragment deletes the `junk.txt` file and then deletes the `dir2` directory. The directory `D:\Garbage\dir\dir1` remains.

If you attempt to delete a file or directory that does not exist using the `delete()` method, an exception of type `NoSuchFileException` is thrown. You can avoid this possibility by using the `deleteIfExists()` method in the `Files` class. When you are deleting a file using this method, no exception is thrown if the file or directory is not there but you can still get the `DirectoryNotEmptyException` exception thrown when you use it to delete a directory.

 WARNING Always take particular care when programming delete operations. Errors can be catastrophic if they result in essential files being removed.

GETTING THE CONTENTS OF A DIRECTORY

The `newDirectoryStream()` method in the `Files` class provides you with the means to access the contents of a directory as a stream of `Path` objects. The method returns a reference of type `java.nio.file.DirectoryStream<Path>`, which is an interface type. You haven't met this form of type syntax before so just take it as given for the time being. This is a *generic type*, which is a parameterized type where the type parameter appears between the angled brackets, so this is a `DirectoryStream` type customized to work with `Path` objects. You learn how to define and use generic types in Chapter 13.

Because the `DirectoryStream<Path>` type implements `Iterable<Path>`, you can use the collection-based `for` loop to access the `Path` objects in the stream. For example:

```
Path currentPath = Paths.get(System.getProperty("user.dir"));
DirectoryStream<Path> paths = null;
try {
  paths = Files.newDirectoryStream(currentPath);
  for(Path path : paths) {
    System.out.println(path.getFileName());
  }
```

```
    } catch(NotDirectoryException e) {
        System.err.println(currentPath + " is not a directory." + e);
    } catch(IOException e) {
        System.err.println("I/O error." + e);
    }
```

This fragment displays the contents of the current directory. The `newDirectoryStream()` method that creates the `DirectoryStream<Path>` stream can throw an exception of type `IOException` if an I/O error occurs, or an exception of type `java.nio.file.NotDirectoryException` if it is called for a `Path` object that does not reference a directory. Note that this fragment only lists the contents of the current directory specified by `currentPath`. The contents of any directories in the current directory are not retrieved, only the directories themselves.

There is another version of the `newDirectoryStream()` method that accepts a second argument of type `String` that specifies a filter for the directory entries that are retrieved. The filter string is a form of regular expression that is referred to as a *glob*, which can contain the special sequences shown in Table 9-5.

TABLE 9-5: Character Sequences for Filtering Directory Streams

CHARACTER SEQUENCE	EFFECT
*	Matches zero or more characters of a name without crossing a directory boundary, that is without passing over a separator character.
**	Matches zero or more characters crossing directory boundaries.
?	Matches a single character in a name.
\	Specifies escape characters that would otherwise be interpreted as special characters in a glob.
[]	Specifies a *bracket expression* that encloses a set of characters where a single character can match any character in the set. The characters *, ?, and \ match themselves in a bracket expression.
-	Used to specify a range, so [a-e] specifies all the lowercase letters a though e.
!	Specifies the negation of a range so [!a-e] specifies that any character other than a through e is a match. The - character matches itself when it is the first character in a bracket expression.
{}	Specifies a set of subpatterns that can be matched where the subpatterns are separated by commas. For example, {exe, txt} matches either exe or txt.

All other characters not in Table 9-5 match themselves. Thus to see only .exe files from a directory stream, you use the glob `"*.exe"`. To see only .exe and .txt files, you could use `"*.{exe,txt}"`. The glob `"*.???"` matches any file with a three-character extension.

CLOSING A STREAM

In the code fragment in the previous section, there is no provision for calling the `close()` method for the `DirectoryStream<Path>` object and there really should be. In general, you should not call the `close()` method for a stream in a `try` block that has other stream operations that also throw exceptions because if such exceptions are thrown, the `close()` method call may be circumvented. Because the `close()` method itself can throw an exception of type `IOException` that must be caught there is the potential for rather messy code to take care of all eventualities. A new version of the `try` block was introduced in Java 7 called a `try` *block-with-resources* that makes it very easy to ensure that a stream is closed when you are done with it.

The `try` block with resources language facility provides the capability for automatically closing streams at the end of executing the code in the `try` block, regardless of how execution of the block terminates. This works with object of any class type that implements the `AutoCloseable` interface.

To call the `close()` method automatically, you must create the stream objects between parentheses that immediately following the `try` keyword. If you need to create multiple stream objects, just separate the statements between the parentheses with semicolons. Stream objects that you create here are implicitly `final` so they cannot be changed within the `try` block. Here's a revised version of the fragment from the previous section using a `try` block with resources:

```
Path currentPath = Paths.get(System.getProperty("user.dir"));
try (DirectoryStream<Path> paths = Files.newDirectoryStream(currentPath)){
  for(Path path : paths) {
    System.out.println(path.getFileName());
  }
} catch(NotDirectoryException e) {
  System.err.println(currentPath + " is not a directory." + e);
} catch(IOException e) {
  System.err.println("I/O error: " + e);
}
```

The `close()` method for `paths` is called after the `try` block code completes, whether or not an exception is thrown from within the block. The `close()` method is not called if `paths` is `null`.

Let's try this out in an example.

TRY IT OUT Listing the Contents of a Directory

In this example, we list the entire contents of a directory and then use a filter to select particular entries.

```
import java.nio.file.*;
import java.io.IOException;

public class ListDirectoryContents {
  public static void main(String[] args) {
    Path currentPath = Paths.get(System.getProperty("user.dir"));
    currentPath = currentPath.getParent();

    // Get the entire directory contents
    filterDirectoryContents(currentPath, null);

    // Now try a filter for .txt files
    System.out.println("\nFilter for .txt:");
    filterDirectoryContents(currentPath, "*.txt");

    // Get files with a 3 character extension begiining with 'j'
    System.out.println("\nFilter for .j??:");
    filterDirectoryContents(currentPath, "*.j??");
  }

  // Filter the contents of a directory
  private static void filterDirectoryContents(Path path, String filter) {
    try (DirectoryStream<Path> paths =
                    filter != null ? Files.newDirectoryStream(path, filter):
                                     Files.newDirectoryStream(path)){
      System.out.println("\n" + path + " directory contains:");
      for(Path p : paths) {
        System.out.println("   " + p.getFileName() +
                            (Files.isDirectory(p) ? " is a directory." : ""));
      }
    } catch(NotDirectoryException e) {
      System.err.println("Path is not a directory." + e);
    } catch(IOException e) {
      System.err.println("I/O error." + e);
    }
  }
}
```

ListDirectoryContents.java

I have engineered the directory path to be one containing a variety of files and directories to get some interesting output. You need to choose a path that references an interesting directory on your computer and adjust the filter strings accordingly. On my system I get the following output:

```
D:\Beginning Java SE 7\Projects\ListDirectoryContents directory contains:
  classes is a directory.
  ListDirectoryContents.jcd
  ListDirectoryContents.jcp
  ListDirectoryContents.jcu
  ListDirectoryContents.jcw
  src is a directory.
  src_listdirectorycontents.txt

Filter for .txt:

D:\Beginning Java SE 7\Projects\ListDirectoryContents directory contains:
  src_listdirectorycontents.txt

Filter for .j??:

D:\Beginning Java SE 7\Projects\ListDirectoryContents directory contains:
  ListDirectoryContents.jcd
  ListDirectoryContents.jcp
  ListDirectoryContents.jcu
  ListDirectoryContents.jcw
```

How It Works

The first two statements in `main()` set up the path to the directory to be explored. The path identified by `"user.dir"` may not be the same when you run the example in which case you may want to modify these statements so that you end up with a path with some interesting contents.

The contents of a directory are output by the static `filterDirectoryContents()` method with the path specified by the first argument and the filter string specified by the second argument. You call this three times — once without a filter and twice subsequently with two different filters. The `DirectoryStream<Path>` object is created in the method by the statement between parentheses following the `try` keyword. If the filter argument is `null`, the statement selects the version of `newDirectoryStream()` that has a single parameter.

The contents of the directory stream is output in the `for` loop. The output statement adds additional text when an entry in the directory is itself a directory, so you can distinguish files and directories in the output. You can see the effects of the filters on the contents of the directory from the output.

MOVING AND COPYING FILES AND DIRECTORIES

The static `move()` method in the `Files` class enables you to move a file or directory. It also enables you to rename a file or directory, as you later see. A directory can only be moved if either it is empty, or if the operation does not require that its contents be moved — that is, essentially renaming the directory.

The method expects two arguments and there is the possibility to add more arguments that specify options for the operation. The first argument is a `Path` object specifying the source path and the second argument is a `Path` object specifying the target or destination. It is easy to misunderstand the target path. It is not the path for the directory that contains the item after the move operation, but the path specification for the item after it has been moved. The optional third or fourth arguments are values of type `CopyOption`. Only two possible `CopyOption` values are applicable to the `move()` method and these are defined in the `java.nio.file.StandardCopyOption` enumeration:

➤ `REPLACE_EXISTING`, which indicates the target file specified by the first argument should be replaced if it exists and is not a non-empty directory

➤ `ATOMIC_MOVE`, which specifies that the move is executed as an atomic operation.

An *atomic operation* is an operation that cannot be interrupted by another thread of execution. If you specify ATOMIC_MOVE, any other CopyOption values that you specify are ignored, so essentially you specify the optional third argument to the move() method as either REPLACE_EXISTING or ATOMIC_MOVE.

If you specify anything other than the two possible options, the method throws an exception of type UnsupportedOperationException. If the copy operation causes a file or directory to be replaced and you have not specified the REPLACE_EXISTING option, an exception of type FileAlreadyExistsException is thrown. If you specify ATOMIC_MOVE and the file cannot be moved as an atomic operation, an exception of type java.nio.file.AtomicMoveNotSupportedException is thrown.

Here's how you could move a file:

```
Path sourcePath = Paths.get("D:/Temp1/output.txt");
Path destinationPath = Paths.get("D:/Temp2/output.txt");
 try {
    sourcePath.moveTo(destinationPath);
} catch(NoSuchFileException e) {
  System.err.println("Move failed." + e);
  } catch(FileAlreadyExistsException e) {
    System.err.println("File already exists." + e);
  } catch(IOException e) {
    System.err.println("I/O error." + e);
  }
```

This moves the output.txt file from the Temp1 directory on the D: drive to Temp2. If the file does not exist in the Temp1 directory, an exception of type NoSuchFileException is thrown. If the file already exists in Temp2, FileAlreadyExistsException is thrown. You can prevent this exception from being thrown by specifying REPLACE_EXISTING as the third argument.

If you want to execute this fragment in a program, first create the directories D:\Temp1and D:\Temp2 and create the file output.txt in the Temp1 directory. (Of course, you could copy any file to the Temp1 directory and change the code accordingly). If you execute the fragment twice, it throws an exception of type NoSuchFileException.

Renaming a File or Directory

A move() operation renames a file or directory if the parent paths of the source and destination paths are the same, and both reference a file or both reference a directory. Here's how you could rename the directory D:\Temp1 to D:\Temp2:

```
Path sourcePath = Paths.get("D:/Temp1");
try {
  Files.move(sourcePath, sourcePath.resolveSibling("Temp2"));
} catch(IOException e) {
  System.err.println("I/O error." + e);
}
```

Renaming a file is essentially the same process. Here's a fragment that creates then renames a directory, creates a new file in it, and then renames the file:

```
Path sourcePath = Paths.get("D:/Temp1/Temp2");
try {
  Files.createDirectories(sourcePath);
  sourcePath = Files.move(sourcePath, sourcePath.resolveSibling("Temp3"));

  Path file = sourcePath.resolve("output.txt");        // The path to the file
  System.out.println(file);
  Files.createFile(file);                    // Create file in renamed directory
  Files.move(file, file.resolveSibling("outputNew.txt")); // Rename the file
} catch(IOException e) {
  System.err.println("I/O error." + e);
}
```

This fragment creates the `Temp1\Temp2` directory on the D: drive, renames it as `Temp1/Temp3`, and then creates an empty file, `output.txt`, in it. The new file is then renamed to `outputNew.txt`.

Copying Files and Directories

The `Files` class defines a static `copy()` method that enables you to copy files and directories. When you use the method to copy a directory that is not empty, only the directory is copied, not the contents. You see how you can copy a directory and its contents in the next section. The `copy()` method usage is similar to that of the `move()` method. The first argument to the `copy()` method is a `Path` object that specifies the item to be copied and the second argument is a `Path` object that specifies the copied item in its new location. There are optional arguments that can be `CopyOption` references, which are the values `REPLACE_EXISTING` and `COPY_ATTRIBUTES`. These are defined by the `java.nio.file.StandardCopyOption` enumeration or the `NOFOLLOW_LINKS` value that is defined by the `java.nio.file.LinkOption` enumeration. These options have the effects on the copy operation shown in Table 9-6.

TABLE 9-6: Options for Copy Operations

OPTION	EFFECT
REPLACE_EXISTING	Causes the target to be replaced if it exists. If the target is a directory, it must be empty for it to be replaced. A symbolic link is replaced, not the target of the link.
COPY_ATTRIBUTES	The attributes of the source file are copied to the target file if possible.
NOFOLLOW_LINKS	Symbolic links are not followed. If a symbolic link is being copied, then the link is copied, not the target of the link.

The `copy()` method can throw the following exceptions:

➤   `UnsupportedOperationException` if you specify an option that is not supported.

➤   `FileAlreadyExistsException` if the target file exists and you have not specified the `REPLACE_EXISTING` option.

➤   `DirectoryNotEmptyException` if the target is a directory that exists and is not empty and you have specified the `REPLACE_EXISTING` option.

Let's try this out in an example along with some of the other file and directory operations I have discussed.

TRY IT OUT   Moving and Copying Files and Directories

This example demonstrates creating and deleting directories and copying and moving files. The source file is `MoveAndCopyFiles.java`. I'm presenting the code piecemeal as separate methods rather than in one big block. The example uses static methods for the operations it uses. Here's the `MoveAndCopyFiles` class method to create a directory:

```
static void createSingleDirectory(Path path) {
  try {
    Files.createDirectories(path);
    System.out.println("\n" + path + " directory created.");
  } catch(IOException e) {
    System.err.println("\nDirectory creation failed:\n" + e);
  }
}
```

MoveAndCopyFiles.java

This method creates a directory from the `Path` object that is passed to it and outputs a message. Any exception that is thrown also results in a message.

The next method checks whether a path is a directory:

```java
static boolean isDirectory(Path path) {
  try {
  BasicFileAttributes attr = Files.readAttributes(
                                    path, BasicFileAttributes.class);
  return attr.isDirectory();
  } catch(IOException e) {
    System.err.println("I/O error in isDirectory method. " + e);
  }
  return false;
}
```

MoveAndCopyFiles.java

The method obtains the attributes for the path by calling the static `readAttributes()` method that is defined in the `Files` class and calls `isDirectory()` for the `BasicFileAttributes` object that is returned to test for a directory. The method returns `true` if the `path` argument references a directory and `false` otherwise.

This method copies files from the `from` directory to the `to` directory:

```java
static boolean copyFiles(Path from, Path to) {
  if(!isDirectory(from)) {
    System.out.println(
                    "Cannot copy files. " + from + " is not a directory.");
    return false;
  } else if(!isDirectory(to)) {
    System.out.println("Cannot copy files. " + to + " is not a directory.");
    return false;
  }

  try (DirectoryStream<Path> files = Files.newDirectoryStream(from, "*.*")) {
    System.out.println("Starting copy...");
    for(Path file : files) {
      Files.copy(file, to.resolve(file.getFileName()));   // Copy the file
      System.out.println("  " + file.getFileName() + " copied.");
    }
  } catch(IOException e) {
    System.err.println("I/O error in copyFiles. " + e);
    return false;
  }
  return true;
}
```

MoveAndCopyFiles.java

The parameters for this method are `Path` references specifying the directory that is the source of files to be copied and the destination directory for the file copies. The method first verifies that both arguments reference directories using the previous method, `isDirectory()`. Remember that the second argument to the `copy()` method for a path is a `Path` object referencing the item after the copy has occurred, not the destination directory. We therefore use the `resolve()` method for the `to` object to combine the destination directory path with the name of the file. The second argument to the `newDirectoryStream()` method is a filter that ensures that the resultant stream only contains files with an extension so directories excluded. The method outputs the name of each file when it has been copied. The method returns `true` if the copy operation is successful and `false` otherwise.

The method to move files from one directory to another is very similar:

```java
static boolean moveFiles(Path from, Path to) {
  if(!isDirectory(from)) {
    System.out.println(
                    "Cannot move files. " + from + " is not a directory.");
    return false;
  } else if(!isDirectory(to)) {
```

```
      System.out.println("Cannot move files. " + to + " is not a directory.");
      return false;
    }
    try (DirectoryStream<Path> files = Files.newDirectoryStream(from, "*.*")) {
      System.out.println("Starting move files...");
      for(Path file : files) {
        Files.move(file, to.resolve(file.getFileName()));     // Move the file
        System.out.println("  " + file.getFileName() + " moved.");
      }
    } catch(IOException e) {
      System.err.println("I/O error in copyFiles. " + e);
      return false;
    }
    return true;
  }
```

MoveAndCopyFiles.java

The next method just pauses the program until the Enter key is pressed:

Available for
download on
Wrox.com

```
    static void waitForEnter() {
      try {
          System.in.read();
      } catch(IOException e) {
          System.err.println(e);
      }
    }
```

MoveAndCopyFiles.java

Pausing the program is achieved by waiting for input from System.in. The read() can throw an exception of type IOException so the method call is in a try block.

The last method you need to complete the example is main():

Available for
download on
Wrox.com

```
import java.nio.file.*;
import java.nio.file.attribute.*;
import java.io.IOException;

public class MoveAndCopyFiles {
  public static void main(String[] args) {
    Path current = Paths.get("D:/Beginning Java SE 7/Projects/MoveAndCopyFiles");
    Path newDir = Paths.get("junkDir");          // New directory for files
    newDir = newDir.toAbsolutePath();            // Make path absolute
    createSingleDirectory(newDir);               // Create directory in current

    // Copy files from current directory to new
    System.out.println("Copying files from " + current + " to " + newDir);
    if(!copyFiles(current, newDir)) {
        System.out.println("Copying files failed.");
        return;
    }

    System.out.println(
          "You can look at the directory to verify that the copy has worked.");
    System.out.println("Press Enter to continue.");
    waitForEnter();

    // Create another subdirectory in current
    Path newDir2 = Paths.get("junkDirBackup");
    newDir2 = newDir2.toAbsolutePath();          // Make path absolute
    createSingleDirectory(newDir2);              // Create directory in current
```

```java
    // Move files from newDir to newDir2
    System.out.println("Moving files from " + newDir + " to " + newDir2);
    if(!moveFiles(newDir, newDir2)) {
        System.out.println("Moving files failed.");
        return;
    }

    System.out.println(
            "You can look at the directory to verify that the move has worked.");
    System.out.println("Press Enter to continue.");
    waitForEnter();

    // Now we can delete newDir because it is empty
    try{
        System.out.println("Deleting " + newDir + "...");
        Files.delete(newDir);
    } catch(IOException e) {
        System.err.println("Deleting " + newDir +" failed:\n" + e);
    }

    // Delete all files from newDir2
    try (DirectoryStream<Path> files =
                            Files.newDirectoryStream(newDir2, "*.*")){
        System.out.println("Deleting files from " + newDir2 + "...");
        for(Path file : files) {
            Files.delete(file);                    // Delete the file
            System.out.println("  " + file.getFileName() + " deleted.");
        }

        // Now delete the directory
        System.out.println("Deleting " + newDir2 + "...");
        Files.delete(newDir2);
    } catch(IOException e) {
        System.err.println("I/O error deleting files. " + e);
    }
}

// Insert the other methods here...
}
```

MoveAndCopyFiles.java

You need to change the path for current in the first statement in main() to something suitable for your environment. On my system I got the following output:

```
D:\Beginning Java SE 7\Projects\MoveAndCopyFiles\classes\junkDir directory created.
Copying files from D:\Beginning Java SE 7\Projects\MoveAndCopyFiles to
                    D:\Beginning Java SE 7\Projects\MoveAndCopyFiles\classes\junkDir
Starting copy...
  MoveAndCopyFiles.jcp copied.
  MoveAndCopyFiles.jcu copied.
  MoveAndCopyFiles.jcw copied.
  src_moveandcopyfiles.txt copied.
You can look at the directory to verify that the copy has worked.
Press Enter to continue.


D:\Beginning Java SE 7\Projects\MoveAndCopyFiles\classes\junkDirBackup
                                                    directory created.
Moving files from D:\Beginning Java SE 7\Projects\MoveAndCopyFiles\classes\junkDir
        to D:\Beginning Java SE 7\Projects\MoveAndCopyFiles\classes\junkDirBackup
Starting move files...
```

```
    MoveAndCopyFiles.jcp moved.
    MoveAndCopyFiles.jcu moved.
    MoveAndCopyFiles.jcw moved.
     src_moveandcopyfiles.txt moved.
You can look at the directory to verify that the move has worked.
Press Enter to continue.

Deleting D:\Beginning Java SE 7\Projects\MoveAndCopyFiles\classes\junkDir...
Deleting files from
          D:\Beginning Java SE 7\Projects\MoveAndCopyFiles\classes\junkDirBackup...
    MoveAndCopyFiles.jcp deleted.
    MoveAndCopyFiles.jcu deleted.
    MoveAndCopyFiles.jcw deleted.
     src_moveandcopyfiles.txt deleted.
Deleting D:\Beginning Java SE 7\Projects\MoveAndCopyFiles\classes\junkDirBackup...
```

After execution finishes successfully, the directories and files that are created by the program will all have been deleted.

How It Works

The main() method first creates a new subdirectory, junkDir, in the current directory by calling the createSingleDirectory() method. All the files in the current directory are then copied to junkDir by using the copyFiles() method. The program then pauses so you can inspect your file system to verify that the copy has indeed been completed.

Another subdirectory to the current directory, junkDirBackup, is created, and all the files in junkDir are moved to junkDirBackup. The program pauses once more to enable you to verify the move.

Finally the main() method deletes junkDir, deletes the files from junkDirBackup, and then deletes junkDirBackup.

Walking a File Tree

The java.nio.file.FileVisitor<T> interface specifies methods that you can use to walk through a tree of directories and files. T is the type of file reference, usually type Path. The java.nio.file .SimpleFileVisitor<T> class implements the methods in the FileVisitor<T> interface that simply visits all files in a tree and rethrows any I/O exceptions that occur. You can extend the SimpleFileVisitor<T> class to override the FileVisitor<T> methods to do what you want.

The methods that are declared in the FileVisitor<Path> interface are called by another method that you call to initiate the process of walking the file tree; this is the static walkFileTree() method that is defined in the Files class. This then calls the FileVisitor<Path> interface methods, which are presented in Table 9-7.

TABLE 9-7: FileVisitor<Path> Interface Methods

METHOD	DESCRIPTION
preVisitDirectory(Path dir, BasicFileAttributes attr)	This is called immediately before the entries in the directory dir are visited. The second argument is the directory's basic attributes. This method provides you with the means of controlling what happens next. You should return one of the following constants defined by the FileVisitResult enum that is in the java.nio.file package. CONTINUE: Entries in dir are visited. SKIP_SIBLINGS or SKIP_SUBTREE : Entries in dir and any subdirectories will not be visited.

METHOD	DESCRIPTION

`postVisitDirectory(`
`    Path dir,`
`    IOException e)`
	This is called after entries in the `dir` directory and their descendants have been visited. This method is also called when visiting entries in the directory is terminated by the `visitFile()` method returning `SKIP_SIBLINGS` or an I/O error occurs. If an I/O error occurs while entries are being visited, `e` references the exception object that was thrown. Otherwise `e` is `null`.

`visitFile(`
`    Path file,`
`    BasicFileAttributes attr)`
	This is called when the `file` file is visited. The `attr` parameter references the attributes for the file.

`visitFileFailed(`
`    Path file,`
`    IOException e)`
	This is called when the attributes for `file` cannot be read or the directory containing the file cannot be opened. `e` references the exception object thrown as a result of an I/O error.

There are two versions of the static `walkFileTree()` method. The simplest accepts two arguments:

➤ A `Path` object specifying the starting directory for the tree to be walked.

➤ A reference to a `FileVisitor` object that implements the methods mentioned earlier to do what you want with the files and directories in the tree.

This version of the method does not follow links and visits all levels in the file tree. The other version of `walkFileTree()` accepts four arguments:

➤ The starting directory path, as before.

➤ A set of `java.nio.file.FileVisitOption` enumeration constants, that contains either `FOLLOW_LINKS` supplied in an `EnumSet` or an empty `EnumSet`. Specifying `FOLLOW_LINKS` causes file links to be followed.

➤ A value of type `int` specifies the maximum depth to be explored in the file tree.

➤ The `FileVisitor` object that implements the methods that are called in the process of walking the file tree.

The class `java.util.EnumSet` defines an object that can store a set of enumeration constants. You learn more about the `EnumSet` class in Chapter 14 so just take it for granted for the moment. To specify an `EnumSet` containing `FOLLOW_LINKS` you can use the expression `EnumSet.of(FOLLOW_LINKS)`. To define an empty `EnumSet` of `FileVisitOption` constants you use the expression `EnumSet.noneOf(FileVisitOption .class)`. The expressions assume that you have imported the constants from the enumeration and you have an import statement for `EnumSet`.

The process for walking a file tree may seem a little hazy at this point, but an example should clarify it.

TRY IT OUT Walking a File Tree

First I will define a class that implements the `FileVisitor<Path>` interface:

Available for
download on
Wrox.com

```java
import static java.nio.file.FileVisitResult.*;      // Import constants
import java.nio.file.*;
import java.nio.file.attribute.*;
import java.io.IOException;

public class ListFiles extends SimpleFileVisitor<Path> {
```

CONFER PROGRAMMER TO PROGRAMMER ABOUT THIS TOPIC.
Visit p2p.wrox.com

```java
    // Output the directory path and set indent for entries
    @Override
    public FileVisitResult preVisitDirectory(
                                    Path dir, BasicFileAttributes attr) {
      System.out.format("\n%sDirectory: %s contains:", indent, dir);
      indent.append("  ");
      return CONTINUE;
    }

    // Note error after walking directory and reset indent
    @Override
    public FileVisitResult postVisitDirectory(Path dir, IOException e) {
        if(e != null) {
          System.out.format(
                      "\n%sError walking directory: %s\n%s", indent, dir, e);
      }
      int len = indent.length();
      indent.delete(len-2, len);
      return CONTINUE;
    }

    // Record file or symbolic link details
    @Override
    public FileVisitResult visitFile(Path file, BasicFileAttributes attr) {
      if(attr.isRegularFile()) {
          System.out.format("\n%sFile: %s", indent, file);
      } else if (attr.isSymbolicLink()) {
        System.out.format("\n%sSymbolic link: %s", indent, file);
      }
      return CONTINUE;
    }

    // Record file visit failure
    @Override
    public FileVisitResult visitFileFailed(Path file, IOException e) {
      System.err.format("\n%sFile attributes could not be read for: %s\n%s",
                                                    indent, file, e);

      return CONTINUE;
    }

    // Indent for entries
    private StringBuilder indent = new StringBuilder("  ");
}
```

Directory "FileTreeWalking"

Our `ListFiles` class extends the `SimpleFileVisitor<Path>` class and implements all the methods in the `FileVisitor<Path>` interface. The `SimpleFileVisitor<Path>` class provides default implementations of all the methods declared in the `FileVisitor<Path>` interface so you can implement a subset if you want.

The class contains the `indent` member of type `StringBuilder` — working with `StringBuilder` objects is faster than using `StringBuffer` objects. The `indent` member provides indentation of the output and is increased by two spaces each time a new directory is visited, which is indicated by the `preVisitDirectory()` being called. When the `postVisitDirectory()` method is called, visiting the entries in a directory is complete so `indent` is shortened by removing the last two characters.

The `visitFile()` method is called for each file or symbolic link in a directory that is visited. This method just outputs the entry name indented by `indent`. If the attributes for a file cannot be obtained, the `visitFileFailed()` method is called, and here you record the problem and continue with the rest of the tree.

Note how the constants in the `FileVisitResult` enumeration are imported using the static import statement. This allows the constants to be used without qualifying them with the name of the enum type.

Here's the code for the application class that uses the `ListFiles` class:

```
import static java.nio.file.FileVisitOption.*;
import java.nio.file.*;
import java.io.IOException;
import java.util.EnumSet;

public class FileTreeWalking {
  public static void main(String[] args) {
    Path treeBase = Paths.get(
             System.getProperty("java.home")).getParent().resolve("sample");
    FileVisitor<Path> listFiles = new ListFiles();
    int depth = 3;
    try {
      Files.walkFileTree(treeBase, EnumSet.of(FOLLOW_LINKS), depth, listFiles);
    } catch(IOException e) {
      e.printStackTrace();
    }
  }
}
```

Directory "FileTreeWalking"

The path for the `treeBase` object will be the directory containing the samples that came with the JDK 7. I set the depth to be explored to 3 in an attempt to keep the volume of output down, but there is still quite a lot of it.

How It Works

Calling the static `getProperty()` method obtains the `Path` object for the Java home directory. Calling `fetParent()` for this path returns the parent directory. Calling `resolve()` with the "sample" argument returns the absolute path to the samples directory that comes with JDK 7.

The `main()` method uses the version of the `walkFileTree()` method that accepts four arguments. I chose to do this because it permits the tree depth to be limited. Note how the set of `FileVisitOption` options is created. In general you can supply any number of arguments to the `of()` method for an `EnumSet<>` object to include them in the set. The last argument to the `walkFileTree()` method is the `FileVisitor` object whose methods will be called in the tree-walking process.

I chose a simple task of listing the contents of a tree, but of course you can implement much more complex operations. You could output the size of each file in addition to its path very easily. You could search for all files of a particular type for example and copy or move them to another directory somewhere. The file-walking mechanism is a very powerful capability that can accommodate most of what you are likely to want to do.

SUMMARY

In this chapter, I discussed how you work with file and directory paths, and the facilities for checking and inspecting physical files and directories. You will use more of the methods defined by the `Files` class in the chapters that follow. The topics discussed here and in the previous chapter provide the foundations for reading and writing files, which you will learn about in the next three chapters.

EXERCISES

You can download the source code for the examples in the book and the solutions to the following exercises from www.wrox.com.

1. Write a program that lists all the directories in a directory defined by a path specified as a command-line argument.

2. Write a program to list all the files with a given extension in a directory. The absolute path for the directory and the extension should be read from the command line. If the extension is absent from the command-line input, the program should list all the files in the specified directory.

3. Write a program that copies all the files in one directory to another with the paths being entered from the command line. The names of the file copies should have _old appended to them and no files in the destination folder should be overwritten.

4. Write a program that outputs a count of the total number of files in each directory in a file tree that is specified by a path entered on the command line and outputs the total number of directories and files in the tree. List the directories by name with each name followed by the file count in that directory.

▶ WHAT YOU LEARNED IN THIS CHAPTER

TOPIC	CONCEPT
File and Directory Paths	The Path class encapsulates a relative or absolute path to a file, a symbolic link, or a directory. The item referenced by a Path object may or may not exist.
Accessing Files and Directories	The Files class provides methods that you can use to determine whether or not there is a physical file or directory corresponding to the path that the object encapsulates.
Checking for a File or Directory	Having established that an entry corresponding to a Path object exists, you can determine whether the entry is a file or directory by examining its attributes.
Accessing Attributes	The attributes for an entry corresponding to a Path object can be obtained by calling the static readBasicFileAttributes() method, which is defined in the Files class. Attributes are returned as an object of type BasicFileAttributes, and the isDirectory() and isRegularFile() methods for the object enable you to determine whether the entry is a directory or a file. The size() attribute method returns the size of a file in bytes.
Creating Files and Directories	The static createFile() or createDirectory() methods in the Files class can create a file or directory for a Path object. The createDirectory() method only creates a single directory.
Creating a Directory Hierarchy	The static createDirectories() method in the Files class creates the directory specified by the Path argument and all necessary parent directories.
Accessing the Entries in a Directory	The newDirectoryStream() method in the Files class returns a stream that contains all the entries in the directory corresponding to a given Path object. You can supply a second argument to the newDirectoryStream() method that filters the entries so the stream only makes available a selected subset of the entries.
Exploring a File Tree	The static walkFileTree() method in the Files class initiates the process of walking a file tree that is headed by a directory specified by a Path object. You receive information about the entries in the file tree by implementing the methods specified in the FileVisitor<Path> interface.

10

Writing Files

WHAT YOU WILL LEARN IN THIS CHAPTER

- ➤ The principles of reading and writing files
- ➤ How you obtain a file channel for a file
- ➤ How you create a buffer and load it with data
- ➤ What view buffers are and how you use them
- ➤ How you use a channel object and buffer objects to write data to a file

In this chapter, you look at ways to write binary or character data to a file. The mechanisms for writing binary data are different from those for writing character data. You'll be writing both types of files in this chapter and reading them back in the next.

FILE I/O BASICS

If you are new to programming file operations, there are a couple of things about how they work that may not be apparent to you and can be a source of confusion, so I'll clarify these before I go any further. If you already know how input and output for disk files work, you can skip this section.

First, let's consider the nature of a file. After you have written data to a file, what you have is just a linear sequence of bytes. The bytes in a file are referenced by their offset from the beginning, so the first byte is byte 0, the next byte is byte 1, the third byte is byte 2, and so on through to the end of the file. If there are n bytes in a file, the last byte is at offset $n - 1$. There is no specific information in the file about how the data originated or what it represents unless you explicitly put it there. Even if there is, you need to know that there is information that tells you how the data is formatted, and read and interpret the data accordingly.

For example, if you write a series of 25 binary values of type `int` to a file, it contains 100 bytes. Nothing in the file indicates that the data consists of 4-byte integers so there is nothing to prevent you from reading the data back as 50 Unicode characters or 10 long values followed by a string, or any other arbitrary collection of data items that corresponds to 100 bytes. Of course, the result is unlikely to be very meaningful unless you interpret the data in the form in which it was originally written. This implies that to read data from a file correctly, you need to have prior knowledge of the structure and format of the data that is in the file.

The form of the data in the file may be recorded or implied in many ways. For example, one way that the format of the data in a file can be communicated is to use a standardized file name extension for data of a particular kind, such as .java for a Java source file or .jpg for a graphical image file or .wav for a sound file. Each type of file has a predefined structure, so from the file extension you know how to interpret the data in the file. Of course, another way of transferring data so that it can be interpreted correctly is to use a generalized mechanism for communicating data and its structure, such as XML. XML files also express form through the file extension .xml. You'll learn more about XML and how to write and read XML files in the last two chapters of the book.

You can access an existing file to read it or write it in two different ways, described as *sequential access* or *random access*. The latter is sometimes referred to as *direct access*. Sequential access to a file is quite straightforward and works pretty much as you would expect. Sequential read access involves reading bytes from the file starting from the beginning with byte 0. Of course, if you are interested only in the file contents starting at byte 100, you can just read and ignore the first 100 bytes. Sequential write access involves writing bytes to the file starting at the beginning if you are replacing the existing data or writing a new file, and writing bytes starting at the end if you are appending new data to an existing file.

The term random access is sometimes misunderstood initially. Just like sequential access, random access is just a way of accessing data in a file and has nothing to do with how the data in the file is structured or how the physical file was originally written. You can access any file randomly for reading and/or writing. When you access a file randomly, you can read one or more bytes from the file starting at any point. For example, you could read 20 bytes starting at the 13th byte in the file (which is the byte at offset 12, of course) and then read 50 bytes starting at the 101st byte or any other point that you choose. Similarly, you can update an existing file in random access mode by writing data starting at any point in the file. In random access mode, the choice of where to start reading or writing and how many bytes you read or write is entirely up to you. You just need to know the offset for the byte where a read or write operation should start. Of course, for these to be sensible and successful operations, you have to have a clear idea of how the data in the file is structured.

> **WARNING** *First a note of caution: Before running any of the examples in this chapter, be sure to set up a separate directory for storing the files that you are using when you are testing programs. It's also not a bad idea to back up any files and directories on your system that you don't want to risk losing. But of course, you do back up your files regularly anyway — right?*

> **WARNING** *The old adage "If anything can go wrong, it will," applies particularly in this context, as does the complementary principle "If anything can't go wrong, it will." Remember also that the probability of something going wrong increases in proportion to the inconvenience it is likely to cause.*

FILE OUTPUT

The Files class provides three ways for you to access a file to write it:

➤ The newOutputStream() method opens or creates a file specified by a Path object. The method returns a reference to an unbuffered OutputStream object encapsulating the file. If you wrap this OutputStream object in a BufferedOutputStream object, you are able to use the write() method for the buffered stream object to write binary data to the file efficiently.

➤ The newBufferedWriter() method opens or creates a file specified by a Path object for writing in text mode. The BufferedWriter object that the method returns provides an efficient way to write textual data to a file.

➤ The newByteChannel() method opens a file specified by a Path object that can be accessed at random for writing and/or reading. The data written or read can be binary or textual data.

The `Files` class also defines two static `write()` methods that can write either a `byte[]` array to a file or an `Iterable` set of lines as characters. I'll concentrate on the three possibilities in the above list because these are the most useful. Let's start by exploring how you can write a file using an `OutputStream` object in more detail.

WRITING A FILE VIA AN OUTPUT STREAM

The `newOutputStream()` method in the `Files` class expects the first argument to be a `Path` object encapsulating the path to the file to be written. You can supply one or more optional arguments to specify open options for the file from the `java.nio.file.StandardOpenOption` enumeration. These determine how the file is opened and where the data goes when you write to it. You can use the options presented in Table 10-1 in this context.

TABLE 10-1: Output Options Defined by the StandardOpenOption Enumeration

OPTION	DESCRIPTION
CREATE	Create a new file if the file does not already exist.
CREATE_NEW	Create a new file, but fail the operation if the file already exists.
DELETE_ON_CLOSE	Delete the file when the stream is closed. This is primarily for use with work files that are only required during execution of your program.
APPEND	Write new data to the end of the file.
TRUNCATE_EXISTING	Truncate the existing file length to 0 so new data is written from the beginning, overwriting any previous data.
WRITE	Open the file for write access.

The enumeration also defines the following constants, as presented in Table 10-2.

TABLE 10-2: Output Options Defined by the StandardOpenOption Enumeration

OPTION	DESCRIPTION
READ	Opens the file for read access.
SPARSE	Provides a hint to improve efficiency for file systems that support sparse files.
SYNC	Requires that all file updates are written synchronously to the storage device. This causes the return from the write method to wait until all data and metadata have been written to the storage device. This is to ensure the integrity of files in the event of a system crash.
DSYNC	This has the same effect as SYNC but only in relation to file data, not metadata.

You use the `READ` option in the next chapter.

If you don't specify any arguments to the `newOutputStream()` method after the first, the default options in effect are `WRITE`, `CREATE`, and `TRUNCATE_EXISTING`. This means that by default a new file is created if it doesn't already exist, and if it does exist, the contents are overwritten. Here's how you can open a file specified by a `Path` object `fileOut` to append data to it if it already exists:

```
OutputStream fileOut = Files.newOutputStream(path, CREATE, APPEND);
```

The `WRITE` option is inferred because the method only creates `OutputStream` objects. Of course, it would be better to use a `BufferedOutputStream` object to write the file because this would make the output operations more efficient. You can create one like this:

```
Path file = Paths.get("D:/Junk/fibonnaci.bin");
BufferedOutputStream fileOut = new BufferedOutputStream(
                Files.newOutputStream(file, CREATE, APPEND));
```

To create a buffered stream, you just pass the OutputStream object returned by the newOutputStream() method to the BufferedOutputStream constructor.

The newOutputStream() method can throw an IOException if an error occurs so it needs to be called in a try block. The stream classes implement the AutoCloseable interface so you can use a try block with resources to automatically close any stream when you are done with it.

A BufferedOutputStream object provides two write() methods:

➤ write(int b) writes a single byte, b, to the internal buffer,.

➤ write(byte[] b, int offset, int length) writes length bytes from the byte array, b, starting at index position offset to the internal buffer.

➤ Both methods can throw IOException. The internal buffer is automatically flushed (written to the stream) when it is full. You can also call the flush() method explicitly to have the buffer contents written to the stream.

Note that flushing the stream does not guarantee that the data is written to the file at that point. Flushing the stream hands over the data to the output operation provided by your operating system and this has its own internal buffers. You see later in this chapter how you can force data to be written to the file.

TRY IT OUT | **Writing a File via a Buffered Stream**

This example generates some binary integer values and writes them to a file:

```java
import java.nio.file.*;
import java.nio.*;
import java.io.*;

public class StreamOutputToFile {

  public static void main(String[] args) {
    final int count = 50;                            // Number of values
    long[] fiboNumbers = {0L,0L};                    // Array of 2 elements
    int index = 0;                                   // Index to fibonumbers
    ByteBuffer buf = ByteBuffer.allocate(count*8);   // Buffer for output
    LongBuffer longBuf = buf.asLongBuffer();         // View buffer for type long
    Path file = Paths.get(System.getProperty("user.home")).
                      resolve("Beginning Java Stuff").resolve("fibonnaci.bin");
    try {
      // Create parent directory if it doesn't exist
      Files.createDirectories(file.getParent());
    } catch(IOException e) {
      System.err.println("Error creating directory: " + file.getParent());
      e.printStackTrace();
      System.exit(1);
    }
    System.out.println("New file is: " + file);

    try(BufferedOutputStream fileOut =
                    new BufferedOutputStream(Files.newOutputStream(file))){
      // Generate Fibonacci numbers in buffer
      for(int i = 0 ; i < count ; ++i) {
        if(i < 2)
          fiboNumbers[index] = i;
        else
          fiboNumbers[index] = fiboNumbers[0] + fiboNumbers[1];
        longBuf.put(fiboNumbers[index]);
        index = ++index%2;
      }
      // Write the numbers to the file
      fileOut.write(buf.array(), 0, buf.capacity());
      System.out.println("File written.");
    } catch(IOException e) {
```

```
        System.err.println("Error writing file: " + file);
        e.printStackTrace();
      }
    }
  }
```

StreamOutputToFile.java

This example generates 50 Fibonacci numbers and writes them to the `fibonacci.bin` file. The only output if everything works as it should is the file path and a message confirming the file has been written.

 NOTE *If you have not come across Fibonacci numbers before, they are not as dull and uninteresting as they might seem. Fibonacci numbers relate to the way many plants grow their leaves and petals and the way spiral seashells grow,. They are even behind the relationship between the height and width of classical buildings.*

 TIP *Don't be too hasty deleting this or other files that you create later in this chapter, as you reuse some of them in the next chapter when you start exploring how to read files.*

How It Works

The first three statements in `main()` set up the variables you need to generate the Fibonacci numbers. The first two Fibonacci numbers are 0 and 1. All subsequent numbers are the sum of the preceding two numbers. The program stores the last two numbers in the `fiboNumbers` array. The `index` variable is used to access this array to store the most recent number.

As the numbers are generated, they are stored in a buffer before they are written to the file. The `ByteBuffer` object, `buf`, is created with a capacity to store `count` numbers. We create a view buffer, `longBuf`, from `buf` to make it easy to store the numbers directly in the buffer. Type `long` is appropriate here because Fibonacci numbers grow quite rapidly. I'll be explaining buffers in more detail later in this chapter, but for the moment, a view buffer allows you to treat a buffer that contains bytes as a sequence of values of some other type, type `long` in this case. Ultimately you have to write a sequence of `long` values (or values of any other type) to a file as bytes, so this enables you set up the `long` values in a buffer, then treat them as bytes when you need to write them to the file.

The `file` object specifies an absolute path to the `fibonacci.bin` file in the `"Beginning Java Stuff"` directory in your home directory. Your home directory is specified by the system property value corresponding to the key `"user.home"`. The `try` block that follows the creation of the `path` object is there to ensure that the directory that is to contain the file exists, or will be created if it doesn't. The `createDirectories()` method creates a directory together with all directories in the path when necessary; if the directory already exists, it does nothing.

The `try` block with resources creates the `BufferedOutputStream` object for the file between the parentheses so it is flushed and closed automatically. Because no options are specified for the `newOutputStream()` method, the file is created when necessary, and the file is always written from the beginning, overwriting any existing contents. This implies that if you run the example more than once, you still end up with the same file contents.

The Fibonacci numbers are created in the loop. As each number is created, it is stored in the `fiboNumbers` array and then written to `longBuf`, which is an overlay of `buf`. The `put()` method automatically increments the current position in the buffer, ready for the next value to be written. The value of index is incremented modulo 2, so it flips between 0 and 1. This has the effect that each number that is generated is stored in the array always replacing the oldest value of the two.

After all the numbers have been written to `longBuf`, the contents of `buf` are converted to a `byte[]` array and written to the file. You can verify that the file has been written by inspecting it and checking the file properties. It should be 400 bytes.

The example writes values of just one type to the file but you can easily deal with sets of values of different fundamental types. You do this with the third mechanism for writing files that you try out later in this chapter. First, you can learn a bit more about using a `Writer` object to write to a file.

WRITING A FILE USING A WRITER

The static `newBufferedWriter()` method in the `Files` class returns a `java.io.BufferedWriter` object that you can use to write to a file. A `BufferedWriter` can only write character data to a file. A `BufferedWriter` has an internal buffer that ensures that strings and even single characters can be written efficiently.

The first argument to the `newBufferedWriter()` method is a `Path` object identifying the file path and the second is a `java.nio.charset.Charset` object that defines a charset. As I explained at the beginning of this chapter, ultimately you are always writing bytes to a file, whatever the type of the original data, and a charset determines how Unicode characters are mapped to the sequences of bytes that are written to the file. There are a range of standard charsets available with Java that offer different mappings for Unicode characters and to create a `Charset` object for one of these, you just pass the name of the standard charset as a string to the static `forName()` method in the `Charset` class. You can also obtain the default charset for the current Java virtual machine by calling the static `defaultCharset()` method. The charset you use when you write a file determines what bytes are written for each Unicode character and of course, when you read a file, you must use the charset that was used when the file was written. In examples that use charsets I use the `"UTF-16"` charset, which is the character encoding for the Java language.

You can optionally specify additional arguments to the `newBufferedWriter()` method that determine how the file is opened. These are the same options that you saw with the `newOutputStream()` method and with the same default options set if you don't specify any.

Here's how you could create a `BufferedWriter` object for a file:

```
Path file = Paths.get("D:/Junk/proverbs.txt");
BufferedWriter fileOut = Files.newBufferedWriter(
                    file, Charset.forName("UTF-16"), CREATE, APPEND);
```

This creates the file if it doesn't already exist and data is appended to the end of the file if it does exist.

A `BufferedWriter` object has the methods shown in Table 10-3.

TABLE 10-3: BufferedWriter Methods

METHOD	DESCRIPTION

`write(`
`    String s,`
`    int offset,`
`    int length)`
	Writes `length` characters from the string `s` starting at position `offset`.

`write(`
`    char[] chars,`
`    int offset,`
`    int length)`
	Writes `length` characters from the `chars` array starting at position `offset`.

`write( int c)`	Write a single character, `c`.
`newLine()`	Writes a newline character as defined by the `line.separator` system property. You should use this method rather than including a `'\n'` character in the text when you need a line separator in the output.
`flush()`	Flushes the stream causing all data in the internal buffer to be written to the file.
`close()`	Closes the stream after flushing it. After the stream has been closed, attempts to write or flush the stream will throw an `IOException`.

All the `BufferedWriter` object methods mentioned here throw an `IOException` if an I/O error occurs.

Because a `BufferedWriter` object can only write strings or single characters, any numerical data must be converted to a string before you can write it to the file. Because all the wrapper classes for the fundamental types provide `toString()` methods, this presents no particular difficulty.

Of course, strings are inherently variable in length so you need to consider how data written by a `BufferedWriter` is going to be read. You either need to record information about the length of strings within the data or make sure there are separator characters that you can use to determine where each data item ends. Let's try an example.

TRY IT OUT   Writing a File Using a Buffered Writer

In this example, you write a series of strings to a file:

Available for
download on
Wrox.com

```java
import java.io.*;
import java.nio.file.*;
import java.nio.charset.Charset;

public class WriterOutputToFile {
  public static void main(String[] args) {
    String[] sayings = {"A nod is as good as a wink to a blind horse.",
                        "Least said, soonest mended.",
                        "There are 10 kinds of people in the world, " +
                        "those that understand binary and those that don't.",
                        "You can't make a silk purse out of a sow's ear.",
                        "Hindsight is always twenty-twenty.",
                        "Existentialism has no future.",
                        "Those who are not confused are misinformed.",
                        "Better untaught that ill-taught."};

    Path file = Paths.get(System.getProperty("user.home")).
                        resolve("Beginning Java Stuff").resolve("Sayings.txt");
    try {
      // Create parent directory if it doesn't exist
      Files.createDirectories(file.getParent());
    } catch(IOException e) {
      System.err.println("Error creating directory: " + file.getParent());
      e.printStackTrace();
      System.exit(1);
    }
    try(BufferedWriter fileOut = Files.newBufferedWriter(
                                    file, Charset.forName("UTF-16"))){
      // Write saying to the file
      for(int i = 0 ; i < sayings.length ; ++i) {
        fileOut.write(sayings[i], 0, sayings[i].length());
        fileOut.newLine();                            // Write separator
      }
    System.out.println("File written.");
    } catch(IOException e) {
      System.err.println("Error writing file: " + file);
      e.printStackTrace();
    }
  }
}
```

WriterOutputToFile.java

The only output is the file path and confirmation that the file was written.

How It Works

As in the previous example, the directory to contain the file is the `"Beginning Java Stuff"` directory in your home directory and you make sure the directory does exist. The `BufferedWriter` class implements the

`AutoCloseable` interface so we create the object in a `try` block with resources. Each element in the sayings array is written to the file in the loop using the `write()` method. The default options are in effect for the `BufferedWriter` object, `WRITE`, `CREATE`, and `TRUNCATE_EXISTING`, so a new file is created if it doesn't already exist and any file contents are overwritten. A newline character is written to the file by calling the `newLine()` method after each saying. This allows the sayings to be separated when the file is read.

The third method for writing files involves the use of *channels*. A channel is a mechanism for transferring data to and from an external source using buffers. Using a channel is considerably more powerful and flexible than using an output stream or a writer so I will spend more time on this than the first two. However, there's something I need to explain before you can use a channel to write file.

All the data that you write to a file using a channel starts out in one or more buffers in memory. Similarly, when you read from a file using a channel, the data from the file ends up in one or more buffers and you access it from there. The Java library provides an extensive range of capabilities for working with buffers, and these are essential when using the `newByteChannel()` route to writing a file. I will explain the various ways in which you can create and use buffers before getting into writing files using channels.

BUFFERS

All the classes that define buffers have the abstract `java.nio.Buffer` class as a base. The `Buffer` class therefore defines the fundamental characteristics common to all buffers. Each buffer class type can store a sequence of elements of a given type, and you can create buffers to hold any primitive data type except for type `boolean`. Thus, you create different types of buffers to store `byte` values, `char` values, `short` values, `int` values, `long` values, `float` values, or `double` values. The classes in Table 10-4 in the `java.nio` package define these buffers.

TABLE 10-4: Classes for Buffers

CLASS	DESCRIPTION
ByteBuffer	A buffer that stores values of type `byte`. You can also store the binary values of any of the other primitive types in this buffer, except for type `boolean`. Each binary value that you store occupies a number of bytes in the buffer determined by the type — values of type `char` or `short` occupy 2 bytes, `int` values occupy 4 bytes, and so on.
CharBuffer	A buffer that stores only values of type `char`.
ShortBuffer	A buffer that stores only values of type `short`.
IntBuffer	A buffer that stores only values of type `int`.
LongBuffer	A buffer that stores only values of type `long`.
FloatBuffer	A buffer that stores only values of type `float`.
DoubleBuffer	A buffer that stores only values of type `double`.

I keep repeating "except for type `boolean`" every so often, so I better address that. There is no buffer type that provides for type `boolean` values, but, of course, you may actually want to record some `boolean` values in a file. In this case, you have to devise a suitable alternative representation. You could use integer values 0 and 1, or perhaps strings `"true"` and `"false"`, or even characters `'t'` and `'f'`. You could even represent each `boolean` value as a single bit and pack eight of them at a time into a single byte, but this is likely to be worthwhile only if you have a lot of them. Which approach you choose depends on what is most convenient in the context in which you are using the `boolean` values.

Although you have seven different classes defining buffers, you use only buffers of type `ByteBuffer` to read or write data. The other types of buffers in the table above are called *view buffers*, because they are usually created as views of an existing buffer of type `ByteBuffer`. The view buffers provide an easy way to get data items of various types into or out of a `ByteBuffer`. You see how a little later in this chapter.

Buffer Capacity

The capacity of a buffer is the maximum number of values it can contain, not the number of bytes — unless, of course, it stores elements of type `byte`. The capacity of a buffer is fixed when you create it and cannot be changed subsequently. You can obtain the capacity for a buffer object as a value of type `int` by calling the `capacity()` method that it inherits from the `Buffer` class. Figure 10-1 shows the capacities of different buffers when each occupies the same amount of memory.

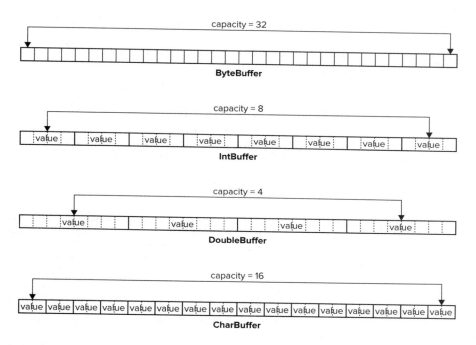

FIGURE 10-1

Of course, for a buffer that stores bytes, the capacity is the maximum number of bytes it can hold, but for a buffer of type `DoubleBuffer`, for example, which stores `double` values, the capacity is the maximum number of values of type `double` you can put in it. Values in a buffer are indexed from zero, so the index position for referencing values in a buffer runs from 0 to `capacity-1`.

Buffer Position and Limit

A buffer also has a *limit* and a *position*, both of which affect data transfer operations to or from the buffer. In the case of a `ByteBuffer`, the position and limit control read and write operations executed by a channel using the buffer.

The *position* is the index position of the next buffer element that is available to be read or written. This may sound a little strange, but keep in mind that a `ByteBuffer` can be for file input or output and you can transfer values into and out of other types of buffer.

Consider a couple of examples. With a `ByteBuffer` that you are using for file output, the position identifies the location in the buffer of the next byte to be written to the file. For a `ByteBuffer` used for file input, the position identifies where the next byte that is read from the file is stored in the buffer. When you transfer one or more values into a `DoubleBuffer` or an `IntBuffer` using methods available for that purpose, the position indicates where the first value is stored in the buffer. When you are extracting values from a buffer, the position indicates the location of the first value to be extracted.

The *limit* is the index position in a buffer of the first value that should not be read or written. Thus, elements can be read or written starting with the element at `position` and up to and including the element at `limit-1`. Thus if you want to fill a buffer, the position must be at zero because this is where the first data item goes, and the limit must be equal to the capacity because the last data item has to be stored at the last element in the buffer, which is `capacity-1`.

You use the position and limit for a `ByteBuffer` to determine what bytes in the buffer are involved in a read or write operation executed by a channel — I'll discuss using a channel later in this chapter, once I have finished with buffers. How the position and limit affect I/O operations is easier to understand if you take a specific example. First consider an operation that writes data from the buffer to a file. This is illustrated in Figure 10-2.

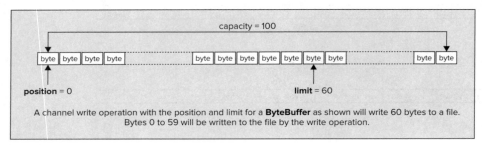

FIGURE 10-2

When a file write operation is executed by a channel using a given `ByteBuffer`, elements from the buffer are written to the file starting at the index specified by the position. Successive bytes are written to the file up to, and including, the byte at index position `limit-1`. Thus with the buffer shown in Figure 10-2, 60 bytes are written to the file. When you want to write all the data from a buffer, you should set the buffer position to 0 and the limit to the buffer capacity. In this case the limit is an index value that is one beyond the index value for the last byte in the buffer, so `limit-1` refers to the last byte.

For a read operation, data that is read from the file is stored in a `ByteBuffer` starting at the byte at the index given by the buffer's position. Assuming that the end of the file is not reached before all the bytes are read, bytes continue to be read up to and including the byte at the index `limit-1`. Thus, the number of bytes read is `limit-position`, and the bytes are stored in the buffer from the byte at `position` up to and including the byte at `limit-1`.

As I said at the beginning of this section, the position and limit are involved when you load data into a buffer before writing it to a file or retrieving data from it after reading from a file. This applies for any type of buffer. The position specifies where the next value is inserted in a buffer or retrieved from it. As you see later, the position is usually automatically incremented to point to the next available position when you insert or extract values in a buffer. The limit acts as a constraint to indicate where the data in a buffer ends, a bit like an end-of-file marker. You cannot insert or extract elements beyond the position specified by the limit.

Because a buffer's position is an index, it must be greater than or equal to zero. You can also deduce that it must also be less than or equal to the limit. Clearly, the limit cannot be greater than the capacity of a buffer. Otherwise, you could be trying to write elements to positions beyond the end of the buffer. However, as you have seen, it can be equal to it. These relationships can be expressed as the following:

```
0 ≤ position ≤ limit ≤ capacity
```

As a general rule, if your code attempts to do things directly or indirectly that result in these relationships being violated, an exception is thrown.

When you create a new buffer that is not a view buffer, its capacity is fixed at the value that you specify. It also has a position of zero and its limit is set to its capacity. When you create a view buffer from an existing `ByteBuffer`, the contents of the view buffer start at the current position for the `ByteBuffer`. The capacity and limit for the view buffer are set to the limit for the original buffer, divided by the number of bytes in an element in the view buffer. The limit and position for the view buffer are subsequently independent of the limit and position for the original buffer.

Setting the Position and Limit

You can set the position and limit for a buffer explicitly by using the methods that are defined in the `Buffer` class, shown in Table 10-5.

TABLE 10-5: Methods that Set Position and Limit for a Buffer

METHOD	DESCRIPTION
`position( int newPosition)`	Sets the position to the index value specified by the argument. The new position value must be greater than or equal to zero, and not greater than the current limit; otherwise, an exception of type `IllegalArgumentException` is thrown. If the buffer's *mark* is defined (I explain the mark in the next section) and greater than the new position, it is discarded.
`limit( int newLimit)`	Sets the limit to the index value specified by the argument. If the buffer's position is greater than the new limit it is set to the new limit. If the buffer's mark is defined and exceeds the new limit, it is discarded. If the new limit value is negative or greater than the buffer's capacity, an exception of type `IllegalArgumentException` is thrown.

Both of these methods return a reference of type `Buffer` for the object for which they were called. This enables you to chain calls to these methods together in a single statement. For example, given a buffer reference `buf`, you could set both the position and the limit with this statement:

```
buf.limit(512).position(256);
```

This assumes the capacity of the buffer is at least 512 elements. If you are explicitly setting both the limit and the position, you should always choose the sequence in which you set them to avoid setting a position that is greater than the limit. If the buffer's limit starts out less than the new position you want to set, attempting to set the position first results in an `IllegalArgumentException` being thrown. Setting the limit first to a value less than the current position has a similar effect. If you want to avoid checking the current limit and position when you want to reset both, you can always do it safely like this:

```
buf.position(0).limit(newLimit).position(newPosition);
```

Of course, the new position and limit values must be legal; otherwise, an exception is still thrown. In other words, `newPosition` must be non-negative and less than `newLimit`. To be 100 percent certain that setting a new position and limit is going to work, you could code it something like this:

```
if(newPosition >= 0 && newLimit > newPosition) {
  buf.position(0).limit(newLimit).position(newPosition);
} else {
  System.err.println("Illegal position:limit settings."
        + "Position: " + newPosition + " Limit: "+ newLimit);
}
```

You can determine whether there are any elements between the position and the limit in a buffer by calling the `hasRemaining()` method for the buffer:

```
if (buf.hasRemaining()) {                 // If limit-position is >0
  System.out.println("We have space in the buffer!");
}
```

You can also find out how many values can currently be accommodated by using the `remaining()` method. For example:

```
System.out.println("The buffer can accommodate " + buf.remaining() +
                    " more elements.");
```

Of course, the value returned by the `remaining()` method is the same as the expression `buf.limit()-buf.position()`.

Creating Buffers

None of the classes that define buffers have public constructors available. Instead, you use a static factory method to create a buffer. You typically create a buffer object of type `ByteBuffer` by calling the static `allocate()` method for the class. You pass a value of type `int` as an argument to the method that defines the capacity of the buffer — the maximum number of bytes that the buffer must accommodate. For example:

```
ByteBuffer buf = ByteBuffer.allocate(1024);   // Buffer of 1024 bytes capacity
```

When you create a new buffer using the `allocate()` method for the buffer class, it has a position of zero, and its limit is set to its capacity. The buffer that the preceding statement creates therefore has a position of 0 and has a limit and capacity of 1024.

You can also create other types of buffers in the same way. For example:

```
// Buffer stores 100 float values
FloatBuffer floatBuf = FloatBuffer.allocate(100);
```

This creates a buffer with a capacity to store 100 values of type `float`. Because each element occupies 4 bytes, the data in this buffer occupies 400 bytes. The buffer's initial position is 0, and its limit and capacity is 100. Note that this is not a view buffer, but an independent buffer to store `float` values.

In practice, you are unlikely to want to create buffers other than `ByteBuffer` objects by calling the static `allocate()` method because you cannot use them directly for I/O operations. You usually create a `ByteBuffer` object first and then create any view buffers that you need from the byte buffer.

Creating View Buffers

You can use a `ByteBuffer` object to create a buffer of any of the other types I have introduced and the new buffer shares all or part of the memory that the original `ByteBuffer` uses to store data. Such a buffer is referred to as a *view buffer* because it provides a view of the contents of the byte buffer as elements of another data type. Data is always transferred to or from a file as a series of bytes, but it typically consists of data values of a mix of types other than type `byte`. A view buffer therefore has two primary uses: for loading data items that are not of type `byte` into a `ByteBuffer` prior to writing it to a file, and for accessing data that has been read from a file as values that are other than type `byte`.

You could create a view buffer of type `IntBuffer` from a `ByteBuffer` object like this:

```
ByteBuffer buf = ByteBuffer.allocate(1024);   // Buffer of 1024 bytes capacity
IntBuffer intBuf = buf.asIntBuffer();         // Now create a view buffer
```

The content of the view buffer, `intBuf`, that you create here start at the byte buffer's current position, which in this case is zero because it is newly created. The remaining bytes in `buf` are effectively shared with the view buffer. At least, the maximum number of them that is a multiple of 4 , because `intBuf` stores elements of type `int` that require 4 bytes each. The view buffer has an initial position of 0 and has a capacity and limit of 256. This is because 256 elements of type `int` completely fill the 1024 bytes remaining in `buf`. If you had allocated `buf` with 1023 bytes, then `intBuf` would have mapped to 1020 bytes of `buf` and would have a capacity and limit of 255.

You could now use this view buffer to load the original buffer with values of type `int`. You could then use the original byte buffer to write the `int` values to a file. As I said at the outset, view buffers have a similar role when you are reading a file. You would have a primary buffer of type `ByteBuffer` into which you read bytes from a file, and then you might access the contents of the `ByteBuffer` through a view buffer of type `DoubleBuffer` to enable you to retrieve the data that is read from the file as values of type `double`.

The `ByteBuffer` class defines the methods for creating view buffers for a byte buffer object shown in Table 10-6.

TABLE 10-6: Methods to Create View Buffers

METHOD	DESCRIPTION
`asCharBuffer()`	Returns a reference to a view buffer of type `CharBuffer`
`asShortBuffer()`	Returns a reference to a view buffer of type `ShortBuffer`
`asIntBuffer()`	Returns a reference to a view buffer of type `IntBuffer`
`asLongBuffer()`	Returns a reference to a view buffer of type `LongBuffer`
`asFloatBuffer()`	Returns a reference to a view buffer of type `FloatBuffer`
`asDoubleBuffer()`	Returns a reference to a view buffer of type `DoubleBuffer`
`asReadOnlyBuffer()`	Returns a reference to a read-only view buffer of type `ByteBuffer`

In each case, the view buffer's contents start at the current position of the original byte buffer. The position of the view buffer itself is initially set to zero, and its capacity and limit are set to the number of bytes remaining in the original byte buffer divided by the number of bytes in the type of element that the view buffer holds. Figure 10-3 illustrates a view buffer of type `IntBuffer` that is created after the initial position of the byte buffer has been incremented by 2, possibly after inserting a value of type `char` into the byte buffer.

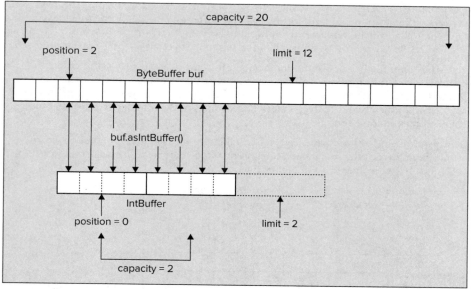

FIGURE 10-3

You can create as many view buffers from a buffer of type `ByteBuffer` as you want, and they can overlap or not as you require. A view buffer always maps to bytes in the byte buffer starting at the current position. You frequently want to map several different view buffers to a single byte buffer so that each provides a view of a different segment of the byte buffer in terms of a particular type of value. Figure 10-4 illustrates this situation.

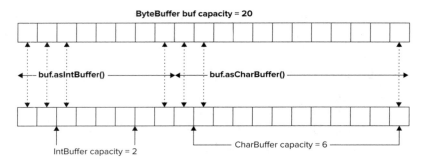

A Byte Buffer with two View Buffers

FIGURE 10-4

The diagram illustrates a byte buffer with a view buffer of type `IntBuffer` mapped to the first 8 bytes, and a view buffer of type `CharBuffer` mapped to the last 12 bytes. All you need to do to achieve this is to ensure that the position of the byte buffer is set appropriately before you create each view buffer.

Duplicating and Slicing Buffers

You can duplicate any of the buffers that I have discussed by calling the `duplicate()` method for the buffer. The method returns a reference to a buffer with the same type as the original, and which shares the contents and memory of the original buffer. The duplicate buffer initially has the same capacity, position, and limit as the original. However, although changes to the contents of the duplicate are reflected in the original, and vice versa, the position and limit for the original buffer and the duplicate are independent of one other. One use for a duplicate buffer is when you want to access different parts of a buffer's contents concurrently. You can retrieve data from a duplicate buffer without affecting the original buffer in any way.

Thus a duplicate buffer is not really a new buffer in memory. It is just a new object that provides an alternative route to accessing the same block of memory that is being used to buffer the data. The `duplicate()` method returns a reference of a new object of the same type as the original, but has no independent data storage. It merely shares the memory that belongs to the original buffer object but with independent position and limit values.

You can also *slice* any of the buffers you have seen. Calling the `slice()` method for a buffer returns a reference to a new buffer object of the same type as the original that shares the elements that remain in the original buffer. Slicing a buffer is illustrated in Figure 10-5.

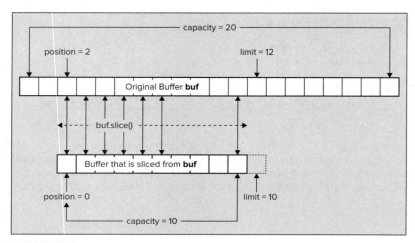

FIGURE 10-5

A buffer produced by the `slice()` method maps to a part of the original buffer starting at the element at its current position, up to and including the element at `limit-1`. Of course, if the position of the original buffer object is zero and the limit is equal to the capacity, the `slice()` method effectively produces the same result as the `duplicate()` method — that is, the buffer memory is shared. Slicing a buffer gives you access to the data in a given part of a buffer through two or more separate routes, each with its own independent position and limit.

Creating Buffers by Wrapping Arrays

You can also create a buffer by wrapping an existing array of the same type as the buffer elements by calling one of the static `wrap()` methods. This method creates a buffer that already contains the data in the array. You saw earlier that you can create a `ByteBuffer` object by wrapping an array of type `byte[]`.

When you create a buffer by wrapping an array, the buffer object does not have memory of its own to store the data. The buffer is backed by the array that you have used to define it, so modifications to the values in the buffer alters the array, and vice versa. The capacity and limit for the buffer are set to the length of the array, and its position is zero.

You can also wrap an array to create a buffer so that the position and limit correspond to a particular sequence of elements in the array. For example:

```
String saying = "Handsome is as handsome does.";
byte[] array = saying.getBytes();       // Get string as byte array
ByteBuffer buf = ByteBuffer.wrap(array, 9, 14);
```

This creates a buffer by wrapping a byte array, but the position and limit are set using the second and third argument. The second and third arguments to the `wrap()` method specify the subsection of the array that is to be read or written next. This is illustrated in Figure 10-6.

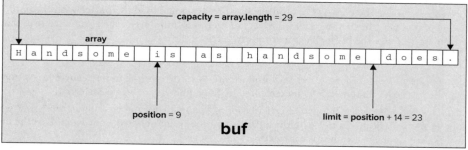

FIGURE 10-6

The buffer's capacity is `array.length` and the position is set to the value of the second argument, 9. The third argument specifies the number of buffer elements that can be read or written so this value is added to the position to define the limit. If either the second argument value or the sums of the second and third argument values do not represent legal index values for the array, then an exception of type `IndexOutOfBoundsException` is thrown.

You can also wrap arrays of values of a primitive type to create a buffer of the corresponding type. For example:

```
long[] numbers = { 1L, 1L, 2L, 3L, 5L, 8L, 13L, 21L, 34L, 55L, 89L};
LongBuffer numBuf = LongBuffer.wrap(numbers);
```

The buffer of type `LongBuffer` that you create here has a capacity of `array.length`, which is 11. The buffer position is set to 0 and the limit is set to the capacity. In a similar manner you can create buffers from arrays of any of the other primitive types with the exception of type `boolean`. Creating buffers other that `ByteBuffer` objects in this way is of little value with channel operations because you cannot use then directly in I/O operations.

Marking a Buffer

You use the *mark* property for a buffer to record a particular index position in the buffer that you want to be able to return to later. You can set the mark to the current position by calling the `mark()` method for a buffer object that is inherited from the `Buffer` class. For example:

```
buf.mark();                          // Mark the current position
```

This method also returns a reference of type `Buffer` so you could chain it with the methods for setting the limit and position:

```
buf.limit(512).position(256).mark();
```

This sets the mark to 256, the same as the position, which is set after the limit has been set to 512.

After a series of operations that alter the position, you can reset the buffer's position to the mark that you have set previously by calling the `reset()` method that is inherited from the `Buffer` class:

```
buf.reset();                         // Reset position to last marked
```

If you have not set the mark, or if it has been discarded by an operation to set the limit or the position, the `reset()` method throws an exception of type `InvalidMarkException`. The mark for a view buffer operates independently of the mark for the buffer from which it was created.

You probably don't need to mark a buffer most of the time. The sort of situation where you could use it is where you are scanning some part of a buffer to determine what kind of data it contains — after reading a file, for example. You could mark the point where you started the analysis, and then return to that point by calling `reset()` for the buffer when you have figured out how to handle the data.

Buffer Data Transfers

Of course, before you can write the contents of a buffer to a file, you must load the buffer with the data. Methods for loading data into a buffer are referred to as *put* methods. Similarly, when you have read data from a file into a buffer, you use the buffer's *get* methods to retrieve the data.

Two kinds of operations transfer data values to or from a buffer.

➤ A *relative* put or get operation transfers one or more values starting at the buffer's current position. In this case, the position is automatically incremented by the number of values transferred.

➤ In an *absolute* put or get operation, you explicitly specify an index for the position in the buffer where the data transfer is to begin. In this case the buffer's position is not updated, so it remains at the index value it was before the operation was executed.

Transferring Data into a Buffer

The `ByteBuffer` class and all the view buffer classes have two `put()` methods for transferring a single value of the buffer's type to the buffer. One is a relative `put()` method that transfers an element to a given index position in the buffer, and the other is an absolute put method that places the element at an index position that you specify as an argument. All the buffer classes also have three relative `put()` methods for bulk transfer of elements of the given type. Let's consider the `put()` methods for a `ByteBuffer` object that are shown in Table 10-7 as an example.

TABLE 10-7: ByteBuffer Class put() Methods

METHOD	DESCRIPTION
put(byte b)	Transfers the byte specified by the argument to the buffer at the current position and increments the position by 1. An exception of type `BufferOverflowException` is thrown if the buffer's position is not less than its limit.
put(int index, byte b)	Transfers the byte specified by the second argument to the buffer at the index position specified by the first argument. The buffer position is unchanged. An exception of type `IndexOutOfBoundsException` is thrown if the index value is negative or greater than or equal to the buffer's limit.

METHOD	DESCRIPTION
put(byte[] array)	Transfers all the elements of `array` to this buffer starting at the current position. The position is incremented by the length of the array. An exception of type `BufferOverflowException` is thrown if there is insufficient space in the buffer to accommodate the contents of the array.

put(
  byte[] array,
  int offset,
  int length)
	Transfers bytes from `array[offset]` to `array[offset+length-1]` inclusive to the buffer. If there is insufficient space for them in the buffer, an exception of type `BufferOverflowException` is thrown.

put(ByteBuffer src)	Transfers the bytes remaining in `src` to the buffer. This is `src.remaining()` elements from the buffer `src` from its position index to `limit-1`. If there is insufficient space to accommodate these, then an exception of type `BufferOverflowException` is thrown. If `src` is identical to the current buffer — you are trying to transfer a buffer to itself,; in other words — , an exception of type `IllegalArgumentException` is thrown.

Each of these methods returns a reference to the buffer for which it was called. If the buffer is read-only, any of these methods throws an exception of type `ReadOnlyBufferException`. You see how a buffer can be read-only when I discuss using view buffers in more detail. Each buffer object that stores elements of a given primitive type — `CharBuffer`, `DoubleBuffer`, or whatever — has `put()` methods analogous to those for `ByteBuffer`, but with arguments of a type appropriate to the type of element in the buffer.

The `ByteBuffer` class has some extra methods that enable you to transfer binary data of other primitive types to the buffer. For example, you can transfer a value of type `double` to a buffer of type `ByteBuffer` with either of the methods in Table 10-8.

TABLE 10-8: ByteBuffer Methods that Transfer double Values

METHOD	DESCRIPTION
putDouble(double value)	Transfers the `double` value specified by the argument to the buffer at the current position and increments the position by 8. If there are fewer than 8 bytes remaining in the buffer, an exception of type `BufferOverflowException` is thrown.

putDouble(
  int index,
  double value)
	Transfers the `double` value specified by the second argument to the buffer starting at the index position specified by the first argument. The buffer's position is unchanged. If there are fewer than 8 bytes remaining in the buffer, an exception of type `BufferOverflowException` is thrown. If `index` is negative or the buffer's limit is less than or equal to `index+7`, the method throws an exception of type `IndexOutOfBoundsException`.

Note that these provide for transferring only single values. If you want to transfer an array of values you must use a loop. Similar pairs of methods to the preceding are defined in the `ByteBuffer` class to transfer values of other primitive types. These are the methods `putChar()`, `putShort()`, `putInt()`, `putLong()`, and `putFloat()`, each of which transfers a value of the corresponding type. Like the other `put()` methods you have seen, these all return a reference to the buffer for which they are called. This is to enable you to chain the calls for these methods together in a single statement if you want. For example:

```
String text = "Value of e = ";
ByteBuffer buf = ByteBuffer.allocate(text.length()+ sizeof(Math.E));
buf.put(text.getBytes()).putDouble(Math.E);
buf.rewind();                  // Reset the current position to zero
```

Here, you write the string to the buffer by converting it to bytes by calling its `getBytes()` method and passing the result to the `put()` method for the buffer. The `put()` method returns a reference to the buffer, buf, so you use that to call the `putDouble()` method to write the 8 bytes for the `double` value, `Math.E`, to the buffer. Of course, `putDouble()` also returns a reference to buf, so you can chain further calls together in the same statement if you wish. Here the buffer capacity has been allocated so that it exactly accommodates the data to be loaded, so the capacity is 21 bytes. Each time you call the put() method for a buffer, the position is moved to the next available position in the buffer. To write the data to the buffer, the position must be set to where the contents to be written start. Calling the rewind() method for a buffer resets the position to zero.

The putDouble() method writes the 8-byte binary double value to the buffer, so you are not going to be able to read this very easily by inspecting the file. If you want to write the value of Math.E as characters, you could use the following code:

```
String text = "Value of e = ";
String eValue = Double.toString(Math.E);
ByteBuffer buf = ByteBuffer.allocate(text.length()+ eValue.length());
buf.put(text.getBytes()).put(eValue.getBytes()).rewind();
```

Now you have the double value written as a string of bytes. The toString() method in the Double class converts the double value to a string. Note that you can chain the rewind() call for the buffer, too.

Note that you are transferring the string characters to the buffer as bytes in the local character encoding in the previous code fragment, not as Unicode characters. To transfer them as the original Unicode characters, you could code the operations like this:

```
String text = "Value of e = ";
char[] array = text.toCharArray();        // Create char[] array from the string
ByteBuffer buf = ByteBuffer.allocate(2*array.length);
// Now use a loop to transfer array elements one at a time
for (char ch : array) {
  buf.putChar(ch);
}
```

Here you use a collection-based for loop to write the elements of the array that you create from text to the buffer.

Retrieving Data from a Buffer

A ByteBuffer object provides get() methods to retrieve data from a buffer that are analogous to the put() methods. You use the get() methods after data has been read into a buffer from an external source and you apply these in the next chapter when you read files. There are four get() method overloads in the ByteBuffer class, as shown in Table 10-9.

TABLE 10-9: ByteBuffer get() Methods

METHOD	DESCRIPTION
get()	This extracts and returns the byte from the current buffer position and increments the position.
get(int index)	Returns the byte at index position index.
get(byte[] bytes)	Retrieves bytes.length bytes from the buffer, starting at position 0. The buffer position is incremented by bytes.length. A reference to the current buffer is returned. The method throws BufferUnderflowException if there are fewer than bytes.length bytes available from the buffer.

get(
  byte[] bytes,
  int offset,
  int length)
	Retrieves length bytes from the buffer starting at the current buffer position and stores them in the bytes array starting at index position offset. The buffer position is incremented by length. A reference to the current buffer is returned. The method throws BufferUnderflowException if there are fewer than length bytes available, or IndexOutOfBoundsException if the values of offset and/or length result in an illegal array index.

Because the last two methods return a reference to the buffer, you can chain calls together to extract data into two or more arrays in a single statement. Each of the view buffer classes have essentially the same four get() methods available for extracting data items of the type that the buffer holds. The ByteBuffer class also has extraction methods for data items that parallel the put methods for fundamental types of data. These are getChar(), getInt(), getLong(), getFloat(), and getDouble(). Each of these comes in two versions, — one without a parameter that retrieves the item at the current position and the other with an index parameter of type int that retrieves the item at the specified position.

Using View Buffers

View buffers are intended to make it easier to transfer data elements of various basic types to or from a ByteBuffer. The only slightly tricky part is that you have to keep track of the position for the original ByteBuffer object yourself when you use a view buffer because operations with the view buffer do not update the position for the backing byte buffer. You could do what the previous code fragment does using view buffers:

```
String text = "Value of e";
ByteBuffer buf = ByteBuffer.allocate(50);   // The original byte buffer
CharBuffer charBuf = buf.asCharBuffer();    // Create view buffer
charBuf.put(text);                          // Transfer string via view buffer

// Update byte buffer position by the number of bytes we have transferred
buf.position(buf.position() + 2*charBuf.position());

buf.putDouble(Math.E);                       // Transfer binary double value
```

Putting data into a view buffer with a relative put() operation updates only the position of the view buffer. The position for the backing ByteBuffer is unchanged, so you must increment it to account for the number of bytes occupied by the Unicode characters that you have written. Because you transfer the eight bytes for the constant Math.E directly using buf, the position in buf is incremented by 8 automatically. Of course, it's essential that you update the buffer's position to account for the characters you have transferred before you transfer the floating-point value. If you don't, you overwrite the first 8 bytes of the character data.

Preparing a Buffer for Output to a File

You have seen that a buffer starts out with its position set to 0 — the first element position — and with its limit set to the capacity. The state of a view buffer reflects the state of the byte buffer from which it is created. Suppose you create a byte buffer with the following statement:

```
ByteBuffer buf = ByteBuffer.allocate(80);
```

You can now create a view buffer from this byte buffer that you can use to store values of type double with the statement:

```
DoubleBuffer doubleBuf = buf.asDoubleBuffer();
```

The view buffer's initial state is shown in Figure 10-7.

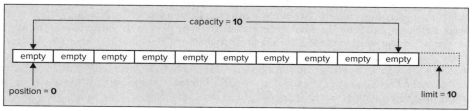

FIGURE 10-7

The limit is automatically set to the capacity, 10, so it points to the position that is one beyond the last value. You could load six values of type `double` into this buffer with the following statements:

```
double[] data = { 1.0, 1.414, 1.732, 2.0, 2.236, 2.449 };
doubleBuf.put(data);          // Transfer the array elements to the buffer
```

The `put()` operation automatically increments the position for the view buffer. Now the buffer is shown in Figure 10-8.

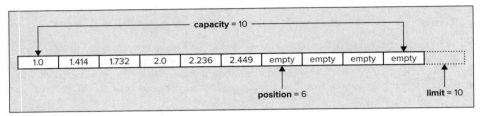

FIGURE 10-8

The position and limit values are now set to values ready for more data to be added to the buffer. The value of `position` points to the first empty element, and `limit` points to one beyond the last empty element. Of course, the position for the backing `ByteBuffer` is still in its original state, but you can update that to correspond with the data you have loaded into the view buffer with the statement:

```
buf.Position(8*doubleBuf.Position());
```

If you now want to write the data you have in the byte buffer to a file, you must change the values for `position` and `limit` in the byte buffer to identify the elements that are to be written. A file write operation writes data elements starting from the element in the buffer at the index specified by `position`, and up to and including the element at the index `limit-1`. To write the data to the file, the limit for the byte buffer needs to be set to the current position, and the position needs to be set back to zero. You could do this explicitly using the methods you have seen. For example:

```
buf.limit(buf.position()).rewind(0);
```

This first sets the limit to the byte referenced by the current position and then resets the position back to the first byte, byte 0. You could call the `position()` method with the argument 0 instead of calling `rewind()`. However, you don't need to specify the operation in such detail. The `Buffer` class conveniently defines the `flip()` method that does exactly this, so you would normally set up the buffer to be written to a file like this:

```
buf.flip();
```

The `flip()` method returns the buffer reference as type `Buffer`, so you can chain this operation on the buffer with others in a single statement. So, after you have loaded your byte buffer with data, don't forget to flip it before you write it to a file. If you don't, your data is not written to the file, but garbage might well be. If you loaded the data using a view buffer, you also have to remember to update the byte buffer's position before performing the flip.

The `clear()` method sets the limit to the capacity and the position to zero, so it restores these values to the state they had when the buffer was created. This doesn't reset the data in the buffer though. The contents are left unchanged. If you want to reset the data you must transfer new data to the buffer. You typically call the `clear()` method when you want to reuse a buffer, either to load new data into it ready to be written, or to read data into it from a channel. The `rewind()` method simply resets the position to zero, leaving the limit unchanged. This enables you to reread the data that is in the buffer. The `clear()` and `rewind()` methods are defined in the base class `Buffer`, and both return a reference to the buffer of type `Buffer`, so you can chain these operations with others that are defined in the `Buffer` class.

Now you have a rough idea of how you can work with buffers, let's investigate how you can apply this knowledge to writing files.

WRITING A FILE USING A CHANNEL

The `java.nio.channels.FileChannel` class encapsulates a *file channel* and a `FileChannel` object provides a connection to a file for writing and/or reading. A channel is simply a path for data to flow to or from an external device. The `FileChannel` class provides the most flexible and powerful way to read, write, or both read and write a file. To write to a file using a channel, you assemble the data that you want to transfer in one or more buffers, and then write the contents of the buffers to the file. Reading a file is the inverse of this process and you learn more about this in the next chapter. The methods that a `FileChannel` object provides for reading and writing files are declared in channel interfaces that the `FileChannel` class implements. All these interfaces are defined in the `java.nio.channels` package.

Channel Interfaces

The channel interfaces are related as illustrated in the hierarchy shown in Figure 10-9.

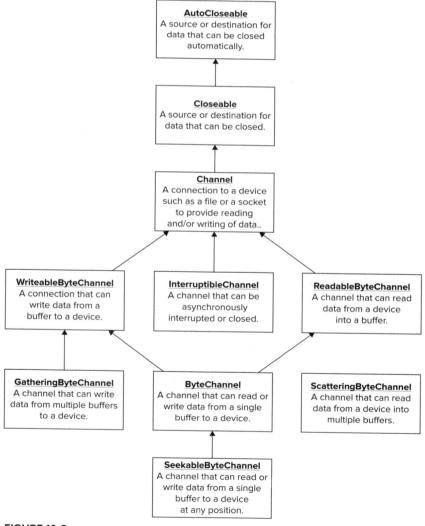

FIGURE 10-9

Each arrow points from a given interface to an interface that it extends. The ReadableByteChannel interface provides for reading from a file into a single ByteBuffer and the WritableByteChannel provides for writing the contents of a ByteBuffer to a file. The ByteChannel interface simply combines the operations specified by the ReadableByteChannel and WritableByteChannel interfaces without declaring any additional methods. The ScatteringByteChannel interface extends the ReadableByteChannel interface by adding methods that allow data to be read and distributed among several separate buffers in a single operation. The GatheringByteChannel interface adds methods to those of the WritableByteChannel interface to permit writing from a number of separate buffers in a single operation.

The SeekableByteChannel interface provides the most comprehensive set of methods for file operations providing random access to a file for both reading and writing.

The InterruptibleChannel interface is implemented by classes encapsulating channels for network sockets and other interruptible devices; I concentrate on file operations in this book, so I won't discuss this interface further.

Channel Operations

The channel interfaces all extend a common interface, java.nio.channels.Channel, which declares two methods:

➤ The close() method, which closes a channel

➤ The isOpen() method, which tests the state of the channel, returning true if it is open and false otherwise

Because the channel interfaces all extend the AutoCloseable interface, all channel objects can be closed automatically if you create them in a try block with resources. The methods that each channel interface in the hierarchy declares are as follows:

ReadableByteChannel interface:

➤ int read(ByteBuffer input): Reads bytes from a channel into the input buffer and returns the number of bytes read, or −1 if the end of the stream is reached.

WritableByteChannel interface:

➤ int write(ByteBuffer output): Writes bytes from the output buffer to the channel and returns the number of bytes written.

➤ ByteChannel interface: This interface just inherits methods from the ReadableByteChannel and WritableByteChannel interfaces. No additional methods are declared.

SeekableByteChannel interface:

➤ long position(): Returns the current position for the channel that corresponds to the current file position.

➤ SeekableByteChannel position(long new)): Sets the channel's position and thus the position in the file to new.

➤ int read(ByteBuffer buf): Reads bytes from the channel into buf and returns the number of bytes read, or −1 if the channel has reached the end of the stream.

➤ int write(ByteBuffer buf): Writes the contents of buf to the channel and returns the number of bytes written.

➤ SeekableByteChannel truncate(long size): Truncates the file to which the channel is connected to size bytes and returns a reference to the channel to permit chaining method calls. If size is greater than the current size then the file is not modified.

➤ long size(): Returns the number of bytes in the file to which the channel is attached.

ScatteringByteChannel interface:

➤ int read(ByteBuffer[] inputs): Reads bytes from the channel into the array of buffers inputs and returns the number of bytes read or −1 if the end of the stream is reached.

➤ int read(ByteBuffer[] inputs, int offset, int length): Reads bytes from the channel into length buffers from the array inputs starting with the buffer inputs[offset].

GatheringByteChannel interface:

➤ int write(ByteBuffer[] outputs): Writes bytes from the array of buffers outputs to the channel, and returns the number of bytes written.

➤ int write(ByteBuffer[] outputs, int offset, int length): Writes bytes to the channel from length buffers from the array outputs starting with the buffer outputs[offset].

All of these methods can throw exceptions of one kind or another, and I go into details on these when you come to apply them. Note that a channel works only with buffers of type ByteBuffer. Other kinds of buffers do exist as you know, but you can't use them directly with the read() and write() methods for a channel.

Obtaining a Channel for a File

To obtain a channel for a file, you call the static newByteChannel() method from the Files class. The first argument is a Path object that encapsulates the file path. The second argument specifies an EnumSet of options from the java.nio.file.StandardOpenOption enumeration that you have already seen. This set of options specifies how you want to work with the file. You used an EnumSet object to hold enum constants in the previous chapter when you implemented walking a file tree, and you learn about the details of the EnumSet class in Chapter 14.

The newByteChannel() method returns a FileChannel object as a reference of type java.nio. channels.SeekableByteChannel. However, ideally you should store the reference returned by the newByteChannel() method in a variable of the interface type that suits what you want to do with the channel and that corresponds with the options you have set. For example, if you are simply writing a file, use WritableByteChannel as the variable type that holds the reference returned by the newByteChannel() method or if you are reading a file use ReadableByteChannel.

 NOTE *Although the* newByteChannel() *method returns a reference to an object of type* FileChannel, *you cannot store the reference directly in a variable of this type. You can only store the reference as type* SeekableByteChannel, *or one of the interface types that the* SeekableByteChannel *interface extends. To store the reference as type* FileChannel, *you must explicitly cast it to that type.*

The following statements create a channel:

```
Path file = Paths.get("D:\Junk\mydata.txt");
WritableByteChannel fileOut = Files.newByteChannel(
                    file, EnumSet.of(WRITE,  CREATE, TRUNCATE_EXISTING));
```

This creates a channel that can write the file specified by the file path. If the file does not exist, it is created and any existing contents are overwritten. The newByteChannel() method can throw several exceptions:

➤ IllegalArgumentException if you supply an invalid set of options.

➤ FileAlreadyExistsException if you specify the CREATE_NEW option and the file already exists.

➤ IOException if an I/O error occurs.

The method can also throw SecurityException if access to the file is prevented by a security manager.

Channel Write Operations

The `WritableByteChannel` interface declares a single method, `write()` that returns the number of bytes written as type `int`. The argument is a `ByteBuffer` object containing the bytes to be written to the file. A channel `write()` operation can throw any of the following exceptions:

➤ `ClosedChannelException`: Thrown if the channel is closed.

➤ `AsynchronousCloseException`: Thrown if another thread closes the channel while the write operation is in progress.

➤ `ClosedByInterruptException`: Thrown if another thread interrupts the current thread while the write operation is in progress.

➤ `IOException`: Thrown if some other I/O error occurs.

The first three are subclasses of `IOException`, which must be caught, so you generally put the `write()` method call in a `try` block. Typically this beis a `try` block with resources in which you create the channel so you get the `close()` method called automatically. If you want to react specifically to one or other of first three exceptions, you need to add a `catch` block for that specific type. Otherwise, you can just include a single `catch` block for type `IOException` to catch all four types of exception.

Let's try a simple example.

TRY IT OUT   Creating a Channel and Writing to a File

This example creates a file and uses a channel to write some text to it:

```java
import static java.nio.file.StandardOpenOption.*;
import java.nio.channels.WritableByteChannel;
import java.io.IOException;
import java.nio.ByteBuffer;
import java.util.EnumSet;
import java.nio.file.*;

public class TryChannel {

  public static void main(String[] args) {
    String[] sayings = {
      "The more you plan the luckier you get.",
      "The time to complete a project is the time " +
            "one person would need to complete it " +
            "multiplied by the number of people on the project.",
      "If at first you don't succeed, remove any evidence that you tried.",
      "A clever person solves problems, a wise person avoids them.",
      "Death is nature's way of telling you to slow down.",
      "A hen is an egg's way of making other eggs.",
      "The earlier you begin coding the later you finish.",
      "Anything you can't understand is intuitively obvious."};

    String separator = System.lineSeparator();

    Path file = Paths.get(System.getProperty("user.home")).
                resolve("Beginning Java Stuff").resolve("MoreSayings.txt");
    try {
      // Create parent directory if it doesn't exist
      Files.createDirectories(file.getParent());
    } catch(IOException e) {
      System.err.println("Error creating directory: " + file.getParent());
      e.printStackTrace();
      System.exit(1);
    }
    System.out.println("New file is: " + file);
```

```
      ByteBuffer buf = null;                          // Buffer to hold a saying
      try(WritableByteChannel channel =
                      Files.newByteChannel(file, EnumSet.of(CREATE, WRITE))){

        // Write sayings to the file
        for(String saying : sayings) {
          // Saying & separator in buffer
          buf = ByteBuffer.wrap((saying + separator).getBytes());
          channel.write(buf);
        }
        System.out.println("File written.");
      } catch (IOException e) {
        e.printStackTrace();
      }
    }
  }
```

TryChannel.java

The `file` path will be created in your user home directory.

The only output is the file path and a message confirming that the file has been written, but you should be able to inspect the contents of the `MoreSayings.txt` file that is created in the `Beginning Java Stuff` directory. If you are using Microsoft Windows, Notepad does it.

How It Works

You obtain the newline separator for the system by calling the static `lineSeparator()` method in the `System` class. You append this to each string to separate the strings in the file. Defining the path and creating the directory if necessary is as you have seen before.

The `FileChannel` object is created in the `try` block using the static `newByteChannel()` method in the `Files` classed. The reference that is returned is stored as type `WritableByteChannel` because the options you specified determine that the file is only opened for writing. Storing the reference as a `WritableByteChannel` reference restricts the methods available to just the `write()` method that the `WritableByteChannel` interface declares.

The data to be written to the file has to be in a `ByteBuffer` object to allow it to be written by the channel. The `getBytes()` method in the `String` class converts the characters in a string to bytes using the default `Charset` for your environment. You apply this method in the loop to each string from the `sayings` array with a line separator appended to it. The static `wrap()` method in the `ByteBuffer` class creates a buffer that wraps the bytes from the `byte` array that you pass as the argument.

The `write()` method for the `FileChannel` object writes the contents of the buffer to the file. When the `try` block ends, the `close()` method for the channel is called automatically to close the channel and release the resources associated with it, including the file.

FILE WRITE OPERATIONS

You have used only the simplest `write()` method for a `FileChannel` object to write all the data contained in a single `ByteBuffer` object to a file. Write operations can be more complicated in three ways:

1. You can arrange that only part of the data in a `ByteBuffer` is written to the file.
2. You can use `write()` methods declared in the `GatheringByteChannel` interface that write data from multiple buffers to a file in a single operation.
3. You can write to random position in a file.

Let's explore each of these possibilities in a little more detail.

Writing Part of a Buffer to a File

So far you have not been concerned with the buffer's limit and position in the examples. As you know, a buffer's position and limit determines the number of bytes written to the file when the `write()` method executes. Bytes are written starting with the byte at the buffer's current position. The number of bytes written is `limit-position`, which is the number returned by the `remaining()` method for the buffer object. The `write()` method that writes a single buffer returns the number of bytes that were actually written as a value of type `int`.

Let's try an example that shows how the buffer's position and limit change during operations with the buffer.

TRY IT OUT Buffer State during a Channel Write

You write the string `"Garbage in, garbage out\n"` to a file with the name `charData.txt` in the `Junk` directory. If you want to write to a file that is different from the example, just change the path accordingly. Here is the code:

Available for
download on
Wrox.com

```
import static java.nio.file.StandardOpenOption.*;
import java.nio.file.*;
import java.nio.channels.*;

import java.util.EnumSet;
import java.io.IOException;
import java.nio.ByteBuffer;

public class BufferStateTrace {
  public static void main(String[] args) {
    String phrase = "Garbage in, garbage out.\n";

    Path file = Paths.get(System.getProperty("user.home")).
                      resolve("Beginning Java Stuff").resolve("charData.txt");
    try {
      // Make sure we have the directory
      Files.createDirectories(file.getParent());
    } catch (IOException e) {
      e.printStackTrace();
      System.exit(1);
    }
    System.out.println("New file is: " + file);

    try (WritableByteChannel channel = Files.newByteChannel(file,
                                         EnumSet.of(WRITE, CREATE))) {
      ByteBuffer buf = ByteBuffer.allocate(1024);
      System.out.printf(
  "\nNew buffer:               position = %1$2d    Limit = %2$4d    capacity = %3$4d",
                            buf.position(), buf.limit(), buf.capacity());
      // Load the data into the buffer
      for(char ch : phrase.toCharArray())
        buf.putChar(ch);
      System.out.printf(
  "\nBuffer after loading: position = %1$2d    Limit = %2$4d    capacity = %3$4d",
                            buf.position(), buf.limit(), buf.capacity());
      buf.flip();                            // Flip the buffer ready for file write
      System.out.printf(
  "\nBuffer after flip:    position = %1$2d    Limit = %2$4d    capacity = %3$4d",
                            buf.position(), buf.limit(), buf.capacity());
      channel.write(buf);                    // Write the buffer to the file channel
      buf.flip();
      channel.write(buf);                    // Write the buffer again to the file channel
      System.out.println("\nBuffer contents written to the file - twice.");
```

```
    } catch (IOException e) {
      e.printStackTrace();
    }
  }
}
```

BufferStateTrace.java

The program produces some command-line output to trace what is going on with the buffer. After you have compiled and run this program, you should see the following output following the file path:

```
New buffer:              position =  0   Limit = 1024   capacity = 1024
Buffer after loading: position = 50   Limit = 1024   capacity = 1024
Buffer after flip:       position =  0   Limit =   50   capacity = 1024
```

You can inspect the contents of the file charData.txt using a plaintext editor. They should look something like the following:

```
G a r b a g e    i n ,    g a r b a g e    o u t . G a r b a g e    i n ,    g a r b a g e    o u t .
```

There are spaces between the characters in the output because the file contents are displayed as 8-bit characters and you are writing Unicode characters to the file where 2 bytes are written for each character in the original string. Your text editor might represent the first of each byte pair as something other than spaces, or possibly not at all, as they are bytes that contain zero. You might even find that your plaintext editor displays only the first 'G'. If so, try to find another editor. If you are using the NetBeans editor, it can display the file contents correctly. If you run the example more than once, the phrase is appended to the file again for each execution of the program.

How It Works

In the try block, you call the static createDirectories() method in the Files class to ensure that the directory is there. This method creates the directory and any subdirectories that are necessary and does nothing if the entry already exists. You then call newByteChannel() in the Files class for the file path to create a channel for the file. Because you have specified the CREATE option, the method creates the file if it does not exist. Specifying the WRITE and APPEND options opens the file for writing with new data being added to the end of the file.

Next, you create a buffer with a capacity of 1024 bytes and output the position, limit, and capacity values for the buffer. You then call putChar() for the buffer object, buf, in a loop, to copy the characters from the array that you create by calling toCharArray() for the String object. The output that follows shows that the buffer position has been changed as a result.

Calling flip() for the buffer object causes the position to be reset to zero and the limit to be set to the end of the data in the buffer, as the next line of output shows.

The FileChannel class has a size() method that returns the length of the file, in bytes, as a value of type long. You could try this out by adding the following statement immediately after the statement that writes the buffer to the channel:

```
System.out.println("\nThe file contains " + ((FileChannel)channel).size() + " bytes.");
```

You have to cast reference in the channel variable to type FileChannel in order to call the size() method. You should see that 50 bytes are written to the file each time, because phrase contains 25 characters. The size() method returns the total number of bytes in the file, so the number grows by 100 each time you run the program.

File Position

The *position* of a file is the index position of where the next byte is to be read or written in the file. The first byte in a file is at position zero so the value for a file's position is the offset of the next byte from the beginning. Don't confuse the *file* position with the position for a *buffer* that I discussed earlier — the two are quite independent.

When you write the contents of a buffer to a file using a channel, the byte at the buffer's current position is written to the file at the file's current position. This is illustrated in Figure 10-10.

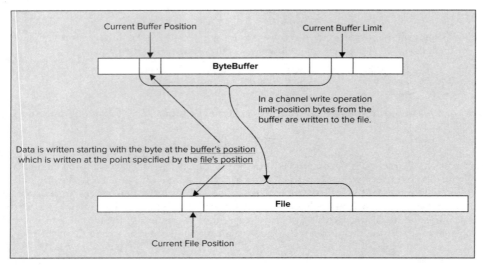

FIGURE 10-10

The file channel object keeps track of the current position in the file. If you created the file stream to append to the file by using a `FileOutputStream` constructor with the append mode argument as `true` then the file position recorded by the channel for the file starts out at the byte following the last byte. Otherwise, the initial file position is the first byte of the file. The file position is generally incremented by the number of bytes written each time you write to the file. There is one exception to this. The `SeekableByteChannel` interface declares a `write()` method that does what is presented in Table 10-10.

TABLE 10-10: SeekableByteChannel write() Method

METHOD	DESCRIPTION

`write(`
  `ByteBuffer buf,`
  `long position)`
	This writes the contents of the buffer, `buf`, to the file at the position specified by the second argument, and not the file position recorded by the channel. Bytes from the buffer are written starting at the buffer's current position, and `buf.remaining()` bytes are written. This does not update the channel's file position.

This method can throw any of the following exceptions:

➤   `IllegalArgumentException`: Thrown if you specify a negative value for the file position.

➤   `NonWritableChannelException`: Thrown if the file was not opened for writing.

➤   `ClosedChannelException`: Thrown if the channel is closed.

➤   `ClosedByInterruptException`: Thrown if another thread interrupts the current thread while the write operation is in progress.

➤   `IOException`: Thrown if any other I/O error occurs.

You might use this version of the `write()` method in a sequence of writes to update a particular part of the file without disrupting the primary sequence of write operations. For example, you might record a count of the number of records in a file at the beginning. As you add new records to the file, you could update the count at the beginning of the file without changing the file position recorded by the channel, which would be pointing to the end of the file where new data is to be written.

A `FileChannel` object has two versions of the `position()` method. The `position()` method without a parameter returns the file position as type `long`. It is of type `long` to provide for large files that could contain more than two billion bytes. You can also set the file position by calling the `position()` method with an argument of type `long` that specifies a new position. This sets the file's position to the new value. For example, if you have a reference to a file channel stored in a variable `outputChannel`, you could alter the file position with the following statements:

```
try {
  outputChannel.position(fileChannel.position() - 100L);
} catch (IOException e) {
  e.printStackTrace();
}
```

This moves the current file position back by 100 bytes. This could be because you have written 100 bytes to the file and want to reset the position so you can rewrite it. The call to the `position()` method should normally be in a `try` block because it can throw an exception of type `IOException` if an I/O error occurs.

You can set the file position beyond the end of the file. If you then write to the file, the bytes between the previous end of the file and the new position contain junk values. If you try to read from a position beyond the end of the file, an end-of-file condition is returned immediately.

Using a View Buffer to Load a Byte Buffer

The code in the previous example is not the only way of writing the string to the buffer. You could have used a view buffer, like this:

```
ByteBuffer buf = ByteBuffer.allocate(1024);
CharBuffer charBuf = buf.asCharBuffer();
charBuf.put(phrase);                    // Transfer string to buffer
buf.limit(2*charBuf.position());        // Update the byte buffer limit
```

You can then write the contents of `buf` to the channel as in the example.

Transferring the string via a view buffer of type `CharBuffer` is much simpler. The only fly in the ointment is that the backing `ByteBuffer` has no knowledge of any data you put in the view buffer. The position for `buf` is still sitting firmly at zero with the limit set as the capacity, so flipping it won't set it up ready to write to the channel. However, all you have to do is set the limit for `buf` to correspond to the number of bytes that you transferred to the view buffer.

Of course, if you were writing the file for use by some other program, writing Unicode characters could be very inconvenient if the other program environment did not understand it. In this case you would write the data as bytes in the local character encoding, as you did in the first example in this chapter.

Writing Varying Length Strings to a File

It is very often the case that you want to write strings of different lengths to a file using a channel. In this case, if you want to recover the strings from the file, you need to provide some information in the file that allows the beginning and/or end of each string to be determined. A `BufferedReader` has a `readLine()` method that enables strings that are separated by line separators to be read easily, but a channel deals with mixed character and binary data so you don't have that luxury.

One possibility is to write the length of each string to the file immediately preceding the string itself. This tells you how many characters there are in a string before you read it. You can use a view buffer to do this. Let's see how that might work in an example.

TRY IT OUT   Writing Multiple Strings to a File

This example just writes a series of useful proverbs to a file:

```java
import static java.nio.file.StandardOpenOption.*;
import java.nio.file.*;
import java.nio.channels.*;

import java.util.EnumSet;
import java.io.IOException;
import java.nio.ByteBuffer;

public class WriteProverbs {
  public static void main(String[] args) {
    String[] sayings = {
      "Indecision maximizes flexibility.",
      "Only the mediocre are always at their best.",
      "A little knowledge is a dangerous thing.",
      "Many a mickle makes a muckle.",
      "Who begins too much achieves little.",
      "Who knows most says least.",
      "A wise man sits on the hole in his carpet."
    };

    Path file = Paths.get(System.getProperty("user.home")).
                        resolve("Beginning Java Stuff").resolve("Proverbs.txt");
    try {
      // Make sure we have the directory
      Files.createDirectories(file.getParent());
    } catch (IOException e) {
      e.printStackTrace();
      System.exit(1);
    }
    System.out.println("New file is: " + file);

    // The buffer must accommodate the longest string
    // so we find the length of the longest string
    int maxLength = 0;
    for (String saying : sayings) {
      if(maxLength < saying.length())
        maxLength = saying.length();
    }

    // The buffer length must hold the longest string
    // plus its length as a binary integer
    // Each character needs 2 bytes and an integer 4 bytes
    ByteBuffer buf = ByteBuffer.allocate(2*maxLength + 4);

    try (WritableByteChannel channel = Files.newByteChannel(
                          file, EnumSet.of(WRITE, CREATE, APPEND))) {

      for (String saying : sayings) {
        buf.putInt(saying.length()).asCharBuffer().put(saying);
        buf.position(buf.position() + 2*saying.length()).flip();
        channel.write(buf);                 // Write the buffer to the file channel
        buf.clear();
      }
      System.out.println("Proverbs written to file.");
    } catch (IOException e) {
      e.printStackTrace();
    }
  }
}
```

When you execute this, it should produce the following rather terse output following the file path specification:

```
Proverbs written to file.
```

You can check the veracity of this assertion by inspecting the contents of the file with a plain text editor. Of course, the length values look strange because they are binary integer values, not characters.

How It Works

You create a `String` array, `sayings[]`, that contains seven proverbs. The same `ByteBuffer` object is used to write all of the strings so it must be large enough to hold the characters from the longest string plus a 4-byte binary integer value for the length of the string.

The strings are written to the file in the `for` loop in the `try` block that creates the `WritableByteChannel` object. You put the length of each proverb in the buffer using the `putInt()` method for the `ByteBuffer` object. You then use a view buffer of type `CharBuffer` to transfer the string to the buffer. The contents of the view buffer, `charBuffer` starts at the current position for the byte buffer. This corresponds to the byte immediately following the string length value because the `putInt()` method increments the buffer position.

Transferring the string into the view buffer causes only the view buffer's position to be updated. The byte buffer's position is still pointing at the byte following the binary string length value where the first character of the string was written. You therefore have to increment the position for the byte buffer by twice the number of characters in the string before flipping it to make it ready to be written to the file.

The first time you run the program, the file doesn't exist, so it is created. You can then look at the contents. If you run the program again, the same proverbs are appended to the file, so there is a second set. Alternatively, you could modify the `sayings[]` array to contain different proverbs the second time around. Each time the program runs, the data is added at the end of the existing file.

After writing the contents of the byte buffer to the file, you call its `clear()` method to reset the position to zero and the limit back to the capacity. This makes it ready for transferring the data for the next proverb on the next iteration. Remember that it doesn't change the contents of the buffer, though.

Using a Formatter Object to Load a Buffer

You saw the `java.util.Formatter` class when I introduced the `printf()` method that you can use with the `System.out` stream object in Chapter 8. The `Formatter` class defines a constructor that accepts a reference of type `java.lang.Appendable` as an argument, and because the `PrintStream` and `PrintWriter` classes implement the `Appendable` interface, you can construct a `Formatter` object that formats data into these objects. The `CharBuffer` class also implements the `Appendable` interface so you can create a `Formatter` object that formats data into a view buffer of type `CharBuffer`. Here's how you might create a `Formatter` object ready for use with a view buffer:

```
ByteBuffer buf = ByteBuffer.allocate(1024);      // Byte buffer
CharBuffer charBuf = buf.asCharBuffer();         // View buffer
Formatter formatter = new Formatter(charBuf);    // Formatter to write view buffer
```

You can now use the `format()` method for the `Formatter` object to format data values into the view buffer `charBuf`. Recall that the `format()` method works just like `printf()` — with the first argument being a format string and the arguments that follow specifying the data values to be formatted. Of course, writing data into the view buffer leaves the backing byte buffer's limit unchanged, so you must update this to reflect the data that is now in the buffer before attempting to write the buffer's contents to the channel. You can see how this works with a simple example.

TRY IT OUT   Using a Formatter Object to Load a Buffer

Here's the code to use a `Formatter` object to prepare the data to be written to a file:

```
import static java.nio.file.StandardOpenOption.*;
import java.nio.file.*;                          // Files  and Path
import java.nio.channels.WritableByteChannel;
import java.nio.*;                               // ByteBuffer and CharBuffer
```

```java
import java.util.*;                               // Formatter and EnumSet
import java.io.IOException;

public class UsingAFormatter {
  public static void main(String[] args) {
    String[] phrases = {"Rome wasn't burned in a day.",
                        "It's a bold mouse that sits in the cat's ear.",
                        "An ounce of practice is worth a pound of instruction."
                       };
    String separator = System.lineSeparator();       // Get line separator
    Path file = Paths.get(System.getProperty("user.home")).
                      resolve("Beginning Java Stuff").resolve("Phrases.txt");
    try {
      // Make sure we have the directory
      Files.createDirectories(file.getParent());
    } catch (IOException e) {
      e.printStackTrace();
      System.exit(1);
    }
    System.out.println("New file is: " + file);

    try (WritableByteChannel channel = Files.newByteChannel(
                            file, EnumSet.of(WRITE, CREATE, APPEND))) {

      ByteBuffer buf = ByteBuffer.allocate(1024);
      CharBuffer charBuf = buf.asCharBuffer(); // Create a view buffer
      System.out.println("Char view buffer:");
      System.out.printf("position = %2d  Limit = %4d  capacity = %4d%n",
                      charBuf.position(),charBuf.limit(),charBuf.capacity());

      Formatter formatter = new Formatter(charBuf);

      // Write to the view buffer using a formatter
      int number = 0;                             // Proverb number
      for(String phrase : phrases) {
        formatter.format("Proverb%2d: %s%s", ++number, phrase, separator);
        System.out.println("\nView buffer after loading:");
        System.out.printf("position = %2d  Limit = %4d  capacity = %4d%n",
                      charBuf.position(), charBuf.limit(),charBuf.capacity());


        charBuf.flip();                           // Flip the view buffer
        System.out.println("View buffer after flip:");
        System.out.printf("position = %2d  Limit = %4d  length = %4d%n",
                        charBuf.position(),charBuf.limit(),charBuf.length());

        buf.limit(2*charBuf.length());            // Set byte buffer limit

        System.out.println("Byte buffer after limit update:");
        System.out.printf("position = %2d  Limit = %4d  length = %4d%n",
                          buf.position(),buf.limit(), buf.remaining());

        channel.write(buf);                       // Write buffer to the channel
        System.out.println("Buffer contents written to file.");
        buf.clear();
        charBuf.clear();
      }
    } catch (IOException e) {
      e.printStackTrace();
    }
  }
}
```

UsingAFormatter.java

With this example I got the following output after the path for the file:

```
Char view buffer:
position =   0  Limit =   512  capacity =   512

View buffer after loading:
position =  41  Limit =   512  capacity =   512
View buffer after flip:
position =   0  Limit =    41  length =    41
Byte buffer after limit update:
position =   0  Limit =    82  length =    82
Buffer contents written to file.

View buffer after loading:
position =  58  Limit =   512  capacity =   512
View buffer after flip:
position =   0  Limit =    58  length =    58
Byte buffer after limit update:
position =   0  Limit =   116  length =   116
Buffer contents written to file.

View buffer after loading:
position =  66  Limit =   512  capacity =   512
View buffer after flip:
position =   0  Limit =    66  length =    66
Byte buffer after limit update:
position =   0  Limit =   132  length =   132
Buffer contents written to file.
```

You can inspect the contents of the file with a plain text editor. Remember that the data is written as Unicode characters.

How It Works

You first create an array of three strings that are written to the file. You can add more to the array if you like. I kept it at three to keep the volume of output down. You've seen the first part of the code that sets up the path and channel before, so I'm going straight to where the buffer is loaded.

You set up the byte buffer and a view buffer holding characters with the statements:

```
ByteBuffer buf = ByteBuffer.allocate(1024);
CharBuffer charBuf = buf.asCharBuffer();
```

After outputting the state of the view buffer `charBuf`, you create the `Formatter` object that you use to load the buffer:

```
Formatter formatter = new Formatter(charBuf);
```

The `format()` method for this `Formatter` object writes data to `charBuf`.

After defining the `number` variable that stores the proverb sequence number, you load the buffer and write to the file in a `for` loop like this:

```
for(String phrase : phrases) {
    // Load the buffer...
    // Write the buffer to the file...
  }
```

This loop iterates over each of the strings in the `phrases` array. You load a proverb from `phrases` into the view buffer with the statement:

```
formatter.format("Proverb%2d: %s%s", ++number, phrase, separator);
```

This transfers the incremented value of `number` followed by the string, `phrase`, and a separator character formatted according to the first argument to the `format()` method. The separator character is useful in separating records when the file is read. Executing this statement updates the position for the view buffer, but not the byte buffer.

You flip the view buffer with the statement:

```
charBuf.flip();                    // Flip the view buffer
```

Flipping the view buffer sets its limit as the current position and resets its position to 0. The `length()` method for the view buffer returns the number of characters in the buffer, which is `limit-position`. You could obtain the same result by calling the `remaining()` method that the `CharBuffer` class inherits from the `Buffer` class. You update the limit for the byte buffer with this statement:

```
buf.limit(2*charBuf.length());     // Set byte buffer limit
```

Because each Unicode character occupies 2 bytes, the statement sets the byte buffer limit to twice the number of characters in `charBuf`.

With the byte buffer set up ready to be written to the channel, you write the data to the file with the statement:

```
channel.write(buf);                // Write buffer to the channel
```

You now need to reset the limit and position for both the byte buffer and the view buffer to be ready for the next proverb to be written. The following two statements do this:

```
buf.clear();
charBuf.clear();
```

Calling the `clear()` method for a buffer sets the buffer's position back to 0 and its limit to the capacity.

This example looks a little more complicated than it really is because of all the statements tracing the states of the buffer. If you delete these, you find the code is quite short.

The output shown for this example was produced on a Microsoft Windows system where a newline is written as two characters, CR and LF. If you are using Linux or other operating systems that represent a newline as a single NL character, the values for `position` after the buffer has been loaded by the `Formatter` object are less.

Direct and Indirect Buffers

When you allocate a byte buffer by calling the static `allocate()` method for the `ByteBuffer` class, you get an *indirect buffer.* An indirect buffer is not used by the native I/O operations, which have their own buffers. Data to be written to a file has to be copied from your indirect buffer to the buffer that the native output routine uses before the write operation can take place. Similarly, after a read operation the data is copied from the input buffer used by your operating system to the indirect buffer that you allocate.

Of course, with small buffers and limited amounts of data being read, using an indirect buffer doesn't add much overhead. With large buffers and lots of data, it can make a significant difference, though. In this case, you can use the `allocateDirect()` method in the `ByteBuffer` class to allocate a *direct buffer.* The JVM tries to make sure that the native I/O operation makes use of the direct buffer, thus avoiding the overhead of the data copying process. The allocation and de-allocation of a direct buffer carries its own overhead, which might outweigh any advantages gained if the buffer size and data volumes are small.

You can test whether a buffer object encapsulates a direct buffer by calling its `isDirect()` method. This returns `true` if it is a direct buffer and `false` otherwise.

You could try this out by making a small change to the `WriteProverbs` example. Just replace the statement

```
ByteBuffer buf = ByteBuffer.allocate(2*maxLength + 4);
```

with the following two statements:

```
ByteBuffer buf = ByteBuffer.allocateDirect(2*maxLength + 4);
System.out.println("Buffer is "+ (buf.isDirect()?"":"not")+"direct.");
```

This outputs a line telling you whether the program is working with a direct buffer or not. If it is, it will produce the following output:

```
Buffer is direct.
Proverbs written to file.
```

Writing Numerical Data Using a Channel

Let's see how you could set up the primes-generating program from Chapter 4 to write the primes to a file instead of outputting them to the command line. You base the new code on the MorePrimes version of the program. Ideally, you could add a command-line argument to specify how many primes you want. This is not too difficult. Here's how the code starts off:

```java
import static java.lang.Math.ceil;
import static java.lang.Math.sqrt;
import static java.lang.Math.min;

public class PrimesToFile {
  public static void main(String[] args) {
    int primesRequired = 100;                      // Default prime count
    if (args.length > 0) {
      try {
        primesRequired = Integer.valueOf(args[0]).intValue();
      } catch (NumberFormatException e) {
        System.out.println("Prime count value invalid. Using default of "
                            + primesRequired);
      }
      // Method to generate the primes...
      // Method to create the file path...
      // Method to write the file...
    }
  }
}
```

Here, if you don't find a command-line argument that you can convert to an integer, you just use a default count of 100. The static import statements enable you to use the static methods in the Math class that you need for the calculation without qualifying their names.

You can now generate the primes with code similar to that in Chapter 4 as follows:

```java
// Calculate enough primes to fill the array
private static long[] getPrimes(long[] primes) {
  primes[0] = 2L;                                // Seed the first prime
  primes[1] = 3L;                                // and the second
  // Count of primes found - up to now, which is also the array index
  int count = 2;
  // Next integer to be tested
  long number = 5L;

  outer:
  for (; count < primes.length ; number += 2) {

    // The maximum divisor we need to try is square root of number
    long limit = (long)ceil(sqrt((double)number));

    // Divide by all the primes we have up to limit
    for (int i = 1; i < count && primes[i] <= limit; ++i)
      if (number % primes[i] == 0L)              // Is it an exact divisor?
        continue outer;                          // yes, try the next number

    primes[count++] = number;                    // We got one!
  }
  return primes;
}
```

Here's how the method to create the file path looks:

```
// Create the path for the named file in the specified directory
// in the user home directory
private static Path createFilePath(String directory, String fileName) {
  Path file = Paths.get(System.getProperty("user.home")).
                    resolve(directory).resolve(fileName);
  try {
    // Make sure we have the directory
    Files.createDirectories(file.getParent());
  } catch (IOException e) {
    e.printStackTrace();
    System.exit(1);
  }
  System.out.println("New file is: " + file);
  return file;
}
```

PrimesToFile.java

Now all you need to do is add the code to write the primes to the file. Let's put this into a working example.

TRY IT OUT   Writing Primes to a File

This program splits the primes calculation, the creation of the file path, and the operations to write the file, into separate methods. Here's the complete example, with the method that writes the file shown shaded:

```
import static java.lang.Math.ceil;
import static java.lang.Math.sqrt;
import static java.lang.Math.min;
import static java.nio.file.StandardOpenOption.*;
import java.nio.file.*;
import java.nio.channels.*;
import java.nio.*;
import java.util.*;
import java.io.IOException;

public class PrimesToFile {
  public static void main(String[] args) {
    int primesRequired = 100;                    // Default count
    if (args.length > 0) {
      try {
        primesRequired = Integer.valueOf(args[0]).intValue();
      } catch (NumberFormatException e) {
        System.out.println("Prime count value invalid. Using default of "
                           + primesRequired);
      }
    }

    long[] primes = new long[primesRequired];    // Array to store primes

    getPrimes(primes);                           // Calculate the primes
    Path file = createFilePath("Beginning Java Stuff", "primes.bin");
    writePrimesFile(primes, file);               // Write the file
  }

  // Calculate enough primes to fill the array
  private static long[] getPrimes(long[] primes) {
    primes[0] = 2L;                              // Seed the first prime
    primes[1] = 3L;                              // and the second
    // Count of primes found - up to now, which is also the array index
```

```
      int count = 2;
      // Next integer to be tested
      long number = 5L;

      outer:
      for (; count < primes.length ; number += 2) {

        // The maximum divisor we need to try is square root of number
        long limit = (long)ceil(sqrt((double)number));

        // Divide by all the primes we have up to limit
        for (int i = 1; i < count && primes[i] <= limit; ++i)
          if (number % primes[i] == 0L)              // Is it an exact divisor?
            continue outer;                          // yes, try the next number

        primes[count++] = number;                    // We got one!
      }
      return primes;
    }

    // Create the path for the named file in the specified directory
    // in the user home directory
    private static Path createFilePath(String directory, String fileName) {
      Path file = Paths.get(System.getProperty("user.home")).
                        resolve(directory).resolve(fileName);
      try {
        // Make sure we have the directory
        Files.createDirectories(file.getParent());
      } catch (IOException e) {
        e.printStackTrace();
        System.exit(1);
      }
      System.out.println("New file is: " + file);
      return file;
    }
    // Write the array contents to file
    private static void writePrimesFile(long[] primes, Path file) {
      final int BUFFERSIZE = 100;                    // Byte buffer size
      try (WritableByteChannel channel = Files.newByteChannel(
                                      file, EnumSet.of(WRITE, CREATE))) {
        ByteBuffer buf = ByteBuffer.allocate(BUFFERSIZE);
        LongBuffer longBuf = buf.asLongBuffer();     // View buffer for type long
        int primesWritten = 0;                       // Count of primes written to file
        while (primesWritten < primes.length) {
          longBuf.put(primes,                        // Array to be written
                    primesWritten,                   // Index of 1st element to write
                    min(longBuf.capacity(), primes.length - primesWritten));
          buf.limit(8*longBuf.position());           // Update byte buffer position
          channel.write(buf);
          primesWritten += longBuf.position();
          longBuf.clear();
          buf.clear();
        }
        System.out.println("File written is " +
                                  ((FileChannel)channel).size() + " bytes.");
      } catch (IOException e) {
        e.printStackTrace();
      }
    }
```

PrimesToFile.java

If you don't supply the number of primes you want as a command-line argument, this program produces the following output:

```
File written is 800 bytes.
```

This looks reasonable because you wrote 100 values of type `long` as binary data and they are 8 bytes each. I ran the program with 150 as the command-line argument.

How It Works

You call the three methods that calculate the primes, create the file path, and write the file in sequence:

```
getPrimes(primes);                                    // Calculate the primes
Path file = createFilePath("Beginning Java Stuff", "primes.bin");
writePrimesFile(primes, file);                        // Write the file
```

You could condense the three statements into one:

```
writePrimesFile(
        getPrimes(primes), createFilePath("Beginning Java Stuff", "primes.bin"));
```

The references returned by the `getPrimes()` and `createFilePath()` methods are the arguments to the `writePrimesFile()` method. This doesn't improve the readability of the code though, so there's no advantage gained by this.

The code to calculate the primes and to create a `Path` object for the specified directory and file name in the user home directory is essentially what you have seen previously so I won't repeat the discussion of these.

Because you don't specify that you want to append to the file when you create the `channel` object, the file is overwritten each time you run the program.

You create the `ByteBuffer` object with a capacity of 100 bytes. This is a poor choice for the buffer size as it is not an exact multiple of 8 — so it doesn't correspond to a whole number of prime values. However, I chose this value deliberately to make the problem of managing the buffer a bit more interesting. You can change the buffer size by changing the value specified for `BUFFERSIZE`.

The primes are transferred to the buffer through a view buffer of type `LongBuffer`. You obtain this from the original byte buffer, `buf`, by calling its `asLongBuffer()` method. Because this buffer is too small to hold all the primes, you have to load it and write the primes to the file in a loop.

The `primesWritten` variable counts how many primes have been written to the file, so you use this to control the `while` loop that writes the primes. The loop continues as long as `primesWritten` is less than the number of elements in the `primes` array. The number of primes that the `LongBuffer` object can hold corresponds to `longBuf.capacity()`. You can transfer this number of primes to the buffer as long as there is that many left in the array still to be written to the file, so you transfer a block of primes to the buffer like this:

```
longBuf.put(primes,                           // Array to be written
            primesWritten,                    // Index of 1st element to write
            min(longBuf.capacity(), primes.length - primesWritten));
```

The first argument to the `put()` method is the array that is the source of the data, and the second argument is the index position of the first element to be transferred. The third argument is the capacity of the buffer as long as there is more than that number of primes still in the array. If there is less than this number on the last iteration, you transfer `primes.length-primesWritten` values to the buffer.

Because you are using a relative put operation, loading the view buffer changes the position for that buffer to reflect the number of values transferred to it. However, the backing byte buffer that you use in the channel write operation still has its limit and position unchanged. You therefore set the limit for the byte buffer with the statement:

```
buf.limit(8*longBuf.position());
```

Each prime occupies 8 bytes, so multiplying the position value for the view buffer by 8 gives you the number of bytes occupied in the primary buffer. You then go ahead and write that buffer to the file and increment primesWritten by the position value for the view buffer, because this corresponds to the number of primes that were written. Before the next iteration, you call clear() for both buffers to reset their positions and limits to their original states — to 0 and the capacity, respectively. When you have written all the primes, the loop ends and you output the length of the file. The channel closes automatically because it was created within the try block with resources.

Because this file contains binary data, you will not want to view it except perhaps for debugging purposes.

Writing Mixed Data to a File

Sometimes, you might want to write more than one kind of binary data to a file. You might want to mix integers with floating-point values with text for example. The text might be descriptive information about each floating-point value, and there could be an integer sequence number. Generally you will want to write floating-point data as binary because the character representation of a value may not be accurate and of course it often makes sense to write text as text.

One way to do this is to use multiple view buffers. You can get an idea of how this works by outputting some text along with each binary prime value in the previous example. Rather than taking the easy route by just writing the same text for each prime value, let's add a character representation of the prime value preceding each binary value. You add something like "prime = nnn" ahead of each binary value.

The first point to keep in mind is that if you ever want to read the file successfully, you can't just dump strings of varying lengths in it. You would have no way to tell where the text ended and where the binary data began. You have to either fix the length of the string so you know how many bytes are characters when you read the file, or you must provide data in the file that specifies the length of the string. Let's therefore choose to write the data corresponding to each prime as three successive data items:

1. A count of the length of the string as binary value (it would sensibly be an integer type, but you'll make it type double because you need the practice).

2. The string representation of the prime value "prime = nnn", where obviously the number of digits vary.

3. The prime as a binary value of type long.

The basic prime calculation does not change at all, so you need only update the shaded method in the previous example that writes the file.

The basic strategy is to create a byte buffer and then create a series of view buffers that map the three different kinds of data into it. A simple approach would be to write the data for one prime at a time, so let's try that first. Setting up the channel is the same, but it is better to change the file extension to .txt so you can look at it as a text file.

```
Path file = createFilePath("Beginning Java Stuff", "primes.txt");
```

Changing the file extension to .txt also differentiates it from the original binary file that you wrote with the previous version so you retain both. You will use of both files when you are looking into file read operations in the next chapter, so don't delete them.

The byte buffer has to be large enough to hold the double value that counts the characters in the string, the string itself, plus the long value for the prime. The original byte buffer with 100 bytes capacity is plenty big enough so let's go with that. You need to create three view buffers from the byte buffer, one that holds the double value for the count, one for the string, and one for the binary prime value, but you have a problem, which is illustrated in Figure 10-11.

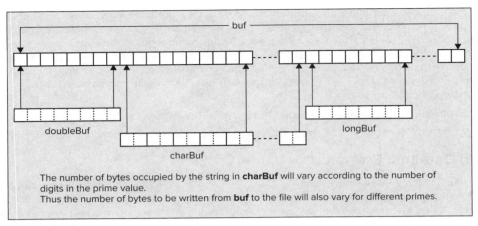

The number of bytes occupied by the string in **charBuf** will vary according to the number of digits in the prime value.
Thus the number of bytes to be written from **buf** to the file will also vary for different primes.

FIGURE 10-11

Because the length of the string depends on the number of decimal digits in the value of each prime, you don't know where it ends. This implies you can't map the last buffer, `longBuf`, to a fixed position in the byte buffer, `buf`. You are going to have to set this buffer up dynamically inside the file-writing loop after you figure out how long the string for the prime is. You can set up the first two view buffers outside the loop, though:

```
DoubleBuffer doubleBuf = buf.asDoubleBuffer();
buf.position(8);
CharBuffer charBuf = buf.asCharBuffer();
```

The first buffer that holds the string length as type `double`, maps to the beginning of the byte buffer, `buf`. The view buffer into which you place the string needs to map to the position in `buf` immediately after the space required for the `double` value — 8 bytes from the beginning of `buf`, in other words. Remember that the first element in a view buffer maps to the current position in the byte buffer. Thus, you can just set the position for `buf` to 8 before creating the view buffer, `charBuf`. All that you need to add is the loop that loads up the first two view buffers, the code to create the third view buffer and load it, and the code to write the file. Let's put the whole thing together as a working example.

TRY IT OUT Using Multiple View Buffers

The code for the loop is shaded in the following complete program:

```
import static java.lang.Math.ceil;
import static java.lang.Math.sqrt;
import static java.lang.Math.min;
import static java.nio.file.StandardOpenOption.*;
import java.nio.file.*;
import java.nio.channels.*;
import java.nio.*;
import java.util.*;
import java.io.IOException;

public class PrimesToFile2 {
  public static void main(String[] args) {
    int primesRequired = 100;                    // Default count
    if (args.length > 0) {
      try {
        primesRequired = Integer.valueOf(args[0]).intValue();
      } catch (NumberFormatException e) {
        System.out.println("Prime count value invalid. Using default of "
                          + primesRequired);
      }
    }
```

```
        long[] primes = new long[primesRequired];    // Array to store primes

        getPrimes(primes);                             // Calculate the primes
        Path file = createFilePath("Beginning Java Stuff", "primes.txt");
        writePrimesFile(primes, file);                 // Write the file
    }

    // getPrimes() method as in the previous example...

    // createFilePath() method as in the previous example...

    // Write the array contents to file
    private static void writePrimesFile(long[] primes, Path file) {
        final int BUFFERSIZE = 100;                    // Byte buffer size
        try (WritableByteChannel channel = Files.newByteChannel(
                                  file, EnumSet.of(WRITE, CREATE))) {
            ByteBuffer buf = ByteBuffer.allocate(BUFFERSIZE);
            DoubleBuffer doubleBuf = buf.asDoubleBuffer();
            buf.position(8);
            CharBuffer charBuf = buf.asCharBuffer();
            LongBuffer longBuf = null;
            String primeStr = null;

            for (long prime : primes) {
                primeStr = "prime = " + prime;                   // Create the string
                doubleBuf.put(0, (double)primeStr.length());     // Store the string length
                charBuf.put(primeStr);                           // Store the string
                buf.position(2*charBuf.position() + 8);          // Position for 3rd buffer
                longBuf = buf.asLongBuffer();                    // Create the buffer
                longBuf.put(prime);                      // Store the binary long value
                buf.position(buf.position() + 8);        // Set position after last value
                buf.flip();                              // and flip
                channel.write(buf);                      // Write the buffer as before

                buf.clear();
                doubleBuf.clear();
                charBuf.clear();
            }
            System.out.println("File written is " +
                                     ((FileChannel)channel).size() + " bytes.");
        } catch (IOException e) {
            e.printStackTrace();
        }
    }
}
```

PrimesToFile2.java

With the default number of primes to be generated, this example should produce the following output following the file path:

```
File written is 3742 bytes.
```

 NOTE *If you run the example to generate a given number of primes and then run it again, the file is overwritten. Of course, if you generate fewer primes when you rerun the program, the file size does not go down!*

How It Works

I'm discussing only the body of the collection-based `for` loop that iterates over the elements in the `primes` array because that's the new functionality in the example. It is shown in bold.

You create the string first because you need to know its length so you can put the length in the buffer first. You insert the length as type `double` in the view buffer, `doubleBuf`. You then put the string into `charBuf` as this buffer already maps to the position starting 8 bytes along from the start of `buf`. Next, you update the position in `buf` to the element following the string. This enables you to map `longBuf` to the correct position in the byte buffer. After creating the third view buffer, `longBuf`, you load the prime value. You then update the position for `buf` to the byte following this value. This is the position as previously set plus 8. Finally, you flip `buf` to set the position and limit for writing, and then write the contents of `buf` to the file channel.

If you inspect the file with a plain text editor you should get an idea of what is in the file. You should be able to see the Unicode strings separated by the binary values you have written to the file. Of course, the binary value doesn't look particularly meaningful when viewed as characters.

This example writes the file one prime at a time, so it's not going to be very efficient. It would be better to use a larger buffer and load it with multiple primes. Let's explore how you might do that with another version of the program.

TRY IT OUT Multiple Records in a Buffer

You load the byte buffer using three different view buffers repeatedly to put data for as many primes into the buffer as you can. The basic idea is illustrated in Figure 10-12.

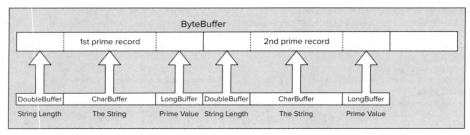

FIGURE 10-12

I'm just showing the new code that replaces the code in the previous example here. This is the code that allocates the buffers and writes the file:

```
// import statements as before...

public class PrimesToFile3 {
  public static void main(String[] args) {
    int primesRequired = 100;                    // Default count
    if (args.length > 0) {
      try {
        primesRequired = Integer.valueOf(args[0]).intValue();
      } catch (NumberFormatException e) {
        System.out.println("Prime count value invalid. Using default of "
                           + primesRequired);
      }
    }

    long[] primes = new long[primesRequired];    // Array to store primes

    getPrimes(primes);                           // Calculate the primes
    Path file = createFilePath("Beginning Java Stuff", "primesAgain.txt");
    writePrimesFile(primes, file);               // Write the file
  }

  // getPrimes() method as in the previous example...
```

```
        // createFilePath() method as in the previous example...

        // Write the array contents to file
        private static void writePrimesFile(long[] primes, Path file) {
          final int BUFFERSIZE = 1024;                   // Buffer size in bytes - bigger!
          try (WritableByteChannel channel = Files.newByteChannel(
                                           file, EnumSet.of(WRITE, CREATE))) {
            ByteBuffer buf = ByteBuffer.allocate(BUFFERSIZE);
            String primeStr = null;
            int primesWritten = 0;

            while (primesWritten < primes.length) {
              while (primesWritten < primes.length) {
                primeStr = "prime = " + primes[primesWritten];
                if ((buf.position() + 2*primeStr.length() + 16) > buf.limit()) {
                  break;
                }
                buf.asDoubleBuffer().put(0, (double)primeStr.length());
                buf.position(buf.position() + 8);
                buf.position(buf.position()
                                  + 2*buf.asCharBuffer().put(primeStr).position());
                buf.asLongBuffer().put(primes[primesWritten++]);
                buf.position(buf.position() + 8);
              }
              buf.flip();
              channel.write(buf);
              buf.clear();
            }
            System.out.println("File written is " +
                                    ((FileChannel)channel).size() + " bytes.");
          } catch (IOException e) {
            e.printStackTrace();
          }
        }
      }
```

PrimesToFile3.java

You should get the same output about the file size as for the previous example here.

How It Works

In the `writePrimesFile()` method, you first create a byte buffer with a capacity of 1024 bytes. All the view buffers are created inside the inner `while` loop. Both loops end when the value of `primesWritten`, which counts the number of primes written to the file, reaches the length of the `primes` array. The inner loop loads up the buffer and the outer loop writes the contents of the buffer to the file.

The first step in the inner loop is to create the prime string. This makes it possible to check whether there is enough free space in the byte buffer to accommodate the string plus the two binary values — the string length as type `double` and the binary prime value of type `long` that together require 16 bytes. If there isn't enough space, the `break` statement is executed so the inner loop ends, and the channel writes the buffer contents to the file after flipping it. After the buffer has been written, the buffer's `clear()` method is called to reset the position to 0 and the limit to the capacity.

When there is space in the byte buffer, the inner loop loads the buffer starting with the statement:

```
        buf.asDoubleBuffer().put(0, (double)primeStr.length());
```

This creates a view buffer of type `DoubleBuffer` and calls its `put()` method to transfer the length of the string to the buffer. You don't save the view buffer reference because you need a different view buffer on the next iteration — one that maps to the position in the byte buffer following the data that you are transferring for the current prime.

The next statement increments the position of the byte buffer by the number of bytes in the string length value. You then execute the statement:

```
buf.position(buf.position()
              + 2*buf.asCharBuffer().put(primeStr).position());
```

This statement is a little complicated so let's dissect it. The expression for the argument to the `position()` method within the parentheses executes first. This calculates the new position for `buf` as the current position, given by `buf.position()`, plus the value resulting from the expression:

```
2*buf.asCharBuffer().put(primeStr).position()
```

The subexpression, `buf.asCharBuffer()`, creates a view buffer of type `CharBuffer`. You call the `put()` method for this buffer to transfer `primeStr` to it, and this returns a reference to the `CharBuffer` object. You use this reference to call the `put()` method for the `CharBuffer` object to transfer the string. You use the reference that the `put()` method returns to call the `position()` method for the `CharBuffer` object, which returns the buffer position after the string has been transferred, so multiplying this value by 2 gives the number of bytes occupied by the string in `buf`. Thus, you update the position for `buf` to the point following the string that you transfer to the buffer.

The last step in the inner loop is to execute the following statements:

```
buf.asLongBuffer().put(primes[primesWritten++]);
buf.position(buf.position() + 8);
```

The first statement here transfers the binary prime value to the buffer via a view buffer of type `LongBuffer` and increments the count of the number of primes written to the file. The second statement updates the position for `buf` to the next available byte. The inner `while` loop then continues with the next iteration to load the data for the next prime into the buffer. This continues until there is insufficient space for data for another prime, whereupon the inner loop ends, and the buffer is written to the file in the outer loop.

Writing from Multiple Buffers

I will introduce one further file channel output capability before you try reading a file — the ability to transfer data to a file from several buffers in sequence in a single write operation. This is called a *gathering-write* operation. The advantage of this capability is that it avoids the necessity to copy information into a single buffer before writing it to a file. A gathering-write operation is one side of what are called *scatter-gather I/O operations*. You look into the other side — the *scattering-read* operation — in the next chapter.

A file channel has two methods declared by the `GatheringByteChannel` interface that performs gathering-write operations from an array of `ByteBuffer` objects:

➤ `write(ByteBuffers[] buffers)`: Writes bytes from each of the buffers in the buffers array to the file in sequence, starting at the channel's current file position.

➤ `write(ByteBuffers[] buffers,
   int offset, int length)`:
   Writes data to the file starting at the channel's current file position from buffers[offset] to buffers [offset+length − 1] inclusive and in sequence.

Both methods can throw the same exceptions as the write method for a single `ByteBuffer` object. The second of these methods can also throw an `IndexOutOfBoundsException` if offset or offset+length−1 is not a legal index value for the `buffers` array.

The data that is written from each buffer to the file is determined from that buffer's position and limit, in the way you have seen. One obvious application of the gathering-write operation is when you are reading data from several different files into separate buffers, and you want to merge the data into a single file. You can also use multiple buffers, each with its own view buffer where necessary, as an alternative to multiple views of a single `ByteBuffer`. You can see how it works by using yet another variation on the primes-writing program.

The Gathering Write

In this example, you set up the string length, the string itself, and the binary prime value in separate byte buffers. You also write the prime string as bytes in the local encoding.

Here's the code:

```java
import static java.lang.Math.ceil;
import static java.lang.Math.sqrt;
import static java.nio.file.StandardOpenOption.*;
import java.nio.file.*;
import java.nio.channels.*;
import java.nio.*;
import java.util.*;
import java.io.IOException;

public class GatheringWrite {
  public static void main(String[] args) {
    int primesRequired = 100;                    // Default count
    if (args.length > 0) {
      try {
        primesRequired = Integer.valueOf(args[0]).intValue();
      } catch (NumberFormatException e) {
        System.out.println("Prime count value invalid. Using default of "
                           + primesRequired);
      }
    }

    long[] primes = new long[primesRequired];    // Array to store primes

    getPrimes(primes);                           // Calculate the primes
    Path file = createFilePath(
                    "Beginning Java Stuff", "GatheringWritePrimes.txt");
    writePrimesFile(primes, file);               // Write the file
  }

  // getPrimes() method as in the previous example...

  // createFilePath() method as in the previous example...

  // Write the array contents to file
  private static void writePrimesFile(long[] primes, Path file) {
    try (GatheringByteChannel channel =
        (FileChannel)(Files.newByteChannel(file, EnumSet.of(WRITE, CREATE)))){
      ByteBuffer[] buffers = new ByteBuffer[3];  // Array of buffer references
      buffers[0] = ByteBuffer.allocate(8);       // To hold a double value
      buffers[2] = ByteBuffer.allocate(8);       // To hold a long value

      String primeStr = null;
      for (long prime : primes) {
        primeStr = "prime = " + prime;
        buffers[0].putDouble((double) primeStr.length()).flip();

        // Create the second buffer to accommodate the string
        buffers[1] = ByteBuffer.allocate(primeStr.length());
        buffers[1].put(primeStr.getBytes()).flip();

        buffers[2].putLong(prime).flip();
        channel.write(buffers);
        buffers[0].clear();
        buffers[2].clear();
      }
```

```
                System.out.println("File written is " +
                                      ((FileChannel)channel).size() + " bytes.");
            } catch (IOException e) {
              e.printStackTrace();
            }
          }
        }
      }
```

GatheringWrite.java

When you execute this with the default of 100 primes generated, it should produce the following output about the file size:

```
    File written is 2671 bytes.
```

The length of the file is considerably less than before, because you are writing the string as bytes rather than Unicode characters. The part of the code that is different is shown shaded and I'll concentrate on explaining that.

How It Works

This time you want the channel variable to be stored as type GatheringByteChannel because that interface declares the gathering write methods. To do this you must first cast the SeekableByteChannel reference that the newByteChannel() method returns to type FileChannel. This is necessary because the SeekableByteChannel interface does not implement the GatheringByteChannel interface, as you can see if you refer to Figure 10-9. Of course, you could also store the reference in a variable of type FileChannel, which would make all the methods in the class available.

You use three byte buffers — one for the string length, one for the string itself, and one for the binary prime value:

```
      ByteBuffer[] buffers = new ByteBuffer[3];    // Array of buffer references
```

You create a ByteBuffer[] array with three elements to hold references to the buffers that you need. The buffers to hold the string length and the prime value are fixed in length so you are able to create those straightaway to hold 8 bytes each:

```
      buffers[0] = ByteBuffer.allocate(8);         // To hold a double value
      buffers[2] = ByteBuffer.allocate(8);         // To hold a long value
```

Because the string length can vary, you have to create the buffer that holds the string dynamically. You do this inside the for loop that iterates over all the prime values you have in the primes array.

After assembling the prime string as primeStr, you transfer the length of this string to the first buffer in the array:

```
        buffers[0].putDouble((double) primeStr.length()).flip();
```

Note that you are able to flip the buffer in the same statement after the data value has been transferred, so it is set up ready to be written to the file. This uses the buffer reference that the putDouble() method returns to call flip().

Next, you create the buffer to accommodate the string, load the byte array equivalent of the string, and flip the buffer:

```
        buffers[1] = ByteBuffer.allocate(primeStr.length());
        buffers[1].put(primeStr.getBytes()).flip();
```

All of the put() methods for the byte buffers you are using in this example automatically update the buffer position, so you can flip each buffer as soon as the data is loaded. As an alternative to allocating this byte buffer directly to accommodate the byte array from the string, you could call the static wrap() method in the ByteBuffer class that wraps a byte array. You could achieve the same as the previous two statements with the following single statement:

```
        buffers[1] = ByteBuffer.wrap(primeStr.getBytes());
```

The `wrap()` method creates a buffer with a capacity that is the same as the length of the array with the position set to zero and the limit to the capacity. Consequently, you don't need to flip the buffer — it is already in a state to be written.

The third buffer in the array holds the binary prime value:

```
buffers[2].putLong(prime).flip();
```

This is essentially the same mechanism as you used to load the first buffer in the array. Here, you use `putLong()` to store the prime value and call `flip()` using the reference that is returned.

The three buffers are ready, so you write the array of buffers to the file like this:

```
channel.write(buffers);
```

This applies the gathering-write operation to write the contents of the three buffers in the `buffers` array to the file.

Finally, you ready the first and third buffers for the next iteration by calling the `clear()` method for each of them:

```
buffers[0].clear();
buffers[2].clear();
```

Of course, the second buffer is re-created on each iteration, so there's no need to clear it. Surprisingly easy, wasn't it?

FORCING DATA TO BE WRITTEN TO A DEVICE

A `write()` method for a channel returns when the write operation is complete, but this does not guarantee that the data has actually been written to the file. Some of the data might still reside in the native I/O buffers in memory. If the data you are writing is critical and you want to minimize the risk of losing it in the event of a system crash, you can force completion of all outstanding output operations to a file that were previously executed by the channel by calling the `force()` method for the `FileChannel` object. The argument to `force()` is a `boolean` value, `false` specifying that only the data needs to be forced to the storage device and `true` specifying both data and metadata must be written. You could use it like this:

```
try( ... create the channel object... ) {
  ...
  for(...) {
    //Write to the channel...
    outputChannel.force(true);            // Force output to the file
    // ...
  }
} catch (IOException e) {
  e.printStackTrace();
}
```

Here, critical data is being written to a file in a loop. Calling the `force()` method after each write operation minimizes the risk of data loss in the event of a system crash. The `force()` method throws a `ClosedChannelException` if the channel is closed, or an `IOException` if some other I/O error occurs. Note that the `force()` method guarantees only that all data is written for a local storage device. If the ultimate destination for the data you are writing using the channel is a storage device elsewhere on a network, you have no direct way to guarantee that the data gets written to the device.

Only one write operation can be in progress for a given file channel at any time. If you call `write()` while a `write()` operation that was initiated by another thread is in progress, your call to the `write()` method blocks until the write that's in progress has been completed.

SUMMARY

In this chapter, you explored the most important facilities for writing basic types of data to a file. The static methods in the Files class create the objects you need for writing files. You now have acquired knowledge of what you need to be able to write files. Reading files is the subject of the next chapter. Writing and reading objects is a little different from regular file input and output, which you learn about in Chapter 12.

EXERCISES

You can download the source code for the examples in the book and the solutions to the following exercises from www.wrox.com.

1. Implement a new version of the example that writes proverbs to a file that writes the proverbs to one file using a `Writer` and the length of each proverb to a separate file using an `OutputStream` object.

2. Write a program that creates an integer array of date values containing month, day, and year as integers for some number of dates (10, say, so the integer array is two-dimensional with 10 rows and 3 columns). The program should write a file with a string representation of each date written as Unicode characters. For example, the date values 3,2,1990 would be written to the file as 2nd March 1990. Make sure that the date strings can be read back, either by using a separator character of some kind to mark the end of each string or by writing the length of each string before you write the string itself.

3. Extend the previous example to write a second file at the same time as the first, but containing the month, day, and year values as binary data. You should have both files open and be writing to both at the same time.

4. Write a program that, for a given `String` object defined in the code, writes strings to a file in the local character encoding (as bytes) corresponding to all possible permutations of the words in the string. For example, for the string `the fat cat`, you would write the strings `the fat cat`, `the cat fat`, `cat the fat`, `cat fat the`, `fat the cat`, and `fat cat the` to the file, although not necessarily in that sequence. (Don't use very long strings; with *n* words in the string, the number of permutations is *n*!, so a string with 10 words has 3,628,800 permutations!).

▶ **WHAT YOU LEARNED IN THIS CHAPTER**

TOPIC	CONCEPT
Channels	A `FileChannel` object encapsulates a connection to a file for reading or writing or both.
Obtaining a Channel for a File	A `FileChannel` object for a file is obtained by calling the static `newByteChannel()` method in the `Files` class with a `Path` object that encapsulates the file path as the first argument. The reference to the object is returned as type `SeekableByteChannel`.
Channel Interfaces	The `FileChannel` class implements several channel interfaces including `WritableByteChannel` that declares the `write()` method that you use to write to a channel, `ReadableByteChannel` that declares the `read()` method that you use to read from a channel, and `SeekableByteChannel` that extends the other two interfaces and declares further methods. The `GatheringWriteChannel` and `GatheringReadChannel` interfaces declare methods that work with arrays of buffers.
Random Access to a File	The `SeekableByteChannel` interface provide the capability for writing to any position in a file.
File Position	A file has a position value that indicates the index position in the file where the next byte is written or read. A `FileChannel` object keeps track of the current file position and enables you to modify it. The position for a file is independent of the position for a buffer.
Buffers	A buffer contains data to be written to a file or data that has been read from a file. Only `ByteBuffer` objects can be used directly in file I/O operations using a channel.
Data in a Buffer	A buffer's position is the index position of the first item of data in the buffer to be written or read. A buffer's limit specifies the index position of the first data item in the buffer that is not to be written or read.
View Buffers	A view buffer is a buffer that allows the data in a backing byte buffer to be viewed as being of a particular basic type.
Transferring Data to and from a Buffer	You insert data into a buffer using its `put()` methods and retrieve data from it using its `get()` methods. Relative `get()` and `put()` methods increment the buffer's position, whereas absolute `get()` and `put()` methods do not.
Writing a Buffer to a Channel	You write the contents of a `ByteBuffer` object to a file using a `write()` method belonging to the `FileChannel` object for the file.
Data Transfer between a Buffer and a Channel	The amount of data transferred between a buffer and a channel in an I/O operation is determined by the buffer's position and limit. Data is read or written starting at the file's current position.

11

Reading Files

WHAT YOU'LL LEARN IN THIS CHAPTER

➤ How to obtain a file channel for reading a file

➤ How to use buffers in file channel read operations

➤ How to read different types of data from a file

➤ How to retrieve data from random positions in a file

➤ How you can read from and write to the same file

➤ How you can do direct data transfer between channels

➤ What a memory-mapped file is and how you can access a memory-mapped file

➤ What a file lock is and how you can lock all or part of a file

In this chapter you investigate how you read files containing basic types of data. You explore how to read files sequentially or at random and how you can open a file for both read and write operations.

FILE READ OPERATIONS

The process for reading a file parallels that of writing a file so if you are comfortable with writing files, this chapter is going to be easy. You have three ways for reading files, all provided by static methods in the `java.nio.file.Files` class:

➤ The `newInputStream()` method returns an `InputStream` object, which you can use to read a binary file.

➤ The `newBufferedReader()` method returns a `BufferedReader` object, which you can use to read a file containing character data.

➤ The `newByteChannel()` method that you used in the Chapter 10 returns a reference to a `FileChannel` object as type `SeekableByteChannel`, which you can use to read a file when the `READ` open option is in effect. You can read binary or character data from the file.

I cover the first two briefly because they are quite simple and then concentrate on the third option, which uses a `FileChannel` object.

Reading a File Using an Input Stream

Here's how you create an input stream to read a given file from the beginning:

```
Path file = Paths.get(System.getProperty("user.home")).
                    resolve("Beginning Java Stuff").resolve("MyFile.txt");
// Make sure we have a directory...

try(BufferedInputStream in =
                  new BufferedInputStream(Files.newInputStream(file))){
  // read the file...
} catch(IOException e) {
  e.printStackTrace();
}
```

The first argument to the `newInputStream()` method is the path to the file. You can supply optional arguments following the first to specify the open options to be in effect when the file is opened. These are the options from the `java.nio.file.StandardOpenOption` enumeration that you saw in the previous chapter. The `newInputStream()` method assumes the READ open option if you do not specify any options. The method can throw the following exceptions:

➤ `IllegalArgumentException` if you specify an invalid combination of options

➤ `UnsupportedOperationException` if you specify an option that is not supported

➤ `IOException` if an I/O error occurs while opening the file

➤ `SecurityException` if the installed security manager determines that you are not permitted to read the file

Wrapping the `InputStream` object that the method returns in a `java.io.BufferedInputStream` object provides more efficient read operations. The stream has an internal buffer of a default size that is automatically filled by reading from the file as you read from the buffered stream. You can create a `BufferedInputStream` object with a buffer of a given size by specifying a second argument to the constructor of type `int` that determines the capacity of the stream buffer in bytes.

Buffered Stream Read Operations

You have two methods that read from a buffered input stream:

➤ `read()` reads a single byte from the stream buffer and returns it as a value of type `int`. If the end-of-file (EOF) is reached, the method returns −1.

➤ `read(byte[] bytes, int offset, int length)` reads up to `length` bytes from the stream and stores them in the `bytes` array starting at index position `offset`. Less than `length` bytes are read if there are fewer than this number of bytes available up to end-of-file. The method returns the actual number of bytes read as type `int` or −1 if no bytes were read because EOF was reached. The method throws a `NullPointerException` if the first argument is null and an `IndexOutOfBoundsException` if `offset` or `length` are invalid or if the `bytes.length-offset` is less than `length`.

Both methods throw an `IOException` if the stream has been closed or if an I/O error occurs.

You can skip over a given number of bytes in the file by calling the `skip()` method for the stream object. You specify the number of bytes that you want to skip as an argument of type `long`. The method returns the actual number of bytes skipped as a `long` value. The method throws an `IOException` if an I/O error occurs or if the underlying stream does not support seek, which means when `mark()` and `reset()` operations are not supported.

The `available()` method for a `BufferedInputStream` returns an estimate of the number of bytes you can read or skip over without blocking as a value of type `int`. A stream can be blocked if another thread of execution is reading from the same file.

Marking a Stream

You can mark the current position in a buffered stream by calling mark() for the stream object. The **argument** to this method is an integer specifying the number of bytes that can be read or skipped before the current mark is invalidated. You can return to the position in the stream that you have marked by calling the reset() method for the stream object. This enables you to read a section of a file repeatedly.

The markSupported() method for a BufferedInputStream object tests if the stream supports marking the stream. It returns true if mark() and reset() are supported and false otherwise.

Let's try an example.

TRY IT OUT   Reading a Binary File

In this example, you read the fibonacci.bin file that you created in the Junk directory in the previous chapter.

Available for
download on
Wrox.com

```java
import java.nio.file.*;
import java.nio.*;
import java.io.*;

public class StreamInputFromFile {
  public static void main(String[] args) {

    Path file = Paths.get(System.getProperty("user.home")).
                       resolve("Beginning Java Stuff").resolve("fibonnaci.bin");

    if(!Files.exists(file)) {
      System.out.println(file + " does not exist. Terminating program.");
      System.exit(1);
    }

    final int count = 6;                          // Number of values to be read each time

    // Buffer to hold count values
    ByteBuffer buf = ByteBuffer.allocate(8*count);

    LongBuffer values = buf.asLongBuffer();
    byte[] bytes = buf.array();                   // Backing array for buf
    int totalRead = 0;                            // Total value read
    try(BufferedInputStream fileIn =
                      new BufferedInputStream(Files.newInputStream(file))){
      int numberRead = 0;
      while(true) {
        numberRead = fileIn.read(bytes, 0, bytes.length);
        if(numberRead == -1)                      // EOF reached
          break;
        totalRead += numberRead/8;                // Increment total

        for(int i = 0 ; i < numberRead/8 ; ++i)   // Access as many as there are
          System.out.format("%12d", values.get());

        System.out.println();                     // New line
        values.flip();                            // Reset for next input
      }
    System.out.format("%d  values read.%n", totalRead);
    } catch(IOException e) {
      System.err.println("Error writing file: " + file);
      e.printStackTrace();
    }
  }
}
```

I got the following output:

```
         0            1            1            2            3            5
         8           13           21           34           55           89
       144          233          377          610          987         1597
      2584         4181         6765        10946        17711        28657
     46368        75025       121393       196418       317811       514229
    832040      1346269      2178309      3524578      5702887      9227465
  14930352     24157817     39088169     63245986    102334155    165580141
 267914296    433494437    701408733   1134903170   1836311903   2971215073
4807526976   7778742049
50   values read.
```

It looks as though I got the same number of values back from the file as I wrote, which is very encouraging.

How It Works

After creating the file path you verify that it does really exist. If the file does not exist, you end the program. After you are sure the file is there, you set up the buffers you use to read the file. A ByteBuffer is convenient here because you can pass the backing byte array to the read() method for the stream to read the data and use a view buffer for values of type long to retrieve the Fibonacci numbers. You create the ByteBuffer with a capacity for 6 values of type long because you can output this many on a single line. The totalRead variable accumulates the number of values that you read from the file.

You create a BufferedInputStream object that wraps the InputStream object that is returned by the getInputStream() method for efficient stream input operations. You don't need to specify any open options for the file because the default option is READ.

You read the file in the indefinite while loop into the bytes array that backs buf. The loop is terminated when the read() method for the stream returns −1, indicating that EOF has been reach. You access the data that was read through the view buffer, values:

```
for(int i = 0 ; i < numberRead/8 ; ++i)    // Access as many as there are
  System.out.format("%12d", values.get());
```

You can't use the value that the hasRemaining() method for the view buffer returns to indicate how many values you have available because the position and limit for the view buffer are not updated when you read data into the bytes array. The read operation does not involve buf or values in any direct way and only the get() and put() methods for a buffer update the position and limit. However, numberRead does reflect the number of bytes actually read from the file, so dividing this by 8 gives you the number of values read for each operation.

Using get() for the view buffer does change its position so you need to call flip() for values to reset its state ready for the next loop iteration.

At the end of the try block, the stream and the file are closed automatically.

If you want to try marking the input stream to re-read it, you could replace the try block in the example with the following code:

```
boolean markIt = true;
while(true) {
  if(markIt)
    fileIn.mark(fileIn.available());

  numberRead = fileIn.read(bytes, 0, bytes.length);
  if(numberRead == -1)                         // EOF reached
    break;

  totalRead += numberRead/8;                   // Increment total

  for(int i = 0 ; i < numberRead/8 ; ++i)      // Read long buffer
    System.out.format("%12d", values.get());

  System.out.println();                        // New line
  values.flip();                               // Reset for next input
```

```
        if(markIt)
          fileIn.reset();

        markIt = !markIt;
      }
    System.out.format("%d  values read.%n", totalRead);
    } catch(IOException e) {
      System.err.println("Error writing file: " + file);
      e.printStackTrace();
    }
```

This uses a `boolean` variable, `markIt`, that flip-flops between `true` and `false` in the `while` loop. When `markIt` is `true`, you call `mark()` to mark the stream and after the input has been processed you call `reset()` to reset the stream to the mark. When `markIt` is `false` you don't reset the stream to the mark. This has the effect of reading and processing each block of input twice. You might want to do this when you were unsure about the format of the data. You could read the input from the stream once and check key items to ascertain whether it had been read correctly. If it has not, you could read it again using a different type of view buffer.

Reading a File Using a Buffered Reader

You can create a `BufferedReader` object that can read a given character file by calling the static `newBufferedReader()` method defined by the `java.nio.file.Files` class. The first argument is a reference to a `Path` object specifying the file that is to be read and the second argument is a reference to a `Charset` object that is the charset to be used for converting the bytes to Unicode characters. I discussed `Charset` objects in the previous chapter so I won't repeat it here. Here's how you might create a buffered reader for reading a file specified by a `Path` object, `path`:

```
BufferedReader inFile = Files.newBufferedReader(path, Charset.forName("UTF-16"));
```

The `newBufferedReader()` method throws an `IOException` if an I/O error occurs when opening the file so it should be in a `try` block.

There are three methods that a `BufferedReader` object provides for reading the file:

➤ `read()` reads a single character from the file and returns it as type `int`. The method returns -1 if EOF is read.

➤ `read(char[] chars, int offset, int length)` attempts to read `length` characters from the file storing them in the `chars` array beginning at index position `offset`. The method returns the number of characters read or −1 if EOF is the first character read.

➤ `readLine()` reads a line of text from the file that is terminated by a line separator character and returns it as type `String`. The method returns null if EOF was reached.

All three methods throw an `IOException` if an I/O error occurs.

You can skip over characters in the file by calling the `skip()` method for the buffered reader. You specify the number of characters to be skipped as an argument of type `long`. It returns the actual number of characters skipped and throws an `IOException` if an I/O error occurs. It throws an `IllegalArgumentException` if you supply a negative argument.

You have `mark()`, `reset()`, and `markSupported()` methods available for a buffered reader that work in the same way as for a buffered input stream. Let's see a `BufferedReader` object in action.

TRY IT OUT   Reading a File Using a Buffered Reader

This example uses a `BufferedReader` object to read the `Sayings.txt` file that you wrote in the previous chapter using a `BufferedWriter` object:

```
import java.io.*;
import java.nio.file.*;
import java.nio.charset.Charset;
```

```
public class ReaderInputFromFile {
  public static void main(String[] args) {
    Path file = Paths.get(System.getProperty("user.home")).
                      resolve("Beginning Java Stuff").resolve("Sayings.txt");
    if(!Files.exists(file)) {
      System.out.println(file + " does not exist. Terminating program.");
      System.exit(1);;
    }

    try(BufferedReader fileIn =
                new BufferedReader(Files.newBufferedReader(
                                      file, Charset.forName("UTF-16")))){
      String saying = null;              // Stores a saying
      int totalRead = 0;                 // Acumulates number of sayings
      // Read sayings until we reach reach EOF
      while((saying = fileIn.readLine()) != null) {
        System.out.println(saying);
        ++totalRead;                     // Increment count
      }
      System.out.format("%d  sayings read.%n", totalRead);
    } catch(IOException e) {
      System.err.println("Error writing file: " + file);
      e.printStackTrace();
    }
  }
}
```

ReaderInputFromFile.java

I got the following output:

```
A nod is as good as a wink to a blind horse.
Least said, soonest mended.
There are 10 kinds of people in the world, those that understand binary
                                               and those that don't.
You can't make a silk purse out of a sow's ear.
Hindsight is always twenty-twenty.
Existentialism has no future.
Those who are not confused are misinformed.
Better untaught that ill-taught.
8  sayings read.
```

The similarity to what was written in the previous chapter is uncanny.

How It Works

Because each saying is terminated by a line separator, it's easy to read the file back. The readLine() method for the BufferedReader object returns either a string, or null when EOF is read. Reading the file and storing the result happens in the loop expression. The while loop, therefore, continues until you reach the end of the file. The loop just writes each saying to standard output and increments the count of the number of lines read. It couldn't be simpler!

READING A FILE USING A CHANNEL

You would use channels for file I/O when high-performance is a primary requirement and when you need multi-threaded to a file. That doesn't apply in our simple examples but they will show you how you can work with a channel. You used the static newByteChannel() method from the Files class in the previous chapter to obtain a FileChannel object that writes a file. If you supply no explicit open option arguments, the READ option is the default. You can then use the channel to read data from the file into one or more buffers. For example:

```
Path file = Paths.get("D:/Junk/MyFile.txt");
// Make sure we have a directory...
try(ReadableByteChannel inCh = Files.newByteChannel(file)){
  // read the file...
} catch(IOException e) {
  e.printStackTrace(System.err);
}
```

This creates a reference to a `FileChannel` object in the `inCh` variable with the file that is specified by the `file` argument opened for reading. Of course, there's no harm in explicitly specifying the READ option when you want to read a file.

File Channel Read Operations

The following three `FileChannel` read operations read bytes starting at the byte indicated by the current position in the file:

➤ `int read(ByteBuffer buf))`: Tries to read `buf.remaining()` bytes (equivalent to `limit-position` bytes) from the file into the buffer, `buf`, starting at the buffer's current position. The number of bytes read is returned, or −1 if the channel reaches the end-of-file during the operation. The buffer position is incremented by the number of bytes read and the buffer's limit is left unchanged.

➤ `int read(ByteBuffer[] buffers))`: Tries to read bytes into each of the buffers in the `buffers` array in sequence. Bytes are read into each buffer starting at the point defined by that buffer's position. The number of bytes read into each buffer is defined by the `remaining()` method for that buffer. The `read()` method returns the total number of bytes read or −1 if the channel reaches the end-of-file during the operation. Each buffer's position is incremented by the number of bytes read into it. Each buffer's limit is unchanged.

➤ `int read(ByteBuffer[] buffers,int offset, int length))`: This operations works in the same way as the previous method except that bytes are read starting with the buffer `buffers[offset]`, up to and including the buffer `buffers[offset+length-1]`. This method throws an exception of type `IndexOutOfBoundsException` if `offset` or `offset+length-1` are not valid index values for the `buffers` array.

As you can see, all three `read()` methods read data into one or more buffers of type `ByteBuffer`. The file position is incremented by the number of bytes read. Because you can use only `ByteBuffer` objects to receive the data read from the file, you can only read data as a series of bytes. How you interpret these bytes afterward, though, is up to you. View buffers provide you with a lot of possibilities.

These methods are distributed among the channel interfaces so the type you use to store the reference to the channel object can be important. The first `read()` method in the list that reads bytes into a single buffer is declared in the `ReadableByteChannel` interface, which the `SeekableByteChannel` interface extends along with the `WritableByteChannel` interface. The other two `read()` methods are declared in the `ScatteringByteChannel` interface that the `FileChannel` class implements. The `newByteChannel()` method returns a reference of type `SeekableByteChannel`, so if you want to use the two latter `read()` methods that work with arrays of buffers, you must cast the reference that these methods return to type `FileChannel`.

All three methods can throw exceptions of any of the following types:

➤ `NonReadableChannelException` is thrown if the file is not opened for reading.

➤ `ClosedChannelException` is thrown if the channel is closed.

➤ `AsynchronousCloseException` is thrown if the channel is closed by another thread while the read operation is in progress.

➤ `ClosedByInterruptException` is thrown if another thread interrupts the current thread while the read operation is in progress.

➤ `IOException` is thrown if some other I/O error occurs.

The third `read()` method that enables you to read data into a subset of buffers from an array can also throw an `IndexOutOfBoundsException` if the index parameters are inconsistent or invalid.

The `FileChannel` object keeps track of the file's current position. This is initially set to zero, which corresponds to the first byte available from the file. Each read operation increments the channel's file position by the number of bytes read, so the next read operation starts at that point, assuming you don't modify the file position by some other means. When you need to change the file position in the channel — to reread the file, for example — you just call the `position()` method for the `FileChannel` object, with the index position of the byte where you want the next read to start as the argument to the method. For example, with a reference to a `FileChannel` object stored in a variable `inChannel`, you could reset the file position to the beginning of the file with the following statements:

```
try (/* ... create channel inCh... */){
  // ...
  inCh.position(0);    // Set file position to first byte

} catch(IOException e) {
  e.printStackTrace();
}
```

This method throws a `ClosedChannelException` if the channel is closed or an `IOException` if some other error occurs, so you need to put the call in a `try` block. It can also throw an `IllegalArgumentException` if the argument you supply to the method is negative. `IllegalArgumentException` is a subclass of `RuntimeException`. You can legally specify a position beyond the end of the file, but a subsequent read operation just returns −1, indicating that the end-of-file has been reached.

Calling the `position()` method with no argument returns the current file position. You can use this to record a file position that you want to return to later in a variable. This version of the method can also throw exceptions of type `ClosedChannelException` and `IOException`, so you must put the call in a `try` block or make the calling method declare the exceptions in a `throws` clause.

The amount of data read from a file into a byte buffer is determined by the position and limit for the buffer when the read operation executes, as Figure 11-1 illustrates. Bytes are read into the buffer starting at the byte in the buffer given by its position; assuming sufficient bytes are available from the file, a total of `limit-position` bytes from the file are stored in the buffer.

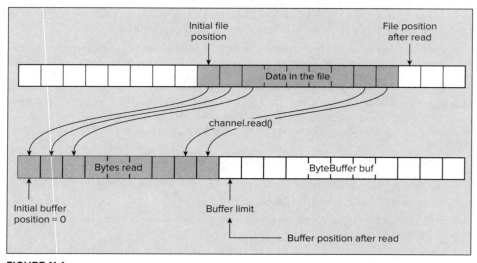

FIGURE 11-1

You'll see some other channel `read()` methods later that you can use to read data from a particular point in a file.

Reading a Text File

You can now attempt to read the `charData.txt` file that you wrote using the `BufferStateTrace` example in the previous chapter. You wrote this file as Unicode characters, so you must take this into account when interpreting the contents of the file. Of course, all files are read as a series of bytes. It's how you interpret those bytes that determines whether or not you get something that makes sense.

Your first steps are to define a `Path` object encapsulating the file path and to create a `FileChannel` object using the process you saw at the beginning of this chapter.

You create a `ByteBuffer` object exactly as you saw previously when you were writing the file in Chapter 10. You know that you wrote 50 bytes at a time to the file — you wrote the string `"Garbage in, garbage out.\n"` that consists of 25 Unicode characters. However, it's possible that you tried appending to the file an arbitrary number of times, so you should provide for reading as many Unicode characters as there are in the file. You can set up the `ByteBuffer` with exactly the right size for the data from a single write operation with the following statement:

```
ByteBuffer buf = ByteBuffer.allocate(50);
```

The code that you use to read from the file needs to allow for an arbitrary number of 25-character strings in the file. Of course, it must also allow for the end-of-file being reached while you are reading the file. You can read from the file into the buffer like this:

```
Path file = Paths.get(System.getProperty("user.home")).
                    resolve("Beginning Java Stuff").resolve("charData.txt");
ByteBuffer buf = ByteBuffer.allocate(50);
try (ReadableByteChannel inCh = file.newByteChannel()){
  while(inCh.read(buf) != -1) {
    // Code to extract the data that was read into the buffer...
    buf.clear();                        // Clear the buffer for the next read
  }
  System.out.println("EOF reached.");
} catch(IOException e) {
  e.printStackTrace();
}
```

The file is read by calling the `read()` method for the `FileChannel` object in the expression that you use for the `while` loop condition. The loop continues to read from the file until the `read()` method returns −1 when the end-of-file is reached. Within the loop you have to extract the data from the buffer, do what you want with it, and then clear the buffer to be ready for the next read operation.

Getting Data from the Buffer

After each read operation, the buffer's position points to the byte following the last byte that was read. Before you attempt to extract any data from the buffer, you therefore need to flip the buffer to reset the buffer position back to the beginning of the data, and the buffer limit to the byte following the last byte of data that was read. One way to extract bytes from the buffer is to use the `getChar()` method for the `ByteBuffer` object. This retrieves a Unicode character from the buffer at the current position and increments the position by two. This could work like this:

```
buf.flip();
StringBuffer str = new StringBuffer(buf.remaining()/2);
while(buf.hasRemaining()) {
  str.append(buf.getChar());
}
System.out.println("String read: "+ str.toString());
```

This code would replace the comment in the previous fragment that appears at the beginning of the `while` loop. You first create a `StringBuffer` object in which you assemble the string. This is the most efficient way to do this — using a `String` object would result in the creation of a new `String` object each time you add a character to the string. Of course, because there's no possibility of multiple threads accessing the string, you could use a `StringBuilder` object here instead of the `StringBuffer` object and gain a little more efficiency.

The remaining() method for the buffer returns the number of bytes read after the buffer has been flipped, so you can just divide this by two to get the number of characters read. You extract characters one at a time from the buffer in the while loop and append them to the StringBuffer object. The getChar() method increments the buffer's position by two each time, so eventually the hasRemaining() method returns false when all the characters have been extracted, and the loop ends. You then just convert the StringBuffer to a String object and output the string on the command line.

This approach works okay, but a better way is to use a view buffer of type CharBuffer. The toString() method for the CharBuffer object gives you the string that it contains directly. Indeed, you can boil the whole thing down to a single statement:

```
System.out.println("String read: " +
                    ((ByteBuffer)(buf.flip())).asCharBuffer().toString());
```

The flip() method returns a reference of type Buffer, so you have to cast it to type ByteBuffer to make it possible to call the asCharBuffer() method for the buffer object. This is necessary because the asCharBuffer() method is defined in the CharBuffer class, not in the Buffer class.

You can assemble these code fragments into a working example.

TRY IT OUT Reading Text from a File

Here's the code for the complete program to read the charData.txt file that you wrote in the previous chapter using the BufferStateTrace.java program:

```java
import java.nio.file.*;
import java.nio.channels.ReadableByteChannel;
import java.io.IOException;
import java.nio.ByteBuffer;

public class ReadAString {

  public static void main(String[] args) {

    Path file = Paths.get(System.getProperty("user.home")).
                       resolve("Beginning Java Stuff").resolve("charData.txt");
    if(!Files.exists(file)) {
      System.out.println(file + " does not exist. Terminating program.");
      System.exit(1);;
    }

    ByteBuffer buf = ByteBuffer.allocate(50);
    try (ReadableByteChannel inCh = Files.newByteChannel(file)){
      while(inCh.read(buf) != -1) {
        System.out.print("String read: " +
                    ((ByteBuffer)(buf.flip())).asCharBuffer().toString());
        buf.clear();                     // Clear the buffer for the next read
      }
      System.out.println("EOF reached.");
    } catch(IOException e) {
      e.printStackTrace();
    }
  }
}
```

ReadAString.java

When you compile and run this, you should get output something like the following:

```
String read: Garbage in, garbage out.
String read: Garbage in, garbage out.
String read: Garbage in, garbage out.

EOF reached.
```

The number of lines of output depends on how many times you ran the example that wrote the file.

How It Works

Nothing is new here beyond what I have already discussed. The file contains new line characters so the `print()` method generates the output that you see.

If you want to output the length of the file, you could add a statement to call the `size()` method for the `inCh` object:

```
System.out.println("File contains " + ((SeekableByteChannel)inCh).size() + " bytes.");
```

For this to compile you will need an `import` statement for `java.nio.channels.SeekableByteChannel`. The `newByteChannel()` method returns a reference of this type, but it was stored as `ReadableByteChannel` (a subinterface of `SeekableByteChannel`) and this type does not specify the `size()` method. Immediately before the `while` loop would be a good place to put it because the `size()` method can throw an `IOException`. You might also like to modify the code to output the buffer's position and limit before and after the read. This shows quite clearly how these change when the file is read.

Of course, this program works because you have prior knowledge of how long the records are in the file. If you didn't have this information, you would have to read a chunk of data from the file and then figure out where each record ended by looking for the `\n` character that appears at the end of each record. You get an idea of how you could deal with this kind of situation a little later in this chapter when I go into reading mixed data from a file.

Reading Binary Data

When you read binary data, you still read bytes from the file, so the process is essentially the same as you used in the previous example. You just use a different type of view buffer to access the data. To read the `primes.bin` file, you have some options for the size of the byte buffer. The number of bytes in the buffer should be a multiple of eight because a prime value is of type `long`, so as long as it's a multiple of eight, you can make it whatever size you like. You could allocate a buffer to accommodate the number of primes that you want to output to the command line — six values, say. This would make accessing the data very easy because you need to set up a view buffer of type `LongBuffer` only each time you read from the file. One thing against this is that reading such a small amount of data from the file in each read operation might not be a very efficient way to read the file. However, in the interests of understanding the mechanics of this, let's see how it would work anyway. The buffer would be created like this:

```
final int PRIMECOUNT = 6;              // Number of primes to read at a time
final int LONG_BYTES = 8;              // Number of bytes for type long
ByteBuffer buf = ByteBuffer.allocate(LONG_BYTES*PRIMECOUNT);
```

You can then read the primes in a `while` loop inside the `try` block that creates the channel using a view buffer of type `LongBuffer`. Calling the `asLongBuffer()` method for the `ByteBuffer` object, `buf`, creates the view buffer. The `LongBuffer` class offers you a choice of four `get()` methods for accessing values of type `long` in the buffer:

➤ `get()` extracts a single value of type `long` from the buffer at the current position and returns it. The buffer position is then incremented by one.

➤ `get(int index)` extracts a single value of type `long` from the buffer position specified by the argument and returns it. The current buffer position is not altered. Remember: The buffer position is in terms of values.

➤ `get(long[] values)` extracts `values.length` values of type `long` from the buffer starting at the current position and stores them in the array `values`. The current position is incremented by the number of values retrieved from the buffer. The method returns a reference to the buffer as type `LongBuffer`. If insufficient values are available from the buffer to fill the array that you pass as the argument — in other words, `limit-position` is less than `values.length` — the method throws an exception of type `BufferUnderflowException`, no values are transferred to the array, and the buffer's position is unchanged.

➤ `get(long[] values, int offset, int length)` extracts `length` values of type `long` from the buffer starting at the current position and stores them in the `values` array, starting at `values[offset]`. The current position is incremented by the number of values retrieved from the buffer. The method returns a reference to the buffer as type `LongBuffer`. If there are insufficient values available from the buffer the method behaves in the same way as the previous version.

The `BufferUnderflowException` class is a subclass of `RuntimeException`, so you are not obliged to catch this exception.

You could access the primes in the buffer like this:

```
LongBuffer longBuf = ((ByteBuffer)(buf.flip())).asLongBuffer();
System.out.println();                      // Newline for the buffer contents
while(longBuf.hasRemaining()) {            // While there are values
  System.out.print("  " + longBuf.get());  // output them on the same line
}
```

If you want to collect the primes in an array, using the form of `get()` method that transfers values to an array is more efficient than writing a loop to transfer them one at a time, but you have to be careful. If the number of primes in the file is not a multiple of the array size, you must take steps to pick up the last few stragglers correctly. If you don't, you see the `BufferUnderflowException` thrown by the `get()` method. Let's see it working in an example.

TRY IT OUT Reading a Binary File

You will read the primes six at a time into an array. Here's the program:

```
import java.nio.file.*;
import java.nio.*;
import java.nio.channels.ReadableByteChannel;
import java.io.IOException;

public class ReadPrimes {
  public static void main(String[] args) {
    Path file = Paths.get(System.getProperty("user.home")).
                              resolve("Beginning Java Stuff").resolve("primes.bin");
    if(!Files.exists(file)) {
      System.out.println(file + " does not exist. Terminating program.");
      System.exit(1);
    }

    final int PRIMECOUNT = 6;
    final int LONG_BYTES = 8;                    // Number of bytes for type long
    ByteBuffer buf = ByteBuffer.allocate(LONG_BYTES*PRIMECOUNT);
    long[] primes = new long[PRIMECOUNT];
    try (ReadableByteChannel inCh = Files.newByteChannel(file)){
      int primesRead = 0;
      while(inCh.read(buf) != -1) {
        LongBuffer longBuf = ((ByteBuffer)(buf.flip())).asLongBuffer();
        primesRead = longBuf.remaining();
        longBuf.get(primes, 0, primesRead);

        // List the primes read on the same line
        System.out.println();
        for(int i = 0 ; i < primesRead ; ++i) {
          System.out.printf("%10d", primes[i]);
        }
        buf.clear();                     // Clear the buffer for the next read
      }
      System.out.println("\nEOF reached.");
```

```
        } catch(IOException e) {
          e.printStackTrace();
        }
      }
    }
```

You should get all the prime values, six to a line, followed by `"EOF reached."`

How It Works

The code to access the primes in the buffer avoids the possibility of buffer underflow altogether. You always transfer the number of values available in `longBuf` by using the `remaining()` method to determine the count so you can't cause the `BufferUnderflowException` to be thrown.

A further possibility is that you could use a buffer large enough to hold all the primes in the file. You can work this out from the value returned by the `size()` method for the channel — which is the length of the file in bytes. You could do that like this:

```
        final int PRIMECOUNT = (int)inCh.size()/LONG_BYTES;
```

Of course, you also must alter the `for` loop that outputs the primes so it doesn't attempt to put them all on the same line. There is a hazard with this though if you don't know how large the file is. Unless your computer is unusually replete with memory, it could be inconvenient if the file contains the first billion primes.

Reading Mixed Data

The `primes.txt` file that you created in the previous chapter contains data of three different types. You have the string length as a binary value of type `double`, which is a strange choice for an integer but good experience, followed by the string itself describing the prime value, followed by the binary prime value as type `long`. Reading this file is a little trickier than it looks at first sight.

To start with you set up the `Path` object appropriately and obtain the channel for the file. Because, apart from the name of the file, this is exactly the same as in the previous example, I won't repeat it here. Of course, the big problem is that you don't know ahead of time exactly how long the strings are. You have two strategies to deal with this:

➤   You can read the string length in the first read operation and then read the string and the binary prime value in the next. The only downside to this approach is that it's not a particularly efficient way to read the file because you have many read operations that each read a very small amount of data.

➤   You can set up a sizable byte buffer of an arbitrary capacity and just fill it with bytes from the file. You can then sort out what you have in the buffer. The problem with this approach is that the buffer's contents may well end partway through one of the data items from the file. You have to do some work to detect this and figure out what to do next, but this is much more efficient than the first approach because you vastly reduce the number of read operations that are necessary to read the entire file.

Let's try the first approach first because it's easier.

To read the string length you need a byte buffer with a capacity to hold a single value of type `double`:

```
    ByteBuffer lengthBuf = ByteBuffer.allocate(8);
```

You can create byte buffers to hold the string and the binary prime value, but you can only create the former after you know the length of the string. Remember, you wrote the string as Unicode characters so you must allow 2 bytes for each character in the original string. Here's how you can define the buffers for the string and the prime value:

```
        ByteBuffer[] buffers = {
                        null,                  // Byte buffer to hold string
                        ByteBuffer.allocate(8) // Byte buffer to hold prime
                          };
```

The first element in the array is the buffer for the string. This is `null` because you redefine this as you read each record.

You need two read operations to get at all the data for a single prime record. A good approach would be to put both read operations in an indefinite loop and use a `break` statement to exit the loop when you hit the end-of-file. Here's how you can read the file using this approach:

```
while(true) {
  if(inCh.read(lengthBuf) == -1)        // Read the string length,
    break;                              // if its EOF exit the loop

  lengthBuf.flip();

  // Extract the length and convert to int
  strLength = (int)lengthBuf.getDouble();

  // Now create the buffer for the string
  buffers[0] = ByteBuffer.allocate(2*strLength);

  if(inCh.read(buffers) == -1) {  // Read the string & binary prime value
    // Should not get here!
    System.err.println("EOF found reading the prime string.");
    break;                              // Exit loop on EOF
  }
  // Output the prime data and clear the buffers for the next iteration...
}
```

After reading the string length into `lengthBuf` you can create the second buffer, `buffers[0]`. The `getDouble()` method for `lengthBuf` provides you with the length of the string. You get the string and the binary prime value the arguments to the output statement. Of course, if you manage to read a string length value, there ought to be a string and a binary prime following, so you have output an error message to signal something has gone seriously wrong if this turns out not to be the case.

Let's see how it works out in practice.

TRY IT OUT   Reading Mixed Data from a File

Here's the complete program code:

```
import java.nio.file.*;
import java.nio.channels.FileChannel;
import java.io.IOException;
import java.nio.ByteBuffer;

public class ReadPrimesMixedData {
  public static void main(String[] args) {
    Path file = Paths.get(System.getProperty("user.home")).
                          resolve("Beginning Java Stuff").resolve("primes.txt");
    if(!Files.exists(file)) {
      System.out.println(file + " does not exist. Terminating program.");
      System.exit(1);;
    }

    try (FileChannel inCh = (FileChannel)Files.newByteChannel(file)){
      ByteBuffer lengthBuf = ByteBuffer.allocate(8);
      int strLength = 0;                            // Stores the string length

      ByteBuffer[] buffers = {
                          null,                     // Byte buffer to hold string
                          ByteBuffer.allocate(8)    // Byte buffer to hold prime
                            };

      while(true) {
        if(inCh.read(lengthBuf) == -1)              // Read the string length,
```

```
        break;                                          // if its EOF exit the loop

      lengthBuf.flip();

      // Extract the length and convert to int
      strLength = (int)lengthBuf.getDouble();

      // Now create the buffer for the string
      buffers[0] = ByteBuffer.allocate(2*strLength);

      if(inCh.read(buffers) == -1) {   // Read the string & binary prime value
        // Should not get here!
        System.err.println("EOF found reading the prime string.");
        break;                                          // Exit loop on EOF
      }

      System.out.printf(
              "String length: %3s  String: %-12s  Binary Value: %3d%n",
              strLength,
              ((ByteBuffer)(buffers[0].flip())).asCharBuffer().toString(),
              ((ByteBuffer)buffers[1].flip()).getLong());

      // Clear the buffers for the next read
      lengthBuf.clear();
      buffers[1].clear();
    }
    System.out.println("\nEOF reached.");
  } catch(IOException e) {
    e.printStackTrace();
  }
 }
}
```

ReadPrimesMixedData.java

The program reads the file that you wrote with `PrimesToFile2.java` in Chapter 10. You should get the following output:

```
String length:   9 String: prime = 2     Binary Value:   2
String length:   9 String: prime = 3     Binary Value:   3
String length:   9 String: prime = 5     Binary Value:   5
```

and so on down to the end:

```
String length:  11 String: prime = 523   Binary Value: 523
String length:  11 String: prime = 541   Binary Value: 541

EOF reached.
```

How It Works

Because you use the channel `read()` method that reads into an array of `ByteBuffer` objects, you cast the reference returned by the `newByteChannel()` method to type `FileChannel`. On each iteration of the loop that reads the file, you first read 8 bytes into `lengthBuf` because this is the length of the string that follows as a value of type `double`. Knowing the length of the string, you are able to create the second buffer, `buffers[0]`, to accommodate the string.

The string and the binary prime value are obtained in the arguments to the `printf()` method:

```
              System.out.printf(
                      "String length: %3s  String: %-12s  Binary Value: %3d%n",
                      strLength,
                      ((ByteBuffer)(buffers[0].flip())).asCharBuffer().toString(),
                      ((ByteBuffer)buffers[1].flip()).getLong());
```

You obtain the string by calling the `asCharBuffer()` method to obtain a `CharBuffer` object from the original `ByteBuffer` and calling its `toString()` method to get the contents as a `String` object. It is necessary to flip the byte buffer before you do this and you have to cast the reference returned by the `flip()` method to type `ByteBuffer` in order to make this possible because `flip()` returns a reference of type `Buffer`. You use a similar mechanism to get the binary prime value.

Finally you clear the buffers for the string length and prime value ready for the next loop iteration.

Compacting a Buffer

Another approach to reading the `primes.txt` file is to read bytes from the file into a large buffer for efficiency and then figure out what is in it. Processing the data needs to take account of the possibility that the last data item in the buffer following a read operation may be incomplete — part of a `double` or `long` value or part of a string. The essence of this approach is therefore as follows:

1. Read from the file into a buffer.

2. Extract the string length, the string, and the binary prime value from the buffer repeatedly until no more complete sets of values are available.

3. Shift any bytes that are left over in the buffer back to the beginning of the buffer. These are some part of a complete set of the string length, the string, and the binary prime value. Go back to point 1 to read more from the file.

The buffer classes provide the `compact()` method for performing the operation you need in the third step here to shift the bytes that are left over in the buffer back to the beginning. An illustration of the action of the `compact()` method on a buffer is shown in Figure 11-2.

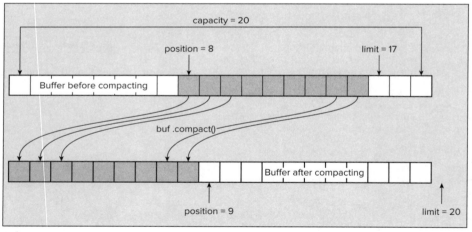

FIGURE 11-2

As you can see, the compacting operation copies everything in the buffer, which are the data elements from the buffer's current position, up to but not including the buffer's limit, to the beginning of the buffer. The buffer's position is then set to the element following the last element that was copied, and the limit is set to the capacity. This is precisely what you want when you have worked partway through the data in an input buffer and you want to add some more data from the file. Compacting the buffer sets the position and limit such that the buffer is ready to receive more data. The next read operation using the buffer adds data at the end of what was left in the buffer.

TRY IT OUT Reading into a Large Buffer

Here is a new version of the previous example that reads data into a large buffer:

```java
import java.nio.file.*;
import java.nio.channels.ReadableByteChannel;
import java.io.IOException;
import java.nio.ByteBuffer;

public class ReadPrimesMixedData2 {
  public static void main(String[] args) {
    Path file = Paths.get(System.getProperty("user.home")).
                         resolve("Beginning Java Stuff").resolve("primes.txt");
    if(!Files.exists(file)) {
      System.out.println(file + " does not exist. Terminating program.");
      System.exit(1);
    }

    try(ReadableByteChannel inCh = Files.newByteChannel(file)) {
      ByteBuffer buf = ByteBuffer.allocateDirect(256);
      buf.position(buf.limit());          // Set the position for the loop operation
      int strLength = 0;                  // Stores the string length
      byte[] strChars = null;             // Array to hold the bytes for the string

      while(true) {
        if(buf.remaining() < 8) {      // Verify enough bytes for string length
          if(inCh.read(buf.compact()) == -1)
            break;                         // EOF reached
          buf.flip();
        }
        strLength = (int)buf.getDouble();  // Get the string length

        // Verify enough bytes for complete string
        if(buf.remaining() < 2*strLength) {
          if(inCh.read(buf.compact()) == -1) {
            System.err.println("EOF found reading the prime string.");
            break;                         // EOF reached
          }
          buf.flip();
        }
        strChars = new byte[2*strLength];  // Array for string bytes
        buf.get(strChars);                 // Get the bytes

        if(buf.remaining()<8) {            // Verify enough bytes for prime value
          if(inCh.read(buf.compact()) == -1) {
            System.err.println("EOF found reading the binary prime value.");
            break;                         // EOF reached
          }
          buf.flip();
        }

        System.out.printf(
                  "String length: %3s  String: %-12s  Binary Value: %3d%n",
                  strLength,
                  ByteBuffer.wrap(strChars).asCharBuffer(),buf.getLong());
      }

      System.out.println("\nEOF reached.");

    } catch(IOException e) {
      e.printStackTrace();
    }
  }
}
```

This should result in the same output as the previous example.

How It Works

I chose a buffer size that would guarantee that we do multiple read operations to read the complete file contents and that we would get bits of a complete record left at the end of the buffer.

All the work is done in the indefinite `while` loop. Before the loop executes you create a direct buffer with a capacity of 256 bytes by calling the `allocateDirect()` method. A direct buffer is faster if you are reading a lot of data from a file, as the data is transferred directly from the file to our buffer. The code within the loop determines whether there are data values left in the buffer by calling the `remaining()` method for the buffer object. You only do another file read when you have processed all the complete prime records that the buffer contains. This is when `remaining()` returns a value that is less than the number of bytes needed to accommodate the next data item. The default initial settings for the buffer are with the position at zero and the limit at the capacity, and this would suggest falsely that there is data in the buffer. Therefore you set the position to the limit initially so that the `remaining()` method returns zero at the beginning of the first loop iteration.

Within the loop you first check whether there are sufficient bytes for the `double` value that specifies the string length. On the first iteration, this is definitely not the case, so the `compact()` method is called to compact the buffer, and the reference to `buf` that is returned is passed to the `read()` method for `inCh` to read data from the file. You then flip the buffer and get the length of the string. Of course, data in the file should be in groups of three items — the string length, the string, the binary prime value — so the end-of-file should be detected trying to obtain the first of these by the `read()` method for the channel returning −1. In this case you exit the loop by executing a `break` statement.

Next you get the string itself, after checking that you have sufficient bytes left in the buffer. You should never find EOF, so you output an error message if EOF is detected. Finally, you obtain the binary prime value in a similar way and output the group of three data items. The loop continues until all data has been read and processed and EOF is recognized when you are looking for a string length value.

COPYING FILES

You have already seen in Chapter 9 how you can use the `copy()` method in the `Files` class to copy a file to another location. There's another way using `FileChannel` objects. A `FileChannel` object connected to an input file can transfer data directly to a `FileChannel` object that is connected to an output file without involving explicit buffers.

The `FileChannel` class defines two methods for direct data transfer between channels that are particularly efficient.

➤ `transferTo(long position, long count, WritableByteChannel dst)`
Attempts to transfer `count` bytes from this channel to the channel `dst`. Bytes are read from this channel starting at the file position specified by `position`. The position of this channel is not altered by this operation, but the position of `dst` is incremented by the number of bytes written. Fewer than `count` bytes are transferred if this channel's file has fewer than `count` bytes remaining, or if `dst` is non-blocking and has fewer than `count` bytes free in its system output buffer. The number of bytes transferred is returned as a value of type `int`.

➤ `transferFrom(ReadableByteChannel src, long position, long count))`
Attempts to transfer `count` bytes to this channel from the channel `src`. Bytes are written to this channel starting at the file position specified by `position`. The position of this channel is not altered by the operation, but the position of `src` is incremented by the number of bytes read from it. If `position` is greater than the size of the file, then no bytes are transferred. Fewer than `count` bytes are transferred if the file corresponding to `src` has fewer than `count` bytes remaining in the file or if it is non-blocking and has fewer than `count` bytes free in its system input buffer. The number of bytes transferred is returned as a value of type `int`.

A channel that was opened for reading supports only the `transferTo()` method. Similarly, a channel that was opened for writing supports only the `transferFrom()` method. Both of these methods can throw any of the following flurry of exceptions:

➤ `IllegalArgumentException` is thrown if either `count` or `position` is negative.

➤ `NonReadableChannelException` is thrown if the operation attempts to read from a channel that was not opened for reading.

➤ `NonWritableChannelException` is thrown if the operation attempts to write to a channel that was not opened for writing.

➤ `ClosedChannelException` is thrown if either channel involved in the operation is closed.

➤ `AsynchronousCloseException` is thrown if either channel is closed by another thread while the operation is in progress.

➤ `ClosedByInterruptException` is thrown if another thread interrupts the current thread while the operation is in progress.

➤ `IOException` is thrown if some other I/O error occurs.

The value of these methods lies in the potential for using the I/O capabilities of the underlying operating system directly. Where this is possible, the operation is likely to be much faster than copying from one file to another in a loop using the `read()` and `write()` methods you have seen.

A file copy program is an obvious candidate for trying out these methods.

TRY IT OUT   Direct Data Transfer between Channels

This example is a program that copies the file that is specified by a command-line argument. You copy the file to a backup file that you create in the same directory as the original. You create the name of the new file by appending "_backup" to the original filename as many times as necessary to form a unique filename. That operation is a good candidate for writing a helper method:

```java
// Method to create a unique backup Path object under MS Windows
public static Path createBackupFilePath(Path file) {
  Path parent = file.getParent();
  String name = file.getFileName().toString();        // Get the file name
  int period = name.indexOf('.');            // Find the extension separator
  if(period == -1) {                         // If there isn't one
    period = name.length();                  // set it to the end of the string
  }
  String nameAdd = "_backup";                 // String to be appended

  // Create a Path object that is a unique
  Path backup = parent.resolve(
             name.substring(0,period) + nameAdd + name.substring(period));
  while(Files.exists(backup)) {              // If the path already exists...
    name = backup.getFileName().toString();  // Get the current file name
    backup = parent.resolve(name.substring(0,period) +        // add _backup
                            nameAdd + name.substring(period));
    period += nameAdd.length();              // Increment separator index
  }
  return backup;
}
```

FileBackup.java

This method assumes the argument has already been validated as a real file. You extract the basic information you need to create the new file first — the parent directory path, the file name, and where the period separator is, if there is one. You then create a `Path` variable, `backup`, that you initialize using the original file path.

The `while` loop continues as long as backup already exists as a file, and an instance of "_backup" is appended to the path until a unique filename is arrived at.

You can now write the `main()` method to use the `createBackupFile()` method to create the destination file for the file backup operation:

```java
import static java.nio.file.StandardOpenOption.*;
import java.nio.file.*;
import java.nio.channels.*;
import java.io.IOException;
import java.util.EnumSet;

public class FileBackup {
  public static void main(String[] args) {
    if(args.length==0) {
      System.out.println("No file to copy. Application usage is:\n" +
                                "java -classpath . FileCopy \"filepath\"" );
      System.exit(1);
    }
    Path fromFile = Paths.get(args[0]);
    fromFile.toAbsolutePath();

    if(Files.notExists(fromFile)) {
      System.out.printf("File to copy, %s, does not exist.", fromFile);
      System.exit(1);
    }

    Path toFile = createBackupFilePath(fromFile);
    try (FileChannel inCh = (FileChannel)(Files.newByteChannel(fromFile));
         WritableByteChannel outCh = Files.newByteChannel(
                                toFile, EnumSet.of(WRITE,CREATE_NEW))){
      int bytesWritten = 0;
      long byteCount = inCh.size();
      while(bytesWritten<byteCount) {
        bytesWritten += inCh.transferTo(bytesWritten,
                                byteCount-bytesWritten,
                                outCh);
      }

      System.out.printf(
              "File copy complete. %d bytes copied to %s%n", byteCount, toFile);
    } catch(IOException e) {
      e.printStackTrace();
    }
  }

  // Code for createBackupFilePath() goes here...
}
```

FileBackup.java

You could try this out by copying the file containing the binary prime values. I supplied the path to my `primes .bin` file as the command-line argument and got the following output:

```
File copy complete. 800 bytes copied to C:\Users\Ivor\Beginning Java Stuff\primes_backup.bin
```

You should be able to verify that the new file's contents are identical to the original by inspecting it, or you could run the earlier example that reads a binary file with the file path to `primes_backup.bin`.

How It Works

You first obtain the command-line argument and create a `Path` object from it with the following code:

```
if(args.length==0) {
  System.out.println("No file to copy. Application usage is:\n"+
                     "java -classpath . FileCopy \"filepath\"" );
  System.exit(1);
}
Path fromFile = Paths.get(args[0]);
```

If there's no command-line argument, you supply a message explaining how to use the program before exiting.

Next, you verify that this is a real file:

```
if(Files.notExists(fromFile)) {
  System.out.printf("File to copy, %s, does not exist.", fromFile);
  System.exit(1);
}
```

If it isn't, there's nothing you can do, so you bail out of the program.

Creating a `Path` object for the backup file is a piece of cake:

```
Path toFile = createBackupFilePath(fromFile);
```

You saw how this helper method works earlier in this chapter.

Next, in the `try` block you create the channel for each file from the `Path` objects:

```
try (FileChannel inCh = (FileChannel)(Files.newByteChannel(fromFile));
     WritableByteChannel outCh = Files.newByteChannel(
                                   toFile, EnumSet.of(WRITE,CREATE_NEW))){
```

There are two `FileChannel` objects that you want to be automatically closed, so you create both between the parentheses following the `try` keyword. The `inCh` file channel has the `READ` option specified by default. You specify the `WRITE` and `CREATE_NEW` options for `outCh`, which guarantees the backup file is a new file. If the backup file already exists, the `getByteChannel()` method would fail. However, this should not happen because you have already verified that the backup file path does not reference a file that already exists.

After you have the channel objects, you transfer the contents of the input file to the output file in the `try` block like this:

```
int bytesWritten = 0;
long byteCount = inCh.size();
while(bytesWritten<byteCount) {
  bytesWritten += inCh.transferTo(bytesWritten,
                                  byteCount-bytesWritten,
                                  outCh);
}
```

You copy the data using the `transferTo()` method for `inCh`. The chances are good that the `transferTo()` method transfers all the data in one go. The `while` loop is there just in case it doesn't. The loop condition checks whether the number of bytes written is less than the number of bytes in the file. If it is, the loop executes another transfer operation for the number of bytes left in the file, with the file position specified as the number of bytes written so far.

RANDOM ACCESS TO A FILE

The `FileChannel` class defines `read()` and `write()` methods that operate at a specified position in the file:

➤ `read(ByteBuffer buf, long position)` reads bytes from the file into `buf` in the same way as you have seen previously except that bytes are read starting at the file position specified by the second argument. The channel's position is not altered by this operation. If `position` is greater than the number of bytes in the file, then no bytes are read.

➤ `write(ByteBuffer buf, long position)` writes bytes from `buf` to the file in the same way as you have seen previously except that bytes are written starting at the file position specified by the second argument. The channel's position is not altered by this operation. If `position` is less than the number of bytes in the file then bytes from that point are overwritten. If `position` is greater than the number of bytes in the file then the file size is increased to this point before bytes are written. In this case the bytes between the original end-of-file and where the new bytes are written contain junk values.

These methods can throw the same exceptions as the corresponding method that accepts a single argument; plus, they might throw an exception of type `IllegalArgumentException` if a negative file position is specified. Obviously, when you want to use a channel to read and write a file, you must specify both the `READ` and `WRITE` open options when you create the `FileChannel` object.

The `SeekableByteChannel` interface that the `FileChannel` class implements also declares an overload of the `position()` method that accepts an argument of type `long`. Calling the method sets the file position for the channel to the position specified by the argument. This version of the `position()` method returns a reference to the channel object as type `FileChannel`. The interface also declares the `size()` method that returns the number of bytes in the file to which the channel is connected. You could use this to decide on the buffer size, possibly reading the whole file in one go if it's not too large.

Let's try an example that demonstrates how you can access a file randomly.

TRY IT OUT   Reading a File Randomly

To show how easy it is to read from random positions in a file, the example extracts a random selection of values from our `primes.bin` file. Here's the code:

```java
import java.nio.file.*;
import java.nio.channels.FileChannel;
import java.io.IOException;
import java.nio.ByteBuffer;

public class RandomFileRead {
  public static void main(String[] args) {
    Path file = Paths.get(System.getProperty("user.home")).
                        resolve("Beginning Java Stuff").resolve("primes.bin");
    if(!Files.exists(file)) {
      System.out.println(file + " does not exist. Terminating program.");
      System.exit(1);
    }

    final int PRIMESREQUIRED = 10;
      final int LONG_BYTES = 8;                 // Number of bytes for type long
    ByteBuffer buf = ByteBuffer.allocate(LONG_BYTES*PRIMESREQUIRED);

    long[] primes = new long[PRIMESREQUIRED];
    int index = 0;                              // Position for a prime in the file

    try (FileChannel inCh = (FileChannel)(Files.newByteChannel(file))){
      // Count of primes in the file
      final int PRIMECOUNT = (int)inCh.size()/LONG_BYTES;

      // Read the number of random primes required
      for(int i = 0 ; i < PRIMESREQUIRED ; ++i) {
        index = LONG_BYTES*(int)(PRIMECOUNT*Math.random());
        inCh.read(buf, index);                 // Read the value
        buf.flip();
        primes[i] = buf.getLong();             // Save it in the array
        buf.clear();
      }

      // Output the selection of random primes 5 to a line in field width of 12
      int count = 0;                           // Count of primes written
```

```
              for(long prime : primes) {
                System.out.printf("%12d", prime);
                if(++count%5 == 0) {
                  System.out.println();
                }
              }

          } catch(IOException e) {
            e.printStackTrace();
          }
        }
      }
```

RandomFileRead.java

When I ran this, I got the following output:

```
        359          107          383          109             7
        173          443          337           17           113
```

You should get something similar but not the same because the random number generator is seeded using the current clock time. The number of random selections is fixed, but you could easily add code for a value to be entered on the command line.

How It Works

You access a random prime in the file by generating a random position in the file with the expression `8*(int)(PRIMECOUNT*Math.random())`. The value of `index` is a pseudo-random integer that can be from 0 to the number of primes in the file minus one, multiplied by 8 because each prime occupies 8 bytes. The prime is read from the file with the statement:

```
        inCh.read(buf, index);            // Read the value at index
```

This calls the `read()` method for the channel object that accepts a file position argument to specify from where in the file bytes are to be read. Because `buf` has a capacity of 8 bytes, only one prime is read each time. You store each randomly selected prime in an element of the `primes` array.

Finally, you output the primes five to a line in a field width of 12 characters.

You could also have used the `read()` method that accepts a single argument together with the `position()` method:

```
        for(int i = 0 ; i<PRIMESREQUIRED ; ++i) {
          index = LONG_BYTES*(int)(PRIMECOUNT*Math.random());
          inCh.position(index).read(buf);              // Read the value
          buf.flip();
          primes[i] = buf.getLong();                   // Save it in the array
          buf.clear();
        }
```

Calling the `position()` method sets the file position to `index` then the `read()` method reads the file starting at that point.

The need to be able to access and update a file randomly arises quite often. Even with a simple personnel file, for example, you are likely to need the capability to update the address or the phone number for an individual. Assuming you have arranged for the address and phone number entries to be of a fixed length, you could update the data for any entry simply by overwriting it. If you want to read from and write to the same file you can just open the channel for reading and writing. Let's try that, too.

TRY IT OUT   Reading and Writing a File Randomly

You can modify the previous example so that you overwrite each random prime that you retrieve from the `primes_backup.bin` file that you created earlier with the value `99999L` to make it stand out from the rest.

This messes up the `primes_backup.bin` file that you use here, but you can always run the program that copies files to copy `primes.bin` if you want to restore it. Here's the code:

```java
import static java.nio.file.StandardOpenOption.*;
import java.nio.file.*;
import java.nio.channels.SeekableByteChannel;
import java.io.IOException;
import java.nio.ByteBuffer;
import java.util.EnumSet;

public class RandomReadWrite {
  public static void main(String[] args)
  {
    Path file = Paths.get(System.getProperty("user.home")).
                   resolve("Beginning Java Stuff").resolve("primes_backup.bin");
    if(!Files.exists(file)) {
      System.out.println(file + " does not exist. Terminating program.");
      System.exit(1);
    }

    final int PRIMESREQUIRED = 10;
    final int LONG_BYTES = 8;
    ByteBuffer buf = ByteBuffer.allocate(LONG_BYTES);

    long[] primes = new long[PRIMESREQUIRED];
    int index = 0;                             // Position for a prime in the file
    final long REPLACEMENT = 99999L;           // Replacement for a selected prime

    try (SeekableByteChannel channel =
                     Files.newByteChannel(file, EnumSet.of(READ, WRITE))){
      final int PRIMECOUNT = (int)channel.size()/8;
      System.out.println("Prime count = "+PRIMECOUNT);
      for(int i = 0 ; i < PRIMESREQUIRED ; ++i) {
        index = LONG_BYTES*(int)(PRIMECOUNT*Math.random());
        channel.position(index).read(buf);     // Read at a random position
        buf.flip();                            // Flip the buffer
        primes[i] = buf.getLong();             // Extract the prime
        buf.flip();                            // Flip to ready for insertion
        buf.putLong(REPLACEMENT);              // Replacement into buffer
        buf.flip();                            // Flip ready to write
        channel.position(index).write(buf);    // Write the replacement to file
        buf.clear();                           // Reset ready for next read
      }

      int count = 0;                           // Count of primes written
      for(long prime : primes) {
        System.out.printf("%12d", prime);
        if(++count%5 == 0) {
          System.out.println();
        }
      }
    } catch(IOException e) {
      e.printStackTrace();
    }
  }
}
```

RandomReadWrite.java

This outputs from the file a set of ten random prime selections that have been overwritten. If you want to verify that you have indeed overwritten these values in the file, you can run the `ReadPrimes` example that you wrote earlier in this chapter with the file name as `"primes_backup.bin"`.

How It Works

All you had to do to write the file as well as read it was to create a `Path` object for the file and create a file channel that is opened for both reading and writing. You can read and write sequentially or at random. You read and write the file using essentially the same mechanism. You call the `position()` method for the `channel` object to set the file position and then you call the `read()` or `write()` method with `buf` as the argument.

You could have used the channel `read()` and `write()` methods that explicitly specify the position where the data is to be read or written as an argument. In this case you would need to cast channel to type `FileChannel`. One problem with the example as it stands is that some of the selections could be `99999L`, which is patently not prime. I got some of these after running the example just three times. You could fix this by checking each value that you store in the `primes` array:

```
for(int i = 0 ; i < PRIMESREQUIRED ; ++i)
{
  while(true)
  {
    index = LONG_BYTES*(int)(PRIMECOUNT*Math.random());
      channel.position(index).read(buf);     // Read at a random position
    buf.flip();                              // Flip the buffer
    primes[i] = buf.getLong();               // Extract the prime
    if(primes[i] != REPLACEMENT) {
      break;                                 // It's good so exit the inner loop
    } else {
      buf.clear();                           // Clear ready to read another
    }
  }
  buf.flip();                                // Flip to ready for insertion
  buf.putLong(REPLACEMENT);                  // Replacement into buffer
  buf.flip();                                // Flip ready to write
    channel.position(index).write(buf);      // Write the replacement to file
  buf.clear();                               // Reset ready for next read
}
```

RandomReadWrite.java

This code fragment is commented out in the download. The `while` loop now continues if the value read from the file is the same as `REPLACEMENT`, so another random file position is selected. This continues until something other than the value of `REPLACEMENT` is found. Of course, if you run the example often enough, you won't have enough primes in the file to fill the array, so the program loops indefinitely looking for something other than `REPLACEMENT`. You could deal with this in several ways. For example, you could count how many iterations have occurred in the `while` loop and bail out if it reaches the number of primes in the file. You could also inspect the file first to see whether there are sufficient primes in the file to fill the array. If there are exactly 10, you can fill the array immediately. I leave it to you to fill in these details.

MEMORY-MAPPED FILES

A memory-mapped file is a file that has its contents mapped into an area of virtual memory in your computer. This enables you to reference or update the data in the file directly without performing any explicit file read or write operations on the physical file yourself. When you reference a part of the file that is not actually in real memory, it is automatically brought in by your operating system. The memory that a file maps to might be paged in or out by the operating system, just like any other memory in your computer, so its immediate availability in real memory is not guaranteed. Because of the potentially immediate availability of the data it contains, a memory-mapped file is particularly useful when you need to access the file randomly. Your program code can reference the data in the file just as though it were all resident in memory.

Mapping a file into memory is implemented by a `FileChannel` object. The `map()` method for a `FileChannel` object returns a reference to a buffer of type `MappedByteBuffer` that maps to a specified part of the channel's file:

```
MappedByteBuffer map(int mode, long position, long size)
```

This method maps a region of the channel's file to a buffer of type `MappedByteBuffer` and returns a reference to the buffer. The file region that is mapped starts at `position` in the file and is of length `size` bytes. The first argument, `mode`, specifies how the buffer's memory may be accessed and can be any of the following three constant values, defined in the `MapMode` class, which is a static nested class of the `FileChannel` class:

➤ `MapMode.READ_ONLY`: This is valid if the channel was opened for reading the file. In this mode the buffer is read-only. If you try to modify the buffer's contents, an exception of type `ReadOnlyBufferException` is thrown.

➤ `MapMode.READ_WRITE`: This is valid if the channel was for both reading and writing. You can access and change the contents of the buffer and any changes to the contents are eventually be propagated to the file. The changes might or might not be visible to other users who have mapped the same file.

➤ `MapMode.PRIVATE`: This mode is for a "copy-on-write" mapping. This option for `mode` is also valid only if the channel was open for both reading and writing. You can access or change the buffer, but changes are not propagated to the file and are not visible to users who have mapped the same file. Private copies of modified portions of the buffer are created and used for subsequent buffer accesses.

When you access or change data in the `MappedByteBuffer` object that is returned when you call the `map()` method, you are effectively accessing the file that is mapped to the buffer. After you have called the `map()` method, the file mapping and the buffer that you have established are independent of the `FileChannel` object. You can close the channel, and the mapping of the file into the `MappedByteBuffer` object is still valid and operational.

Because the `MappedByteBuffer` class is a subclass of the `ByteBuffer` class, you have all the `ByteBuffer` methods available for a `MappedByteBuffer` object. This implies that you can create view buffers for a `MappedByteBuffer` object, for instance.

The `MappedByteBuffer` class defines three methods of its own to add to those inherited from the `ByteBuffer` class:

TABLE 11-1: MappedByteBuffer Class Methods

METHOD	DESCRIPTION
`force()`	If the buffer was mapped in `MapMode.READ_WRITE` mode, this method forces any changes that you make to the buffer's contents to be written to the file and returns a reference to the buffer. For buffers created with other access modes, this method has no effect.
`load()`	Tries on a "best efforts" basis to load the contents of the buffer into memory and returns a reference to the buffer.
`isLoaded()`	Returns true if it is likely that this buffer's contents are available in physical memory and `false` otherwise.

The `load()` method is dependent on external operating system functions executing to achieve the desired result, so the result cannot in general be guaranteed. Similarly, when you get a `true` return from the `isLoaded()` method, this is an indication of a probable state of affairs rather than a guarantee. This doesn't imply any kind of problem. It just means that accessing the data in the mapped byte buffer may take longer that you might expect in some instances.

Unless the file is large, using a mapped byte buffer is typically slower than using the `read()` and `write()` methods for a channel. Using a memory-mapped file through a `MappedByteBuffer` is simplicity itself though, so let's try it.

TRY IT OUT Using a Memory-Mapped File

You will access and modify the `primes_backup.bin` file using a `MappedByteBuffer`, so you might want to rerun the file copy program to restore it to its original condition. Here's the code:

```java
import static java.nio.file.StandardOpenOption.*;
import static java.nio.channels.FileChannel.MapMode.READ_WRITE;
import java.nio.file.*;
import java.nio.channels.FileChannel;
import java.io.IOException;
import java.nio.MappedByteBuffer;
import java.util.EnumSet;

public class MemoryMappedFile {
  public static void main(String[] args) {
    Path file = Paths.get(System.getProperty("user.home")).
                    resolve("Beginning Java Stuff").resolve("primes_backup.bin");
    if(!Files.exists(file)) {
      System.out.println(file + " does not exist. Terminating program.");
      System.exit(1);
    }

    final int PRIMESREQUIRED = 10;
    final int LONG_BYTES = 8;
    long[] primes = new long[PRIMESREQUIRED];

    int index = 0;                          // Position for a prime in the file
    final long REPLACEMENT = 999999L;       // Replacement for a selected prime

    try {
      FileChannel channel =
            (FileChannel)(Files.newByteChannel(file, EnumSet.of(READ, WRITE)));
      final int PRIMECOUNT = (int)channel.size()/LONG_BYTES;
      MappedByteBuffer buf = channel.map(
                                  READ_WRITE, 0L, channel.size()).load();
      channel.close();                      // Close the channel

      for(int i = 0 ; i < PRIMESREQUIRED ; ++i) {
        index = LONG_BYTES*(int)(PRIMECOUNT*Math.random());
        primes[i] = buf.getLong(index);
        buf.putLong(index, REPLACEMENT);
      }
      int count = 0;                        // Count of primes written
      for(long prime : primes) {
        System.out.printf("%12d", prime);
        if(++count%5 == 0) {
          System.out.println();
        }
      }
    } catch(IOException e) {
      e.printStackTrace();
    }
  }
}
```

MemoryMappedFile.java

This should output ten randomly selected primes, but some or all of the selections may turn out to be 99999L, the value of REPLACEMENT, if you have not refreshed the contents of `primes_backup.bin`.

How It Works

The statements of interest are those that are different to the previous example.

You have an `import` statement for the `MappedByteBuffer` class name, and you import the static member of the `MapMode` nested class to the `FileChannel` class that you use in the code.

You get the file channel with the following statement:

```
FileChannel channel =
        (FileChannel)(Files.newByteChannel(file, EnumSet.of(READ, WRITE)));
```

This stores the reference that the `newByteChannel()` method as type `FileChannel` because you want to call the `map()` method that the `FileChannel` class defines. Opening the channel for both reading and writing is essential here because you want to access and change the contents of the `MappedByteBuffer` object. Notice that the program uses a regular `try` block instead of a `try` block with resources. This is because you want to close the channel as soon as the memory mapping is established so as to demonstrate that it works independently from the channel.

You create and load a `MappedByteBuffer` object with the statement:

```
MappedByteBuffer buf =
                channel.map(READ_WRITE, 0L, channel.size()).load();
```

The buffer is created with the `READ_WRITE` mode specified, which permits the buffer to be accessed and modified. The buffer maps to the entire file because you specify the start file position as zero, and the length that is mapped is the length of the file. The `map()` method returns a reference to the `MappedByteBuffer` object that is created, and you use this to call its `load()` method to request that the contents of the file be loaded into memory immediately. The `load()` method also returns the same buffer reference, and you store that in `buf`.

Note that you are not obliged to call the `load()` method before you access the data in the buffer. If the data is not available when you try to access it through the `MappedByteBuffer` object, it is loaded for you. Try running the example with the call to `load()` removed. It should work the same as before.

The next statement closes the file channel because it is no longer required:

```
channel.close();                         // Close the channel
```

It is not essential to close the channel, but doing so demonstrates that memory-mapped file operations are independent of the channel after the mapping has been established.

Inside the `for` loop, you retrieve a value from the buffer at a random position, `index`:

```
primes[i] = buf.getLong(index);
```

You have no need to execute any explicit `read()` operations. The file contents are available directly through the buffer and any read operations that need to be executed to make the data you are accessing available are initiated automatically.

Next, you change the value at the position from which you retrieved the value that you store in `primes[i]`:

```
buf.putLong(index, REPLACEMENT);
```

This statement changes the contents of the buffer, and this change is subsequently written to the file at some point. When this occurs depends on the underlying operating system.'

Finally, you output the contents of the `primes` array. You have been able to access and modify the contents of the file without having to execute any explicit I/O operations on the file. For large files where you are transferring large amounts of data, this is potentially much faster than using explicit read and write operations. How much faster depends on how efficiently your operating system handles memory-mapped files and whether the way in which you access the data results in a large number of page faults.

Memory-mapped files have one risky aspect that you need to consider, and you will look at that in the next section.

Locking a File

You need to take care that an external program does not modify a memory-mapped file that you are working with, especially if the file could be truncated externally while you are accessing it. If you try to access a part of the file through a `MappedByteBuffer` that has become inaccessible because a segment has been chopped off the end of the file by another program, then the results are somewhat unpredictable. You may get a junk value back that your program may not recognize as such, or an exception of some kind may be thrown. You can acquire a *lock* on the file to try to prevent this sort of problem. A *shared lock* allows several processes to have concurrent read access to the file. An *exclusive lock* gives you exclusive access to the file; no one else can access the file while you have the exclusive lock. A file lock simply ensures your right of access to the file and might also inhibit the ability of others to change or possibly access the file as long as your lock is in effect. This facility is available only if the underlying operating system supports file locking.

 WARNING *Some operating systems may prevent the use of memory mapping for a file if a mandatory lock on the file is acquired and vice versa. In such situations using a file lock with a memory-mapped file does not work.*

A lock on a file is encapsulated by an object of the `java.nio.channels.FileLock` class. The `lock()` method for a `FileChannel` object tries to obtain an exclusive lock on the channel's file. Acquiring an exclusive lock on a file ensures that another program cannot access the file at all, and is typically used when you want to write to a file, or when any modification of the file by another process causes you problems. Here's one way to obtain an exclusive lock on a file specified by a `Path` object, `file`:

```
try (FileChannel fileChannel =
        (FileChannel)(Files.newByteChannel(file, EnumSet.of(READ, WRITE)));
    FileLock fileLock = channel.lock()){

  // Work with the locked file...

} catch (IOException e) {
  e.printStackTrace();
}
```

The `lock()` method attempts to acquire an exclusive lock on the channel's entire file so that no other program or thread can access the file while this channel holds the lock. A prerequisite for obtaining an exclusive lock is that the file has been opened for both reading and writing. If another program or thread already has a lock on the file, the `lock()` method blocks (i.e., does not return) until the lock on the file is released and can be acquired by this channel. The lock that is acquired is owned by the channel, `channel`, and is automatically released when the channel is closed. The `FileLock` class implements the `AutoClosable` interface so its `close()` method is called at the end of the `try` block to release the lock. You can also release the lock on a file by explicitly calling the `release()` method for the `FileLock` object.

You can call the `isValid()` method for a `FileLock` object to determine whether it is valid. A return value of `true` indicates a valid lock; otherwise, `false` is returned indicating that the lock is not valid. Note that once created, a `FileLock` object is immutable. It also has no further effect on file access after it has been invalidated. If you want to lock the file a second time, you must acquire a new lock.

The previous fragment hangs until a lock on the file is acquired. Having your program hang until a lock is acquired is not an ideal situation because it is quite possible a file could be locked permanently — at least until the computer is rebooted. This could be because a programming error in another program has locked the file, in which case your program hangs indefinitely. The `tryLock()` method for a channel offers an alternative way of requesting a lock that does not block. It either returns a reference to a valid `FileLock` object or returns `null` if the lock could not be acquired. This gives your program a chance to do something else or retire gracefully:

```
try (FileChannel fileChannel =
        (FileChannel)(Files.newByteChannel(file, EnumSet.of(READ, WRITE)))){
```

```
FileLock  fileLock = channel.tryLock();
  if(fileLock == null) {
    System.out.println("The file's locked - again!! Oh, I give up...");
    System.exit(1);
  }

  // Work with the locked file...
} catch (IOException e) {
  e.printStackTrace();
}
```

You will later see a better response to a lock than this in an example, but you should get the idea.

Locking Part of a File

Overloaded versions of the `lock()` and `tryLock()` methods enable you to specify just the part of the file you want to obtain a lock on so you don't lock the whole file and enable you to request a shared lock:

➤ `lock(long position, long size, boolean shared)`
   Requests a lock on the region of this channel's file starting at `position` and of length `size`. If the last argument is `true`, the lock requested is a shared lock. If it is `false`, the lock requested is an exclusive lock. If the lock cannot be obtained for any reason, the method blocks until the lock can be obtained or the channel is closed by another thread.

➤ `tryLock(long position, long size, boolean shared)`
   Works in the same way as the previous method, except that `null` is returned if the requested lock cannot be acquired. This avoids the potential for hanging your program indefinitely.

The effect of a shared lock is to prevent an exclusive lock being acquired by another program that overlaps the region that is locked. However, a shared lock does permit another program to acquire a shared lock on a region of the file that may overlap the region to which the original shared lock applies. This implies that more than one program may be accessing the same region of the file, so the effect of a shared lock is simply to ensure that your code is not prevented from doing whatever it is doing by some other program with a shared lock on the file. Some operating systems do not support shared locks, in which case the request is always treated as an exclusive lock regardless of what you requested. Microsoft Windows 7 supports shared locks.

Note that a single Java Virtual Machine (JVM) does not allow overlapping locks, so different threads running on the same JVM cannot have overlapping locks on a file. However, the locks within two or more JVMs on the same computer can overlap. If another program changing the data in a file would cause a problem for you then the safe thing to do is to obtain an exclusive lock on the file you are working with. If you want to test for the presence of an overlapping lock, you can call the `overlaps()` method for your lock object.

Practical File Locking Considerations

You can apply file locks in any context, not just with memory-mapped files. The fact that all or part of a file can be locked by a program means that you cannot ignore file locking when you are writing a real-world Java application that may execute in a context where file locking is supported. You need to include at least shared file locks for regions of a file that your program uses. In some instances, though, you should use exclusive locks because external changes to a file's contents can still be a problem even when the parts you are accessing cannot be changed. As I've said, you can obtain an exclusive lock only on a channel that is open for both reading and writing; a `NonReadableChannelException` or `NonWritableChannelException` is thrown, as appropriate, if you have opened the file just for input or just for output. This means that if you really must have an exclusive lock on a file, you have to have opened it for reading and writing.

You don't need to obtain a lock on an entire file. Generally, if it is likely that other programs will be using the same file concurrently, it is not reasonable practice to lock everyone else out, unless it is absolutely necessary, such as a situation in which you may be performing a transacted operation that must either succeed or fail entirely. Circumstances where it would be necessary are when the correctness of your program result is dependent on the entire file's contents not changing. If you were computing a checksum for a file, for example, you need to lock the entire file. Any changes made while your checksum calculation is in progress are likely to make it incorrect.

Most of the time it is quite sufficient to lock the portion of the file you are working with and then release it when you are done with it. You can get an idea of how you might do this in the context of the program that lists the primes from the `primes.bin` file.

TRY IT OUT   Using a File Lock

You will lock the region of the `primes.bin` file that you intend to read and then release it after the read operation is complete. You will use the `tryLock()` method because it does not block and try to acquire the lock again if it fails to return a reference to a `FileLock` object. To do this sensibly you need to be able to pause the current thread rather than roaring round a tight loop frantically calling the `tryLock()` method. I bring forward a capability from Chapter 16 to do this for you. You can pause the current thread by 200 milliseconds with the following code:

```
try {
  Thread.sleep(200);      // Wait for 200 milliseconds

} catch(InterruptedException e) {
  e.printStackTrace();
}
```

The static `sleep()` method in the `Thread` class causes the current thread to sleep for the number of milliseconds specified by the argument. While the current thread is sleeping, other threads can execute, so whoever has a lock on our file has a chance to release it.

Here's the code for the complete example:

Available for
download on
Wrox.com

```
import java.nio.file.*;
import java.nio.channels.*;
import java.io.IOException;
import java.nio.*;

public class LockingPrimesRead {
  public static void main(String[] args) {
    Path file = Paths.get(System.getProperty("user.home")).
                    resolve("Beginning Java Stuff").resolve("primes.bin");
    final int PRIMECOUNT = 6;
    final int LONG_BYTES = 8;
    ByteBuffer buf = ByteBuffer.allocate(LONG_BYTES*PRIMECOUNT);
    long[] primes = new long[PRIMECOUNT];

    try (FileChannel inCh = (FileChannel)(Files.newByteChannel(file))){
      int primesRead = 0;
      FileLock inLock = null;

      // File reading loop
      while(true) {
        int tryLockCount = 0;

        // Loop to get a lock on the file region you want to read
        while(true) {
          inLock = inCh.tryLock(inCh.position(), buf.remaining(), true);
          if(inLock != null) {              // If you have a lock
           System.out.println("\nAcquired file lock.");
           break;                          // exit the loop
          }
```

```
            if(++tryLockCount >= 100) {        // If you've tried too often
              System.out.printf("Failed to acquire lock after %d tries." +
                                            "Terminating...%n", tryLockCount);
              System.exit(1);                   // end the program
            }

            // Wait 200 msec before the next try for a file lock
            try {
                  Thread.sleep(200);            // Wait for 200 milliseconds
            } catch(InterruptedException e) {
                e.printStackTrace();
            }
          }

          // You have a lock so now read the file
          if(inCh.read(buf) == -1) {
            break;
          }
          inLock.release();                     // Release lock as read is finished
          System.out.println("Released file lock.");

          LongBuffer longBuf = ((ByteBuffer)(buf.flip())).asLongBuffer();
          primesRead = longBuf.remaining();
          longBuf.get(primes,0, longBuf.remaining());
          for(int i = 0 ; i < primesRead ; ++i) {
            if(i%6 == 0) {
              System.out.println();
            }
            System.out.printf("%12d", primes[i]);
          }
          buf.clear();                          // Clear the buffer for the next read
        }

      System.out.println("\nEOF reached.");
    } catch(IOException e) {
      e.printStackTrace();
    }
  }
}
```

LockingPrimesRead.java

This outputs primes from the file just as the ReadPrimes example does, but interspersed with comments showing where you acquire and release the file lock.

How It Works

The overall while loop for reading the file is now indefinite because you need to obtain a file lock before reading the file. You attempt to acquire the file lock in the inner while loop with the following statement:

```
inLock = inCh.tryLock(inCh.position(), buf.remaining(), true);
```

This requests a shared lock on buf.remaining() bytes in the file starting with the byte at the current file position. You can't get an exclusive lock on a file unless it has been opened for both reading and writing, and this doesn't apply here. Acquiring a shared lock on just the part of the file that you want to read ensures that other programs are not prevented from accessing the file, but the bit you are working with cannot be changed externally. Another program cannot acquire an exclusive overlapping lock, but it can acquire a shared overlapping lock.

You have to test the value returned by the tryLock() method for null to determine whether you have obtained a lock or not. The if statement that does this is quite simple:

```
if(inLock != null) {              // If you have a lock
  System.out.println("\nAcquired file lock.");
  break;                          // exit the loop
}
```

If `inLock` is not `null`, you have a lock on the file, so you exit the loop to acquire the lock. If `inLock` is `null`, you then check how often you have tried to acquire a lock and failed:

```
if(++tryLockCount >= 100) {       // If you've tried too often
  System.out.printf("Failed to acquire lock after %d tries. " +
                             "Terminating...%n", tryLockCount);
  System.exit(1);                 // end the program
}
```

The only reason for the `String` concatenation here is that the string won't fit in the width of the page. If you have already tried 100 times to obtain a lock, you give up and exit the program. If it's fewer tries than this, you're prepared to give it another try, but first you pause the current thread:

```
try {
    Thread.sleep(200);           // Wait for 200 milliseconds
} catch(InterruptedException e) {
    e.printStackTrace();
}
```

This pauses the current thread for 200 milliseconds, which provides an opportunity for the program that has an exclusive lock on the file to release it. After returning from the `sleep()` method, the `while` loop continues for another try at acquiring a lock.

After you have acquired a lock, you read the file in the usual way and release the lock:

```
if(inCh.read(buf) == -1) {
  break;
}
inLock.release();                 // Release lock as read is finished
System.out.println("Released file lock.");
```

By releasing the lock immediately after reading the file, you ensure that the amount of time the file is blocked is a minimum. Of course, if the `read()` method returns −1 because EOF has been reached, you won't call the `release()` method for the `FileLock` object here because you exit the outer loop. However, after exiting the outer `while` loop you exit the `try` block, which closes the channel, and closing the channel releases the lock.

SUMMARY

In this chapter, I discussed the various ways in which you can read basic types of data from a file. You can now transfer data of any of the basic types to or from a file. In the next chapter you will learn how to transfer objects of class types that you have defined to or from a file.

EXERCISES

You can download the source code for the examples in the book and the solutions to the following exercises from www.wrox.com.

1. Write a program to read back the contents of the files written by the first exercise in the previous chapter and output the proverb length that was read and the proverb itself for each of the proverbs.

2. Extend the `ReadPrimes` example that you produced in this chapter to optionally display the *n*th prime, when *n* is entered from the keyboard.

3. Extend the `ReadPrimes` program further to output a given number of primes, starting at a given number. For example, output 15 primes starting at the 30th. The existing capabilities should be retained.

4. Write a program that outputs the contents of a file to the command line as groups of eight hexadecimal digits with five groups to a line, each group separated from the next by a space.

5. Write a program that allows either one or more names and addresses to be entered from the keyboard and appended to a file, or the contents of the file to be read back and output to the command line.

6. Modify the previous example to store an index to the name and address file in a separate file. The index file should contain each person's second name, plus the position where the corresponding name and address can be found in the name and address file. Provide support for an optional command argument allowing a person's second name to be entered. When the command-line argument is present, the program should then find the name and address and output it to the command line.

▶ **WHAT YOU LEARNED IN THIS CHAPTER**

TOPIC	CONCEPT
File Input/Output	All file input and output is in terms of bytes. When you read bytes from a file, you must then interpret the bytes as the types of data items that were written to the file.
Accessing a File	You can obtain a FileChannel object connected to a file for reading, writing, or both by calling the static newByteChannel() method in the Files class for the Path object that encapsulates the path to the file. The method returns a reference of type SeekableByteChannel.
Reading and Writing a File	The argument to the newByteChannel() method determines whether you open the file for reading, writing, or both. The argument can be one or more of the constants defined by the StandardOpenOption enumeration.
File Read Operations	You call the read() method for a FileChannel object connected to a file to read() from the file.
Reading Data from a File	The data that you read from a file is stored in a buffer of type ByteBuffer.
Interpreting Data from a File	You can call one of the get methods for a ByteBuffer object to retrieve bytes from the buffer interpreted as a given basic type.
Using View Buffers	A view buffer interprets the contents of a ByteBuffer as a sequence of data items of a given type. You can use view buffers to interpret the bytes read from a file into a ByteBuffer as any basic type other than boolean. You obtain a view buffer corresponding to a ByteBuffer object for a given data type by calling the appropriate ByteBuffer class method.
Memory-Mapped Files	A memory-mapped file enables you to access data in the file as though it were resident in memory. You access a memory-mapped file through a MappedByteBuffer object that you obtain by calling the map() method for a FileChannel object.
File Locking	You can lock all or part of the contents of a file by acquiring a file lock. A file lock can be an exclusive lock that locks the entire file for your use, or it can be a shared lock that locks part of a file while you are accessing it.
Exclusive File Locks	You can obtain an exclusive lock only on a file you have opened for both reading and writing. You obtain an exclusive lock by calling the lock() method for the FileChannel object that is connected to the file.
Shared File Locks	You obtain a shared file lock by calling the tryLock() method for the FileChannel object that is connected to the file.

12

Serializing Objects

WHAT YOU WILL LEARN IN THIS CHAPTER

➤   What serialization is and how you make a class serializable

➤   How to write objects to a file

➤   What transient fields in a class are

➤   How to write basic types of data to an object file

➤   How to implement the Serializable interface

➤   How to read objects from a file

➤   How to implement serialization for classes containing objects that are not
    serializable by default

In this chapter, you see how you can transfer objects to and from a stream. This greatly simplifies file I/O in your object-oriented programs. In most circumstances, the details of writing all the information that makes up an object is taken care of completely and automatically. Similarly, objects are typically reconstructed automatically from what you wrote to the file.

STORING OBJECTS IN A FILE

The process of storing and retrieving objects in an external file is called *serialization*. Writing an object to a file is referred to as *serializing*, and reading an object from a file is called *deserializing*. Serialization is concerned with writing objects and the fields they contain to a stream, so static member data is not included. Static fields have whatever values are assigned by default in the class definition. Note that an array of any type is an object and can be serialized—even an array of values of a primitive type, such as type int or type double.

I think you might be surprised at how easy this is. Perhaps the most impressive aspect of the way serialization is implemented in Java is that you can generally read and write objects of almost any class type, including objects of classes that you have defined yourself, without adding any code to the classes involved to support this mechanism. For the most part, everything is taken care of automatically.

Two classes from the java.io package are used for serialization. An ObjectOutputStream object manages the writing of objects to a file, and reading the objects back is handled by an object of the class ObjectInputStream. As Figure 12-1 illustrates, these classes are derived from OutputStream and InputStream, respectively.

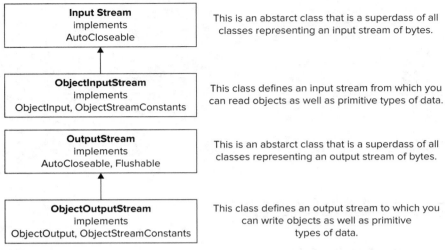

Input Stream
implements
AutoCloseable

This is an abstarct class that is a superdass of all classes representing an input stream of bytes.

ObjectInputStream
implements
ObjectInput, ObjectStreamConstants

This class defines an input stream from which you can read objects as well as primitive types of data.

OutputStream
implements
AutoCloseable, Flushable

This is an abstarct class that is a superdass of all classes representing an output stream of bytes.

ObjectOutputStream
implements
ObjectOutput, ObjectStreamConstants

This class defines an output stream to which you can write objects as well as primitive types of data.

FIGURE 12-1

The `ObjectInput` and `ObjectOutput` interfaces extend the `DataInput` and `DataOutput` interfaces that declare methods for reading and writing data of the primitive types and add the methods for reading and writing objects. The `ObjectInputStream` class implements `ObjectInput` and `ObjectOutputStream` implements `ObjectOutput`. Both object stream classes implement the `ObjectStreamConstants` interface, which defines constants that are used to identify elements of an object in the stream. They both implement the `AutoClosable` interface so they can be closed automatically if you create the objects within a `try` block with resources.

WRITING AN OBJECT TO A FILE

To write objects to a file, the constructor for the `ObjectOutputStream` class requires a reference to an `OutputStream` object as an argument, and this object defines the stream that encapsulates the file in which you intend to store your objects. You can create an `ObjectOutputStream` object from a channel with the following statements:

```
Path file = Paths.get("MyObjectFile");
// Check out the file path...

// Create the object output stream for the file
try (ObjectOutputStream objectOut =
                    new ObjectOutputStream(Files.newOutputStream(file))){

  // Write to the object output stream...

} catch(IOException e) {
  e.printStackTrace();
}
```

I discussed the static `newOutputStream()` method that the `Files` class defines in Chapter 10. Here you have not specified any open options so the default options assumed are `WRITE`, `CREATE`, and `TRUNCATE_EXISTING`. The `ObjectOutputStream` constructor throws an exception of type `IOException` if an error occurs while the stream header is being written to the file.

Although the previous code fragment works perfectly well, it does not result in a stream that is particularly efficient because the output stream returned by `newOutputStream()` is unbuffered, so each output operation writes directly to the file. In practice you probably want to buffer write operations to the file in memory, in which case you would create the `ObjectOutputStream` object between the `try` block parentheses like this:

```
try(ObjectOutputStream objectOut =
           new ObjectOutputStream(new BufferedOutputStream(
                                      Files.newOutputStream(file)))) {
   ...
} catch(IOException e) {
   e.printStackTrace();
}
```

The `BufferedOutputStream` constructor creates an object that buffers the `OutputStream` object that is passed to it, so here you get a buffered `OutputStream` object for the file that you pass to the `ObjectOutputStream` constructor. The `BufferedOutputStream` object writes the data to an internal buffer. Data from the buffer is written to the file whenever the buffer is full, or when the stream is closed. By default, the buffer has a capacity of 2048 bytes. If you want to use a buffer of a different size, you can use the `BufferedOutputStream` constructor that accepts a second argument of type `int` that defines the size of the buffer in bytes.

To write an object to the file, you call the `writeObject()` method for `objectOut` with a reference to the object to be written as the argument. Because this method accepts a reference of type `Object` as an argument, you can pass a reference of any class type to the method and this includes `enum` types and arrays. Three basic conditions have to be met for an object to be written to a stream:

➤   The class must be declared as `public`.

➤   The class must implement the `Serializable` interface.

➤   If the class has a direct or indirect base class that is not serializable, then that base class must have a default constructor — that is, a constructor that requires no arguments. The derived class must take care of transferring the base class data members to the stream. I'll explain how a little later in this chapter.

It is also very desirable that the class defines a member of type long with the name `serialVersionUID`. For example, you could define the member of the class like this:

```
private static final long serialVersionUID = 9002L;
```

This defines the member as `private`, but any access modifier is acceptable. This variable identifies a version number for the class that is used to verify that the same class definition is used during the deserialization process when objects are read from the file as when objects were written to the file. The specific value you assign to the `serialVersionUID` variable is not important. What is important is that you change the value if you modify the class definition, which ensures that using the incorrect version of the class to read objects from a file is flagged. Other than this, implementing the `Serializable` interface is a lot less difficult than it sounds; you see how in a moment. I come back to the question of how to deal with a non-serializable base class later in this chapter.

If `myObject` is an instance of a public class that implements `Serializable`, then to write `myObject` to the stream that you defined previously, you use the following statement:

```
try (ObjectOutputStream objectOut =
             new ObjectOutputStream(
                 new BufferedOutputStream(Files.newOutputStream(file)))){

   objectOut.writeObject(myObject);

} catch(IOException e) {
   e.printStackTrace();
}
```

The `writeObject()` method can throw any of the following exceptions:

➤   `InvalidClassException` is thrown when there is something wrong with the class definition for the object being written. This might be because the class is not `public`, for instance.

➤   `NotSerializableException` is thrown if the object's class, or the class of a data member of the class, does not implement the `Serializable` interface.

➤   `IOException` is thrown when a file output error occurs.

The first two exception classes here are subclasses of `ObjectStreamException`, which is itself a subclass of `IOException`. Thus, you can catch any of them with a `catch` block for `IOException`. Of course, if you want to take some specific action for any of these then you can catch them individually. Just be sure to put the `catch` blocks for the first two types of exception before the one for `IOException`.

The call to `writeObject()` takes care of writing everything to the stream that is necessary to reconstitute the object later in a read operation. This includes information about the class and all its superclasses, including their version IDs, as well as the contents and types of the data members of the class. Remarkably, this works even when the data members are themselves class objects as long as they are objects of classes that implement the `Serializable` interface. Our `writeObject()` call causes the `writeObject()` method to be called for each object that is a data member, and this mechanism continues recursively until everything that makes up our object has been written to the stream. Each independent object that you write to the stream requires a separate call to the `writeObject()` method, but the objects that are members of an object are taken care of automatically. This is not completely foolproof in that the relationships between the class objects can affect this process, but for the most part this is all you need to do.

Writing Primitive Data Types to an Object Stream

You can write data of any of the primitive types using the methods declared in the `DataOutput` interface and defined in the `ObjectOutputStream` class for this purpose. For writing individual items of data of various types, you have the following methods:

`write(int byte)`	`writeByte(int byte)`
`writeFloat(float x)`	`writeDouble(double x)`
`writeShort(int n)`	`writeInt(int n)`
`writeLong(long n)`	`writeChar(int ch`
`writeBoolean(boolean val)`	

The `write()` and `writeByte()` methods both write a single byte to the stream. None of the listed methods returns a value, and they can all throw an `IOException` because they are output operations.

When you want to write a `String` object to the file as an object, you normally use the `writeObject()` method. You can also write a string to the file as a sequence of bytes using the `writeBytes()` method by passing a reference to a `String` as the argument to the method. In this case, each character in the string is converted to a byte using the default charset. You can write a string simply as a sequence of Unicode characters by using the `writeChars()` method, again with a reference of type `String` as the argument. This writes each Unicode character in the string as two bytes. Note that the `writeBytes()` and `writeChars()` methods write just a sequence of bytes or characters. No information about the original `String` object is written so the fact that these characters belonged to a string is lost.

You have two methods defined in the `ObjectOutputStream` class that apply to arrays of bytes:

➤   `write(byte[] array)` writes the contents of array to the file as bytes.

➤   `write(byte[] array, int offset, int length)` writes `length` elements from array to the file starting with `array[offset]`.

In both cases just bytes are written to the stream as binary data, not the array object itself. An array of type `byte[]` is written to the stream as an object by default, so you need to use these methods only if you do not want an array of type `byte[]` written as an object.

You can mix writing data of the basic types and class objects to the stream. If you have a mixture of objects and data items of basic types that you want to store in a file, you can write them all to the same `ObjectOutputStream`. You just have to make sure that you read everything back in the sequence and form in which it was written.

Implementing the Serializable Interface

A necessary condition for objects of a class to be serializable is that the class implements the `Serializable` interface, but this may not be sufficient, as you see later. In most instances, you need only declare that the class implements the `Serializable` interface to make the objects of that class type serializable and preferably define the `serialVersionUID` member that I introduced earlier. If you don't define this member of the class, a default is created by the serialization runtime, but this is not foolproof and can result in an exception of type `InvalidClassException` being thrown during deserialization. No other code is necessary. For example, the following declares a class that implements the interface:

```
public MyClass implements Serializable {
  // Definition of the rest of the class...
  private static final long serialVersionUID = 9002L;
}
```

As long as all the fields in `MyClass` are serializable then simply declaring that the class implements the `Serializable` interface and defining `serialVersionUID` as a final static class member is sufficient to make objects of type `MyClass` serializable. If your class is derived from another class that implements the `Serializable` interface, then your class also inherits the implementation of `Serializable`, so you don't have to declare that this is the case. Let's try this out on a simple class to verify that it really works.

TRY IT OUT   Writing Objects to a File

You first define a serializable class that has some arbitrary fields with different data types:

```
import java.io.Serializable;

public class Junk implements Serializable {
  private static java.util.Random generator = new java.util.Random();
  private int answer;                                 // The answer
  private double[] numbers;                           // Valuable data
  private String thought;                             // A unique thought
  private static final long serialVersionUID = 9001L;

  public Junk(String thought) {
    this.thought = thought;
    answer = 42;                                      // Answer always 42

    numbers = new double[3+generator.nextInt(4)]; // Array size 3 to 6
    for(int i = 0 ; i<numbers.length ; ++i) {     // Populate with
      numbers[i] = generator.nextDouble();        // random values
    }
  }

  @Override
  public String toString() {
    StringBuffer strBuf = new StringBuffer(thought);
    strBuf.append('\n').append(String.valueOf(answer));
    for(int i = 0 ; i<numbers.length ; ++i) {
      strBuf.append("\nnumbers[")
            .append(String.valueOf(i))
            .append("] = ")
            .append(numbers[i]);
    }
    return strBuf.toString();
  }
}
```

Directory "SerializeObjects"

An object of type `Junk` has three instance fields: A simple integer that is always 42, a `String` object, and an array of `double` values. The `toString()` method provides a `String` representation of a `Junk` object that you can output to the command line. The static field `generator` is not written to the stream when an object of type `Junk` is serialized. The only provision you have made for serializing objects of type `Junk` is to declare that the class implements the `Serializable` interface.

You can write objects of this class type to a file with the following program:

```java
import java.io.*;
import java.nio.file.*;
import java.io.IOException;

public class SerializeObjects {
  public static void main(String[] args) {
    Junk obj1 = new Junk("A green twig is easily bent.");
    Junk obj2 = new Junk("A little knowledge is a dangerous thing.");
    Junk obj3 = new Junk("Flies light on lean horses.");

    Path file = Paths.get(System.getProperty("user.home")).
                    resolve("Beginning Java Stuff").resolve("JunkObjects.bin");
    try {
      // Make sure we have the directory
      Files.createDirectories(file.getParent());
    } catch (IOException e) {
      e.printStackTrace();
      System.exit(1);
    }

    try (ObjectOutputStream objectOut = new ObjectOutputStream(
                new BufferedOutputStream(Files.newOutputStream(file)))){
      // Write three objects to the file
      objectOut.writeObject(obj1);              // Write object
      objectOut.writeObject(obj2);              // Write object
      objectOut.writeObject(obj3);              // Write object
      System.out.println("\n\nobj1:\n" + obj1
                        +"\n\nobj2:\n" + obj2
                        +"\n\nobj3:\n" + obj3);

    } catch(IOException e) {
      e.printStackTrace();
    }
  }
}
```

Directory "SerializeObjects"

When I ran this, I got the following output:

```
obj1:
A green twig is easily bent.
42
numbers[0] = 0.2639251629586685
numbers[1] = 0.7212385629586818
numbers[2] = 0.9652574768726307
numbers[3] = 0.4347419118504684
numbers[4] = 0.38425335784130443

obj2:
A little knowledge is a dangerous thing.
42
numbers[0] = 0.20540865153372645
numbers[1] = 0.14819027494615766
numbers[2] = 0.966333475583602

obj3:
Flies light on lean horses.
```

```
42
numbers[0] = 0.582505845190295
numbers[1] = 0.7568767131705605
numbers[2] = 0.031276131457401934
numbers[3] = 0.22867560732800996
numbers[4] = 0.030591566057953434
```

You should get something vaguely similar.

How It Works

You first create three objects of type `Junk` in the `main()` method .Within the `try` block you create the `ObjectOutputStream` object that you use to write objects to the file `D:/Junk/JunkObjects.bin` via a buffered output stream. Each `Junk` object is written to the file by passing it to the `writeObject()` method for the `ObjectOutputStream` object. Each object is written to the file, including the values of its three instance fields, answer, thought, and numbers. The `String` object and the array are written to the file as objects. This is taken care of automatically and requires no special provision within the code. The static field `generator` is not written to the file.

The stream is closed automatically at the end of the `try` block. You read the objects back from the file a little later in this chapter.

Conditions for Serialization

In general, you could encounter a small fly in the ointment. For implementing the `Serializable` interface to be sufficient to make objects of the class serializable, all the fields in the class must be serializable (or transient—which I come to), and all superclasses of the class must also be serializable. This implies that the fields must be either of primitive types or of class types that are themselves serializable.

If a superclass of your class is not serializable, it still might be possible to make your class serializable. The conditions that must be met for this to be feasible are:

➤ Each superclass that is not serializable must have a public no-arg constructor—a constructor with no parameters.

➤ Your class must be declared as implementing the `Serializable` interface.

➤ Your class must take responsibility for serializing and deserializing the fields for the superclasses that are not serializable.

This is usually the case for your own classes, but one or two classes that come along with Java do not implement the `Serializable` interface. What's more, you can't make them serializable because they do not have a public default constructor. The `Graphics` class in the package `java.awt` is an example of such a class—you see more of this class when you get into programming using windows. All is not lost, however. You have an escape route. As long as you know how to reconstruct any fields that were not serializable when you read an object back from a stream, you can still serialize your objects by declaring the non-serializable fields as `transient`.

Transient Data Members of a Class

If your class has fields that are not serializable, or that you just don't want to have written to the stream, you can declare them as `transient`. For example:

```
public class MyClass implements Serializable {
  private static final long serialVersionUID = 8001L;
  transient protected Graphics g;    // Transient class member

  // Rest of the class definition
}
```

Declaring a data member as `transient` prevents the `writeObject()` method from attempting to write the data member to the stream. When the class object is read back, the object is created properly, including any members that you declared as `transient`. The transient class members just won't have their values set, because they were not written to the stream. Unless you arrange for something to be done about it, the transient fields are `null`.

You may well want to declare some data members of a class as `transient`. You would do this when they have a value that is not meaningful long term or out of context—objects that represent the current time, or today's date, for example. You must either provide code to explicitly reconstruct the members that you declare as `transient` when the object that contains them is read from the stream or accept the defaults for these that apply when the objects are re-created.

READING AN OBJECT FROM A FILE

Reading objects back from a file is just as easy as writing them. First, you need to create an `ObjectInputStream` object for the file. To do this you just pass a reference to an `InputStream` object that encapsulates the file to the `ObjectInputStream` class constructor:

```
Path file = Paths.get(System.getProperty("user.home")).
                      resolve("Beginning Java Stuff").resolve("JunkObjects.bin");
// Verify that the file exists...

try (ObjectInputStream objectIn =
           new ObjectInputStream(new BufferedInputStream(
                                      Files.newInputStream(file)))){
  // Read objects from the file...

} catch(IOException e) {
  e.printStackTrace();
}
```

The `ObjectInputStream` constructor throws an exception of type `StreamCorruptedException`—a subclass of `IOException`—if the stream header is not correct, or of type `IOException` if an error occurs while reading the stream header. Calling `newInputStream()` from the `Files` class with the `Path` object, `file`, as the argument creates an input stream for the file. This is exactly as you saw in Chapter 11. As you know, the default open option that is assumed is `READ`.

After you have created the `ObjectInputStream` object, you call its `readObject()` method to read an object from the file:

```
try (ObjectInputStream objectIn =
    new ObjectInputStream(new BufferedInputStream(Files.newInputStream(file)))){
  Object myObject = objectIn.readObject();

} catch(ClassNotFoundException|IOException e){
  e.printStackTrace();
}
```

The `readObject()` method can throw the following exceptions:

➤   `ClassNotFoundException`: Thrown if the class for an object read from the stream cannot be found.

➤   `InvalidClassException`: Thrown if something is wrong with the class for an object. Often this is caused by using a class definition when you read an object from a stream that is different from the class definition in effect when you wrote it.

➤   `StreamCorruptedException`: When objects are written to the stream, additional control data is written so that the object data can be validated when it is read back. This exception is thrown when the control information in the stream violates consistency checks.

➤   `OptionalDataException`: Thrown when basic types of data are read rather than an object. For example, if you wrote a `String` object using the `writeChars()` method and then attempted to read it back using the `readObject()` method, this exception would be thrown.

➤   `EOFException`: Thrown if the end-of-file is read.

➤   `IOException`: Thrown if an error occurred reading the stream.

Clearly, if you do not have a full and accurate class definition for each type of object that you want to read from the stream, the stream object does not know how to create the object and the read fails. The last five of the six possible exceptions are flavors of `IOException`, so you can use that as a catchall as you have in the preceding code fragment. However, `ClassNotFoundException` is derived from `Exception`, so you must provide for catching this exception, too. Otherwise, the code does not compile. Here, you catch either exception type in the same `catch` block because you have the same action for both.

As the code fragment implies, the `readObject()` method returns a reference to the object as type `Object`, so you need to cast it to the appropriate class type to use it. Note that arrays are considered to be objects and are treated as such during serialization, so if you explicitly read an array from a file, you have to cast it to the appropriate array type.

For example, if the object in the previous code fragment was of type `MyClass`, you could read it back from the file with the statement:

```
MyClass theObject = (MyClass)(objectIn.readObject());
```

This casts the reference that is returned by the `readObject()` method to type `MyClass`.

Armed with the knowledge of how the `readObject()` method works, you can now read the file that you wrote in the previous example.

TRY IT OUT   Deserializing Objects

You can read the file containing `Junk` objects with the following code:

Available for
download on
Wrox.com

```
import java.io.*;
import java.nio.file.*;

class DeserializeObjects {
  public static void main(String args[]) {
    Path file = Paths.get(System.getProperty("user.home")).
                      resolve("Beginning Java Stuff").resolve("JunkObjects.bin");
    if(Files.notExists(file)) {
      System.out.printf("\nFile %s does not exist.", file);
      System.exit(1);
    }

    int objectCount = 0;                       // Number of objects read
    try (ObjectInputStream objectIn =
          new ObjectInputStream(new BufferedInputStream(
                                      Files.newInputStream(file)))){
      // Read from the stream until we hit the end
      Junk object = null;                      // Stores an object reference
      while(true) {
        object = (Junk)objectIn.readObject(); // Read an object
        ++objectCount;                         // Increment the count
        System.out.println(object);            // Output the object
      }

    } catch(EOFException e) {  // This will execute when we reach EOF
      System.out.println("EOF reached. "+ objectCount + " objects read.");

    } catch(IOException|ClassNotFoundException e) {
      e.printStackTrace();
    }
  }
}
```

I got the following output from this example:

```
A green twig is easily bent.
42
numbers[0] = 0.2639251629586685
numbers[1] = 0.7212385629586818
numbers[2] = 0.9652574768726307
numbers[3] = 0.4347419118504684
numbers[4] = 0.38425335784130443
A little knowledge is a dangerous thing.
42
numbers[0] = 0.20540865153372645
numbers[1] = 0.14819027494615766
numbers[2] = 0.966333475583602
Flies light on lean horses.
42
numbers[0] = 0.582505845190295
numbers[1] = 0.7568767131705605
numbers[2] = 0.031276131457401934
numbers[3] = 0.22867560732800996
numbers[4] = 0.030591566057953434
EOF reached. 3 objects read.
```

You should get output corresponding to the objects that were written to your file.

How It Works

You first define the `Path` object that encapsulates the path to the file containing the objects to be read and verify that it does indeed exist. You use the `objectCount` variable to accumulate a count of the total number of objects read from the stream.

To make the program a little more general, the read operation is in a loop to show how you might read the file when you don't know how many objects there are in it. The `object` variable stores the reference to each object that you read. To read each object, you just call the `readObject()` method for the input stream and cast the reference that is returned to type `Junk` before storing it in `object`.

So you can see what you have read from the file, the string representation of each object is displayed on the command line. The `while` loop continues to read objects from the stream indefinitely. When the end of the file is reached, an exception of type `EOFException` is thrown. This effectively terminates the loop, and the code in the `catch` block for this exception executes. This outputs a message to the command line showing the number of objects that were read. In spite of the `try` block being terminated by an exception being thrown, the stream is still closed automatically. The `catch` block for `EOFException` must precede the block that catches `IOException` because `EOFException` is a subclass of `IOException`.

As you can see, you get back all the objects that you wrote to the file originally. This is obviously very encouraging—getting fewer objects than you wrote would be inconvenient to say the least, and getting more would be worrying.

Determining the Class of a Deserialized Object

The `readObject()` method returns the object that it reads from the stream as type `Object` so you need to know what the original type of the object was to be able to cast it to its actual type. For the most part, you will know what the class of the object is when you read it back. It is possible that in some circumstances you won't know exactly, but you will have a rough idea, in which case you can test it. To bring the problem into sharper focus, consider a hypothetical situation.

Suppose you have a file containing objects that represent employees. The basic characteristics of all employees are defined in a base class, `Person`, but various different types of employee are represented by subclasses of `Person`. You might have subclasses `Manager`, `Secretary`, `Admin`, and `ShopFloor`, for example. The file can contain any of the subclass types in any sequence. Of course, you can cast any object read from the file to type `Person` because that is the base class, but you want to know precisely what each object is so you can call some type-specific methods. Because you know what the possible types are, you can check the type of the object against each of these types and cast accordingly:

```
Person person = null;
try ( ... ){
  Person person = (Person)objectIn.readObject();
  if(person instanceof Manager)
    processManager((Manager)person);
  else if(person instanceof Secretary)
    processSecretary((Secretary)person);

    // and so on...

} catch (IOException e){
    e.printStackTrace();
}
```

Here you determine the specific class type of the object read from the file before calling a method that deals with that particular type of object. Don't forget though that the `instanceof` operator does not guarantee that the object being tested is actually of the type tested for—`Manager`, say. The object could also be of any type that is a subclass of `Manager`. In any event, the cast to type `Manager` is perfectly legal.

Where you need to be absolutely certain of the type, you can use a different approach:

```
String className = person.getClass().getName();
if(className.equals("Manager"))
   processManager((Manager)person);
 else if(className.equals(Secretary))
     processSecretary((Secretary)person);

   // and so on...
```

This calls the `getClass()` method (inherited from `Object`) for the object that was read from the file and that returns a reference to the `Class` object that represents the class of the object. Calling the `getName()` method for the `Class` object returns the fully qualified name of the class. This approach guarantees that the object is of the type for which you are testing, and is not a subclass of that type.

Another approach would be to just execute a cast to a particular type, and catch the `ClassCastException` that is thrown when the cast is invalid. This is fine if you do not expect the exception to be thrown under normal conditions, but if on a regular basis the object read from the stream might be other than the type to which you are casting, you are much better off with code that avoids the need to throw and catch the exception because this adds quite a lot of overhead.

Reading Basic Data from an Object Stream

The `ObjectInputStream` class defines the methods that are declared in the `DataInput` interface for reading basic types of data back from an object stream and binary values. They are:

`readBoolean()`	`readByte()`
`readFloat()`	`readDouble()`
`readShort ()`	`readInt()`
`readLong()`	`readChar()`

They each return a value of the corresponding type, and they can all throw an `IOException` if an error occurs or can throw an `EOFException` if the end-of-file is reached. There is also a `read()` method with no parameter that reads a single byte from the stream and returns it as type `int`. This returns −1 when EOF is reached and does not throw the exception.

Just to make sure that the process of serializing and deserializing objects is clear, let's try it again in another simple example.

Using Object Serialization

In Chapter 6, you produced an example that created `PolyLine` objects containing `Point` objects in a generalized linked list. This is a good basis for demonstrating how effectively serialization takes care of handling objects that are members of objects. You can create an example that writes `PolyLine` objects to a file using serialization.

TRY IT OUT   Serializing a Linked List

The classes `PolyLine`, `Point`, and `LinkedList` and the inner class `ListItem` are the same as in Chapter 6 except that you need to implement the `Serializable` interface in each of them.

The `PolyLine` definition needs to be amended to the following:

Available for download on Wrox.com

```java
import java.io.Serializable;

public final class PolyLine implements Serializable  {
    // Class definition as before...
    private static final long serialVersionUID = 7001L;
}
```

Directory "TryPolyLineObjects"

The `Point` definition needs a similar change:

Available for download on Wrox.com

```java
import java.io.Serializable;

public class Point implements Serializable {
    // Class definition as before...
    private static final long serialVersionUID = 7001L;
}
```

Directory "TryPolyLineObjects"

The `LinkedList` class and its inner class likewise:

Available for download on Wrox.com

```java
import java.io.Serializable;

public class LinkedList implements Serializable {
    // Class definition as before...
    private static final long serialVersionUID = 7001L;

    private class ListItem implements Serializable {
        // Inner class definition as before...
        private static final long serialVersionUID = 7001L;
    }
}
```

Directory "TryPolyLineObjects"

The class to write `PolyLine` objects to a stream looks like this:

Available for download on Wrox.com

```java
import java.io.*;
import java.nio.file.*;

public class TryPolyLineObjects {
    public static void main(String[] args) {
        // Create an array of coordinate pairs
```

```
        double[][] coords = { {1., 1.}, {1., 2.}, { 2., 3.},
                             {-3., 5.}, {-5., 1.}, {0., 0.} };

    Path file = Paths.get(System.getProperty("user.home")).
                    resolve("Beginning Java Stuff").resolve("Polygons.bin");
    try {
      Files.createDirectories(file.getParent()); // Make sure we have directory
    } catch (IOException e) {
      e.printStackTrace();
      System.exit(1);
    }

    // Create the polyline objects and write them to the file
    System.out.println("Writing objects to file.");
    try (ObjectOutputStream objectOut = new ObjectOutputStream(
                    new BufferedOutputStream(Files.newOutputStream(file)))){

      // Create a polyline from the coordinates
      PolyLine polygon1 = new PolyLine(coords);
      System.out.println(polygon1);
      objectOut.writeObject(polygon1);          // Write first object

      PolyLine polygon2 = new PolyLine(coords);
      polygon2.addPoint(10., 10.);
      System.out.println(polygon2);             // Add a point
      objectOut.writeObject(polygon2);          // Write second object

      PolyLine polygon3 = new PolyLine(coords);
      polygon3.addPoint(10., 15.);
      System.out.println(polygon3);             // Add a point
      objectOut.writeObject(polygon3);          // Write third object
      System.out.println("File written.");
    } catch(IOException e) {
      e.printStackTrace();
      System.exit(1);
    }

    // Read the objects back from the file
    PolyLine polylines[] = new PolyLine[3];
    System.out.println("\nReading objects from the file:");
    try (ObjectInputStream objectIn =
                new ObjectInputStream(
                        new BufferedInputStream(Files.newInputStream(file)))){
      for(int i = 0 ; i<polylines.length ; ++i) {
        polylines[i] = (PolyLine)objectIn.readObject();
      }
    } catch(ClassNotFoundException  e) {
      System.err.println("Class not found.");
      e.printStackTrace();
    } catch(IOException e){
      e.printStackTrace();
    }
    // Display the objects read from the file
    for(int i = 0 ; i<polylines.length ; ++i)
      System.out.println(polylines[i]);
  }
}
```

Directory "TryPolyLineObjects"

This produces the following output:

```
Writing objects to file.
Polyline: (1.0,1.0) (1.0,2.0) (2.0,3.0) (-3.0,5.0) (-5.0,1.0) (0.0,0.0)
```

```
Polyline: (1.0,1.0) (1.0,2.0) (2.0,3.0) (-3.0,5.0) (-5.0,1.0) (0.0,0.0) (10.0,10.0)
Polyline: (1.0,1.0) (1.0,2.0) (2.0,3.0) (-3.0,5.0) (-5.0,1.0) (0.0,0.0) (10.0,15.0)
File written.

Reading objects from the file:
Polyline: (1.0,1.0) (1.0,2.0) (2.0,3.0) (-3.0,5.0) (-5.0,1.0) (0.0,0.0)
Polyline: (1.0,1.0) (1.0,2.0) (2.0,3.0) (-3.0,5.0) (-5.0,1.0) (0.0,0.0) (10.0,10.0)
Polyline: (1.0,1.0) (1.0,2.0) (2.0,3.0) (-3.0,5.0) (-5.0,1.0) (0.0,0.0) (10.0,15.0)
```

How It Works

In the second `try` block you create an `ObjectOutputStream` for the file, `Polygons.bin`, in the `Beginning Java Stuff` directory that is in your home directory. You create `objectOut` from a buffered output stream that you create from the `Path` object for the file. You then create three `PolyLine` objects and write each of them to the file using the `writeObject()` method for `objectOut`.

You don't need to explicitly write the `LinkedList` and `Point` objects to the stream. These are part of the `PolyLine` object, so they are taken care of automatically. The same goes for when you read the `PolyLine` objects back. All the subsidiary objects are reconstructed automatically.

To read the file, you create an `ObjectInputStream` object for `Polygons.bin` in the third `try` block. You read the objects using the `readObject()` method and store the references in the `polylines` array. After the `try` block you output the objects to the standard output stream. It couldn't be simpler really, could it?

Serializing Classes Yourself

Earlier, I identified situations where the default serialization that you used in the example won't work. One such situation occurs if your class has a superclass that is not serializable. As I said earlier, to make it possible to overcome this, the superclass must have a default constructor, and you must take care of serializing the fields that are inherited from the superclass yourself. If the superclass does not have a default constructor and you do not have access to the original definition of the superclass, you have a problem with no obvious solution.

Another situation where the default serialization mechanism isn't satisfactory is where your class has fields that don't travel well. If you use the `hashCode()` method that your classes inherit from `Object` then the hashcode for an object is derived from its internal address. When you read the object back from a file its address is different and therefore so is its hashcode. You may have a class with significant numbers of fields with zero values or values such as dates and times that can be obsoleted, for example, that you might not want to have automatically written to the file as part of an object. These are all cases where do-it-yourself serialization is needed.

To implement and control the serialization of a class yourself, you must implement two `private` methods in the class: one for input from an `ObjectInputStream` object and the other for output to an `ObjectOutputStream` object. The `readObject()` and `writeObject()` methods for the stream call these methods to perform I/O on the stream if you implement them.

Even though it isn't necessary in this class, let's take the `PolyLine` class as a demonstration vehicle for how this works. To do your own serialization, the class would be:

```java
class PolyLine implements Serializable {
  // Serialized input method
  private void readObject(ObjectInputStream in) throws IOException {
    // Code to do the serialized input...
  }

  // Serialized output method
  private void writeObject(ObjectOutputStream out)
    throws IOException, ClassNotFoundException {
    // Code to do the serialized output...
  }
  // Class definition as before...
}
```

These two methods must have exactly the same signature in any class where they are required, and they must be declared as `private`.

In a typical situation, you should use the default serialization operations provided by the object stream and just add your own code to fix up the data members that you want to take care of—or have to in the case of a non-serialized base class. To get the default serialization done on input, you just call the `defaultReadObject()` method for the stream in your serialization method:

```
private void readObject(ObjectInputStream in) throws IOException {
  in.defaultReadObject();                        // Default serialized input
  // Your code to do serialized input...
}
```

You can get the default serialized output operation in a similar fashion by calling the `defaultWriteObject()` method for the stream object that is passed to your output method. Obviously, you must read back the data in exactly the same sequence as it was written, so the two methods have essentially mirror operations on the same sequence of data items.

Serialization Problems and Complications

For most classes and applications, serialization works in a straightforward fashion. You will have situations that can cause confusion, though. One such situation is when you want to write several versions of the same object to a file. You need to take care to ensure that the result is what you want. Suppose you write an object to a file—a `PolyLine` object, say. A little later in your code, you modify the `PolyLine` object in some way, by moving a point perhaps, and you now write the same object to the file again in its modified state. What happens? Does the file contain the two versions of the object? The answer—perhaps surprisingly—is no. Let's explore this in a little more detail with a revised version of the `TryPolylineObjects` example.

TRY IT OUT Serializing Variations on an Object

The only change to the previous example is in the `TryPolylineObjects` class. Instead of creating the variables `polygon1`, `polygon2`, and `polygon3` that hold the references to the objects that are written to the file, you can use a single variable, `polygon`:

Available for download on Wrox.com

```
public class TryPolyLineObjects2 {
    public static void main(String[] args) {
        // Create an array of coordinate pairs
        double[][] coords = { {1., 1.}, {1., 2.}, { 2., 3.},
                              {-3., 5.}, {-5., 1.}, {0., 0.} };

        // Create the path object as before...

        // Create the polyline objects and write them to the file
        System.out.println("Writing objects to file.");
        try (ObjectOutputStream objectOut =
                      new ObjectOutputStream(
                          new BufferedOutputStream(Files.newOutputStream(file)))){

            // Create a polyline from the coordinates
            PolyLine polygon = new PolyLine(coords);
            System.out.println(polygon);
            objectOut.writeObject(polygon);                // Write first object

            polygon.addPoint(10., 10.);
            System.out.println(polygon);                   // Add a point
            objectOut.writeObject(polygon);                // Write second object

            polygon.addPoint(10., 15.);
            System.out.println(polygon);                   // Add a point
            objectOut.writeObject(polygon);                // Write third object
            System.out.println("File written.");
```

```
        } catch(IOException e) {
          e.printStackTrace();
          System.exit(1);
        }

        // Read the objects from the file and display them as before...
    }
}
```

Directory "TryPolyLineObjects2"

Executing this version of the previous program produces the following output:

```
Writing objects to file.
Polyline: (1.0,1.0) (1.0,2.0) (2.0,3.0) (-3.0,5.0) (-5.0,1.0) (0.0,0.0)
Polyline: (1.0,1.0) (1.0,2.0) (2.0,3.0) (-3.0,5.0) (-5.0,1.0) (0.0,0.0) (10.0,10.0)
Polyline: (1.0,1.0) (1.0,2.0) (2.0,3.0) (-3.0,5.0) (-5.0,1.0) (0.0,0.0)
                                                      (10.0,10.0) (10.0,15.0)
File written.

Reading objects from the file:
Polyline: (1.0,1.0) (1.0,2.0) (2.0,3.0) (-3.0,5.0) (-5.0,1.0) (0.0,0.0)
Polyline: (1.0,1.0) (1.0,2.0) (2.0,3.0) (-3.0,5.0) (-5.0,1.0) (0.0,0.0)
Polyline: (1.0,1.0) (1.0,2.0) (2.0,3.0) (-3.0,5.0) (-5.0,1.0) (0.0,0.0)
```

All three objects that you read from the file are equal and identical to the first object that was written. From the output it is clear that you did modify `polygon` twice so there should have been three different objects. This seems rather strange and unexpected so let's try to understand what is happening here.

How It Works

As you know, all variables of a class type store references, not objects, and in general you might have several different variables referring to the same object in your program. For this reason, the serialization output process keeps track of the objects that are written to the stream. Any attempt to write the same object to the stream doesn't result in duplicates of the object being written. Only a *handle*, which is a sort of reference, is written to the stream for each duplicate of an object, and this points to the first occurrence of the object in the stream.

Consequently , the modified versions of the `polygon` object in the example are not written to the file. The first write operation writes the original object referenced by `polygon` to the stream. For the second and third write operations, the serialization process detects that you are writing an object that has previously been written to the file, and so only a handle that refers back to the original unmodified version of the object is written. The result is that the changes to the object are lost. This explains why, when you read the three objects back from the file, they all turn out to be identical. This is not at all what you intended in this case, so how can you avoid this?

Resetting an Object Output Stream

The appropriate course of action in such situations is obviously going to be application-dependent, but in the previous example it is clear—you want each version of `polygon` explicitly written to the file. You can make the `ObjectOutputStream` object forget the objects it has previously written to a stream by calling its `reset()` method:

```
    objectOut.reset();                              // Reset the stream
```

This clears the record that is kept within the stream object of what has been written and writes a **reset marker** to the stream to record that the object stream was rest at this point. Following this the output stream object has no knowledge of what was previously written and so it will write an object that otherwise would be ignored as a duplicate reference.

When an `ObjectInputStream` object reads a "reset marker" it too clears its record of what has been read, so that subsequent object read operations are as if the stream started at that point. You can use this to make sure that multiple versions of the same object exist in the stream when you need it. It's your code, so you know what you want to do. To make the example work as you want, you can reset the stream before each output operation after the first call to writeObject(), like this:

```
PolyLine polygon = new PolyLine(coords);
System.out.println(polygon);
objectOut.writeObject(polygon);          // Write first object
objectOut.reset();                           // Reset the stream

polygon.addPoint(10., 10.);
System.out.println(polygon);             // Add a point
objectOut.writeObject(polygon);          // Write second object
objectOut.reset();                           // Reset the stream
polygon.addPoint(10., 15.);
System.out.println(polygon);             // Add a point
objectOut.writeObject(polygon);          // Write third object
```

If you insert the calls to reset() in the original code and run the example again, you should get the output you were expecting.

For more complex situations, it is possible to take complete control of the serialization process within your classes by implementing the Externalizable interface. This is important when the class definition for the object involves change over time. With careful programming you can accommodate modifications to classes without invalidating existing serialized objects. A detailed discussion of what is involved in this is outside the scope of this book.

SUMMARY

In this chapter you explored how you can write objects to a file and read them back. Making your class serializable makes it very easy to save your application data in a file. Although what I have discussed is by no means exhaustive, you now know enough to deal with straightforward object serialization.

EXERCISES

You can download the source code for the examples in the book and the solutions to the following exercises from www.wrox.com.

1. Define a Person class to encapsulate a person's name and address, with the name and address being fields of type Name and Address. Write a program to allow names and addresses to be entered from the keyboard and stored as Person objects in a file. After the file exists new entries should be appended to the file.

2. Extend the previous example to optionally list all the names and addresses contained within the file on the command line.

3. Extend the previous example to add an index based on the person's name for each person entered at the keyboard to locate the corresponding Person object in the object file. The index file contains entries of type IndexEntry, each of which encapsulates a name and a file position in the object file. The index file should be a separate file from the original file containing Person objects.

Note: You might find it easiest to delete the previous file before you run this example so that the object file can be reconstructed along with the index file. You can't get the file position in an object stream in the same way as you can with a channel. However, you can use the sequence number for an object as the index—the first object being 1, the second being 2, and so on.

4. Use the index file to provide random direct access to the object file for querying random names entered from the keyboard. Entering a name from the keyboard should result in the address for the individual, or a message indicating the entry is not present in the file. The process is to first search the index file for an object with a name field matching the keyboard entry. When an IndexEntry is found, you use the sequence number it contains to retrieve the appropriate Person object.

▶ WHAT YOU LEARNED IN THIS CHAPTER

TOPIC	CONCEPT
Making a Class Serializable	To make objects of a class serializable the class must implement the `Serializable` interface.
Class Version ID	The deserialization process checks the version ID for the class definition used to read objects to verify that the class is the same as that used when the file was written. You should define explicitly the variable `serialVersionUID` as static and final in your serializable classes to ensure deserialization works without difficulty.
Base Classes Not Serializable	If a class has a superclass that does not implement the `Serializable` interface then the superclass must have a public default constructor if it is to be possible to serialize the class.
Object Streams	Objects are written to a file using an `ObjectOutputStream` object and read from a file using an `ObjectInputStream` object.
Creating Object Streams	You can create an object input stream by calling the `newInputStream()` method for a `Path` object. Calling the `newOutputStream()` method for a `Path` object creates an object output stream.
Writing Objects to a File	Objects are written to a file by calling the `writeObject()` method for the `ObjectOutputStream` object corresponding to the file.
Reading Objects from a File	Objects are read from a file by calling the `readObject()` method for the `ObjectInputStream` object corresponding to the file.
Writing Versions of an Object	To write different versions of the same object to an object output stream you need to call the `reset()` method for the stream before you write each object version after the first. If you don't call reset, only the first version of the object is written to the stream and subsequent versions are written as handles referencing the first object instance that was written.

13

Generic Class Types

WHAT YOU WILL LEARN IN THIS CHAPTER:

➤ What a generic type is

➤ How you define a generic type

➤ How you specify type parameters for a generic type

➤ What parameter type bounds are and how you use them

➤ What wildcard type specifications are and how you use them

➤ How you define bounds for a wildcard

➤ How you define and use parameterized methods

Generic class types are not a separate capability from the class and interface types that you have seen in earlier chapters. The facility for defining generic class and interface types is an extension of the ordinary definition of classes and interfaces that you are familiar with that enables you to define families of classes and interfaces.

WHAT ARE GENERIC TYPES?

A *generic type*, which is also referred to as a *parameterized type*, is a class or interface type definition that has one or more type parameters. You define an actual class or interface type from a generic type by supplying a type argument for each of the type parameters that the generic type has. It'll be easier to understand what this means with a concrete example of where and how you could apply the concept.

I'm sure you recall the LinkedList class that you first saw in Chapter 6 and used in an example in Chapter 12. You used the LinkedList class to encapsulate a linked list of Point objects, but the idea of a linked list applies to any set of objects that you want to organize in this way. A linked list is just one example of classes that define objects for organizing other objects of a given type into a collection in some way. Such classes are described as *collection classes* for obvious reasons, and in Chapter 14 you see a variety of these that are defined in the java.util package. Of course, you have already seen the EnumSet collection class in use for file I/O, and you learn more about this class later in Chapter 14, too.

The LinkedList class that you implemented in Chapter 6 can organize objects of any given type into a linked list. This clearly has the advantage that the code for a single class defines a linked list class that you can use for objects of any kind, but it has significant disadvantages, too. When you were adding Point objects to a LinkedList object, nothing in the code prevented you from adding a Line object, or indeed any type of object, to the same linked list. Of course, if you were to do this inadvertently, the result would be a disaster, because when you retrieved objects from the list, you would not know that some of the objects were not of type Point. If you attempt to use an object as a Point object that was actually type Line or type String, your program fails.

To avoid such problems, ideally what you need is a LinkedList class that is type safe. By type safe I mean that when you are using a LinkedList object to store Point objects, no possibility of any other type of object being added exists. In other words, you want a class that always prevents you from accidentally adding objects of the wrong type. Of course, you can define a LinkedList class that works only with objects of type Point. You just use parameters of type Point in the methods that you use to add objects to the list and to retrieve them. The problem with this solution is that you must write a new LinkedList class for every type of object that you want to organize in this way, so you end up with a LinkedLineList class, a LinkedPointList class, a LinkedElephantList class—well, you can see the problem.

That's *exactly* where generic types come in. Generic types provide a way for you to define a generic LinkedList class that can transform itself into a class that defines a type safe LinkedList class for objects of any type that you want to organize in a linked list. Broadly, a *generic type* can assume the guise of any particular class from the set or family of classes that it represents. You just supply the appropriate type arguments for the parameters in the generic type and it behaves as that particular class. Let's see how that works in practice.

DEFINING A GENERIC CLASS TYPE

I'm using the LinkedList class as a model for showing how you define a generic type because you already know how a linked list works. A definition of a generic class type looks very much like the definition of an ordinary class, but with a parameter specification added following the class name. Here's how the LinkedList class from Chapter 6 looks as an outline of a generic type:

```
public class LinkedList<T> {                    // T is the type parameter
  // Generic type definition...
}
```

The parameter that appears between the angled brackets, <>, that follows the generic type name, LinkedList, is called a *type parameter*. The name, T, identifies the type parameter, and you use the parameter name in the definition of the methods and fields in the generic type where there is a dependency on the argument value for this parameter in the implementation detail. Occurrences of the type parameter name in the definition of a generic type are called *type variables* because they are replaced by a value that is a type in a similar way to how method parameters are replaced by the arguments that you supply.

Although I've used a single letter, T, as the type parameter name to indicate that the argument should be a Type, you can use any legal identifier. For example, you could use InsertYourTypeHere as the parameter name, but this would make the code in the body of the generic type definition rather cumbersome. It's generally best to keep the parameter names as short as possible—ideally as a single letter. The convention in Java is to use single letters as type parameter names so it is advantageous to adopt this in your code. Typically, T is used to indicate a parameter is a type, N is used for a parameter that is a numerical value, K is used for a parameter that is a key, and V is used for a type parameter that is a value. You read about K and V type parameters later in this chapter.

Within the text I'm appending angled brackets to a generic type name to differentiate when I'm referring to a generic type such as LinkedList<> from when I'm referring to an ordinary class or interface type. Although the LinkedList<> example is a generic *class* type, you can equally well define generic *interface* types, and you find quite a number of these in the standard packages. You work with the Iterable<> and Comparable<> generic interface types from the java.lang package later in this chapter.

To create a class from the generic type, LinkedList<>, you just supply an appropriate argument for the parameter between the angled brackets. All occurrences of the type variable, T, that appear in the definition are replaced by the type argument that you supply. This results in a class type that you can use to create an object that implements a linked list that stores objects of the type that you specified, as illustrated in Figure 13-1.

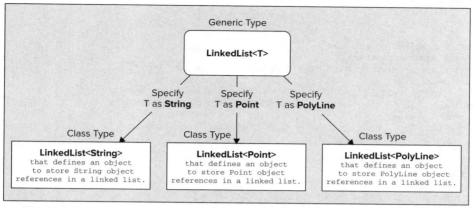

FIGURE 13-1

Thus, a generic type essentially defines a set of types, the set being produced by different arguments for the parameters for the generic type. Note that although Figure 13-1 shows three *types* being defined, there aren't three classes. There's just the generic class type to which you supply a type argument to produce a particular type. The three types in Figure 13-1 are produced by plugging the three type arguments shown into the generic type.

You can supply only a class or interface type such as type String or type Point as an argument for a type parameter in a generic type. In other words, you cannot use a primitive type such as int or type double as an argument, although, of course, you can use type Integer or type Double because these are class types that wrap the corresponding primitive types. When you create a particular type from the generic type definition by supplying an argument value for T, the argument is substituted for every occurrence of T in the generic type specification. This applies to fields as well as the definitions of methods in the generic type.

You put a generic type definition in a source file with the extension .java, just like an ordinary class, so you could save the code for the preceding outline generic type as LinkedList.java. It even compiles as it is, although it's not very useful at the moment.

Implementing a Generic Type

You can easily convert the definition of the LinkedList class you were working with earlier into a generic type. Here's how an initial stab at a LinkedList<> generic type definition looks:

```
public class LinkedList<T> {
  // Default constructor - creates an empty list
  public LinkedList() {}

  // Constructor to create a list containing one object
  public LinkedList(T item) {
    if(item != null) {
      current=end=start=new ListItem(item);     // item is the start and end
    }
  }

  // Construct a linked list from an array of objects
  public LinkedList(T[] items) {
    if(items != null) {
      // Add the items to the list
      for(int i = 0 ; i < items.length ; ++i) {
        addItem(items[i]);
      }
      current = start;
```

```
    }
  }

  // Add an item object to the list
  public void addItem(T item) {
    ListItem newEnd = new ListItem(item);  // Create a new ListItem
    if(start == null) {                     // Is the list empty?
      start = end = newEnd;                 // Yes, so new element is start and end
    } else {                                // No, so append new element
      end.next = newEnd;                    // Set next variable for old end
      end = newEnd;                         // Store new item as end
    }
  }
  // Get the first object in the list
  public T getFirst() {
    current = start;
    return start == null ? null : start.item;
  }

  // Get the next object in the list
  public T getNext() {
    if(current != null) {
      current = current.next;               // Get the reference to the next item
    }
    return current == null ? null : current.item;
  }

  private ListItem start = null;            // First ListItem in the list
  private ListItem end = null;              // Last ListItem in the list
  private ListItem current = null;          // The current item for iterating

  private class ListItem {

    // Constructor
    public ListItem(T item) {
      this.item = item;                     // Store the item
      next = null;                          // Set next as end point
    }

    // Return class name & object
    @Override
    public String toString() {
      return "ListItem " + item ;
    }

    ListItem next;                          // Refers to next item in the list
    T item;                                 // The item for this ListItem
  }
}
```

The bold lines reflect changes to the original LinkedList class definition that you created in Chapter 6. Each of the lines that have been modified in the body of the generic type definition replace type Object by the type variable, T. The item field in the ListItem inner class is now of type T, for example, and the return type for the getNext() method is also type T. All the methods that use the parameter T in their definitions are customized by the argument type that is supplied for T when you define a type from the generic type. A generic type can include ordinary methods that do not involve any parameters in their definitions. This just means that the ordinary methods are not customized for particular instances of the generic type.

You now have a generic LinkedList<T> type that you can use to create a new LinkedList class for storing objects of any type that you want. Let's look at how you use it.

Instantiating a Generic Type

You use the generic type name followed by a class or interface type name between angled brackets to define a new type. For example:

```
       LinkedList<String> strings;                // A variable of type LinkedList<String>
```

This declares a variable with the name `strings` of type `LinkedList<String>`, which is from the generic type that you defined in the previous section. The compiler uses the type argument `String` that you supplied to replace every instance of the type variable, `T`, in the generic type definition to arrive at the notional class type definition for `LinkedList<String>`.

Of course, you can initialize an object when you declare the variable, like this:

```
       LinkedList<String> strings = new LinkedList<String>();
```

This calls the default constructor for the `LinkedList<String>` class type to define an object that implements a linked list of `String` objects. A reference to this object is stored in `strings`.

There's some redundancy in the previous statement. The type of the `strings` variable determines the type of elements that the list it references can store, and this information is repeated on the right side of the statement. You can avoid typing the list element type twice by writing the statement as:

```
       LinkedList<String> strings = new LinkedList<>();
```

> **NOTE** *The angled brackets without a type specification between are often referred to as the diamond operator, although it's not really an operator within the Java language. If you include spaces between the angled brackets, your code still compiles, but it is recommended that you don't do this.*

The argument that you supply to a generic type could also be a type that you define using a generic type. Look at this example:

```
       LinkedList<LinkedList<String>> texts = new LinkedList<>();
```

Here you have created an object that implements a linked list in which you can store objects that are themselves linked lists of type `LinkedList<String>`. Thus, you have defined a linked list of linked lists!

To apply the new generic `LinkedList<>` type that you have defined in a working context, let's repeat the `TryPolyLine` example from Chapter 6 using a type that is generated from the `LinkedList<>` type.

TRY IT OUT   Using a Generic Linked List Type

First you need a modified version of the `PolyLine` class that uses the `LinkedList<T>` generic type:

```
public class PolyLine {
  // Construct a polyline from an array of coordinate pairs
  public PolyLine(double[][] coords) {
    Point[] points = new Point[coords.length];   // Array to hold points

    // Create points from the coordinates
    for(int i = 0 ; i < coords.length ; ++i) {
      points[i] = new Point(coords[i][0], coords[i][1]);
    }

    // Create the polyline from the array of points
    polyline = new LinkedList<>(points);          // Create list of Point objects
  }

  // Construct a polyline from an array of points
  public PolyLine(Point[] points) {
    polyline = new LinkedList<>(points);          // Create list of Point objects
  }

  // Add a Point object to the list
  public void addPoint(Point point) {
```

```
      polyline.addItem(point);                     // Add the point to the list
    }

    // Add a point from a coordinate pair to the list
    public void addPoint(double x, double y) {
      polyline.addItem(new Point(x, y));            // Add the point to the list
    }

    // String representation of a polyline
    @Override
    public String toString() {
      StringBuffer str = new StringBuffer("Polyline:");
      Point point = polyline.getFirst();
                                                    // Set the 1st point as start
      while(point != null) {
        str.append(" (" + point + ")");             // Append the current point
        point = polyline.getNext();                 // Make the next point current
      }
      return str.toString();
    }

    private LinkedList<Point> polyline;             // The linked list of points
  }
```

Directory "TryGenericLinkedList"

I have bolded all the lines that have been changed from the original version—yes, all five of them! Two of the changes remove now redundant casts to type `Point`. The constructor calls that create objects implementing a linked list now use the `LinkedList<T>` generic type. I use the diamond operator so the compiler infers that the type argument is `Point` because `polyline` is now of type `LinkedList<Point>`.

Put this source file in a directory along with the `Point` class source file that you created in Chapter 6 and the source file containing the `LinkedList<>` generic type. You can then add the following source file that tries out the new version of the `PolyLine` class:

```
public class TryGenericLinkedList {
    public static void main(String[] args) {
      // Create an array of coordinate pairs
      double[][] coords = { {1, 1}, {1, 2}, { 2, 3},
                            {-3, 5}, {-5, 1}, {0, 0} };

      // Create a polyline from the coordinates and display it
      PolyLine polygon = new PolyLine(coords);
      System.out.println(polygon);
      // Add a point and display the polyline again
      polygon.addPoint(10, 10);
      System.out.println(polygon);

      // Create Point objects from the coordinate array
      Point[] points = new Point[coords.length];
      for(int i = 0 ; i < points.length ; ++i) {
        points[i] = new Point(coords[i][0],coords[i][1]);
      }
      // Use the points to create a new polyline and display it
      PolyLine newPoly = new PolyLine(points);
      System.out.println(newPoly);
    }
}
```

Directory "TryGenericLinkedList"

Apart from the class name, this is the same as the `TryPolyLine` class that you created in Chapter 6. Compiling this program results in five `.class` files. Two are the result of compiling `LinkedList.java`. The source for the generic type compiles into `LinkedList.class` plus the `LinkedList$ListItem.class` corresponding to the inner class. When you execute this example, it produces the same output as the example in Chapter 6.

How It Works

The `PolyLine` class creates the `LinkedList<Point>` type from the `LinkedList<T>` generic type that implements a linked list of `Point` objects because of this statement:

```
    private LinkedList<Point> polyline;                // The linked list of points
```

The class type that results from this is produced by passing `Point` as the argument for the type variable `T` in the `LinkedList<T>` generic type definition. This process is described as *type erasure* because all occurrences of the type variable `T` are eliminated, so you end up with a notional class with the following definition:

```java
public class LinkedList {
  // Default constructor - creates an empty list
  public LinkedList() {}

  // Constructor to create a list containing one object
  public LinkedList(Object item) {
    if(item != null) {
      current=end=start=new ListItem(item); // item is the start and end
    }
  }

  // Construct a linked list from an array of objects
  public LinkedList(Object[] items) {
    if(items != null) {
      // Add the items to the list
      for(int i = 0 ; i < items.length ; ++i) {
        addItem(items[i]);
      }
      current = start;
    }
  }

  // Add an item object to the list
  public void addItem(Object item) {
    ListItem newEnd = new ListItem(item);   // Create a new ListItem
    if(start == null) {                     // Is the list empty?
      start = end = newEnd;                 // Yes, so new element is start and end
    } else {                                // No, so append new element
      end.next = newEnd;                    // Set next variable for old end
      end = newEnd;                         // Store new item as end
    }
  }
  // Get the first object in the list
  public Object getFirst() {
    current = start;
    return start == null ? null : start.item;
  }

  // Get the next object in the list
  public Object getNext() {
    if(current != null) {
      current = current.next;               // Get the reference to the next item
    }
    return current == null ? null : current.item;
  }

  private ListItem start = null;            // First ListItem in the list
  private ListItem end = null;              // Last ListItem in the list
```

```
     private ListItem current = null;         // The current item for iterating

     private class ListItem {

       // Constructor
       public ListItem(Object item) {
         this.item = item;                     // Store the item
         next = null;                          // Set next as end point
       }

       // Return class name & object
       @Override
       public String toString() {
         return "ListItem " + item ;
       }

       ListItem next;                          // Refers to next item in the list
       Object item;                            // The item for this ListItem
     }
   }
```

The type parameter following the class name in the original generic type definition has been removed, and all occurrences of the type variable Point within the class definition have been replaced by type Object. The bold lines are the one affected. Type Object is chosen by the compiler to replace the type variable because type Object is the ultimate superclass class from which type Point is derived. The type that the compiler selects to replace a type variable is the *leftmost bound* of the type variable. Type Object is the default leftmost bound that applies to any class type because all classes have type Object as their ultimate superclass. You see later in the chapter how you can specify a different leftmost bound for a type parameter and what the reasons are for doing this.

Of course, this class doesn't exist as a separate entity. The preceding code represents a description of how the generic type behaves when you supply a type argument as type Point. Looking at the class that now works with references of type Object, you may wonder what the advantage of being able to specify the type parameter is; after all, you can supply a reference to an object of any type for a parameter of type Object. The answer is that the type variable you supply is used by the compiler to ensure compile-time type safety. When you use an object of type LinkedList<Point> in your code, the compiler checks that you use it only to store objects of type Point and flags any attempt to store objects of other types as an error. When you call methods for an object of type LinkedList<Point>, the compiler ensures that you supply references only of type Point where the original method parameter was specified as the type parameter.

You use the methods in the parameterized type in the same way as those in the original LinkedList class. Everything is very straightforward, and you now have a PolyLine implementation that uses a type safe linked list. I think you'll agree that the essentials of defining and using a generic type could be described as a piece of cake.

Using Primitive Type Wrapper Class Types as Arguments

On occasion you will want to store values of a primitive type in a collection such as a linked list. In this situation you use the generic type with one of the wrapper classes for primitive types as the type argument—these are the classes Integer, Short, Double, and so on that are defined in the java.lang package. Here's how you could use the LinkedList<T> generic type to hold values of type double:

```
LinkedList<Double> temperatures = new LinkedList<>();
```

Here you have created a linked list that stores objects of type Double, and the autoboxing facility that you met in Chapter 5 enables you to use the LinkedList<Double> object directly with values of type double. For example, to add a value of type double to the linked list you have just created, you could write the following:

```
temperatures.addItem(10.5);
```

Because the parameter type for this method for the LinkedList<Double> object is of type Double, the compiler automatically inserts a boxing conversion to convert the double value 10.5 to an object of type

`Double` that encapsulates it. Thus, the creation of the appropriate wrapper class object is taken care of automatically, so you can use the linked list object as though it stored values of the primitive type.

Let's see if the linked list type can really take the heat.

TRY IT OUT Autoboxing with Generic Types

In this example you create an instance of the `LinkedList<T>` generic type and use it to store random temperature values of type `double`:

Available for
download on
Wrox.com

```
public class TryAutoboxing {
  public static void main(String[] args) {
    LinkedList<Double> temperatures = new LinkedList<>();

    // Insert 6 temperature values 0 to 25 degress Centigrade
    for(int i = 0 ; i < 6 ; ++i) {
      temperatures.addItem(25.0*Math.random());
    }

    Double value = temperatures.getFirst();
    while(value != null) {
      System.out.printf("%.2f degrees Fahrenheit%n", toFahrenheit(value));
      value=temperatures.getNext();
    }
  }

  // Convert Centigrade to Fahrenheit
  public static double toFahrenheit(double temperature) {
    return 1.8*temperature+32.0;
  }
}
```

Directory "TryAutoboxing"

Of course, you need to copy the `LinkedList.java` source file to the directory for this example. This program outputs something similar to the following:

```
72.88 degrees Fahrenheit
32.80 degrees Fahrenheit
38.36 degrees Fahrenheit
65.76 degrees Fahrenheit
65.92 degrees Fahrenheit
67.56 degrees Fahrenheit
```

How It Works

You create an object of type `LinkedList<Double>` from the parameterized type to store elements of type `Double` in the linked list. When you pass a value of type `double` to the `addItem()` method, the compiler inserts a boxing conversion to type `Double` because that's the argument type that the method requires.

When you extract `Double` objects from the linked list and pass them to the `toFahrenheit()` method, the compiler automatically inserts an unboxing conversion to extract the original `double` values and those are passed to the method. You could equally well use the reference returned by `getFirst()` or `getNext()` in an arithmetic expression; you would get the same unboxing conversion provided automatically.

You can see how the `printf()` method is helpful in making the output more readable by limiting the display of temperature values to two decimal places after the decimal point.

The Runtime Type of Generic Type Instances

Suppose you create two different types from the `LinkedList<T>` generic type:

```
LinkedList<Double> numbers = new LinkedList<>();      // List to store numbers
LinkedList<String> proverbs = new LinkedList<>();     // List to store strings
```

Clearly the variables `numbers` and `proverbs` are instances of different class types. One type represents a linked list that stores values of type `Double`, and the other represents a linked list that stores values of type `String`. However, things are not quite as straightforward as that. Because you have only one generic type, both classes share the same `Class` object at runtime, which is the `Class` object that corresponds to the generic type, so their class type names are identical. Indeed, *all* types that you generate from a given generic type share the same class name at run time. You can demonstrate this with the following example.

TRY IT OUT   The Run Time Types of Generic Type Instances

In this example you create two different instances of the `LinkedList<T>` generic type and see what their type names are.

```java
public class TestClassTypes {
  public static void main(String[] args) {
    LinkedList<String> proverbs = new LinkedList<>();
    LinkedList<Double> numbers = new LinkedList<>();
    System.out.println("numbers class name " + numbers.getClass().getName());
    System.out.println("proverbs class name " + proverbs.getClass().getName());
    System.out.println("Compare Class objects: " +
                         numbers.getClass().equals(proverbs.getClass()));
  }
}
```

Directory "TestClassTypes"

This code produces the following output:

```
numbers class name LinkedList
proverbs class name LinkedList
Compare Class objects: true
```

How It Works

You call the `getClass()` method that is inherited from the `Object` class to obtain the `Class` objects for the objects referenced by `proverbs` and `numbers`. You then call the `getName()` method for the `Class` object to get the runtime type name. In both instances the type name is `LinkedList`. The fact that the runtime types are identical is further confirmed by the comparison of the `Class` objects for the `LinkedList<String>` and `LinkedList<Double>` objects, and the output shows they are identical.

Thus, you have the unavoidable conclusion that all instances of a given type share the same `Class` object at runtime, and therefore the same runtime type. Of course, this does not mean that the objects are the same type. For example, the following statement does not compile:

```
proverbs = (LinkedList<String>)numbers; // Illegal cast - will not compile
```

The compiler knows that these objects are really of different types and does not allow you to do this.

However, not a lot prevents you from doing the following:

```
Object obj = (Object)numbers;
proverbs = (LinkedList<String>)obj;      // Will result in a compiler warning
```

Here the cast of `numbers` to type `Object` is legal—every class has `Object` as a base so the compiler allows this. With the second statement, though, the compiler knows only that you are casting a reference of type `Object` and therefore cannot identify this as an illegal operation. However, you will get a warning about unsafe operations.

At runtime this operation is not checked because the runtime type of the reference stored in `obj` is `LinkedList`, the same as that of `proverbs`. This means that you end up with a reference to an object that is really of type `LinkedList<Double>` in a variable of type `LinkedList<String>`. You discover that this is a problem only when you attempt to call methods for the object. If you want to verify that this is the case, you can add the following code to the end of the example:

```
Object obj = (Object)numbers;
System.out.println("obj class name " + obj.getClass().getName());
proverbs = (LinkedList<String>)obj;
System.out.println("obj in proverbs class name " + obj.getClass().getName());
```

After some warnings from the compiler the example then produces the following output when you execute it:

```
numbers class name LinkedList
proverbs class name LinkedList
Compare Class objects: true
obj class name LinkedList
obj in proverbs class name LinkedList
```

Where the compiler recognizes unsafe casts, you get a warning message to indicate that you have a potential problem. You should use such casts only when they are absolutely necessary, and you should always double-check that the cast is valid. Of course, situations arise where such casts are unavoidable. One example is when you are deserializing objects that are instances of a class produced from a generic type. You try this later in this chapter.

 NOTE *One further point to keep in mind about types that you create from a generic type: Because all types that you produce from a generic type have the same runtime type, you cannot use the* `instanceof` *operator to test for such types.*

Relationships between Generic Type Instances

It's easy to be misled about whether types that you create from a generic type are related. Suppose you create an object as follows:

```
LinkedList<String> strings = new LinkedList<>();           // A list of strings
```

You have created a linked list that store objects of type `String`. Suppose you now create another linked list:

```
LinkedList<Object> things = new LinkedList<>();           // A list of objects
```

This stores objects of type `Object` organized as a linked list. Of course, it also stores objects of any type that is a subclass of `Object`, so any class type is acceptable. Is there any relationship between the type of `things`, which is `LinkedList<Object>`, and the type of `strings`, which is `LinkedList<String>`? Superficially, you might jump to the conclusion that there is; after all, `Object` is a superclass of every class type, including type `String`. However, if you think about it, the relationship between the type arguments is an irrelevancy, and the conclusion would be wrong. The types just happen to be produced by a single generic type, `LinkedList<>`, but there's no reason why the type argument that you use should establish any relationship between these types, no more than there would be between two ordinary collection classes that you might define to store `String` objects and `Object` objects.

Multiple Type Parameters

The `LinkedList<T>` type has a single type parameter, but in general you can define a generic type with as many type parameters as you wish. Suppose that you want to define a generic type that defines a set of classes that encapsulate a pair of objects of arbitrary types. This would typically arise where one object is used as a key to access another object that represents a value in a collection. For example, you might store `Person` objects in a collection that encapsulates personal details such as the name, the address, and the phone number. You could associate each `Person` object with a `Name` object that you use as a key to retrieve the `Person` object. One way of establishing the association between an object and its key is to encapsulate both in another object—of type `Pair`, say.

Here's how you might define a generic type, `Pair<K,V>`, to be used for defining classes that encapsulate a key/value pair of any type:

```
public class Pair <KeyType, ValueType> {
  // Constructor
  public Pair(KeyType aKey, ValueType aValue) {
    key = aKey;
    value = aValue;
  }

  // Get the key for this pair
  public getKey() {
    return key;
  }

  // Get the value for this pair
  public getValue() {
    return value;
  }

  // Set the value for this pair
  public setValue(ValueType aValue) {
   value = aValue;
  }

  private KeyType key;
  private ValueType value;
}
```

Obviously, a practical definition would be more complicated than this—you'd need a means of comparing key objects, for example—but it suffices to show how you can use two parameters in the definition of a generic type.

Here's an example of how you could use this generic type:

```
Pair<String, String> entry = new Pair<>("Fred Thrump", "212 222 3333");
```

This creates an object of type `Pair<String, String>` and stores a reference to it in `entry`. The element type parameters in the constructor call are inferred from the type of the variable on the left of the assignment, just as for generic types with a single type parameter.

Type Parameter Scope

The scope of a type parameter is the entire generic class definition, but excluding any static members or initializers in the class. This implies that you cannot specify the type of a static field within a generic type definition as any of the type parameters for the generic type. Similarly, static methods cannot have parameters or return types that correspond to a class type parameter, and you must not use the class type parameters in the bodies of static method definitions.

This does not mean that static methods cannot be parameterized—I am talking only about types for variables in a static method corresponding to any of the parameter types in a generic type definition. You see later in this chapter that you can define *generic methods* that have their own independent parameterized definitions involving their own set of parameters, and such parameterized methods may be static or non-static.

Static Fields in a Generic Type

All types produced from a given generic type share the same runtime type. Consequently they do not have their own independent static fields. Any static fields you define in a generic type are shared among all instances of it. For example, suppose you add a static field—count, say—of type `int` to the `LinkedList<>` type definition to record the number of objects created. You then add a statement to each constructor to increment `count` each time it was called. Each type instance, such as `LinkedList<String>`

or `LinkedList<Point>`, would share a single copy of `count`, so the static `count` member of the `LinkedList<String>` type would reflect the number of times the `LinkedList<T>` constructor had been called; in our example this would be two. Static fields in generic type definitions are best avoided.

Type Parameter Bounds

In some situations you define a generic type where you want to constrain the type arguments that are supplied to define a class instance so that they extend a particular class, or implement specific interfaces, or even both. The reason for this is that your generic type has to make some assumptions about the capabilities of the objects an instance of the type is dealing with. Such constraints are called *type parameter bounds*.

The first bound that you specify for a type parameter can be either a class type or an interface type. Any additional bounds after the first for a type parameter can be interface types only. If you don't specify any bounds for a type parameter, it has type `Object` as its implicit bound because all classes have this type as their ultimate base class.

To understand how you specify a type parameter bound, consider a simple example of where this applies. Suppose that you want to modify the `LinkedList<T>` generic type that you saw earlier so that objects of classes produced by this type would be serializable. Not only would `LinkedList<T>` need to implement the `Serializable` interface, but type `T` would also have to implement `Serializable`. The definition for the generic type would therefore look like this:

```
import java.io.Serializable;
class LinkedList<T extends Serializable> implements Serializable {
  // Default constructor - creates an empty list
  public LinkedList() {}

  // Constructor to create a list containing one object
  public LinkedList(T item) {
    if(item != null) {
      current=end=start=new ListItem(item); // item is the start and end
    }
  }

  // Construct a linked list from an array of objects
  public LinkedList(T[] items) {
    if(items != null) {
      // Add the items to the list
      for(int i = 0; i < items.length; i++) {
        addItem(items[i]);
      }
      current = start;
    }
  }

  // Add an item object to the list
  public void addItem(T item) {
    ListItem newEnd = new ListItem(item);   // Create a new ListItem
    if(start == null) {                      // Is the list empty?
      start = end = newEnd;                  // Yes, so new element is start and end
    } else {                                 // No, so append new element
      end.next = newEnd;                     // Set next variable for old end
      end = newEnd;                          // Store new item as end
    }
  }
  // Get the first object in the list
  public T getFirst() {
    current = start;
    return start == null ? null : start.item;
  }

  // Get the next object in the list
```

```
    public T getNext() {
      if(current != null) {
        current = current.next;              // Get the reference to the next item
      }
      return current == null ? null : current.item;
    }

    private ListItem start = null;           // First ListItem in the list
    private ListItem end = null;             // Last ListItem in the list
    private ListItem current = null;         // The current item for iterating
    private static final long serialVersionUID = 1001L;

    private class ListItem implements Serializable {

      // Constructor
      public ListItem(T item) {
        this.item = item;                    // Store the item
        next = null;                         // Set next as end point
      }

      // Return class name & object
      @Override
      public String toString() {
        return "ListItem " + item ;
      }

      ListItem next;                         // Refers to next item in the list
      T item;                                // The item for this ListItem
      private static final long serialVersionUID = 1001L;
    }
  }
```

The changes from the previous version of the generic type are the bold lines. Notice how you use the extends keyword regardless of whether the type parameter bound is a class or an interface. Of course, this applies only to bounds for type parameters in a generic type. Where the generic type itself implements an interface, you use the implements keyword, and where it extends a class you use the extends keyword, just as you would for an ordinary class type. Of course, the ListItem inner class must also implement the Serializable interface because you need ListItem objects to be serializable.

Where you need to specify a type parameter that has several bounds, you use a special notation. You put & between the type names that are bounds following the extends keyword. Here's how that looks:

```
class MyType<T extends FancyClass & Serializable & MyInterface> {
  // Code defining the generic type…
}
```

The parameter for the MyType<> generic type has three bounds: the FancyClass class and the interfaces Serializable and MyInterface. All type arguments for T to the MyType<T> parameterized type must extend the FancyClass class and implement both the Serializable and the MyInterface interfaces.

Let's see if the serializable LinkedList<> generic type works.

TRY IT OUT   Using Parameter Bounds in a Generic Type

This example exercises the last version of the LinkedList<> generic type by serializing a list of integers and then deserializing it:

Available for
download on
Wrox.com

```
import static java.lang.Math.random;
import java.nio.file.*;
import java.io.*;

public class TrySerializableLinkedList {
```

```java
public static void main(String[] args) {
  Path file = Paths.get("D:/Junk/Numbers.bin");
  try {
    // Create parent directory if it doesn't exist
    Files.createDirectories(file.getParent());
  } catch(IOException e) {
    System.err.println("Error creating directory: " + file.getParent());
    e.printStackTrace();
  }

  // Create a list containing random integers
  LinkedList<Integer> numbers = new LinkedList<>();
  for(int i = 0 ; i < 10 ; ++i) {
    // Add ten random integers 1 to 100
    numbers.addItem(1 + (int)(100.0*random()));
  }

  System.out.println("\nnumbers list contains:");
  listAll(numbers);                             // List contents of numbers

  // Now serialize the list to a file
  try (ObjectOutputStream objOut = new ObjectOutputStream(
                new BufferedOutputStream(Files.newOutputStream(file)))){
    objOut.writeObject(numbers);
  } catch(IOException e) {
    e.printStackTrace();
    System.exit(1);
  }

  LinkedList<Integer> values = null;  // Variable to store list from the file

  // Deserialize the list from the file
  try (ObjectInputStream objIn = new ObjectInputStream(
                new BufferedInputStream(Files.newInputStream(file)))){
    values = (LinkedList<Integer>)(objIn.readObject());
  } catch(ClassNotFoundException|IOException e) {
    e.printStackTrace();
    System.exit(1);
  }

  System.out.println("\nvalues list contains:");
  listAll(values);                              // List contents of values
}

// Helper method to list the contents of a linked list
static void listAll(LinkedList<Integer> list) {
  Integer number = list.getFirst();
  int count = 0;
  do {
    System.out.printf("%5d", number);
    if(++count%5 == 0) {
      System.out.println();
    }
  } while((number = list.getNext()) != null);
}
}
```

Directory "TrySerializableLinkedList"

Include the source file for `LinkedList<>` in the same directory as this source file. When you compile this program, you get a warning message from the compiler relating to an unchecked cast. This example produces output along the following lines:

```
numbers list contains:
   56   79   36   64   43
   78   81    3   36   56

values list contains:
   56   79   36   64   43
   78   81    3   36   56
```

How It Works

You first create a linked list of type `LinkedList<Integer>` that stores objects of type `integer`:

```
LinkedList<Integer> numbers = new LinkedList<>();
```

You populate this list with ten `Integer` objects that encapsulate random integer values from 1 to 100 in the `for` loop:

```
for(int i = 0 ; i < 10 ; ++i) {
  // Add ten random integers 1 to 100
  numbers.addItem(1 + (int)(100.0*random()));
}
```

This relies on autoboxing to create the `Integer` objects to be passed as arguments to the `addItem()` method.

The static `listAll()` method is a helper method that lists the contents of a linked list of integers, and you call that to output what is stored in the `numbers` linked list.

Because the linked list is now supposed to be serializable, you demonstrate that this is the case by writing the `numbers` object to a file in the way that you saw in the previous chapter. You then read it back and store a reference to the list that you read from the file in a new variable, `values`. The statement in the `try` block that reads the object from the file is:

```
values = (LinkedList<Integer>)(objIn.readObject());
```

The `readObject()` method returns a reference of type `Object`, so you must cast it to type `LinkedList<Integer>` before storing it in `values`. The compiler recognizes that this cast is unchecked at run time, so you get a warning message as a result of this statement. However, you have no alternative to casting in this instance.

Having read the `LinkedList<Integer>` from the file, you demonstrate that it is indeed the same as the original by listing its contents via a call to the `listAll()` method. The output shows that the serialization and deserialization operations were successful.

 NOTE *When you have code where you know you will get a compiler warning that you are going to ignore, you can prevent the warning being issued by using an annotation. The annotation can be placed before the definition of a method that causes the warning or before a class definition. You could place the following line immediately preceding the TrySerializableLinkedList class definition to prevent the unchecked cast warning being issued:*

`@SuppressWarnings("unchecked")`

The identifier for the warning message you want to suppress goes between the parentheses. It appears in the warning message between square brackets. You should only use this to suppress warnings you are sure are redundant for your code.

GENERIC TYPES AND GENERIC INTERFACES

A generic type can implement one or more interface types, including generic interface types. The syntax that you use for this is the same as for ordinary class and interface types, the only difference being that each generic type name is followed by its type parameter list between angled brackets. For example:

```
public class MyClass<T> implements MyInterface<T> {
  // Details of the generic type definitions
}
```

You can see how this works by taking a look at practical example.

Enabling the Collection-Based for Loop for a Container Class

The `for` loop that you have been using to extract the elements stored in a linked list, such as in the `TryAutoboxing` example at the beginning of this chapter, was rather cumbersome. Wouldn't it be nice if you could use the collection-based `for` loop with the classes produced from the `LinkedList<>` generic type? It's not that difficult to implement, so let's see how to do it.

For an object of a container class type to be usable with the collection-based `for` loop, the class must fulfill just one requirement—it must implement the generic `java.lang.Iterable<>` interface. The `Iterable<T>` interface is a generic type that declares a single method, `iterator()`, that returns a reference of type `Iterator<T>`. All your class has to do then is to declare that it implements the `Iterable<T>` interface and provide an implementation for the `iterator()` method.

Here's the outline of what you need to add to the `LinkedList<>` generic type that you developed at the beginning of this chapter to make it usable with the collection-based `for` loop:

```
import java.util.Iterator;

public class LinkedList<T> implements Iterable<T> {

  // Returns an iterator for this list
  public Iterator<T> iterator() {
    // Code to return an Iterator<T> reference for this list...
  }

  // Rest of the LinkedList<T> generic type definition as before...
}
```

The generic `LinkedList<>` class type now implements the generic `Iterable<>` interface type, and they share a common type parameter. The type argument that you supply for `LinkedList<>` also applies to `Iterable<>`. You can see why the `Iterable<>` and `Iterator<>` interfaces need to be generic types. The type parameter allows them to be automatically adapted to work with objects of any type. Because these interfaces are defined as generic types, you can define classes that contain sets of objects of any type and provide the capability for iterating over the contents using the collection-based `for` loop simply by implementing the `Iterable<>` interface. The interface is automatically customized to work with whatever type of object a particular container contains.

The `Iterator<T>` type is a generic interface type that is defined in the `java.util` package. Your implementation of the `iterator()` method must return an object of a class type that implements the `Iterator<T>` interface. This is easy to do. The methods in the `Iterator<T>` interface provide a mechanism for iterating once over each of the elements of type `T` in a collection in turn and may also provide the ability to remove elements. These methods are the following:

> ➤ `T next()` returns a reference of type `T` to the next object that is available from the iterator and throws an exception of type `java.util.NoSuchElementException` if no further elements are available. `T` is the type parameter for the generic interface and corresponds to the type of objects stored in the container. Note that you'll also see `E` used as the type parameter that represents `Element` instead of `T` for `Type`.

➤ boolean hasNext() returns true if at least one more element is available from the iterator. When this is the case, calling the next() method for the iterator returns a reference to the next object in the container. The method returns false if no more elements are available from the iterator. Thus this method provides a way for you to check whether calling the next() method for the iterator returns a reference or throws an exception.

➤ void remove() is an optional operation that removes the last element that was retrieved by the next() method from the collection. If the remove operation is not supported, this method must be implemented to throw an exception of type java.lang.UnsupportedOperationException. It must also throw an exception of type java.lang.IllegalStateException if the next() method has not been called for the iterator object prior to calling the remove() method.

The first two methods provide a mechanism for iterating over all the elements in a collection such as a generic linked list. Suppose that you have a LinkedList<String> reference stored in a variable, strings, where LinkedList<> is the version that implements Iterable<>. You could use the iterator like this:

```
Iterator<String> iter = strings.iterator();   // Get an iterator
String str = null;                             // Stores an element from the list
while(iter.hasNext()) {                        // If there are more elements
  str = iter.next();                           // Get the next one...
  // Do something with str...
}
```

The while loop continues to retrieve elements from iter as long as the hasNext() method returns true. Within the loop, successive elements are retrieved by calling the next() method. You don't need to put this loop in a try block because the exception that the next() method can throw is of a type derived from RuntimeException. Removing an element would just involve calling the remove() method for strings after a call of the next() method, typically after you have analyzed the object retrieved to determine that you really do want to remove it. The exceptions that the remove() method can throw are also derived from RuntimeException so you are not obliged to catch them.

Of course, you can also iterate over the strings in the list like this:

```
for(String string : strings) {
  // Do something with string...
}
```

Implementing an Iterator Capability

As I said in the previous section, the iterator() method in the LinkedList<T> type must return an object reference as type Iterator<T>, so the class type for the iterator object should implement the Iterator<T> interface. An iterator is a one-time use object so you need to recreate it each time. You could define a class representing an iterator as an inner class to LinkedList<T>:

```
import java.util.Iterator;

public class LinkedList<T> implements Iterable<T> {

  // Returns an iterator for this list
  public Iterator<T> iterator() {
    return new ListIterator();          // Create iterator of the inner class type
  }

  // Inner class defining iterator objects for this linked list
  private class ListIterator implements Iterator<T> {
    // Constructor
    public ListIterator() {
      // Code to initialize the iterator...
    }

    // Method to test whether more elements are available
    public boolean hasNext() {
```

```
      // Code to determine if there are more elements...
    }

    // Method to return the next available object from the linked list
    public T next() {
      // Code to return the next element...
    }

    // Method to remove the last element retrieved from the linked list
    public void remove() {
      // Code to remove the element last accessed by next()...
    }

    // Any other members needed for ListIterator<T>...
  }
  // Rest of the LinkedList<T> generic type definition as before...
}
```

You have added a nested class to define an iterator object for a linked list. The `ListIterator` class defines the methods declared in the `Iterator<T>` interface plus a constructor. Note that you do not need to specify a type parameter for the `ListIterator` class. Only the interface that is implemented by the `ListIterator` class is parameterized, and that uses the type variable name for the outer class. The type argument you supply for the container type also applies to the methods declared by the `Iterator<T>` interface that are implemented by `ListIterator`.

A `ListIterator` object is able to access the members of its parent `LinkedList<T>` object directly, but because it must provide a one-pass iteration through the elements in the linked list, it needs to track what is happening during successive calls of the `next()` method. You can provide this by adding a field of type `T` to the `ListIterator` class to record the element from the linked list that is available when the `next()` method is called. You can easily initialize such a field in the constructor and then implement the other methods to make use of it. The inner class definition would then look like this:

```
private class ListIterator implements Iterator<T> {
  // Constructor
  public ListIterator() {
    nextElement = getFirst();
  }

  // Method to test whether more elements are available
  public boolean hasNext() {
    return nextElement != null;
  }

  // Method to return the next available object from the linked list
  public T next() {
    T element = nextElement;
    if(element == null) {
      throw new java.util.NoSuchElementException();
    }
    nextElement = getNext();
    return element;
  }

  // Method to remove the last element retrieved from the linked list
  // You don't want to support this operation so just throw the exception
  // If you did support this operation, you would need to include a check
  // that next() has been called, and if not,
  // throw IllegalStateException
  public void remove() {
    throw new UnsupportedOperationException(
                        "Remove not supported for LinkedList<>");
  }

  private T nextElement;
}
```

If you add this inner class to the definition of LinkedList<>, you can use a new version of the TryAutoboxing example to try it out.

TRY IT OUT Using the Collection-Based for Loop

Here's a version of the original TryAutoboxing example that has been modified to use the collection-based for loop:

```
public class TryAutoboxing2 {
  public static void main(String[] args) {
    LinkedList<Double> temperatures = new LinkedList<>();

    // Insert 6 temperature values 0 to 25 degrees Centigrade
    for(int i = 0 ; i < 6 ; ++i) {
      temperatures.addItem(25.0*Math.random());
    }

    // Collection-based for loop used with LinkedList<Double>
    for(Double value : temperatures) {
      System.out.printf("%.2f degrees Fahrenheit%n", toFahrenheit(value));
    }
  }

  // Convert Centigrade to Fahrenheit
  public static double toFahrenheit(double temperature) {
    return 1.8*temperature + 32.0;
  }
}
```

Directory "TryAutoboxing2"

Put the source file for this class in the same directory as the new version of LinkedList<T> that implements the Iterable<T> interface. If you use the old version, the program does not compile.

The output is similar to the previous version of TryAutoboxing.

How It Works

The collection-based for loop requires an iterator of type Iterator<T> that it uses to iterate over the members of a collection or an array. Clearly, all arrays implement the Iterator<T> interface; otherwise, you couldn't use them with this form of for loop. Because the LinkedList<T> type now implements Iterable<T>, you can use the collection-based for loop with any LinkedList<T> collection, as the example demonstrates.

A Parameterized Type for Binary Trees

Let's consider another kind of container as a candidate for being a generic type. A *binary tree* is a structure for organizing data in the form of a tree, where each node in the tree has at most two child nodes. Binary tree algorithms have a wide range of applications including language parsing and searching. Another very interesting application of a binary tree is for sorting. This is an easily understood context, so let's use that to explore how you might implement a generic binary tree class. Figure 13-2 shows an example of integers organized in a binary tree structure.

The first node in a binary tree is called the *root node* because this node is the starting point for accessing all

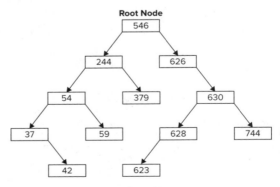

A Binary Tree of Integers

FIGURE 13-2

the other nodes in the tree. Each node in a binary tree, including the root node, can have two child nodes, usually referred to as the *left child node* and the *right child node*. Thus, each node in a binary tree may have zero, one, or two child nodes. Figure 13-2 contains examples of all three possibilities. A *parent node* is a node that has at least one child node and a *leaf node* is a node with no child nodes. The root node is the only node with no parents.

You can construct a binary tree so that for each node, the object stored as the left child node is always less than the object stored in the node and the object in the right child node is always greater. With this form of tree you'll be able to extract the objects that are stored in it so that they are in sequence. The tree shown in Figure 13-2 has been constructed like this, and it's a very simple process.

Adding a node involves starting with the root node and seeing whether the new node is less than or greater than the current node. This establishes whether it is a potential left or right child node for the root node. If the root node already has a child node in the position where the new node might belong, you repeat the comparison process with that child node. Eventually you'll find a node that has no child node where the new node fits, so that's where you put it. Implementing this as a recursive method helps to make the code very concise.

Given that you have constructed a tree in this manner, starting with the root node you can work your way through all the nodes in the tree by following the left and right child nodes in an orderly fashion to extract all the objects from the tree in sequence. Because all the nodes are similar, the use of recursion simplifies the implementation of this process, too.

Because a binary tree is a structure you can apply to organizing objects of any type, it is an obvious candidate for being a generic type. It also provides another example of where being able to constrain the type parameter is important. The way the tree is constructed implies that you must be able to compare objects that are added to a tree. This means that every object in the tree must have a method available for comparing it to objects of the same type. Making the object type implement an interface that declares a method that compares objects is the way to do this. A binary tree implementation also provides an example of a situation where you can apply the power of recursion to very good effect.

Defining the Generic Type

You can come to some general conclusions about what the characteristics of your `BinaryTree<T>` class are going to be by considering how it will work. Objects of type `Node` are going to be a fundamental part of a binary tree. The `Node` objects in the tree are really part of the inner workings of the container so they don't need to be known about or accessible externally. It is therefore appropriate to define `Node` objects by a private inner class to the `BinaryTree<T>` class. All nodes in a binary tree must be different, but you can allow for duplicates of existing data items to be added to a tree by providing for a count of the number of identical objects to be recorded within a `Node` object. As a minimum, a `BinaryTree<T>` object has to store the `Node` object that is the root node for the tree as a member and provide a method for adding new nodes. Ideally it also provides a means for returning all the data that is stored in the tree in sequence as a single object, which requires a facility that can package this collection of data. The generic `LinkedList<T>` type from the previous example provides a convenient facility for this.

You need to be able to decide whether an object to be stored in a tree is greater or less than existing objects so bjects that are to be added to the tree must be of a type that has a method for comparing objects. The `java.lang.Comparable<T>` interface declares a single method, the `compareTo()` method, that fits the bill. The method returns a negative integer if the object for which it is called is less than the argument, 0 if it equals the argument, and a positive integer if it is greater, so it does precisely what you need for placing new values in a `BinaryTree<T>` class object. If you specify the `Comparable<T>` interface as a constraint on the type parameter for the `BinaryTree<T>` class, it ensures that all objects added to a `BinaryTree<T>` object are of a class type that implements the `compareTo()` method. Because `Comparable<T>` is a parameterized type, it fits exactly with what you want here.

Here's a first stab at outlining the `BinaryTree<T>` generic type:

```
public class BinaryTree<T extends Comparable<T>> {

  // Add a value to the tree
  public void add(T value) {
```

```
        // Add a value to the tree...
    }

    // Create a list containing the values from the tree in sequence
    public LinkedList<T> sort() {
        // Code to extract objects from the tree in sequence
        // and insert them in a LinkedList object and return that...
    }

    private Node root;                          // The root node

    // Private inner class defining nodes
    private class Node {
        Node(T value) {
            obj = value;
            count = 1;
        }

        T obj;                                  // Object stored in the node
        int count;                              // Count of identical nodes
        Node left;                              // The left child node
        Node right;                             // The right child node
    }
}
```

No `BinaryTree<T>` constructor is defined explicitly because the default constructor suffices. The default no-arg constructor creates an object with the root node as `null`. Thus, all objects are added to the tree by calling the `add()` method. The `sort()` method returns a `LinkedList<T>` object that contain the objects from the tree in ascending sequence.

The inner `Node` class has four fields that store the value, the count of the number of identical values in the current node, and references to its left and right child nodes. The constructor just initializes the `obj` and `count` fields in the `Node` object that is created, leaving `left` and `right` with their default values of `null`. Of course, when a `Node` object is first created, it doesn't have any child nodes, and the count of identical objects in the tree is 1. Let's look at how objects are inserted into a tree.

Inserting Objects in a Binary Tree

It's easy to see how adding an object to the tree can be a recursive operation in general. The process is illustrated in Figure 13-3.

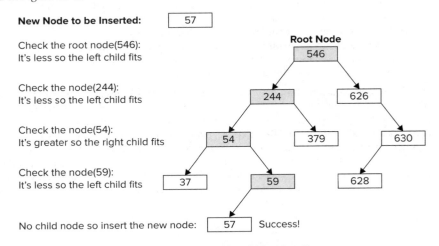

Inserting a New Object in a Tree

FIGURE 13-3

The shaded nodes in Figure 13-3 are the ones that have to be considered in the process of inserting the value 57 in the tree. To find where the new node for an object should be placed in relation to the existing nodes, you start with the root node to see which of its child nodes represents a potential position for the new node. If the candidate child node that you choose already exists then you must repeat the process you've just gone through with the root node with the chosen child node. Of course, this child node may itself have child nodes so the process may need to be repeated again. You should be able to visualize how this can continue until either you find a child node that contains an object that is identical to the one contained in the new node, or you find a vacant child node position where the new node fits.

You can implement the add() method in the BinaryTree<T> class like this:

```java
public void add(T value) {
  if(root == null) {              // If there's no root node
    root = new Node(value);       // store it in the root
  } else {                        // Otherwise...
    add(value, root);             // add it recursively
  }
}
```

If the root node is null, the add() method creates a new root node containing the value to be inserted. If root is not null then the node where it fits in the tree must be found, and this is the function performed by another version of the add() method that accepts two arguments specifying the value to be inserted into the tree and the node where it might be inserted. The second argument allows the method to be called recursively. This method can be private as it does not need to be accessed externally. You could implement it like this:

```java
private void add(T value, Node node) {
  int comparison = node.obj.compareTo(value);
  if(comparison == 0) {              // If value is equal to the current node
    ++node.count;                    // just increment the count
    return;
  }
  if(comparison > 0) {               // If value less than the current node
    if(node.left == null) {          // and the left child node is null
      node.left = new Node(value);   // Store it as the left child node
    } else {                         // Otherwise...
      add(value, node.left);         // ...call add() again at the left node
    }
  } else {                           // It must be greater than the current node
    if(node.right == null) {         // so it must go to the right...
      node.right = new Node(value);  // store it as the right node
    } else {                         // ...or when right node is not null
      add(value, node.right);        // ...call add() again at the right node
    }
  }
}
```

This method is called only with a non-null second argument. The first step is to compare the object to be inserted, which is the first argument, value, with the object stored in the current node, specified by the second argument, node. If the new object equals the one stored in the current node, you need to update the count only for the current node.

If the new object is not equal to that stored in the current node, you first check whether it's less. Remember that the compareTo() method returns a positive integer when the object for which it is called is *greater* than the argument, so if the result of a comparison is positive then it means that the argument is *less than* that in the current node. That makes it a candidate for the left child node of the current node, but only if the left child node is null. If the left child node is not null, you call the add() method recursively to add the object relative to the left node. You've tested for zero and positive values of comparison, so the only other possibility is that the comparison value is negative. In this case you repeat the same procedure, but with the right child node. This process finds the place for the new node so that each node has only a left child that is less than the current node and a right child that is greater. In fact, for any node, the values stored in the whole left subtree are less than the current node, and the values in the whole right subtree are greater. Now that you have objects in the tree, you have to figure out how you're going to get them out again.

Extracting Objects from the Binary Tree

Calling the `sort()` method for a `BinaryTree<>` object should return a `LinkedList<>` object containing the objects from the tree in ascending sequence. The process for selecting the objects to be inserted into the linked list is also recursive. You can define `sort()` like this:

```
public LinkedList<T> sort() {
  LinkedList<T>values = new LinkedList<>();      // Create a linked list
  treeSort(root);                                // Sort the objects into the list
  return values;
}
```

You create a new `LinkedList<T>` object when the `sort()` method executes to hold the sorted values from the tree. The `sort()` method could be called several times for a `BinaryTree<T>` object, with the contents of the binary tree being changed in the intervening period, so you must create the linked list from scratch each time. The real work of inserting the objects from the tree into the linked list, `values`, is going to be done by the recursive `treeSort()` method. You can get an inkling of how this works if you recall that the left child node object of every node is less than the current node, which is less than the right child node. Therefore, you want to access the objects in the sequence:

```
left child node : node : right child node
```

Of course, the child nodes may themselves have child nodes, *but the same applies to them.* Take the left child node, for example. The objects here should be accessed in the sequence:

```
left child of left child node : left child node : right child of left child node
```

The same goes for the right child node and its children. All you have to do is express this as code, and you can do that like this:

```
private void treeSort(Node node, LinkedList<T> values) {
  if(node != null) {                         // If the current node isn't null
    treeSort(node.left, values);             // process its left child node

    // List the duplicate objects for the current node
    for(int i = 0 ; i < node.count ; ++i) {
      values.addItem(node.obj);
    }
    treeSort(node.right, values);            // Now process the right child node
  }
}
```

If the node that is passed to the `treeSort()` method is `null`, nothing further is left to do so the method returns. If the argument is not `null`, you first process the left child node, then the node that was passed as the argument, and finally the right child node—just as you saw earlier. That does it all. The actual insertion of an object into the linked list that is passed as the second argument always occurs in the `for` loop. This loop typically executes one iteration because most of the time, no duplicate objects are in the tree. The value of the left child node, if it exists, is always added to the linked list before the value of the current node because you don't add the value from the current node until the `treeSort()` method call for the left child returns. Similarly, the value from the right child node is always added to the linked list after that of the current node.

You're ready to give the generic `BinaryTree<T>` type a whirl.

TRY IT OUT   **Sorting Using a Binary Tree**

You need to create a directory to hold the three source files for this program. When you've set that up, copy the `LinkedList.java` source file from the previous example to the new directory. You can then add the `BinaryTree.java` source file containing the following code to the directory:

```
public class BinaryTree<T extends Comparable<T>> {

  // Add a value to the tree
  public void add(T value) {
    if(root == null) {                    // If there's no root node
      root = new Node(value);             // store it in the root
    } else {                              // Otherwise...
      add(value, root);                   // add it recursively
    }
  }

  // Recursive insertion of an object
  private void add(T value, Node node) {
    int comparison = node.obj.compareTo(value);
    if(comparison == 0) {                 // If it is equal to the current node
      ++node.count;                       // just increment the count
      return;
    }
    if(comparison > 0) {                  // If it's less than the current node
      if(node.left == null) {             // and the left child node is null
        node.left = new Node(value);      // Store it as the left child node
      } else {                            // Otherwise...
        add(value, node.left);            // ... call add() again at the left node
      }
    } else {                              // It must be greater than the current node
      if(node.right == null) {            // so it must go to the right...
        node.right = new Node(value);     // store it as the right node
      } else {                            // ...or when right node is not null
        add(value, node.right);           // ...call add() again at the right node
      }
    }
  }

  // Create a list containing the values from the tree in sequence
  public LinkedList<T> sort() {
    LinkedList<T> values = new LinkedList<>();      // Create a linked list
    treeSort(root);                                  // Sort the objects into the list
    return values;
  }

  // Extract the tree nodes in sequence
  private void treeSort(Node node, LinkedList<T> values) {
    if(node != null) {                    // If the current node isn't null
      treeSort(node.left);                // process its left child node

      // List the duplicate objects for the current node
      for(int i = 0 ; i < node.count ; ++i) {
        values.addItem(node.obj);
      }
      treeSort(node.right);               // Now process the right child node
    }
  }

  private Node root;                      // The root node

  // Private inner class defining nodes
  private class Node {
    Node(T value) {
      obj = value;
      count = 1;
    }

    T obj;                                // Object stored in the node
```

```
      int count;                      // Count of identical objects
      Node left;                      // The left child node
      Node right;                     // The right child node
    }
  }
```

Directory "TryBinaryTree"

You can try out sorting integers and strings using `BinaryTree<>` objects with the following code:

```java
public class TryBinaryTree {
  public static void main(String[] args) {
    int[] numbers = new int[30];
    for(int i = 0 ; i < numbers.length ; ++i) {
      numbers[i] = (int)(1000.0*Math.random());   // Random integers 0 to 999
    }

    // List starting integer values
    int count = 0;
    System.out.println("Original values are:");
    for(int number : numbers) {
      System.out.printf("%6d", number);
      if(++count%6 == 0) {
        System.out.println();
      }
    }

    // Create the tree and add the integers to it
    BinaryTree<Integer> tree = new BinaryTree<>();
    for(int number:numbers) {
      tree.add(number);
    }

    // Get sorted values
    LinkedList<Integer> values = tree.sort();
    count = 0;
    System.out.println("\nSorted values are:");
    for(Integer value : values) {
      System.out.printf("%6d", value);
      if(++count%6 == 0) {
        System.out.println();
      }
    }

    // Create an array of words to be sorted
    String[] words = {"vacillate", "procrastinate", "arboreal", "syzygy",
                      "xenocracy", "zygote"        , "mephitic", "soporific",
                      "grisly"   , "gristly" };

    // List the words
    System.out.println("\nOriginal word sequence:");
    for(String word : words) {
      System.out.printf("%-15s", word);
      if(++count%5 == 0) {
        System.out.println();
      }
    }

    // Create the tree and insert the words
    BinaryTree<String> cache = new BinaryTree<>();
    for(String word : words) {
      cache.add(word);
    }

    // Sort the words
```

```
      LinkedList<String> sortedWords = cache.sort();

      // List the sorted words
      System.out.println("\nSorted word sequence:");
      count = 0;
      for(String word : sortedWords) {
        System.out.printf("%-15s", word);
        if(++count%5 == 0) {
          System.out.println();
        }
      }
    }
  }
}
```

Directory "TryBinaryTree"

The output should be along the lines of the following:

```
Original values are:
   110   136   572   589   605   832
   565   765   514   616   347   724
   152   527   124   324    42   508
   621   653   480   236     1   793
   324    31   127   170   724   546

Sorted values are:
     1    31    42   110   124   127
   136   152   170   236   324   324
   347   480   508   514   527   546
   565   572   589   605   616   621
   653   724   724   765   793   832

Original word sequence:
vacillate        procrastinate   arboreal        syzygy          xenocracy
zygote           mephitic        soporific       grisly          gristly

Sorted word sequence:
arboreal         grisly          gristly         mephitic        procrastinate
soporific        syzygy          vacillate       xenocracy       zygote
```

How It Works

You have defined BinaryTree<T> with a type parameter that is constrained to implement the parameterized interface type Comparable<T>. Thus, any type argument that you use with the BinaryTree<T> type must implement the Comparable<T> interface. If it doesn't, the code doesn't compile. This ensures that all objects added to a BinaryTree<T> object have the compareTo() method available.

The definition for BinaryTree<T> also demonstrates that a generic type can include references to other generic types—LinkedList<T> in the sort() method for example and the second parameter to the treeSort() method. The type of the LinkedList<T> return value is determined by the type argument supplied to the BinaryTree<T> generic type. The same would apply if you had fields with generic types parameterized by T.

After creating and displaying an array of 30 random integer values, you define a BinaryTree<Integer> object that stores objects of type Integer. The following statement does this:

```
      BinaryTree<Integer> tree = new BinaryTree<>();
```

You then insert the integers into the binary tree in a loop:

```
      for(int number:numbers) {
        tree.add(number);
      }
```

The parameter type for the add() method is type Integer, but autoboxing automatically takes care of converting your arguments to objects of type Integer.

Calling the sort() method for tree returns the objects from the tree contained in a LinkedList<Integer> object:

```
LinkedList<Integer> values = tree.sort();
```

The Integer objects in the linked list container are ordered in ascending sequence. You list these in a for loop:

```
for(Integer value : values) {
  System.out.printf("%6d", value);
  if(++count%6 == 0) {
    System.out.println();
  }
}
```

You are able to use the collection-based for loop here because the LinkedList<T> type implements the Iterable<T> interface; this is the sole prerequisite on a container for it to allow you to apply this for loop to access the elements.

Just to demonstrate that BinaryTree<> works with more types than just Integer, you create an object of type BinaryTree<String> that you use to store a series of String objects. You use essentially the same process as you used with the integers to obtain the words sorted in ascending sequence. Note the use of the '-' flag in the format specifier for the strings in the first argument to the printf() method. This outputs the string left-justified in the output field, which makes the output of the strings look tidier.

Hidden Constraints in the BinaryTree<> Type

So the BinaryTree<T> class works well? Well, not as well as it might. The parameterized type has a built-in constraint that was not exposed by the examples storing String and Integer objects. Suppose you define a Person class like this:

```
public class Person implements Comparable<Person> {
  public Person(String name) {
    this.name = name;
  }

  public int compareTo(Person person) {
    if( person == this) {
      return 0;
    }
    return this.name.compareTo(person.name);
  }

  @Override
  public String toString() {
    return name;
  }

  protected String name;
}
```

This is a simple class representing a person. It implements the Comparable<Person> interface so you can use a BinaryTree<Person> object to store and sort objects of type Person. This works just as well as the BinaryTree<String> and BinaryTree<Integer> examples.

However, you might possibly subclass the Person type like this:

```
public class Manager extends Person {
  public Manager(String name, int level) {
    super(name);
```

```
      this.level = level;
    }

    @Override
    public String toString() {
      return "Manager " + super.toString() + " level: " + level;
    }

    protected int level;
  }
```

This class defines a special kind of Person—a manager no less! You have just one extra field specifying the level that reflects where the manager sits in the corporate pecking order. You also have a version of the toString() method that presents the Person as a manager with his or her level. The class inherits the implementation of the Comparable<Person> interface from the base class. If that's sufficient for differentiating two persons, it should be okay for separating two managers. However, it's not good enough for the BinaryTree<T> type. You could try adding Manager objects to a binary tree like this:

```
      BinaryTree<Manager> people = new BinaryTree<>();
      Manager[] managers = { new Manager("Jane",1), new Manager("Joe",3), new Manager("Freda",3)};
      for(Manager manager: managers){
        people.add(manager);
      }
```

However, it doesn't work. If you insert this fragment at the end of main() in the previous example, you get a compiler error message relating to the statement that creates the BinaryTree<Manager> object; it says something along the lines of "type parameter Manager is not within its bound."

The problem is that your BinaryTree<T> class requires that the Manager class should implement the Comparable<Manager> interface. The inherited implementation of Comparable<Person> is not acceptable. Obviously, this is a serious constraint. You don't want the binary tree implementation to be as rigid as that. As long as there's an implementation of Comparable<T> in a class that allows objects to be compared, that should suffice. What you really want is for your BinaryTree<T> type to accept any type argument that is of a type that implements Comparable<T> for the type itself, or for any superclass of the type. You don't have the tools to deal with this at this point, but I'll return to the solution to this problem a little later in this chapter.

VARIABLES OF A RAW TYPE

You have seen that the runtime type of all instances of a generic type is the same and is just the generic type name without any parameters. You can use the generic type name by itself to define variables. For example:

```
      LinkedList list = null;
```

This creates a variable with the name list that is of type LinkedList from the LinkedList<T> generic type. This type that results from eliminating the parameters from the generic type is referred to as a *raw type*.

The class that corresponds to the raw type is produced by removing the type parameters from the generic type definition and replacing each instance of a type variable in the definition by the leftmost bound of its corresponding type parameter. This process of mapping from a generic type to a non-generic type is called *type erasure* because all occurrences of the type variable are effectively erased from the generic class definition. A raw type exists as a consequence of implementing generic types using type erasure.

In the absence of any explicit type parameter bounds, every type parameter T is implicitly bounded by type Object, so all occurrences of T in a generic type definition are replaced by Object to produce the raw type. This is important for interface types such as Iterable<T> and Comparable<T> in the standard packages. Interfaces in the standard packages that define methods are generally defined as generic types for maximum flexibility. When you implement such an interface in an ordinary class without specifying a type argument, your class is implementing the raw type, so the methods in the interface are declared with parameters and/or return types of type Object.

Suppose you have specified that the type parameter T for a parameterized type is bounded by the type Comparable<T>. This is the case for the BinaryTree<T> type that you implemented earlier. In the raw type for the parameterized type, all occurrences of the type variable T are replaced by Comparable. The raw type corresponding to Comparable<T> is produced by using type Object as the replacement for the type parameter because no parameter constraints are specified for the Comparable<T> type. Thus for the BinaryTree<T> type, the raw type definition is produced by substituting Comparable in place of the type variable, T. This may be what you want for a valid raw type in this case. The parameter type to the add() method is Comparable, so you can pass an object of any class type that implements the Comparable interface to it. However, in other instances where methods with a return type are specified by a type parameter, you may want the raw type to be produced using Object as the upper bound for the type parameter. This applies to the serializable version of the LinkedList<T> generic type where the bound on the type parameter is Serializable. It might be better to have the getFirst() and getNext() methods return a reference of type Object instead of type Serializable. You can accomplish this quite easily by simply defining the first bound for the type parameter as type Object, like this:

```
class LinkedList<T extends Object & Serializable> implements Serializable {

    // Class definition as before...
}
```

Now the leftmost bound for the type parameter is type Object, so the raw type is produced by replacing the type variable T by Object in the generic type definition.

> **NOTE** *You can store a reference of any of the types produced from a generic type in a variable of the corresponding raw type. For example, you could write:*
>
> LinkedList list = new LinkedList<String>();
>
> *This is legal for compatibility with code written before generic types were available in Java. However, you should not regard it as part of your normal programming repertoire as it's an inherently risky practice.*

WILDCARDS AS TYPE PARAMETER ARGUMENTS

You express a particular type from the set defined by a generic type by supplying a type argument for each of its type parameters. For example, to specify the BinaryTree<T> type that stores objects of type String, you specify the type argument as String—so the type is BinaryTree<String>. Instead of supplying a specific type as the type argument for a generic type, you can specify the argument as ?, in which case you have specified the type argument as a *wildcard*. A wildcard type represents any class or interface type.

You can declare variables of a generic type using a wildcard type argument. For example:

```
BinaryTree<?> tree = new BinaryTree<Double>();
```

The tree variable is of type BinaryTree<?> so you can store a reference to any type of BinaryTree<> object in it. In this instance you have stored a reference to an object of type BinaryTree<Double>, but BinaryTree<String> or BinaryTree<AnyType> is equally acceptable—as long as the type argument is not a primitive type. You can think of the use of a variable of a wildcard type as loosely paralleling the use of a variable of type Object. Because tree is the result of a wildcard type argument, the actual type of the reference stored is not known, so you cannot use this variable to call methods specific to the object that it references.

So what is the difference between using a wildcard type argument to a generic type and using a raw type that you are supposed to avoid? The compiler applies much stricter rules to the wildcard parameterized type than to the corresponding raw type. Operations performed on the raw type that result in "unchecked" warnings from the compiler are rejected as errors so the code won't compile. Consequently, using a wildcard type parameter is much safer than using a raw type.

You can use a wildcard type argument to specify a method parameter type where there is no dependency in the code on the actual type argument for the generic type. If you specify the type of a parameter to a method as `BinaryTree<?>` then the method accepts an argument of type `BinaryTree<String>`, `BinaryTree<Double>`, or indeed any `BinaryTree<>` type. To make this clearer, let's consider a specific situation where you might use a wildcard as an argument for a method parameter of a generic type.

In the previous example, the `main()` method listed the objects in the `LinkedList<>` object that the `sort()` method returns by executing a specific loop for each of the two cases—`Integer` objects and `String` objects. You could write a static method that would list the items stored in a linked list, whatever they are. Here's how you could define such a method as a static member of the `TryBinaryTree` class:

```
public static void listAll(LinkedList<?> list) {
  for(Object obj : list) {
    System.out.println(obj);
  }
}
```

The parameter type for the `listAll()` method uses a wildcard specification instead of an explicit type argument. Thus, the method accepts an argument of any `LinkedList<>` type. Because every object has a `toString()` method regardless of the actual type, the argument passed to `println()` in the body of the method is always valid. Now you could list the integers in the `values` object that is of type `LinkedList<Integer>` with the statement:

```
listAll(values);
```

You could also list the contents of the `sortedWords` object of type `LinkedList<String>` with the statement:

```
listAll(sortedWords);
```

You can plug these code fragments, including the definition of the method, of course, into the `TryBinaryTree` class and recompile to see it working.

TRY IT OUT Using a Wildcard Type Argument

Here's a modified version of the previous example:

```
public class TryWildCard {
  public static void main(String[] args) {
    int[] numbers = new int[30];
    for(int i = 0 ; i < numbers.length ; ++i) {
      numbers[i] = (int)(1000.0*Math.random());    // Random integers 0 to 999
    }
    // List starting integer values
    int count = 0;
    System.out.println("Original values are:");
    for(int number : numbers) {
      System.out.printf("%6d", number);
      if(++count%6 == 0) {
        System.out.println();
      }
    }

    // Create the tree and add the integers to it
    BinaryTree<Integer> tree = new BinaryTree<>();
    for(int number:numbers) {
      tree.add(number);
    }

    // Get sorted values
    LinkedList<Integer> values = tree.sort();
    System.out.println("\nSorted values are:");
```

```
    listAll(values);

    // Create an array of words to be sorted
    String[] words = {"vacillate", "procrastinate", "arboreal",
                      "syzygy", "xenocracy", "zygote",
                      "mephitic", "soporific", "grisly", "gristly" };

    // List the words
    System.out.println("\nOriginal word sequence:");
    for(String word : words) {
      System.out.printf("%-15s", word);
      if(++count%5 == 0) {
        System.out.println();
      }
    }

    // Create the tree and insert the words
    BinaryTree<String> cache = new BinaryTree<>();
    for(String word : words) {
      cache.add(word);
    }

    // Sort the words
    LinkedList<String> sortedWords = cache.sort();

    // List the sorted words
    System.out.println("\nSorted word sequence:");
    listAll(sortedWords);
  }

  // List the elements in any linked list
  public static void listAll(LinkedList<?> list) {
    for(Object obj : list) {
      System.out.println(obj);
    }
  }
}
```

Directory "TryWildCard"

You should get essentially the same output as before except that the sorted data is listed with each item on a separate line.

How It Works

You have a static method defined in the TryWildCard class that lists the elements in any LinkedList<> object. You use this to list the contents of objects of type LinkedList<Integer> and LinkedList<String>. The listAll() method relies only on the toString() method being implemented for the objects retrieved from the linked list. This is the case for any type of object because the toString() method is always inherited from the Object class. Of course, relying on the inherited toString() method to represent an object in output is not ideal in many cases.

Constraints on a Wildcard

It may be the case that you'd like to limit a wildcard specification to some extent—after all, allowing any non-primitive type is an incredibly wide specification. You can explicitly constrain a wildcard specification. One possibility is to specify that it extends another type. This type of constraint is described as an *upper bound* of the wildcard type because it implies that any subclass of the type that the wildcard extends is acceptable, including the type itself, of course.

Defining an Upper Bound

Suppose that you want to implement a method that serializes the objects stored in a `LinkedList<>` object. A prerequisite is that the objects in the list implement the `Serializable` interface, whatever type they are. You could define a static method to do this using an upper bound on the wildcard type specification:

```
public static void saveAll(LinkedList<? extends java.io.Serializable>  list) {
  // Serialize the objects from the list...
}
```

The parameter to the `saveAll()` method is of type:

```
LinkedList<? extends java.io.Serializable>
```

This says that the argument to the `saveAll()` method can be a linked list of objects of any type as long as they implement the `Serializable` interface. Knowing that the objects in the list implement the `Serializable` interface means that you can serialize them without knowing exactly what type they are. You can just pass an object reference to the `writeObject()` method for the stream, and everything is taken care of.

To make the upper bound for a wildcard type `Object`, you just write it as:

```
? extends Object
```

You might think that specifying a wildcard with an upper bound that is type `Object` is stating the obvious and not a useful thing to do. However, it does have a very useful effect. It forces the specification to represent only class types, and not interface types, so you can use this when you want to specify any type, as long as it's a class type.

Defining a Lower Bound

You can constrain a wildcard type specification by specifying that it is a superclass of a given type. In this case you use the `super` keyword to define a *lower bound* for the wildcard. Here's an example:

```
public static void analyze(LinkedList<? super MyClass> list) {

  // Code to do whatever with the list...
}
```

Here you are saying that the elements in the list that is passed as the argument to the `analyze()` method must be of type `MyClass`, or of a type that `MyClass` extends or implements. This should ring a bell in relation to the `BinaryTree<T>` generic type from earlier in this chapter. A wildcard that is a superclass of a given type sounds like a good candidate for what you were looking for to make the `BinaryTree<T>` type more flexible, and it would accept a type argument that possibly inherited an implementation of the `Comparable<T>` interface. You could modify the definition to the following to allow this:

```
public class BinaryTree<T extends Comparable<? super T>> {

  // Details exactly as before...
}
```

The only change that you have made to the `BinaryTree<>` type is that you've changed the type parameter for the `Comparable<T>` interface to a wildcard that is a superclass of `T`, the type parameter for `BinaryTree<>`. The effect is to allow any type argument to be accepted that implements the `Comparable<T>` interface or inherits an implementation of it. This should allow the `BinaryTree<>` type to be used with classes such as the `Manager` class, which could not be used as a type argument in the previous `BinaryTree<T>` implementation. Let's prove it.

CONFER PROGRAMMER TO PROGRAMMER ABOUT THIS TOPIC.
Visit p2p.wrox.com

A More Flexible Binary Tree

You need the definition of the Person and Manager classes that you saw earlier. The Person class definition is the following:

```java
public class Person implements Comparable<Person> {
  public Person(String name) {
    this.name = name;
  }

  public int compareTo(Person person) {
    if( person == this) {
      return 0;
    }
    return this.name.compareTo(person.name);
  }

  @Override
  public String toString() {
    return name;
  }

  protected String name;
}
```

Directory "TryFlexibleBinaryTree"

The Manager class definition is the following:

```java
public class Manager extends Person {
  public Manager(String name, int level) {
    super(name);
    this.level = level;
  }

  @Override
  public String toString() {
    return "Manager " + super.toString() + " level: " + level;
  }

  protected int level;
}
```

Directory "TryFlexibleBinaryTree"

You can put the Person and Manager class definitions in the same directory as the following source file, which stores Manager objects in a BinaryTree<Manager> object:

```java
public class TryFlexibleBinaryTree {
  public static void main(String[] args) {

    BinaryTree<Manager> people = new BinaryTree<>();
    Manager[] managers = { new Manager("Jane", 1), new Manager("Joe", 3),
                           new Manager("Freda", 3), new Manager("Albert", 2)};
    for(Manager manager: managers){
      people.add(manager);
      System.out.println("Added "+ manager);
    }
    System.out.println();
    listAll(people.sort());
  }
```

```
    // List the elements in any linked list
    public static void listAll(LinkedList<?> list) {
      for(Object obj : list) {
        System.out.println(obj);
      }
    }
  }
```

Directory "TryFlexibleBinaryTree"

You also need the modified version of BinaryTree<> and the source file for LinkedList<>. The output should be:

```
Added Manager Jane level: 1
Added Manager Joe level: 3
Added Manager Freda level: 3
Added Manager Albert level: 2

Manager Albert level: 2
Manager Freda level: 3
Manager Jane level: 1
Manager Joe level: 3
```

How It Works

The output demonstrates that the BinaryTree<T> type works with a type argument that implements Comparable<T> even when the implementation is inherited. The use of a wildcard with a lower bound as the parameter for the constraint adds the flexibility to allow inherited implementations of the constraint type. This is usually what you want for any constraint on a type argument for a parameterized type, so you should always use this pattern with constraints for all your generic types unless you have a reason not to.

More on the Class Class

I mentioned in Chapter 6 that the Class class is not an ordinary class type; rather, it's defined as a parameterized type. The Class<> object for a given type such as Person or java.lang.String in your application is produced by supplying the type as the argument for the generic type parameter, so of type Class<Person> and Class<java.lang.String> in these two instances. Because these class types are produced from a generic type, many of the methods have parameters or return types that are specifically the type argument—Person or java.lang.String in the two examples I've cited.

The Class<T> type defines a lot of methods, but I'm mentioning only a few of them here as their application is beyond the scope of this book. You'll probably find that the primary use you have for Class<> is obtaining the class of an object by calling the getClass() method for the object. However, you also get a number of other useful methods with an object of a Class<> type, as shown in Table 13-1.

TABLE 13-1: Class<T> Methods

METHOD	PURPOSE
forName()	This is a static method that you can use to get the Class<T> object for a known class or interface type T. You pass the fully qualified name of the type as a String object to this method, and it returns the Class<> object for the type that has the name you have supplied (for example, Class<String> by specifying forName("java.lang.String")). If no class or interface of the type you specify exists, a ClassNotFoundException exception is thrown.

continues

TABLE 13-1 *(continued)*

METHOD	PURPOSE
newInstance()	This method calls the default constructor for the class that the current Class<T> object represents and returns a new object of type T. When things don't work as they should, this method can throw exceptions of type IllegalAccessException if class T or its no-arg constructor is not accessible or of type InstantiationException if T represents an abstract class, an interface, an array type, a primitive type, or void, or if T does not have a no-arg constructor. It can also throw an exception of type ExceptionInInitializerError if the object initialization fails, or of SecurityException if no permission for creating the new object exists.
getSuperclass()	This method returns a Class<> object for the superclass of the class represented by the current Class<T> object. Where the type represented is an array type, the method returns an object of type Class<Object>. If the current Class<T> object represents the Object class or a primitive type or void, then null is returned.
isInterface()	This method returns true if the current Class<T> object represents an interface.
getInterfaces()	This method returns an array of type Class<?>[] containing objects that represent the interfaces implemented by the class or interface type corresponding to the current Class<> object. If the class or interface does not implement any interfaces, the array that is returned has a length of 0.
toString()	This method returns a String object representing the current Class<T> object.

As I said, the list of methods in Table 13-1 for the Class<T> type is not exhaustive. A number of other methods defined in the class enable you to find out details of the contents of a class—the fields, the public methods defined in the class, or even classes that are defined within the class. If you need this kind of capability, you can find out more by browsing the API documentation relating to the Class<T> generic type.

ARRAYS AND PARAMETERIZED TYPES

Arrays of elements that are of a type produced from a generic type are not allowed. For example, although it looks quite reasonable, the following statement is not permitted and results in a compiler error message:

```
LinkedList<String>[] lists = new LinkedList<>[10];        // Will not compile!!!
```

Although you can declare a field in a generic type by specifying the type using a type parameter, you are not allowed to create arrays of elements using a type parameter. For example, you can define a data member like this:

```
public class MyType<T> {
  // The methods and data members of the type…
  private T[] data;                                       // This is OK
}
```

Although defining the data field as being of type T[] is legal and will compile, the following is not legal and will not compile:

```
public class MyType<T> {
  // Constructor
  public MyType() {
    data = new T[10];                                     // Not allowed!!
  }

  // The methods and data members of the type…
  private T[] data;                                       // This is OK
}
```

In the constructor you are attempting to create an array of elements of the type given by the type parameter T, and this is not permitted.

However, you can define arrays of elements of a generic type where the element type is the result of an unbounded wildcard type argument. For example, you can define the following array:

```
LinkedList<?>[] lists = new LinkedList<?>[10];              // OK
```

Each element in the array can store a reference to any specific `LinkedList<>` type, and they could all be different types. Just so that you can believe it, let's try it.

TRY IT OUT   A Wildcard Array

You can modify the previous `TryWildcard` example to demonstrate using a wildcard type in an array:

Available for
download on
Wrox.com

```java
public class TryWildCardArray {
  public static void main(String[] args) {
    BinaryTree<?>[] trees = {new BinaryTree<Integer>(), new BinaryTree<String>()};
    LinkedList<?>[] lists = new LinkedList<?>[trees.length];

    int[] numbers = new int[30];
    for(int i = 0 ; i < numbers.length ; ++i) {
      numbers[i] = (int)(1000.0*Math.random());    // Random integers 0 to 999
    }
    // List starting integer values
    int count = 0;
    System.out.println("Original values are:");
    for(int number : numbers) {
      System.out.printf("%6d", number);
      if(++count%6 == 0) {
        System.out.println();
      }
    }

    // Add the integers to first tree
    for(int number: numbers) {
      ((BinaryTree<Integer>)trees[0]).add(number);
    }

    // Create an array of words to be sorted
    String[] words = {"vacillate", "procrastinate", "arboreal", "syzygy",
                      "xenocracy", "zygote", "mephitic", "soporific",
                      "grisly", "gristly" };

    // List the words
    System.out.println("\nOriginal word sequence:");
    for(String word : words) {
      System.out.printf("%-15s", word);
      if(++count%5 == 0) {
        System.out.println();
      }
    }

    // Insert the words into second tree
    for(String word : words) {
      ((BinaryTree<String>)trees[1]).add(word);
    }

    // Sort the values in both trees
    for(int i = 0 ; i < lists.length ; ++i){
```

```
        lists[i] = trees[i].sort();
    }

    // List the sorted values from both trees
    for(LinkedList<?> list : lists){
      System.out.println("\nSorted results:");
      listAll(list);
    }
  }

  // List the elements in any linked list
  public static void listAll(LinkedList<?> list) {
    for(Object obj : list) {
      System.out.println(obj);
    }
  }
}
```

Directory "TryWildcardArray"

You should copy the `BinaryTree.java` and `LinkedList.java` source files from the previous example to the directory containing `TryWildcardArray.java`. When you compile this program, you get two warnings from the compiler from the statements that involve explicit casts. Note that to see both warmings, you must specify the `-Xlint:unchecked` compiler option. The output will is similar to that from the previous example. The sorted lists of values is output one value per line because that's how the `listAll()` method displays them.

How It Works

You create two arrays using wildcard type specifications:

```
BinaryTree<?>[] trees = {new BinaryTree<Integer>(), new BinaryTree<String>()};
LinkedList<?>[] lists = new LinkedList<?>[trees.length];
```

The length of the `trees` array is determined by the number of values in the initializing list—two in this case. You can see that you can happily initialize the array with references to objects of different specific types as long as they are produced from the generic type `BinarayTree<>`. The `lists` array is of type `LinkedList<?>[]` and is defined as having the same number of elements as the `trees` array. You store the `LinkedList<>` references returned by the `sort()` method in these elements eventually.

After creating the array of random integer values, you add them to a binary tree in a loop:

```
for(int number:numbers) {
  ((BinaryTree<Integer>)trees[0]).add(number);
}
```

You can't call the `add()` method while the reference stored in `trees[0]` is of type `BinaryTree<?>` because the compiler cannot decide on the form of the `add()` method without having a specific type argument available. The type argument determines the parameter type for the method. Without that there's no way to decide how the argument to the method is to be passed. You must cast the reference to a specific type, `BinaryTree<Integer>` in this case, to allow the `add()` method for that type to be called. You get a warning from the compiler at this point because the compiler cannot verify that this cast is valid. If it isn't, calling the `add()` method causes an exception to be thrown at run time so you have to accept responsibility for it. In this example it works, and the integer values are converted automatically to type `Integer`.

You then create an array of `String` objects as you did in the previous version and add these to the second binary tree:

```
for(String word : words) {
  ((BinaryTree<String>)trees[1]).add(word);
}
```

Again it is necessary to cast the reference in `trees[1]` to type `BinaryTree<String>`, which results in the second warning from the compiler.

You sort the contents of the binary trees in another loop:

```
for(int i = 0 ; i < lists.length ; ++i){
  lists[i] = trees[i].sort();
}
```

Sorting a tree is not dependent on a specific type. You can call the `sort()` method without a cast because the operation does not depend on a type argument. The method returns a `LinkedList<>` reference of a specific type, `LinkedList<Integer>` in the first call and `LinkedList<String>` in the second, but the `lists` array is of type `LinkedList<?>` so you can store references of any `LinkedList<>` type in it.

You list the sorted values stored in the lists that result from calls to the `sort()` method for the `BinaryTree<>` objects in a loop:

```
for(LinkedList<?> list : lists){
  System.out.println("\nSorted results:");
  listAll(list);
}
```

The loop variable is of a wildcard type, `LinkedList<?>`, and it iterates over the elements in the `lists` array. This is fine here because the static `listAll()` method does not require a particular type of `LinkedList<>` reference as the argument; it works for `LinkedList` types created from the `LinkedList<>` generic type using any type argument.

Note that you can create arrays of a generic type only using a wildcard specification that is unbounded. If you specify an upper or lower bound for a wildcard type argument when defining an array type, it is flagged by the compiler as an error.

PARAMETERIZED METHODS

You can define a method with its own independent set of one or more type parameters, in which case you have a *parameterized method*, which is also referred to as a *generic method*. You can define parameterized methods in an ordinary class. Methods within a generic type definition can also have independent type parameters.

You could modify the `listAll()` method that you defined in the `TryWildcardArray` class in the previous example so that it is a parameterized method. Here's how that would look:

```
public static <T> void listAll(LinkedList<T> list) {
  for(T obj : list) {
    System.out.println(obj);
  }
}
```

The `<T>` following the `public` and `static` keywords is the type parameter list for the generic method. Here you have only one type parameter, `T`, but you could have more. The type parameter list for a generic method always appears between angled brackets and should follow any modifiers such as `public` and `static`, as you have here, and should precede the return type.

Not that calling this version of the `listAll()` method does not require the type argument to be supplied explicitly. The type argument is deduced from the type of the argument to the method when the method is called. If you replace the `listAll()` code in the previous example by the version here, you should find that it works just as well. No other changes to the program are necessary to make use of it.

You could also gain some advantage by using parameterized methods in the `BinaryTree<>` type definition. With the present version of this type, the `add()` method accepts an argument of type `T`, which is the type argument for the generic class type. In general, you might want to allow objects that are of types that are subclasses of `T` to be added to a `BinaryTree<T>` object. Harking back to the `Person` and `Manager` classes that you saw earlier, it might well be the case that you would want to add `Manager` objects and objects of any subclass of `Person` to a `BinaryTree<Person>` container. You could accommodate this by redefining the `add()` method in the class as an independently parameterized method:

Available for
download on
Wrox.com

```
public <E extends T> void add(E value) {
  if(root == null) {                     // If there's no root node
    root = new Node(value);              // store it in the root
  } else {                               // Otherwise...
    add(value, root);                    // add it recursively
  }
}
```

Directory "TryParameterizedMethods"

Now the method has an independent type, `E`, for the method parameter. This type has an upper bound, which in this case is the type parameter for `BinaryTree<T>`. Thus, you are saying here that the `add()` method accepts an argument of any type that is type `T`, or a subclass of `T`. This clearly adds flexibility to the use of `BinaryTree<T>` objects. You have no need to change the body of the method in this case. All the flexibility is provided by the way you have defined the method parameter.

Of course, you must also alter the other version of the `add()` method that is defined in the `BinaryTree<>` class to have an independent parameter:

Available for
download on
Wrox.com

```
private <E extends T> void add(E value, Node node) {
  int comparison = node.obj.compareTo(value);
  if(comparison == 0) {                  // If it is equal to the current node
    ++node.count;                        // just increment the count
    return;
  }
  if(comparison > 0) {                   // If it's less than the current node
    if(node.left == null) {              // and the left child node is null
      node.left = new Node(value);       // Store it as the left child node
    } else {                             // Otherwise...
      add(value, node.left);             // ...add it to the left node
    }
  } else {                               // It must be greater than the current node
    if(node.right == null) {             // so it must go to the right...
      node.right = new Node(value);      // store it as the right node
    } else {                             // ...or when right node is not null
      add(value, node.right);            // ...call add() again at the right node
    }
  }
}
```

Directory "TryParameterizedMethods"

Although you have used the same identifier, `E`, as the type parameter, it has nothing to do with the `E` that you used as the parameter for the previous version of `add()`. The scope of a type parameter for a method is the method itself, so the two `E`s are quite separate and independent of one another. You could use `K` or some other parameter name here if you want to make it absolutely obvious. Let's give it a whirl.

TRY IT OUT Using Parameterized Methods

First, create a directory to hold the source files for this example and copy the files containing the `Person` and `Manager` class definitions to it. You also need the `BinaryTree.java` file containing the version with the parameterized `add()` methods and the source file for the `LinkedList<>` generic type. Here's the program to make use of these:

Available for
download on
Wrox.com

```
public class TryParameterizedMethods {
  public static void main(String[] args) {

    BinaryTree<Person> people = new BinaryTree<>();

    // Create and add some Manager objects
```

```
         Manager[] managers = { new Manager("Jane",1), new Manager("Joe",3),
                                               new Manager("Freda",3)};
      for(Manager manager : managers){
        people.add(manager);
      }

      // Create and add some Person objects
      Person[] persons = {
                    new Person("Will"), new Person("Ann"), new Person("Mary"),
                    new Person("Tina"), new Person("Stan")};
      for(Person person : persons) {
        people.add(person);
      }

      listAll(people.sort());   // List the sorted contents of the tree
    }

    // Parameterized method to list the elements in any linked list
    public static <T> void listAll(LinkedList<T> list) {
      for(T obj : list) {
        System.out.println(obj);
      }
    }
  }
```

Directory "TryParameterizedMethods"

The output should be as follows:

```
Ann
Manager Freda level: 3
Manager Jane level: 1
Manager Joe level: 3
Mary
Stan
Tina
Will
```

How It Works

You create an object of a BinaryTree type that stores Person objects:

```
BinaryTree<Person> people = new BinaryTree<>();
```

You then define an array of Manager objects and add those to the people binary tree:

```
Manager[] managers = { new Manager("Jane",1), new Manager("Joe",3),
                                               new Manager("Freda",3)};
for(Manager manager : managers){
  people.add(manager);
}
```

The add() method is defined as a parameterized method in the BinaryTree<> type definition, where the method's parameter, E, has an upper bound that is the type variable for the BinaryTree<> type. This enables the add() method to accept arguments that are of a type that can be type Person or any subclass of Person. You defined the Manager class with Person as the base class so the add() method happily accepts arguments of type Manager.

Just to demonstrate that you can, you create an array of Person objects and add those to the people binary tree:

```
Person[] persons = {
                    new Person("Will"), new Person("Ann"), new Person("Mary"),
                    new Person("Tina"), new Person("Stan")};
for(Person person : persons) {
  people.add(person);
}
```

You now have a mix of `Person` and `Manager` objects in the binary tree. You list the contents of the binary tree in ascending alphabetical order by calling the parameterized `listAll()` method that you defined as a static member of the `TryParameterizedMethods` class:

```
listAll(people.sort());  // List the sorted contents of the tree
```

The argument to the `listAll()` method is of type `BinaryTree<Person>`, so the compiler supplies `Person` as the type argument to the method. This means that within the method, the loop iterates over an array of `Person` references using a loop variable of type `Person`. The output demonstrates that the mix of `Person` and `Manager` objects were added to the binary tree correctly and are displayed in the correct sequence.

Generic Constructors

As you know, a constructor is a specialized kind of method and you can define class constructors with their own independent parameters. You can define parameterized constructors for both ordinary classes and generic class types. Let's consider an example.

Suppose you want to add a constructor to the `BinaryTree<T>` type definition that accepts an argument that is an array of items to be added to the binary tree. In this case, defining the constructor as a parameterized method gives you the same flexibility that you have with the `add()` method. Here's how the constructor definition looks:

```
public <E extends T> BinaryTree(E[] items) {
  for(E item : items) {
    add(item);
  }
}
```

The constructor type parameter is `E`. You have defined this with an upper bound of `T`, so the argument to the constructor can be an array of elements of the type specified by the type parameter `T` or any subclass of `T`. For example, if you define a binary tree of type `BinaryTree<Person>`, then you can pass an array to the constructor with elements of type `Person` or any type that is a subclass of `Person`.

Let's try it.

TRY IT OUT   Using a Parameterized Constructor

The definition of `BinaryTree<>` is now as follows:

```
public class BinaryTree<T extends Comparable<? super T>> {

  // No-arg constructor
  public BinaryTree() {}

  // Parameterized constructor
  public <E extends T> BinaryTree(E[] items) {
    for(E item : items) {
      add(item);
    }
  }

  // Rest of the code the same as in the BinaryTree definition
  // in the previous example...

}
```

Directory "TryParameterizedConstructor"

The only changes from the previous version are the addition of the constructor that accepts an array as an argument and the definition of the no-arg constructor, which is not supplied by the compiler when you explicitly define a constructor of your own. Put this source file in a new directory and copy the `LinkedList.java`, `Person.java`, and `Manager.java` files from the previous example to this directory.

You can add the following source file to try out the parameterized constructor:

```java
public class TryParameterizedConstructor {
    public static void main(String[] args) {
        Manager[] managers = {new Manager("Jane",1), new Manager("Joe",3),
                              new Manager("Freda",3), new Manager("Bert", 2),
                              new Manager("Ann", 2),new Manager("Dave", 2)};

        // Create the tree with an array of managers
        BinaryTree<Person> people = new BinaryTree<>(managers);

        // Create and add some Person objects
        Person[] persons = {
                    new Person("Will"), new Person("Ann"), new Person("Mary"),
                    new Person("Tina"), new Person("Stan")};

        for(Person person : persons) {
          people.add(person);
        }

        listAll(people.sort());
    }

    // List the elements in any linked list
    public static <T> void listAll(LinkedList<T> list) {
      for(T obj : list) {
        System.out.println(obj);
      }
    }
}
```

Directory "TryParameterizedConstructor"

The output is

```
Manager Ann level: 2
Manager Ann level: 2
Manager Bert level: 2
Manager Dave level: 2
Manager Freda level: 3
Manager Jane level: 1
Manager Joe level: 3
Mary
Stan
Tina
Will
```

How It Works

After you create an array of `Manager` objects you create a `BinaryTree<Person>` object with the contents of the managers array as the initial contents of the binary tree:

```java
BinaryTree<Person> people = new BinaryTree<>(managers);
```

Because the constructor has an independent parameter and that parameter has the type variable for the `BinaryTree<>` type as its upper bound, the constructor accepts the managers array as the argument because it is a subclass of `Person`, the type argument that you use to specify the type of the binary tree object.

You then add the non-management personnel to the tree as you did in the previous example.

The output shows that the array elements were added to the binary tree and were successfully extracted and stored in sequence in a linked list by the `sort()` method. However, there's something wrong with the output. There is Ann the manager and Ann the lowly worker, and somehow in the output there are two managers called Ann and Ann the non-manager has disappeared. The problem is the `compareTo()` method in the `Person` class compares `Person` objects without reference to their position in the company that is reflected in their class type. A non-manager is the equal of a manager and this cannot be right. You can fix this by changing the `compareTo()` method definition in the `Person` class to the following:

```
public int compareTo(Person person) {
   if( person == this) {
     return 0;
   }

   if(this.getClass().getName().equals(person.getClass().getName())) {
     return this.name.compareTo(person.name);
   } else if(this.getClass().getName().equals("Manager")) {
     return 1;
   } else {
     return -1;
   }
}
```

Directory "TryParameterizedConstructor"

With this change, the output puts Ann the non-managerial person in her place. What's more, the managers are listed after the non-managers as it should be, since they are higher up the tree.

PARAMETERIZED TYPES AND INHERITANCE

You can define a class as a subclass of an instance of a generic type. For example, you could derive a new class from `LinkedList<Person>` or from type `BinaryTree<String>`. Methods and fields are inherited from the base class in the usual way. However, you can encounter complications because of the way the compiler translates methods that involve type arguments into bytecodes, so let's first understand that process.

Each method that involves parameters and/or the return value type specified by a type argument is translated by the compiler to a method with the same name, but with the type of each parameter whose type is a type variable replaced by its leftmost bound. Where the type of the return value is a type variable, then that, too, is replaced by its leftmost bound. Casts are inserted in the body of the translated method where necessary to produce the actual types required. An example will help clarify this.

Earlier you saw a version of the `LinkedList<>` type defined as:

```
public LinkedList<T extends Object & Serializable> {
   public void addItem(T item) {
     // Code for the method...
   }

   // More code for the type definition...
}
```

If you define an object of type `LinkedList<String>`, notionally the `addItem()` method for the object looks like this:

```
public void addItem(String item) {

   // Code for the method...
}
```

However, the compiler translates the `addItem()` method to the following:

```
public void addItem(Object item) {

  // Code for the method...

  // References to fields originally of type T will be cast to type String
  // as will values returned by method calls originally of type T.
}
```

Normally you don't need to be aware of this, but suppose you derive a new class from type `LinkedList<String>`:

```
public class SpecialList extends LinkedList<String> {

  // Override base class version of addItem() method
  @Override
  public void addItem(String item) {
    // New code for the method...
  }

  // Rest of the code for SpecialList...
}
```

Here you are trying to override the version of `addItem()` that your class inherits from `LinkedList<String>`. Because the compiler chooses to compile the method to bytecodes with a different signature, as your method is written it doesn't override the base class method at all. The base class method parameter is of type `Object`, whereas the parameter for your version of the method is of type `String`. To fix the problem the compiler creates a *bridge method* in your derived `SpecialList` class that looks like this:

```
public void addItem(Object item) {
  addItem((String)item);                // Call derived class version
}
```

The effect of the bridge method is to convert any calls to the inherited version of `addItem()` to a call to your version, thus making your attempt at overriding the base class method effective.

However, the approach adopted by the compiler has implications for you. You must take care not to define methods in your derived class that have the same signature as an inherited method. Because the compiler changes the parameter types and return types involving type variables to their bounds, you must consider the inherited methods in these terms when you are defining your derived class methods. If a method in a class that you have derived from a generic type has the same signature as the erasure of an inherited method, your code does not compile.

SUMMARY

In this chapter you learned the essentials of how generic types are defined and used. Generic types add a powerful capability to your Java programming armory. In the next chapter you see how the `java.util` package provides you with an extensive range of standard generic types that you can use in your programs for managing collections of data items.

EXERCISES

You can download the source code for the examples in the book and the solutions to the following exercises from www.wrox.com.

1. A stack is a container that stores objects in a manner indicated by its name—a vertical stack where only the object at the top of the stack is accessible. It works rather like a sprung stack of plates in a cafeteria. Only the top plate is at counter level and, therefore, is the only one you can access. When you add a plate to the stack, the existing plates are pushed down so the new plate is now the one that you can access.

Define a generic Stack<> type with a method push() that adds the object that is passed as an argument to the top of the stack, and with a method pop() that removes and returns the object that is currently at the top of the stack. The pop() method should return null when the stack is empty. Demonstrate the operation of your Stack<> implementation by storing and retrieving 10 strings and 10 Double objects in stacks of a suitable type.

2. Implement and demonstrate a listAll() method in the Stack<> class definition that will list the objects in the stack.

3. Modify your Stack<> type to make it serializable. Demonstrate that this is the case by creating a Stack<String> object, adding 10 strings to it, serializing and deserializing the Stack<String> object, and listing the contents of the deserialized stack.

▶ WHAT YOU LEARNED IN THIS CHAPTER

TOPIC	CONCEPT
Generic Types	A generic type, which is also referred to as a parameterized type, defines a family of classes or interfaces using one or more type parameters. Container classes are typically defined as generic types.
Using a Generic Type	You define a specific type from a generic type by supplying a type argument for each type parameter. You can omit the type arguments for the type parameters in a constructor call for a generic type and the compiler infers the parameter arguments from the type of variable you use to store the reference.
Generic Type Arguments	The argument that you supply for a type parameter can be a class type or an interface type. It cannot be a primitive type.
Type Parameter Bounds	You can limit the scope of type arguments for a given type parameter by specifying one or more bounds for the parameter using the `extends` keyword. The first bound can be a class or interface type; the second and subsequent bounds must be interface types.
Runtime Type of Generic Type Instances	All types produced from a given generic type share the same runtime type.
Parameterized Methods	A parameterized method defines a family of methods using one or more independent type parameters. A parameterized method can be a member of an ordinary class type or a generic type.
Wildcard Type Arguments	A wildcard type argument matches any type. This allows you to specify a method parameter type as any instance of a generic type. For example a parameter of type `Iterator<?>` accepts a reference of type `Iterator<T>` type for any `T`.
Wildcard Type Argument Bounds	You can constrain a wildcard type argument with either an upper bound that you specify using the `extends` keyword or with a lower bound that you specify using the `super` keyword.

14

The Collections Framework

WHAT YOU WILL LEARN IN THIS CHAPTER

➤ What sets, sequences, and maps are, and how they work

➤ The capabilities of the `EnumSet<E>` collection class

➤ What a `Vector<T>` collection object is and how to use `Vector<T>` objects in your programs

➤ How to manage `Vector<T>` objects so that storing and retrieving elements is typesafe

➤ What a `Stack<T>` collection is and how you use it

➤ How you use the `LinkedList<T>` collections

➤ How you store and retrieve objects in a hash table represented by a `HashMap<K,V>` object

➤ How you can generate hashcodes for your own class objects

In this chapter you look at the Java collections framework, which consists of generic types that represent sets of collection classes. These types are defined in the `java.util` package, and they provide you with a variety of ways for structuring and managing collections of objects in your programs. In particular, the collection types enable you to deal with situations where you don't know in advance how many objects you need to store, or where you need a bit more flexibility in the way in which you access an object other than by the indexing mechanism provided by an array.

UNDERSTANDING THE COLLECTIONS FRAMEWORK

The Java collections framework is a set of generic types that you use to create *collection classes* that support various ways for you to store and manage objects of any kind in memory. Recall from Chapter 13 that a collection class is simply a class that organizes a set of objects of a given type in a particular way, such as in a linked list or a pushdown stack. The majority of types that make up the collections framework are defined in the `java.util` package.

Using a generic type for your collections means that you get static checking by the compiler for whatever types of objects you want to manage. This ensures that you do not inadvertently attempt to store objects of the wrong type in a collection. The collections framework includes a professional implementation of a generic linked list type, which is vastly superior to the linked list that you took so much trouble to develop for yourself first as an ordinary class in Chapter 6 and later as a generic type in Chapter 13. However, the effort wasn't entirely wasted because you now have a good idea of how linked lists work and how generic types are defined.

You'll find that the collections framework is a major asset in most of your programs. When you want an array that automatically expands to accommodate however many objects you throw into it, or you need to be able to store and retrieve an object based on what it is rather than using an index or a sequence number, then look no further. You get all this and more in the generic types implemented within the collections framework.

The collections framework involves too much for me to discuss it in complete detail, but you look at how you apply some representative examples of collections that you're likely to need most often. You explore the capabilities provided by the following generic types in detail:

➤ The `Iterator<T>` interface type declares methods for iterating through elements of a collection, one at a time. You met this interface in the previous chapter.

➤ The `Vector<T>` type supports an array-like structure for storing objects. The number of objects that you can store in a `Vector<T>` object increases automatically as necessary.

➤ The `Stack<T>` type supports the storage of objects in a pushdown stack.

➤ The `LinkedList<T>` type supports the storage of objects in a doubly-linked list, which is a list that you can iterate through forward or backward.

➤ The `EnumSet<E>` type stores constants of a given enum type, `E`, in a set. You have already used this collection class in file I/O operations.

➤ The `HashMap<K, V>` type supports the storage of objects of type `V` in a hash table, sometimes called a map. An object is stored using an associated key object of type `K`. To retrieve an object you just supply its associated key.

Let's start by looking in general terms at the various types of collections you can use.

COLLECTIONS OF OBJECTS

In Chapter 13 you put together a generic type that defined a linked list. An object of type `LinkedList<T>` represented an example of a *collection* of objects of type `T`, where `T` could be any class or interface type as long as the type met the conditions required by the collection. A *collection* is the term used to describe any object that represents a set of objects grouped together and organized in a particular way in memory. A class that defines collections of objects is often referred to as a *container class*. A linked list is just one of a number of ways of organizing objects together in a collection.

There are three main groups of collections that organize objects in different ways, called *sets*, *sequences*, and *maps*. Let's first get an understanding of how these kinds of collections work in principle and then look at the specific classes that implement versions of these. One point I'd like to emphasize about the following discussion is that when I talk about a collection of objects, I mean a collection of *references* to objects. In Java, collections store references only—the objects themselves are external to the collection.

Sets

A *set* is probably the simplest kind of collection you can have. Here the objects are not ordered in any particular way at all, and objects are simply added to the set without any control over where they go. It's a bit like putting things in your pocket—you just put things in and they rattle around inside your pocket in no particular order but at least you know roughly where they are. Figure 14-1 illustrates the idea of a set.

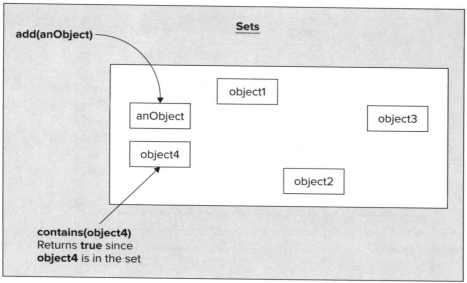

FIGURE 14-1

You can add objects to a set and iterate over all the objects in a set. You can also check whether a given object is a member of the set or not. For this reason you cannot have duplicate objects in a set—each object in a set must be unique. Of course, you can remove a given object from a set, but only if you know what the object is in the first place—in other words, if you have a reference to the object in the set.

There are variations on the basic set that I have described here. For example, sets can be ordered, so objects added to a set are inserted into a sequence ordered according to some comparison criterion. Such sets require that the objects to be stored are of a type that implements the `Comparable<T>` interface.

Sequences

The linked list that you have already explored to some extent is an example of a more general type of collection called a *sequence*. A primary characteristic of a sequence is that the objects are stored in a linear fashion, not necessarily in any particular order, but organized in an arbitrary fixed sequence with a beginning and an end. This contrasts with the set discussed in the previous section, where there may be no order at all. An ordinary array is basically another example of a sequence, but it is more limited than the equivalent collection because it holds a fixed number of elements.

Collections generally have the capability to expand to accommodate as many elements as necessary. The `Vector<T>` type, for example, is an example of a sequence that provides similar functionality to an array, but also has the capability to accommodate as many new elements as you want to add to it. Figure 14-2 illustrates the organization of objects in the various types of sequence collections that you have available.

Because a sequence is linear, you are able to add a new object only at the beginning or at the end, or insert a new object following a given object position in the sequence—after the fifth, say. Generally, you can retrieve an object from a sequence in several ways. You can select the first or the last; you can get the object at a given position—as in indexing an array; or you can search for an object identical to a given object by checking all the objects in the sequence either backward or forward. You can also iterate through the sequence backward or forward accessing each object in turn. You didn't implement all these capabilities in the linked list class in Chapter 6, but you could have.

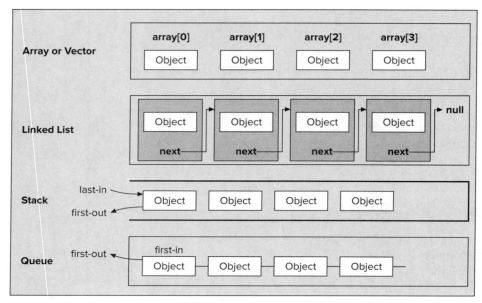

FIGURE 14-2

You have essentially the same options for deleting objects from a sequence as you have for retrieving them; that is, you can remove the first or the last, you can delete the object at a particular position in the sequence, or you can remove an object that is equal to a given object. Sequences have the facility to store several copies of the same object at different places in the sequence. This is not true of all types of collections, as is you already know from the outline of a set in the previous section.

A *stack*, which is a last-in, first-out (LIFO) storage mechanism, is also considered to be a sequence, as is a *queue*, which is usually a first-in, first-out (FIFO) mechanism. The Java collections framework implements a range of different queues including a *priority queue* in which elements in the queue are ordered, which implies that FIFO doesn't apply. The elements in a priority queue are in ascending sequence from the head of the queue, so it's more a case of "lowest in, first out."

It's easy to see that a linked list can act as a stack because using the methods to add and remove objects at the end of a list makes the list operate as a stack. Similarly, only adding objects by using the method to add an object to the end of a linked list, and only retrieving objects from the head of the list, makes it operate as a FIFO queue.

Maps

A *map* is rather different from a set or a sequence collection because each entry involves a pair of objects. A map is sometimes referred to as a *dictionary* because of the way it works. Each object that is stored in a map has an associated *key* object, and the object and its key are stored together as a pair. The key determines where the object is stored in the map, and when you want to retrieve an object, you must supply its key—so the key acts as the equivalent of a word that you look up in a regular dictionary. Figure 14-3 shows how a map works.

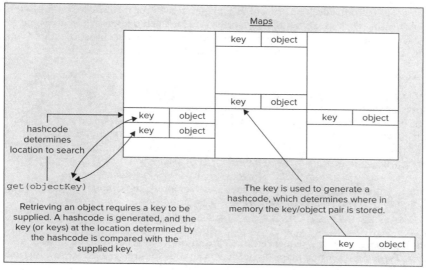

Maps

hashcode
determines
location to search

get(objectKey)

Retrieving an object requires a key to be
supplied. A hashcode is generated, and the
key (or keys) at the location determined by
the hashcode is compared with the
supplied key.

The key is used to generate a
hashcode, which determines where in
memory the key/object pair is stored.

FIGURE 14-3

A key can be any kind of object that you want to use to reference the stored objects. Because a key has to uniquely identify an object, all the keys in a map must be different. To put this in context, suppose you were creating a program to provide an address book. You might store all the details of each person—the name, address, phone number, or whatever—in a single object of type Entry, perhaps, and store a reference to the object in a map. The key is the mechanism for retrieving objects, so assuming that all names are different, a person's name is a natural choice for the key. Thus the entries in the map in this case would be Name/Entry pairs. You would supply a Name object as the key and get back the Entry object corresponding to the key, which might encapsulate data such as the address and/or the phone number. You might also have another map in this application where entries were keyed on the phone number. Then you could retrieve an entry corresponding to a given number. Of course, in practice, names are not unique—hence, the invention of such delightful attachments to the person as Social Security numbers.

Hashing

Where a key/object pair is stored in a map is determined from the key by a process known as *hashing*. Hashing processes the key object to produce an integer value called a *hashcode*. A basic requirement for hashing is that you get the same hashcode from repeatedly hashing the same object.

The hashCode() method that is defined in the Object class produces a hashcode of type int for an object based on the object's location in memory. The hashcode for a key is typically used to calculate an offset from the start of the memory that has been allocated within the map for storing objects, and the offset determines the location where the key/object pair is stored.

Ideally the hashing process should result in values that are uniformly distributed within a given range, and every key should produce a different hashcode. In general, this may not be the case. However, there are ways of dealing with hashcodes that don't turn out to be ideal, so it is not a major problem. The implementations for map collections usually have provision for dealing with the situation where two or more different key objects produce the same hashcode. I explain keys and hashcodes in a little more detail later in this chapter when I discuss using maps.

Now let's look at how you can move through the objects in a collection.

ITERATORS

In the LinkedList<T> class that you developed in Chapter 13 you implemented the Iterable<> interface for getting the objects from the list. This resulted in your LinkedList<T> type being able to make an *iterator* available. As you know, an iterator is an object that you can use once to retrieve all the objects in a collection one by one. Someone dealing cards from a deck one by one is acting as an iterator for the card deck—without the shuffle, of course. Implementing the `Iterable<T>` interface was a much better approach to accessing the members of a list than the technique that you originally implemented, and it made the collection usable with a collection-based `for` loop. An *iterator* is a standard mechanism for accessing elements in a collection.

 NOTE *It is worth noting at this point that Java also provides something called an enumerator that is defined by any class that implements the* `java.util.Enumeration<T>` *generic interface type. An enumerator provides essentially the same capability as an iterator, but it is recommended in the Java documentation that you use an iterator in preference to an enumerator for collections. There's nothing particularly wrong with enumerators — it's just that the* `Iterator<T>` *interface declares an optional* `remove()` *method that the* `Enumeration<T>` *interface does not, and the methods in the* `Iterator<T>` *interface have shorter names than those in the* `Enumeration<T>` *interface, so code that uses them is less cluttered.*

Any collection object that represents a set or a sequence can create an object of type `java.util.Iterator<>` that behaves as an iterator. Types representing maps do not have methods for creating iterators. However, a map class provides methods to enable the keys or objects, or indeed the key/object pairs, to be viewed as a set, so you can then obtain an iterator to iterate over the objects in the set view of the map.

An `Iterator<>` object encapsulates references to all the objects in the original collection in some sequence, and they can be accessed one by one using the `Iterator<>` interface methods that you saw in the previous chapter. In other words, an iterator provides an easy way to get at all the objects in a collection one at a time. Just to remind you, the basic mechanism for using an iterator in Java is illustrated in Figure 14-4.

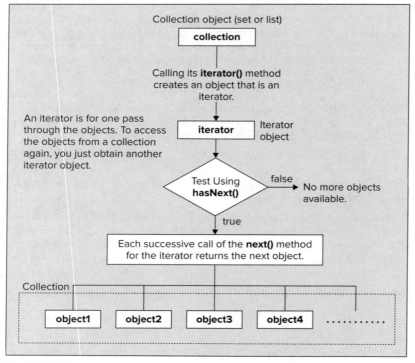

FIGURE 14-4

As you saw in the previous chapter, the Iterator<T> interface declares three methods: next(), hasNext(), and remove().

> **NOTE** *Don't confuse the* Iterable<T> *interface with the* Iterator<T> *interface.* Iterable<T> *defines a method that returns a reference of type* Iterator<T>; *in other words, a class that implements* Iterable<T> *can make an iterator available.* Iterator<T> *defines the methods that enable the iterator mechanism.*

Calling the next() method for an iterator returns successive objects from the collection starting with the first, so you can progress through all the objects in a collection very easily with a loop such as the following:

```
MyClass item;                       // Stores an object from the collection
while(iter.hasNext()) {             // Check that there's another
  item = iter.next();               // Retrieve next object
  // Do something with item...
}
```

This fragment assumes that iter is of type Iterator<MyClass> and stores a reference to an object obtained from whatever collection class you were using.

Most collection classes provide an iterator() method that returns an iterator for the current contents of the collection. The next() method returns an object as the original type so there's no need for casting. As long as the hasNext() method returns true, there is at least one more object available from the iterator. When all the objects have been accessed, the hasNext() method will return false. You must obtain a new iterator each time you need to go through the objects in a collection because an iterator is a "use once" object.

The iterator that you have seen here is a single-use one-way street—you can go through the objects in a collection one at a time, in sequence, once, and that's it. This is fine for many purposes but not all, so you have other possibilities for accessing the entire contents of a collection. You can access the objects in any collection that implements the Iterable<T> interface directly using the collection-based for loop. If this is not enough, there's another kind of iterator that is more flexible than the one you have seen—called a *list iterator*.

List Iterators

The java.util.ListIterator<T> interface declares methods that you can use to traverse a collection of objects backward or forward. You don't have to choose a particular direction either. You can change from forward to backward and *vice versa* at any time, so an object can be retrieved more than once.

The ListIterator<> interface extends the Iterator<> interface type so the iterator methods you have already seen and used still apply. The additional methods that the ListIterator<> interface declares for moving through a collection are:

➤ int nextIndex(): Returns the index of the object that is returned by the next call to next() as type int, or returns the number of elements in the list if the ListIterator<> object is at the end of the list.

➤ T previous(): Returns the previous object in sequence in the list. You use this method to run backward through the list.

➤ boolean hasPrevious(): Returns true if the next call to previous() returns an object.

➤ int previousIndex()(): Returns the index of the object that is returned by the next call to previous(), or returns −1 if the ListIterator<> object is at the beginning of the list.

You can alternate between calls to next() and previous() to go backward and forward through the list. Calling previous() immediately after calling next(), or *vice versa*, returns the same element.

In addition to the remove() method, a ListIterator<> object provides methods that can add and replace objects:

➤ void add(T obj): Adds the argument immediately before the object that would be returned by the next call to next(), and after the object that would be returned by the next call to previous(). The call to next() after the add() operation returns the object that was added. The next call to previous() is not affected. This method throws an UnsupportedOperationException if objects cannot be added, a ClassCastException if the class of the argument prevents it from being added, and IllegalOperationException if there is some other reason why the add cannot be done.

➤ void set(T obj): Replaces the last object retrieved by a call to next() or previous(). If neither next() nor previous() have been called, or add() or remove() have been called most recently, an IllegalStateException is thrown. If the set() operation is not supported for this collection, an UnsupportedOperationException is thrown. If the class of the reference passed as an argument prevents the object from being stored, a ClassCastException is thrown. If some other characteristic of the argument prevents it from being stored, an IllegalArgumentException is thrown.

Now that you know more about iterators, you need to find out a bit about the collection classes themselves to make use of them.

COLLECTION CLASSES

The classes in java.util that support collections that are sets, lists, queues, and maps include the following:

Collection Classes That Are Sets

➤ HashSet<T>: Implements a set using HashMap<T> under the covers. Although a set is by definition unordered, there has to be some way to find an object reasonably efficiently. Using a HashMap<T> object to implement the set enables store and retrieve operations to be done in a constant time. However, the order in which elements of the set are retrieved might vary over time.

➤ LinkedHashSet<T>: Implements a set using a hash table with all the entries in a doubly-linked list. This class can be used to make a copy of any set such that iteration ordering is preserved—something that does not apply to a HashSet<>.

➤ TreeSet<T>: Implements a set that orders the objects in ascending sequence. This means that an iterator obtained from a TreeSet<T> object provides the objects in ascending sequence. You can also search the set for the closest match to a given item.

➤ EnumSet<E extends Enum<E>>: Implements a specialized set that stores enum values from a single enum type, E.

Collection Classes That Are Lists

➤ Vector<T>: Implements a list as an array that automatically increases in size to accommodate as many elements as you need. Objects are stored and retrieved using an integer index. You can also use an iterator to retrieve objects from a Vector<>. The Vector<> type is synchronized—that is, it is well behaved when concurrently accessed by two or more threads. I will discuss threads and synchronization in Chapter 16.

➤ ArrayList<T>: Implements an array that can vary in size and can also be accessed as a linked list. This provides a similar function to the Vector<T> generic type but is unsynchronized, so it is not safe for use by multiple threads.

➤ Stack<T>: This class is derived from Vector<T> and adds methods to implement a stack—a last-in, first-out storage mechanism.

➤ LinkedList<T>>: Implements a linked list. The linked list defined by this class can also be used as a stack or a queue.

Collection Classes That Are Queues

➤ ArrayDeque<T>: Implements a resizable array as a double-ended queue.

➤ PriorityQueue<T>>: Implements a priority queue in which objects are ordered in ascending sequence from the head of the queue. The order is determined either by a Comparator<T> object supplied to the constructor for the collection class, or through the compareTo() method declared in the Comparable<T> interface that the object type implements.

Collection Classes That Are Maps

➤ `Hashtable<K,V>`: Implements a map with keys of type K and values of type V where all keys must be non-null. The key class must implement the `hashcode()` and `equals()` methods to work effectively. This type, like `Vector<T>`, is synchronized, so it's safe for concurrent use by two or more threads.

➤ `HashMap<K,V>`: Implements a map where objects of type V are stored using keys of type K. This collection allows `null` objects to be stored and allows a key to be `null` (only one of course, because keys must be unique). The map is not synchronized.

➤ `LinkedHashMap<K,V>`: Implements a map storing values of type V using keys of type K with all of its entries in a doubly-linked list. This class can be used to create a copy of a map of any type such that the order of the entries in the copy is the same as the original.

➤ `WeakHashMap<K,V>`: Implements a map storing values of type V using keys of type K such that if a reference to a key no longer exists outside the map, the key/object pair is discarded. This contrasts with `HashMap<>` where the presence of the key in the map maintains the life of the key/object pair, even though the program using the map no longer has a reference to the key and therefore cannot retrieve the object.

➤ `IdentityHashMap<K,V>`: Implements a map storing values of type V using keys of type K using a hash table where comparisons in searching the map for a key or a value compares references, not objects. This implies that two keys are equal only if they are the same key. The same applies to values. This is a specialized collection class for situations where reference equality is required for both keys and objects.

➤ `TreeMap<K,V>`: Implements a map storing values of type V using keys of type K such that the objects are arranged in ascending key order.

This is not an exhaustive list; it is just the classes that are most commonly used. In addition, the `java.util.concurrent` package defines further collection classes that are specifically designed to support concurrent operations by multiple threads.

The generic types representing sets, lists, and queues are related in the manner shown in Figure 14-5.

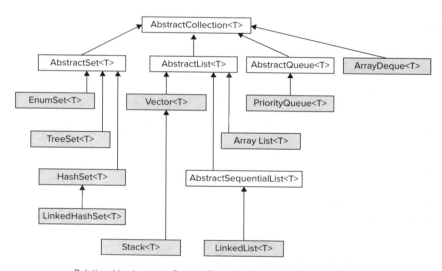

Relationships between Generic Types Defining Sets, Lists, and Queues

FIGURE 14-5

The shaded boxes identify generic types that you use to define collections. The others are abstract types that you cannot instantiate. All types that define sequences share a common base class, `AbstractCollection<T>`. This class defines methods for the operations that are common to sets, lists, and queues. The operations provided by the `AbstractCollection<T>` class include adding objects to a collection, removing objects, providing an iterator for a collection, and testing for the presence of one or more objects in a collection.

The parameterized types that define maps of various kinds are related as shown in Figure 14-6.

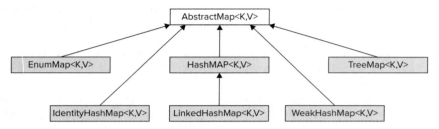

Relationships between Generic Types Defining Maps

FIGURE 14-6

All the concrete types that define maps have AbstractMap<K,V> as a common base class. This provides an outline implementation of operations that apply to maps, thus simplifying the definitions of the more specialized types of maps.

I don't have the space to go into all these collection classes in detail, but to show you some examples of how and where these can be applied, I'll describe the three generic types that you are likely to find most useful: Vector<T>, LinkedList<T>, and HashMap<K,V>. These are representative examples of the most frequently used collections. After you have worked with these, you should have little difficulty with the others. I also explain the EnumSet<E> collection class that you have already used in more detail. Before I get into the specifics of using these classes, I introduce the interfaces that they implement, because these define the operations that they support and thus define the ways in which you can apply them.

Collection Interfaces

The java.util package defines eight generic collection interface types that determine the methods that you use to work with each type of collection class. These interfaces are related in the manner shown in Figure 14-7.

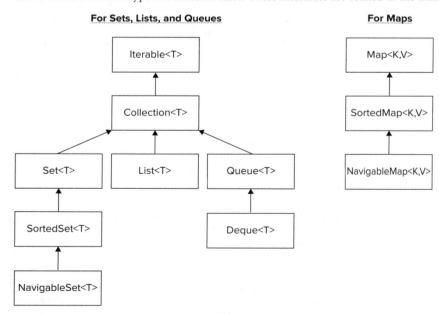

Interfaces for Collections

FIGURE 14-7

These are not all the interfaces defined in the `java.util` package, just the ones that relate to the topics in this chapter. You can see that the interfaces for maps have no connection to the interfaces implemented by sets and lists. You can also see that the map interfaces do not implement the `Iterable<T>` interface, so you cannot use the collection-based `for` loop to iterate over the objects in a map. However, the `Map<K,V>` interface declares a `values()` method that returns a collection view of the objects in a map as type `Collection<V>`. You can use the `Collection<V>` reference with a collection-based `for` loop to access the contents of the map because the `Collection<V>` type extends `Iterable<T>`.

There are four basic collection interfaces—the `Set<T>`, `List<T>`, `Queue<T>`, and `Map<K,V>` interfaces— that relate to the fundamental organization of objects in a collection. The first three inherit the members of `Iterable<T>` and `Collection<T>`, so sets, lists, and queues share the characteristics specified by these two interfaces. `SortedSet<T>` and `SortedMap<K,V>` are specialized versions of their respective superinterfaces that add methods for ordering objects within a collection. The `NavigableSet<T>` and `NavigableMap<K,V>` interfaces provide further specialization that defines the capability for finding the closest match for a given search target in a collection. Don't confuse the `Collection<T>` interface with the `Collections` class (with an *s*) that you will see later.

These interfaces are implemented by the classes from the `java.util` package that I have introduced, as shown in Table 14-1:

TABLE 14-1: java.util Package Classes

INTERFACE TYPE	IMPLEMENTED BY
`Set<T>`	`HashSet<T>`, `LinkedHashSet<T>`, `EnumSet<T>`
`SortedSet<T>`	`TreeSet<T>`
`List<T>`	`Vector<T>`, `Stack<T>`, `ArrayList<T>`, `LinkedList<T>`
`Queue<T>`	`PriorityQueue<T>`, `LinkedList<T>`
`Deque<T>`	`LinkedList<T>`, `ArrayDeque<T>`
`Map<K,V>`	`Hashtable<K,V>`, `HashMap<K,V>`, `LinkedHashMap<K,V>`, `WeakHashMap<K,V>`, `IdentityHashMap<K,V>`, `EnumMap<K extends Enum<K>,V>`
`SortedMap<K,V>`	`TreeMap<K,V>`
`NavigableMap<K,V>`	`TreeMap<K,V>`

The `LinkedList<T>` type implements the `List<T>`, the `Queue<T>`, and the `Deque<T>` interfaces, so it really does have multiple personalities in that you can regard a `LinkedList<T>` object as a linked list, as a queue, or as a double-ended queue.

Keep in mind that any collection class object that implements the `Collection<T>` interface can be referenced using a variable of type `Collection<T>`. This means that any of the list or set collections can be referenced in this way; only the map class types are excluded (but not entirely, as you can obtain a set from a map, and the classes implementing a map can provide a view of the values stored as a `Collection<T>` reference). You see that using a parameter of type `Collection<T>` is a standard way of passing a list or a set to a method.

These interfaces involve quite a large number of methods, so rather than go through them in the abstract, let's see them at work in the context of some specific collection class types.

USING ENUMSET

The `EnumSet<E>` collection class enables you to store one or more enumeration constants of a given type, `E`. A primary use for this collection class is as you saw in the context of file I/O. It provides a convenient way of packaging an arbitrary number of enumeration constants so they can be passed to a method as a single argument. There are no constructors for this class. You create an `EnumSet<E>` object by using one of the static factory methods that the class defines.

> **NOTE** *A factory method is a static method that is not a constructor, but nonetheless creates objects. A factory method can provide advantages over a constructor in some situations. For example, it makes it possible to limit the number of objects that may be created. It allows caching of objects so objects may be reused. It also allows a reference to be returned that is an interface type that the object implements. You saw this with static methods in the* `Files` *class.*

The static `of()` method in the `EnumSet<E>` generic class is the factory method that you have already used, and the one you are likely to use most often. It comes in six overloaded versions. Five accept one, two, three, four, or five arguments of type `E` to be stored in the collection. The sixth method uses a varargs parameter list to permit an arbitrary number of arguments of type `E`. The reason for implementing the `of()` method as a set of overloads like this is to maximize efficiency when you put a small number of enumeration constants in a set. The varargs parameter list slows things down, and the overloads for one to five arguments ensure that performance is excellent in the majority of situations.

Assuming you have a static import statement for the constants from the `StandardOpenOption` enumeration, you could define an `EnumSet<>` object like this:

```
EnumSet<StandardOpenOption> set = EnumSet.of(CREATE,WRITE);
```

The more common usage is to create an `EnumSet<>` object in the argument expression, like this:

```
WritableByteChannel fileOut = Files.newByteChannel(
                    file, EnumSet.of(WRITE,  CREATE, TRUNCATE_EXISTING));
```

You have seen this usage several times before in Chapter 10.

After you have the `EnumSet<StandardOpenOption>` object, `set`, you can create another `EnumSet<>` object that represents the set of constants that are not in `set`:

```
EnumSet<StandardOpenOption> setComplement = EnumSet.complementOf(set);
```

`setComplement` contains all the constants from the `StandardOpenOption` enumeration that are not in `set`.

You might want to create an empty set that can hold enumeration constants of a given type:

```
EnumSet<StandardOpenOption> options = EnumSet.noneOf(StandardOpenOption.class);
```

The static `noneOf()` method creates an empty set that can hold constants of the type you specify as the argument. The expression `StandardOpenOption.class` specifies the class type for the `StandardOpenOption` enumeration. You can test for an empty set by calling the `isEmpty()` method for the object.

To add a constant to an existing set, you use the `add()` method:

```
options.add(READ);
```

This adds the `StandardOpenOption.READ` constant to `options`.

The static `copyOf()` method returns a set that is the copy of its argument. The static `allOf()` method returns a set that contains all of the constants of the enumeration type you specify as the argument. For example:

```
EnumSet<StandardOpenOption> optionsCopy = EnumSet.copyOf(options);
EnumSet<StandardOpenOption> allOptions = EnumSet.allOf(StandardOpenOption.class);
```

The `optionsCopy` variable references a new set identical to `options`. The `allOptions` variable references a set containing all the constants from the `StandardOpenOption` enumeration.

Next, I'll present a collection class, which you will note is close to the notion of an array, as you've now become very familiar with arrays.

ARRAY COLLECTION CLASSES

There are two collection classes that emulate arrays: `Vector<T>` and `ArrayList<T>`. Both types define a sequence collection of elements of any type `T`. They work rather like an array, but with the additional feature that they can grow automatically when you need more capacity. They also implement the `List<T>` interface, so you can also access the contents of containers of these types as a list.

These collection classes are similar in function and operation. They have the same base class and implement the same set of interfaces, so understanding the differences between them is useful.

➤ `Vector<T>` is synchronized so it is safe for concurrent use by more than one thread. `ArrayList<T>` is not synchronized so you should not allow it to be accessed by more than one thread. You can convert an `ArrayList<T>` into a synchronized list using the static `synchronizedList()` method in the `Collections` class.

➤ You can specify how a `Vector<T>` object should increase its capacity when it is necessary whereas with an `ArrayList<T>` you cannot. You can have some control over how an `ArrayList<T>` increases in capacity by using its `ensureCapacity()` method that sets a given capacity.

➤ You can discover the current capacity of a `Vector<T>` by calling its `capacity()` method. You have no way to know the current capacity of an `ArrayList<T>` unless you have set its capacity explicitly.

➤ `ArrayList<T>` is faster in general than a `Vector<T>` because it does not include the overhead for synchronized operation. However, beware of default increments in capacity with an `ArrayList<T>`.

I describe how you use array collection classes in the context of the `Vector<T>` class. However, except where noted, the methods and usage are the same with the `ArrayList<T>` class.

 WARNING *Like arrays, array collection class objects hold object references, not actual objects. To keep the text simple I refer to a collection as holding "objects," rather than saying "references to objects." However, you should keep in mind that all the collection classes hold references.*

Creating a Vector

The default constructor creates an empty `Vector<>` object with the capacity to store objects of the type argument that you supply. The default capacity of a `Vector<>` object is 10 objects, and the capacity doubles when you add an object when the container is full. For example:

```
Vector<String> transactions = new Vector<>();
```

This statement creates an empty vector with a capacity for storing references to 10 `String` objects. You can set the initial capacity of the `Vector<>` object explicitly when you create it by using a different constructor. You just specify the capacity you require as an argument of type `int`. For example:

```
Vector<String> transactions = new Vector<>(100);
```

The object you're defining here will have the capacity to store 100 strings initially. It also doubles in capacity each time you exceed the current capacity. The process of doubling the capacity of a vector when more space is required can be quite inefficient. For example, if you add 7,000 `String` object references to the vector you have just defined, it actually has space for 12,800 object references. The capacity-doubling mechanism means that the capacity is always a value of the form 100×2^n, and the smallest n to accommodate 7,000 references is 128. As each object reference requires 4 bytes (on a 32-bit JVM), you are occupying more than 20K bytes unnecessarily.

You have a way of avoiding this with a `Vector<T>` that is not available with the `ArrayList<T>` class. You can specify the amount by which the vector should be incremented as well as the initial capacity when you create it. Both arguments to the constructor are of type `int`. For example

```
Vector<String> transactions = new Vector<>(100,10);
```

This object has an initial capacity of 100, but the capacity is only increased by 10 elements when more space is required.

 NOTE Why not increment the vector object by one each time then? The process of incrementing the capacity takes time because it involves copying the contents of the vector to a new area of memory. The bigger the vector is, the longer the copy takes, and that affects your program's performance if it happens very often.

You can create a vector or an array list collection that contains objects from another collection. You pass the collection to the constructor as an argument of type `Collection<>`. Because all the set and list collection classes implement the `Collection<>` interface, the constructor argument can be of any set or list class type, including another `Vector<>`. The objects are stored in the new collection class object in the sequence in which they are returned from the iterator for the argument.

Let's see a vector working.

TRY IT OUT   Using a Vector

I take a very simple example here, just storing a few strings in a vector:

```java
import java.util.Vector;

public class TrySimpleVector {
  public static void main(String[] args) {
    Vector<String> names = new Vector<>();
    String[] firstnames = { "Jack", "Jill", "John",
                            "Joan", "Jeremiah", "Josephine"};

    // Add the names to the vector
    for(String firstname : firstnames) {
      names.add(firstname);
    }

    // List the contents of the vector
    for(String name : names) {
      System.out.println(name);
    }
  }
}
```

TrySimpleVector.java

If you compile and run this, it lists the names that are defined in the program. The code works just as well with `Vector` replaced by `ArrayList`.

How It Works

You first create a vector to store strings using the default constructor:

```java
Vector<String> names = new Vector<>();
```

This vector has the default capacity to store ten references to strings. You copy the references to the `Vector<String>` object, `names`, in the first `for` loop. The `add()` method adds the object to the vector at the next available position.

The second `for` loop iterates over the `String` references in the vector:

```
for(String name : names) {
  System.out.println(name);
}
```

All collection classes that are sequences implement the `Iterable<>` interface so you can always use the collection-based `for` loop to access their contents. Of course, you could also use an iterator. The following code produces the same result as the `for` loop:

```
java.util.Iterator<String> iter = names.iterator();
while(iter.hasNext()) {
    System.out.println(iter.next());
}
```

The `iter` object provides a one-time pass through the contents of the `names` collection. The `boolean` value returned by the `hasNext()` method determines whether or not the loop should continue. The `next()` method returns the object reference as the type that you used to create the vector so no casting is necessary.

You are spoiled for choice when accessing elements because you have a third mechanism you can use. The `get()` method returns the reference at the index position specified by the argument to the method. The argument is a zero-based index, just like an array. To iterate over all the index values for elements in a vector you need to know how many elements are stored in it and the `size()` method supplies this as a value of type `int`. You could access the elements like this:

```
for(int i = 0 ; i < names.size() ; ++i) {
  System.out.println(names.get(i));
}
```

The collection-based `for` loop is the simplest and clearest mechanism for iterating over the contents of a vector. However, the `get()` method is useful for accessing an element stored at a particular index position.

Capacity and Size

Although I said earlier that `Vector<>` and `ArrayList<>` collections work like arrays, you can now appreciate that this isn't strictly true. One significant difference is in the information you can get about the storage space provided. An array has a single measure, its length, which is the count of the total number of elements it can reference. Vectors and array lists have two measures relating to the space they provide: the *capacity* and the *size*. However, the capacity of an `ArrayList<>` object is not accessible.

Obtaining and Ensuring Capacity

The *capacity* is the maximum number of objects that a vector or array list can hold at any given instant. Of course, the capacity can vary over time because when you store an object in a `Vector<>` container that is full, its capacity automatically increases. For example, the `Vector<>` object `transactions` that you defined in the last of the constructor examples earlier had an initial capacity of 100. You also specified the capacity increment as 10. After you've stored 101 objects in it, its capacity is 110 objects. A vector typically contains fewer objects than its capacity.

The `capacity()` method returns the current capacity of a vector as a value of type `int`. For example:

```
int namesMax = names.capacity();          // Get current capacity
```

If this statement follows the definition you have for `names` in the previous example, the variable `namesMax` has the value 10. The `capacity()` method is not available in the `ArrayList<>` class.

You can ensure that a vector or an array list has sufficient capacity for your needs by calling its `ensureCapacity()` method. For example:

```
names.ensureCapacity(150);                // Set minimum capacity to 150
```

If the capacity of names is less than 150, it is increased to that value. If it's already 150 or greater, it is unchanged by this statement. The argument you specify is of type int. There's no return value.

Changing the Size

When you first create a Vector<> object , it is empty. The space allocated is occupied after you've stored references in it. The number of elements you have stored in a Vector<> is referred to as its *size*. The size of a Vector<> clearly can't be greater than the capacity. As you have seen, you can obtain the size as a value of type int by calling the size() method. You could use the size() method in conjunction with the capacity() method to calculate the number of free entries in a Vector<> object transactions with the following statement:

```
int freeCount = names.capacity() - names.size();
```

Storing an object in a vector increases its size, but you can also change the size of a vector directly by calling a method; this does not apply to an array list. Using the method setSize(), you can increase and decrease the size. For example:

```
names.setSize(50);                       // Set size to 50
```

The size of the names vector is set to the argument value (of type int). If the names vector has fewer than 50 elements stored, the additional elements up to 50 are filled with null references. If it already contains more than 50 objects, all object references in excess of 50 are discarded. The objects themselves may still be available if other references to them exist.

Looking back to the situation I discussed earlier, you saw how the effects of incrementing the capacity by doubling each time the current capacity was exceeded could waste memory. A Vector<> or an ArrayList<> object provides you with a direct way of dealing with this—the trimToSize() method. This changes the capacity to match the current size. For example:

```
names.trimToSize();                      // Set capacity to size
```

If the size of the names vector is 30 when this statement executes, then the capacity is set to 30. Of course, you can still add more objects to the Vector<> object, and it grows to accommodate them by whatever increment is in effect.

Storing Objects

The simplest way to store an object is to use the add() method, as you did in the last example. To store a name in the names vector, you could write the following:

```
names.add(aName);
```

This adds a reference to the object aName to the Vector<> object called names. The new entry is added at the end of the vector, and the size is increased by one. All the objects that were already stored in the vector remain at their previous index position.

You can also store an object at a particular index position using another version of add(). The first argument is the index position and the second is the object to be stored. The index must be less than or equal to the size of the vector, which implies that either there is already an object reference at this position, or it is the position at the end of the vector that is next in line to receive one. The index is the same as for an array—an offset from the first element—so you reference the first element using an index value of zero. For example, to insert the object aName as the third entry in names, you would write the following:

```
names.add(2, aName);
```

The index is of type int and represents the position of the new object. The new object, aName, is inserted in front of the object that was previously at index position 2, so objects stored at index values equal to or greater than 2 are shifted along so their indexes increase by 1. If you specify an index argument that is negative, or greater than the size of the vector, an ArrayIndexOutOfBoundsException is thrown.

To replace an element in a vector or array list you use the `set()` method. This accepts two arguments. The first is the index position where the object specified by the second argument is to be stored. To change the third element in the vector `names` to newName, you write:

```
names.set(2, newName);
```

The method returns a reference to the object that was previously stored at this position. This gives you a chance to hang on to the displaced object if you want to keep it. If the first argument is negative, or is greater than or equal to the current size of the vector, an `ArrayIndexOutOfBoundsException` is thrown.

You can add all the objects from another collection, either at the end or following a given index position. For example, to append the contents of a `LinkedList<>` object, myNamesList—and here I'm referring to the `java.util.LinkedList<>` type, not the homemade version—to a vector, `names`, you would write:

```
names.addAll(myNamesList);
```

The parameter to the method is of type `Collection<? extends T>`, so because the `names` vector is of type `Vector<String>`, the argument must be of type `Collection<String>`. Here, this implies that myNamesList is of type `LinkedList<String>`.

To insert the collection of objects at a particular position , you specify the insertion position as the first argument. So to insert the objects from myNamesList in the `names` vector starting at index position i, you would write:

```
names.addAll(i, myNamesList);
```

The objects originally at and following index position i are all shifted along to make room for the new objects. If the index value passed as the first argument is negative, or is greater than the size of `names`, an `ArrayIndexOutOfBoundsException` object is thrown. Adding a collection increases the size of the vector by the number of objects added.

Retrieving Objects

As you saw in the simple example earlier, if you have the index for an element in a vector, you can obtain the element at that position by using the `get()` method. For the `names` vector you could write the following:

```
String name = names.get(4);
```

This statement retrieves the fifth element in the `names` vector. The return type for the `get()` method is determined by the type argument you used to create the `Vector<>` object.

The `get()` method throws an `ArrayIndexOutOfBoundsException` if the argument is an illegal index value. The index must be non-negative and less than the size of the vector.

You can retrieve the first element in a vector using the `firstElement()` method. For example:

```
String name = names.firstElement();
```

You can retrieve the last element in a vector by using the `lastElement()` method in a similar manner. Neither method is implemented in the `ArrayList<>` class. However, both a vector and an array list have the flavor of a list about them, and if you want to process the objects like a list, you can obtain an iterator.

Accessing Elements in a Vector through a List Iterator

You've already seen how you can obtain all the elements in a vector using an `Iterator<>` object, so I won't repeat it. You can also obtain a `ListIterator` reference by calling the `listIterator()` method:

```
ListIterator<String> listIter = names.listIterator();
```

Now you can go backward or forward though the objects in `names` using the `ListIterator` methods that you saw earlier.

It is also possible to obtain a `ListIterator<>` object that encapsulates just a part of a vector, using a `listIterator()` overload that accepts an argument specifying the index position in the vector of the first element in the iterator:

```
ListIterator<String> listIter = names.listIterator(2);
```

This statement results in a list iterator that encapsulates the elements from `names` from index position 2 to the end. If the argument is negative or greater than the size of `names`, an `IndexOutOfBoundsException` is thrown. Take care not to confuse the interface name `ListIterator`, with a capital *L*, with the method of the same name, with a small *l*.

Additionally, you can retrieve an internal subset of the objects as a collection of type `List<>` using the `subList()` method:

```
List<String> list = names.subList(2, 5); // Extract elements 2 to 4 as a sublist
```

The first argument is the index position of the first element from the vector to be included in the list, and the second index is the element at the upper limit — *not* included in the list. Thus this statement extracts elements 2 to 4, inclusive. Both arguments must be positive. The first argument must be less than the size of the vector and the second argument must not be greater than the size; otherwise, an `IndexOutOfBoundsException` is thrown. If the first argument is greater than the second argument, `IllegalArgumentException` is thrown.

You have lots of ways of using the `subList()` method in conjunction with other methods, for example:

```
ListIterator<String> listIter = names.subList(5, 15).listIterator(2);
```

The call to `subList()` returns a `List<String>` object that encapsulates the elements from `names` at index positions 5 to 14, inclusive. You then call the `listIterator()` method for this object, which returns a list iterator of type `ListIterator<String>` for elements in the `List<String>` collection from index position 2 to the end. This corresponds to elements 7 to 14, inclusive, from the original `names` vector. You can use this iterator to roam backward and forward through elements 7 to 14 from the `names` vector to your heart's content.

Extracting All the Elements from a Vector

A `Vector<>` object provides you with tremendous flexibility in use, particularly with the capability to automatically adjust its capacity. Of course, the flexibility you get comes at a price. There is always some overhead involved when you're retrieving elements. For this reason, there might be times when you want to retrieve the elements contained in a `Vector<>` object as a regular array. The `toArray()` method that both array collections implement does this for you. You typically use the method like this:

```
String[] data = names.toArray(new String[names.size()]);
```

The argument to the `toArray()` method must be an array of the same type or a supertype of the type of elements in the vector. If it isn't, an `ArrayStoreException` is thrown. If the argument is `null`, then a `NullPointerException` is thrown. If the array argument is not large enough to accommodate all the elements in the vector, then a new array is created, and a reference to that is returned. The `toArray()` method here returns an array of type `String[]` containing all the elements from `names` in the correct sequence.

It's worth noting that the `java.util.Arrays` class you first saw in Chapter 3 defines a static parameterized method, `asList()`, that converts an array of a given type, `T`, into a `List<T>` collection. The argument is the array of type `T` that you want to convert, and the reference returned is of type `List<T>`. For example:

```
String[] people = { "Brian", "Beryl", "Belinda", "Barry", "Bill", "Barbara" };
List<String> nameList = java.util.Arrays.asList(people);
```

Note that the `List<>` object that is returned does not have storage independent of the array. The `List<>` object is backed by the array you pass as the argument. From the interface hierarchy that you saw earlier you know that a `List<String>` reference is also a `Collection<String>` reference. You can therefore pass it as an argument to a `Vector<String>` constructor. For example:

```
Vector<String> names = new Vector<>( java.util.Arrays.asList(people));
```

Here you are calling the constructor that accepts an argument of type `Collection<>`. You thus have a way to create a `Vector<>` object containing the elements from a predefined array. Of course, the type of elements in the array must be consistent with the type argument for the vector you are creating.

Removing Objects

You can remove the reference at a particular index position by calling the `remove()` method with the index position of the object as the argument. For example:

```
names.remove(3);
```

This removes the fourth element from the `names` vector. The elements that follow the one that was removed are now at index positions that are one less than they were before, so what was previously the fifth element is now at index position 3. Of course, the index value that you specify must be legal for the vector, so it must be greater than or equal to 0 and less than the size of the vector, or an `ArrayIndexOutOfBoundsException` is thrown. The `remove()` method returns a reference to the object removed, so you can retain a reference to the object after you remove it:

```
String name = names.remove(3);
```

Here you save the reference to the object that was removed in `name`.

Sometimes, you want to remove a particular reference, rather than the reference at a given index. If you know what the object is that you want to remove, you can use another version of the `remove()` method to delete it:

```
boolean deleted = names.remove(aName);
```

This searches the `names` vector from the beginning to find the first reference to the object `aName` and removes it. If the object is found and removed from the vector, the method returns `true`; otherwise, it returns `false`. When you are not sure that the element to be removed is present in the vector, you can test the value returned by the `remove()` method.

Another way to remove a single element is to use the `removeElementAt()` method, which requires an argument specifying the index position of the element to be removed. This is similar to the version of `remove()` that accepts an index as an argument, the difference being that here the return type is `void`. This is because the element is always removed if the index you supply is valid, and an `ArrayIndexOutOfBoundsException` is thrown if it isn't.

The `removeAll()` method accepts an argument of type `Collection<>` and removes elements from the collection that you pass to the method if they are present in the vector. The method returns `true` if the `Vector` object is changed by the operation—that is, if at least one element was removed. You could use this in conjunction with the `subList()` method to remove a specific set of elements:

```
names.removeAll(names.subList(5,15));
```

This removes elements 5 to 14, inclusive, from the `Vector<String>` object `names`, plus any duplicates of those objects that are in the vector.

The `removeRange()` method expects two arguments, an index for the first element to be removed, and an index to one past the last element to be removed. So you could apply this to names like this:

```
names.removeRange(5, 15);
```

This removes elements with index values from 5 to 14 inclusive. This is different from the previous statement in that duplicates of these elements will not be removed.

The `retainAll()` method provides a backhanded removal mechanism. You pass a reference of type `Collection<>` as the argument that contains the elements to be retained. Any elements not in the collection you pass to the method are removed. For example, you could keep the elements at index positions

5 to 14, inclusive, plus any duplicates of these elsewhere in the vector, and discard the rest with the following statement:

```
names.retainAll(names.subList(5,15));
```

The method returns `true` if the vector has been changed—in other words, if at least one element has been removed. The method throws a `NullPointerException` if the argument is `null`.

If you want to discard all the elements in a `Vector`, you can use the `removeAllElements()` method to empty the `Vector` in one go:

```
names.removeAllElements();      // Dump the whole lot
```

This removes all the elements from the `names` vector and sets the size to zero. The `clear()` method that is declared in the `List<>` interface is identical in function so you can use that to empty a vector if you prefer.

With all these ways of removing elements from a `Vector<>` object, there's a lot of potential for ending up with an empty container. It's often handy to know whether or not a vector contains elements, particularly if there's been a lot of adding and deleting of elements. You can determine whether a vector contains elements by calling its `isEmpty()` method. This returns `true` if the vector's size is zero and `false` otherwise.

> **NOTE** *Note that if a* `Vector<>` *or* `ArrayList<>` *object contains only* `null` *references, it doesn't mean the* `size()` *is zero or that the* `isEmpty()` *method returns* `true`. *To empty a container you must actually remove all the elements, not just set the elements to* `null`.

Searching for Objects

You get the index position of an object stored in a vector if you pass the object as an argument to the `indexOf()` method. For example:

```
int position = names.indexOf(aName);
```

This searches the `names` vector from the beginning for `aName` using the `equals()` method for the argument, so your `aName` class type needs to have a proper implementation of `equals()` for this to work. The variable `position` contains either the index of the first reference to the object in `names`, or −1 if the object isn't found. The `lastIndexOf()` method works in a similar fashion, but the search is starting from the last element back to the first.

Another version of the `indexOf()` method that is not available for an `ArrayList<>` accepts a second argument specifying the index position where the search for the object should begin. The main use for this arises when an object can be referenced more than once in a vector. You can use the method in this situation to recover all occurrences of any particular object, as follows:

```
String aName = "Fred";                                // Name to be found
int count = 0;                                        // Number of occurrences
int position = -1;                                    // Search starting index
while(++position < names.size()) {                    // Search with a valid index
  if((position = names.indexOf(aName, position)) < 0) {  // Find next
    break;
  }
  ++count;
}
```

This counts the number of occurrences of a `Name` in the `names` vector. The `while` loop continues as long as the `indexOf()` method returns a valid index value and the index isn't incremented beyond the end of the vector names. Figure 14-8 shows how this works.

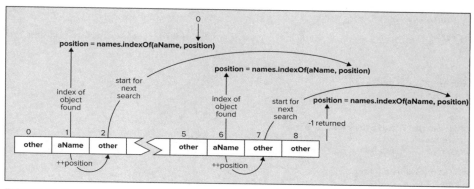

FIGURE 14-8

On each loop iteration, the indexOf() method searches names from the element given by the index stored in position. The initial value of -1 is incremented in the while loop condition, so on the first iteration it is 0. On subsequent iterations, as long as indexOf() finds an occurrence of aName, the loop condition increments position to the next element, ready for the next search. When no further references to the object can be found from the position specified by the second argument, the method returns -1 and the loop ends by executing the break statement. If aName is found in the last element in the vector at index position size-1, the value of position is incremented to size by the loop condition expression, so the expression is false and the loop ends.

When you just want to know whether or not a particular element is stored, and don't really need to know where it is, you can use the contains() method that returns true if the object you pass as the argument is in the container and returns false otherwise. The Vector<> and ArrayList<> containers also have the containsAll() method. You pass a collection to this method as an argument of type Collection and the method returns true if all the objects in the argument collection are also in the vector or array list.

Applying Vectors

Let's implement a simple example to see a Vector<> container working in practice. You write a program to model a collection of people, where you can add the names of the persons that you want in the crowd from the keyboard. You first define a class to represent a person:

```java
public class Person {
  // Constructor
  public Person(String firstName, String surname) {
    this.firstName = firstName;
    this.surname = surname;
  }

  @Override
  public String toString() {
    return firstName + " " + surname;
  }

  private String firstName;                 // First name of person
  private String surname;                   // Second name of person
}
```

The only data members are the String members to store the first and second names for a person. You override the inherited version of the toString() method to get better output when Person class objects are used as arguments to the println() method. Now you can define an example with which you can try your skills as a casting director.

TRY IT OUT Creating the Crowd

You can now add a class containing a `main()` method to try storing `Person` objects in a vector. You can call it `TryVector`:

```java
import java.util.Vector;
import java.util.ListIterator;
import java.io.*;

public class TryVector {
  public static void main(String[] args) {
    Person aPerson = null;                    // A person object
    Vector<Person> filmCast = new Vector<>();

    // Populate the film cast
    while(true) {                             // Indefinite loop
      aPerson = readPerson();                 // Read in a film star
      if(aPerson == null) {                   // If null obtained...
        break;                                // We are done...
      }
      filmCast.add(aPerson);                  // Otherwise, add to the cast
    }

    int count = filmCast.size();
    System.out.println("You added " + count +
                  (count == 1 ? " person": " people") + " to the cast:");
    // Show who is in the cast using an iterator
    ListIterator<Person> thisLot = filmCast.listIterator();

    while(thisLot.hasNext()) {                // Output all elements
      System.out.println( thisLot.next());
    }
    System.out.println("\nThe vector currently has room for " +
                  (filmCast.capacity() - count) + " more people.");
  }

  // Read a person from the keyboard
  static Person readPerson() {
    // Read in the first name and remove blanks front and back
    String firstName = null;
    String surname = null;
    System.out.println("\nEnter first name or ! to end:");
    try {
      firstName = keyboard.readLine().trim();   // Read and trim a string

      if(firstName.charAt(0) == '!') {          // Check for ! entered
        return null;                            // If so, we are done...
      }

      // Read in the surname, also trimming blanks
      System.out.println("Enter surname:");
      surname = keyboard.readLine().trim();     // Read and trim a string
    } catch(IOException e) {
      System.err.println("Error reading a name.");
      e.printStackTrace();
      System.exit(1);
    }
    return new Person(firstName,surname);
  }

  static BufferedReader keyboard = new BufferedReader(
                                    new InputStreamReader(System.in));
}
```

Directory "TryVector"

With a huge film budget, I got the following output (my input is in bold):

```
Enter first name or ! to end:
Johnny
Enter surname:
Depp

Enter first name or ! to end:
George
Enter surname:
Clooney

Enter first name or ! to end:
Judy
Enter surname:
Dench

Enter first name or ! to end:
Jennifer
Enter surname:
Aniston

Enter first name or ! to end:
!
You added 4 people to the cast:
Johnny Depp
George Clooney
Judy Dench
Jennifer Aniston

The vector currently has room for 6 more people.
```

How It Works

Here you be assembling an all-star cast for a new blockbuster. The `main()` method creates a `Person` variable, which is used as a temporary store for an actor or actress, and a `Vector<Person>` object, `filmCast`, to hold the entire cast.

The `while` loop uses the `readPerson()` method to obtain the necessary information from the keyboard and create a `Person` object. If `!` is entered from the keyboard, `readPerson()` returns `null`, and this ends the input process for cast members.

You output the number of stars entered with these statements:

```
int count = filmCast.size();
System.out.println("You added " + count +
            (count == 1 ? " person": " people") + " to the cast:");
```

The `size()` method returns the number of objects in the vector, which is precisely what you want. The complication introduced by the conditional operator is just to make the grammar in the output sentence correct.

Just to try it out you output the members of the cast using a `ListIterator<Person>` object. You could do the job just as well with an `Iterator<Person>` object or even a collection-based `for` loop. Using an iterator is still relatively simple:

```
ListIterator<Person> thisLot = filmCast.listIterator();

while(thisLot.hasNext()) {          // Output all elements
  System.out.println( thisLot.next());
}
```

Instead of an iterator, you could have used the `get()` method for the `filmCast` object to retrieve the actors:

```
for(int i = 0 ; i < filmCast.size() ; ++i) {
  System.out.println(filmCast.get(i));
}
```

The collection-based `for` loop is the simplest way of all for listing the contents of the vector:

```
for(Person person : filmCast) {
  System.out.println(person);
}
```

To output the space remaining in the vector, you calculate the difference between the capacity and the size:

```
System.out.println("\nThe vector currently has room for "
                + (filmCast.capacity() - count) + " more people.");
```

This is interesting but irrelevant because the vector accommodates as many stars as you care to enter.

The static `readPerson()` method is a convenient way of managing the input. The input source is the static class member defined by the following statement:

```
static BufferedReader keyboard = new BufferedReader(
                                  new InputStreamReader(System.in));
```

The keyboard object is `System.in` wrapped in an `InputStreamReader` object that is wrapped in a `BufferedReader` object. The `InputStreamReader` object provides conversion of the input from the byte stream `System.in` to characters. The `BufferedReader` object buffers the data read from the `InputStreamReader`. Because the input consists of a series of strings entered one to a line, the `readLine()` method does everything you need. The calls to `readLine()` is in a `try` block because it can throw an `IOException`. The call to the `trim()` method for the `String` object returned by the `readLine()` method removes leading or trailing blanks.

Sorting a Collection

The output from the last example appears in the sequence in which you enter it. If you want to arrange them in alphabetical order you could write your own method to sort `Person` objects in the `filmCast` object, but it is a lot less trouble to take advantage of another feature of the `java.util` package, the `Collections` class—not to be confused with the `Collection<>` interface. The `Collections` class defines a variety of handy static utility methods that you can apply to collections, and one of them happens to be a `sort()` method.

The `sort()` method only sorts lists—that is, collections that implement the `List<>` interface. Obviously there has to be some way for the `sort()` method to determine the order of objects from the list that it is sorting—in your case, `Person` objects. The most suitable way to do this is to implement the `Comparable<>` interface in the `Person` class. As you know, the `Comparable<>` interface declares only one method, `compareTo()`. You saw this method in the previous chapter so you know it returns –1, 0, or +1 depending on whether the current object is less than, equal to, or greater than the argument. If the `Comparable<>` interface is implemented for the type of object stored in a collection, you can just pass the collection object as an argument to the `sort()` method. The collection is sorted in place so there is no return value.

You can implement the `Comparable<>` interface very easily for your `Person` class, as follows:

```
public class Person implements Comparable<Person> {
  // Constructor
  public Person(String firstName, String surname) {
    this.firstName = firstName;
    this.surname = surname;
  }

  @Override
  public String toString() {
    return firstName + " " + surname;
  }

  // Compare Person objects
  public int compareTo(Person person) {
    int result = surname.compareTo(person.surname);
```

```
        return result == 0 ? firstName.compareTo(person.firstName) : result;
    }

    private String firstName;      // First name of person
    private String surname;        // Second name of person
}
```

Directory "TryVector"

You use the `compareTo()` method in the `String` class to compare the surnames, and if the surnames are equal, the result is determined from the first names.

You can just pass your `Vector<Person>` object to the `sort()` method, and this uses the `compareTo()` method in the `Person` class to compare members of the list.

Let's see if it works for real.

TRY IT OUT   Sorting the Stars

You can now add statements to the `main()` method in `TryVector` to sort the cast members:

Available for download on Wrox.com

```
public static void main(String[] args) {
    // Code as previously...

    // Now sort the vector contents and list it
    Collections.sort(filmCast);
    System.out.println("\nThe cast in ascending sequence is:\n");
    for(Person person : filmCast) {
        System.out.println(person);
    }
}
```

Directory "TryVector"

You'll need to add the following `import` statement to the `TryVector.java` file:

import java.util.Collections;

If you run the example with these changes, you get additional output with the cast in alphabetical order. Here's what I got when I entered the same data as last time:

```
Input record and output exactly as before...

The cast in ascending sequence is:
Jennifer Aniston
George Clooney
Judy Dench
Johnny Depp
```

How It Works

Passing the `filmCast` object to the static `sort()` method in the `Collections` class sorts the objects in the vector in place. Like shelling peas!

The `sort()` method is actually a parameterized method so it works for any type that implements the `Comparable<>` interface. The way the type parameter for the method is defined is interesting:

```
static <T extends Comparable<? super T>> void sort(List<T> list)
```

Recall from the discussion of parameterized types in the previous chapter that using a wildcard with the superclass constraint that you see here specifies that the type argument can be any type that implements the `Comparable<>` interface or inherits an implementation from a superclass.

The method parameter is of type `List<T>` rather than `Collection<T>` because the `List<T>` interface provides methods that allow the position where elements are inserted to be determined. It also provides the `listIterator()` method that returns a `ListIterator<T>` object that allows iteration forward and backward through the objects in the collection.

Stack Storage

A stack is a storage mechanism that works on a last-in, first-out basis, which, as you know, is often abbreviated to LIFO. Don't confuse this with FIFO, which is first-in, first-out, or FIFI, which is a name for a poodle. The operation of a stack is analogous to the plate stack you see in some self-service restaurants and is illustrated in Figure 14-9. The stack of plates is supported by a spring that allows the stack of plates to sink into a hole in the countertop so that only the top plate is accessible. The plates come out in the reverse order to the way they went in, so the cold plates are at the bottom, and the hot plates, fresh from the dishwasher, are at the top, which is not so good if you want something chilled.

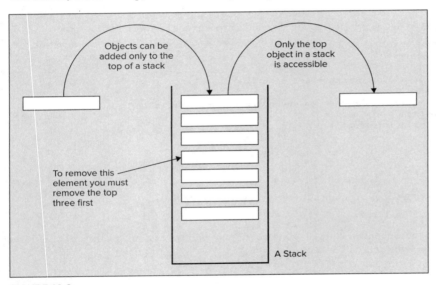

FIGURE 14-9

A stack in Java doesn't have a spring, but it does have all the facilities of a vector because the generic `Stack<>` type is derived from the `Vector<>` type. Of course, you know the `Vector<>` class implements the `List<>` interface so a `Stack<>` object is also a `List<>`.

The `Stack<T>` class adds five methods to those inherited from `Vector<T>`, two of which provide you with the LIFO mechanism; the other three give you extra capabilities. These methods are:

➤ `T push(T obj)`: Pushes `obj` onto the top of the stack. It also returns the `obj` reference.

➤ `T pop()`: Pops the object off the top of the stack and returns it. This removes the reference from the stack. If the stack contains no references when you call this method, an `EmptyStackException` is thrown.

➤ `T peek()`: Returns the object reference at the top of the stack without removing it. Like the previous method, this method can throw an `EmptyStackException`.

➤ `int search(Object obj)`: Returns a value that is the position of `obj` on the stack. The reference at the top of the stack is at position 1, the next reference is at position 2, and so on. Note that this is quite different from referencing elements in a `Vector<>` or an array, where indexes start at 0. If the object isn't found on the stack, −1 is returned.

➤ `boolean empty()`: Returns `true` if the stack is empty and returns `false` otherwise.

The only constructor for a `Stack<>` object is the no-arg constructor. This calls the default constructor for the base class, `Vector<>`, so you always get an initial capacity for 10 objects. Because it's basically a vector a stack grows automatically in the same way.

One possible point of confusion is the relationship between the top of a `Stack<>` object and the elements in the underlying `Vector<>` object. Intuitively, you might think that the top of the stack is going to correspond to the first element in the vector, with index 0. If so, you would be totally *wrong*! The `push()` method for a `Stack<>` object is analogous to `add()` for a `Vector<>`, which adds an object to the end of the vector. Thus, the top of the stack corresponds to the end of the vector.

Let's try a `Stack<>` object out in an example so you get a feel for how the methods are used.

TRY IT OUT   Dealing Cards

You can use a `Stack<>` object along with another useful method from the `Collections` class to simulate dealing cards from a card deck. You need a way of representing a card's suit and face value or rank. An `enum` type works well because it has a fixed set of constant values. Here's how you can define the suits:

```java
public enum Suit {
    CLUBS, DIAMONDS, HEARTS, SPADES
}
```

Directory "TryDeal"

The sequence in which the suits are defined here determines their sort order, so CLUBS is the lowest and SPADES is the highest. Save this source file as `Suit.java` in a new directory for the files for this example.

You can define the possible card face values just as easily:

```java
public enum Rank {
    TWO,   THREE, FOUR, FIVE, SIX,   SEVEN,
    EIGHT, NINE,  TEN,  JACK, QUEEN, KING, ACE
}
```

Directory "TryDeal"

TWO is the lowest card face value, and ACE is the highest. You can save this as `Rank.java`. You're now ready to develop the class that represents cards. Here's an initial outline:

```java
public class Card {
    public Card(Rank rank, Suit suit) {
        this.rank = rank;
        this.suit = suit;
    }

    private Suit suit;
    private Rank rank;
}
```

Directory "TryDeal"

Your `Card` class has two data members that are both enumeration types. One defines the suit and the other defines the face value of the card.

You will undoubtedly need to display a card, so you need a `String` representation of a `Card` object. The `toString()` method can do this for you:

```java
public class Card {
    @Override
    public String toString() {
        return rank + " of " + suit;
```

```
    }

    // Other members as before...
}
```

Directory "TryDeal"

The `String` representation of an `enum` constant is the name you assign to the constant, so the `String` representation of a `Card` object with the `suit` value as `CLUBS` and the `rank` value as `FOUR` is `"FOUR of CLUBS"`.

In general, you probably want to compare cards, so you could also make the `Card` class implement the `Comparable<>` interface:

```
public class Card implements Comparable<Card> {

  // Compare two cards
  public int compareTo(Card card) {
    if(suit.equals(card.suit)) {                    // First compare suits
      if(rank.equals(card.rank)) {                  // So check face values
        return 0;                                   // They are equal
      }
      return rank.compareTo(card.rank) < 0 ? -1 : 1;
    } else {                                        // Suits are different
      return suit.compareTo(card.suit) < 0 ? -1 : 1; // Sequence is C<D<H<S
    }
  }

  // Other members as before...
}
```

Directory "TryDeal"

You can see the benefit of the `Comparable<>` interface being a generic type. The `Card` class implements the `Comparable<Card>` interface, so the `compareTo()` method works with `Card` objects and no cast is necessary in the operation. The suit first determines the card sequence. If the two cards are of the same suit, then you compare the face values. To compare `enum` values for equality you use the `equals()` method. The `Enum<>` class that is the base for all `enum` types implements the `Comparable<>` interface so you can use the `compareTo()` method to determine the sequencing of `enum` values.

You could represent a hand of cards that is dealt from a deck as an object of type `Hand`. A `Hand` object needs to accommodate an arbitrary number of cards, depending on the game the hand is intended for. You can define the `Hand` class using a `Vector<Card>` object to store the cards:

```
// Class defining a hand of cards
import java.util.Vector;

public class Hand {
  // Add a card to the hand
  public void add(Card card) {
    hand.add(card);
  }

  @Override
  public String toString() {
    StringBuilder str = new StringBuilder();
    boolean first = true;
    for(Card card : hand) {
      if(first) {
        first = false;
      } else {
```

```
          str.append(", ");
        }
        str.append(card);
      }
      return str.toString();
    }

    private Vector<Card> hand = new Vector<>();        // Stores a hand of cards
  }
```

Directory "TryDeal"

The default constructor generated by the compiler creates a Hand object containing an empty Vector<Card> member, hand. The add() member adds the Card object passed as an argument by adding it to the hand vector. You also have implemented a toString() method in the Card class that creates a string that combines the rank name with the suit name. You use the collection-based for loop to traverse the cards in the hand and construct a string representation of the complete hand.

It might be good to provide a way to sort the cards in a hand. You could do this by adding a sort() method to the Hand class:

```
import java.util.Vector;
import java.util.Collections;

public class Hand {
  // Sort the hand
  public Hand sort() {
    Collections.sort(hand);
    return this;
  }

  // Rest of the class as before...
}
```

Directory "TryDeal"

The Card class implements the Comparable<> interface, so you can use the static sort() method in the Collections class to sort the cards in the hand. In order to return the current Hand object after it has been sorted, the sort() method in the class returns this. This makes the use of the sort() method a little more convenient, as you see when you put the main() method together.

You might well want to compare hands in general, but this is completely dependent on the context. The best approach to accommodate this when required is to derive a game-specific class from Hand—a PokerHand class, for example—and make it implement its own version of the compareTo() method in the Comparable<> interface.

The last class that you define represents a deck of cards and is able to deal a hand:

```
import java.util.Stack;

public class CardDeck {
  // Create a deck of 52 cards
  public CardDeck() {
    for(Suit suit : Suit.values())
      for(Rank rank : Rank.values())
        deck.push(new Card(rank, suit));
  }

  // Deal a hand
  public Hand dealHand(int numCards) {
```

```
      if(deck.size() < numCards) {
        System.err.println("Not enough cards left in the deck!");
        System.exit(1);
      }
      Hand hand = new Hand();
      for(int i = 0 ; i < numCards ; ++i) {
        hand.add(deck.pop());
      }
      return hand;
    }

    private Stack<Card> deck = new Stack<>();
  }
```

Directory "TryDeal"

The card deck is stored as a `Stack<Card>` object, `deck`. In the constructor, the nested `for` loops create the cards in the deck. For each suit in turn, you generate all the `Card` objects for each rank and push them onto the `Stack<>` object, `deck`. The `values()` method for an `enum` type returns a collection containing all the `enum` constants so that's how the loop iterates over all possible suits and ranks.

The `dealHand()` method creates a `Hand` object, and then pops `numCards` `Card` objects off the deck stack and adds each of them to `hand`. The `Hand` object is then returned. At the moment your deck is completely sequenced. You need a method to shuffle the deck before you deal:

```
import java.util.Stack;
import java.util.Collections;

public class CardDeck {
  // Shuffle the deck
  public void shuffle() {
    Collections.shuffle(deck);
  }

  // Rest of the class as before...
}
```

Directory "TryDeal"

With the aid of another `static` parameterized method from the `Collections` class it couldn't be easier. The `shuffle()` method in `Collections` shuffles the contents of any collection that implements the `List<>` interface. The `Stack<>` class implements `List<>` so you can use the `shuffle()` method to produce a shuffled deck of `Card` objects. For those interested in the details of shuffling, this `shuffle()` method randomly permutes the list by running backward through its elements swapping the current element with a randomly chosen element between the first and the current element. The time taken to complete the operation is proportional to the number of elements in the list.

An overloaded version of the `shuffle()` method enables you to supply an object of type `Random` as the second argument, which is used for selecting elements at random while shuffling.

The final piece of the example is a class that defines `main()`:

```
class TryDeal {
  public static void main(String[] args) {
    CardDeck deck = new CardDeck();
    deck.shuffle();

    Hand myHand = deck.dealHand(5).sort();
    Hand yourHand = deck.dealHand(5).sort();
    System.out.println(„\nMy hand is:\n" + myHand);
```

```
        System.out.println(„\nYour hand is:\n" + yourHand);
  }
}
```

Directory "TryDeal"

I got the following output:

```
My hand is:
THREE of CLUBS, TWO of DIAMONDS, SEVEN of DIAMONDS, FOUR of SPADES, JACK of SPADES

Your hand is:
FOUR of CLUBS, FIVE of CLUBS, TWO of HEARTS, ACE of HEARTS, THREE of SPADES
```

You will almost certainly get something different.

How It Works

Your code for `main()` first creates a `CardDeck` object and calls its `shuffle()` method to randomize the sequence of `Card` objects. You then create two `Hand` objects of five cards with the following statements:

```
Hand myHand = deck.dealHand(5).sort();
Hand yourHand = deck.dealHand(5).sort();
```

The `dealHand()` method returns a `Hand` object that you use to call its `sort()` method. Because the `sort()` method returns a reference to the `Hand` object after sorting, you are able to call it in a single statement like this. The `Hand` object that the `sort()` method returns is stored in the local variable, either `myHand` or `yourHand` as the case may be. The output statements just display the hands that were dealt.

A `Stack<>` object is particularly well suited to dealing cards because you want to remove each card from the deck as it is dealt, and this is done automatically by the `pop()` method that retrieves an object. When you need to go through all the objects in a stack without removing them, you can use a collection-based `for` loop, just as you did for the `Vector<Card>` object in the `toString()` method in the `Hand` class. Of course, because the `Stack<>` class is derived from `Vector<>`, all the `Vector<>` class methods are available for a stack when you need them.

I think you'll agree that using a stack is very simple. A stack is a powerful tool in many different contexts. A stack is often applied in applications that involve syntactical analysis, such as compilers and interpreters—including those for Java.

LINKED LISTS

The `LinkedList<T>` type implements the `List<>` interface and defines a generalized linked list. You have already seen quite a few of the methods that the class implements, as the members of the `List<>` interface are implemented in the `Vector<>` class. Nonetheless, here I quickly review the methods that the `LinkedList<>` class implements. There are two constructors: a default constructor that creates an empty list and a constructor that accepts a `Collection<>` argument that creates a `LinkedList<>` object that contains the objects from the collection that is passed to it.

To add objects to a list you have the `add()` and `addAll()` methods, exactly as I discussed for a `Vector<>` object. You can also add an object at the beginning of a list using the `addFirst()` method, and you can add one at the end using `addLast()`. Both methods accept an argument of a type corresponding to the type argument you supplied when you created the `LinkedList<>` object, and neither return a value. Of course, the `addLast()` method provides the same function as the `add()` method.

To retrieve an object at a particular index position in the list, you can use the get() method, as in the Vector<> class. You can also obtain references to the first and last objects by using the getFirst() and getLast() methods, respectively. To remove an object you use the remove() method with an argument that is either an index value or a reference to the object that is to be removed. The removeFirst() and removeLast() methods do what you would expect.

Replacing an existing element in the list at a given index position is achieved by using the set() method. The first argument is the index and the second argument is the new object at that position. The old object is returned, and the method throws an IndexOutOfBoundsException if the index value is not within the limits of the list. The size() method returns the number of elements in the list.

As with a Vector<> object, you can obtain an Iterator<> object by calling iterator(), and you can obtain a ListIterator<> object by calling listIterator(). Recall that an Iterator<> object enables you only to go forward through the elements, whereas a ListIterator<> object enables you to iterate backward and forward.

You could change the TryPolyLine example from Chapter 6 to use a LinkedList<> collection object rather than your homemade version.

TRY IT OUT   Using a Genuine Linked List

Put this example in a new directory, TryPolyLine. You can use the TryPolyLine class that contains main() and the Point class exactly as they are, so if you still have them, copy the source files to the new directory. You just need to change the PolyLine class definition:

```java
import java.util.LinkedList;

public class PolyLine {
  // Construct a polyline from an array of points
  public PolyLine(Point[] points) {
    // Add the  points
    for(Point point : points) {
      polyline.add(point);
    }
  }
  // Construct a polyline from an array of coordinates
  public PolyLine(double[][] coords) {
    for(double[] xy : coords) {
      addPoint(xy[0], xy[1]);
    }
  }

  // Add a Point object to the list
  public void addPoint(Point point) {
    polyline.add(point);                 // Add the new point
  }

  // Add a point to the list
  public void addPoint(double x, double y) {
    polyline.add(new Point(x, y));
  }

  // String representation of a polyline
  @Override
  public String toString() {
    StringBuffer str = new StringBuffer("Polyline:");

    for(Point point : polyline) {
      str.append(" " + point);           // Append the current point
    }
    return str.toString();
```

```
      }

      private LinkedList<Point> polyline = new LinkedList<>();
}
```

Directory "TryPolyLine"

The class is a lot simpler because the `LinkedList<>` class provides all the mechanics for operating a linked list. Because the interface to the `PolyLine` class is the same as the previous version, the original version of `main()` runs unchanged and produces exactly the same output.

How It Works

The only interesting bit is the change to the `PolyLine` class. `Point` objects are now stored in the linked list implemented by the `LinkedList<>` object, `polyline`. You use the `add()` method to add points in the constructors, and the `addPoint()` methods. Using a collection class makes the `PolyLine` class very straightforward.

I changed the implementation of the second constructor in the `PolyLine` class to illustrate how you can use the collection-based `for` loop with a two-dimensional array:

```
public PolyLine(double[][] coords) {
  for(double[] xy : coords) {
    addPoint(xy[0], xy[1]);
  }
}
```

The `coords` parameter to the constructor is a two-dimensional array of elements of type `double`. This is effectively a one-dimensional array of references to one-dimensional arrays that have two elements each, corresponding to the *x* and *y* coordinate values for a point. Thus, you can use the collection-based `for` loop to iterate over the array of arrays. The loop variable is `xy`, which is of type `double[]` and has two elements. Within the loop, you pass the elements of the array `xy` as arguments to the `addPoint()` method. This method then creates a `Point` object and adds it to the `LinkedList<Point>` collection, `polyline`.

USING MAPS

As you saw at the beginning of this chapter, a *map* is a way of storing data that minimizes the need for searching when you want to retrieve an object. Each object is associated with a key that is used to determine where to store the reference to the object, and both the key and the object are stored in the map. Given a key, you can always go more or less directly to the object that has been stored in the map based on the key. It's important to understand a bit more about how the storage mechanism works for a map, and in particular what the implications of using the default hashing process are. You explore the use of maps primarily in the context of the `HashMap<K,V>` generic class type.

The Hashing Process

The implementation of a map in the Java collections framework that is provided by the `HashMap<K,V>` class sets aside an array in which it stores key and object pairs of type `K` and `V` respectively. The index to this array is produced from the key object by using the hashcode for the object to compute an offset into the array for storing the key/object pair. By default, this uses the `hashCode()` method for the key object. This is inherited in all classes from `Object` so this is the method that produces the basic hashcode unless the `hashCode()` method is redefined in the class for the key. The `HashMap<>` class does not assume that the basic hashcode is adequate. To try to ensure that the hashcode that is used has the characteristics required for an efficient map, the basic hashcode is further transformed within the `HashMap<>` object.

An entry in the table that is used to store key/value pairs is called a *bucket*. The hashcode produced from a key selects a particular bucket in which the key/value pair should be stored. This is illustrated in Figure 14-10.

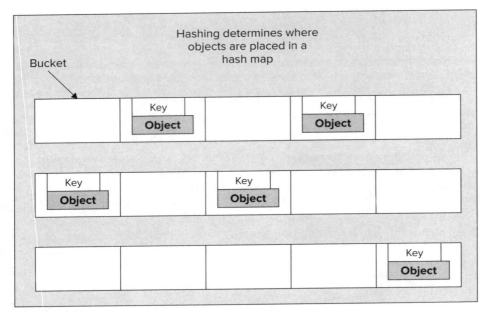

FIGURE 14-10

Note that, although every key must be unique, each key doesn't have to result in a unique hashcode. When two or more keys produce the same hash value, it's called a *collision*. A HashMap<> object deals with collisions by storing all the key/object pairs that have the same hash value in a linked list. If this occurs often, it is obviously going to slow down the process of storing and retrieving data. Retrieving an object that resulted in a collision when it was stored is a two-stage process. The key is hashed to find the location where the key/object pair should be. The linked list then has to be searched to sort out the key you are searching on from all the others that have the same hash value. There is therefore a strong incentive to minimize collisions, and the price of reducing the possibility of collisions in a hash table is having plenty of empty space in the table.

The Object class defines the hashCode() method so any object can be used as a key and it hashes by default. The method as it is implemented in Object in Java, however, isn't a panacea. Because it usually uses the memory address where an object is stored to produce the hash value, distinct objects always produce different hash values. In one sense this is a plus, because the more likely it is that a unique hash value is produced for each key, the more efficient the operation of the hash map is going to be. The downside is that different objects that have identical data produce different hash values, so you can't compare them.

This becomes a nuisance if you use the default hashCode() method for objects that you're using as keys. In this case, an object stored in a hash map can never be retrieved using a different key object instance, even though that key object may be identical in all other respects. Yet this is precisely what you want to do in many cases.

Consider an application such as a simple address book. You might store map entries keyed on the names of the people to whom the entries relate, and you would want to search the map based on a name that was entered from the keyboard. However, the object representing the newly entered name is inevitably going to be distinct from that used as a key for the entry. Using the former, you won't be able to find the entry corresponding to the name.

The solution to this problem is to create a hashcode from the instance variables of the object. Then, by comparing the hashcode produced from the data members of the new name object with the hashcodes for the name objects used as keys in the hash map, you are able to make a match.

Using Your Own Class Objects as Keys

For objects of one of your own classes to be usable as keys in a hash table, you must override the `equals()` method of the `Object` class. In its default form, `equals()` accepts an object of the same class as an argument and returns a `boolean` value. The `equals()` method is used by methods in the `HashMap<>` class to determine when two keys are equal, so in order to enable the changes discussed in the previous section, your version of this method should return `true` when two different objects contain identical data values.

You can also override the default `hashCode()` method, which returns the hash value for the object as type `int`. The `hashCode()` method is used to generate the value that determines where a key/object pair is located. Your `hashCode()` method should produce hashcodes that are reasonably uniform over the possible range of keys and is generally unique for each key.

Generating Hashcodes

The various techniques for generating hashcodes form a big topic, and I can barely scratch the surface here. How you write the `hashCode()` method for your class is up to you, but it needs to meet certain requirements if it is to be effective. A hashcode is returned by the `hashCode()` method as a value of type `int`. You should aim to return a hashcode that has a strong probability of being unique to the object, and the hashcodes that you produce for the range of different objects that you are working with should be as widely distributed across the range of `int` values as possible.

To achieve the uniqueness, you typically want to combine the values of all the data members in an object to produce the hashcode, so the first step is to produce an integer corresponding to each data member. You must then combine these integers to generate the return value that is the hashcode for the object. One technique you can use to do this is to multiply each of the integers corresponding to the data members by a different prime number and then sum the results. This should produce a reasonable distribution of values that have a good probability of being different for different objects. It doesn't matter which prime numbers you use as multipliers, as long as:

➤ They aren't so large as to cause the result to fall outside the range of type `int`.

➤ You use a different one for each data member.

So how do you get from a data member of a class to an integer? Generating an integer for data members of type `String` is easy: you just call the `hashCode()` method for the member. This has been implemented in the `String` class to produce good hashcode values that are the same for identical strings (take a look at the source code if you want to see how). You can use integer data members as they are, but floating-point data members need a bit of judgment. If they have a small range in integer terms, you need to multiply them by a value that's going to result in a unique integer when they are cast to type `int`. If they have a very large range in integer terms you might need to scale them down.

Suppose you intended to use a `Person` object as a key in a hash table, and the class data members were `firstName` and `surname` of type `String` and `age` of type `int`. You could implement the `hashCode()` method for the class as the following:

```
public int hashCode() {
  return 13*firstName.hashCode() + 17*surname.hashCode() + 19*age;
}
```

Wherever a data member is an object of another class rather than a variable of one of the basic types, you need to implement the `hashCode()` method for that class. You can then use that in the computation of the hashcode for the key class.

Creating a HashMap Container

As you saw earlier in this chapter, all map classes implement the `Map<>` interface, so an object of any map class can be referenced using a variable of type `Map<>`. You look in detail at the `HashMap<>` class because it is good for most purposes. There are four constructors to create a `HashMap<K, V>` object:

➤ HashMap() creates a map with the capacity to store a default number of objects. The default capacity is 16 objects, and the default load factor (more on the load factor below) is 0.75.

➤ HashMap(int capacity) creates a map with the capacity to store the number of objects you specify in the argument and a default load factor of 0.75.

➤ HashMap(int capacity, float loadFactor) creates a map with the capacity and load factor that you specify.

➤ HashMap(Map<? extends K, ? extends V> map) creates a map with the mappings, capacity and load factor of the Map object passed as the argument.

To create a map using the default constructor, you can write something like this:

```
HashMap<String,Person> theMap = new HashMap<>();
```

This statement creates a HashMap<> object that can store Person objects with associated keys of type String.

The *capacity* for a map is simply the number of key/object pairs it can store. The capacity increases automatically as necessary, but this is a relatively time-consuming operation. The capacity value of the map is combined with the hashcode for the key that you specify to compute the index that determines where an object and its key are to be stored. To make this computation produce a good distribution of index values, you should ideally use prime numbers for the capacity of a hash table when you specify it yourself. For example:

```
HashMap myMap<String,Person> = new HashMap<>(151);
```

This map has a capacity for 151 objects and their keys, although the number of objects stored can never actually reach the capacity. You must always have spare capacity in a map for efficient operation. With too little spare capacity, you have an increased likelihood that keys generate the same bucket index, so collisions become more likely.

The *load factor* is used to decide when to increase the size of the hash table. When the size of the table reaches a value that is the product of the load factor and the capacity, the capacity is increased automatically to twice the old capacity plus one — the plus one ensuring it is at least odd, if not prime. The default load factor of 0.75 is a good compromise, but if you want to reduce it you could do so by using the third constructor:

```
// Create a map with a 60% load factor
HashMap<String,Person> aMap = new HashMap<>(151, 0.6f);
```

This map works a bit more efficiently than the current default, but at the expense of having more unoccupied space. When 90 objects have been stored, the capacity is increased to 303, $(2 \times 151 + 1)$.

Storing, Retrieving, and Removing Objects

Storing, retrieving, and removing objects in a HashMap<> is very simple. The methods involved in these operations are the following:

➤ V put(K key, V value): Stores the object value in the map using the key specified by the first argument. value replaces any existing object associated with key, and a reference to the previous object for the key is returned. If no object was previously stored for key or the key was used to store null as an object, null is returned.

➤ void putAll(Map<? extends K,? extends V> map): Transfers all the key/object pairs from map to the current map, replacing any objects that exist with the same keys.

➤ V get(Object key): Returns the object stored with the same key as the argument. If no object was stored with this key or null was stored as the object, null is returned. Note that the object remains in the map.

➤ V remove(Object key): Removes the entry associated with key if it exists and returns a reference to the object. A null is returned if the entry does not exist, or if null was stored using key.

If you attempt to retrieve an object using `get()` and a `null` is returned, it is still possible that a `null` was stored as the object associated with the key that you supplied to the `get()` method. You can determine if this is the case by passing your key object to the `containsKey()` method for the map. This returns `true` if the key is stored in the map.

You should ensure that the value returned from the `put()` method is `null`. If you don't, you may unwittingly replace an object that was stored in the table earlier using the same key. The following code fragment illustrates how you might do that:

```java
HashMap<String,Integer> aMap = new HashMap<>();
String myKey = "Goofy";
int value = 12345;
Integer oldValue = null;
for (int i = 0 ; i < 4 ; ++i) {
  if((oldValue = aMap.put(myKey, value++)) != null) {
    System.out.println("Uh-oh, we bounced an object: " + oldValue);
  }
}
```

Of course, you could throw your own exception here instead of displaying a message on the command line. The second parameter to the `put()` method for the `aMap` object is of type `Integer`, so the compiler supplies an autoboxing conversion for the `int` value that is passed as the argument.

If you execute this fragment, it generates the following output:

```
Uh-oh, we bounced an object: 12345
Uh-oh, we bounced an object: 12346
Uh-oh, we bounced an object: 12347
```

When the first value is stored, there's nothing stored in the map for the key, so there's no message. For all subsequent attempts to store objects, the previous object is replaced, and a reference to it is returned.

Note that the `get()` operation returns a reference to the object associated with the key, but it does not remove it from the table. To retrieve an object and delete the entry containing it from the table, you must use the `remove()` method. This removes the object corresponding to the key and returns a reference to it:

```java
int objectValue = aMap.remove(myKey);
```

As noted previously, if there's no stored object corresponding to `myKey`, or `null` was stored as the object, `null` is returned. If you were to append this statement to the previous fragment, a reference to an `Integer` object encapsulating the value 12348 would be returned. Because you store it in a variable of type `int`, the compiler inserts an unboxing conversion for the return value.

Processing All the Elements in a Map

The `Map<>` interface provides three ways of obtaining a collection view of the contents of a map. You can obtain all the keys from a `Map<K,V>` object as an object of type `Set<K>`.You can also get a `Collection<V>` object that contains all the values in the map. Key/object pairs are stored in a map as objects of a type that implements the `Map.Entry<K,V>` interface. This is a generic interface type that is defined within the `Map<K,V>` interface. You can get all the key/object pairs from the map as an object of type `Set<Map.Entry<K,V>>`.

Note that the `Set<>` or `Collection<>` object that you get is essentially a view of the contents of a map, so changes to a `HashMap<>` object are reflected in the associated `Set<>` or `Collection<>`, and *vice versa*. The three methods involved are the following:

➤ `Set<K> keySet()`: Returns an object containing all the keys from the map.

➤ `Set<Map.Entry<K,V>> entrySet()`: Returns an object containing the key/object pairs—each pair being an object of type `Map.Entry<K,V>`.

➤ `Collection<V> values()`: Returns an object containing all the values stored in the map.

Let's first see how you can use a set of keys. The `keySet()` method for a `HashMap<K,V>` object returns a `Set<K>` object containing the set of keys that you can either use directly to access the keys or use indirectly to get at the objects stored in the map. For a `HashMap<String, Integer>` object aMap, you could get the set of all the keys in the map with the following statement:

```
Set<String> keys = aMap.keySet();
```

Now you can get an iterator for this set of keys with this statement:

```
Iterator<String> keyIter = keys.iterator();
```

You can use the `iterator()` method for the object keys to iterate over all the keys in the map. Of course, you can combine these two operations to get the iterator directly. For example:

```
Iterator<String> keyIter = aMap.keySet().iterator();  // Get the iterator

while(keyIter.hasNext()) {                             // Iterate over the keys
   System.out.println(keyIter.next());
}
```

This iterates over all the keys and outputs them.

The `Set<>` interface has `Iterable<>` as a superinterface, so you can use the collection-based `for` loop directly with the object that the `keySet()` method returns:

```
for(String key : aMap.keySet()) {
   System.out.println(key);
}
```

That's much neater than messing about with an iterator, isn't it? In general, the collection-based `for` loop provides you with code that is easier to understand than an iterator.

Of course, you could use the keys to extract the values but the `Collection<>` object that is returned by the `values()` method provides you with a more direct way of doing this. Here's how you could list the values stored in aMap, assuming it is of type `HashMap<String,Integer>`:

```
Collection<Integer> collection = aMap.values();
for(Integer i : collection) {
   System.out.println(i);
}
```

This uses a collection-based `for` loop to iterate over the elements in the collection of values that the `values()` method returns.

The `entrySet()` method returns a `Set<Map.Entry<K,V>>` object containing the key/object pairs. In a similar way to that used for the set of keys, you use a `for` loop to access the `Map.Entry<>` objects. Each `Map.Entry<K,V>` object contains the following methods:

➤ `K getKey()`: Returns the key for the `Map.Entry<K,V>` object.

➤ `V getValue()`: Returns the value for the `Map.Entry<K,V>` object.

➤ `V setValue(V new)`: Sets the value for this `Map.Entry<K,V>` object to the argument and returns the original value. Remember that this alters the original map. This method throws:

　➤ `UnsupportedOperationException` if `put()` is not supported by the underlying map.

　➤ `ClassCastException` if the argument cannot be stored because of its type.

　➤ `IllegalArgumentException` if the argument is otherwise invalid.

　➤ `NullPointerException` if the map does not allow `null` objects to be stored and the argument is null. This last exception does not apply to `HashMap<>`.

A `Map.Entry<>` object also needs an `equals()` method for comparisons with another `Map.Entry<>` object passed as an argument and a `hashCode()` method to compute a hashcode for the `Map.Entry` object. With a set of `Map.Entry<>` objects you can obviously access the keys and the corresponding values using a collection-based `for` loop, and you can modify the value part of each key/value pair if you need to.

You have waded through a lot of the theory for `HashMap<>` objects; let's put together an example that applies it.

You can create a very simple phone book that uses a map. We won't worry too much about error recovery so as not to bulk up the code. You'll use a variation of the last version of the `Person` class that you saw earlier in this chapter in the example where you were sorting objects in a vector. Copy the source file to a new directory called `TryPhoneBook` or something similar. Besides the `Person` class, you need to create a `PhoneNumber` class and a `BookEntry` class that represents an entry in your phone book combining a name and a number. You could add other stuff such as the address, but this is not necessary to show the principles. You'll also define a `PhoneBook` class to represent the phone book.

<hr>

TRY IT OUT   Using a HashMap Map

You need to improve your old `Person` class to make `Person` objects usable as keys in the map that you use— to store the phone book entries. You must add an `equals()` method to do this, and you override the default `hashCode()` method just to show how this can work. The extended version of the class is as follows:

```java
import java.io.*;

public class Person implements Comparable<Person>, Serializable {
  @Override
  public boolean equals(Object person) {
    return compareTo((Person)person) == 0;
  }

  @Override
  public int hashCode() {
    return 7*firstName.hashCode()+13*surname.hashCode();
  }

  // The rest of the class as before...
  private static final long serialVersionUID = 1001L;
}
```

Directory "TryPhoneBook 1"

You've added to the previous version of the class two methods that override the `equals()` and `hashCode()` methods inherited from `Object` and defined `serialVersionUID` for the class. Because the `String` class defines a good `hashCode()` method, you can easily produce a hash code for a `Person` object from the data members. To implement the `equals()` method you just call the `compareTo()` method that you implemented for the `Comparable<>` interface. You have also made the class serializable just in case it comes in useful at some point.

There's another thing you can do that is definitely useful. You can add a `static` method to the `Person` class that reads data for a `Person` object from the keyboard:

```java
import java.io.*;

public class Person implements Comparable<Person>, Serializable {
  // Read a person from the keyboard
  public static Person readPerson() {
    String firstName = null;
    String surname = null;
    try {
      System.out.print("Enter first name: ");
      firstName = keyboard.readLine().trim();
      System.out.print("Enter surname: ");
      surname = keyboard.readLine().trim();
    } catch(IOException e) {
      System.err.println("Error reading a name.");
      e.printStackTrace();
      System.exit(1);
    }
    return new Person(firstName,surname);
```

```
    }

    // Rest of the class as before...
    private static BufferedReader keyboard = new BufferedReader(
                                    new InputStreamReader(System.in));
  }
```

Directory "TryPhoneBook 1"

You should have no trouble seeing how this works because it's almost identical to the readPerson() method that you used previously in this chapter.

You can make the PhoneNumber class very simple:

Available for download on Wrox.com

```
import java.io.*;

class PhoneNumber implements Serializable {
  public PhoneNumber(String areacode, String number) {
    this.areacode = areacode;
    this.number = number;
  }

  @Override
  public String toString() {
    return areacode + " " + number;
  }

  private String areacode;
  private String number;
  private static final long serialVersionUID = 1001L;
}
```

Directory "TryPhoneBook 1"

You could do a whole lot of validity checking of the number here, but it's not important for the example.

However, you could use a static method to read a number from the keyboard, so let's add that, too:

Available for download on Wrox.com

```
import java.io.*;

class PhoneNumber implements Serializable {
  // Read a phone number from the keyboard
  public static PhoneNumber readNumber() {
    String area = null;                              // Stores the area code
    String localcode = null;                         // Stores the local code
    try {
      System.out.print("Enter area code: ");
      area = keyboard.readLine().trim();
      System.out.print("Enter local code: ");
      localcode = keyboard.readLine().trim();
      System.out.print("Enter the number: ");
      localcode += " " + keyboard.readLine().trim();
    } catch(IOException e) {
      System.err.println("Error reading a phone number.");
      e.printStackTrace();
      System.exit(1);
    }
    return new PhoneNumber(area,localcode);
  }

  // Rest of the class as before...
  private static BufferedReader keyboard = new BufferedReader(
                                    new InputStreamReader(System.in));
}
```

Directory "TryPhoneBook 1"

This is again very similar to the `readPerson()` method. You don't need a separate variable to store the number that is entered. You just append the string that is read to `localcode`, with a space character inserted to make the output look nice. In practice, you certainly want to verify that the input is valid, but you don't need this to show how a hash map works.

An entry in the phone book combines the name and the number and probably includes other things such as the address. You can get by with the basics:

```java
import java.io.Serializable;

class BookEntry implements Serializable {
  public BookEntry(Person person, PhoneNumber number) {
    this.person = person;
    this.number = number;
  }

  public Person getPerson() {
    return person;
  }

  public PhoneNumber getNumber() {
    return number;
  }

  @Override
  public String toString() {
    return person.toString() + '\n' + number.toString();
  }

  // Read an entry from the keyboard
  public static BookEntry readEntry() {
    return new BookEntry(Person.readPerson(), PhoneNumber.readNumber());
  }

  private Person person;
  private PhoneNumber number;
  private static final long serialVersionUID = 1001L;
}
```

Directory "TryPhoneBook 1"

This is all pretty standard stuff. In the `static readEntry()` method, you just make use of the methods that create `Person` and `PhoneNumber` objects using input from the keyboard, so this becomes very simple.

The class that implements the phone book is next—called the `PhoneBook` class, of course:

```java
import java.io.Serializable;
import java.util.HashMap;

class PhoneBook implements Serializable {
  public void addEntry(BookEntry entry) {
    phonebook.put(entry.getPerson(), entry);
  }

  public BookEntry getEntry(Person key) {
    return phonebook.get(key);
  }

  public PhoneNumber getNumber(Person key) {
    BookEntry entry = getEntry(key);
    if(entry != null) {
    return entry.getNumber();
```

```
      } else {
        return null;
      }
  }

  private HashMap<Person,BookEntry> phonebook = new HashMap<>();
  private static final long serialVersionUID = 1001L;
}
```

Directory "TryPhoneBook 1"

To store `BookEntry` objects you use a `HashMap<Person, BookEntry>` member, `phonebook`. You use the `Person` object corresponding to an entry as the key, so the `addEntry()` method has to retrieve only the `Person` object from the `BookEntry` object that is passed to it and use that as the first argument to the `put()` method for `phonebook`.

All you need now is a class containing `main()` to test these classes:

Available for download on Wrox.com

```
public class TryPhoneBook {
  public static void main(String[] args) {
    PhoneBook book = new PhoneBook();                    // The phone book
    FormattedInput in = new FormattedInput();            // Keyboard input
    Person someone;
    while(true) {
      System.out.println("Enter 1 to enter a new phone book entry\n" +
                         "Enter 2 to find the number for a name\n" +
                         "Enter 9 to quit.");
      int what = 0;                                      // Stores input selection
      try {
        what = in.readInt();

      } catch(InvalidUserInputException e) {
        System.out.println(e.getMessage() + "\nTry again.");
        continue;
      }

      switch(what) {
        case 1:
          book.addEntry(BookEntry.readEntry());
          break;
        case 2:
          someone = Person.readPerson();
          BookEntry entry = book.getEntry(someone);
          if(entry == null) {
            System.out.println(
                          "The number for " + someone + " was not found.");
          } else {
            System.out.println(
                    "The number for " + someone + " is " + entry.getNumber());
          }
          break;
        case 9:
          System.out.println("Ending program.");
          return;
        default:
          System.out.println("Invalid selection, try again.");
          break;
      }
    }
  }
}
```

Directory "TryPhoneBook 1"

You're using the `FormattedInput` class that you developed in Chapter 8 to read the input values, so copy the source file for this class along with the source file for the `InvalidUserInputException` class, which is also from Chapter 8, to the directory for this example.

This is what the example produces with my input:

```
Enter 1 to enter a new phone book entry
Enter 2 to find the number for a name
Enter 9 to quit.
1
Enter first name: Algernon
Enter surname: Lickspittle
Enter area code: 914
Enter local code: 321
Enter the number: 3333
Enter 1 to enter a new phone book entry
Enter 2 to find the number for a name
Enter 9 to quit.
2
Enter first name: Algernon
Enter surname: Lickspittle
The number for Algernon Lickspittle is 914 321 3333
Enter 1 to enter a new phone book entry
Enter 2 to find the number for a name
Enter 9 to quit.
9
Ending program.
```

Of course, you can try it with several entries if you have the stamina.

How It Works

The values in the map that represents a phone book are `BookEntry` objects to allow for more information to be stored about a person. If you wanted to keep it really simple, you could use `PhoneNumber` objects as values in the map.

The `main()` method runs an ongoing loop that continues until a 9 is entered. When a 1 is entered, the `addEntry()` method for the `PhoneBook` object is called with the expression `BookEntry.readEntry()` as the argument. The `static` method `readEntry()` calls the `static` methods in the `Person` class and the `PhoneNumber` class to read from the keyboard and create objects of these classes. The `readEntry()` method then passes these objects to the constructor for the `BookEntry` class, and the object that is created is returned. This object is added to the `HashMap` member of the `PhoneBook` object.

If a 2 is entered, the `getEntry()` method is called. The `readPerson()` member of the `Person` class is called to obtain the `Person` object corresponding to the name entered from the keyboard. This object is then used to retrieve an entry from the map in the `PhoneBook` object. Of course, if there is no such entry `null` is returned, so you have to check for it and display an appropriate message.

`String` comparisons are case sensitive so searching for "algernon lickspittle" will not find an entry. You could convert both strings to the same case if you wanted to have comparisons that were not case sensitive.

TRY IT OUT   Storing a Map in a File

This phone book is not particularly useful. The process of echoing what you just keyed in doesn't hold one's interest for long. What you need is a phone book that is held in a file. That's not difficult. You just need to add a constructor and another method to the `PhoneBook` class:

```java
import java.nio.file.*;
import java.io.*;
import java.util.*;

class PhoneBook implements Serializable {
```

```java
public PhoneBook() {
  if(Files.exists(file)) {                        // If there's a phone book in a file...
    try (ObjectInputStream in = new ObjectInputStream(
                  new BufferedInputStream(Files.newInputStream(file)))){
      phonebook = (HashMap<Person, BookEntry>)in.readObject();    //...read it in.

    } catch(ClassNotFoundException| IOException e) {
      e.printStackTrace();
      System.exit(1);
    }
  }
}

public void save() {
  try {
    Files.createDirectories(file.getParent()); // Make sure we have the directory
  } catch (IOException e) {
    System.err.println("I/O error creating directory. " + e.getMessage());
    e.printStackTrace();
    System.exit(1);
  }
  try (ObjectOutputStream out = new ObjectOutputStream(
                    new BufferedOutputStream(Files.newOutputStream(file)))){
    System.out.println("Saving phone book");
    out.writeObject(phonebook);
    System.out.println("Done");
  } catch(IOException e) {
    System.err.println("I/O error saving phone book. " + e.getMessage());
    e.printStackTrace();
    System.exit(1);
  }
}
// Other members of the class as before...

private Path file = Paths.get(System.getProperty("user.home")).
                 resolve("Beginning Java Stuff").resolve("Phonebook.bin");}
```

Directory "TryPhoneBook 2"

The new private data member `file` defines the path for the file where the map holding the phone book entries is to be stored. The `file` object is used in the constructor that now reads the `HashMap<>` object from the file if it exists. If it doesn't exist, the constructor does nothing, and the `PhoneBook` object uses the default empty `HashMap` object. The cast of the reference returned by the `readObject()` method to type `HashMap<Person, BookEntry>` causes the compiler to issue a warning message to the effect that you have an unchecked cast. There is no way around this because the compiler cannot know what the type of the object that is read from the file is. Everything is fine as long as you know what you are doing!

The `save()` method provides for storing the map away, so you need to call this method before ending the program.

To make the program a little more interesting you could add a method to the `PhoneBook` class that lists all the entries in a phone book. Ideally, the entries should be displayed in alphabetical order by name. One way to do this would be to create a linked list containing the entries and use the static `sort()` method that the `Collections` class defines to sort them. The `sort()` method expects an argument that is of type `List<>`, where the type of elements in the list implements the `Comparable<>` interface. Thus, to be able to sort the entries in the phone book, the `BookEntry` class must implement the `Comparable<>` interface. This is quite easy to arrange:

```java
import java.io.Serializable;

class BookEntry implements Comparable<BookEntry>, Serializable {
  public int compareTo(BookEntry entry) {
    return person.compareTo(entry.getPerson());
```

```
      }
      // Rest of the class as before...
    }
```

Directory "TryPhoneBook 2"

When sorting the entries, you want the sort order of the `Person` objects to determine the sort order of the `BookEntry` objects. Because the `Person` class already implements the `Comparable<>` interface, you can implement the `compareTo()` method in the `BookEntry` class by calling the method for the `Person` object in the entry.

Now you can implement the `listEntries()` method in the `PhoneBook` class to list the entries in alphabetical order:

```
import java.nio.file.*;
import java.io.*;
import java.util.*;
class PhoneBook implements Serializable {
  // List all entries in the book
  public void listEntries() {
    // Get the entries as a linked list
    LinkedList<BookEntry> entries = new LinkedList<>(phonebook.values());
    Collections.sort(entries);                      // Sort the entries

    for(BookEntry entry : entries) {
      System.out.println(entry);
    }
  }
  // Other members as before...
}
```

Directory "TryPhoneBook 2"

Listing the entries in name sequence is relatively simple. Calling the `values()` method for the phonebook object returns the objects in the map, which are `BookEntry` objects, as a `Collection<>`. You pass this to the constructor for the `LinkedList<BookEntry>` class to obtain a list of entries. The `LinkedList<>` class implements the `List<>` interface, so you can pass the `entries` object to the `sort()` method to sort the values. It's then a simple matter of using the collection-based `for` loop to iterate through the sorted values to output them.

You can update `main()` to take advantage of the new features of the `PhoneBook` class:

```
public class TryPhoneBook2 {
  public static void main(String[] args) {
    PhoneBook book = new PhoneBook();                  // The phone book
    FormattedInput in = new FormattedInput();          // Keyboard input
    Person someone;

    while(true) {
      System.out.println("Enter 1 to enter a new phone book entry\n"+
                         "Enter 2 to find the number for a name\n"+
                         "Enter 3 to list all the entries\n" +
                         "Enter 9 to quit.");
      int what = 0;
      try {
        what = in.readInt();

      } catch(InvalidUserInputException e) {
        System.out.println(e.getMessage() + "\nTry again.");
        continue;
      }

      switch(what) {
        case 1:
```

```
            book.addEntry(BookEntry.readEntry());
            break;
        case 2:
            someone = Person.readPerson();
            BookEntry entry = book.getEntry(someone);
            if(entry == null) {
              System.out.println(
                            "The number for " + someone + " was not found.");
            } else {
              System.out.println(
                    "The number for " + someone + " is " + entry.getNumber());

            }
            break;
        case 3:
            book.listEntries();
            break;
        case 9:
            book.save();
            System.out.println("Ending program.");
            return;
        default:
            System.out.println("Invalid selection, try again.");
            break;
      }
    }
  }
}
```

Directory "TryPhoneBook 2"

How It Works

The first changes here are an updated prompt for input and a new case in the `switch` to list the entries in the phone book. The other change is to call the `save()` method to write the map that stores the phone book to a file before ending the program.

> **WARNING** Beware of the default `hashCode()` method in the `Object` class when storing maps in a file. As you know, the hashcodes are generated from the address of the object, so the hashcode for a key is entirely dependent on where it is stored in memory. Getting a key back from a file in exactly the same place in memory where it was originally stored is about as likely as finding hairs on a frog. The result is that when you read a map back from a file, the hashcode generated from a key you now use to access the map is different from what was originally produced when you stored the object with the key, so you will never find the entry in the map to which it corresponds.
>
> There is a solution to the problem. You must override the default `hashCode()` method so that the hashcodes for keys are produced from the data members of the key objects. This ensures that the hashcode for a given key is always the same. The `Person` class does exactly this by overriding the `hashCode()` method.

The first time you run `TryPhoneBook2` it creates a new file and stores the entire phone book in it. On subsequent occasions the `PhoneBook` constructor reads from the file, so all the previous entries are available.

In the next chapter you move on to look at some of the other components from the `java.util` package.

SUMMARY

All of the classes in this chapter will be useful sooner or later when you're writing your own Java programs. You apply many of them in examples throughout the remainder of the book. Collection classes have been implemented in other languages such as C++, so the concepts you have learned here about ways of storing and organizing objects applicability are applicable in other situations.

EXERCISES

You can download the source code for the examples in the book and the solutions to the following exercises from www.wrox.com.

1. Implement a version of the program to calculate prime numbers that you saw in Chapter 4 to use a `Vector<>` object instead of an array to store the primes. (Hint: Remember the `Integer` class.)

2. Write a program to store a deck of 52 cards in a linked list in random sequence using a `Random` class object. You can represent a card as a two-character string— `"1C"` for the ace of clubs, `"JD"` for the jack of diamonds, and so on. Output the cards from the linked list as four hands of 13 cards.

3. Extend the program from this chapter that used a map to store names and telephone numbers such that you can enter a number to retrieve the name.

4. Implement a phone book so that just a surname can be used to search and have all the entries corresponding to the name display.

▶ WHAT YOU LEARNED IN THIS CHAPTER

TOPIC	CONCEPT
Collections Framework	The Java collections framework provides you with a range of collection classes implemented as generic types. These enable you to organize your data in various ways.
EnumSet<E>	The EnumSet<> collection class enables you to aggregate one or more constants from a given enumeration type into a set so they can be passed to a method as a single argument.
Vector<T>	You can use a Vector<> object as a kind of flexible array that expands automatically to accommodate any number of objects stored.
ArrayList<T>	An ArrayList<> is very similar to a vector. The primary difference between them is that a Vector<> is thread-safe, whereas an ArrayList<> is not.
Stack<T>	The Stack<> class is derived from the Vector class and implements a pushdown stack.
HashMap<K, V>	The HashMap<> class defines a hash map in which objects are stored based on an associated key.
Iterators	An Iterator<> is an interface for retrieving objects from a collection sequentially. An Iterator<> object enables you to access all the objects it contains serially—but only once. There's no way to go back to the beginning.
List Iterators	The ListIterator<> interface provides methods for traversing the objects in a collection backward and forward.
Using Iterators	Objects stored in any type of collection can be accessed using Iterator<> objects.
Using List Iterators	Objects stored in a Vector<>, a Stack<>, or a LinkedList<> can be accessed using ListIterator<> objects.

15

A Collection of Useful Classes

WHAT YOU WILL LEARN IN THIS CHAPTER

➤ How to use the static methods in the `Arrays` class for filling, copying, comparing, sorting, and searching arrays

➤ How to use the `Observable` class and the `Observer` interface to communicate between objects

➤ What facilities the `Random` class provides

➤ How to create and use `Date` and `Calendar` objects

➤ What regular expressions are and how you can create and use them

➤ What a `Scanner` class does and how you use it

In this chapter you look at some more useful classes in the `java.util` package, but this time they are not collection classes—just a collection of classes. You also look at the facilities provided by classes in the `java.util.regex` package that implement regular expressions in Java. Support for regular expressions is a very powerful and important feature of Java.

UTILITY METHODS FOR ARRAYS

The `java.util.Arrays` class defines a set of static methods for operating on arrays. You have methods for sorting and searching arrays, as well as methods for comparing arrays of elements of a basic type. You also have methods for filling arrays with a given value. Let's look at the simplest method first, the `fill()` method for filling an array.

Filling an Array

The need to fill an array with a specific value arises quite often, and you already met the static `fill()` method that is defined in the `Arrays` class in Chapter 4. The `fill()` method comes in a number of overloaded versions of the form

```
fill(type[] array, type value)
```

Here `type` is a placeholder for the types supported by various versions of the method. The method stores `value` in each element of `array`. The return type is `void` so there is no return value. There are versions supporting `type` as any of the following:

boolean	byte	char	float	double
short	int	long	Object	

Here's how you could fill an array of integers with a particular value:

```
long[] values = new long[1000];
java.util.Arrays.fill(values, 888L);  // Every element as 888
```

It's quite easy to initialize multidimensional arrays, too. To initialize a two-dimensional array, for example, you treat it as an array of one-dimensional arrays. For example:

```
int[][] dataValues = new int[10][20];
for(int[] row : dataValues) {
  Arrays.fill(row, 99);
}
```

The for loop sets every element on the dataValues array to 99. The loop iterates over the 10 arrays of 20 elements that make up the dataValues array. If you want to set the rows in the array to different values, you could do it like this:

```
int initial = 0;
int[][] dataValues = new int[10][20];
for(int[] row : dataValues) {
  Arrays.fill(row, ++initial);
}
```

This results in the first row of 20 elements being set to 1, the second row of 20 elements to 2, and so on through to the last row of 20 elements that is set to 10.

The version of fill() that accepts an argument of type Object[] obviously processes an array of any class type. You could fill an array of Person objects like this:

```
Person[] people = new Person[100];
java.util.Arrays.fill(people, new Person("John", "Doe"));
```

This inserts a reference to the object passed as the second argument to the fill() method in every element of the people array. Note that there is only one Person object that all the array elements reference.

Another version of fill() accepts four arguments. This is of the form:

```
fill(type[] array, int fromIndex, int toIndex, type value)
```

This fills part of array with value, starting at array[fromIndex] up to and including array[toIndex-1]. There are versions of this method for the same range of types as the previous set of fill() methods. This variety of fill() throws an IllegalArgumentException if fromIndex is greater than toIndex. It also throws an ArrayIndexOutOfBoundsException if fromIndex is negative or toIndex is greater than array.length. Here's an example of using this form of the fill() method:

```
Person[] people = new Person[100];
java.util.Arrays.fill(people, 0, 50, new Person("Jane", "Doe"));
java.util.Arrays.fill(people, 50, 100, new Person("John", "Doe"));
```

This sets the first 50 elements to reference one Person object and the second 50 elements to reference another.

Copying an Array

You can copy an array of any type using the static copyOf() method in the Arrays class. Here's an example:

```
String[] decisions = {"yes", "no", "maybe", "definitely not"};
String[] copyDecisions = Arrays.copyOf(decisions, decisions.length);
```

copyDecisions references a new array that is returned by the copyOf() method that is a duplicate of decisions because the second argument specifies the same length as decisions. If the second argument to `copyOf()` is negative, a `NegativeArraySizeException` is thrown. If the first argument is `null`, a `NullPointerException` is thrown. Both exceptions have `RuntimeException` as a base class and therefore need not be caught.

You can arrange for the array copy to be truncated, or to have an increased number of elements by specifying a different value for the second argument. For example:

```
String[]copyDecisions1 = Arrays.copyOf(decisions, decisions.length - 2);
String[]copyDecisions2 = Arrays.copyOf(decisions, decisions.length + 5);
```

Here `copyDecisions1` has just two elements corresponding to the first two elements of `decisions`. The `copyDecisions2` array has nine elements. The first four are identical to that of the first argument, `decisions`, and the last five are set to `null`.

You can also create a new array from part of an existing array. For example:

```
String[]copyDecisions = Arrays.copyOfRange(decisions, 1, 3);
```

The new array that is created contains two elements, `"no"` and `"maybe"`. The second and third arguments specify the index values for the first element to be copied and one beyond the last element to be copied respectively. The second argument must be between zero and the length of the array that is the first argument, otherwise an `ArrayIndexOutOfBoundsException` is thrown. If the second argument is not less than the third argument, an `IllegalArgumentException` is thrown. The third argument can be greater than the length of the array being copied, in which case the excess elements are supplied as the equivalent of null — that is, `null` for an array containing objects and zero for numerical elements. If the first argument is `null`, a `NullPointerException` is thrown. All the exceptions that the `copyOfRange()` method can throw are subclasses of `RuntimeException` so you are not obliged to catch them.

Comparing Arrays

There are nine overloaded versions of the static `equals()` method for comparing arrays defined in the `Arrays` class, one for each of the types that apply to the `fill()` method. All versions of `equals()` are of the form:

```
boolean equals(type[] array1, type[] array2)
```

The method returns `true` if `array1` is equal to `array2` and `false` otherwise. The two arrays are equal if they contain the same number of elements and the values of all corresponding elements in the two arrays are equal. If `array1` and `array2` are both `null`, they are also considered to be equal.

When floating-point arrays are compared, `0.0` is considered to be equal to `-0.0`, and elements that contain NaN are also considered to be equal. Array elements of a class type are compared by calling their `equals()` method. If you have not implemented the `equals()` method in your own classes, then the version inherited from the `Object` class is used. This compares references, not objects, and so returns `true` only if both references refer to the same object.

Here's how you can compare two arrays:

```
String[] numbers = {"one", "two", "three", "four" };
String[] values = {"one", "two", "three", "four" };
if(java.util.Arrays.equals(numbers, values)) {
  System.out.println("The arrays are equal");
} else {
  System.out.println("The arrays are not equal");
}
```

In this fragment both arrays are equal so the `equals()` method returns `true`.

Sorting Arrays

The static `sort()` method in the `Arrays` class sorts the elements of an array that you pass as the argument into ascending sequence. The method is overloaded for eight of the nine types (`boolean` is excluded) you saw for the `fill()` method, for each of two versions of `sort()`:

```
void sort(type[] array)
void sort(type[] array, int fromIndex, int toIndex)
```

The first variety sorts the entire array into ascending sequence. The second sorts the elements from `array[fromIndex]` to `array[toIndex-1]` into ascending sequence. This throws an `IllegalArgumentException` if `fromIndex` is greater than `toIndex`. It throws an `ArrayIndexOutOfBoundsException` if `fromIndex` is negative or `toIndex` is greater than `array.length`.

You can pass an array of elements of any class type to the versions of the `sort()` method that have the first parameter as type `Object[]`. If you are using either variety of the `sort()` method to sort an array of objects, then the objects must support the `Comparable<>` interface because the `sort()` method uses the `compareTo()` method.

Here's how you can sort an array of strings:

```
String[] numbers = {"one", "two", "three", "four", "five",
                    "six", "seven", "eight"};
java.util.Arrays.sort(numbers);
```

After executing these statements, the elements of the `numbers` array contain:

```
"eight" "five" "four" "one" "seven" "six" "three" "two"
```

Two additional versions of the `sort()` method that sort arrays of objects are parameterized methods. These are for sorting arrays in which the order of elements is determined by an external comparator object. The class type of the comparator object must implement the `java.util.Comparator<>` interface. One advantage of using an external comparator is that you can have several comparators that can impose different orderings depending on the circumstances. For example, in some cases you might want to sort a name file ordering by first name within second name. On other occasions you might want to sort by second name within first name. You can't do this using the `Comparable<>` interface implemented by the class. The first version of the `sort()` method that makes use of a comparator is:

```
<T>void sort(T[] array, Comparator<? super T> comparator)
```

This sorts all the elements of `array` using the comparator you pass as the second argument.

The second version of the `sort()` method using a comparator is:

```
<T>void sort(T[] array, int fromIndex, int toIndex, Comparator<? super T>  comparator)
```

This sorts the elements of `array` from index position `fromIndex` up to but excluding the element at index position `toIndex`.

The wildcard parameter to the `Comparator<>` type specifies that the type argument to the comparator can be `T` or any superclass of `T`. This implies that the `sort()` method can sort an array of elements of type `T` using a `Comparator<>` object that can compare objects of type `T` or objects of any superclass of `T`. To put this in a specific context, this means that you can use an object of type `Comparator<Person>` to sort an array of objects of type `Manager`, where `Manager` is a subclass of `Person`.

The `Comparator<T>` interface declares two methods. First is the `compare()` method, which the `sort()` method uses for comparing elements of the array of type `T[]`. The method compares two objects of type `T` that are passed as arguments, so it's of the form:

```
int compare(T obj1, T obj2)
```

The method returns a negative integer, zero, or a positive integer, depending on whether obj1 is less than, equal to, or greater than obj2. The method throws a ClassCastException if the types of the argument you pass are such that they cannot be compared by the comparator.

The second method in the Comparator<T> interface is equals(), which is used for comparing Comparator<> objects for equality. The method is of the form:

```
boolean equals(Object comparator)
```

This compares the current Comparator<> object with another object of a type that also implements the Comparator<> interface that you pass as the argument. It returns a boolean value indicating whether the current comparator object and the argument impose the same ordering on a collection of objects. I think it would be a good idea to see how sorting using a Comparator<> object works in practice.

TRY IT OUT Sorting an Array Using a Comparator

You can borrow the version of the Person class that implements the Comparable<> interface from the TryVector example in Chapter 14 for this example. Copy the Person.java file to the directory you set up for this example. The comparator needs access to the first name and the surname for a Person object to make comparisons, so you need to add methods to the Person class to allow that:

Available for download on Wrox.com

```java
public class Person implements Comparable<Person> {
  public String getFirstName() {
    return firstName;
  }
  public String getSurname() {
    return surname;
  }
  // Rest of the class as before...
}
```

Directory "TrySortingWithComparator"

You can now define a class for a comparator that applies to Person objects:

Available for download on Wrox.com

```java
import java.util.Comparator;

public class ComparePersons implements Comparator<Person> {
  // Method to compare Person objects - order is descending
  public int compare(Person person1, Person person2) {
    int result = -person1.getSurname().compareTo(person2.getSurname());
    return result == 0 ?
           -person1.getFirstName().compareTo(person2.getFirstName()) : result;
  }

  // Method to compare with another comparator
  public boolean equals(Object comparator) {
    if(this == comparator) {          // If argument is the same object
      return true;                    // then it must be equal
    }
    if(comparator == null) {          // If argument is null
      return false;                   // then it can't be equal
    }
    // Class must be the same for equal
    return getClass() == comparator.getClass();
  }
}
```

Directory "TrySortingWithComparator"

Just to make it more interesting and to demonstrate that it's this comparator and not the `compareTo()` method in the `Person` class that's being used by the `sort()` method, this comparator establishes a descending sequence of `Person` objects. By switching the sign of the value that the `compareTo()` method returns, you invert the sort order. Thus, sorting using this comparator sorts `Person` objects in descending alphabetical order by surname and then by first name within surname.

You can try this out with the following program:

```java
import java.util.Arrays;

public class TrySortingWithComparator {
  public static void main(String[] args) {
    Person[] authors = {
      new Person("Danielle", "Steel"),    new Person("John", "Grisham"),
      new Person("Tom", "Clancy"),        new Person("Christina", "Schwartz"),
      new Person("Patricia", "Cornwell"), new Person("Bill", "Bryson")
                       };

    System.out.println("Original order:");
    for(Person author : authors) {
      System.out.println(author);
    }

    Arrays.sort(authors, new ComparePersons()); // Sort using comparator

    System.out.println("\nOrder after sorting using comparator:");
    for(Person author : authors) {
      System.out.println(author);
    }

    Arrays.sort(authors);                        // Sort using compareTo() method

    System.out.println("\nOrder after sorting using compareTo() method:");
    for(Person author : authors) {
      System.out.println(author);
    }
  }
}
```

Directory "TrySortingWithComparator"

This example produces the following output:

```
Original order:
Danielle Steel
John Grisham
Tom Clancy
Christina Schwartz
Patricia Cornwell
Bill Bryson

Order after sorting using comparator:
Danielle Steel
Christina Schwartz
John Grisham
Patricia Cornwell
Tom Clancy
Bill Bryson

Order after sorting using compareTo() method:
Bill Bryson
Tom Clancy
```

```
Patricia Cornwell
John Grisham
Christina Schwartz
Danielle Steel
```

How It Works

After defining the `authors` array of `Person` objects, you sort them with the statement:

```
Arrays.sort(authors, new ComparePersons());   // Sort using comparator
```

The second argument is an instance of the `ComparePersons` class, which is a comparator for `Person` objects because it implements the `Comparator<Person>` interface. The `sort()` method calls the `compare()` method to establish the order between `Person` objects, and you defined this method like this:

```
public int compare(Person person1, Person person2) {
    int result = -person1.getSurname().compareTo(person2.getSurname());
    return result == 0 ?
               -person1.getFirstName().compareTo(person2.getFirstName()):
               result;
}
```

The primary comparison is between surnames and returns a result that is the opposite of that produced by the `compareTo()` method for `String` objects. Because the order established by the `compareTo()` method is ascending, your `compare()` method establishes a descending sequence. If the surnames are equal, the order is determined by the first names, again inverting the sign of the value returned by the `compareTo()` method to maintain descending sequence. Of course, you could have coded this method by switching the arguments, `person1` and `person2`, instead of reversing the sign:

```
public int compare(Person person1, Person person2) {
    int result = person2.getSurname().compareTo(person1.getSurname());
    return result == 0 ?
               person2.getFirstName().compareTo(person1.getFirstName()) : result;
}
```

This would establish a descending sequence for `Person` objects.

You call the `sort()` method a second time with the statement:

```
Arrays.sort(authors);                          // Sort using compareTo() method
```

Because you have not supplied a comparator, the `sort()` method expects the class type of the elements to be sorted to have implemented the `Comparable<>` interface. Fortunately your `Person` class does, so the authors get sorted. This time the result is in ascending sequence because that's what the `compareTo()` method establishes.

Searching Arrays

The static `binarySearch()` method in the `Arrays` class searches the elements of a sorted array for a given value using the binary search algorithm. This works only if the elements of the array are in ascending sequence, so if they are not, you should call the `sort()` method before calling `binarySearch()`. The binary search algorithm works by repeatedly subdividing the sequence of elements to find the target element value, as illustrated in Figure 15-1.

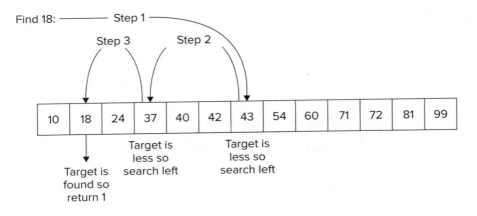

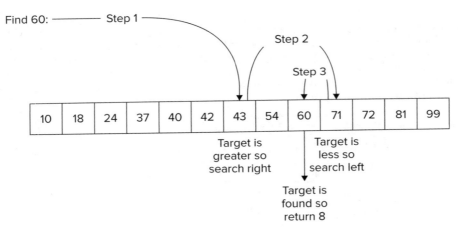

FIGURE 15-1

The figure shows two searches of an array of integers. The first step is always to compare the target with the element at the approximate center of the array. The second step is to examine the element at the approximate center of the left or right half of the array, depending on whether the target is less than or greater than the element. This process of subdividing and examining the element at the middle of the interval continues until the target is found, or the interval consists of a single element that is different from the target. When the target is found, the result is the index position of the element that is equal to the target. You should be able to see that the algorithm implicitly assumes that the elements are in ascending order.

You have eight overloaded versions of the `binarySearch()` method supporting the range of types that you saw with `fill()`:

```
binarySearch(type[] array, type value)
```

The second argument is the value you are searching for. You have an additional version of the method for searching an array of type `T[]` for which you can supply a reference to a `Comparator<? super T>` object as the third argument; the second argument is the value sought. You also have a version that will search a part of an array:

```
binarySearch(T[] array, int from, int to, T value, Comparator<? super T> c)
```

This searches the elements from `array[from]` to `array[to-1]` inclusive for `value`.

All versions of the `binarySearch()` method return a value of type `int` that is the index position in `array` where `value` was found. Of course, it is possible that the value is not in the array. In this case a negative integer is returned. This is produced by taking the value of the index position of the first element that is greater than the value, reversing its sign, and subtracting 1. For example, suppose you have an array of integers containing the element values 2, 4, 6, 8, and 10:

```
int[] numbers = {2, 4, 6, 8, 10};
```

You could search for the value 7 with the following statement:

```
int position = java.util.Arrays.binarySearch(numbers, 7);
```

The value of `position` is -4 because the element at index position 3 is the first element that is greater than 7. The return value is calculated as -3-1, which is -4. This mechanism guarantees that if the value sought is not in the array then the return value is always negative, so you can always tell whether a value is in the array by examining the sign of the result. The magnitude of the value returned when the search fails is the index position where you could insert the value you were looking for and still maintain the order of the elements in the array.

Unless you are using a method that uses a comparator for searching arrays of objects, the class type of the array elements must implement the `Comparable<>` interface. Here's how you could search for a string in an array of strings:

```
String[] numbers = {"one", "two", "three", "four", "five", "six", "seven"};

java.util.Arrays.sort(numbers);
int position = java.util.Arrays.binarySearch(numbers, "three");
```

You must sort the `numbers` array; otherwise, the binary search doesn't work. After executing these statements the value of `position` is 5.

TRY IT OUT   **In Search of an Author**

You could search the `authors` array from the previous example. Copy the source file for the `Person` class from the previous example to a new directory for this example. Here's the code to try a binary search:

Available for download on Wrox.com

```java
import java.util.Arrays;

public class TryBinarySearch {
  public static void main(String[] args) {
    Person[] authors = {
        new Person("Danielle", "Steel"), new Person("John", "Grisham"),
        new Person("Tom", "Clancy"),     new Person("Christina", "Schwartz"),
        new Person("Patricia", "Cornwell"), new Person("Bill", "Bryson")
                    };

    Arrays.sort(authors);                         // Sort using compareTo() method

    System.out.println("\nOrder after sorting into ascending sequence:");
    for(Person author : authors) {
      System.out.println(author);
    }

    // Search for authors
    Person[] people = {
        new Person("Christina", "Schwartz"), new Person("Ned", "Kelly"),
        new Person("Tom", "Clancy"),         new Person("Charles", "Dickens")
                    };
    int index = 0;
    System.out.println("\nIn search of authors:");
    for(Person person : people) {
```

```
      index = Arrays.binarySearch(authors, person);
      if(index >= 0) {
        System.out.println(person + " was found at index position " + index);
      } else {
        System.out.println(person + " was not found. Return value is " + index);
      }
    }
  }
}
```

Directory "TryBinarySearch"

This example produces the following output:

```
Order after sorting into ascending sequence:
Bill Bryson
Tom Clancy
Patricia Cornwell
John Grisham
Christina Schwartz
Danielle Steel

In search of authors:
Christina Schwartz was found at index position 4
Ned Kelly was not found. Return value is -5
Tom Clancy was found at index position 1
Charles Dickens was not found. Return value is -4
```

How It Works

You create and sort the authors array in the same way as you did in the previous example. The elements in the authors array are sorted into ascending sequence because you use the sort() method without supplying a comparator, and the Comparable<> interface implementation in the Person class imposes ascending sequence on objects.

You create the people array containing Person objects that might or might not be authors. You use the binarySearch() method to check whether the elements from the people array appear in the authors array in a loop:

```
for(Person person : people) {
  index = Arrays.binarySearch(authors, person);
  if(index >= 0) {
    System.out.println(person + " was found at index position " + index);
  } else {
    System.out.println(person + " was not found. Return value is " + index);
  }
}
```

The person variable references each of the elements in turn. If the person object appears in the authors array, the index is non-negative, and the first output statement in the if executes; otherwise, the second output statement executes. You can see from the output that everything works as expected.

Array Contents as a String

The Arrays class defines several static overloads of the toString() method that return the contents of an array you pass as the argument to the method as a String object. There are overloads of this method for each of the primitive types and for type Object. The string that the methods return is the string representation of each of the array elements separated by commas, between square brackets. This is very useful when you when to output an array in this way. For example:

```
int[] numbers = {1, 2, 3, 4, 5, 6, 7, 8, 9, 10, 11, 12};
System.out.println(Arrays.toString(numbers));
```

Executing this code fragment produces the output:

```
[1, 2, 3, 4, 5, 6, 7, 8, 9, 10, 11, 12]
```

For presenting a multidimensional array as a string, the `Arrays` class defines the static `deepToString()` method that has a parameter of type `Object[]`. The method works for arrays of any number of dimensions and array elements of any type, including primitive types. If the array elements are references, the string representation of the element is produced by calling its `toString()` method.

Here's an example:

```
String[][] folks = {
                    {"Ann", "Arthur",  "Arnie"},
                    { "Bill", "Barbara", "Ben", "Brenda", "Brian"},
                    {"Charles", "Catherine"}};
System.out.println(Arrays.deepToString(folks));
```

The output produced by this fragment is:

```
[[Ann, Arthur, Arnie], [Bill, Barbara, Ben, Brenda, Brian], [Charles, Catherine]]
```

OBSERVABLE AND OBSERVER OBJECTS

The `Observable` class provides an interesting mechanism for communicating a change in one class object to a number of other class objects. One use for this mechanism is in graphical user interface (GUI) programming where you often have one object representing all the data for the application—a text document, for example, or a geometric model of a physical object—and several other objects that represent views of the data displayed in separate windows, where each shows a different representation or perhaps a subset of the data. This is referred to as the *document/view architecture* for an application, or sometimes the *model/view architecture*. This is a contraction of something referred to as the model/view/controller architecture, and I come back to this when I discuss creating *GUIs*. The document/view terminology is applied to any collection of application data—geometry, bitmaps, or whatever. It isn't restricted to what is normally understood by the term *document*. Figure 15-2 illustrates the document/view architecture.

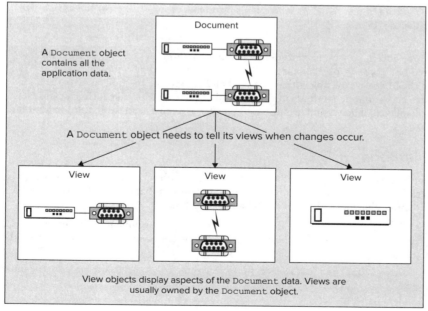

FIGURE 15-2

When the `Document` object changes, all the views need to be notified that a change has occurred, because they may well need to update what they display. The document is *observable*, and the views are *observers*. This is exactly what the `Observable` class is designed to achieve when used in combination with the `Observer` interface. A document can be considered to be an `Observable` object, and a view can be thought of as an `Observer` object. This enables a view to respond to changes in the document.

The document/view architecture portrays a many-to-many relationship. A document may have many observers, and a view may observe many documents.

Defining Classes of Observable Objects

You use the `java.util.Observable` class in the definition of a class of objects that may be observed. You simply derive the class for objects to be monitored—`Document`, say—from the `Observable` class.

Any class that may need to be notified when a `Document` object changes must implement the `Observer` interface. This doesn't in itself cause the `Observer` objects to be notified when a change in an observed object occurs; it just establishes the potential for this to happen. You need to do something else to link the observers to the observable, which I come to in a moment.

The definition of the class for observed objects could be of the form:

```
public class Document extends Observable {

  // Details of the class definitions...
}
```

The `Document` class inherits methods that operate the communications to the `Observer` objects from the `Observable` class.

A class for observers could be defined as the following:

```
public class View implements Observer {
  // Method for the interface
  public void update(Observable theObservableObject, Object arg) {
    // This method is called when the observed object changes
  }

  // Rest of the class definition...
}
```

To implement the `Observer` interface, you need to define just one method, `update()`. This method is called when an associated `Observable` object changes. The first argument that is passed to the `update()` method is a reference to the `Observable` object that changed and caused the method to be called. This enables the `View` object to access public methods in the associated `Observable` object that would be used to access the data to be displayed. The second argument to `update()` conveys additional information to the `Observer` object.

Observable Class Methods

The `Observable` class maintains an internal record of all the `Observer` objects related to the object to be observed. Your class, derived from `Observable`, inherits the data members that deal with this. Your class of observable objects also inherits nine methods from the `Observable` class:

➤   void addObserver(Observer o): Adds the object you pass as the argument to the internal record of observers. Only `Observer` objects in the internal record are notified when a change in the `Observable` object occurs.

➤   void deleteObserver(Observer o): Deletes the object you pass as the argument from the internal record of observers.

➤ void deleteObservers(): Deletes all observers from the internal record of observers.

➤ void notifyObservers(Object arg): Calls the update() method for all of the Observer objects in the internal record if the current object has been set as changed. The current object is set as changed by calling the setChanged() method. The current object and the argument passed to the notifyObservers() method are passed to the update() method for each Observer object. The clearChanged() method for the Observable is called to reset its status.

➤ void notifyObservers(): Calling this method is equivalent to calling the previous method with a null argument.

➤ int countObservers(): Returns the number of Observer objects for the current object.

➤ void setChanged(): Sets the current object as changed. You must call this method before calling the notifyObservers() method. Note that this method is protected.

➤ boolean hasChanged(): Returns true if the object has been set as changed and returns false otherwise.

➤ void clearChanged(): Resets the changed status of the current object to unchanged. Note that this method is also protected. This method is called automatically after notifyObservers() is called.

It's fairly easy to see how these methods are used to manage the relationship between an Observable object and its observers. To connect an observer to an Observable object, the Observer object must be registered with the Observable object by calling its addObserver() method. The Observer is then notified when changes to the Observable object occur. An Observable object is responsible for adding Observer objects to its internal record through the addObserver() method. In practice, the Observer objects are typically created as objects that are dependent on the Observable object, and then they are added to the record, so there's an implied ownership relationship.

This makes sense if you think about how the mechanism is often used in an application using the document/ view architecture. A document has permanence because it represents the data for an application. A view is a transient presentation of some or all of the data in the document, so a document object should naturally create and own its view objects. A view is responsible for managing the interface to the application's user, but the update of the underlying data in the document object would be carried out by methods in the document object, which would then notify other view objects that a change has occurred.

Of course, you're in no way limited to using the Observable class and the Observer interface in the way in which I described here. You can use them in any context where you want changes that occur in one class object to be communicated to others. We can exercise the process in a frightening example.

TRY IT OUT **Observing the Observable**

We first define a class for an object that can exhibit change:

```java
import java.util.Observable;

public class JekyllAndHyde extends Observable {
  public void drinkPotion() {
    name = "Mr.Hyde";
    setChanged();
    notifyObservers();
  }

  public String getName() {
    return name;
  }

  private String name = "Dr. Jekyll";
}
```

Directory "Horrific"

Now we can define the class of person who's looking out for this kind of thing:

```java
import java.util.Observer;
import java.util.Observable;

public class Person implements Observer {
  // Constructor
  public Person(String name, String says) {
    this.name = name;
    this.says = says;
  }

  // Called when observing an object that changes
  public void update(Observable thing, Object o) {
    System.out.println("It's " + ((JekyllAndHyde)thing).getName() +
                       "\n" + name + ": " + says);
  }

  private String name;                       // Person's identity
  private String says;                       // What they say when startled
}
```

Directory "Horrific"

We can gather a bunch of observers to watch Dr. Jekyll with the following class:

```java
// Try out observers
import java.util.Observer;

public class Horrific {
  public static void main(String[] args) {
    JekyllAndHyde man = new JekyllAndHyde();        // Create Dr. Jekyll

    Observer[] crowd = {
     new Person("Officer","What's all this then?"),
     new Person("Eileen Backwards", "Oh, no, it's horrible Ð those teeth!"),
     new Person("Phil McCavity", "I'm your local dentist Ð here's my card."),
     new Person("Slim Sagebrush", "What in tarnation's goin' on here?"),
     new Person("Freaky Weirdo", "Real cool, man. Where can I get that stuff?")
                        };

    // Add the observers
    for(Observer observer : crowd) {
      man.addObserver(observer);
    }
    man.drinkPotion();                              // Dr. Jekyll drinks up
  }
}
```

Directory "Horrific"

If you compile and run this, you should get the following output:

```
It's Mr.Hyde
Freaky Weirdo: Real cool, man. Where can I get that stuff?
It's Mr.Hyde
Slim Sagebrush: What in tarnation's goin' on here?
It's Mr.Hyde
Phil McCavity: I'm your local dentist - here's my card.
It's Mr.Hyde
Eileen Backwards: Oh, no, it's horrible - those teeth!
```

```
It's Mr.Hyde
Officer: What's all this then?
```

How It Works

JekyllAndHyde is a very simple class with just two methods. The drinkPotion() method encourages Dr. Jekyll to do his stuff and change into Mr. Hyde, and the getName() method enables anyone who is interested to find out who he now is. The class extends the Observable class, so you can add observers for a JekyllAndHyde object.

The revamped Person class implements the Observer interface, so an object of this class can observe an Observable object. When notified of a change in the object being observed, the update() method is called. Here, it just outputs who the person is and what he or she says.

In the Horrific class, after defining Dr. Jekyll in the variable man, you create an array, crowd, of type Observer[] to hold the observers—which are of type Person, of course. You can use an array of type Observer[] because the Person class implements the Observer interface. You pass two arguments to the Person class constructor: a name and a string indicating what the person says when he sees a change in Dr. Jekyll. You add each of the observers for the man object in the for loop.

Calling the drinkPotion() method for man causes the internal name to be changed, the setChanged() method to be called for the man object, and the notifyObservers() method that is inherited from the Observable class to be called. This results in the update() method for each of the registered observers being called, which generates the output. If you comment out the setChanged() call in the drinkPotion() method, and compile and run the program again, you get no output. Unless setChanged() is called, the observers aren't notified.

Now let's move on to look at the java.util.Random class.

GENERATING RANDOM NUMBERS

You have already used the Random class a little, but let's investigate this in more detail. The Random class enables you to create multiple random number generators that are independent of one another. Each object of the class is a separate random number generator. Any Random object can generate pseudo-random numbers of types int, long, float, or double. These numbers are created using an algorithm that takes a *seed* and *grows* a sequence of numbers from it. Initializing the algorithm twice with the same seed produces the same sequence because the algorithm is deterministic.

The integer values that are generated are uniformly distributed over the complete range for the type, and the floating-point values are uniformly distributed over the range 0.0 to 1.0 for both types. You can also generate numbers of type double with a *Gaussian* (or normal) distribution that has a mean of 0.0 and a standard deviation of 1.0. This is the typical bell-shaped curve that represents the probability distribution for many random events. Figure 15-3 illustrates the principle flavors of random number generators that you can define.

In addition to the methods shown in Figure 15-3, nextBoolean() returns either true or false with equal probability, and nextBytes() that fills the byte[] array you supply as the argument with a sequence of bytes with random values; NullPointerException is thrown if the argument is null.

There are two constructors for a Random object. The default constructor creates an object that uses the current time from your computer clock as the seed value for generating pseudo-random numbers. The other constructor accepts an argument of type long that is used as the seed.

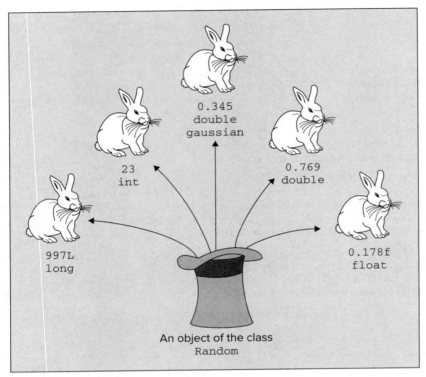

FIGURE 15-3

```
Random lottery = new Random();            // Sequence not repeatable
Random repeatable = new Random(997L);     // Repeatable sequence
```

If you use the default constructor, the sequence of numbers that is generated is different each time a program is run, although beware of creating two generators in the same program with the default constructor. The time resolution can be down to nanoseconds but it is only guaranteed to be no greater than 1 millisecond. If you create two objects in successive statements they may generate the same sequence because the times used for the starting seed values were identical.

Random objects that you create using the same seed always produce the same sequence, which can be very important when you are testing a program. Testing a program where the output is not repeatable can be a challenge! A major feature of random number generators you create using a given seed in Java is that not only do they always produce the same sequence of pseudo-random numbers, but they also do so on totally different computers.

Random Operations

The public methods provided by a Random object are the following:

➤ `int nextInt()`: Returns a pseudo-random number integer. Values are uniformly distributed across the range of possible values of type `int`.

➤ `int nextInt(int limit)`: Returns a pseudo-random number integer that is greater than or equal to 0, and less than `limit`—very useful for creating random array index values.

➤ `long nextLong()()`: The same as `nextInt()` except values are of type `long`.

➤ `float nextFloat()`: Returns a pseudo-random `float` value. Values are uniformly distributed across the range 0.0f to 1.0f, excluding 1.0f.

➤ `double nextDouble()`: Returns a pseudo-random number of type `double`. Values are uniformly distributed across the range 0.0 to 1.0, excluding 1.0.

➤ `double nextGaussian()`: Returns a pseudo-random number selected from a Gaussian distribution. Values generated have a mean of 0.0 and a standard deviation of 1.0.

➤ `void nextBytes(byte[] bytes)`: Fills the array, `bytes`, with pseudo-random values.

➤ `boolean nextBoolean()`: Returns a pseudo-random `boolean` value with `true` and `false` being equally probable.

➤ `void setSeed(long seed)`: Resets the random number generator to generate values using the value passed as an argument as a starting seed for the algorithm.

To produce a pseudo-random number of a particular type, you just call the appropriate method for a `Random` object. You can repeat a sequence of numbers that has been generated by a `Random` object with a given seed by calling the `setSeed()` method with the original seed value as the argument.

You can give the `Random` class an outing with a simple program that simulates throwing a pair of dice. The program allows you six throws to try to get a double six.

TRY IT OUT Using Random Objects

Here's the program:

Available for download on Wrox.com

```java
import java.util.Random;
import java.io.IOException;

public class Dice {
  public static void main(String[] args) {
    System.out.println("You have six throws of a pair of dice.\n" +
                "The objective is to get a double six. Here goes...\n");

    Random diceValues = new Random();              // Random number generator
    String[] goes = {"First",  "Second", "Third",
                    "Fourth", "Fifth",  "Sixth"};
    int die1 = 0;                                  // First die value
    int die2 = 0;                                  // Second die value

    for(String go : goes)  {
      die1 = 1 + diceValues.nextInt(6);            // Number from 1 to 6
      die2 = 1 + diceValues.nextInt(6);            // Number from 1 to 6
      System.out.println(go + " throw: " + die1 + ", " + die2);

      if(die1 + die2 == 12) {                      // Is it double 6?
        System.out.println("     You win!!");      // Yes !!!
        return;
      }
    }
    System.out.println("Sorry, you lost...");
    return;
  }
}
```

Dice.java

If you compile this program you should get output that looks something like this:

```
You have six throws of a pair of dice.
The objective is to get a double six. Here goes...

First throw: 3, 2
```

```
Second throw: 1, 1
Third throw: 1, 2
Fourth throw: 5, 3
Fifth throw: 2, 2
Sixth throw: 6, 4
Sorry, you lost...
```

How It Works

You use a random number generator that you create using the default constructor, so it is seeded with the current time and produces a different sequence of values each time the program is run. You simulate throwing the dice in the `for` loop. For each throw you need a random number between 1 and 6 to be generated for each die. The easiest way to produce this is to add 1 to the value returned by the `nextInt()` method when you pass 6 as the argument. If you want to make a meal of it, you could obtain the same result by using the following statement:

```
die1 = 1 + abs(diceValues.nextInt())%6;                    // Number from 1 to 6
```

Remember that the pseudo-random integer values that you get from the version of the `nextInt()` method you are using here is uniformly distributed across the whole range of possible values for type `int`, positive and negative. That's why you need to use the `abs()` method from the `Math` class here to make sure you end up with a positive die value. The remainder after dividing the value resulting from `abs(diceValues.nextInt())` by 6 is between 0 and 5. Adding 1 to this produces the result you want.

 NOTE *Remember that the odds against a double six are 36:1, so on average you only succeed once out of every six times you run the example.*

DATES AND TIMES

Quite a few classes in the `java.util` package are involved with dates and times, including the `Date` class, the `Calendar` class, and the `GregorianCalendar` class. In spite of the class name, a `Date` class object actually defines a particular instant in time to the nearest millisecond, measured from January 1, 1970, 00:00:00 GMT. Because it is relative to a particular instant in time, it also corresponds to a date. The `Calendar` class is the base class for `GregorianCalendar`, which represents the sort of day/month/year calendar everybody is used to and also provides methods for obtaining day, month, and year information from a `Date` object. A `Calendar` object is always set to a particular date—a particular instant on a particular date to be precise—but you can change it by various means. From this standpoint a `GregorianCalendar` object is more like one of those desk calendars that just show one date, and you can flip over the days, months, or years to show another date.

You also have the `TimeZone` class that defines a time zone that can be used in conjunction with a calendar and that you can use to specify the rules for clock changes due to daylight saving time. The ramifications of handling dates and times are immense so you are only able to dabble here, but at least you get the basic ideas. Let's look at `Date` objects first.

The Date Class

A `Date` class object represents a given date and time. You have two `Date` constructors:

➤ `Date()` creates an object based on the current time of your computer clock to the nearest millisecond.

➤ `Date(long time)` creates an object based on `time`, which is the number of milliseconds since 00:00:00 GMT on January 1, 1970.

With either constructor, you create an object that represents a specific instant in time to the nearest millisecond. Carrying dates around as the number of milliseconds since the dawn of the year 1970 won't grab you as being incredibly user-friendly—but I come back to how you can better interpret a Date object in a moment. The Date class provides three methods for comparing objects that return a boolean value:

➤ after(Date earlier) returns true if the current object represents a date that's later than the date represented by the argument and returns false otherwise.

➤ before(Date later) returns true if the current object represents a date that's earlier than the date represented by the argument and returns false otherwise.

➤ equals(Object aDate) returns true if the current object and the argument represent the same date and time and returns false otherwise.

The Date class implements the Comparable<Date> interface so you have the compareTo() method available. As you've seen in other contexts, this method returns a negative integer, zero, or a positive integer depending on whether the current object is less than, equal to, or greater than the argument. The presence of this method in the class means that you can use the sort() method in the Arrays class to sort an array of Date objects, or the sort() method in the Collections class to sort a collection of dates. Because the hashCode() method is also implemented for the class, you have all you need to use Date objects as keys in a hash map.

Interpreting Date Objects

The DateFormat class is an abstract class that you can use to create meaningful String representations of Date objects. It isn't in the java.util package though—it's defined in the package java.text. You have four standard representations for the date and the time that are identified by constants defined in the DateFormat class. The effects of these vary in different countries, because the representation for the date and the time reflects the conventions of those countries. The constants in the DateFormat class defining the four formats are shown in Table 15-1.

TABLE 15-1: Date Formats

DATE FORMAT	DESCRIPTION
SHORT	A completely numeric representation for a date or a time, such as 2/2/97 or 4:15 a.m.
MEDIUM	A longer representation than SHORT, such as 5-Dec-97
LONG	A longer representation than MEDIUM, such as December 5, 1997
FULL	A comprehensive representation of the date or the time such as Friday, December 5, 1997 AD or 4:45:52 PST (Pacific Standard Time)

A java.util.Locale object identifies information that is specific to a country, a region, or a language. You can define a Locale object for a specific country, for a specific language, for a country and a language, or for a country and a language and a variant, the latter being a vendor- or browser-specific code such as WIN or MAC. When you are creating a Locale object, you use ISO codes to specify the language or the country (or both). The language codes are defined by ISO-639. Countries are specified by the country codes in the standard ISO-3166. You can find the country codes on the Internet at www.iso.org/iso/country_codes.

You can also get a list of the country codes as an array of String objects by calling the static getISOCountries() method. For example:

```
String[] countryCodes = java.util.Locale.getISOCountries();
```

You can find the language codes at www.loc.gov/standards/iso639-2/php/English_list.php.

You can also get the language codes that are defined by the standard in a String object:

```
String[] languages = java.util.Locale.getISOLanguages();
```

For some countries, the easiest way to specify the locale, if you don't have the ISO codes on the tip of your tongue, is to use one of the static `Locale` objects defined within the `Locale` class:

US	CANADA	CANADA_FRENCH	PRC
UK	GERMANY	FRANCE	ITALY
JAPAN	KOREA	CHINA	TAIWAN

The `Locale` class also defines static `Locale` objects that represent languages:

CHINESE	ENGLISH	FRENCH	GERMAN
ITALIAN	JAPANESE	KOREAN	
SIMPLIFIED_CHINESE		TRADITIONAL_CHINESE	

Because the `DateFormat` class is `abstract`, you can't create objects of the class directly, but you can obtain `DateFormat` objects by using static methods that are defined in the class, each of which returns a value of type `DateFormat`. A `DateFormat` object encapsulates a `Locale` and an integer date style. The style is defined by one of the constants defined in the `DateFormat` class, `SHORT`, `MEDIUM`, `LONG`, or `FULL` that you saw earlier.

Each `Locale` object has a default style that matches conventions that apply for the country or language it represents.

You can create `DateFormat` instances that can format a `Date` object as a time, as a date, or as a date and a time. The static methods that create `DateFormat` objects of various kinds are `getTimeInstance()` that returns a time formatter, `getDateInstance()` that returns a date formatter, and `getDateTimeInstance()` that returns an object that can format the date and the time. The first two come in three flavors, a no-arg version where you get a formatter for the default locale and style, a single argument version where you supply the style for the default locale, and a version that accepts a style argument and a `Locale` argument. The `getDateTimeInstance()` also comes in three versions, the no-arg version that creates a formatter for the default locale and the default date and time style, a version where you supply two arguments that are the date style and the time style, and a version that requires three arguments that are the date style, the time style, and a `Locale` object for the locale.

When you've obtained a `DateFormat` object for the country and the style that you want, and the sort of data you want to format—the date or the time or both—you're ready to produce a `String` from the `Date` object.

You just pass the `Date` object to the `format()` method for the `DateFormat` object. For example:

```
Date today = new Date();                   // Object for now - today's date
DateFormat fmt = DateFormat.getDateTimeInstance(DateFormat.FULL,  // Date style
                                                DateFormat.FULL,  // Time style
                                                Locale.US);       // Locale

String formatted = fmt.format(today);
```

The first statement creates a `Date` object that represents the instant in time when the call to the `Date` constructor executes. The second statement creates a `DateFormat` object that can format the date and time encapsulated by a `Date` object. In this case you specify the formatting style for the data and the time to be the same, the `FULL` constant in the `DateFormat` class. This provides the most detailed specification of the date and time. The third argument, `Locale.US`, determines that the formatting should correspond to that required for the United States. The `Locale` class defines constants for other major countries and languages. The third statement applies the `format()` method of the `fmt` object to the `Date` object. After executing these statements, the `String` variable `formatted` contains a full representation of the date and the time when the `Date` object `today` was created.

You can try out some dates and formats in an example.

TRY IT OUT   Producing Dates and Times

This example shows the four different date formats for four countries:

```
// Trying date formatting
import java.util.Locale;
import java.text.DateFormat;
import java.util.Date;
import static java.util.Locale.*;          // Import names of constants
import static java.text.DateFormat.*;      // Import names of constants

public class TryDateFormats {
  public enum Style {FULL, LONG, MEDIUM, SHORT}

  public static void main(String[] args) {
    Date today = new Date();
    Locale[] locales = {US, UK, GERMANY, FRANCE};

    // Output the date for each locale in four styles
    DateFormat fmt = null;
    for(Locale locale : locales) {
      System.out.println("\nThe Date for " +
                           locale.getDisplayCountry() + ":");
      for (Style style : Style.values()) {
        fmt = DateFormat.getDateInstance(style.ordinal(), locale);
        System.out.println( "  In " + style +
                            " is " + fmt.format(today));
      }
    }
  }
}
```

TryDateFormats.java

When I compiled and ran this it produced the following output:

```
The Date for United States:
  In FULL is Monday, June 27, 2011
  In LONG is June 27, 2011
  In MEDIUM is Jun 27, 2011
  In SHORT is 6/27/11

The Date for United Kingdom:
  In FULL is Monday, 27 June 2011
  In LONG is 27 June 2011
  In MEDIUM is 27-Jun-2011
  In SHORT is 27/06/11

The Date for Germany:
  In FULL is Montag, 27. Juni 2011
  In LONG is 27. Juni 2011
  In MEDIUM is 27.06.2011
  In SHORT is 27.06.11

The Date for France:
  In FULL is lundi 27 juin 2011
  In LONG is 27 juin 2011
  In MEDIUM is 27 juin 2011
  In SHORT is 27/06/11
```

How It Works

By statically importing the constants from the `Locale` and `DateFormat` classes, you obviate the need to qualify the constants in the program and thus make the code a little less cluttered. The nested `Styles` enum defines the four possible styles. The program creates a `Date` object for the current date and time and an array of `Locale` objects for four countries using values defined in the `Locale` class.

The output is produced in the nested `for` loops. The outer loop iterates over the countries, and the inner loop is a collection-based for loop that iterates over the styles for each country in the `Styles` enum. The `ordinal()` method for an enum value returns the ordinal for the value in the enumeration. You use this to specify the style as the first argument to the `getDateInstance()` method. A `DateFormat` object is created for each style and country combination. Calling the `format()` method for the `DateFormat` object produces the date string in the inner call to `println()`.

You could change the program in a couple ways. You could initialize the `locales[]` array with `DateFormat.getAvailableLocales()`. This returns an array of type `Locale` containing all of the supported locales, but be warned—there are a lot of them. You may find that the characters won't display for some countries because your machine doesn't support the country-specific character set. You could also use the method `getTimeInstance()` or `getDateTimeInstance()` instead of `getDateInstance()` to see what sort of output they generate.

Under the covers, a `DateFormat` object contains a `DateFormatSymbols` object that contains all the strings for the names of days of the week and other fixed information related to time and dates. This class is also in the `java.text` package. Normally you don't use the `DateFormatSymbols` class directly, but it can be useful when all you want are the days of the week.

Obtaining a Date Object from a String

The `parse()` method for a `DateFormat` object interprets a `String` object argument as a date and time, and returns a `Date` object corresponding to the date and the time. The `parse()` method throws a `ParseException` if the `String` object can't be converted to a `Date` object, so you must call it within a `try` block.

The `String` argument to the `parse()` method must correspond to the country and style that you used when you obtained the `DateFormat` object. For example, the following code parses the string properly:

```
Date aDate;
DateFormat fmt = DateFormat.getDateInstance(DateFormat.FULL, Locale.US);
try {
  aDate = fmt.parse("Saturday, July 4, 1998 ");
  System.out.println("The Date string is: " + fmt.format(aDate));

} catch(java.text.ParseException e) {
  System.out.println(e);
}
```

This works because the string is what would be produced by the locale and style. If you omit the day from the string, or you use the `LONG` style or a different locale, a `ParseException` is thrown.

Gregorian Calendars

The Gregorian calendar is the calendar generally in use today in the western world and is represented by an object of the `GregorianCalendar` class. A `GregorianCalendar` object encapsulates time zone information, as well as date and time data. You have no less than seven constructors for `GregorianCalendar` objects, from the default that creates a calendar with the current date and time in the default locale for your machine through to a constructor specifying the year, month, day, hour, minute, and second. The default suits most situations:

```
GregorianCalendar calendar = new GregorianCalendar();
```

This object is set to the current instant in time, and you can access this as a `Date` object by calling its `getTime()`:

```
Date now = calendar.getTime();
```

You can create a `GregorianCalendar` object encapsulating a specific date and/or time with any of the following constructors:

```
GregorianCalendar(int year, int month, int day)
GregorianCalendar(int year, int month, int day, int hour, int minute)
GregorianCalendar(int year, int month, int day, int hour, int minute, int second)
```

The `day` argument is the day within the month, so the value can be from 1 to 28, 29, 30, or 31, depending on the month and whether it's a leap year or not. The `month` value is zero-based so January is 0 and December is 11.

The `GregorianCalendar` class is derived from the abstract `Calendar` class from which it inherits a large number of methods and static constants for use with these methods. The constants include month values with the names JANUARY to DECEMBER so you could create a calendar object with the statement:

```
GregorianCalendar calendar = new GregorianCalendar(1967, Calendar.MARCH, 10);
```

If you statically import the constant members of the `GregorianCalendar` class you are able to use constants such as MARCH and DECEMBER without the need to qualify them with the class name. The time zone and locale is the default for the computer on which this statement executes. If you want to specify a time zone, there is a GregorianCalendar constructor that accepts an argument of type `java.util.TimeZone`. You can get the default `TimeZone` object by calling the static `getDefault()` method, but if you are going to the trouble of specifying a time zone, you probably want something other than the default. To create a particular time zone you need to know its ID. This is a string specifying a region or country plus a location. For example, here are some examples of time zone IDs:

`"Europe/Stockholm"`	`"Asia/Novosibirsk"`
`"Pacific/Guam"`	`"Antarctica/Palmer"`
`"Atlantic/South_Georgia"`	`"Africa/Accra"`
`"America/Chicago"`	`"Europe/London"`

To obtain a reference to a `TimeZone` object corresponding to a given time zone ID, you pass the ID to the static `getTimeZone()` method. For example, we could create a `Calendar` object for the Chicago time zone like this:

```
GregorianCalendar calendar =
        new GregorianCalendar(TimeZone.getTimeZone("America/Chicago"));
```

If you want to know what all the time zones IDs are, you could list them like this:

```
String[] ids = TimeZone.getAvailableIDs();
for(String id : ids) {
  System.out.println(id);
}
```

Be prepared for a lot of output though. There are well more 500 time zone IDs.

The calendar created from a `TimeZone` object has the default locale. If you want to specify the locale explicitly, you have a constructor that accepts a `Locale` reference as the second argument. For example:

```
GregorianCalendar calendar =
        new GregorianCalendar(TimeZone.getTimeZone("America/Chicago"), Locale.US);
```

You can also create a `Calendar` object from a locale:

```
GregorianCalendar calendar = new GregorianCalendar(Locale.UK);
```

This creates a calendar set to the current time in the default time zone within the UK.

Setting the Date and Time

If you have a `Date` object available, you can pass it to the `setTime()` method for a `GregorianCalendar` object to set it to the time specified by the `Date` object:

```
GregorianCalendar calendar = new GregorianCalendar();
calendar.setTime(date);
```

More typically you will want to set the date and/or time with explicit values such as day, month, and year, and you have several overloaded versions of the `set()` method for setting various components of the date and time. These are inherited in the `GregorianCalendar` class from its superclass, the `Calendar` class. You can set a `GregorianCalendar` object to a particular date like this:

```
GregorianCalendar calendar = new GregorianCalendar();
calendar.set(1995, 10, 29);                    // Date set to 29th November 1995
```

The three arguments to the `set()` method here are the year, the month, and the day as type `int`. You need to take care with this method because it's easy to forget that the month is zero-based, with January specified by 0. Note that the fields reflecting the time setting within the day are not changed. They remain at whatever they were. You can reset all fields for a `GregorianCalendar` object to undefined by calling its `clear()` method.

The other versions of the `set()` method are:

```
set(int year, int month, int day, int hour, int minute)
set(int year, int month, int day, int hour, int minute, int second)
set(int field, int value)
```

It's obvious what the first two of these do. In each case the fields not explicitly set are left at their original values. The third version of `set()` sets a field specified by one of the integer constants defined in the `Calendar` class for this purpose (shown in Table 15-2):

TABLE 15-2: Calendar Field Setting Options

FIELD	VALUE
AM_PM	Can have the values AM or PM, which correspond to values of 0 and 1
DAY_OF_WEEK	Can have the values SUNDAY, MONDAY, and so on, through to SATURDAY, which correspond to values of 1 to 7
DAY_OF_WEEK_IN_MONTH	Ordinal number for the day of the week in the current month.
DAY_OF_YEAR	Can be set to a value from 1 to 366
MONTH	Can be set to a value of JANUARY, FEBRUARY, and so on, through to DECEMBER, corresponding to values of 0 to 11
DAY_OF_MONTH or DATE	Can be set to a value from 1 to 31
WEEK_OF_MONTH	Can be set to a value from 1 to 6
WEEK_OF_YEAR	Can be set to a value from 1 to 54
HOUR_OF_DAY	A value from 0 to 23
HOUR	A value from 1 to 12 representing the current hour in the a.m. or p.m.
MINUTE	The current minute in the current hour—a value from 0 to 59
SECOND	The second in the current minute, 0 to 59
MILLISECOND	The millisecond in the current second, 0 to 999
YEAR	The current year—for example, 2011
ERA	Can be set to either `GregorianCalendar.BC` or `GregorianCalendar.AD` (both values being defined in the `GregorianCalendar` class)

FIELD	VALUE
`ZONE_OFFSET`	A millisecond value indicating the offset from GMT
`DST_OFFSET`	A millisecond value indicating the offset for daylight saving time in the current time zone

Qualifying the names of these constants with the class name `GregorianCalendar` can make the code look cumbersome but you can use static import for the constants to simplify things:

```
import static java.util.Calendar.*;
import static java.util.GregorianCalendar.*;
```

The static `import` statement imports only the names of static data members that are defined in a class, not the names of inherited members. Therefore, you need two `import` statements if you want access to all the constants you can use with the `GregorianCalendar` class.

With these two `import` statements in effect, you can write statements like this:

```
GregorianCalendar calendar = new GregorianCalendar();
calendar.set(DAY_OF_WEEK, TUESDAY);
```

Getting Date and Time Information

You can get information such as the day, the month, and the year from a `GregorianCalendar` object by using the `get()` method and specifying what you want by the argument. The possible arguments to the `get()` method are those defined in the earlier table of constants identifying calendar fields. All values returned are of type `int`. For example, you could get the day of the week with the statement:

```
int day = calendar.get(calendar.DAY_OF_WEEK);
```

You could now test this for a particular day using the constants defined in the class:

```
if(day == calendar.SATURDAY)
    // Go to game...
```

Because the values for `day` are integers, you could equally well use a `switch` statement:

```
switch(day) {
  case Calendar.MONDAY:
  // do the washing...
  break;
  case Calendar.TUESDAY:
  // do something else...
  break;
  // etc...
}
```

Modifying Dates and Times

Of course, you might want to alter the current instant in the calendar, and for this you have the `add()` method. The first argument determines what units you are adding in, and you specify this argument using the same field designators as in the previous list. For example, you can add 14 to the year with the statement:

```
calendar.add(calendar.YEAR, 14);  // 14 years into the future
```

To go into the past, you just make the second argument negative:

```
calendar.add(calendar.MONTH, -6);  // Go back 6 months
```

You can increment or decrement a field of a calendar by 1 using the `roll()` method. This method modifies the field specified by the first argument by +1 or –1, depending on whether the second argument is `true` or `false`. For example, to decrement the current month in the object `calendar`, you would write the following:

```
calendar.roll(calendar.MONTH, false);  // Go back a month
```

The change can affect other fields. If the original month were January, rolling it back by one would make the date December of the previous year.

Another version of the `roll()` method allows you to roll a field by a specified signed integer amount as the second argument. A negative value rolls down and a positive value rolls up.

Of course, having modified a `GregorianCalendar` object, you can get the current instant back as a `Date` object using the `getTime()` method that we saw earlier. You can then use a `DateFormat` object to present this in a readable form.

Comparing Calendars

Checking the relationship between dates represented by `Calendar` objects is a fairly fundamental requirement and you have four methods available for comparing them (shown in Table 15-3):

TABLE 15-3: Methods for Comparing Calendar Objects

METHOD	DESCRIPTION
`before()`	Returns `true` if the current object corresponds to a time before that of the `Calendar` object passed as an argument. Note that this implies a `true` return can occur if the date is the same but the time is different.
`after()`	Returns `true` if the current object corresponds to a time after that of the `Calendar` object passed as an argument.
`equals()`	Returns `true` if the current object corresponds to a time that is identical to that of the `Calendar` object passed as an argument.
`compareTo(Calendar c)`	Returns a value of type `int` that is negative, zero, or positive depending on whether the time value for the current object is less than, equal to, or greater than the time value for the argument.

These are very simple to use. To determine whether the object `thisDate` defines a time that precedes the time defined by the object `today`, you could write:

```
if(thisDate.before(today)) {
   // Do something...
}
```

Alternatively you could write the same thing as:

```
if(today.after(thisDate)) {
   // Do something...
}
```

It's time to look at how we can use calendars.

TRY IT OUT   Using a Calendar

This example deduces important information about when you were born. It uses the `FormattedInput` class from Chapter 8 to get input from the keyboard, so copy this class and the source file for the `InvalidUserInputException` class to a new directory for the source files for this example. Here's the code:

Available for download on Wrox.com

```
import java.util.GregorianCalendar;
import java.text.DateFormatSymbols;
import static java.util.Calendar.*;

class TryCalendar {
  public static void main(String[] args) {
    FormattedInput in = new FormattedInput();

    // Get the date of birth from the keyboard
    int day = 0, month = 0, year = 0;
```

```
      System.out.println("Enter your birth date as dd mm yyyy: ");
      try {
        day = in.readInt();
        month = in.readInt();
        year = in.readInt();
      } catch(InvalidUserInputException e) {
        System.out.println("Invalid input - terminating...");
        System.exit(1);
      }

      // Create birth date calendar - month is 0 to 11
      GregorianCalendar birthdate = new GregorianCalendar(year, month-1,day);
      GregorianCalendar today = new GregorianCalendar();          // Today's date

      // Create this year's birthday
      GregorianCalendar birthday = new GregorianCalendar(
                                     today.get(YEAR),
                                     birthdate.get(MONTH),
                                     birthdate.get(DATE));

      int age = today.get(YEAR) - birthdate.get(YEAR);

      String[] weekdays = new DateFormatSymbols().getWeekdays(); // Get day names

      System.out.println("You were born on a " +
                          weekdays[birthdate.get(DAY_OF_WEEK)]);
      System.out.println("This year you " +
                          (birthday.after(today)    ?"will be " : "are ") +
                          age + " years old.");
      System.out.println("In " + today.get(YEAR) + " your birthday " +
                          (today.before(birthday)? "will be": "was") +
                          " on a "+ weekdays[birthday.get(DAY_OF_WEEK)] +".");
    }
  }
```

TryCalendar.java

I got the following output:

```
Enter your birth date as dd mm yyyy:
05 12 1974
You were born on a Thursday
This year you will be 37 years old.
In 2011 your birthday will be on a Monday.
```

How It Works

You start by prompting for the day, month, and year for a date of birth to be entered through the keyboard as integers. You then create a `GregorianCalendar` object corresponding to this date. Note the adjustment of the month—the constructor expects January to be specified as 0. You need a `GregorianCalendar` object for today's date so you use the default constructor for this. To compute the age this year, you just have to subtract the year of birth from this year, both of which you get from the `GregorianCalendar` objects.

To get at the strings for the days of the week, you create a `DateFormatSymbols` object and call its `getWeekdays()` method. This returns an array of eight `String` objects, the first of which is empty to make it easy to index using day numbers from 1 to 7. The second element in the array contains `"Sunday"`. You can also get the month names using the `getMonths()` method.

To display the day of the week for the date of birth, you call the `get()` method for the `GregorianCalendar` object `birthdate` and use the result to index the `weekdays[]` array. To determine the appropriate text in the next two output statements, you use the `after()` and `before()` methods for `Calendar` objects to compare today with the birthday date this year.

REGULAR EXPRESSIONS

You saw some elementary capability for searching strings when I discussed the `String` class in Chapter 4. You have much more sophisticated facilities for analyzing strings using search patterns known as *regular expressions*. Regular expressions are not unique to Java. Perl is perhaps better known for its support of regular expressions and C++ supports them too. Many word processors, especially on UNIX, support regular expressions, and there are specific utilities for regular expressions, too. Many IDEs such as JCreator and Microsoft Visual Studio also support regular expressions.

So what is a regular expression? A regular expression is simply a string that describes a pattern that you use to search for matches within some other string. It's not simply a passive sequence of characters to be matched, though. A regular expression is essentially a mini-program for a specialized kind of computer called a *state-machine*. This isn't a real machine but a piece of software specifically designed to interpret a regular expression and analyze a given string based on the operations implicit in a regular expression.

The regular expression capability in Java is implemented through two classes in the `java.util.regex` package: the `Pattern` class, which defines objects that encapsulate regular expressions, and the `Matcher` class, which defines an object that encapsulates a state-machine that can search a particular string using a given `Pattern` object. The `java.util.regex` package also defines the `PatternSyntaxException` class, which defines exception objects that are thrown when a syntax error is found when compiling a regular expression to create a `Pattern` object.

Using regular expressions in Java is basically very simple:

1. You create a `Pattern` object by passing a string containing a regular expression to the static `compile()` method in the `Pattern` class.

2. You then obtain a `Matcher` object, which can search a given string for the pattern, by calling the `matcher()` method for the `Pattern` object with the string that is to be searched as the argument.

3. You call the `find()` method (or some other methods, as you later see) for the `Matcher` object to search the string.

4. If the pattern is found, you query the `Matcher` object to discover the whereabouts of the pattern in the string and other information relating to the match.

Although this is a straightforward process that is easy to code, the hard work is in defining the pattern to achieve the result that you want. This is an extensive topic because in their full glory regular expressions are immensely powerful and can be very complicated. There are books devoted entirely to this, so my aim is to give you enough of a bare-bones understanding of how regular expressions work that you are in a position to look into the subject in more depth if you need to. Although regular expressions can look quite fearsome, don't be put off. They are always built step-by-step, so although the result may look complicated and obscure, they are not necessarily difficult to put together. Regular expressions are a lot of fun and a sure way to impress your friends and maybe confound your enemies.

Defining Regular Expressions

You may not have heard of regular expressions before reading this book and, therefore, may think you have never used them. If so, you are almost certainly wrong. Whenever you search a directory for files of a particular type, `"*.java"`, for example, you are using a form of regular expression. However, to say that regular expressions can do much more than this is something of an understatement. To get an understanding of what you can do with regular expressions, you start at the bottom with the simplest kind of operation and work your way up to some of the more complex problems they can solve.

Creating a Pattern

In its most elementary form, a regular expression just does a simple search for a substring. For example, if you want to search a string for the word *had*, the regular expression is exactly that. The string that defines this particular regular expression is `"had"`. Let's use this as a vehicle for understanding the programming mechanism for using regular expressions. You create a `Pattern` object for the expression `"had"` like this:

```
Pattern had = Pattern.compile("had");
```

The static `compile()` method in the `Pattern` class returns a reference to a `Pattern` object that contains the compiled regular expression. The method throws a `PatternSyntaxException` if the argument is invalid. You don't have to catch this exception as it is a subclass of `RuntimeException` and therefore is unchecked, but it is a good idea to do so to make sure the regular expression pattern is valid. The compilation process stores the regular expression in a `Pattern` object in a form that is ready to be processed by a `Matcher` state-machine.

A further version of the `compile()` method enables you to control more closely how the pattern is applied when looking for a match. The second argument is a value of type `int` that specifies one or more of the following flags that are defined in the `Pattern` class (shown in Table 15-4):

TABLE 15-4: Flags Controlling Pattern Operation

FLAG	DESCRIPTION
CASE_INSENSITIVE	Matches ignoring case, but assumes only US-ASCII characters are being matched.
MULTILINE	Enables the beginning or end of lines to be matched anywhere. Without this flag only the beginning and end of the entire sequence is matched.
UNICODE_CASE	When this is specified in addition to CASE_INSENSITIVE, case-insensitive matching is consistent with the Unicode standard.
DOTALL	Makes the expression (which you see shortly) match any character, including line terminators.
LITERAL	Causes the string specifying a pattern to be treated as a sequence of literal characters, so escape sequences, for example, are not recognized as such.
CANON_EQ	Matches taking account of canonical equivalence of combined characters. For example, some characters that have diacritics may be represented as a single character or as a single character with a diacritic followed by a diacritic character. This flag treats these as a match.
COMMENTS	Allows whitespace and comments in a pattern. Comments in a pattern start with # so from the first # to the end of the line is ignored.
UNIX_LINES	Enables UNIX lines mode, where only '\n' is recognized as a line terminator.
UNICODE_CHARACTER_CLASS	Enables the Unicode version of predefined character classes.

All these flags are unique single-bit values within a value of type `int` so you can combine them by ORing them together or by simple addition. For example, you can specify the `CASE_INSENSITIVE` and the `UNICODE_CASE` flags with the following expression:

```
Pattern.CASE_INSENSITIVE | Pattern.UNICODE_CASE
```

Or you can write this as:

```
Pattern.CASE_INSENSITIVE + Pattern.UNICODE_CASE
```

Beware of using addition when you want to add a flag to a variable representing an existing set of flags. If the flag already exists, addition produces the wrong result because adding the two corresponding bits results in a carry to the next bit. ORing always produces the correct result.

If you want to match `"had"` ignoring case, you could create the pattern with the following statement:

```
Pattern had = Pattern.compile("had", Pattern.CASE_INSENSITIVE);
```

In addition to the exception thrown by the first version of the method, this version throws an `IllegalArgumentException` if the second argument has bit values set that do not correspond to any of the flag constants defined in the `Pattern` class.

Creating a Matcher

After you have a `Pattern` object, you can create a `Matcher` object that can search a specified string, like this:

```
String sentence = "Smith, where Jones had had 'had', had had 'had had'.";
Matcher matchHad = had.matcher(sentence);
```

The first statement defines the string `sentence` that you want to search. To create the `Matcher` object, you call the `matcher()` method for the `Pattern` object with the string to be analyzed as the argument. This returns a `Matcher` object that can analyze the string that was passed to it. The parameter for the `matcher()` method is actually of type `CharSequence`. This is an interface that is implemented by the `String`, `StringBuffer`, and `StringBuilder` classes so you can pass a reference of any of these types to the method. The `java.nio.CharBuffer` class also implements `CharSequence`, so you can pass the contents of a `CharBuffer` to the method, too. This means that if you use a `CharBuffer` to hold character data you have read from a file, you can pass the data directly to the `matcher()` method to be searched.

An advantage of Java's implementation of regular expressions is that you can reuse a `Pattern` object to create `Matcher` objects to search for the pattern in a variety of strings. To use the same pattern to search another string, you just call the `matcher()` method for the `Pattern` object with the new string as the argument. You then have a new `Matcher` object that you can use to search the new string.

You can also change the string that a `Matcher` object is to search by calling its `reset()` method with a new string as the argument. For example:

```
matchHad.reset("Had I known, I would not have eaten the haddock.");
```

This replaces the previous string, `sentence`, in the `Matcher` object, so it is now capable of searching the new string. Like the `matcher()` method in the `Pattern` class, the parameter type for the `reset()` method is `CharSequence`, so you can pass a reference of type `String`, `StringBuffer`, `StringBuilder`, or `CharBuffer` to it.

Searching a String

Now that you have a `Matcher` object, you can use it to search the string. Calling the `find()` method for the `Matcher` object searches the string for the next occurrence of the pattern. If it finds the pattern, the method stores information about where it was found in the `Matcher` object and returns `true`. If it doesn't find the pattern, it returns `false`. When the pattern has been found, calling the `start()` method for the `Matcher` object returns the index position in the string where the first character in the pattern was found. Calling the `end()` method returns the index position following the last character in the pattern. Both index values are returned as type `int`. Therefore, you could search for the first occurrence of the pattern like this:

```
if(m.find()) {
   System.out.println("Pattern found. Start: " + m.start() + " End: " + m.end());
} else {
   System.out.println("Pattern not found.");
}
```

Note that you must not call `start()` or `end()` for the `Matcher` object before you have succeeded in finding the pattern. Until a pattern has been matched, the `Matcher` object is in an undefined state and calling either of these methods results in an exception of type `IllegalStateException` being thrown.

You usually want to find all occurrences of a pattern in a string. When you call the `find()` method, searching starts either at the beginning of this matcher's region, or at the first character not searched by a previous call to `find()`. Thus, you can easily find all occurrences of the pattern by searching in a loop like this:

```
while(m.find()) {
  System.out.println(" Start: " + m.start() + " End: " + m.end());
}
```

At the end of this loop the index position is at the character following the last occurrence of the pattern in the string. If you want to reset the index position to zero, you just call an overloaded version of `reset()` for the `Matcher` object that has no arguments:

```
m.reset();                              //Reset this matcher
```

This resets the `Matcher` object to its state before any search operations were carried out. To make sure you understand the searching process, let's put it all together in an example.

TRY IT OUT Searching for a Substring

Here's a complete example to search a string for a pattern:

```
import java.util.regex.Matcher;
import java.util.regex.Pattern;
import java.util.Arrays;

class TryRegex {
  public static void main(String args[]) {
    //  A regex and a string in which to search are specified
    String regEx = "had";
    String str = "Smith, where Jones had had 'had', had had 'had had'.";

    // The matches in the output will be marked (fixed-width font required)
    char[]  marker = new char[str.length()];
    Arrays.fill(marker,' ');
    //  So we can later replace spaces with marker characters

    //  Obtain the required matcher
    Pattern pattern = Pattern.compile(regEx);
    Matcher m = pattern.matcher(str);

    // Find every match and mark it
    while( m.find() ){
      System.out.println(
                "Pattern found at Start: " + m.start() + " End: " + m.end());
      Arrays.fill(marker,m.start(),m.end(),'^');
    }

    // Show the object string with matches marked under it
    System.out.println(str);
    System.out.println(marker);
  }
}
```

TryRegex.java

This produces the following output:

```
Pattern found at Start: 19 End: 22
Pattern found at Start: 23 End: 26
Pattern found at Start: 28 End: 31
Pattern found at Start: 34 End: 37
Pattern found at Start: 38 End: 41
```

```
Pattern found at Start: 43 End: 46
Pattern found at Start: 47 End: 50
Smith, where Jones had had 'had', had had 'had had'.
                  ^^^ ^^^  ^^^   ^^^ ^^^  ^^^ ^^^
```

How It Works

You first define a string, regEx, containing the regular expression, and a string, str, that you search:

```
String regEx = "had";
String str = "Smith, where Jones had had 'had', had had 'had had'.";
```

You also create an array, marker, of type char[] with the same number of elements as str, that you use to indicate where the pattern is found in the string:

```
char[]  marker = new char[str.length()];
```

You fill the elements of the marker array with spaces initially using the static fill() method from the Arrays class:

```
Arrays.fill(marker,' ');
```

Later you replace some of the spaces in the array with '^' to indicate where the pattern has been found in the original string.

After compiling the regular expression regEx into a Pattern object, pattern, you create a Matcher object, m, from pattern, which applies to the string str:

```
Pattern pattern = Pattern.compile(regEx);
Matcher m = pattern.matcher(str);
```

You then call the find() method for m in the while loop condition:

```
while( m.find() ){
  System.out.println(
        "Pattern found at Start: " + m.start() + " End: " + m.end());
  Arrays.fill(marker, m.start(), m.end(), '^');
}
```

This loop continues as long as the find() method returns true. On each iteration you output the index values returned by the start() and end() methods, which reflect the index position where the first character of the pattern was found, and the index position following the last character. You also insert the '^' character in the marker array at the index positions where the pattern was found—again using the fill() method. The loop ends when the find() method returns false, implying that there are no more occurrences of the pattern in the string.

When the loop ends you have found all occurrences of the pattern, so you output str with the contents of the marker array immediately below it. As long as the command-line output uses a fixed-width font, the '^' characters mark the positions where the pattern appears in the string.

You reuse this example as you delve into further options for regular expressions by plugging in different definitions for regEx and the string that is searched, str. The output is more economical if you delete or comment out the statement in the while loop that outputs the start and end index positions.

Matching an Entire String

On some occasions you want to try to match a pattern against an entire string—in other words, you want to establish that the complete string you are searching is a match for the pattern. Suppose you read an input value into your program as a string. This might be from the keyboard or possibly through a dialog box managing the entry data in the graphical user interface for an application. You might want to be sure that the input string is an integer, for example. If input should be of a particular form, you can use a regular expression to determine whether it is correct or not.

The `matches()` method for a `Matcher` object tries to match the entire input string with the pattern and returns `true` only if there is a match. The following code fragment demonstrates how this works:

```
String input = null;
// Read into input from some source...

Pattern yes = Pattern.compile("yes");
Matcher m = yes.matcher(input);

if(m.matches()) {                              // Check if input matches "yes"
  System.out.println("Input is yes.");
} else {
  System.out.println("Input is not yes.");
}
```

Of course, this illustration is trivial, but later you see how you can define more sophisticated patterns that can check for a range of possible input forms.

Defining Sets of Characters

A regular expression can be made up of ordinary characters, which are upper- and lowercase letters and digits, plus sequences of *meta-characters*, which are characters that have a special meaning. The pattern in the previous example was just the word `"had"`, but what if you wanted to search a string for occurrences of `"hid"` or `"hod"` as well as `"had"`, or even any three-letter word beginning with `"h"` and ending with `"d"`?

You can deal with any of these possibilities with regular expressions. One option is to specify the middle character as a wildcard by using a period; a period is one example of a meta-character. This meta-character matches any character except end-of-line, so the regular expression `"h.d"`, represents any sequence of three characters that starts with `"h"` and ends with `"d"`. Try changing the definitions of `regEx` and `str` in the previous example to

```
String regEx = "h.d";
String str = "Ted and Ned Hodge hid their hod and huddled in the hedge.";
```

If you recompile and run the example again, the last two lines of output are

```
Ted and Ned Hodge hid their hod and huddled in the hedge.
                ^^^     ^^^ ^^^          ^^^
```

You can see that you didn't find `"Hod"` in `Hodge` because of the capital `"H"`, but you found all the other 3-letter sequences beginning with `"h"` and ending with `"d"`.

Of course, the regular expression `"h.d"` would also have found `"hzd"` or `"hNd"` if they had been present, which is not what you want. You can limit the possibilities by replacing the period with just the collection of characters you are looking for between square brackets, like this:

```
String regEx = "h[aio]d";
```

The `[aio]` sequence of meta-characters defines what is called a *simple class* of characters, consisting in this case of `"a"`, `"i"`, or `"o"`. Here the term *class* is used in the sense of a set of characters, not a class that defines a type. If you try this version of the regular expression in the previous example, the last two lines of output are:

```
Ted and Ned Hodge hid their hod and huddled in the hedge.
                ^^^     ^^^
```

The regular expression now matches all 3-letter sequences that begin with `"h"` and end with `"d"` and have a middle letter of `"a"` or `"i"` or `"o"`.

You can define character classes in a regular expression in a variety of ways. Table 15-5 gives some examples of the more useful forms:

TABLE 15-5: Character Classes in a Regular Expression

CLASS	DESCRIPTION
`[aeiou]`	This is a simple class that any of the characters between the square brackets match — in this example, any lowercase vowel. You used this form in the earlier code fragment to search for variations on `"had"`.
`[^aeiou]`	This represents any character except those appearing to the right of the ^ character between the square brackets. Thus, here you have specified any character that is not a lowercase vowel. Note this is any *character*, not any letter, so the expression `"h[^aeiou]d"` looks for `"h!d"` or `"h9d"` as well as `"hxd"` or `"hWd"`. Of course, it rejects `"had"` or `"hid"` or any other form with a lowercase vowel as the middle letter.
`[a-e]`	This defines an inclusive range — any of the letters `"a"` to `"e"` in this case. You can also specify multiple ranges. For example: `[a-cs-zA-E]` This corresponds to any of the characters from `"a"` to `"c"`, from `"s"` to `"z"`, or from `"A"` to `"E"`. If you want to specify that a position must contain a digit, you could use `[0-9]`. To specify that a position can be a letter or a digit, you could express it as `[a-zA-Z0-9]`.

You can use any of these in combination with ordinary characters to form a regular expression. For example, suppose you want to search some text for any sequence beginning with `"b"`, `"c"`, or `"d"`, with `"a"` as the middle letter, and ending with `"d"` or `"t"`. You could define the regular expression to do this as:

```
String regEx = "[b-d]a[dt]";
```

This expression matches any occurrence of `"bad"`, `"cad"`, `"dad"`, `"bat"`, `"cat"`, or `"dat"`.

Logical Operators in Regular Expressions

You can use the `&&` operator to combine classes that define sets of characters. This is particularly useful when you use it combined with the negation operator, `^`, that appears in the second row of the table in the preceding section. For example, if you want to specify that any lowercase consonant is acceptable, you could write the expression that matches this as:

```
"[b-df-hj-np-tv-z]"
```

However, this can much more conveniently be expressed as the following pattern:

```
"[a-z&&[^aeiou]]"
```

This produces the intersection (in other words, the characters common to both sets) of the set of characters `"a"` through `"z"` with the set that is not a lowercase vowel. To put it another way, the lowercase vowels are subtracted from the set `"a"` through `"z"` so you are left with just the lowercase consonants.

The `|` operator is a logical OR that you use to specify alternatives. A regular expression to find `"hid"`, `"had"`, or `"hod"` could be written as `"hid|had|hod"`. You can try this in the previous example by changing the definition of regEx to:

```
String regEx = "hid|had|hod";
```

Note that the `|` operation means either the whole expression to the left of the operator or the whole expression to the right, not just the characters on either side as alternatives.

You could also use the `|` operator to define an expression to find sequences beginning with an uppercase or lowercase `"h"`, followed by a lowercase vowel, and ending in `"d"`, like this:

```
String regEx = "[h|H][aeiou]d";
```

The first pair of square brackets encloses the choice of "h" or "H". The second pair of square brackets determines that the next character is any lowercase vowel. The last character must always be "d". With this as the regular expression in the example, the "Hod" in Hodge is found as well as the other variations.

Predefined Character Sets

You also have a number of predefined character classes that provide you with a shorthand notation for commonly used sets of characters. Table 15-6 gives some that are particularly useful:

TABLE 15-6: Predefined Character Classes

CHARACTER CLASS	DESCRIPTION
.	This represents any character, as you have already seen.
\d	This represents any digit and is therefore shorthand for [0-9].
\D	This represents any character that is not a digit. It is therefore equivalent to [^0-9].
\s	This represents any whitespace character. A whitespace character is a space, a tab '\t', a newline character '\n', a form feed character '\f', a carriage return '\r', or a page break 'x0B'.
\S	This represents any non-whitespace character and is therefore equivalent to [^\s].
\w	This represents a word character, which corresponds to an upper- or lowercase letter, a digit, or an underscore. It is therefore equivalent to [a-zA-Z_0-9].
\W	This represents any character that is not a word character, so it is equivalent to [^\w].

Note that when you are using any of the sequences that start with a backslash in a regular expression, you need to keep in mind that Java treats a backslash as the beginning of an escape sequence. Therefore, you must specify the backslash in the regular expression as \\. For example, to find a sequence of three digits, the regular expression would be "\\d\\d\\d". This is peculiar to Java because of the significance of the backslash in Java strings, so it doesn't necessarily apply to other environments that support regular expressions, such as Perl.

Obviously, you may well want to include a period, or any of the other meta-characters, as part of the character sequence you are looking for. To do this you can use an escape sequence starting with a backslash in the expression to define such characters. Because Java strings interpret a backslash as the start of a Java escape sequence, the backslash itself has to be represented as \\, the same as when using the predefined character sets that begin with a backslash. Thus, the regular expression to find the sequence "had." would be "had\\.".

The earlier search you tried with the expression "h.d" found embedded sequences such as "hud" in the word huddled. You could use the \s set that corresponds to any whitespace character to prevent this by defining regEx like this:

```
String regEx = "\\sh.d\\s";
```

This searches for a five-character sequence that starts and ends with any whitespace character. The output from the example is now:

```
Ted and Ned Hodge hid their hod and huddled in the hedge.
                 ^^^^^       ^^^^^
```

You can see that the marker array shows the five-character sequences that were found. The embedded sequences are now no longer included, as they don't begin and end with a whitespace character.

To take another example, suppose you want to find hedge or Hodge as words in the sentence, bearing in mind that there's a period at the end. You could do this by defining the regular expression as:

```
String regEx = "\\s[h|H][e|o]dge[\\s|\\.]";
```

The first character is defined as any whitespace by \\s. The next character is defined as either "h" or "H" by [h|H]. This can be followed by either "e" or "o" specified by [e|o]. This is followed by plaintext dge with either a whitespace character or a period at the end, specified by `[\\s|\\.]`. This doesn't cater to all possibilities. Sequences at the beginning of the string are not found, for example, nor are sequences followed by a comma. You see how to deal with these next.

Matching Boundaries

So far you have been trying to find the occurrence of a pattern anywhere in a string. In many situations you will want to be more specific. You may want to look for a pattern that appears at the beginning of a line in a string but not anywhere else, or maybe just at the end of any line. As you saw in the previous example, you may want to look for a word that is not embedded—you want to find the word `"cat"` but not the `"cat"` in `"cattle"` or in `"Popacatapetl"`, for example. The previous example worked for the string you were searching but would not produce the right result if the word you were looking for was followed by a comma or appeared at the end of the text. However, you have other options for specifying the pattern. You can use a number of special sequences in a regular expression when you want to match a particular boundary. For example, those presented in Table 15-7 are especially useful:

TABLE 15-7: Boundary Matching in a Regular Expression

SEQUENCE	BOUNDARY MATCHED
^	Specifies the beginning of a line. For example, to find the word Java at the beginning of any line you could use the expression `"^Java"`.
$	Specifies the end of a line. For example, to find the word Java at the end of any line you could use the expression `"Java$"`. Of course, if you were expecting a period at the end of a line the expression would be `"Java\\.$"`.
\b	Specifies a word boundary. To find three-letter words beginning with `'h'` and ending with `'d'`, you could use the expression `"\\bh.d\\b"`.
\B	A non-word boundary — the complement of \b.
\A	Specifies the beginning of the string being searched. To find the word The at the very beginning of the string being searched, you could use the expression `"\\AThe\\b"`. The `\\b` at the end of the regular expression is necessary to avoid finding Then or There at the beginning of the input.
\z	Specifies the end of the string being searched. To find the word hedge followed by a period at the end of a string, you could use the expression "`\\bhedge\\.\\z`".
\Z	The end of input except for the final terminator. A final terminator is a newline character (`'\n'`) if `Pattern.UNIX_LINES` is set. Otherwise, it can also be a carriage return (`'\r'`), a carriage return followed by a newline character, a next-line character (`'\u0085'`), a line separator (`'\u2028'`), or a paragraph separator (`'\u2029'`).

Although you have moved quite a way from the simple search for a fixed substring offered by the `String` class methods, you still can't search for sequences that may vary in length. If you wanted to find all the numerical values in a string, which might be sequences such as `1234` or `23.45` or `999.998`, for example, you don't yet have the ability to do that. You can fix that now by taking a look at *quantifiers* in a regular expression and what they can do for you.

Using Quantifiers

A quantifier following a subsequence of a pattern determines the possibilities for how that subsequence of a pattern can repeat. Let's take an example. Suppose you want to find any numerical values in a string. If you take the simplest case, we can say an integer is an arbitrary sequence of one or more digits. The quantifier for one or more is the meta-character `"+"`. You have also seen that you can use \d as shorthand for any digit (remembering, of course, that it becomes \\d in a Java `String` literal), so you could express any sequence of digits as the regular expression:

```
"\\d+"
```

Of course, a number may also include a decimal point and may be optionally followed by further digits. To indicate something can occur just once or not at all, as is the case with a decimal point, you can use the ? quantifier. You can write the pattern for a sequence of digits followed by an optional decimal point as:

```
"\\d+\\.?"
```

To add the possibility of further digits, you can append `\\d+` to what you have so far to produce the expression:

```
"\\d+\\.?\\d+"
```

This is a bit untidy. You can rewrite this as an integral part followed by an optional fractional part by putting parentheses around the bit for the fractional part and adding the ? operator:

```
"\\d+(\\.\\d+)?"
```

However, this isn't quite right. You can have 2. as a valid numerical value, for example, so you want to specify zero or more appearances of digits in the fractional part. The * quantifier expresses that, so maybe you should use:

```
"\\d+(\\.\\d*)?"
```

You are still missing something, though. What about the value .25 or the value -3? The optional sign in front of a number is easy, so let's deal with that first. To express the possibility that + or - can appear, you can use `[+|-]`, and because this either appears or it doesn't, you can extend it to `[+|-]?`. So to add the possibility of a sign, you can write the expression as:

```
"[+|-]?\\d+(\\.\\d*)?"
```

You have to be careful how you allow for numbers beginning with a decimal point. You can't allow a sign followed by a decimal point or just a decimal point by itself to be interpreted as a number, so you can't say a number starts with zero or more digits or that the leading digits are optional. You could define a separate expression for numbers without leading digits like this:

```
"[+|-]?\\.\\d+"
```

Here then is an optional sign followed by a decimal point and at least one digit. With the other expression there is also an optional sign, so you can combine these into a single expression to recognize either form, like this:

```
"[+|-]?(\\d+(\\.\\d*)?)|(\\.\\d+)"
```

This regular expression identifies substrings with an optional plus or minus sign followed by either a substring defined by `"\\d+(\\.\\d*)?"` or a substring defined by `"\\.\\d+"`. You might be tempted to use square brackets instead of parentheses here, but this would be quite wrong as square brackets define a set of characters, so any single character from the set is a match.

That was probably a bit more work than you anticipated, but it's often the case that things that look simple at first sight can turn out to be a little tricky. Let's try that out in an example.

TRY IT OUT Finding Numbers

This is similar to the code we have used in previous examples except that here we just list each substring that is found to correspond to the pattern:

Available for
download on
Wrox.com

```java
import java.util.regex.Pattern;
import java.util.regex.Matcher;

public class FindingNumbers {
  public static void main(String args[]) {
    String regEx = "[+|-]?(\\d+(\\.\\d*)?)|(\\.\\d+)";
    String str = "256 is the square of 16 and -2.5 squared is 6.25 " +
                                      "and -.243 is less than 0.1234.";
    Pattern pattern = Pattern.compile(regEx);
    Matcher m = pattern.matcher(str);
    String subStr = null;
```

```
    while(m.find()) {
      System.out.println(m.group());              // Output the substring matched
    }
  }
}
```

This produces the following output:

```
256
16
-2.5
6.25
.243
0.1234
```

How It Works

Well, you found all the numbers in the string, so our regular expression works well, doesn't it? You can't do that with the methods in the `String` class. The only new code item here is the method, `group()`, that you call in the `while` loop for the `Matcher` object, m. This method returns a reference to a `String` object that contains the subsequence corresponding to the last match of the entire pattern. Calling the `group()` method for the `Matcher` object m is equivalent to the expression `str.substring(m.start(), m.end())`.

Tokenizing a String

You saw in Chapter 4 that you could tokenize a string using the `split()` method for a `String` object. As I mentioned then, the `split()` method does this by applying a regular expression—in fact, the first argument to the method is interpreted as a regular expression. This is because the expression `text.split(str, limit)`, where text is a `String` variable, is equivalent to the expression:

```
Pattern.compile(str).split(text, limit)
```

This means that you can apply all of the power of regular expressions to the identification of delimiters in the string. To demonstrate that this is the case, I will repeat the example from Chapter 4, but modify the first argument to the `split()` method so only the words in the text are included in the set of tokens.

TRY IT OUT | Extracting the Words from a String

Here's the code for the modified version of the example:

Available for download on Wrox.com

```
public class StringTokenizing {
  public static void main(String[] args) {
    String text =
               "To be or not to be, that is the question."; // String to segment
    String delimiters = "[^\\w]+";

    // Analyze the string
    String[] tokens = text.split(delimiters);

    // Output the tokens
    System.out.println("Number of tokens: " + tokens.length);
    for(String token : tokens) {
      System.out.println(token);
    }
  }
}
```

Now you should get the following output:

```
Number of tokens: 10
To
be
or
not
to
be
that
is
the
question
```

How It Works

The program produces 10 tokens in the output, which is the number of words in the text. The original version in Chapter 4 treated a comma followed by a space as two separate tokens and produced an empty token as a result. The pattern `"[^\\w]+"` matches one or more characters that are not word characters; i.e., not uppercase or lowercase letters, or digits. This means the delimiters pattern includes one or more spaces, periods, exclamations marks and question marks, and all the words in `text` are found.

Search and Replace Operations

You can implement a search and replace operation very easily using regular expressions. Whenever you call the `find()` method for a `Matcher` object, you can call the `appendReplacement()` method to replace the subsequence that was matched. You create a revised version of the original string in a new `StringBuffer` object that you supply to the method. The arguments to the `appendReplacement()` method are a reference to the `StringBuffer` object that is to contain the new string, and the replacement string for the matched text. You can see how this works by considering a specific example.

Suppose you define a string to be searched as:

```
String joke = "My dog hasn't got any nose.\n" +
              "How does your dog smell then?\n" +
              "My dog smells horrible.\n";
```

You now want to replace each occurrence of `"dog"` in the string by `"goat"`. You first need a regular expression to find `"dog"`:

```
String regEx = "dog";
```

You can compile this into a pattern and create a `Matcher` object for the string `joke`:

```
Pattern doggone = Pattern.compile(regEx);
Matcher m = doggone.matcher(joke);
```

You are going to assemble a new version of `joke` in a `StringBuffer` object that you can create like this:

```
StringBuffer newJoke = new StringBuffer();
```

This is an empty `StringBuffer` object ready to receive the revised text. You can now find and replace instances of `"dog"` in `joke` by calling the `find()` method for `m` and calling `appendReplacement()` each time it returns `true`:

```
while(m.find()) {
  m.appendReplacement(newJoke, "goat");
}
```

Each call of `appendReplacement()` copies characters from `joke` to `newJoke` starting at the character where the previous `find()` operation started and ending at the character preceding the first character matched: at `m.start()-1`, in other words. The method then appends the string specified by the second argument to `newJoke`. This process is illustrated in Figure 15-4.

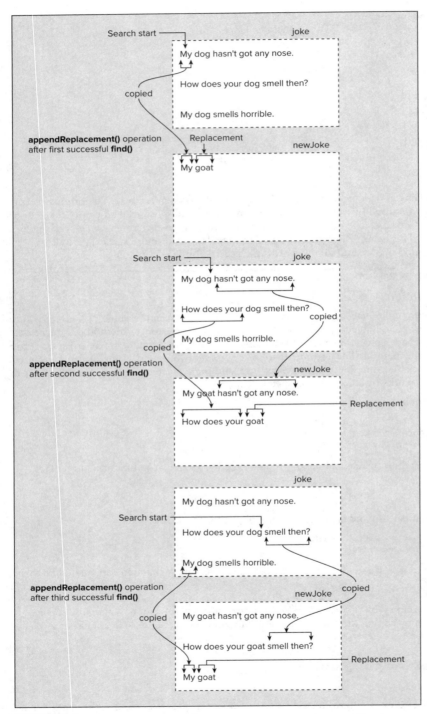

FIGURE 15-4

The find() method returns true three times, once for each occurrence of "dog" in joke. When the three steps shown in the diagram have been completed, the find() method returns false on the next iteration, terminating the loop. This leaves newJoke in the state shown in the last box in Figure 15-4. All you now need to complete newJoke is a way to copy the text from joke that comes after the last subsequence that was found. The appendTail() method for the Matcher object does that:

```
m.appendTail(newJoke);
```

This copies the text starting with the m.end() index position from the last successful match through to the end of the string. Thus this statement copies the segment "smells horrible." from joke to newJoke. You can put all that together and run it.

TRY IT OUT   Search and Replace

Here's the code I have just discussed assembled into a complete program:

```java
import java.util.regex.Pattern;
import java.util.regex.Matcher;

class SearchAndReplace {
  public static void main(String args[]) {
    String joke = "My dog hasn't got any nose.\n"
                  +"How does your dog smell then?\n"
                  +"My dog smells horrible.\n";
    String regEx = "dog";

    Pattern doggone = Pattern.compile(regEx);
    Matcher m = doggone.matcher(joke);

    StringBuffer newJoke = new StringBuffer();
    while(m.find()) {
      m.appendReplacement(newJoke, "goat");
    }
    m.appendTail(newJoke);
    System.out.println(newJoke);
  }
}
```

SearchAndReplace.java

When you compile and execute this you should get the following output:

```
My goat hasn't got any nose.
How does your goat smell then?
My goat smells horrible.
```

How It Works

Each time the find() method in the while loop condition returns true, you call the appendReplacement() method for the Matcher object m. This copies characters from joke to newJoke, starting at the index position where find() started searching, and ending at the character preceding the first character in the match, which is at m.start()-1. The method then appends the replacement string, "goat", to newJoke.

After the loop finishes, the appendTail() method copies characters from joke to newJoke, starting with the character following the last match at m.end() through to the end of joke. Thus, you end up with a new string similar to the original, but which has each instance of "dog" replaced by "goat".

You can use the search and replace capability to solve some string manipulation problems very easily. For example, if you want to make sure that any sequence of one or more whitespace characters is replaced by a single space, you can define the regular expression as "\\s+" and the replacement string as a single space " ". To eliminate all spaces at the beginning of each line, you can use the expression "^\\s+" and define the replacement string as empty, "". You must specify Pattern.MULTILINE as the flag for the compile() method for this to work.

Using Capturing Groups

Earlier you used the `group()` method for a `Matcher` object to retrieve the subsequence matched by the entire pattern defined by the regular expression. The entire pattern represents what is called a *capturing group* because the `Matcher` object captures the subsequence corresponding to the pattern match. Regular expressions can also define other capturing groups that correspond to parts of the pattern. Each pair of parentheses in a regular expression defines a separate capturing group in addition to the group that the whole expression defines. In the earlier example, you defined the regular expression by the following statement:

```
String regEx = "[+|-]?(\\d+(\\.\\d*)?)|(\\.\\d+)";
```

This defines three capturing groups other than the whole expression: one for the subexpression `(\\d+(\\.\\d*)?)`, one for the subexpression `(\\.\\d*)`, and one for the subexpression `(\\.\\d+)`. The `Matcher` object stores the subsequence that matches the pattern defined by each capturing group, and what's more, you can retrieve them.

To retrieve the text matching a particular capturing group, you need a way to identify the capturing group that you are interested in. To this end, capturing groups are numbered. The capturing group for the whole regular expression is always number 0. Counting their opening parentheses from the left in the regular expression numbers the other groups. Thus, the first opening parenthesis from the left corresponds to capturing group 1, the second corresponds to capturing group 2, and so on for as many opening parentheses as there are in the whole expression. Figure 15-5 illustrates how the groups are numbered in an arbitrary regular expression.

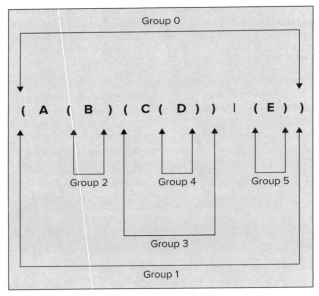

FIGURE 15-5

As you see, it's easy to number the capturing groups as long as you can count left parentheses. Group 1 is the same as Group 0 because the whole regular expression is parenthesized. The other capturing groups in sequence are defined by `(B)`, `(C(D))`, `(D)`, and `(E)`.

To retrieve the text matching a particular capturing group after the `find()` method returns `true`, you call the `group()` method for the `Matcher` object with the group number as the argument. The `groupCount()` method for the `Matcher` object returns a value of type `int` that specifies the number of capturing groups within the pattern—that is, excluding group 0, which corresponds to the whole pattern. Therefore, you have all you need to access the text corresponding to any or all of the capturing groups in a regular expression.

TRY IT OUT Capturing Groups

Let's modify our earlier example to output the text matching each group:

Available for
download on
Wrox.com

```java
import java.util.regex.Pattern;
import java.util.regex.Matcher;

public class TryCapturingGroups {
    public static void main(String args[]) {
        String regEx = "[+|-]?(\\d+(\\.\\d*)?)|(\\.\\d+)";
        String str = "256 is the square of 16 and -2.5 squared is 6.25 " +
                                            "and -.243 is less than 0.1234.";
        Pattern pattern = Pattern.compile(regEx);
        Matcher m = pattern.matcher(str);
        while(m.find()) {
            for(int i = 0; i <= m.groupCount() ; i++) {
                System.out.println(
                            "Group " + i + ": " + m.group(i)); // Group i substring
            }
        }
    }
}
```

TryCapturingGroups.java

This produces the following output:

```
Group 0: 256
Group 1: 256
Group 2: null
Group 3: null
Group 0: 16
Group 1: 16
Group 2: null
Group 3: null
Group 0: -2.5
Group 1: 2.5
Group 2: .5
Group 3: null
Group 0: 6.25
Group 1: 6.25
Group 2: .25
Group 3: null
Group 0: .243
Group 1: null
Group 2: null
Group 3: .243
Group 0: 0.1234
Group 1: 0.1234
Group 2: .1234
Group 3: null
```

How It Works

The regular expression here defines four capturing groups:

➤ Group 0: The whole expression
➤ Group 1: The subexpression "(\\d+(\\.\\d*)?)"
➤ Group 2: The subexpression "(\\.\\d*)"
➤ Group 3: The subexpression "(\\.\\d+)"

After each successful call of the `find()` method for m, you output the text captured by each group by passing the index value for the group to the `group()` method. Note that because you want to output group 0 as well as the other groups, you start the loop index from 0 and allow it to equal the value returned by `groupCount()` so as to index over all the groups.

You can see from the output that group 1 corresponds to numbers beginning with a digit, and group 3 corresponds to numbers starting with a decimal point, so either one or the other of these is always `null`. Group 2 corresponds to the sub-pattern within group 1 that matches the fractional part of a number that begins with a digit, so the text for this can be non-`null` only when the text for group 1 is non-`null` and the number has a decimal point.

Juggling Captured Text

Because you can get access to the text corresponding to each capturing group, you can move such blocks of text around. The `appendReplacement()` method has special provision for recognizing references to capturing groups in the replacement text string. If $n, where n is an integer, appears in the replacement string, it is interpreted as the text corresponding to group n. You can therefore replace the text matched to a complete pattern by any sequence of your choosing of the subsequences corresponding to the capturing groups in the pattern. That's hard to describe in words, so let's demonstrate it with an example.

TRY IT OUT   Rearranging Captured Group Text

I'm sure you remember that the `Math.pow()` method requires two arguments; the second argument is the power to which the first argument must be raised. Thus, to calculate 16^3 you can write:

```
double result = Math.pow(16.0, 3.0);
```

Let's suppose a weak programmer on your team has written a Java program in which the two arguments have mistakenly been switched, so in trying to compute 16^3 the programmer has written:

```
double result = Math.pow(3.0, 16.0);
```

Of course, this computes 3^{16}, which is not quite the same thing. Let's suppose further that this sort of error is strewn throughout the source code and in every case the arguments are the wrong way round. You would need a month of Sundays to go through manually and switch the argument values, so let's see if regular expressions can rescue the situation.

What you need to do is find each occurrence of `Math.pow()` and switch the arguments around. The intention here is to understand how you can switch things around, so I'll keep it simple and assume that the argument values to `Math.pow()` are always a numerical value or a variable name.

The key to the whole problem is to devise a regular expression with capturing groups for the bits you want to switch—the two arguments. Be warned: This is going to get a little messy, not difficult though—just messy.

You can define the first part of the regular expression that finds the sequence `"Math.pow("` at any point, and where you want to allow an arbitrary number of whitespace characters, you can use the sequence `\\s*`. Recall that `\\s` in a Java string specifies the predefined character class `\s`, which is whitespace. The `*` quantifier specifies zero or more of them. If you allow for whitespace between `Math.pow` and the opening parenthesis for the arguments, and some more whitespace after the opening parenthesis, the regular expression is:

```
"(Math.pow)\\s*\\(\\s*"
```

You have to specify the opening parenthesis by `"\\("`. An opening parenthesis is a meta-character, so you have to write it as an escape sequence.

The opening parenthesis is followed by the first argument, which I said could be a number or a variable name. You created a regular expression to identify a number earlier:

```
"[+|-]?(\\d+(\\.\\d*)?)|(\\.\\d+)"
```

To keep things simple, you assume that a variable name is just any sequence of letters, digits, or underscores that begins with a letter or an underscore. This avoids getting involved with qualified names. You can match a variable name with the expression:

```
"[a-zA-Z_]\\w*"
```

You can therefore match either a variable name or a number with the pattern:

```
"(([a-zA-Z_]\\w*)|([+|-]?(\\d+(\\.\\d*)?)|(\\.\\d+)))"
```

This just ORs the two possibilities together and parenthesizes the whole thing so it is a capturing group.

A comma that may be surrounded by zero or more whitespace characters on either side follows the first argument. You can match that with the pattern:

```
\\s*,\\s*
```

The pattern to match the second argument will be exactly the same as the first:

```
"(([a-zA-Z_]\\w*)|([+|-]?(\\d+(\\.\\d*)?)|(\\.\\d+)))"
```

Finally, this must be followed by a closing parenthesis that may or may not be preceded by whitespace:

```
\\s*\\)
```

You can put all this together to define the entire regular expression as the value for a `String` variable:

```
String regEx = "(Math.pow)" +                                         // Math.pow
    "\\s*\\(\\s*" +                                                    // Opening (
    "(([a-zA-Z_]\\w*)|([+|-]?(\\d+(\\.\\d*)?)|(\\.\\d+)))" +           // First argument
    "\\s*,\\s*" +                                                      // Comma
    "(([a-zA-Z_]\\w*)|([+|-]?(\\d+(\\.\\d*)?)|(\\.\\d+)))" +           // Second argument
    "\\s*\\)";                                                         // Closing )
```

Here you assemble the string literal for the regular expression by concatenating six separate string literals. Each of these corresponds to an easily identified part of the method call. If you count the left parentheses, excluding the escaped parenthesis of course, you can also see that capturing group 1 corresponds with the method name, group 2 is the first method argument, and group 8 is the second method argument.

You can put this in the following example:

```java
import java.util.regex.Pattern;
import java.util.regex.Matcher;

public class RearrangeText {
  public static void main(String args[]) {
    String regEx = "(Math.pow)"                                          // Math.pow
      + "\\s*\\(\\s*"                                                     // Opening (
      + "(([a-zA-Z_]\\w*)|([+|-]?(\\d+(\\.\\d*)?)|(\\.\\d+)))"            // First argument
      + "\\s*,\\s*"                                                       // Comma
      + "(([a-zA-Z_]\\w*)|([+|-]?(\\d+(\\.\\d*)?)|(\\.\\d+)))"            // Second argument
      + "\\s*\\)";                                                        // Closing )

    String oldCode =
        "double result = Math.pow( 3.0, 16.0);\n" +
        "double resultSquared = Math.pow(2 ,result );\n" +
        "double hypotenuse = Math.sqrt(Math.pow(2.0, 30.0)+Math.pow(2 , 40.0));\n";
    Pattern pattern = Pattern.compile(regEx);
    Matcher m = pattern.matcher(oldCode);

    StringBuffer newCode = new StringBuffer();
    while(m.find()) {
      m.appendReplacement(newCode, "$1\\($8,$2\\)");
    }
    m.appendTail(newCode);
```

```
        System.out.println("Original Code:\n" + oldCode);
        System.out.println("New Code:\n" + newCode);
      }
    }
```

RearrangeText.java

You should get the following output:

```
Original Code:
double result = Math.pow( 3.0, 16.0);
double resultSquared = Math.pow(2 ,result );
double hypotenuse = Math.sqrt(Math.pow(2.0, 30.0)+Math.pow(2 , 40.0));

New Code:
double result = Math.pow(16.0,3.0);
double resultSquared = Math.pow(result,2);
double hypotenuse = Math.sqrt(Math.pow(30.0,2.0)+Math.pow(40.0,2));
```

How It Works

You have defined the regular expression so that separate capturing groups identify the method name and both arguments. As you saw earlier, the method name corresponds to group 1, the first argument to group 2, and the second argument to group 8. You therefore define the replacement string to the appendReplacement() method as "$1\\($8,$2\\)". The effect of this is to replace the text for each method call that is matched by the following items in Table 15-8, in sequence:

TABLE 15-8: Matching a Method Call

ITEM	TEXT THAT IS MATCHED
$1	The text matching capturing group 1 — the method name
\\(	A left parenthesis
$8	The text matching capturing group 8 — the second argument
,	A comma
$2	The text matching capturing group 2 — the first argument
\\)	A right parenthesis

The call to appendTail() is necessary to ensure that any text left at the end of oldCode following the last match for regEx gets copied to newCode.

In the process, you have eliminated any superfluous whitespace that was lying around in the original text.

USING A SCANNER

The java.util.Scanner class defines objects that use regular expressions to scan character input from a variety of sources and present the input as a sequence of tokens of various primitive types or as strings. For example, you can use a Scanner object to read data values of various types from a file or a stream, including the standard stream System.in. Indeed, using a Scanner object would have saved you the trouble of developing the FormattedInput class in Chapter 8 — still, it was good practice, wasn't it?

The facilities provided by the Scanner class are quite extensive, so I'm not able to go into all of it in detail because of space limitations. I just provide you with an idea of how the scanner mechanisms you are likely to find most useful can be applied. After you have a grasp of the basics, I'm sure you'll find the other facilities quite easy to use.

Creating Scanner Objects

A `Scanner` object can scan a source of text and parse it into tokens using regular expressions. You can create a `Scanner` object by passing an object that encapsulates the source of the data to a `Scanner` constructor. You can construct a `Scanner` from any of the following types:

```
InputStream  File  Path  ReadableByteChannel  Readable  String
```

The `Scanner` object that is created is able to read data from whichever source you supply as the argument to the constructor. `Readable` is an interface implemented by objects of type such as `BufferedReader`, `CharBuffer`, `InputStreamReader`, and a number of other readers, so you can create a `Scanner` object that scans any of these. For input from an external source, such as an `InputStream` or a file identified by a `Path` object or a `File` object, bytes are converted into characters either using the default charset in effect or using a charset that you specify as a second argument to the constructor.

Of course, read operations for `Readable` sources may also result in an `IOException` being thrown. If this occurs, the `Scanner` object interprets this as signaling that the end of input has been reached and does not rethrow the exception. You can test whether an `IOException` has been thrown when reading from a source by calling the `ioException()` method for the `Scanner` object; the method returns the exception object if the source has thrown an `IOException`.

Let's take the obvious example of a source from which you might want to interpret data. To obtain a `Scanner` object that scans input from the keyboard, you could use the following statement:

```
java.util.Scanner keyboard = new java.util.Scanner(System.in);
```

Creating a `Scanner` object to read from a file is a little more laborious because of the exception that might be thrown:

```
Path file = Paths.get("TryScanner.java");
try (Scanner fileScan = new Scanner(file)){
  // Scan the input...
} catch(IOException e) {
  e.printStackTrace();
  System.exit(1);
}
```

This creates a `Scanner` object that you can use to scan the file `TryScanner.java`. The `Scanner` class implements `AutoClosable` so you can create it in the form of a `try` block with resources.

Getting Input from a Scanner

By default, a `Scanner` object reads tokens assuming they are delimited by whitespace. Whitespace corresponds to any character for which the `isWhitespace()` method in the `Character` class returns `true`. Reading a token therefore involves skipping over any delimiter characters until a non-delimiter character is found and then attempting to interpret the sequence of non-delimiter characters in the way you have requested. You can read tokens of primitive types from the scanner source using the methods found in Table 15-9.

TABLE 15-9: Methods That Read a Token

METHOD	DESCRIPTION
`nextByte()`	Reads and returns the next token as type `byte`
`nextShort()`	Reads and returns the next token as type `short`
`nextInt()`	Reads and returns the next token as type `int`
`nextLong()`	Reads and returns the next token as type `long`
`nextFloat()`	Reads and returns the next token as type `float`
`nextDouble()`	Reads and returns the next token as type `double`
`nextBoolean()`	Reads and returns the next token as type `boolean`

The first four methods each have an overloaded version that accepts an argument of type int specifying the radix to be used in the interpretation of the value. All of these methods throw a java.util .InputMismatchException if the input does not match the regular expression for the input type being read or a java.util.NoSuchElementException if the input is exhausted. Note that type NoSuchElementException is a superclass of type InputMismatchException, so you must put a catch clause for the latter first if you intend to catch both types of exceptions separately. The methods can also throw an exception of type IllegalStateException if the scanner is closed.

If the input read does not match the token you are trying to read, the invalid input is left in the input buffer, so you have an opportunity to try an alternative way of matching it. Of course, if it is simply erroneous input, you should skip over it before continuing. In this case you can call the next() method for the Scanner object, which reads the next token up to the next delimiter in the input and returns it as a String object.

The Scanner class also defines nextBigInteger() and nextBigDecimal() methods that read the next token as a java.math.BigInteger object or a java.math.BigDecimal object, respectively. The BigInteger class defines objects that encapsulate integers with an arbitrary number of digits and provides the methods you need to work with such values. The BigDecimal class does the same thing for non-integral values.

You have enough knowledge to try out a scanner, so let's do it.

Available for download on Wrox.com

TRY IT OUT Using a Scanner

Here's a simple example that just reads a variety of input from the standard input stream and displays what was read from the keyboard:

```java
import java.util.Scanner;
import java.util.InputMismatchException;

public class TryScanner {
  public static void main(String[] args) {
    Scanner kbScan = new Scanner(System.in);       // Create the scanner
    int selectRead = 1;                            // Selects the read operation
    final int MAXTRIES = 3;                        // Maximum attempts at input
    int tries = 0;                                 // Number of input attempts

    while(tries < MAXTRIES) {
      try {
        switch(selectRead) {
          case 1:
          System.out.print("Enter an integer: ");
          System.out.println("You entered: " + kbScan.nextLong());
          ++selectRead;                            // Select next read operation
          tries = 0;                               // Reset count of tries

          case 2:
          System.out.print("Enter a floating-point value: ");
          System.out.println("You entered: " + kbScan.nextDouble());
          ++selectRead;                            // Select next read operation
          tries = 0;                               // Reset count of tries

          case 3:
          System.out.print("Enter a boolean value(true or false): ");
          System.out.println("You entered: " + kbScan.nextBoolean());
        }
        break;
      } catch(InputMismatchException e) {
        String input = kbScan.next();
        System.out.println("\"" + input + "\" is not valid input.");
        if(tries<MAXTRIES) {
          System.out.println("Try again.");
        } else {
```

```
                System.out.println(" Terminating program.");
                System.exit(1);
            }
        }
    }
}
```

You probably get a compiler warning about possible fall-through in the `switch` case statements, but it is intentional. With my limited typing skills, I got the following output:

```
Enter an integer: 1$
"1$" is not valid input.
Try again.
Enter an integer: 14
You entered: 14
Enter a floating-point value: 2e1
You entered: 20.0
Enter a boolean value(true or false): tree
"tree" is not valid input.
Try again.
Enter a boolean value(true or false): true
You entered: true
```

How It Works

You use a scanner to read values of three different types from the standard input stream. The read operations take place in a loop to allow multiple attempts at correct input. Within the loop you have a rare example of a `switch` statement that doesn't require a `break` statement after each case. In this case you want each case to fall through to the next. The `selectRead` variable that selects a `switch` case provides the means by which you manage subsequent attempts at correct input, because it records the case label currently in effect.

If you enter invalid input, an `InputMismatchException` is thrown by the `Scanner` method that is attempting to read a token of a particular type. In the `catch` block, you call the `next()` method for the `Scanner` object to retrieve and thus skip over the input that was not recognized. You then continue with the next `while` loop iteration to allow a further attempt at reading the token.

Testing for Tokens

The `hasNext()` method for a `Scanner` object returns `true` if another token is available from the input source. You can use this in combination with the `next()` method to read a sequence of tokens of any type from a source, delimited by whitespace. For example:

```
Path file = Paths.get("TryScanner.java");
try (Scanner fileScan = new Scanner(file)){
  String token = null;
  while(fileScan.hasNext()) {
    token = fileScan.next();
    // Do something with the token read...
  }
} catch(IOException e) {
  e.printStackTrace();
  System.exit(1);
}
```

Here you are just reading an arbitrary number of tokens as strings. In general, the `next()` method can throw an exception of type `NoSuchElementException`, but this cannot happen here because you use the `hasNext()` method to establish that there is another token to be read before you call the `next()` method.

The `Scanner` object can do better than this. In addition to the `hasNext()` method that checks whether a token of any kind is available, you have methods such as `hasNextInt()` and `hasNextDouble()` for testing for the availability of any of the types that you can read with methods such as `nextInt()` and `nextDouble()`. This enables you to code so that you can process tokens of various types, even when you don't know ahead of time the sequence in which they will be received. For example:

```
while(fileScan.hasNext()) {
  if(fileScan.hasNextInt()) {
  // Process integer input...

  } else if(fileScan.hasNextDouble()) {
  // Process floating-point input...

  } else if(fileScan.hasNextBoolean()) {
  // Process boolean input...

  }
}
```

The `while` loop continues as long as there are tokens of any kind available from the scanner. The `if` statements within the loop decide how the next token is to be processed, assuming it is one of the ones that you are interested in. If you want to skip tokens that you don't want to process within the loop, you call the `next()` method for `fileScan`.

Defining Your Own Patterns for Tokens

The `Scanner` class provides a way for you to specify how a token should be recognized. You use one of two overloaded versions of the `next()` method to do this. One version accepts an argument of type `Pattern` that you produce by compiling a regular expression in the way you saw earlier in this chapter. The other accepts an argument of type `String` that specifies a regular expression that identifies the token. In both cases the token is returned as type `String`.

There are also overloaded versions of the `hasNext()` method that accept either a `Pattern` argument, or a `String` object containing a regular expression that identifies a token. You use these to test for tokens of your own specification. You could see these in action in an example that scans a string for a token specified by a simple pattern.

TRY IT OUT Scanning a String

This example scans a string looking for occurrences of `"had"`:

```
import java.util.Scanner;
import java.util.regex.Pattern;

public class ScanString {
  public static void main(String[] args) {
    String str = "Smith , where Jones had had 'had', had had 'had had'.";
    String regex = "had";
    System.out.println("String is:\n" + str + "\nToken sought is: " + regex);

    Pattern had = Pattern.compile(regex);
    Scanner strScan = new Scanner(str);
    int hadCount = 0;
    while(strScan.hasNext()) {
      if(strScan.hasNext(had)) {
        ++hadCount;
        System.out.println("Token found!: " + strScan.next(had));
      } else {
        System.out.println("Token is     : " + strScan.next());
      }
    }
```

```
        }
        System.out.println(hadCount + " instances of \"" + regex +  "\" were found.");
    }
}
```

ScanString.java

This program produces the following output:

```
String is:
Smith , where Jones had had 'had', had had 'had had'.
Token sought is: had
Token is     : Smith
Token is     : ,
Token is     : where
Token is     : Jones
Token found!: had
Token found!: had
Token is     : 'had',
Token found!: had
Token found!: had
Token is     : 'had
Token is     : had'.
4 instances of "had" were found.
```

How It Works

After defining the string to be scanned and the regular expression that defines the form of a token, you compile the regular expression into a `Pattern` object. Passing a `Pattern` object to the `hasNext()` method (or the `next()` method) is more efficient than passing the original regular expression when you are calling the method more than once. When you pass a regular expression as a `String` object to the `hasNext()` method, the method must compile it to a pattern before it can use it. If you compile the regular expression first and pass the `Pattern` object as the argument, the compile operation occurs only once.

You scan the string, `str`, in the `while` loop. The loop continues as long as there is another token available from the string. Within the loop, you check for the presence of a token defined by `regex` by calling the `hasNext()` method with the `had` pattern as the argument:

```
if(strScan.hasNext(had)) {
    ++hadCount;
    System.out.println("Token found!: " + strScan.next(had));
} else {
    System.out.println("Token is     : " + strScan.next());
}
```

If `hasNext()` returns `true`, you increment `hadCount` and output the token returned by `next()` with the argument as `had`. Of course, you could just as well have used the `next()` method with no argument here. If the next token does not correspond to `had`, you read it anyway with the `next()` method. Finally, you output the number of times your token was found.

From the output you can see that only four instances of `"had"` were found. This is because the scanner assumes the delimiter is one or more whitespace characters. If you don't like this you can specify another regular expression that the scanner should use for the delimiter:

```
strScan.useDelimiter("[^\\w*]");
```

The `useDelimiter()` method expects an argument of type `String` that specifies a regular expression for recognizing delimiters. In this case the expression implies a delimiter is any number of characters that are not uppercase or lowercase letters, or digits. If you add this statement following the creation of the `Scanner` object the program should find all the `"had"` tokens.

SUMMARY

This chapter has been a brief canter through some of the interesting and useful classes available in the `java.util` package. The ones I chose to discuss are those that seem to me to be applicable in a wide range of application contexts, but there's much more to this package than I have had the space to discuss here. You should find it is a rewarding exercise to delve into the contents of this package a little further.

You can download the source code for the examples in the book and the solutions to the following exercises from www.wrox.com.

1. Define a static method to fill an array of type `char[]` with a given value passed as an argument to the method.

2. For the adventurous gambler—use a stack and a `Random` object in a program to simulate a game of Blackjack for one player using two decks of cards.

3. Write a program to display the sign of the Zodiac corresponding to a birth date entered through the keyboard.

4. Write a program using regular expressions to remove spaces from the beginning and end of each line in a file.

5. Write a program using a regular expression to reproduce a file with a sequential line number starting at "0001" inserted at the beginning of each line in the original file. You can use a copy of your Java source file as the input to test this.

6. Write a program using a regular expression to eliminate any line numbers that appear at the beginning of lines in a file. You can use the output from the previous exercise as a test for your program.

▶ **WHAT YOU LEARNED IN THIS CHAPTER**

TOPIC	CONCEPTS
The Arrays Class	The java.util.Arrays class provides static methods for sorting, searching, filling, copying, and comparing arrays.
The Random Class	Objects of type java.util.Random can generate pseudo-random numbers of type int, long, float, and double. The integers are uniformly distributed across the range of the type int or long. The floating-point numbers are between 0.0 and 1.0. You can also generate numbers of type double with a Gaussian distribution with a mean of 0.0 and a standard deviation of 1.0 and random boolean values.
The Observable Class	Classes derived from the java.util.Observable class can signal changes to classes that implement the Observer interface. You define the Observer objects that are to be associated with an Observable class object by calling the addObserver() method. This is primarily intended to be used to implement the document/view architecture for applications in a GUI environment.
The Date Class	You can create java.util.Date objects to represent a date and time that you specify in milliseconds since January 1, 1970, 00:00:00 GMT or as the current date and time from your computer clock.
The DateFormat Class	You can use a java.util.DateFormat object to format the date and time for a Date object as a string. The format is determined by the style and the locale that you specify.
The GregorianCalendar Class	A java.util.GregorianCalendar object represents a calendar set to an instant in time on a given date.
Regular Expressions	A regular expression defines a pattern that is used for searching text.
Patterns and Matchers	In Java, a regular expression is compiled into a java.util.Pattern object that you can then use to obtain a java.util.Matcher object that scans a given string looking for the pattern.
Making Pattern Substitutions	The appendReplacement() method for a Matcher object enables you to make substitutions for patterns found in the input text.
Capturing Groups	A capturing group in a regular expression records the text that matches a sub-pattern. By using capturing groups you can rearrange the sequence of substrings in a string matching a pattern.
The Scanner Class	A java.util.Scanner object uses a regular expression to segment data from a variety of sources into tokens.

16

Threads

WHAT YOU WILL LEARN IN THIS CHAPTER

➤ What a thread is and how to create threads in your programs

➤ How to control interactions between threads

➤ What synchronization means and how to apply it in your code

➤ What deadlocks are and how to avoid them

➤ What an executor is and how to use an executor to start and manage threads

➤ How to create threads that return a value

➤ How to set thread priorities

In this chapter you investigate the Java facilities that enable you to overlap the execution of segments of a single program. As well as ensuring your programs run more efficiently, this capability is particularly useful when your program must, of necessity, do a number of things at the same time: for example, a server program on a network that needs to communicate with multiple clients. As you see in Chapter 18, threads are also fundamental to any Java application that uses a graphical user interface (GUI), so it's essential that you understand how threads work.

UNDERSTANDING THREADS

Most programs of a reasonably large size contain some code segments that are more or less independent of one another and that might execute more efficiently if the code segments could be overlapped in time. *Threads* provide a way to do this. A *thread* of execution is a serial sequence of instructions that is reasonably independent of other code segments in a program so its execution can be controlled independently. If you have a machine with two or more processors then as many computations as you have processors can be executing concurrently. This allows the possibility for more than one program to be executing at any given instant. It also allows multiple threads of execution in a single program to be executing at the same time. All the program examples you have seen so far in the book consist of a single thread of execution. Graphical applications have two or more threads. Other kinds of applications can benefit from having more than one thread.

Of course, if your computer has only one processor, you can't execute more than one computation at any instant, but you can still overlap input/output operations with processing. You can also have multiple threads in progress at one time. In this case the operating system manages the transfer of execution control between them and determines when each thread gets access to the processor and for how long.

Using threads you can allow processes in a program that need to run continuously, such as a continuously running animation, to be overlapped with other activities in the same program. Java applets in a web page are executed under the control of a single program—your browser—and threads make it possible for multiple applets to be executing concurrently. In this case the threads serve to segment the activities running under the control of the browser so that they appear to run concurrently. If you have only one processor, this is an illusion created by your operating system because only one thread can actually be executing instructions at any given instant, but it's a very effective illusion. To produce animation, you typically put some code that draws a succession of still pictures in a loop that runs indefinitely. The code to draw the picture generally runs under the control of a timer so that it executes at a fixed rate—for example, 20 times per second. Of course, nothing else can happen in the same thread while the loop is running. If you want to have another animation running, it must be in a separate thread. Then the multitasking capability of your operating system can allow both threads to share the available processor time, thus allowing both animations to run.

Let's get an idea of the principles behind how threads operate. Consider a simple program that consists of three activities:

➤ Reading a number of blocks of data from a file

➤ Performing some calculation on each block of data

➤ Writing the results of the calculation to another file

You could organize the program as a single sequence of activities. In this case the activities—read file, process, write file—run in sequence, and the sequence is repeated for each block to be read and processed. You could also organize the program so that reading a block from the file is one activity, performing the calculation is a second activity, and writing the results is a third activity. Both of these situations are illustrated in Figure 16-1.

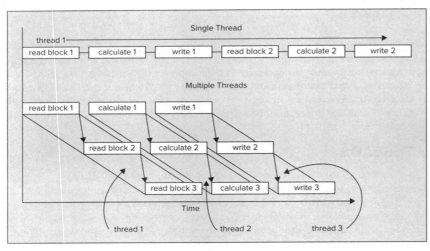

FIGURE 16-1

After a block of data has been read, the computation process can start, and as soon as the computation has been completed, the results can be written out. With the program executing each step in sequence (that is, as a single thread), as shown in the top half of Figure 16-1, the total time for execution is the sum of the times for each of the individual activities. However, suppose you were able to execute each of the activities independently, as illustrated in the lower half of Figure 16-1. In this case, reading the second block of data can start as soon as the first block has been read, and in theory you can have all three activities executing concurrently. This is possible even though you have only one processor because the input and output operations are likely to require relatively little processor time while they are executing, so the processor can be doing other things while they are in progress. This can reduce the total execution time for the program.

These three processes that run more or less independently of one another—one to read the file, another to process the data, and a third to write the results—are separate threads. Of course, the first example at the top of Figure 16-1 has just one thread that does everything in sequence. Every Java program has at least one thread. However, the three threads in the lower example in Figure 16-1 aren't completely independent of one another. After all, if they were, you might as well make them independent programs. You have practical limitations, too—the potential for overlapping these threads is dependent on the capabilities of your hardware and your operating system. However, if you *can* get some overlap in the execution of the threads, the program is likely to run faster. You'll find no magic in using threads, though. Your computer has only a finite capacity for executing instructions, and if you have many threads running, you may in fact increase the overall execution time because of the overhead implicit in managing the switching of control between threads.

An important consideration when you have a single program running as multiple threads is that the threads are unlikely to have identical execution times, and when one thread is dependent on another, you can't afford to have one overtaking the other—otherwise, you have chaos. Before you can start calculating in the example in Figure 16-1, you need to be sure that the block of data that the calculation uses has been read, and before you can write the output, you need to know that the calculation is complete. This necessitates having some means for the threads to communicate with one another.

The way I have shown the threads executing in Figure 16-1 isn't the only way of organizing the program. You could have three threads, each of which reads the file, calculates the results, and writes the output, as shown in Figure 16-2.

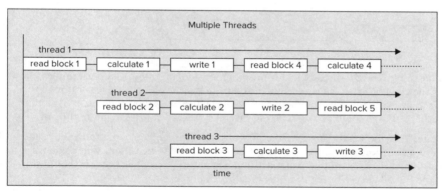

FIGURE 16-2

Now there's a different sort of contention between the threads. They are all competing to read the file and write the results, so there needs to be some way of preventing one thread from getting at the input file while another thread is already reading from it. The same goes for the output file. There's another aspect of this arrangement that is different from the previous version. For example, if one thread, *thread 1,* reads a block, *block 4,* that needs a lot of time to compute the results, another thread, *thread 2,* could conceivably read a following block, *block 5,* and calculate and write the results for *block 5* before *thread 1* has written the results for *block 4.* If you don't want the results appearing in a different sequence from the input, you should do something about this. However, before I delve into the intricacies of making sure that the threads don't get tangled or knotted, let's first look at how you create a thread.

Creating Threads

Your program always has at least one thread: the one created when the program begins execution. In a normal Java application program, this thread starts at the beginning of main(). With an applet, the browser is the main thread. That means that when your program creates a thread, it is in addition to the main thread of execution that created it. As you might have guessed, creating an additional thread involves using an object of a class, and the class is `java.lang.Thread`. Each additional thread that your program creates is represented by an object of the class `Thread`, or of a subclass of `Thread`. If your program is to have three additional threads, you need to create three such objects.

To start the execution of a thread, you call the `start()` method for the `Thread` object. The code that executes in a new thread is always a method called `run()`, which is `public`, accepts no arguments, and doesn't return a value. Threads other than the main thread in a program always start in the `run()` method for the object that represents the thread. A program that creates three threads is illustrated diagrammatically in Figure 16-3.

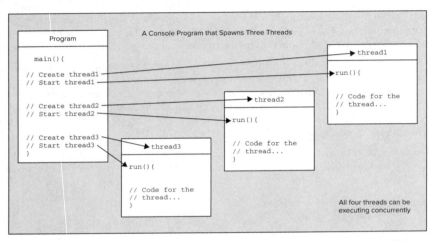

FIGURE 16-3

If a class that you define to represent a thread in your program is to do anything, you must implement the `run()` method for the class because the version inherited from the `Thread` class does nothing. Your implementation of `run()` can call any other methods you want. Figure 16-3 shows the `main()` method creating all three threads, but that doesn't have to be the case. Any thread can create more threads.

Now here comes the bite: You don't call the `run()` method to start a thread, you call the `start()` method for the object representing the thread, and that causes the `run()` method to be called. When you want to stop the execution of a thread that is running, you must signal to the `Thread` object that it should stop itself by setting a field that the thread checks at regular intervals, for example.

The reason you must start a thread in the way I have described is somewhat complex, but basically it boils down to this: Threads are always owned and managed by the operating system, and only the operating system can create and start a new thread. If you were to call the `run()` method yourself, it would simply operate like any other method, running in the same thread as the program that calls it.

When you call the `start()` method for a `Thread` object, you are calling a native code method that causes the operating system to initiate another thread from which the `run()` method for the `Thread` object executes.

In any case, it is not important to understand exactly how this works. Just remember: Always start your thread by calling the `start()` method. If you call the `run()` method directly, you have not created a new thread and your program does not work as you intended.

You can define a class that is to represent a thread in two ways:

➤ You can define a subclass of `Thread` that provides a definition of the `run()` method that overrides the inherited method.

➤ You can define your class as implementing the `Runnable` interface, which declares the `run()` method, and then creates a `Thread` object in your class when you need it.

You explore the advantages of both approaches in a little more detail. You can see how deriving a subclass of `Thread` works by using an example.

TRY IT OUT   Deriving a Subclass of Thread

You define a single class, `TryThread`, which you derive from `Thread`. As always, execution of the application starts in the `main()` method. Here's the code:

```java
import java.io.IOException;

public class TryThread extends Thread {
  public TryThread(String firstName, String secondName, long delay) {
    this.firstName = firstName;                          // Store the first name
    this.secondName = secondName;                        // Store the second name
    aWhile = delay;                                      // Store the delay
    setDaemon(true);                                     // Thread is daemon
  }

  public static void main(String[] args) {
    // Create three threads
    Thread first = new TryThread("Hopalong ", "Cassidy ", 200L);
    Thread second = new TryThread("Marilyn ", "Monroe ", 300L);
    Thread third = new TryThread("Slim ", "Pickens ", 500L);

    System.out.println("Press Enter when you have had enough...\n");
    first.start();                                       // Start the first thread
    second.start();                                      // Start the second thread
    third.start();                                       // Start the third thread

    try {
      System.in.read();                                  // Wait until Enter key pressed
      System.out.println("Enter pressed...\n");

    } catch (IOException e) {                             // Handle IO exception
      System.out.println(e);                             // Output the exception
    }
    System.out.println("Ending main()");
    return;
  }

  // Method where thread execution will start
  @Override
  public void run() {
    try {
      while(true) {                                      // Loop indefinitely...
        System.out.print(firstName);                     // Output first name
        sleep(aWhile);                                   // Wait aWhile msec.
        System.out.print(secondName + "\n");             // Output second name
      }
    } catch(InterruptedException e) {                    // Handle thread interruption
      System.out.println(firstName + secondName + e);    // Output the exception
    }
  }

  private String firstName;                              // Store for first name
  private String secondName;                             // Store for second name
  private long aWhile;                                   // Delay in milliseconds
}
```

TryThread.java

If you compile and run the code, you see something like this:

```
Press Enter when you have had enough...

Hopalong Marilyn Slim Cassidy
Hopalong Monroe
```

```
Marilyn Cassidy
Hopalong Pickens
Slim Monroe
Marilyn Cassidy
Hopalong Cassidy
Hopalong Monroe
Marilyn Pickens
Slim Cassidy
Hopalong Monroe
Marilyn Cassidy
Hopalong Cassidy
Hopalong Monroe
Marilyn Pickens
Slim Cassidy
Hopalong Cassidy
Hopalong Monroe
Marilyn
Enter pressed...

Ending main()
```

How It Works

You have three instance variables in the `TryThread` class, and these are initialized in the constructor. The two `String` variables hold first and second names, and the variable `aWhile` stores a time period in milliseconds. The constructor for the class, `TryThread()`, automatically calls the default constructor, `Thread()`, for the base class.

The class containing the `main()` method is derived from `Thread` and implements `run()`, so objects of this class represent threads. The fact that each object of your class has access to the method `main()` is irrelevant—the objects are perfectly good threads. The method `main()` creates three such objects: `first`, `second`, and `third`.

Daemon and User Threads

The call to `setDaemon()`, with the argument `true` in the `TryThread` constructor, makes the thread that is created a *daemon thread*. A daemon thread is simply a background thread that is subordinate to the thread that creates it, so when the thread that created it ends, the daemon thread dies with it. In this case, the `main()` method creates the daemon threads so that when `main()` returns and ends the main thread, all the threads it has created also end. If you run the example a few times pressing Enter at random, you should see that the daemon threads die after the `main()` method returns, because, from time to time, you get some output from one or another thread after the last output from `main()`.

A thread that isn't a daemon thread is called a *user thread*. The diagram in Figure 16-4 shows two daemon threads and a user thread that are created by the main thread of a program.

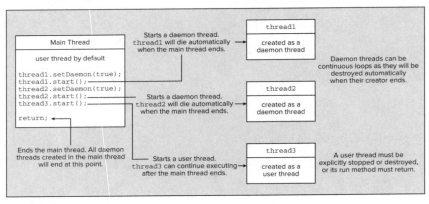

FIGURE 16-4

A user thread has a life of its own that is not dependent on the thread that creates it. It can continue execution after the thread that created it has ended. The default thread that contains `main()` is a user thread, as shown in the diagram, but `thread3` shown in the diagram could continue to execute after `main()` has returned. Threads that run for a finite time are typically user threads, but there's no reason why a daemon thread can't be finite. Threads that run indefinitely should usually be defined as daemon threads simply because you need a means of stopping them. A hypothetical example might help you to understand this, so let's consider how a network server handling transactions of some kind might work in principle.

A network server might be managed overall by a user thread that starts one or more daemon threads to listen for requests. When the server starts up, the operator starts the management thread, and this thread creates daemon threads to listen for requests. Each request that is recognized by one of these daemon threads might be handled by another thread that is created by the listening thread, so that each request is handled independently. Where processing a transaction takes a finite time, and where it is important that the requests are completed before the system shuts down, the thread to handle the request might be created as a user thread to ensure that it runs to completion, even if the listening thread that created it stops. Generally you would not want a program to be able to create an unlimited number of threads because the more threads there are running, the greater the operating system overhead there is in managing the threads. For this reason, a program often makes use of a *thread pool* of a specified fixed number of threads. When a new thread is required for a particular task, such as servicing a request, one of the threads in the thread pool is allocated to the task. If all the threads in the pool have been allocated, then a new thread cannot be started until one of the threads that is currently running terminates. The class libraries provide help in the creation and management of thread pools through the `java.util.concurrent.ThreadPoolExecutor` class. When the time comes to shut the system down, the operator doesn't have to worry about how many listening threads are running. When the main thread is shut down all the listening threads also shut down because they are daemon threads. Any outstanding threads dealing with specific transactions then run to completion.

Note that you can call `setDaemon()` for a thread only before it starts; if you try to do so afterward, the method throws an `IllegalThreadStateException` exception. Also, a thread that is itself created by a daemon thread is a daemon by default.

Creating Thread Objects

In the `main()` method you create three `Thread` variables that store three different objects of type `TryThread`. As you can see, each object has an individual name pair as the first two arguments to its constructor, and a different delay value passed as the third argument. All objects of the class `TryThread` are daemon threads because you call `setDaemon()` with the argument `true` in the constructor. Because the output can continue indefinitely, you display a message to explain how to stop it.

After you've created a thread, it doesn't start executing by itself. You need to set it going. As I said earlier, you don't call the `run()` method for the `Thread` object to do this, you call its `start()` method. Thus, you start the execution of each of the threads represented by the objects `first`, `second`, and `third` by calling the `start()` method that is inherited from `Thread` for each object. The `start()` method starts the object's `run()` method executing and then returns to the calling thread. Eventually, all three threads are executing in parallel with the original application thread, `main()`.

Implementing the run() Method

The `run()` method contains the code for thread execution. The code in this case is a single, infinite `while` loop that you have put in a `try` block because the `sleep()` method that is called in the loop can throw the `InterruptedException` exception that is caught by the `catch` block. The code in the loop outputs the first name, calls the `sleep()` method that is inherited from `Thread`, and then outputs the second name. The `sleep()` method suspends execution of the thread for the number of milliseconds that you specify in the argument. This gives any other threads that have previously been started a chance to execute. This allows the output from the three threads to become a little jumbled.

With a multicore processor as many PCs have these days, multiple threads will be executing concurrently. Each time a thread calls the `sleep()` method, one of the waiting threads jumps in and starts executing.

You can see the sequence in which the threads execute from the output. From the names in the output you can deduce that they execute in the sequence first, second, third, first, first, second, second, first, first, third, and so on. The actual sequence depends on your operating system scheduler and the number of processors that you have, so this is likely to vary from machine to machine. The execution of the read() method that is called in main() is blocked until you press Enter, but all the while the other threads continue executing. The output stops when you press Enter because this allows the main thread to continue and execute the return. Executing return ends the thread for main(), and because the other threads are daemon threads, they also die when the thread that created them dies, although as you may have seen, they can run on a little after the last output from main().

Stopping a Thread

If you did not create the threads in the last example as daemon threads, they would continue executing independently of main(). If you are prepared to terminate the program yourself (use Ctrl+C in a Windows command-line session running Java), you can demonstrate this by commenting out the call to setDaemon() in the constructor. Pressing Enter ends main(), but the other threads continue indefinitely.

A thread can signal another thread that it should stop executing by calling the interrupt() method for that Thread object. This in itself doesn't stop the thread; it just sets a flag in the thread that indicates an interruption has been requested. This flag must be checked in the run() method to have any effect and the thread should then terminate itself. The isInterrupted() method that the Thread class defines returns true if the interrupted flag has been set. The method does not reset the flag, but calling the interrupted() method tests the flag and resets it if it was set.

As it happens, the sleep() method checks whether the thread has been interrupted and throws an InterruptedException if it has been. You can see that in action by altering the previous example a little.

TRY IT OUT Interrupting a Thread

Make sure the call to the setDaemon() method is still commented out in the constructor and modify the main() method as follows:

Available for
download on
Wrox.com

```
public static void main(String[] args) {
  // Create three threads
  Thread first = new TryThread("Hopalong ", "Cassidy ", 200L);
  Thread second = new TryThread("Marilyn ", "Monroe ", 300L);
  Thread third = new TryThread("Slim ", "Pickens ", 500L);

  System.out.println("Press Enter when you have had enough...\n");
  first.start();                        // Start the first thread
  second.start();                       // Start the second thread
  third.start();                        // Start the third thread
  try {
    System.in.read();                   // Wait until Enter key pressed
    System.out.println("Enter pressed...\n");

    // Interrupt the threads
    first.interrupt();
    second.interrupt();
    third.interrupt();
  } catch (IOException e) {              // Handle IO exception
    System.out.println(e);              // Output the exception
  }
  System.out.println("Ending main()");
  return;
}
```

TryThreadInterrupted.java

I created this as a new example in the download called `TryThreadInterrupted`. Of course, some of the code in `main()` has to be changed accordingly. Now the program produces output that is something like the following:

```
Press Enter when you have had enough...

Slim Hopalong Marilyn Cassidy
Hopalong Monroe
Marilyn Cassidy
Hopalong Pickens
Slim Cassidy
Hopalong Monroe
Marilyn
Enter pressed...


Ending main()
Marilyn Monroe java.lang.InterruptedException: sleep interrupted
Slim Pickens java.lang.InterruptedException: sleep interrupted
Hopalong Cassidy java.lang.InterruptedException: sleep interrupted
```

How It Works

Because the `main()` method calls the `interrupt()` method for each of the threads after you press the Enter key, the `sleep()` method that is called in each thread registers the fact that the thread has been interrupted and throws an `InterruptedException`. This is caught by the `catch` block in the `run()` method and produces the new output that you see. Because the `catch` block is outside the `while` loop, the `run()` method for each thread returns and each thread terminates.

You can check whether a thread has been interrupted by calling the `isInterrupted()` method for the thread. This returns `true` if `interrupt()` has been called for the thread in question. Because this is an instance method, you can use this in one thread to determine whether another thread has been interrupted. For example, in `main()` you could write:

```
if(first.isInterrupted()) {
    System.out.println("First thread has been interrupted.");
}
```

Note that this determines only whether the interrupted flag has been set by a call to `interrupt()` for the thread—it does not determine whether the thread is still running. A thread could have its interrupt flag set and continue executing—it is not obliged to terminate because `interrupt()` is called. To test whether a thread is still operating, you can call its `isAlive()` method. This returns `true` if the thread has not terminated.

The instance method `isInterrupted()` in the `Thread` class has no effect on the interrupt flag in the thread—if it was set, it remains set. However, the static `interrupted()` method in the `Thread` class is different. It tests whether the currently executing thread has been interrupted, and if it has, it clears the interrupted flag in the current `Thread` object and returns `true`.

When an `InterruptedException` is thrown, the flag that registers the interrupt in the thread is cleared, so a subsequent call to `isInterrupted()` or `interrupted()` returns `false`.

Connecting Threads

If in one thread you need to wait until another thread dies, you can call the `join()` method for the thread that you expect isn't long for this world. Calling the `join()` method with no arguments halts the current thread for as long as it takes the specified thread to die:

```
thread1.join();            // Suspend the current thread until thread1 dies
```

You can also pass a `long` value to the `join()` method to specify the number of milliseconds you're prepared to wait for the death of a thread:

```
thread1.join(1000);        // Wait up to 1 second for thread1 to die
```

If this is not precise enough, you have a version of `join()` with two parameters. The first is a time in milliseconds and the second is a time in nanoseconds. The current thread waits for the duration specified by the sum of the arguments. Of course, whether or not you get nanosecond resolution depends on the capability of your hardware.

The `join()` method can throw an `InterruptedException` if the current thread is interrupted by another thread, so you should put a call to `join()` in a `try` block and catch the exception.

Thread Scheduling

The scheduling of threads depends to some extent on your operating system, but each thread certainly gets a chance to execute while the others are "asleep," that is, when they've called their `sleep()` methods. If your operating system uses preemptive multitasking (Microsoft Windows and Linux both support preemptive multitasking), or your hardware has multiple processors that are supported by the operating system, the program works without the call to `sleep()` in the `run()` method (you should also remove the `try` and `catch` blocks if you remove the `sleep()` call). However, if your operating system doesn't schedule in this way, without the `sleep()` call in `run()`, the `first` thread hogs a single processor and continues indefinitely.

Figure 16-5 illustrates how four threads might share a single processor over time by calling the `sleep()` method to relinquish control.

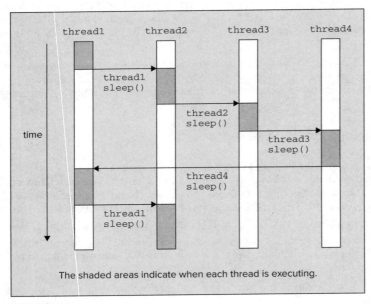

The shaded areas indicate when each thread is executing.

FIGURE 16-5

Note that there's another method, `yield()`, defined in the `Thread` class, that gives other threads a chance to execute. You use this when you just want to allow other threads a look-in if they are waiting, but you don't want to suspend execution of the current thread for a specific period of time. When you call the `sleep()` method for a thread, the thread does not continue for at least the time you have specified as an argument, even if no other threads are waiting. Calling `yield()`, on the other hand, causes the current thread to resume immediately if no threads are waiting.

Implementing the Runnable Interface

As an alternative to defining a new subclass of `Thread`, you can implement the `Runnable` interface in a class. You'll find that this is generally much more convenient than deriving a class from `Thread` because you can derive your class from a class other than `Thread` and it can still represent a thread. Because Java allows only a single base class, if you derive your class from `Thread`, it can't inherit functionality from any other class. The `Runnable` interface declares only one method, `run()`, and this is the method that is executed when the thread is started.

To see how this works in practice, you can write another version of the previous example. I've called this version of the program `JumbleNames`:

```java
import java.io.IOException;

public class JumbleNames implements Runnable {
  // Constructor
  public JumbleNames(String firstName, String secondName, long delay) {
    this.firstName = firstName;                    // Store the first name
    this.secondName = secondName;                  // Store the second name
    aWhile = delay;                                // Store the delay
  }

  // Method where thread execution will start
  public void run() {
    try {
      while(true) {                                // Loop indefinitely...
        System.out.print(firstName);              // Output first name
        Thread.sleep(aWhile);                     // Wait aWhile msec.
        System.out.print(secondName+"\n");        // Output second name
      }
    } catch(InterruptedException e) {              // Handle thread interruption
      System.out.println(firstName + secondName + e); // Output the exception
    }
  }

  public static void main(String[] args) {
    // Create three threads
    Thread first = new Thread(new JumbleNames("Hopalong ", "Cassidy ", 200L));
    Thread second = new Thread(new JumbleNames("Marilyn ", "Monroe ", 300L));
    Thread third = new Thread(new JumbleNames("Slim ", "Pickens ", 500L));

    // Set threads as daemon
    first.setDaemon(true);
    second.setDaemon(true);
    third.setDaemon(true);
    System.out.println("Press Enter when you have had enough...\n");
    first.start();                                 // Start the first thread
    second.start();                                // Start the second thread
    third.start();                                 // Start the third thread
    try {
      System.in.read();                            // Wait until Enter key pressed
      System.out.println("Enter pressed...\n");

    } catch (IOException e) {                       // Handle IO exception
      System.err.println(e);                       // Output the exception
    }
    System.out.println("Ending main()");
    return;
  }

  private String firstName;                        // Store for first name
  private String secondName;                       // Store for second name
  private long aWhile;                             // Delay in milliseconds
}
```

How It Works

You have the same data members in this class as you had in the previous example. The constructor is almost the same as previously, too. You can't call `setDaemon()` in this class constructor because the class isn't derived from `Thread`. Instead, you need to do that in `main()` after you've created the objects that represent the threads and before you call the `run()` method. The `run()` method implementation is also very similar. The class doesn't have `sleep()` as a member, but because it's a `public static` member of the `Thread` class, you can call it in the `run()` method by using the class name as the qualifier.

In the `main()` method you still create a `Thread` object for each thread of execution, but this time you use a constructor that accepts an object of type `Runnable` as an argument. You pass an object of our class `JumbleNames` to it. This is possible because the `JumbleNames` class implements `Runnable`.

Thread Names

Threads have a name, which in the case of the `Thread` constructor you're using in the example is a default name composed of the string `"Thread*"` with a sequence number appended. If you want to choose your own name for a thread, you can use a `Thread` constructor that accepts a `String` object specifying the name you want to assign to the thread. For example, you could have created the `Thread` object `first` with the following statement:

```
Thread first = new Thread(new JumbleNames("Hopalong ", "Cassidy ", 200L), "firstThread");
```

This assigns the name `"firstThread"` to the thread. Note that this name is used only when displaying information about the thread. It has no relation to the identifier for the `Thread` object, and there's nothing, apart from common sense, to prevent several threads being given the same name.

You can obtain the name assigned to a thread by calling the `getName()` method for the `Thread` object. The name of the thread is returned as a `String` object. You can also change the name of a thread by calling the `setName()` method defined in the class `Thread` and passing a `String` object to it.

After you've created the three `Thread` objects in the example, you call the `setDaemon()` method for each of them. The rest of `main()` is the same as in the original version of the previous example, and you should get similar output when you run this version of the program.

An object of a class that implements `Runnable` might need access to the `Thread` object that encapsulates the thread in which it is executing. The static `currentThread()` method in the `Thread` class returns a reference to the current thread so that provides access when you need it.

MANAGING THREADS

In all the examples you've seen so far in this chapter, the threads are launched and then left to compete for computer resources. Because all three threads compete in an uncontrolled way for a processor, the output from the threads gets muddled. This isn't normally a desirable feature in a program. In most instances where you use threads, you need to manage the way in which they execute so that their activities are coordinated and they don't interfere with each other.

Of course, in our examples, the programs are deliberately constructed to release control of the processor part way through outputting a name. While this is very artificial, similar situations can arise in practice, particularly where threads are involved in a repetitive operation. It is important to appreciate that a thread can be interrupted while a source statement is executing. For example, imagine that a bank teller is crediting a check to an account and at the same time the customer with that account is withdrawing some cash through an ATM. This might happen in the following way:

➤ The bank teller checks the balance of the customer's account, which is $500.

➤ The ATM asks for the account balance.

➤ The teller adds the value of the check, $100, to the account balance to give a figure of $600.

➤ The ATM takes $50 off the balance of $500, which gives a figure of $450, and spits out five $10 bills.

➤ The teller assigns the value of $600 to the account balance.

➤ The ATM assigns the value $450 to the account balance.

Here you can see the problem very well. The account balance should be $550, so the customer has lost $100. Asking the account for its balance and assigning a new balance to the account are two different operations that are totally unconnected. As long as this is the case, you can never guarantee that this type of problem will not occur. Of course, I'm talking about programming here, not banks. Everyone knows that banks *never* make mistakes.

Where two or more threads share a common resource, such as a file or a block of memory, you'll need to take steps to ensure that one thread doesn't modify a resource while that resource is still being used by another thread. Having one thread update a record in a file while another thread is partway through retrieving the same record is a recipe for disaster. One way of managing this sort of situation is to use *synchronization* for the threads involved. I will discuss the basic synchronization capabilities provided by the Java language in this chapter, but note that the concurrency library provided as the `java.util.concurrent`, `java.util.concurrent.atomic`, and `java.util.concurrent.locks` packages contains classes that implement specialized thread management facilities.

Synchronization

The objective of synchronization is to ensure that when several threads want access to a single resource, only one thread can access it at any given time. You can use synchronization to manage your threads of execution in two ways:

➤ **You can manage code at the method level.** This involves synchronizing methods.

➤ **You can manage code at the block level.** This uses synchronizing blocks.

Let's look at how you can use synchronized methods first.

Synchronized Methods

You can make a subset (or indeed all) of the methods for any class object mutually exclusive, so that only one of the methods can execute at any given time. You make methods mutually exclusive by declaring them in the class using the keyword `synchronized`. For example:

```
class MyClass {
  synchronized public void method1() {
    // Code for the method...
  }

  synchronized public void method2() {
    // Code for the method...
  }

  public void method3() {
    // Code for the method...
  }
}
```

Now, only one of the synchronized methods in a class object can execute at any one time. Only when the currently executing synchronized method for an object has ended can another synchronized method start for the same object. The idea here is that each synchronized method has guaranteed exclusive access to the object while it is executing, at least so far as the other synchronized methods for the class object are concerned.

The synchronization process makes use of an internal *lock* that every object has associated with it. The lock is a kind of flag that is set by a process, referred to as *locking* or a lock action, when a synchronized method starts execution. Each synchronized method for an object checks to see whether the lock has been set by another method. If it has, it does not start execution until the lock has been reset by an *unlock action*. Thus, only one synchronized method can be executing at one time, because that method has set the lock that prevents any other synchronized method from starting.

 NOTE *There is no constraint here on simultaneously executing synchronized methods for two different objects of the same class. It's only concurrent access to any one object that is controlled by synchronization.*

Of the three methods in myClass, two are declared as synchronized, so for any object of the class, only one of these methods can execute at one time. The method that isn't declared as synchronized, method3(), can always be executed by a thread, regardless of whether a synchronized method is executing in some other thread.

It's important to keep clear in your mind the distinction between an object that has instance methods that you declared as synchronized in the class definition and the threads of execution that might use them. A hypothetical relationship between three threads and two objects of the class myClass is illustrated in Figure 16-6.

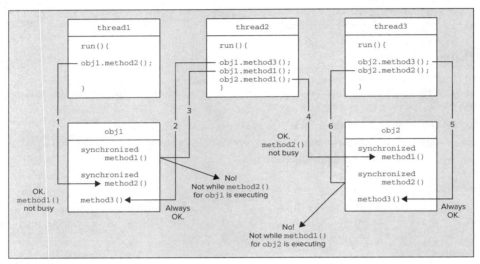

FIGURE 16-6

The numbers on the arrows in the figure indicate the sequence of events. **No!** indicates that the thread waits until the method is unlocked so it can execute it. While method1() in obj2 is executing, method2() for the same object can't be executed. The synchronization of these two instance methods in an object provides a degree of protection for the object, in that only one synchronized method can mess with the data in the object at any given time.

However, each object is independent of any other object when it comes to synchronized instance methods. When a thread executes a synchronized method for an object, it is assured exclusive access to the object insofar as the synchronized methods in that object are concerned. Another thread, though, can still call the same method for a different object. While method1() is being executed for obj1, this doesn't prevent method1() for obj2 being executed by some other thread. Also, if there's a method in an object that has not been declared as synchronized—method3() in obj1, for example—any thread can call that at any time, regardless of the state of any synchronized methods in the object.

If you apply synchronization to static methods in a class, only one of those static methods in the class can be executing at any point in time; this is per-class synchronization, and the class lock is independent of any locks for objects of the class.

An important principle that you need to understand is that only the `run()` method is necessarily part of a thread of execution in a class object that represents a thread. Other methods for the same class object are only part of the thread of execution if they are called directly or indirectly by the `run()` method. All the methods that are called directly or indirectly from the `run()` method for an object are all part of the same thread, but they clearly don't have to be methods for the same `Thread` object. Indeed, they can be methods that belong to any other objects, including other `Thread` objects that have their own `run()` methods.

Using Synchronized Methods

To see how synchronization can be applied in practice, you construct a program that provides a simple model of a bank. This particular bank is a very young business with only one customer account initially, but you have two clerks, each working flat out to process transactions for the account, one handling debits and the other handling credits. The objects in the program are illustrated in Figure 16-7.

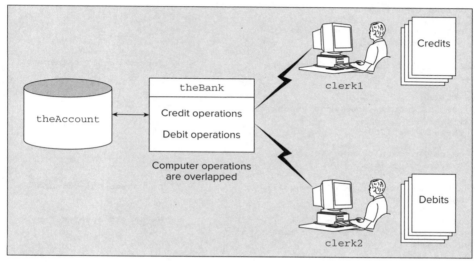

FIGURE 16-7

The bank in the model is actually a computer that performs operations on the account, and the account is stored separately. Each clerk can communicate directly with the bank. You define four classes that you use in the program to model banking operations:

➤ A `Bank` class to represent the bank's computer

➤ An `Account` class to represent the account at the bank

➤ A `Transaction` class to represent a transaction on the account—a debit or a credit, for example

➤ A `Clerk` class to represent a bank clerk

You also define a class containing the method `main()` that starts the process off and determines how it all works.

 WARNING *As you develop the code, you won't necessarily get it right the first time, but you will improve as you find out more about how to program using threads. This will expose some of the sorts of errors and complications that can arise when you're programming using threads. I've included the incremental changes to the example as separate programs in the code download numbered sequentially.*

TRY IT OUT   Defining a Bank Class

The bank computer is the agent that performs the operations on an account so you start with that. You can define the Bank class that represents the bank computer as follows:

Available for
download on
Wrox.com

```
// Define the bank

public class Bank {
  // Perform a transaction
  public void doTransaction(Transaction transaction) {
    int balance = transaction.getAccount().getBalance(); // Get current balance

    switch(transaction.getTransactionType()) {
      case CREDIT:
        // Credits require a lot of checks...
        try {
          Thread.sleep(100);

        } catch(InterruptedException e) {
          System.out.println(e);
        }
        balance += transaction.getAmount();              // Increment the balance
        break;

      case DEBIT:
        // Debits require even more checks...
        try {
          Thread.sleep(150);

        } catch(InterruptedException e) {
          System.out.println(e);
        }
        balance -= transaction.getAmount();              // Decrement the balance
        break;

      default:                                           // We should never get here
        System.out.println("Invalid transaction");
        System.exit(1);
    }
    transaction.getAccount().setBalance(balance);        // Restore the A/C balance
  }
}
```

Directory "BankOperation 1"

How It Works

The Bank class is very simple. It keeps no records of anything locally as the accounts are identified separately, and it has only one method that carries out a transaction. The Transaction object provides all the information about what the transaction is and the account to which it applies. You can define the possible types of transactions with the following enumeration:

```
// Bank account transaction types
public enum TransactionType {DEBIT, CREDIT }
```

You have provided only for debit and credit operations on an account, but the enum type and the switch statement could easily be extended to accommodate other types of transactions. Both of the transactions supported involve some delay while the standard nameless checks and verifications that all banks have are carried out. The delay is simulated by calling the sleep() method belonging to the Thread class.

Of course, during this time, other things in other threads may be going on. There are no instance variables to initialize in a Bank object, so you don't need a constructor. Because the Bank object works using a Transaction object, let's define the class for that next.

TRY IT OUT   Defining a Transaction on an Account

The `Transaction` class can represent any transaction on an account. You can define the class as follows:

```java
public class Transaction {
  // Constructor
  public Transaction(Account account, TransactionType type, int amount) {
    this.account = account;
    this.type = type;
    this.amount = amount;
  }

  public Account getAccount() {
    return account;
  }

  public TransactionType getTransactionType() {
    return type;
  }

  public int getAmount() {
    return amount;
  }

  @Override
  public String toString() {
    return type + " A//C: " + account + ": $" + amount;
  }

  private Account account;
  private int amount;
  private TransactionType type;
}
```

Directory "BankOperation 1"

How It Works

The type of transaction is specified by the `TransactionType` enumeration. A transaction records the amount for the transaction and a reference to the account to which it applies, so a `Transaction` object specifies a complete transaction. The methods are very straightforward, just accessor methods for the data members that are used by the `Bank` object, plus the `toString()` method overload in case you need it.

TRY IT OUT   Defining a Bank Account

You can define an account by the following class type:

```java
// Defines a customer account
public class Account {
  // Constructor
  public Account(int accountNumber, int balance) {
    this.accountNumber = accountNumber;        // Set the account number
    this.balance = balance;                    // Set the initial balance
  }

  // Return the current balance
  public int getBalance() {
    return balance;
  }

  // Set the current balance
  public void setBalance(int balance) {
    this.balance = balance;
  }
```

```
    public int getAccountNumber() {
      return accountNumber;
    }

    @Override
    public String toString() {
      return "A/C No. " + accountNumber + " : $" + balance;
    }

    private int balance;                        // The current account balance
    private int accountNumber;                  // Identifies this account
  }
```

Directory "BankOperation 1"

How It Works

The `Account` class is also very simple. It just maintains a record of the amount in the account as a balance and provides methods for retrieving and setting the current balance. Operations on the account are performed externally by the `Bank` object. You have a bit more than you need in the `Account` class at the moment, but the methods you don't use in the current example might be useful later.

TRY IT OUT Defining a Bank Clerk

A clerk is a slightly more complicated animal. He or she retains information about the bank and details of the current transaction, and is responsible for initiating debits and credits on an account by communication with the central bank. Each clerk works independently of the others so they are each a separate thread:

Available for
download on
Wrox.com

```
public class Clerk implements Runnable {
  // Constructor
  public Clerk(Bank theBank) {
    this.theBank = theBank;              // Who the clerk works for
    inTray = null;                       // No transaction initially
  }

  // Receive a transaction
  public void doTransaction(Transaction transaction) {
    inTray = transaction;
  }

  // The working clerk...
  public void run() {
    while(true) {                        // Non-stop work...
      while(inTray == null) {            // No transaction waiting?
        try {
          Thread.sleep(150);             // Then take a break...

        } catch(InterruptedException e) {
          System.out.println(e);
        }
      }

      theBank.doTransaction(inTray);
      inTray = null;                     // In-tray is empty
    }
  }

  // Busy check
  public boolean isBusy() {
    return inTray != null;               // A full in-tray means busy!
  }
```

```
      private Bank theBank;              // The employer - an electronic marvel
      private Transaction inTray;        // The in-tray holding a transaction
    }
```

Directory "BankOperation 1"

How It Works

A `Clerk` object is a thread because it implements the `Runnable` interface. Each clerk has an in-tray, capable of holding one transaction, and although the in-tray is not `null`, the clerk is clearly busy. A clerk needs to be aware of the `Bank` object that is employing him or her, so a reference is stored in `theBank` when a `Clerk` object is created. A transaction is placed in the in-tray for a clerk by calling his or her `doTransaction()` method. You can check whether a clerk is busy by calling the `isBusy()` member, which returns `true` if a transaction is still in progress.

The real work is actually done in the `run()` method. If the in-tray is empty, indicated by a `null` value in `inTray`, then there's nothing for the clerk to do, so after sleeping a while, the loop goes around again to give the clerk another look at the in-tray. When a transaction has been recorded in the in-tray, the method in `theBank` object is called to carry it out, and the `inTray` is reset to `null`.

All you need now is the class to drive our model world, which you can call `BankOperation`. This class requires only the method `main()`, but there are quite a lot of things to do in this method so you put it together piece by piece.

TRY IT OUT Defining the Operation of the Bank

Apart from setting everything up, the `main()` method has to originate transactions on the accounts and pass them on to the clerks to be expedited. You start with just one account and a couple of clerks. Here's the basic structure:

```
import java.util.Random;

public class BankOperation {
   public static void main(String[] args) {
      int initialBalance = 500;     // The initial account balance
      int totalCredits = 0;         // Total credits on the account
      int totalDebits =0;           // Total debits on the account
      int transactionCount = 20;    // Number of debits and credits

      // Create the account, the bank, and the clerks...

      // Create the threads for the clerks as daemon, and start them off

      // Generate the transactions of each type and pass to the clerks

      // Wait until both clerks are done

      // Now output the results
   }
}
```

Directory "BankOperation 1"

The `import` for the `Random` class is there because you need it for code you add a little later. To create the `Bank` object, the clerks, and the account, you need to add the following code:

```
      // Create the account, the bank, and the clerks...
      Bank theBank = new Bank();                    // Create a bank
      Clerk clerk1 = new Clerk(theBank);            // Create the first clerk
      Clerk clerk2 = new Clerk(theBank);            // Create the second clerk
      Account account = new Account(1, initialBalance);// Create an account
```

The next step is to add the code to create the threads for the clerks and start them going:

```
                  // Create the threads for the clerks as daemon, and start them off
                  Thread clerk1Thread = new Thread(clerk1);
                  Thread clerk2Thread = new Thread(clerk2);
                  clerk1Thread.setDaemon(true);              // Set first as daemon
                  clerk2Thread.setDaemon(true);              // Set second as daemon
                  clerk1Thread.start();                      // Start the first
                  clerk2Thread.start();                      // Start the second
```

The code to generate the transactions looks like a lot but is quite repetitive:

```
                  // Generate transactions of each type and pass to the clerks
                  Random rand = new Random();                // Random number generator
                  Transaction transaction;                   // Stores a transaction
                  int amount = 0;                            // stores an amount of money
                  for(int i = 1 ; i <= transactionCount ; ++i) {
                    amount = 50 + rand.nextInt(26);          // Generate amount of $50 to $75
                    transaction = new Transaction(account,   // Account
                                      TransactionType.CREDIT, // Credit transaction
                                          amount);           //   of amount
                    totalCredits += amount;                  // Keep total credit tally

                    // Wait until the first clerk is free
                    while(clerk1.isBusy()) {
                      try {
                        Thread.sleep(25);                    // Busy so try later

                      } catch(InterruptedException e) {
                        System.out.println(e);
                      }
                    }
                    clerk1.doTransaction(transaction);       // Now do the credit

                    amount = 30 + rand.nextInt(31);          // Generate amount of $30 to $60
                    transaction = new Transaction(account,   // Account
                                      TransactionType.DEBIT, // Debit transaction
                                          amount);           //   of amount
                    totalDebits += amount;                   // Keep total debit tally
                    // Wait until the second clerk is free
                    while(clerk2.isBusy()) {
                      try {
                        Thread.sleep(25);                    // Busy so try later

                      } catch(InterruptedException e) {
                        System.out.println(e);
                      }
                    }
                    clerk2.doTransaction(transaction);       // Now do the debit
                  }
```

After all the transactions have been processed, you can output the results. However, the clerks could still be busy after you exit from the loop, so you need to wait for both of them to be free before outputting the results. You can do this with a while loop:

```
                  // Wait until both clerks are done
                  while(clerk1.isBusy() || clerk2.isBusy()) {
                    try {
                      Thread.sleep(25);

                    } catch(InterruptedException e) {
                      System.out.println(e);
                    }
                  }
```

Lastly, you output the results:

```
// Now output the results
System.out.println(
            "Original balance : $" + initialBalance+"\n" +
            "Total credits    : $" + totalCredits+"\n" +
            "Total debits     : $" + totalDebits+"\n" +
            "Final balance    : $" + account.getBalance() + "\n" +
            "Should be        : $" + (initialBalance + totalCredits - totalDebits));
```

How It Works

The variables in the main() method track the total debits and credits, and record the initial account balance. They are there to help you figure out what has happened after the transactions have been processed. The number of times you debit and then credit the account is stored in transactionCount, so the total number of transactions is twice this value. You have added five further blocks of code to perform the functions indicated by the comments, so let's now go through each of them in turn.

The Account object is created with the account number as 1 and with the initial balance stored in initialBalance. You pass the bank object, theBank, to the constructor for each of the Clerk objects, so that they can record it.

The Thread constructor requires an object of type Runnable, so you can just pass the Clerk objects in the argument. There's no problem in doing this because the Clerk class implements the Runnable interface. You can always implicitly cast an object to a type that is any superclass of the object or any interface type that the object class implements.

All the transactions are generated in the for loop. The handling of debits is essentially the same as the handling of credits, so I go through the code only for the latter in detail. A random amount between $50 and $75 is generated for a credit transaction by using the nextInt() method for the rand object of type Random that you create. You recall that nextInt() returns an int value in the range 0 to one less than the value of the argument, so by passing 26 to the method, you get a value between 0 and 25 returned. You add 50 to this and, presto, you have a value between 50 and 75. You then use this amount to create a Transaction object that represents a credit for the account. To keep a check on the work done by the clerks, you add this credit to the total of all the credits generated, which is stored in the variable totalCredits. This enables you to verify whether or not the account has been updated properly.

Before you pass the transaction to clerk1, you must make sure that he or she isn't busy. Otherwise, you would overwrite the clerk's in-tray. The while loop does this. As long as the isBusy() method returns true, you continue to call the sleep() method for a 25-millisecond delay, before you go round and check again. When isBusy() returns false, you call the doTransaction() method for the clerk, with the reference to the transaction object as the argument. The for loop runs for 20 iterations, so you generate 20 random transactions of each type.

The third while loop works in the same way as the previous check for a busy clerk—the loop continues if either of the clerks is busy.

Lastly, you output the original account balance, the totals of credits and debits, and the final balance, plus what it should be for comparison. That's all you need in the method main(), so you're ready to give it a whirl. Remember that all four classes need to be in the same directory.

Running the Example

Now, if you run the example, the final balance is wrong. You should get results something like the following:

```
Original balance : $500
Total credits    : $1295
Total debits     : $880
Final balance    : $212
Should be        : $915
```

Of course, your results won't be the same as this, but they should be just as wrong. The customer will not be happy. His account balance is seriously off—in the bank's favor, of course, as always. So how has this come about?

The problem is that both clerks are operating on the same account at the same time. Both clerks call the doTransaction() method for the Bank object, so this method is executed by both clerk threads. Separate calls on the same method are overlapping.

TRY IT OUT   Synchronizing Methods

One way you can fix this is by simply declaring the method that operates on an account as synchronized. This prevents one clerk getting at the method for an account while it is still in progress with the other clerk. To implement this you should amend the Bank class definition as follows:

```
// Define the bank
public class Bank {
  // Perform a transaction
  synchronized public void doTransaction(Transaction transaction) {
    // Code exactly as before...
  }
}
```

Directory "BankOperation 2 - Synchronized Methods"

How It Works

Declaring this method as synchronized prevents a call to it from being executed while another is still in operation. If you run the example again with this change, the result is something like:

```
Original balance : $500
Total credits    : $1279
Total debits     : $932
Final balance    : $847
Should be        : $847
```

The amounts might be different because the transaction amounts are random, but your final balance should be the same as adding the credits to the original balance and subtracting the debits.

As you saw earlier, when you declare methods in a class as synchronized, it prevents concurrent execution of those methods within a single object, *including concurrent execution of the same method*. It is important not to let the fact that there is only one copy of a particular method confuse you. A given method can be potentially executing in any number of threads—as many threads as there are in the program, in fact. If it were not synchronized, the doTransaction() method could be executed concurrently by any number of clerks.

Although this fixes the problem in that the account balance is now correct, the bank is still amazingly inefficient. Each clerk is kicking his or her heels while another clerk is carrying out a transaction. At any given time a maximum of one clerk is working. On this basis the bank could fire them all bar one and get the same throughput. You can do better, as you see later.

Synchronizing Code Blocks

In addition to being able to synchronize methods on a class object, you can also specify a statement or a block of code in your program as synchronized, which is more powerful because you specify which particular object is to benefit from the synchronization of the statement or code block, not just the object that contains the code as in the case of a synchronized method. Here you can set a lock on any object for a given statement block. When the block that is synchronized on the given object is executing, no other code block or method that is synchronized on the same object can execute. To synchronize a statement, you just write:

```
synchronized(theObject)
  statement;                 // Synchronized with respect to theObject
```

No other statements or statement blocks in the program that are synchronized on the object theObject can execute while this statement is executing. This applies even when the statement is a call to a method, which may in turn call other methods. The statement here could equally well be a block of code between braces. This is powerful stuff. Now you can lock a particular object while the code block that is working is running.

To see precisely how you can use this in practice, let's create a modification of the last example. Let's up the sophistication of our banking operation to support multiple accounts. To extend our example to handle more than one account, you just need to make some changes to main(). You add one extra account to keep the output modest, but you modify the code to handle any number of accounts.

TRY IT OUT   Handling Multiple Accounts

You can modify the code in main() that creates the account and sets the initial balance to create multiple accounts as follows:

Available for download on Wrox.com

```java
public class BankOperation3 {
  public static void main(String[] args) {
    int[] initialBalance = {500, 800};                      // The initial account balances
    int[] totalCredits = new int[initialBalance.length];    // Two cr totals
    int[] totalDebits = new int[initialBalance.length];     // Two db totals
    int transactionCount = 20;                              // Number of debits and credits

    // Create the bank and the clerks...
    Bank theBank = new Bank();                              // Create a bank
    Clerk clerk1 = new Clerk(theBank );                    // Create the first clerk
    Clerk clerk2 = new Clerk(theBank );                    // Create the second clerk

    // Create the accounts, and initialize total credits and debits
    Account[] accounts = new Account[initialBalance.length];
    for(int i = 0 ; i < initialBalance.length ; ++i) {
      accounts[i] = new Account(i+1, initialBalance[i]); // Create accounts
      totalCredits[i] = totalDebits[i] = 0;
    }

    // Create the threads for the clerks as daemon, and start them off

    // Create transactions randomly distributed between the accounts...

    // Wait until both clerks are done

    // Now output the results...
  }
}
```

Directory "BankOperation 3 - Multiple Accounts"

The shaded lines are where the changes occur. You now create an array of accounts in a loop, the number of accounts being determined by the number of initial balances in the initialBalance array. Account numbers are assigned successively starting from 1. The code for creating the bank and the clerks and for creating the threads and starting them is exactly the same as before. The shaded comments that follow the code indicate the other segments of code in main() that you need to modify.

The next piece you need to change is the creation and processing of the transactions:

Available for download on Wrox.com

```java
// Create transactions randomly distributed between the accounts
Random rand = new Random();
Transaction transaction;                        // Stores a transaction
int amount = 0;                                 // Stores an amount of money
int select = 0;                                 // Selects an account
for(int i = 1 ; i <= transactionCount ; ++i) {
  // Choose an account at random for credit operation
  select = rand.nextInt(accounts.length);
  amount = 50 + rand.nextInt(26);               // Generate amount of $50 to $75
```

```
      transaction = new Transaction(accounts[select],    // Account
                            TransactionType.CREDIT,       // Credit transaction
                                  amount);                //   of amount
      totalCredits[select] += amount;                     // Keep total credit tally

      // Wait until the first clerk is free
      while(clerk1.isBusy()) {
        try {
          Thread.sleep(25);                               // Busy so try later
        } catch(InterruptedException e) {
          System.out.println(e);
        }
      }
      clerk1.doTransaction(transaction);                  // Now do the credit

      // choose an account at random for debit operation
      select = rand.nextInt(accounts.length);
      amount = 30 + rand.nextInt(31);                     // Generate amount of $30 to $60
      transaction = new Transaction(accounts[select],     // Account
                            TransactionType.DEBIT,        // Debit transaction
                                  amount);                //   of amount
      totalDebits[select] += amount;                      // Keep total debit tally

      // Wait until the second clerk is free
      while(clerk2.isBusy()) {
        try {
          Thread.sleep(25);                               // Busy so try later
        } catch(InterruptedException e) {
          System.out.println(e);
        }
      }
      clerk2.doTransaction(transaction);                  // Now do the debit
    }
```

Directory "BankOperation 3 - Multiple Accounts"

The last modification you must make to the method `main()` is for outputting the results. You now do this in a loop, as you have to process more than one account:

Available for
download on
Wrox.com

```
// Now output the results
for(int i = 0 ; i < accounts.length ; ++i) {
  System.out.println("Account Number:"+accounts[i].getAccountNumber() + "\n" +
     "Original balance    : $" + initialBalance[i] + "\n" +
     "Total credits       : $" + totalCredits[i] + "\n" +
     "Total debits        : $" + totalDebits[i] + "\n" +
     "Final balance       : $" + accounts[i].getBalance() + "\n" +
     "Should be           : $" + (initialBalance[i]
                               + totalCredits[i]
                               - totalDebits[i]) + "\n");
}
```

Directory "BankOperation 3 - Multiple Accounts"

This is much the same as before except that you now extract values from the arrays you have created. If you run this version it works perfectly, of course. A typical set of results is:

```
Account Number:1
Original balance   : $500
Total credits      : $659
Total debits       : $614
Final balance      : $545
Should be          : $545
```

```
Account Number:2
Original balance    : $800
Total credits       : $607
Total debits        : $306
Final balance       : $1101
Should be           : $1101
```

How It Works

You now allocate arrays for the initial account balances, the totals of credits and debits for each account, and for the accounts themselves. The number of initializing values in the `initialBalance[]` array determines the number of elements in each of the arrays. In the `for` loop, you create each of the accounts with the appropriate initial balance and initialize the `totalCredits[]` and `totalDebits[]` arrays to zero.

In the modified transactions loop, you select the account from the array for both the debit and the credit transactions by generating a random index value that you store in the variable `select`. The index `select` is also used to keep a tally of the total of the transactions of each type.

This is all well and good, but by declaring the methods in the class `Bank` as `synchronized`, you're limiting the program quite significantly. No operation of any kind can be carried out while any other operation is in progress. This is unnecessarily restrictive because there's no reason to prevent a transaction on one account while a transaction for a different account is in progress. What you really want to do is constrain the program to prevent overlapping of operations on the same account, and this is where declaring blocks of code to be synchronized on a particular object can help.

Let's consider the methods in the class `Bank` once more. What you really want is the code in the `doTransaction()` method to be synchronized so that simultaneous processing of the same account is prevented, not so that processing of different accounts is inhibited. What you need to do is synchronize the processing code for a transaction on the `Account` object that is involved.

TRY IT OUT   Applying Synchronized Code Blocks

You can do this with the following changes:

Available for
download on
Wrox.com

```java
public class Bank {
  // Perform a transaction
  public void doTransaction(Transaction transaction) {
    switch(transaction.getTransactionType()) {
      case CREDIT:
        synchronized(transaction.getAccount()) {
          // Get current balance
          int balance = transaction.getAccount().getBalance();
          // Credits require a lot of checks...
          try {
            Thread.sleep(100);

          } catch(InterruptedException e) {
            System.out.println(e);
          }
          balance += transaction.getAmount();              // Increment the balance
          transaction.getAccount().setBalance(balance); // Restore A/C balance
          break;
        }

      case DEBIT:
        synchronized(transaction.getAccount()) {
          // Get current balance
          int balance = transaction.getAccount().getBalance();

          // Debits require even more checks...
          try {
            Thread.sleep(150);
```

```
          } catch(InterruptedException e) {
            System.out.println(e);
          }
          balance -= transaction.getAmount();              // Decrement the balance...
          transaction.getAccount().setBalance(balance);// Restore A/C balance
          break;
        }

      default:                                             // We should never get here
        System.out.println("Invalid transaction");
        System.exit(1);
      }
    }
  }
}
```

Directory "BankOperation 4 - Synchronized Code Blocks"

How It Works

The expression in parentheses following the keyword `synchronized` specifies the object for which the synchronization applies. Once one synchronized code block is entered with a given account object, no other code block or method can be entered that has been synchronized on the same object. For example, if the block performing credits is executing with a reference to the object `accounts[1]` returned by the `getAccount()` method for the transaction, the execution of the block carrying out debits cannot be executed for the same object, but it could be executed for a different account.

The object in a synchronized code block acts rather like a baton in a relay race that serves to synchronize the runners in the team. Only the runner with the baton is allowed to run. The next runner in the team can run only after he gets hold of the baton. Of course, in any race you have several different batons so you can have several sets of runners. In the same way, you can specify several different sets of `synchronized` code blocks in a class, each controlled by a different object. It is important to realize that code blocks that are synchronized with respect to a particular object don't have to be in the same class. They can be anywhere in your program where the appropriate object can be specified.

Note how you had to move the code to access and restore the account balance inside both synchronized blocks. If you hadn't done this, accessing or restoring the account balance could occur while a synchronized block was executing. This could obviously cause confusion because a balance could be restored by a debit transaction after the balance had been retrieved for a credit transaction. This would cause the effect of the debit to be wiped out.

If you want to verify that we really are overlapping these operations in this example, you can add output statements to the beginning and end of each method in the class `Bank`. Outputting the type of operation, the amount, and whether it is the start or end of the transaction is sufficient to identify them. For example, you could modify the `doTransaction()` method in the `Bank` class to:

```
// Perform a transaction
public void doTransaction(Transaction transaction) {
  switch(transaction.getTransactionType()) {
    case CREDIT:
      synchronized(transaction.getAccount()) {
        System.out.println("Start credit of " +
                transaction.getAccount() + " amount: " +
                transaction.getAmount());

        // code to process credit...

        System.out.println("  End credit of " +
                transaction.getAccount() + " amount: " +
                transaction.getAmount());
        break;
      }
```

```
      case DEBIT:
        synchronized(transaction.getAccount()) {
          System.out.println("Start debit of " +
                  transaction.getAccount() + " amount: " +
                  transaction.getAmount());
          // code to process debit...
          System.out.println("  End debit of " +
                  transaction.getAccount() + " amount: " +
                  transaction.getAmount());
          break;
        }

      default:                                      // We should never get here
        System.out.println("Invalid transaction");
        System.exit(1);
    }
  }
}
```

This produces quite a lot of output, but you can always comment it out when you don't need it. You should be able to see how a transaction for an account that is currently being worked on is always delayed until the previous operation on the account is completed. You can also see from the output that operations on different accounts do overlap. Here's a sample of what I got:

```
Start debit of A/C No. 2 : $800 amount: 34
Start credit of A/C No. 1 : $500 amount: 72
  End credit of A/C No. 1 : $572 amount: 72
  End debit of A/C No. 2 : $766 amount: 34
Start credit of A/C No. 2 : $766 amount: 69
  End credit of A/C No. 2 : $835 amount: 69
Start debit of A/C No. 2 : $835 amount: 43
  End debit of A/C No. 2 : $792 amount: 43
Start credit of A/C No. 2 : $792 amount: 59
  End credit of A/C No. 2 : $851 amount: 59
Start debit of A/C No. 1 : $572 amount: 45
  End debit of A/C No. 1 : $527 amount: 45
Start credit of A/C No. 1 : $527 amount: 52
  End credit of A/C No. 1 : $579 amount: 52
Start debit of A/C No. 1 : $579 amount: 45
Start credit of A/C No. 2 : $851 amount: 64
...
```

You can see from the first two lines here that a credit for account 1 starts before the preceding debit for account 2 is complete, so the operations are overlapped. The overlapping of operations is affected by the number of processors in your PC. If you want to force overlapping debits and credits on the same account, you can comment out the calculation of the value for select for the debit operation in the for loop in main(). This modification is shown in bold:

```
// Generate a random account index for debit operation
// select = rand.nextInt(accounts.length);
totalDebits[select] += amount;                // Keep total debit tally
```

This makes the debit transaction apply to the same account as the previous credit, so the transactions are always contending for the same account.

Of course, this is not the only way of getting the operations to overlap. Another approach would be to equip accounts with methods to handle their own credit and debit transactions and declare these as synchronized methods.

Although testing that you have synchronization right is relatively easy in our example, in general it is extremely difficult to be sure you have adequately tested a program that uses threads. Getting the design right first is essential, and you really have no substitute for careful design in programs that have multiple threads (or indeed any real-time program that has interrupt handlers). You can never be sure that a real-world program is 100 percent correct—only that it works correctly most of the time!

Deadlocks

Because you can synchronize code blocks for a particular object virtually anywhere in your program, there's potential for a particularly nasty kind of bug called a *deadlock*. This involves a mutual interdependence between two threads. One way this arises is when one thread executes some code synchronized on a given object, theObject, say, and then needs to execute another method that contains code synchronized on another object, theOtherObject, say. Before this occurs, though, a second thread executes some code synchronized to theOtherObject and needs to execute a method containing code synchronized to the first object, theObject. This situation is illustrated in Figure 16-8.

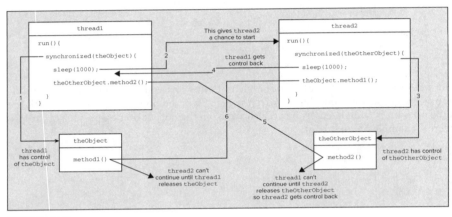

FIGURE 16-8

The sequence of events is as follows:

➤ thread1 starts first and synchronizes on theObject. This prevents any methods for theObject being called by any other thread.

➤ thread1 then calls sleep() so thread2 can start.

➤ thread2 starts and synchronizes on theOtherObject. This prevents any methods for theOtherObject being called by any other thread.

➤ thread2 then calls sleep(), allowing thread1 another go.

➤ thread1 wakes up and tries to call method2() for theOtherObject, but it can't until the code block in thread2 that is synchronized on theOtherObject completes execution.

➤ thread2 gets another go because thread1 can't proceed and tries to call method1() for theObject. This can't proceed until the code block in thread1 that is synchronized on theObject completes execution.

Neither thread has any possibility of continuing—they are deadlocked. Finding and fixing this sort of problem can be very difficult, particularly if your program is complicated and has other threads that continue to execute.

You can create a trivial deadlock in the last example by making the for loop in main() synchronized on one of the accounts. For example:

```
synchronized(accounts[1]) {
  for(int i = 1 ; i <= transactionCount ; ++i) {
    // code for generating transactions etc...
  }
}
```

A deadlock occurs as soon as a transaction for accounts[1] arises because the doTransaction() method in the theBank object that is called by a Clerk object to handle the transaction is synchronized to the same object and can't execute until the loop ends. Of course, the loop can't continue until the method in the theBank object terminates, so the program hangs.

In general, ensuring that your program has no potential deadlocks is extremely difficult. If you intend to do a significant amount of programming using threads, you need to study the subject in much more depth than I can deal with here.

USING EXECUTORS

An *executor* is an object that you can use to start and manage threads. This can make thread programming much easier and more efficient. An executor can execute a `Runnable` task, which is the kind of task that is already familiar to you. It can also execute a `Callable<V>` task, which is a task that can execute in a separate thread, just like a `Runnable` task, but which also returns a value on completion. The type parameter, `V`, for the interface is the type of the value to be returned by the class, so a `Callable<>` class type must implement the interface with the appropriate type specified.

The `Callable<>` interface specifies just one method, `call()`, that a `Callable<>` object must implement. The `call()` method is the equivalent of the `run()` method in the `Runnable` interface, but in addition returns a value when the method terminates. Thus you can define a task that you want to execute as a separate thread either by a class that implements the `Runnable` interface, or by a class that implements the `Callable<>` interface when you want the task to return a value.

The `java.util.concurrent.Executors` class provides static factory methods for creating executor objects. I introduce you to `java.util.concurrent.ExecutorService` objects as an example of how you can use an executor. You can create an `ExecutorService` object like this:

```
ExecutorService threadPool = Executors.newCachedThreadPool();
```

This creates an object that creates new threads as required. Each time you use the `threadPool` object to start another task, either an existing thread in the pool that is currently no longer running is used, or a new thread is created and added to the thread pool. If you want to limit the number of threads that might be created, you can create a thread pool with a fixed number of threads, like this:

```
int nThreads = 5;
ExecutorService threadPool = Executors.newFixedThreadPool(nThreads);
```

This fragment creates a thread pool that contains up to `nThreads` threads. Starting a new task using the `threadPool` object results in the task being executed in a new thread as long as there are fewer than `nThreads` threads already in operation. If all threads in the pool have been allocated, the new task is placed in a queue to wait until one of the existing threads becomes free. All the threads in the pool continue to exist until `threadPool` is shut down. The method throws an exception of type `IllegalArgumentException` if you specify the maximum number of threads to be less than 1.

`ExecutorService` is an interface type that is implemented by several classes in the `java.util.concurrent` package. Both of the methods from the `Executors` class that I have introduced return a reference to an object of type `ThreadPoolExecutor`, and the functionality is described by the `ExecutorService` interface. Let's look at how you use a `ThreadPoolExecutor` object.

Working with an Executor

The methods specified by the `ExecutorService` interface enable you to submit new tasks to be executed in a new thread or an existing unused thread within a thread pool. The interface declares three versions of the `submit()` method: two for starting tasks that are `Runnable` objects and one for starting `Callable<>` tasks. You start a `Runnable` task like this:

```
ExecutorService threadPool = Executors.newCachedThreadPool();
Future<?> future = threadPool.submit(clerk1);
```

This fragment starts the `Runnable` task, `clerk1`, that is a `Clerk` object from the previous example. In general, the `submit()` method returns a reference of type `java.util.concurrent.Future<V>` that reflects the state of the task at any time, and eventually encapsulates the result of executing a task, the result being of type `V`. A `Runnable` task does not return a result so the value returned by submit will be of type `Future<?>`.

The second submit() method for a `Runnable` task accepts a second argument of type V that specifies the result that is to be returned when the task completes. This enables you to ensure that the result you specify is encapsulated by the `Future<V>` object when the task finishes.

I'll discuss the other version of the `submit()` method and then return to the question of what you can do with a `Future<V>` object.

Executing Callable<V> Tasks

A task that executes in a thread and returns a result must implement the `Callable<>` interface that declares the `call()` method. The result that the `call()` method returns is the result of executing the task. You can execute a `Callable<>` task in a thread pool like this:

```
Future<String> future = threadPool.submit(callableTask);
```

This statement executes the task, `callableTask`, and the `future` object encapsulates the result of executing the task that, in this instance, is an object of type `String`.

All versions of the `submit()` method throw an exception of type `NullPointerException` if the task argument is `null` and throw an exception of type `java.util.concurrent.RejectedExecutionException` if the task cannot be executed for some reason.

Future<V> Object Methods

The `Future<>` reference that the `submit()` method returns is returned immediately, before the task completes execution. The `Future<>` object therefore provides a way to access the executing task and determine its state. You can use the `Future<>` object to cancel execution of the task to which it relates:

```
if(future.cancel(true)) {
  System.out.println("Task has been cancelled.");
} else {
  System.out.println("Task could not be cancelled.");
}
```

The argument to the `cancel()` method should be specified as `true` if the task should be interrupted. If you specify the argument as `false` and the task is still executing, it is allowed to continue. The method returns `false` if the task could not be cancelled and `true` otherwise.

You can call the `isCancelled()` method for a `Future<>` object to determine whether or not the task was canceled before it completed normally. The method returns `true` if the task was canceled and `false` otherwise. If the task has ended, calling the `isDone()` method returns `true`; it returns `false` if the task is still running.

You obtain the result of executing a task by calling the `get()` method for the `Future<>` object that relates to it. There are two versions of `get()`. The first has no parameters and you call it like this:

```
String result = null;
try {
  result = future.get();
} catch(CancellationException e) {
  System.out.println("Task was cancelled before a result was obtained.");
} catch(InterruptedException e) {
  System.out.println(
             "Current thread was interrupted while awaiting a result.");
} catch(ExecutionException e) {
  System.out.println("Task threw an exception: ");
  Throwable cause = e.getCause();
  if(cause == null) {
    System.out.println("Cause could not be determined.");
  } else {
    System.out.println(cause);
  }
}
```

The `future` reference here relates to a `Callable<String>` task that returns a `String` object. The `get()` method will block if the task is still running and returns the result when the task has completed. The method throws `java.util.concurrent.CancellationException` if the task was canceled so the result cannot be returned. This exception has `RuntimeException` as a base class and need not be caught. The method can also throw an exception of type `ExecutionException` if the task threw an exception, and, in this case, calling `getCause()` for the exception object returns a `Throwable` reference identifying the cause of the exception or `null` if the cause could not be determined. The method throws an exception of type `InterruptedException` if the current thread was interrupted while waiting for the task to complete.

The second version of `get()` enables you to avoid the possibility of the method blocking indefinitely. It requires two arguments, a value of type `long` specifying the maximum number of time units the method should wait for the task to complete before returning, and a constant from the `java.util.concurrent.TimeUnit` enumeration that specifies the time unit for the first argument. The enumeration defines the following constants:

NANOSECONDS	MICROSECONDS	MILLISECONDS	SECONDS
MINUTES	HOURS	DAYS	

Obviously, you are most likely to be using `MILLISECONDS` or possibly `SECONDS` as the value for the second argument to the `get()` method.

Shutting down a Thread Pool

Calling `shutdown()` for an `ExecutorService` object starts the process of shutting down a thread pool by closing it to new tasks. Existing tasks continue to run. You typically want to wait for tasks in a thread pool to complete before closing it and the `awaitTermination()` method does that. Here's how you might use it:

```
threadPool.shutdown();
try {
  if(threadPool.awaitTermination(100L, TimeUnit.MILLISECONDS)) {
    System.out.println("All tasks completed.");
  } else {
    System.out.println("Tasks failed to complete.");
  }
} catch(InterruptedException e) {
  System.out.println("Current thread interrupted awaiting termination.");
}
```

The `awaitTermination()` waits for tasks in the thread pool to complete for the time you specify by the two arguments. The method returns `false` if all the tasks did not complete in that timeframe.

You can shut down the tasks in a thread pool by calling its `shutdownNow()` method:

```
List<Runnable> tasks = threadPool.shutdownNow();
```

This attempts to shut down all the tasks in the thread pool although the result is not guaranteed. The method cancels tasks that are running by calling `interrupt()` for each thread so tasks that do not respond to being interrupted do not shut down. The method returns a reference to a list containing references to those tasks in the thread pool that were waiting to start execution when shut down occurred.

You can test whether all tasks in a thread pool have been shut down by calling the `isTerminated()` method for the `ExecutorService` object. This method returns `true` if either `shutdown()` or `shutdownNow()` has been called and all tasks have ended. The `isShutdown()` method returns `true` if the executor has been shut down.

Let's try an executor in an example.

TRY IT OUT Using an Executor

This example implements a version of the bank using an executor to execute the treads. The `Account` and `Transaction` classes and the `TransactionType` enum are the same as for the previous example. I call the class that defines the `main()` method `UsingExecutors`.

In this version of the bank, you create debit and credit transactions as tasks executing in separate threads that submit transactions to the clerks. The tasks that create transactions are `Callable<>` tasks because they need to return the total value of the debit or credit transactions that have been created for each account.

Generating Transactions

Here's a definition of the class identifying a source of transactions:

```java
// Generates transactions for clerks
import java.util.Random;
import java.util.Vector;
import java.util.concurrent.Callable;

public class TransactionSource implements Callable<int[]> {

  // Constructor
  public TransactionSource(TransactionType type, int maxTrans,
                               Vector<Account> accounts, Vector<Clerk> clerks) {
    this.type = type;
    this.maxTrans = maxTrans;
    this.accounts = accounts;
    this.clerks = clerks;
    totals = new int[accounts.size()];
  }

  // The source of transactions
  public int[] call() {
    // Create transactions randomly distributed between the accounts
    Random rand = new Random();
    Transaction transaction = null;          // Stores a transaction
    int amount = 0;                          // Stores an amount of money
    int select = 0;                          // Selects an account
    boolean done = false;
    for(int i = 1 ; i <= maxTrans ; ++i) {
      // Generate a random account index for  operation
      select = rand.nextInt(accounts.size());
      amount = 50 + rand.nextInt(26);          // Generate amount $50 to $75
      transaction = new Transaction(accounts.get(select), // Account
                                    type,                 // Transaction type
                                    amount);              //   of amount
      totals[select] += amount;                // Keep total tally for account
      done = false;
      while(true) {
        // Find a clerk to do the transaction
        for(Clerk clerk : clerks) {
          if(done = clerk.doTransaction(transaction))
            break;
        }
        if(done) {
          break;
        }

        // No clerk was free so wait a while
        try {
          Thread.sleep(10);
        } catch(InterruptedException e) {
          System.out.println(" TransactionSource\n" + e);
          return totals;
        }
      }
      if(Thread.interrupted()) {
        System.out.println("Interrupt flag for "+ type +
                                    " transaction source set. Terminating.");
```

```
            return totals;
        }
    }
    return totals;
}

    private TransactionType type;
    private int maxTrans;
    private Vector<Account> accounts;
    private Vector<Clerk> clerks;
    private int[] totals;
}
```

Directory "UsingExecutors"

The class implements Callable<int[]> because a task returns an array of values of type int. The constructor expects four arguments: the type of transactions to be generated, DEBIT or CREDIT, the maximum number of transactions to be created, a reference to a Vector<Account> containing the accounts, and a reference to a Vector<Clerk> containing the clerks. The constructor just stores these in the object and creates an array of the appropriate size to store the total value of the transactions created for each account.

The call() method returns a reference of type int[], which is a reference to the array of totals. The for loop generates the transactions in much the same way as the previous example. Having created a transaction, the method tries to assign the transaction to a clerk in an indefinite while loop. It searches through the clerks vector to find a clerk that can accept a transaction; you implement the doTransaction() method for a Clerk object to return true if the transaction can be accepted and false otherwise. If a clerk accepts the transaction, the indefinite while loop is terminated and the outer for loop continues.

If no clerk is free, the method calls sleep() to wait a while before trying again to see if a clerk has become free. This continues until a clerk does become free or until the thread is interrupted.

On each iteration of the outer for loop that generates transactions, you call the static interrupted() method for the Thread class to allow the possibility for the thread to be canceled externally. If you don't do this, the only possibility for canceling the thread is while it is sleeping. When the call() method ends, it returns a reference to the totals array.

Defining a Clerk

Each clerk also runs as a separate thread, but because a clerk does not need to return a value, you can define it as a Runnable class:

```
import java.util.List;
import java.util.Collections;
import java.util.LinkedList;

public class Clerk implements Runnable {
  // Constructor
  public Clerk(int ID, Bank theBank) {
    this.ID = ID;
    this.theBank = theBank;                 // Who the clerk works for
  }

  // Receive a transaction
  synchronized public boolean doTransaction(Transaction transaction) {
    if(inTray.size() >= maxTransactions)
      return false;
    inTray.add(transaction);                // Add transaction to the list
    return true;
  }

  // The working clerk...
  public void run() {
```

```
    while(true) {
      while(inTray.size() == 0) {        // No transaction waiting?
        try {
          Thread.sleep(200);             // then take a break
          if(inTray.size() != 0)
            break;
          else
            return;
        } catch(InterruptedException e) {
          System.out.println("Clerk " + ID + "\n" + e);
          return;
        }
      }
      theBank.doTransaction(inTray.remove(0));
      if(Thread.interrupted()) {
        System.out.println(
                    "Interrupt flag for Clerk " + ID + " set. Terminating.");
        return;
      }
    }
  }

  int ID;
  private Bank theBank;
  private List<Transaction> inTray =     // The in-tray holding transactions
                  Collections.synchronizedList(new LinkedList<Transaction>());
  private int maxTransactions = 8;       // Maximum transactions in the in-tray
}
```

Directory "UsingExecutors"

The Clerk constructor requires two arguments: an integer value that identifies a particular clerk and a reference to the bank. Transactions are stored in a List<Transaction> collection that is the in-tray for a clerk. The List<Transaction> object is created as a synchronized list from a LinkedList<Transaction> object using a static utility method that is defined in the Collections class. Using a synchronized list ensures that there is no concurrent access to the list by a transaction source thread, which involves the doTransaction() method for a Clerk object, and a Clerk thread, which is the run() method for a Clerk object.

A clerk has an in-tray of a limited size specified by the maxTransactions member and does not accept transactions if the in-tray is full. The doTransaction() method returns true if the transaction can be added to the in-tray returns false otherwise. The doTransaction() method is also synchronized to ensure that only one transaction source can communicate with a given clerk at one time.

In the run() method, a clerk sleeps if there are no transaction in inTray. Each time a clerk completes a transaction, the interrupted() method is called to allow for cancellation of the Clerk thread.

Defining the Bank

The bank is defined by the Bank class, much as you have seen earlier:

```
public class Bank {
  // Perform a transaction
  public void doTransaction(Transaction transaction) {
    synchronized(transaction.getAccount()) {
      int balance = 0;
      switch(transaction.getTransactionType()) {
        case CREDIT:
          System.out.println("Start credit of " +
                  transaction.getAccount() + " amount: " +
                  transaction.getAmount());

          // Get current balance
          balance = transaction.getAccount().getBalance();
```

```
          // Credits require a lot of checks...
          try {
            Thread.sleep(100);

          } catch(InterruptedException e) {
            System.out.println(e);
          }
          balance += transaction.getAmount();              // Increment the balance
          transaction.getAccount().setBalance(balance);// Restore A/C balance
          System.out.println("  End credit of " +
                  transaction.getAccount() + " amount: " +
                  transaction.getAmount());
          break;
        case DEBIT:
          System.out.println("Start debit of " +
                  transaction.getAccount() + " amount: " +
                  transaction.getAmount());

          // Get current balance
          balance = transaction.getAccount().getBalance();

          // Debits require even more checks...
          try {
            Thread.sleep(150);

          } catch(InterruptedException e) {
            System.out.println(e);
          }
          balance -= transaction.getAmount();              // Decrement the balance...
          transaction.getAccount().setBalance(balance);// Restore A/C balance

          System.out.println("  End debit of " +
                  transaction.getAccount() + " amount: " +
                  transaction.getAmount());
          break;

      default:                                             // We should never get here
        System.out.println("Invalid transaction");
        System.exit(1);
    }
  }
}
```

Directory "UsingExecutors"

The `doTransaction()` method for the `Bank` object is executed in a `Clerk` thread. The code in the `doTransaction()` method for the bank is synchronized on the account to which the transaction applies. This ensures that only one clerk can access any given account at a time. As before, debits take longer than credits to process. The `doTransaction()` method includes output for each transaction that is processed so you can see all the details of what goes on in the bank before that final accounts are displayed.

Running Banking Operations

The `main()` method creates and initiates all the threads that operate the bank. Here's the class definition:

Available for download on Wrox.com

```
import java.util.Vector;
import java.util.concurrent.Executors;
import java.util.concurrent.ExecutorService;
import java.util.concurrent.Future;
import java.util.concurrent.ExecutionException;
import java.util.concurrent.TimeUnit;
```

```java
public class UsingExecutors {

    public static void main(String[] args) {
        int[] initialBalance = {500, 800};           // The initial account balances
        int[] totalCredits = new int[initialBalance.length]; // Two cr totals
        int[] totalDebits = new int[initialBalance.length];  // Two db totals
        int transactionCount = 20;                   // Number of debits and of credits
        int clerkCount = 2;

        // Create the account, the bank, and the clerks...
        Bank theBank = new Bank();                   // Create a bank
        Vector<Clerk> clerks = new Vector<Clerk>();  // Stores the clerk
        Vector<Account> accounts = new Vector<Account>();  // Stores the accounts

        for(int i = 0 ; i < clerkCount ; ++i) {
            clerks.add(new Clerk(i+1, theBank));     // Create the clerks
        }

        for(int i = 0 ; i < initialBalance.length ; ++i) {
            accounts.add(new Account(i+1, initialBalance[i])); // Create accounts
            totalCredits[i] = totalDebits[i] = 0;
        }

        ExecutorService threadPool = Executors.newCachedThreadPool();

        // Create and start the transaction source threads
        Future<int[]> credits = threadPool.submit(new TransactionSource(
                    TransactionType.CREDIT, transactionCount, accounts, clerks));
        Future<int[]> debits = threadPool.submit(new TransactionSource(
                    TransactionType.DEBIT, transactionCount, accounts, clerks));

        // Create and start the clerk threads
        for(Clerk clerk : clerks) {
            threadPool.submit(clerk);
        }
        try {
            totalCredits = credits.get();
            totalDebits = debits.get();
        } catch(ExecutionException e) {
            System.out.println(e.getCause());
        } catch(InterruptedException e) {
            System.out.println(e);
        }

        // Orderly shutdown when all threads have ended
        threadPool.shutdown();
        try {
            threadPool.awaitTermination(10L, TimeUnit.SECONDS);
        } catch(InterruptedException e) {
            System.out.println(e);
        }

        if(threadPool.isTerminated()) {
            System.out.println("\nAll clerks have completed their tasks.\n");
        } else {
            System.out.println("\nClerks still running - shutting down anyway.\n");
            threadPool.shutdownNow();
        }


        // Now output the results
```

```
for(int i = 0 ; i < accounts.size() ; ++i) {
  System.out.println("Account Number:"+accounts.get(i).getAccountNumber()+"\n"+
      "Original balance    : $" + initialBalance[i] + "\n" +
      "Total credits       : $" + totalCredits[i] + "\n" +
      "Total debits        : $" + totalDebits[i] + "\n" +
      "Final balance       : $" + accounts.get(i).getBalance() + "\n" +
      "Should be           : $" + (initialBalance[i]
                                + totalCredits[i]
                                - totalDebits[i]) + "\n");
    }
  }
}
```

Directory "UsingExecutors"

When I ran the example, I got the following output:

```
Start credit of A/C No. 2 : $800 amount: 62
  End credit of A/C No. 2 : $862 amount: 62
Start debit of A/C No. 1 : $500 amount: 66
Start credit of A/C No. 2 : $862 amount: 54
  End credit of A/C No. 2 : $916 amount: 54
Start debit of A/C No. 2 : $916 amount: 53
  End debit of A/C No. 1 : $434 amount: 66
Start credit of A/C No. 1 : $434 amount: 56
  End credit of A/C No. 1 : $490 amount: 56
  End debit of A/C No. 2 : $863 amount: 53
Start debit of A/C No. 1 : $490 amount: 58
  End debit of A/C No. 1 : $432 amount: 58
Start credit of A/C No. 1 : $432 amount: 61
Start credit of A/C No. 2 : $863 amount: 61
  End credit of A/C No. 1 : $493 amount: 61
  End credit of A/C No. 2 : $924 amount: 61
Start debit of A/C No. 1 : $493 amount: 51
  End debit of A/C No. 1 : $442 amount: 51
Start credit of A/C No. 2 : $924 amount: 72
Start debit of A/C No. 1 : $442 amount: 53
  End credit of A/C No. 2 : $996 amount: 72
Start debit of A/C No. 2 : $996 amount: 50
  End debit of A/C No. 1 : $389 amount: 53
  End debit of A/C No. 2 : $946 amount: 50
Start credit of A/C No. 1 : $389 amount: 67
Start credit of A/C No. 2 : $946 amount: 62
  End credit of A/C No. 1 : $456 amount: 67
  End credit of A/C No. 2 : $1008 amount: 62
Start debit of A/C No. 2 : $1008 amount: 65
Start debit of A/C No. 1 : $456 amount: 50
  End debit of A/C No. 1 : $406 amount: 50
  End debit of A/C No. 2 : $943 amount: 65
Start credit of A/C No. 2 : $943 amount: 51
  End credit of A/C No. 2 : $994 amount: 51
Start debit of A/C No. 2 : $994 amount: 66
  End debit of A/C No. 2 : $928 amount: 66
Start credit of A/C No. 1 : $406 amount: 71
Start credit of A/C No. 2 : $928 amount: 64
  End credit of A/C No. 2 : $992 amount: 64
Start credit of A/C No. 2 : $992 amount: 53
  End credit of A/C No. 1 : $477 amount: 71
Start credit of A/C No. 1 : $477 amount: 72
  End credit of A/C No. 2 : $1045 amount: 53
  End credit of A/C No. 1 : $549 amount: 72
```

```
Start debit of A/C No. 1 : $549 amount: 58
  End debit of A/C No. 1 : $491 amount: 58
Start debit of A/C No. 1 : $491 amount: 54
  End debit of A/C No. 1 : $437 amount: 54
Start credit of A/C No. 2 : $1045 amount: 73
Start credit of A/C No. 1 : $437 amount: 55
  End credit of A/C No. 2 : $1118 amount: 73
  End credit of A/C No. 1 : $492 amount: 55
Start credit of A/C No. 1 : $492 amount: 50
  End credit of A/C No. 1 : $542 amount: 50
Start debit of A/C No. 2 : $1118 amount: 65
Start credit of A/C No. 1 : $542 amount: 69
  End credit of A/C No. 1 : $611 amount: 69
Start credit of A/C No. 1 : $611 amount: 69
  End debit of A/C No. 2 : $1053 amount: 65
  End credit of A/C No. 1 : $680 amount: 69
Start credit of A/C No. 2 : $1053 amount: 60
Start debit of A/C No. 1 : $680 amount: 67
  End credit of A/C No. 2 : $1113 amount: 60
  End debit of A/C No. 1 : $613 amount: 67
Start debit of A/C No. 1 : $613 amount: 55
  End debit of A/C No. 1 : $558 amount: 55
Start credit of A/C No. 2 : $1113 amount: 71
Start debit of A/C No. 1 : $558 amount: 75
  End credit of A/C No. 2 : $1184 amount: 71
Start debit of A/C No. 2 : $1184 amount: 59
  End debit of A/C No. 1 : $483 amount: 75
  End debit of A/C No. 2 : $1125 amount: 59
Start debit of A/C No. 1 : $483 amount: 54
Start debit of A/C No. 2 : $1125 amount: 72
  End debit of A/C No. 1 : $429 amount: 54
  End debit of A/C No. 2 : $1053 amount: 72
Start debit of A/C No. 2 : $1053 amount: 66
  End debit of A/C No. 2 : $987 amount: 66
Start debit of A/C No. 1 : $429 amount: 63
  End debit of A/C No. 1 : $366 amount: 63

All clerks have completed their tasks.

Account Number:1
Original balance    : $500
Total credits       : $570
Total debits        : $704
Final balance       : $366
Should be           : $366

Account Number:2
Original balance    : $800
Total credits       : $683
Total debits        : $496
Final balance       : $987
Should be           : $987
```

When you run the example, you will almost certainly see different output.

How It Works

The initialization in `main()` that occurs before the `ExecutorService` object is created is much the same as the previous example. The principle difference is that the clerks and accounts are now stored in `Vector<>` collection objects. You have the possibility of specifying an arbitrary number of accounts by increasing the number of values in the `initialBalance` array and increasing the number of clerks by changing the value specified for `clerkCount`. If you want more transactions, just change the value of `transactionCount`. I kept the number low for everything to keep the volume of output at modest levels.

After the accounts and clerks have been created, you obtain an `ExecutorService` reference to an executor object by calling the `newCachedThreadPool()` factory method from the `Executors` class:

```
ExecutorService threadPool = Executors.newCachedThreadPool();
```

This provides as many threads as you require.

You create the `TransactionSource` objects in the arguments to the `submit()` method for the `ExecutorService` object:

```
Future<int[]> credits = threadPool.submit(new TransactionSource(
        TransactionType.CREDIT, transactionCount, accounts, clerks));
Future<int[]> debits = threadPool.submit(new TransactionSource(
        TransactionType.DEBIT, transactionCount, accounts, clerks));
```

You only need references to the `Future<>` objects that are returned by the `submit()` method because these give you access to the value returned by the `Callable<>` threads as well as the means of controlling their execution. The type parameter for the `Future<>` type specification corresponds to the type of value that each thread returns. After executing these statement, you have two new threads running.

You create and start the `Clerk` threads in a loop:

```
for(Clerk clerk : clerks) {
   threadPool.submit(clerk);
}
```

This creates and starts a thread for each `Clerk` object in the `clerks` vector. After executing this loop you have a total of five threads running, including the main thread.

You retrieve the values returned by the `TransactionSource` threads by calling the `get()` method for the `Future<>` object that is returned when you call `submit()` for the `ExecutorService` object. This occurs in a `try` block to deal with the exceptions that can be thrown.

Before producing the final output summarizing the status of each account, you shut down the threads and the thread pool in an orderly fashion. The first step is to call `shutdown()` for the `threadPool` object to ensure no further threads can start. You then call `awaitTermination()` to wait for the threads to terminate. The method waits for up to 10 seconds for all the threads to end and continues execution if they do not. If all the clerks have not completed their tasks after 10 seconds, you shut down the thread pool anyway and output the results.

THREAD PRIORITIES

All threads have a priority that determines which thread is executed when several threads are waiting for their turn. This makes it possible to give one thread more access to processor resources than another. Let's consider an elementary example of how this could be used. Suppose you have one thread in a program that requires all the processor resources—some solid long-running calculation—and some other threads that require relatively few resources. By making the thread that requires all the resources a low-priority thread, you ensure that the other threads are executed promptly while the processor bound thread can make use of the processor cycles that are left over after the others have had their turn.

The possible values for thread priority are defined in `static` data members of the class `Thread`. These members are of type `int` and are declared as `final`. The maximum thread priority is defined by the member `MAX_PRIORITY`, which has the value 10. The minimum priority is `MIN_PRIORITY`, defined as 1. The value of the default priority that is assigned to the main thread in a program is `NORM_PRIORITY`, which is set to 5. When you create a thread, its priority is the same as that of the thread that created it.

You can modify the priority of a thread by calling the `setPriority()` method for the `Thread` object representing the thread. This method accepts an argument of type `int` that defines the new priority for the thread. An `IllegalArgumentException` is thrown if you specify a priority that is less than `MIN_PRIORITY` or greater than `MAX_PRIORITY`.

If you're going to be messing about with the priorities of the threads in your program, you need to be able to find out the current priority for a thread. You can do this by calling the getPriority() method for the Thread object. This returns the current priority for the thread as a value of type int.

You need to keep in mind that the actual execution priority of a thread that you set by calling setPriority() depends on the mapping between Java thread priorities and the native operating system priorities. The thread scheduling algorithm that your operating system uses also affects how your Java threads execute and what proportion of the processor time they are allocated.

Using Thread Priorities

In the last example, you could set priorities for the threads by modifying the Clerk and TransactionSource class constructors to accept an extra argument of type int. This would provide you with a program to play with the effect of setting different thread priorities and you could experiment with different delays for doing transactions in the bank. For example, you could change the Clerk class constructor to:

```
public Clerk(int ID, Bank theBank, int priority) {
  this.ID = ID;
  this.theBank = theBank;           // Who the clerk works for
  this.priority = priority;
}
```

You also need to add a new data member to the class to store the priority for the thread:

```
private int priority;
```

Of course, you *can't* set the thread priority in the *constructor*. This is an easy mistake to make if you don't think about what is going on. The constructor is executed in the main thread, not in the working clerk thread. The place to set the priority for the clerk thread is at the beginning of the run() method. You need to add the following as the first statement in the run() method:

```
Thread.currentThread().setPriority(priority); // Set priority for thread
```

This obtains a reference to the current thread by calling the static currentThread() method and then uses that to call setPriority() for the thread.

The TransactionSource class constructor could be changed in a similar way:

```
public TransactionSource(TransactionType type, int maxTrans,
              Vector<Account> accounts, Vector<Clerk> clerks, int priority) {
  this.type = type;
  this.maxTrans = maxTrans;
  this.accounts = accounts;
  this.clerks = clerks;
  this.priority = priority;
  totals = new int[accounts.size()];
}
```

You also need to add the priority member to the class. Setting the priority for the thread should be the first statement in the call() method—it's the same statement as in the run() method in the Clerk class.

The main() method needs to be changed so the constructor calls pass a value for the priority of each thread. Here's how you might set priorities for the clerk threads:

```
int priority = 0;
for(int i = 0 ; i < clerkCount ; ++i) {
  priority = i%2 == 0 ? Thread.MIN_PRIORITY + (i + 1) : Thread.MAX_PRIORITY - (i + 1);
  if(priority < Thread.MIN_PRIORITY || priority > Thread.MAX_PRIORITY)
    priority = Thread.NORM_PRIORITY;
  clerks.add(new Clerk(i+1, theBank, priority));    // Create the clerks
}
```

This assigns priorities alternating between high and low priorities to get a large divergence between the threads. If the number of clerks was set greater than MAX_PRIORITY−1, you could end up with invalid priority values so the if statement verifies that everything is legal and sets NORM_PRIORITY in place of invalid values.

You could amend the calls to the TransactionSource constructor to the following:

```
Future<int[]> credits = threadPool.submit(
        new TransactionSource(
                TransactionType.CREDIT, transactionCount,
                accounts, clerks, Thread.MAX_PRIORITY−1));
Future<int[]> debits = threadPool.submit(
                new TransactionSource(
                TransactionType.DEBIT, transactionCount,
                accounts, clerks, Thread.MIN_PRIORITY+1));
```

I won't go through this in detail as the example really is just for experimenting with threads. The complete example is in the download in the SettingThreadPriorities directory. This includes some changes to track which clerk is doing each transaction. Whether or not thread priorities have any effect depends on your operating system. If it doesn't support thread priorities, then setting thread priorities in your Java code has no effect. Try out the program to see what happens.

SUMMARY

In this chapter you learned about threads and the basics of how you can create and manage them. You use threads from time to time in examples later in this book, so be sure you don't move on from here without being comfortable with the basic ideas of how you create and start a thread.

In general, thread programming is not for the faint-hearted. Thread programming is difficult, even for experienced programmers. It is hard for most people to visualize clearly what is happening when multiple threads are executing and it is easy to get things wrong, sometimes in very subtle ways. It is therefore something to venture into only when there are clear performance benefits to be gained.

EXERCISES

You can download the source code for the examples in the book and the solutions to the following exercises from www.wrox.com.

1. Modify the UsingExecutors example in the chapter so that each transaction is a debit or a credit at random.

2. Modify the result of the previous exercise to allow an arbitrary number of transaction source objects to be in effect.

3. Extend the result of the previous exercise to incorporate two supervisors for two teams of clerks, where the supervisors each run in their own thread. The supervisor threads should receive transactions from transaction sources and pass them to the clerks they supervise. The supervisors' work should result in a variable time delay in transferring transaction to the clerks of between 100 and 500 milliseconds.

CONFER PROGRAMMER TO PROGRAMMER ABOUT THIS TOPIC.
Visit p2p.wrox.com

▶ WHAT YOU LEARNED IN THIS CHAPTER

TOPIC	CONCEPT
Threads	Threads are subtasks in a program that can be executing concurrently.
Thread Objects	A thread is represented by an object of the class `Thread`. Execution of a thread begins with the execution of the `run()` method defined in the class `Thread`.
Thread Code	You define the code to be executed in a thread by implementing the `run()` method in a class derived from `Thread`, or in a class that implements the interface `Runnable`.
Daemon Threads	A thread specified as daemon ceases execution when the thread that created it ends.
User Threads	A thread that isn't a daemon thread is called a user thread. A user thread is not terminated automatically when the thread that created it ends.
Starting a Thread	You can start execution of a thread by calling the `start()` method for its `Thread` object. If you need to halt a thread before normal completion, you can stop execution of a thread by calling the `interrupt()` method for its `Thread` object.
Synchronized Methods	Methods can be declared as `synchronized`. Only one `synchronized` instance method for an object can execute at any given time. Only one `synchronized static` method for a class can execute at one time.
Synchronized Code Blocks	A code block can be declared as `synchronized` on an object. Only one synchronized code block for an object can execute at any given time.
Deadlocks	A deadlock is a situation in which two threads are both waiting for the other to complete some action. Deadlocks can occur in subtle ways in multi-threaded applications, which makes such applications difficult to debug.
Executors	An executor is an object that can create, manage, and start threads.
Creating an Executor	You create an executor object by calling one of the static methods defined in the `Executors` class.
Thread Pools	You can create executors that provide a thread pool with a fixed number of threads that may be reused or with an unlimited number of threads.
Threads Returning a Value	A thread that returns a value is defined by a class that implements the `Callable<V>` interface. This interface defines the `call()` method that returns a value of type `V`.
`Future<V>` Objects	A `Future<V>` object is returned by the `submit()` method for an `ExecutorService` object that starts a thread. You can use the object returned to manage the thread and to obtain the result of a `Callable<>` thread.
Thread Priorities	You can modify the relative priority of a thread by calling its `setPriority()` method. This has an effect on execution only in environments that support priority scheduling.

17

Creating Windows

WHAT YOU WILL LEARN IN THIS CHAPTER

➤ How you create and display a resizable window
➤ What components and containers are
➤ How you can add components to a window
➤ How you can control the layout of components
➤ How you create a menu bar and menus for a window
➤ What a menu shortcut is and how you can add a shortcut for a menu item
➤ What the restrictions on the capabilities of an applet are
➤ How to convert an application into an applet

Until now, the programs you have been creating have perhaps not been what you may instinctively think of as useful programs. You can't expect a user to be prepared to enter all the input and get all the output on the command line. A more practical program is window-based, with one or more windows that provide the interface between the user and the application. These windows, and the environment that the user interacts with, are known as the *graphical user interface (GUI)*.

In this chapter you investigate how to create a window for a Java application, and you take a first look at some of the components you can assemble to create a graphical user interface in Java.

GRAPHICAL USER INTERFACES IN JAVA

There is a vast amount of functionality in the Java class libraries devoted to supporting graphical user interface (GUI) creation and management, far more than it is feasible to cover in a single book — even if it is big. Just the JFrame class, which you begin to explore in a moment, contains more than 200 methods when you include those inherited from superclasses! I therefore have to be selective in what I cover in detail in terms of both the specific classes that I discuss and their methods. However, I cover the basic operations that you need to understand to create your own applications and applets. With a good grasp of the basics, you should be able to explore other areas of the Java class library beyond those I discuss without too much difficulty.

The fundamental elements that you need to create a GUI reside in two packages: java.awt and javax.swing. The java.awt package was the primary repository for classes you would use to create a GUI way back in Java 1.1—awt being an abbreviation for Abstract Windowing Toolkit—but many of the classes this package defines have been superseded by javax.swing. Note that I said many of the classes, not all. Most of the classes in the javax.swing package define GUI elements, referred to as *Swing components*, that provide much-improved alternatives to components defined by classes in java.awt. You look into the JButton class in the Swing set that defines a button, rather than the Button class in java.awt. However, the Swing component classes are generally derived from, and depend on, fundamental classes that are defined within the java.awt package, so you can't afford to ignore these.

The Swing classes are part of a more general set of GUI programming capabilities that are collectively referred to as the *Java Foundation Classes*, or *JFC* for short. JFC covers not only the Swing component classes, such as those defining buttons and menus, but also classes for 2D drawing from the java.awt.geom package and classes that support drag-and-drop capability in the java.awt.dnd package. The JFC also includes an application program interface (API) defined in the javax.accessibility package that allows applications to be implemented that provide for users with disabilities.

The Swing component classes are more flexible than the component classes defined in the java.awt package because they are implemented entirely in Java. The java.awt components depend on native code to a great extent and are, therefore, restricted to a "lowest common denominator" set of interface capabilities. Because Swing components are pure Java, they are not restricted by the characteristics of the platform on which they run. Apart from the added functionality and flexibility of the Swing components, they also provide a feature called *pluggable look-and-feel* that makes it possible to change the appearance of a component. You can programmatically select the look-and-feel of a component from those implemented as standard, or you can create your own look-and-feel for components if you want. The pluggable look-and-feel of the Swing components has been facilitated by designing the classes in a particular way, called the Model-View-Controller architecture.

Model-View-Controller (MVC) Architecture

The design of the Swing component classes is loosely based on something called the *Model-View-Controller architecture*, or *MVC*. This is not of particular consequence in the context of applying the Swing classes, but it's important to be aware of it if you want to modify the pluggable look-and-feel of a component. MVC is not new and did not originate with Java. In fact, the idea of MVC emerged some time ago within the context of the SmallTalk programming language. MVC is an idealized way of modeling a component as three separate parts:

➤ The **model** that stores the data that defines the component

➤ The **view** that creates the visual representation of the component from the data in the model

➤ The **controller** that deals with user interaction with the component and modifies the model and/or the view in response to a user action as necessary

Figure 17-1 illustrates the relationships between the model, the view, and the controller.

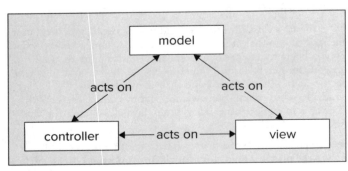

FIGURE 17-1

In object-oriented terms, each of the three logical parts for a component—the model, the view, and the controller—is ideally represented by a different class type. In practice this turns out to be difficult because of the dependencies between the view and the controller. Because the user interacts with the physical representation of the component, the controller operation is highly dependent on the implementation of the view. For this reason, the view and controller are typically represented by a single composite object that corresponds to a view with an integrated controller. In this case the MVC concept degenerates into the document/view architecture that I introduced when I discussed the `Observable` class and `Observer` interface. Sun calls it the *Separable Model architecture*, as illustrated in Figure 17-2.

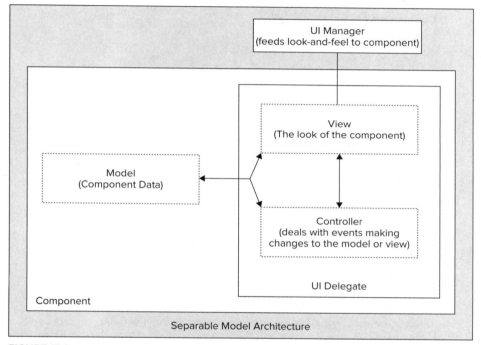

FIGURE 17-2

The Swing components provide for a pluggable look-and-feel by making the visual appearance of a component and the interface to the user the responsibility of an independent object called the *UI delegate*. This is the view+controller part of the MVC model. Thus, a different UI delegate can provide a component with a new look-and-feel.

The details of how you modify the look-and-feel of a component are beyond the scope of this book, but I introduce how you can set one of the standard looks-and-feels that are distributed with the Java Development Kit (JDK). It is as well to be aware of the MVC architecture on which the Swing components are based because it appears quite often in the literature around Java, and you may want to change the look-and-feel of a component at some time.

CREATING A WINDOW

A basic window in Java is represented by an object of the `Window` class, which is defined in the `java.awt` package. Objects of the `Window` class are hardly ever used directly because borders and a title bar are fairly basic prerequisites for a typical application window, and this class provides neither. The library class `JFrame` that is defined in the `javax.swing` package is a much more useful class for creating a window because, in addition to a title bar and a border, it provides a wealth of other facilities. Its superclasses are shown in Figure 17-3.

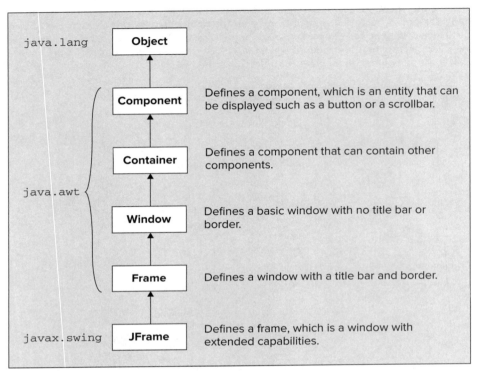

FIGURE 17-3

The Component class is the grandmother of all component classes—it defines the basic properties and methods shared by all components. You see later that all the Swing components have the Component class as a base. The Container class adds the capability for a Component object to contain other components, which is a frequent requirement. Because JFrame has Container as a superclass, a JFrame object can contain other components. Beyond the obvious need for a window to be able to contain the components that represent the GUI, a menu bar should contain menus, for example, which in turn contains menu items; a toolbar obviously contains toolbar buttons; and there are many other examples. For this reason the Container class is also a base for all the classes that define Swing components.

The Window class adds methods to the Container class that are specific to a window, such as the capability to handle events arising from user interaction with the window. The Frame class is the original class in java.awt that provided a proper window with a title bar and a border, with which everyone is familiar. The JFrame class adds functionality to the Frame class to support much more sophisticated facilities for drawing and displaying other components. You can deduce from the hierarchy in the diagram how a JFrame object can easily end up with its 200+ methods, as it has five superclasses from which it inherits members. You aren't going to trawl through all these classes and methods. You just look into the ones you need in context as you go along, and then see how they are applied in some examples. This teaches you the most important methods in this class.

Framing a Window

You can display an application window simply by creating an object of type JFrame, calling a method for the object to set the size of the window, and then calling a method to display the window. Executing the following code fragment creates a window object and displays the window that it represents:

```
JFrame aWindow = new JFrame("This is the Window Title");
int windowWidth = 400;                          // Window width in pixels
int windowHeight = 150;                         // Window height in pixels
aWindow.setBounds(50, 100,                      // Set position
                  windowWidth, windowHeight);   // and size
aWindow.setDefaultCloseOperation(JFrame.EXIT_ON_CLOSE);
aWindow.setVisible(true);                        // Display the window
```

The window is encapsulated by the `JFrame` object, `aWindow`. The `setBounds()` method for the `aWindow` object determines the size and position of the application window. Calling `setVisible()` causes the window to be displayed. If you plug this code directly into the `main()` method, it surely displays the window, but this is not the way to do it.

Preventing Deadlocks in GUI Code

Preparing the application window and any components it contains and displaying it is described as *realizing* the window. Calling `setVisible()` for an application window object realizes the window. After the GUI for an application has been realized, modifying or querying it on the main thread can cause deadlocks. Methods for Swing components are not thread-safe so they must all execute in a separate thread from the main thread to avoid the kinds of problems I described in Chapter 16. The thread in which you create the GUI and in which all interactions with the GUI are dealt with is called the *Swing event dispatching thread*. Let's see how you create an application window in an example.

TRY IT OUT   Creating an Application Window

Here's the code to create and display an application window:

```java
import javax.swing.JFrame;
import javax.swing.SwingUtilities;

public class TryWindow {
  public static void createWindow(){
    JFrame aWindow = new JFrame("This is the Window Title");
    int windowWidth = 400;                          // Window width in pixels
    int windowHeight = 150;                         // Window height in pixels
    aWindow.setBounds(50, 100,                      // Set position
                      windowWidth, windowHeight);   // and size
    aWindow.setDefaultCloseOperation(JFrame.EXIT_ON_CLOSE);
    aWindow.setVisible(true);                        // Display the window
  }

  public static void main(String[] args) {
    SwingUtilities.invokeLater(new Runnable() {
          public void run() {
              createWindow();
          }
      });
  }
}
```

TryWindow.java

Under Microsoft Windows, the program displays the window shown in Figure 17-4.

How It Works

The first `import` statement adds the `JFrame` class in the `javax.swing` package to the program. From now on most of your programs use the components defined in this package. The second adds the `SwingUtilities` class that you use in the `main()` method.

FIGURE 17-4

The code to create and display the application window is in the static `createWindow()` method. The method `setBounds()` defines the size and position of the window; the first pair of arguments correspond to the x and y coordinates of the top-left corner of the application window relative to the top-left corner of the display screen, and the second pair of arguments specify the width and height of the window in pixels. The screen coordinate system has the origin point, (0, 0), at the top-left corner of the screen, with the positive x-axis running left to right and the positive y-axis from top to bottom. The positive y-axis in screen coordinates is therefore in the opposite direction to that of the usual Cartesian coordinate system. The coordinate system for screen coordinates is illustrated in Figure 17-5.

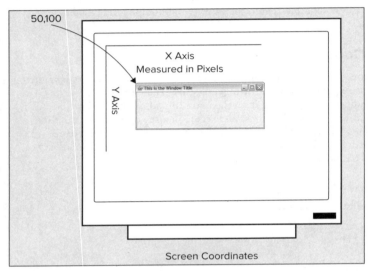

FIGURE 17-5

You have specified the top-left corner of the application window at position (50,100) on the screen, which is 50 pixels to the right and 100 pixels down. Because the window is 400 pixels wide and 150 pixels high, the bottom-right corner is at position (450,250). The actual physical width and height of the window, as well as its position relative to the edge of the screen, depends on the size of your screen and the display resolution. For a given screen size, the higher the display resolution, the smaller the window is and the closer it is to the top left-hand corner, simply because the pixels on the screen are closer together. You see how you can get around this potential problem later in this chapter.

Window Close Options

The `setDefaultCloseOperation()` method for the `JFrame` object determines what happens when you close the window by either clicking on the X icon or selecting Close from the menu that is displayed when you click the Java icon in the top-left corner of the window. There are four possible argument values you can use here. The constant you have used as the argument to the method is `EXIT_ON_CLOSE`, which is defined in the `JFrame` class. The effect of this is to close the window, dispose of the window resources and those of any components it contains, and finally to terminate the application. There are three other argument values you could use with the `setDefaultCloseOperation()` method that are defined in the `WindowConstants` interface that is implemented by the `JFrame` class. These values are shown in Table 17-1:

TABLE 17-1: Argument Values for setDefaultCloseOperation()

ARGUMENT	DESCRIPTION
DISPOSE_ON_CLOSE	This causes the frame and any components it contains to be destroyed but doesn't terminate the application.
DO_NOTHING_ON_CLOSE	This makes the close operation for the frame window ineffective.

ARGUMENT	DESCRIPTION
HIDE_ON_CLOSE	This just hides the window by calling its setVisible() method with an argument of false. This is the default action if you don't call the setDefaultCloseOperation() method with a different argument value. When a window is hidden, you can always display the window again later by calling setVisible() with an argument of true.

Of course, you might want to take some action beyond the options I have discussed here when the user chooses to close the window. If the program involves entering a lot of data for instance, you may want to ensure that the user is prompted to save the data before the program ends. This involves handling an event associated with the Close menu item or the Close button, and you investigate this in the next chapter.

Creating and Displaying the Application Window

The setVisible() method with the argument set to true displays the application window on top of any other windows that are currently visible on the screen. If you want to hide a window at some point during the execution of an application, you would call setVisible() with the argument set to false.

The createWindow() method is called by the run() method in the anonymous Runnable class object that is created in main(). The SwingUtilities class that is defined in the javax.swing package contains several static utility methods, including the invokeLater() method that you call here. This method executes the run() method for the Runnable object that you pass as the argument on the event dispatching thread, which is exactly what you want if you are to avoid problems with handling user interactions with the application window.

Window Look-and-Feel

The application displays the default look-and-feel on my system, and it may well be the same on yours. It corresponds to the Java cross-platform look-and-feel that is distributed with the JDK. Each look-and-feel is defined by a class, and on my system the following look-and-feel classes are installed:

```
javax.swing.plaf.metal.MetalLookAndFeel
javax.swing.plaf.nimbus.NimbusLookAndFeel
com.sun.java.swing.plaf.motif.MotifLookAndFeel
com.sun.java.swing.plaf.windows.WindowsLookAndFeel
com.sun.java.swing.plaf.windows.WindowsClassicLookAndFeel
```

The first class corresponds to the standard Java look-and-feel, which used to be known as the Metal look-and-feel. It is intended to provide a uniform cross-platform look-and-feel, and you can use it on any platform that supports the JFC. The second is the Nimbus look-and-feel that is implemented using Java 2D vector graphics and has a very small footprint. The third class defines the Motif look-and-feel that is for use on UNIX systems. The last two classes can be used only with Microsoft Windows.

The UIManager class that is defined in the javax.swing package deals with setting the look-and-feel of a Java application. You could list the names of the look-and-feel classes that are installed with the JDK on your system on the console by adding the following code at the beginning of main() in the example:

```
UIManager.LookAndFeelInfo[] looks = UIManager.getInstalledLookAndFeels();
for(UIManager.LookAndFeelInfo look : looks) {
  System.out.println(look.getClassName());
}
```

For this to work, you need to add the following import statement:

```
import javax.swing.UIManager;
```

You can set a look-and-feel by passing the fully qualified name of one of your look-and-feel classes to the static setLookAndFeel() method that is defined in the UIManager class. This method can throw a ClassNotFoundException if the look-and-feel class cannot be found, plus other exceptions, so you should put the method call in a try block and arrange to catch the exception. For example:

```
try {
  UIManager.setLookAndFeel("javax.swing.plaf.nimbus.NimbusLookAndFeel");
  javax.swing.SwingUtilities.updateComponentTreeUI(aWindow);
} catch(Exception e) {
  System.err.println("Look and feel not set.");
}
```

You can put this code in the createWindow() method in the example to try it out. Calling the static updateComponentTreeUI() method in the SwingUtilities class causes the frame window to be updated with the look-and-feel that is currently set.

The class name for the cross-platform look-and-feel is returned by the static getCrossPlatformLook AndFeelClassName() method in the UIManager class, so you can set this explicitly using the following code:

```
try {
  UIManager.setLookAndFeel( UIManager.getCrossPlatformLookAndFeelClassName() );
  javax.swing.SwingUtilities.updateComponentTreeUI(aWindow);
} catch(Exception e) {
  System.err.println("Look and feel not set.");
}
```

Alternatively, you can make your application adopt the look-and-feel for the platform on which it is running by calling the static getSystemLookAndFeelClassName() method in the UIManager class and passing the class name that it returns to the setLookAndFeel() method.

The window for the example is fully operational. You could try resizing the window for the example by dragging a border or a corner with the mouse. You can also try minimizing the window by clicking on the icons to the right of the title bar. Everything should work okay so you are getting quite a lot for so few lines of code. You can close the application by clicking on the X icon.

 WARNING *This example terminates okay if you have entered the code correctly; however, errors could prevent this. If an application doesn't terminate properly for any reason, you have to get the operating system to end the task. Under MS Windows 7, pressing Ctrl+Shift+Esc brings up the Task Manager window from which you can terminate the application.*

The example creates a very *nice* window, but it's not overly useful. All you can do with it is move it, resize it, and changes its width and or height. You can drag the borders and maximize and minimize it. The Close icon works because you elected to dispose of the window and exit the program when the close operation is selected by setting the appropriate option through the setDefaultCloseOperation() method. If you omitted this method call, you would get the default action, HIDE_ON_CLOSE, whereby the window would be hidden, but the program would not terminate.

The setBounds() and setVisible() methods are members of the JFrame class inherited from the Component class, so these are available for any component. However, you don't normally set the size and position of other components, as you see later. The setDefaultCloseOperation() method is defined in the JFrame class so this method only applies to JFrame window objects.

Before you expand the example, you need to look a little deeper into the makeup of the component classes.

COMPONENTS AND CONTAINERS

A component represents a graphical entity of one kind or another that can be displayed on the screen. A component is any object of a class that is a subclass of Component. As you have seen, a JFrame window is a component, but there are many others. Before getting into specifics, let's first get a feel for the general relationship between the groups of classes that represent components. Part of the class hierarchy with Component as a base is shown in Figure 17-6. The arrows in the diagram point toward the superclass.

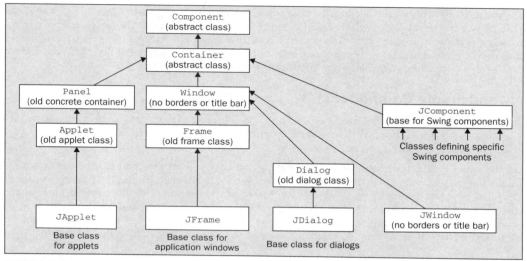

FIGURE 17-6

This shows some of the subclasses of Component—the ones that are important to you at the moment. I discussed the chain through to JFrame earlier, but the other branches are new. The classes that you use directly are all the most commonly derived classes.

Table 17-2 summarizes how you typically use the key classes in this hierarchy:

TABLE 17-2: Using Component subclasses

CLASS	USE
JFrame	This is used as the basic Java application window. An object of this class has a title bar and provision for adding a menu. You can also add other components to it. You usually subclass this class to create a window class specific to your application. You then are able to add GUI components or draw in this window if required, as you later see.
JWindow	An object of this class type is a window with no title bar or window management icons. One typical use for a JWindow object is for a subsidiary application window that is displayed on a secondary display where two or more displays are attached to a system.
JDialog	You use this class to define a dialog window that is used for entering data into a program in various ways. You usually code the creation of a dialog in response to some menu item or button being selected.
JApplet	This is the base class for a Java 2 applet—which is a program designed to run embedded in a web page. All your Java 2 applets have this class as a base. You can draw in a JApplet and also add menus and other components.
JComponent	The subclasses of JComponent define a range of standard components such as menus, buttons, checkboxes, and so on. You use these classes to create the GUI for your application or applet.

All the classes derived from Container can contain other objects of any of the classes derived from Component and are referred to generically as *containers*. Because the Container class is a subclass of the Component class, every container object is a Component, too, so a container can contain other containers. The exception is the Window class and its subclasses, as objects of type Window (or of a subclass type) can't be contained in another container. If you try to do this, an exception is thrown. The JComponent class is the base for all the Swing components used in a window as part of the GUI, and because this class is derived from Container, all of the Swing components are also containers.

As you can see, the JApplet class, which is a base class for all Swing applets, is derived from Component via the Container class. An applet does therefore inherit methods from the Container and Component classes.

It also inherits methods from the old `Applet` class, which it extends. Note that the `JApplet`, `JFrame`, and `JDialog` classes and the `JComponent` class and its subclasses are all in the package `javax.swing`. The `Applet` class is in `java.applet`, and all the others are in `java.awt`. The package `java.applet` is tiny — it contains only the one class plus three related interfaces, but you don't need to use it directly. You always use the `JApplet` class to define an applet, as it's significantly better than `Applet`.

Window and Frame Components

The basic difference between a `JFrame` object and a `Window` object is that a `JFrame` object represents the main window for an application, whereas a `Window` object does not — you always need a `JFrame` object before you can create a `Window` object.

Because the `JDialog` class is derived directly from the `Window` class, you can create a `JDialog` object in an application only in the context of a `JFrame` object. Apart from the default constructor, the constructors for the `JDialog` class generally require a `JFrame` object to be passed as an argument. This `JFrame` object is referred to as the *parent* of the `JDialog` object. A `JFrame` object has a border, is resizable, and has the ability to hold a built-in menu bar. Because a `JFrame` object is the top-level window in an application, its size and location are defined relative to the screen. A `JDialog` object with a `JFrame` object as a parent is located relative to its parent.

As I said, the `JApplet`, `JFrame`, and `JDialog` classes are all containers because they have `Container` as a base class and therefore, in principle, can contain any kind of component. They are also all components themselves because they are derived ultimately from the `Component` class. However, things are not quite as simple as that. You don't add the components for your application or applet GUI *directly* to the `JFrame` or `JApplet` object for your program. Let's look at how it actually works in practice.

Window Panes

When you want to add GUI components or draw in a window displayed from a `JFrame` object, you add the components to, or draw on, a *window pane* that is managed by the `JFrame` object. The same goes for an applet. Broadly speaking, window panes are container objects that represent an area of a window, and they come in several different types.

You use a window pane called the *content pane* most of the time, but there are others. The relationship between the `contentPane` object, other window panes, and the application window itself is shown in Figure 17-7.

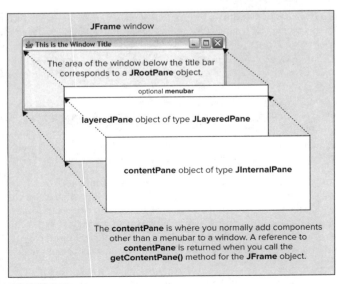

FIGURE 17-7

As you see, the area below the title bar in a JFrame window corresponds to a JRootPane object. This contains another pane, the layeredPane object in the illustration, which is of type JLayeredPane. This pane corresponds to the whole of the area occupied by the JRootPane object in the window and manages the menu bar if the window has one. The area in the layeredPane below the menu bar corresponds to the contentPane object, and it's here that you typically add GUI components. You also display text or do any drawing in the area covered by the content pane.

The layeredPane object has special properties for advanced applications that permit groups of components to be managed in separate layers that overlay one another within the pane. With this capability you can control how components are displayed relative to one another, because the layers are displayed in a particular order from back to front. The components in a layer at the front appear on the screen in front of those in a layer that is towards the back.

There is also an additional pane not shown in Figure 17-7. This is the glassPane object, which also corresponds to the complete JRootPane area. The contents of the glassPane object displays on top of all the other panes, so this is used to display components that you always want to display on top of anything else displayed in the window—such as drop-down menus. You can also use the glassPane object to display graphics that need to be updated relatively frequently—such as when you create an animation. When part of what is displayed is to be animated, a static background can be displayed independently via the contentPane. Because this doesn't need to be reprocessed each time the animated objects need to be redrawn, the whole process can be much more efficient.

The JFrame class defines methods to provide you with a reference to any of the panes (shown in Table 17-3):

TABLE 17-3: JFrame Class Methods

METHOD	DESCRIPTION
getRootPane()	Returns the root pane as type JRootPane.
getLayeredPane()	Returns the layered pane as type JLayeredPane.
getContentPane()	Returns the content pane as type Container. This is the method you use most frequently because you normally add components to the content pane.
getGlassPane()	Returns the glass pane as type Component.

All the classes here that represent panes are themselves Swing components, defined in the javax.swing package. A JApplet object has the same arrangement of panes as a JFrame object, so adding components to an applet, or drawing on it, works in exactly the same way. An applet defined as a JApplet object can also have a menu bar just like an application window.

All the panes, as well as the menu bar, are components, so before I start delving into how to add a menu bar or other components to a window, let's unearth a little more about the makeup of components in general.

BASICS OF COMPONENTS

You need to understand several basic concepts common to all components before you can apply them properly. They also have uses in many different contexts. Although this section may seem like something of a catalog of classes and methods without much in the way of practical application, please stay with it. You use most of these capabilities later. To understand the fundamental things you can do with Swing components, you need to explore the functionality the Swing components inherit from the Component and Container classes.

When a component is contained within another component, the outer object is referred to as the *parent*. You can obtain a reference to the parent object of any given component by calling its getParent() method. This method is inherited from the Component class, and it returns the parent as type Container because only a subclass of Container can hold other components. If there is no parent, as is the case with a JFrame component, this method returns null.

Component Attributes

The Component class defines attributes, which record the following information about an object:

➤ The **position** is stored as (x, y) coordinates. This fixes where the object is in relation to its container in the coordinate system of the container object.

➤ The **name** of the component is stored as a String object.

➤ The **size** is recorded as values for the width and the height of the object.

➤ The **foreground color** and **background color** that apply to the object are used when the object is displayed.

➤ The **font** used by the object when text is displayed.

➤ The **cursor** for the object—this defines the appearance of the cursor when it is over the object.

➤ Whether the object is **enabled** or not—when a component is enabled, its enabled state is true, and it has a normal appearance. When a component is disabled it is grayed out. Note that a disabled component can still originate events, which I will discuss in Chapter 18.

➤ Whether the object is **visible** on the screen or not—if an object is not marked as visible, it is not drawn on the screen.

➤ Whether the object is valid or not—if an object is not valid, the layout of the entities that make up the object has not been determined. This is the case before an object is made visible. You can make a Container object invalid by changing its contents. It then needs to be validated before it is displayed correctly.

You can only modify the characteristics of a Component object by calling its methods or affecting it indirectly in some way because all of the data members that store its characteristics are private. For example, you can change the name of a Component object myWindow with the statement:

```
myWindow.setName("The Name");
```

To retrieve the name of a component you use the getName() method, which returns the name as a String object. For example:

```
String theName = myWindow.getName();
```

The isVisible(), isEnabled(), and isValid() methods return true if the component is visible, enabled, and valid, respectively. Calling validate() for a components makes it valid. You can set a component as visible or enabled by passing the value true to the methods setVisible() and setEnabled(), respectively.

A common misconception with Swing components is that calling setEnabled(false) inhibits events such as mouse clicks from a component. This is not the case. All it does is to set the internal enabled status for the component to false, causing the component to be grayed out. To prevent events from a disabled component having an effect, you must call isEnabled() for the component in your event handling code to determine whether the component is enabled or not. You can then choose to do nothing when the isEnabled() method returns false.

Let's see how you can change the size and position of a Component object.

The Size and Position of a Component

Position is defined by x and y coordinates of type int, or by an object of type java.awt.Point. A Point object has two public data members, x and y, corresponding to the x and y coordinate values. Size is defined by width and height, also values of type int, or by an object of type java.awt.Dimension. The Dimension class has two public members of type int, namely width and height. The size and position of a component are often specified together by an object of type java.awt.Rectangle. A Rectangle object has public data members, x and y, defining the top-left corner of the rectangle, with width and height members defining its size. All these are of type int.

Components have a "preferred" size defined by a java.awt.Dimension object encapsulating values for the width and the height. The preferred size varies depending on the particular object. For example, the preferred size of a JButton object that defines a button is the size that accommodates the label for the button. Note that the size of a component is managed automatically when it has a parent component. I explain how this works later in this chapter. A component also has a minimum size and a maximum size. The size of the component lies within the range from the minimum to the maximum, and if the space available to it is less than the minimum size, the component is not displayed. You can set the preferred size for a component as well as the minimum and maximum size. This provides a way for you to influence the size of a component when it is displayed.

The methods defined in the `Component` class that retrieve the size and position are the following:

➤ `Rectangle getBounds()`: Returns the position and size of the object as an object of type `Rectangle`.

➤ `Rectangle getBounds(Rectangle rect)`: Stores the position and size in the `Rectangle` object that you pass as the argument and returns a reference to rect. This version of the method enables you to reuse an existing `Rectangle` object to store the bounds. If rect is null, a new `Rectangle` object is created by the method.

➤ `Dimension getSize()`: Returns the current size of the `Component` object as a `Dimension` object.

➤ `Dimension getSize(Dimension dim)`: Stores the current size in dim and returns a reference to dim. This enables you to reuse an existing `Dimension` object.

➤ `Point getLocation()`: Returns the position of the `Component` object as an object of type `Point`.

➤ `Point getLocation(Point p)`: Stores the coordinates of the current position of the component in the argument, *p*, and returns a reference to *p*. This enables you to reuse an existing `Point` object to store the position.

You can also change the size and/or position of a component by using the following methods:

➤ `void setBounds(int x, int y,int width, int height)`:
Sets the position of the Component object to the coordinates (*x,y*) and the width and height of the object to the values defined by the third and fourth arguments.

➤ `void setBounds(Rectangle rect)`: Sets the position and size of the `Component` object to be that of the `Rectangle` argument rect.

➤ `void setSize(Dimension d)`: Sets the width and height of the `Component` object to the values stored in the members of the object d.

➤ `setLocation(int x, int y)`: Sets the position of the component to the point defined by (*x,y*).

➤ `setLocation(Point p)`: Sets the position of the component to the point p.

You can also set the parameters that determine the range of variation in size that is possible for a component with the following methods:

➤ `void setMinimumSize(Dimension d)`: Sets the minimum size of the `Component` object to the dimensions specified by the argument d. A null argument restores the default minimum size for the component.

➤ `void setMaximumSize(Dimension d)`: Sets the maximum size of the `Component` object to the dimensions specified by the argument d. A null argument restores the default maximum size for the component.

➤ `void setPreferredSize(Dimension d)`: Sets the preferred size of the `Component` object to the dimensions specified by the argument d. A null argument restores the default preferred size for the component.

Another important method defined in the `Component` class is `getToolkit()`. This returns an object of type `Toolkit` that contains information about the environment in which your application is running, including the screen size in pixels. You can use the `getToolkit()` method to help set the size and position of a window on the screen. You can modify the previous example to demonstrate this.

TRY IT OUT   Sizing Windows with Toolkit

You use the `Toolkit` object to display the window in the center of the screen (or primary monitor if you have more than one), with the width and height set as half of the screen width and height:

Available for download on Wrox.com

```
import javax.swing.JFrame;
import javax.swing.SwingUtilities;
import java.awt.Toolkit;
```

```
import java.awt.Dimension;

public class TryWindow2 {
  public static void createWindow(){
    JFrame aWindow = new JFrame("This is the Window Title");
    Toolkit theKit = aWindow.getToolkit();                  // Get the window toolkit
    Dimension wndSize = theKit.getScreenSize();             // Get screen size

    // Set the position to screen center & size to half screen size
    aWindow.setBounds(wndSize.width/4, wndSize.height/4,    // Position
                      wndSize.width/2, wndSize.height/2);   // Size
    aWindow.setDefaultCloseOperation(JFrame.EXIT_ON_CLOSE);
    aWindow.setVisible(true);                               // Display the window
  }

  public static void main(String[] args) {
    SwingUtilities.invokeLater(new Runnable() {
        public void run() {
          createWindow();
        }
      });
  }
}
```

TryWindow2.java

If you try this example, you should see the application window centered on your primary display with a width and height of half that of the screen. Of course, you could set the window to any position and dimensions you like.

How It Works

You obtain the `Toolkit` object, `theKit`, by calling the `getToolkit()` method for the `JFrame` object, `aWindow`. This object represents the environment on your computer, so it encapsulates all the properties and capabilities of that environment as far as Java is concerned, including the screen resolution and size.

 NOTE *You can't create a* Toolkit *object directly because* Toolkit *is an* abstract *class. There is only one* Toolkit *object in an application—the one that you get a reference for when you call* getToolkit() *for a component.*

The `getScreenSize()` method that is a member of the `Toolkit` object returns an object of type `Dimension` containing data members `width` and `height`. These hold the number of pixels for the width and height of your primary display. You use these values to set the coordinates for the position of the window and the width and height of the window through the `setBounds()` method. Of course, you can use this approach to position the application window anywhere relative to the screen.

This is not the only way of centering a window. A `java.awt.GraphicsEnvironment` object contains information about the graphics devices attached to a system, including the display—or displays in systems with more than one. You can obtain a reference to a `GraphicsEnvironment` object that encapsulates information about the graphics devices on the local machine by calling the static `getLocalGraphicsEnvironment()` method in the `GraphicsEnvironment` class, like this:

```
GraphicsEnvironment localGE = GraphicsEnvironment.getLocalGraphicsEnvironment();
```

This requires the following import:

```
import java.awt.GraphicsEnvironment;
```

You can now call this object's `getCenterPoint()` method to obtain a `java.awt.Point` object containing the coordinates of the center of the screen:

```
        Point center = localGE.getCenterPoint();
```

You can now pass the coordinates of `center` to the `setBounds()` method:

```
        aWindow.setBounds(center.x-wndSize.width/2, center.y- wndSize.height/2,
                                          wndSize.width, wndSize.height);
```

An even simpler mechanism is to call the `setLocationRelativeTo()` method that a `JFrame` object inherits from the `Window` class. This method centers the window at the center of another component that you pass as the argument. If the argument is `null`, the method centers the window relative to the primary display.

You could try this with a variation on the original version of the example.

TRY IT OUT Centering a Window

Here's the code:

Available for
download on
Wrox.com

```
import javax.swing.JFrame;
import javax.swing.SwingUtilities;

public class TryWindow3 {
    public static void createWindow(){
        JFrame aWindow = new JFrame("This is the Window Title");
        int windowWidth = 400;                          // Window width in pixels
        int windowHeight = 150;                         // Window height in pixels
        aWindow.setSize(windowWidth, windowHeight);     // Set window size
        aWindow.setLocationRelativeTo(null);            // Center window

        aWindow.setDefaultCloseOperation(JFrame.EXIT_ON_CLOSE);
        aWindow.setVisible(true);                       // Display the window
    }

    public static void main(String[] args) {
        SwingUtilities.invokeLater(new Runnable() {
                public void run() {
                    createWindow();
                }
            });
    }
}
```

TryWindow3.java

When you execute this, you should see the window displayed centered on your primary display.

How It Works

This example calls the `setSize()` method for `aWindow` to specify the dimension for the window. Calling `setLocationRelativeTo()` with a `null` argument centers the window relative to the primary monitor.

Points and Rectangles

Before continuing with the `Component` class methods, let's digress briefly into more detail concerning the `Point` and `Rectangle` classes, as they are going to come up quite often. As you've seen, both these classes are defined in `java.awt`. You will find many of the methods provided by the `Point` and `Rectangle` classes very useful when drawing in a window. Entities displayed in a window typically have `Rectangle` objects associated with them that define the areas within the window that they occupy. `Point` objects are used in the definition of other geometric entities such as lines and circles, and to specify their position in a window.

Note that neither `Point` nor `Rectangle` objects have any built-in representation on the screen. They aren't components; they are abstract geometric entities. If you want to display a rectangle you have to draw it. You see how to do this in Chapter 19 when you read about other classes that define geometric shapes that can be displayed.

Point Objects

As I said, the `Point` class defines a point by two `public` data members of type `int`, `x` and `y`, so you can access them directly. Let's look at the methods that the class provides.

TRY IT OUT   **Playing with Point Objects**

Try the following code:

```java
import java.awt.Point;

public class PlayingWithPoints {
  public static void main(String[] args) {
    Point aPoint = new Point();            // Initialize to 0,0
    Point bPoint = new Point(50,25);
    Point cPoint = new Point(bPoint);
    System.out.println("aPoint is located at: " + aPoint);
    aPoint.move(100,50);                   // Change to position 100,50

    bPoint.x = 110;
    bPoint.y = 70;

    aPoint.translate(10,20);               // Move by 10 in x and 20 in y
    System.out.println("aPoint is now at: " + aPoint);

    if(aPoint.equals(bPoint))
      System.out.println("aPoint and bPoint are at the same location.");
  }
}
```

PlayingWithPoints.java

If you run the program, you should see the following output produced:

```
aPoint is located at: java.awt.Point[x=0,y=0]
aPoint is now at: java.awt.Point[x=110,y=70]
aPoint and bPoint are at the same location.
```

How It Works

You apply the three constructors that the `Point` class provides in the first few lines. You then manipulate the `Point` objects you've instantiated.

You change a `Point` object to a new position with the `move()` method. Alternatively, you can use the `setLocation()` method to set the values of the `x` and `y` members. The `setLocation()` method behaves exactly the same as the `move()` method. It's included in the `Point` class for compatibility with the `setLocation()` method for a component. For the same reason, there's also a `getLocation()` method in the `Point` class that returns a copy of the current `Point` object. As the example shows, you can translate a `Point` object by specified distances in the *x* and *y* directions using the `translate()` method.

Lastly, you compare two `Point` objects using the `equals()` method. This compares the *x* and *y* coordinates of the two `Point` objects and returns `true` if both are equal. The final output statement is executed because the `Point` objects are equal.

Note that this is not the only class that represents points. You see other classes that define points in Chapter 19 when I discuss how you draw in a window.

Rectangle Objects

As I mentioned earlier, the `java.awt.Rectangle` class defines four `public` data members, all of type `int`. The position of a `Rectangle` object is defined by the members `x` and `y`, and its size is defined by `width` and `height`. As they are all `public`, you can retrieve or modify these directly, but your code may be a little more readable if you use the methods provided to access them.

There are no less than seven constructors that you can use:

➤ `Rectangle()` creates a rectangle at (0,0) with zero width and height.

➤ `Rectangle(int x, int y, int width, int height)` creates a rectangle at (x,y) with the specified width and height.

➤ `Rectangle(int width, int height)` creates a rectangle at (0,0) with the specified width and height.

➤ `Rectangle(Point p, Dimension d)` creates a rectangle at point p with the width and height specified by d. A `java.awt.Dimension` object has two public fields, `width` and `height`.

➤ `Rectangle(Point p)` creates a rectangle at point p with zero width and height.

➤ `Rectangle(Dimension d)` creates a rectangle at (0,0) with the width and height specified by d.

➤ `Rectangle(Rectangle r)` creates a rectangle with the same position and dimensions as the rectangle r.

You can retrieve or modify the position of a `Rectangle` object using the `getLocation()` method that returns a `Point` object, and `setLocation()`, which comes in two versions, one of which requires *x* and *y* coordinates of the new position as arguments and the other of which requires a `Point` object. You can also apply the `translate()` method to a `Rectangle` object in the same way as to a `Point` object.

To retrieve or modify the size of a `Rectangle` object, you use the methods `getSize()`, which returns a `Dimension` object, and `setSize()`, which requires either a `Dimension` object specifying the new size as an argument or two arguments corresponding to the new width and height values as type `int`.

You can also use several methods to combine `Rectangle` objects and to extend a `Rectangle` object to enclose a point. The effects of each of these methods are shown in Figure 17-8.

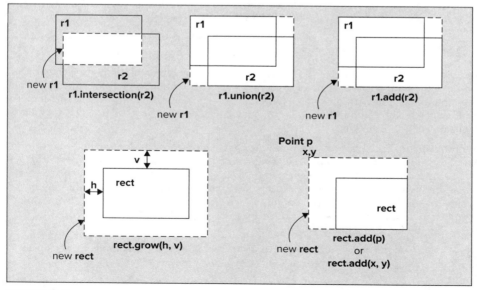

FIGURE 17-8

The rectangle that results from each operation is shown with dashed line boundaries. The details of the operations provided by the methods illustrated in Figure 17-8 are as follows:

➤ `Rectangle intersection(Rectangle r):` Returns a `Rectangle` object that is the intersection of the current object and the argument. If the two rectangles do not intersect, the `Rectangle` object returned is at position (0,0), and the `width` and `height` members are zero, so the rectangle is empty.

➤ `Rectangle union(Rectangle r):` Returns the smallest `Rectangle` object enclosing both the current Rectangle object and the Rectangle object r, passed as an argument.

➤ `void add(Rectangle r):` Expands the current `Rectangle` object to enclose the argument `Rectangle`.

➤ `void add(Point p):` Expands the current `Rectangle` object to enclose the `Point` object p. The result is the smallest rectangle that encloses the original rectangle and the point.

➤ `void add(int x, int y):` Expands the current `Rectangle` object to enclose the point at (x, y).

➤ `void grow(int h, int v):` Enlarges the current `Rectangle` object by moving the boundary out from the center by h horizontally and v vertically.

You can also test and compare `Rectangle` objects in various ways with the following methods:

➤ `boolean isEmpty():` Returns `true` if the `width` and `height` members of the current `Rectangle` object are zero and returns `false` otherwise.

➤ `boolean equals(Object rect):` Returns `true` if the `Rectangle` object passed as an argument is equal to the current `Rectangle` object, and `false` otherwise. The two rectangles are equal if they are at the same position and have the same width and height. If the argument is not a `Rectangle` object, `false` is returned.

➤ `boolean intersects(Rectangle rect):` Returns `true` if the current `Rectangle` object intersects rect and returns `false` otherwise.

➤ `boolean contains(Point p):` Returns `true` if the current `Rectangle` object encloses p and returns `false` otherwise.

➤ `boolean contains(int x, int y):` Returns `true` if the current `Rectangle` object encloses the point (x, y) and returns `false` otherwise.

These methods are useful when you are dealing with the contents of the client area of the application window. You work with points and rectangles relating to the items drawn in the window. You meet other classes that define rectangles when you start drawing in a window in Chapter 19.

Visual Characteristics of a Component

Two things determine the visual appearance of a Swing component: the representation of the component created by the code in the component class that is executed when the component is displayed, and whatever you draw on the component. You draw on a `Component` object by implementing its `paint()` method. You used this method in Chapter 1 to output the text for an applet. The `paint()` method is called automatically when the component needs to be drawn.

The need to redraw a component can arise quite often for a variety of reasons—for example, your program may request that the area that the component occupies should be redrawn, or the user may resize the window containing the component. Your implementation of this method must include code to generate whatever you want drawn within the `Component` object. Note that the component itself—the `JButton` or `JFrame` or whatever—is drawn for you. You only need to override the `paint()` method for anything additional that you want to draw on it. You override the `paint()` method in Chapter 19 to draw in a window, so I'm leaving further discussion of it until then.

You can alter some aspects of the appearance of the basic component by calling methods for the object. The following methods have an effect on the appearance of a `Component` object:

➤ `void setBackground(Color aColor):` Sets the background color to aColor. The background color is the color used for the basic component. You must use a different color from the background when you draw if you want what you have drawn to be visible.

➤ `Color getBackground()`: Returns the component's current background color. This is useful when you want to verify that the color you plan to use for drawing on a component is different from the background.

➤ `void setForeground(Color bColor)`: Sets the foreground color to `bColor`. The foreground color is the color used by default for anything you draw on the component.

➤ `Color getForeground()`: Returns the component's current foreground color.

➤ `void setCursor(Cursor aCursor)`: Sets the cursor for the component to `aCursor`. This determines the appearance of the cursor within the area occupied by the component.

➤ `void setFont(Font aFont)`: Sets the font for the `Component` object. This is the default font when you draw text on the component.

➤ `Font getFont()`: Returns the current font for the component.

To be able to make use of these properly, you need to understand what `Color` objects are, and you need to know how to create `Cursor` and `Font` objects.

Defining Colors

A screen color is represented by a `java.awt.Color` object. You define a color value as a combination of the three primary colors: red, green, and blue. They are usually expressed in that sequence, and are often referred to as *RGB values*. There are other ways of specifying colors in Java, but I discuss only RGB. You can specify the intensity of each primary color to be a value from 0 to 255. If the intensities of all three are 0, you have the color black, and if all three are 255 you have white. If only one intensity value is positive and the others are zero, you have a pure primary color; for example, (0, 200, 0) is a shade of green. You could define variables corresponding to these colors with the following statements:

```
ck = new Color(0,0,0);                   // Color black
Color myWhite = new Color(255,255,255);  // Color white
Color myGreen = new Color(0,200,0);      // A shade of green
```

The three arguments to the constructor correspond to the intensities of the red, green, and blue components of the color, respectively. The `Color` class defines a number of standard color constants as `public final static` variables, whose RGB values are given in parentheses:

WHITE	(255, 255, 255)	RED	(255, 0, 0)
PINK	(255, 175, 175)	LIGHT_GRAY	(192, 192, 192)
ORANGE	(255, 200, 0)	MAGENTA	(255, 0, 255)
GRAY	(128, 128, 128)	YELLOW	(255, 255, 0)
CYAN	(0, 255, 255)	DARK_GRAY	(64, 64, 64)
GREEN	(0, 255, 0)	BLUE	(0, 0, 255)
BLACK	(0, 0, 0,)		

There is an identical set of members of the `Color` class with the same names, but in lowercase, so you can use either an upper- or lowercase name to reference a standard color.

If you want the window in the previous example to have a pink background, you could add the following statement to the `createWindow()` method:

```
aWindow.setBackground(Color.PINK);
```

When you have created a `Color` object, you can brighten or darken the color it represents by calling its `brighter()` or `darker()` methods, which increase or decrease the intensity of the color components by a predefined factor:

```
thisColor.brighter();                    // Brighten the color
thatColor.darker();                      // Darken the color
```

The intensities of the component colors always remain between 0 and 255. When you call `brighter` and a color component is already at 255, it remains at that value. The other component intensities are increased if they are less than 255. In a similar way, the `darker()` method does not change a component intensity if it is zero. The factor used for darkening a color component is 0.7. To brighten a color component, the intensity is increased by 1/0.7.

You can obtain only the colors available within the computer and the operating system environment on which your Java program is running. If you have a limited range of colors, the `brighter()` and `darker()` methods may appear to have no effect. Although you can create `Color` objects that are supposed to represent all kinds of colors, if your computer is a valuable antique that supports only 16 colors, you always end up with one of your 16. If your graphics card supports 24-bit or more colors, and this is supported in your system environment, then everything should be fine and dandy.

You can obtain any of the component intensities by calling `getRed()`, `getGreen()`, or `getBlue()` for a `Color` object. A color can also be obtained as a value of type `int` that is a composite of the red, green, and blue components of the color by calling the `getRGB()` method. You can also create a `Color` object from a single RGB value of type `int`.

To compare two `Color` objects you use the `equals()` method. For example, to compare two color objects `colorA` and `colorB`, you could write the following:

```
if(colorA.equals(colorB)) {
  // Do something...
}
```

The `equals()` method returns `true` if all three components of the two `Color` objects are equal. As with object references in general, don't use the `==` operator to compare `Color` objects. If you do, you are just determining whether the two `Color` object references refer to the same object. Applying the `==` operator to two different `Color` objects that represent the same color results in `false`.

You could also use the `getRGB()` method for a `Color` object when you are comparing colors:

```
if(colorA.getRGB() == colorB.getRGB()) {
  // Do something....
}
```

This compares the two integer RGB values for equality, so here the `==` operator produces the correct result.

 NOTE Note that the `Color` class also supports color transparency by storing an alpha compositing value in the range 0 to 255, where 0 is completely transparent and 255 is completely opaque. You also have `Color` constructors that accept color component values between 0.0 and 1.0.

System Colors

The `java.awt` package defines the class `SystemColor` as a subclass of the `Color` class. The `SystemColor` class encapsulates the standard colors that the native operating system uses for displaying various components. The class contains definitions for 26 `public final static` variables of type `SystemColor` that specify the standard system colors used by the operating system for a range of GUI components. For example, the system colors for a window are referenced by the following:

`window`	Defines the background color for a window
`windowText`	Defines the text color for a window
`windowBorder`	Defines the border color for a window

You can find the others covering colors used for menus, captions, controls, and so on, if you need them, by looking at the documentation for the `SystemColor` class.

If you want to compare a `SystemColor` value with a `Color` object, then you must use the `getRGB()` method in the comparison. This is because the `SystemColor` class stores the colors internally in a way that uses the fields it inherits from the `Color` class differently from a normal `Color` object. For example, to see whether `colorA` corresponds to the system background color for a window, you could write:

```
if(colorA.getRGB() == SystemColor.window.getRGB()) {
  // colorA is the window background color...
}
```

Of course, because `SystemColor` is a subclass of the `Color` class, it inherits all the members of that class, including all the color constants that you saw in the previous section.

Creating Cursors

An object of the `java.awt.Cursor` class encapsulates a bitmap representation of the mouse cursor. The `Cursor` class contains a range of `final static` constants that specify standard cursor types. You use these to select or create a particular cursor. The standard cursor types are the following:

DEFAULT_CURSOR	N_RESIZE_CURSOR	NE_RESIZE_CURSOR
CROSSHAIR_CURSOR	S_RESIZE_CURSOR	NW_RESIZE_CURSOR
WAIT_CURSOR	E_RESIZE_CURSOR	SE_RESIZE_CURSOR
TEXT_CURSOR	W_RESIZE_CURSOR	SW_RESIZE_CURSOR
HAND_CURSOR	MOVE_CURSOR	

The resize cursors are the ones that you see when you resize a window by dragging its boundaries. Note that these are not like the `Color` constants, which are `Color` objects—these constants are of type `int`, not type `Cursor`, and are intended to be used as arguments to a `Cursor` constructor. To create a `Cursor` object representing a text cursor you could write:

```
Cursor myCursor = new Cursor(Cursor.TEXT_CURSOR);
```

Alternatively, you can retrieve a predefined cursor using a `static` class method:

```
Cursor myCursor = Cursor.getPredefinedCursor(Cursor.TEXT_CURSOR);
```

This method is particularly useful when you don't want to store the `Cursor` object, but just want to pass it to a method, such as `setCursor()` for a `Component` object.

If you want to see what the standard cursors look like, you could add a cursor to an application window, along with a pink background.

TRY IT OUT Color and Cursors

You can change the background color of the content pane for the application window and try out a different cursor:

Available for download on Wrox.com

```
import javax.swing.JFrame;
import javax.swing.SwingUtilities;
import java.awt.Toolkit;
import java.awt.Dimension;
import java.awt.Color;
import java.awt.Cursor;

public class TryWindow4 {
  public static void createWindow(){
    JFrame aWindow = new JFrame("This is the Window Title");
    Toolkit theKit = aWindow.getToolkit();          // Get the window toolkit
    Dimension wndSize = theKit.getScreenSize();      // Get screen size

    // Set the position to screen center & size to half screen size
    aWindow.setSize(wndSize.width/2, wndSize.height/2);   // Set window size
```

```
        aWindow.setLocationRelativeTo(null);                    // Center window
        aWindow.setDefaultCloseOperation(JFrame.EXIT_ON_CLOSE);

        aWindow.setCursor(Cursor.getPredefinedCursor(Cursor.CROSSHAIR_CURSOR));
        aWindow.getContentPane().setBackground(Color.PINK);

        aWindow.setVisible(true);                               // Display the window
    }

    public static void main(String[] args) {
        SwingUtilities.invokeLater(new Runnable() {
            public void run() {
                createWindow();
            }
        });
    }
}
```

TryWindow4.java

When you move the mouse cursor into the application window, you see the crosshair cursor against a pink background. You can try all the cursors by plugging in each of the standard cursor names in turn. You could also try out a few variations on the background color.

 NOTE *You also have the capability to create your own custom cursor. The* createCustomCursor() *method for a* Toolkit *object enables you to create a cursor with a cursor image that you supply to the method along with the coordinates of the cursor hotspot and the cursor name.*

Selecting Fonts

An object of type java.awt.Font represents a font. The Font class is actually quite complicated, so I only scratch the surface of the class enough for your needs here. The Font class differentiates between a *character*—the letter uppercase Q, say—and a *glyph*, which is the shape defining its appearance when it is displayed or printed. In general, a given character in one font has a different glyph in a different font. With fonts for many languages—German, French, or Finnish, for example—a character may involve more than one glyph to display it. This is typically the case for characters that involve *diacritic marks*, which are additional graphics attached to a character. The letter *ä*, for example, combines the normal letter *a* with an umlaut, the two dots over it, so it may be represented by two glyphs, one for the letter and the other for the umlaut. A Font object contains a table that maps the Unicode value for each character to the glyph code or codes that create the visual representation of the character.

To create a Font object you must supply the font name, the style of the font, and the point size. For example, consider the following statement:

```
    Font myFont = new Font("Serif", Font.ITALIC, 12);
```

This defines a 12-point italic font that is a *logical font*. Logical fonts are five families of fonts defined by the Java platform and are therefore supported in any Java runtime. The other options you could use for the font style are PLAIN and BOLD. The name you have given to the font here, "Serif", is a *logical font name*. The other logical font names you could have used are "Dialog", "DialogInput", "Monospaced", or "SansSerif".

Instead of a logical font name, you can supply a *physical font* face name such as "Times New Roman" or "Palatino". A physical font is a font from a font library and includes fonts that are TrueType or Postscript fonts. Swing components work with either logical fonts or physical fonts, whereas AWT components can use only logical fonts. Logical fonts have the advantage that they work on any platform, so you can use a logical font without needing to verify its availability. However, the appearance of a logical font may vary from one platform to another. Using physical fonts provides a lot more flexibility, but the font you are using must be available on the platform on which your code is executing. Using logical fonts is easy to program and you can be sure that the code works anywhere.

It's a bit more difficult to program for using physical fonts than logical. Although your programs can create strings of Japanese or Tibetan characters, if your operating system doesn't have fonts for these you can't display or print them. Therefore, to display or print text in the way that you want, you need to know what font face names are available in the system on which your code is running. I come back to this in a moment.

You can specify a combination of font styles by ORing them together because each style is a single-bit integer. If you want `myFont` to be `BOLD` and `ITALIC` you would write:

```
Font myFont = new Font("Serif", Font.ITALIC | Font.BOLD, 12);
```

You retrieve the style and size of an existing `Font` object by calling its methods `getStyle()` and `getSize()`, both of which return a value of type `int`. You can also check the individual font style for a `Font` object with the methods `isPlain()`, `isBold()`, and `isItalic()`. Each of these methods returns a `boolean` value indicating whether or not the `Font` object has that style.

Before you create a physical font, you need to know whether the font is available on the system where your code is executing. You can use the `getAllFonts()` method in the `java.awt.GraphicsEnvironment` class to obtain an array of the fonts available as follows:

```
GraphicsEnvironment e = GraphicsEnvironment.getLocalGraphicsEnvironment();
Font[] fonts = e.getAllFonts();                    // Get the fonts
```

You get a reference to the `GraphicsEnvironment` object for the current machine by calling the `static` method `getLocalGraphicsEnvironment()`. You then use the reference that is returned to call its `getAllFonts()` method. The `getAllFonts()` method returns an array of `Font` objects consisting of those available on the current system. You can then check this list for the font you want to use. Each of the `Font` instances in the array are of a 1-point size. Characters with a point size of 1 are approximately 1/72 of an inch, or 0.353 mm, so you should change this unless your screen and eyesight are really exceptional. To change the size and/or style of a font, you call its `deriveFont()` method. This method comes in six versions but I'll only discuss three of them:

➤ `Font deriveFont(int Style)`: Returns a new `Font` object with the style specified— one of `PLAIN`, `BOLD`, `ITALIC`, or `BOLD+ITALIC`.

➤ `Font deriveFont(float size)`: Returns a new `Font` object with the specified point size.

➤ `Font deriveFont(int Style, float size)`: Returns a new `Font` object with the specified style and point size.

You could use the last font from the array of `Font` objects to create an equivalent 12-point font with the following statement:

```
Font newFont = fonts[fonts.length-1].deriveFont(12.0f);
```

Of the three other versions of `deriveFont()`, two involve an object of type `java.awt.geom.Affine Transform`, but I'm deferring discussion of `AffineTransform` objects until Chapter 20. The third makes use of a `Map` collection object containing special iterator objects for text attributes, but I don't discuss these.

Getting a `Font` object for every physical font in the system can be a time-consuming process if you have many fonts installed. A much faster alternative is to get the physical font names and then use one of these to create the `Font` object that you require. You can get the face names for all the fonts in a system like this:

```
GraphicsEnvironment e = GraphicsEnvironment.getLocalGraphicsEnvironment();
String[] fontnames = e.getAvailableFontFamilyNames();
```

The array `fontnames` contains the names of all the font faces available, and you can use one or more of these to create the `Font` objects you need.

TRY IT OUT Getting the List of Fonts

This program outputs your primary display's size and resolution, as well as the list of font family names installed on your machine:

Available for download on Wrox.com

```java
import java.awt.Toolkit;
import java.awt.GraphicsEnvironment;
import java.awt.Font;
import java.awt.Dimension;

public class FontInfo {
  public static void main(String[] args) {
    Toolkit theKit = Toolkit.getDefaultToolkit();

    System.out.println("\nScreen Resolution: "
                      + theKit.getScreenResolution() + " dots per inch");

    Dimension screenDim = theKit.getScreenSize();
    System.out.println("Screen Size: "
                      + screenDim.width + " by "
                      + screenDim.height + " pixels");

    GraphicsEnvironment e = GraphicsEnvironment.getLocalGraphicsEnvironment();
    String[] fontnames = e.getAvailableFontFamilyNames();
    System.out.println("\nFonts available on this platform: ");
    int count = 0;
    for (String fontname : fontnames) {
      System.out.printf("%-30s", fontname);
      if(++count % 3 == 0) {
        System.out.println();
      }
    }
  }
}
```

FontInfo.java

On my system I get the following output:

```
Screen Resolution: 96 dots per inch
Screen Size: 1920 by 1080 pixels

Fonts available on this platform:
Aharoni                Andalus                Angsana New
AngsanaUPC             Aparajita              Arabic Typesetting
Arial                  Arial Black            Arial Narrow
Arial Unicode MS       Batang                 BatangChe
Berling Antiqua        Blackadder ITC         Book Antiqua
Bookdings              Bookman Old Style      Bookshelf Symbol 7
Bradley Hand ITC       BRAZIL                 Browallia New
BrowalliaUPC           Calibri                Cambria
Cambria Math           Candara                CENA
  . . .
```

with many more font names in the list.

How It Works

You first get a `Toolkit` object by calling the `static` method `getDefaultToolkit()` —this is the key to the other information. The `getScreenResolution()` method returns the number of pixels per inch as a value of type `int`. The `getScreenSize()` method returns a `Dimension` object that specifies the width and height of the screen in pixels.

You use the `getAvailableFontFamilyNames()` method to get a `String` array containing the names of the fonts, which you output to the console.

Font Metrics

Every component has a `getFontMetrics()` method that you can use to retrieve *font metrics*—a wealth of dimensional data about a font. You pass a `Font` object as an argument to the method, and it returns an object of type `FontMetrics` that you can use to obtain data relating to the particular font. For example, if `aWindow` is a `Frame` object and `myFont` is a `Font` object, you could obtain a `FontMetrics` object corresponding to the font with the following statement:

```
FontMetrics metrics = aWindow.getFontMetrics(myFont);
```

You could use the `getFont()` method for a component to explore the characteristics of the font that the component contains. For example:

```
FontMetrics metrics = aWindow.getFontMetrics(aWindow.getFont());
```

You can now call any of the following `FontMetrics` methods for the object to get at the basic dimensions of the font:

➤ `int getAscent()`: Returns the *ascent* of the font, which is the distance from the baseline to the top of the majority of the characters in the font. The *baseline* is the line on which the characters rest. Depending on the font, some characters can extend beyond the ascent.

➤ `int getMaxAscent()`: Returns the maximum ascent for the font. No character exceeds this ascent.

➤ `int getDescent()`: Returns the *descent* of the font, which is the distance from the baseline to the bottom of most of the font characters that extend below the baseline. Depending on the font, some characters may extend beyond the descent for the font.

➤ `int getMaxDescent()`: Returns the maximum descent of the characters in the font. No character exceeds this descent.

➤ `int getLeading()`: Returns the *leading* for the font, which is the line spacing for the font—that is the spacing between the bottom of one line of text and the top of the next. The term originated when type was actually made of lead, and there was a strip of lead between one line of type and the next when a page was typeset.

➤ `int getHeight()`: Returns the height of the font, which is defined as the sum of the ascent, the descent, and the leading.

Figure 17-9 shows how the dimensions relate to the font.

FIGURE 17-9

The *advance width* for a character is the distance from the reference point of the character to the reference point of the next character. The *reference point* for a character is on the baseline at the left edge of the character. Each character has its own advance width, which you can obtain by calling a `FontMetrics` method `charWidth()`. For example, to obtain the advance width for the character `'X'`, the following statement could be used:

```
int widthX = metrics.charWidth('X');
```

You can also obtain the advance widths for the first 256 characters in the font as an array of type `int` with the method `getWidths()`:

```
int[] widths = metrics.getWidths();
```

If you just want the maximum advance width for the characters in the font, you can call the method `getMaxAdvance()`. Lastly, you can get the total advance width for a `String` object by passing the object to the method `stringWidth()`. The advance width is returned as a value of type `int`. It's important to appreciate that the advance width for a string is not necessarily the sum of the widths of the characters that it contains.

Although you now know a great deal about how to create and manipulate fonts, you haven't actually created and used one. You remedy this after you get a feel for what Swing components can do and have learned a little about using containers.

Swing Components

Swing components all have the `JComponent` class as a base, which itself extends the `Component` class to add the following capability:

➤ Support for pluggable look-and-feel for components, allowing you to change the look-and-feel programmatically, or implement your own look-and-feel for all components displayed.

➤ Support for tooltips—a *tooltip* being a message describing the purpose of a component when the mouse cursor lingers over it. Tooltips are defined by the `JToolTip` class.

➤ Support for automatic scrolling in a list, a table, or a tree when a component is dragged with the mouse.

➤ Component class extensions to enable you to create your own custom components.

All the Swing component classes are defined in the `javax.swing` package and have class names that begin with `J`. There are quite a few Swing components, so I'll give you an overview of the most used classes and how they relate to one another. I will go into the detail of particular Swing components when I use them in examples.

Buttons

The Swing button classes in the `javax.swing` package define various kinds of buttons operated by clicking with a mouse. The button classes have the `AbstractButton` class as a base, as shown in Figure 17-10.

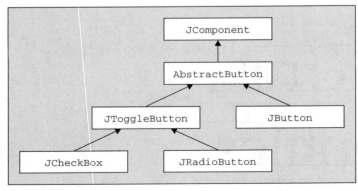

FIGURE 17-10

The JButton class defines a regular pushbutton that you would use as a dialog button—OK and Cancel buttons, for example, that you are sure to have seen and used—or in a toolbar, where the buttons might provide alternatives to using menu items. There are two subclasses of JButton, BasicArrowButton that is a button with an arrow on it and MetalComboBoxButton, which is a helper class for creating the metal look-and-feel. I won't be going into these in detail.

The JToolBar class is used in conjunction with the JButton class to create a toolbar containing buttons. A toolbar is dockable without any additional programming effort on your part, as you later see.

The JToggleButton class defines a two-state button, pressed or not, and two more specialized versions are defined by JCheckBox and JRadioButton. Radio buttons defined as JRadioButton objects generally operate in a group so that only one button can be in the pressed state at any one time. This grouping is established by adding the JRadioButton object to a ButtonGroup object that takes care of the state of the buttons in the group.

A JCheckBox object is a button with a square checkbox to the left. Clicking on the checkbox changes its state from checked to unchecked or vice versa.

All the buttons can be displayed with a text label, an icon, or both.

Menus

The Swing components include support for pop-up or context menus as well as menu bars. The classes defining elements of a menu are shown in Figure 17-11.

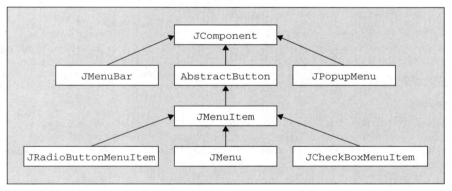

FIGURE 17-11

The JMenuBar class defines a *menu bar* usually found at the top of an application window. A JMenu object represents a top-level menu item on a menu bar that drops down a list of menu items when it is clicked. The items in a menu are defined by the JMenuItem class. The JPopupMenu class defines a context menu that is typically implemented to appear at the current cursor position when the right mouse button is clicked. A JCheckBoxMenuItem component is a menu item with a checkbox that is ticked when the item is selected. The JRadioButtonMenuItem class defines a menu item that is part of a group where only one item can be selected at any time. The group is created by adding JRadioButtonMenuItem objects to a ButtonGroup object. You implement a menu in an application and an applet later in this chapter.

Text Components

The capability of the Swing text components is very wide indeed. The classes in the javax.swing packages that represent text components are shown in Figure 17-12. Like all Swing components, they have the JComponent class as a base.

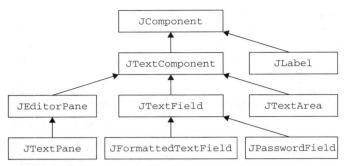

FIGURE 17-12

The most elementary text component is a JLabel object, which displays as a single line of text. A JLabel component is passive and does not react to input events so you can't edit it. A JTextField component looks similar to a label in that it displays a single line of text, but in this case it is editable. A JFormattedTextField component is a JTextField component that can control and format the data that is displayed or entered. It can supply automatic formatting in many instances so it can automatically display a Date object as a date for example. A JPasswordField component allows entry of a password as a single line of input and prevents the characters in the password from being seen.

The JTextArea class defines a component that allows editing of multiline text that is contained within a given area. A JTextArea component does not support scrolling directly, but it's easy to add scrollbars by placing the JTextArea component in a JScrollPane container.

The JEditorPane and JTextPane components are a different order of complexity from the others and enable you to implement sophisticated editing facilities relatively easily. The JEditorPane supports editing of plaintext, text in HTML, and RTF (Rich Text Format). The JTextPane class extends JEditorPane and enables you to embed images or other components within the text managed by the component.

Other Swing Components

Other Swing components you use regularly include the JPanel component. The JPanel class defines something like a physical panel that you can use as a container to group a set of components. For example, you might use two JPanel objects to support two separate groups of JButton components in the content pane of an application window.

The JList<E> and JTable components are also very useful. A JList<E> component displays a list of items of type E with one item per line from which a user can select an item. The list of items displayed by a JList<E> component is maintained in an object of type javax.swing.ListModel<E>, where ListModel<> is a generic interface type. You can create a JList<E> component from a javax.swing. DefaultListModel<E> object in which you store the items you want to have displayed in the list. A DefaultListModel<> object is much like a vector<> container. You add items to the list model by calling the addElement() member and you can add an item at a particular index position by calling the add() method where the first argument is the index position and the second is the item to be added.

A JTable component displays items in a rectangular table with column headers with the items stored in a table model. You can create your own table model class by using the javax.swing.table.AbstractTableModel class as a base. A user can edit a single cell, or relocate or delete an entire row or column. A JTable component automatically takes care of reordering the columns when a column is dragged to a new position using the mouse.

In principle, you can add a border to any component, and the javax.swing.borders package contains eight classes that represent different kinds of borders you can use for a component. However, you can also place a component to which you want to add a border in a JPanel container, and add the border to the JPanel object. You use JPanel containers quite a lot throughout the rest of the book.

I have not introduced all the Swing component classes by any means, and you meet a few more as you progress through the rest of the chapters.

USING SWING CONTAINERS

A Swing container is any component of a type that has the `Container` class as a base, so all the Swing components are containers. The `Container` class is the direct base class for the `Window` class, and it provides the capability for a window to contain other components. Because the `Container` class is an `abstract` class, you cannot create instances of `Container`. Instead, it's objects of the subclasses such as `Window`, `JFrame`, or `JDialog` that inherit the capability to contain other components.

> **NOTE** *A container cannot contain an object of the* `Window` *class, or an object of any of the classes derived from* `Window`. *An object of any other class that is derived from* `Component` *can be added to a container.*

The components within a container are displayed within the area occupied by the container on the display screen. A dialog box, for example, might contain a `JList<>` object offering some options, `JCheckbox` objects offering other options, and `JButton` objects representing buttons enabling the user to end the dialog or enter the selections—all these components would appear within the boundaries of the dialog box. Of course, for the contained components to be visible, the container must itself be displayed because the container effectively "owns" its components. The container also controls how its embedded components are laid out by means of an object called a *layout manager*.

Before I introduce you to what a layout manager is and how the layout of the components in a container is determined, let's consider the basic methods that the `Container` class defines that are available to all containers.

You can find out about the components in a `Container` object by using the following methods that are defined in the `Container` class:

➤ `int getComponentCount()`: Returns a count of the number of components contained by the current container.

➤ `Component getComponent(int index)`: Returns the component identified by the `index` value. `index` is an array index so it must be between 0 and one less than the number of components contained; otherwise, an `ArrayIndexOutOfBoundsException` is thrown.

➤ `Component[] getComponents()`: Returns an array of all the components in the current container.

You can also obtain a reference to a component that contains a given point within the area occupied by the container by calling the `getComponentAt()` method, with the *x* and *y* coordinates of the point as arguments. If more than one component contains the point, a reference to the component closest to index 0 in the container is returned.

If you have a `Container` object, `content`, perhaps the content pane of a `JFrame` window, you could iterate through the components in the `Container` with the following statements:

```
Component component = null;                           // Stores a Component
int numComponents = content.getComponentCount();      // Get the count

for(int i = 0 ; i < numComponents ; ++i) {
  component = content.getComponent(i);                // Get each component
  // Do something with component...
}
```

This retrieves the components in `content` one at a time in the `for` loop. Alternatively, you could retrieve them from the container all at once:

```
Component[] theComponents = content.getComponents();  // Get all components

for(Component component : theComponents) {
  // Do something with component...
}
```

The `getComponent()` method returns all the components in the container as an array of elements of type `Component`. You can then use the collection-based `for` loop to iterate over the components in the array.

Adding Components to a Container

The components that you add to a container are recorded in a list within the `Container` object. To add a component to a container, you use the `add()` method. The `Container` class defines the following four overloaded versions of the `add()` method:

➤ `Component add(Component c)`: Adds `c` to the end of the list of components stored in the container. The return value is `c`.

➤ `Component add(Component c, int index)`: Adds `c` to the list of components in the container at the position specified by `index`. If `index` is −1, the component is added to the end of the list. If the value of `index` is not −1, it must be less than the number of components in the container and greater than or equal to 0. The return value is `c`.

➤ `void add(Component c, Object constraints)`: Adds `c` to the end of the list of components stored in the container. The position of the component relative to the container is subject to the constraints defined by the second parameter. You learn about constraints in the next section.

➤ `void add(Component c, Object constraints, int index)`: Adds `c` to the list of components in the container at the position specified by `index` and the position subject to `constraints`. If `index` is −1, the component is added to the end of the list. If the value of `index` is not −1, it must be less than the number of components in the container and greater than or equal to 0.

Note that a component can be in only one container at a time. Adding a component to a container that is already in another container removes it from the original container.

Before you can try adding components to a container, you need to understand the constraints that appear in some of the `add()` methods and look at how the layout of components in a container is controlled.

CONTAINER LAYOUT MANAGERS

As I said, an object called a *layout manager* determines the way that components are arranged in a container. All containers have a default layout manager, but you can choose a different layout manager when necessary. Many layout manager classes are provided in the `java.awt` and `javax.swing` packages, so I introduce those that you are most likely to need. It is also possible to create your own layout manager classes, but creating layout managers is beyond the scope of this book. The layout manager for a container determines the position and size of all the components in the container, so you should not generally change the size and position of such components yourself; just let the layout manager take care of it.

Because the classes that define layout managers all implement the `LayoutManager` interface, you can use a variable of type `LayoutManager` to reference any of them. I introduce six layout manager classes in a little more detail. The names of these classes and the basic arrangements that they provide are as follows:

➤ `FlowLayout` places components in successive rows in a container, fitting as many on each row as possible and starting on the next row as soon as a row is full. This works in much the same way as your text processor places words on a line. Its primary use is for arranging buttons, although you can use it with other components. It is the default layout manager for `JPanel` objects.

➤ `BorderLayout` places components against any of the four borders of the container and in the center. The component in the center fills the available space. This layout manager is the default for the content pane in a `JFrame`, `JDialog`, or `JApplet` object.

➤ `CardLayout` places components in a container one on top of the other—like a deck of cards. Only the "top" component is visible at any one time.

➤ GridLayout places components in the container in a rectangular grid with the number of rows and columns that you specify.

➤ GridBagLayout also places the components into an arrangement of rows and columns, but the rows and columns can vary in length. This is a complicated layout manager with a lot of flexibility in how you control where components are placed in a container.

➤ BoxLayout arranges components either in a row or in a column. In either case the components are clipped to fit if necessary, rather than wrapping to the next row or column. The BoxLayout manager is the default for the Box container class.

➤ SpringLayout allows components to have their positions defined by "springs" or "struts" fixed to an edge of the container or other components in the container.

The BoxLayout, SpringLayout, and Box classes are defined in the javax.swing package. The other layout manager classes in the preceding list are defined in java.awt.

One question you might ask is why do you need layout managers at all? Why can't you just place components at some given position in a container? The basic reason is to ensure that the GUI elements for your Java program are displayed properly in every possible Java environment. Layout managers automatically adjust the size and positions of components to fit within the space available. If you fix the size and position of each of the components, they could run into one another and overlap if the screen area available to your application window is reduced.

You call the setLayout() method for a Container object to set the layout manager. For example, you could change the layout manager for the JFrame object aWindow from its default BorderLayout layout manager to flow layout with the following statements:

```
FlowLayout flow = new FlowLayout();
aWindow.getContentPane().setLayout(flow);
```

Remember that components that you want to display in the client area of a JFrame object should be added to its content pane. The same goes for JDialog and JApplet objects. In fact, if you use the add() method for a JFrame, JDialog, or JApplet object to add a component, it is redirected to the content pane, so everything is as it should be. This convenience facility is there for consistency with similar AWT components. However, for some other operations—setting the background color, for example—you *must* call the method belonging to the content pane object for things to turn out as you expect. For this reason I think it's better to explicitly perform all operations on the content pane rather than rely on redirection by the parent frame object. That way you won't forget that it's the content pane you are working with.

With some containers you can set the layout manager in the constructor for that container, as you see in later examples. Let's look at how the layout managers work, and some examples of how you might use them in practice.

 NOTE *Several Java IDEs provide a great deal of support for laying out components and relieve you of the drudgery of working with the detail of a flow layout manager. However, it is still useful to understand what is going on.*

The Flow Layout Manager

The flow layout manager places components in a row, and when the row is full, it automatically spills components onto the next row. The default positioning of the row of components is centered in the container, and the default orientation is from left to right. You have five possible row-positioning options that you specify by constants of type int that are defined in the FlowLayout class. These are LEFT, RIGHT, CENTER, LEADING, and TRAILING. LEADING and TRAILING specify the edge of the component to which the row should be justified. The effects of the first three on the alignment of a row of components are what you would expect. The CENTER option is the default. By default, components in a row are separated by a five-unit gap and successive rows are separated by the same distance.

The flow layout manager is very easy to use, so let's jump straight in and see it working in an example.

Using a Flow Layout Manager

As I said earlier, this layout manager is used primarily to arrange a few components whose relative position is unimportant. Let's implement a `TryFlowLayout` program based on the `TryWindow4` example:

Available for
download on
Wrox.com

```java
import javax.swing.JFrame;
import javax.swing.SwingUtilities;
import java.awt.Toolkit;
import java.awt.Dimension;
import javax.swing.JButton;
import java.awt.Container;
import java.awt.FlowLayout;

public class TryFlowLayout {
  // Create the application window
  public static void createWindow(){
    JFrame aWindow = new JFrame("This is the Window Title");
    Toolkit theKit = aWindow.getToolkit();              // Get the window toolkit
    Dimension wndSize = theKit.getScreenSize();         // Get screen size

    // Set the position to screen center & size to half screen size
    aWindow.setSize(wndSize.width/2, wndSize.height/2);   // Set window size
    aWindow.setLocationRelativeTo(null);                  // Center window
    aWindow.setDefaultCloseOperation(JFrame.EXIT_ON_CLOSE);

    FlowLayout flow = new FlowLayout();                   // Create a layout manager
    Container content = aWindow.getContentPane(); // Get the content pane
    content.setLayout(flow);                              // Set the container layout mgr

    // Now add six button components
    for(int i = 1; i <= 6; ++i)
      content.add(new JButton("Press " + i));      // Add a Button to content pane

    aWindow.setVisible(true);                             // Display the window
  }

  public static void main(String[] args) {
    SwingUtilities.invokeLater(new Runnable() {
        public void run() {
            createWindow();
        }
      });
  }
}
```

TryFlowLayout.java

The new code that is of interest is in bold.

How It Works

You create a `FlowLayout` object and make this the layout manager for `aWindow` by calling `setLayout()`. You then add six `JButton` components of a default size to `aWindow` in the loop.

If you compile and run the program, you should get a window similar to the one shown in Figure 17-13.

CONFER PROGRAMMER TO PROGRAMMER ABOUT THIS TOPIC.
Visit p2p.wrox.com

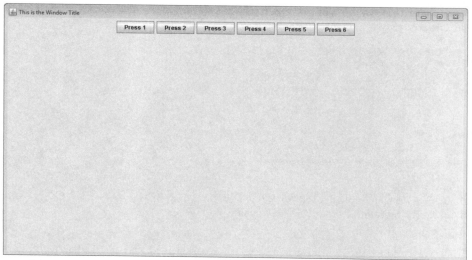

FIGURE 17-13

The Button objects are positioned by the layout manager flow. As you can see, they have been added to the first row in the window, and the row is centered. You can confirm that the row is centered and see how the layout manger automatically spills the components onto the next row after a row is full by reducing the size of the window by dragging the window boundaries. I reduced the height of the window to take up less space in the book. The result on my computer is shown in Figure 17-14.

FIGURE 17-14

Here the second row is clearly centered. Each button component has been set to its preferred size, which comfortably accommodates the text for the label. The centering is determined by the alignment constraint for the layout manager, which defaults to CENTER.

It can also be set to RIGHT or LEFT by using a different constructor. For example, you could have created the layout manager with the statement:

```
FlowLayout flow = new FlowLayout(FlowLayout.LEFT);
```

The flow layout manager then left aligns each row of components in the container. If you run the program with this definition and resize the window, you should be able to make it look like Figure 17-15.

Now the buttons are clearly left aligned. I have reduced the width of the window so two of the buttons have spilled from the first row to the second because there is insufficient space across the width of the window to accommodate them all.

FIGURE 17-15

Changing the Gap

The flow layout manager in the previous examples applies a default gap of 5 pixels between components in a row, and between one row and the next. You can choose values for the horizontal and vertical gaps by using yet another FlowLayout constructor. You can set the horizontal gap to 20 pixels and the vertical gap to 30 pixels in the last example with the statement:

```
FlowLayout flow = new FlowLayout(FlowLayout.LEFT, 20, 30);
```

If you rerun the program with this definition of the layout manager and resize the window, you should see a window with the buttons arranged as in Figure 17-16.

FIGURE 17-16

You can also set the gaps between components and rows explicitly by calling the setHgap() or the setVgap() method. To set the horizontal gap to 35 pixels, you would write:

```
flow.setHgap(35);                    // Set the horizontal gap
```

Don't be misled by this. You can't get differential spacing between components by setting the gap before adding each component to a container. The last values for the gaps between components that you set for a layout manager apply to all the components in a container. This is because the layout is recalculated dynamically each time the container is displayed. Of course, many different events may necessitate a container being redisplayed while an application is running. The methods getHgap() and getVgap() return the current setting for the horizontal or vertical gap as a value of type int.

The initial size at which the application window is displayed is determined by the values you pass to the setBounds() method for the JFrame object. If you want the window to assume a size that just accommodates the components it contains, you can call the pack() method for the JFrame object. Add the following line immediately before the call to setVisible():

```
aWindow.pack();
```

If you recompile and run the example again, the application window should fit the components and appear as shown in Figure 17-17.

FIGURE 17-17

As I've said, you add components to an applet created as a JApplet object in the same way as for a JFrame application window. You can verify this by adding some buttons to an example of an applet. You can try out a Font object and add a border to the buttons to brighten them up a bit at the same time.

TRY IT OUT   Adding Buttons to an Applet

You can define the class for an applet displaying buttons as follows:

```
import javax.swing.JButton;
import javax.swing.JApplet;
import javax.swing.SwingUtilities;
import javax.swing.border.BevelBorder;
import java.awt.Font;
import java.awt.Container;
import java.awt.FlowLayout;

public class TryApplet extends JApplet {
```

```
@Override
public void init() {
  try {
    SwingUtilities.invokeAndWait(new Runnable() {
        public void run() {
          createAppletGUI();
        }
    });
  } catch (Exception e) {
      System.err.println("Applet GUI creation failed.");
  }
}

private void createAppletGUI() {
  // Set layout for content pane
  getContentPane().setLayout(new FlowLayout(FlowLayout.RIGHT, 20, 30));

  JButton button;                                        // Stores a button
  Font[] fonts = { new Font("Serif", Font.ITALIC, 10),   // Two fonts
                   new Font("Dialog", Font.PLAIN, 14)
                 };

  BevelBorder edge = new BevelBorder(BevelBorder.RAISED); // Bevelled border

  // Add the buttons using alternate fonts
  for(int i = 1; i <= 6; ++i) {
    add(button = new JButton("Press " + i));             // Add the button
    button.setFont(fonts[i%2]);                          // One of our own fonts
    button.setBorder(edge);                              // Set the button border
  }
}
}
```

Directory "TryApplet"

Of course, to run the applet you need an .html file containing the following:

```
<html>  <head>  </head>
  <body bgcolor="000000">
    <center>
      <applet
        code = "TryApplet.class"
        width = "500"
        height = "300"
      >
      </applet>
    </center>
  </body>
</html>
```

This specifies the width and height of the applet—you can use your own values here if you want. You can save the file as TryApplet.htm.

After you have compiled the applet source code using javac, you can execute it with the appletviewer program by entering the following command from the folder containing the .htm file and the .class file:

```
appletviewer TryApplet.html
```

You should see the Applet Viewer window displaying the applet as in Figure 17-18.

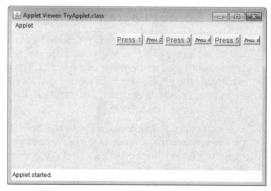

FIGURE 17-18

The arrangement of the buttons is now right-justified in the flow layout. You have the button labels alternating between the two fonts that you created. The buttons also look more like buttons with a beveled edge.

How It Works

As you saw in Chapter 1, an applet is executed rather differently from a Java program, and it is not really an independent program at all. The browser (or appletviewer in this case) initiates and controls the execution of the applet. An applet does not require a main() method. To execute the applet, the browser first creates an instance of our applet class, TryApplet and then calls the init() method for it. This method is inherited from the Applet class (the base for JApplet) and you typically override this method to start the applet on the event dispatch thread. To do this you use the invokeAndWait() method from the SwingUtilities class to start a Runnable thread where the run() method calls createAppletGUI() for the JApplet object that is created by the browser to create the GUI for the applet.

It is not strictly necessary to use invokeAndWait() in this example; you could use invokeLater(). There is a significant difference between the methods. The invokeLater() method executes the run() method asynchronously and allows it to be called after all pending events on the dispatch thread have been processed. It allows run() to return even though there may be dispatch thread events still outstanding. The invokeAndWait() method executes the run() method synchronously and prevents run() from returning until there are no events outstanding on the event dispatch thread. Thus you should use invokeAndWait() for an applet when the initialization code involves handling dispatch thread events. This is not the case here but applets can often involve dealing with events during the initialization phase, particularly when image files have to be loaded.

In the createAppletGUI() method you set the layout manager for the applet's content pane to be a flow layout. Before creating the buttons, you create a BevelBorder object that you use to specify the border for each button. To add the buttons, you use the add() method for the JApplet object. This method adds a component to the content pane for the applet. In the loop that adds the buttons, you select one or other of the Font objects you have created, depending on whether the loop index is even or odd and then set edge as the border by calling the setBorder() member. This would be the same for any component.

Note how the size of each button is automatically adjusted to accommodate the button label. Of course, the fonts in the example are both logical fonts, so they are available on every system. If you want to try physical fonts, choose two from those that you have installed on your system.

The buttons look much better with raised edges. If you wanted them to appear sunken, you would specify BevelBorder.LOWERED as the constructor argument. You might like to try out a SoftBevelBorder, too. All you need to do is use the class name, SoftBevelBorder, when creating the border. Don't forget the import statement for the class name; the border classes are defined in the javax.swing.border package.

Using a Border Layout Manager

The border layout manager is intended to place up to five components in a container. With this layout manager you can place components on any of the four borders of the container and in the center. Only one component can be at each position. If you add a component at a position that is already occupied, the previous component is displaced. A border is selected by specifying a constraint that can be NORTH, SOUTH, EAST, WEST, or CENTER. These are all final static constants defined in the BorderLayout class.

You can't specify the constraints in the BorderLayout constructor because a different constraint has to be applied to each component. You specify the position of each component in a container when you add it using the add() method. You can modify the earlier application example to add five buttons to the content pane of the application window in a border layout.

TRY IT OUT   Testing the BorderLayout Manager

This a variation on the `TryFlowLayout.java` example to try out the border layout manager and exercise another border class:

```java
import javax.swing.*;
import javax.swing.SwingUtilities;
import java.awt.*;
import javax.swing.border.EtchedBorder;

public class TryBorderLayout {

  public static void createWindow(){
    JFrame aWindow = new JFrame("This is the Window Title");
    Toolkit theKit = aWindow.getToolkit();           // Get the window toolkit
    Dimension wndSize = theKit.getScreenSize();       // Get screen size

    // Set the position to screen center & size to half screen size
    aWindow.setSize(wndSize.width/2, wndSize.height/2);   // Set window size
    aWindow.setLocationRelativeTo(null);              // Center window
    aWindow.setDefaultCloseOperation(JFrame.EXIT_ON_CLOSE);

    BorderLayout border = new BorderLayout();             // Create a layout manager
    Container content = aWindow.getContentPane();       // Get the content pane
    content.setLayout(border);                          // Set the container layout mgr
    EtchedBorder edge = new EtchedBorder(EtchedBorder.RAISED); // Button border

    // Now add five JButton components and set their borders
    JButton button;
    content.add(button = new JButton("EAST"), BorderLayout.EAST);
    button.setBorder(edge);
    content.add(button = new JButton("WEST"), BorderLayout.WEST);
    button.setBorder(edge);
    content.add(button = new JButton("NORTH"), BorderLayout.NORTH);
    button.setBorder(edge);
    content.add(button = new JButton("SOUTH"), BorderLayout.SOUTH);
    button.setBorder(edge);
    content.add(button = new JButton("CENTER"), BorderLayout.CENTER);
    button.setBorder(edge);

    aWindow.setVisible(true);                              // Display the window
  }

  public static void main(String[] args) {
    SwingUtilities.invokeLater(new Runnable() {
          public void run() {
              createWindow();
          }
       });
  }
}
```

TryBorderLayout.java

If you compile and execute the example, you see the window shown in Figure 17-19.

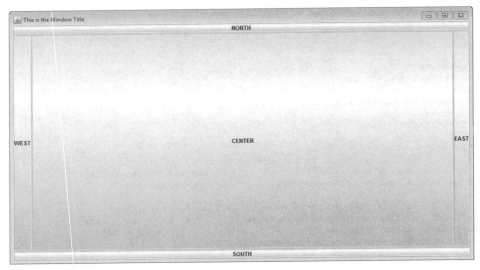

FIGURE 17-19

You can see here how a raised `EtchedBorder` edge to the buttons looks.

How It Works

Components laid out with a border layout manager are extended to fill the space available in the container. The `"NORTH"` and `"SOUTH"` buttons are the full width of the window and the `"EAST"` and `"WEST"` buttons occupy the height remaining unoccupied once the `"NORTH"` and `"SOUTH"` buttons are in place. It always works like this, regardless of the sequence in which you add the buttons—the `"NORTH"` and `"SOUTH"` components occupy the full width of the container and the `"CENTER"` component takes up the remaining space. If there are no `"NORTH"` and `"SOUTH"` components, the `"EAST"` and `"WEST"` components extend to the full height of the container.

The width of the `"EAST"` and `"WEST"` buttons is determined by the space required to display the button labels. Similarly, the `"NORTH"` and `"SOUTH"` buttons are determined by the height of the characters in the labels.

You can alter the spacing between components by passing arguments to the `BorderLayout` constructor—the default gaps are zero. For example, you could set the horizontal gap to 20 pixels and the vertical gap to 30 pixels with the following statement:

```
content.setLayout(new BorderLayout(20, 30));
```

Like the flow layout manager, you can also set the horizontal and vertical gaps individually by calling the methods `setHgap()` and `setVgap()` for the `BorderLayout` object. For example:

```
BorderLayout border = new BorderLayout();    // Construct the object
content.setLayout(border);                    // Set the layout
border.setHgap(20);                           // Set horizontal gap
```

This sets the horizontal gap between components to 20 pixels and leaves the vertical gap at the default of zero. You can also retrieve the current values for the gaps with the `getHgap()` and `getVgap()` methods.

Using a Card Layout Manager

The card layout manager generates a stack of components, one on top of the other. The first component that you add to the container is at the top of the stack, and therefore visible, and the last one is at the bottom. You can create a `CardLayout` object with the default constructor, `CardLayout()`, or you can specify horizontal and vertical gaps as arguments to the constructor. The gaps in this case are between the edge of the component and the boundary of the container. You can see how this works in an applet.

TRY IT OUT | Dealing Components

Because of the way a card layout works, you need a way to interact with the applet to switch from one component to the next. You will implement this by enabling mouse events to be processed, but I won't explain the code that does this in detail here. I'm leaving that to the next chapter.

Try the following code:

Available for download on Wrox.com

```java
import javax.swing.JButton;
import javax.swing.*;
import java.applet.*;
import javax.swing.border.BevelBorder;
import java.awt.*;
import java.awt.event.ActionEvent;            // Class defining events
import java.awt.event.ActionListener;         // Interface for receiving events

public class TryCardLayout extends JApplet implements ActionListener {

  @Override
  public void init() {
    try {
      SwingUtilities.invokeAndWait(new Runnable() {
            public void run() {
               createAppletGUI();
            }
         });
    } catch (Exception e) {
        System.err.println("Applet GUI creation failed.");
    }
  }

  private void createAppletGUI() {
    Container content = getContentPane();
    content.setLayout(card);                         // Set card as the layout mgr
    JButton button;                                  // Stores a button
    for(int i = 1; i <= 6; ++i) {
      // Add a button
      content.add(button = new JButton(" Press " + i), "Card" + i);
      button.addActionListener(this);                // Add listener for button
    }
    card.show(content, "Card5");                      // Show the 5th card to start
  }

  // Handle button events
  public void actionPerformed(ActionEvent e) {
    card.next(getContentPane());                      // Switch to the next card
  }

  private CardLayout card = new CardLayout(50,50);// The layout manager
}
```

Directory "TryCardLayout"

You need an HTML file to execute the applet containing the following:

```html
<html>
  <head> </head>
  <body bgcolor="000000">
    <center>
```

```
        <applet
          code = "TryCardLayout.class"
          width = "500"
          height = "300"
          >
        </applet>
      </center>
    </body>
  </html>
```

If you run the program using `appletviewer`, the applet should be as shown in Figure 17-20. Click the button showing to display the next button.

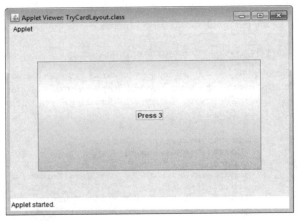

FIGURE 17-20

How It Works

You create the `CardLayout` object, `card`, with horizontal and vertical gaps of 50 pixels as a member of the class because you need to access it in two class methods. In the `createAppletGUI()` method for the applet, you set `card` as the layout manager and add six buttons to the content pane. Note that you have two arguments to the `add()` method, the first being the reference to the component you are adding to the container, the second being a String object to identify the card. Using card layout requires that you identify each component by an object of some class type and you supply this via the second argument to the `add()` method—the method parameter is of type `Object`. In this example, you pass a `String` object as the second argument to the `add()` method consisting of the string `"Card"` with the sequence number of the button appended to it. You could use this string to identify a particular card to be displayed by calling the show() method for the `CardLayout` object. For example:

```
        card.show(content, "Card5");
```

Executing this statement displays the fifth card in `content`. You could put this statement as the last in the `createAppletGUI()` method to see it working.

Within the loop you call the `addActionListener()` method for each button to identify the applet object as the object that handles events generated for the button (such as clicking on it with the mouse). You learn a lot more about action listeners and handling events in the next chapter. When you click on a button, the `actionPerformed()` method for the applet object is called. This just calls the `next()` method for the layout object to move the next component in sequence to the top. You look at event handling in much more detail in the next chapter so just accept it for now.

The argument to the `next()` method identifies the container as the `TryCardLayout` object that is created when the applet starts. The `CardLayout` class has other methods that you can use for selecting from the stack of components. They all have a void return type:

➤ `previous(Container parent)` selects the previous component in `parent`.

➤ `first(Container parent)` selects the first component in `parent`.

➤ `last(Container parent)` selects the last component in `parent`.

You can cycle through the components repeatedly using the `next()` or `previous()` methods because the next component after the last is the first, and the component before the first is the last.

Using a Grid Layout Manager

A grid layout manager arranges components in a rectangular grid within the container. You have three constructors for creating `GridLayout` objects:

➤ `GridLayout()`: Creates a grid layout manager that arranges components in a single row (that is, a single column per component) with no gaps between components.

➤ GridLayout(`int rows, int cols`): Creates a grid layout manager that arranges components in a grid with `rows` rows and `cols` columns, and with no gaps between components.

➤ GridLayout(
    `int rows,int cols,int hgap,int vgap`):
  Creates a grid layout manager that arranges components in a grid with `rows` rows and `cols` columns, and with horizontal and vertical gaps between components of `hgap` and `vgap` pixels, respectively.

In the second and third constructors, you can specify either the number of rows or the number of columns as zero (but not both). If you specify the number of rows as zero, the layout manager provides as many rows in the grid as are necessary to accommodate the number of components you add to the container. Similarly, setting the number of columns to zero indicates an arbitrary number of columns. If you fix both the rows and the columns, and add more components to the container than the grid accommodates, the number of columns is increased.

You can try out a grid layout manager in a variation of a previous example.

TRY IT OUT Gridlocking Buttons

Here's the code to demonstrate a `GridLayout` layout manager in action:

Available for
download on
Wrox.com

```java
import javax.swing.*;
import java.awt.*;
import javax.swing.border.EtchedBorder;

public class TryGridLayout {

  public static void createWindow(){
    JFrame aWindow = new JFrame("This is the Window Title");
    Toolkit theKit = aWindow.getToolkit();                // Get the window toolkit
    Dimension wndSize = theKit.getScreenSize();           // Get screen size

    // Set the position to screen center & size to half screen size
    aWindow.setSize(wndSize.width/2, wndSize.height/2);   // Set window size
    aWindow.setLocationRelativeTo(null);                  // Center window
    aWindow.setDefaultCloseOperation(JFrame.EXIT_ON_CLOSE);

    GridLayout grid = new GridLayout(3,4,30,20);     // Create a layout manager
    Container content = aWindow.getContentPane();    // Get the content pane
    content.setLayout(grid);                         // Set the container layout mgr
    EtchedBorder edge = new EtchedBorder(EtchedBorder.RAISED); // Button border

    // Now add ten Button components
    JButton button = null;                                  // Stores a button
    for(int i = 1 ; i <= 10 ; ++i) {
      content.add(button = new JButton(" Press " + i));   // Add a Button
      button.setBorder(edge);                             // Set the border
    }
    aWindow.pack();                                       // Size for components
    aWindow.setVisible(true);                             // Display the window
  }

  public static void main(String[] args) {
    SwingUtilities.invokeLater(new Runnable() {
        public void run() {
            createWindow();
        }
    });
  }
}
```

TryGridLayout.java

When you run this example, the application window appears as shown in Figure 17-21.

How It Works

You create a grid layout manager, grid, for three rows and four columns, and with horizontal and vertical gaps between components of 30 and 20 pixels, respectively. You set grid as the layout manager for

FIGURE 17-21

the content pane of the application window. You add ten buttons, each with a raised etched border, in the for loop. The layout manager causes the buttons to be arranged in a rectangular grid arrangement, with gaps of 30 units between buttons in a row and a gap of 20 units between rows. When you need a rectangular grid arrangement for your components, the GridLayout manager makes it very easy.

Using a BoxLayout Manager

The javax.swing.BoxLayout class defines a layout manager that arranges components in either a single row or a single column. You specify whether you want a row-wise or a columnar arrangement when creating the BoxLayout object. The BoxLayout constructor requires two arguments. The first is a reference to the container to which the layout manager applies, and the second is a constant that can be either BoxLayout. X_AXIS for a row-wise arrangement or BoxLayout.Y_AXIS for a column-wise arrangement.

Components are added from left to right in a row, or from top to bottom in a column. Components in a given row or column do not spill onto the next row or column when the row or column is full. When you add more components to a row or column than can be accommodated within the space available, the layout manager reduces the size of the components or even clips them if necessary to keep them all in a single row or column. With a row of components, the box layout manager tries to make all the components the same height and tries to set a column of components to the same width.

The javax.swing.Box container class is particularly convenient when you want to use a box layout because it has a BoxLayout manager built in. It also has some additional facilities that provide more flexibility in the arrangement of components than is provided by other containers such as JPanel objects. The Box constructor accepts a single argument that specifies the orientation as either BoxLayout.X_AXIS or BoxLayout.Y_AXIS. The class also has two static methods, createHorizontalBox() and createVerticalBox(), that each return a reference to a Box container with the orientation implied.

As I said earlier, a container can contain another container, so you can easily place one Box container inside another to get any arrangement of rows and columns that you want. Let's try that out.

TRY IT OUT   Boxes Containing Boxes

In this example you create an application that has a window containing a column of radio buttons on the left, a column of checkboxes on the right, and a row of buttons across the bottom. Here's the code:

```
import javax.swing.*;
import java.awt.*;
import javax.swing.border.*;

public class TryBoxLayout {

  public static void createWindow(){
    JFrame aWindow = new JFrame("This is the Window Title");
    Toolkit theKit = aWindow.getToolkit();          // Get the window toolkit
    Dimension wndSize = theKit.getScreenSize();      // Get screen size

    // Set the position to screen center & size to half screen size
    aWindow.setSize(wndSize.width/2, wndSize.height/2);   // Set window size
```

```
   aWindow.setLocationRelativeTo(null);                      // Center window
   aWindow.setDefaultCloseOperation(JFrame.EXIT_ON_CLOSE);

   // Create left column of radio buttons
   Box left = Box.createVerticalBox();
   ButtonGroup radioGroup = new ButtonGroup();              // Create button group
   JRadioButton rbutton;                                    // Stores a button
   radioGroup.add(rbutton = new JRadioButton("Red"));       // Add to group
   left.add(rbutton);                                       // Add to Box
   radioGroup.add(rbutton = new JRadioButton("Green"));
   left.add(rbutton);
   radioGroup.add(rbutton = new JRadioButton("Blue"));
   left.add(rbutton);
   radioGroup.add(rbutton = new JRadioButton("Yellow"));
   left.add(rbutton);

   // Create right columns of checkboxes
   Box right = Box.createVerticalBox();
   right.add(new JCheckBox("Dashed"));
   right.add(new JCheckBox("Thick"));
   right.add(new JCheckBox("Rounded"));

   // Create top row to hold left and right
   Box top = Box.createHorizontalBox();
   top.add(left);
   top.add(right);
   // Create bottom row of buttons
   JPanel bottomPanel = new JPanel();
   Border edge = BorderFactory.createRaisedBevelBorder();   // Button border
   JButton button;
   Dimension size = new Dimension(80,20);
   bottomPanel.add(button = new JButton("Defaults"));
   button.setBorder(edge);
   button.setPreferredSize(size);
   bottomPanel.add(button = new JButton("OK"));
   button.setBorder(edge);
   button.setPreferredSize(size);
   bottomPanel.add(button = new JButton("Cancel"));
   button.setBorder(edge);
   button.setPreferredSize(size);

   // Add top and bottom panel to content pane
   Container content = aWindow.getContentPane();            // Get content pane
   content.setLayout(new BorderLayout());                   // Set border layout manager
   content.add(top, BorderLayout.CENTER);
   content.add(bottomPanel, BorderLayout.SOUTH);

   aWindow.pack();                                          // Size for components
   aWindow.setVisible(true);                                // Display the window
 }

 public static void main(String[] args) {
   SwingUtilities.invokeLater(new Runnable() {
         public void run() {
             createWindow();
         }
     });
 }
}
```

TryBoxLayout.java

When you run this example and try out the radio buttons and checkboxes, it should produce a window something like the one shown in Figure 17-22.

It's not an ideal arrangement, but you'll improve on it later.

FIGURE 17-22

How It Works

The bold code is of interest—the rest you have seen before. The first bold block in `createWindow()` creates the left column of radio buttons providing a color choice. You use a `Box` object with a vertical orientation to contain the radio buttons. If you try clicking the radio buttons, you find that only one of them can be selected at a time. Each time you click on a radio button to select it, any other button that is selected becomes deselected. This is the effect of the `ButtonGroup` object. To ensure that radio buttons operate properly, you must add them to a `ButtonGroup` object.

Note that a `ButtonGroup` object is not a component—it's just a logical grouping of radio buttons—so you can't add it to a container. You must add the buttons to the `Box` container that manages their physical arrangement. The `Box` object for the right-hand group of `JCheckBox` objects works in the same way as that for the radio buttons.

Both the `Box` objects holding the columns are added to another `Box` object that implements a horizontal arrangement to position them side-by-side. Note how the vertical `Box` objects adjust their widths to match that of the largest component in the column. That's why the two columns are bunched toward the left side. You see how to improve on this in a moment.

You use a `JPanel` object to hold the buttons. This has a flow layout manager by default. Calling the `setPreferredSize()` method for each button sets the preferred width and height to that specified by the `Dimension` object `size`. This ensures that, space permitting, each button is 80 pixels wide and 20 pixels high.

I have introduced another way of obtaining a border for a component here. The `javax.swing.BorderFactory` class contains static methods that return standard borders. The `createBevelBorder()` method returns a reference to a `BevelBorder` object as type `Border`—`Border` being an interface that all border objects implement. You use this border for each of the buttons. You try more methods in the `BorderFactory` class later.

To improve the layout of the application window, you can make use of some additional facilities provided by a `Box` container.

Struts and Glue

The `Box` class contains static methods to create an invisible component called a *strut*. A vertical strut has a given height in pixels and zero width. A horizontal strut has a given width in pixels and zero height. The purpose of these struts is to enable you to insert space between your components, either vertically or horizontally. By placing a horizontal strut between two components in a horizontally arranged `Box` container, you fix the distance between the components. By adding a horizontal strut to a vertically arranged `Box` container, you can force a minimum width on the container. You can use a vertical strut in a horizontal box to force a minimum height. The way in which you might use struts to fix the vertical spacing between radio buttons is illustrated in Figure 17-23.

Note that although vertical struts have zero width, they have no maximum width so they can expand horizontally to have a width that takes up any excess space. Similarly, the height of a horizontal strut expands when excess vertical space is available.

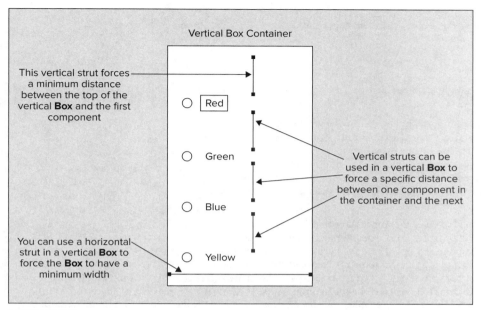

Vertical Box Container

This vertical strut forces a minimum distance between the top of the vertical **Box** and the first component

○ Red

Vertical struts can be used in a vertical **Box** to force a specific distance between one component in the container and the next

○ Green

○ Blue

You can use a horizontal strut in a vertical **Box** to force the **Box** to have a minimum width

○ Yellow

FIGURE 17-23

A vertical strut is returned as an object of type `Component` by the static `createVerticalStrut()` method in the `Box` class. The argument to the method specifies the height of the strut in pixels. To create a horizontal strut, you use the `createHorizontalStrut()` method.

You can space out the radio buttons in the previous example by inserting struts between them:

```
// Create left column of radio buttons
Box left = Box.createVerticalBox();
left.add(Box.createVerticalStrut(30));                // Starting space
ButtonGroup radioGroup = new ButtonGroup();           // Create button group
JRadioButton rbutton;                                 // Stores a button
radioGroup.add(rbutton = new JRadioButton("Red"));    // Add to group
left.add(rbutton);                                    // Add to Box
left.add(Box.createVerticalStrut(30));                // Space between
radioGroup.add(rbutton = new JRadioButton("Green"));
left.add(rbutton);
left.add(Box.createVerticalStrut(30));                // Space between
radioGroup.add(rbutton = new JRadioButton("Blue"));
left.add(rbutton);
left.add(Box.createVerticalStrut(30));                // Space between
radioGroup.add(rbutton = new JRadioButton("Yellow"));
left.add(rbutton);
```

TryBoxLayout2.java

The extra statements add a 30-pixel vertical strut at the start of the columns, and a further strut of the same size between each radio button and the next. You can do the same for the checkboxes:

```
// Create right columns of checkboxes
Box right = Box.createVerticalBox();
right.add(Box.createVerticalStrut(30));               // Starting space
right.add(new JCheckBox("Dashed"));
right.add(Box.createVerticalStrut(30));               // Space between
```

```
      right.add(new JCheckBox("Thick"));
      right.add(Box.createVerticalStrut(30));              // Space between
      right.add(new JCheckBox("Rounded"));
```

If you run the example with these changes, the window looks like the one shown in Figure 17-24.

It's better, but far from perfect. The columns are now equally spaced in the window because the vertical struts have assumed a width to take up the excess horizontal space. The distribution of surplus space vertically is different in the two columns because the number of components is different. You can control where surplus space goes in a `Box` object with *glue*. Glue is an invisible component that has the sole function of taking up surplus space in a `Box` container.

Although the name *glue* gives the impression that it binds components together, in fact glue provides an elastic connector between two components that can expand or contract as necessary, so it acts more like a spring. You can place glue components between the components

FIGURE 17-24

in the `Box` and at either or both ends. Any surplus space that arises after the actual components have been accommodated is distributed between the glue components. If you want all the surplus space to be at the beginning of a `Box` container, for example, you should first add a single glue component in the container.

You create a component that represents glue by calling the `createGlue()` method for a `Box` object. You then add the glue component to the `Box` container in the same way as any other component wherever you want surplus space to be taken up. You can add glue at several positions in a row or column, and spare space is distributed between the glue components. You can add glue after the last component in each column to make all the spare space appear at the end of each column of buttons. For the radio buttons you can add the following statement:

```
      // Statements adding radio buttons to left Box object...
      left.add(Box.createGlue());                          // Glue at the end
```

You can do the same for the right box:

```
      // Statements adding check boxes to right Box object...
      right.add(Box.createGlue());                         // Glue at the end
```

The glue component at the end of each column of buttons takes up all the surplus space in each vertical `Box` container. This makes the buttons line up at the top. Running the program with added glue results in the application window shown in Figure 17-25.

It's better now, but let's put together a final version of the example with some additional embroidery.

FIGURE 17-25

TRY IT OUT   **Embroidering Boxes**

You use some `JPanel` objects with a new kind of border to contain the vertical `Box` containers:

```
      import javax.swing.*;
      import java.awt.*;
      import javax.swing.border.*;

      public class TryBoxLayout4 {
        public static void createWindow(){
```

```
    // Set up the window as before...

    // Create left column of radio buttons with struts and glue as above...
    // Create a panel with a titled border to hold the left Box container
    JPanel leftPanel = new JPanel(new BorderLayout());
    leftPanel.setBorder(new TitledBorder(
                                new EtchedBorder(),      // Border to use
                                "Line Color"));          // Border title
    leftPanel.add(left, BorderLayout.CENTER);

    // Create right columns of checkboxes with struts and glue as above...
    // Create a panel with a titled border to hold the right Box container
    JPanel rightPanel = new JPanel(new BorderLayout());
    rightPanel.setBorder(new TitledBorder(
                                new EtchedBorder(),      // Border to use
                                "Line Properties"));     // Border title
    rightPanel.add(right, BorderLayout.CENTER);

    // Create top row to hold left and right
    Box top = Box.createHorizontalBox();
    top.add(leftPanel);
    top.add(Box.createHorizontalStrut(5));          // Space between vertical boxes
    top.add(rightPanel);

    // Create bottom row of buttons
    JPanel bottomPanel = new JPanel();
    bottomPanel.setBorder(new CompoundBorder(
          BorderFactory.createLineBorder(Color.black, 1),        // Outer border
          BorderFactory.createBevelBorder(BevelBorder.RAISED))); // Inner border
    // Create and add the buttons as before...

    // Add top and bottom panel to content pane
    Container content = aWindow.getContentPane(); // Set container layout mgr
    BoxLayout box = new BoxLayout(content, BoxLayout.Y_AXIS);
                                                    // Vertical for content pane
    content.setLayout(box);                         // Set box layout manager
    content.add(top);
    content.add(bottomPanel);
    aWindow.pack();
    aWindow.setVisible(true);                        // Display the window
  }

  // main() method definition as before
}
```

TryBoxLayout4.java

The example now displays the window shown in Figure 17-26.

How It Works

Both vertical boxes are now contained within a JPanel container.
Because JPanel objects are Swing components, you can add a border to them,
and this time you add a TitledBorder border that you create directly using
the constructor. A TitledBorder is a combination of the border that you
specify by the first argument to the TitledBorder constructor and a title that
is a String object you specify as the second argument to the constructor. You
use a border of type EtchedBorder here, but you can use any type of border.

You introduce space between the two vertically aligned Box containers by
adding a horizontal strut to the Box container that contains them. If you
wanted space at each side of the window, you could add struts to the container
before and after the components.

FIGURE 17-26

The last improvement is to the panel holding the buttons along the bottom of the window. You now have a border that is composed of two borders, one inside the other: a `LineBorder` and a `BevelBorder`. A `CompoundBorder` object defines a border that is a composite of two border objects, the first argument to the constructor being the outer border and the second being the inner border. The `LineBorder` class defines a border consisting of a single line of the color specified by its first constructor argument and a thickness in pixels specified by the second. There is a static method defined for the `LineBorder` class, `createBlackLineBorder()`, that creates a black line border that is one pixel wide, so you could have used that here.

Using a GridBagLayout Manager

The `java.awt.GridBagLayout` manager is much more flexible than the other layout managers you have seen and, consequently, rather more complicated to use. The basic mechanism arranges components in an arbitrary rectangular grid, but the rows and columns of the grid are not necessarily the same height or width. A component is placed at a given cell position in the grid specified by the coordinates of the cell, where the cell at the top-left corner is at position (0,0). You can spread a component over several cells in a row and/or column in the grid, but a component always occupies a rectangular group of cells.

Each component in a `GridBagLayout` has its own set of constraints. These are defined by an object of type `GridBagConstraints` that you associate with each component before adding the component to the container. The location of each component, its relative size, and the area it occupies in the grid are all determined by its associated `GridBagConstraints` object.

A `GridBagConstraints` object has no less than 11 public instance variables that may be set to define the constraints for a component. Because they also interact with each other, there's more entertainment here than with a Rubik's cube. Let's first get a rough idea of what these instance variables in a `GridBagConstraints` object do (as listed in Table 17-4):

TABLE 17-4: GridBagConstraints Object Instances

INSTANCE VARIABLE	DESCRIPTION
`gridx` and `gridy`	Determines the position of the component in the container as coordinate positions of cells in the grid, where (0,0) is the top-left position in the grid.
`gridwidth` and `gridheight`	Determines the size of the area occupied by the component in the container.
`weightx` and `weighty`	Determines how free space is distributed between components in the container.
`anchor`	Determines where a component is positioned within the area allocated to it in the container.
`ipadx` and `ipady`	Determines by how much the component size is to be increased above its minimum size.
`fill`	Determines how the component is to be enlarged to fill the space allocated to it.
`insets`	Specifies the free space that is to be provided around the component within the space allocated to it in the container.

All that should seem straightforward enough. You can now explore the possible values you can set for these and then try them out.

GridBagConstraints Instance Variables

A component occupies at least one grid position, or *cell*, in a container that uses a `GridBagLayout` object, but it can occupy any rectangular array of cells. The total number of rows and columns, and thus the cell size, in the grid for a container is variable and determined by the constraints for all of the components in the container. Each component has a specified position in the grid plus the area it is allocated within the grid defined by a number of horizontal and vertical grid positions. This is illustrated in Figure 17-27.

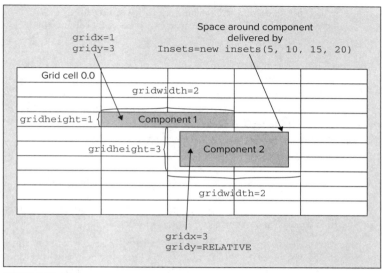

FIGURE 17-27

The top-left cell in a layout is at position (0,0). You specify the position of a component by defining where the top-left cell that it occupies is, either relative to the grid origin or relative to the last component that was added to the container. You specify the position of the top-left cell that a component occupies in the grid by setting the gridx and gridy members of the GridBagConstraints object to appropriate values of type int. The default value for gridx is GridBagConstraints.RELATIVE—a constant that places the top-left grid position for the component in the column immediately to the right of the previous component. The same value is the default for gridy, which places the next component immediately below the previous one.

You specify the number of cells to be occupied by a component horizontally and vertically by setting values for the gridwidth and gridheight instance variables for the GridBagConstraints object. The default value for both of these is 1. You can use two constants as values for these variables. The GridBagConstraints.REMAINDER value makes the component the last one in the row or column and occupies the remaining cells. If you specify the value as GridBagConstraints.RELATIVE, the component is the penultimate one in the row or column.

If the preferred size of the component is less than the display area, you can control how the size of the component is adjusted to fit the display area by setting the fill and insets instance variables for the GridBagConstraints object, as shown in Table 17-5:

TABLE 17-5: Variables for Adjusting Component to Display Area

VARIABLE	DESCRIPTION
fill	The value for this variable is of type int, and it determines how the size of the component is adjusted in relation to the array of cells it occupies. The default value of GridBagConstraints. NONE means that the component is not resized.
	A value of GridBagConstraints.HORIZONTAL adjusts the width of the component to fill the display area.
	A value of GridBagConstraints.VERTICAL adjusts the height of the component to fill the display area.
	A value of GridBagConstraints.BOTH adjusts the height and the width to completely fill the display area.
insets	This variable stores a reference to an object of type Insets. An Insets object defines the space allowed between the edges of the components and boundaries of the display area it occupies. Four parameter values to the class constructor define the top, left-side, bottom, and right-side padding from the edges of the component. The default value is Insets(0, 0, 0, 0).

If you don't intend to expand a component to fill its display area, you may still want to enlarge the component from its minimum size. You can adjust the dimensions of the component by setting the following `GridBagConstraints` instance variables:

TABLE 17-6: Variables for Enlarging the Component Size

VARIABLE	DESCRIPTION
ipadx	An int value that defines the number of pixels by which the top and bottom edges of the component are to be expanded. The default value is 0.
ipady	An int value that defines the number of pixels by which the left and right edges of the component are to be expanded. The default value is 0.

If the component is still smaller than its display area in the container, you can specify where it should be placed in relation to its display area by setting a value for the `anchor` instance variable of the `GridBagConstraints` object. Possible values are NORTH, NORTHEAST, EAST, SOUTHEAST, SOUTH, SOUTHWEST, WEST, NORTHWEST, and CENTER, all of which are defined in the `GridBagConstraints` class.

The last `GridBagConstraints` instance variables to consider are `weightx` and `weighty`, which are of type `double`. These determine how space in the container is distributed between components in the horizontal and vertical directions. You should always set a value for these; otherwise, the default of 0 causes the components to be bunched together in the center of the container. The absolute values for `weightx` and `weighty` are not important. It's the relative values that matter. If you set all the values the same (but not zero), the space for each component is distributed uniformly. Space is distributed between components in the proportions defined by the values of `weightx` and `weighty`.

For example, if three components in a row have `weightx` values of 1.0, 2.0, and 3.0, the first gets 1/6 of the total in the *x* direction, the second gets 2/6, which is 1/3, and the third gets 3/6, which is half. The proportion of the available space that a component gets in the x direction is the `weightx` value for the component divided by the sum of the `weightx` values in the row. This also applies to the `weighty` values for allocating space in the y direction.

I'm starting with a simple example of placing two buttons in a window and introducing another way of obtaining a standard border for a component.

TRY IT OUT   Applying the GridBagConstraints Object

You can compile and execute the following program to try out the `GridBagLayout` manager:

```
import javax.swing.JFrame;
import javax.swing.SwingUtilities;

import java.awt.Toolkit;
import java.awt.Dimension;
import java.awt.GridBagLayout;
import java.awt.GridBagConstraints;
import javax.swing.JButton;
import javax.swing.BorderFactory;
import javax.swing.border.Border;

public class TryGridBagLayout {
  public static void createWindow(){
    JFrame aWindow = new JFrame("This is the Window Title");
    Toolkit theKit = aWindow.getToolkit();                  // Get the window toolkit
    Dimension wndSize = theKit.getScreenSize();             // Get screen size

    // Set the position to screen center & size to half screen size
    aWindow.setBounds(wndSize.width/4, wndSize.height/4,    // Position
                      wndSize.width/2, wndSize.height/2);   // Size
```

```
        aWindow.setDefaultCloseOperation(JFrame.EXIT_ON_CLOSE);

        GridBagLayout gridbag = new GridBagLayout();     // Create a layout manager
        GridBagConstraints constraints = new GridBagConstraints();
        aWindow.getContentPane().setLayout(gridbag);     // Set container layout mgr

        // Set constraints and add first button
        constraints.weightx = constraints.weighty = 10.0;
        constraints.fill = GridBagConstraints.BOTH;        // Fill the space
        addButton(" Press ", constraints, gridbag, aWindow);   // Add the button

        // Set constraints and add second button
        constraints.gridwidth = GridBagConstraints.REMAINDER;  // Rest of the row
        addButton("GO", constraints, gridbag, aWindow);        // Create and add button

        aWindow.setVisible(true);                          // Display the window
    }

    static void addButton(String label,
                          GridBagConstraints constraints,
                          GridBagLayout layout,
                          JFrame window) {
      // Create a Border object using a BorderFactory method
      Border edge = BorderFactory.createRaisedBevelBorder();

      JButton button = new JButton(label);                 // Create a button
      button.setBorder(edge);                              // Add its border
      layout.setConstraints(button, constraints);    // Set the constraints
      window.getContentPane().add(button);           // Add button to content pane
    }

    public static void main(String[] args) {
      SwingUtilities.invokeLater(new Runnable() {
            public void run() {
                createWindow();
            }
        });
    }
}
```

TryGridBagLayout.java

The program window looks like that shown in Figure 17-28.

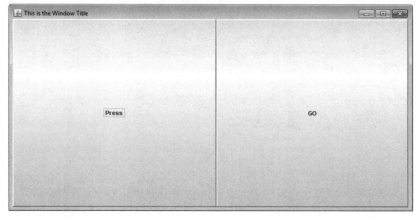

FIGURE 17-28

As you see, the left button is slightly wider than the right button. This is because the length of the button label affects the size of the button.

How It Works

Because the process is the same for every button that you add, you have implemented a helper method, `addButton()`. This method creates a `Button` object, associates the `GridBagConstraints` object with it in the `GridBagLayout` object, and then adds it to the content pane of the frame window.

After creating the layout manager and `GridBagConstraints` objects, you set the values for `weightx` and `weighty` to 10.0. A value of 1.0 or 100.0 would have the same effect because it is the relative values that these variables have for the constraints on components in a column or row, not their absolute values. You set the `fill` constraint to `BOTH` to make the component fill the space it occupies. When `setConstraints()` is called to associate the `GridBagConstraints` object with the button object, it creates a copy of the `constraints` object that you pass as the argument, and a reference to the copy is stored in the layout—not a reference to the object that you created. This enables you to change the `constraints` object that you created and use it for the second button without affecting the constraints for the first.

The buttons are more or less equal in size in the *x* direction (they would be exactly the same size if the labels were the same length) because the `weightx` and `weighty` values are the same for both. Both buttons fill the space available to them because the `fill` constraint is set to `BOTH`. If `fill` was set to `HORIZONTAL`, for example, the buttons would be the full width of the grid positions they occupy, but just high enough to accommodate the label because they would have no preferred size in the *y* direction.

If you alter the constraints for the second button to

```
// Set constraints and add second button
constraints.weightx = 5.0;                               // Weight half of first
constraints.insets = new java.awt.Insets(10, 30, 10, 20); // Left 30 & right 20
constraints.gridwidth = GridBagConstraints.RELATIVE;     // Rest of the row
addButton("GO", constraints, gridbag);                   // Add button to content pane
```

TryGridBagLayout2.java

the application window is as shown in Figure 17-29.

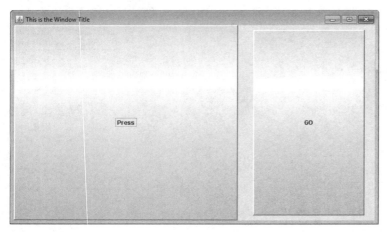

FIGURE 17-29

Now the second button occupies one third of the space in the *x* direction—that corresponds to $5/(5 + 10)$ of the total space in *x* that is available—and the first button occupies two-thirds. Note that the buttons still occupy one grid cell each—the default values for `gridwidth` and `gridheight` of 1 apply—but the `weightx` constraint values have altered the relative sizes of the cells for the two buttons in the *x* direction.

The second button is also within the space allocated—10 pixels at the top and bottom, 30 pixels on the left, and 20 on the right (set by the `insets` constraint). You can see that for a given window size here, the size of a grid position depends on the number of objects. The more components there are, the less space each is allocated.

Suppose you wanted to add a third button, the same width as the Press button, and immediately below it. You could do that by adding the following code immediately after that for the second button:

Available for download on Wrox.com

```
// Set constraints and add third button
constraints.insets = new java.awt.Insets(0,0,0,0);   // No insets
constraints.gridx = 0;                               // Begin new row
constraints.gridwidth = 1;                           // Width as "Press"
addButton("Push", constraints, gridbag, aWindow);    // Add button to content pane
```

TryGridBagLayout3.java

You reset the `gridx` constraint to zero to put the button at the start of the next row. It has a default `gridwidth` of one cell, like the others. The window would now look like the one shown in Figure 17-30.

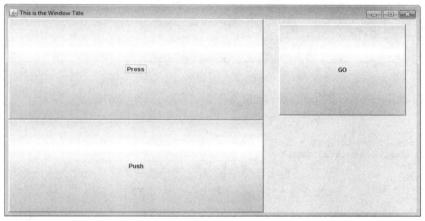

FIGURE 17-30

Having seen how it looks now, clearly it would be better if the GO button were the height of Press and Push combined. To arrange them like this, you need to make the height of the GO button twice that of the other two buttons. The height of the Press button is 1 by default, so by making the height of the GO button 2, and resetting the `gridheight` constraint of the Push button to 1, you should get the desired result. Modify the code for the second and third buttons to:

Available for download on Wrox.com

```
// Set constraints and add second button
constraints.weightx = 5.0;                               // Weight half of first
constraints.insets = new java.awt.Insets(10, 30, 10, 20); // Left 30 & right 20
constraints.gridwidth = GridBagConstraints.RELATIVE;     // Rest of the row
constraints.gridheight = 2;                              // Height 2x "Press"
addButton("GO", constraints, gridbag);                   // Add button to content pane

// Set constraints and add third button
constraints.insets = new java.awt.Insets(0, 0, 0, 0);    // No insets
constraints.gridx = 0;                                   // Begin new row
constraints.gridwidth = 1;                               // Width as "Press"
constraints.gridheight = 1;                              // Height as "Press"
addButton("Push", constraints, gridbag);                 // Add button to content pane
```

TryGridBagLayout4.java

With these code changes, the window is as shown in Figure 17-31.

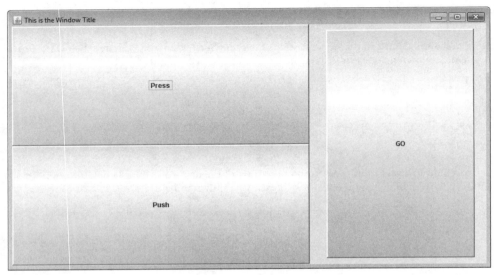

FIGURE 17-31

You could also see the effect of padding the components out from their preferred size by altering the button constraints a little:

```
// Set constraints and add first button
constraints.weightx = constraints.weighty = 10.0;
constraints.fill = GridBagConstraints.NONE;
constraints.ipadx = 30;                                 // Pad 30 in x
constraints.ipady = 10;                                 // Pad 10 in y
addButton("Press", constraints, gridbag, aWindow);      // Add button to content pane

// Set constraints and add second button
constraints.weightx = 5.0;                              // Weight half of first
constraints.fill = GridBagConstraints.BOTH;             // Expand to fill space
constraints.ipadx = constraints.ipady = 0;              // No padding
constraints.insets = new Insets(10, 30, 10, 20);        // Left 30 & right 20
constraints.gridwidth = GridBagConstraints.RELATIVE;    // Rest of the row
constraints.gridheight = 2;                             // Height 2x "Press"
addButton("GO", constraints, gridbag, aWindow);         // Add button to content pane

// Set constraints and add third button
constraints.gridx = 0;                                  // Begin new row
constraints.fill = GridBagConstraints.NONE;
constraints.ipadx = 30;                                 // Pad component in x
constraints.ipady = 10;                                 // Pad component in y
constraints.gridwidth = 1;                              // Width as "Press"
constraints.gridheight = 1;                             // Height as "Press"
constraints.insets = new Insets(0, 0, 0, 0);            // No insets
addButton("Push", constraints, gridbag, aWindow);       // Add button to content pane
```

TryGridBagLayout5.java

With the constraints for the buttons as before, the window looks as shown in Figure 17-32.

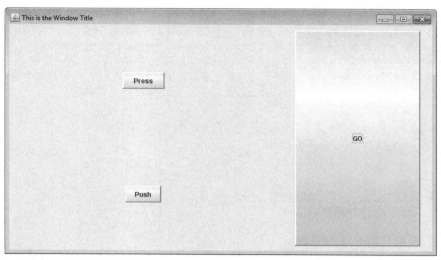

FIGURE 17-32

Both the Push and the Press button occupy the same space in the container, but because `fill` is set to `NONE` they are not expanded to fill the space in either direction. The `ipadx` and `ipady` constraints specify by how much the buttons are to be expanded from their preferred size—by 30 pixels on the left and right and 10 pixels on the top and bottom. The overall arrangement remains the same.

You need to experiment with using `GridBagLayout` and `GridBagConstraints` to get a good feel for how the layout manager works because it's only with experience that you can appreciate what you can do with it.

Using a SpringLayout Manager

You can set the layout manager for the content pane of a `JFrame` object, `aWindow`, to be a `javax.swing.` `SpringLayout` manager like this:

```
SpringLayout layout = new SpringLayout();          // Create a layout manager
Container content = aWindow.getContentPane();      // Get the content pane
content.setLayout(layout);
```

The layout manager defined by the `SpringLayout` class determines the position and size of each component in the container according to a set of constraints that are defined by `javax.swing.Spring` objects. Every component within a container using a `SpringLayout` manager has an object associated with it of type `SpringLayout.Constraints` that defines constraints on the position of each of the four edges of the component. Before you can access the `SpringLayout.constraints` object for a component object, you must first add the component to the container. For example:

```
JButton button = new JButton("Press Me");
content.add(button);
```

Now you can call the `getConstraint()` method for the `SpringLayout` object to obtain the object encapsulating the constraints:

```
SpringLayout.Constraints constraints = layout.getConstraints(button);
```

The argument to the `getConstraints()` method identifies the component in the container for which you want to access the `constraints` object. To constrain the location and size of the `button` object, you call methods for the `constraints` object to set individual constraints.

Understanding Spring Constraints

The top, bottom, left, and right edges of a component are referred to by their compass points: north, south, west, and east. When you need to refer to a particular edge in your code—for setting a constraint, for example—you use constants that are defined in the `SpringLayout` class, `NORTH`, `SOUTH`, `WEST`, and `EAST`, respectively. This is shown in Figure 17-33.

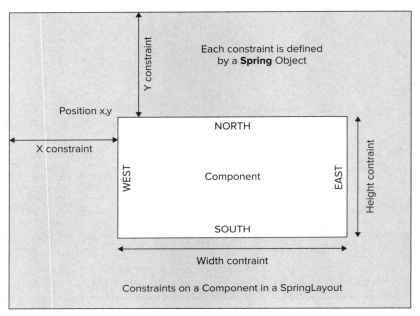

FIGURE 17-33

As Figure 17-33 shows, the position of a component is determined by a horizontal constraint on the *x* coordinate of the component and a vertical constraint on the *y* coordinate. These obviously also determine the location of the `WEST` and `NORTH` edges of the component because the position determines where the top-left corner is located. The width and height are determined by horizontal constraints that relate the position of the `EAST` and `SOUTH` edges to the positions of the `WEST` and `NORTH` edges, respectively. Thus, the constraints on the positions of the `EAST` and `SOUTH` edges are determined by constraints that are derived from the others, as follows:

```
EAST_constraint = X_constraint + width_constraint
SOUTH_constraint = Y_constraint + height_constraint
```

You can set the `X`, `Y`, `width`, and `height` constraints independently, as you see in a moment, and you can set a constraint explicitly for any edge. Obviously, it is possible to set constraints such that the preceding relationships between the constraints may be violated. In this case, the layout manager adjusts one or other of the constraints so that the preceding relationships still apply. The constraint that is adjusted depends on which constraint you set to potentially cause the violation, as shown in Table 17–7:

TABLE 17-7: Constraint Relationships

IF YOU SET A CONSTRAINT FOR A COMPONENT ON:	THE LAYOUT MANAGER MAKES THE ADJUSTMENT:
X or the WEST edge	width value set to EAST − X
The width	EAST edge is set to X + width
EAST edge	X is set to EAST − width

IF YOU SET A CONSTRAINT FOR A COMPONENT ON:	THE LAYOUT MANAGER MAKES THE ADJUSTMENT:
Y or the NORTH edge	height is set to SOUTH − Y
The height	SOUTH edge is set to Y + height
The SOUTH edge	Y is set to SOUTH − height

The SpringLayout manager automatically adds Spring constraints that control the width and height of a component based on the component's minimum, maximum, and preferred sizes. The width or height is set to a value between the maximum and minimum for the component. These sizes are obtained dynamically by calling the getMinimumSize(), getMaximumSize(), and getPreferredSize() methods for the component. Normally these constraints on the width and height expand or contract the component as the size of the container changes, but when the getPreferredSize() and getMaximumSize() methods return the same value, the layout manager does not alter the width and height of the component as the container size is changed.

Defining Spring Constraints

The Spring class in the javax.swing package defines an object that represents a constraint. A Spring object is defined by three integer values that relate to the notional length of the spring: the minimum length, the preferred length, and the maximum length. A Spring object also has an actual length value that lies between the minimum and the maximum, and that determines the location of the edge to which it applies. You can create a Spring object like this:

```
Spring spring = Spring.constant(10, 30, 50);    // min=10, pref=30, max=50
```

The static constant() method in the Spring class creates a Spring object from the three arguments that are the minimum, preferred, and maximum values for the Spring object. If all three values are equal, the object is called a strut because its value is fixed at the common value you set for all three. There's an overloaded version of the constant() method for creating struts that has just one parameter:

```
Spring strut = Spring.constant(40); // min, pref, and max all set to 40
```

The Spring class also defines static methods that operate on Spring objects:

➤ Spring sum(Spring spr1, Spring spr2): Returns a reference to a new object that has minimum, preferred, and maximum values that are the sum of the corresponding values of the arguments.

➤ Spring minus(Spring spr): Returns a reference to a new object with minimum, preferred, and maximum values that are the same magnitude as those of the argument but with opposite signs.

➤ Spring max(Spring spr1, Spring spr2): Returns a reference to a new object that has minimum, preferred, and maximum values that are the maximum of the corresponding values of the arguments.

Setting Constraints for a Component

The setX() and setY() methods for a SpringLayout.Constraints object set the constraints for the WEST and NORTH edges of the component, respectively. For example:

```
SpringLayout.Constraints constraints = layout.getConstraints(button);
Spring xSpring = Spring.constant(5,10,20);         // Spring we'll use for X
Spring ySpring = Spring.constant(3,5,8);           // Spring we'll use for Y
constraints.setX(xSpring);                         // Set the WEST edge constraint
constraints.setY(xSpring);                         // Set the NORTH edge constraint
```

The layout variable references a SpringLayout object that has been set as the layout manager for the container that contains the button component. The setX() method defines a constraint between the WEST edge of the container and the WEST edge of the button component. Similarly, the setY() method defines a constraint between the NORTH edge of the container and the NORTH edge of the button component. This fixes the location of the component relative to the origin of the container, as illustrated in Figure 17-34.

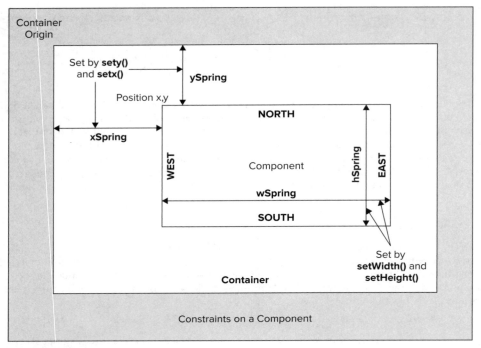

FIGURE 17-34

To set the width and height of the component, you call the `setWidth()` and `setHeight()` methods for its `SpringLayout.Constraints` object and supply a `Spring` object that you want to control the dimension. Here's how you could specify specific `Spring` objects of your choosing:

```
Spring wSpring = Spring.constant(30,50,70);   // Spring we'll use for width
Spring hSpring = Spring.constant(15);         // Strut we'll use for height
constraints.setWidth(wSpring);                // Set component width constraint
constraints.setHeight(hSpring);               // Set component height constraint
```

The width constraint is applied between the WEST and EAST edges and the height constraint applies between the component's NORTH and SOUTH edges. Because you have specified a strut for the height, there is no leeway on this constraint; its value is fixed at 15.

The `Spring` class defines the static methods `width()` and `height()` that return a `Spring` object based on the minimum, maximum, and preferred sizes of the component that you pass as the argument to the method. These are the constraints that the layout manager applies to the width and height by default, but there may be circumstances where you want to reapply them. You could use these methods to create `Spring` objects to control the width and height of the `button` object like this:

```
constraints.setWidth(Spring.width(button));  // Set component width constraint
constraints.setHeight(Spring.width(button)); // Set component height constraint
```

The springs you have set here adjust the width and height based on the component's minimum, maximum, and preferred sizes.

If you want to explicitly set an edge constraint for a component, you call the `setConstraint()` method for the component's `SpringLayout.Constraints` object:

```
layout.getConstraints(newButton).setConstraint(
                  StringLayout.EAST, Spring.sum(xSpring, wSpring));
```

This ties the EAST edge of the newButton component to the WEST edge of the container by a Spring object that is the sum of xSpring and wSpring.

You can also set constraints between pairs of vertical or horizontal edges, where one edge can belong to a different component from the other. For example, you could add another button to the container like this:

```
JButton newButton = new JButton("Push");
content.add(newButton);
```

You can now constrain its WEST and NORTH edges by tying the edges to the EAST and SOUTH edges of the button component that you added to the container previously. You use the putConstraint() method for the SpringLayout object to do this:

```
SpringLayout.Constraints newButtonConstr = layout.getConstraints(newButton);
layout.putConstraint(SpringLayout.WEST,
                     newButton,
                     xSpring,
                     SpringLayout.EAST,
                     button);
```

The first two arguments to the putConstraint() method for the layout object are the edge specification and a reference to the dependent component, respectively. The third argument is a Spring object defining the constraint. The fourth and fifth arguments specify the edge and a reference to the component to which the dependent component is anchored. Obviously, because constraints can only be horizontal or vertical, both edges should have the same orientation. There is an overloaded version of the putConstraint() method for which the third argument is a value of type int that defines a fixed distance between the edges.

Let's look at a simple example using a SpringLayout object as the layout manager.

TRY IT OUT   Using a SpringLayout Manager

Here's the code for an example that displays six buttons in a window:

Available for
download on
Wrox.com

```
import javax.swing.*;
import java.awt.*;

public class TrySpringLayout {

  public static void createWindow(){
    JFrame aWindow = new JFrame("This is the Window Title");
    Toolkit theKit = aWindow.getToolkit();          // Get the window toolkit
    Dimension wndSize = theKit.getScreenSize();      // Get screen size

    // Set the position to screen center & size to half screen size
    aWindow.setBounds(wndSize.width/4, wndSize.height/4,     // Position
                      wndSize.width/2, wndSize.height/2);    // Size
    aWindow.setDefaultCloseOperation(JFrame.EXIT_ON_CLOSE);

    SpringLayout layout = new SpringLayout();              // Create a layout manager
    Container content = aWindow.getContentPane();          // Get the content pane
    content.setLayout(layout);                             // Set the container layout mgr

    JButton[] buttons = new JButton[6];                    // Array to store buttons
    SpringLayout.Constraints constr = null;
    for(int i = 0; i < buttons.length; ++i) {
      buttons[i] = new JButton("Press " + (i+1));
      content.add(buttons[i]);                             // Add a Button to content pane
    }

    Spring xSpring = Spring.constant(5,15,25);             // x constraint for 1st button
    Spring ySpring = Spring.constant(10,30, 50);           // y constraint for 1st button

    // Connect x,y for first button to left and top of container by springs
```

```
      constr = layout.getConstraints(buttons[0]);
      constr.setX(xSpring);
      constr.setY(ySpring);

      // Hook buttons together with springs
      for(int i = 1 ; i < buttons.length ; ++i) {
        constr = layout.getConstraints(buttons[i]);
        layout.putConstraint(SpringLayout.WEST, buttons[i],
                             xSpring,SpringLayout.EAST, buttons[i-1]);
        layout.putConstraint(SpringLayout.NORTH, buttons[i],
                             ySpring,SpringLayout.SOUTH, buttons[i-1]);
      }

      aWindow.setVisible(true);                       // Display the window
    }

  public static void main(String[] args) {
    SwingUtilities.invokeLater(new Runnable() {
          public void run() {
              createWindow();
          }
      });
    }
  }
```

TrySpringLayout.java

When you compile and run this, you should get a window with the buttons laid out as shown in Figure 17-35.

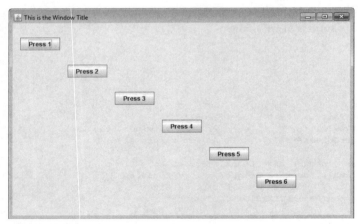

FIGURE 17-35

How It Works

You first create a variable that stores a reference to a SpringLayout.Constraints object and array to hold references to JButton objects:

```
JButton[] buttons = new JButton[6];              // Array to store buttons
SpringLayout.Constraints constr = null;
```

You create and add six buttons to the content pane of the window in a loop:

```
for(int i = 0 ; i < buttons.length ; ++i) {
  buttons[i] = new JButton("Press " + (i+1));
  content.add(buttons[i]);                      // Add a Button to content pane
}
```

As each button is added to the container, the layout manager applies the constraints to the height and width of the container that I discussed earlier. Unless these are overridden because the component is overconstrained, these constraints adjust the size of the button based on the minimum, maximum, and preferred sizes for the component.

After adding six buttons to the content pane of the window, you define two Spring objects that you use to position the first button relative to the container:

```
Spring xSpring = Spring.constant(5,15,25);    // x constraint for 1st button
Spring ySpring = Spring.constant(10,30, 50); // y constraint for 1st button
```

You then set the location of the first button relative to the container:

```
constr = layout.getConstraints(buttons[0]);
constr.setX(xSpring);
constr.setY(ySpring);
```

This fixes the top-left corner of the first button. You can define the positions of each of the remaining buttons relative to its predecessor. You do this by adding constraints between the NORTH and WEST edges of each button and the SOUTH and EAST edges of its predecessor. This is done in the for loop:

```
for(int i = 1 ; i< buttons.length ; ++i) {
  constr = layout.getConstraints(buttons[i]);
  layout.putConstraint(SpringLayout.WEST, buttons[i],
                       xSpring,SpringLayout.EAST, buttons[i-1]);
  layout.putConstraint(SpringLayout.NORTH, buttons[i],
                       ySpring,SpringLayout.SOUTH, buttons[i-1]);
}
```

This places each component after the first relative to the bottom-right corner of its predecessor, so the buttons are laid out in a cascade fashion.

Relating the Container Size to the Components

Of course, the size of the application window in our example is independent of the components within it. If you resize the window the springs do not change. If you call pack() for the aWindow object before calling its setVisible() method, the window shrinks to a width and height just accommodating the title bar so you don't see any of the components. This is because SpringLayout does not adjust the size of the container by default so the effect of pack() is as though the content pane were empty.

You can do much better than this. You can set constraints on the edges of the content pane using springs that control its size. You can therefore place constraints on the height and width of the content pane in terms of the springs that you used to determine the size and locations of the components. This has the effect of relating all the springs that determine the size and position of the buttons to the size of the application window. Try adding the following code to the example, immediately preceding the call to setVisible() for the window object:

```
SpringLayout.Constraints constraint = layout.getConstraints(content);
constraint.setConstraint(SpringLayout.EAST,
                  Spring.sum(constr.getConstraint(SpringLayout.EAST),
                  Spring.constant(15)));
constraint.setConstraint(SpringLayout.SOUTH,
                  Spring.sum(constr.getConstraint(SpringLayout.SOUTH),
                  Spring.constant(10)));
aWindow.pack();
```

This sets the constraint on the EAST edge of a container that is the Spring constraining the EAST edge of the last button plus a strut 15 units long. This positions the right edge of the container 15 units to the right of the right edge of the last button. The bottom edge of the container is similarly connected by a fixed link, 10 units long, to the bottom edge of the last button. If you recompile with these additions and run the example again, you should find that not only is the initial size of the window set to accommodate all the buttons, but when you resize the window the size and positions of the buttons adapt accordingly. Isn't that nice?

Note how the width and height of each button is maintained as you resize the window, even when the content pane is too small to accommodate all the buttons. This is because a JButton object returns a maximum size that is the same as the preferred size, so the layout manager does not alter the width or the height.

The SpringLayout manager is extremely flexible and can do much of what the other layout mangers can do if you choose the constraints on the components appropriately. It's well worth experimenting to see the effect of various configurations of springs on your application.

ADDING A MENU TO A WINDOW

As you know, a JMenuBar object represents the menu bar that is placed at the top of a window. You can add JMenu or JMenuItem objects to a JMenuBar object, and these are displayed on the menu bar. A JMenu object is a menu with a label that can display a list of menu items when clicked. A JMenuItem object represents a menu item with a label within a menu that results in some program action when clicked—such as opening a dialog. A JMenuItem object can have an icon in addition to, or instead of, a String label. Each item in a JMenu object can be of type JMenu, JMenuItem, JCheckBoxMenuItem, or JRadioButtonMenuItem. If an item in a menu is a JMenu object then it represents a second level of menu containing further menu items.

A JCheckBoxMenuItem is a simple menu item with a checkbox associated with it. The checkbox can be checked and unchecked and typically indicates that that menu item was selected last time the drop-down menu was displayed. You can also add separators in a drop-down menu. These are simply bars to separate one group of menu items from another. A JRadioButtonMenuItem is a menu item much like a radio button in that it is intended to be one of a group of like menu items added to a ButtonGroup object. Both JCheckBoxMenuItem and JRadioButtonMenuItem objects can have icons.

Creating JMenu and JMenuItem

To create a menu you call a JMenu class constructor and pass a String object to it that specifies the label. For example, to create a File menu you could write:

```
JMenu fileMenu = new JMenu("File");
```

The string that is passed as the argument is the text that appears.

Creating a menu item is much the same as creating a menu:

```
JMenuItem openMenu = new JMenuItem("Open");
```

The argument is the text that appears on the menu item.

If you create a JCheckboxMenuItem object by passing just a String argument to the constructor, the object represents a checkbox menu item that is initially unchecked. For example, you could create an unchecked item with the following statement:

```
JCheckboxMenuItem circleItem = new JCheckboxMenuItem("Circle");
```

Another constructor for this class enables you to set the check mark by specifying a second argument of type boolean. For example:

```
JCheckboxMenuItem lineItem = new JCheckboxMenuItem("Line", true);
```

This creates an item with the label, Line, which is checked initially. You can, of course, also specify that you want an item to be unchecked by setting the second argument to false.

A JRadioButtonMenuItem object is created in essentially the same way:

```
JRadioButtonMenuItem item = new JRadioButtonMenuItem("Curve", true);
```

This creates a radio button menu item that is selected.

If you want to use a menu bar in your application window, you must create your window as a JFrame object because the JFrame class incorporates the capability to manage a menu bar. You can also add a menu bar to JDialog and JApplet objects. Let's explore how you create a menu on a menu bar.

Creating a Menu

To create a window with a menu bar, you need to define your own window class as a subclass of JFrame. This provides a much more convenient way to manage all the details of the window compared to using a JFrame object directly. By extending the JFrame class, you can add your own members that customize a JFrame window to your particular needs. You can also override the methods defined in the JFrame class to modify their behavior, if necessary.

You add functionality to this example over several chapters, so create a directory for it with the name Sketcher. You develop this program into a window-based sketching program that enables you to create sketches using lines, circles, curves, and rectangles, and to annotate them with text. By building an example in this way, you gradually create a much larger Java program than the examples seen so far, and you also gain experience in combining many of the capabilities of javax.swing and other standard packages in a practical situation. Note that this is not a smooth progression. From time to time you might backtrack on function in Sketcher to implement it better. The final version ends up combining the major techniques you have learned for implementing an interactive application in Java.

TRY IT OUT   Building a Menu

To start with, you have two class files in the Sketcher program. The file Sketcher.java contains the main() method where execution of the application starts, and the SketcherFrame.java file contains the class defining the application window.

You can define a preliminary version of the window class as follows:

Available for download on Wrox.com

```java
// Main window for the Sketcher application
import javax.swing.*;

public class SketcherFrame extends JFrame {
  // Constructor
  public SketcherFrame(String title) {
    setTitle(title);                          // Set the window title
    setDefaultCloseOperation(EXIT_ON_CLOSE);

    setJMenuBar(menuBar);                     // Add the menu bar to the window

    JMenu fileMenu = new JMenu("File");       // Create File menu
    JMenu elementMenu = new JMenu("Elements"); // Create Elements menu

    menuBar.add(fileMenu);                     // Add the file menu
    menuBar.add(elementMenu);                  // Add the element menu
  }

  private JMenuBar menuBar = new JMenuBar();   // Window menu bar
}
```

Directory "Sketcher 1"

Save this code as SketcherFrame.java in the Sketcher directory. Because JFrame is serializable, the compiler expects SketcherFrame to be serializable too. The compiler issues a warning message that there is no definition for serialVersionUID. Because you have no plans to serialize the SketcherFrame class, you can ignore the warning. If you find getting the warning message each time you recompile irritating, you can suppress a particular compiler warning by using an annotation. You could add the following annotation before the SketcherFrame class definition to suppress the serial warning:

```java
@SuppressWarnings("serial")
```

The name of the warning that you want suppressed appears as a string between the parentheses. The warnings that can be suppressed depends on your compiler. `"fallthrough"` suppresses messages about missing `break` statements in a `switch` statement and `"all"` suppresses all compiler warning messages. However, compiler warnings are very helpful in many instances so don't suppress them all.

Next, you can enter the code for the `Sketcher` class in a separate file:

```java
// Sketching application
import javax.swing.*;
import java.awt.*;

public class Sketcher {
  public static void main(String[] args) {
    SwingUtilities.invokeLater(new Runnable() {
        public void run() {
            createWindow();
        }
      });
  }

  public static void createWindow(){
    window = new SketcherFrame("Sketcher");          // Create the app window
    Toolkit theKit = window.getToolkit();            // Get the window toolkit
    Dimension wndSize = theKit.getScreenSize();      // Get screen size

    // Set the position to screen center & size to half screen size
    aWindow.setSize(wndSize.width/2, wndSize.height/2);   // Set window size
    aWindow.setLocationRelativeTo(null);                  // Center window
    aWindow.setDefaultCloseOperation(JFrame.EXIT_ON_CLOSE);

    window.setVisible(true);
  }

  private static SketcherFrame window;               // The application window
}
```

Directory "Sketcher 1"

Save this file as `Sketcher.java` in the `Sketcher` directory. If you compile and run `Sketcher`, you should see the window shown in Figure 17-36.

How It Works

The `Sketcher` class has a `SketcherFrame` variable, `window`, as a data member that you use to store the application window object. You must declare this variable as `static` as there are no instances of the `Sketcher` class around. The `window` variable is initialized in the method `createWindow()` that is called when the application execution begins on the event dispatch thread. After the `window` object exists, you set the size of

FIGURE 17-36

the window based on the screen size in pixels, which you obtain using the `Toolkit` object. This is exactly the same process that you saw earlier in this chapter. Finally, you call the `setVisible()` method for the window object with the argument `true` to display the application window.

In the constructor for the `SketcherFrame` class, you could pass the title for the window to the superclass constructor to create the window with the title bar directly. However, later when you have developed the application a bit more, you should modify the title, so you call the `setTitle()` member to set the window title here. Next you call the `setJMenuBar()` method that is inherited from the `JFrame` class to specify `menuBar` as the menu bar for the window. To define the two menus that are to appear on the menu bar, you create one `JMenu` object with the label `"File"` and another with the label `"Elements"`. These labels are displayed on the menu bar. You add the `fileMenu` and `elementMenu` objects to the menu bar by calling the `add()` method for the `menuBar` object.

The `menuBar` field that you have defined represents the menu bar. Both items on the menu bar are of type `JMenu` and are therefore menus, so you add menu items to each of them. The File menu provides the file input, file output, and print options, and you eventually use the Elements menu to choose the kind of geometric figure you want to draw. Developing the menu further, you can now add the menu items.

Adding Menu Items to a Menu

Both menus on the menu bar need menu items to be added—they can't do anything by themselves because they are of type `JMenu`. You use a version of the `add()` method that is defined in the `JMenu` class to add items to a menu.

The simplest version of the `add()` method creates a menu item with the label that you pass as an argument. For example:

```
JMenuItem newMenu = fileMenu.add("New");              // Add the menu item "New"
```

This creates a menu item as a `JMenuItem` object with the label `"New"`, adds it to the menu represented by the `fileMenu` object, and returns a reference to the menu item. You need the reference to the menu item to enable the program to react to the user clicking the item.

You can also create the `JMenuItem` object explicitly and use another version of the `add()` method for the `JMenu` object to add it:

```
JMenuItem newMenu = new JMenuItem("New");             // Create the item
fileMenu.add(newMenu);                                // and add it to the menu
```

You can operate on menu items by using the following `JMenuItem` class methods:

➤ `void setEnabled(boolean b)`: If `b` has the value `true`, the menu item is enabled; `false` makes it. The default state is enabled.

➤ `void setText(String label)`: Sets the menu item label to the string stored in the label.

➤ `String getText()`: Returns the current menu item label.

Because the `JMenu` class is a subclass of `JMenuItem`, these methods also apply to `JMenu` objects.

To add a separator to a menu you call the `addSeparator()` method for the `JMenu` object. The separator appears following the previous menu item that you added to the menu.

Let's now create the drop-down menus for the File and Element menus on the menu bar in the Sketcher application and try out some of the menu items.

TRY IT OUT | **Adding Drop-Down Menus**

You can change the definition of our `SketcherFrame` class to do this:

Available for download on Wrox.com

```
// Frame for the Sketcher application
import javax.swing.*;

public class SketcherFrame extends JFrame {
  // Constructor
  public SketcherFrame(String title) {
    setTitle(title);                                 // Set the window title
    setDefaultCloseOperation(EXIT_ON_CLOSE);

    setJMenuBar(menuBar);                            // Add the menu bar to the window

    JMenu fileMenu = new JMenu("File");              // Create File menu
    JMenu elementMenu = new JMenu("Elements");       // Create Elements menu
```

```
      // Construct the file drop-down menu
      newItem = fileMenu.add("New");              // Add New item
      openItem = fileMenu.add("Open");            // Add Open item
      closeItem = fileMenu.add("Close");          // Add Close item
      fileMenu.addSeparator();                    // Add separator
      saveItem = fileMenu.add("Save");            // Add Save item
      saveAsItem = fileMenu.add("Save As...");    // Add Save As item
      fileMenu.addSeparator();                    // Add separator
      printItem = fileMenu.add("Print");          // Add Print item

      // Construct the Element drop-down menu
      elementMenu.add(lineItem = new JRadioButtonMenuItem("Line", true));
      elementMenu.add(rectangleItem = new JRadioButtonMenuItem(
                                              "Rectangle", false));
      elementMenu.add(circleItem = new JRadioButtonMenuItem("Circle", false));
      elementMenu.add(curveItem = new JRadioButtonMenuItem("Curve", false));
      ButtonGroup types = new ButtonGroup();
      types.add(lineItem);
      types.add(rectangleItem);
      types.add(circleItem);
      types.add(curveItem);

      elementMenu.addSeparator();

      elementMenu.add(redItem = new JCheckBoxMenuItem("Red", false));
      elementMenu.add(yellowItem = new JCheckBoxMenuItem("Yellow", false));
      elementMenu.add(greenItem = new JCheckBoxMenuItem("Green", false));
      elementMenu.add(blueItem = new JCheckBoxMenuItem("Blue", true));
      menuBar.add(fileMenu);                      // Add the file menu
      menuBar.add(elementMenu);                   // Add the element menu
    }

    private JMenuBar menuBar = new JMenuBar();       // Window menu bar

    // File menu items
    private JMenuItem newItem,    openItem,    closeItem,
                      saveItem, saveAsItem, printItem;

    // Element menu items
    private JRadioButtonMenuItem lineItem,  rectangleItem, circleItem,  // Types
                                 curveItem, textItem;
    private JCheckBoxMenuItem    redItem,    yellowItem,                 // Colors
                                 greenItem, blueItem ;
  }
```

Directory "Sketcher 2 with menus"

If you recompile `Sketcher` once more, you can run the application again to try out the menus. If you extend the File menu by clicking on it, you see that it has the menu items that you have added. The window is shown in Figure 17-37.

Now if you extend the Elements menu it should appear with the Line and Blue items checked.

How It Works

You have defined the fields that store references to the menu items for the drop-down menus as private members of the class. For the File menu, the menu items are of type `JMenuItem`. In

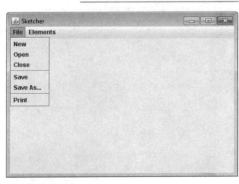

FIGURE 17-37

the Element menu the items select a type of shape to be drawn, and because these are clearly mutually exclusive, you use objects of type `JRadioButtonMenuItem` for them. You would normally use objects of the same type for the element color menu items, but to try it out you are using the `JCheckBoxMenuItem` type.

To create the items in the File menu, you pass the `String` object for the label for each menu item to the `add()` method and leave it to the `JMenu` object to create the `JMenuItem` object. The `add()` method returns a reference to the object that it creates and you store the reference in one of the fields you have defined for that purpose. You need access to the menu item objects later when you add code to service events that arise from the user clicking a menu item.

The first group of Elements menu items are `JRadioButtonMenuItem` objects, and you create each of these in the argument to the `add()` method. To ensure only one is checked at a time, you also add them to a `ButtonGroup` object. The color menu items are of type `JCheckBoxMenuItem`, so the current selection is indicated by a check mark on the menu. To make Line the default element type and Blue the default color, you set both of these as checked by specifying `true` as the second argument to the constructor.

The other items are unchecked initially because you have specified the second argument as `false`. You could have omitted the second argument to leave these items unchecked by default. It then means that you need to remember the default to determine what is happening, so it is better to set the checks explicitly.

You can see the effect of the `addSeparator()` method from the `JMenu` class. It produces the horizontal bar separating the items for element type from those for color. If you select any of the unchecked element type items on the Elements drop-down menu, they are checked automatically, and only one can appear checked. More than one of the color items can be checked at the moment, but you add some code in the next chapter to make sure only one of these items is checked at any given time.

You could try putting the color selection item in an additional drop-down menu. You can do this by changing the code that follows the statement adding the separator in the Elements menu as follows:

```
elementMenu.addSeparator();
JMenu colorMenu = new JMenu("Color");            // Color submenu
elementMenu.add(colorMenu);                       // Add the submenu
colorMenu.add(redItem = new JCheckBoxMenuItem("Red", false));
colorMenu.add(yellowItem = new JCheckBoxMenuItem("Yellow", false));
colorMenu.add(greenItem = new JCheckBoxMenuItem("Green", false));
colorMenu.add(blueItem = new JCheckBoxMenuItem("Blue", true));
```

Directory "Sketcher 3 with Color submenu"

Now you add a `JMenu` object, `colorMenu`, to the drop-down menu for Elements. This has its own drop-down menu consisting of the color menu items. The Color item is displayed on the Elements menu with an arrow to show that a further drop-down menu is associated with it. If you run the application again and extend the drop-down menus, the window should be as shown in Figure 17-38.

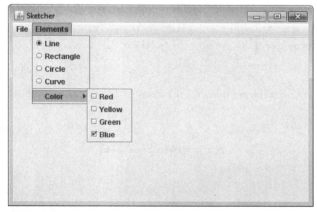

FIGURE 17-38

Whether you choose this menu structure or the previous one is a matter of taste. It might even be better to have a separate item on the menu bar, but let's leave it at that for now. You see in the next chapter that the programming necessary to deal with menu selections by the user is the same in either case.

Adding Menu Shortcuts and Accelerators

A *shortcut* is a unique key combination used to select a menu on the menu bar directly from the keyboard to display the drop-down menu. A typical shortcut under Microsoft Windows would be the Alt key plus a letter from the menu item label, so the shortcut for the File menu item might be Alt+F. When you enter this key combination the menu is displayed. You can add shortcuts for the File and Elements menu items by adding the following statements after you add the menu items to the menu bar:

```
fileMenu.setMnemonic('F');                    // Create shortcut
elementMenu.setMnemonic('E');                 // Create shortcut
```

The `setMnemonic()` method is inherited from the `AbstractButton` class, so all subclasses of this class inherit this method. The argument is a character from the label for the item that is to be the shortcut character—under Windows, the File menu would then pop up if you key Alt+F. The effect of `setMnemonic()` is to implement the shortcut and underline the shortcut character letter in the menu label. The shortcut for each menu on the menu bar must be a unique key combination.

An *accelerator* is a key combination that you can enter to select an item from a drop-down menu without having to go through the process of displaying the menu. Under Windows, the Ctrl key is frequently used in combination with a letter as an accelerator for a menu item, so Ctrl+L might be the combination for the Line item in the Elements menu. To define the accelerator for a menu item, you call the `setAccelerator()` method for the object that encapsulates the menu item. For example, for the Line menu item you could write the following:

```
lineItem.setAccelerator(KeyStroke.getKeyStroke('L', InputEvent.CTRL_DOWN_MASK));
```

The `javax.swing.KeyStroke` class defines a keystroke combination. The static method `getKeyStroke()` in the `KeyStroke` class returns the `KeyStroke` object corresponding to the arguments. The first argument is a character in the keystroke combination and the second argument specifies one or more modifier keys. Only use uppercase letters to identify a letter for a keystroke. Lowercase letters select the non-alphabetic keys, such as the numeric keypad and the function keys. The modifier keys are specified as a combination of single-bit constants that are defined in the `InputEvent` class that appears in the `java.awt.event` package. The `InputEvent` class defines constants that identify control keys on the keyboard and mouse buttons. In this context, the constants you are interested are `SHIFT_DOWN_MASK`, `ALT_DOWN_MASK`, `META_DOWN_MASK`, and `CTRL_DOWN_MASK`. If you want to express a combination of the Alt and Ctrl keys for example, you can combine them as shown in the following expression:

```
InputEvent.ALT_DOWN_MASK | InputEvent.CTRL_DOWN_MASK
```

Of course, when you add accelerators for menu items, if the accelerators are to work properly, you must make sure that each accelerator key combination is unique. Let's see how this works in practice.

TRY IT OUT   **Adding Menu Shortcuts**

You can add some shortcuts to Sketcher by amending the statements that add the items to the File menu in the `SketcherFrame` class constructor:

```
// Frame for the Sketcher application
import javax.swing.*;
import static java.awt.event.InputEvent.*;          // For modifier constants

public class SketcherFrame extends JFrame {
  // Constructor
```

```
public SketcherFrame(String title) {
    setTitle(title);                                  // Call the base constructor
    setDefaultCloseOperation(EXIT_ON_CLOSE);
    setJMenuBar(menuBar);                             // Add the menu bar to the window

    JMenu fileMenu = new JMenu("File");              // Create File menu
    JMenu elementMenu = new JMenu("Elements");       // Create Elements menu
    fileMenu.setMnemonic('F');                       // Create shortcut
    elementMenu.setMnemonic('E');                    // Create shortcut
    // Construct the file drop-down menu as before...
    // Add File menu accelerators
    newItem.setAccelerator(KeyStroke.getKeyStroke('N',CTRL_DOWN_MASK ));
    openItem.setAccelerator(KeyStroke.getKeyStroke('O', CTRL_DOWN_MASK));
    saveItem.setAccelerator(KeyStroke.getKeyStroke('S', CTRL_DOWN_MASK));
    printItem.setAccelerator(KeyStroke.getKeyStroke('P', CTRL_DOWN_MASK));
    // Construct the Element drop-down menu as before...
    // Add element type accelerators
    lineItem.setAccelerator(KeyStroke.getKeyStroke('L', CTRL_DOWN_MASK));
    rectangleItem.setAccelerator(KeyStroke.getKeyStroke('E', CTRL_DOWN_MASK));
    circleItem.setAccelerator(KeyStroke.getKeyStroke('I', CTRL_DOWN_MASK));
    curveItem.setAccelerator(KeyStroke.getKeyStroke('V', CTRL_DOWN_MASK));

    elementMenu.addSeparator();

    // Create the color submenu as before...

    // Add element color accelerators
    redItem.setAccelerator(KeyStroke.getKeyStroke('R', CTRL_DOWN_MASK));
    yellowItem.setAccelerator(KeyStroke.getKeyStroke('Y', CTRL_DOWN_MASK));
    greenItem.setAccelerator(KeyStroke.getKeyStroke('G', CTRL_DOWN_MASK));
    blueItem.setAccelerator(KeyStroke.getKeyStroke('B', CTRL_DOWN_MASK));

    menuBar.add(fileMenu);                           // Add the file menu
    menuBar.add(elementMenu);                        // Add the element menu
}

    // File menu items and the rest of the class as before...
}
```

Directory "Sketcher 4 with shortcuts and accelerators"

If you save SketcherFrame.java after you have made the changes, you can recompile Sketcher and run it again. The file menu now appears as shown in Figure 17-39.

How It Works

You have added a static import statement for the constants in the InputEvent class. The names of the constants are already quite wordy and importing the names saves having to add qualifiers to them.

You use the setMnemonic() method to set the shortcuts for the menu bar items, and the setAccelerator() method to add accelerators to the

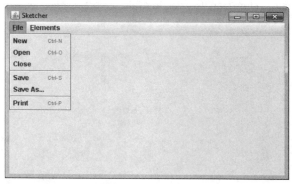

FIGURE 17-39

submenu items. You must make sure that you do not use duplicate key combinations, and the more menu items that you have accelerators for, the trickier this gets. The File menu here defines the standard

Windows accelerators. You can see that the `setAccelerator()` method adds the shortcut key combination to the item label.

The menus don't actually work at the moment, but at least they look good! You start adding the code to implement menu operations in the next chapter.

SUMMARY

In this chapter you learned how to create an application window and how to use containers in the creation of the GUI for a program. You also learned about the primary layout managers for arranging components within a container. You know how to create menus in a menu bar, and how you define drop-down menus. You should also be comfortable with creating buttons and grouping radio buttons and checkboxes to ensure that only one can be selected at any given time.

In the next chapter you move on to look at events—that is, how you associate program actions with menu items and components within a window.

EXERCISES

You can download the source code for the examples in the book and the solutions to the following exercises from `www.wrox.com`.

1. Create an application with a square window in the center of the screen that is half the height of the screen by deriving your own window class from `JFrame`.

2. Add six buttons to the application in the previous example in a vertical column on the left side of the application window.

3. Add a menu bar containing the items File, Edit, Window, and Help.

4. Add a drop-down menu for Edit containing two groups of items of your own choice with a separator between them.

5. Add another item to the Edit drop-down menu, which itself has a drop-down menu, and provide accelerators for the items in the menu.

6. Here's an exercise to tickle the brain cells—use a `SpringLayout` to obtain the button arrangement shown in Figure 17-40 in an application window.

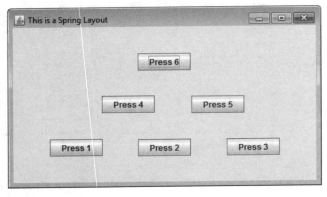

FIGURE 17-40

▶ **WHAT YOU LEARNED IN THIS CHAPTER**

TOPIC	CONCEPT
GUI Classes	The package `javax.swing` provides classes for creating a graphical user interface.
Components	A component is an object that is used to form part of the GUI for a program. All components have the class `Component` as a superclass.
Containers	A container is a component that can contain other components. A container object is created with a class that is a subclass of `Container`. The classes `JPanel`, `JApplet`, `JWindow`, `JFrame`, and `JDialog` are containers.
Defining Applets	The class `JApplet` is the base class for an applet. The `JFrame` class is a base class for an application window with a title bar, borders, and a menu.
Layout Managers	The arrangement of components in a container is controlled by a layout manager.
Default Layout Managers	The default layout manager for the content pane of `JFrame`, `JApplet`, and `JDialog` objects is `BorderLayout`.
Spring Layout Manager	A layout manager of type `SpringLayout` arranges components by applying constraints in the form of `Spring` objects to their edges.
Box Containers	A `Box` container can be used to arrange components or containers in rows and columns. A `Box` container has `BoxLayout` as its layout manager. You can use multiple nested `Box` containers in combination to easily create complex arrangements that otherwise might require `GridBagLayout` to be used.
Creating Menus	A menu bar is represented by a `JMenuBar` object. Menu items can be objects of type `JMenu`, `JMenuItem`, `JCheckBoxMenuItem`, or `JRadioButtonMenuItem`.
Drop-down Menus	You associate a drop-down menu with an object of type `JMenu`.
Menu Shortcuts and Accelerators	You can create a shortcut for a menu by calling its `setMnemonic()` method, and you can create an accelerator key combination for a menu item by calling its `setAccelerator()` method.

18

Handling Events

WHAT YOU WILL LEARN IN THIS CHAPTER:

➤ What an event is

➤ What an event-driven program is and how it is structured

➤ How events are handled in Java

➤ How events are categorized in Java

➤ How components handle events

➤ What an event listener is and how you create one

➤ What an adapter class is and how you can use it to make programming the handling of events easier

➤ What actions are and how you use them

➤ How to create a toolbar

In this chapter you learn how a window-based Java application is structured and how to respond to user actions in an application or an applet. This is the fundamental mechanism you use in virtually all of your graphical Java programs. When you understand how user actions are handled in Java, you are equipped to implement the application-specific code that is necessary to make your program do what you want.

INTERACTIVE JAVA PROGRAMS

Before you get into the programming specifics of interactive window-based applications you need to understand a little of how such programs are structured, and how they work. There are fundamental differences between the console programs that you have been producing up to now and an interactive program with a graphical user interface (GUI). With a console program, you start the program and the program code determines the sequences of events. Generally everything is predetermined. You enter data when required, and the program outputs data when it wants. At any given time, the specific program code that executes next is generally known.

A window-based application, or an applet for that matter, is quite different. The operation of the program is driven by what you do with the GUI. Selecting menu items or buttons using the mouse, or through the keyboard, causes particular actions within the program. At any given moment, the user has a whole range of possible interactions available, each of which results in a different program action. Until you do something, the specific program code that is to be executed next is not known.

Event-Driven Programs

Your actions when you're using the GUI for a window-based program or an applet—clicking a menu item or a button, moving the mouse, and so on—are first recognized by the operating system. For each action, the operating system determines which of the programs currently running on your computer should know about it and passes the action on to that program. When you click a mouse button, it's the operating system that registers this and notes the position of the mouse cursor on the screen. It then decides which application controls the window where the cursor was when you pressed the button and communicates the mouse button-press to that program. The signals that a program receives from the operating system as a result of your actions are called *events*. The basic idea of how actions and events are communicated to your program code is illustrated in Figure 18-1.

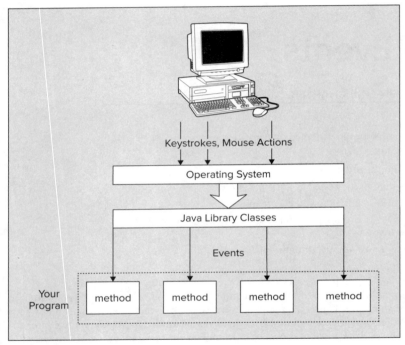

FIGURE 18-1

A program is not obliged to respond to any particular event. If you just move the mouse, for example, the program need not invoke any code to react to that. If it doesn't, the event is quietly disposed of. Each event that the program does recognize is associated with one or more methods, and when the event occurs—when you click a menu item, for example—the appropriate methods are called automatically. A window-based program is called an *event-driven program* because the sequence of events created as a result of your interaction with the GUI drives and determines what happens in the program.

> **NOTE** *Events are not limited to window-based applications—they are a quite general concept. Most programs that control or monitor things in the real world are event-driven. Any occurrence external to a program, such as a switch closing or a preset temperature being reached, can be registered as an event. In Java you can even create events within your program to signal some other part of the code that something noteworthy has happened. However, I'm going to concentrate on the kinds of events that occur when a user interacts with a program through its GUI.*

THE EVENT-HANDLING PROCESS

To manage the user's interaction with the components that make up the GUI for a program, you must understand how events are handled in Java. To get an idea of how this works, let's consider a specific example. Don't worry too much about the class names and other details here. Just try to get a feel for how things connect.

Suppose the user clicks a button in the GUI for your program. The button is the source of this event. The event that is generated as a result of the mouse click is associated with the `JButton` object in your program that represents the button on the screen. An event always has a source object—in this case the `JButton` object. When the button is clicked, it creates a new object that represents and identifies this event—in this case an object of type `ActionEvent`. This object contains information about the event and its source. Any event that is passed to a Java program is represented by a particular event object—and this object is passed as an argument to the method that is to handle the event. Figure 18-2 illustrates this mechanism.

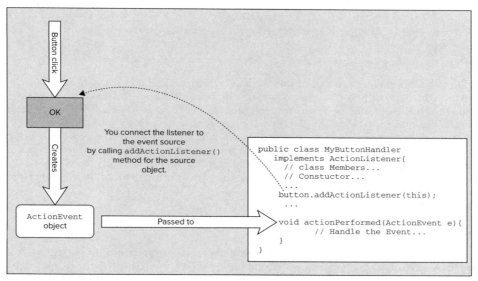

FIGURE 18-2

The event object corresponding to the button click is passed to any *listener object* that has previously registered an interest in this kind of event—a listener object being simply an object that listens for particular events. A listener is also called a *target* for an event. Here, "passing the event to the listener" just means the object that is the event source calls a particular method in the listener object and passes the event object to it as an argument. A listener object can listen for events for a particular object—just a single button, for example—or it can listen for events for several different objects—a group of menu items, for example. Which approach you take when you define a class representing listeners depends on the context and which is most convenient from a programming point of view. Your programs often involve both.

So how do you define a class that represents a listener? You can make the objects of any class listener objects by making the class implement a *listener interface*. You find quite a variety of listener interfaces to cater for different kinds of events. In the case of our button click, an object of a type that implements the `ActionListener` interface needs to be created to receive the event from the button. The code that is to receive this event object and respond to the event is implemented in a method declared in the listener interface. In this example, the `actionPerformed()` method in the `ActionListener` interface is called when the event occurs, and the event object is passed as an argument. Each kind of listener interface defines particular methods for receiving the events that that listener has been designed to deal with.

Simply implementing a listener interface isn't sufficient to link the listener object to an event source. You still have to connect the listener object to the source, or sources, of the events that you want it to deal with. You register a listener object with a source by calling a particular method in the source object. To register a listener to listen for button-click events, you call the `addActionListener()` method for the `JButton` object and pass the listener object as the argument to the method.

This mechanism for handling events using listeners is very flexible and efficient, particularly for GUI events. Any number of listeners can receive a particular event. However, a particular event is passed only to the listeners that have registered to receive it, so only interested parties are involved in responding to each event. Because being a listener only requires a suitable interface to be implemented, you can receive and handle events virtually anywhere among the classes that make up your application. The way in which events are handled in Java, using listener objects, is referred to as the *delegation event model*. This is because the responsibility for responding to events for a component, such as a button or a menu item, is not handled by the objects that originated the events themselves—but is delegated to separate listener objects.

 NOTE *Not all event handling necessarily requires a separate listener. A component can handle its own events, as you see a little later in this chapter.*

A important point to keep in mind when writing code to handle events is that all such code executes in the event-dispatching thread, which as you know is separate from the thread in which `main()` executes. This implies that while one event is being dealt with, no other events can be processed. The code to handle the next event starts executing only when the current event-handler finishes. Thus, the responsiveness of your program to the user is dependent on how long your event-handling code takes to execute. For snappy performance, your event handlers must take as little time as possible to execute. Also, because events are processed in a separate thread from the main thread, you must not modify or query the GUI for an application from the main thread after the GUI has been displayed or is ready to be displayed. Otherwise, a deadlock may result.

EVENT CLASSES

Your program might need to respond to many different kinds of events—from menus, from buttons, from the mouse, from the keyboard, and from a number of other components. To have a structured approach to handling events, the events are broken down into subsets. At the topmost level, there are two broad categories of events in Java:

> **Low-Level Events:** These are system-level events that arise from the keyboard or from the mouse, or events associated with operations on a window, such as reducing it to an icon or closing it. The meaning of a low-level event is something like "the mouse was moved," "this window has been closed," or "this key was pressed."

> **Semantic Events:** These are specific GUI component-level events such as selecting a button by clicking it to cause some program action or adjusting a scrollbar. They originate, and you interpret them, in the context of the GUI you have created for your program. The meaning of a semantic event is typically along the lines of "the OK button was pressed," or "the Save menu item was selected." Each kind of component, a button or a menu item, for example, can generate a particular kind of semantic event.

These two categories can seem to be a bit confusing as they overlap in a way. If you click a button, you create a semantic event as well as a low-level event. The click produces a low-level event object in the form of "the mouse was clicked" as well as a semantic event "the button was pushed." In fact it produces more than one mouse event, as you later see. Whether your program handles the low-level events or the semantic events, or possibly both kinds of events, depends on what you want to do.

Most of the events relating to the GUI for a program are represented by classes that are in the `java.awt.event` package. This package also defines the listener interfaces for various kinds of events. The package `javax.swing.event` defines classes for events that are specific to Swing components.

Low-Level Event Classes

You can elect to handle four kinds of low-level events in your programs. They are represented by the classes in the `java.awt.event` package that are shown in Table 18-1.

TABLE 18-1 Classes for Low-Level Events

EVENT	DESCRIPTION
FocusEvent	Objects of this class represent events that originate when a component gains or loses the focus. Only the component that has the focus can receive input, so it is usually highlighted or has the cursor displayed.
MouseEvent	These are events that result from user actions with the mouse, such as moving the mouse or pressing a mouse button. You learn how you deal with these events in Chapter 19.
KeyEvent	These represent events that arise from pressing keys on the keyboard.
WindowEvent	Objects of this class represent events that relate to a window, such as activating or deactivating it, reducing it to its icon, or closing it. These events relate to objects of type `Window` or any subclass of `Window`.

The `MouseEvent` class has two subclasses that identify more specialized mouse events. One is the `MenuDragMouseEvent` class that defines events that signal when the mouse is dragged over a menu item. The other is the `MouseWheelEvent` class that defines events indicating when the mouse wheel is rotated.

 WARNING *Just so that you know, this isn't an exhaustive list of all of the low-level event classes. It's a list of the ones you need to know about. For example, there's also the `PaintEvent` class that is concerned with the internals of how components are painted on the screen. There's also another low-level event class, `ContainerEvent`, that defines events relating to a container, such as adding or removing components. You can ignore these classes, as these events are handled automatically.*

Each of these event classes defines methods that enable you to analyze an event. For a `MouseEvent` object, for example, you can get the coordinates of the cursor when the event occurred. These low-level event classes also inherit methods from their superclasses and are related in the manner shown in Figure 18-3.

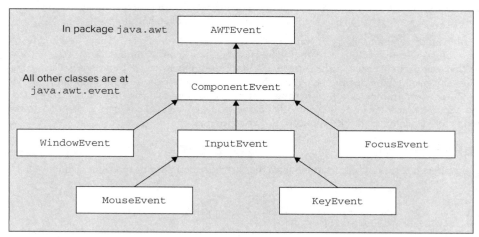

FIGURE 18-3

`AWTEvent` is derived from `java.util.EventObject`. The `EventObject` class implements the `Serializable` interface, so all objects of the event classes in the diagram are serializable. It also defines a `getSource()` method that returns the source of an event as type `Object`. All the event classes shown inherit this method.

The `AWTEvent` class defines constants that are public final values identifying the various kinds of events. These constants are named for the sake of consistency as the event name in capital letters, followed by `_MASK`. The constants identifying the low-level events that you are most likely to be interested in are the following:

MOUSE_EVENT_MASK	MOUSE_MOTION_EVENT_MASK
MOUSE_WHEEL_EVENT_MASK	KEY_EVENT_MASK
ADJUSTMENT_EVENT_MASK	WINDOW_EVENT_MASK
WINDOW_FOCUS_EVENT_MASK	WINDOW_STATUS_EVENT_MASK
TEXT_EVENT_MASK	ITEM_EVENT_MASK
FOCUS_EVENT_MASK	

Each constant is a value of type `long` with a single bit set to 1. Because they are defined this way you can combine them using a bitwise OR operator and you can separate a particular constant out from a combination by using a bitwise AND.

 WARNING *The provided list of event masks is not exhaustive. There are masks for component events represented by objects of the class* `ComponentEvent` *and for container events. These events occur when a component is moved or resized, or a component is added to a container, for example. There is also a mask for events associated with components that receive text input. You won't normally need to get involved in these events so I don't discuss them further.*

You use the identifiers for event masks to enable a particular group of events in a component object. You call the `enableEvents()` method for the component and pass the identifier for the events you want enabled as an argument. However, you do this only when you aren't using a listener. Registering a listener automatically enables the events that the listener wants to hear, so you don't need to call the `enableEvents()` method. The circumstance when you might do this is when you want an object to handle some of its own events, although you can achieve the same result using a listener.

Making a Window Handle Its Own Events

Using listener objects is the preferred way of handling events because it is easier than enabling events directly for an object, and the code is clearer. Nonetheless, you should take a look at how events are dealt with after calling `enableEvents()` in case you come across it elsewhere. An example of where you might want to call `enableEvents()` exists in the `SketcherFrame` class in the Sketcher program.

As you may recall from the previous chapter, you used the `setDefaultCloseOperation()` method to determine what happens when you close the window by clicking the X icon. Although the `EXIT_ON_CLOSE` argument value that you used disposed of the frame and closed the application, it didn't provide any opportunity to do any checking or cleanup before causing the program to exit. You can respond to the close icon being clicked in the program yourself, rather than letting the `JFrame` facilities handle the associated event within the window object itself. This eventually enables you to prompt the user to save any data that has been created before shutting down the application. Let's give it a try.

TRY IT OUT Closing a Window

You need to modify the `SketcherFrame` class definition from the Sketcher example in the previous chapter as follows:

```
// Frame for the Sketcher application
import javax.swing.*;
import static java.awt.event.InputEvent.*;        // For modifier constants
import java.awt.event.WindowEvent;

public class SketcherFrame extends JFrame {
```

```
    // Constructor
    public SketcherFrame(String title) {
      setTitle(title);                                 // Set the window title
      //   setDefaultCloseOperation(EXIT_ON_CLOSE);
      // rest of code as before...

      menuBar.add(fileMenu);                           // Add the file menu
      menuBar.add(elementMenu);                        // Add the element menu
      enableEvents(WINDOW_EVENT_MASK);                 // Enable window events
    }

    // Handle window events
    protcted void processWindowEvent(WindowEvent e) {
      if (e.getID() == WindowEvent.WINDOW_CLOSING) {
        dispose();                                     // Release resources
        System.exit(0);                                // Exit the program
      }
      super.processWindowEvent(e);                     // Pass on the event
    }

    private JMenuBar menuBar = new JMenuBar();         // Window menu bar

    // File menu items
    private JMenuItem newItem,  openItem,   closeItem,
                   saveItem, saveAsItem, printItem;

    // Elements menu items
    private JRadioButtonMenuItem lineItem,  rectangleItem, circleItem,  // Types
                          curveItem, textItem;
    private JCheckBoxMenuItem    redItem,   yellowItem,                 // Colors
                          greenItem, blueItem ;
  }
```

Directory "Sketcher 1 handling its own closing event"

You add the call to `enableEvents()` as the last in the constructor. Note that the statement that sets EXIT_ON_CLOSE as the close option for the window is commented out. You could delete the statement if you want. When you compile `SketcherFrame` and run Sketcher again, you are able to close the window as before, and the program shuts down gracefully. However, this time it's your method that's doing it.

How It Works

The additional import statement makes the `WindowEvent` class name available to your source file without the need to qualify it with the package name. You call `enableEvents()` in the constructor with WINDOW_EVENT_MASK as the argument to enable window events. This enables all the window events represented by the `WindowEvent` class. An object of this class can represent one of a number of different window events that are each identified by an event ID, which is a constant defined within the `WindowEvent` class. The event IDs for the `WindowEvent` class are shown in Table 18-2:

TABLE 18-2 Event IDs for the WindowEvent Class

EVENT ID	DESCRIPTION
WINDOW_OPENED	The event that occurs the first time a window is made visible.
WINDOW_CLOSING	The event that occurs as a result of the close icon being selected or Close being selected from the window's system menu.
WINDOW_CLOSED	The event that occurs when the window has been closed.

continues

TABLE 18-2 *(continued)*

EVENT ID	DESCRIPTION
WINDOW_ACTIVATED	The event that occurs when the window is activated—obtains the focus, in other words. When another GUI component has the focus, you could make the window obtain the focus by clicking on it, for example.
WINDOW_DEACTIVATED	The event that occurs when the window is deactivated—loses the focus, in other words. Clicking on another window would cause this event, for example.
WINDOW_GAINED_FOCUS	The event that occurs when the window gains the focus. This implies that the window or one of its components receives keyboard events.
WINDOW_LOST_FOCUS	The event that occurs when the window loses the focus. This implies that keyboard events are not delivered to the window or any of its components.
WINDOW_ICONIFIED	The event that occurs when the window is minimized and reduced to an icon.
WINDOW_DEICONIFIED	The event that occurs when the window is restored from an icon.
WINDOW_STATE_CHANGED	The event that occurs when the window state changes—when it is maximized or minimized, for instance.

If any of these events occur, your `processWindowEvent()` method is called. Your version of the method overrides the base class method that is inherited from `Window` and is responsible for passing the event to any listeners that have been registered. The argument of type `WindowEvent` that is passed to the method contains the event ID that identifies the event that occurred. To obtain the ID of the event, you call the `getID()` method for the event object and compare that with the ID that identifies the `WINDOW_CLOSING` event. If the event is `WINDOW_CLOSING`, you call the `dispose()` method for the window to close the window and release the system resources it is using. You then close the application by calling the `exit()` method defined in the `System` class. If you need convincing that it is your method closing the application, put an output statement immediately before the call to exit.

 NOTE *The* `getID()` *method is defined in the* `AWTEvent` *class, which is a superclass of all the low-level event classes I have discussed, so all event objects that encapsulate low-level events have this method.*

In the `SketcherFrame` class, the `dispose()` method is inherited from the `Window` class via the base class `JFrame`. This method releases all the resources for the window object, including those for all components owned by the object. Calling the `dispose()` method doesn't affect the window object itself. It just tells the operating system that the resources used to display the window and the components it contains are no longer required. The window object is still around together with its components, so you could call its methods or even open it again.

 WARNING *Note that you call the* `processWindowEvent()` *method in the superclass if it is not the closing event. It is very important that you do this as it allows the event to be passed on to any listeners that have been registered for these events. If you don't call* `processWindowEvent()` *for the superclass, any events that you do not handle in your* `processWindowEvent()` *method are lost.*

If you had not removed the call to the `setDefaultCloseOperation()` method, your `processWindowEvent()` method would still have been called when the close icon was clicked. with the call to `setDefaultCloseOperation()` in effect, you would not need to call `dispose()` and `exit()` in the method. This would all have been taken care of automatically after your `processWindowEvent()` method had finished executing. This would be preferable as it means there would be less code in your program, and the code to handle the default close action is there in the `JFrame` class anyway.

Enabling Other Low-Level Events

The `enableEvents()` method is inherited from the `Component` class. This means that any component can elect to handle its own events. You just call the `enableEvents()` method for the component and pass an argument defining the events you want the component to handle. If you want to enable more than one type of event for a component, you just combine the event masks from `AWTEvent` that you saw earlier by linking them with a bitwise OR. To make the window object handle mouse events as well as window events, you could write the following:

```
enableEvents(WINDOW_EVENT_MASK | MOUSE_EVENT_MASK);
```

Of course, you must now also implement the `processMouseEvent()` method for the `SketcherFrame` class. Like the `processWindowEvent()` method, this method is protected and has `void` as the return type. It receives the event as an argument of type `MouseEvent`. There are two other methods specific to the `Window` class that handle events, shown in Table 18-3.

These methods and the `processWindowEvent()` method are available only for objects of type `Window` or a subclass of `Window`, so don't try to enable window events on other components.

TABLE 18-3 Window Class Methods for Handling Window Events

EVENT-HANDLING METHODS	DESCRIPTION
`processWindowFocusEvent(` `        WindowEvent e)`	This is called for any window focus events that arise as long as such events are enabled for the window.
`processWindowStateEvent(` `        WindowEvent e)`	This is called for events resulting from the window changing state.

The other event-handling methods in the window that you can override to handle component events are show in Table 18-4.

TABLE 18-4 Window Class Methods for Handling Component Events

EVENT-HANDLING METHODS	DESCRIPTION
`processEvent(AWTEvent e)`	This is called first for any events that are enabled for the component. If you implement this and fail to call the base class method, none of the methods for specific groups of events are called.
`processFocusEvent(FocusEvent e)`	This is called for focus events, if they are enabled for the component.
`processKeyEvent(KeyEvent e)`	This is called for key events, if they are enabled for the component.
`processMouseEvent(MouseEvent e)`	This is called for mouse button events, if they are enabled for the component.
`processMouseMotionEvent(MouseEvent e)`	This is called for mouse move and drag events, if they are enabled for the component.
`processMouseWheelEvent(MouseWheelEvent e)`	This is called for mouse wheel rotation events, if they are enabled for the component.

All the event-handling methods for a component are protected methods that have a return type of `void`. The default behavior implemented by these methods is to dispatch the events to any listeners registered for the component. If you don't call the base class method when you override these methods, this behavior is lost.

WARNING *Although it seems convenient to handle the window-closing event in the* SketcherFrame *class by implementing* processWindowEvent(), *as a general rule you should use listeners to handle events. Using listeners is the recommended approach to handling events in the majority of circumstances. Separating the event handling from the object that originated the event results in a simpler code structure that is easier to understand and is less error prone. You change the handling of the window-closing event in Sketcher to use a listener later in this chapter.*

Low-Level Event Listeners

A class that defines an event listener must implement a listener interface. All event listener interfaces extend the interface java.util.EventListener. This interface doesn't declare any methods, though — it's just used to identify event listener objects. You can use a variable of type EventListener to hold a reference to any kind of event listener object.

There are many event listener interfaces. You consider just eight at this point concerned with low-level events. The following sections describe these interfaces and the methods they declare.

The WindowListener Interface

The WindowListener interface declares methods to respond to events reflecting changes in the state of a window (shown in Table 18-5).

TABLE 18-5 WindowListener Methods

METHOD	DESCRIPTION
windowOpened(WindowEvent e)	Called the first time a window is opened.
windowClosing(WindowEvent e)	Called when the system menu Close item or the window close icon is selected.
windowClosed(WindowEvent e)	Called when a window has been closed.
windowActivated(WindowEvent e)	Called when a window is activated — by clicking on it, for example.
windowDeactivated(WindowEvent e)	Called when a window is deactivated — by clicking on another window, for example.
windowIconified(WindowEvent e)	Called when a window is minimized and reduced to an icon.
windowDeiconified(WindowEvent e)	Called when a window is restored from an icon.

The WindowFocusListener Interface

The WindowFocusListener interface declares methods (shown in Table 18-6) to respond to a window gaining or losing the focus. When a window has the focus, one of its child components can receive input from the keyboard. When it loses the focus, keyboard input via a child component of the window is not possible.

TABLE 18-6: WindowFocusListener Methods

METHOD	DESCRIPTION
windowGainedFocus(WindowEvent e)	Called when a window gains the focus such that the window or one of its components can receive keyboard events.
windowLostFocus(WindowEvent e)	Called when a window loses the focus. After this event, neither the window nor any of its components receive keyboard events.

The WindowStateListener Interface

The WindowStateListener interface declares a method to respond to any change in the state of a window (see Table 18-7).

TABLE 18-7 WindowStateListener Method

METHOD	DESCRIPTION
windowStateChanged(WindowEvent e)	Called when the window state changes—when it is maximized or iconified, for example.

The MouseListener Interface

The MouseListener interface declares methods (shown in Table 18-7) to respond to events arising when the mouse cursor is moved into or out of the area occupied by a component, or one of the mouse buttons is pressed, released, or clicked.

TABLE 18-8 MouseListener Methods

METHOD	DESCRIPTION
mouseClicked(MouseEvent e)	Called when a mouse button is clicked when the cursor is on a component—that is, when the button is pressed and released.
mousePressed(MouseEvent e)	Called when a mouse button is pressed when the cursor is on a component.
mouseReleased(MouseEvent e)	Called when a mouse button is released when the cursor is on a component.
mouseEntered(MouseEvent e)	Called when the mouse cursor enters the area occupied by a component.
mouseExited(MouseEvent e)	Called when the mouse cursor exits the area occupied by a component.

The MouseMotionListener Interface

The MouseMotionListener interface declares methods (shown in Table 18-9) that are called when the mouse is moved or dragged with a button pressed.

TABLE 18-9 MouseMotionListener Methods

METHOD	DESCRIPTION
mouseMoved(MouseEvent e)	Called when the mouse is moved when the cursor is on a component.
mouseDragged(MouseEvent e)	Called when the mouse is moved when the cursor is on a component while a mouse button is held down.

The MouseWheelListener Interface

The `MouseWheelListener` interface declares a method (shown in Table 18-10) to respond to the mouse wheel being rotated. This is frequently used to scroll information that is displayed, but you can use it in any way that you want.

TABLE 18-10 MouseWheelListener Method

METHOD	DESCRIPTION
mouseWheelMoved(MouseWheelEvent e)	Called when the mouse wheel is rotated.

The KeyListener Interface

The `KeyListener` interface declares methods (shown in Table 18-11) to respond to events arising when a key on the keyboard is pressed or released.

TABLE 18-11 KeyListener Methods

METHOD	DESCRIPTION
keyTyped(KeyEvent e)	Called when a key is pressed and then released.
keyPressed(KeyEvent e)	Called when a key is pressed.
keyReleased(KeyEvent e)	Called when a key is released.

The FocusListener Interface

The `FocusListener` interface declares methods (shown in Table 18-12) to respond to a component gaining or losing the focus. You might implement these methods to change the appearance of the component to reflect whether or not it has the focus.

TABLE 18-12 FocusListener Methods

METHOD	DESCRIPTION
focusGained(FocusEvent e)	Called when a component gains the focus.
focusLost(FocusEvent e)	Called when a component loses the focus.

There is a further listener interface, `MouseInputListener`, that is defined in the `javax.swing.event` package. This listener implements both the `MouseListener` and `MouseMotionListener` interfaces so it declares methods for all possible mouse events in a single interface.

The `WindowListener`, `WindowFocusListener`, and `WindowStateListener` interfaces declare methods corresponding to each of the event IDs defined in the `WindowEvent` class that you saw earlier. If you deduced from this that the methods in the other listener interfaces correspond to event IDs for the other event classes, well, you're right. All the IDs for mouse events are defined in the `MouseEvent` class. These are:

MOUSE_CLICKED	MOUSE_PRESSED	MOUSE_DRAGGED
MOUSE_ENTERED	MOUSE_EXITED	MOUSE_RELEASED
MOUSE_MOVED	MOUSE_WHEEL	

The `MOUSE_MOVED` event corresponds to just moving the mouse. The `MOUSE_DRAGGED` event arises when you move the mouse while keeping a button pressed.

The event IDs that the `KeyEvent` class defines are:

| KEY_TYPED | KEY_PRESSED | KEY_RELEASED |

Those defined in the `FocusEvent` class are:

| FOCUS_GAINED | FOCUS_LOST |

To implement a listener for a particular event type, you just need to implement the methods declared in the corresponding interface. You could handle some of the window events for the `SketcherFrame` window by making the application class the listener for window events. You must then create a `Sketcher` object that is the listener for the events.

TRY IT OUT Implementing a Low-Level Event Listener

First, delete the call to the `enableEvents()` method in the `SketcherFrame()` constructor. Then delete the definition of the `processWindowEvent()` method. Now you can modify the `Sketcher` class in the Sketcher application so that it is a listener for window events:

Available for
download on
Wrox.com

```java
// Sketching application
import javax.swing.*;
import java.awt.*;
import java.awt.event.*;

public class Sketcher implements WindowListener {
  public static void main(String[] args) {
    theApp = new Sketcher();                             // Create the application object
    SwingUtilities.invokeLater(
      new Runnable() {                                   // Anonymous Runnable class object
                     public void run() {                 // Run method executed in thread
                            theApp.createGUI();           // Call GUI creator
                     }
                  });
  }

  // Method to create the application GUI
  private void createGUI() {
    window = new SketcherFrame("Sketcher");              // Create the app window
    Toolkit theKit = window.getToolkit();               // Get the window toolkit
    Dimension wndSize = theKit.getScreenSize();         // Get screen size

    // Set the position to screen center & size to half screen size
    window.setSize(wndSize.width/2, wndSize.height/2);  // Set window size
    window.setLocationRelativeTo(null);                 // Center window
    window.addWindowListener(this);                     // theApp as window listener
    window.setVisible(true);
  }

  // Handler for window closing event
  public void windowClosing(WindowEvent e) {
    window.dispose();                                   // Release the window resources
    System.exit(0);                                     // End the application
  }

  // Listener interface methods you must implement - but don't need
  public void windowOpened(WindowEvent e) {}
  public void windowClosed(WindowEvent e) {}
  public void windowIconified(WindowEvent e) {}
```

```
        public void windowDeiconified(WindowEvent e) {}
        public void windowActivated(WindowEvent e) {}
        public void windowDeactivated(WindowEvent e) {}

        private SketcherFrame window;                    // The application window
        private static Sketcher theApp;                  // The application object
    }
```

Directory "Sketcher 2 implementing a low-level listener"

If you run the Sketcher program again, you see it works just as before, but now the `Sketcher` class object is handling the close operation.

How It Works

You have added an import statement for the names in the `java.awt.event` package, which includes `WindowEvent` and `WindowListener`. The `Sketcher` class now implements the `WindowListener` interface, so an object of type `Sketcher` can handle window events. The `main()` method now creates a `Sketcher` object and stores the reference in the static class member `theApp`.

I changed the name of the `createWindow()` method to `createGUI()` because this reflects better what it does. It is now an instance method. It is called on the event-dispatching thread using the application object, `theApp`. The `createGUI()` method creates the application window object as before, but now the reference is stored in a field that is called `theApp`.

After setting up the window components, the `createGUI()` method calls the `addWindowListener()` method for the window object. The argument to the `addWindowListener()` method is a reference to the listener object that is to receive window events. Here it is the variable `this`, which refers to the application object, `theApp`. If you had other listener objects that you wanted to register to receive this event, you would just need to add more calls to the `addWindowListener()` method—one call for each listener.

When you implement the `WindowListener` interface in the `Sketcher` class, you must implement all seven methods that are declared in the interface. If you failed to do this, the class would be abstract and you could not create an object of type `Sketcher`. Only the `windowClosing()` method contains code here—the bodies of all the other methods are empty because you don't need to use them. The `windowClosing()` method does the same as the `processWindowEvent()` method that you implemented for the previous version of the `SketcherFrame` class, but here you don't need to check the object passed to it because the `windowClosing()` method is called only for a `WINDOW_CLOSING` event. You don't need to pass the event on either; this is necessary only when you handle events in the manner I discussed earlier. Here, if there were other listeners around for the window events, they would automatically receive the event.

You have included the code that calls `dispose()` and `exit()` here, but if you set the default close operation in `SketcherFrame` to `EXIT_ON_CLOSE`, you could omit these, too. You really only need to put your application cleanup code in the `windowClosing()` method, and this typically displays a dialog to just prompt the user to save any application data. You get to that eventually.

Having to implement six methods that you don't need is rather tedious. But you have a way to avoid this—by using what is called an adapter class to define a listener.

Using Adapter Classes

An adapter class is a term for a class that implements a listener interface with methods that have no content, so they do nothing. The idea of this is to enable you to derive your own listener class from any of the adapter classes that are provided and then implement just the methods that you are interested in. The other empty methods are inherited from the adapter class so you don't have to worry about them.

The `MouseInputAdapter` adapter class that is defined in the `javax.swing.event` package defines the methods for the `MouseInputListener` interface. There are five further adapter classes defined in the `java.awt`.

event package that cover the methods in the other low-level listener interfaces you have seen. Here's the complete set:

FocusAdapter   WindowAdapter   KeyAdapter
MouseAdapter   MouseMotionAdapter MouseInputAdapter

The WindowAdapter class implements all the methods declared in the WindowListener, WindowFocusListener, and WindowStateListener interfaces. The other five adapter classes each implement the methods in the corresponding listener interface.

To handle the window closing event for the Sketcher application, you could derive your own class from the WindowAdapter class and just implement the windowClosing() method. If you also make it a nested class to the Sketcher class, it automatically has access to the members of the Sketcher object regardless of their access specifiers. Let's change the structure of the Sketcher class once more to make use of an adapter class.

TRY IT OUT   Implementing an Adapter Class

The version of the Sketcher class to implement this is as follows, with changes to the previous version highlighted:

Available for download on Wrox.com

```java
// Sketching application
import javax.swing.*;
import java.awt.*;
import java.awt.event.*;

public class Sketcher {
  public static void main(String[] args) {
    theApp = new Sketcher();                   // Create the application object
    SwingUtilities.invokeLater(new Runnable() {
                    public void run() {
                      theApp.creatGUI();              // Call static GUI creator
                    }
                  });
  }

  // Method to create the application GUI
  private void creatGUI() {
    window = new SketcherFrame("Sketcher");        // Create the app window
    Toolkit theKit = window.getToolkit();          // Get the window toolkit
    Dimension wndSize = theKit.getScreenSize();    // Get screen size

    // Set the position to screen center & size to half screen size
    window.setSize(wndSize.width/2, wndSize.height/2);  // Set window size
    window.setLocationRelativeTo(null);            // Center window
    window.addWindowListener(new WindowHandler());  // Add window listener
    window.setVisible(true);                       // Display the window
  }

  // Handler class for window events
  class WindowHandler extends WindowAdapter {
    // Handler for window closing event
    @Override
    public void windowClosing(WindowEvent e) {
      window.dispose();                            // Release the window resources
      System.exit(0);                              // End the application
    }
  }

  private SketcherFrame window;                     // The application window
  private static Sketcher theApp;                   // The application object
}
```

Directory "Sketcher 3 using an Adapter class"

This example displays the same application window as the previous example.

How It Works

As the `Sketcher` class is no longer the listener for `window`, it doesn't need to implement the `WindowListener` interface. The `WindowHandler` class is the listener class for `window` events. Because the `WindowHandler` class is an inner class to the `Sketcher` class, it has access to all the members of the class, so calling the `dispose()` method for the `window` object is still quite straightforward—you just access the `window` field of the top-level class.

The `WindowAdapter` object that is the listener for the window object is created in the argument to the `addWindowListener()` method for `window`. You don't need an explicit variable to contain it because it is stored in a data member of the `SketcherFrame` class that is inherited from the `Window` class.

> **WARNING** *It is very important to use the* `@Override` *annotation when you are using adapter classes. An easy mistake to make when you're using adapter classes is to misspell the name of the method that you are using to implement the event—typically by using the wrong case for a letter. If you have not specified the* `@Override` *annotation for your method, you won't get any indication of this. You aren't overriding the adapter class method at all; you're adding a new method. Your code should compile perfectly well but your program does not handle any events. They are all passed to the method in the adapter class with the name your method should have had—which does nothing, of course.*

You haven't finished with low-level events yet by any means, and you return to handling more low-level events in the next chapter when you begin to add drawing code to the Sketcher program. In the meantime, let's start looking at how you can manage semantic events.

Semantic Events

As you saw earlier, semantic events relate to operations on the components in the GUI for your program. If you select a menu item or click a button, for example, a semantic event is generated. Three classes represent the basic semantic events you deal with most of the time, and they are derived from the `AWTEvent` class, as shown in Figure 18-4.

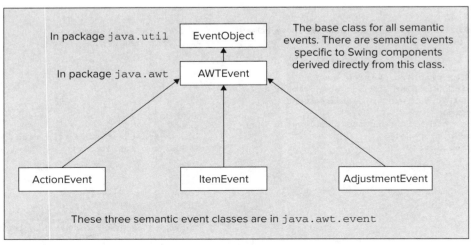

FIGURE 18-4

An `ActionEvent` is generated when you perform an action on a component such as clicking on a menu item or a button. An `ItemEvent` occurs when a component is selected or deselected, and an `AdjustmentEvent` is produced when an adjustable object, such as a scrollbar, is adjusted.

Different kinds of components can produce different kinds of semantic events. Some of the components that can originate the three types of event in Figure 18-4 are the following:

➤ `ActionEvent`

Buttons: `JButton`, `JToggleButton`, `JCheckBox`

Menus: `JMenuItem`, `JMenu`, `JCheckBoxMenuItem`, `JRadioButtonMenuItem`

➤ `ItemEvent`

Buttons: `JButton`, `JToggleButton`, `JCheckBox`

Menus: `JMenuItem`, `JMenu`, `JCheckBoxMenuItem`, `JRadioButtonMenuItem`

➤ `AdjustmentEvent`

Scrollbar: `JScrollbar`

These three types of event are also generated by the old AWT components, but I won't go into these because you'll only use Swing components. Of course, any class you derive from these component classes to define your own customized components can be the source of the event that the base class generates. If you define your own class for buttons—`MyFancyButton`, say—your class has `JButton` as a base class and inherits all of the methods from the `JButton` class, and objects of your class originate events of type `ActionEvent` and `ItemEvent`.

As with low-level events, the most convenient way to handle semantic events is to use listeners, so I delve into the listener interfaces for semantic events next.

Semantic Event Listeners

You have a listener interface defined for each of the three semantic event types that I have introduced so far, and they each declare a single method:

➤ `ActionListener` defines `actionPerformed(ActionEvent e)`.

➤ `ItemListener` defines `itemStateChanged(ItemEvent e)`.

➤ `AdjustmentListener` defines `adjustmentValueChanged(AdjustmentEvent e)`.

All three methods have a `void` return type. Because each of these semantic event listener interfaces declares only one method, there's no need for corresponding adapter classes. The adapter classes for the low-level events were there only because of the number of methods involved in each listener interface. To define your semantic event listener objects, you just define a class that implements the appropriate listener interface. You can try that out by implementing a simple applet now, and then see how you can deal with semantic events in a more complicated context by adding to the Sketcher program later.

SEMANTIC EVENT HANDLING IN APPLETS

Event handling in an applet is exactly the same as in an application, but you ought to see it for yourself. Let's see how you might handle events for buttons in an applet. You can create an applet that uses some buttons that have listeners. To make this example a bit more gripping, I'm throwing in the possibility of monetary gain. That's interesting to almost everybody.

Let's suppose you want to implement an applet that creates a set of random numbers for a lottery entry. The requirement is to generate six different random numbers between 1 and 49. It would also be nice to be able to change a single number if you don't like it, so you add that capability as well. Because the local lottery may not be like this, you implement the applet to make it easily adaptable to fit local requirements.

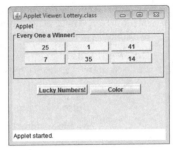

By displaying the six selected numbers on buttons, you can provide for changing one of the choices by processing the action event for that button. Thus, clicking a button provides another number. You also add a couple of control buttons, one to make a new selection for a complete set of lottery numbers, and another just for fun to change the button color. Figure 18-5 shows how the applet looks when running under `appletviewer`.

FIGURE 18-5

You can outline the broad structure of the applet's code as follows:

```java
// Applet to generate lottery entries
import javax.swing.*;
import java.awt.*;
import java.awt.event.*;
import java.util.Random;                                        // For random number generator

public class Lottery extends JApplet {
  // Initialize the applet
  @Override
  public void init() {
    // Create interface components on event dispatch thread...
  }

  // Create User Interface for applet
  public void createGUI() {
    // Set up the lucky numbers buttons...

    // Set up the control buttons...
  }

  // Class defining custom buttons showing lottery selection
  private class Selection extends JButton implements ActionListener {
    // Constructor...
    public Selection(int value) {
      // Create the button showing the value...
    }

    // Handle selection button event
    public void actionPerformed(ActionEvent e) {
      // Change the current selection value to a new selection value
    }
    // Details of the rest of the selection class definition...
  }

  // Class defining a handler for a control button
  private class HandleControlButton implements ActionListener {
    // Constructor...

    // Handle button click
    public void actionPerformed(ActionEvent e) {
      // Handle button click for a particular button...
    }

    // Rest of the inner class definition...
  }

  final static int NUMBER_COUNT = 6;                            // Number of lucky numbers
```

```
final static int MIN_VALUE = 1;                           // Minimum in range
final static int MAX_VALUE = 49;                          // Maximum in range

// Array of possible VALUES
final static int[] VALUES = new int[MAX_VALUE-MIN_VALUE+1];
static {                                                  // Initialize array
  for(int i = 0 ; i<VALUES.length ; ++i)
    VALUES[i] = i + MIN_VALUE;
}

// An array of custom buttons for the selected numbers
private Selection[] luckyNumbers = new Selection[NUMBER_COUNT];

private static Random choice = new Random();              // Random number generator
}
```

Directory "Lottery 1"

How It Works

The applet class is called `Lottery`, and it contains two inner classes: `Selection` and `HandleControlButton`. The `Selection` class provides a custom button that shows a number as its label, the number being passed to the constructor as an argument. You can make an object of the `Selection` class listen for its own action events. As I said at the outset, an event for a selection button changes the label of the button to a different value, so of course, you need to make sure this doesn't duplicate any of the values for the other buttons.

The two control buttons use separate listeners to handle their action events, and the response to an event is quite different for each of them. One control button creates a new set of lucky numbers and the other control button just changes the color of the buttons.

The `NUMBER_COUNT` member of the `Lottery` class sets the number of values that is created. The `MIN_VALUE` and `MAX_VALUE` members specify the range of possible values that lottery numbers can have. The possible values for selections are stored in the `VALUES` array, and this is set up in the static initialization block. The `Lottery` class has an array of `Selection` objects as a data member — you can have arrays of components just like arrays of any other kind of object. Because the `Selection` buttons are all the same, it's very convenient to create them as an array, and having an array of components enables you to set them up in a loop. You also have a `Random` object as a class member that you use to generate random integers. You can now set about filling in the sections of the program that you have roughed out.

Filling in the Details

The generation of `maxCount` random values from the elements in the `values` array is quite independent of everything else here, so you can define a static method in the `Lottery` class to do this:

```
public class Lottery extends JApplet {
  // Generate NUMBER_COUNT random selections from the VALUES array
  private static int[] getNumbers() {
    // Store for the numbers to be returned
    int[] numbers = new int[NUMBER_COUNT];

    int candidate = 0;                              // Stores a candidate selection
    for(int i = 0 ; i < NUMBER_COUNT ; ++i) {       // Loop to find the selections

      search:
      // Loop to find a new selection different from any found so far
      while(true) {
        candidate = VALUES[choice.nextInt(VALUES.length)];
        for(int j = 0 ; j < i ; ++j) {              // Check against existing selections
          if(candidate==numbers[j]) {               // If it is the same
            continue search;                        // get another random selection
```

```
        }
      }
      numbers[i] = candidate;        // Store the selection in numbers array
      break;                         // and go to find the next
    }
  }
  return numbers;                    // Return the selections
}

// Plus the rest of the class definition...
}
```

Directory "Lottery 1"

The `getNumbers()` method returns a reference to an array of values of type `int` that represent the selections—which must all be different, of course. You start the process by creating an array to hold the selections, and a variable, `candidate`, to hold a potential selection for the `values` array. You generate a new selection for each iteration of the outer loop. The process for finding an acceptable selection is quite simple. In the indefinite `while` loop with the label `search`, you choose a random value from the `values` array using the random number generator and then check its value against any selections already stored in the `numbers` array. If it is the same as any of them, the labeled `continue` statement goes to the next iteration of the indefinite `while` loop. This continues until a selection is found that is different from the others. In this way you ensure that you end up with a set of selections that are all different.

Let's implement the `init()` method and the `createGUI()` method for the `Lottery` class next, as these set up the `Selection` buttons and the rest of the applet.

TRY IT OUT Setting Up the Lucky Number Buttons

The `init()` method has to execute only the `createGUI()` method on the event-dispatching thread:

```
// Initialize the applet
@Override
public void init() {
  SwingUtilities.invokeLater(          // Create interface components
    new Runnable() {                   // on the event dispatching thread
      public void run() {
        createGUI();
      }
    });
}
```

Directory "Lottery 1"

In the class outline, you identified two tasks for the `createGUI()` method. The first was setting up the lucky number buttons to be contained in the `luckyNumbers` array.

Here is the code to do that:

```
// Create User Interface for applet
public void creatGUI() {
  // Set up the selection buttons
  Container content = getContentPane();
  content.setLayout(new GridLayout(0,1)); // Set the layout for the applet

  // Set up the panel to hold the lucky number buttons
  JPanel buttonPane = new JPanel();      // Add the pane containing numbers
```

```
          // Let's have a fancy panel border
          buttonPane.setBorder(BorderFactory.createTitledBorder(
                          BorderFactory.createEtchedBorder(Color.cyan,
                                                           Color.blue),
                                                           "Every One a Winner!"));

          int[] choices = getNumbers();              // Get initial set of numbers
          for(int i = 0 ; i < NUMBER_COUNT ; ++i) {
            luckyNumbers[i] = new Selection(choices[i]);

            // Button is it's own listener
            luckyNumbers[i].addActionListener(luckyNumbers[i]);
            buttonPane.add(luckyNumbers[i]);
          }
          content.add(buttonPane);

        // Set up the control buttons...
      }
```

Directory "Lottery 1"

How It Works

The init() method uses the invokeLater() method from the SwingUtilities class to execute the createGUI() method on the event-dispatching thread. This guarantees that there is no possibility of a deadlock arising in the GUI construction process. This is the same technique that you used in the previous example.

The first step in the createGUI() method is to define the layout manager for the applet. To make the layout easier, you use one panel to hold the selection buttons and another to hold the control buttons. You position these panels one above the other by specifying the layout manager for the content pane of the applet as a grid layout with one column. The top panel contains the lucky number buttons and the bottom panel contains the control buttons.

The buttonPane panel that holds the lucky number buttons is of type JPanel, so it has a FlowLayout object as its layout manager by default. A flow layout manager allows components to assume their "natural" or "preferred size," so you set the preferred size for the buttons in the Selection class constructor. You decorate the panel with a border by calling its setBorder() method. The argument is the reference that is returned by the static createTitledBorder() method from the BorderFactory class. The first argument to createTitledBorder() is the border to be used, and the second is the title.

You use an etched border that is returned by another static method in the BorderFactory class. The two arguments to this method are the highlight and shadow colors to be used for the border. A big advantage of using the BorderFactory methods rather than creating border objects from the border class constructors directly is that border objects are shared where possible, so you can use a particular border in various places in your code and only one object is created.

The buttons to display the chosen numbers are of type Selection, and you get to the detail of this inner class in a moment. You call the static getNumbers() method to obtain the first set of random values for the buttons. You then create and store each button in the luckyNumbers array and add it to the panel in the for loop. Because these buttons are going to listen for their own events, you call the addActionListener() method for each button with a reference to the button as the argument. The last step here is to add the buttonPane panel to the content pane for the applet.

You can now add the code for the control buttons to the createGUI() method.

TRY IT OUT Setting Up the Control Buttons

The listeners for each of the control buttons are of the same class type, so the listener object needs some way to determine which button originated a particular event. One way to do this is to use constants as IDs to identify the control buttons and pass the appropriate ID to the class constructor for the listener object.

You can define the constants PICK_LUCKY_NUMBERS and COLOR as fields in the Lottery class for this purpose. The COLOR control button also references a couple of variables of type Color, startColor, and flipColor. You can add the following statements to the Lottery class after the definition of the luckyNumbers array:

```
// An array of custom buttons for the selected numbers
private Selection[] luckyNumbers = new Selection[NUMBER_COUNT];

final public static int PICK_LUCKY_NUMBERS = 1;          // Select button ID
final public static int COLOR = 2;                       // Color button ID

// swap colors
Color flipColor = new Color(Color.YELLOW.getRGB()^Color.RED.getRGB());

Color startColor = Color.YELLOW;                         // start color
```

Directory "Lottery 1"

The startColor field is initialized with the YELLOW color from the Color class. The flipColor field is set to the color that results from EORing the colors YELLOW and RED. Of course, to get a sensible color as a result you must EOR the RGB values that you obtain from the Color objects, not the references to the Color objects! You use the flipColor field to change the color of the buttons.

The code to add the other panel and the control buttons is as follows:

```
// Create User Interface for applet
public void createGUI() {
    // Setting up the selections buttons as previously...

    // Add the pane containing control buttons
    JPanel controlPane = new JPanel(new FlowLayout(FlowLayout.CENTER, 5, 10));

    // Add the two control buttons
    JButton button;                                  // A button variable
    Dimension buttonSize = new Dimension(100,20);    // Button size

    controlPane.add(button = new JButton("Lucky Numbers!"));
    button.setBorder(BorderFactory.createRaisedBevelBorder());
    button.addActionListener(new HandleControlButton(PICK_LUCKY_NUMBERS));
    button.setPreferredSize(buttonSize);

    controlPane.add(button = new JButton("Color"));
    button.setBorder(BorderFactory.createRaisedBevelBorder());
    button.addActionListener(new HandleControlButton(COLOR));
    button.setPreferredSize(buttonSize);

    content.add(controlPane);
}
```

Directory "Lottery 1"

How It Works

You create another JPanel object to hold the control buttons and just to show that you can, you pass a layout manager object to the constructor. It's a FlowLayout manager again, but this time you explicitly specify that the components are to be centered and the horizontal and vertical gaps are to be 5 and 10 pixels, respectively.

You declare the button variable to use as a temporary store for the reference to each button while you set it up. You also define a Dimension object that you use to set a common preferred size for the buttons. The buttons in this case are JButton components, not custom components, so you must set each of them up here with a listener and a border. You add a raised bevel border to each button to make them look like buttons—again using a BorderFactory method.

The listener for each button is an object of the inner class HandleControlButton, and you pass the appropriate button ID to the constructor for reasons that are apparent when you define that class. To set the preferred size for each button object, you call its setPreferredSize() method. The argument is a Dimension object that specifies the width and height. Finally, after adding the two buttons to controlPane, you add that to the content pane for the applet.

The inner class HandleControlButton defines the listener object for each control button, so let's implement that next.

TRY IT OUT   Defining the Control Button Handler Class

You have already determined that the HandleControlButton class constructor accepts an argument that identifies the particular button for which it is listening. This is to enable the actionPerformed() method in the listener class to choose the course of action appropriate to the button that originated the event. Here's the inner class definition to do that:

Available for
download on
Wrox.com

```java
private class HandleControlButton implements ActionListener {
  // Constructor
  public HandleControlButton(int buttonID) {
    this.buttonID = buttonID;                        // Store the button ID
  }

  // Handle button click
  public void actionPerformed(ActionEvent e) {
    switch(buttonID) {
      case PICK_LUCKY_NUMBERS:
        int[] numbers = getNumbers();                // Get maxCount random numbers
        for(int i = 0 ; i < NUMBER_COUNT ; ++i) {
          luckyNumbers[i].setValue(numbers[i]);      // Set the button VALUES
        }
        break;
      case COLOR:
        Color color = new Color(
              flipColor.getRGB()^luckyNumbers[0].getBackground().getRGB());
        for(int i = 0 ; i < NUMBER_COUNT ; ++i)
          luckyNumbers[i].setBackground(color);      // Set the button colors
        break;
    }
  }

  private int buttonID;
}
```

Directory "Lottery 1"

How It Works

The constructor stores its argument value in the buttonID field so each listener object has the ID for the button available. The actionPerformed() method uses the button ID to select the appropriate code to execute for a particular button. Each case in the switch statement corresponds to a different button. You could extend this to enable the class to handle as many different buttons as you want by adding case statements. Because of the way you have implemented the method, each button must have a unique ID associated with it. Of course, this isn't the only way to do this, as you'll see in a moment.

For the PICK_LUCKY_NUMBERS button event, you just call the getNumbers() method to produce a set of numbers and then call the setValue() method for each selection button and pass a number to it. You implement the setValue() method when you define the Selection class in detail.

For the COLOR button event, you create a new color by exclusive ORing (that is, XOR) the RGB value of flipColor with the current button color. Recall from the discussion of the ^ operator (in Chapter 2) that you can use it to exchange two values, and that is what you are doing here. You defined flipColor as the result of exclusive ORing the two colors, Color.YELLOW and Color.RED, together. Exclusive ORing flipColor with either color produces the other color, so you flip from one color to the other automatically for each button by exclusive ORing the background and flipColor. As I said earlier, you must get the RGB value for each color and operate on those—you can't apply the ^ operator to the object references. You then turn the resulting RGB value back into a Color object.

Let's now add the inner class, Selection, which defines the lucky number buttons.

TRY IT OUT Defining the Selection Buttons

Each button needs to store the value shown on the label, so the class needs a data member for this purpose. The class also needs a constructor, a setValue() method to set the value for the button to a new value, and a method to compare the current value for a button to a given value. You need to be able to set the value for a button for two reasons—you need the capability when you set up all six selections in the listener for the control button, and you want to reset the value for a button to change it individually.

The method to compare the value set for a button to a given integer enables you to exclude a number that was already assigned to a button when you are generating a new set of button values. You also need to implement the actionPerformed() method to handle the action events for the button, as the buttons are going to handle their own events. Here's the basic code for the class definition:

Available for download on Wrox.com

```java
private class Selection extends JButton implements ActionListener {
  // Constructor
  public Selection(int value) {
    super(Integer.toString(value));  // Call base constructor and set the label
    this.value = value;                            // Save the value
    setBackground(startColor);
    setBorder(BorderFactory.createRaisedBevelBorder());    // Add button border
    setPreferredSize(new Dimension(80,20));
  }

  // Handle selection button event
  public void actionPerformed(ActionEvent e) {
    // Change this selection to a new selection
    int candidate = 0;
    while(true) {                                  // Loop to find a different selection
      candidate = VALUES[choice.nextInt(VALUES.length)];
      if(!isCurrentSelection(candidate)) {         // If it is different
        break;                                     // end the loop
      }
    }
    setValue(candidate);                           // We have one so set the button value
  }
  // Set the value for the selection
  public void setValue(int value) {
    setText(Integer.toString(value));              // Set value as the button label
    this.value = value;                            // Save the value
  }

  // Check the value for the selection
  boolean hasValue(int possible) {
    return value==possible;                        // Return true if equals current value
  }

  // Check the current choices
  boolean isCurrentSelection(int possible) {
    for(int i = 0 ; i < NUMBER_COUNT ; ++i) {      // For each button
      if(luckyNumbers[i].hasValue(possible)) {     // check against possible
        return true;                               // Return true for any =
      }
    }
  }
```

```
        return false;                      // Otherwise return false
    }

        private int value;                 // Value for the selection button
    }
```

Directory "Lottery 1"

How It Works

The constructor calls the base class constructor to set the initial label for the button. It also stores the value of type int that is passed as an argument. The setValue() method just updates the value for a selection button with the value passed as an argument and changes the button label by calling the setText() method, which is inherited from the base class, JButton. The hasValue() method returns true if the argument value passed to it is equal to the current value stored in the data member value and returns false otherwise.

The actionPerformed() method has a little more meat to it, but the technique is similar to that in the getNumbers() method. To change the selection, you must create a new random value for the button from the numbers in the VALUES array, but excluding all the numbers currently assigned to the six buttons. To do this you just check each candidate against the six existing selections by calling the isCurrentSelection() method and continue choosing a new candidate until you find one that's different.

In the isCurrentSelection() method, you just work through the array of Selection objects, luckyNumbers, comparing each value with the possible argument using the hasValue() method. If any button has the same value as possible, the method returns true; otherwise, it returns false.

You're ready to start generating lottery entries. If you compile the Lottery.java file, you can run the applet using appletviewer. You need an HTML file, of course. The following contents for the file do the job:

```html
<html>
  <head>
  </head>
    <body bgcolor="000000">
      <center>
        <applet
          code = "Lottery.class"
          width  = "300"
          height = "200"
          >
        </applet>
      </center>
    </body>
</html>
```

You can adjust the width and height values to suit your monitor resolution if necessary.

The applet should produce a selection each time you click the left control button. Clicking any of the selection buttons generates an action event that causes a new value to be created for the button. This enables you to replace any selection that you know to be unlucky with an alternative.

NOTE *Undoubtedly, anyone who profits from using this applet will have immense feelings of gratitude and indebtedness towards the author, who will not be offended in the slightest by any offers of a portion of that success, however large!*

Alternative Event-Handling Approaches

As I indicated in the discussion, there are various approaches to implementing listeners. Let's look at a couple of other ways in which you could have dealt with the control button events.

Instead of passing a constant to the listener class constructor to identify which button was selected, you could have exploited the fact that the event object has a method, getSource(), that returns a reference to the object that is the source of the event. To make use of this, references to both button objects would need to be available to the actionPerformed() method to enable you to determine which button was clicked. You could easily arrange for this to be the case by adding a couple of fields to the Lottery class:

```
JButton pickButton = new JButton("Lucky Numbers!");
JButton colorButton = new JButton("Color");
```

The inner class could then be defined as follows:

```
class HandleControlButton implements ActionListener {
  // Handle button click
  public void actionPerformed(ActionEvent e) {
    Object source = e.getSource();                      // Get source object reference

    if(source == pickButton) {                          // Is it the pick button?
        int[] numbers = getNumbers();                   // Get maxCount random numbers
        for(int i = 0 ; i < NUMBER_COUNT ; ++i) {
          luckyNumbers[i].setValue(numbers[i]);         // Set the button values
        }
    } else if(source == colorButton) {                  // Is it the color button?
      Color color = new Color(
              flipColor.getRGB()^luckyNumbers[0].getBackground().getRGB());
      for(int i = 0 ; i < NUMBER_COUNT ; ++i) {
        luckyNumbers[i].setBackground(color);           // Set the button colors
      }
    }
  }
}
```

You no longer need to define a constructor, as the default is sufficient. The actionPerformed() method now decides what to do by comparing the reference returned by the getSource() method for the event object with the two button references in the JButton fields of the Lottery class. With the previous version of the listener class, you stored the ID as a data member, so a separate listener object was needed for each button. In this case there are no data members in the listener class, so you can use one listener object for both buttons. This is clearly a better way of handling the button events that the previous approach.

The code to add these buttons in the createGUI() method would then be the following:

```
// Add the two control buttons
Dimension buttonSize = new Dimension(100,20);
pickButton.setPreferredSize(buttonSize);
pickButton.setBorder(BorderFactory.createRaisedBevelBorder());

colorButton.setPreferredSize(buttonSize);
colorButton.setBorder(BorderFactory.createRaisedBevelBorder());

HandleControlButton controlHandler = new HandleControlButton();
pickButton.addActionListener(controlHandler);
colorButton.addActionListener(controlHandler);

controlPane.add(pickButton);
controlPane.add(colorButton);
content.add(controlPane);
```

The only fundamental difference here is that you use one listener object for both buttons.

There is another possible way to implement listeners for these buttons. You could define a separate class for each listener—this would not be unreasonable, as the actions to be performed in response to the semantic events for each button are quite different. You could use anonymous classes in this case—as I discussed in Chapter 6. You could do this by adding the listeners for the button objects in the createGUI() method like this:

```
// Add the two control buttons
Dimension buttonSize = new Dimension(100,20);
pickButton.setPreferredSize(buttonSize);
pickButton.setBorder(BorderFactory.createRaisedBevelBorder());

colorButton.setPreferredSize(buttonSize);
colorButton.setBorder(BorderFactory.createRaisedBevelBorder());

pickButton.addActionListener(
    new ActionListener() {
      public void actionPerformed(ActionEvent e) {
        int[] numbers = getNumbers();
        for(int i = 0 ; i < NUMBER_COUNT ; ++i) {
          luckyNumbers[i].setValue(numbers[i]);
        }
      }
    });

colorButton.addActionListener(
    new ActionListener() {
      public void actionPerformed(ActionEvent e) {
        Color color = new Color(
                flipColor.getRGB()^luckyNumbers[0].getBackground().getRGB());
        for(int i = 0 ; i < NUMBER_COUNT ; ++i) {
          luckyNumbers[i].setBackground(color);
        }
      }
    });

controlPane.add(pickButton);
controlPane.add(colorButton);
content.add(controlPane);
```

Now the two listeners are defined by anonymous classes, and the implementation of the `actionPerformed()` method in each just takes care of the particular button for which it is listening. This is a very common technique when the action to be performed in response to an event is simple, as it is in this case.

Handling Low-Level and Semantic Events

I said earlier in this chapter that a component generates both low-level and semantic events, and you could handle both if you want. I can demonstrate this quite easily with a small extension to the `Lottery` applet. Suppose you want to change the cursor to a hand cursor when it is over one of the selection buttons. This would be a good cue that you can select these buttons individually. You can do this by adding a mouse listener for each button.

TRY IT OUT   A Mouse Listener for the Selection Buttons

There are many ways in which you could define the listener class. Here you define it as a separate class called `MouseHandler`:

Available for download on Wrox.com

```
// Mouse event handler for a selection button
import java.awt.Cursor;
import java.awt.event.*;

class MouseHandler extends MouseAdapter {
  Cursor handCursor = new Cursor(Cursor.HAND_CURSOR);
  Cursor defaultCursor = new Cursor(Cursor.DEFAULT_CURSOR);

  // Handle mouse entering the selection button
  @Override
  public void mouseEntered(MouseEvent e) {
    e.getComponent().setCursor(handCursor);              // Switch to hand cursor
  }
```

```
// Handle mouse exiting the selection button
@Override
public void mouseExited(MouseEvent e) {
    e.getComponent().setCursor(defaultCursor);        // Change to default cursor
    }
}
```

Directory "Lottery 2 with mouse listener"

All you need to do to expedite this is to add a mouse listener for each of the six selection buttons. You need only one listener object and after creating this you only need to change the loop in the createGUI() method for the applet to add the mouse listener:

Available for download on Wrox.com

```
int[] choices = getNumbers();                         // Get initial set of numbers
MouseHandler mouseHandler = new MouseHandler();       // Create the listener
for(int i = 0 ; i < NUMBER_COUNT ; ++i) {
    luckyNumbers[i] = new Selection(choices[i]);

    // Button is it's own listener
    luckyNumbers[i].addActionListener(luckyNumbers[i]);
    luckyNumbers[i].addMouseListener(mouseHandler);
    buttonPane.add(luckyNumbers[i]);
}
```

Directory "Lottery 2 with mouse listener"

How It Works

The mouseEntered() method is called when the mouse enters the area of the component with which the listener is registered, and the method then changes the cursor for the component to a hand cursor. When the cursor is moved out of the area occupied by the component, the mouseExited() method is called, which restores the default cursor.

Just two extra statements in createGUI() create the listener object and then add it for each selection button within the loop. If you recompile the applet and run it again, a hand cursor should appear whenever the mouse is over the selection buttons. Of course, you are not limited to just changing the cursor in the event handler. You could highlight the button by changing its color for instance. You could apply the same technique for any kind of component where the mouse is the source of actions for it.

SEMANTIC EVENT LISTENERS IN AN APPLICATION

The Sketcher program is an obvious candidate for implementing semantic event listeners to support the operation of the menu bar in the SketcherFrame class. When you click on an item in one of the drop-down menus, a semantic event is generated that you can listen for and then use to determine the appropriate program action.

Listening to Menu Items

Let's start with the Elements menu. This is concerned with identifying the type of graphic element to be drawn next, and the color in which it will be drawn. You won't be drawing them for a while, but you can put in the infrastructure to set the type and color for an element without worrying about how it will actually be created and drawn.

To identify the type of element, you can define constants that act as IDs for the four types of element you have provided for in the menu so far. This helps with the operation of the listeners for the menu item as well as provides a way to identify a particular type of element. Because you'll accumulate quite a number of application-wide constants, it is convenient to define them as static fields in a class from which they can be imported statically. To be able to import the static fields, the class must be in a named package, so let's set that up. To put the class in a package with the name Constants, you need to set up a directory with this name at a suitable location on your disk, and then use the -classpath option when you compile the class in the Constants package to identify the path to the Constants directory. Here's the initial definition, including constants to define line, rectangle, circle, and curve elements:

```
// Defines application wide constants
package Constants;

public class SketcherConstants {
  // Element type definitions
  public final static int LINE      = 101;
  public final static int RECTANGLE = 102;
  public final static int CIRCLE    = 103;
  public final static int CURVE     = 104;

  // Initial conditions
  public final static int DEFAULT_ELEMENT_TYPE = LINE;
}
```

Save this as SketcherConstants.java in the Constants directory you have created. Each element type ID in the class is an integer constant with a unique value, and you can obviously extend the variety of element types if necessary. Of course, you could also have defined the element IDs as enumeration constants, but because you will be adding other types of constants to Sketcher later, you would have more than one class involved in the definition of constants for Sketcher.

You have defined the DEFAULT_ELEMENT_TYPE constant to specify the initial element type to apply when the Sketcher application starts. You could do the same thing for the Color submenu and supply a constant that specifies the default initial element color:

Available for download on Wrox.com

```
// Defines application wide constants
package Constants;
import java.awt.Color;

public class SketcherConstants {
  // Element type definitions
  public final static int LINE      = 101;
  public final static int RECTANGLE = 102;
  public final static int CIRCLE    = 103;
  public final static int CURVE     = 104;

  // Initial conditions
  public final static int DEFAULT_ELEMENT_TYPE = LINE;
  public final static Color DEFAULT_ELEMENT_COLOR = Color.BLUE;
}
```

Directory "Sketcher 4 with element type listeners"

You have defined the DEFAULT_ELEMENT_COLOR field as type Color, so you have added an import statement for the Color class name. When you want to change the default startup color or element type, you just need to change the values of the constants in the SketcherConstants class. This automatically takes care of setting things up—as long as you implement the program code appropriately.

You can add fields to the SketcherFrame class to store the current element type and color because these are application-wide values and are not specific to a view:

```
private Color elementColor = DEFAULT_ELEMENT_COLOR;   // Current element color
private int elementType = DEFAULT_ELEMENT_TYPE;        // Current element type
```

You can now use these to ensure that the menu items are checked appropriately when the application starts. Of course, for the class to compile, you also want the names of the constants from the SketcherConstants class imported into the `SketcherFrame` class, so make the following changes to the `SketcherFrame` class definition:

```
import javax.swing.*;
import static java.awt.event.InputEvent.*;      // For modifier constants
import java.awt.Color;
import static java.awt.Color.*;
import static Constants.SketcherConstants.*;

public class SketcherFrame extends JFrame {
  // Constructor
  public SketcherFrame(String title) {
    setTitle(title);                             // Set the window title
    setJMenuBar(menuBar);                        // Add the menu bar to the window
    setDefaultCloseOperation(EXIT_ON_CLOSE);

    // Code to create the File menu...

    // Construct the Elements drop-down menu
    elementMenu.add(lineItem = new JRadioButtonMenuItem(
                                      "Line", elementType==LINE));
    elementMenu.add(rectangleItem = new JRadioButtonMenuItem(
                               "Rectangle", elementType==RECTANGLE));
    elementMenu.add(circleItem = new JRadioButtonMenuItem(
                                    "Circle", elementType==CIRCLE));
    elementMenu.add(curveItem = new JRadioButtonMenuItem(
                                     "Curve", elementType==CURVE));
    ButtonGroup types = new ButtonGroup();

    // ...plus the rest of the code for grouping the element types as before...
    // ...and the code for accelerators for the element types as before...

    elementMenu.addSeparator();

    elementMenu.add(colorMenu);                          // Add the sub-menu
    colorMenu.add(redItem = new JCheckBoxMenuItem(
                                  "Red", elementColor.equals(RED)));
    colorMenu.add(yellowItem = new JCheckBoxMenuItem(
                               "Yellow", elementColor.equals(YELLOW)));
    colorMenu.add(greenItem = new JCheckBoxMenuItem(
                                "Green", elementColor.equals(GREEN)));
    colorMenu.add(blueItem = new JCheckBoxMenuItem(
                                 "Blue", elementColor.equals(BLUE)));

    // Add element color accelerators...
    // ... plus the rest of the constructor as before...
  }

  // ...plus the rest of the class as before...
  private Color elementColor = DEFAULT_ELEMENT_COLOR;   // Current element color
  private int elementType = DEFAULT_ELEMENT_TYPE;       // Current element type
}
```

Directory "Sketcher 4 with element type listeners"

You have imported static constants from the `Color` class, so you can use the names of the standard color objects that the class defines without qualifying them. When you construct the element objects, you use the `elementType` and `elementColor` members to set the state of each menu item. Only the element type menu item corresponding to the default type set in `elementType` is checked because that's the only comparison that produces a true result as an argument to the `JRadioButtonMenuItem` constructor. The mechanism is the same for the color menu items, but note that you use the `equals()` method defined in the `Color` class for a valid comparison of `Color` objects. You might just get away with using `==` because you are using only constant `Color` values that are defined in the class, but as soon as you use a color that is not one of these, this would no longer work. Of course, you have to use `==` for the element type items because the IDs are of type `int`.

At this point it would be a good idea to recompile Sketcher to make sure everything is as it should be. Because you now have your own package containing the `SketcherConstants` class definition, you must use the `-classpath` option to tell the compiler where to find it. Assuming the `Constants` directory is a subdirectory of the `C:/Packages` directory, for example, and the current directory is the one containing `Sketcher.java` and `SketcherFrame.java`, you can use the following command to compile Sketcher:

```
javac -classpath ".;C:/Packages" Sketcher.java
```

The `-classpath` option defines two paths: the current directory, which is specified by the period, and `C:/Packages`, which is the path to the `Constants` directory that contains the `SketcherConstants.java` source file. This command should compile everything, including your package.

Having got that sorted out, you can have a go at implementing the listeners for the `Elements` menu, starting with the type menu items.

TRY IT OUT   Handling Events for the Element Type Menu

You add an inner class to `SketcherFrame` that defines listeners for the menu items specifying the element type. This class implements the `ActionListener` interface because you want to respond to actions on these menu items. Add the following definition as an inner class to `SketcherFrame`:

Available for download on Wrox.com

```java
// Handles element type menu items
class TypeListener implements ActionListener {
  // Constructor
  TypeListener(int type) {
    this.type = type;
  }

  // Sets the element type
  public void actionPerformed(ActionEvent e) {
    elementType = type;
  }

  private int type;                       // Store the type for the menu
}
```

Directory "Sketcher 4 with element type listeners"

Now you can use objects of this class as listeners for the menu items. Add the following code to the `SketcherFrame` constructor, after the code that sets up the type menu items for the `Elements` menu just before the last two lines of the constructor:

Available for download on Wrox.com

```java
// Add type menu item listeners
lineItem.addActionListener(new TypeListener(LINE));
rectangleItem.addActionListener(new TypeListener(RECTANGLE));
circleItem.addActionListener(new TypeListener(CIRCLE));
curveItem.addActionListener(new TypeListener(CURVE));

menuBar.add(fileMenu);                         // Add the file menu
menuBar.add(elementMenu);                      // Add the element menu
}
```

Directory "Sketcher 4 with element type listeners"

It is also necessary to add an `import` statement to the source file for the `SketcherFrame` class for `ActionListener` and `ActionEvent`:

```
import java.awt.event.*;
```

Recompile Sketcher and see how it looks.

How It Works

The application window won't look any different, as the listeners just set the current element type in the `SketcherFrame` object. The listener class is remarkably simple. Each listener object stores the type corresponding to the menu item that is passed as the constructor argument. When an event occurs, the `actionPerformed()` method just stores the type in the listener object in the `elementType` member of the `SketcherFrame` object.

Now you can do the same for the color menu items.

TRY IT OUT | **Implementing Color Menu Item Listeners**

You define another inner class to `SketcherFrame` that defines listeners for the `Color` menu items:

```
// Handles color menu items
class ColorListener implements ActionListener {
  public ColorListener(Color color) {
    this.color = color;
  }

  public void actionPerformed(ActionEvent e) {
    elementColor = color;
  }

  private Color color;
}
```

Directory "Sketcher 5 with element color listeners"

You just need to create listener objects and add them to the color menu items. Add the following code at the end of the `SketcherFrame` constructor after the code that sets up the `Color` submenu:

```
// Add color menu item listeners
redItem.addActionListener(new ColorListener(RED));
yellowItem.addActionListener(new ColorListener(YELLOW));
greenItem.addActionListener(new ColorListener(GREEN));
blueItem.addActionListener(new ColorListener(BLUE));

  menuBar.add(fileMenu);                    // Add the file menu
  menuBar.add(elementMenu);                 // Add the element menu
}
```

Directory "Sketcher 5 with element color listeners"

This adds a listener object for each menu item in the `Color` menu. The listeners don't do anything yet, but they will, eventually. You could add an output statement to the `actionPerformed()` method if you wanted confirmation of when it is executed:

```
System.out.println("Color event " + e.toString());
```

How It Works

The `ColorListener` class works in the same way as the `TypeListener` class. Each class object stores an identifier for the menu item for which it is listening—in this case a `Color` object corresponding to the color the menu item sets up. The `actionPerformed()` method just stores the `Color` object from the listener object in the `elementColor` member of the `SketcherFrame` object.

Of course, the menu doesn't quite work as it should. The `Color` menu item check marks are not being set correctly, as you can see in Figure 18-6. You want an exclusive check, as with the radio buttons; having more than one color checked at one time doesn't make sense.

FIGURE 18-6

Fixing the Color Menu Check Marks

One way to deal with the problem is to make the listener object for a color menu item set the check marks for all the menu items. You could code this in the `ColorListener` inner class to `SketcherFrame`:

```
class ColorListener implements ActionListener {
  public void actionPerformed(ActionEvent e) {
    elementColor = color;
    // Set the checks for all menu items
    redItem.setState(color.equals(RED));
    greenItem.setState(color.equals(GREEN));
    blueItem.setState(color.equals(BLUE));
    yellowItem.setState(color.equals(YELLOW));
  }
  // Rest of the class as before...
}
```

This calls the `setState()` method for each menu item. If the argument to the method is `true`, the check mark is set, and if it is `false`, it isn't. Clearly this sets the check mark only for the item that corresponds to the color referenced by `color`. This is quite straightforward, but there is a better way.

A `ButtonGroup` object works with `JCheckBoxMenuItem` objects because they have `AbstractButton` as a base class. Therefore, you could add these menu items to their own button group in the `SketcherFrame` constructor, and it is all taken care of for you. The `ButtonGroup` object tracks the state of all of the buttons in the group. When any button is turned on, all the others are turned off, so only one button in the group can be on at one time. Add the following code—it could go anywhere after the items have been created but place it following the code that adds the items to the `Color` menu for consistency with the element type code:

Available for download on Wrox.com

```
ButtonGroup colors = new ButtonGroup();      // Color menu items button group
colors.add(redItem);
colors.add(yellowItem);
colors.add(greenItem);
colors.add(blueItem);
```

Directory "Sketcher 5 with element color listeners"

Now the `Color` menu check marks are set automatically, so you can forget about them.

USING ACTIONS

One difficulty with the code that you have added to support the menus is that it is very menu specific. What I mean by this is that if you are going to do a proper job on the Sketcher application, you undoubtedly want it to have a toolbar. The toolbar will surely have a whole bunch of buttons that perform exactly the same actions as the menu items you have just implemented, so you'll be in the business of doing the same thing all over again in the toolbar context. Of course, the only reason I brought it up, as I'm sure you've anticipated, is that there is another way of working with menus, and that is to use an `Action` object.

An `Action` object is a bit of a strange beast. It can be quite hard to understand at first, so I'm taking it slowly. First of all let's look at what is meant by an "action" here, as it is a precise term in this context. An action is an object of any class that implements the `javax.swing.Action` interface. This interface declares methods that operate on an `Action` object—for example, storing properties relating to the action, enabling it, and disabling it. The `Action` interface happens to extend the `ActionListener` interface, so an `Action` object is a listener as well as an action. Now that you know an `Action` object can get and set properties and is also a listener, how does that help us in implementing the Sketcher GUI?

One answer is in the last capability of an `Action` object. Some Swing components, including those of type `JMenu` and `JToolBar`, have an `add()` method that accepts an argument of type `Action`. When you add an `Action` object to these components using the `add()` method, the method creates a component from the `Action` object that is automatically of the right type. If you add an `Action` object to a `JMenu` object, a `JMenuItem` is created and returned by the `add()` method. On the other hand, when you add exactly the same `Action` object to a `JToolBar` object, an object of type `JButton` is created and returned. This means that you can add the very same `Action` object to both a menu and a toolbar, and because the `Action` object is its own listener, you automatically get both the menu item and the toolbar button supported by the same action. Clever, eh?

There's more. You can construct any type of menu item, including those of type `JCheckBoxMenuItem` and `JRadioButtonMenuItem`, from `Action` objects, so if you want to have these on your menus, you can. You just add the menu items you create from your `Action` objects to a menu in the way you have seen. First, you need to look at the `Action` interface.

The Action Interface

In general, *properties* are items of information that relate to a particular object and are stored as part of the object. Properties are often stored in a map, where a key identifies a particular property, and the value corresponding to that property can be stored in association with the key. The `Properties` class that is defined in the `java.util` package does exactly that. The `Action` interface has provision for storing several basic standard properties that relate to an `Action` object. These properties are accessed through keys of type `String`. The identifiers for the keys that are defined in the `Action` interface and the corresponding values are the following:

- ➤ `NAME`: A `String` object that is the label for a menu item or a toolbar button.
- ➤ `SMALL_ICON`: A `javax.Swing.Icon` reference to a small icon for a menu item (typically a `javax.Swing.ImageIcon` object).
- ➤ `LARGE_ICON_KEY`: An `Icon` reference to a large icon for a toolbar button (typically an `ImageIcon` object).
- ➤ `SHORT_DESCRIPTION`: A `String` object that is a tooltip.
- ➤ `LONG_DESCRIPTION`: A `String` object that is a context-sensitive help message.
- ➤ `ACCELERATOR_KEY`: A `javax.swing.KeyStroke` object that represents a key combination is the accelerator for the action.

➤ DISPLAYED_MNEMONIC_INDEX_KEY: An Integer object indicating where in the NAME property value the decoration (which is an underline) for a mnemonic should be rendered. You use this to create a visual cue to the character for the accelerator.

➤ MNEMONIC_KEY: An Integer that corresponds to a KeyEvent key code.

➤ SELECTED_KEY: A Boolean object that records the selected or unselected state.

➤ ACTION_COMMAND_KEY: A String object that is the command string for the action.

Just so you are aware of them I have included the complete set here, but you will only use a few of them in Sketcher. You are not obliged to provide for all of these properties in your action classes, but the Action interface provides the framework for it. There is another key defined in the interface with the name DEFAULT, but this is not used currently.

Action Methods

The Action interface also declares the following methods:

➤ void putValue(String key,Object value): Stores the object value associated with the key constant key in the action object. To store the name of an action within a class method, you might write:

```
putValue(NAME, "Save All");
```

This stores the string "Save All" as the object corresponding to the standard key NAME. A menu item created from the action object displays "Save All" as the menu item text.

➤ Object getValue(String key): This retrieves the object from the map corresponding to the key key. To retrieve a small icon from an action object, action, you can write:

```
ImageIcon lineIcon = (ImageIcon)(action.getValue(SMALL_ICON));
```

➤ boolean isEnabled(): This returns true if the action object is enabled and false otherwise.

➤ void setEnabled(boolean state): This sets the Action object as enabled if state is true and disabled if it is false. This operates on both the toolbar button and the menu item if they have been created using the same Action object.

➤ void addPropertyChangeListener(PropertyChangeListener listener): This adds the listener passed as an argument, which listens for changes to properties such as the enabled state of the object. This is used by a container for an Action object to track property changes.

➤ void removePropertyChangeListener(PropertyChangeListener listener): This removes the listener passed as an argument. This is also for use by a Container object.

Of course, because the Action interface extends the ActionListener interface, it also incorporates the ActionPerformed() method that you are already familiar with. So far, all you seem to have gained with this interface is a license to do a lot of work in implementing it, but it's not as bad as that. The javax.swing package defines the AbstractAction class that already implements the Action interface. If you extend this class to create your own action class, you get a basic infrastructure for free, including the ability to handle events. Let's try it out in the context of Sketcher.

Using Actions as Menu Items

Using Action objects involves major surgery on the SketcherFrame class. Although you throw away all those fancy varieties of menu items you spent so much time putting together, at least you know how they work now, and you end up with much less code after re-engineering the class, as you later see. As the saying goes, you've got to crack a few eggs to make a soufflé.

You go back nearly to square one and reconstruct the class definition. First you delete a lot of code from the existing class definition. Comments show where you add code to re-implement the menus using actions. Get your definition of the SketcherFrame class to the following state:

```
// Frame for the Sketcher application
import javax.swing.*;
import java.awt.event.*;
import java.awt.Color;

import static java.awt.event.InputEvent.*;
import static java.awt.AWTEvent.*;
import static java.awt.Color.*;
import static Constants.SketcherConstants.*;

public class SketcherFrame extends JFrame {
  // Constructor
  public SketcherFrame(String title) {
    setTitle(title);                               // Set the window title
    setJMenuBar(menuBar);                          // Add the menu bar to the window
    setDefaultCloseOperation(EXIT_ON_CLOSE);       // Default is exit the application

    createFileMenu();                              // Create the File menu
    createElementMenu();                           // Create the element menu
    createColorMenu();                             // Create the color menu
  }

  // You will add helper methods that create Action objects here...

  // You will add helper methods that create the menus here...

  // You will add inner classes that define action objects here...

  // You will add action objects as members here...

  private JMenuBar menuBar = new JMenuBar();       // Window menu bar
  // You will add members to store menubar menus here...
  private Color elementColor = DEFAULT_ELEMENT_COLOR;  // Current element color
  private int elementType = DEFAULT_ELEMENT_TYPE;      // Current element type
}
```

Directory "Sketcher 6 using Action objects"

In the previous version of Sketcher, Color was a submenu of Elements. This was useful in demonstrating how you create a submenu, but color has no particular connection to the type of element, so perhaps it would be better with Color as an independent menu item on the menu bar in the new version. The three method calls in the constructor create the menus.

You have restored the statement to set the default close operation as EXIT_ON_CLOSE, so you won't need to call dispose() and exit() in the window event handler. Now would be a good time to delete the statements from the windowClosing() method in the inner WindowHandler class to the Sketcher class. The old inner classes in SketcherFrame have been deleted, as well as the fields storing references to menu items. All the code to create the menu items has been wiped as well, along with the code that added the listeners. You are ready to begin reconstruction. You *can* rebuild it! Stronger! Faster! Invincible!

Defining Action Classes

You need three inner classes defining actions: one for the File menu items, another for the element type menu items, and the third for element colors. You derive each of these classes from the javax.swing. AbstractAction class that already implements the Action interface. The AbstractAction class has three constructors. The no-arg constructor creates an object with a default name and icon. You can supply just a name argument as type String, and you get a default icon. Finally you can supply both a name and an icon as type Icon.

The AbstractAction class definition already provides the mechanism for storing action properties. For the last two constructors, the argument values are stored using the standard keys in the Action interface that I described earlier. For the moment, you use the constructor with just a name argument and leave icons until a little later.

Actions for File Menu Items

You can define the `FileAction` inner class as follows:

```
// Inner class defining Action objects for File menu items
class FileAction extends AbstractAction {
  // Create action with a name
  FileAction(String name) {
    super(name);
  }

  // Create action with a name and accelerator
  FileAction(String name, char ch, int modifiers) {
    super(name);
    putValue(ACCELERATOR_KEY, KeyStroke.getKeyStroke(ch, modifiers));

    // Now find the character to underline
    int index = name.toUpperCase().indexOf(ch);
    if(index != -1) {
      putValue(DISPLAYED_MNEMONIC_INDEX_KEY, index);
    }
  }

  // Event handler
  public void actionPerformed(ActionEvent e) {
    // You will add action code here eventually...
  }
}
```

Directory "Sketcher 6 using Action objects"

You have two constructors. The first just stores the name for the action as the NAME property by calling the base class constructor. The second stores the name by calling the first constructor and then creates and stores the accelerator keystroke in the Action object as the value for the ACCELERATOR_KEY property. You create the KeyStroke object from the ch and modifiers arguments. The character, ch, must always be an uppercase letter because lowercase letters are used to identify non-alphabetic keys in a keystroke. You find the index of the character in the name that corresponds to ch and use that as the value for the DISPLAYED_MNEMONIC_INDEX_KEY property. This causes the character at that index position in the name to be underlined.

Because the class is an action listener, you have implemented the `actionPerformed()` method in it. You don't yet know what you are going to do with the File menu item actions, so you can leave it open for now and let the `actionPerformed()` method do nothing. Alternatively you could add a statement to output something so you know when it is called. Add the `FileAction` class as an inner class to `SketcherFrame` where the comment indicated.

The `SketcherFrame` class needs a data member of type `FileAction` for each menu item that you intend to add to the File menu, so add the following statement to the `SketcherFrame` class definition where the comment indicated:

```
// File actions
private FileAction newAction, openAction, closeAction,
                   saveAction, saveAsAction, printAction, exitAction;
private FileAction[] fileActions;            // File actions as an array
```

Directory "Sketcher 6 using Action objects"

Note the additional `exitAction` member for a menu item to exit Sketcher. The `fileActions` array allows you to process all the menu actions in the in a loop when necessary.

Actions for Elements Menu Items

You can define an inner class for the Elements menu next:

```
// Inner class defining Action objects for Element type menu items
class TypeAction extends AbstractAction {
  // Create action with just a name property
  TypeAction(String name, int typeID) {
    super(name);
    this.typeID = typeID;
  }

  // Create action with a name and an accelerator
  private TypeAction(String name,int typeID, char ch, int modifiers) {
    this(name, typeID);
    putValue(ACCELERATOR_KEY, KeyStroke.getKeyStroke(ch, modifiers));

    // Now find the character to underline
    int index = name.toUpperCase().indexOf(ch);
    if(index != -1) {
      putValue(DISPLAYED_MNEMONIC_INDEX_KEY, index);
    }
  }

  public void actionPerformed(ActionEvent e) {
    elementType = typeID;
  }

  private int typeID;
}
```

Directory "Sketcher 6 using Action objects"

Add this definition to the `SketcherFrame` class following the previous inner class. In this class you retain the `typeID` to identify the element type. This makes the listener operation simple and fast. Because each object corresponds to a particular element type, there is no need for any testing of the event in the `actionPerformed()` method—you just store the `typeID` as the new element type in the `elementType` member of the `SketcherFrame` class.

Add the following statement to the `SketcherFrame` class to define members that store references to `TypeAction` objects, following the statement that defines the members storing `FileAction` references:

```
// Element type actions
private TypeAction lineAction, rectangleAction, circleAction, curveAction;
private TypeAction[] typeActions;            // Type actions as an array
```

Directory "Sketcher 6 using Action objects"

You have a convenience array here for `Action` objects, too.

Actions for Color Menu Items

The third inner class to `SketcherFrame` defining `Action` objects for the Color menu items is just as simple:

```
// Handles color menu items
class ColorAction  extends AbstractAction {
  // Create an action with a name and a color
  public ColorAction(String name, Color color) {
    super(name);
    this.color = color;
```

```
  }

  // Create an action with a name, a color, and an accelerator
  public ColorAction(String name, Color color, char ch, int modifiers) {
    this(name, color);
    putValue(ACCELERATOR_KEY, KeyStroke.getKeyStroke(ch, modifiers));

    // Now find the character to underline
    int index = name.toUpperCase().indexOf(ch);
    if(index != -1) {
      putValue(DISPLAYED_MNEMONIC_INDEX_KEY, index);
    }
  }

  public void actionPerformed(ActionEvent e) {
    elementColor = color;

    // This is temporary - just to show it works...
    getContentPane().setBackground(color);
  }

  private Color color;
}
```

Directory "Sketcher 6 using Action objects"

You use the idea that you used in the listener class for the `Color` menu items in the previous implementation of `SketcherFrame` to show when it works. You have a statement in the `actionPerformed()` method that sets the background color of the content pane to the element color. When you click on a color menu item, the background color of the content pane changes. You remove this code later.

Add the following statement to the `SketcherFrame` class for the color action members, following the `TypeAction` fields:

Available for
download on
Wrox.com

```
// Element color actions
  private ColorAction redAction, greenAction, blueAction, yellowAction;
  private ColorAction[] colorActions;                 // Color actions as an array
```

Directory "Sketcher 6 using Action objects"

You can try these action classes out now to reconstruct the menus in Sketcher.

TRY IT OUT   Actions in Action

To break up the code into more manageable chunks, you can add three helper methods to the `SketcherFrame` class to initialize the `Action` objects for the menu items. Here's how you can create the File menu actions:

Available for
download on
Wrox.com

```
private void createFileMenuActions() {
    newAction = new FileAction("New", 'N', CTRL_DOWN_MASK);
    openAction = new FileAction("Open", 'O', CTRL_DOWN_MASK);
    closeAction = new FileAction("Close");
    saveAction = new FileAction("Save", 'S', CTRL_DOWN_MASK);
    saveAsAction = new FileAction("Save As...");
    printAction = new FileAction("Print", 'P', CTRL_DOWN_MASK);
    exitAction = new FileAction("Exit", 'X', CTRL_DOWN_MASK);

    // Initialize the array
    FileAction[] actions = {openAction, closeAction, saveAction,
                            saveAsAction, printAction, exitAction};
    fileActions = actions;
  }
```

Directory "Sketcher 6 using Action objects"

Each `FileAction` object has a `NAME` field value. Only the actions for the Close and Save As menu items do not have accelerator keys. You initialize the `fileActions` array so it holds all the file action references.

The helper method in the `SketcherFrame` class to create the actions for the type menu items in the Elements menu looks like this:

```
private void createElementTypeActions() {
    lineAction = new TypeAction("Line", LINE, 'L', CTRL_DOWN_MASK);
    rectangleAction = new TypeAction("Rectangle", RECTANGLE, 'R', CTRL_DOWN_MASK);
    circleAction =  new TypeAction("Circle", CIRCLE,'C', CTRL_DOWN_MASK);
    curveAction = new TypeAction("Curve", CURVE,'U', CTRL_DOWN_MASK);

    // Initialize the array
    TypeAction[] actions = {lineAction, rectangleAction, circleAction, curveAction};
    typeActions = actions;
}
```

Directory "Sketcher 6 using Action objects"

This is very similar to the previous method. Each of the actions has a name value and the accelerator key combination.

Here the code for the helper method to create actions for the Color menu:

```
private void createElementColorActions() {
    redAction = new ColorAction("Red", RED, 'R', CTRL_DOWN_MASK|ALT_DOWN_MASK);
    yellowAction = new ColorAction(
                        "Yellow", YELLOW, 'Y', CTRL_DOWN_MASK|ALT_DOWN_MASK);
    greenAction = new ColorAction(
                        "Green", GREEN, 'G', CTRL_DOWN_MASK|ALT_DOWN_MASK);
    blueAction = new ColorAction(
                        "Blue", BLUE, 'B', CTRL_DOWN_MASK|ALT_DOWN_MASK);

    // Initialize the array
    ColorAction[] actions = {redAction, greenAction, blueAction, yellowAction};
    colorActions = actions;
}
```

Directory "Sketcher 6 using Action objects"

I used a combination of modifiers, the Ctrl and Alt keys, for the accelerators for the Color menu item actions. This enables me to retain R, G, and B as the letters in the key combinations to set the corresponding colors.

Now you can implement the methods that create the menus, starting with the `createFileMenu()` method:

```
private void createFileMenu() {
    JMenu fileMenu = new JMenu("File");        // Create File menu
    fileMenu.setMnemonic('F');                 // Create shortcut
    createFileMenuActions();                   // Create Actions for File menu items

    // Construct the file drop-down menu
    fileMenu.add(newAction);                   // New Sketch menu item
    fileMenu.add(openAction);                  // Open sketch menu item
    fileMenu.add(closeAction);                 // Close sketch menu item
    fileMenu.addSeparator();                   // Add separator
    fileMenu.add(saveAction);                  // Save sketch to file
    fileMenu.add(saveAsAction);                // Save As menu item
    fileMenu.addSeparator();                   // Add separator
    fileMenu.add(printAction);                 // Print sketch menu item
    fileMenu.addSeparator();                   // Add separator
    fileMenu.add(exitAction);                  // Print sketch menu item
    menuBar.add(fileMenu);                     // Add the file menu
}
```

Directory "Sketcher 6 using Action objects"

You can't use the array of file actions very comfortably here because of the separators. First you create the File menu item on the menu bar and set its mnemonic as `'F'`. You then call the `createFileMenuActions()` helper method to create the `FileAction` objects you use to create the menu items. You create each menu item by passing the appropriate `FileAction` object to the `JMenuItem` class constructor. The resulting reference you pass to the `add()` method for the `JMenu` object, `fileMenu`. The properties you have set in a `FileAction` object determine the appearance and behavior of the menu item that you create from it. Finally you add the menu to the menu bar.

The other two menu bars are a little different because they are going to be radio buttons. We need to access these menus later to set the correct menu item checked, so add `JMenu` members to `SketcherFrame` to store references to them:

```
private JMenu elementMenu;                            // Elements menu
private JMenu colorMenu;                              // Color menu
```

Directory "Sketcher 6 using Action objects"

These statements can go following the definition of `menuBar`.

Here's the `createElementMenu()` method implementation:

```
private void createElementMenu() {
  createElementTypeActions();
  elementMenu = new JMenu("Elements");               // Create Elements menu
  elementMenu.setMnemonic('E');                      // Create shortcut
  createRadioButtonDropDown(elementMenu, typeActions, lineAction);
  menuBar.add(elementMenu);                           // Add the element menu
}
```

Directory "Sketcher 6 using Action objects"

This creates the menu items for element types. It uses another helper method, `createRadioButtonDropDown()`, to create the menu items in the drop-down as radio button menu items.

The helper method code to create the menu items is as follows:

```
private void createRadioButtonDropDown(
                          JMenu menu, Action[] actions, Action selected) {
  ButtonGroup group = new ButtonGroup();
  JRadioButtonMenuItem item = null;
  for(Action action : actions) {
    group.add(menu.add(item = new JRadioButtonMenuItem(action)));
    if(action == selected) {
      item.setSelected(true);                        // This is default selected
    }
  }
}
```

Directory "Sketcher 6 using Action objects"

The first parameter is the menu to which the items are to be added. This makes use of an array of actions that is passed to it as the second argument, and the third argument is an `Action` reference that identifies the menu item that is to be selected initially. The loop iterates over the actions in the array. Each iteration creates a menu item from the action and adds it to the menu. The `add()` method for `JMenu` returns a reference to the item that was added so this reference is passed to the `add()` method for `group` to add it to the button group. Each action is compared with the one supplied as the third argument to identify the menu item to be set as selected.

You use the `createRadioButtonDropDown()` in the creation of the Color menu, too:

```
private void createColorMenu() {
  createElementColorActions();
  colorMenu = new JMenu("Color");                    // Create Elements menu
  colorMenu.setMnemonic('C');                        // Create shortcut
  createRadioButtonDropDown(colorMenu, colorActions, blueAction);
  menuBar.add(colorMenu);                             // Add the color menu
}
```

Directory "Sketcher 6 using Action objects"

This is almost identical to the method that creates the Elements menu.

If you recompile and run Sketcher after you have made the changes I have described, you get a window that looks like the one shown in Figure 18-7.

FIGURE 18-7

How It Works

This works much as before but with some embroidery to the GUI. The menu items in the drop-downs have accelerator keys that are shown on the menu items. You can see that the corresponding letter in the menu item text has been underlined. You can access any menu using the mouse, or you can go directly to the menu item using the accelerator key combination. The appropriate default menu item is selected in the Elements and Color menus.

If you try out the color menus either by selecting from the drop-down or using the accelerator you should see the background color change. If it doesn't, there's something wrong somewhere. After you have verified the color menus work, you can delete the statement that sets the background color from the `actionPerformed()` method in the `ColorAction` class. Now that you have the menus set up using `Action` objects, you are ready to tackle the next stage, adding a toolbar to the Sketcher application.

ADDING A TOOLBAR

A toolbar is a bar in an application window, usually positioned at the top edge of the content pane below the menu bar, that contains buttons that provide more direct routes to menu options. You could add a toolbar to the Sketcher program for the menu items that are likely to be most popular. Just so that you know where you are heading, the kind of toolbar you end up with ultimately is shown in Figure 18-8.

The four buttons in the first group are for the most frequently used functions in the File menu. The other two groups of four buttons select the element type and element color, respectively. So how are you going to put this toolbar together?

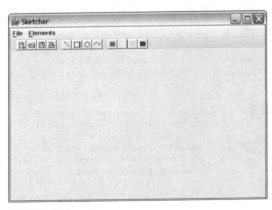

FIGURE 18-8

Adding the toolbar itself couldn't be easier. A toolbar is a Swing component defined by the `javax.swing.JToolBar` class. You can add a member to the `SketcherFrame` class for a toolbar by adding the following field to the class definition:

```
private JToolBar toolBar = new JToolBar();          // Window toolbar
```

You can position this following the declaration of the `menuBar` member. It simply creates a `JToolBar` object as a member of the class. Of course, you need to add an `import` statement to the `SketcherFrame` class for `javax.swing.JToolbar`.

To add the toolbar to the application window, you need to add the following statement after the existing code in the `SketcherFrame` constructor:

```
getContentPane().add(toolBar, BorderLayout.NORTH);
```

This adds the (currently empty) toolbar to the top of the content pane for the frame window. The content pane has the `BorderLayout` manager as the default, which is very convenient. You add a `JToolBar` object to a `Container` using the `BorderLayout` manager because it is normally positioned at one of the four sides of a component. The other three sides of the content pane would be identified by the SOUTH, EAST, and WEST constants in the `BorderLayout` class. An empty toolbar is not much use so let's see how you add buttons to it.

Adding Buttons to a Toolbar

The `JToolBar` class inherits the `add()` methods from the `Container` class, so you can create `JButton` objects and add them to the toolbar using this method. The `JButton` class defines a constructor that accepts an argument of type `Action`, and creates a button based on the `Action` object that is passed to it. You can use this to create buttons for any of the `Action` objects that you created for the menus, and have the toolbar button events taken care of without any further work.

For example, you could add a button you create from the `openAction` object corresponding to the Open menu item in the File menu with the following statements:

```
JButton button = new JButton(openAction);   // Create button from Action
toolBar.add(button);                         // Add a toolbar button
```

That's all you need basically. The `JButton` constructor creates a `JButton` object based on the `Action` object that you pass as the argument. The properties defined in the `Action` object apply to the button, so this matches the Open menu item in the File menu. More than that, because the button and the menu item share a single `Action` object, clicking on either the menu item or the toolbar button calls the same `actionPerformed()` method, which is the one you have defined for the `Action` object. The `add()` method for `toolBar` adds the `JButton` object to the toolbar.

A nice feature of a `JToolBar` object is that it can highlight the button that the mouse cursor is over with a mechanism that is referred to as *rollover action*. To switch on this feature you can call `setRollover()` for the `JToolBar` object with the argument as `true`:

```
toolBar.setRollover(true);
```

Add this statement to the `SketcherFrame` constructor, immediately before you add the toolbar to the content pane. Calling the `setRollover()` method with `false` as the argument switches off rollover action. You will see button highlighting in operation in Sketcher.

Inhibiting Text on a Toolbar Button

Because a toolbar button is created using the `Action` object properties that you have defined for the corresponding menu item, it has a NAME value, and the text for the name displays on the toolbar button by default. This is not want you want in most cases. You can prevent the name from being displayed by calling the `setHideActionText()` for a `JButton` toolbar button with an argument value `true`:

```
button.setHideActionText(true);
```

Calling this method with a `false` argument would cause the text to be displayed, so you can switch the text on and off. What you really want, though, is to be able to display an icon on a toolbar button instead of displaying the text.

Adding Icons to Toolbar Buttons

A reference to an icon is generally stored in a variable of type `javax.swing.Icon`, which is an interface that declares methods that return the height and width of an icon in pixels—`getHeight()` and `getWidth()` methods, respectively. The `Icon` interface also declares the `paint()` method that paints the icon image on a component. The `javax.swing.ImageIcon` class implements the `Icon` interface and you use this class to create an icon object in your program from a file that contains the data defining the icon image.

The `ImageIcon` class has several constructors, and the one you use accepts a `String` argument that specifies the path for the file in which the icon image is found. The `String` object that you pass as the argument can be just the file name, in which case the file should be in the current directory when Sketcher executes. You can also supply a string that specifies the full path to the file containing the image. I'm putting the files containing the icons for the Sketcher application in a directory with the path `D:\Sketcher\Images` and specifying the full path to the location of each icon. You can put them elsewhere if you want, on your C: drive perhaps.

The `ImageIcon` constructors accept icon files in PNG format (Portable Network Graphics format, which have the extension `.png`), GIF format (Graphics Interchange Format, or `.gif` files), or JPEG format (Joint Photographic Experts Group format, or `.jpg` files) formats. I'm assuming GIF files in the Sketcher code. If you want to use files in one of the other formats, just modify the code for the example accordingly.

A large icon in an `Action` object applies to a toolbar button. This is identified by the `LARGE_ICON_KEY` key. A large icon is usually 24 × 24 pixels, whereas a small icon that might be used on a menu item is usually 16 × 16 pixels. Obviously, a large icon can have more detail in the image.

If you add a static import statement interface to `SketcherFrame.java`, for the keys that are defined in the `Action` you don't have to qualify the action property keys in the code:

```
import static javax.swing.Action.*;
```

To create a large icon for the `openAction` object from an image in a file `Open24.gif`, you could write the following:

```
openAction.putValue(
          LARGE_ICON_KEY, new ImageIcon("D:/Sketcher/Images/Open24.gif"));
```

This creates the `ImageIcon` object from the GIF file and stores it in the `Action` object; the icon is associated with the `LARGE_ICON_KEY` key. The key identifies the icon as that to be used for a toolbar button. If the `ImageIcon` constructor cannot find the file, the object created does not contain an image; you get no indication of this. The icon specified by the `Open24.gif` file is 24 × 24 pixels, so is ideally suited for use as a toolbar button. Of course, if you have already created the Icon object, you can pass the reference to the `putValue()` method.

 NOTE *You can use the GIF files containing the icons for the toolbar buttons that are in the code download for the book or create some for yourself. You can download the code from the Wrox Press website:* www.wrox.com.

You can use any graphics editor that can save files in the GIF format to create your own—Paint Shop Pro, Microsoft Paint, or GIMP, for example. Menu item icons should be 16 × 16 pixels and toolbar button icons 24 × 24 pixels.

You can also download icons for a variety of applications from the Java look-and-feel graphics repository at http://java.sun.com/developer/techDocs/hi/repository. *These icons have been designed specifically to go with the Java look-and-feel. The icons are available as 16 × 16 pixels and 24 × 24 pixels. The first four icons on the toolbar shown at the beginning of this section are icons from this set—the others I created for myself.*

Let's add some toolbar buttons to Sketcher.

TRY IT OUT   Adding Toolbar Buttons for the File Menu

I assume that you have added the declaration for the `toolBar` object to the `SketcherFrame` class and the statements to the constructor that add it to the GUI:

Available for
download on
Wrox.com

```
public SketcherFrame(String title) {
    // Constructor code as before...
    createToolbar();
    toolBar.setRollover(true);
    getContentPane().add(toolBar, BorderLayout.NORTH);
}
```

Directory "Sketcher 7 with File toolbar buttons"

The icons for toolbar buttons, or anything else in Sketcher, can be created and stored as constants in the `SketcherConstants` class, and they are available to any part of the program. Amend the class definition as follows:

Available for
download on
Wrox.com

```
package Constants;
import java.awt.Color;
import javax.swing.*;

public class SketcherConstants {
    // Path for images
    public final static String imagePath = "D:/Sketcher/Images/";

    // Toolbar icons
    public final static Icon NEW24 = new ImageIcon(imagePath + "New24.gif");
    public final static Icon OPEN24 = new ImageIcon(imagePath + "Open24.gif");
    public final static Icon SAVE24 = new ImageIcon(imagePath + "Save24.gif");
    public final static Icon SAVEAS24 = new ImageIcon(imagePath + "SaveAs24.gif");
    public final static Icon PRINT24 = new ImageIcon(imagePath + "Print24.gif");

    // Rest of the class as before...
}
```

Directory "Sketcher 7 with File toolbar buttons"

Now the icons are generally available. The `imagePath` object defines the path to where the .gif files for the icons are stored. If you are storing them in a different location, just change the definition of `imagePath`.

The next step is to amend the `createFileMenuActions()` method in `SketcherFrame` to add large icons to the action objects:

Available for
download on
Wrox.com

```
private void createFileMenuActions() {
    // Code to create action objects as before...
    // Add toolbar icons
    newAction.putValue(LARGE_ICON_KEY, NEW24);
    openAction.putValue(LARGE_ICON_KEY, OPEN24);
    saveAction.putValue(LARGE_ICON_KEY, SAVE24);
    saveAsAction.putValue(LARGE_ICON_KEY, SAVEAS24);
    printAction.putValue(LARGE_ICON_KEY, PRINT24);
}
```

Directory "Sketcher 7 with File toolbar buttons"

Only five of the menu items have corresponding toolbar buttons so you only add large icons to the `Action` objects you use to create these.

Next you need add another method in the `SketcherFrame` class that adds buttons to the toolbar:

```
private void createToolbar() {
    for(FileAction action: fileActions){
        if(action != exitAction && action != closeAction)
            addToolbarButton(action);                      // Add the toolbar button
    }
}
```

Directory "Sketcher 7 with File toolbar buttons"

This adds a toolbar button using a helper method, `addToolbarButton()`. You add a toolbar button for each action object you used to create the File menu items except for those for the Close and Exit menu items.

You can now add the helper method to the `SketcherFrame` class that creates a button and adds it to the toolbar:

```
private void addToolbarButton(Action action) {
    JButton button = new JButton(action);                  // Create from Action
    button.setBorder(BorderFactory.createCompoundBorder(   // Add button border
        new EmptyBorder(2,5,5,2),                          // Outside border
        BorderFactory.createRaisedBevelBorder()));         // Inside border
    button.setHideActionText(true);                        // No label on the button
    toolBar.add(button);                                   // Add the toolbar button
}
```

Directory "Sketcher 7 with File toolbar buttons"

You need to add the following `import` statements to the `SketcherFrame` class:

```
import javax.swing.border.*;
import static javax.swing.Action.*;
```

Directory "Sketcher 7 with File toolbar buttons"

The first makes the border class names available without qualifiers and the second imports member names in the `Action` class that define keys.

If you recompile Sketcher and run it, the window should look like that shown in Figure 18-9.

How It Works

Calling `putValue()` for an `Action` object stores the value you specify by the second argument with the key you supply as the first argument. The new statements in the `createFileMenuActions()` method add an `Icon` object from the `SketcherConstants` class as the value corresponding to the `LARGE_ICON_KEY` key for each of the actions except for those

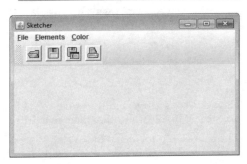

FIGURE 18-9

corresponding to the Close and Exit menu items. The icons are 24 × 24 pixels, a standard size for use on the toolbar. You could use icons of any size and the toolbar adjusts in height to accommodate them. Of course, if the icons are very big, this limits how many you can have in a single row.

The `addToolBarButton()` method creates a single button and adds it to the toolbar. It creates the `JButton` object from the `Action` object that is passed as the argument. The `setBorder()` method adds the border specified by the argument to a button. You add a compound border that you create by calling the `createCompoundBorder()` method from the `BorderFactory` class. The first argument is the outside border. This is an empty border so it determines the space between buttons on the toolbar and between the buttons and the top and bottom of the toolbar. The integer arguments to the `EmptyBorder` class constructor correspond to the widths of the bottom, left, right, and top edges of the border.

The `createToolBar()` method that you added calls the `addToolBarButton()` method for each of the actions for which you want a toolbar button. Calling this method in the `SketcherFrame` constructor adds the buttons to the toolbar.

A feature that comes for free with a `JToolBar` object is that it is automatically dockable and can float as an independent window. You can drag the toolbar using the mouse by holding mouse button 1 down with the cursor in the gray area to the left of the button and then dragging it to a new position. The toolbar turns into a free-floating window, as Figure 18-10 shows.

FIGURE 18-10

You can also drag the toolbar to any of the four edges of the content pane, or to its original docked position again at the top of the content pane. You must drag with the cursor in the gray area of the toolbar to redock it. Dragging with the cursor in the toolbar title area just moves the window.

It's not always convenient to have the toolbar floating. You can inhibit the capability to drag the toolbar around by calling the `setFloatable()` method for the `JToolBar` object with the argument specified as `false`. If you want to try this out in Sketcher, add the following statement to the `SketcherFrame` constructor before the statement that adds the toolbar to the content pane:

```
      toolBar.setFloatable(false);                   // Inhibit toolbar floating
      getContentPane().add(toolBar, BorderLayout.NORTH);
    }
```

A `true` argument to the `setFloatable()` method allows the toolbar to float, so you can switch this on and off in an application as you wish. You can also test whether a toolbar can float by calling the `isFloatable()` method for the `JToolBar` object. This returns `true` if the toolbar is floatable and `false` otherwise. If you recompile `SketcherFrame` and run Sketcher again you see that the gray bit at the left-hand end of the toolbar is no longer there, and you cannot drag the toolbar around.

Adding More Toolbar Buttons with Icons

Now that you know how it works with the File menu, you can easily add toolbar buttons with icons corresponding to the Elements and Color menus. The process is the same—first you add a large icon to each of the Action objects and then you create the toolbar buttons from the Action objects.

Adding Large Icons for Element Type Selection Buttons

First add definitions for the icons as constants in the `SketcherConstants` class:

```
      public final static Icon LINE24 = new ImageIcon(imagePath + "Line24.gif");
      public final static Icon RECTANGLE24 = new ImageIcon(imagePath + "Rectangle24.gif");
      public final static Icon CIRCLE24 = new ImageIcon(imagePath + "Circle24.gif");
      public final static Icon CURVE24 = new ImageIcon(imagePath + "Curve24.gif");
```

Directory "Sketcher 8 with toolbar buttons and menu icons"

Now you can add icons for the Elements menu action items like this:

```
      private void createElementTypeActions() {
        // Code as before...

        // Add toolbar icons
        lineAction.putValue(LARGE_ICON_KEY, LINE24);
        rectangleAction.putValue(LARGE_ICON_KEY, RECTANGLE24);
```

```
        circleAction.putValue(LARGE_ICON_KEY, CIRCLE24);
        curveAction.putValue(LARGE_ICON_KEY, CURVE24);
    }
```

Directory "Sketcher 8 with toolbar buttons and menu icons"

Adding Large Icons for Color Selection Buttons

You add the icons for the Color menu in the same way. First, add the icon definitions to
`SketcherConstants`:

```
    public final static Icon RED24 = new ImageIcon(imagePath + "Red24.gif");
    public final static Icon GREEN24 = new ImageIcon(imagePath + "Green24.gif");
    public final static Icon BLUE24 = new ImageIcon(imagePath + "Blue24.gif");
    public final static Icon YELLOW24 = new ImageIcon(imagePath + "Yellow24.gif");
```

Directory "Sketcher 8 with toolbar buttons and menu icons"

All the GIF files are in the same directory. I created very simple 24 × 24 icons for the Elements and Color
menus and these are in the code download. You might like to create some fancier versions.

Now update the method that creates the actions for the Color menu:

```
    private void createElementColorActions() {
        // Code as before...
        // Add toolbar icons
        redAction.putValue(LARGE_ICON_KEY, RED24);
        greenAction.putValue(LARGE_ICON_KEY, GREEN24);
        blueAction.putValue(LARGE_ICON_KEY, BLUE24);
        yellowAction.putValue(LARGE_ICON_KEY, YELLOW24);
    }
```

Directory "Sketcher 8 with toolbar buttons and menu icons"

Creating the Toolbar Buttons

You create the new toolbar buttons in the `createToolbar()` method in `SketcherFrame`:

```
    private void createToolbar() {
        // Code for File menu buttons as before...

        toolBar.addSeparator();

        // Create Color menu buttons
        for(ColorAction action:colorActions){
            addToolbarButton(action);                    // Add the toolbar button
        }
        toolBar.addSeparator();

        // Create Elements menu buttons
        for(TypeAction action:typeActions){
            addToolbarButton(action);                    // Add the toolbar button
        }
    }
```

Directory "Sketcher 8 with toolbar buttons and menu icons"

Both sets of buttons are created from the corresponding `Action` objects in the same way. If you recompile
Sketcher, you should see a more comprehensive toolbar when you execute it. However, there's a problem. If
you click a toolbar button for a new color or a new element type, the menu item checks don't get updated.

Fixing Menu Checks

You did not store the menu items or the toolbar buttons. Updating the status of menu items you have not stored is a little tricky, but possible. The key to fixing the selected status of the menu items lies with the Action objects you used to create them. You used the same Action objects to create the toolbar buttons. If you can use this to match the toolbar button that was clicked with the corresponding menu item, you are almost there. I explain how it works and then give you the code.

The actionPerformed() method for an Action object receives an event as an object of type ActionEvent that records information about the source of the event. You can get a reference to the menu item or toolbar button that originated the event by calling getSource() for the ActionEvent object. The getSource() method returns a reference of type Object, but you can easily determine whether or not it is a JButton object using the instanceof operator. A JMenu object has a getItem() method that returns the menu item at a given index position. You have the elementMenu and colorMenu objects available so this gives you a way to get to the menu items in the drop-down.

Both menu item or toolbar button objects provide a getAction() method that returns a reference to the Action object that originated them. Thus you can get the Action object for a JButton that originates an action event and compare it with the Action objects for the menu items. If you have a match, then the toolbar button that corresponds to the menu item that has the same Action object was clicked.

Applying all that I have discussed about actions to the code that sets menu item checks when a color toolbar button is clicked looks like this:

```
public void actionPerformed(ActionEvent e) {
    elementColor = color;
    setChecks(colorMenu, e.getSource());
}
```

Directory "Sketcher 8 with toolbar buttons and menu icons"

This method is in the ColorAction class. It passes the JMenu item for the menu and a reference to the object that originated to a new method that sets the menu checks when appropriate. Using a separate method for this allows the same code to set checks for both the Elements menu and the Color menu. You can implement this as a SketcherFrame method:

```
private void setChecks(JMenu menu, Object eventSource) {
    if(eventSource instanceof JButton){
        JButton button = (JButton)eventSource;
        Action action = button.getAction();
        for(int i = 0 ; i < menu.getItemCount() ; ++i) {
            JMenuItem item = menu.getItem(i);
            item.setSelected(item.getAction() == action);
        }
    }
}
```

Directory "Sketcher 8 with toolbar buttons and menu icons"

Make sure you don't place it inside one of the inner classes inadvertently. The method first tests whether or not the event originated with a JButton object. If it does then it's certainly from one of the color toolbar buttons. You can then compare the Action object for the button with the Action object for each item in the menu. The getItemCount() method for a JMenu object returns the number of menu items it contains. You combine this with the getItem() method that returns the menu item at the index position specified by the argument to access each of the menu items in turn. The setSelected() method for a menu item sets the item as checked when the argument is true. This is only the case for the menu item that has the same Action object as the button.

The actionPerformed() method for the TypeAction class is essentially the same as that for the ColorAction class:

```
public void actionPerformed(ActionEvent e) {
  elementType = typeID;
  setChecks(elementMenu, e.getSource());
}
```

Directory "Sketcher 8 with toolbar buttons and menu icons"

Just one extra statement. With these changes clicking a color or element type toolbar button updates the menus.

ADDING MENU ICONS

It would be nice to have as many GUI features in Sketcher as possible, so let's add icons for the menu items, too, to complement the toolbar icons. This is very easy. All you need to do is add `IconImage` objects as values for the `SMALL_ICON` key in the `Action` objects that you use to create the menu items. You can implement this by first adding definitions for the icons for menu items to `SketcherConstants`:

```
// Menu item icons
public final static Icon NEW16 = new ImageIcon(imagePath + "new16.gif");
public final static Icon OPEN16 = new ImageIcon(imagePath + "Open16.gif");
public final static Icon SAVE16 = new ImageIcon(imagePath + " Save16.gif");
public final static Icon SAVEAS16 = new ImageIcon(imagePath + "SaveAs16.gif");
public final static Icon PRINT16 = new ImageIcon(imagePath + "print16.gif");

public final static Icon LINE16 = new ImageIcon(imagePath + "Line16.gif");
public final static Icon RECTANGLE16 = new ImageIcon(imagePath + "Rectangle16.gif");
public final static Icon CIRCLE16 = new ImageIcon(imagePath + "Circle16.gif");
public final static Icon CURVE16 = new ImageIcon(imagePath + "Curve16.gif");

public final static Icon RED16 = new ImageIcon(imagePath + "Red16.gif");
public final static Icon GREEN16 = new ImageIcon(imagePath + "Green16.gif");
public final static Icon BLUE16 = new ImageIcon(imagePath + "Blue16.gif");
public final static Icon YELLOW16 = new ImageIcon(imagePath + "Yellow16.gif");
```

Directory "Sketcher 8 with toolbar buttons and menu icons"

The icons are 16 × 16 pixels to go with the menu items. Now you can add code to `createFileMenuActions()` to use these:

```
private void createFileMenuActions() {
  // Code to create action objects as before...
  // Code to add large icons to the action objects as before...
  // Add menu item actions
  newAction.putValue(SMALL_ICON, NEW16);
  openAction.putValue(SMALL_ICON, OPEN16);
  saveAction.putValue(SMALL_ICON, SAVE16);
  saveAsAction.putValue(SMALL_ICON,SAVEAS16);
  printAction.putValue(SMALL_ICON, PRINT16);
}
```

Directory "Sketcher 8 with toolbar buttons and menu icons"

Adding icons for the Elements menu items is similar. Add the following statements to the end of the `createElementTypeActions()` method:

```
lineAction.putValue(SMALL_ICON, LINE16);
rectangleAction.putValue(SMALL_ICON, RECTANGLE16);
circleAction.putValue(SMALL_ICON, CIRCLE16);
curveAction.putValue(SMALL_ICON, CURVE16);
```

Directory "Sketcher 8 with toolbar buttons and menu icons"

You can add similar statements to the createElementColorActions() method in SketcherFrame:

```
redAction.putValue(SMALL_ICON, RED16);
blueAction.putValue(SMALL_ICON, BLUE16);
greenAction.putValue(SMALL_ICON, GREEN16);
yellowAction.putValue(SMALL_ICON, YELLOW16);
```

Directory "Sketcher 8 with toolbar buttons and menu icons"

That's all you need to do. Let's see it working.

TRY IT OUT Implementing Menu Item Icons

If you amend the createFileMenuActions() method as described, when you recompile Sketcher and execute it, the application window appears as in Figure 18-11.

How It Works

It works exactly as expected. If there is a value for the SMALL_ICON key in an action, the image is displayed on the menu item that you create from it.

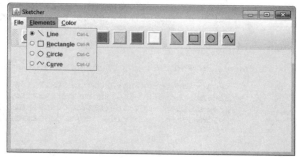

It could be that you create a menu item from an Action object that has a value for the SMALL_ICON key, but you don't want the icon displayed on the menu item. You can prevent the icon from being shown on a menu item like this:

FIGURE 18-11

```
menuItem.setIcon(null);
```

The JMenuItem class has a setIcon() method that accepts a reference of type Icon to set an icon for a menu item. If you want to remove the icon for a menu item, you just call its setIcon() method with the argument as null. You could also use the method to change the icon.

ADDING TOOLTIPS

I'm sure you have seen tooltips in operation. These are the little text prompts that appear automatically when you let the mouse cursor linger over certain GUI elements on the screen for a second or two. They disappear automatically when you move the cursor. I think you will be surprised at how easy it is to implement support for tooltips in Java.

The secret is again in the Action objects that you are using. Action objects have a built-in capability to store tooltip text because it is already provided for with the SHORT_DESCRIPTION key. All you have to do is store the tooltip text as the value for the key.

TRY IT OUT Implementing Tooltips

You can provide for tooltip text in each of the inner classes by adding a little more code to the createFileMenuActions() method in SketcherFrame:

```
private void createFileMenuActions() {
    // Code to create action objects as before...
    // Code to add large icons to the action objects as before...
    // Code to add small icons to the action objects as before...
    // Add tooltip text
    newAction.putValue(SHORT_DESCRIPTION, "Create a new sketch");
    openAction.putValue(SHORT_DESCRIPTION, "Read a sketch from a file");
```

```
        saveAction.putValue(SHORT_DESCRIPTION, "Save the current sketch to file");
        saveAsAction.putValue(SHORT_DESCRIPTION, "Save the current sketch to a new file");
        printAction.putValue(SHORT_DESCRIPTION, "Print the current sketch");
    }
```

Directory "Sketcher 9 with tooltips"

The `String` value for the `SHORT_DESCRIPTION` key represents the tooltip text for an object you create from an action. You should keep the tooltip text short because it is displayed on the fly. Add the following statements to the end of the `createElementTypeActions()` method:

Available for
download on
Wrox.com

```
        lineAction.putValue(SHORT_DESCRIPTION, "Draw lines");
        rectangleAction.putValue(SHORT_DESCRIPTION, "Draw rectangles");
        circleAction.putValue(SHORT_DESCRIPTION, "Draw circles");
        curveAction.putValue(SHORT_DESCRIPTION, "Draw curves");
```

Directory "Sketcher 9 with tooltips"

The statements you add to `createElementColorActions()` method to implement tooltips are much the same:

Available for
download on
Wrox.com

```
        redAction.putValue(SHORT_DESCRIPTION, "Draw in red");
        blueAction.putValue(SHORT_DESCRIPTION, "Draw in blue");
        greenAction.putValue(SHORT_DESCRIPTION, "Draw in green");
        yellowAction.putValue(SHORT_DESCRIPTION, "Draw in yellow");
```

Directory "Sketcher 9 with tooltips"

You can try the tooltips out. Just recompile the `SketcherFrame` class and run Sketcher again. You should be able to see the tooltip when you let the cursor linger over a button, as Figure 18-12 illustrates.

How It Works

`Action` objects act as a repository for the tooltip text for components that implement the actions, so this works for the toolbar buttons in Sketcher. If an `Action` object contains a tooltip property, a toolbar button that you create from it automatically has the tooltip operational. Try lingering the cursor over a menu item. Because the menu items are created from `Action` items, tooltips are available for them, too.

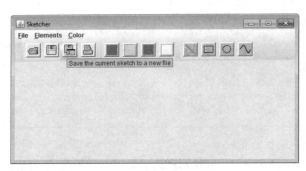

FIGURE 18-12

DISABLING ACTIONS

You don't want to have all of the menu items and toolbar buttons in Sketcher enabled all of the time. For example, while there is no sketch active, the `Save` and `Print` menu items should not be operational, and neither should the corresponding buttons. The `Action` objects provide a single point of control for enabling or disabling menu items and the corresponding toolbar buttons. To disable an action, you call the `setEnabled()` method for the `Action` object with an argument of `false`. You can restore the enabled state by calling the method with a `true` argument. The `isEnabled()` method for an `Action` object returns `true` if the action is enabled, and `false` otherwise.

You use the ability to disable actions in Sketcher when you implement more operational details. In the meantime you can see how disabled toolbar buttons and menu items look by adding statements temporarily to the `SketcherFrame` constructor to disable some actions.

SUMMARY

In this chapter you have learned how to handle events in your applications and in your applets. Events are fundamental to all window-based applications, as well as most applets, so you can apply the techniques you have seen in this chapter throughout the rest of the book.

You also now know how to create menu items and toolbar buttons from `Action` objects. This is a very powerful technique that simplifies the management of events for these GUI components. You now have a version of Sketcher that is an application of around 400 lines of code. It doesn't do a lot yet, though. You enhance the function of Sketcher and increase the number of lines of code a great deal in subsequent chapters.

EXERCISES

You can download the source code for the examples in the book and the solutions to the following exercises from www.wrox.com.

1. Modify the `Lottery` applet to present the six numbers selected in ascending sequence.

2. Replace the action listener for the selection buttons in the `Lottery` applet with a mouse listener and use the `mousePressed()` method to update the selection with a new value.

3. Modify the `Lottery` applet to implement the mouse listener for a selection button as an inner class to the `Lottery` class.

4. Modify the `Lottery` applet to implement the control buttons on a toolbar based on `Action` objects.

5. Change the `Lottery` applet to handle the `MOUSE_ENTERED` and `MOUSE_EXITED` events within the toolbar buttons you added in the previous exercise and display a hand cursor.

6. Add tooltips to the lucky number buttons and the toolbar buttons in the `Lottery` applet. (You can make the tooltip the same for each of the lucky number buttons.)

▶ WHAT YOU LEARNED IN THIS CHAPTER

TOPIC	CONCEPT
Events	A user interaction generates an event in the context of a component.
Event Categories	Two categories of events are associated with a component: low-level events from the mouse or keyboard, or window system events such as opening or closing a window; and semantic events that represent component actions such as pressing a button or selecting a menu item.
Event Occurrences	Both low-level and semantic events can arise simultaneously.
Handling Events	An event for a component can be handled by the component object itself, or by a separate object that implements a listener interface corresponding to the event type.
Component Event Handling	A component that is to handle its own events does so by calling its `enableEvents()` method and implementing the class method to process the kind of event that has been enabled.
Registered Listeners	A listener object that is registered with a component receives notification of the events originating with the component that correspond to the type(s) of events the listener can handle.
Low-level Event Listeners	A listener for low-level events requires several event-handling methods to be implemented.
Semantic Event Listeners	A listener for semantic events only requires a single event-handling method to be implemented.
Adapter Classes	An adapter class defines a set of empty methods for one or more low-level event interfaces. You can create your own class defining a low-level event listener by deriving your class from an adapter class and then implementing the event-handling methods in which you are interested.
Action Objects	An `Action` object is an object of a class that implements the `Action` interface. `Action` objects can be used to create menu items and associated toolbar buttons.
Action Object Properties	You can set `Action` object properties by setting values associated with standard property keys. The properties you can set include name text and icons for menu items and toolbar buttons, and text for tooltips.
Action Objects and Menus	You can create a menu item from an `Action` object. The appearance of the menu item is determined by the properties set for the `Action` object.
Action objects and Toolbars	You can create a toolbar button from an Action object. The appearance of the button is determined by the properties you have set for the Action object.
Events and Action Objects	An `Action` object is automatically the listener for events arising for the menu item and toolbar button that are created from it. In this way, events arising from a toolbar button and a menu item click event can be processed by the same method in the `Action` object.

YOU CAN DOWNLOAD THE CODE FOUND IN THIS BOOK. VISIT WROX.COM AND SEARCH FOR ISBN 9780470404140.

19

Drawing in a Window

WHAT YOU WILL LEARN IN THIS CHAPTER:

➤ How you can implement Sketcher using the model/view architecture

➤ How coordinates are defined for drawing on a component

➤ How you implement drawing on a component

➤ How to structure the components in a window for drawing

➤ What kinds of shapes you can draw on a component

➤ How you implement mouse listener methods to enable interactive drawing operations

In this chapter you look at how you can draw using the Java 2D facilities that are part of the Java Foundation Classes (JFC). You explore how you draw on a component in an applet and in an application. You investigate how you can combine the event-handling capability that you learned about in Chapter 18 with the drawing facilities you explore in this chapter to implement an interactive graphical user interface for creating a sketch.

USING THE MODEL/VIEW ARCHITECTURE

You need to develop an idea of how you're going to manage the data for a sketch in the Sketcher program before you start drawing a sketch, because this affects where and how you handle events. You already have a class that defines an application window, `SketcherFrame`, but this class would not be a very sensible place to store the underlying data that defines a sketch. For one thing, you'll want to save a sketch in a file, and serialization is the easiest way to do that. If you're going to use serialization to store a sketch, you don't want all the fields in the implementation of the `SketcherFrame` class muddled up with the data relating to the sketch you have created. For another thing, it makes the program easier to implement if you separate the basic data defining a sketch from the definition of the GUI. This is along the lines of the **Model-View-Controller** (MVC) architecture that I first mentioned in Chapter 17, a variant of which is used in the definition of Swing components. Ideally, you should manage the sketch data in a class designed specifically for that purpose. This class is the model for a sketch.

A class that represents a view of the data in the model displays the sketch and handles user interactions, so this class combines viewing methods with a sketch controller. The general GUI creation and operations that are not specific to a view are dealt with in the `SketcherFrame` class. This is not the only way of implementing the things you want in the Sketcher program, but it's quite a good way.

The model object contains a mixture of text and graphics that make up a sketch. You can call the model class `SketcherModel`, and the class that represents a view of the model can have the name `SketcherView`, although you won't be adding the view to the program until the next chapter. Figure 19-1 illustrates the relationships between the classes you have in Sketcher.

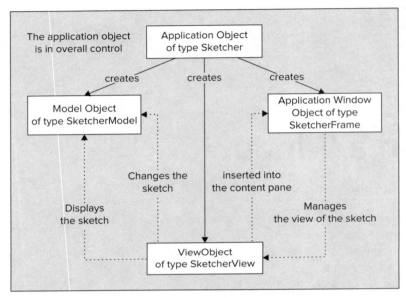

FIGURE 19-1

The application object has overall responsibility for managing links between the other objects involved in the program. Any object that has access to the application object is to communicate with any other object as long as the application class has methods to make each of the objects available. Thus, the application object acts as the communication channel between objects.

Note that `SketcherFrame` is not the view class — it just defines the application window and the GUI components associated with that. When you create a `SketcherView` object, you arrange to insert the `SketcherView` object into the content pane of the `SketcherFrame` object and manage it using the layout manager for the content pane. By defining the view class separately from the application class, you separate the view of a sketch from the menus and other components that you use to interact with the program. One benefit of this is that the area in which you display a sketch has its own coordinate system, independent of that of the application window.

To implement the foundations for the model/view design in Sketcher, you need to define classes for the model and the view, at least in outline. You can define in skeleton form the class to encapsulate the data that defines a sketch:

```
import java.io.Serializable;
import java.util.Observable;

public class SketcherModel extends Observable implements Serializable {
  // Detail of the rest of class to be filled in later...
  private final static long serialVersionUID = 1001L;
}
```

This is going to be `Serializable` because you want to save a sketch to a file. You obviously have a bit more work to do on this class to make it effective! You add to this as you go along. Because the `SketcherModel` class extends the `Observable` class, you are able to register the view class with it as an observer and automatically notify the view of any changes to the model. This facility comes into its own when you have multiple views of a sketch.

You can define the view class as a component by deriving it from the JComponent class. This builds in all the methods for operating as a Swing component and you are able to override any of these when necessary. You will be using Swing components throughout, so when I refer to a component, I mean a Swing component. The view class also needs to implement the Observer interface so that you can register it with the model to receive notification when the model changes. Here's the outline:

```
import javax.swing.JComponent;
import java.util.*;

public class SketcherView extends JComponent implements Observer {
  public SketcherView(Sketcher theApp) {
    this.theApp = theApp;
  }

  // Method called by Observable object when it changes
  public void update(Observable o, Object rectangle) {
    // Code to respond to changes in the model...
  }

  private Sketcher theApp;               // The application object
}
```

Directory "Sketcher 1 drawing a 3D rectangle"

The view needs access to the model to display it, but rather than store a reference to the model in the view, the constructor has a parameter to enable the application object to be passed to it. The view object is able to use the application object to access the model object, and the application window if necessary.

The view is registered as an observer for the model. If a completely different object represents the model because, for example, a new file is loaded, the view object is automatically notified by the model that it has changed and is able to respond by redrawing the view.

To integrate a model and its view into the Sketcher application, you just need to add some code to the Sketcher class that defines the application object:

```
import javax.swing.*;
import java.awt.*;
import java.awt.event.*;

public class Sketcher {
  public static void main(String[] args) {
    theApp = new Sketcher();                              // Create the application object
    SwingUtilities.invokeLater(new Runnable() {
            public void run() {
                          theApp.createGUI();             // Call GUI creator
            }
         });

    // Method to create the application GUI
    private void createGUI() {
      window = new SketcherFrame("Sketcher", this);        // Create the app window
      Toolkit theKit = window.getToolkit();                // Get the window toolkit
      Dimension wndSize = theKit.getScreenSize();          // Get screen size

      // Set the position to screen center & size to half screen size
      window.setSize(wndSize.width/2, wndSize.height/2);   // Set window size
      window.setLocationRelativeTo(null);                  // Center window
      window.addWindowListener(new WindowHandler());       // Add window listener

      sketch = new SketcherModel();                        // Create the model
      view = new SketcherView(this);                       // Create the view
      sketch.addObserver(view);                            // Register view with the model
```

```
        window.getContentPane().add(view, BorderLayout.CENTER);
        window.setVisible(true);
    }

    // Return a reference to the application window
    public SketcherFrame getWindow() {
        return window;
    }

    // Return a reference to the model
    public SketcherModel getModel() {
        return sketch;
    }

    // Return a reference to the view
    public SketcherView getView() {
        return view;
    }

    // Handler class for window events
    class WindowHandler extends WindowAdapter {
      // Handler for window closing event
      @Override
      public void windowClosing(WindowEvent e) {
        // Code to be added here later...
      }
    }

    private SketcherModel sketch;          // The data model for the sketch
    private SketcherView view;             // The view of the sketch
    private static SketcherFrame window;   // The application window
    private static Sketcher theApp;        // The application object
}
```

Directory "Sketcher 1 drawing a 3D rectangle"

The `SketcherFrame` constructor that you defined in the previous chapter needs to be modified as follows:

Available for
download on
Wrox.com

```
    public SketcherFrame(String title, Sketcher theApp) {
        setTitle(title);                        // Set the window title
        this.theApp = theApp;                   // Save app. object reference
        setJMenuBar(menuBar);                   // Add the menu bar to the window
        setDefaultCloseOperation(EXIT_ON_CLOSE); // Default is exit the application

        // Rest of the constructor as before...
    }
```

Directory "Sketcher 1 drawing a 3D rectangle"

You can add a field to the `SketcherFrame` class that stores the reference to the application object:

```
    private Sketcher theApp;                // The application object
```

There are new methods in the `Sketcher` class that return a reference to the application window, the model, and the view, so all of these are now accessible from anywhere in the Sketcher application code where you have a reference to the application object available.

After creating the model and view objects in the `createGUI()` method in the `Sketcher` class, you register the view as an observer for the model to enable the model to notify the view when any changes occur. You then add the view to the content pane of the window object, which is the main application window. Because you add the view in the center using the `BorderLayout` manager for the content pane, it occupies all the remaining space in the pane.

You now know roughly the direction in which you are heading, so let's move on down the road.

COMPONENT COORDINATE SYSTEMS

In Chapter 17, you saw how your computer screen has a coordinate system that is used to define the position and size of a window. You also saw how you can add components to a container with their position established by a layout manager. The coordinate system that is used by a container to position components within it is analogous to the screen coordinate system. The origin is at the top-left corner of the container, with the positive *x*-axis running horizontally from left to right, and the positive *y*-axis running from top to bottom. The positions of buttons in a `JWindow` or a `JFrame` object are specified as a pair of (*x,y*) coordinates, relative to the origin at the top-left corner of the container object on the screen. In Figure 19-2 you can see the coordinate system for the `Sketcher` application window.

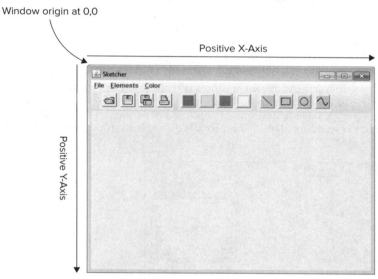

FIGURE 19-2

Of course, the layered pane for the window object has its own coordinate system, with the origin in the top-left corner of the pane, and this is used to position the menu and the content pane. The content pane has its own coordinate system, too, which is used to position the components that it contains.

It's not just containers and windows that have their own coordinate system: Each `JButton` object also has its own system, as do `JToolBar` objects. In fact, every component has its own coordinate system, and an example is shown in Figure 19-3.

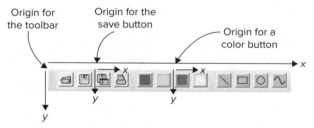

FIGURE 19-3

The toolbar and the buttons each have their own independent coordinate systems with the origin in the top-left corner. It's clear that a container needs a coordinate system for specifying the positions of the components it contains. You also need a coordinate system to draw on a component — to draw a line, for example, you need to be able to specify where it begins and ends in relation to the component. Although the coordinate system you use for drawing on a component is similar to that used for positioning components in a container, it's not exactly the same. It's more complicated when you are drawing — but for very good reasons. Let's see how the coordinate system for drawing works.

DRAWING ON A COMPONENT

Before I get into the specifics of how you draw on a Swing component, I will explain the principle ideas behind it. When you draw on a component using the Java 2D capabilities, two coordinate systems are involved. When you draw something — a line or a curve, for example — you specify the line or the curve in a device-independent logical coordinate system called the *user coordinate system* for the component, or *user space*. By default, this coordinate system has the same orientation as the system that I discussed for positioning components in containers. The origin is at the top-left corner of the component; the positive *x*-axis runs from left to right, and the positive *y*-axis from top to bottom. Coordinates are usually specified as floating-point values, although you can also use integers.

A particular graphical output device has its own device coordinate system, or device space, as illustrated in Figure 19-4. This coordinate system has the same orientation as the default user coordinate system, but the coordinate units depend on the characteristics of the device. Your display, for example, has a different device coordinate system for each configuration of the screen resolution, so the coordinate system when your display is set to a resolution 1024 × 768 pixels is different from the coordinate system for 1920× 1080 pixels.

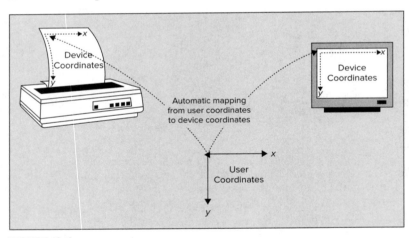

FIGURE 19-4

 NOTE *Incidentally, the drawing process is often referred to as* rendering. *Graphical output devices are generally raster devices that display an image as a rectangular array of pixels and drawing elements such as lines, rectangles, text, and so on need to be rendered into a rasterized representation before they can be output to the device.*

Having a device-independent coordinate system for drawing means that you can use essentially the same code for writing graphical information to a variety of different devices — to your display screen, for example, or to your printer — even though these devices themselves have quite different coordinate systems with different resolutions. The fact that your screen might have 90 pixels per inch and your printer may have 600 dots per inch is automatically taken care of. Java 2D deals with converting your user coordinates to the device coordinate system that is specific to the output device you are using.

Graphics Contexts

The user coordinate system for drawing on a component using Java 2D is encapsulated in an object of type `java.awt.Graphics2D`, which is usually referred to as a *graphics context*. It provides all the tools you need to draw whatever you want on the surface of the component. A graphics context enables you to draw lines, curves, shapes, filled shapes, as well as images, and gives you a great deal of control over the drawing process.

The `Graphics2D` class is derived from the `java.awt.Graphics` class and references to graphics contexts are usually passed around as type `Graphics`, so you need to be aware of it. This is because the `Component` class defines a `getGraphics()` method that returns a reference to a graphics context as type `Graphics` and the Swing component classes, which are subclasses of `Component`, typically override this method. Note that both the `Graphics` and `Graphics2D` classes are abstract classes, so you can't create objects of either type directly. An object representing a graphics context is entirely dependent on the component to which it relates, so a graphics context is always obtained for use with a particular component.

The `Graphics2D` object for a component takes care of mapping user coordinates to device coordinates, so it contains information about the device that is the destination for output as well as the user coordinates for the component. The information required for converting user coordinates to device coordinates is encapsulated in objects of three different types that are defined in the `java.awt` package:

➤ A `GraphicsEnvironment` object encapsulates all the graphics devices (as `GraphicsDevice` objects) and fonts (as `Font` objects) that are available to a Java application on your computer.

➤ A `GraphicsDevice` object encapsulates information about a particular device, such as a screen or a printer, and stores it in one or more `GraphicsConfiguration` objects.

➤ A `GraphicsConfiguration` object defines the characteristics of a particular device, such as a screen or a printer. Your display screen typically has several `GraphicsConfiguration` objects associated with it, each corresponding to a particular combination of screen resolution and number of displayable colors.

The graphics context also maintains other information necessary for drawing operations, such as the drawing color, the line style, and the specification of the fill color and pattern for filled shapes. You see how to work with these attributes in examples later in this chapter.

Because a graphics context defines the drawing context for a specific component, you must have a reference to the graphics context object for a component before you can draw on the component. For the most part, you draw on a component by implementing the `paint()` method that is inherited from `JComponent`. This method is called whenever the component needs to be reconstructed. A reference to an object representing the graphics context for the component is passed as an argument to the `paint()` method, and you use this object to do the drawing. The graphics context includes all the methods that you use to draw on a component, and I'll introduce you to many of these in this chapter.

The `paint()` method is not the only way of drawing on a component. You can obtain a graphics context for a component at any time just by calling its `getGraphics()` method. You can then use methods for the `Graphics` object to specify the drawing operations.

There are occasions when you want to get a component redrawn while avoiding a direct call of the `paint()` method. In such cases you should call `repaint()` for the component, versions of which are inherited in a Swing component class from the `Component` and `JComponent` classes. This situation arises when you make a succession of changes to what is drawn on a component, but want to defer redrawing the component until all the changes have been made. Five versions of the `repaint()` method are available; here are four of them:

➤ `repaint()` causes the entire component to be repainted by calling its `paint()` method after all the currently outstanding events have been processed.

➤ `repaint(long msec)` requests that a call to `paint()` should occur within `msec` milliseconds.

➤ `repaint(int msec, int x, int y, int width, int height)` adds the region specified by the arguments to the dirty region list if the component is visible. The *dirty region list* is simply a list of areas of the component that need to be repainted. The component is repainted by calling its `paint()`

method when all currently outstanding events have been processed, or within msec milliseconds. The region is the rectangle at position (x, y), with the width and height as specified by the last two arguments.

➤ `repaint(Rectangle rect)` adds the rectangle specified by `rect` to the dirty region list if the component is visible. The dirty region is the area to be repainted when the component is next redrawn.

You will find that the first and the last methods are the ones you use most of the time.

That's enough theory for now. It's time to get a bit of practice. Let's get an idea of how you can draw on a component by drawing on the `SketcherView` object that you added to Sketcher. All you need to do is implement the `paint()` method in the `SketcherView` class that you added earlier in this chapter.

TRY IT OUT Drawing in a View

You are going to modify Sketcher temporarily to make it display a 3D rectangle. Add the following implementation of the `paint()` method to the `SketcherView` class:

```java
import javax.swing.JComponent;
import java.util.*;
import java.awt.*;

class SketcherView extends JComponent implements Observer {
  // Method to draw on the view
  @Override
  public void paint(Graphics g) {
    // Temporary code to be replaced later...
    Graphics2D g2D = (Graphics2D)g;                        // Get a Java 2D device context

    g2D.setPaint(Color.RED);                               // Draw in red
    g2D.draw3DRect(50, 50, 150, 100, true);                // Draw a raised 3D rectangle
    g2D.drawString("A nice 3D rectangle", 60, 100);        // Draw some text
  }
  // Rest of the class as before...
}
```

Directory "Sketcher 1 drawing a 3D rectangle"

If you recompile the `SketcherFrame.java` file and run Sketcher once again, you can see what the `paint()` method produces. You should see the window shown in Figure 19-5.

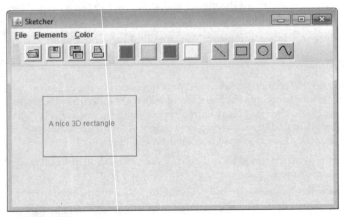

FIGURE 19-5

Okay, it's not 3D in the usual sense and you probably can't see the effect in the book. In this case, the edges of the rectangle are highlighted so that they appear to be beveled and lift from the top left-hand corner (or the coordinate origin).

How It Works

The graphics context is passed as the argument to the paint() method as type Graphics, the base class for Graphics2D, so to use the methods defined in the Graphics2D class you must first cast it to that type.

After you have cast the graphics context object, you set the color in which you draw by calling the setPaint() method for the Graphics2D object with the drawing color as the argument. All subsequent drawing operations are now in the color Color.RED. You can change this with another call to setPaint() whenever you want to draw in a different color.

Next, you call the draw3DRect() method for the Graphics2D object, and this draws the 3D rectangle. The first two arguments are integers specifying the *x* and *y* coordinates of the top-left corner of the rectangle to be drawn, relative to the user space origin of the component, which in this case is the top-left corner of the view object in the content pane. The third and fourth arguments are integers specifying the width and height of the rectangle respectively, also in units determined by the user coordinate system. The fifth argument is a boolean value that makes the rectangle appear to be raised when the value is true.

The drawString() method draws the string specified as the first argument at the position determined by the second and third arguments — these are the *x* and *y* coordinates in user coordinates of the bottom-left corner of the first letter of the string. The string is drawn by obtaining the glyphs for the current Font object in the device context corresponding to the characters in the string. As I said when I discussed Font objects, the glyphs for a font define the physical appearance of the characters.

However, there's more to drawing than is apparent from this example. The graphics context has information about the line style to be drawn, as well as the color, the font to be used for text, and more besides. Let's dig a little deeper into what is going on.

The Drawing Process

A Graphics2D object maintains a whole heap of information that determines how things are drawn. Most of this information is contained in six attributes within a Graphics2D object:

➤ **Paint:** Determines the drawing color for lines. It also defines the color and pattern to be used for filling shapes. The paint attribute is set by calling the setPaint(Paint paint) method for the graphics context. java.awt.Paint is an interface that is implemented by the Color class that defines a color. It is also implemented by the java.awt.GradientPaint and java.awt.TexturePaint classes, which represent a color pattern and a texture, respectively. You can therefore pass references of any of these types to the setPaint() method. The default paint attribute is the color of the component.

➤ **Stroke:** Defines a pen that determines the line style, such as solid, dashed, or dotted lines, and the line thickness. It also determines the shape of the ends of lines. The stroke attribute is set by calling the setStroke(Stroke s) method for a graphics context. The default stroke attribute defines a square pen that draws a solid line with a thickness of one user coordinate unit. The ends of the line are square, and joins are mitered (i.e., the line ends are beveled where lines join so they fit together). The java.awt.Stroke interface is implemented by the java.awt.BasicStroke class, which defines a basic set of attributes for rendering lines.

➤ **Font:** Determines the font to be used when drawing text. The font attribute is set by calling the setFont(Font font) method for the graphics context. The default font is the font set for the component.

➤ **Transform:** Defines the transformations to be applied during the rendering process. What you draw can be translated, rotated, and scaled as determined by the transforms currently in effect. There are several methods for applying transforms to what is drawn, as you see later. The default transform is the identity transform, which leaves things unchanged.

➤ **Clip:** Defines the boundary of an area on a component. Rendering operations are restricted so that drawing takes place only within the area enclosed by the clip boundary. The clip attribute is set by calling one of the two `setClip()` methods for a graphics context. With one version of `setClip()` you define the boundary of the area to be rendered as a rectangle that you specify by the coordinates of its top-left corner and the width and height of the rectangle. The other `setClip()` method expects the argument to be a reference of type `java.awt.Shape`. The `Shape` interface is implemented by a variety of classes in the `java.awt.geom` package that define geometric shapes of various kinds, such as lines, circles, polygons, and curves. The default clip attribute is the whole component area.

➤ **Composite:** Determines how overlapping shapes are drawn on a component. You can alter the transparency of the fill color of a shape so an underlying shape shows through. You set the composite attribute by calling the `setComposite(Composite comp)` method for the graphics context. The default composite attribute causes a new shape to be drawn over whatever is already there, taking account of the transparency of any of the colors used.

All the objects that represent attributes are stored as references within a `Graphics2D` object. Therefore, you must always call a `setXXX()` method to alter an attribute in a graphics context, not try to modify an external object directly. If you externally alter an object that has been used to set an attribute, the results are unpredictable.

 NOTE *You can also affect how the rendering process deals with "jaggies" when drawing lines. The process to eliminate jaggies on sloping lines is called* antialiasing, *and you can change the antialiasing that is applied by calling one of the two* `setRenderingHints()` *methods for a graphics context. I don't go into this aspect of drawing further, though.*

There's a huge amount of detail on attributes under the covers. Rather than going into all that here, you explore how to apply new attributes to a graphics context piecemeal where it is relevant to the various examples you create.

Rendering Operations

You have the following basic methods available with a `Graphics2D` object for rendering various kinds of graphic entities:

➤ `draw(Shape shape)` renders a shape using the current attributes for the graphics context. I discuss what a shape is next.

➤ `fill(Shape shape)` fills a shape using the current attributes for the graphics context. You see how to do this later in this chapter.

➤ `drawString(String text)` renders a text string using the current attributes for the graphics context. You apply this further in the next chapter.

This is very much a subset of the methods available in the `Graphics2D` class. I concentrate on those that draw shapes and strings that I have identified here. Let's see what shapes are available; they'll help make Sketcher a lot more useful.

SHAPES

Classes that define geometric shapes are contained in the `java.awt.geom` package, but the `Shape` interface that these classes implement is defined in `java.awt`. Objects that represent shapes are often passed around as references of type `Shape`, so you often need to import class names from both packages into your source file. Any class that implements the Shape interface defines a shape, and visually a shape is some composite of straight lines and curves. Straight lines, rectangles, ellipses, and curves are all shapes.

A graphics context knows how to draw objects of a type that implements the Shape interface. To draw a shape on a component, you just need to pass the object defining the shape to the draw() method for the Graphics2D object for the component. To explore this in detail, I split the shapes into three groups: straight lines and rectangles, arcs and ellipses, and freeform curves. First, though, you must take a look at how points are defined.

Classes Defining Points

Two classes in the java.awt.geom package define points: Point2D.Float and Point2D.Double. From the class names you can see that these are both inner classes to the Point2D class, which also happens to be an abstract base class for both classes, too. The Point2D.Float class defines a point from a pair of (*x,y*) coordinates of type float, whereas the Point2D.Double class defines a point as a coordinate pair of type double. The Point class in the java.awt package also defines a point, but in terms of a coordinate pair of type int. The Point class also has Point2D as a base, and the hierarchy of classes that represents points is shown in Figure 19-6.

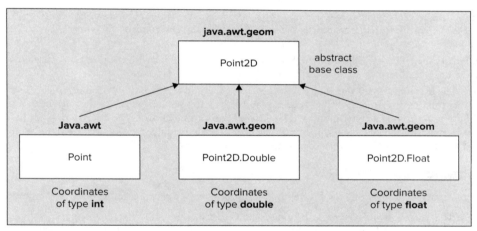

FIGURE 19-6

The Point class actually predates the Point2D class, but the Point class was redefined to make it a subclass of Point2D when Point2D was introduced, hence the somewhat unusual class hierarchy with only two of the subclasses as static nested classes. The merit of this arrangement is that all of the subclasses inherit the methods defined in the Point2D class, so operations on each of the three kinds of point are the same. Objects of all three concrete types that represent points can be passed around as references of type Point2D.

The three subclasses of Point2D define a default constructor that defines the point (0,0) and a constructor that accepts a pair of coordinates of the type appropriate to the class type.

Each of the three concrete point classes inherits the following operations:

1. **Accessing coordinate values:** The getX() and getY() methods return the *x* and *y* coordinates of a point as type double, regardless of how the coordinates are stored. These are abstract methods in the Point2D class, so they are defined in each of the subclasses. Although you get coordinates as values of type double from all three concrete classes via these methods, you can always access the coordinates with their original type directly because the coordinates are stored in public fields with the same names, x and y, in each case.

2. **Calculating the distance between two points:** You have no less than three overloaded versions of the `distance()` method for calculating the distance between two points and returning it as type `double`:

   ➤ `distance(double x1,double y1, double x2,double y2)`: This is a static version of the method that calculates the distance between the points (x1, y1) and (x2, y2).

   ➤ `distance(double xNext,double yNext)`: This calculates the distance from the current point (the object for which the method is called) and the point (xNext, yNext).

   ➤ `distance(Point2D nextPoint)`: This calculates the distance from the current point to the point `nextPoint`. The argument can be any of the subclass types, `Point`, `Point2D.Float`, or `Point2D.Double`.

   Here's how you might calculate the distance between two points:

   ```
   Point2D.Double p1 = new Point2D.Double(2.5, 3.5);
   Point p2 = new Point(20, 30);
   double lineLength = p1.distance(p2);
   ```

   You can also calculate this distance without creating the points by using the static method:

   ```
   double lineLength = Point2D.distance(2.5, 3.5, 20, 30);
   ```

   Corresponding to each of the three `distance()` methods is a convenience method, `distanceSq()`, with the same parameter list that returns the square of the distance between two points as a value of type `double`.

3. **Comparing points:** The `equals()` method compares the current point with the point object referenced by the argument and returns `true` if they are equal and `false` otherwise.

4. **Setting a new location for a point:** The `setLocation()` method comes in two versions. One accepts an argument that is a reference of type `Point2D` and sets the coordinate values of the current point to those of the point passed as an argument. The other accepts arguments of type `double` that are the *x* and *y* coordinates of the new location. The `Point` class also defines a version of `setLocation()` that accepts two arguments of type `int` to define the new coordinates.

Lines and Rectangles

The `java.awt.geom` package contains the following classes for shapes that are straight lines and rectangles:

➤ `Line2D`: This is an abstract base class defining a line between two points. Two concrete subclasses — `Line2D.Float` and `Line2D.Double` — define lines in terms of user coordinates of type `float` and `double`, respectively. You can see from their names that the subclasses are nested classes to the abstract base class `Line2D`.

➤ `Rectangle2D`: This is the abstract base class for the `Rectangle2D.Double` and `Rectangle2D.Float` classes that define rectangles. A rectangle is defined by the coordinates of the position of its top-left corner plus its width and height. The `Rectangle2D` class is also the abstract base class for the `Rectangle` class in the `java.awt` package, which stores the position coordinates and the height and width as values of type `int`.

➤ `RoundRectangle2D`: This is the abstract base class for the `RoundRectangle2D.Double` and `RoundRectangle2D.Float` classes, which define rectangles with rounded corners. The rounded corners are specified by a width and height.

Like the `java.awt.Point` class, the `java.awt.Rectangle` class predates the `Rectangle2D` class, but the definition of the `Rectangle` class was changed to make `Rectangle2D` a base for compatibility reasons. Note that there is no equivalent to the `Rectangle` class for lines defined by integer coordinates. If you are browsing the documentation, you might notice there is a `Line` interface, but this declares operations for an audio channel and has nothing to do with geometry.

Figure 19-7 illustrates how, lines, rectangles, and round rectangles are defined.

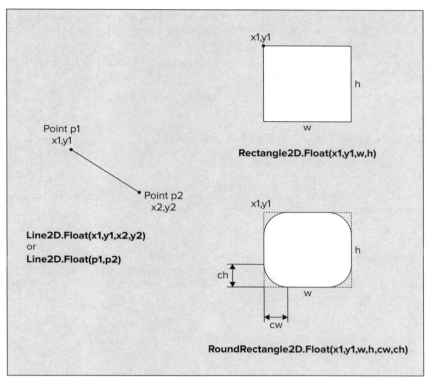

FIGURE 19-7

You can define a line by supplying two `Point2D` objects to a constructor, or two pairs of (*x,y*) coordinates. For example, here's how you define a line by two coordinate pairs:

```
Line2D.float line = new Line2D.Float(5.0f, 100.0f, 50.0f, 150.0f);
```

This draws a line from the point (5.0, 100.0) to the point (50.0, 150.0). You could also create the same line using `Point2D.Float` objects, like this:

```
Point2D.Float p1 = new Point2D.Float(5.0f, 100.0f);
Point2D.Float p2 = new Point2D.Float(50.0f, 150.0f);
Line2D.float line = new Line2D.Float(p1, p2);
```

You draw a line on a component using the `draw()` method for a `Graphics2D` object. For example:

```
g2D.draw(line);                         // Draw the line
```

To create a rectangle, you specify the coordinates of its top-left corner, and the width and height of the rectangle:

```
float width = 120.0f;
float height = 90.0f;
Rectangle2D.Float rectangle = new Rectangle2D.Float(50.0f, 150.0f, width, height);
```

The default constructor creates a rectangle at the origin with a zero width and height. You can set the position, width, and height of a rectangle by calling its `setRect()` method. There are three versions of this method. One of them accepts arguments for the coordinates of the top-left corner and the width and height as values of type `float`, exactly as in the constructor. Another accepts arguments with the same meaning but of type `double`. The third `setRect()` method accepts an argument of type `Rectangle2D`, so you can pass any type of rectangle object to it.

A `Rectangle2D` object has `getX()` and `getY()` methods for retrieving the coordinates of the top-left corner, and `getWidth()` and `getHeight()` methods that return the width and height of the rectangle, respectively.

A round rectangle is a rectangle with rounded corners. The corners are defined by a width and a height and are essentially a quarter segment of an ellipse (I get to the details of ellipses later). Of course, if the corner width and height are equal, then the corner is a quarter of a circle.

You can define a round rectangle using coordinates of type `double` with the following statements:

```
Point2D.Double position = new Point2D.Double(10, 10);
double width = 200.0;
double height = 100;
double cornerWidth = 15.0;
double cornerHeight = 10.0;
RoundRectangle2D.Double roundRect = new RoundRectangle2D.Double(
                        position.x, position.y,          // Position of top-left
                        width, height,                   // Rectangle width & height
                        cornerWidth, cornerHeight);      // Corner width & height
```

The only difference between this and defining an ordinary rectangle is the addition of the width and height to be applied for the corner rounding.

Combining Rectangles

You can combine two rectangles to produce a new rectangle that is either the union of the two original rectangles or the intersection. The union of two rectangles is the smallest rectangle enclosing both. The intersection is the rectangle that is common to both. Let's take a couple of specifics to see how this works. You can create two rectangles with the following statements:

```
float width = 120.0f;
float height = 90.0f;
Rectangle2D.Float rect1 = new Rectangle2D.Float(50.0f, 150.0f, width, height);
Rectangle2D.Float rect2 = new Rectangle2D.Float(80.0f, 180.0f, width, height);
```

You can obtain the intersection of the two rectangles with the following statement:

```
Rectangle2D.Float rect3 = rect1.createIntersection(rect2);
```

The effect is illustrated in Figure 19-8 by the shaded rectangle. Of course, the result is the same if you call the method for `rect2` with `rect1` as the argument. If the rectangles don't overlap, the rectangle that is returned is the rectangle from the bottom right of one rectangle to the top right of the other that does not overlap either of the original rectangles.

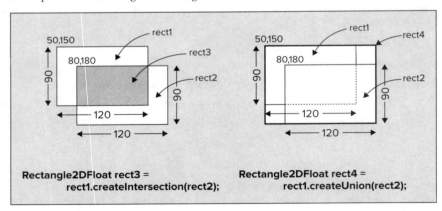

FIGURE 19-8

The following statement produces the union of the two rectangles:

```
Rectangle2D.Float rect3 = rect1.createUnion(rect2);
```

The result is shown in Figure 19-8 by the rectangle with the heavy boundary that encloses the other two.

Testing Rectangles

Perhaps the simplest test you can apply to a Rectangle2D object is for an empty rectangle. The isEmpty() method that is implemented in all the rectangle classes returns true if the Rectangle2D object is empty — which is when either the width or the height (or both) are zero.

You can also test whether a point lies inside any type of rectangle object by calling its contains() method. There are contains() methods for all the rectangle classes that accept either a Point2D argument, or a pair of (*x*,*y*) coordinates of a type matching that of the rectangle class: They return true if the point lies within the rectangle and false otherwise. Every shape class defines a getBounds2D() method that returns a Rectangle2D object that encloses the shape.

The getBounds2D() method is frequently used in association with the contains() method to provide an efficient test of whether the cursor lies within a particular shape. Testing whether the cursor is within the enclosing rectangle is a lot faster in general than testing whether it is within the precise boundary of the shape and is good enough for many purposes — for example, when you are selecting a particular shape on the screen to manipulate it in some way.

You also have versions of the contains() method to test whether a given rectangle lies within the area occupied by a rectangle object — this obviously enables you to test whether a shape lies within another shape. You can pass the given rectangle to the contains() method as the coordinates of its top-left corner, and its height and width as type double, or as a Rectangle2D reference. The method returns true if the rectangle object completely contains the given rectangle.

Let's try drawing a few simple lines and rectangles by inserting some code in the paint() method for the view in Sketcher.

TRY IT OUT Drawing Lines and Rectangles

Begin by adding an import statement to SketcherView.java for the class names from the java.awt.geom package:

```
import java.awt.geom.*;
```

Now you can replace the previous code in the paint() method in the SketcherView class with the following:

Available for
download on
Wrox.com

```
@Override
public void paint(Graphics g) {
    // Temporary code - to be deleted later...
    Graphics2D g2D = (Graphics2D)g;                    // Get a Java 2D device context

    g2D.setPaint(Color.RED);                           // Draw in red

    // Position width and height of first rectangle
    Point2D.Float p1 = new Point2D.Float(50.0f, 10.0f);
    float width1 = 60;
    float height1 = 80;

    // Create and draw the first rectangle
    Rectangle2D.Float rect = new Rectangle2D.Float(p1.x, p1.y, width1, height1);
    g2D.draw(rect);

    // Position width and height of second rectangle
    Point2D.Float p2 = new Point2D.Float(150.0f, 100.0f);
    float width2 = width1 + 30;
    float height2 = height1 + 40;

    // Create and draw the second rectangle
    g2D.draw(new Rectangle2D.Float((float)(p2.getX()), (float)(p2.getY()), width2, height2));
    g2D.setPaint(Color.BLUE);                          // Draw in blue

    // Draw lines to join corresponding corners of the rectangles
    Line2D.Float line = new Line2D.Float(p1,p2);
```

```
        g2D.draw(line);

        p1.setLocation(p1.x + width1, p1.y);
        p2.setLocation(p2.x + width2, p2.y);
        g2D.draw(new Line2D.Float(p1,p2));

        p1.setLocation(p1.x, p1.y + height1);
        p2.setLocation(p2.x, p2.y + height2);
        g2D.draw(new Line2D.Float(p1,p2));

        p1.setLocation(p1.x - width1, p1.y);
        p2.setLocation(p2.x - width2, p2.y);
        g2D.draw(new Line2D.Float(p1, p2));

        p1.setLocation(p1.x, p1.y - height1);
        p2.setLocation(p2.x, p2.y - height2);
        g2D.draw(new Line2D.Float(p1, p2));

        g2D.drawString("Lines and rectangles", 60, 250); // Draw some text
    }
```

Directory "Sketcher 2 drawing lines and rectangles"

If you type this code in correctly and recompile the `SketcherView` class, the Sketcher window looks like the one shown in Figure 19-9.

How It Works

After casting the graphics context object that is passed to the `paint()` method to type `Graphics2D`, you set the drawing color to red. All subsequent drawing that you do is in red until you change the color with another call to `setPaint()`. You define a `Point2D.Float` object to represent the position of the first rectangle, and you define variables to hold the width and height of the rectangle. You use these to create the rectangle by passing them as arguments to the constructor that you saw earlier in this chapter and display the rectangle by passing the `rect` object to the `draw()` method for the

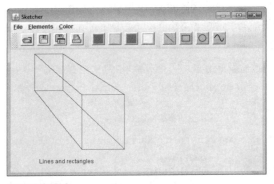

FIGURE 19-9

graphics context, `g2D`. The second rectangle is defined by essentially the same process, except that this time you create the `Rectangle2D.Float` object in the argument expression for the `draw()` method.

Note that you have to cast the values returned by the `getX()` and `getY()` members of the `Point2D` object, as they are returned as type `double`. It is generally more convenient to reference the *x* and *y* fields directly as you do in the rest of the code.

You change the drawing color to blue so that you can see quite clearly the lines you are drawing. You use the `setLocation()` method for the point objects to move the point on each rectangle to successive corners and draw a line at each position. The caption also appears in blue because that is the color in effect when you call the `drawString()` method to output the text string.

Arcs and Ellipses

There are shape classes defining both arcs and ellipses. The abstract class representing a generic ellipse is:

➤ `Ellipse2D`: This is the abstract base class for the `Ellipse2D.Double` and `Ellipse2D.Float` classes that define ellipses. An ellipse is defined by the top-left corner, width, and height of the rectangle that encloses it.

➤ Arc2D: This is the abstract base class for the `Arc2D.Double` and `Arc2D.Float` classes that define arcs as a portion of an ellipse. The full ellipse is defined by the position of the top-left corner and the width and height of the rectangle that encloses it. The arc length is defined by a start angle measured in degrees counterclockwise relative to the horizontal axis of the full ellipse, plus an angular extent measured anticlockwise from the start angle in degrees. You can specify an arc as OPEN, which means the ends are not connected; as CHORD, which means the ends are connected by a straight line; or as PIE, which means the ends are connected by straight lines to the center of the whole ellipse. These constants are defined as static members of the `Arc2D` class.

Arcs and ellipses are closely related because an arc is just a segment of an ellipse. Constructors for the `Ellipse2D.Float` and `Arc2d.Float` classes are shown in Figure 19-10. To define an ellipse you supply the data necessary to define the enclosing rectangle — the coordinates of the top-left corner, the width, and the height. To define an arc you supply the data to define the ellipse, plus additional data that defines the segment of the ellipse that you want. The seventh argument to the arc constructor determines the type, whether OPEN, CHORD, or PIE.

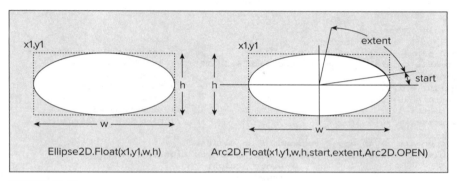

FIGURE 19-10

You could define an ellipse with the following statements:

```
Point2D.Double position = new Point2D.Double(10,10);
double width = 200.0;
double height = 100;
Ellipse2D.Double ellipse = new Ellipse2D.Double(
                    position.x, position.y,  // Top-left corner
                    width, height);          // width & height of rectangle
```

You could define an arc that is a segment of the previous ellipse with this statement:

```
Arc2D.Double arc = new Arc2D.Double(
                    position.x, position.y,  // Top-left corner
                    width, height,           // width & height of rectangle
                    0.0, 90.0,               // Start and extent angles
                    Arc2D.OPEN);             // Arc is open
```

This defines the upper-right quarter segment of the whole ellipse as an open arc. The angles are measured counterclockwise from the horizontal in degrees. As shown in Figure 19-10, the first angular argument is where the arc starts, and the second is the angular extent of the arc.

Of course, a circle is just an ellipse for which the width and height are the same, so the following statement defines a circle with a diameter of 150:

```
double diameter = 150.0;
Ellipse2D.Double circle = new Ellipse2D.Double(
                    position.x, position.y,  // Top-left corner
                    diameter, diameter);     // width & height of rectangle
```

This presumes the point `position` is defined somewhere. You often want to define a circle by its center and radius — adjusting the arguments to the constructor a little does this easily:

```
Point2D.Double center = new Point2D.Double(200, 200);
double radius = 150;
Ellipse2D.Double newCircle = new Ellipse2D.Double(
        center.x-radius, center.y-radius,     // Top-left corner
        2*radius, 2*radius);                  // width & height of rectangle
```

The fields that stores the coordinates of the top-left corner of the enclosing rectangle and the width and height are public members of `Ellipse2D` and `Arc2D` objects. They are x, y, width, and height, respectively. An `Arc2D` object also has public members, start and extent, that store the angles.

TRY IT OUT   Drawing Arcs and Ellipses

Let's modify the `paint()` method in `SketcherView.java` once again to draw some arcs and ellipses. Replace the code in the body of the `paint()` method with the following:

```
@Override
public void paint(Graphics g) {
    // Temporary code - to be deleted later...
    Graphics2D g2D = (Graphics2D)g;                          // Get a 2D device context
    Point2D.Double position = new Point2D.Double(50,10);     // Initial position
    double width = 150;                                      // Width of ellipse
    double height = 100;                                     // Height of ellipse
    double start = 30;                                       // Start angle for arc
    double extent = 120;                                     // Extent of arc
    double diameter = 40;                                    // Diameter of circle

    // Define open arc as an upper segment of an ellipse
    Arc2D.Double top = new Arc2D.Double(position.x, position.y,
                                width, height,
                                start, extent,
                                Arc2D.OPEN);

    // Define open arc as lower segment of ellipse shifted up relative to 1st
    Arc2D.Double bottom = new Arc2D.Double(
                        position.x, position.y - height + diameter,
                        width, height,
                        start + 180, extent,
                        Arc2D.OPEN);

    // Create a circle centered between the two arcs
    Ellipse2D.Double circle1 = new Ellipse2D.Double(
                        position.x + width/2 - diameter/2,position.y,
                        diameter, diameter);

    // Create a second circle concentric with the first and half the diameter
    Ellipse2D.Double circle2 = new Ellipse2D.Double(
                    position.x + width/2 - diameter/4, position.y + diameter/4,
                    diameter/2, diameter/2);

    // Draw all the shapes
    g2D.setPaint(Color.BLACK);                               // Draw in black
    g2D.draw(top);
    g2D.draw(bottom);

    g2D.setPaint(Color.BLUE);                                // Draw in blue
    g2D.draw(circle1);
    g2D.draw(circle2);
    g2D.drawString("Arcs and ellipses", 80, 100);           // Draw some text
}
```

Directory "Sketcher 3 drawing arcs and ellipses"

Running Sketcher with this version of the `paint()` method in `SketcherView` produces the window shown in Figure 19-11.

How It Works

This time you create all the shapes first and then draw them. The two arcs are segments of ellipses of the same height and width. The lower arc segment is shifted up with respect to the first arc segment so that they intersect, and the distance between the top of the rectangle for the first arc and the bottom of the rectangle for the second arc is `diameter`, which is the diameter of the first circle you create.

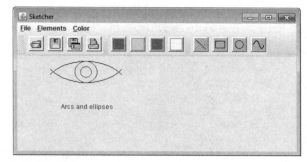

FIGURE 19-11

Both circles are created centered between the two arcs and are concentric. Finally, you draw all the shapes — the arcs in black and the circles in blue.

Next time you change the code in Sketcher, you build the application as it should be, so you can now remove the temporary code from the `paint()` method and, if you haven't done so already, also remove the code that sets the background color in the `ColorAction` inner class to the `SketcherFrame` class.

Curves

There are two classes that define arbitrary curves, one defining a quadratic or second-order curve, and the other defining a cubic curve. These arbitrary curves are parametric curves defined by a sequence of curve segments. A quadratic curve segment is defined by an equation that includes squares of the independent variable, x. A cubic curve is defined by an equation that includes cubes of the independent variable, x. The cubic curve just happens to be a Bézier curve (so called because it was developed by a Frenchman, Monsieur Pierre Bézier, and first applied in the context of defining contours for programming numerically controlled machine tools for manufacturing car body forms).

The classes defining these curves are:

➤ `QuadCurve2D`: This is the abstract base class for the `QuadCurve2D.Double` and `QuadCurve2D.Float` classes that define a quadratic curve segment. The curve is defined by its end points plus a control point that defines the tangent at each end. The tangents are the lines from the end points to the control point.

➤ `CubicCurve2D`: This is the abstract base class for the `CubicCurve2D.Double` and `CubicCurve2D.Float` classes that define a cubic curve segment. The curve is defined by its end points plus two control points that define the tangent at each end. The tangents are the lines from the end points to the corresponding control point.

Figure 19-12 illustrates how the control points relate to the curves in each case. In general, there are many other methods for modeling arbitrary curves, but the two defined in Java have the merit that they are both easy to understand, and the effect on the curve segment when you move a control point is quite intuitive.

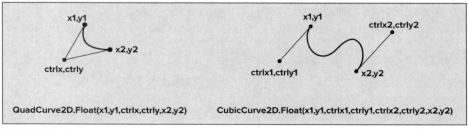

FIGURE 19-12

An object of a curve type defines a curve segment between two points. The control points — one for a QuadCurve2D curve and two for a CubicCurve2D curve — control the direction and magnitude of the tangents at the end points. A QuadCurve2D curve constructor has six parameters corresponding to the *x* and *y* coordinates of the starting point for the segment, the *x* and *y* coordinates of the control point, and the *x* and *y* coordinates of the end point. You can define a QuadCurve2D curve from a point start to a point end, plus a control point, control, with the following statements:

```
Point2D.Double startQ = new Point2D.Double(50, 150);
Point2D.Double endQ = new Point2D.Double(150, 150);
Point2D.Double control = new Point2D.Double(80,100);

QuadCurve2D.Double quadCurve = new QuadCurve2D.Double(
                    startQ.x, startQ.y,       // Segment start point
                    control.x, control.y,     // Control point
                    endQ.x, endQ.y);          // Segment end point
```

The QuadCurve2D subclasses have public members storing the end points and the control point so you can access them directly. The coordinates of the start and end points are stored in the fields x1, y1, x2, and y2. The coordinates of the control point are stored in ctrlx and ctrly.

Defining a cubic curve segment is very similar — you just have two control points, one for each end of the segment. The arguments are the (*x,y*) coordinates of the start point, the control point for the start of the segment, the control point for the end of the segment, and finally the end point. You could define a cubic curve with the following statements:

```
Point2D.Double startC = new Point2D.Double(50, 300);
Point2D.Double endC = new Point2D.Double(150, 300);
Point2D.Double controlStart = new Point2D.Double(80, 250);
Point2D.Double controlEnd = new Point2D.Double(160, 250);

CubicCurve2D.Double cubicCurve = new CubicCurve2D.Double(
                startC.x, startC.y,                   // Segment start point
                controlStart.x, controlStart.y,       // Control point for start
                controlEnd.x, controlEnd.y,           // Control point for end
                endC.x, endC.y);                      // Segment end point
```

The cubic curve classes also have public members for all the points: x1, y1, x2, and y2 for the end points and ctrlx1, ctrly1, ctrlx2, and ctrly2 for the corresponding control points. You could therefore use the default constructor to create a curve object with all the fields set to 0 and set them yourself. The following statements create the same curve as the previous fragment:

```
CubicCurve2D.Double cubicCurve = new CubicCurve2D.Double();
cubicCurve.x1 = 50;
cubicCurve.y1 = 300;
cubicCurve.x2 = 150;
cubicCurve.y2 = 300;
cubicCurve.ctrlx1 = 80;
cubicCurve.ctrly1 = 250;
cubicCurve.ctrlx2 = 160;
cubicCurve.ctrly2 = 250;
```

Of course, you could use the same approach to create a quadratic curve.

You can understand these curve classes better if you try them out. This time let's do it with an applet.

Drawing Curves

You can define an applet to display the curves that I used as examples in the previous section:

```
import javax.swing.*;
import java.awt.*;
import java.awt.geom.*;

@SuppressWarnings("serial")
public class CurveApplet extends JApplet {
```

```java
  // Initialize the applet
  @Override
  public void init() {
    pane = new CurvePane();                   // Create pane containing curves
    Container content = getContentPane();     // Get the content pane

    // Add the pane displaying the curves to the content pane for the applet
    content.add(pane);                        // BorderLayout.CENTER is default position
  }

  // Class defining a pane on which to draw
  class CurvePane extends JComponent {
    // Constructor
    public CurvePane() {
      quadCurve = new QuadCurve2D.Double(     // Create quadratic curve
                    startQ.x, startQ.y,       // Segment start point
                    control.x, control.y,     // Control point
                    endQ.x, endQ.y);          // Segment end point

      cubicCurve = new CubicCurve2D.Double(   // Create cubic curve
                    startC.x, startC.y,       // Segment start point
                    controlStart.x, controlStart.y, // Control pt for start
                    controlEnd.x, controlEnd.y,     // Control point for end
                    endC.x, endC.y);          // Segment end point
    }

    @Override
    public void paint(Graphics g) {
      Graphics2D g2D = (Graphics2D)g;         // Get a 2D device context

      // Draw the curves
      g2D.setPaint(Color.BLUE);
      g2D.draw(quadCurve);
      g2D.draw(cubicCurve);
    }
  }

  // Points for quadratic curve
  private Point2D.Double startQ = new Point2D.Double(50, 75);       // Start point
  private Point2D.Double endQ = new Point2D.Double(150, 75);        // End point
  private Point2D.Double control = new Point2D.Double(80, 25);      // Control point

  // Points for cubic curve
  private Point2D.Double startC = new Point2D.Double(50, 150);      // Start point
  private private Point2D.Double endC = new Point2D.Double(150, 150);// End point
  private Point2D.Double controlStart = new Point2D.Double(80, 100); // 1st cntrl pt
  private Point2D.Double controlEnd = new Point2D.Double(160, 100);  // 2nd cntrl pt
  private QuadCurve2D.Double quadCurve;                             // Quadratic curve
  private CubicCurve2D.Double cubicCurve;                           // Cubic curve
  private CurvePane pane = new CurvePane();                         // Pane to contain curves
}
```

Directory "CurveApplet 1"

You need an HTML file to run the applet. The contents can be something like:

```html
<html>
  <head>
  </head>
  <body bgcolor="000000">
    <center>
      <applet
        code = "CurveApplet.class"
        width = "300"
        height = "300"
```

```
        >
      </applet>
    </center>
  </body>
</html>
```

If you run the applet using `appletviewer`, you get a window that looks like the one shown in Figure 19-13.

How It Works

To display the curves, you need an object of your own class type so that you can implement the `paint()` method for it. You define the inner class, `CurvePane`, for this purpose with `JComponent` as the base class so it is a Swing component. You create an object of this class (which is a member of the `CurveApplet` class) and add it to the content pane for the applet using its inherited `add()` method. The layout manager for the content pane is `BorderLayout`, and the default positioning is `BorderLayout.CENTER` so the `CurvePane` object fills the content pane.

FIGURE 19-13

The points defining the quadratic and cubic curves are defined as fields in the `CurveApplet` class and the fields that store references to the curve objects are used in the `paint()` method for the `CurvePane` class to display curves. The fields that store points are used in the `CurvePane` class constructor to create the objects encapsulating curves. You draw the curves in the `paint()` method by calling the `draw()` method for the `Graphics2D` object and passing a reference to a curve object as the argument. The classes that define curves implement the `Shape` interface so any curve object can be passed to the `draw()` method that has a parameter of type `Shape`.

It's hard to see how the control points affect the shape of the curve, so let's add some code to draw the control points.

TRY IT OUT **Displaying the Control Points**

You can mark the position of each control point by drawing a small circle around it that I'll call a marker. You will be able to move a control point around by dragging the marker with the mouse and see the effect on the curve. You can define a marker using an inner class of `CurveApplet` that you can define as follows:

Available for
download on
Wrox.com

```java
// Inner class defining a control point marker
private class Marker {
  public Marker(Point2D.Double control)  {
    center = control;                    // Save control point as circle center

    // Create circle around control point
    circle = new Ellipse2D.Double(control.x-radius, control.y-radius,
                                  2.0*radius, 2.0*radius);
  }

  // Draw the marker
  public void draw(Graphics2D g2D) {
    g2D.draw(circle);
  }

  // Get center of marker - the control point position
  Point2D.Double getCenter() {
    return center;
  }

  Ellipse2D.Double circle;              // Circle around control point
  Point2D.Double center;                // Circle center - the control point
  static final double radius = 3;       // Radius of circle
}
```

Directory "CurveApplet 2 displaying control points"

The argument to the constructor is the control point that is to be marked. The constructor stores this control point in the member `center` and creates an `Ellipse2D.Double` object that is the circle to mark the control point. The class also has a method, `draw()`, to draw the marker using the `Graphics2D` object reference that is passed to it, so `Marker` objects can draw themselves, given a graphics context. The `getCenter()` method returns the center of the marker as a `Point2D.Double` reference. You use the `getCenter()` method when you draw tangent lines from the end points of a curve to the corresponding control points.

You can now add fields to the `CurveApplet` class to define the `Marker` objects for the control points. These definitions should follow the members that define the points:

```
// Markers for control points
private Marker ctrlQuad = new Marker(control);
private Marker ctrlCubic1 = new Marker(controlStart);
private Marker ctrlCubic2 = new Marker(controlEnd);
```

Directory "CurveApplet 2 displaying control points"

You can now add code to the `paint()` method for the `CurvePane` class to draw the markers and the tangents from the end points of the curve segments:

```
@Override
public void paint(Graphics g) {
    // Code to draw curves as before...
    // Create and draw the markers showing the control points
    g2D.setPaint(Color.red);                    // Set the color
    ctrlQuad.draw(g2D);
    ctrlCubic1.draw(g2D);
    ctrlCubic2.draw(g2D);
    // Draw tangents from the curve end points to the control marker centers
    Line2D.Double tangent = new Line2D.Double(startQ, ctrlQuad.getCenter());
    g2D.draw(tangent);
    tangent = new Line2D.Double(endQ, ctrlQuad.getCenter());
    g2D.draw(tangent);

    tangent = new Line2D.Double(startC, ctrlCubic1.getCenter());
    g2D.draw(tangent);
    tangent = new Line2D.Double(endC, ctrlCubic2.getCenter());
    g2D.draw(tangent);
}
```

Directory "CurveApplet 2 displaying control points"

If you recompile the applet with these changes, when you execute it again you should see the window shown in Figure 19-14.

How It Works

In the `Marker` class constructor, the top-left corner of the rectangle enclosing the circle for a control point is obtained by subtracting the radius from the x and y coordinates of the control point. You then create an `Ellipse2D.Double` object with the width and height as twice the value of `radius` — which is the diameter of the circle.

In the `paint()` method, you call the `draw()` method for each of the `Marker` objects to draw a red circle around each control point. The tangents to the curves are just lines from the end points of each curve segment to the centers of the corresponding `Marker` objects.

FIGURE 19-14

It would be good to see what happens to a curve segment when you move the control points around. Then you could really see how the control points affect the shape of the curve. That's not as difficult to implement as it might sound, so let's give it a try.

Moving the Control Points

You arrange to allow a control point to be moved by positioning the cursor on it, pressing a mouse button, and dragging it around. Releasing the mouse button stops the process for that control point, so the user then is free to manipulate another control point. To implement this functionality in the applet you add another inner class to `CurveApplet` that handles mouse events:

```java
private class MouseHandler extends MouseInputAdapter {
  @Override
  public void mousePressed(MouseEvent e) {
    // Check if the cursor is inside any marker
    if(ctrlQuad.contains(e.getX(), e.getY())) {
      selected = ctrlQuad;
    }
    else if(ctrlCubic1.contains(e.getX(), e.getY())) {
      selected = ctrlCubic1;
    }
    else if(ctrlCubic2.contains(e.getX(), e.getY())) {
      selected = ctrlCubic2;
    }
  }

  @Override
  public void mouseReleased(MouseEvent e) {
    selected = null;                       // Deselect any selected marker
  }

  @Override
  public void mouseDragged(MouseEvent e) {
    if(selected != null) {                 // If a marker is selected
      // Set the marker to current cursor position
      selected.setLocation(e.getX(), e.getY());
      pane.repaint();                      // Redraw pane contents
    }
  }

  private Marker selected;                 // Stores reference to selected marker
}
```

Directory "CurveApplet 3 moving the control points"

You need to add two `import` statements to the beginning of the source file, one because you reference the `MouseInputAdapter` class and the other because you refer to the `MouseEvent` class:

```java
import javax.swing.event.MouseInputAdapter;
import java.awt.event.MouseEvent;
```

Directory "CurveApplet 3 moving the control points"

The `mousePressed()` method calls a `contains()` method for a `Marker` that should test whether the point defined by the arguments is inside the marker. You can implement this in the `Marker` class like this:

```java
// Test if a point x,y is inside the marker
public boolean contains(double x, double y) {
  return circle.contains(x,y);
}
```

Directory "CurveApplet 3 moving the control points"

This just calls the `contains()` method for the circle object that is the marker. This returns `true` if the point (*x*,*y*) is inside the circle, and `false` if it isn't.

The `mouseDragged()` method calls a `setLocation()` method for the selected `Marker` object that is supposed to move the marker to a new position, so you need to implement this in the `Marker` class, too:

```
// Sets a new control point location
public void setLocation(double x, double y) {
  center.x = x;                    // Update control point
  center.y = y;                    // coordinates
  circle.x = x-radius;             // Change circle position
  circle.y = y-radius;             // correspondingly
}
```

Directory "CurveApplet 3 moving the control points"

After updating the coordinates of the point `center`, you also update the position of the circle by setting its data member directly. You can do this because `x` and `y` are public members of the `Ellipse2D.Double` class and store the coordinates of the center of the ellipse.

You can create a `MouseHandler` object in the `init()` method for the applet and set it as the listener for mouse events for the `pane` object:

```
@Override
public void init() {
  pane = new CurvePane();                        // Create pane containing curves
  Container content = getContentPane();          // Get the content pane

  // Add the pane displaying the curves to the content pane for the applet
  content.add(pane);                             // BorderLayout.CENTER is default position

  MouseHandler handler = new MouseHandler();     // Create the listener
  pane.addMouseListener(handler);                // Monitor mouse button presses
  pane.addMouseMotionListener(handler);          // as well as movement
}
```

Directory "CurveApplet 3 moving the control points"

Of course, to make the effect of moving the control points apparent, you must update the curve objects before you draw them. You can add the following code to the `paint()` method to do this:

```
@Override
public void paint(Graphics g) {
  Graphics2D g2D = (Graphics2D)g;                // Get a 2D device context

  // Update the curves with the current control point positions
  quadCurve.ctrlx = ctrlQuad.getCenter().x;
  quadCurve.ctrly = ctrlQuad.getCenter().y;
  cubicCurve.ctrlx1 = ctrlCubic1.getCenter().x;
  cubicCurve.ctrly1 = ctrlCubic1.getCenter().y;
  cubicCurve.ctrlx2 = ctrlCubic2.getCenter().x;
  cubicCurve.ctrly2 = ctrlCubic2.getCenter().y;
  // Rest of the method as before...
```

Directory "CurveApplet 3 moving the control points"

You can update the data members that store the control point coordinates for the curves directly because they are public members of each curve class. You get the coordinates of the new positions for the control points from their markers by calling the `getCenter()` method for each `Marker` object. You can then use the appropriate data member of the `Point2D.Double` object that is returned to update the fields for the curve objects.

If you recompile the applet with these changes and run it again you should get something like the window shown in Figure 19-15.

You should be able to drag the control points around with the mouse and see the curves change shape. If you find it's a bit difficult to select the control points, just make the value of `radius` a bit larger. Note how the angle of the tangent as well as its length affects the shape of the curve.

How It Works

The `mousePressed()` method in the `MouseHandler` class is called when you press a mouse button. In this method you check whether the current cursor position is within any of the markers enclosing the control points. You do this by calling the `contains()` method for each `Marker` object and passing the coordinates of the cursor position to it. The `getX()` and `getY()` methods for the `MouseEvent` object supply the coordinates of the current cursor position. If one of the markers does enclose the cursor, you store a reference to the `Marker` object in the `selected` member of the `MouseHandler` class for use by the `mouseDragged()` method.

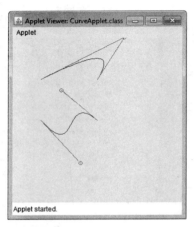

FIGURE 19-15

In the `mouseDragged()` method, you set the location for the `Marker` object referenced by `selected` to the current cursor position, and call `repaint()` for the pane object. The `repaint()` method causes the `paint()` method to be called for the component, so everything is redrawn, taking account of the modified control point position.

Releasing the mouse button causes the `mouseReleased()` method to be called. In here you just set the `selected` field back to `null` so no `Marker` object is selected. Remarkably easy, wasn't it?

Complex Paths

You can define a more complex geometric shape as an object of type `GeneralPath`. A `GeneralPath` object can be a composite of lines, `Quad2D` curves, and `Cubic2D` curves, or even other `GeneralPath` objects.

In general, closed shapes such as rectangles and ellipses can be filled with a color or pattern quite easily because they consist of a closed path enclosing a region. In this case, whether a given point is inside or outside a shape can be determined quite simply. With more complex shapes such as those defined by a `GeneralPath` object, it can be more difficult. Such paths may be defined by an exterior bounding path that encloses interior "holes," and the "holes" may also enclose further interior paths. Therefore, it is not necessarily obvious whether a given point is inside or outside a complex shape. In these situations, the determination of whether a point is inside or outside a shape is made by applying a *winding rule*. When you create a `GeneralPath` object, you have the option of defining one of two winding rules that are then used to determine whether a given point is inside or outside the shape. The winding rules that you can specify are defined by static constants that are inherited in the `GeneralPath` class from `Path2D`:

➤ `WIND_EVEN_ODD`: A point is interior to a `GeneralPath` object if the boundary is crossed an odd number of times by a line from a point exterior to the `GeneralPath` to the point in question. When you use this winding rule for shapes with holes, a point is determined to be interior to the shape if it is enclosed by an odd number of boundaries.

➤ `WIND_NON_ZERO`: Whether a point is inside or outside a path is determined by considering how the path boundaries cross a line drawn from the point in question to infinity, taking account of the direction in which the path boundaries are drawn.

Looking along the line from the point, the point is interior to the GeneralPath object if the difference between the number of times the line is crossed by a boundary from left to right, and the number of times the line is crossed from right to left, is non-zero. When you use this rule for shapes bounded by more than one contiguous path — with holes, in other words — the result varies depending on the direction in which each path is drawn. If an interior path is drawn in the opposite direction to the outer path, the interior of the inner path is determined as not being interior to the shape.

The way these winding rules affect the filling of a complex shape is illustrated in Figure 19-16.

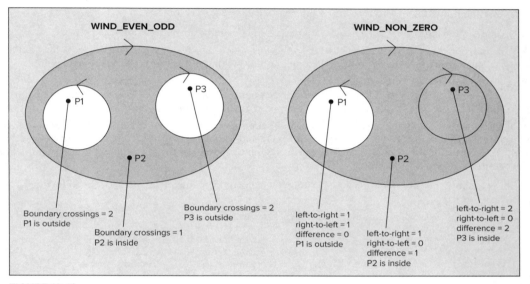

FIGURE 19-16

The region of the shape that is determined as being inside the shape is shown shaded in Figure 19-16. The directions in which the boundaries are drawn are indicated by the arrows on the boundaries. As you can see, the region where P3 lies is determined as being outside the shape by the WIND_EVEN_ODD rule, and as being inside the shape by the WIND_NON_ZERO rule.

You have four constructors available for creating GeneralPath objects:

➤ GeneralPath(): Defines a general path with a default winding rule of WIND_NON_ZERO.

➤ GeneralPath(int rule): Creates an object with the winding rule specified by the argument. You can specify the argument as WIND_NON_ZERO or WIND_EVEN_ODD.

➤ GeneralPath(int rule, int capacity): Creates an object with the winding rule specified by the first argument and the number of path segments specified by the second argument. In any event, the capacity is increased when necessary.

➤ GeneralPath(Shape shape): Creates an object from the Shape object that is passed as the argument.

You can create a GeneralPath object with the following statement:

```
GeneralPath p = new GeneralPath(GeneralPath.WIND_EVEN_ODD);
```

A GeneralPath object embodies the notion of a *current point* of type Point2D from which the next path segment is drawn. You set the initial current point by passing a pair of (*x,y*) coordinates as values of type `float` to the `moveTo()` method for the `GeneralPath` object. For example, for the object generated by the previous statement, you could set the current point with the following statement:

```
p.moveTo(10.0f,10.0f);          // Set the current point to 10,10
```

When you add a segment to a general path, the segment is added starting at the current point, and the end of the segment becomes the new current point that is used as the starting point for the next segment. Of course, if you want disconnected segments in a path, you can call `moveTo()` to move the current point to wherever you want before you add a new segment. If you need to get the current position at any time, you can call the `getCurrentPoint()` method that returns it as a reference of type `Point2D`.

You can use the following methods to add segments to a `GeneralPath` object:

➤ `void lineTo(float x, float y)`: Draws a line from the current point to the point (x, y).

➤ `void quadTo(float ctrlx, float ctrly, float x2, float y2)`: Draws a quadratic curve segment from the current point to the point (x2, y2) with (ctrlx, ctrly) as the control point.

➤ `void curveTo(float ctrlx1, float ctrly1, float ctrlx2, float ctrly2, float x2, float y2)`: Draws a Bezier curve segment from the current point with control point (ctrlx1, ctrly1) to (x2, y2) with (ctrlx2, ctrly2) as the control point.

Each of these methods updates the current point to be the end of the segment that is added. A path can consist of several subpaths because a new subpath is started by a `moveTo()` call. The `closePath()` method closes the current subpath by connecting the current point at the end of the last segment to the point defined by the previous `moveTo()` call.

I can illustrate how this works with a simple example. You could create a triangle with the following statements:

```
GeneralPath p = new GeneralPath(GeneralPath.WIND_EVEN_ODD);
p.moveTo(50.0f, 50.0f);                 // Start point for path
p.lineTo(150.0f, 50.0f);                // Line from 50,50 to 150,50
p.lineTo(150.0f, 250.0f);               // Line from 150,50 to 150,250
p.closePath();                          // Line from 150,250 back to start
```

The first line segment starts at the current position set by the `moveTo()` call. Each subsequent segment begins at the end point of the previous segment. The `closePath()` call joins the latest end point to the point set by the previous `moveTo()` call — which in this case is the beginning of the path. The process is much the same using `quadTo()` or `curveTo()` method calls, and of course you can intermix them in any sequence you like. You can remove all the segments in a path by calling the `reset()` method for the `GeneralPath` object. This empties the path.

The `GeneralPath` class implements the `Shape` interface, so a `Graphics2D` object knows how to draw a path. You just pass a reference to a `GeneralPath` object as the argument to the `draw()` method for the graphics context. To draw the path, p, that was defined in the preceding example in the graphics context g2D, you would write the following:

```
g2D.draw(p);                            // Draw path p
```

Let's try an example.

TRY IT OUT **Reaching for the Stars**

You won't usually want to construct a `GeneralPath` object as I did in the preceding example. You probably want to create a particular shape — a triangle or a star, say — and then draw it at various points on a component. You might think you can do this by subclassing `GeneralPath`, but the `GeneralPath` class is declared as `final` so subclassing is not allowed. However, you can always add a `GeneralPath` object as a member of your class. You can try drawing some stars using your own `Star` class. You'll use a `GeneralPath` object to create the star shown in Figure 19-17.

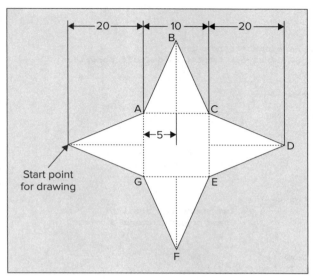

FIGURE 19-17

Here's the code for a class that can create a path for a star:

```
import java.awt.geom.*;

public class Star {
  // Return a path for a star at x,y
  public static GeneralPath starAt(float x, float y) {
    Point2D.Float point = new Point2D.Float(x, y);
    p = new GeneralPath(GeneralPath.WIND_NON_ZERO);
    p.moveTo(point.x, point.y);
    p.lineTo(point.x + 20.0f, point.y - 5.0f);        // Line from start to A
    point = (Point2D.Float)p.getCurrentPoint();
    p.lineTo(point.x + 5.0f, point.y - 20.0f);        // Line from A to B
    point = (Point2D.Float)p.getCurrentPoint();
    p.lineTo(point.x + 5.0f, point.y + 20.0f);        // Line from B to C
    point = (Point2D.Float)p.getCurrentPoint();
    p.lineTo(point.x + 20.0f, point.y + 5.0f);        // Line from C to D
    point = (Point2D.Float)p.getCurrentPoint();
    p.lineTo(point.x - 20.0f, point.y + 5.0f);        // Line from D to E
    point = (Point2D.Float)p.getCurrentPoint();
    p.lineTo(point.x - 5.0f, point.y + 20.0f);        // Line from E to F
    point = (Point2D.Float)p.getCurrentPoint();
    p.lineTo(point.x - 5.0f, point.y - 20.0f);        // Line from F to g
    p.closePath();                                    // Line from G to start
    return p;                                         // Return the path
  }

  private static GeneralPath p;                       // Star path
}
```

Directory "StarApplet 1"

You can now define an applet that draw stars:

```
import javax.swing.*;
import java.awt.*;

@SuppressWarnings("serial")
public class StarApplet extends JApplet {
```

```
                // Initialize the applet
                @Override
                public void init() {
                  StarPane pane = new StarPane();   // Pane containing stars
                  getContentPane().add(pane);       // BorderLayout.CENTER is default position
                }

                // Class defining a pane on which to draw
                class StarPane extends JComponent {
                  @Override
                  public void paint(Graphics g) {
                    Graphics2D g2D = (Graphics2D)g;
                    float delta = 60f;                       // Increment between stars
                    float starty = 0f;                       // Starting y position

                    // Draw 3 rows of stars
                    for(int yCount = 0; yCount < 3; yCount++) {
                      starty += delta;                       // Increment row position
                      float startx = 0f;                     // Start x position in a row

                      // Draw a row of 4 stars
                      for(int xCount = 0; xCount<4; xCount++) {
                        g2D.draw(Star.starAt(startx += delta, starty));
                      }
                    }
                  }
                }
              }
```

Directory "StarApplet 1"

The HTML file for this applet could contain:

```
        <html>
          <head>
          </head>
          <body bgcolor="000000">
            <center>
              <applet
                code = "StarApplet.class"
                width = "360"
                height = "240"
                >
              </applet>
            </center>
          </body>
        </html>
```

This is large enough to accommodate our stars. If you compile and run the applet, you should see the Applet Viewer window shown in Figure 19-18.

How It Works

The Star class has a GeneralPath object, p, as a static member that references the path for a star. There's no need to create Star objects as all we are interested in is the path to draw a star.

The static starAt() method creates the path for a star at the position point that is defined by the arguments. The first line is drawn relative to the start point that is set by the call to moveTo() for p. For each subsequent line, you retrieve the current position by calling

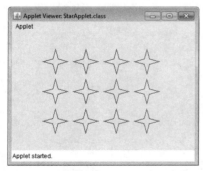

FIGURE 19-18

getCurrentPoint() for p and drawing the line relative to that. The last line to complete the star is drawn by calling closePath(). A reference to the GeneralPath object, p, that results is returned.

The StarApplet class draws stars on a component defined by the inner class StarPane. You draw the stars using the paint() method for the StarPane object, which is a member of the StarApplet class. Each star is drawn in the nested loop with the position specified by (x,y). The y coordinate defines the vertical position of a row, so this is incremented by delta on each iteration of the outer loop. The coordinate x is the position of a star within a row so this is incremented by delta on each iteration of the inner loop.

FILLING SHAPES

After you know how to create and draw a shape, filling it is easy. You just call the fill() method for the Graphics2D object and pass a reference of type Shape to it. This works for any shape, but for sensible results the boundary should be closed. The way the enclosed region is filled is determined by the window rule in effect for the shape.

Let's try it out by modifying the applet example that displayed stars.

TRY IT OUT Filling Stars

To fill the stars you just need to call the fill() method for each star in the paint() method of the StarPane object. Modify the paint() method as follows:

Available for download on Wrox.com

```java
@Override
public void paint(Graphics g) {
  Graphics2D g2D = (Graphics2D)g;
  float delta = 60;                                // Increment between stars
  float starty = 0;                                // Starting y position

  // Draw 3 rows of 4 stars
  GeneralPath star = null;
  for(int yCount = 0 ; yCount<3; yCount++) {
    starty += delta;                               // Increment row position
    float startx = 0;                              // Start x position in a row

    // Draw a row of 4 stars
    for(int xCount = 0 ; xCount<4; xCount++) {
      star = Star.starAt(startx += delta, starty);
      g2D.setPaint(Color.GREEN);                   // Color for fill is green
      g2D.fill(star);                              // Fill the star
      g2D.setPaint(Color.BLUE);                    // Drawing color blue
      g2D.draw(star);
    }
  }
}
```

Directory "StarApplet 2 filled stars"

You also need an import statement for the GeneralPath class name in the StarApplet.java source file:

```java
import java.awt.geom.GeneralPath;
```

Now the applet window looks something like that shown in Figure 19-19, but in color, of course.

CONFER PROGRAMMER TO PROGRAMMER ABOUT THIS TOPIC.
→ Visit p2p.wrox.com ←

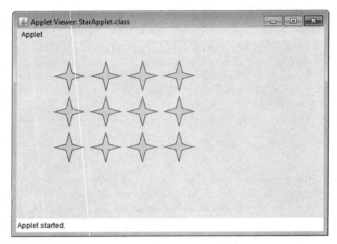

FIGURE 19-19

How It Works

You set the color for drawing and filling the stars differently, simply to show that you can get the outline as well as the fill. The stars are displayed in green with a blue boundary. It is important to draw the outline after the fill, otherwise the fill might encroach on the outline. You can fill a shape without drawing a boundary for it — just call the `fill()` method. You could amend the example to do this by deleting the last two statements in the inner loop. Now all you get is the green fill for each shape — no outline.

Gradient Fill

You are not limited to filling a shape with a uniform color. You can create a `java.awt.GradientPaint` object that represents a graduation in shade from one color to another and pass that to the `setPaint()` method for the graphics context. There are four `GradientPaint` class constructors:

➤ `GradientPaint(Point2D p1, Color c1, Point2D p2, Color c2)`

Defines a gradient from point p1 with the color c1 to the point p2 with the color c2. The color varies linearly from color c1 at point p1 to color c2 at point p2

➤ `GradientPaint(float x1, float y1, Color c1, float x2, float y2, Color c2)`

By default the gradient is acyclic, which means the color variation applies only between the two points. Beyond either end of the line the color is the same as the nearest end point.

➤ `GradientPaint(Point2D p1, Color c1, Point2D p2, Color c2, boolean cyclic)`

This does same as the previous constructor but with the points specified by their coordinates. With `cyclic` specified as `false`, this is identical to the first constructor. If you specify `cyclic` as `true`, the color gradation repeats cyclically off either end of the line — that is, you get repetitions of the color gradient in both directions.

➤ `GradientPaint(float x1, float y1, Color c1,`
`                float x2, float y2, Color c2,`
`                boolean cyclic)`

This is the same as the previous constructor except for the explicit point coordinates.

Points that are off the line defining the color gradient have the same color as the normal (that is, right-angle) projection of the point onto the line. This stuff is easier to demonstrate than to describe, so Figure 19-20 shows the output from the example you're going to try out next.

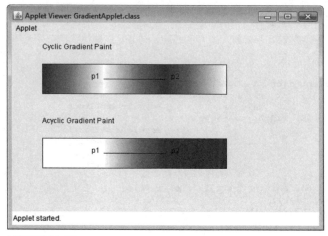

FIGURE 19-20

You can see that points along lines at right angles to the line defined by p1 and p2 have the same color as the point on the line. The window shows both cyclic and acyclic gradient fill.

TRY IT OUT Color Gradients

You will create an example similar to the star applet except that the applet draws rectangles with GradientPaint fills. Here's the complete code:

```java
import javax.swing.*;
import java.awt.*;
import java.awt.geom.*;

@SuppressWarnings("serial")
public class GradientApplet extends JApplet {
  // Initialize the applet
  @Override
  public void init() {
    GradientPane pane = new GradientPane(); // Pane contains filled rectangles
    getContentPane().add(pane);             // BorderLayout.CENTER is default position
  }

  // Class defining a pane on which to draw
  class GradientPane extends JComponent {
    @Override
    public void paint(Graphics g) {
      Graphics2D g2D = (Graphics2D)g;

      Point2D.Float p1 = new Point2D.Float(150.f, 75.f); // Gradient line start
      Point2D.Float p2 = new Point2D.Float(250.f, 75.f); // Gradient line end
      float width = 300;
      float height = 50;
      GradientPaint g1 = new GradientPaint(p1, Color.WHITE,
                                           p2, Color.DARK_GRAY,
                                           true);          // Cyclic gradient
      Rectangle2D.Float rect1 = new Rectangle2D.Float(p1.x-100, p1.y-25, width,height);
```

```
          g2D.setPaint(g1);                                    // Gradient color fill
          g2D.fill(rect1);                                     // Fill the rectangle
          g2D.setPaint(Color.BLACK);                           // Outline in black
          g2D.draw(rect1);                                     // Fill the rectangle
          g2D.draw(new Line2D.Float(p1, p2));
          g2D.drawString("Cyclic Gradient Paint", p1.x-100, p1.y-50);
          g2D.drawString("p1", p1.x-20, p1.y);
          g2D.drawString("p2", p2.x+10, p2.y);

          p1.setLocation(150, 200);
          p2.setLocation(250, 200);
          GradientPaint g2 = new GradientPaint(p1, Color.WHITE,
                                               p2, Color.DARK_GRAY,
                                               false);         // Acyclic gradient
          rect1.setRect(p1.x-100, p1.y-25, width, height);
          g2D.setPaint(g2);                                    // Gradient color fill
          g2D.fill(rect1);                                     // Fill the rectangle
          g2D.setPaint(Color.BLACK);                           // Outline in black
          g2D.draw(rect1);                                     // Fill the rectangle
          g2D.draw(new Line2D.Float(p1, p2));
          g2D.drawString("Acyclic Gradient Paint", p1.x-100, p1.y-50);
          g2D.drawString("p1", p1.x-20, p1.y);
          g2D.drawString("p2", p2.x+10, p2.y);

        }

      }
    }
```

Directory "GradientApplet 1"

If you run this applet with the following HTML, you should get the window previously shown in Figure 19-20:

```
<html>
  <head>
  </head>
  <body bgcolor="000000">
    <center>
      <applet
        code = "GradientApplet.class"
        width = "400"
        height = "280"
        >
      </applet>
    </center>
  </body>
</html>
```

Note that to get a nice smooth color gradation, your monitor needs to be set up for at least 16-bit colors (65536 colors), and preferably 24-bit colors (16.7 million colors).

How It Works

The applet displays two rectangles, and they are annotated to indicate which is which. The applet also displays the gradient lines, which lie in the middle of the rectangles. You can see the cyclic and acyclic gradients quite clearly. You can also see how points off the gradient line have the same color as the normal projection onto the line.

The first block of code in the paint() method creates the upper rectangle where the GradientPaint object that is used is g1. This is created as a cyclic gradient between the points p1 and p2, and varying from white to dark gray. I chose these shades because the book is printed in black and white, but you can try the example with any color combination you like. To set the color gradient for the fill, you call setPaint() for the Graphics2D object and pass g1 to it. Any shapes that are drawn and/or filled subsequent to this call use the gradient color, but here you just fill the rectangle, rect1.

To make the outline and the annotation clearer, you set the current color back to black before calling the `draw()` method to draw the outline of the rectangle and the `drawString()` method to annotate it.

The code for the lower rectangle is essentially the same as that for the first. The only important difference is that you specify the last argument to the constructor as `false` to get an acyclic gradient fill pattern. This causes the colors of the ends of the gradient line to be the same as the end points. You could have omitted the `boolean` parameter here, getting an acyclic gradient by default.

The applet shows how points off the gradient line have the same color as the normal projection onto the line. This is always the case, regardless of the orientation of the gradient line. You could try changing the definition of `g1` for the upper rectangle to:

```
GradientPaint g1 = new GradientPaint(p1.x, p1.y - 20, Color.WHITE,
                                     p2.x, p2.y + 20, Color.DARK_GRAY,
                                     true);              // Cyclic gradient
```

You also need to draw the gradient line in its new orientation:

```
g2D.draw(rect1);                                   // Fill the rectangle
//g2D.draw(new Line2D.Float(p1, p2));
g2D.draw(new Line2D.Float(p1.x, p1.y - 20, p2.x, p2.y + 20));
```

The annotation for the end points also have to be moved:

```
g2D.drawString("p1",p1.x - 20,p1.y - 20);
g2D.drawString("p2",p2.x + 10,p2.y + 20);
```

If you run the applet with these changes, you can see in Figure 19-21 how the gradient is tilted and how the color of a point off the gradient line matches that of the point that is the orthogonal projection onto it.

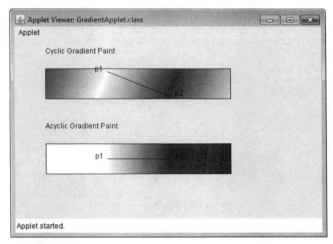

FIGURE 19-21

MANAGING SHAPES

When you create shapes in Sketcher, you have no idea of the sequence of shape types that will occur. This is determined totally by the person using the program to produce a sketch. You therefore need to be able to draw shapes and perform other operations on them without knowing what they are — and of course polymorphism can help here.

You don't want to use the shape classes defined in `java.awt.geom` directly because you want to add your own attributes such as color or line style for the shapes and store them as part of your shape objects. You could consider using the shape classes as base classes for your shapes, but you couldn't use the `GeneralPath` class in this scheme of things because, as I said earlier, the class has been defined as `final` and therefore cannot be subclassed. You could define an interface that all your shape classes would implement. However, some methods have a common implementation in all your shape classes, which would mean that you would need to repeat this code in every class.

Taking all of this into account, the easiest approach might be to define a common base class for the Sketcher shape classes and include a member in each class to store a `java.awt.geom` shape object of one kind or another. You are then able to store a reference to any of your shape class objects as the base class type and get polymorphic behavior.

You can start by defining a base class, `Element`, from which you derive the classes defining specific types of shapes for Sketcher. The `Element` class has data members that are common to all your shape types, and contains all the methods that you want to be able to execute polymorphically. Each shape class that is derived from the `Element` class might need its own implementation of some or all of these methods.

Figure 19-22 shows the initial members that you define in the `Element` base class. The class is serializable because you want to write a sketch to a file eventually. There are three fields: the `color` member to store the color of a shape, the `position` member to store the location of a shape, and the `serialVersionUID` member for serialization. The `getBounds()` method returns a rectangle that completely encloses the element. This is for use in paint operations. The `draw()` method draws an element. The `getBounds()` and `draw()` methods are abstract here because the `Element` class is not intended to define a shape. They need to be included in the `Element` class to be able to call them polymorphically for derived class objects. You can implement the `getColor()` and `getPosition()` methods in this class though.

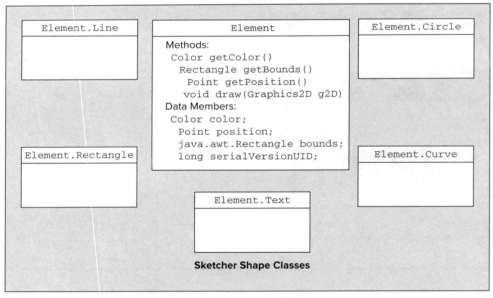

Sketcher Shape Classes

FIGURE 19-22

Initially, you define the five classes shown Figure 19-22 that represent shapes, with the `Element` class as a base. They provide objects that represent straight lines, rectangles, circles, freehand curves, and blocks of text. These classes inherit the fields that you define for the `Element` class and they are serializable.

As you can see from the names of the Sketcher shape classes in Figure 19-22, they are all nested classes to the `Element` class. The `Element` class serves as the base class, as well as housing the shape classes. This helps to avoid any possible confusion with other classes in the Java libraries that might have the same names. Because there are no `Element` objects around, you declare the inner shape classes as static members of the `Element` class.

You can now define the base class, `Element`. This won't be the final version because you will add more functionality in later chapters. Here's the code for `Element.java`:

Available for download on Wrox.com

```
import java.awt.*;
import java.io.Serializable;

public abstract class Element implements Serializable {
  protected Element(Point position, Color color) {
    this.position = position;
    this.color = color;
  }

  public Color getColor() {
    return color;
  }

  public Point getPosition() {
    return position;
  }

  public java.awt.Rectangle getBounds() {
    return bounds;
  }

  public abstract void draw(Graphics2D g2D);
  public abstract void modify(Point start, Point last);

  protected Point position;                           // Position of a shape
  protected Color color;                              // Color of a shape
  protected java.awt.Rectangle bounds;                // Bounding rectangle
  private final static long serialVersionUID = 1001L;
}
```

Directory "Sketcher 4 drawing sketch line and rectangle elements"

Put this file in the same directory as `Sketcher.java`. You have defined a constructor to initialize the `color` and `position` data member and the `get` methods to provide access to these. The `bounds` member is created by the subclasses and it also has a `get` method. The member and return type must be qualified by the package name to distinguish it from the inner class type `Rectangle`. The constructor is `protected` because it is only called by inner class constructors.

The return type for the `getBounds()` method that makes the bounding rectangle for an element available is fully qualified by the package name. This is to avoid confusion with your own `Rectangle` class that you add as an inner class later in this chapter.

There are two `abstract` methods that must be implemented by the subclasses. This means that the `Element` class must be declared as `abstract`. An implementation of the `draw()` method draws an element using the `Graphics2D` object that is passed to it. The `modify()` method alters the definition of an element using the `Point` objects that are passed to it as defining points.

Storing Shapes in the Model

Even though you haven't defined the classes for the shapes that Sketcher creates, you can implement the mechanism for storing them in the `SketcherModel` class. You'll store all of them as objects of type `Element`, so you can use a `LinkedList<Element>` collection class object to hold an arbitrary number of `Element` objects. The container for `Element` references needs to allow deletion as well as additions to the contents, and you will want to remove items and rearrange the order of items, too. This makes a linked list the best choice. A map container just doesn't apply to Sketcher data. An `ArrayList<>` or a `Vector<>` container doesn't really fit the bill. Neither is it very efficient when you want to remove items on a regular basis whereas deleting a shape from a linked list is fast.

You can add a member to the `SketcherModel` class that you defined earlier in the Sketcher program to store elements:

```
import java.io.Serializable;
import java.util.*;

public class SketcherModel extends Observable implements Serializable {
  // Detail of the rest of class to be filled in later...
  protected LinkedList<Element> elements = new LinkedList<>();
  private final static long serialVersionUID = 1001L;
}
```

You definitely want methods to add and delete `Element` objects. It is also very useful if the `SketcherModel` class implements the `Iterable<Element>` interface because that allows a collection-based `for` loop to be used to iterate over the `Element` objects stored in the model. Here's how the class looks to accommodate that:

```
import java.io.Serializable;
import java.util.*;

public class SketcherModel extends Observable
                           implements Serializable, Iterable<Element> {
  //Remove an element from the sketch
  public boolean remove(Element element) {
    boolean removed = elements.remove(element);
    if(removed) {
      setChanged();
      notifyObservers(element.getBounds());
    }
    return removed;
  }

  //Add an element to the sketch
  public void add(Element element) {
    elements.add(element);
    setChanged();
    notifyObservers(element.getBounds());
  }

  // Get iterator for sketch elements
  public Iterator<Element> iterator() {
    return elements.iterator();
  }

  protected LinkedList<Element> elements = new LinkedList< >();
  private final static long serialVersionUID = 1001L;
}
```

Directory "Sketcher 4 drawing sketch line and rectangle elements"

All three methods make use of methods that are defined for the `LinkedList<Element>` object, `elements`, so they are very simple. When you add or remove an element, the model is changed, so you call the `setChanged()` method inherited from `Observable` to record the change and the `notifyObservers()` method to communicate this to any observers that have been registered with the model. The observers are the views that display the sketch. You pass the `java.awt.Rectangle` object that is returned by `getBounds()` for the element to `notifyObservers()`. Each of the shape classes defined in the `java.awt.geom` package implements the `getBounds()` method to return the rectangle that bounds the shape. You are able to use this in the view to specify the area that needs to be redrawn.

In the `remove()` method, it is possible that the element was not removed — because it was not there, for example — so you test the `boolean` value that is returned by the `remove()` method for the `LinkedList<Element>` object. You also return this value from the `remove()` method in the `SketcherModel` class, as the caller may want to know if an element was removed or not.

The `iterator()` method returns an iterator of type `Iterator<Element>` for the linked list that holds the elements in the sketch. This can be used to iterate over all the elements in a sketch. It also allows an element to be removed using the `remove()` method that is declared in the `Iterator<>` interface.

Even though you haven't defined any of the element classes that Sketcher supports, you can still make provision for displaying them in the view class.

Drawing Shapes

You draw the shapes in the `paint()` method for the `SketcherView` class, so if you haven't already done so, remove the old code from the `paint()` method now. You can replace it with code for drawing Sketcher shapes like this:

Available for download on Wrox.com

```
import javax.swing.JComponent;
import java.util.*;
import java.awt.*;

class SketcherView extends JComponent implements Observer {
  public SketcherView(Sketcher theApp) {
    this.theApp = theApp;
  }

  // Method called by Observable object when it changes
  public void update(Observable o, Object rectangle) {
    // Code to respond to changes in the model...
  }

  @Override
  public void paint(Graphics g) {
    Graphics2D g2D = (Graphics2D)g;                // Get a 2D device context
    for(Element element: theApp.getModel()) {  // For each element in the model
      element.draw(g2D);                        // ...draw the element
    }
  }

  private Sketcher theApp;                          // The application object
}
```

Directory "Sketcher 4 drawing sketch line and rectangle elements"

The `getModel()` method that you implemented in the `Sketcher` class returns a reference to the `SketcherModel` object, and because `SketcherModel` implements the `Iterable<>` interface, you can use it in a collection-based `for` loop to iterate over all the `Element` objects in the sketch. For each element, you call its `draw()` method with `g2D` as the argument. This draws any type of element because the `draw()` method is polymorphic. In this way you draw all the elements that are stored in the model. You should be able to compile Sketcher successfully, even though the `Element` class does not have any inner classes defined for elements.

It's time you put in place the mechanism for creating Sketcher elements. This determines the data that you use to define the location and dimensions of an element.

DRAWING USING THE MOUSE

You've drawn shapes in examples just using data internal to a program so far. The Sketcher program must be able to draw a shape from user input and then store the finished shape in the model. You provide mechanisms for a user to draw any shape using the mouse.

Ideally, the process should be as natural as possible, so to achieve this you will allow a user to draw by pressing the left mouse button (more accurately, button 1 — if you have a left-handed setup for the mouse it is the right button, but still button 1) and dragging the cursor to draw the selected type of shape. So for a line, the point where you depress the mouse button is the start point for the line, and the point where you release the button is the end point. This process is illustrated in Figure 19-23.

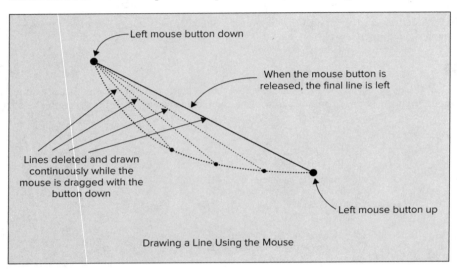

FIGURE 19-23

As the user drags the mouse with the button down, Sketcher displays the line as it looks at that point. Thus, the line is displayed dynamically all the time the mouse cursor is being dragged with the left button pressed. This process is called *rubber-banding*.

You can use essentially the same process of pressing the mouse button and dragging the cursor for all four of the geometric shapes you saw when I discussed the `Element` class. Two points define a line, a rectangle, or a circle — the cursor position where the mouse button is pressed and the cursor position where the mouse button is released. For a line the two points are the end points, for a rectangle they are opposite corners, and for a circle they are the center and a point on the circumference. This implies that the constructors for these have three parameters, corresponding to the two points and the color. A curve is a little more complicated in that many more than two points are involved, so I'm deferring discussion of that until later.

All the operations that deal with the mouse in your program involve handling events that the mouse generates. Let's look at how you handle mouse events to make drawing lines, rectangles, and circles work.

Handling Mouse Events

Because all the drawing operations for a sketch are accomplished using the mouse, you must implement the process for creating elements within the methods that handle the mouse events. The mouse events you're interested in originate in the `SketcherView` object because the mouse events that relate to drawing shapes originate in the content pane for the application window, which is the view object. You make the view responsible for handling all its own events, which includes events that occur in the drawing process as well as interactions with existing shapes.

Drawing a shape, such as a line, interactively involves you in handling three different kinds of mouse event. Table 19-1 is a summary of what they are and what you need to do in Sketcher when they occur:

TABLE 19-1: Mouse Events for Drawing Shapes

EVENT	ACTION
Button 1 Pressed	Save the cursor position somewhere as the starting point for the shape. This is the first point on a line, a corner of a rectangle, or the center of a circle. You store this in a data member of the inner class to SketcherView that you create to define listeners for mouse events.
Mouse Dragged	Save the current cursor position somewhere as the end point for a shape. This is the end of a line, the opposite corner of a rectangle, or a point on the circumference of a circle. Erase any previously drawn temporary shape, and create a new temporary shape from the starting point that was saved initially. Draw the new temporary shape.
Button 1 Released	If there's a reference to a temporary shape stored, add it to the sketch model and redraw it.

The shape that is created is determined by the value stored in the elementType member of the SketcherFrame class. The color of the shape is the color stored in the elementColor member. Both can be changed by the user at any time using the menu items and toolbar buttons you added in the previous chapter.

Remember from Chapter 18 that there are two mouse listener interfaces: MouseListener, which has methods for handling events that occur when any of the mouse buttons are pressed or released, and MouseMotionListener, which has methods for handling events that arise when the mouse is moved. Also recall that the MouseInputAdapter class implements both, and because you need to implement methods from both interfaces, you add an inner class to the SketcherView class that extends the MouseInputAdapter class.

Because there's quite a lot of code involved in this, you first define the bare bones of the class to handle mouse events and then continue to add the detail incrementally until it does what you want.

Implementing a Mouse Listener

Add the following class outline as an inner class to SketcherView:

```
import javax.swing.JComponent;
import java.util.*;
import java.awt.*;
import java.awt.event.MouseEvent;
import javax.swing.event.MouseInputAdapter;

class SketcherView extends JComponent implements Observer {
  // Rest of the SketcherView class as before...

  class MouseHandler extends MouseInputAdapter {
    @Override
    public void mousePressed(MouseEvent e)  {
      // Code to handle mouse button press...
    }

    @Override
    public void mouseDragged(MouseEvent e) {
      // Code to handle the mouse being dragged...
    }

    @Override
    public void mouseReleased(MouseEvent e) {
      // Code to handle the mouse button being release...
```

```
    }

    private Point start;                    // Stores cursor position on press
    private Point last;                     // Stores cursor position on drag
    private Element tempElement;            // Stores a temporary element
  }
  private Sketcher theApp;                  // The application object
}
```

Directory "Sketcher 4 drawing sketch line and rectangle elements"

You have implemented the three methods that you need to create an element.

The `mousePressed()` method will store the position of the cursor in the `start` member of the `MouseHandler` class, so this point is available to the `mouseDragged()` method that is called repeatedly when you drag the mouse cursor with the button pressed.

The `mouseDragged()` method creates an element using the current cursor position together with the position previously saved in `start`. It stores a reference to the element in the `tempElement` member. The `last` member of the `MouseHandler` class is used to store the cursor position when `mouseDragged()` is called. Both `start` and `last` are of type `Point` because this is the type that you get for the cursor position, but remember that `Point` is a subclass of `Point2D`, so you can always cast a `Point` reference to `Point2D` when necessary.

The `mouseReleased()` method is called when you release the mouse button. This method stores the element in the sketch and cleans up where necessary.

An object of type `MouseHandler` is the listener for mouse events for the view object, so you can put this in place in the `SketcherView` constructor. Add the following code at the end of the existing code:

```
public SketcherView(Sketcher theApp) {
  this.theApp = theApp;
  MouseHandler handler = new MouseHandler();      // create the mouse listener
  addMouseListener(handler);                       // Listen for button events
  addMouseMotionListener(handler);                 // Listen for motion events
}
```

Directory "Sketcher 4 drawing sketch line and rectangle elements"

You call the `addMouseListener()` and `addMotionListener()` methods and pass the same listener object as the argument to both because the `MouseHandler` class deals with both types of event. Both methods are inherited in the `SketcherView` class from the `Component` class, which also defines an `addMouseWheelListener()` method for when you want to handle mouse wheel events.

Let's go for the detail of the `MouseHandler` class now, starting with the `mousePressed()` method.

Handling Mouse Button Press Events

First, you need to find out which button is pressed. It is generally a good idea to make mouse button operations specific to a particular button. That way you avoid potential confusion when you extend the code to support more functionality. The `getButton()` method for the `MouseEvent` object that is passed to a handler method returns a value of type `int` that indicates which of the three mouse buttons changed state. The value is one of four constants that are defined in the `MouseEvent` class:

BUTTON1   BUTTON2   BUTTON3   NOBUTTON

On a two-button mouse or a wheel mouse, BUTTON1 for a right-handed user corresponds to the left button and BUTTON2 corresponds to the right button. BUTTON3 corresponds to the middle button when there is one. NOBUTTON is the return value when no button has changed state.

You can record the button state in the handler object. First add a member to the `MouseHandler` class to store the button state:

```
private int buttonState = MouseEvent.NOBUTTON;    // Records button state
```

You can record which button is pressed by using the following code in the `mousePressed()` method:

```
public void mousePressed(MouseEvent e) {
  buttonState = e.getButton();              // Record which button was pressed
  if(buttonState == MouseEvent.BUTTON1) {
    // Code to handle button 1 press...
  }
}
```

By recording the button state, you make it available to the `mouseDragged()` method. The button state won't change during a mouse dragged event so if you don't record it when the mouse pressed event occurs, the information about which button is pressed is lost.

The `MouseEvent` object that is passed to all mouse handler methods records the current cursor position, and you can get a `Point` reference to it by calling the `getPoint()` method for the object. For example:

```
public void mousePressed(MouseEvent e) {
  start = e.getPoint();                     // Save the cursor position in start
  buttonState = e.getButton();              // Record which button was pressed
  if(buttonState == MouseEvent.BUTTON1) {
    // Code to handle button 1 press...
  }
}
```

The `mouseDragged()` method is going to be called very frequently, and to implement rubber-banding of the element, the element must be redrawn each time so it needs to be very fast. You don't want to have the whole view redrawn each time, as this carries a lot of overhead. You need an approach that redraws just the element.

Using XOR Mode

One way to implement rubber-banding is to draw in *XOR mode*. You set XOR mode by calling the `setXORMode()` method for a graphics context and passing a color to it — usually the background color. In this mode the pixels are not written directly to the screen. The color in which you are drawing is combined with the color of the pixel currently displayed together with a third color that you specify, by exclusive ORing them together, and the resultant pixel color is written to the screen. The third color is usually set to be the background color, so the color of the pixel that is written is the result of the following operation:

```
resultant_Color = foreground_color^background_color^current_color
```

If you remember the discussion of the exclusive OR operation back in Chapter 2, you realize that the effect of this is to flip between the drawing color and the background color. The first time you draw a shape, the result is in the current element color. When you draw the same shape a second time, the result is the background color so the shape disappears. Drawing a third time makes it reappear.

Based on the way XOR mode works, you can now implement the `mousePressed()` method for the `MouseHander` class like this:

```
public void mousePressed(MouseEvent e) {
    start = e.getPoint();                     // Save the cursor position in start
    buttonState = e.getButton();              // Record which button was pressed
    if(buttonState == MouseEvent.BUTTON1) {
      g2D = (Graphics2D)getGraphics();        // Get graphics context
      g2D.setXORMode(getBackground());        // Set XOR mode
  }
}
```

The `getGraphics()` method that you call in this method is for the view object; the `MouseHandler` class has no such method. The method is inherited in the `SketcherView` class from the `Component` class. If button 1 was pressed, you obtain a graphics context for the view and store it in `g2D`, so you must add `g2D` as a field in the `MouseHandler` class:

```
    private Graphics2D g2D = null;            // Temporary graphics context
```

You pass the color returned by the `getBackground()` method for the view object to the `setXORMode()` method for `g2D`. This causes objects that you redraw in a given color to switch between the origin color and the background color. You are able to use this mode in the `mouseDragged()` method to erase a previously drawn shape.

With the code in place to handle a button pressed event, you can have a go at implementing `mouseDragged()`.

Handling Mouse Dragged Events

You obtain the cursor position in the `mouseDragged()` method by calling `getPoint()` for the event object that is passed as the argument, so you could write:

```
last = e.getPoint();                    // Get cursor position
```

But you want to handle drag events only for button 1, so you make this conditional upon the `buttonState` field having the value `MouseEvent.BUTTON1`.

When `mouseDragged()` is called for the first time, you won't have created an element. In this case you can just create one from the points stored in `start` and `last` and then draw it using the graphics context saved by the `mousePressed()` method. The `mouseDragged()` method is called lots of times while you drag the mouse though, and for every occasion other than the first, you must redraw the old element so that you effectively erase it before creating and drawing the new one. Because the graphics context is in XOR mode, drawing the element a second time displays it in the background color, so it disappears from the view. Here's how you can do all that:

```java
public void mouseDragged(MouseEvent e) {
    last = e.getPoint();                              // Save cursor position

    if(buttonState == MouseEvent.BUTTON1) {
        if(tempElement == null) {                     // Is there an element?
            tempElement = Element.createElement(      // No, so create one
                          theApp.getWindow().getElementType(),
                          theApp.getWindow().getElementColor(),
                          start, last);
        } else {
            tempElement.draw(g2D);                    // Yes - draw to erase it
            tempElement.modify(start, last);          // Now modify it
        }
        tempElement.draw(g2D);                        // and draw it
    }
}
```

Directory "Sketcher 4 drawing sketch line and rectangle elements"

This method is only called when a button is pressed, and if button 1 is pressed, you are interested. You first check for an existing element by comparing the reference in `tempElement` with `null`. If it is `null`, you create an element of the current type by calling a `createElement()` method that you will add to the `Element` class in a moment. You save a reference to the element that is created in the `tempElement` member of the listener object. You pass the element type and color to the `createElement()` method. You obtain these using the application object to access the application window so you can then call methods for the `SketcherFrame` object to retrieve them. These methods don't exist in `SketcherFrame` yet, but it's not difficult to implement them:

```java
// Return the current drawing color
public Color getElementColor() {
    return elementColor;
}

// Return the current element type
public int getElementType() {
    return elementType;
}
```

Directory "Sketcher 4 drawing sketch line and rectangle elements"

If `tempElement` is not `null` in the `mouseDragged()` method, an element already exists, so you draw over it in the application window by calling its `draw()` method. Because you are in XOR mode, this effectively erases the element. You then modify the existing element to incorporate the latest cursor position by calling the method `modify()` for the element object. Finally, you draw the latest version of the element that is referenced by `tempElement`.

You can implement the `createElement()` method as a static member of the `Element` class. The parameters for the method are the current element type and color and the two points that are used to define each element. Here's the code:

```
public static Element createElement(int type, Color color, Point start, Point end) {
  switch(type) {
    case LINE:
      return new Line(start, end, color);
    case RECTANGLE:
      return new Rectangle(start, end, color);
    case CIRCLE:
      return new Circle(start, end, color);
    case CURVE:
      return new Curve(start, end, color);
    default:
      assert false;                            // We should never get to here
  }
  return null;
}
```

Directory "Sketcher 4 drawing sketch line and rectangle elements"

Because you refer to the constants that identify element types here, you must import the static members of the `SketcherConstants` class that you defined in the `Constants` package into the `SketcherView.java` source file. Add the `import` statement to the `Element` class file:

```
import static Constants.SketcherConstants.*;
```

The `createElement()` method returns a reference to a shape as type `Element`. You determine the type of shape to create by retrieving the element type ID stored in the `SketcherFrame` class by the menu item listeners that you put together in the previous chapter.

The `switch` statement in the `createElement()` method selects the constructor to be called, and as you see, they are all essentially of the same form. If the code falls through the switch with an ID that you haven't provided for, you return `null`. Of course, none of these shape class constructors exists in the Sketcher program yet, so if you want to try compiling the code you have so far, you need to comment out each of the return statements. Because you are calling the constructors from a static method in the `Element` class, the element classes must be static, too. You implement these very soon, but first let's add the next piece of mouse event handling that's required — handling button release events.

Handling Button Release Events

When the mouse button is released, you have created an element. In this case all you need to do is to add the element that is referenced by the `tempElement` member of the `MouseHandler` class to the `SketcherModel` object that represents the sketch. One thing you need to consider, though: someone might click the mouse button without dragging it. In this case there won't be an element to store. In this case you just clean up the data members of the `MouseHandler` object:

```
public void mouseReleased(MouseEvent e) {
  if(e.getButton() == MouseEvent.BUTTON1) {
    buttonState = MouseEvent.NOBUTTON;        // Reset the button state

    if(tempElement != null) {                 // If there is an element...
      theApp.getModel().add(tempElement);     // ...add it to the model...
```

```
        tempElement = null;             // ...and reset the field
    }
    if(g2D != null) {                   // If there's a graphics context
        g2D.dispose();                  // ...release the resource...
        g2D = null;                     // ...and reset field to null
    }
    start = last = null;                // Remove any points
    }
}
```

Directory "Sketcher 4 drawing sketch line and rectangle elements"

When button 1 for the mouse is released it changes state, so you can use the getButton() method here to verify that this occurred. Of course, once button 1 is released, you should reset buttonState.

If there is a reference stored in tempElement, you add it to the model by calling the add() method that you defined for the SketcherModel class and set tempElement back to null. It is most important that you set tempElement back to null here. Failing to do that would result in the old element reference being added to the model when you click the mouse button.

Another important operation that the mouseReleased() method carries out is to call the dispose() method for the g2D object. Every graphics context makes use of system resources. If you use a lot of graphics context objects and you don't release the resources they use, your program consumes more and more resources. When you call dispose() for a graphics context object, it can no longer be used, so you set g2D back to null to be on the safe side.

When you add the new element to the model, the view is notified as an observer, so the update() method for the view object is called. You can implement the update() method in the SketcherView class like this:

```
public void update(Observable o, Object rectangle) {
    if(rectangle != null) {
        repaint((Rectangle)rectangle);
    } else {
        repaint();
    }
}
```

Directory "Sketcher 4 drawing sketch line and rectangle elements"

If the reference passed to update() is not null, then you have a reference to a Rectangle object that was provided by the notifyObservers() method call in the add() method for the SketcherModel object. This rectangle is the area occupied by the new element, so when you pass this to the repaint() method for the view object, just this area is added to the area to be redrawn on the next call of the paint() method. The rectangle needs to completely enclose what you want painted. In particular, points on the right and bottom boundaries of the rectangle are not included. If rectangle is null, you call the version of repaint() that has no parameter to redraw the whole view.

You have implemented the three methods that you need to draw shapes. You could try it out if only you had a shape to draw, but before I get into that I'm digressing briefly to introduce another class that you can use to get information about where the mouse cursor is. This is just so you know about this class. You aren't using it in any examples.

Using MouseInfo Class Methods

The java.awt.MouseInfo class provides a way for you to get information about the mouse at any time. The MouseInfo class defines a static method, getPointerInfo(), that returns a reference to an object of type java.awt.PointerInfo, which encapsulates information about where the mouse cursor was when the method was called. To find the location of the mouse cursor from a PointerInfo object you call its getLocation()

method. This method returns a reference to a `Point` object that identifies the mouse cursor location. Thus you can find out where the mouse cursor is at any time like this:

```
Point position = MouseInfo.getPointerInfo().getLocation();
```

After executing this code fragment, the `position` object contains the coordinates of the mouse cursor at the time you call the `getPointerInfo()` method. Note that the `PointerInfo` object that this method returns does not get updated when the mouse cursor is moved, so there's no point in saving it. You must always call the `getPointerInfo()` method each time you want to find out where the cursor is.

When you have two or more display devices attached to your computer, you can find out which display the mouse cursor is on by calling the `getDevice()` method for the `PointerInfo` object. This returns a reference to a `java.awt.GraphicsDevice` object that encapsulates the display that shows the cursor.

The `MouseInfo` class also defines a static method `getNumberOfButtons()`, which returns a value of type `int` that specifies the number of buttons on the mouse. This is useful when you want to make your code adapt automatically to the number of buttons on the mouse. You can make your program take advantage of the second or third buttons on the mouse when they are present, and adapt to use alternative GUI mechanisms when they are not available — by using an existing mouse button combined with keyboard key presses to represent buttons that are absent, for example.

Most of the time you will want to find the cursor location from within a mouse event-handling method. In these cases you find it is easiest to obtain the mouse cursor location from the `MouseEvent` object that is passed to the method handling the event. However, when you don't have a `MouseEvent` object available, you still have the `MouseInfo` class methods to fall back on.

Now, I return to the subject of how you can define shapes.

DEFINING YOUR OWN SHAPE CLASSES

All the classes that define shapes in Sketcher are static nested classes of the `Element` class. As I said earlier, as well as being a convenient way to keep the shape class definitions together, this also avoids possible conflicts with the names of standard classes such as the `Rectangle` class in the `java.awt` package.

It will be helpful later if each shape class defines a shape with its own origin, like a Swing component. The process for drawing a shape in a graphics context is to move the origin of the graphics context to the position recorded for the shape and then draw the shape relative to the new origin. You can start with the simplest type of Sketcher shape — a class representing a line.

Defining Lines

A line is defined by two points and its color. The origin is the first point on the line, so all line objects have their first point as (0,0). This is used in all the shape classes in Sketcher, so add a new member to the `Element` class:

```
static final Point origin = new Point();
```

The default constructor for `Point` creates a point at the origin.

You can define the `Line` class as a nested class in the base class `Element` as follows:

```
import java.awt.*;
import java.io.Serializable;
import static Constants.SketcherConstants.*;
import java.awt.geom.*;

public abstract class Element implements Serializable {
  // Code defining the base class...
  // Nested class defining a line
  public static class Line extends Element {
```

```
    public Line(Point start, Point end, Color color) {
      super(start, color);

      line = new Line2D.Double(origin.x,               origin.y,
                               end.x - position.x , end.y - position.y);
      bounds = new java.awt.Rectangle(
                  Math.min(start.x ,end.x),    Math.min(start.y, end.y),
                  Math.abs(start.x - end.x)+1, Math.abs(start.y - end.y)+1);
    }

    // Change the end point for the line
    public void modify(Point start, Point last) {
      line.x2 = last.x - position.x;
      line.y2 = last.y - position.y;
      bounds = new java.awt.Rectangle(
                  Math.min(start.x ,last.x),    Math.min(start.y, last.y),
                  Math.abs(start.x - last.x)+1, Math.abs(start.y - last.y)+1);
    }

    // Display the line
    public  void draw(Graphics2D g2D) {
      g2D.setPaint(color);                       // Set the line color
      g2D.translate(position);                   // Move origin
      g2D.draw(line);                            // Draw the line
      g2D.translate(-position.x, -position.y);   // Move context origin back
    }

    private Line2D.Double line;
    private final static long serialVersionUID = 1001L;
  }
  // Abstract methods & fields in Element class...
}
```

Directory "Sketcher 4 drawing sketch line and rectangle elements"

The Line constructor has three parameters: the two end points of the line as type Point and the color. You use type Point because all the points you work with originate from mouse events as type Point. Calling the base class constructor records the position and color of the line in the members of the Line class inherited from Element. You create the line shape as a Line2D.Double object in the Line class constructor using the Line2D.Double constructor that accepts the coordinates of the two points that define the line. You then store the reference in the line member of the class. The coordinates of the first point on the line is the origin point so you must adjust the coordinates of the second point to be relative to origin at (0,0). You can easily do this by subtracting the x and y coordinates of position from the corresponding coordinates of end.

The constructor creates the bounds rectangle from the two points that define the line. The position of the rectangle is the top-left corner. This is the point corresponding to the minimum x and minimum y of the two defining points. The rectangle width and height are the differences between the x and the y coordinates, respectively. However, when an area specified by a rectangle is painted, the pixels that lie on the right and bottom edges of the rectangle are not included. To ensure that the entire line lies within the rectangle you add 1 to the width and height.

The modify() method is called when an end point of the line changes when the mouse is being dragged to define the line. The end point of a Line2D.Double object is stored in its public members, x2 and y2. The modify() method updates these by subtracting the corresponding members of last to adjust for the first point being at origin. The method then updates the bounds member to accommodate the new end point.

The draw() method sets the line color in the device context by passing it to the setPaint() method and then moves the origin of the device context to position by calling its translate() method. It then draws a line relative to the new origin by calling draw() for the g2D object. You call translate() once more to reset the origin back to its original state at `position`. It is essential to do this because the `mouseDragged()` method executes many times and calls `draw()` using the same device context. If you don't reset the origin for the device context, it is moved further and further each time you draw another instance of an element.

 NOTE *The* `translate()` *method you are using here to move the origin of the device context has two parameters of type* `int`*. The* `Graphics2D` *class defines another version of this method that has two parameters of type* `double` *and has a slightly different role in drawing operations. I'll introduce you to the second version of* `translate()` *in Chapter 20.*

Defining Rectangles

The interactive mechanism for drawing a rectangle is similar to that for a line. When you are drawing a rectangle, the point where the mouse is pressed defines one corner of the rectangle, and as you drag the mouse, the cursor position defines an opposite corner, as illustrated in Figure 19-24.

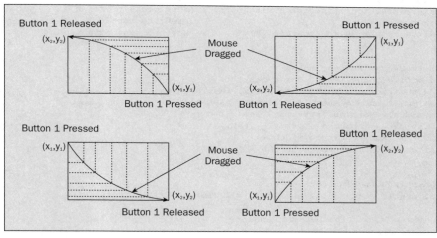

FIGURE 19-24

Releasing the mouse button establishes the final rectangle shape to be stored in the model. As you can see, the cursor position when you press the mouse button can be any corner of the rectangle. This is fine from a usability standpoint, but our code needs to take account of the fact that a `Rectangle2D` object is always defined by the top-left corner, plus a width and a height.

Figure 19-24 shows the four possible orientations of the mouse path as it is dragged in relation to the rectangle drawn. The top-left corner has coordinates that are the minimum x and the minimum y from the points at the ends of the diagonal. The width is the absolute value of the difference between the x coordinates for the two ends, and the height is the absolute value of the difference between the y coordinates. From that you can define the `Rectangle` class for Sketcher.

TRY IT OUT **The Element.Rectangle Class**

Here's the definition of the class for a rectangle object:

```java
import java.awt.*;
import java.io.Serializable;
import static Constants.SketcherConstants.*;
import java.awt.geom.*;
```

```
class Element implements Serializable {
    // Code for the base class definition...

    // Nested class defining a line...

    // Nested class defining a rectangle
    public static class Rectangle extends Element {
        public Rectangle(Point start, Point end, Color color) {
            super(new Point(
                        Math.min(start.x, end.x), Math.min(start.y, end.y)), color);
            rectangle = new Rectangle2D.Double(
                origin.x, origin.y,                          // Top-left corner
                Math.abs(start.x - end.x), Math.abs(start.y - end.y));// Width & height
            bounds = new java.awt.Rectangle(
                        Math.min(start.x ,end.x),     Math.min(start.y, end.y),
                        Math.abs(start.x - end.x)+1, Math.abs(start.y - end.y)+1);
        }

        // Display the rectangle
        public  void draw(Graphics2D g2D) {
            g2D.setPaint(color);                        // Set the rectangle color
            g2D.translate(position.x, position.y);      // Move context origin
            g2D.draw(rectangle);                        // Draw the rectangle
            g2D.translate(-position.x, -position.y);    // Move context origin back
        }

        // Method to redefine the rectangle
        public void modify(Point start, Point last) {
            bounds.x = position.x = Math.min(start.x, last.x);
            bounds.y = position.y = Math.min(start.y, last.y);
            rectangle.width = Math.abs(start.x - last.x);
            rectangle.height = Math.abs(start.y - last.y);
            bounds.width = (int)rectangle.width +1;
            bounds.height = (int)rectangle.height + 1;
        }

        private Rectangle2D.Double rectangle;
        private final static long serialVersionUID = 1001L;
    }
    // Abstract methods & fields in Element class...
}
```

Directory "Sketcher 4 drawing sketch line and rectangle elements"

If you comment out the lines in the createElement() method that creates circles and curves you should be able to recompile the Sketcher program and draw rectangles as well as lines — in various colors, too. A typical high-quality artistic sketch that you are now able to create is shown in Figure 19-25.

How It Works

The code that enables lines and rectangles to be drawn work in essentially the same way. You can drag the mouse in any direction to create a rectangle or a line. Both types rubber-band as you drag the mouse with button 1 down.

The type of element that is created is determined as a line by default, but you can select Rectangle from the

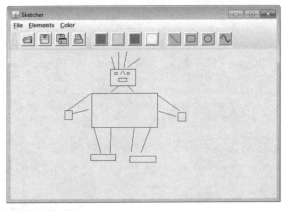

FIGURE 19-25

Element menu. When you are creating a rectangle, the constructor sorts out the correct coordinates for the top-left corner. This is necessary because the rectangle is being defined from any of its diagonals, because the rectangle is always displayed from the point where the mouse button was pressed to the current cursor position. The point where the mouse button is pressed can be at any of the four corners of the rectangle. Because the top-left corner always defines the position of a `Rectangle2D` object, you have to work out where that is.

The `getBounds()` method in the `Element.Rectangle` class calls the `getBoundingRectangle()` method inherited from the base class, `Element`. You can see why it is necessary to increase the width and height of the bounding rectangle if you temporarily comment out the statements that do this. You see that rectangles are drawn with the right and bottom edges missing.

Defining Circles

The most natural mechanism for drawing a circle is to make the point where the mouse button is pressed the center, and the point where the mouse button is released the end of the radius — that is, on the circumference. You need to do a little calculation to make it work this way.

Figure 19-26 illustrates the drawing mechanism for a circle. Circles are drawn dynamically as the mouse is dragged, with the cursor position being on the circumference of the circle. You have the center of the circle and a point on the circumference available in the methods that handle the mouse events, but the `Ellipse2D` class that you use to define a circle expects it to be defined by the coordinates of the point on the top-right corner of the rectangle that encloses the circle plus its height and width. This means you have to calculate the position, height, and width of the rectangle from the center and radius of the circle.

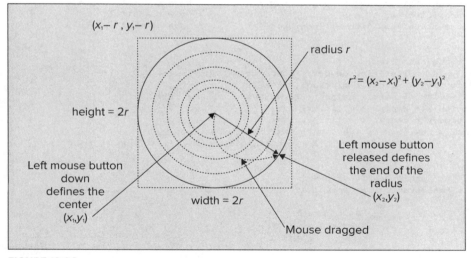

FIGURE 19-26

Pythagoras' theorem provides the formula that you might use to calculate the radius of the circle from the point at the center and any point on the circumference, and this is shown in Figure 19-26. The formula may look a little complicated, but Java makes this easy. Remember the `distance()` method defined in `Point2D` class? That does exactly what is shown here, so you are able to use that to obtain the radius directly from the two defining points. When you have the radius, you can then calculate the coordinates of the top-left point by subtracting the radius value from the coordinates of the center. The height and width of the enclosing rectangle for the circle are just twice the radius.

Here's how this is applied in the definition of the `Element.Circle` class:

```java
import java.awt.*;
import java.io.Serializable;
import static Constants.SketcherConstants.*;
import java.awt.geom.*;

public abstract class Element implements Serializable{
  // Code defining the base class...
  // Nested class defining a line...
  // Nested class defining a rectangle...
  // Nested class defining a circle
  public static class Circle extends Element {
    public Circle(Point center, Point circum, Color color) {
      super(color);

      // Radius is distance from center to circumference
      double radius = center.distance(circum);
      position = new Point(center.x - (int)radius, center.y - (int)radius);
      circle = new Ellipse2D.Double(origin.x, origin.y, 2.*radius, 2.*radius);
      bounds = new java.awt.Rectangle(position.x, position.y,
                            1 + (int)circle.width, 1+(int)circle.height);
    }

    // Display the circle
    public  void draw(Graphics2D g2D) {
      g2D.setPaint(color);                          // Set the circle color
      g2D.translate(position.x, position.y);        // Move context origin
      g2D.draw(circle);                             // Draw the circle
      g2D.translate(-position.x, -position.y);      // Move context origin back
    }

    // Recreate this circle
    public void modify(Point center, Point circum) {
      double radius = center.distance(circum);
      circle.width = circle.height = 2*radius;
      position.x = center.x - (int)radius;
      position.y = center.y - (int)radius;
      bounds = new java.awt.Rectangle(position.x, position.y,
                            1 + (int)circle.width, 1+(int)circle.height);
    }

    private Ellipse2D.Double circle;
    private final static long serialVersionUID = 1001L;
  }
  // Abstract methods & fields in Element class...
}
```

You can't use the base class constructor that requires two arguments because you have to calculate the position for a circle first. A base class constructor call must appear as the first statement in the body of the derived class constructor. Add the following constructor to the `Element` class:

```java
protected Element(Color color) {
  this.color = color;
}
```

This just initializes the color member.

If you amend the `createElement()` method in the `MouseHandler` class by uncommenting the line that creates `Element.Circle` objects and recompile the Sketcher program, you are ready to draw circles. You are now equipped to produce artwork of the astonishing sophistication shown in Figure 19-27.

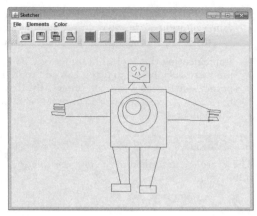

FIGURE 19-27

How It Works

The circle is generated by the button down point defining the center and the cursor position while dragging as a point on the circumference. A circle is a special case of an ellipse, and a shape that is an ellipse is defined by the top-left corner and the width and height of the rectangle that encloses it. The `distance()` method that is defined in the `Point2D` class calculates the radius, and this value is used to calculate the coordinates of the top-left corner of the enclosing rectangle, which is stored in `position`. The width and height of the rectangle enclosing the circle are just twice the radius value, so the circle is stored as an `Ellipse2D.Double` object at `origin` with a width and height as twice the radius.

Because of the way a circle is drawn, the `modify()` method has to recalculate the `position` coordinates as well as the width and height. The other methods in the `Element.Circle` class are much the same as you have seen previously.

Drawing Curves

Curves are a bit trickier to deal with than the other shapes. You want to be able to create a freehand curve by dragging the mouse, so that as the cursor moves the curve extends. This needs to be reflected in how you define the `Element.Curve` class. Let's first consider how the process of drawing a curve is going to work and define the `Element.Curve` class based on that.

The `QuadCurve2D` and `CubicCurve2D` classes are not very convenient or easy to use here. These are applicable when you have curves that you define by a series of points together with control points that define tangents to the curve. A curve in Sketcher is going to be entered freehand, and the data that you get is a series of points that are relatively close together, but you don't know ahead of time how many there are going to be; as long as the mouse is being dragged you collect more points. You won't have any control points either. This gives us a hint as to an approach you could adopt for creating a curve that keeps it as simple as possible. Figure 19-28 illustrates the approach you could take.

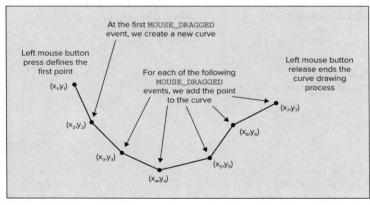

FIGURE 19-28

Successive points that define the freehand curve are quite close together, so you could create a visual representation of the curve by joining the points to form a series of connected line segments. Because the lengths of the line segments are short, it should look like a reasonable curve.

Implementing this looks like a job for a GeneralPath object. A GeneralPath object can handle any number of segments, and you can add to it. You can construct an initial path as soon as you have two points — which is when you process the first MOUSE_DRAGGED event. You can extend the curve by calling the modify() method to add another segment to the path using the point that you get for each of the subsequent MOUSE_DRAGGED events.

TRY IT OUT The Element.Curve Class

The approach described in the previous section means that the outline of the Curve class is going to be the following:

Available for download on Wrox.com

```
import java.awt.*;
import java.io.Serializable;
import static Constants.SketcherConstants.*;

public abstract class Element implements Serializable {
    // Code defining the base class...
    // Nested class defining a line...
    // Nested class defining a rectangle...
    // Nested class defining a circle...
    // Nested class defining a curve
    public static class Curve extends Element {
        public Curve(Point start, Point next, Color color) {
            super(start, color);
            curve = new GeneralPath();
            curve.moveTo(origin.x, origin.y);            // Set current position as origin
            curve.lineTo(next.x - position.x, next.y - position.y);  // Add segment
            bounds = new java.awt.Rectangle(
                        Math.min(start.x ,next.x),     Math.min(start.y, next.y),
                        Math.abs(next.x - start.x)+1, Math.abs(next.y - start.y)+1);
        }

        // Add another segment
        public void modify(Point start, Point next) {
            curve.lineTo(next.x - position.x, next.y - position.y);  // Add segment
            bounds.add(new java.awt.Rectangle(next.x,next.y, 1, 1));  // Extend bounds
        }


        // Display the curve
        public  void draw(Graphics2D g2D) {
          g2D.setPaint(color);                             // Set the curve color
          g2D.translate(position.x, position.y);           // Move context origin
          g2D.draw(curve);                                 // Draw the curve
          g2D.translate(-position.x, -position.y);         // Move context origin back
        }

        private GeneralPath curve;
        private final static long serialVersionUID = 1001L;
    }
    // Abstract methods & fields in Element class...
}
```

Directory "Sketcher 6 drawing sketch curve elements"

The Curve class constructor creates a GeneralPath object and adds a single line segment to it by moving the current point for the path to start by calling moveTo() and then calling the lineTo() method for the GeneralPath object with next as the argument. You compute an initial bounding rectangle here that encloses the first two points. As always, the height and width of the rectangle are increased by one to ensure all points are enclosed.

Additional curve segments are added by the `modify()` method. This calls `lineTo()` for the `GeneralPath` member of the class with the new point, `next`, as the argument. This adds a line from the end of the last segment that was added to the new point. The bounding rectangle is extended, if necessary, by adding a 1× 1 rectangle at `next` to bounds. Adding a 1× 1 rectangle, rather than just the `next` point, is necessary to ensure that the new point lies within bounds and not on its boundary.

Of course, you need to uncomment the line creating an `Element.Curve` object in the `createElement()` method in the `MouseHandler` inner class to `SketcherFrame`. Then you're ready to roll again. If you recompile Sketcher you are able to give freehand curves a whirl and produce elegant sketches such as that in Figure 19-29.

FIGURE 19-29

How It Works

Drawing curves works in essentially the same way as drawing the other elements. The use of XOR mode is superfluous with drawing a curve because you only extend it, but it would be quite a bit of work to treat it as a special case. This would be justified only if drawing curves were too slow and produced excessive flicker.

You might be wondering if you can change from XOR mode back to the normal mode of drawing in a graphics context. Certainly you can: Just call the `setPaintMode()` method for the graphics context object to get back to the normal drawing mode.

Figure 19-29 is mainly curves. In the next chapter you add a facility for adding text to a sketch. Don't draw too many masterpieces yet. You won't be able to preserve them for the nation and posterity by saving them in a file until Chapter 21.

CHANGING THE CURSOR

As a last flourish in this chapter, you can make the cursor change to a crosshair cursor in the content pane of the window. All that is necessary to do this is to implement the `mouseEntered()` and `mouseExited()` methods in the `MouseHandler` inner class to the `SketcherView` class:

```
@Override
public void mouseEntered(MouseEvent e) {
  setCursor(Cursor.getPredefinedCursor(Cursor.CROSSHAIR_CURSOR));
```

```
    }

    @Override
    public void mouseExited(MouseEvent e) {
      setCursor(Cursor.getDefaultCursor());
    }
```

Directory "Sketcher 7 with a crosshair cursor"

The `mouseEntered()` method is called each time the mouse cursor enters the area occupied by a component, the view in this case. You set the cursor to the crosshair cursor by calling `setCursor()` for the view object. The argument is the `Cursor` object returned by the static `getPredefinedCursor()` method in the `Cursor` class. For the `mouseExited()` method that is called when the mouse cursor leaves a component, you set the cursor back to the default cursor. With these changes, you should have a crosshair cursor available when you are drawing shapes.

SUMMARY

In this chapter you learned how to draw on components and how you can use mouse listeners to implement a drawing interface. You saw how you can derive your own class from the `Component` class and add it to the content pane for a window to allow text and geometric shapes to be displayed.

The easy way to deal with mouse events is to derive your own class from an adapter class. When you do that, you should use the `@Override` annotation for each method that you implement to make sure that your method matches the signature of a method in the adapter class.

EXERCISES

You can download the source code for the examples in the book and the solutions to the following exercises from www.wrox.com.

1. Add code to the Sketcher program to support drawing an ellipse.

2. Modify the Sketcher program to include a button for switching fill mode on and off.

3. Extend the classes defining rectangles, circles, and ellipses to support filled shapes.

4. Extend the curve class to support filled shapes.

5. (Harder — for curve enthusiasts!) Implement an applet to display a curve as multiple `CubicCurve2D` objects from points on the curve entered by clicking the mouse. The applet should have two buttons — one to clear the window and allow points on the curve to be entered and the other to display the curve. Devise your own scheme for default control points.

6. (Also harder!) Modify the previous example to ensure that the curve is continuous — this implies that the control points on either side of an interior point, and the interior point itself, should be on a straight line. Allow control points to be dragged with the mouse, but still maintain the continuity of the curve.

7. Modify Sketcher so that the mouse cursor changes to a hand cursor when it is over any of the toolbar buttons.

CONFER PROGRAMMER TO PROGRAMMER ABOUT THIS TOPIC.

→ Visit p2p.wrox.com ←

► **WHAT YOU LEARNED IN THIS CHAPTER**

TOPIC	CONCEPT
Device Context	A Graphics2D object represents the drawing surface of a component when the component is displayed on a device such as a display or printer. This is called a device context.
Drawing on a Component	You draw on a component by calling methods provided by its Graphics2D object.
Implementing paint()	You normally draw on a component by implementing its paint() method. The paint() method is passed a Graphics2D object that is the graphics context for the component but as type Graphics. You must cast the Graphics object to type Graphics2D to be able to access the Graphics2D class methods. The paint() method is called whenever the component needs to be redrawn,
Drawing Coordinate Systems	The user coordinate system for drawing on a component has the origin in the top-left corner of the component by default, with the positive x-axis from left to right, and the positive y-axis from top to bottom. This is automatically mapped to the device coordinate system, which is in the same orientation.
Obtaining a Graphics Context	You can't create a Graphics2D object. If you want to draw on a component outside of the paint() method, you can obtain a Graphics2D object for the component by calling its getGraphics() method.
Drawing Modes	There is more than one drawing mode that you can use. The default mode is paint mode, where drawing overwrites the background pixels with pixels of the current color. Another mode is XOR mode, where the current color is combined with the background color. This is typically used to alternate between the current color and a color passed to the setXORMode() method.
Defining Geometric Shapes	The java.awt.geom package defines classes that represent 2D shapes.
Drawing Geometric Shapes	The Graphics2D class defines methods for drawing outline shapes as well as filled shapes.
Drawing Using the Mouse	You can create mechanisms for drawing on a component using the mouse by implementing methods that handle mouse events.

20

Extending the GUI

WHAT YOU WILL LEARN IN THIS CHAPTER:

- ➤ How to create a status bar
- ➤ How to create a dialog
- ➤ What a modal dialog is and how it differs from a modeless dialog
- ➤ How to create a message box dialog
- ➤ How you can use components in a dialog to receive input
- ➤ What a pop-up menu is
- ➤ How you can apply and use transformations to the user coordinate system when drawing on a component
- ➤ What context menus are and how you can implement them

In this chapter you investigate how you can improve the graphical user interface (GUI) for Sketcher. After adding a status bar, you create dialogs and explore how you can use them to communicate with the user and manage input. You look at context menus, which are pop-up menus that vary depending on the context in which they are displayed. You use context menus to enhance the functionality of the Sketcher application. All of this gives you a lot more practice in implementing event listeners, and much more besides.

CREATING A STATUS BAR

One limitation of the Sketcher program as it stands is that you have no direct feedback on what the current element type is and what its color is. As a gentle start to this chapter, let's fix that now. A window status bar at the bottom of an application window is a common and very convenient way of displaying the status of various application parameters, each in its own pane.

There is no Swing class that defines a status bar, so you have to make up your own StatusBar class. Ideally you would design a class for a general-purpose status bar and customize it for Sketcher, but as space in the book is limited I'm taking the simple approach of showing how you can design a class that is specific to Sketcher. The JPanel class is a good basis for the StatusBar class because it represents a panel, and you can add objects to it that represent status bar panes. You use the JLabel class as a base for defining status bar panes and add sunken borders to them to give them a distinctive appearance.

A Status Bar Class for Sketcher

Let's start with a status bar at the bottom of the Sketcher application that contains two panes for showing the current element type and color. Then the user will know exactly what they are about to draw. You can start by defining the `StatusBar` class that represents the status bar in the application window. The `StatusPane` class that defines a region within the status bar can be an inner class to `StatusBar`.

Here's an initial stab at the definition for the `StatusBar` class that you can add to the Sketcher application:

Available for
download on
Wrox.com

```java
// Class defining a status bar
import javax.swing.*;
import java.awt.*;
import javax.swing.border.BevelBorder;
import static Constants.SketcherConstants.*;

class StatusBar extends JPanel {
  // Constructor
  public StatusBar() {
    setLayout(new FlowLayout(FlowLayout.LEFT, 10, 3));
    setBackground(Color.LIGHT_GRAY);
    setBorder(BorderFactory.createLineBorder(Color.DARK_GRAY));
    colorPane = new StatusPane("BLUE", BLUE16);
    setColorPane(DEFAULT_ELEMENT_COLOR);
    setTypePane(DEFAULT_ELEMENT_TYPE);
    add(colorPane);                          // Add color pane to status bar
    add(typePane);                           // Add type pane to status bar
  }
  // Set color pane contents
  public void setColorPane(Color color) {
    // Code to set the color pane contents...
  }

  // Set type pane contents
  public void setTypePane (int elementType) {
    // Code to set the type pane contents...
  }

  // Panes in the status bar
  private StatusPane colorPane;
  private StatusPane typePane;

  // Class defining a status bar pane
  class StatusPane extends JLabel {
    // Rest of the class implementation...
  }
}
```

Directory "Sketcher 1 with a status bar"

Because the `StatusBar` class imports the names of static members of the `SketcherConstants` class from the `Constants` package, all the constants that represent possible element types and colors and the icons used for toolbar buttons and menu items are available. This outline version of `StatusBar` has two fields of type `StatusPane` that are the panes showing the current color and element type.

The `StatusPane` objects will be left-justified when they are added to the status bar, as a result of the first argument to the `setLayout()` method call in the `StatusBar` constructor. The layout manager leaves a 10-pixel horizontal gap between successive panes in the status bar and a 3-pixel vertical gap between rows of components. The border for the status bar is a single dark gray line that you add using the static `createLineBorder()` method in the `BorderFactory` class.

The panes in the status bar need to display only a small amount of text, so you derive the `StatusPane` class from the `JLabel` class; a pane for the status bar is a specialized kind of `JLabel`. The `StatusBar` constructor updates the information to be displayed in each pane initially by calling the `setColorPane()` and `setTypePane()` methods. This ensures that the `StatusPane` objects display the default color and element type that you defined for the application at startup. One or other of these methods is called whenever it is necessary to update the status bar. You will complete the definitions for `setColorPane()` and `setTypePane()` when you've defined the detail of the `StatusPane` class.

The `StatusPane` class that is nested in `StatusBar` is derived from `JPanel`. A `JPanel` object can display text, or an icon, or both. You can provision for status bar panes in Sketcher that display text, or text with an icon. You need two constructors to accommodate this. Here's the inner class definition:

```java
class StatusPane extends JLabel {
  // Constructor - text only
  public StatusPane(String text) {
    super(text, LEFT);
    setupPane();
  }

  // Constructor - text with an icon
  public StatusPane(String text, Icon icon) {
    super(text, icon, LEFT);
    setupPane();
  }

  // Helper method for use by constructors
  private void setupPane() {
    setBackground(Color.LIGHT_GRAY);                              // Set background color
    setForeground(Color.BLACK);                                  // Set foreground color
    setFont(paneFont);                                           // Set the fixed font
    setBorder(BorderFactory.createCompoundBorder(
      BorderFactory.createBevelBorder(BevelBorder.LOWERED),      // Outside border
      BorderFactory.createEmptyBorder(0,5,0,3)));                //  Inside border
    setPreferredSize(new Dimension(80,20));
  }


  private Font paneFont =
                 new Font("Serif", Font.PLAIN, 10);   // Font for pane text
}
```

Directory "Sketcher 1 with a status bar"

The `StatusPane` constructors call different `JLabel` constructors, one with and one without an `Icon` argument. The last argument to the `JLabel` constructors is a value of type `int` that determines the alignment of what is displayed in the label. You can set the contents to be aligned left, centered, or aligned right by specifying the `LEFT`, `CENTER`, or `RIGHT` constants from the `SwingConstants` interface that the `JLabel` class implements. I'm choosing left-alignment for the status bar pane content in both cases.

The `StatusPane` constructors call a helper method, `setupPane()`, that contains code that is common to both. This sets up the physical appearance of a pane. It first sets the background and foreground colors, the latter being the color of any text that is displayed. It then sets the font for displayed text to be the class member, `font`. This is a standard 10-point serif font, but you could choose a different font if you like.

The panes have a compound border. The outside border is a lowered bevel border that distinguishes each pane clearly. The inside border is an empty border that serves to set the distance of the contents that you display in a pane from the outside border. The four arguments in sequence specify the distances from the top, left, bottom, and right edges respectively.

If you can maintain a fixed width for each pane, it prevents the size of the pane from jumping around when you change the text. To do this you call the inherited `setPreferredSize()` method. The argument is a `java.awt.Dimension` object, and the first argument to the constructor is the width and the second argument is the height. The values are such to accommodate the maximum length of contents you want to display with the specified font.

Now you know the detail of the `StatusPane` class, you can update the definitions of the `colorPane` and `typePane` members of the `StatusBar` class:

```
private StatusPane colorPane = new StatusPane("BLUE", BLUE16);
private StatusPane typePane = new StatusPane("LINE");
```

The `colorPane` member has text and an icon as the contents. The icon is the one you used on the corresponding menu item. These are 16 × 16 so they fit within the height of a pane. The `typePane` member just displays the current element type as text. The longest text to be displayed is "Rectangle," and this fits within the width of a pane as a 10-point font. They are created to correspond with the initial element type and color.

Updating the Panes

You can code the `setColorPane()` method as follows:

Available for download on Wrox.com

```
// Set color pane contents
public void setColorPane(Color color) {
    String text = null;                          // Text for the color pane
    Icon icon = null;                            // Icon to be displayed
    if(color.equals(Color.RED)) {
      text = "RED";
      icon = RED16;
    } else if(color.equals(Color.YELLOW)) {
      text = "YELLOW";
      icon = YELLOW16;
    } else if(color.equals(Color.GREEN)) {
      text = "GREEN";
      icon = GREEN16;
    } else if(color.equals(Color.BLUE)) {
      text = "BLUE";
      icon = BLUE16;
    } else {
      text = "CUSTOM COLOR";
    }
    colorPane.setIcon(icon);
    colorPane.setText(text);                     // Set the pane text
}
```

Directory "Sketcher 1 with a status bar"

This sets the text and selects an icon for a color pane based on the `Color` argument that is passed to it. The icons are available from the `SketcherConstants` class and these are imported statically so you can reference them without qualification. The text and icon to be displayed in the color pane are selected in the series of `if-else` statements. They each compare the color that is passed as the argument with the standard colors you use in Sketcher and set the `text` and `icon` variables accordingly. The last `else` should never be reached at the moment, but it is obvious if it is. This provides the possibility of adding more flexibility in the choice of drawing color later on. The `setText()` and `setIcon()` methods that set the text and icon to be displayed are inherited from the `JLabel` class.

In the code for the `setTypePane()` method, you can use a `switch` statement rather than `if` statements to test the parameter value because it is of type `int`:

Available for download on Wrox.com

```
public void setTypePane(int elementType) {
    String text = null;                          // Text for the type pane
    switch(elementType) {
      case LINE:
        text = "LINE";
        break;
      case RECTANGLE:
```

```
          text = "RECTANGLE";
          break;
      case CIRCLE:
          text = "CIRCLE";
          break;
      case CURVE:
          text = "CURVE";
          break;
      default:
          assert false;
      }
      typePane.setText(text);                              // Set the pane text
  }
```

Directory "Sketcher 1 with a status bar"

The method selects the text to be displayed in the pane based on the argument. If something goes wrong somewhere that results in an invalid element type, the program asserts through the default case.

You can implement the status bar in the `SketcherFrame` class now. For this you must add a field to the `SketcherFrame` class that stores a reference to the status bar, modify the `SketcherFrame` class constructor to add the status bar to the content pane of the window, and extend the `actionPerformed()` methods in the `TypeAction` and `ColorAction` classes to update the status bar when the element type or color is altered.

TRY IT OUT   The Status Bar in Action

You can add the following statement to the `SketcherFrame` class to define the status bar as a data member, following the members that define the menu bar and toolbar:

```
      private StatusBar statusBar = new StatusBar();            // Window status bar
```

You create `statusBar` as a data member so that it can be accessed throughout the class definition, including from within the `Action` classes. You need to add one statement to the end of the `SketcherFrame` class constructor:

```
      public SketcherFrame(String title, Sketcher theApp) {
        // Constructor code as before...
        getContentPane().add(statusBar, BorderLayout.SOUTH);       // Add the statusbar
      }
```

Directory "Sketcher 1 with a status bar"

This adds the status bar to the bottom of the application window. To update the status bar when the element type changes, you can add one statement to the `actionPerformed()` method in the inner class `TypeAction`:

```
      public void actionPerformed(ActionEvent e) {
        elementType = typeID;
        setChecks(elementMenu, e.getSource());
        statusBar.setTypePane(typeID);
      }
```

Directory "Sketcher 1 with a status bar"

The type pane is updated by calling the `setTypePane()` method for the status bar and passing the current element type to it as an argument. You can add a similar statement to the `actionPerformed()` method in the `ColorAction` inner class to update the color pane:

```
      public void actionPerformed(ActionEvent e) {
        elementColor = color;
        setChecks(colorMenu, e.getSource());
        statusBar.setColorPane(color);
      }
```

Directory "Sketcher 1 with a status bar"

If you now recompile and run Sketcher again, you see the status bar in the application, as shown in Figure 20-1.

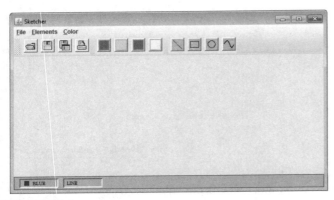

FIGURE 20-1

As you change the element type and color through the menus or toolbar buttons, the status bar is updated automatically.

USING DIALOGS

A dialog is a window that is displayed within the context of another window—its parent. You use dialogs to manage input that can't be handled conveniently through interaction with the view—selecting from a range of options, for example, or enabling data to be entered from the keyboard. You can also use dialogs for information messages or warnings. The `JDialog` class in the `javax.swing` package defines dialogs, and a `JDialog` object is a specialized sort of `Window`. A `JDialog` object typically contains one or more components for displaying information or allowing data to be entered, plus buttons for selecting dialog options (including closing the dialog), so there's quite a bit of work involved in putting one together. However, for many of the typical dialogs that you might want to use, the `JOptionPane` class provides an easy shortcut to creating dialogs. Figure 20-2 shows a dialog that you will create later in this chapter using just one statement.

FIGURE 20-2

You use this dialog to provide a response to clicking on a Help/About menu item that you will add to Sketcher in a moment. First, though, you need to understand a little more about how dialogs work.

Modal and Modeless Dialogs

There are two different kinds of dialog that you can create, and they have distinct operating characteristics. You have a choice of creating either a *modal dialog* or a *modeless dialog*.

There are three varieties of modal dialog:

➤ **Application-modal dialogs:** Prevent user interaction with all other windows in the same application except for windows that are created by the dialog object. Interaction with other application windows is restored when an application modal dialog closes.

➤ **Document-modal dialogs:** Block all ancestor windows of the dialog window that share a common root. The windows in the hierarchy each have an owner except for the root window.

➤ **Toolkit-modal dialogs:** Prevent interaction with all other windows that execute in the same toolkit. When a web page has several applets running, they all share the same toolkit so a dialog created by one applet can prevent interaction with other applets in the same web page.

A modeless dialog can be left on the screen for as long as you want, because it doesn't block interaction with other windows in the application. You can also switch the focus back and forth between a modeless dialog and any other application windows that are on the screen. I only discuss modeless and application-modal dialogs in this book. I'll refer to application-modal dialogs simply as modal dialogs.

You display a modal dialog typically by selecting a menu item or clicking a button. The dialog in Figure 20-2 that displays a message is a modal dialog. The dialog window retains the focus as long as it is displayed, and the application cannot continue until you click the OK button. Modal dialogs that manage input normally have at least two buttons: an OK button, which you use to accept whatever input has been entered and then close the dialog, and a Cancel button to just close the dialog and abort the entry of the data. Dialogs that manage input are almost always modal dialogs, simply because you don't generally want to allow other interactions to be triggered until your user's input is complete.

Whether you create a modal or a modeless dialog is determined either by an argument to a dialog class constructor, or by which constructor you choose, because some constructors create modeless dialogs by default. The default, no-argument `JDialog` constructor creates a modeless dialog with an empty title bar. Because you have no provision for specifying a parent window for the dialog with the no-argument constructor, a shared hidden frame will be assigned as the parent in this case. You have a choice of five constructors for creating a `JDialog` object where the parent can be a window of type `Frame` or `JFrame`:

➤ `JDialog(Frame parent)`: Creates a modeless dialog with an empty title bar.

➤ `JDialog(Frame parent, String title)`: Creates a modeless dialog with the `title` string in the title bar.

➤ `JDialog(Frame parent, boolean modal)`: Creates a dialog with an empty title bar. If `modal` is `true` then the dialog is modal.

➤ `JDialog(Frame parent, String title, boolean modal)`: Creates a dialog with the `title` string in the title bar. If `modal` is `true` then the dialog is modal.

➤ `JDialog(Frame parent, String title, boolean modal, GraphicsConfiguration gc)`: Creates a dialog with the `title` string in the title bar. If `modal` is `true` then the dialog is modal. The `gc` parameter describes the characteristics (resolution, color depth, and so on) of the device on which the dialog is to be displayed.

Because the first parameter to these constructors is of type `Frame`, you can supply a reference of type `Frame` or of type `JFrame` to identify the parent window. There are a further five constructors for creating `JDialog` objects with a `Dialog` or `JDialog` object as the parent. The only difference between these and the ones in the preceding list is that the type of the first parameter is `Dialog` rather than `Frame`. Any of these constructors can throw an exception of type `HeadlessException` if the system on which the code is executing does not have a display attached.

After you've created a `JDialog` object, you can switch the dialog window it produces between modal and modeless by calling the `setModal()` method for the object. With a `true` argument to the method the dialog is modal, and `false` makes it modeless. The `isModal()` method for a `JDialog` object returns `true` if it represents a modal dialog and `false` otherwise.

All `JDialog` objects are initially invisible, so to display them you must call the `setVisible()` method for the `JDialog` object with the argument `true`. This method is inherited from the `Component` class via the `Container` and `Window` classes. If you call `setVisible()` with the argument `false`, the dialog window is removed from the screen. After you've displayed a modal dialog window, the user can't interact with any of the other application windows until you call `setVisible()` for the dialog object with the argument `false`, so you typically do this in the event handler that is called to close the dialog. Note that the `setVisible()` method affects only the visibility of the dialog. You still have a perfectly good `JDialog` object. When you want to display the dialog again, you just call its `setVisible()` method with the argument `true`. Of course, if you call `dispose()` for the `JDialog` object, or set the default close operation to `DISPOSE_ON_CLOSE`, then you aren't able to use the `JDialog` object again.

You can set or change the title bar for a dialog by passing a `String` object to the `setTitle()` method for the `JDialog` object. The `getTitle()` method for a dialog returns a reference to a `String` object that contains the title bar string.

Dialog windows are resizable by default, so you can change the size of a dialog window by dragging its boundaries. If you don't want to allow a dialog window to be resized, you can inhibit this by calling the `setResizable()` method for the `JDialog` object with the argument as `false`. An argument value of `true` enables the resizing capability.

A Simple Modal Dialog

The simplest kind of dialog just displays some information. You could see how this works by adding a Help menu with an About menu item and then displaying an About dialog to provide information about the application.

Defining the AboutDialog Class

You derive your own dialog class from `JDialog` so you can create an About dialog. `AboutDialog` seems like a good name for the new class.

The constructor for the `AboutDialog` class needs to accept three arguments—the parent `Frame` object, which is the application window in Sketcher; a `String` object defining what should appear on the title bar; and a `String` object for the message that you want to display. There is only one button in the dialog window, an OK button to close the dialog. You can make the whole thing self-contained by making the `AboutDialog` class the action listener for its OK button, and because it's relevant only in the context of the `SketcherFrame` class, you can define it as a nested class to `SketcherFrame`:

```
// Import statements as before...

public class SketcherFrame extends JFrame {
  // SketcherFrame class as before...

  // Class defining a general purpose message box
  class AboutDialog extends JDialog implements ActionListener    {
    public AboutDialog(JFrame parent, String title, String message)    {
      super(parent, title, true);
      // If there was a parent, set dialog position inside
      if(parent != null) {
        Dimension parentSize = parent.getSize(); // Parent size
        Point p = parent.getLocation();          // Parent position
        setLocation(p.x + parentSize.width/4,p.y + parentSize.height/4);
      }

      // Create the message pane
      JPanel messagePane = new JPanel();
      messagePane.add(new JLabel(message));
      getContentPane().add(messagePane);

      // Create the button pane
      JPanel buttonPane = new JPanel();
      JButton button = new JButton("OK");         // Create OK button
      buttonPane.add(button);                     // add to content pane
      button.addActionListener(this);
      getContentPane().add(buttonPane, BorderLayout.SOUTH);
      setDefaultCloseOperation(DISPOSE_ON_CLOSE);
      pack();                                     // Size window for components
      setVisible(true);
    }

    // OK button action
    public void actionPerformed(ActionEvent e)    {
```

```
        setVisible(false);                    // Set dialog invisible
        dispose();                            // Release the dialog resources
    }
}
```

Directory "Sketcher 2 displaying an About dialog"

The constructor first calls the base `JDialog` class constructor to create a modal dialog with the title bar given by the `title` argument. It then defines the position of the dialog relative to the position of the frame.

> **NOTE** *When you create an instance of the `AboutDialog` class in the Sketcher program a little later in this chapter, you specify the `SketcherFrame` object as the parent for the dialog. The parent relationship between the application window and the dialog implies a lifetime dependency. When the `SketcherFrame` object is destroyed, the `AboutDialog` object is, too, because it is a child of the `SketcherFrame` object. This doesn't just apply to `JDialog` objects — any `Window` object can have another `Window` object as a parent.*

By default the `AboutDialog` window is positioned relative to the top-left corner of the screen. To position the dialog in a more sensible position relative to the application window, you set the coordinates of the top-left corner of the dialog as one quarter of the distance across the width of the application window, and one quarter of the distance down from the top-left corner of the application window.

You add the components you want to display in a dialog to the content pane for the `JDialog` object. The content pane has a `BorderLayout` manager by default, just like the content pane for the application window, and this is quite convenient for the `AboutDialog` layout. The dialog contains two `JPanel` objects that are created in the constructor, one to hold a `JLabel` object for the message that is passed as an argument to the constructor and the other to hold the OK button that closes the dialog. The `messagePane` object is added so that it fills the center of the dialog window. The `buttonPane` position is specified as `BorderLayout.SOUTH`, so it is at the bottom of the dialog window. Both `JPanel` objects have a `FlowLayout` manager by default.

You want the `AboutDialog` object to be the listener for the OK button so you pass the `this` variable as the argument to the `addActionListener()` method call for the button.

The `pack()` method is inherited from the `Window` class. This method packs the components in the window, setting the window to an optimal size for the components it contains before laying out the components. Note that if you don't call `pack()` here, the size for your dialog is not set and you aren't able to see it.

The `actionPerformed()` method is called when the OK button is selected. This just disposes of the dialog by calling the `dispose()` method for the `AboutDialog` object so the dialog window disappears from the screen and the resources it was using are released.

Creating an About Menu Item

To add a Help menu with an About item to the Sketcher application, you need to insert some code into the `SketcherFrame` class constructor. You can make the `SketcherFrame` object the listener for the About menu item by making it implement the `ActionListener` interface and adding the `actionPerformed()` method implementation. Let's see it working.

TRY IT OUT   Displaying an About Dialog

First, add `ActionListener` as an interface implemented by the `SketcherFrame` class:

```
public class SketcherFrame extends JFrame implements ActionListener {
```

The changes to the `SketcherFrame` class constructor to add the Help menu are:

```
public SketcherFrame(String title , Sketcher theApp) {
  setTitle(title);                                  // Set the window title
  this.theApp = theApp;                             // Save app. object reference
  setJMenuBar(menuBar);                             // Add the menu bar to the window
  setDefaultCloseOperation(EXIT_ON_CLOSE);          // Default is exit the application

  createFileMenu();                                 // Create the File menu
  createElementMenu();                              // Create the element menu
  createColorMenu();                                // Create the element menu
  createToolbar();
  toolBar.setRollover(true);
  JMenu helpMenu = new JMenu("Help");               // Create Help menu
  helpMenu.setMnemonic('H');                        // Create Help shortcut

  // Add the About item to the Help menu
  aboutItem = new JMenuItem("About");               // Create About menu item
  aboutItem.addActionListener(this);                // Listener is the frame
  helpMenu.add(aboutItem);                          // Add item to menu
  menuBar.add(helpMenu);                            // Add Help menu to menu bar
  getContentPane().add(toolBar, BorderLayout.NORTH); // Add the toolbar
  getContentPane().add(statusBar, BorderLayout.SOUTH); // Add the statusbar
}
```

Directory "Sketcher 2 displaying an About dialog"

Add `aboutMenu` as a private member of the `SketcherFrame` class:

```
private JMenuItem aboutItem;                        // About menu item
```

Lastly, you need to implement the method in the `SketcherFrame` class to handle the About menu item's events:

```
// Handle About menu events
public void actionPerformed(ActionEvent e)  {
  if(e.getSource() == aboutItem) {
    // Create about dialog with the app window as parent
    AboutDialog aboutDlg = new AboutDialog(this, "About Sketcher",
                                  "Sketcher Copyright Ivor Horton 2011");

  }
}
```

Directory "Sketcher 2 displaying an About dialog"

You can now recompile `SketcherFrame.java` to try out your smart new dialog, which you can see in Figure 20-3.

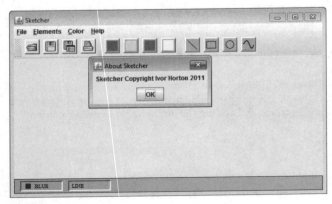

FIGURE 20-3

The dialog pops up when you select the About item in the Help menu. Until you select the OK button in the About Sketcher dialog, you can't interact with the application window because you created this as a modal dialog. By changing the last argument in the call to the superclass constructor in the AboutDialog constructor, you can make it modeless and see how that works. This kind of dialog is usually modal, though.

If you resize the application window before you display the About dialog, you will see that the position of the dialog relative to the application window is adjusted accordingly.

How It Works

This is stuff that should be very familiar to you by now. You create a JMenu object for the Help item on the menu bar, and add a shortcut for it by calling its setMnemonic() member. You create a JMenuItem object, which is the About menu item, and call its addActionListener() method to make the SketcherFrame object the listener for the item. After adding the menu item to the Help menu, you add the helpMenu object to the menuBar object.

You create an AboutDialog object in the actionPerformed() method for the SketcherFrame object, as this method is called when the About menu item is clicked. Before you display the dialog, you verify that the source of the event is the menu item, aboutItem. This is not important now, but you will add other menu items later, and you will handle their events using the same actionPerformed() method. The dialog object is self-contained and disposes of itself when the OK button is clicked. The dialog that you want to display here always displays the same message, so there's no real point in creating and destroying it each time you want to display it. You could arrange for the dialog box object to be created once and the reference stored as a member of the SketcherFrame class. Then you could make it visible in the actionPerformed() method for the menu item and make it invisible in the actionPerformed() method responding to the dialog OK button event.

This is all very well, but it was a lot of work just to get a dialog with a message displayed. Deriving a class from JDialog gives you complete flexibility as to how the dialog works, but you didn't really need it in this case. Didn't I say there was an easier way?

Instant Message Dialogs

The JOptionPane class in the javax.swing package defines static methods that create and display standard modal dialogs for you. The simplest dialog you can create this way is a message dialog rather like the About message dialog in the previous example. The static methods in the JOptionPane class, shown in Table 20-1, produce message dialogs:

TABLE 20-1: Static Method in the JOptionPane Class

DIAL-A-DIALOG METHODS	DESCRIPTION

showMessageDialog(
        Component parent,
        Object message)
	This displays a modal dialog with the default title "Message". The first argument is the parent for the dialog that is used to position the dialog. If the first argument is null, a default Frame object is created and used to position the dialog centrally on the screen.
	The second argument specifies what is to be displayed in addition to the default OK button. This can be a String object specifying the message, an Icon object defining an icon to be displayed, or a Component reference to an object. If you pass some other type of object reference as the second argument, then its toString() method is called, and the String object that is returned is displayed. You usually get a default icon for an information message along with your message.

continues

TABLE 20-1 (*continued*)

DIAL-A-DIALOG METHODS	DESCRIPTION

showMessageDialog(
        Component parent,
        Object message,
        String title,
        int messageType)
	This displays a dialog just as the first method in this table, but with the title specified by the third argument. The fourth argument, messageType, can be:
	    ERROR_MESSAGE
	    INFORMATION_MESSAGE
	    WARNING_MESSAGE
	    QUESTION_MESSAGE
	    PLAIN_MESSAGE
	These static JOptionPane fields determine the style of the message constrained by the current look-and-feel. This usually includes a default icon, such as a question mark for QUESTION_MESSAGE.

showMessageDialog(
        Component parent,
        Object message,
        String title,
        int messageType,
        Icon icon)
	This displays a dialog as the second method in this table, except that the icon is what you pass as the fifth argument. Specifying a null icon argument produces a dialog just as the second method in this table.

You could have used one of these for the About dialog instead of all that messing about with inner classes. Let's see how.

TRY IT OUT   An Easy About Dialog

Delete the AboutDialog inner class from SketcherFrame—you don't need that any longer. Change the implementation of the actionPerformed() method in the SketcherFrame class to the following:

```
public void actionPerformed(ActionEvent e) {
  if(e.getSource() == aboutItem) {
    // Create about dialog with the app window as parent
    JOptionPane.showMessageDialog(this,                       // Parent
                    "Sketcher Copyright Ivor Horton 2011",    // Message
                    "About Sketcher",                         // Title
                    JOptionPane.INFORMATION_MESSAGE);         // Message type
  }
}
```

Directory "Sketcher 3 with an easy About dialog"

If you recompile SketcherFrame and run Sketcher once more, you should get something like the window shown in Figure 20-4 when you click the Help/About menu item.

FIGURE 20-4

The pretty little icon comes for free.

How It Works

All the work is done by the static `showMessageDialog()` method in the `JOptionPane` class. What you get is controlled by the arguments that you supply, and the Swing look-and-feel that is in effect. By default this corresponds to the cross-platform look-and-feel, and this is what Figure 20-4 shows. You get the icon that you see in the dialog because you specified the message type as `INFORMATION_MESSAGE`. You can try plugging in the other message types to see what you get.

Instant Input Dialogs

`JOptionPane` has four static methods that you can use to create standard modal dialogs for user input:

```
showInputDialog(Object message)
```

This method displays a default modal input dialog with a text field for input. The message you pass as the argument is set as the caption for the input field, and the default also supplies an OK button, a Cancel button, and Input as a title. For example, if you pass the message `"Enter Input:"` as the argument, as in the following statement:

```
String input = JOptionPane.showInputDialog("Enter Input:");
```

the dialog shown in Figure 20-5 is displayed.

FIGURE 20-5

When you click the OK button, whatever you entered in the text field is returned by the `showInputDialog()` method and stored in `input`; this is `"This is the input..."` in this case. If you click the Cancel button, `null` is returned. Note that this is not the same as *no* input. If you click OK without entering anything in the text field, a reference to an empty `String` object is returned.

You could also use the overloaded version of the method that has the following form:

```
String showInputDialog(Component parent, Object message)
```

This version produces the same dialog as the previous method, but with the component you specify as the first argument as the parent.

Another possibility is to use the method with the following form:

```
String showInputDialog(Component parent, Object message,
                                    String title, int messageType)
```

In this case the title of the dialog is supplied by the third argument, and the style of the message is determined by the fourth argument. The values for the fourth argument can be any of those I discussed earlier in the context of message dialogs. For example, you could display the dialog shown in Figure 20-6 with the following statement:

FIGURE 20-6

```
String input = JOptionPane.showInputDialog(this, "Enter Input:",
                                    "Dialog for Input",
                                    JOptionPane.WARNING_MESSAGE);
```

Because of the fourth argument specification, the dialog displays a warning icon. The data that you enter in the text field is returned by the `showInputDialog()` method when the OK button is pressed as before.

You also have a version that accepts seven arguments:

```
Object showInputDialog(Component parent, Object message,
                       String title, int messageType,
                       Icon icon, Object[] selections,
                       Object initialSelection)
```

This version of the method displays a dialog with a list of choices in a drop-down list box. You pass the items that are the set of choices as the sixth argument to the method in the form of an array, and it can be an array of elements of any class type. The initial selection to be shown when the dialog is first displayed is specified by the seventh argument. Whatever is chosen when the OK button is clicked is returned as type `Object`, and if the Cancel button is clicked, `null` is returned. You can specify your own icon to replace the default icon by passing a reference of type `Icon` as the fifth argument. The following statements display the dialog shown in Figure 20-7:

```
String[] choices = {"Money", "Health",    "Happiness",
                    "Power", "Notoriety", "Anonymity"};
String input = (String)JOptionPane.showInputDialog(null, "Choose now...",
                              "The Choice of a Lifetime",
                              JOptionPane.QUESTION_MESSAGE,
                              null,            // Use default icon
                              choices,         // Array of choices
                              choices[1]);     // Initial choice
```

Note that you have to cast the reference returned by this version of the `showInputDialog()` method to the type of choice value you have used. Here you are using type `String`, but the selections could be type `Icon`, or whatever you want. Clicking the down arrow displays the list of choices.

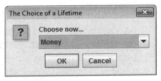

FIGURE 20-7

USING A DIALOG TO CREATE TEXT ELEMENTS

It would be good if our Sketcher program provided a means of adding text to a picture—after all, you might want to put your name to a sketch. A dialog is the obvious way to provide the mechanism for entering the text when you create text elements, and the one that generated Figure 20-6 is a good candidate. This could be generated by one or other of the mouse event handler methods to get input for a text element. You must put the infrastructure in place to deal with text elements, though.

For consistency with other types of elements in Sketcher, you need to add a `Text` menu item to the `Elements` menu and a toolbar button. You also have to define a class to represent text elements, which is the `Element.Text` class with `Element` as the base class. Let's start with the GUI elements, as they are quite easy to implement.

Defining the Menu Item and Toolbar Button for Text

To start, add a `textAction` member of type `TypeAction` to the `SketcherFrame` class:

Available for download on Wrox.com

```
private TypeAction lineAction, rectangleAction, circleAction,
                   curveAction, textAction;
```

You can initialize the `Action` object for text in the `createElementTypeAction()` method in `SketcherFrame`:

```
private void createElementTypeActions() {
   // Other type action definitions...
   textAction = new TypeAction("Text", TEXT,'T', CTRL_DOWN_MASK);

   // Initialize the array
   TypeAction[] actions = {lineAction, rectangleAction, circleAction,
                           curveAction, textAction};
   typeActions = actions;

   // Add toolbar icons
   // Toolbar icons for existing actions...
```

```
    textAction.putValue(LARGE_ICON_KEY, TEXT24);

    // Add menu item icons
    // Menu item icons for existing actions...
    textAction.putValue(SMALL_ICON, TEXT16);

    // Add tooltip text
    // tooltip text for existing actions...
    textAction.putValue(SHORT_DESCRIPTION, "Draw text");
}
```

Directory "Sketcher 4 creating text elements"

You create the `Action` object for a text element and add values to specify the icons to be used for the menu item and the toolbar button, plus the tooltip text. The `SketcherConstants` class needs some additional members to provide for text elements:

```
package Constants;
import java.awt.*;
import javax.swing.*;

public class SketcherConstants {
    // Path for images
    public final static String imagePath = "D:/Sketcher/Images/";
    // Toolbar icons for File menu items as before...

    // Toolbar icons for Type menu items as before...
    public final static Icon TEXT24 = new ImageIcon(imagePath + "Text24.gif");

    // Toolbar icons for Color menu items as before...

    // Icons for the items in the File menu as before...

    // Icons for Element menu items as before...
    public final static Icon TEXT16 = new ImageIcon(imagePath + Text16.gif");

    // Toolbar icons for Color menu items as before...

    // Element type definitions
    public final static int LINE      = 101;
    public final static int RECTANGLE = 102;
    public final static int CIRCLE    = 103;
    public final static int CURVE     = 104;
    public final static int TEXT      = 105;

    // Initial conditions
    public final static int DEFAULT_ELEMENT_TYPE = LINE;
    public final static Color DEFAULT_ELEMENT_COLOR = Color.BLUE;
    public final static Font DEFAULT_FONT = new Font("Serif", Font.BOLD, 12);
}
```

Directory "Sketcher 4 creating text elements"

There are now icons defined for the text menu item and toolbar button, and there's a constant, `TEXT`, that identifies the text element type. There's also a default `Font` object that you can use to initialize a `Font` member of the `SketcherFrame` class. Add the following member to `SketcherFrame`:

```
    private Font textFont = DEFAULT_FONT;          // Default font for text elements
```

The `textFont` member stores the current font for text elements. You add a mechanism for changing the font later. The view class wants access to the `textFont` member for creating text elements, so add the following method to the `SketcherFrame` class:

```
public Font getFont() {
  return textFont;
}
```

Directory "Sketcher 4 creating text elements"

This complements the methods that provide access to the `SketcherFrame` members that record the current element type and color.

You don't need any more code to add the menu item for text to the Element menu or to add a text button to the toolbar. The existing code in the `createRadioButtonDropDown()` and `createToolbar()` methods take care of these. The event handling by `textAction` object deals with setting the element type and updating the menu checks.

You do have to do something about the status bar though. You must add an extra case for TEXT to the `switch` statement in the `setTypePane()` member of the `StatusBar` class:

```
public void setTypePane(int elementType) {
  String text = null;                        // Text for the type pane
  switch(elementType) {
      // Case statements for other element types as before...
      case TEXT:
      text = "TEXT";
      break;
    default:
      assert false;
  }
  typePane.setText(text);                     // Set the pane text
}
```

Directory "Sketcher 4 creating text elements"

This code is analogous to that of the other types. All that is necessary is to set the `typePane` to display `"TEXT"`. You can define the class for a text element next. Then you are able to complete the mechanism for adding text elements to a sketch.

Defining the Text Class

You can use the `drawString()` method for the `Graphics2D` object to display text on a sketch. You have to figure out the bounding rectangle for a text element that you use when you want it redrawn. With `Shape` objects, you can use the `getBounds()` method supplied by the 2D shape classes in `java.awt.geom` to obtain a bounding rectangle, but for text you have to do a bit more work.

The bounding rectangle for a text string is dependent on the length of the string, the font used in a given graphics context, and the characters in the string, because some characters are wider and higher than others. You therefore need a `Graphics2D` object, the string, and the font used to display the string available to get the bounding rectangle. A `java.awt.FontMetrics` object can help you get the bounding rectangle, and calling `getFontMetrics()` for a `Graphics2D` object with a `Font` object as the argument provides one. The `stringWidth()` method for the `FontMetrics` object provides an estimate of the width of the bounding rectangle and the `getHeight()` method provides an estimate of the height. The estimates for the width and height are not totally accurate, so it's a good idea to increase these a little to ensure the text is completely inside the rectangle.

Here's the definition for the inner `Text` class in `Element`:

```
public static class Text extends Element  {
  public Text(String text, Point start, Color color, FontMetrics fm) {
    super(start, color);
    this.text = text;
```

```
      this.font = fm.getFont();
        maxAscent = fm.getMaxAscent();
        bounds = new java.awt.Rectangle(position.x, position.y,
                 fm.stringWidth(text) + 4, maxAscent+ fm.getMaxDescent() + 4);
               System.out.println(bounds);
  }

  public void draw(Graphics2D g2D)  {
    g2D.setPaint(highlighted ? HIGHLIGHT_COLOR : color);
    Font oldFont = g2D.getFont();                       // Save the old font
    g2D.setFont(font);                                  // Set the new font
    // Reference point for drawString() is the baseline of the 1st character
    g2D.drawString(text, position.x + 2, position.y + maxAscent + 2);
    g2D.setFont(oldFont);                               // Restore the old font
  }

  public void modify(Point start, Point last) {
    // No code is required here, but you must supply a definition
  }

  private Font font;                                   // The font to be used
  private int maxAscent;                               // Maximum ascent
  private String text;                                 // Text to be displayed
  private final static long serialVersionUID = 1001L;
}
```

Directory "Sketcher 4 creating text elements"

The constructor calls the superclass constructor to store the position and color for the element and then stores the text string and the font in members of the Text class. The font is obtained from the FontMetrics object that is passed as the last constructor argument. The getMaxAscent() method that the constructor calls for the FontMetrics object returns the maximum ascent, and this is stored in a class member for later use by the draw() method. You create the bounding rectangle in the constructor using information provided by the FontMetrics object. The stringWidth() method provides the width of the string passed as the argument and the getMaxDescent() method returns the maximum descent for the characters in the font.

The position member defines the top-left corner of the enclosing rectangle for the text. Figure 20-8 illustrates how the rectangle is defined based on information from the FontMetrics object.

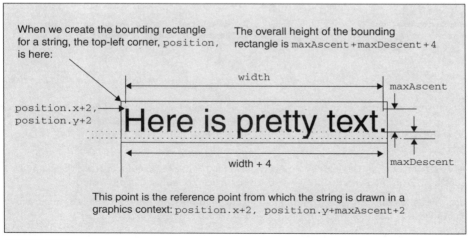

When we create the bounding rectangle for a string, the top-left corner, position, is here:

The overall height of the bounding rectangle is maxAscent+maxDescent+4

position.x+2, position.y+2

width

width + 4

maxAscent

maxDescent

Here is pretty text.

This point is the reference point from which the string is drawn in a graphics context: position.x+2, position.y+maxAscent+2

FIGURE 20-8

The coordinates that you supply to the drawString() method in the draw() method for the Text class specifies the baseline of the first character in the string, so you must add the maximum character ascent to the y coordinate of position and add 2 to get this. This is because you increase the overall width and height of the rectangle by 4 to be sure the text is fully enclosed.

Creating Text Elements

Text is a little tricky. For one thing, you can't treat it just like another geometric element. The mouse won't be used in the same way. The existing process for creating shapes through the mouse event handlers has to be changed to accommodate text. Basically, the process for creating an element when text mode is in effect is to click the mouse to set the location for the text and then enter the string that is to be displayed through a dialog. This suggests that implementing the mouseClicked() event handler may be a good way to go. The mouseClicked() handler is only invoked when button 1 is pressed then released. It is *not* called if you drag the mouse between pressing and releasing button 1.

TRY IT OUT   Creating Text Elements

The mouseClicked() method in the WindowHandler inner class to SketcherView creates Text elements:

Available for
download on
Wrox.com

```
@Override
public void mouseClicked(MouseEvent e) {
  // Only if it's TEXT and button 1 was clicked
  if(theApp.getWindow().getElementType() == TEXT &&
                               buttonState == MouseEvent.BUTTON1) {
    String text = JOptionPane.showInputDialog(
                     theApp.getWindow(),"Enter Input:",
                     "Create Text Element", JOptionPane.PLAIN_MESSAGE);

    if(text != null && !text.isEmpty()) {       // Only if text was entered
      g2D = (Graphics2D)getGraphics();

      tempElement = new Element.Text(text, start,
                      theApp.getWindow().getElementColor(),
                      g2D.getFontMetrics(theApp.getWindow().getFont()));
      g2D.dispose();
      g2D = null;
      if(tempElement != null) {
        theApp.getModel().add(tempElement);
      }
    }
    tempElement = null;              // Reset for next element creation
    start = null;                    // Reset for next element
  }
}
```

Directory "Sketcher 4 creating text elements"

This method does something only if the element type is TEXT and button 1 was clicked. The dialog for entering text is displayed using the showInputDialog() method. You only want to create an element if text is not null and not empty. If the dialog Cancel button is selected, text is null, and text is empty if OK is selected without entering any text.

You obtain a Graphics2D object from the view so you can obtain a FontMetrics object from the graphics context for the current font. You then create an Element.Text object by calling its constructor.

Because you reference the TEXT constant here, you must add a static import for the SketcherConstants class members to the SketcherView class file:

```
import static Constants.SketcherConstants.*;
```

You also need to add an import for `javax.swing.JOptionPane`, or you can change the import for `JComponent` to import all names from the package.

A mouse clicked event occurs when the mouse is pressed and then immediately released. Of course, this also causes mouse pressed and mouse released events to occur as well. You rely on the `mousePressed()` method to record the `start` point and the button state, but you must prevent this method and the `mousedDragged()` and `mouseReleased()` methods from doing anything else when the element type is `TEXT`. Add the following statement after the statement that records the start point in `mousePressed()`:

```
public void mousePressed(MouseEvent e)  {
  start = e.getPoint();                   // Save the cursor position in start
  buttonState = e.getButton();            // Record which button was pressed
  if(theApp.getWindow().getElementType() == TEXT) return;
  // Rest of the code as before...
}
```

Directory "Sketcher 4 creating text elements"

The `mouseDragged()` implementation can be:

```
public void mouseDragged(MouseEvent e) {
  last = e.getPoint();                         // Save cursor position
  if(theApp.getWindow().getElementType() == TEXT) return;
  // Rest of the method code as before...
}
```

Directory "Sketcher 4 creating text elements"

You could place the check for the `TEXT` element type before the current cursor position is stored in `last`, but you need the cursor position available in `last` later for another purpose later in this chapter.

In the `mouseReleased()` method, you must make sure that the `start` and `last` members are reset to `null` if `last` is not null when the element type is `TEXT`:

```
public void mouseReleased(MouseEvent e) {
  if(theApp.getWindow().getElementType() == TEXT) {
    if(last != null) {
      start = last = null;
    }
    return;
  }
  // Rest of the method code as before...
}
```

Directory "Sketcher 4 creating text elements"

This covers the situation when the element type is `TEXT` and the mouse is dragged. In this situation the mouse clicked event does not occur, but there are mouse pressed and mouse dragged events, which store `Point` references in `start` and `last`.

How It Works

The `mouseClicked()` handler is called when a mouse button is clicked without dragging the mouse. The method responds to mouse button 1 being clicked when the element type is `TEXT`. This method is called after the `mouseReleased()` method has been called. Within the `if` statement that determines that button 1 was clicked and the current element is of type `TEXT`, you create a dialog to receive the text input by calling the static `showInputDialog()` in the `JOptionPane` class. If the Cancel button is clicked in the dialog, `text` is `null`, so in this case you do nothing. You also do nothing if `text` is an empty string. If `text` is not `null` and not an empty string, you create an `Element.Text` object at the current cursor position containing the text string that was entered in the dialog. You then add this to the model, as long as the reference is not `null`. You reset the `start` and `tempElement` members back to `null` to avoid any potential confusion in subsequent event-handling operations. You can try it out after you have recompiled Sketcher. Just click the mouse where you want the text displayed, type the text in the dialog, and click the OK button. The text is displayed starting at the point in the view where you clicked the mouse button. You can draw text in any of the colors—just like the geometric elements. The application window may look something like Figure 20-9 when the text dialog is displayed.

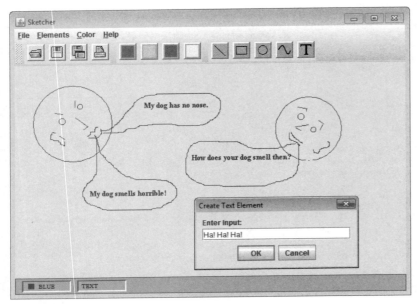

FIGURE 20-9

> **NOTE** *Although there isn't a method to detect double-clicks on the mouse button, it's easy to implement. The* `getClickCount()` *method for the* `MouseEvent` *object that is passed to the* `mouseClicked()` *method returns the click count. To respond to a double-click, you could write the following in the* `mouseClicked()` *implementation:*
>
> ```
> if(e.getClickCount() == 2) {
>   //Response to double-click...
> }
> ```

A FONT SELECTION DIALOG

You don't really want to be stuck with a 12-point serif font. You need to be able to release your creativity with all kinds of fonts and sizes so your sketches astound and delight! A font dialog that pops up in response to a click on a suitable menu item could enable you to change the font for text elements to any of those available on the system. Implementing this gives you a chance to see how you can get at and process the fonts that are available. You also learn more about how to add components to a dialog window. The first step is to establish what the font dialog does.

You want to be able to choose the font name from those available on the system on which the application is executing. You also want to select the style of the font, whether plain, bold, or italic, as well as the point size. It would also be nice to see what a font looks like before you decide to use it. The dialog therefore needs to obtain a list of the fonts available and display them in a component. It also needs a component to allow the point size to be selected and some means for choosing the style for the font.

This is not going to be a wimpy, pathetic excuse for a dialog like those you have seen so far. This is going to be a real, chunky Java programmer's dialog. You drag in a diversity of components here, just for the experience. Because it involves quite a lot of code, you build it step-by-step. Just so that you know where you're headed, the finished dialog is shown in Figure 20-10.

The component that provides the choice of font in Figure 20-10 is a Swing component of type `javax.swing.JList<T>` that can display a list of objects of type `T`. Below that is a panel holding a `JLabel` object, which displays a sample of the current font. The list of font names and the panel below are displayed in a split pane that is defined by the `JSplitPane` class. Here the pane is split vertically, but a `JSplitPane` object can also hold two panels side by side.

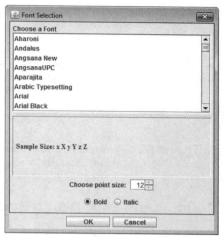

FIGURE 20-10

The point size is displayed in another Swing component called a spinner, which is an object of type `javax.swing.JSpinner`. The choice for the font style options is provided by two radio buttons, and either, neither, or both may be selected, so they won't be in a button group. Finally, you have two buttons to close the dialog.

You can set the foundations by defining the `FontDialog` class with its data members and its constructor, and then build on that.

The FontDialog Class

Most of the work is in the dialog class constructor, which sets up all the GUI elements as well as the necessary listeners to respond to user interactions with the dialog. The dialog object needs access to the `SketcherFrame` object that represents the Sketcher application window and is the dialog's parent, so you pass a `SketcherFrame` reference to the constructor.

Here's the code for the outline of the `FontDialog` class:

```java
// Class to define a dialog to choose a font
import java.awt.*;
import javax.swing.*;

public class FontDialog extends JDialog {
  // Constructor
  public FontDialog(SketcherFrame window) {
    // Code to initialize the data members...

    // Code to create buttons and the button panel...

    // Code to create the data input panel...

    // Code to create font choice and add it to the input panel...

    // Code to create font size choice and add it to the input panel...

    // Code to create font style checkboxes and add them to the input panel...

    // ...and then some!
  }
  private Font font;                              // Currently selected font
}
```

Directory "Sketcher 5 displaying a font dialog"

You add more data members shortly, but at least you know you need the one that is shown here. You can initialize the `font` member from the font that is stored in the `SketcherFrame` object:

```
public FontDialog(SketcherFrame window) {
    // Call the base constructor to create a modal dialog
    super(window, "Font Selection", true);
    font = window.getFont();                    // Get the current font
    // Plus the code for the rest of the constructor...
}
```

Directory "Sketcher 5 displaying a font dialog"

You call the base class constructor and pass the `window` object to it as the parent. The second argument is the title for the dialog, and the third argument determines that the dialog is modal. The `getFont()` method returns the font stored in the `window` object, so this is the default setting the first time you open the dialog.

Creating the Font Dialog Buttons

Next you can add the code to the constructor that creates the button panel with the OK and Cancel buttons. You can place the button panel at the bottom of the content pane for the dialog using the default `BorderLayout` manager:

```
public FontDialog(SketcherFrame window) {
    // Initialization as before...
    // Create the dialog button panel
    JPanel buttonPane = new JPanel();                      // Create a panel to hold buttons

    // Create and add the buttons to the buttonPane
    buttonPane.add(ok = createButton("OK"));               // Add the OK button
    buttonPane.add(cancel = createButton("Cancel"));       // Add the Cancel button
    getContentPane().add(buttonPane, BorderLayout.SOUTH);  // Add pane
    // Plus the code for the rest of the constructor...
}
```

Directory "Sketcher 5 displaying a font dialog"

The `buttonPane` object has a `FlowLayout` manager by default, so this takes care of positioning the buttons. You add the button pane to the dialog content pane using the `BorderLayout.SOUTH` specification to place it at the bottom of the window. Because creating each button involves several steps that are the same for both buttons, you are using a helper method, `createButton()`, that requires only the button label as an argument. The code implies that you store each button reference in a class field, so you must add these members to the `FontDialog` class:

```
private JButton ok;         // OK button
private JButton cancel;     // Cancel button
```

You use these fields in the listener for the button events.

You can code the `createButton()` method as a member of the `FontDialog` class as follows:

```
JButton createButton(String label) {
    JButton button = new JButton(label);            // Create the button
    button.setPreferredSize(new Dimension(80,20));  // Set the size
    button.addActionListener(this);                 // Listener is the dialog
    return button;                                  // Return the button
}
```

Directory "Sketcher 5 displaying a font dialog"

You set the preferred size of the button here to ensure that the buttons are all of the same size. Without this call, each button would be sized to fit its label, so the dialog would look a bit untidy. The listener is the

FontDialog class object, so the FontDialog class must implement the ActionListener interface, which implies that an actionPerformed() method must be defined in the class:

Available for download on Wrox.com

```java
import java.awt.*;
import javax.swing.*;
import java.awt.event.*;

class FontDialog extends JDialog implements ActionListener {
  // Constructor definition...
  // createButton() definition...
  public void actionPerformed(ActionEvent e) {
    if(e.getSource()== ok)  {                          // If it's the OK button
      ((SketcherFrame)getOwner()).setFont(font);      // ...set selected font
    } else {
      font = ((SketcherFrame)getOwner()).getFont();   // Restore the current font
      fontDisplay.setFont(font);
      chooseSize.setValue(font.getSize());            // Restore the point size
      fontList.setSelectedValue(font.getName(),true);
      int style = font.getStyle();
      bold.setSelected((style & Font.BOLD) > 0);      // Restore the
      italic.setSelected((style & Font.ITALIC) > 0);  // style options
    }
    // Now hide the dialog - for ok or cancel
    setVisible(false);
  }
  // Plus the rest of the class definition...
}
```

Directory "Sketcher 5 displaying a font dialog"

The getSource() member of the ActionEvent object e returns a reference to the object that originated the event, so you can use this to determine the button that originated the event. You just compare the source object reference with the OK button reference to determine whether it was clicked. If it is the OK button, you call the setCurrentFont() method in the SketcherFrame object that is the parent for this dialog to set the font. You then just hide the dialog so Sketcher can continue. When the Cancel button is selected for the dialog, you must restore the dialog to the state it was in when it opened. The user may have changed some of the selections before clicking Cancel, so you set things back so they correspond to the font stored in the SketcherFrame object. The getOwner() method for the dialog returns a reference to the parent window.

Of course, you must add the definition of setFont() to the SketcherFrame class:

Available for download on Wrox.com

```java
// Method to set the current font
public void setFont(Font font) {
  textFont = font;
}
```

Directory "Sketcher 5 displaying a font dialog"

Now let's get back to the FontDialog constructor.

Adding the Data Pane

You can now add a panel to contain the components that receive input. You use a JList<String> object for the font names, a JSpinner object for the point size of the font, and two JRadioButton objects for selecting the font style. You can add the code to create the panel first:

Available for download on Wrox.com

```java
public FontDialog(SketcherFrame window) {
  // Initialization as before...
  // Button panel code as before...
  // Code to create the data input panel
  JPanel dataPane = new JPanel();                   // Create the data entry panel
```

```
            dataPane.setBorder(BorderFactory.createCompoundBorder( // Pane border
                           BorderFactory.createLineBorder(Color.black),
                           BorderFactory.createEmptyBorder(5, 5, 5, 5)));
        GridBagLayout gbLayout = new GridBagLayout();            // Create the layout
        dataPane.setLayout(gbLayout);                            // Set the pane layout
        GridBagConstraints constraints = new GridBagConstraints();
        // Plus the code for the rest of the constructor...
    }
```

Directory "Sketcher 5 displaying a font dialog"

Here you use a `GridBagLayout` manager so you can set constraints for each component that you add to the `dataPane` container. You also set a black line border for `dataPane` with an inset empty border 5 pixels wide. This uses the `BorderFactory` static methods that you have seen before. You have many other possible layout managers that you could use here. `BoxLayout` managers, for example, are very easy to use to lay out components in vertical columns and horizontal rows.

The first component that you add to `dataPane` is a label that prompts for the font selection:

Available for
download on
Wrox.com

```
    public FontDialog(SketcherFrame window) {
        // Initialization as before...
        // Button panel code as before...
        // Set up the data input panel to hold all input components as before...
        // Create the font choice and add it to the input panel
        JLabel label = new JLabel("Choose a Font");
        constraints.fill = GridBagConstraints.HORIZONTAL;
        constraints.gridwidth = GridBagConstraints.REMAINDER;
        gbLayout.setConstraints(label, constraints);
        dataPane.add(label);

        // Plus the code for the rest of the constructor...
    }
```

Directory "Sketcher 5 displaying a font dialog"

With the `fill` constraint set as `HORIZONTAL`, the components in a row fill the width of the `dataPane` container, but without affecting the height. With the width constraint set to `REMAINDER`, the `label` component fills the width of the row.

Implementing the Font List

You add the `JList<String>` object that displays the list of fonts next, but you won't add this directly to the `dataPane` panel because the list is likely to be long enough to need scrolling capability. You can obtain the list of fonts using the `GraphicsEnvironment` object that encapsulates information about the system in which the application is running. Recall that you call a `static` method in the `GraphicsEnvironment` class to get the `GraphicsEnvironment` object. Here's the code to create the list of font names:

Available for
download on
Wrox.com

```
    public FontDialog(SketcherFrame window) {
        // Initialization as before...
        // Button panel code as before...
        // Set up the data input panel to hold all input components as before...
        // Add the font choice prompt label as before...
        // Code to set up font list choice component
        GraphicsEnvironment e = GraphicsEnvironment.getLocalGraphicsEnvironment();
        String[] fontNames = e.getAvailableFontFamilyNames();  // Get font names

        fontList = new JList<>(fontNames);                     // Create list of font names
        fontList.setValueIsAdjusting(true);                    // single event selection
        fontList.setSelectionMode(ListSelectionModel.SINGLE_SELECTION);
        fontList.setSelectedValue(font.getFontName(),true);
        fontList.addListSelectionListener(this);
```

```
fontList.setToolTipText("Choose a font");
JScrollPane chooseFont = new JScrollPane(fontList);  // Scrollable list
chooseFont.setMinimumSize(new Dimension(400,100));
chooseFont.setWheelScrollingEnabled(true);               // Enable mouse wheel scroll

// Plus the code for the rest of the constructor...
}
```

Directory "Sketcher 5 displaying a font dialog"

You obtain the list of font family names by calling the `getAvailableFontFamilyNames()` method for the `GraphicsEnvironment` object. The `fontList` variable needs to be accessible in the method that handles events for the list, so this is another data member of the `FontDialog` class:

```
private JList<String> fontList;                        // Font list
```

A `JList<>` component doesn't support scrolling directly, but it is scrolling "aware." To get a scrollable list with scrollbars, you just pass the `JList<>` object to the `JScrollPane` constructor. A `JScrollPane` object creates a pane with scrollbars—either vertical, horizontal, or both—as necessary—for whatever it contains. You set a minimum size for the `JScrollPane` object to limit how small it can be made in the split pane into which you insert it in a moment. Note how easy it is to get the mouse wheel supported for scrolling here. You just call the `setWheelScrollingEnabled()` method for the scroll pane with the argument as `true`, and it's done. You don't really need it here, but just because you can, you set a tooltip for the `fontList` object. Any component can have a tooltip set.

Working with JList<T> Components

You can create a `JList<>` object by passing an array or a `Vector<>` object that contains the objects you want in the list to the constructor. The `fontNames` array holds `String` objects, but you can create a `JList<>` object for any kind of object, including images, for example. It is possible to allow multiple entries from a list to be selected. Calling `setSelectionMode()` with the argument `SINGLE_SELECTION` ensures that only one font name can be selected.

You have two multiple selection modes that you can enable for a `JList<>` object. Passing the value `SINGLE_INTERVAL_SELECTION` to the `setSelectionMode()` method allows a series of consecutive items to be selected. Passing `MULTIPLE_SELECTION_INTERVAL` provides you with total flexibility and allows any number of items anywhere to be selected. The initial selection in the list is set by the `setSelectedValue()` call. You pass the name for the current font as the argument specifying the initial selection. There is a complementary method, `getSelectedValue()`, that you use in the event handler.

Handling JList<T> Component Events

There's a special kind of listener for `JList<>` selection events that is an object of a class type that implements the `javax.swing.event.ListSelectionListener` interface. You set the `FontDialog` object as the listener for the list in the call to the `addListSelectionListener()` method, so you had better make sure the `FontDialog` class implements the interface:

```
class FontDialog extends JDialog
                implements ActionListener,           // For buttons etc.
                           ListSelectionListener {    // For list box
```

There's only one method in the `ListSelectionListener` interface, and you can implement it in the `FontDialog` class like this:

```
// List selection listener method
public void valueChanged(ListSelectionEvent e) {
  if(!e.getValueIsAdjusting()) {
    font = new Font(fontList.getSelectedValue(),
                            font.getStyle(), font.getSize());
```

```
        fontDisplay.setFont(font);
        fontDisplay.repaint();
    }
}
```

Directory "Sketcher 5 displaying a font dialog"

This method is called when you select an item in the list. You have only one list, so you don't need to check which object was the source of the event. If you were handling events from several lists, you could call the `getSource()` method for the event object that is passed to `valueChanged()`, and compare it with the references to the `JList<>` objects being used.

The `ListSelectionEvent` object that is passed to the `valueChanged()` method contains the index positions of the list items that changed. You can obtain these as a range by calling the `getFirstIndex()` method for the event object to get the first in the range, and the `getLastIndex()` method returns the last. You don't need to worry about any of this in the `FontDialog` class. Because you have disallowed multiple selections, you only get one index.

You have to be careful, though. Because you start out with an item already selected, selecting another font name from the list causes two events—one for deselecting the original font name and the other for selecting the new name. To make sure that you deal only with the last event, you call the `getValueIsAdjusting()` method for the event object in the `if` expression. This returns `false` for the event when all changes due to a selection are complete, and `true` if things are still changing when the event occurred. Thus your implementation of the `valueChanged()` method does nothing when the `getValueIsAdjusting()` method returns `true`.

You are sure nothing further is changing when `getValueIsAdjusting()` returns `false`, so you retrieve the selected font name from the list by calling its `getSelectedValue()` method. You create a new `Font` object using the selected family name and the current values for `fontStyle` and `fontSize`. You store the new font in the data member `font` and call the `setFont()` member of a data member, `fontDisplay`, that you haven't added to the `FontDialog` class yet. This is a `JLabel` object displaying a sample of the current font. After you've set the new font, you call `repaint()` for the `fontDisplay` label to get it redrawn with the new font.

You need another import statement for the `ListSelectionListener` and `ListSelectionEvent` types:

```
import javax.swing.event.*;
```

Displaying the Selected Font

You display the selected font in a `JLabel` object that you place in another `JPanel` pane. Adding the following code to the constructor does this:

```
public FontDialog(SketcherFrame window) {
    // Initialization as before...
    // Button panel code as before...
    // Set up the data input panel to hold all input components as before...
    // Add the font choice prompt label as before...
    // Set up font list choice component as before...
    // Panel to display font sample
    JPanel display = new JPanel(true);
    fontDisplay = new JLabel("Sample Size: x X y Y z Z");
    fontDisplay.setFont(font);
    fontDisplay.setPreferredSize(new Dimension(350,100));
    display.add(fontDisplay);
    // Plus the code for the rest of the constructor...
}
```

Directory "Sketcher 5 displaying a font dialog"

You create the `JPanel` object `display` and add the `JLabel` object `fontDisplay` to it. The `JPanel` constructor with a `true` argument makes it double-buffered. This ensures flicker-free updating at the expense of using more memory. Remember, you update this object in the `valueChanged()` handler for selections from the list of font names. You also update it when the font size or style is changed. The `fontDisplay` object just presents some sample text in the chosen font. You can choose different sample text if you like, but make sure the preferred size is large enough to accommodate it at the maximum point size.

It's not strictly necessary here, but just for the experience you use a split pane to hold the scroll pane containing the list, `chooseFont`, and the `display` panel.

Using a Split Pane

A `JSplitPane` object represents a pane with a movable horizontal or vertical split, so that it can hold two components. The split pane divider can be adjusted by dragging it with the mouse. Here's the code to do that:

```
public FontDialog(SketcherFrame window) {
    // Initialization as before...
    // Button panel code as before...
    // Set up the data input panel to hold all input components as before...
    // Add the font choice prompt label as before...
    // Set up font list choice component as before...
    // Panel to display font sample as before...
    //Create a split pane with font choice at the top
    // and font display at the bottom
    JSplitPane splitPane = new JSplitPane(JSplitPane.VERTICAL_SPLIT,
                                    true,
                                    chooseFont,
                                    display);
    gbLayout.setConstraints(splitPane, constraints);   // Split pane constraints
    dataPane.add(splitPane);                           // Add to the data pane
    // Plus the code for the rest of the constructor...
}
```

Directory "Sketcher 5 displaying a font dialog"

The `JSplitPane` constructor does it all. The first argument specifies that the pane supports two components, one above the other. You can probably guess that for side-by-side components you specify `JSplitPane.HORIZONTAL_SPLIT`. If the second constructor argument is `true`, the components are redrawn continuously as the divider is dragged. If it is `false` the components are not redrawn until you stop dragging the divider.

The third argument is the component to go at the top, or to the left for `HORIZONTAL_SPLIT`, and the fourth argument is the component to go at the bottom, or to the right, as the case may be.

NOTE *You don't need to do it here, but you can change the components in a split pane. You have four methods to do this:* `setLeftComponent()` *and* `setRightComponent()` *for a horizontal arrangement of the panes, and* `setTopComponent()` *and* `setBottomComponent()` *for a vertical arrangement of the panes. You just pass a reference to the component you want to set to whichever method you want to use. There are also corresponding* `get` *methods to retrieve the components in a split pane. You can even change the orientation by calling the* `setOrientation()` *method and passing either* `JSplitPane.HORIZONTAL_SPLIT` *or* `JSplitPane.VERTICAL_SPLIT` *to it.*

There is a facility to provide a widget on the divider to collapse and restore either pane. You don't need it, but if you want to try this here, you can add the following statement after the `JSplitPane` constructor call:

```
splitPane.setOneTouchExpandable(true);
```

Calling this method with the argument as `false` removes the widget.

After you have created the `splitPane` object, you add it to the `dataPane` panel with constraints that make it fill the full width of the container.

Next you can add the font size selection mechanism.

Using a Spinner

You could use another list for this, but to broaden your horizons you use another Swing component, a `javax.swing.JSpinner` object. A JSpinner object displays a sequence of numbers or objects, and the user can select any one from the set. The spinner displays up and down arrows at the side of the spinner for stepping through the list. You can also use the keyboard up and down arrow keys for this.

The sequence of choices in a spinner is managed by a `javax.swing.SpinnerModel` object. There are three concrete spinner model classes defined in the `javax.swing` package. The one you use depends on what sort of items you are choosing from:

➤ `SpinnerNumberModel` is a model for a sequence of numbers. Numbers are stored internally and returned as type `Number`, which is the superclass of the classes that encapsulate the primitive numerical types — `Integer`, `Long`, `Double`, and so on. `Number` is also the superclass of other classes such as `BigDecimal`, but only the classes corresponding to the primitive types are supported.

➤ `SpinnerListModel` is a model for a sequence defined by an array of objects of any type, or by a `java.util.List<>` object. You could use this to use a sequence of strings as the choices in the spinner.

➤ `SpinnerDateModel` is a model for a sequence of dates specified as `java.util.Date` objects.

I'm not able to go through all the detail on these, so let's just take a `JSpinner` object using a `SpinnerNumberModel` class to contain the sequence, as that fits with selecting a font size.

You use a fixed range of point sizes to choose from, so let's add some constants to the `SketcherConstants` class to define this:

```
public final static int POINT_SIZE_MIN = 8;      // Minimum font point size
public final static int POINT_SIZE_MAX = 24;     // Maximum font point size
public final static int POINT_SIZE_STEP = 2;     // Point size step  public
```

Thus the smallest point size that can be chosen is 8, the largest is 24, and the step from 8 onward is 2.

You create a `JSpinner` object by passing a `SpinnerModel` reference to it. For example:

```
JSpinner spinner = new JSpinner(spinnerModel);
```

In the font dialog, the spinner model is of type `SpinnerNumberModel`, and the constructor you use to create the object expects four arguments: a current value that is the one displayed initially, a minimum value, a maximum value, and the step size. Here's how you can create that for the font dialog:

Available for download on Wrox.com

```
public FontDialog(SketcherFrame window) {
    // Initialization as before...
    // Button panel code as before...
    // Set up the data input panel to hold all input components as before...
    // Add the font choice prompt label as before...
    // Set up font list choice component as before...
    // Panel to display font sample as before...
    // Create a split pane with font choice at the top as before...
    // Set up the size choice using a spinner
    JPanel sizePane = new JPanel(true);                  // Pane for size choices
    label = new JLabel("Choose point size: ");           // Prompt for point size
```

```
        sizePane.add(label);                                    // Add the prompt

        chooseSize = new JSpinner(new SpinnerNumberModel(font.getSize(),
                           POINT_SIZE_MIN, POINT_SIZE_MAX, POINT_SIZE_STEP));
        chooseSize.setValue(font.getSize());                    // Set current font size
        chooseSize.addChangeListener(this);
        sizePane.add(chooseSize);

          // Add spinner to pane
        gbLayout.setConstraints(sizePane, constraints);         // Set pane constraints
        dataPane.add(sizePane);                                 // Add the pane
        // Plus the code for the rest of the constructor...
    }
```

Directory "Sketcher 5 displaying a font dialog"

Add a static `import` statement for the constants in the `SketcherConstants` class:

```
import static Constants.SketcherConstants.*;
```

You again create a panel to contain the spinner and its associated prompt to make the layout easier. The default `FlowLayout` in the panel is fine for what you want. You had better add a couple more members to the `FontDialog` class to store the references to the `chooseSize` and `fontDisplay` objects:

```
private JSpinner chooseSize;                     // Font size options
private JLabel fontDisplay;                       // Font sample
```

A spinner generates an event of type `ChangeEvent` when an item is selected that is sent to listeners of type `ChangeListener`. Both types are defined in the `javax.swing.event` package. The listener for our spinner is the `FontDialog` object, so you need to specify that it implements the `ChangeListener` interface:

```
class FontDialog extends JDialog
                 implements ActionListener,           // For buttons etc.
                        ListSelectionListener,         // For list box
                        ChangeListener {               // For the spinner
```

The `ChangeListener` interface defines one method, `stateChanged()`, which has a parameter of type `ChangeEvent`. You obtain a reference to the source of the event by calling `getSource()` for the event object. You then need to cast the reference to the type of the source—in this case, `JSpinner`. For example, you could code it like this:

```
public void stateChanged(ChangeEvent e) {
  JSpinner source = (JSpinner)e.getSource();
  // ...plus code to deal with the spinner event for source...
}
```

Directory "Sketcher 5 displaying a font dialog"

Of course, you want the value that is now selected in the spinner, and the `getValue()` method returns a reference to this as type `Object`. Because you are using a `SpinnerNumberModel` object as the spinner model, the object encapsulating the value is actually of type `Number`, so you can cast the reference returned by `getValue()` to this type. You can get a little closer to what you want by amending our `stateChanged()` method to:

```
public void stateChanged(ChangeEvent e) {
  Number value = (Number)((JSpinner)e.getSource()).getValue();
}
```

Directory "Sketcher 5 displaying a font dialog"

You're not really interested in a `Number` object, though. What you want is the integer value it contains, so you can store it in the `fontSize` member of the dialog and then derive a new font. The `intValue()` method for the Number object produces that. You can therefore arrive at the final version of setChanged() that does what you want:

```
public void stateChanged(ChangeEvent e) {
    int fontSize = ((Number)(((JSpinner)e.getSource()).getValue())).intValue();
    font = font.deriveFont((float)fontSize);
    fontDisplay.setFont(font);
    fontDisplay.repaint();
}
```

Directory "Sketcher 5 displaying a font dialog"

That first statement looks quite daunting, but because you put it together one step at a time, you should see that it isn't really difficult—there are just a lot of parentheses to keep in sync.

Using Radio Buttons to Select the Font Style

Two JRadioButton objects provide the means for selecting the font style. One selects bold or not, and the other selects italic or not. A plain font is simply one that is neither bold nor italic. You could use JCheckBox objects here if you prefer—they would work just as well. The radio buttons need to be fields in the dialog class because you update them in the actionPerformed() method. Add them to the FontDialog class:

```
private JRadioButton bold;          // Bold style button
private JRadioButton italic;        // Italic style button
```

Here's the code to set them up:

```
public FontDialog(SketcherFrame window) {
    // Initialization as before...
    // Button panel code as before...
    // Set up the data input panel to hold all input components as before...
    // Add the font choice prompt label as before...
    // Set up font list choice component as before...
    // Panel to display font sample as before...
    // Create a split pane with font choice at the top as before...
    // Set up the size choice using a spinner as before...

    // Set up style options using radio buttons
    bold = new JRadioButton("Bold", (font.getStyle() & Font.BOLD) > 0);
    italic = new JRadioButton("Italic", (font.getStyle() & Font.ITALIC) > 0);
    bold.addItemListener(new StyleListener(Font.BOLD));  // Add button listeners
    italic.addItemListener(new StyleListener(Font.ITALIC));
    JPanel stylePane = new JPanel(true);               // Create style pane
    stylePane.add(bold);                               // Add buttons
    stylePane.add(italic);                             // to style pane...
    gbLayout.setConstraints(stylePane, constraints);   // Set pane constraints
    dataPane.add(stylePane);                           // Add the pane

    getContentPane().add(dataPane, BorderLayout.CENTER);
    pack();
    setVisible(false);
}
```

Directory "Sketcher 5 displaying a font dialog"

It looks like a lot of code, but it's repetitive, as you have two radio buttons. The second argument to the JRadioButton constructor sets the state of the button. If the existing style of the current font is BOLD and/or ITALIC, the initial states of the buttons are set accordingly. You add a listener of type StyleListener for each button, and you add a definition for StyleListener as an inner class to FontDialog in a moment.

Note that you pass the style constant that corresponds to the set state of the button to the constructor for the listener.

The `stylePane` object presents the buttons using the default `FlowLayout` manager, and this pane is added as the last row to `dataPane`. The final step is to add the `dataPane` object as the central pane in the content pane for the dialog. The call to `pack()` lays out the dialog components with their preferred sizes if possible, and the `setVisible()` call with the argument `false` means that the dialog is initially hidden. Because this is a complex dialog, you don't want to create a new object each time you want to display the font dialog. You just call the `setVisible()` method for the dialog object with the argument `true` when you want to display it.

Listening for Radio Buttons

The inner class, `StyleListener`, in the `FontDialog` class works on principles that you have seen before. A radio button (or a checkbox) generates events of type `java.awt.ItemEvent`, and the listener class must implement the `java.awt.ItemListener` interface:

Available for download on Wrox.com

```
class StyleListener implements ItemListener {
  public StyleListener(int style) {
    this.style = style;
  }

  public void itemStateChanged(ItemEvent e) {
    int fontStyle = font.getStyle();
    if(e.getStateChange()==ItemEvent.SELECTED) {  // If style was selected
      fontStyle |= style;                          // turn it on in the font style
    } else {
      fontStyle &= ~style;                         // otherwise turn it off
    }
    font = font.deriveFont(fontStyle);             // Get a new font
    fontDisplay.setFont(font);                     // Change the label font
    fontDisplay.repaint();                         // repaint
  }
    private int style;                             // Style for this listener
}
```

Directory "Sketcher 5 displaying a font dialog"

The constructor accepts an argument that is the style for the button, so the value of the member, `style`, is the value you want to set in the `fontStyle` member that you use to create a new `Font` object, either `Font.BOLD` or `Font.ITALIC`. You initialize the `fontStyle` variable with the current font style. Because the listener for a particular button already contains the corresponding style, the `itemStateChanged()` method that is called when an item event occurs just switches the value of `style` in `fontStyle` either on or off, depending on whether the radio button was selected or deselected. It then derives a font with the new style, sets it in the `fontDisplay` label, and repaints the label.

You have now completed the `FontDialog` class. If you have been creating the code yourself, now would be a good time to try compiling the class to see what is missing—`import` statements, usually. All you need now is some code in the `SketcherFrame` class to make use of it.

TRY IT OUT Using the Font Dialog

To get the font dialog operational in Sketcher, you can add an Options menu to the menu bar with a Choose font . . . menu item, and install a listener for the menu item. First, add `SketcherFrame` members to store the `JMenu` object for the Options menu and an instance of the font dialog:

```
private JMenu optionsMenu;            // Options menu
private FontDialog fontDlg;           // The font dialog
```

You can also add a member to store the menu item in the Options menu:

```
private JMenuItem fontItem;                      // Font chooser menu item
```

Now you can create the Options menu with the following code in the `SketcherFrame` constructor:

```
public SketcherFrame(String title, Sketcher theApp) {
  setTitle(title);                               // Set the window title
  this.theApp = theApp;                          // Save app. object reference
  setJMenuBar(menuBar);                          // Add the menu bar to the window
  setDefaultCloseOperation(EXIT_ON_CLOSE);       // Default is exit the application

  createFileMenu();                              // Create the File menu
  createElementMenu();                           // Create the element menu
  createColorMenu();                             // Create the element menu
  JMenu optionsMenu = new JMenu("Options");      // Create options menu
  optionsMenu.setMnemonic('O');                  // Create shortcut
  menuBar.add(optionsMenu);                       // Add options to menu bar

  // Add the font choice item to the options menu
  fontItem = new JMenuItem("Choose font...");
  fontItem.addActionListener(this);
  optionsMenu.add(fontItem);
  fontDlg = new FontDialog(this);                // Create the font dialog
  // Rest of the constructor code as before...
}
```

Directory "Sketcher 5 displaying a font dialog"

You create the `FontDialog` object in the `SketcherFrame` constructor. You are able to reuse the `FontDialog` object as often as you want. When you need to display it, you simply call its `setVisible()` method.

The `actionPerformed()` method in the `SketcherFrame` class can handle the events for the new menu item:

```
public void actionPerformed(ActionEvent e) {
  if(e.getSource() == aboutItem) {
    // Create about dialog with the app window as parent
    JOptionPane.showMessageDialog(this,                       // Parent
                    "Sketcher Copyright Ivor Horton 2011",    // Message
                    "About Sketcher",                          // Title
                    JOptionPane.INFORMATION_MESSAGE);          // Message type
  } else if(e.getSource() == fontItem) {                       // Set the dialog window position
    Rectangle bounds = getBounds();
    fontDlg.setLocationRelativeTo(this);
    fontDlg.setVisible(true);                                  // Show the dialog
  }
}
```

Directory "Sketcher 5 displaying a font dialog"

The new `else if` block makes the dialog visible after setting its location in relation to the application window. Calling the `setLocationRelativeTo()` method that is inherited from the `Window` class in `JDialog` makes the center of the dialog coincide with the center of the component passed as the argument, which in this case is the application window. If you want to position it differently, you could call the `setLocation()` method with specific coordinates for where you want the top-left corner of the dialog to be.

If you recompile Sketcher, you are able to play with fonts to your heart's content. Figure 20-11 shows what I mean.

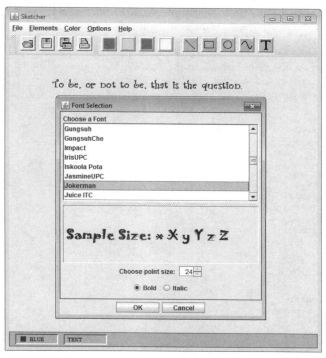

FIGURE 20-11

How It Works

This last piece is relatively trivial. The additional menu is added to the menu bar just like the other menus. The menu item is a `JMenuItem` object rather than an `Action` object and the `actionPerformed()` method is called when the Choose font . . . menu item is clicked. This sets the top-left corner of the dialog window one-third of the way in from the top and left sides of the application window. It then calls `setVisible()` for the dialog object to display it.

POP-UP MENUS

The `javax.swing` package defines the `JPopupMenu` class, which represents a menu that you can pop up at any position within a component. Conventionally you display a pop-up menu at the current mouse cursor position when a particular mouse button is pressed, usually button 2. There are two constructors in the `PopupMenu` class: one to which you pass a `String` object that defines a name for the menu, and a default constructor that defines a menu without a name. If you specify a name for a pop-up menu with a statement such as:

```
generalPopup = new PopupMenu("General");
```

the name you supply is primarily for identification purposes and is not always displayed when the menu is popped up; it depends on your environment. Under Microsoft Windows, for example, it doesn't appear. This is different from a menu on a menu bar where the string you pass to the constructor is what appears on the menu bar. Don't forget to add an `import` statement for `javax.swing.JPopupMenu`.

Let's add a pop-up menu to the `SketcherFrame` class by adding a data member of type `JPopupMenu`:

```
private JPopupMenu popup = new JPopupMenu("General");          // Window pop-up
```

To populate a pop-up menu with menu items, you add JMenuItem objects by passing each of them to the add() method for the JPopupMenu object. If you're using Action objects because you also want to implement toolbar buttons, you can create the JMenuItem object using a constructor that accepts a reference of type Action, and then pass it to the add() method for the pop-up menu object. You can also pass a String object to add(), which creates a JMenuItem object and adds it to the pop-up. A reference to the menu item object is always returned by the various overloaded add() methods. Handling the events for the menu items is a process identical to that for regular menu items, and Action objects handle their own events, as you have seen.

You now add menu items to the pop-up that you have created as a member of a SketcherFrame object by adding the following method to the SketcherFrame class:

Available for
download on
Wrox.com

```
// Create pop-up menu
private void createPopupMenu() {
  // Element menu items
  popup.add(new JMenuItem(lineAction));
  popup.add(new JMenuItem(rectangleAction));
  popup.add(new JMenuItem(circleAction));
  popup.add(new JMenuItem(curveAction));
  popup.add(new JMenuItem(textAction));

  popup.addSeparator();

  // Color menu items
  popup.add(new JMenuItem(redAction));
  popup.add(new JMenuItem(yellowAction));
  popup.add(new JMenuItem(greenAction));
  popup.add(new JMenuItem(blueAction));
}
```

Directory "Sketcher 5 displaying a font dialog"

This adds the element menu items to the pop-up. You can call this method from the SketcherFrame constructor:

Available for
download on
Wrox.com

```
public SketcherFrame(String title, Sketcher theApp) {
  setTitle(title);                                  // Set the window title
  this.theApp = theApp;                             // Save app. object reference
  setJMenuBar(menuBar);                             // Add the menu bar to the window
  setDefaultCloseOperation(EXIT_ON_CLOSE);          // Default is exit the application

  createFileMenu();                                 // Create the File menu
  createElementMenu();                              // Create the element menu
  createColorMenu();                                // Create the element menu
  JMenu optionsMenu = new JMenu("Options");         // Create options menu
  optionsMenu.setMnemonic('O');                     // Create shortcut
  menuBar.add(optionsMenu);                         // Add options to menu bar

  createPopupMenu();                                // Create popup
  // Rest of the constructor code as before...
}
```

Directory "Sketcher 5 displaying a font dialog"

You might want to add the font choice menu item to the pop-up, but you must not try to add the same JMenuItem object to two different menus. You could create an Action object that would display the font dialog and create two menu item objects from that. Alternatively, you could create another menu item that did the same as the original and add that to the pop-up. The former approach would be better, because a single Action object would handle events from either menu item.

Displaying a Pop-Up Menu

You can display a pop-up within the coordinate system of any component by calling the `show()` method for the `JPopupMenu` object. The method requires three arguments to be specified: a reference to the parent component that is the context for the pop-up, and the *x* and *y* coordinates where the menu is to be displayed relative to the origin of the parent. For example:

```
generalPopup.show(view, xCoord, yCoord);
```

This displays the pop-up at position (`xCoord`, `yCoord`) in the coordinate system for the `view` component.

A pop-up menu is usually implemented as a *context menu*. The principal idea of a context menu is that it's not just a single menu. A context menu displays a different set of menu items depending on the context—that is, what is under the mouse cursor when the button is clicked. The mouse button that you press to display a context menu is sometimes called a *pop-up trigger*, simply because pressing it triggers the display of the pop-up. On systems that support the notion of a pop-up trigger, the pop-up trigger is fixed, but it can be different between systems. It is usually the right mouse button on a two- or three-button mouse for right-handed users. On systems with a one-button mouse, you typically have to hold down a modifier key while pressing the mouse button to fire the pop-up trigger.

The `MouseEvent` class has a special method, `isPopupTrigger()`, that returns `true` when the event should display a pop-up menu. This method returns `true` only in the `mousePressed()` or `mouseReleased()` methods. It always returns `false` in methods responding to other mouse events. This method helps solve the problem of different mouse buttons being used on different systems to display a pop-up. If you use this method to decide when to display a pop-up, you have them covered—well, almost. You typically use this with the following code to display a pop-up:

```
public void mouseReleased(MouseEvent e) {
  if(e.isPopupTrigger()) {
    // Code to display the pop-up menu...
  }
}
```

I have shown conceptual code for the `mouseReleased()` method here. This would be fine for Windows, but unfortunately it may not work on some other systems—Solaris, for example. This is because in some operating system environments, the `isPopupTrigger()` returns `true` only when the button is pressed, not when it is released. The pop-up trigger is not just a particular button—it is a either a mouse-pressed event or a mouse-released event associated with a particular button. This implies that if you want your code to work on a variety of systems using the "standard" mouse button to trigger the pop-up in every case, you must implement the code to call `isPopupTrigger()` and pop the menu in both the `mousePressed()` and `mouseReleased()` methods. The method returns `true` only in one or the other. Of course, you could always circumvent this by ignoring convention and pop the menu for a specific button press with code like this:

```
if((e.getButton() == e.BUTTON3) {
  // Code to display the pop-up menu...
}
```

With this code, the pop-up operates only with button 3, regardless of the convention for the underlying operating system. However, the user might not be happy about having to use a different pop-up trigger for your Java program compared to other applications on the same system.

You implement a pop-up menu in Sketcher so it works in any environment. The logic in the mouse event handlers gets a little convoluted because there are several possible combinations of states. Let's try to put it together.

TRY IT OUT Displaying a Pop-Up Menu

In Sketcher, the pop-up menu would sensibly operate in the area where the sketch is displayed—in other words, triggering the pop-up menu has to happen in the view. Of course, you could have different pop-up menus for other components in the application window, such as the toolbar.

Assuming you have already added the code to `SketcherFrame` that creates the pop-up menu as I discussed earlier, you just need to add a method to `SketcherFrame` to make the pop-up available to the view:

Available for
download on
Wrox.com

```
// Retrieve the pop-up menu
public JPopupMenu getPopup() {
  return popup;
}
```

Directory "Sketcher 5 displaying a font dialog"

Now the `SketcherView` object can get a reference to the pop-up menu object that is stored in the `SketcherFrame` object by using the application object to get to this method.

To maintain proper cross-platform operation for Sketcher, you implement the pop-up triggering in both the `mousePressed()` and the `mouseReleased()` methods in the `MouseHandler` inner class to `SketcherView`. The `mousePressed()` method looks like this:

Available for
download on
Wrox.com

```
public void mousePressed(MouseEvent e)  {
   start = e.getPoint();                          // Save the cursor position in start
   buttonState = e.getButton();                   // Record which button was pressed
   if(e.isPopupTrigger()) {
      theApp.getWindow().getPopup().show(SketcherView.this, start.x, start.y);
      start = null;
      buttonState = MouseEvent.NOBUTTON;
      return;
   }
   if(theApp.getWindow().getElementType() == TEXT) return;

   if(buttonState == MouseEvent.BUTTON1) {
      g2D = (Graphics2D)getGraphics();            // Get graphics context
      g2D.setXORMode(getBackground());            // Set XOR mode
   }
}
```

Directory "Sketcher 5 displaying a font dialog"

You obtain a reference to the `JPopupMenu` object from the application window object, which you access via the application object reference that is stored in the view. You then call the `show()` method for the pop-up menu object, passing a reference to the source of the event as the parent.

This is one of the rare occasions when you want to reference the outer class object from an inner class. As you know, you use the keyword `this` to refer to the current class object, so here `this` references the `MouseHandler` object. To reference the outer class object from an inner class object you qualify `this` with the class name, so here you use `SketcherView.this`.

The cursor position is the point stored in `start`. You reset `start` and `buttonState` here because you cannot be certain they will be reset in event handlers that are called subsequently. Button 2 down is the pop-up trigger, and the code in the `mouseDragged()` and `mouseReleased()` methods are executed only when button 1 is down.

Here's how the `mouseReleased()` method can be implemented:

Available for
download on
Wrox.com

```
public void mouseReleased(MouseEvent e) {
   if(e.isPopupTrigger()) {
      if(last != null) {                          // If mouse was dragged
         start = last;                            // show popup at last cursor position
      }
      theApp.getWindow().getPopup().show(SketcherView.this, start.x, start.y);
      start = last = null;
      buttonState = MouseEvent.NOBUTTON;
      return;
   }

   if(theApp.getWindow().getElementType() == TEXT) {
```

```
        if(last != null) {
          start = last = null;
        }
        return;
      }

      if(e.getButton() == MouseEvent.BUTTON1) {
        buttonState = MouseEvent.NOBUTTON;              // Reset the button state

        if(tempElement != null) {                       // If there is an element...
          theApp.getModel().add(tempElement);           // ...add it to the model...
          tempElement = null;                           // ...and reset the field
        }
        if(g2D != null) {                               // If there's a graphics context
          g2D.dispose();                                // ...release the resource...
          g2D = null;                                   // ...and reset field to null
        }
        start = last = null;                            // Remove any points
      }
    }
```

Directory "Sketcher 5 displaying a font dialog"

The method checks for a pop-up trigger event. If that's what the event is, the method displays the pop-up menu either at `last` if it is not `null`, or at `start`. You could use the position that was stored in `start` by the `mousePressed()` method to display the pop-up, but if the pop-up is associated with the mouse released event and the user drags the cursor before releasing the button, the menu appears at a different position from where the button was released. This might look a little odd.

The `start`, `last`, and `buttonState` fields are reset before returning from the method. If it's not the pop-up trigger event, the method executes exactly as before. No changes are necessary to the `mouseDragged()` method. `mouseClicked()` only responds to button 1 clicks when `TEXT` is the element type, so that stays the same, too. If you recompile Sketcher and run it again, the pop-up menu should appear in response to a right-button click, or whatever button triggers a context menu on your system. The way it looks on my system is shown in Figure 20-12.

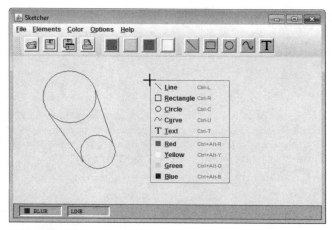

FIGURE 20-12

Note how you get the icons, the label and the accelerator key combination, for each of the menu items. This is because both are defined in the `Action` objects that were used to generate the menu. You could remove the icons by calling the `setIcon()` method for the menu items with the argument `null`.

How It Works

The isPopupTrigger() method for the MouseEvent object returns true when the button corresponding to a context menu is pressed or released. In this case you call the processPopupTrigger() method that you implemented to display the pop-up menu. When you click on a menu item in the pop-up, or click elsewhere, the pop-up menu is automatically hidden. Now any element type or color is a couple of clicks away.

This is just a pop-up menu, not really a context menu. A context menu should display a different menu depending on what's under the cursor. You now look more closely at how you could implement a proper context menu capability in Sketcher.

Implementing a Context Menu

As a context menu displays a different menu depending on the context, it follows that the program needs to know what is under the cursor at the time the pop-up trigger button is pressed. Let's take the specific instance of the view in Sketcher where you are listening for mouse events. You could define two contexts for the cursor in the view — one when an element in the view is under the cursor and another when there is no element under the cursor. In the first context, you could display a special pop-up menu that provides operations that apply specifically to the element under the cursor — to delete or move the element, for example. In the second context, when there is no element under the cursor, you could display the pop-up menu that you created in the previous example. The context menu that is displayed when an element is under the cursor is going to look like that shown in Figure 20-13.

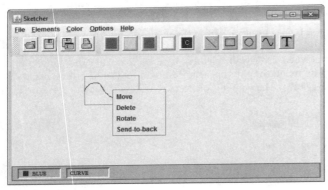

FIGURE 20-13

That's where you're headed, but there are a few bridges to be crossed on the way. For starters, if the context menu is to be really useful, users need to know which element is under the cursor before they pop up the context menu; otherwise they can't be sure to which element the pop-up menu operations apply, particularly when elements overlap on the screen. Deleting the wrong element could be irritating, to say the least.

What you need is some visual feedback to show when an element is under the cursor — highlighting the element under the cursor by changing its color, for example.

Highlighting an Element

You could draw an element in magenta rather than its normal color to highlight that it's the one under the mouse cursor. Every element needs a boolean field to indicate whether it is highlighted or not, so the object knows which color to use in the draw() method when drawing the element. You can add this variable as a field in the Element class:

```
protected boolean highlighted = false;        // Highlight flag
```

You can add this line immediately following the statement for the other data members in the `Element` class definition. The `highlighted` field is inherited by all of the subclasses of `Element`.

You need a method to set the `highlighted` flag in the `Element` class:

```
// Set or reset highlight color
public void setHighlighted(boolean highlighted) {
  this.highlighted = highlighted;
}
```

Directory "Sketcher 6 highlighting elements"

This method is also inherited by all of the subclasses of `Element`.

You can define the color to be used for highlighting in the `SketcherConstants` class as:

public final static Color HIGHLIGHT_COLOR = Color.MAGENTA;

To implement the basis for getting highlighting to work, you need to change one line in the `draw()` method for each of the subclasses of `Element`—that is, `Element.Line`, `Element.Circle`, `Element.Curve`, `Element.Rectangle`, and `Element.Text`. The line to change is the one that sets the drawing color—it's the first line in each of the `draw()` methods. You should change it to:

g2D.setPaint(highlighted ? HIGHLIGHT_COLOR : color);

Now each element can potentially be highlighted.

The `setHighlighted()` method accepts a `boolean` value as an argument and stores it in the data member `highlighted`. When you want an element to be highlighted, you just call this method with the argument as `true`. To switch highlighting off for an element, you call this method with the argument `false`.

Previously, the `setPaint()` statement just set the color stored in the data member `color` as the drawing color. Now, if `highlighted` is `true`, the color is set to magenta, and if `highlighted` is `false`, the color stored in the data member `color` is used.

To make use of highlighting to provide the visual feedback necessary for a user-friendly implementation of the context menu, you need to determine at all times what is under the cursor. This means you must track and analyze all mouse moves *all the time*!

Tracking Mouse Moves

Whenever the mouse is moved, the `mouseMoved()` method in the `MouseMotionListener` interface is called. You can therefore track mouse moves by implementing this method in the `MouseHandler` class that you defined as an inner class to the `SketcherView` class. Before I get into that, I need to define what I mean by an element being "under the mouse cursor," and more crucially, how you are going to find out to which element, if any, this applies at any time.

It's not going to be too difficult. You can arbitrarily decide that an element is "under the mouse cursor" when the cursor position is inside the bounding rectangle for an element. This is not too precise a method, but it has the great attraction that it is extremely simple. Precise hit-testing on an element would carry considerably more processing overhead. Electing to add any greater complexity does not help you to understand the principles here, so you will stick with the simple approach.

So what is going to be the methodology for finding the element under the mouse cursor? Brute force, basically: Whenever the mouse is moved, you can just search through the bounding rectangles for each of the elements in the model until you find one that encloses the current cursor position. You then arrange for the first element that you find to be highlighted. If you check all the elements in the model without finding a bounding rectangle that encloses the cursor, then there isn't an element under the cursor. The mechanism for the various geometric elements is illustrated in Figure 20-14.

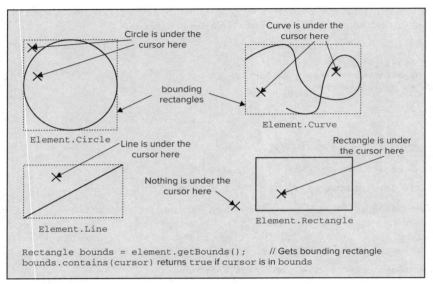

FIGURE 20-14

At most one element can be highlighted at any given time. You need to remember which element is highlighted when there is one so you can reset its highlighting when it isn't under the cursor. To record a reference to the element that is under the cursor, you add a data member of type Element to the SketcherView class. When there isn't an element under the cursor, you make sure that this data member is null.

TRY IT OUT Highlighting to Elements

Add the following statement after the statement that declares the theApp data member in the SketcherView class definition:

```
private Element highlightElement;                          // Highlighted element
```

The mouseMoved() method in MouseHandler is going to be called very frequently, so you must make sure it executes as quickly as possible. This means that for any given set of conditions, you execute the minimum amount of code. Here's the implementation of the mouseMoved() method in the MouseHandler class in SketcherView:

```
// Handle mouse move events
@Override
public void mouseMoved(MouseEvent e) {
  Point cursor = e.getPoint();                         // Get current cursor position

  for(Element element : theApp.getModel()) {  // Go through the list...
    if(element.getBounds().contains(cursor)) {  // ...under the cursor
      if(element==highlightElement) {          // If it's already highlighted
        return;                                 // we are done
      }

      // Un-highlight any existing highlighted element
      if(highlightElement!= null) {             // If an element is highlighted
        highlightElement.setHighlighted(false); // un-highlight it and
        repaint(highlightElement.getBounds());  //... redraw it
      }

      element.setHighlighted(true);             // Set highlight for new element
      highlightElement = element;               // Store new highlighted element
        repaint(highlightElement.getBounds());
```

```
        return;
      }
    }

    // Here there is no element under the cursor so...
    if(highlightElement!=null)    {              // If an element is highlighted...
      highlightElement.setHighlighted(false);    // ...turn off highlighting...
      repaint(highlightElement.getBounds());     // ... and redraw the element
      highlightElement = null;                   // No element highlighted
    }
  }
```

Directory "Sketcher 6 highlighting elements"

To check that highlighting works, recompile Sketcher and run it again. If you draw a few elements, you should see them change color as the cursor moves over them.

How It Works

This method is a fair amount of code, so let's work through it step by step. The first statement saves the current cursor position in the local variable currentCursor. You use a collection-based for loop to iterate over all the elements in the model. In the loop, you obtain the bounding rectangle for each element by calling its getBounds() method, and then call the contains() method for the rectangle that is returned with the current cursor position as the argument. This returns true if the rectangle encloses the point and returns false if it doesn't.

When you find an element under the cursor, it is quite possible that the element is already highlighted because the element was found and highlighted the last time the mouseMoved() method was called. This occurs when you move the cursor within the rectangle bounding an element. In this case you don't need to do anything, so you return from the method.

If the element found is not the same as last time, you check whether the highlightElement variable is null—it is null if the cursor newly entered the rectangle for an element and previously none were highlighted. If highlightElement is not null, you must restore the normal color to the old element before you highlight the new one. To do this you call the setHighlighted() method for the old element with the argument false, and then call the repaint() method for the view with the bounding rectangle for the element as the argument. This causes the area occupied by the old element to be repainted.

To highlight the new element, you call its setHighlighted() method with the argument true, and then store a reference to the element in highlightElement. You then call repaint() for the view to get the element drawn in the highlight color.

The next block of code in the method executes if you exit the for loop because no element is under the cursor. In this case you must check if there was an element highlighted last time around. If there was, you unhighlight it, repaint the element bounding rectangle in the view to redraw the element in its normal color, and reset highlightElement to null.

Defining the Other Context Menu

You already have the menu defined in SketcherFrame for when the cursor is not over an element. It's sensible to keep it there, because the menu items are a subset of those from the application windows menus. The context menu when the cursor is over an element has a new set of menu items, specific to operating on individual elements, so it can be defined in the view. All you need is the code to define the new context menu—plus the code to decide which menu to display when isPopupTrigger() returns true for a mouse event.

You already know from Figure 20-13 that you have four menu items in the element context menu:

> **Move:** This moves the element under the cursor to a new position. This operation works by dragging it with the left mouse button down (button 1).

➤ **Delete** This operation deletes the element under the cursor.

➤ **Rotate:** This operation enables you to rotate the element under the cursor about the top-left corner of its bounding rectangle by dragging it while holding button 1 (normally the left mouse button) down.

➤ **Send-to-back:** This operation overcomes the problem of an element being impossible to highlight because it is masked by the bounding rectangle of another element.

Because you highlight an element by searching the list from the beginning, an element is never highlighted if the rectangle for an earlier element in the list completely encloses it. Moving the earlier element in the list that is hogging the highlighting to the end of the list allows the formerly masked element to be highlighted. This is what the Send-to-back operation does.

TRY IT OUT Creating Context Menus

The element operations can be handled entirely within the view, so add a data member to the SketcherView class that stores the element pop-up menu reference:

```
private JPopupMenu elementPopup = new JPopupMenu("Element Operations");
```

You can create the elementPopup context menu in the SketcherView constructor and also provide the framework for handling events from the menu items:

Available for
download on
Wrox.com

```
public SketcherView(Sketcher theApp) {
    this.theApp = theApp;
    MouseHandler handler = new MouseHandler();      // create the mouse listener
    addMouseListener(handler);                      // Listen for button events
    addMouseMotionListener(handler);                // Listen for motion events

    // Add the pop-up menu items
    JMenuItem moveItem = elementPopup.add(new JMenuItem("Move"));
    JMenuItem deleteItem = elementPopup.add(new JMenuItem("Delete"));
    JMenuItem rotateItem = elementPopup.add(new JMenuItem("Rotate"));
    JMenuItem sendToBackItem = elementPopup.add(new JMenuItem("Send-to-back"));

    // Create the menu item listeners
    moveItem.addActionListener(new ActionListener(){
      public void actionPerformed(ActionEvent e){
        // Handle the move event...
      }
    });
    deleteItem.addActionListener(new ActionListener(){
      public void actionPerformed(ActionEvent e){
        // Handle the delete event...
      }
    });
    rotateItem.addActionListener(new ActionListener(){
      public void actionPerformed(ActionEvent e){
        // Handle the rotate event...
      }
    });
    sendToBackItem.addActionListener(new ActionListener(){
      public void actionPerformed(ActionEvent e){
        sendToBack();                               // Handle the send-to-back event
      }
    });
}
```

Directory "Sketcher 7 with element context menus"

You add the menu items using the add() method that accepts a JMenuItem argument, and returns a reference to the JMenuItem object that it creates. You create each JMenuItem object in the expression that is the argument to the add() method. You then create the listener object for each menu item in the pop-up as an instance of an anonymous class. This simplifies the code for handling each event, because each menu item has a dedicated listener object.

The only listener that is implemented at this point is for the Send To Back menu item, and this calls a `SketcherView` method that you can implement like this:

```
private void sendToBack() {
  if(highlightElement != null) {
    SketcherModel sketch = theApp.getModel();
    if(sketch.remove(highlightElement)) {
      sketch.add(highlightElement);
    } else {
      JOptionPane.showMessageDialog(
                  SketcherView.this,"Element not found to remove.",
                  "Remove Element from Sketch",
                  JOptionPane.ERROR_MESSAGE);
    }
  }
}
```

Directory "Sketcher 7 with element context menus"

To cover the `ActionEvent` and `ActionListener` types, modify the `import` statement for `java.awt.event.MouseEvent` in the `SketcherView.java` file to the following:

```
import java.awt.event.*;
```

To display the context menu, you need to modify the code in the `mousePressed()` and `mouseReleased()` methods in the `MouseHandler` inner class. Here's the former:

```
public void mousePressed(MouseEvent e)  {
  start = e.getPoint();                      // Save the cursor position in start
  buttonState = e.getButton();               // Record which button was pressed
  if(showContextMenu(e)) {
    start = null;
    buttonState = MouseEvent.NOBUTTON;
    return;
  }

  if(theApp.getWindow().getElementType() == TEXT) return;

  if(buttonState == MouseEvent.BUTTON1) {
    g2D = (Graphics2D)getGraphics();         // Get graphics context
    g2D.setXORMode(getBackground());         // Set XOR mode
  }
}
```

Directory "Sketcher 7 with element context menus"

This just adds an `if` statement that calls the `showContextMenu()` method as the condition. This method displays the appropriate menu depending on whether there is a highlighted element, and returns `true` when it displays a menu and `false` otherwise. You can add a definition for this to the `MouseHandler` class:

```
private boolean showContextMenu(MouseEvent e) {
  if(e.isPopupTrigger()){
    if(last != null) {                       // If mouse was dragged
      start = last;                          // show popup at last cursor position
    }
    if(highlightElement == null) {           // If there is no highlighted element
      // Show the  popup menu from the app window
      theApp.getWindow().getPopup().show(SketcherView.this, start.x, start.y);
    } else {                                 // Otherwise...
```

```
        // Show the element operations context menu
        elementPopup.show(SketcherView.this, start.x, start.y);
      }
      return true;
    }
    return false;
  }
```

Directory "Sketcher 7 with element context menus"

The `mouseReleased()` method makes use of this method, too:

```
public void mouseReleased(MouseEvent e) {
  if(showContextMenu(e)) {
    start = last = null;
    return;
  }

  // Check for TEXT being the element type
  if(theApp.getWindow().getElementType() == TEXT) {
    if(last != null) {
      start = last = null;
    }
    return;
  }

  // Rest of the method code as before...
}
```

Directory "Sketcher 7 with element context menus"

If you recompile Sketcher you should get a different context menu in response to a button 2 click, depending on whether or not an element is under the cursor. If you draw a few concentric circles, you can try out the Send To Back operation, too.

How It Works

Using an anonymous class for each menu item means that the implementation of the `actionPerformed()` method for a listener only has to deal with the event for a specific menu item. As you see from the implementation of the Send To Back operation, it becomes very easy. The `sendToBack()` method that is called just calls `remove()` for the sketch object to remove the highlighted element and then calls `add()` for the sketch to add it back at the end of the list. The effect is that the element is only found by the highlighting mechanism if no other element in the list is found to qualify for highlighting. The checks in the method are belt and suspenders, really. You don't expect not to find the highlighted element in the sketch object.

Where the implementation of an anonymous class method needs access to fields in the containing class, it is often easiest to put the implementation in an outer class method that the anonymous class method can call, as you have done here. This is because there are restrictions on accessing outer class fields from an anonymous class. In general, outer class fields must be declared as `final` if you want to access them from an anonymous inner class.

The `showContextMenu()` method in the `MouseHandler` inner class now pops one or another of the two pop-ups you have, depending on whether or not the reference in `highlightElement` is `null`. It returns `true` if the pop-up trigger was recognized and `false` otherwise, so the caller method can respond appropriately. The method is called by the `mousePressed()` method and the `mouseReleased()` method, and which method receives the pop-up trigger event depends on how the pop-up trigger is defined in your environment.

You can select items from the general pop-up to set the color or the element type, but in the element pop-up menu only Send To Back works at present. It just needs a few lines of code somewhere to do element moves, rotations and deletions. Don't worry—it'll be like falling off a log, but not so painful.

NOTE *Anonymous classes can be very helpful in simplifying code, but they don't come entirely free. The more classes you have in your application, the more memory it requires, and the time to start up your application also increases with the number of classes.*

Deleting Elements

Let's take another easy element operation next—deleting an element. All that's involved here is calling `remove()` for the sketch object. Let's give it a try.

TRY IT OUT   Deleting Elements

You can add the following method to the `SketcherView` class to delete an element:

```
private void deleteElement() {
    if(highlightElement != null) {
      if(!theApp.getModel().remove(highlightElement)) {
        JOptionPane.showMessageDialog(
                       SketcherView.this,"Element not found to remove.",
                       "Remove Element from Sketch",
                       JOptionPane.ERROR_MESSAGE);
      }
    }
  }
```

Directory "Sketcher 8 with delete element operation"

Now you can change the listener for the Delete menu item in the `SketcherView` constructor to call this method:

```
deleteItem.addActionListener(new ActionListener(){
    public void actionPerformed(ActionEvent e){
      deleteElement();
    }
  });
```

Directory "Sketcher 8 with delete element operation"

Recompile Sketcher, create a few elements, and then watch them disappear before your very eyes when you select Delete from the pop-up.

How It Works

After verifying in the `deleteElement()` method that `highlightElement` is not `null`, you call the `remove()` method that you added in the `SketcherModel` class way back. This will delete the element from the list, so when the view is repainted, it is no longer displayed. The repaint occurs automatically because the `update()` method for the view—the method that you implemented for the `Observer` interface—is called because the model has changed. Of course, you must remember to set `highlightElement` to `null`, too; otherwise, it could get drawn by a mouse handler even though it is no longer in the model.

You have run out of easy operations. You must now deal with a not quite so easy one—the move operation. To handle this you look into a new topic—transforming the user coordinate system. If you are not of a mathematical bent, some of what I discuss here might sound complicated. But even if your math is very rusty, you should not have too many problems. Like a lot of things, it's the unfamiliarity of the jargon that makes it seem more difficult than it is.

TRANSFORMING THE USER COORDINATE SYSTEM

I said when you started learning how to draw on a component that the drawing operations are specified in a user coordinate system, and the user coordinates are converted to a device coordinate system. The conversion of coordinates from the user system to the device system is taken care of by the methods in the graphics context object that you use to do the drawing, and they do this by applying a *transformation* to the user coordinates. The term *transformation* refers to the computational operations that perform the conversion.

By default, the origin, the (0,0) point in the user coordinate system, corresponds to the (0,0) point in the device coordinate system. The axes are also coincident, too, with positive *x* heading from left to right, and positive *y* from top to bottom. As you know, you can move the origin of the user coordinate system relative to its default position. Such a move is called a *translation*, and this is illustrated in Figure 20-15.

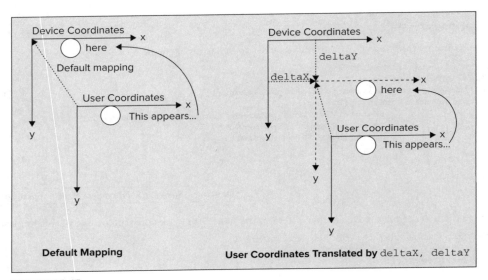

FIGURE 20-15

A fixed value, `deltaX`, say, is added to each *x* coordinate, and another value, `deltaY`, say, is added to every *y* coordinate, and the effect of this is to move the origin of the user coordinate system relative to the device coordinate system: Everything is shifted to the right and down compared to where it would have been without the translation. Of course, the `deltaX` and `deltaY` values can be negative, in which case it would shift things to the left and up. In the element classes, you move the origin of the user coordinate system so you can to draw all elements at the same position, (0,0). This was not necessary up to now, but it turns out to be very handy when you want to rotate elements.

A translation is one kind of *affine transformation*. (*Affine* is a funny word. Some say its origin goes back to Laurel and Hardy, where Ollie says, "This is affine mess you've got us into," but I don't subscribe to that theory.) An affine transformation is actually a linear transformation that leaves straight lines still straight and parallel lines still parallel. As well as translations, there are three other kinds of affine transformation that you can define:

➤ **Rotation**: The user coordinates system is rotated through a given angle about its origin.

➤ **Scale**: The *x* and *y* coordinates are each multiplied by a scaling factor, and the multipliers for *x* and *y* can be different. This enables you to enlarge or reduce something in size. If the scale factor for one coordinate axis is negative, then objects are reflected in the other axis. Setting the scale factor for *x* coordinates to −1, for example, makes all positive coordinates negative and vice versa, so everything is reflected in the *y* axis.

➤ **Shear**: This is perhaps a less familiar operation. It adds to each x coordinate a value that depends on the y coordinate, and adds to each y coordinate a value that depends on the x coordinate. You supply two values to specify a shear, sX and sY, say, and they change the coordinates in the following way:

> ➤ Each x coordinate becomes (x + sX * y)
>
> ➤ Each y coordinate becomes (y + sY * x)

You can visualize the effect of a shear transformation most easily if you first imagine a rectangle that is drawn normally. A shearing transform can squash it by tilting the sides—rather like when you flatten a carton—but keep the top and bottom straight and parallel. Figure 20-16 illustrates the three affine transformations that I've just described.

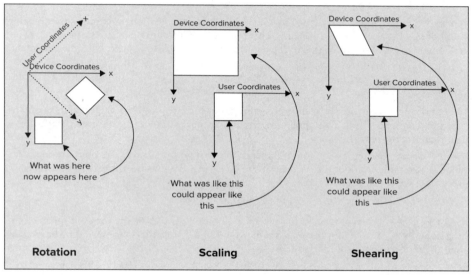

FIGURE 20-16

Figure 20-16 shows the following:

➤ A rotation of $-\pi/4$ radians, which is the same as a rotation of -45 degrees. Rotation angles are expressed in radians, and a positive angle rotates everything from the positive x-axis toward the positive y-axis—therefore clockwise. The rotation in Figure 20-16 is negative and therefore counterclockwise.

➤ A scaling transformation corresponding to an x scale of 2.5 and a y scale of 1.5.

➤ A shearing operation where only the x coordinates have a shear factor. The factor for the y coordinates is 0 so they are unaffected, and the transformed shape is the same height as the original.

The AffineTransform Class

The AffineTransform class in the java.awt.geom package represents an affine transformation. Every Graphics2D object contains an AffineTransform object. The default AffineTransform object in a graphics context is the *identity transform*, which leaves user coordinates unchanged. The transform is applied to the user coordinate system anyway for everything you draw, but all the coordinates for an entity that is displayed are unaltered by default. You can retrieve a copy of the current transform object for a graphics context object by calling its getTransform() method. For example:

```
AffineTransform at = g2D.getTransform();    // Get current transform
```

Although this retrieves a copy of the current transform for a graphics context, you can also replace it by another transform object:

```
g2D.setTransform(at);
```

You can retrieve the transform currently in effect with `getTransform()`, set it to some other operation before you draw some shapes, and then restore the original transform later with `setTransform()` when you're finished. The fact that `getTransform()` returns a reference to a copy, rather than a reference to the original transform object, is important. It means you can replace the existing transform with one of your own and then restore the copy later.

Although the default transform object for a graphics context leaves everything unchanged, you could change it to make it do something by calling one of its member functions:

➤ `void setToTranslation(double deltaX, double deltaY)`: This method makes the transform a translation of `deltaX` in *x* and `deltaY` in *y*. This replaces whatever the previous transform was for the graphics context. You could apply this to the transform for a graphics context with the statements:

```
// Save current transform and set a new one
AffineTransform at = g2D.getTransform();
at.setToTranslation(5.0, 10.0);
```

➤ The effect of the new transform is to shift everything that is drawn in the graphics context g2D 5.0 to the right and down by 10.0. This applies to everything that is drawn in g2D subsequent to the statement that sets the new transform.

➤ `void setToRotation(double angle)`: You call this method for a transform object to make it a rotation of `angle` radians about the origin. This replaces the previous transform. To rotate the axes 30 degrees clockwise, you could write:

```
g2D.getTransform().setToRotation(30*Math.PI/180);
```

➤ This statement gets the current transform object for g2D and sets it to be the rotation specified by the expression `30*Math.PI/180`. Because π radians is 180 degrees, this expression produces the equivalent of 30 degrees measured in radians.

➤ `void setToScale(double scaleX, double scaleY)`: This method sets the transform object to scale the *x* coordinates by `scaleX`, and the *y* coordinates by `scaleY`. To draw everything half scale you could set the transformation with the following statement:

```
g2D.getTransform().setToScale(0.5, 0.5);
```

➤ `void setToShear(double shearX, double shearY)`: The *x* coordinates are converted to `x+shearX*y`, and the *y* coordinates are converted to `y+shearY*x`.

All of these methods replace the transform in an `AffineTransform` object. You can modify the existing transform object in a graphics context, too, and this make it possible for a transform to change the user coordinate system in more than one way.

Modifying the Transformation for a Graphics Context

Modifying the current transform for a `Graphics2D` object involves calling a method for the `Graphics2D` object. The `setToXXX()` methods in the `AffineTransform` class that I introduced in the previous section *replace* the current transform. The effect of the `Graphics2D` methods in this section is to *add* whatever transform you are applying with the method to whatever the transform did before. You can add a translate, rotate, scale, or shear transform to the existing transform in a graphics context by using the following `Graphics2D` class methods:

```
void translate(double deltaX, double deltaY)
void translate(int deltaX, int deltaY)
void rotate(double angle)
void rotate(double angle, double deltaX, double deltaY)
void scale(double scaleX, double scaleY)
void shear(double shearX, double shearY)
```

Each of these adds or *concatenates* the transform specified to the existing transform object for a `Graphics2D` object. Therefore, you can cause a translation of the coordinate system followed by a rotation about the new origin position with the following statements:

```
g2D.translate(5, 10);              // Translate the origin
g2D.rotate(Math.PI/3);             // Clockwise rotation 60 degrees
g2D.draw(line);                    // Draw in translate and rotated space
```

Of course, you can apply more than two transforms to the user coordinate system; you can apply as many as you like. However, it is important to note that the order in which you apply the transforms matters. To see why, look at the example shown in Figure 20-17.

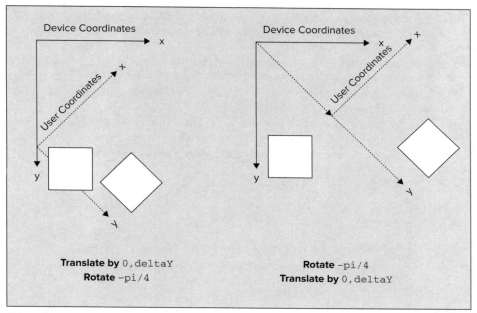

FIGURE 20-17

The figure shows just two transforms in effect, but it should be clear that the sequence in which they are applied makes a big difference. This is because the second transform is applied relative to the new position of the coordinate system after the first transform has been applied. If you need more convincing that the order in which you apply transforms matters, you can apply some transforms to yourself. Stand with your back to any wall in the room. Now apply a translation—take three steps forward. Next apply a rotation—turn 45 degrees clockwise. Make a mental note of where you are. If you now go back and stand with your back to the wall in the original position and first turn 45 degrees before you take the three steps forward, you are clearly in quite a different place in the room than you were the first time around.

Next on your affine tour—how you can create completely new `AffineTransform` objects.

Creating AffineTransform Objects

Of course, there are constructors for `AffineTransform` objects: the default "identity" constructor and a number of other constructors, but I don't have space to go into them here. The easiest way to create transform objects is to call a `static` member of the `AffineTransform` class. There are nine static methods, each of which returns an `AffineTransform` object containing the transform that has the effect described:

➤ `getTranslateInstance(double deltaX, double deltaY)`: Translates the origin to the point (deltaX, deltaY).

➤ `getRotateInstance(double angle)`: Rotates the coordinate system about the origin through `angle` radians.

➤ `getRotateInstance(double angle, double pX, double pY)`: Rotates the coordinate system about the point (pX, pY) through `angle` radians.

➤ `getRotateInstance(double vectorX, double vectorY)`: Rotates the coordinate system about the origin so that the point (vectorX, vectorY) lies on the x-axis.

➤ `getRotateInstance(double vectorX, double vectorY, pX, pY)`: Rotates the coordinate system about the point (pX,pY) so that the x-axis is parallel to a line from the origin to the point (vectorX,vectorY) lies on the x-axis.

➤ `getQuadrantRotateInstance(int nQuadrants)`: Rotates the coordinate system about the origin through `nQuadrants` quadrants, where a quadrant is $\pi/2$ radians, which is 90 degrees. A positive argument specifies a clockwise rotation and a negative argument specifies an anticlockwise rotation.

➤ `getQuadrantRotateInstance(int nQuadrants, double pX, double pY)`: This is similar to the previous transform except that the rotation is about the point (pX,pY).

➤ `getScaleInstance(double scaleX, double scaleY)`: Scales the coordinate system by `scaleX` for x-coordinates and `scaleY` for y-coordinates.

➤ `getShearInstance(double shearX, double shearY)`: Shears the coordinate system so that each x coordinate becomes `(x + shearX*y)` and each y coordinate becomes `(y + shearY*x)`.

For example, to create a transform to rotate the user space clockwise by 90 degrees, you could write the following:

```
AffineTransform at = AffineTransform.getRotateInstance(Math.PI/2);
```

Alternatively you could write:

```
AffineTransform at = AffineTransform.getQuadrantRotateInstance(1);
```

An argument of −1 would rotate the coordinate system counterclockwise by 90 degrees.

After you have created an `AffineTransform` object, you can apply it to a graphics context by passing it as an argument to the `setTransform()` method.

Transforming Shapes

An `AffineTransform` object has another use, too: You can use it to transform a `Shape` object. The `createTransformedShape()` method for the `AffineTransform` object does this. Suppose you define a `Rectangle` object with the following statement:

```
Rectangle rect = new Rectangle(10, 10, 100, 50);
```

You now have a rectangle that is 100 wide by 50 high, at position (10,10). You can create a transform object with the statement:

```
AffineTransform at = getTranslateInstance(25, 30);
```

The `at` object represents a translation of 25 in *x* and of 30 in *y*. You can create a new `Shape` object from the original rectangle with the statement:

```
Shape transRect = at.createTransformedShape(rect);
```

The new `transRect` object looks the same as the original rectangle but is translated by 25 in *x* and 30 in *y*, so its top-left corner is now at (35, 40). Figure 20-18 illustrates this operation.

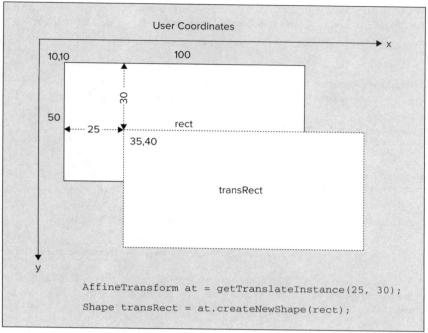

```
AffineTransform at = getTranslateInstance(25, 30);

Shape transRect = at.createNewShape(rect);
```

FIGURE 20-18

However, although `transRect` looks like a rectangle, it is not a `Rectangle` object. The `createTrans-formedShape()` method always returns a `GeneralPath` object because it has to work with any transform. Some transformations deform a shape so the shape cannot be an instance of the original shape type. Applying a shear to a rectangle, for example, results in a shape that is no longer a rectangle. The method has to be able to apply any transform to any `Shape` object, and returning a `GeneralPath` shape makes this possible.

Let's try some of this out with the Sketcher shape classes. At the moment, you translate the origin explicitly by calling the `translate()` method before you draw each shape or text element. Let's use an `AffineTransform` object to do the translation of the coordinate system before the element is drawn.

Translating Sketcher Elements using a Transform

Because you already draw elements at the origin, this is going to be close to trivial. Here's how you could use a transform object in the `draw()` method for the `Element.Line` class:

```
public void draw(Graphics2D g2D) {
  g2D.setPaint(highlighted ? Color.MAGENTA : color);    // Set the line color
  AffineTransform old = g2D.getTransform();              // Save the current transform
  AffineTransforn new = AffineTransform.getTranslateInstance(
                        position.x, position.y);         // Translate to position
  g2D.setTransform(new);                                 // Set the new transform
  g2D.draw(line);                                        // Draw the line
  g2D.setTransform(old);                                 // Restore original transform
}
```

Directory "Sketcher 9 using affine transforms to draw elements"

Saving a copy of the old transform is most important, because that enables you to restore the original scheme after you've drawn the line. If you don't do this, subsequent draw operations in the same graphics context have more and more translations applied cumulatively, so objects get further and further away from where they should be. This occurs in the `mouseDragged()` handler that deals with creating geometric shapes.

Only one line of code involves the element itself and that is the following statement:

```
g2D.draw(line);                                    // Draw the line
```

All the rest are common to all the geometric shapes—`Element.Text` is the sole exception. You could economize on the amount of code by adding an overloaded `draw()` method to the `Element` base class that you can define like this:

Available for download on Wrox.com

```
protected void draw(Graphics2D g2D, Shape element) {
    g2D.setPaint(highlighted ? HIGHLIGHT_COLOR : color); // Set the element color
    AffineTransform old = g2D.getTransform();        // Save the current transform

    // Add a translation to current transform
    g2D.translate((double)position.x, (double)position.y);

    g2D.draw(element);                               // Draw the element
    g2D.setTransform(old);                           // Restore original transform
}
```

Directory "Sketcher 9 using affine transforms to draw elements"

This method is inherited in all the derived classes. The `translate()` method that accepts `double` arguments adds a translation to the existing transform in the graphics context. Thus this `draw()` method draws any `Shape` object after applying a translation to the point `position`. You can now call this method from the `draw()` method in the `Element.Line` class:

Available for download on Wrox.com

```
public void draw(Graphics2D g2D) {
    draw(g2D, line);                                 // Call base draw method
}
```

Directory "Sketcher 9 using affine transforms to draw elements"

You can now go ahead and implement the `draw()` method in exactly the same way for all the nested classes to `Element`, with the exception of the `Element.Text` class. Just pass the underlying `Shape` reference for each class as the second argument to the overloaded `draw()` method. You can't use the base class helper method in the `Element.Text` class because text is not a `Shape` object. You have to treat the class defining text as a special case.

Translating Text

The only changes that you need to make to use a transform to draw a `Text` element are to the `draw()` method in the `Element.Text` class:

Available for download on Wrox.com

```
public void draw(Graphics2D g2D) {
    g2D.setPaint(highlighted ? HIGHLLIGHT_COLOR : color);
    Font oldFont = g2D.getFont();                    // Save the old font
    g2D.setFont(font);                               // Set the new font

    AffineTransform old = g2D.getTransform();        // Save the current transform

    // Add translation transform to current
    g2D.translate((double)position.x, (double)position.y);
    g2D.drawString(text, origin.x, origin.y+(int)bounds.getHeight());
    g2D.setTransform(old);                           // Restore original transform

    g2D.setFont(oldFont);                            // Restore the old font
}
```

Directory "Sketcher 9 using affine transforms to draw elements"

This doesn't seem to have moved things any further forward compared to the code that was there before, so why is this useful? Well, you want to be able to move and rotate all the elements, including `Text` elements, and introducing an affine transform into the drawing process makes this possible.

TRY IT OUT   Using Affine Transforms in Drawing Operations

You can now recompile Sketcher for another trial. If you have done everything right it should still work as before.

How It Works

The draw methods all apply a transform to move the coordinate system to the point stored in `position` before drawing the element. The `draw()` methods then restore the original transform to leave the graphics context unchanged. Each of the `getBounds()` methods returns a bounding rectangle in the original untransformed coordinate system, because that is the context in which it is used. You are now ready to try moving elements around.

Moving Elements

Now you can implement the move operation that you provided for in the context menu. Taking the trouble to define all the elements relative to the origin and using a transform to position them correctly really pays off when you want to apply other transformations to the elements. You can add a `move()` method to the base class `Element` that moves any element:

```
// Move an element
public void move(int deltaX, int deltaY) {
   position.translate(deltaX, deltaY);
   bounds.translate(deltaX, deltaY);
}
```

Directory "Sketcher 10 moving and rotating elements"

This makes use of the `translate()` methods that the `Point` and `Rectangle` classes define, which conveniently moves the x and y coordinates of a point or rectangle by the increments supplied as the arguments. When an element is moved, the bounding rectangle must move with it. The transform in the graphics context makes sure the element is drawn at the right position.

Let's review the process that you are implementing to move an element. From a user's point of view, to move an element you just click on the Move menu item in the context menu and then drag the highlighted element to where you want it to be with button 1 held down.

In programming terms, moving an element is initiated in the `actionPerformed()` method in the anonymous class that defines the listener for the Move menu item selection. When the Move menu item is clicked, you set the Sketcher operating mode to what you define as MOVE mode. You can check for this in the mouse handler methods that expedite a move. The Rotate menu operation works in exactly the same way by setting the mode to ROTATE. To accommodate this you add a new member, `mode`, of type `String` to the `SketcherView` class that stores the current operating mode. You could use type `int`, but let's use strings to be different. By default, the mode is NORMAL.

Add the following member declaration to `SketcherView`:

```
private String mode = NORMAL;                      // Sketching mode
```

You add the definitions of the constants that identify these operating modes to the `SketcherConstants` class in the `Constants` package by adding the following statements:

```
// Operating modes
public final static String NORMAL = "Normal";
public final static String MOVE   = "Move";
public final static String ROTATE = "Rotate";
```

When you set the operating mode to other than NORMAL, the highlighted element is the one to which the mode applies. However, the mouse cursor may be moved after selecting a menu item, which could cause the element to become unhighlighted, so add a member to `SketcherView` to record the selected element for a move or rotate operation:

```
private Element selectedElement;              // Element for move or rotate
```

Now you can change the `actionPerformed()` method in anonymous classes that define listeners for the Move and Rotate menu items in the `SketcherView` class as follows:

```
moveItem.addActionListener(new ActionListener(){
  public void actionPerformed(ActionEvent e){
    mode = MOVE;
    selectedElement = highlightElement;
  }
});
rotateItem.addActionListener(new ActionListener(){
  public void actionPerformed(ActionEvent e){
    mode = ROTATE;
    selectedElement = highlightElement;
  }
});
```

Directory "Sketcher 10 moving and rotating elements"

Moving the selected element is managed in the `mouseDragged()` method in the `MouseHandler` inner class to `SketcherView`. Figure 20-19 illustrates how it works.

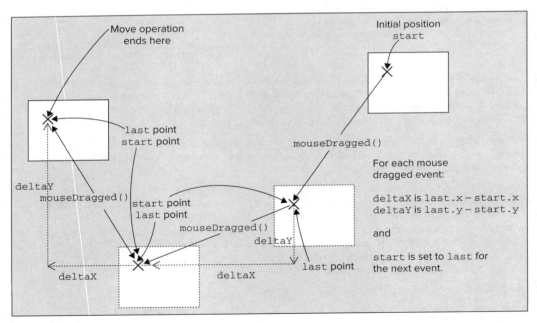

FIGURE 20-19

Expediting a move operation after clicking the Move menu item involves dragging the selected element to its new position with button 1 down. Each move is from the previous cursor position stored in `start` to the current cursor position when the MOUSE_DRAGGED event occurred. After each mouse dragged event has been processed, the current cursor position in `last` is stored in the variable `start`, ready for the next event. For each MOUSE_DRAGGED event, you move the element the distance between successive cursor positions.

Moving Elements

Because the element classes are equipped to move, and you have equiped `SketcherView` to handle the menu item action, you just need to add the code to the methods in `MouseHandler`. The `mousePressed()` method records the start point for a move, and it also sets up the XOR mode for drawing. However, you don't need this to move or rotate existing elements, so you only want the `mousePressed()` method to set XOR drawing mode when the sketching mode is NORMAL. This is simple to fix:

```java
public void mousePressed(MouseEvent e)  {
    start = e.getPoint();                              // Save the cursor position in start
    buttonState = e.getButton();                       // Record which button was pressed
    if(showContextMenu(e)) {
        start = null;
        buttonState = MouseEvent.NOBUTTON;
        return;
    }

    if(theApp.getWindow().getElementType() == TEXT) return;

    if(buttonState == MouseEvent.BUTTON1 && mode == NORMAL) {
        g2D = (Graphics2D)getGraphics();               // Get graphics context
        g2D.setXORMode(getBackground());               // Set XOR mode
    }
}
```

Directory "Sketcher 10 moving and rotating elements"

It's only necessary to verify that the sketching mode is NORMAL and button 1 is down before you set XOR mode. You may wonder why it is not necessary to use the `equals()` method to compare mode with NORMAL. You should use `equals()` to compare arbitrary strings but here, mode is not arbitrary. It can only be a reference to one of the `String` objects you defined in the `SketcherConstants` class. This allows you to compare the `String` references for equality.

You have to test for the setting of mode in the `mouseDragged()` method, and execute different code depending on its value. You have three possibilities: NORMAL, where you do as you did before; MOVE, where you execute a move operation; and ROTATE, where you execute a rotate operation, which you implement later. Here's the new version of `mouseDragged()` to accommodate moving elements:

```java
public void mouseDragged(MouseEvent e) {
    last = e.getPoint();                               // Save cursor position
    if(theApp.getWindow().getElementType() == TEXT && mode == NORMAL) return;

    // Select operation based on sketching mode
    switch(mode){
      case NORMAL:
        // Creating an element
        if(buttonState == MouseEvent.BUTTON1) {
          if(tempElement == null) {                    // Is there an element?
            tempElement = Element.createElement(       // No, so create one
                              theApp.getWindow().getElementType(),
                              theApp.getWindow().getElementColor(),
                              start, last);
          } else {
            tempElement.draw(g2D);                     // Yes - draw to erase it
            tempElement.modify(start, last);           // Now modify it
          }
          tempElement.draw(g2D);                       // and draw it
        }
        break;
      case MOVE:
        // Moving an element
        if(buttonState == MouseEvent.BUTTON1 && selectedElement != null) {
```

```
                        selectedElement.move(last.x-start.x, last.y-start.y);  // Move it
                        repaint();
                        start = last;                                // Make start current point
                    }
                    break;
                case ROTATE:
                    // Rotating an element
                    // Execute rotate...
                    break;
            }
        }
```

Directory "Sketcher 10 moving and rotating elements"

Now the method only executes the previous code in NORMAL mode. For MOVE mode, if button 1 is down and there is an element selected to move, you move it by calling its move() method and repainting the view. The current last is start for the next MOUSE_DRAGGED event.

The final alterations to the code occur in the mouseReleased() method:

Available for download on Wrox.com

```
public void mouseReleased(MouseEvent e) {
    if(mode == MOVE || mode == ROTATE) {
        selectedElement = null;
        start = last = null;
        mode = NORMAL;
        return;
    }
    // Rest of the code as before...
}
```

Directory "Sketcher 10 moving and rotating elements"

There is a new if condition at the beginning that checks for the sketching mode being MOVE or ROTATE. If it is either of these, you only have to reset start, last, and selectedElement to null, and set mode back to NORMAL. g2D is not created if the mode is not NORMAL so you don't need to reset that.

If you recompile Sketcher and rerun it, you can now produce sketches like the one shown in Figure 20-20.

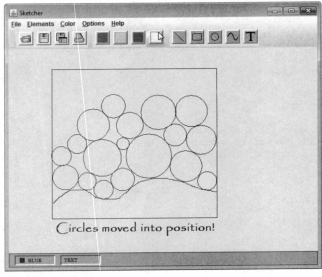

FIGURE 20-20

Note how you can move an element by dragging the mouse from any position. If the cursor is outside the element bounding rectangle when the mouse button is pressed, the element is moved unhighlighted.

How It Works

Using a transform to position each element means that expediting a move operation consists of just altering the position member of an element and its bounding rectangle. The move operation depends on setting a MOVE mode for the mouse event-handling methods to respond to. A move for each element is the same: moving the element and then repainting the view.

Now that you have made Move work, Rotate should be a piece of cake.

Enabling Elements to Rotate

For elements to rotate they need to store their rotation angle. Add the following member to the Element base class:

```
protected double angle = 0.0;                              // Element rotation
```

This stores the angle in radians through which the element is rotated from its default orientation. The rotation angle for an element is only set after the element has been created, because all elements are created initially in the default orientation with a rotation angle of zero.

You can add the following methods to the Element class to get and set the rotation angle for an element:

Available for
download on
Wrox.com

```
// Rotate an element
public void setRotation(double angle) {
   this.angle = angle;
}

// Get the rotation angle
public double getRotation() {
   return angle;
}
```

Directory "Sketcher 10 moving and rotating elements"

The methods are inherited in all the derived element classes.

For the geometric elements, you can arrange to draw them rotated through angle radians about position by modifying the draw() method that is implemented in the Element class:

Available for
download on
Wrox.com

```
protected void draw(Graphics2D g2D, Shape element) {
   g2D.setPaint(highlighted ? Color.MAGENTA : color); // Set the element color
   AffineTransform old = g2D.getTransform(); // Save copy of current transform

   // Add a translation to current transform
   g2D.translate((double)position.x, (double)position.y);

   g2D.rotate(angle);                           // Rotate about position
   g2D.draw(element);                           // Draw the element
   g2D.setTransform(old);                       // Restore original transform
}
```

Directory "Sketcher 10 moving and rotating elements"

Just one line of code does it. The additional statement adds a rotation through angle radians to the current transform in the graphics context. Thus the transform performs a translation of the origin to the point position, followed by a rotation about the origin through angle radians before the element is drawn.

Element.Text objects are a special case, because they take care of drawing themselves. Updating the draw() method for Text elements is not a great challenge either:

```
public void draw(Graphics2D g2D)  {
    g2D.setPaint(highlighted ? HIGHLIGHT_COLOR : color);
    Font oldFont = g2D.getFont();                      // Save the old font
    g2D.setFont(font);                                 // Set the new font

    AffineTransform old = g2D.getTransform();   // Save the current transform

    // Add translation transform to current
    g2D.translate((double)position.x, (double)position.y);

    g2D.rotate(angle);                                 // Rotate about position
    // Reference point for drawString() is the baseline of the 1st character
    g2D.drawString(text, origin.x + 2, maxAscent + 2);
    g2D.setTransform(old);                             // Restore original transform
    g2D.setFont(oldFont);                              // Restore the old font
}
```

Directory "Sketcher 10 moving and rotating elements"

A single line of code does it here, too. Implementing the GUI process for rotating elements is a bit harder.

Rotating Elements

You have implemented the mechanism for the elements to be drawn rotated, so all you need to figure out is the mechanics of how the user accomplishes the rotation of an element, and how this is communicated to the Element object.

The first step is already in place—the actionPerformed() method in the anonymous class for the Rotate listener already sets ROTATE mode, and saves the reference to the highlighted element in selectedElement in response to the Rotate menu action. The user then drags the element to the angle required with the mouse while holding button 1 down. You need to work out the rotation angle for each MOUSE_DRAGGED event. Figure 20-21 shows what happens when the mouse is dragged for a rotation.

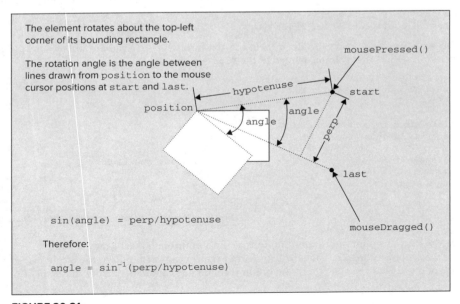

FIGURE 20-21

The concept behind rotating an element is very simple. Imagine a rigid rod between `position` and the mouse cursor. The rod is fixed to `position` but free to rotate about that point, and the cursor can slide up and down the rod as it is dragged. The element to be rotated is bonded to the rod and therefore rotates with it about `position` as the cursor is dragged. The angle in Figure 20-21 is exaggerated so you can see what is going on during a single mouse, dragged event. The `mousePressed()` method is called when the button is first pressed at some arbitrary position, and the cursor position is recorded in `start`. When the `mouseDragged()` method is called, you record the cursor position in `last`, and you now need to calculate `angle`. You must apply a little high school math to get this, which you can ignore if your recall of trigonometry is nonexistent.

You can get the length of the perpendicular from the point `start` in Figure 20-21 to the line from `position` to `last` by using a static method in the `Line2D` class:

```
double perp = Line2D.ptLineDist(position.x, position.y,
                                last.x, last.y,
                                start.x, start.y);
```

The `ptLineDist()` method calculates the perpendicular distance of the point specified by the last two arguments to the line specified by the first four arguments as a value of type `double`. The first pair of arguments are the coordinates of the beginning of the line, and the second pair are the coordinates of the end point.

You know how to get the distance from `position` to `start`. You just apply the `distance()` method that is defined in the `Point` class:

```
double hypotenuse = position.distance(start);
```

From Figure 20-21 you can see that you can calculate `angle` as:

$$\sin^{-1}(perp/hypotenuse)$$

This comes from the definition of what the sine of an angle is. The `Math` class provides the `asin()` method to calculate $\sin^{-1}$ values (also called arcsine values), so you can calculate `angle` as

```
double angle = Math.asin(perp/hypotenuse);
```

The `asin()` method returns an angle in radians between $-\pi/2$ and $\pi/2$, which is fine for the situation you are dealing with in Sketcher. You are unlikely to create an angle outside this range for a single `mouseDragged()` event unless there is something seriously awry with your PC.

Of course, you need to know which way the rotation is going, clockwise or counterclockwise. Another static method in the `Line2D` class can help out here. The `relativeCCW()` method determines where a point lies with respect to a line. If you have to rotate the line clockwise to reach the point, the method returns -1, and if you have to rotate the line counterclockwise, it returns $+1$. It returns zero if the points are collinear. You can use this method to test whether the point `last` is clockwise or counterclockwise with respect to the line from `position` to `start`. Because angles rotating the coordinate system clockwise are positive, you can calculate a suitably signed value for `angle` with the following statement:

```
double angle = -Line2D.relativeCCW(position.x, position.y,
                                   start.x, start.y,
                                   last.x, last.y)*Math.asin(perp/hypotenuse);
```

The minus sign is necessary because the method returns -1 when `last` is clockwise with respect to the line from `position` to `start`. That's all the math you need. Let's do it.

TRY IT OUT   **Rotating Elements**

You need to record the original rotation angle for an element and the new angle through which it is rotated by mouse dragged events in the `MouseHandler` class. Add the following members to the class:

```
private double oldAngle = 0.0;          // Initial element rotation
private double angle = 0.0;             // Additional rotation
```

The `mousePressed()` method sets values for these when the mode is ROTATE:

```
public void mousePressed(MouseEvent e)  {
  start = e.getPoint();                        // Save the cursor position in start
  buttonState = e.getButton();                 // Record which button was pressed

  if(showContextMenu(e)) {
    start = null;
    buttonState = MouseEvent.NOBUTTON;
    return;
  }

  if(theApp.getWindow().getElementType() == TEXT && mode == NORMAL) return;

  // Initialize rotation angles when mode is ROTATE
  if(mode == ROTATE && selectedElement != null) {
    oldAngle = selectedElement.getRotation();
    angle = 0.0;
  }

  if(buttonState == MouseEvent.BUTTON1 && mode == NORMAL) {
    g2D = (Graphics2D)getGraphics();           // Get graphics context
    g2D.setXORMode(getBackground());           // Set XOR mode
  }
}
```

Directory "Sketcher 10 moving and rotating elements"

The check for the element type being TEXT now has an additional condition for a return from the method; it must be NORMAL mode, too.

When the mode is ROTATE and there is a selected element, the current element rotation angle is recorded in the oldAngle member of the MouseHandler object. The angle member that records any additional rotation is set to zero.

To deal with ROTATE mode in the mouseDragged() method, you can add code to the ROTATE case in the switch statement:

```
case ROTATE:
  // Rotating an element
  if(buttonState == MouseEvent.BUTTON1 && selectedElement != null) {
    angle += getAngle(selectedElement.getPosition(), start, last);
    if(angle != 0.0) {                         // If there is rotation...
     // ...rotate the element
      selectedElement.setRotation(oldAngle + angle);
      repaint();                               // Repaint the view
      start = last;                            // last is start next time
    }
  }
  break;
```

Directory "Sketcher 10 moving and rotating elements"

This uses a helper method, getAngle(). You can add it to the MouseHandler class as:

```
// Helper method for calculating the rotation angle
double getAngle(Point position, Point start, Point last) {
  // Get perpendicular distance from last to line from position to start
  double perp = Line2D.ptLineDist(position.x, position.y,
                                  last.x, last.y, start.x, start.y);

  // Get the distance from position to start
```

```
        double hypotenuse = position.distance(start);

        if(perp < 1.0 || hypotenuse < 1.0) return 0.0;   // Ensure sensible values

        // Angle is the arc sine of perp/hypotenuse. Clockwise is positive angle
        return -Line2D.relativeCCW(position.x, position.y, start.x, start.y,
                                    last.x, last.y)*Math.asin(perp/hypotenuse);
    }
```

Directory "Sketcher 10 moving and rotating elements"

This is basically just an assembly of the code fragments in the last section for calculating the angle. The only addition is the `if` statement that returns a zero angle if either of the lengths are very small—less than 1. This is to avoid complications in the angle calculation.

You need an `import` statement for `Line2D` in the source file for `SketcherView`:

```
        import java.awt.geom.Line2D;
```

Recompile Sketcher and try out the new context menus. Having a rotate capability adds a lot of flexibility, and with the move operation giving you much more precision in positioning elements relative to one another, this should enable a massive leap forward in the quality of your artwork. Figure 20-22 shows the sort of standard you might be able to achieve after many months of practice.

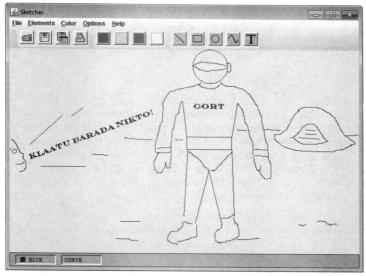

FIGURE 20-22

How It Works

The total rotation angle for a Rotate operation is accumulated in `angle` throughout a sequence of successive mouse dragged events. The total rotation during each event is added to any existing rotation for the element that is obtained by calling `getRotation()` for the element. The result is set as the element's rotation by calling `setRotation()` for the element before repainting the view to present the element in its new orientation.

Enabling elements to be rotated just involves adding an extra transform following the translation transform before each element is drawn. Because you a transform and draw each element at the origin, rotating an element becomes extremely simple. The only real work was implementing the GUI process.

CHOOSING CUSTOM COLORS

It is rather boring only having four colors for elements. It would be a shame to limit Sketcher like this, so let's add a GUI capability to enable any color to be chosen. This is going to be easier than you might imagine, but it's not trivial. Along the way you not only learn about a new standard dialog for choosing colors, you also learn how to modify icon images programmatically and how to get information about text layout.

First, add new icons to the SketcherConstants class:

```
public final static ImageIcon CUSTOM24 =
        new ImageIcon(new BufferedImage(24, 24, BufferedImage.TYPE_INT_ARGB));
public final static ImageIcon CUSTOM16 =
        new ImageIcon(new BufferedImage(16, 16, BufferedImage.TYPE_INT_ARGB));
```

These are the icons you use with the menu item and toolbar button for custom color selection. You display CUSTOM16 in the status bar when the element color is a selected color. The icon references are of type java.swing.ImageIcon rather than type Icon like the others, because you are calling some of the methods that the ImageIcon class defines. Of course, you could make all of the icon references type ImageIcon if you want. These statements create ImageIcon objects from a java.awt.image.BufferedImage object. Although CUSTOM16 and CUSTOM24 are declared as final, you can still call their methods, and the getImage() method returns a reference to the image the icon contains as type Image, which is an abstract class type. Because the image reference is a BufferedImage, you can cast it to that type and then do all kinds of things with it, including modifying it. Although the CUSTOM16 and CUSTOM24 objects are immutable, the images they contain are not.

You must add the following import statement to SketcherConstants.java:

```
import java.awt.image.BufferedImage;
```

Using a Buffered Image

The arguments to the BufferedImage constructor you are using are the width of the image, the height of the image, and the image type. All three arguments are values of type int. You can create a BufferedImage object with a variety of different representations for the underlying image. A range of standard types are defined as static fields of type int in the BufferedImage class. The one you use to create the underlying images for the custom color icons is TYPE_INT_ARGB, which represents each pixel as four 8-bit bytes in an integer that are the alpha channel, and the red, green, and blue color components. The alpha channel determines the transparency, 0 being completely transparent and 255 being completely opaque. There are 13 other types, including types with no alpha channel and grayscale images.

The createGraphics() method for a BufferedImage object returns a reference to a Graphics2D object that is the graphics context for the image. You can then use the Graphics2D methods that you have already seen to draw the image. For the custom color menu item icon, you just want a color rectangle on the image that is the custom color. You could produce this with the following statements:

```
BufferedImage image = (BufferedImage)(CUSTOM16.getImage());
Graphics2D g2D = image.createGraphics();
g2D.setPaint(color);
g2D.fillRect(3,3,10,10);                    // Fill 10x10 rectangle
g2D.dispose();
```

These obtain the underlying image from the CUSTOM16 ImageIcon object by calling its getImage() method. You cast the reference to its original type, BufferedImage, so you can call its createGraphics() method. You use the Graphics2D object to set the paint color to color, and to draw a filled rectangle in that color on the image using the fillRect() method. The image is 16×16 pixels, so in the 10×10 filled area you draw a 10×10 pixel rectangle with the top-left corner at (3,3). Thus the rectangle is inset from the boundaries of the image by 3 pixels all round.

For the custom color toolbar button, you should draw a larger filled rectangle because the button icon is larger than the menu item icon, but other than that the code for the rectangle is similar to the previous fragment. It would be a good idea to distinguish it in some way from the other color toolbar buttons, and one way of doing this is to draw text on it. This isn't difficult because you can draw text using a Graphics2D object.

Using a JColorChooser Dialog

A JColorChooser object is a pane for choosing colors. You can add color chooser panes to your own window to provide a color choosing mechanism, but the class also provides static methods for creating a complete dialog for choosing a color. This is the route you will follow.

The static createDialog() method in the JColorChooser class returns a JDialog object containing a JColorChooser pane that you create using a JColorChooser constructor and pass to the method. The method requires six arguments:

➤ The parent component for the dialog.

➤ A String object specifying the contents of the dialog's title bar.

➤ A boolean value that is true when you want a modal dialog and false for a modeless dialog.

➤ A reference to a JColorChooser pane.

➤ An ActionListener reference to handle events from the OK button.

➤ An ActionListener reference to handle events from the Cancel button.

The default JColorChooser constructor creates a pane with white as the default color. You can also specify the initial color as an argument to the constructor.

You could construct a color chooser dialog with the following statement:

```
JDialog chooseColor = JColorChooser.createDialog(
                        this, "Choose a Custom Color", true,
                        new JColorChooser(elementColor), this, this);
```

The statement creates a modal dialog with current window as the parent and as the listener for both dialog buttons. The default color for the chooser pane in the dialog is elementColor.

A simpler alternative to creating a dialog is to use another static JColorChooser method to display a standard customizable dialog:

```
Color color = JColorChooser.showDialog(this, "Select Custom Color", customColor);
```

This statement displays a dialog with the current window as the parent and with the default color as customColor. If the OK dialog button is clicked, the color that was selected is returned. If the dialog is closed without choosing a color, by clicking the Cancel button for example, null is returned. We use this approach in Sketcher.

Adding the Custom Color GUI

You add a menu item to the Color menu, a toolbar button to the toolbar, and a menu item to the general pop-up menu. First, you need to add an additional Action member to the SketcherFrame class:

```
private ColorAction redAction, yellowAction,greenAction,
                    blueAction, customAction;
```

The Action objects for colors are set up in the createElementColorActions() method in SketcherFrame:

```
private void createElementColorActions() {
    // Create color Action objects as before...
    customAction = new ColorAction("Custom...", BLUE, 'C', CTRL_DOWN_MASK|ALT_DOWN_MASK);

    // Initialize the array
    ColorAction[] actions = {redAction, greenAction, blueAction,
```

```
                                    yellowAction, customAction};
        colorActions = actions;

        // Add toolbar icons as before...
        customAction.putValue(LARGE_ICON_KEY, CUSTOM24);

        // Add menu item icons as before...
        customAction.putValue(SMALL_ICON, CUSTOM16);

        // Add tooltip text to actions as before...
        customAction.putValue(SHORT_DESCRIPTION, "Draw in custom color");
    }
```

You set up the new `Action` object for custom color GUI components and equip it with large and small icons and the text for a tooltip.

The icons for the `customAction` object need to be created in the `SketcherFrame` constructor, ready for use in the `Action` object:

```
public SketcherFrame(String title, Sketcher theApp) {
    setTitle(title);                              // Set the window title
    this.theApp = theApp;                         // Save app. object reference
    setJMenuBar(menuBar);                         // Add the menu bar to the window
    setDefaultCloseOperation(EXIT_ON_CLOSE);      // Default is exit the application

    setCustomIconColor(CUSTOM16,customColor);     // Setup small custom color icon
    setCustomIconColor(CUSTOM24,customColor);     // Setup large custom color icon
    // Rest of the constructor code as before...
}
```

A new method in the `SketcherFrame` class sets up the icons, so add the implementation for that next:

```
private void setCustomIconColor(ImageIcon icon, Color color) {
    BufferedImage image = (BufferedImage)(icon.getImage());
    int width = image.getWidth();                 // Image width
    int indent =  width == 16 ? 3 : 2;            // Indent for filled rectangle
    int rectSize = width - 2*indent;              // Filled rectangle size
    Graphics2D g2D = image.createGraphics();
    g2D.setPaint(color);
    g2D.fillRect(indent,indent,rectSize,rectSize);   // Fill centered rectangle
    if(width == 24) {
      TextLayout textLayout = new TextLayout("C", g2D.getFont(), g2D.getFontRenderContext());
      Rectangle2D.Float rect = (Rectangle2D.Float)textLayout.getBounds();
      g2D.setPaint(
      new Color(255-color.getRed(),255-color.getGreen(), 255-color.getBlue()));
      g2D.drawString("C", (width-rect.width)/2, (width+rect.height)/2);
    }
    g2D.dispose();
}
```

Add the following import statements to `SketcherFrame.java` for the new types introduced in this method:

```
import java.awt.image.BufferedImage;
import java.awt.font.TextLayout;
import java.awt.geom.Rectangle2D;
```

You could have implemented two separate helper methods for setting up the CUSTOM16 and CUSTOM24 icons, but there's quite a lot of common code so I made it one method. The first step is to obtain the BufferedImage object that the icon argument contains. The getImage() method returns a reference of type Image, so you need to cast it to the proper type. The getWidth() method for image returns the width of the image, which in this particular case is the same as the height. There's a getHeight() method for when they differ. You want to draw a filled rectangle indented from the boundaries of the image, but the indents need to be different for the 16 × 16 and 24 × 24 images so that the menu item and toolbar button appear similar to the others in the same set.

The createGraphics() method returns a Graphics2D object that you can use to draw on the image. In both cases you draw a filled rectangle in the color specified by the second argument. The differences for the two sizes of image are the dimensions of the rectangle and the position of its top-left corner.

For a 24 × 24 image that is used on a toolbar button, you draw a capital 'C' for "Custom" centrally on the image to distinguish the custom color toolbar button from those that are used to set the standard colors. To determine the position for the text on the image, you create a java.awt.font.TextLayout object that provides information about styled text. In this case the text is just a single character "C" that you pass to the TextLayout constructor. The second argument is the font used to draw the text and the third argument is a FontRenderContext object that encapsulates the context in which the text is rendered, and you obtain both by calling methods for g2D. The TextLayout object needs all this information to determine the layout of the text. The getBounds() method for textLayout returns a rectangle that encloses the text. You use the height and width of this rectangle in conjunction with the width of the filled rectangle to determine the position where the text is to be drawn. Finally the drawString() method draws "C" on the image.

Note how the color for drawing the text is set. If you were to use a fixed color, the user might choose the same color as a custom color, in which case the text would be invisible. To contrast the text with the background, you subtract the RGB values for the filled rectangle color from 255 and use these to create a new Color object for the text. The only instance in which this won't produce a contrasting color is if the RGB component values are all 128, but this color is an unlikely shade of mid-gray anyway. If you want to take care of this, you could check for these RGB values, and use Color.BLACK for the text in this case.

Displaying the Color Chooser Dialog

Add a field to SketcherFrame to hold the current custom color:

```
private Color customColor = DEFAULT_ELEMENT_COLOR;      // Current custom color
```

It is initialized with the default color at the outset. This needs to be a field that is independent of elementColor because you want to remember the last custom color that was chosen, even when the element color is changed to one of the standard colors.

Events from the custom color menu items and toolbar button are handled by the actionPerformed() member of the ColorAction class.

Available for
download on
Wrox.com

```
public void actionPerformed(ActionEvent e) {
  if(this == customAction) {
    // This could be a new custom color
    Color newColor = JColorChooser.showDialog(
                       SketcherFrame.this, "Select Custom Color", customColor);
    if(newColor != null) {
      elementColor = customColor = newColor;

      // Setup small custom color icons
      setCustomIconColor(CUSTOM16,customColor);
      setCustomIconColor(CUSTOM24,customColor);
      toolBar.repaint();                                 // Repaint the toolbar
    }
  } else {
    // This is just a standard color change
```

```
        elementColor = color;
    }
    statusBar.setColorPane(elementColor);        // Update the status bar
    setChecks(colorMenu, e.getSource());         // Set Color menu checks
}
```

Directory "Sketcher 11 with custom colors"

If the current `Action` object is `customAction` when the method is called, you know a custom color component initialed the event. You display the color chooser dialog using the static `showDialog()` method. The first argument is the parent component, and you qualify `this` with `SketcherFrame` to reference the outer class object. If the dialog returns a non-null reference, this is the new custom color. You store it in `customColor` so next time the dialog is created, this is the selected color, and in `elementColor` for new elements. Both icons must be updated to reflect the new color, and you use the helper method that you added to `SketcherFrame` for this. You then call `repaint()` for the toolbar. The toolbar is visible all the time and you must call `repaint()` to ensure it reflects the new custom color immediately.

If it's not a custom color event, you just store the current `color` member of the `ColorAction` object as the new color. Finally you update the status bar and the Color menu checks.

Assuming you have put all that together correctly you can try it out.

TRY IT OUT   Choosing a Custom Color

Recompile Sketcher with the changes I have described. You should be able to produce something like Figure 20-23, but in glorious color.

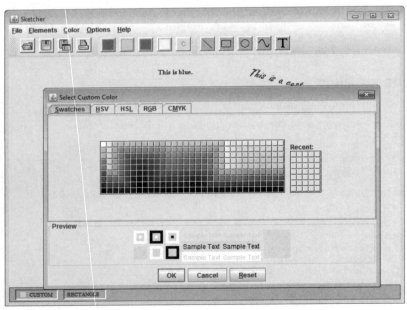

FIGURE 20-23

How It Works

The `Action` object that you create for custom color operations takes care of virtually everything you need. Custom color choosing is dealt with in the `actionPerformed()` method for the `Action` object that you use to create custom color menu items and the toolbar button. Using the `ImageIcon` class as the basis for the menu item and toolbar button icons is the key to being able to customize these for custom colors. You could have created all the icons used in Sketcher programmatically. If you really wanted to go to town, you could draw the icons for the element types in the current color!

The JColorChooser class defines a complete color-choosing facility that you can use in your own dialog, or you can create a complete modal dialog by calling the static method showDialog() as you have done here. The arguments to showDialog() are a reference to the parent component for the dialog, the title for the dialog, and the initial color selection. You can choose a color using any of the three tabs, which provide different mechanisms for defining the color that you want. When you click OK, the color that you chose is returned as type Color. If you exit the dialog by any means other than selecting the OK button, the dialog returns null. You just store the color that is returned in elementColor and set it in the status bar pane. Subsequent sketching operations are in the custom color.

SUMMARY

In this chapter you learned how to use dialogs to manage data input. You have also learned how to implement context menus, which can bring a professional feel to the GUI in your applications. You have applied scrollbars to varying data values as well as scrolled a window, so you should be in a position to use them in whatever context you need.

There are many more components in the Swing library classes than I have the space to discuss in the book, but if you have managed to get Sketcher working with all the features of this chapter, you should have no difficulty working with other Swing components.

EXERCISES

You can download the source code for the examples in the book and the solutions to the following exercises from www.wrox.com.

1. Implement a dialog initiated from a toolbar button to select the current element color.

2. Add a menu item to the Element context menu that displays information about the element at the cursor in a dialog—what it is and its basic defining data.

3. Display a special context menu when the cursor is over a TEXT object that provides a menu option to edit the text through a dialog.

4. Change the implementations of the element classes to make use of the combined translate and rotate operation.

5. Add a toolbar button to switch highlighting on and off. The same button should turn it on when it is off and vice versa, so you need to change the button label appropriately.

6. Add a Scale menu item to the element context menu that allows a geometric element to be scaled by dragging the mouse cursor.

7. Implement a main menu item and a toolbar button for choosing a custom color.

CONFER PROGRAMMER TO PROGRAMMER ABOUT THIS TOPIC.
Visit p2p.wrox.com

▶ WHAT YOU LEARNED IN THIS CHAPTER

TOPIC	CONCEPT
Modal Dialogs	A modal dialog blocks input from other windows in the same application as long as it is displayed.
Modeless Dialogs	A modeless dialog does not block input to other windows. You can switch the focus between a modeless dialog and other windows in the application whenever necessary.
Status Bars	A status bar can appear at the bottom of an application window and displays application parameter values of interest to the user. You can define a class to represent a status bar very easily.
The JOptionPane class	The JOptionPane class provides static methods for creating simple dialogs.
Pop-up Menus	A pop-up menu is a menu that can be displayed at any point within the coordinate system of a component.
Context Menus	A context menu is a pop-up menu that varies depending on what lies at the point where the menu is displayed—so the contents of the menu depend on the context.
Pop-up Trigger	A context menu is displayed as a result of a pop-up trigger, which is usually a left mouse-button click for a right-handed mouse setup.
Device Contexts	An object of the Graphics or Graphics2D type encapsulates device context. You use the device context for a component to draw on the component.
Affine Transforms	The AffineTransform class defines an affine transformation that can be applied to a graphics context. A Graphic2D object always contains an AffineTransform object, and the default transform leaves coordinates unchanged.
Transforming Coordinates	The transform for a graphics context applies to the user coordinate system and is applied immediately before the user coordinates for a shape you are drawing are converted to device coordinates.
Types of Transforms	You can create four kinds of transforms: translations, rotations, scaling, and shearing. You can combine any number of transforms in a single AffineTransform object.
Color Choosers	The JColorChooser class encapsulates panes you can incorporate into a dialog to allow a color to be chosen. The class also provides static methods that create and display predefined dialogs for choosing a color.

YOU CAN DOWNLOAD THE CODE FOUND IN THIS BOOK. VISIT WROX.COM AND SEARCH FOR ISBN 9780470404140.

21

Filing and Printing Documents

WHAT YOU WILL LEARN IN THIS CHAPTER:

➤ How to use the `JFileChooser` class

➤ How to save a sketch in a file as objects

➤ How to implement the Save As menu mechanism

➤ How to open a sketch stored in a file and integrate it into the application

➤ How to create a new sketch and integrate it into the application

➤ How to ensure that the current sketch is saved before the application is closed or a new sketch is loaded

➤ How printing in Java works

➤ How to print in landscape orientation rather than portrait orientation

➤ How to implement multipage printing

➤ How to output Swing components to your printer

In this chapter, you explore serializing and printing documents in an application, and you add these capabilities as the finishing touches to the Sketcher program. Neither serialization nor printing are available to an untrusted applet for security reasons, so everything I cover in this chapter applies only to applications and trusted applets. Although you have already covered serialization in Chapter 12, you'll find that there is quite a difference between understanding how the basic methods for object input and output work and applying them in a practical context.

SERIALIZING THE SKETCH

The Sketcher program can be considered to be a practical application only if you can save sketches in a file and retrieve them later—in other words, you need to implement serialization for a `SketcherModel` object and use that to make the File menu work. Ideally, you want to be able to write the model for a sketch to a file and be able to read it back at a later date and reconstruct exactly the same model object. The basics are already in place. You have declared that the `SketcherModel` class and the `Element` class, and therefore its subclasses implement the `Serializable` interface. You now need to make sure that the other conditions for serialization are met; namely that all the fields in the classes meet the requirements of serialization, too.

Implementing Serialization

For a class to be serializable, all its data members must be either serializable or declared as `transient`. If this is not the case, then an exception of type `NotSerializableException` is thrown when you try to serialize an object. To avoid this, you must trawl through the data members of the `SketcherModel` class and make sure they either implement the `Serializable` interface or are declared as `transient`.

You cannot assume that objects of a standard class type are serializable, because some most definitely are not. It's a fairly quick fishing trip though, because the `SketcherModel` class has only one data member — the linked list of elements that make up the sketch. If the `SketcherModel` object is to be serializable, you simply need to make sure the `elements` field is serializable.

Serializing the List of Elements

If you look through the JDK documentation, you'll see that the `LinkedList<>` generic class implements the `Serializable` interface, so all you need to worry about are the elements you store in the list.

Class fields of any of the basic types are always serializable. The data members of our `Element` class that are object references are of types `java.awt.Color`, `java.awt.Point`, and `java.awt.Rectangle`. You can verify from the JDK documentation that all three classes are serializable, so our `Element` class is serializable. Now you need to look at the subclasses of `Element`.

Subclasses of `Element` inherit the implementation of the `Serializable` interface, so they are all declared to be serializable by default. All of the concrete classes in the `java.awt.geom` package that implement the `java.awt.Shape` interface are already serializable, as is the `java.awt.Font` field in the `Element.Text` class. All the other fields in the classes that define sketch elements are of basic types. This means that *all* the sketch element types are serializable without any further effort on your part, so writing a sketch to a file is going to be fairly trivial.

BASIC INFRASTRUCTURE FOR SAVING SKETCHES

Putting in place the graphical user interface functionality for saving a sketch on disk and reading it back from a file is significantly more work than implementing serialization for the model. The logic of opening and saving files so as not to lose anything accidentally can get rather complex. Before you get into that, there are some fundamental points that need to be addressed.

For starters, a sketch doesn't have a name. You should at least make provision for assigning a file name to a sketch, and maybe displaying the name of the current sketch in the title bar of the application window. You also need ways to record the file name for a sketch and the directory where it is stored. Let's name that sketch first.

Assigning a Document Name

The sketch is going to have a name, and because you intend to store it somewhere, let's define a default directory to hold sketches. Add the following lines to the end of the `SketcherConstants` class that you defined in the `Constants` package:

```
public final static Path DEFAULT_DIRECTORY =
        Paths.get(System.getProperty("user.home")).resolve("Sketches");
```

The default directory for storing sketches is the `Sketches` directory in your `user.home` directory. If you want to store your sketches in a different directory, set the definition of `DEFAULT_DIRECTORY` to suit your needs. The file extension `.ske` to identify sketches is also arbitrary. You can change this if you prefer to use a different extension.

You should store information related to saving a sketch, and the application window object is a suitable repository for it, so add the following data members to the `SketcherFrame` class definition:

```
private String frameTitle;          // Frame title
private Path currentSketchFile;     // Current sketch file on disk
```

The `frameTitle` member records the basic title for the Sketcher application window. You append the file name for the sketch to it when there is one and display the result in the title bar. The `currentSketchFile` object is only non-null when a sketch has been saved. The value for the `currentSketchFile` member is set by the event handling for the File menu items as follows:

➤ The New menu item event sets it to `null`.

➤ The Save menu item event sets it to the path for the file where the sketch was saved if it was not previously saved. It leaves the member unchanged if the sketch was previously saved.

➤ The Save As menu item event sets it to the path where the sketch was saved.

➤ The Open menu item event sets it to the path for the file that was read.

You can add import statements to `SketcherFrame.java` that cover `Path` and other types you use for file I/O:

```
import java.nio.file.*;
import java.io.*;
```

Validating the Directory for Sketches

You must make sure that `DEFAULT_DIRECTORY` exists. If it doesn't exist, you need to create it so sketches can be saved. You can add the following method to the `SketcherFrame` class to do this:

```
private void checkDirectory(Path directory) {
  if(Files.notExists(directory)) {
    JOptionPane.showMessageDialog(null,
                      "Creating directory: " + directory,
                      "Directory Not Found",
                      JOptionPane.INFORMATION_MESSAGE);
    try {
      Files.createDirectories(directory);
    } catch(IOException e) {
      e.printStackTrace();
      JOptionPane.showMessageDialog(null,
          "Cannot create: " + directory + ". Terminating Sketcher.",
          "Directory Creation Failed",
          JOptionPane.ERROR_MESSAGE);
      System.exit(1);
    }
  }
}
```

Directory "Sketcher 1 saving a sketch to a file"

You have seen this sort of code for ensuring a directory exists back in Chapter 9. This method checks whether the directory passed as the argument exists. If it doesn't, it pops an information dialog telling the user the directory is created. The first argument to the `showMessageDialog()` method is `null` because the `SketcherFrame` object has not been created when the `checkDirectory()` method is called from the `SketcherFrame` constructor. The `null` argument causes a default frame to be used to position the dialog window.

It is possible that the `createDirectories()` method could fail and throw an exception. In this case, another message dialog is displayed and the stack trace is recorded on the command line before terminating Sketcher. You can test that this all works and see what the stack trace looks like by specifying a string for `DEFAULT_DIRECTORY` that is not a valid path.

You can call the new method from the constructor with the following code:

```
public SketcherFrame (String title, Sketcher theApp) {
  checkDirectory(DEFAULT_DIRECTORY);
  setTitle(title);                                // Set the window title
  frameTitle = title;                             // Remember original title
  // Rest of the code in the constructor as before...
}
```

Directory "Sketcher 1 saving a sketch to a file"

After calling the method that verifies the directory is available, you record the window title in `frameTitle`.

When you close Sketcher, there should be a means of checking whether the sketch needs to be saved. Otherwise, it is all too easy to close the application and lose the brilliant sketch that you have spent many hours crafting. Checking whether the sketch needs to be saved isn't difficult. You just need to record the fact that the model has changed.

Recording Changes to a Sketch

To provide the means of recording whether or not a sketch has been changed, you can add a `boolean` field to the `SketcherFrame` class that you set to `true` when the `SketcherModel` object changes and set to `false` when it is in a new and original condition—as is the case when it has just been loaded or saved in a file. Add the following data member definition to the `SketcherFrame` class:

```
private boolean sketchChanged = false;          // Model changed flag
```

Directory "Sketcher 1 saving a sketch to a file"

This sort of variable is sometimes referred to as a "dirty" flag for the model because it records when something has been done to sully the pristine state of the model data. The flag is `false` by default because the sketch is empty and therefore unchanged by definition. Any change that the user makes to the model should result in the flag being set to `true`, and whenever the model is written to a file, the flag should be reset to `false`. By checking the state of this flag you can avoid unnecessary Save operations while the sketch in memory remains unchanged.

You already have in place the means to signal changes to a sketch because the `SketcherModel` class has `Observable` as a base class. As you know, an `Observable` object can automatically notify any registered `Observer` objects when a change takes place. All you need to do is to make the `SketcherFrame` class implement the `Observer` interface and register the application window as an observer of the sketch object:

```
public class SketcherFrame  extends JFrame implements ActionListener, Observer {
  // Constructor and other methods as before...
  // Method called by SketcherModel object when it changes
  public void update(Observable o, Object obj) {
    sketchChanged = true;
  }

  // Rest of the class as before...
}
```

Directory "Sketcher 1 saving a sketch to a file"

The `update()` member of `SketcherFrame` will be called by the `sketch` object whenever the sketch changes in some way. You record the change by setting `sketchChanged` to `true`. This implies that the sketch in its current state has not been saved, and when the sketch is saved, you must set `sketchChanged` back to `false`.

The `Observer` interface and the `Observable` class are defined in the `java.util` package, so you must import the class names into the `SketcherFrame.java` file with the following statement:

```
import java.util.*;
```

You can register the application window as an observer for the `SketcherModel` object by adding one statement to the `createGUI()` method in the `Sketcher` class:

```
private void createGUI() {
// Code as before...
  sketch = new SketcherModel();           // Create the model
  view = new SketcherView(this);          // Create the view
  sketch.addObserver(view);               // Register view with the model
  sketch.addObserver(window);             // Register window with the model
```

```
            window.getContentPane().add(view, BorderLayout.CENTER);
            window.setVisible(true);
        }
```

The `window` field in the `Sketcher` object stores a reference to the application window. Whenever an element is added to the sketch, or deleted from it, the application window object is notified. You can now press ahead with serializing the model for a sketch.

Handling File Menu Events

To support the menu items in the File menu, you must add some code to the `actionPerformed()` method in the `FileAction` class. This single method definition supports events for all of the items in the File menu. You need to figure out what action originated the event.

You know how to do this because you have done it before in the `ColorAction` class. All the `FileAction` references are stored as members of the `SketcherFrame` object. All you need to do is compare the `this` reference with each of the `FileAction` references. An outline of the `actionPerformed()` method in the `FileAction` class looks like this:

```
    public void actionPerformed(ActionEvent e) {
      if(this == saveAction) {
        // Code to handle file Save operation...

      } else if(this == saveAsAction) {
        // Code to handle file Save As operation...

      } else if(this == openAction) {
        // Code to handle file Open operation...

      } else if(this == closeAction) {
        // Code to handle close operation...

      } else if(this == newAction){
        // Code to handle file New operation...

      } else if(this == printAction) {
        // Code to handle Print operation...

      } else if(this == exitAction) {
        // Code to handle Exit operation...

      }
    }
```

It really could not be much simpler. You have one `if` or `else-if` block for each action, and you develop the code for these one by one.

Many of these operations involve dialogs. In particular you should get at the file system and display the list of directories and files to choose from, for an Open operation for instance. It sounds like a lot of work, and it certainly would be, if it weren't for a neat facility provided by the `javax.swing.JFileChooser` class.

USING A FILE CHOOSER

The `JFileChooser` class in the `javax.swing` package provides an easy-to-use mechanism for creating file dialogs for opening and saving files. The `JFileChooser` class is slightly out of kilter with the new I/O capability in that it uses `java.io.File` objects to encapsulate file paths, rather than `java.nio.file.Path` objects that you use with the new I/O. A `File` object encapsulates an absolute or relative path string for a file or directory, similar to a `Path` object. Producing `Path` objects from `File` objects and vice versa is very easy, so having to work with both `File` and `Path` objects doesn't represent a problem.

You can use a single object of this class to create all the file dialogs you need, so you can add a member to the `SketcherFrame` class now to store a reference to a `JFileChooser` object that you create in the constructor:

```
private JFileChooser fileChooser;                    // File chooser dialog
```

There are several `JFileChooser` constructors, but I'm discussing only a couple of them here. The default constructor creates an object with the current directory as the default directory, but that won't quite do for our purposes. What you want in the first instance is for the default directory to be the one specified by the `DEFAULT_DIRECTORY` path that you defined in the `SketcherConstants` class. There is no `JFileChooser` constructor that accepts a `Path` object reference, so you use the constructor that accepts an argument of type `String` that specifies the directory that the dialog displays initially. You can call the `toString()` method for `DEFAULT_DIRECTORY` to get the path as a `String` and pass that to the constructor that accepts a `String` reference to specify the directory. Add the following statement to the `SketcherFrame` constructor, following the statements that you added earlier that verified `DEFAULT_DIRECTORY` actually existed on the hard drive:

```
fileChooser = new JFileChooser(DEFAULT_DIRECTORY.toString());
```

The dialog that the `fileChooser` object encapsulates displays the contents of the directory specified by `DEFAULT_DIRECTORY`. The dialog has two buttons, one to approve a selection from the directory contents and the other to cancel the dialog. You can now use the `fileChooser` object to implement the event handling for the `File` menu. During use of the dialog, the user may well change the current directory to something else. As long as you are using the same `JFileChooser` object to display the dialogs for choosing a file, the current directory is remembered between displaying one file chooser dialog and the next.

There are a considerable number of methods in the `JFileChooser` class, so rather than trying to discuss them all, which would take many pages of text and be incredibly boring, I'm leaving you to explore these at your leisure and will just introduce the ones that you can apply to Sketcher to support the `File` menu.

Displaying a File Save Dialog

In most cases you'll want to display a modal file save dialog when the Save menu item or toolbar button is selected. As luck would have it, the `JFileChooser` class has a `showSaveDialog()` method that does precisely what you want. All you have to do is call the method with a reference to the `Component` object that is the parent for the dialog to be displayed as the argument. The method returns a value indicating how the dialog was closed. You could display a save dialog in a method for a `FileAction` object with the following statement:

```
int result = fileChooser.showSaveDialog(SketcherFrame.this);
```

This automatically creates a file save dialog with the `SketcherFrame` object as parent, and with Save and Cancel buttons. The `SketcherFrame.this` notation is used to refer to the `this` member for the `SketcherFrame` object from within a method of an inner class object of type `FileAction`. Just to remind you, you reference the `this` variable for an outer class object from a non-static inner class object by qualifying `this` with the outer class name. The file chooser dialog is displayed centered in the parent component, which is the `SketcherFrame` object here. If you specify the parent component as `null`, the dialog is centered on the screen. This also applies to all the other methods I discuss that display file chooser dialogs.

Displaying a File Open Dialog

When you need a file open dialog, you can call the `showOpenDialog()` member of a `JFileChooser` object. Don't be fooled here, though. A save dialog and an open dialog are essentially the same. They differ only in minor details—the title bar and one of the button labels. The sole purpose of both dialogs is simply to enable the user to select a file—for whatever purpose. If you want to be perverse, you could pop up a save dialog to open a file and vice versa!

You can also display a customized dialog from a `JFileChooser` object. Although it's not strictly necessary for the Sketcher application—the standard file dialogs are quite adequate—you adopt a custom approach so you get some experience of using a few more `JFileChooser` methods.

You display a custom dialog by calling the showDialog() method for the JFileChooser object supplying two arguments. The first argument is the parent component for the dialog window, and the second is the approve button text—the approve button being the button that you click to expedite the operation rather than cancel it. You could display a dialog with an Open button with the following statement:

```
int result = fileChooser.showDialog(SketcherFrame.this, "Open");
```

If you pass null as the second argument here, the button text is whatever was set previously—possibly the default. The value that the method returns can be one of three constants that are defined in the JFileChooser class:

➤ APPROVE_OPTION if the approve button was clicked

➤ CANCEL_OPTION if the cancel button was clicked

➤ ERROR_OPTION if an error occurred or if the dialog window was closed

You can compare the value that showDialog() returns with these constants to determine how the dialog was closed.

Customizing a File Chooser Dialog

Before you display a custom dialog, you would normally do a bit more customizing of what is to be displayed by the dialog. You use the following JFileChooser methods to customize the dialogs for Sketcher:

➤ setDialogTitle(String text): Sets the String object that you pass as the argument as the dialog's title bar text.

➤ setApproveButtonText(String text): Sets the String object that you pass as the argument as the approve button label.

➤ setApproveButtonToolTipText(String text): Sets the String object that you pass as the argument as the approve button tooltip.

➤ addChoosableFileFilter(FileFilter filter): Filters the file list using the file filter you supply as the argument.

➤ setSelectedFile(File file):Sets file as the file preselected when the dialog opens.

Contents of the File List

You can set a file chooser dialog to display files, directories, or both. You determine what is displayed in a dialog by calling the setFileSelectionMode() method. The argument must be one of the int constants FILES_ONLY, DIRECTORIES_ONLY, and FILES_AND_DIRECTORIES that are defined as static members of the JFileChooser class. FILES_ONLY is the default selection mode. The getFileSelectionMode() method returns the current selection mode.

By default a user can select only one file or directory, but you can allow multiple selections to be made from the list in the file dialog if you call the setMultiSelectionEnabled() method for your JFileChooser object with the argument true.

Preselecting a File

If you want the dialog to have a particular file selected when it opens, you pass a java.io.File object to the setSelectedFile() method for the JFileChooser object. This will preselect the file in the file list if the file already exists, and inserts the file name in the file name field if it doesn't. You can create a File object from a Path object by calling its toFile() method. If you have enabled multiple selections in the dialog, you can pass an array of File objects to the setSelectedFiles() method to have several files preselected when the dialog opens.

Updating the File List

The file list is created when you create the JFileChooser object, but naturally files may be added or deleted over time, and when this occurs you need to reconstruct the file list in the dialog object. Calling the `rescanCurrentDirectory()` method before you display the dialog does this for you. You can change the current directory at any time by passing a `File` object specifying the directory you want to make current to the `setCurrentDirectory()` method.

Filtering the File List

You can supply a file filter for the sketch files. The default file filter in a `JFileChooser` object accepts any file or directory, but you can add one or more filters of your own to select a subset of the files in the current directory. A file filter object is of a type that has the `javax.swing.filechooser.FileFilter` class as a superclass. The `FileFilter` class declares two methods, both of which are abstract, so your file filter class must implement them:

> ➤ The `accept(File file)` method: Returns `true` if the file represented by `file` is accepted by the file filter and returns `false` otherwise.

> ➤ The `getDescription()` method: Returns a `String` object that describes the filter — "Sketch files," for example.

The `JFileChooser` class works with `File` objects rather than `Path` objects, so the filter has to work with `File` objects, too.

You limit the files in the list in the dialog to display only the files you want by calling the `addChoosableFileFilter()` method, with an object of your file filter class as the argument.

You can define your own file filter class for use with the Sketcher program as follows:

```java
import javax.swing.filechooser.FileFilter;
import java.io.File;

public class ExtensionFilter extends FileFilter {
  public ExtensionFilter(String ext, String descr) {
    extension = ext.toLowerCase();          // Store the extension as lower case
    description = descr;                     // Store the description
  }

  public boolean accept(File file) {
    return(file.isDirectory() || file.getName().toLowerCase().endsWith(extension));
  }

  public String getDescription() {
    return description;
  }

  private String description;               // Filter description
  private String extension;                 // File extension
}
```

Directory "Sketcher 1 saving a sketch to a file"

Add the `ExtensionFilter.java` source file to the Sketcher program directory. The `accept()` method determines whether or not a file is displayed in a file chooser list. A file is accepted if either of the operands for the `||` operator in the method evaluates to `true`. The `isDirectory()` method for a `File` object returns `true` if the object represents a directory and not a file. This is the first operand for the `||` operator, so all directories are displayed in the list by this filter. The second operand is `true` when the extension for a file path in the `File` object is `extension`. The `getName()` method for a `File` object is the equivalent of the `getFileName()` method for a `Path` object; it returns the name of the file as a `String` object without the root path. After converting it to lowercase, calling `endsWith()` for the `String` object results in `true` if the string ends with the argument `extension`, so all files with that extension are included in the list.

To identify a filter for files with the extension `.ske`, you could add a field to the `SketcherFrame` class:

Available for download on Wrox.com

```
private ExtensionFilter sketchFilter = new ExtensionFilter(
                                     ".ske", "Sketch files (*.ske)");
```

Directory "Sketcher 1 saving a sketch to a file"

You use this object when you implement file operations for a sketch.

> **NOTE** *There is a* `java.io.FileFilter` *interface that is easily confused with the* `javax .swing.filechooser.FileFilter` *class, especially if you make use of * to import all the names in a package.*

Querying a File Chooser Dialog

You obviously need to be able to discover which file or directory the user selected in the dialog. When the dialog is closed with the approve button, you can call `getSelectedFile()` for the dialog object. This returns the file as a `File` object. You don't need it for Sketcher, but if you have enabled multiple selections in the dialog, calling the `getSelectedFiles()` method for the dialog object returns an array of `File` objects corresponding to the selected files.

That's enough detail on the `JFileChooser` class for now. Let's return to what you need to implement in Sketcher for File menu operations.

IMPLEMENTING FILE OPERATIONS

You need to implement the capability to respond to events for the Save, Save As, and New menu items in the File menu. Although these are independent operations, they have quite a lot of function in common. Where a dialog is required, it is a `JFileChooser` dialog customized to the requirements of a given operation. Let's implement a customized file dialog capability in Sketcher first of all.

Creating a Customized File Dialog

You can add a method to the `SketcherFrame` class to display a customized file dialog and return a `String` object encapsulating the path for the file that has been selected:

Available for download on Wrox.com

```
// Display a custom file dialog
private Path showDialog(String dialogTitle,
                        String approveButtonText,
                        String approveButtonTooltip,
                        ExtensionFilter filter,
                        Path file) {             // Current file path - if any
  fileChooser.setDialogTitle(dialogTitle);
  fileChooser.setApproveButtonText(approveButtonText);
  fileChooser.setApproveButtonToolTipText(approveButtonTooltip);
  fileChooser.setFileSelectionMode(JFileChooser.FILES_ONLY);
  fileChooser.addChoosableFileFilter(filter);    // Add the filter
  fileChooser.setFileFilter(filter);             // and select it

  fileChooser.rescanCurrentDirectory();
  Path selectedFile = null;
  if(file == null) {
    selectedFile = Paths.get(
              fileChooser.getCurrentDirectory().toString(), DEFAULT_FILENAME);
  } else {
    selectedFile = file;
  }
  fileChooser.setSelectedFile(selectedFile.toFile());
```

```
// Show the file save dialog
int result = fileChooser.showDialog(this, null);
return (result == JFileChooser.APPROVE_OPTION) ?
              Paths.get(fileChooser.getSelectedFile().getPath()) : null;
```

Directory "Sketcher 1 saving a sketch to a file"

The method requires five arguments to customize the dialog—the dialog title, the button label, the button tooltip, the file filter object, and the `Path` object representing the file path for the current sketch. Each of the options is set using the methods for the `JFileChooser` object that I discussed earlier. The last argument is used to select a file from the file list initially. If the last argument is `null`, a file with the default file name is selected. The `showDialog()` method returns `null` if no file was selected when the dialog closes.

Note that you reconstruct the file list for the dialog by calling the `rescanCurrentDirectory()` method before you display the dialog. This is to ensure that you always display an up-to-date list of files. If you didn't do this, the dialog would display the list of files that were in the directory when you created the `JFileChooser` object. Any subsequent changes to the contents of the directory would not be taken into account.

The value that is returned by the `showDialog()` member of the `JFileChooser` object indicates whether or not the approve button was selected. If it was, you return the `Path` object corresponding to the `File` object that the dialog returns. Otherwise, you return `null`. A method that calls your `showDialog()` method to display the dialog can determine whether or not a file was chosen by testing the return value for `null`.

You can now use this method when you implement handling of a Save menu item action event. A save operation is a little more complicated than you might imagine at first sight, so let's consider it in a little more detail.

Implementing the Save Operation

If `sketchChanged` is `false` when a Save event occurs, either the sketch is new and unchanged, or it has not been changed since it was last saved; in either case, you do nothing. What happens in a Save operation when `sketchChanged` is `true` depends on whether the current sketch has been saved before.

You have to consider two basic possibilities: The current sketch has been previously saved, or it hasn't. Let's elaborate on what needs to happen for each case:

1. The current sketch has been saved previously, indicated by `currentSketchFile` being non-`null`:
   ➤ Save the sketch immediately using the file path that is in `currentSketchFile`.
   ➤ Set `sketchChanged` to `false`.
   ➤ End the operation.
2. The current sketch has never been saved, indicated by `currentSketchFile` being `null`:
   ➤ Display the file chooser dialog.
   ➤ If the dialog returns `null` when it closes, end the operation.
   ➤ If a non-null `File` reference is returned from the dialog, check whether the selected file exists:
   a. If the file does not exist:
      ➤ Save the sketch with the selected file path.
      ➤ Record the file path in `currentSketchFile`.
      ➤ Set `sketchChanged` to `false`.
   b. If the file does exist:
      ➤ Display a dialog asking if the file is to be overwritten.
      ➤ If NO, end the operation.
      ➤ If YES, write the sketch with the selected path, record the path in `currentSketch-File`, set `sketchChanged` to `false`.

All the complications arise with a new sketch that has never been saved. You can package up these checks for when you need to save and for when you should display the dialog in another method in the SketcherFrame class. You can call it saveOperation() and make it a private member of the SketcherFrame class:

```
// Save the sketch if it is necessary
private void saveOperation() {
  if(!sketchChanged) {                       // If the sketch is unchanged...
    return;                                   // ... do nothing
  }

  if(currentSketchFile != null) {            // If the sketch has been saved...
    if(saveSketch(currentSketchFile)) {      // .. just save it.
      sketchChanged = false;                  // Write successful
    }
    return;
  }

  // Here, the sketch was never saved...
  Path file = showDialog("Save Sketch",      // ...so display Save dialog
                         "Save",
                         "Save the sketch",
                         sketchFilter,
                         Paths.get(DEFAULT_FILENAME));
  if(file == null) {                         // No file selected...
    return;                                   // ... so we are done.
  }

  file = setFileExtension(file, "ske");      // Make sure extension is .ske

  if(Files.exists(file) &&                   // If the path exists and...
       JOptionPane.NO_OPTION ==              // .. NO selected in dialog...
           JOptionPane.showConfirmDialog(
                           this,
                           file.getFileName() + " exists. Overwrite?",
                           "Confirm Save As",
                           JOptionPane.YES_NO_OPTION,
                           JOptionPane.WARNING_MESSAGE)) {
          return;                             // ...do nothing
  }
  if(saveSketch(file)) {                      // Save the sketch
      currentSketchFile = file;              // Save successful
      setTitle(frameTitle + " - " + currentSketchFile);  // Update title bar
      sketchChanged = false;                  // Sketch now unchanged
  }
}
```

Directory "Sketcher 1 saving a sketch to a file"

You first check the sketchChanged flag. If the flag is false, either the sketch is empty or it hasn't been changed since the last save. Either way, there's no point in writing the sketch to disk, so you return immediately.

If the sketchChanged flag is true, you check the reference stored in currentSketchFile. If it is not null, then you just call the saveSketch() method to write the sketch to the file specified by currentSketchFile—you will implement the saveSketch() method in a moment. You don't need to update the title bar here because it already shows the sketch file path.

The sketch was never saved if currentSketchFile is null, in which case you display the file chooser dialog with the default file name selected. If the showDialog() method returns null, then the dialog was closed without choosing a file so you end the save operation.

You also need to check whether the file exists. If it does, you want to give the user the option not to overwrite it with the current sketch. The condition tested in the `if` looks rather complicated, but this is primarily due to the plethora of arguments in the `showConfirmDialog()` call. You can break the condition down into its component parts quite easily. The condition comprises two logical expressions separated by the `&&` operator. So if both expressions are `true` then you execute a `return`. The first expression results in `false` if `file` does not exist, so if this is the case, you return immediately.

When `file` references a file that already exists, , the second expression in the `if` is evaluated, otherwise it isn't. The second expression is `true` if the value returned from the `showConfirmDialog()` method is `JOptionPane.NO_OPTION`. The confirm dialog just warns of the overwrite potential, so if `JOptionPane.NO_OPTION` is returned, then the user has elected not to overwrite the file.

Remember that if the left operand for the `&&` operator is `false`, then the right operand is not evaluated. This means that the `showConfirmDialog()` method is called only when `file` references a file that already exists. Thus if the NO option is chosen in the dialog, the return is executed and the sketch is not saved. If the YES option is selected, then you don't execute the return statement in the `if` block, but you continue to execute the code that follows, which calls `saveSketch()` with `file` as the argument. After successfully saving the sketch, you update `currentSketchFile` to contain the new file path, set `sketchChanged` to `false` because the sketch has not yet been changed relative to the file contents, and record the path for the current sketch file in the title bar for the application window.

If `showDialog()` returns a non-null reference, the path should end in `.ske`. It won't if the user keys a new name for the file in the dialog without the `.ske` extension. The user might have added their own extension, in which case you want to leave it as it is. However, if the path string does not end in `.ske` and there is no other extension (indicated by the presence of a period in the file name), you should append `.ske`. You achieve this by calling the following method:

```
// Set the extension for a file path
private Path setFileExtension(Path file, String extension) {
  StringBuffer fileName = new StringBuffer(file.getFileName().toString());
  if(fileName.indexOf(extension) >= 0) {
    return file;
  }
  int index = fileName.lastIndexOf(".");
  if(index < 0) {                              // No extension
    fileName.append(".").append(extension);    // so append one
  }
  return file.getParent().resolve(fileName.toString());
}
```

If there is no extension, `.ske` is appended. If there is an extension, check if it is `.ske` or some other choice of the user. In either case we leave it as it is. You could have done this easily with inline code, but this method is more general and is useful later. Add this method definition to the `SketcherFrame` class.

Writing a Sketch to a File

Writing a sketch to a file just involves making use of what you learned about writing objects to a file. You have already made sure that a `SketcherModel` object is serializable, so you can write the sketch to an `ObjectOutputStream` with the following method in the `SketcherFrame` class:

```
// Write a sketch to file path file
private boolean saveSketch(Path file) {
try (ObjectOutputStream out = new ObjectOutputStream(
               new BufferedOutputStream(Files.newOutputStream(file)))) {
    out.writeObject(theApp.getModel());   // Write the sketch to the stream
  } catch(IOException e) {
    System.err.println(e);
    JOptionPane.showMessageDialog(this,
                          "Error writing a sketch to " + file,
                          "File Output Error",
                          JOptionPane.ERROR_MESSAGE);
```

```
            return false;              // Serious error - file not written
        }
        return true;
    }
```

Directory "Sketcher 1 saving a sketch to a file"

The `saveSketch()` method writes the current `SketcherModel` object to the object output stream that you create from the `Path` object that is passed to it. It returns `true` if the write was successful and `false` if there was a problem. This enables the calling program to determine whether or not the file was written.

If an error occurs, an exception of type `IOException` is thrown, in which case you write the exception to the standard error output stream for diagnostic purposes and pop up a dialog indicating that an error has occurred. You assume that the user might want to retry the operation, so you just return `false` from the method rather than terminating the application.

You can now put together the code that handles the Save menu item event.

TRY IT OUT   Saving a Sketch

The code to initiate handling the Save menu item event goes in the `actionPerformed()` method of the `FileAction` inner class. You have done all the real work by implementing the `saveOperation()` and `saveSketch()` methods, so it amounts to just one statement:

Available for download on Wrox.com

```
            public void actionPerformed(ActionEvent e) {
        if(this == saveAction) {
            saveOperation();
            return;
    // else if blocks as before...
    }
```

Directory "Sketcher 1 saving a sketch to a file"

You can recompile Sketcher and run it again. The Save menu item and toolbar button should now be working. When you select either of them, you should get the dialog displayed in Figure 21-1, as long as you have created a sketch to save. Note that you cannot save a new empty sketch because it is unchanged.

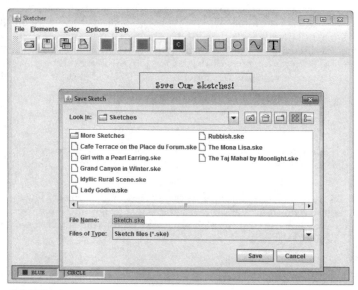

FIGURE 21-1

All the buttons in the dialog are fully operational. Go ahead and try them out, and then save the sketch using the default name. Next time you save the sketch, the dialog doesn't appear. Be sure to check out the button tooltips.

After you have created a few sketch files, you should get the warning shown in Figure 21-2 if you attempt to overwrite an existing sketch file with a new one.

FIGURE 21-2

You can now save any sketch in a file—regardless of its complexity—with protection against accidentally overwriting existing files. I hope you agree that the save operation was relatively easy to implement.

How It Works

When the event is for the `saveAction` object, the `actionPerformed()` method calls the `saveOperation()` method that you defined in the `SketcherFrame` class. This carries out the save operation that writes the `SketcherModel` object to a file.

The file filter `sketchFilter` that you create and pass to the `showDialog()` method is added to the list of available filters in the `JFileChooser` object by passing a reference to the `addChoosableFileFilter()` method. You set this filter as the one in effect by calling the `setFileFilter()` method. The `JFileChooser` object checks each file in the file list by passing each `File` object to the `accept()` method for the file filter object that is in effect. The new file filter you have created returns `true` only for directories, or files with the extension `.ske`, so only those files are displayed in the dialog. The description of the filter is obtained by the `JFileChooser` object calling the `getDescription()` method for the Sketcher `FileFilter` object, and this description is displayed in the dialog.

Of course, the available list of file filters includes the "accept all" filter that is there by default. You might want to suppress this in some situations, and there is a method defined in the `JFileChooser` class to do this:

```
files.setAcceptAllFileFilter(false);        // Remove 'all files' filter
```

Of course, passing an argument of `true` to this method restores the filter to the list. You can also discover whether the "all files" filter is in effect for the dialog by calling the `isAcceptAllFileFilterUsed()` method that returns `true` if it is, or `false` if it isn't.

You can also remove specific `FileFilter` objects from the list maintained by the `JFileChooser` object. This enables you to adapt a `JFileChooser` object to suit circumstances at different points in a program. To remove a filter, just pass a `FileFilter` reference to the `removeChoosableFileFilter()` method for your file chooser object. For example:

```
files.removeChoosableFileFilter(sketchFilter);   // Removes our filter
```

This would remove the filter you have defined for Sketcher files.

Implementing the Save As Operation

For Save As operations, you always want to display a save dialog, regardless of whether the file has been saved before, and ignoring the state of the `sketchChanged` flag. Apart from that and some cosmetic differences in the dialog itself, the operation is very similar to the Save menu item event handling. With the `showDialog()` method that you have added to the `SketcherFrame` class, the implementation becomes quite easy.

File Save As Operations

You can do the trivial bit first. The code in the `else if` block in the `actionPerformed()` method in the `FileAction` class for this operation is:

```
else if(this == saveAsAction) {
    saveAsOperation();
    return;
}
```

Directory "Sketcher 2 with Save As capability"

Now the bit with more meat—the implementation of the `saveAsOperation()` method in the `SketcherFrame` class:

```
private void saveAsOperation() {
    Path file = showDialog("Save Sketch As",
                           "Save",
                           "Save the sketch",
                           sketchFilter,
                           currentSketchFile == null ?
                           Paths.get(DEFAULT_FILENAME): currentSketchFile);

    if(file == null) {                                // No file selected...
        return;                                       // ...so we are done.
    }

    file = setFileExtension(file, "ske");             // Make sure extension is .ske

    if(Files.exists(file) &&
            !file.equals(currentSketchFile) &&
                JOptionPane.NO_OPTION ==               // Overwrite warning
                  JOptionPane.showConfirmDialog(this,
                                     file.getFileName() + " exists. Overwrite?",
                                     "Confirm Save As",
                                     JOptionPane.YES_NO_OPTION,
                                     JOptionPane.WARNING_MESSAGE)) {
        return;                                       // No file selected
    }

    if(saveSketch(file)) {                            // Save the sketch
        currentSketchFile = file;                     // Save successful
        setTitle(frameTitle + " - " + currentSketchFile); // Update title bar
        sketchChanged = false;                        // Sketch now unchanged
    }
}
```

Directory "Sketcher 2 with Save As capability"

If you recompile Sketcher with these additions, you have a working Save As option on the File menu.

How It Works

You have a fancy expression as the last argument to the `showDialog()` method. This is because the Save As operation could be used with a sketch that has been saved previously or with a sketch that has never been saved. The expression passes `currentSketchFile` as the argument if it is not `null` and creates a new `Path` object as the argument from the default file name if `currentSketchFile` is `null`. If you get a `Path` object back from the `showDialog()` method that is null, you know there was no file selected by the user, so you are done.

If `file` is not `null` you must check for a potential overwrite of an existing file, and if there is a conflict you must ask the user if he wants to continue. This is the case if the selected file exists and is also different from `currentSketchFile`. In this instance you want to display a YES/NO dialog warning of this. Checking whether the file exists, whether it is the same as the current file, and displaying the dialog, are all carried out in the `if` expression. If they are all `true` you just return from the method. The three checks are combined with `&&` operators, so from left to right the first check that results in `false` results in `false` for the whole expression, and prevents subsequent operands from being evaluated.

If the selected file does not exist, or if it exists but is not the same as the current file, or if it exists and is the same as the current file and YES was selected in the warning dialog, you want to write the sketch to the file. Thus if any of the three operands are `false`, you save the current sketch in the file.

Because you can record sketches in files, you are ready to look at implementing the operation for the Open menu item where you read them back.

Implementing the File Open Operation

Supporting the file open operation is in some ways a little more complicated than save. You have to consider the currently displayed sketch, first of all. Opening a new sketch replaces it, so does it need to be saved before the file open operation? If it does, you must deal with that before you can read a new sketch from the file. Fortunately, most of this is already done by the `saveOperation()` method that you have implemented in the `SketcherFrame` class. You just need to add a prompt for the save operation when necessary. You could put this in a `checkForSave()` method that you can implement in the `SketcherFrame` class as:

Available for download on Wrox.com

```
// Prompt for save operation when necessary for File Open
public void checkForSave() {
  if(sketchChanged && JOptionPane.YES_OPTION ==
          JOptionPane.showConfirmDialog(this,
                         "Current file has changed. Save current file?",
                         "Confirm Save Current File",
                         JOptionPane.YES_NO_OPTION,
                         JOptionPane.WARNING_MESSAGE)) {
    saveOperation();
  }
}
```

Directory "Sketcher 3 opening sketch files"

This method will be useful outside the `SketcherFrame` class a little later on, so you have defined it as a `public` member of the class. If the `sketchChanged` flag is `true`, the expression that is the right operand for the `&&` operator is evaluated. This pops up a confirmation dialog to verify that the sketch needs to be saved. If it does, you call the `saveOperation()` method to do just that. Of course, if `sketchChanged` has the value `false`, the right operand to the `&&` operator is not evaluated, and so the dialog isn't displayed.

When you get to the point of reading a sketch from the file, some further complications arise. You must replace the existing `SketcherModel` object and its view in the application with a new `SketcherModel` object and its view.

With those few thoughts, you should be ready to make it happen.

TRY IT OUT Implementing the Open Menu Item Operation

The file open process is similar to a save operation, but instead of writing the file, it reads it. You add another helper method, `openSketch()`, to the `SketcherFrame` class that does the reading, given a `Path` object identifying the source of the data. Using this method, the code to handle the `Open` menu item event in the `actionPerformed()` method for the `FileAction` class is:

```
    } else if(this == openAction) {
      // Save current sketch if we need to
      checkForSave();

      // Now open a sketch file
      Path file = showDialog(
                        "Open Sketch File",        // Dialog window title
                        "Open",                    // Button label
                        "Read a sketch from file", // Button tooltip text
                        sketchFilter,              // File filter
                        null);                     // No file selected
      if(file != null) {                           // If a file was selected
        if(openSketch(file)) {                     // ...then read it
          currentSketchFile = file;                // Success!
          setTitle(frameTitle + " - " + currentSketchFile);
          sketchChanged = false;
        }
        return;
      }
    }
```

Directory "Sketcher 3 opening sketch files"

You can implement the `openSketch()` method in the `SketcherFrame` class as follows:

```
// Method for opening a sketch file and creating the model
public boolean openSketch(Path file) {
  try (ObjectInputStream in = new ObjectInputStream(
                  new BufferedInputStream(Files.newInputStream(file)))){
    theApp.insertModel((SketcherModel)in.readObject());
    currentSketchFile = file;
    setTitle(frameTitle+" - "+currentSketchFile);    // Update the window title
    sketchChanged = false;                           // Status is unchanged
  } catch(Exception e) {
    System.err.println(e);
    JOptionPane.showMessageDialog(this,
                          "Error reading a sketch file.",
                          "File Input Error",
                          JOptionPane.ERROR_MESSAGE);
    return false;
  }
  return true;
}
```

Directory "Sketcher 3 opening sketch files"

This method returns `true` if the file read operation is successful and returns `false` if an error occurs. You pass the `SketcherModel` object that is read from the file to a new method in the `Sketcher` class, `insertModel()`. This method has to replace the current sketch with the new one that is passed as the argument.

You can implement the `insertModel()` method in the `Sketcher` class like this:

```
// Insert a new sketch model
public void insertModel(SketcherModel newSketch) {
  sketch = newSketch;                    // Store the new sketch
  sketch.addObserver(view);              // Add the view as observer
  sketch.addObserver(window);            // Add the app window as observer
  view.repaint();                        // Repaint the view
}
```

Directory "Sketcher 3 opening sketch files"

After you have loaded the new model, you update the window title bar and record the status as unchanged in the SketcherFrame object. If you compile Sketcher once more, you can give the file open operation a workout. The Open dialog should be as shown in Figure 21-3.

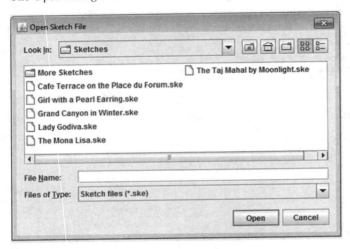

FIGURE 21-3

Don't forget to try out the tooltip for the Open button.

How It Works

After dealing with saving the current sketch in the actionPerformed() member of the FileAction class, you call the showDialog() method that you defined in the SketcherFrame class to display a file open dialog. The showDialog() method is all-purpose—you can put any kind of label on the button or any title in the title bar, so you can use it to display all of the dialogs you need for file operations.

If a file was chosen in the dialog that was displayed by the actionPerformed() method, you pass the Path object that the showDialog() returns to the openSketch() member of the SketcherFrame object to read a new sketch from the file. The openSketch() method creates an ObjectInputStream object from the Path object that was passed to it, and reads a SketcherModel object from the stream by calling the readObject() method. The object returned by the readObject() method has to be cast to the appropriate type—SketcherModel in this case.

You pass this SketcherModel object to the insertModel() method for the application object. This replaces the current sketch reference in the sketch member of the application object with a reference to the new sketch, and then sets the view and the application window as observers. Calling repaint() for the view object displays the new sketch. The paint() method for the view object obtains a reference to the current model by calling the getModel() member of the application object, which returns the reference to the new model.

Starting a New Sketch

The File ⇨ New menu item simply starts a new sketch. This is quite similar to the open operation, except that you must create an empty sketch rather than read a new one from disk. The processes of checking for the need to save the current sketch and inserting the new SketcherModel object into the application are the same.

TRY IT OUT Implementing the New Operation

You need to place the code to create a new empty sketch in the `else-if` block corresponding to the `newAction` object event. This is in the `actionPerformed()` method in the `FileAction` inner class:

Available for
download on
Wrox.com

```
else if(this == newAction) {
    checkForSave();
    theApp.insertModel(new SketcherModel());      // Insert new empty sketch
    currentSketchFile = null;                     // No file for it
    setTitle(frameTitle);
    sketchChanged = false;                        // Not changed yet
    return;
}
```

Directory "Sketcher 4 creating a new sketch"

With this addition to Sketcher you can create a new sketch.

How It Works

All the saving of the existing sketch is dealt with by the `checkForSave()` method that you added to the `SketcherFrame` class. The new part is the last five lines of the highlighted code. You call the `SketcherModel` constructor to create a new empty sketch, and pass it to the `insertModel()` method for the application object. This inserts the new sketch into the application and gets the view object to display it. You then update the data members of the window that record information about the file for the current sketch and its status. You also set the `sketchChanged` flag to `false`, as it's an empty sketch.

Preventing Data Loss on Close

At the moment, the application shuts down immediately when you click the window close icon. This means you could lose hours of work in an instant if you forget to save the sketch. But the solution is very simple. You just need to get the event handler for the window closing event to call the `checkForSave()` method for the window object.

TRY IT OUT Prompting for Save on Close

To implement this you can use the `WindowListener` object for the application window that you have already added in the `Sketcher` class. This listener receives notification of events associated with opening and closing the window, as well as minimizing and maximizing it. You just need to add some code to the body of the `windowClosing()` method for the listener. You require one extra line in the Sketcher class definition:

Available for
download on
Wrox.com

```
// Handler class for window events
  class WindowHandler extends WindowAdapter {
    // Handler for window closing event
    public void windowClosing(WindowEvent e) {
      window.checkForSave();
    }
  }
```

Directory "Sketcher 5 checking for save on close and exit"

This ensures that a sketch is not lost when you click on the close icon for the application window.

How It Works

The `WindowHandler` class is a subclass of the `WindowAdapter` class. In the subclass you just define the methods you are interested in to override the empty versions in the adapter class. You saw in Chapter 18 that the `WindowListener` interface declares seven methods corresponding to various window events, but you need just the `windowClosing()` method.

Clearly, using the `WindowAdapter` class as a base saves a lot of time and effort. Without it you would have to define all seven of the methods declared in the interface in our class. Because the `WindowHandler` class is an inner class, its methods can access the fields of the `Sketcher` class, so the `windowClosing()` method can call the `checkForSave()` method for the `window` member of the `Sketcher` class object.

Now if you close the application window without having saved your sketch, you are prompted to save it.

Defining the `WindowHandler` inner class explicitly with just one method is not the only way to do this. You could use an anonymous class, as the method is so simple. If you removed the `WindowHandler` inner class from the Sketcher class, you could replace the statement that adds the window listener for the window object with the following statement:

```
window.addWindowListener(new WindowAdapter() {   // Add window listener
                           public void windowClosing(WindowEvent e) {
                             window.checkForSave();
                           }
                         } );
```

This defines an anonymous class derived from the `WindowHandler` class in the expression that is the argument to the `addWindowListener()` method. The syntax is exactly the same as if you were defining an anonymous class that implements an interface. The class defines just one method, the `windowClosing()` method that you defined previously in the `WindowHandler` class.

This makes use of the code that you implemented for the save operation, packaged in the `checkForSave()` method. This does everything necessary to enable the sketch to be saved before the application window is closed. Defining methods judiciously makes for economical coding.

This still leaves you with the File ⇨ Close and File ⇨ Exit items to tidy up. Closing a sketch is not really any different from the File ⇨ New function, so you could implement it in exactly the same way. You could combine handling the `closeAction` event with the `newAction` event by changing the `if-else` block for `newAction` in the definition of `actionPerformed()` in the `FileAction` inner class to:

Available for download on Wrox.com

```
} else if(this == newAction || this == closeAction){
  checkForSave();
  theApp.insertModel(new SketcherModel());     // Insert new empty sketch
  currentSketchFile  = null;                   // No file for it
  setTitle(frameTitle);
  sketchChanged = false;                       // Not changed yet
  return;
} else if(this == printAction) {
```

Directory "Sketcher 5 checking for save on close and exit"

The Exit menu item terminates the application, so handling the event for this just involves calling `checkForSave()` to make sure the current sketch is not lost inadvertently:

```
} else if(this == exitAction) {
  checkForSave();
  System.exit(0);
}
```

Directory "Sketcher 5 checking for save on close and exit"

All but one of the file menu items are now operable. To complete the set you just need to get printing up and running.

PRINTING IN JAVA

Printing is always a messy business—inevitably so, because you have to worry about tedious details such as the size of a page, the margin sizes, and how many pages you're going to need for your output. As you might expect, there are differences between the process for printing an image and printing text, but the basic mechanism is the same. You may have the added complication of several printers with different capabilities being available, so with certain types of documents you need to select an appropriate printer. The way through this is to take it one step at a time. Let's understand the general principles first.

There are five packages dedicated to supporting printing capabilities in Java:

➤ `javax.print`: Defines classes and interfaces that enable you to determine what printers are available and what their capabilities are. It also enables you to identify types of documents to be printed.

➤ `javax.print.attribute`: Defines classes and interfaces supporting the definition of sets of printing attributes. For example, you can define a set of attributes required by a particular document when it is printed, such as color output and two-sided printing.

➤ `javax.print.attribute.standard`: Defines classes that identify a set of standard printing attributes.

➤ `javax.print.event`: Defines classes that identify events that can occur while printing and interfaces that identify listeners for printing events.

➤ `java.awt.print`: Defines classes and attributes for expediting the printing of 2D graphics and text.

The first four make up what is called the *Print Service API*. This allows printing on all Java platforms and has facilities for discovering and using multiple printers with varying capabilities. Because in all probability you have just a single printer available, I'm concentrating on explaining the classes and interfaces defined in the `java.awt.print` package that carry out print operations on a given printer, and stray into classes and interfaces from the other packages when necessary.

Four classes are defined in the `java.awt.print` package, and you use all of them eventually:

➤ `PrinterJob` objects: Control printing to a particular print service (such as a printer or fax capability).

➤ `PageFormat` objects: Define information about a page to be printed, such as its dimensions, margin sizes, and orientation.

➤ `Paper` objects: Define the size and printable area of sheets of paper.

➤ `Book` objects: Define a multipage documents where pages may have different formats and require different rendering processes.

The `PrinterJob` class drives the printing process. Don't confuse this with the `PrintJob` class in the `java.awt` package—this is involved in the old printing process that was introduced in Java 1.1, and the `PrinterJob` class now supersedes this. A `PrinterJob` object provides the interface to a printer in your environment, and you use `PrinterJob` class methods to set up and initiate the printing process for a particular document. You start printing off one or more pages in a document by calling the `print()` method for the `PrinterJob` object.

You'll get into the details of how you work with the other types of objects in the list a little later in this chapter.

There are three interfaces in the `java.awt.print` package:

➤ `Printable` : Implemented by a class to print a single page.

➤ `Pageable`: Implemented by a class to print a multipage document, where each page may be printed by a different `Printable` object. This allows pages in a document to have independent specifications, such as orientation and margin sizes.

➤ `PrinterGraphics`: Declares a method for obtaining a reference to the `PrinterJob` object for use in a method that is printing a page.

When you print a page, an object of a class that implements the `Printable` interface determines what is actually printed. Such an object is referred to as a *page painter*. Figure 21-4 illustrates the basics of how the printing process works.

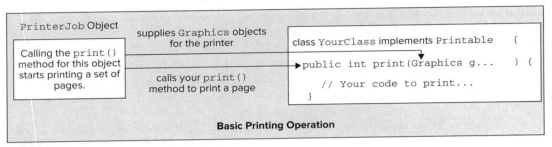

FIGURE 21-4

The `Printable` interface defines only one method, `print()`, which is called by a `PrinterJob` object when a page should be printed, so this method prints a page. Note that I have mentioned two `print()` methods, one defined in the `PrinterJob` class that you call to starting the printing process and another declared in the `Printable` interface. You implement the latter in your class that is to do the printing legwork for a single page.

The printing operation that you must code when you implement the `Printable` interface works through a graphics context object that provides the means for writing data to your printer. The first argument passed to your `print()` method when it is called by a `PrinterJob` object is a reference of type `Graphics` that represents the graphics context for the printer. The object that it references is actually of type `Graphics2D`, which parallels the process you are already familiar with for drawing on a component. You use the methods defined in the `Graphics` and `Graphics2D` classes to print what you want, and the basic mechanism for printing 2D graphics or text on a page is identical to drawing on a component. The `Graphics` object for a printer implements the `PrinterGraphics` interface (not to be confused with the `PrintGraphics` interface in the `java.awt` package!) that declares just one method, `getPrinterJob()`. You call this method to obtain a reference to the object that is managing the print process. You do this if you need to call `PrinterJob` methods to extract information about the print job, such as the job name or the user name.

A class that implements the `Pageable` interface defines an object that represents a set of pages to be printed, rather than a single page. You would implement this interface for more complicated printing situations in which a different page painter may print each page using an individual `PageFormat` object. It's the job of the `Pageable` object to supply information to the `PrinterJob` object about which page painter and `PageFormat` object should be used to print each page. The `Pageable` interface declares three methods:

➤   `getNumberOfPages()`: Returns the number of pages to be printed as type `int`, or the constant value `UNKNOWN_NUMBER_OF_PAGES` if the number of pages is not known. This constant is defined in the `Pageable` interface.

➤   `getPageFormat(int pageIndex)`: Returns a `PageFormat` object describing the size and orientation of the page specified by the argument. An exception of type `IndexOutOfBoundsException` is thrown if the page does not exist.

➤   `getPrintable(int pageIndex)`: Returns a reference to the `Printable` object responsible for printing the page specified by the argument. An exception of type `IndexOutOfBoundsException` is thrown if the page does not exist.

A `Book` object also encapsulates a document that consists of a number of pages, each of which may be processed individually for printing. The difference between this and an object of a class that implements the `Pageable` interface is that you can add individual pages to a `Book` object programmatically, whereas an object of a class that implements `Pageable` encapsulates all the pages. You look at how both of these options work later in this chapter.

Creating and Using PrinterJob Objects

Because the `PrinterJob` class encapsulates and manages the printing process for a given physical printer that is external to the Java Virtual Machine (JVM), you can't create an object of type `PrinterJob` directly using a constructor. You obtain a reference to a `PrinterJob` object for the default printer on a system by calling the static method `getPrinterJob()` that is defined in the `PrinterJob` class:

```
PrinterJob printJob = PrinterJob.getPrinterJob(); // For the default printer
```

The `printJob` object provides the interface to the default printer and controls each print job that you send to it.

A printer is encapsulated by a `javax.print.PrintService` object, and you can obtain a reference of type `PrintService` to an object encapsulating the printer that is used by a `PrinterJob` object by calling its `getPrintService()` method:

```
PrintService printer = printJob().getPrintService();
```

You can query the object that is returned for information about the capabilities of the printer and the kinds of documents it can print, but I won't divert down that track for the moment. One point you should keep in mind is that sometimes a printer may not be available on the machine on which your code is running. In this case the `getPrintService()` method returns `null`, so it's a good idea to call the method and test the reference that is returned, even if you don't want to obtain details of the printer.

If multiple print services are available, such as several printers or perhaps a fax capability, you can obtain an array of `PrintService` references for them by calling the static `lookupPrintServices()` method that is defined in the `PrinterJob` class. For example:

```
PrintService[] printers = PrinterJob.lookupPrintServices();
```

The `printers` array has one element for each print service that is available. If no print services are available, the array has zero length. If you want to select a specific printer for the `PrinterJob` object to work with, you just pass the array element corresponding to the print service of your choice to the `setPrintService()` method for the `PrinterJob` object. For example:

```
if(printers.length>0) {
  printJob.setPrintService(printers[0]);
}
```

The `if` statement checks that there are some print services before attempting to set the print service. Without this you could get an `IndexOutOfBoundsException` exception if the `printers` array has no elements. Of course, more realistically, you would use methods defined in the `PrintService` interface to query the printers, and use the results to decide which printer to use.

Displaying a Print Dialog

When you want to provide the user with control over the printing process, you can display a print dialog by calling the `printDialog()` method for a `PrinterJob` object. This method displays the modal dialog that applies to your particular print facility. There are two versions of the `printDialog()` method. The version without arguments displays the native dialog if the `PrinterJob` object is printing on a native printer, so I'm introducing that first and return to the other version later.

If the print dialog is closed using the button that indicates printing should proceed, the `printDialog()` method returns `true`; otherwise, it returns `false`. The method throws a `java.awt.HeadlessException` if there is no display attached to the system. Thus, to initiate printing, you can call the `printDialog()` method to put the decision to proceed in the hands of the user, and if the method returns `true`, call the `print()` method for the `PrinterJob` object to start printing. Note that the `print()` method throws a `java.awt.print.PrinterException` if an error in the printing system causes the operation to be aborted.

Of course, the `PrinterJob` object has no prior knowledge of what you want to print, so you have to call a method to tell the `PrinterJob` object where the printed pages are coming from before you initiate printing. The simplest way to do this is to pass a reference to an object of a class that implements the `Printable` interface to the `setPrintable()` method.

In Sketcher, the obvious candidate to print a sketch is the `SketcherView` object, and you could provide for the possibility of sketches being printed by making the `SketcherView` class implement the `Printable` interface. You could then set the source of the printed output by passing a reference to the view to the `setPrintable()` method for a `PrinterJob` object. You might consider the `SketcherModel` object to be a candidate to do the printing, but printing is really no more related to a sketch than plotting it or displaying it on the screen. The model is the input to the printing process, not the owner of it. It is generally better to keep the model dedicated to encapsulating the data that represents the sketch.

Starting the Printing Process

You can use what you now know about printing to add some code to the `actionPerformed()` method in the `FileAction` inner class to `SketcherFrame`. This handles the event for the `printAction` object:

```
if(this == printAction) {
  // Get a printing object
  PrinterJob printJob = PrinterJob.getPrinterJob();
  PrintService printer = printJob.getPrintService();
  if(printer == null) {                            // See if there is a printer
    JOptionPane.showMessageDialog(SketcherFrame.this,
                                  "No default printer available.",
                                  "Printer Error",
                                  JOptionPane.ERROR_MESSAGE);
    return;
  }
  // The view is the page source
  printJob.setPrintable(theApp.getView());

  if(printJob.printDialog()) {                     // Display print dialog

    try {                                          // and if true is returned...
      printJob.print();                            // ...then print
    } catch(PrinterException pe) {
      System.out.println(pe);
      JOptionPane.showMessageDialog(SketcherFrame.this,
                                    "Error printing a sketch.",
                                    "Printer Error",
                                    JOptionPane.ERROR_MESSAGE);

    }
  }
} else if(this == exitAction) {
  checkForSave();
  System.exit(0);
}
```

Directory "Sketcher 6 printing a sketch"

The code here obtains a `PrinterJob` object and, after verifying that there is a printer to print on, sets the view as the printable source. You don't need access to the `PrinterService` object to print, but it's one way of verifying that a printer is available. The expression for the second `if` displays a print dialog, and if the return value from the `printDialog()` method call is `true`, you call the `print()` method for the `printJob` object to start the printing process. This is one of two overloaded `print()` methods that the `PrinterJob` class defines. You look into the other one when you try out the alternative `printDialog()` method a little later in this chapter.

Two more `import` statements are needed in the `SketcherFrame.java` file:

```
import javax.print.PrintService;
import java.awt.print.*;
```

The `SketcherFrame` class still doesn't compile at the moment because you haven't made the `SketcherView` class implement the `Printable` interface yet.

Printing Pages

The object that you pass to the `setPrintable()` method is responsible for all the details of the printing process. The object class type must implement the `Printable` interface, which implies defining the `print()` method in the class. You can make the `SketcherView` class implement the `Printable` interface like this:

```
// Import statements as before...
import java.awt.print.*;

class SketcherView extends JComponent implements Observer, Printable {
    // Constructor code etc. as before...
    // Print the sketch on a local printer
    public int print(Graphics g,                // Graphics context for printing
                     PageFormat pageFormat,     // The page format
                     int pageIndex)             // Index number of current page
                 throws PrinterException {
      // Code to do the printing...
    }

    // Rest of the class definition as before...
}
```

The code that you added to the `actionPerformed()` method in the `FileAction` inner class to `SketcherFrame` identified the `SketcherView` object to the `PrinterJob` object as responsible for executing the printing of a page. The `PrinterJob` object therefore calls the `print()` method that you have defined here for each page to be printed. This process starts when you call the `print()` method for the `PrinterJob` object that has overall control of the printing process.

You can see that the `print()` method in `SketcherView` can throw an exception of type `PrinterException`. If you identify a problem within your `print()` method code, the way to signal the problem to the `PrinterJob` object is to throw an exception of this type.

 NOTE *Keep in mind that you cannot assume that the* `PrinterJob` *object calls the* `print()` *method for your* `Printable` *object just once per page. In general, the* `print()` *method is likely to be called several times for each page because the output to the printer is buffered within the Java printing system, and the buffer is not necessarily large enough to hold a complete page. You don't need to worry about this unduly. Just don't build any assumptions into your code about how often* `print()` *is called for a given page.*

Of course, the `PrinterJob` object in the `actionPerformed()` method code has no way of knowing how many pages need to be printed. When you call the `PrinterJob` object's `print()` method, it continues calling the `SketcherView` object's `print()` method until the value returned indicates there are no more pages to be printed. You can return one of two values from the `print()` method in the `Printable` interface—either `PAGE_EXISTS`, to indicate you have rendered a page, or `NO_SUCH_PAGE` when there are no more pages to be printed. Both constants are defined in the `Printable` interface. The `PrinterJob` object continues calling the `print()` method for the `Printable` object until the method returns the value `NO_SUCH_PAGE`. If you don't make sure that the `print()` method returns this value at some point, you have an indefinite loop in the program.

Three arguments are passed to the print() method in the Printable interface. The first is the graphics context that you must use to write to the printer. The reference is to an object of type Graphics2D, so you typically cast it to this type before using it—just as you did within the paint() method for a component. In the print() method in the view class, you could draw the sketch on the printer with the following statements:

```
public int print(Graphics g,                  // Graphics context for printing
                 PageFormat pageFormat,        // The page format
                 int pageIndex)                // Index number of current page
              throws PrinterException {
   Graphics2D g2D = (Graphics2D) g;
   paint(g2D);
   return PAGE_EXISTS;
}
```

This works after a fashion, but you have more work to do before you can try this out. At the moment, it prints the same page over and over, indefinitely, so let's take care of that as a matter of urgency!

The third argument to print() is an index value for the page. The first page in a print job has index value 0, the second has index value 1, and so on for as long as there are more pages to be printed. If you intend to print a sketch on a single page, you can stop the printing process by checking the page index:

```
public int print(Graphics g,                  // Graphics context for printing
                 PageFormat pageFormat,        // The page format
                 int pageIndex)                // Index number of current page
              throws PrinterException {
   if(pageIndex > 0) {
     return NO_SUCH_PAGE;
   }
   Graphics2D g2D = (Graphics2D) g;
   paint(g2D);                                 // Draw the sketch
   return PAGE_EXISTS;
}
```

You want to print only one page, so if the value passed as the third parameter is greater than 0, you return NO_SUCH_PAGE to stop the printing process.

Although you won't now print endlessly, you still won't get the output formatted the way you want it. You must use the information provided by the second argument that is passed to the print() method, the PageFormat object, to position the sketch properly on the paper.

The PageFormat Class

The PageFormat reference that is passed as the second argument to the print() method provides details of the page size, the position and size of the printable area on the page, and the orientation—portrait or landscape.

Perhaps the most important pieces of information is where the top-left corner of the printable area (or *imageable area* to use the terminology of the method names) is on the page and its width and height, because this is the area you have available for printing your output. The printable area on a page is simply the area within the current margins that are defined for your printer. The position of the printable area is returned by the methods getImageableX() and getImageableY(). These return the *x* and *y* coordinates of the top-left corner of the printable area in user coordinates for the printing context as values of type double, which happen to be in units of 1/72 of an inch, which, as luck would have it, corresponds to a *point*—as in *point* size for a font. The width and height of the printable area are returned in the same units by the getImageableWidth() and getImageableHeight() methods for the PageFormat object.

The origin of the page coordinate system, the point (0,0), corresponds initially to the top-left corner of the paper. If you want the output to be placed in the printable area on the page, the first step is to move the origin of the graphics context that you use for writing to the printer to the position of the top-left corner of the printable area. Figure 21-5 illustrates the way you do this.

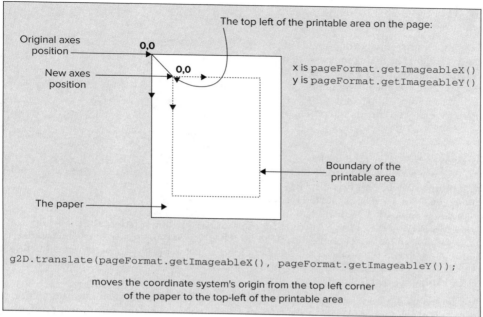

FIGURE 21-5

You know how to do this; it's exactly what you have been doing in the draw() method for each of our element classes. You call the translate() method for the graphics context to move the origin for the user coordinate system. Here's how this would work for the print() method in the SketcherView class:

Available for download on Wrox.com

```java
public int print(Graphics g,                    // Graphics context for printing
                 PageFormat pageFormat,         // The page format
                 int pageIndex)                 // Index number of current page
                 throws PrinterException {
  if(pageIndex>0) {
    return NO_SUCH_PAGE;
  }
  Graphics2D g2D = (Graphics2D) g;

  // Move origin to page printing area corner
  g2D.translate(pageFormat.getImageableX(), pageFormat.getImageableY());

  paint(g2D);                                   // Draw the sketch
  return PAGE_EXISTS;
}
```

Directory "Sketcher 6 printing a sketch"

Calling the translate() method for the Graphics2D object moves the user coordinate system so that the (0,0) point is positioned at the top-left corner of the printable area on the page.

Let's see if that works in practice.

TRY IT OUT Printing a Sketch

You should have added the code you saw earlier to the actionPerformed() method in the FileAction inner class to SketcherView to handle the Print menu item event, and added the code to SketcherView to implement the Printable interface. If you compile and run Sketcher, you should be able to print a sketch.

On my system, when I select the toolbar button to print, I get the dialog shown in Figure 21-6.

This is the standard dialog for my printer. You should get a dialog for your default printer. The dialog indicates that there are 9999 pages to be printed. Because you haven't specified how many pages there are, the maximum is assumed. You only print the number of pages that the `print()` method allows though, and this should be 1.

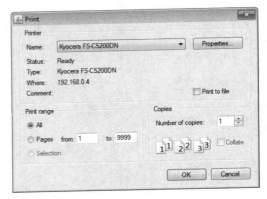

How It Works

The code in the `actionPerformed()` method in the `FileAction` class executes when you click the toolbar button or menu item to print a sketch. This first displays the print dialog by calling the `printDialog()` method for the `PrinterJob` object that you obtain. Clicking the OK

FIGURE 21-6

button causes the dialog to close and the `print()` method for the `PrinterJob` object to be called. This in turn causes the `print()` method in the `SketcherView` class to be called one or more times for each page that is to be printed, and once more to end the process. The number of pages that are printed is determined by the `print()` method in the `SketcherView` class. Only when this method returns the value `NO_SUCH_PAGE` does the `PrinterJob` object cease calling the method.

In the `print()` method in `SketcherView`, you adjust the origin of the user coordinate system for the graphics context so that its position is at the top-left corner of the printable area on the page. Only one page is printed because you return `NO_SUCH_PAGE` when the page index value that is passed to the `print()` method is greater than 0. Incidentally, if you want to see how many times the `print()` method is called for a page, just add a statement at the beginning of the method to output some trace information to the console.

I used the print facility to print the sketch shown in Figure 21-7, and frankly, I was disappointed.

FIGURE 21-7

The picture that I get printed on the paper is incomplete. The flowers and rocks to the right are not in in view, and that interesting cross between a rabbit and a cat is missing. I was hoping to see the picture in its full glory.

If you think about it, though, it's very optimistic to believe that you could automatically get the whole sketch printed. First of all, neither the `PrinterJob` object nor the view object has any idea how big the sketch is.

That's a fairly fundamental piece of data if you want a complete sketch printed. Another consideration is that the sketch might be wider than it is high, and you are printing in portrait orientation. Moreover, in general parts of the sketch might be outside the screen area—when you draw a circle with the center close to the edge of the application window for instance. Let's see how you might deal with some of these problems.

> **NOTE** *Note that material change to the* `Element` *subclasses cause problems in retrieving old sketches. Sketches that were serialized before the changes do not deserialize afterward, because the class definition you use to read the data is different from the class definition when you wrote it. You should always change the value of* `serialVersionUID` *when you change the class definition.*

Printing the Whole Sketch

A starting point is to figure out the extent of the sketch. Ideally you need a rectangle that encloses all the elements in the sketch. It's really surprisingly easy to get that. Every element has a `getBounds()` method that returns a `java.awt.Rectangle` object enclosing the element. As you saw in Chapter 17, the `Rectangle` class defines an `add()` method that combines the `Rectangle` object that you pass as the argument with the `Rectangle` object for which you called the method, and returns the smallest `Rectangle` object that encloses both; this is referred to as the *union* of the two rectangles. With these two bits of information and by accessing the elements in the list in the `SketcherModel` object, you can get a rectangle that encloses the entire sketch by implementing the following method in the `SketcherModel` class:

Available for download on Wrox.com

```
// Get the rectangle enclosing an entire sketch
Rectangle getModelExtent() {
  Rectangle rect = new Rectangle();          // An empty rectangle
  for(Element element : elements) {          // Go through the list
    rect.add(element.getBounds());           // Expand union
  }
  if(rect.width == 0) {                      // Make sure width
    rect.width = 2;                          // is non-zero
  }
  if(rect.height == 0) {                     // and the height
    rect.height = 2;
  }
  return rect;
}
```

Directory "Sketcher 7 printing the whole sketch"

Don't forget to add an `import` statement for the `Rectangle` class name to the `SketcherModel` source file:

```
import java.awt.Rectangle;
```

Using the collection-based `for` loop to iterate over the elements in the list, you generate the union of the bounding rectangles for all the elements, so you end up with a rectangle that bounds everything in the sketch. A zero width or height for the rectangle is unlikely, but you want to be sure it can't happen because you use these values as divisors later. A minimum width and height of 2 ensures that the rectangle has an interior.

You can see from Figure 21-8 how the rectangle returned by the `getModelExtent()` method is simply the rectangle that encloses all the bounding rectangles for the individual elements. If you visualize the origin of the user coordinate system being placed at the top-left corner of the printable area on the page, you can appreciate that a section of the sketch in the illustration is hanging out to the left outside the printable area. This can arise quite easily in Sketcher—when you are drawing a circle with the center close to either of the axes, for example, or if you move a shape so this is the case. You can avoid missing part of the sketch from the printed output by first translating the origin of the graphics context to the top-left corner of the printable area on the page and then translating the origin of the coordinate system to the top-left corner of `rect`.

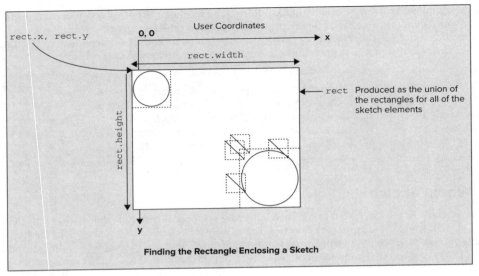

Finding the Rectangle Enclosing a Sketch

FIGURE 21-8

The following code in the print() method in the SketcherView class does this:

```
public int print(Graphics g,                    // Graphics context for printing
                 PageFormat pageFormat,          // The page format
                 int pageIndex)                  // Index number of current page
            throws PrinterException {
  if(pageIndex>0) {
    return NO_SUCH_PAGE;
  }
  Graphics2D g2D = (Graphics2D) g;
  // Get sketch bounds
  Rectangle rect = theApp.getModel().getModelExtent();

  // Move origin to page printing area corner
  g2D.translate(pageFormat.getImageableX(), pageFormat.getImageableY());
  g2D.translate(-rect.x, -rect.y);       // Move origin to rect top left
  paint(g2D);                             // Draw the sketch
  return PAGE_EXISTS;
}
```

You get the rectangle bounding the sketch by calling the getModelExtent() method that you put together just now. You move the origin for the graphics context so that it corresponds to the top-left corner of the printable area on the page. You then use rect to position the new origin at the top-left corner of rect. You could have combined these two translations into one, but it's better in this instance to keep them separate, first to make it easier to see what is going on, and second because you'll later be adding some other transformations in between these translations. There is a potentially puzzling aspect to the second translation—why are the arguments to the translate() method negative to move the origin to the top-left corner of rect?

To understand this, it is important to be clear about what you are doing. It's easy to get confused, so I'm taking it step by step. First of all, the paper is a physical entity with given dimensions, and its coordinate system just defines where each point ends up on the paper when you print something. Of course, you can move the coordinate system for the paper about, and you can scale or even rotate it to get something printed where you want. None of this affects what you are printing. If you have a rectangle object at (5,5) with a width of 20 and a height of 10, that is what it will always be, unless you change the object. You always print it at position (5,5). If you want this object to appear at the top-left corner of the paper then the coordinates of the top-left corner of the paper must be (5,5).

Now consider our sketch. The point (`rect.x`, `rect.y`) is the top-left corner of the rectangle bounding our sketch, the area you want to transfer to the page, and this point is fixed—you can't change it. With the current paper coordinates at the top-left corner of the printable area, it might print something like that shown in Figure 21-9.

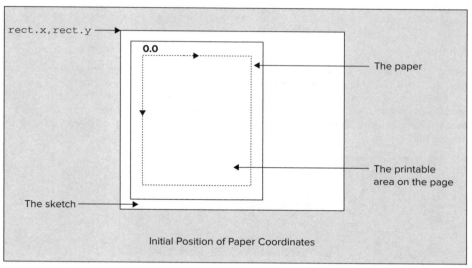

FIGURE 21-9

When you print a sketch you really want the point (`rect.x`, `rect.y`) to end up at the top-left corner of the printable area on the page. In other words, you have to move the origin of the coordinate system for the paper so that the point (`rect.x`, `rect.y`) in the new coordinate system is the top-left corner of the printable area. To do this you must move the origin to the new position shown in Figure 21-10.

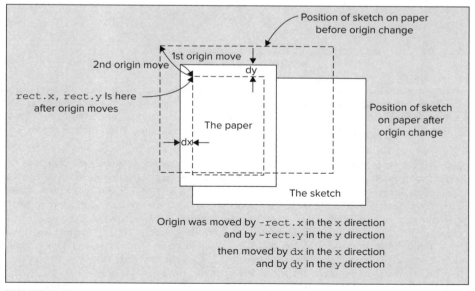

FIGURE 21-10

A translation of the paper origin to the top-left corner of the printable area, followed by a translation of the new origin to point (-rect.x, -rect.y) makes the position (rect.x,rect.y) the top-left corner of the printable area on the paper.

You have the sketch in the right place on the page, but it won't necessarily fit into the space available on the paper. You must scale the sketch so that it doesn't hang out beyond the right side or below the bottom of the printable page area.

Scaling the Sketch to Fit

You saw earlier that you can get the width and height of the printable area on a page by calling the getImageableWidth() and getImageableHeight() methods for the PageFormat object that is passed to the print() method. You also have the width and height of the rectangle that encloses the entire sketch. This provides the information that you need to scale the sketch to fit on the page. There are a couple of tricky aspects that you need to think about, though. Figure 21-11 shows what happens when you scale up by a factor of 2, for example.

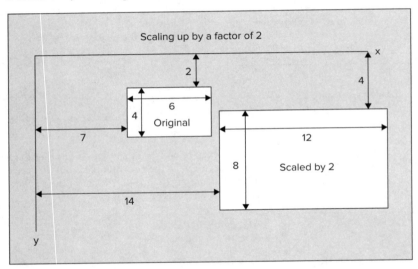

FIGURE 21-11

First, note that when you scale a coordinate system, a unit of length along each of the axes changes so things move relative to the origin as well as relative to one another. When you scale up with a factor greater than 1, everything moves away from the origin. You can see in Figure 21-11 how scaling up by a factor of 2 causes the dimensions of the rectangle to double, and the distances of the new rectangle from each of the axes are also doubled.

The reverse happens with scale factors less than 1. You want to make sure that you scale the sketch to fit the page while keeping its top-left corner at the top left of the printable area. This means that you can't just apply the scaling factor necessary to make the sketch fit the page in the new coordinate system I showed in the previous illustration. If you were to scale with this coordinate system, the sketch would move in relation to the origin, away from it if you are scaling up, as is the case in Figure 21-11, or toward it if you are scaling down. As a consequence, the top-left corner of the sketch would no longer be at the top left of the printable area. Thus you must apply the scaling operation to make the sketch fit on the page *after* you have translated the paper origin to the top-left corner of the printable area, but *before* you translate this origin point to make the top-left corner of the sketch appear at the top-left corner of the printable area. This ensures that the sketch is scaled to fit the page, and the top-left corner of the sketch stays at the top-left corner of the printable area on the page and doesn't move to some other point.

Secondly, you want to make sure that you scale *x* and *y* by the same factor. If you apply different scales to the *x* and *y* axes in the user coordinate system, the relative proportions of a sketch are not maintained and circles become ellipses and squares become rectangles.

You can calculate the scale factors you need to apply to get the sketch to fit within the printable area of the page with the following statements:

```
// Calculate the x and y scales to fit the sketch to the page
double scaleX = pageFormat.getImageableWidth()/rect.width;
double scaleY = pageFormat.getImageableHeight()/rect.height;
```

You are using variables of type `double` for the scale factors here because the `getImageableWidth()` and `getImageableHeight()` methods return values of type `double`. The scale factor for the *x*-axis needs to be such that when you multiply the width of the sketch, `rect.width`, by the scale factor, the result is no greater than the width of the printable area on the page, and similarly for scaling the *y*-axis. Because you want to apply the same scale to both axes, you should calculate the minimum of the scale factors `scaleX` and `scaleY`. If you then apply this minimum to both axes, the sketch fits within the width and height of the page and is still in proportion.

TRY IT OUT Printing the Whole Sketch

You just need to add some code to the `print()` method in `SketcherView` to calculate the required scale factor, and then use the `scale()` method for the `Graphics2D` object to apply the scaling transformation:

Available for
download on
Wrox.com

```
public int print(Graphics g,                    // Graphics context for printing
                 PageFormat pageFormat,         // The page format
                 int pageIndex)                 // Index number of current page
                 throws PrinterException {
  if(pageIndex>0) {
    return NO_SUCH_PAGE;
  }
  Graphics2D g2D = (Graphics2D) g;
  // Get sketch bounds
  Rectangle rect = theApp.getModel().getModelExtent();

  // Calculate the scale to fit sketch to page
  double scaleX = pageFormat.getImageableWidth()/rect.width;
  double scaleY = pageFormat.getImageableHeight()/rect.height;

  // Get minimum scale factor
  double scale = Math.min(scaleX, scaleY);

  // Move origin to page printing area corner
  g2D.translate(pageFormat.getImageableX(), pageFormat.getImageableY());

  g2D.scale(scale, scale);                      // Apply scale factor

  g2D.translate(-rect.x, -rect.y);              // Move origin to rect top left

  paint(g2D);                                   // Draw the sketch
  return PAGE_EXISTS;
}
```

Directory "Sketcher 7 printing the whole sketch"

If you compile and run Sketcher with these changes, you should now be able to print each sketch within a page.

How It Works

You calculate the scaling factors for each axis as the ratio of the dimension of the printable area on the page to the corresponding dimension of the rectangle enclosing the sketch. You then take the minimum of these two scale factors as the scale to be applied to both axes. As long as the scale transformation is applied before the translation of the top-left corner of `rect` to the top-left corner of the printable page area, one or other dimension of the sketch fits exactly within the printable area of the page.

The output is now fine, but if the width of the sketch is greater than the height, you waste a lot of space on the page. Ideally in this situation you should print with a landscape orientation rather than the default portrait orientation. Let's see what possibilities you have for doing that.

Printing in Landscape Orientation

You can easily determine when a landscape orientation would be preferable by comparing the width of a sketch with its height. If the width is larger than the height, a landscape orientation makes better use of the space on the paper and you get a larger-scale picture.

You can set the orientation of the output in relation to the page by calling the `setOrientation()` method for the `PageFormat` object. You can pass one of three possible argument values to this method, which are defined within the `PageFormat` class (shown in Table 21-1):

TABLE 21-1: setOrientation() Method Arguments

ARGUMENT VALUE	DESCRIPTION
PORTRAIT	The origin is at the top-left corner of the page, with the positive *x*-axis running from left to right and the positive *y*-axis running from top to bottom. This is the Microsoft Windows and Postscript portrait definition.
LANDSCAPE	The origin is at the bottom-left corner of the page, with the positive *x*-axis running from bottom to top and the positive *y*-axis running from left to right.
REVERSE_LANDSCAPE	The origin is at the top-right corner of the page, with the positive *x*-axis running from top to bottom and the positive *y*-axis running from right to left. This is the Apple Macintosh landscape definition.

In each case the long side of the paper is in the same orientation as the y-axis, but note that an Apple Macintosh landscape specification has the origin at the top-right corner of the page rather than the top-left or bottom-left.

You might think that you can incorporate `LANDSCAPE` orientation into the `print()` method in `SketcherView` by changing the `PageFormat` object:

```
public int print(Graphics g,              // Graphics context for printing
                 PageFormat pageFormat,    // The page format
                 int pageIndex)            // Index number of current page
          throws PrinterException {
  if(pageIndex>0) {
    return NO_SUCH_PAGE;
  }
  Graphics2D g2D = (Graphics2D) g;
```

```
                // Get sketch bounds
                Rectangle rect = theApp.getModel().getModelExtent();

                // If the width is more than the height, set landscape - not effective!
                if(rect.width>rect.height) {
                  pageFormat.setOrientation(pageFormat.LANDSCAPE);
                }

                // Rest of the code as before...
            }
```

Having set the orientation for the PageFormat object, the methods returning the coordinates for the position of the printable area, and the width and height all return values consistent with the orientation. Thus the width of the printable area is greater than the height if the orientation has been set to LANDSCAPE. Everything looks fine until you try it out. It just doesn't work. The PageFormat object that is passed to the print() method here is a carrier of information—the information that the PrinterJob method used when it created the graphics context object. The coordinate system in the graphics context has already been set up with whatever paper orientation was set in the PageFormat object, and changing it here is too late. The solution is to make sure the PrinterJob object that controls the printing process works with a PageFormat object that has the orientation set the way that you want.

If you had known ahead of time, back in the actionPerformed() method in the FileAction inner class to SketcherFrame, you could have set up the PageFormat object for the print job before the print() method for the view object ever gets called. You can still do this by modifying the code that initiates printing in the actionPerformed() method like this:

```
                // Get a printing object
                PrinterJob printJob = PrinterJob.getPrinterJob();
                PrintService printer = printJob.getPrintService();
                if(printer == null) {
                  JOptionPane.showMessageDialog(SketcherFrame.this,
                                                "No default printer available.",
                                                "Printer Error",
                                                JOptionPane.ERROR_MESSAGE);
                  return;
                }
                PageFormat pageFormat = printJob.defaultPage();
                Rectangle rect = theApp.getModel().getModelExtent(); // Get sketch bounds

                // If the sketch width is greater than the height, print landscape
                if(rect.width>rect.height) {
                  pageFormat.setOrientation(PageFormat.LANDSCAPE);
                }
                printJob.setPrintable(theApp.getView(), pageFormat);

                if(printJob.printDialog()) {                            // Display print dialog
                  try {                                                 // and if true is returned...
                    printJob.print();                                   // ...then print
                  } catch(PrinterException pe) {
                    System.out.println(pe);
                    JOptionPane.showMessageDialog(SketcherFrame.this,
                                                  "Error printing a sketch.",
                                                  "Printer Error",
                                                  JOptionPane.ERROR_MESSAGE);
                  }
```

Directory "Sketcher 8 printing landscape automatically"

Calling the defaultPage() method for a PrinterJob object returns a reference to the default page for the current printer. You can then change that to suit the conditions that you want to apply in the printing operation and pass the reference to an overload of the setPrintable() method. The call to setPrintable() here makes the printJob object use the SketcherView object as the Printable object, and supplies the PageFormat object to be used when the print() method for the view is called. With this code you don't need to worry about the orientation in the print() method for the Printable object. It is taken care of before print() ever gets called.

If you recompile and try printing a sketch that is wider than it is long, it should come out automatically in landscape orientation. Although everything works, there is a better way to implement printing. The PrinterJob and PrintService objects are re-created every time the event handler executes. This has a detrimental effect on the performance of the printing event handler in the FileAction class, and what's more, it's not necessary. You will fix this in the next section.

Improving the Printing Facilities

Of course, there are many situations where choosing the best orientation from a paper usage point of view might not be what the user wants. Instead of automatically setting landscape or portrait orientation based on the dimensions of a sketch, you could leave it to the user with a dialog to select the page setup parameters in the print dialog that you display. The mechanism for the user to set the job parameters is already in place in Sketcher. Clicking the Properties button on the dialog usually displays an additional dialog in which you can set the parameters for the print job, including whether the output is portrait or landscape. Whatever is set in the print dialog overrides the orientation that you determine programmatically in the actionPerformed() method in the FileAction class.

However, the printing facilities in Sketcher are not always implemented in this way for an application. The toolbar button and the File ⇨ Print menu item do exactly the same thing, but often it's the menu item that pops a print dialog, and the toolbar button just initiates printing of the current document. Also, there's often a separate menu item that enables the page to be set up for printing, independent of the process of printing a document. You can fix that without too much difficulty, though.

In the actionPerformed() method in the FileAction class, you need to be able to determine whether it was the toolbar button or the menu item that initiated the event. You can get a reference to the object that originated the event by calling the getSource() method for the ActionEvent object that is passed to the actionPerformed() method. You can easily check whether the source object is of type JButton. If it is, it's the toolbar button that originated the event, and if it isn't, it was the menu item.

You can now update the code in the actionPerformed() method in the FileAction inner class so you get the print dialog displayed only when the menu item is selected:

Available for
download on
Wrox.com

```
      // The view is the page source
      printJob.setPrintable(theApp.getView(), pageFormat);
      boolean printIt = true;

      // If it's not a toolbar button...
      if(!(e.getSource() instanceof JButton)) {
        printIt = printJob.printDialog();      // ...display the print dialog
      }
      if(printIt) {                            // If printIt is true...
        try {
          printJob.print();                    // ...then print
        } catch(PrinterException pe) {
          System.out.println(pe);
          JOptionPane.showMessageDialog(SketcherFrame.this,
                              "Error printing a sketch.",
                              "Printer Error",
                              JOptionPane.ERROR_MESSAGE);

        }
      }
```

Directory "Sketcher 9 Printing landscape with toolbar and menu different"

The value of the `printIt` flag you have defined is `true` by default. It may be reset to `false` by the value returned by the `printDialog()` method, which is the case if the user cancels the dialog. The `printDialog()` method only gets called when the menu item caused the event for printing, not when the toolbar button is clicked.

If you've completed all the changes I've described, recompile Sketcher and run it again. You should now get different behavior depending on whether you use the toolbar button or the menu item for printing.

Implementing Page Setup

You can add a menu item to the File menu to provide for setting up the printer page. Because you are not going to add a toolbar button for this, you don't need to use an `Action` object. `Action` objects carry more overhead than a simple component, so it's best not to use them unless you need the capability they provide. Although this is somewhat inconsistent with the way you have created the rest of the File menu, you also see how you can combine both techniques.

Add the boldfaced code to the `createFileMenu()` method in the `SketcherFrame` class to create the `JMenuItem` object for the new `printSetupItem` menu item and add the menu item to the File menu:

Available for
download on
Wrox.com

```java
private void createFileMenu() {
  JMenu fileMenu = new JMenu("File");          // Create File menu
  fileMenu.setMnemonic('F');                   // Create shortcut
  createFileMenuActions();                     // Create Actions for File menu item

  // Create print setup menu item
  JMenuItem printSetupItem = new JMenuItem("Print Setup...");
  printSetupItem.setToolTipText("Setup the page for the printer");
  printSetupItem.addActionListener(new ActionListener() {
          public void actionPerformed(ActionEvent e) {
            // update the page format
            pageFormat = printJob.pageDialog(pageFormat);
          }
  });
  // Construct the file drop-down menu
  fileMenu.add(newAction);                     // New Sketch menu item
  fileMenu.add(openAction);                    // Open sketch menu item
  fileMenu.add(closeAction);                   // Close sketch menu item
  fileMenu.addSeparator();                     // Add separator
  fileMenu.add(saveAction);                    // Save sketch to file
  fileMenu.add(saveAsAction);                  // Save As menu item
  fileMenu.addSeparator();                     // Add separator
  fileMenu.add(printAction);                   // Print sketch menu item
  fileMenu.add(printSetupItem);                // Print page setup menu item
  fileMenu.addSeparator();                     // Add separator
  fileMenu.add(exitAction);                    // Print sketch menu item
  menuBar.add(fileMenu);                       // Add the file menu
}
```

Directory "Sketcher 10 with printer page setup"

The new menu item has a tooltip. The action events for the `printSetupItem` are handled by an anonymous class object. It references the `printJob` object to call its `pageDialog()` method, which displays a dialog for setting up the printed page. Data from the `PageFormat` object you supply as the argument is used to set the values in controls in the dialog. The `PageFormat` object that `pageDialog()` returns is stored in `pageFormat`. This is the updated `PageFormat` object if the user makes changes and selects the OK button, or the original object that was the argument if the dialog is canceled.

For the `printJob` and `pageFormat` objects to be accessible here, you can make them members of the `SketcherFrame` class, along with the `PrintService` object. Add the following class members to `SketcherFrame`:

```
private PrinterJob printJob;          // The current printer job
private PageFormat pageFormat;        // The printing page format
private PrintService printer;         // The printer to be used
```

Directory "Sketcher 10 with printer page setup"

You can initialize the first two fields in the `SketcherFrame` constructor. Add the following statements at the beginning of the code in the constructor:

```
printJob = PrinterJob.getPrinterJob();     // Get a printing object
pageFormat = printJob.defaultPage();       // Get the page format
printer = printJob.getPrintService();      // Get the default printer
```

Directory "Sketcher 10 with printer page setup"

The fields concerned with printing are now accessible from anywhere in the `SketcherFrame` class code, including the inner classes such as the `FileAction` class.

You need to change the code in the `actionPerformed()` method in the `FileAction` class to make use of the fields you have just added to the `SketcherFrame` class. This involves deleting the first two statements in the block dealing with `printAction` events that initialize `printJob` and `printService`, and deleting the statement that follows the first `if` statement that creates the `pageFormat` object. These are all taken care of elsewhere now. You can also remove the statements that set the page orientation, because this is dealt with by the page dialog that is displayed when the "Print Setup..." menu item is clicked. The code now looks like this:

```
    } if(this == printAction) {
      // Get a printing object
      if(printer == null) {                      // See if there is a printer
        JOptionPane.showMessageDialog(SketcherFrame.this,
                                "No default printer available.",
                                "Printer Error",
                                JOptionPane.ERROR_MESSAGE);

        return;
      }

      printJob.setPrintable(theApp.getView(), pageFormat);
      boolean printIt = true;

      // If it's not a toolbar button
      if(!(e.getSource() instanceof JButton)) {
        printIt = printJob.printDialog();        // ...display the print dialog
      }

      if(printIt) {                              // If printIt is true...
        try {
          printJob.print();                      // ...then print
        } catch(PrinterException pe) {
          System.err.println(pe);
          JOptionPane.showMessageDialog(SketcherFrame.this,
                                "Error printing a sketch.",
                                "Printer Error",
                                JOptionPane.ERROR_MESSAGE);

        }
      }
    } else if(this == exitAction) {
      checkForSave();
      System.exit(0);
    }
```

Directory "Sketcher 10 with printer page setup"

On my system, the `pageDialog()` method displays the dialog shown in Figure 21-12.

As you can see, with my printer I can select the paper size and the source tray. I can also set the margin sizes as well as select portrait or landscape orientation. When the dialog is closed normally with the OK button, the method returns a new `PageFormat` object that incorporates the values set by the user in the dialog. If the Cancel button is used to close the dialog, the original reference that was passed as an argument is returned. The printing operations that are initiated in the `actionPerformed()` method in the `FileAction` class use the updated `PageFormat` object. You achieve this by passing `pageFormat` as the second argument to the overloaded `setPrintable()` method with two parameters. The first argument is the object that implements the `Printable` interface and thus carries out the printing, and the second is the `PageFormat` object that is to be used.

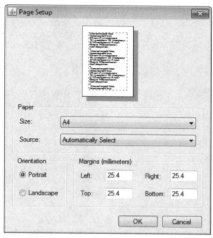

FIGURE 21-12

Using the Java Print Dialog

The overloaded version of the `printDialog()` method that I sidestepped earlier generates a Java-based print dialog instead of using the native dialog. This method requires a single argument of type `PrintRequestAttributeSet`. This interface type is defined in the `javax.print.attribute` package and declares methods for adding attributes relating to a print request to a set. These attributes specify things such as the number of copies to be printed, the orientation of the image on the paper, or the media or media tray to be selected for the print job. The `HashPrintRequestAttributeSet` class that is defined in the same package implements this interface and encapsulates a set of print request attributes stored as a hash map. It is useful if you can define a set of attributes that have some persistence in Sketcher so they can be carried forward from one print request to the next. You can add a member to store an initially empty set of print request attributes to the `SketcherFrame` class like this:

```
private HashPrintRequestAttributeSet printAttr = new HashPrintRequestAttributeSet();
```

Directory "Sketcher 11 using the Java print dialog"

There are other `HashPrintRequestAttributeSet` class constructors that create non-empty attribute sets, but this suffices for Sketcher. You need an `import` statement for the class in the `SketcherFrame.java` file:

```
import javax.print.attribute.HashPrintRequestAttributeSet;
```

Directory "Sketcher 11 using the Java print dialog"

Now that you have a print request attribute set object available, you can modify the code for printing in the `actionPerformed()` method in the `FileAction` inner class to use the Java print dialog:

```
// Get a printing object
if(printer == null) {                          // See if there is a printer
    JOptionPane.showMessageDialog(SketcherFrame.this,
                          "No default printer available.",
                          "Printer Error",
                          JOptionPane.ERROR_MESSAGE);
    return;
}

// The view is the page source
printJob.setPrintable(theApp.getView(), pageFormat);
boolean printIt = true;
```

```
          // If it's not a toolbar button
          if(!(e.getSource() instanceof JButton)) {
            // ...display the print dialog
            printIt = printJob.printDialog(printAttr);
          }
          if(printIt) {                                 // If printIt is true...
            try {
              printJob.print(printAttr);                // ...then print
            } catch(PrinterException pe) {
              System.err.println(pe);
              JOptionPane.showMessageDialog(SketcherFrame.this,
                                     "Error printing a sketch.",
                                     "Printer Error",
                                     JOptionPane.ERROR_MESSAGE);
            }
          }
        }
```

Directory "Sketcher 11 using the Java print dialog"

Note that you also use an overloaded version of the `print()` method for the `PrinterJob` object to which you pass the print request attribute set. Thus the print operation uses whatever attributes were set or modified in the print dialog displayed by the `printDialog()` method.

As you are using print attributes when printing, you should make the page dialog that is displayed in response to the "Print Setup…" menu item use them, too. There's a slight complication in that the behavior of the `pageDialog()` method that has a parameter of type `PrintRequestAttributeSet` is different from that of the method with a parameter of type `PageFormat` when the Cancel button in the dialog is clicked. The former version returns `null`, whereas the latter version returns a reference to the `PageFormat` object that was passed as the argument. If you don't take account of this, canceling the page setup dialog causes printing to fail, because the `pageFormat` field in `SketcherFrame` is set to `null`. You therefore must modify the code in the `actionPerformed()` method in the anonymous `ActionListener` class for the `printSetupMenuItem` menu item. This is in the `createFileMenu()` method in `SketcherFrame`:

```
          public void actionPerformed(ActionEvent e) {
            PageFormat pf = printJob.pageDialog(printAttr);
            if(pf != null) {
              pageFormat = pf;                   // update the page format
            }
          }
        }
```

Directory "Sketcher 11 using the Java print dialog"

Now you update `pageFormat` only when the value returned by the `pageDialog()` method is not `null`.

If you run Sketcher with these changes you should see a dialog with three tabs when you print a sketch, similar to that shown in Figure 21-13.

Now you have the ability to set attributes on any of the tabs in the dialog, and the attributes are stored in the `PrintAttr` member of the `SketcherFrame` class that you passed to the `printDialog()` method. Because you also pass this reference to the `print()` method for the `PrinterJob` object, the print request is executed using these attributes. This is accomplished by passing a `PageFormat` object to the `Printable` object, which prints a page that has its size, orientation, and other attributes set from the print request attributes defined by `PrintAttr`. You can see that the page

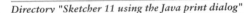

FIGURE 21-13

count has been set to 1 by default in this dialog. You can set attributes related to a print job and store them in the `PrintRequestAttributeSet` object that you pass to the `printDialog()` method. Let's explore that a little further.

Setting Print Request Attributes Programmatically

Print request attributes are specifications of the kinds of options displayed in the dialog you just saw. They specify things like the number of copies, whether printing is in color or monochrome, the page margin sizes, and so on. Each print request attribute is identified by a class that implements the `PrintRequestAttribute` interface, and the `javax.print.attributes.standard` package defines a series of classes for standard print request attributes, as well as classes for other types of print attributes. There is a large number of standard classes for print request attributes, and I don't have the space to go into the details of them all here. So I'm just picking one to show how you can query and set them.

All the classes that implement the `PrintRequestAttribute` interface are identified in the interface documentation. You can use the `Copies` class in the `javax.print.attributes.standard` package that specifies the number of printed copies to be produced.

You add an instance of the `Copies` class to your `PrintAttr` object to specify the number of copies to be printed, and this is displayed by the print dialog. You can create an object specifying the number of copies to be produced by extending the code relating to printer setup in the `SketcherFrame` constructor, like this:

```
// Set up the printer and page format objects
printJob = PrinterJob.getPrinterJob(); // Get a printing object
pageFormat = printJob.defaultPage();   // Get the page format
printer = printJob.getPrintService(); // Get the default printer
Copies twoCopies = new Copies(2);
if (printer.isAttributeCategorySupported(twoCopies.getCategory())) {
  printAttr.add(twoCopies);
}
```

The argument to the `Copies` class constructor specifies the number of copies to be produced. Our object specifies just two copies, but you can go for more if you have the paper, the time, and the inclination.

Before you add this object to the print request attribute set, you verify that the printer does actually support the production of multiple copies. Obviously, it only makes sense to set an attribute for a printer that has the appropriate capability—you won't be able to print in color on a monochrome printer, for instance. You can call the `isAttributeCategorySupported()` method for the `PrintService` object that you obtained from the `PrinterJob` object to do this.

The `isAttributeCategorySupported()` method requires an argument of type `Class` to identify the attribute category that you are querying, and you obtain this by calling the `getCategory()` method for the `Copies` object. If the attribute is supported, you add the `twoCopies` object to the set encapsulated by `printAttr` by calling its `add()` method.

You should add an `import` statement for the `Copies` class to `SketcherFrame.java`:

```
import javax.print.attribute.standard.Copies;
```

If you recompile and run Sketcher once more, the print dialog should come up with two copies set initially.

Of course, setting things such as margin sizes and page orientation once and for all for every page in a document might not be satisfactory in many cases. It is easy to imagine situations where you may want to print some pages in a document in portrait orientation while you need to print others, perhaps containing illustrations, in landscape orientation. You look at how you can handle that in Java next, but before going any further, delete the following code from the `SketcherFrame` constructor:

```
Copies twoCopies = new Copies(2);
if (printer.isAttributeCategorySupported(twoCopies.getCategory())) {
  printAttr.add(twoCopies);
}
```

You can remove the `import` statement for the `Copies` class name, too.

Multipage Document Printing

If you need to print a document that contains several pages, you can allow for this possibility in the implementation of the print() method in the SketcherView class. The PrinterJob object continues to call this method until the value NO_SUCH_PAGE is returned. However, this won't be convenient in every case. In a more complicated application than Sketcher, as well as having different page orientations, you might want to have different class objects printing different kinds of pages—rendering the same data as graphical or textual output, for instance. You can't do this conveniently with just one class implementing the Printable interface. You also need something that is more flexible than just passing a class object that does printing to the PrinterJob object by calling its setPrintable() method.

The solution is to implement the Pageable interface in a class, and call the setPageable() method for the PrinterJob object instead of setPrintable(). The essential difference between the Printable and Pageable interfaces is that a Printable object is intended to encapsulate a single page to be printed, whereas a Pageable object encapsulates multiple pages. Each page that is to be printed by a Pageable object is encapsulated by a Printable object though.

Implementing the Pageable Interface

A class that implements the Pageable interface defines a set of pages to be printed. A Pageable object must be able to supply the PrinterJob object with a count of the number of pages for a job, a reference of type Printable for the object that is to print each page, plus a PageFormat object defining the format of each page. The PrinterJob object acquires this information by calling the three methods declared in the Pageable interface:

➤ int getNumberOfPages(): Returns the number of pages to be printed. If the number of pages cannot be determined, then the UNKNOWN_NUMBER_OF_PAGES constant that is defined in the Pageable interface should be returned.

➤ PageFormat getPageFormat(int pageIndex): Returns a PageFormat object for the page specified by the page index that is passed to it.

➤ Printable getPrintable(int pageIndex): Returns a reference to the object responsible for printing the page specified by the page index that is passed to it.

At the start of a print job that was initiated by a call to the setPageable() method for a PrinterJob object, the PrinterJob object calls the getNumberOfPages() method for the Pageable object to determine how many pages are to be printed. If you return the value UNKNOWN_NUMBER_OF_PAGES, then the process relies on a Printable object returning NO_SUCH_PAGE at some point to stop printing. It is therefore a good idea to supply the number of pages when it can be determined.

The PrinterJob object assumes each page in a print job is associated with a page index value, with page index values starting at 0. For each page index, the PrinterJob object calls the getPageFormat() method to obtain the PageFormat object to be used to print the page, and then calls getPrintable() for the Pageable object to obtain a reference to the Printable object that does the printing. Of course, just because you *can* supply a different Printable object for each page doesn't mean that you *must*. You can use as many or as few as you need for your application, and control how different pages are printed by making the getPageFormat() method for the Pageable object return different PageFormat objects. Remember, though, that the print() method for a Printable object may be called more than once by the PrinterJob object to print a particular page, and the same page should be rendered each time the same page index is passed as an argument to the print() method, so you must not code the method in a way that presumes otherwise.

Creating PageFormat Objects

As you saw earlier, you can get the default PageFormat object for the print service you are using by calling the defaultPage() method for the PrinterJob object. You could use the default PageFormat class constructor to create an object that is portrait-oriented, but in this case you have no guarantee that the object is compatible with the current print service. A PageFormat object encapsulates information about the size of the paper and the margins in effect, so the object produced by the default constructor may not correspond with your printer setup. If you want to go this route, you can pass a reference to a `PageFormat` object to the `validatePage()` method for a `PrinterJob` object. For example:

```
// Object for current printer
PrinterJob printJob = PrinterJob.getPrinterJob();

// Validated page
PageFormat pageFormat = printJob.validatePage(new PageFormat());
```

Note that the `validatePage()` method does not return the reference that you pass as the argument. The method clones the object that was passed to it and returns a reference to the clone, which has been modified where necessary to suit the current printer. Because it does not modify the object in place, you always need to store the reference that is returned. This is obviously well suited to multipage printing because you can create a series of distinct `PageFormat` objects from the same argument.

Fundamentally, a `PageFormat` object encapsulates all the information needed to print on a page, as Figure 21-14 illustrates.

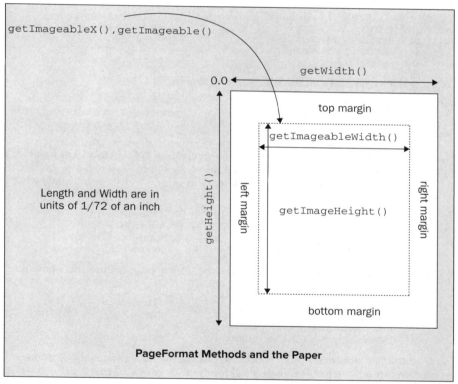

FIGURE 21-14

After you have a `PageFormat` object, you can modify the orientation of the page by calling its `setOrientation()` method as you know, the possible values for the argument being LANDSCAPE, PORTRAIT, or REVERSE_LANDSCAPE. The `PageFormat` class defines several methods to retrieve information about the paper—you have seen that you can get the position and size of the printable area on the page, for instance, by calling the `getImageableX()`, `getImageableY()`, `getImageableWidth()`, and `getImageableHeight()` methods. You also have `getWidth()` and `getHeight()` methods in the `PageFormat` class that return the overall width and height of the page, respectively. These are all properties of the paper itself, which is represented by an object of the `java.awt.print.Paper` class that is associated with a `PageFormat` object. You can also work with the `Paper` object for a `PageFormat` object directly.

Dealing with Paper

The `Paper` class encapsulates the size of the paper and the size and position of the printable area on the page. The default constructor for the `Paper` class creates an American letter-sized sheet with one-inch margins—the printable area being the area inside the margins. You can change the size of the paper by calling the `setSize()` method for the `Paper` object, as you see in a moment.

Rather than creating an independent `Paper` object, you would normally retrieve a reference to the `Paper` object for a `PageFormat` object by calling its `getPaper()` method. If you then want to change the size of the paper, or the printable area—the page margins, in other words—you can call the `setSize()` or the `setImageableArea()` method for the `Paper` object. You can restore the paper details by passing an object of type `Paper` back to the `PageFormat` object by calling its `setPaper()` method with a reference to the `Paper` object as the argument.

The `setSize()` method for a `Paper` object has two parameters of type `double` that specify the width and height of the paper in units of 1/72 of an inch. If you use A4 paper, you could specify the size of the paper for a `PageFormat` object with the following statements:

```
Paper paper = pageFormat.getPaper();
final double MM_TO_PAPER_UNITS = 72.0/25.4;              // 25.4 mm to an inch
final double widthA4 = 210*MM_TO_PAPER_UNITS;
final double heightA4 = 297*MM_TO_PAPER_UNITS;
paper.setSize(widthA4, heightA4);
```

If you use letter size paper that is 8.5 by 11 inches, it's somewhat simpler:

```
Paper paper = pageFormat.getPaper();
final double widthLetterSize = 72.0*8.5;
final double heightLetterSize = 72.0*11.0;
paper.setSize(widthLetterSize, heightLetterSize);
```

The `setImageableArea()` method expects you to supply four arguments of type `double`. The first two are the coordinates of the top-left corner of the printable area and the next two are the width and the height. All these values are in units of 1/72 of an inch. To set 20 mm margins on your A4 sheet you could write the following:

```
double marginSize = 20.0* MM_TO_PAPER_UNITS;            // 20 mm wide
paper.setImageableArea(marginSize, marginSize,          // Top left
                       widthA4-2.0*marginSize,          // Width
                       heightA4-2.0*marginSize);        // Height
```

If you are printing on letter-size paper, a one-inch margin might be more appropriate, so you would write this:

```
double marginSize = 72.0;                               // 1 inch wide
paper.setImageableArea(marginSize, marginSize,          // Top left
                       widthLetterSize-2.0*marginSize,  // Width
                       heightLetterSize-2.0*marginSize);// Height
```

Of course, there's no reason why a class that implements the `Pageable` interface cannot also implement `Printable`, so you could do this in Sketcher just to get a feel for the `Pageable` interface in action.

TRY IT OUT Using the Pageable Interface

You just print two pages in a print job in Sketcher, a cover page with a title for the sketch plus the sketch itself, which may be portrait or landscape, of course. You could produce both pages in `SketcherView`, but to make it more interesting, let's define a separate class to represent a `Printable` object for the cover page:

```
import java.awt.*;
import java.awt.geom.*;
import java.awt.print.*;
import java.awt.font.TextLayout;
```

```
public class SketchCoverPage implements Printable {
  public SketchCoverPage(String sketchName) {
    this.sketchName = sketchName;
  }

  // Print the cover page
  public int print(Graphics g,
                   PageFormat pageFormat,
                   int pageIndex)
                   throws PrinterException {
    // If it's page 0 print the cover page...
  }

  private String sketchName;
}
```

Directory "Sketcher 12 using the Pageable interface"

You will use the `TextLayout` class in the implementation of the `print()` method.

The name of the sketch to print on the cover page is passed to the `SketchCoverPage` constructor. Because the need has come up, you should add a `getSketchName()` method to the `SketcherFrame` class that supplies a reference to a `String` object containing the file name:

Available for
download on
Wrox.com

```
// Method to return the name of the current sketch
public String getSketchName() {
  return currentSketchFile == null ? DEFAULT_FILENAME.toString() :
                          currentSketchFile.getFileName().toString();
}
```

Directory "Sketcher 12 using the Pageable interface"

You can use this method when you create a `SketchCoverPage` object. The `print()` method in the `SketchCoverPage` class needs to recognize when it is being called to print the first page—that is, when the page index is zero—and then print the cover page. You could do whatever you like here to produce a fancy cover page, but I'm just putting the code to draw a line border inset from the page and put the sketch file name in the middle in a box. Here's how you could do that:

Available for
download on
Wrox.com

```
public int print(Graphics g,
                 PageFormat pageFormat,
                 int pageIndex)
           throws PrinterException {
  if(pageIndex > 0) {
    return NO_SUCH_PAGE;
  }
  Graphics2D g2D = (Graphics2D) g;
  float x = (float)pageFormat.getImageableX();
  float y = (float)pageFormat.getImageableY();

  GeneralPath path = new GeneralPath();
  path.moveTo(x+1, y+1);
  path.lineTo(x+(float)pageFormat.getImageableWidth()-1, y+1);
  path.lineTo(x+(float)pageFormat.getImageableWidth()-1,
              y+(float)pageFormat.getImageableHeight()-1);
  path.lineTo(x+1, y+(float)pageFormat.getImageableHeight()-1);
  path.closePath();

  g2D.setPaint(Color.red);
  g2D.draw(path);

  // Get a 12 pt bold version of the default font
  Font font = g2D.getFont().deriveFont(12.f).deriveFont(Font.BOLD);
```

```
      g2D.setFont(font);                              // Set the new font
      Rectangle2D textRect =
        new TextLayout(sketchName, font, g2D.getFontRenderContext()).getBounds();
      double centerX = pageFormat.getWidth()/2;
      double centerY = pageFormat.getHeight()/2;
      Rectangle2D.Double surround = new Rectangle2D.Double(
                                        centerX-textRect.getWidth(),
                                        centerY-textRect.getHeight(),
                                        2*textRect.getWidth(),
                                        2*textRect.getHeight());

      g2D.draw(surround);

      // Draw text in the middle of the printable area
      g2D.setPaint(Color.blue);
      g2D.drawString(sketchName, (float)(centerX-textRect.getWidth()/2),
                                 (float)(centerY+textRect.getHeight()/2));

      return PAGE_EXISTS;
    }
```

Directory "Sketcher 12 using the Pageable interface"

To center the file name on the page, you need to know the width and height of the text string when it is printed. The getStringBounds() method in the Font class returns the rectangle bounding the string. The second argument is a reference to an object of type FontRenderContext that the getFontRenderContext() method for g2D returns. A FontRenderContext object contains all the information the getStringBounds() method needs to figure out the rectangle bounding the text when it is printed. This includes information about the size of the font as well as the resolution of the output device—the printer, in this case.

You can now implement the Pageable interface in the SketcherView class. You must add three methods to the class: getNumberOfPages(), which returns the number of pages to be printed; getPrintable(), which returns a reference to a Printable object that prints a page with a given index; and getPageFormat(), which returns a reference to a PageFormat object corresponding to a particular page:

```
// Import statements as before...

class SketcherView extends JComponent
                    implements Observer, ActionListener, Printable, Pageable {
  // Constructor and othe code as before...
  // Method to return page count - always two pages
  public int getNumberOfPages() {
    return 2;
  }

  // Method to return the Printable object that will render the page
  public Printable getPrintable(int pageIndex) {
    if(pageIndex == 0) {                              // For the first page
      // return the cover page
      return new SketchCoverPage(theApp.getWindow().getSketchName());
    } else {
      return this;
    }
  }

  public PageFormat getPageFormat(int pageIndex) {
    // Code to define the PageFormat object for the page...
  }

  // Print the sketch on a local printer
  public int print(Graphics g,                    // Graphics context for printing
                   PageFormat pageFormat,         // The page format
                   int pageIndex)                 // Index number of current page
            throws PrinterException {
    // Code to test pageIndex must be removed...
    //if(pageIndex > 0) {
```

```
//   return NO_SUCH_PAGE;
//}      Graphics2D g2D = (Graphics2D) g;

 // Get sketch bounds
 Rectangle rect = theApp.getModel().getModelExtent();
 // Rest of the code as before...
}

 // Plus the rest of the class as before...
}
```

Directory "Sketcher 12 using the Pageable interface"

The first two methods are already fully defined here. You always print two pages, the first page being printed by a SketchCoverPage object and the second page by the view object. The print() method should now print the page when called without testing the pageIndex value for zero. The page with index 0 is printed by the SketchCoverPage object.

Let's see how you can produce the PageFormat object for a page. You should use the PageFormat object that's stored as a field in the application window, so add a method to the SketcherFrame class to make it accessible from another class:

Available for
download on
Wrox.com

```
// Method to return a reference to the current PageFormat object
public PageFormat getPageFormat() {
   return pageFormat;
}
```

Directory "Sketcher 12 using the Pageable interface"

To exercise some of the methods in the Paper class that I've discussed, you can arbitrarily double the size of the margins for the cover page but leave the margins for the other page at their default sizes. You can also set the cover page to landscape orientation, but leave the second page as whatever is set in the pageFormat field of the application object. Here's the code for the getPageFormat() method in the SketcherView class that does that:

Available for
download on
Wrox.com

```
public PageFormat getPageFormat(int pageIndex) {
   if(pageIndex == 0) {                 // If it's the cover page...
                                        // ...make the margins twice the size
      // Create a duplicate of the current page format
      PageFormat pageFormat =
                 (PageFormat)(theApp.getWindow().getPageFormat().clone());
      Paper paper = pageFormat.getPaper();

      // Get top and left margins - x & y coordinates of top-left corner
      // of imageable area are the left & top margins
      double leftMargin = paper.getImageableX();
      double topMargin = paper.getImageableY();

      // Get right and bottom margins
      double rightMargin = paper.getWidth()-paper.getImageableWidth()-leftMargin;
      double bottomMargin = paper.getHeight()-paper.getImageableHeight()-topMargin;

      // Double the margin sizes
      leftMargin *= 2.0;
      rightMargin *= 2.0;
      topMargin *= 2.0;
      bottomMargin *= 2.0;

      // Set new printable area for the paper
      paper.setImageableArea(leftMargin, topMargin,
                             paper.getWidth() - leftMargin - rightMargin,
                             paper.getHeight() - topMargin-bottomMargin);
```

```
    pageFormat.setPaper(paper);                          // Restore the paper
    pageFormat.setOrientation(PageFormat.LANDSCAPE);
    return pageFormat;                                    // Return the page format
  }
  // For pages after the first, use the object from the app window
  return theApp.getWindow().getPageFormat();
}
```

Directory "Sketcher 12 using the Pageable interface"

You don't want to mess up the PageFormat object from the application window for use when you are printing the cover page, so you duplicate it by calling its clone() method. The PageFormat class specifically overrides the clone() method that it inherits from the Object class with a public member to allow a PageFormat object to be duplicated. The clone() method returns a reference of type Object, so you must cast it to the correct type.

The sizes for the left and top margins correspond to the values of the *x* and *y* coordinates of the top-left corner of the imageable area for the page, so you call the methods for the Paper object to retrieve these values. You calculate the size of the right margin by subtracting the width of the imageable area and the value for the left margin from the overall width of the page. You produce the value for the size of the bottom margin in a similar way. After doubling the margin sizes, you redefine the position and size of the imageable area for the Paper objects from these and then restore the modified Paper object in the PageFormat object.

If it's not the cover page, you just return a reference to the PageFormat object that is stored in the application window object.

The last thing you need to do is alter the code in the actionPerformed() method for the inner class FileAction in SketcherFrame. You must replace the setPrintable() method call with a setPageable() call:

```
  } if(this == printAction) {
    // Get a printing object
    if(printer == null) {                               // See if there is a printer
      JOptionPane.showMessageDialog(SketcherFrame.this,
                              "No default printer available.",
                              "Printer Error",
                              JOptionPane.ERROR_MESSAGE);

      return;
    }

    // The view is the page source
    printJob.setPageable(theApp.getView());
    boolean printIt = true;

    // If it's not the toolbar button...
    if(!(e.getSource() instanceof JButton)) {
      printIt = printJob.printDialog();    // ...display the print dialog
    }
    if(printIt) {                                       // If printIt is true...
      try {
        printJob.print();                               // ...then print
      } catch(PrinterException pe) {
        System.err.println(pe);
        JOptionPane.showMessageDialog(SketcherFrame.this,
                                "Error printing a sketch.",
                                "Printer Error",
                                JOptionPane.ERROR_MESSAGE);

      }
    }
  } else if(this == exitAction) {
    checkForSave();
    System.exit(0);
  }
```

Directory "Sketcher 12 using the Pageable interface"

This code is the earlier version that uses the `printDialog()` method without an argument to show the effect in this context. If you comment out the most recent code, you can try both versions by juggling the commented-out code. On my system, the print dialog now shows that pages numbered from 1 to 2 should be printed, courtesy of the `Pageable` interface implementation that you added to Sketcher. You can see my print dialog in Figure 21-15.

How It Works

The `PrinterJob` object now calls methods in the `Pageable` interface that you have implemented in the `SketcherView` class that defines the view object. The number of pages in the document is now determined by the `getNumberOfPages()` method, and the `PageFormat` and `Printable` objects are now obtained individually for each page.

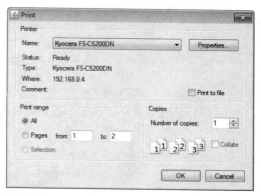

FIGURE 21-15

If you switch the code back to using the `printDialog()` and `print()` methods with an argument of type `PrintRequestAttributeSet`, the print operation runs in the same way. The print attributes passed to the `print()` method do not override those specified in the `PageFormat` object returned by the `getPageFormat()` method for the `Pageable` object. If the attribute set passed to the print method includes attributes not determined by the `Pageable` object—such as a `Copies` attribute object—these have an effect on the printing process. Similarly, if you set the page orientation to landscape using the dialog displayed by the Print Setup menu item, the second page that contains the sketch prints in landscape orientation.

Printing Using a Book

A `Book` object is a repository for a collection of pages where the pages may be printed using different formats. The page painter for a page in a book is represented by a `Printable` object, and each `Printable` object within a book can print one or possibly several pages with a given format. Figure 21-16 shows an example of a `Book` object that uses three `Printable` objects to print a total of seven pages.

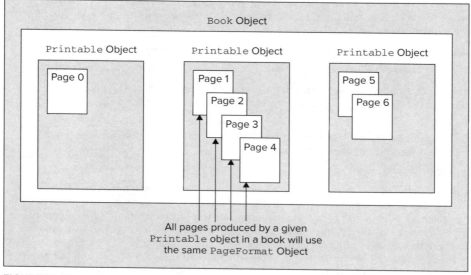

FIGURE 21-16

Because the `Book` class implements the `Pageable` interface, you print a book in the same way as you print a `Pageable` object. After you have assembled all the pages you want in a `Book` object, you just pass a reference to it to the `setPageable()` method for your `PrinterJob` object. Let's take it from the top.

The `Book` class has only a default constructor and that creates an empty book. Thus, you create a book like this:

```
Book sketchBook = new Book();
```

You add a page to a book by calling the `append()` method for the `Book` object. There are two overloaded versions of `append()`: one to add a `Printable` object that represents a single page, and the other to add a `Printable` object that represents several pages. In the latter case, all the pages are printed using the same `PageFormat` object.

The first version of `append()` accepts two arguments: a reference to the `Printable` object and a reference to an associated `PageFormat` object. This means each page in a book can have its own formatting. Suppose you want to create a `Book` object for Sketcher, and the object would be created in the `SketcherFrame` object somewhere. You could add the cover page of a sketch just as in the previous example to the `sketchBook` object like this:

```
PageFormat pageFormat = pageFormat.clone();
Paper paper = pageFormat.getPaper();

double leftMargin = paper.getImageableX();      // Top left corner is indented
double topMargin = paper.getImageableY();       // by the left and top margins
double rightMargin = paper.getWidth()-paper.getImageableWidth()-leftMargin;
double bottomMargin = paper.getHeight()-paper.getImageableHeight()-topMargin;
leftMargin *= 2.0;                              // Double the left margin...
rightMargin *= 2.0;                            // ...and the right...
topMargin *= 2.0;                              // ...and the top...
bottomMargin *= 2.0;                           // ...and the bottom

paper.setImageableArea(leftMargin, topMargin,  // Set new printable area
                   paper.getWidth()-leftMargin-rightMargin,
                   paper.getHeight()-topMargin-bottomMargin);
pageFormat.setPaper(paper);                     // Restore the paper
sketchBook.append(new SketchCoverPage(theApp), pageFormat);
```

Apart from the first statement and the last statement that appends the `Printable` object that represents the page painter, all this code is essentially the same as the code in the previous example for creating the `PageFormat` object for the cover page.

To add the second page of the sketch to the `Book` object, you could write the following:

```
sketchBook.append(theApp.getView(), pageFormat);
```

The arguments to the `append()` method specify that the view object prints the page, and that the `PageFormat` object that should be used is the one stored in the `pageFormat` field in the `SketcherFrame` class.

Now that you have assembled the book containing the two pages for the print job, you can tell the `PrinterJob` object that you want to print the book:

```
printJob.setPageable(sketchBook);              // The book is the source of pages
```

All you need to do is call the `print()` method for the `PrinterJob` object to start printing. To expedite printing, the `PrinterJob` object communicates with the `Book` object to get the number of pages to be printed and to get the page painter and page format appropriate to print each page. The total number of pages is returned by the `getNumberOfPages()` method for the `Book` object. In this case it always returns 2 because a printed sketch consists of just a cover page plus the sketch. A reference to the `Printable` object for a given page index is returned by the `getPrintable()` method for the `Book` object, and the `PageFormat` object for a given page index is returned by the `getPageFormat()` method. Obviously, in the case of

Sketcher, using a `Book` object doesn't offer much advantage over the `Pageable` object that you used in the previous example. In situations where you have more complex documents with a lot of pages with diverse formats, it can make things much easier.

You use the other version of `append()` for a `Book` object to add a given number of pages to a book that is produced by a single `Printable` object, and where all the pages have the same format. Here's an example:

```
Book book = new Book();
book.append(painter, pageFormat, pageCount);
```

Here the `painter` argument is a reference of type `Printable` that prints `pageCount` pages all with the same format, `pageFormat`. A typical instance where you might use this might be a long text document. The document could consist of many pages, but they all are printed with the same page format. The view object for the document typically provides a method to figure out the number of pages that are necessary to output the document.

Printing Swing Components

Printing components is easier than you might think. Swing components are particularly easy to print because they already know how to draw themselves. You should not call a Swing component's `paint()` method when you want to print it, though. Rendering of Swing components is buffered by default to improve the efficiency of displaying them but printing one by calling its `paint()` method adds a lot of unnecessary overhead to the printing operation. Instead you should call the `print()` method that is defined in the `JComponent` class. This renders the component directly to the graphics context that is passed as an argument, so there is no buffering of the output. The method automatically prints any child components that the component contains, so you need to call `print()` directly only for a top-level component.

The `print()` method for a Swing component that has `JComponent` as a base calls three protected methods to actually carry out the printing. The `printComponent()` method prints the component, the `printBorder()` method prints the component border, and the `printChildren()` method prints components that are children of the component. They each have a `Graphics` parameter.

If you want to customize how a Swing component is printed, you can subclass the component and override any or all of these. This doesn't apply to a `JFrame` component, though. The `JFrame` class is a subclass of `Frame` and does not have `JComponent` as a superclass. However, you can still call the `print()` method for a `JFrame` component to print it. In this case it's inherited from the `Container` class.

Let's implement a capability to print the Sketcher application window to see how this can be done.

TRY IT OUT   Printing the Sketcher Window

You can set up a menu item for this in the `createFileMenu()` method in the `SketcherFrame` class:

```
private void createFileMenu() {
  JMenu fileMenu = new JMenu("File");                // Create File menu
  fileMenu.setMnemonic('F');                         // Create shortcut
  createFileMenuActions();                           // Create Actions for File menu item

  // Code to create print setup menu item...

  // Menu item to print the application window
  JMenuItem printWindowItem = new JMenuItem("Print Window");
  printWindowItem.addActionListener(new ActionListener() {
          public void actionPerformed(ActionEvent e) {
            if(printer == null) {
              JOptionPane.showMessageDialog(SketcherFrame.this,
                                "No default printer available.",
                                "Printer Error",
                                JOptionPane.ERROR_MESSAGE);

              return;
            }
```

```
                    // The app window is the page source
                    printJob.setPrintable(SketcherFrame.this, pageFormat);
                    try {
                      printJob.print();
                    } catch(PrinterException pe) {
                      System.out.println(pe);
                      JOptionPane.showMessageDialog(SketcherFrame.this,
                                   "Error printing the application window.",
                                   "Printer Error",
                                   JOptionPane.ERROR_MESSAGE);
                    }
                  }
              });

            // Construct the file drop-down menu
            // Code to add file menu items as before...
            fileMenu.addSeparator();                 // Add separator
            fileMenu.add(printAction);               // Print sketch menu item
            fileMenu.add(printSetupItem);            // Print page setup menu item
            fileMenu.add(printWindowItem);           // Print window menu item
            fileMenu.addSeparator();                 // Add separator
            fileMenu.add(exitAction);                // Print sketch menu item
            menuBar.add(fileMenu);                   // Add the file menu
        }
```

Directory "Sketcher 13 printing the application window"

Note that you must qualify this in the actionPerformed() method. If you don't, this refers to the anonymous class object, and not the SketcherFrame object.

The application window is responsible for printing the window because it is obviously best placed to do this, so you must make the SketcherFrame class implement the Printable interface. Change the first line of the class definition to the following:

```
public class SketcherFrame   extends JFrame
                         implements ActionListener, Observer, Printable {
```

Directory "Sketcher 13 printing the application window"

Now you can add the definition of the print() method to the SketcherFrame class:

```
// Print the window
public int print(Graphics g,
                 PageFormat pageFormat,
                 int pageIndex)
            throws PrinterException {

  if(pageIndex > 0)                                // Only one page page 0 to be printed
    return NO_SUCH_PAGE;

  // Scale the component to fit
  Graphics2D g2D = (Graphics2D) g;

  // Calculate the scale factor to fit the window to the page
  double scaleX = pageFormat.getImageableWidth()/getWidth();
  double scaleY = pageFormat.getImageableHeight()/getHeight();

  double scale = Math.min(scaleX,scaleY);     // Get minimum scale factor

  // Move paper origin to page printing area corner
  g2D.translate(pageFormat.getImageableX(), pageFormat.getImageableY());
  g2D.scale(scale,scale);                          // Apply the scale factor
```

```
    print(g2D);                        // Draw the component
    return PAGE_EXISTS;
}
```

Directory "Sketcher 13 printing the application window"

The getWidth() and getHeight() methods you are calling here are inherited in the SketcherFrame class from the Component class, and they return the width and height of the window, respectively.

If you recompile and run Sketcher once more, the File ⇨ Print Window menu item should be operational.

How It Works

The menu operation and the printing mechanism function as I have already discussed. The SketcherFrame object is the page painter for the window, so the print() method is where it all happens. After checking the page index value and casting the Graphics reference passed to the method to Graphics2D, you calculate the scaling factor to fit the window to the page. The getWidth() and getHeight() methods inherited in our SketcherFrame class return the width and height of the window, respectively. You then apply the scale just as you did for printing a sketch. The coordinates of the top-left corner of the window are at (0, 0) so you can just print it once you have applied the scaling factor. Calling the inherited print() method with g2D as the argument does this.

I'm sure you have noticed that the output has deficiencies. The title bar and window boundary are missing. Of course, a JFrame object is a top-level window, and because it is derived from the Frame class, it is a heavyweight component with its appearance determined by its native peer, which is outside the Java code. The print() method for the JFrame object that you call to print the window does not include the peer elements of the window (peer elements are the native GUI elements). The printAll() method that the JFrame class inherits from the Component class does though. Modify the code in the print() method in SketcherFrame to call printAll() rather than print(), like this:

Available for download on Wrox.com

```
    printAll(g2D);                     // Draw the component
    return PAGE_EXISTS;
```

Directory "Sketcher 13 printing the application window"

Now you should get the whole application window printed.

SUMMARY

In this chapter you have added full support for the File menu to the Sketcher application for both sketch storage and retrieval and for printing. You should find that the techniques that you have used here are readily applicable in other Java applications. The approach to saving and restoring a model object is not usually dependent on the kind of data it contains. Of course, if your application is a word processor, you have a little more work to do taking care that the number of lines printed on each page is a whole number of lines. In other words, you have to make sure you avoid having the top half of a line of text on one page and the bottom half on the next. There are other Java classes to help with that and I don't really have the space to discuss them here, but look them up—the javax.swing.text package is a veritable gold mine for text handling!

If you have been following all the way with Sketcher, you now have an application that consists of well more than 1,500 lines of code, so you should be pretty pleased with yourself. And you're not finished with Sketcher yet—you add the capability to export and import sketches in XML over the next two chapters.

CONFER PROGRAMMER TO PROGRAMMER ABOUT THIS TOPIC.
Visit p2p.wrox.com

EXERCISES

You can download the source code for the examples in the book and the solutions to the following exercises from wrox.com.

1. Modify the Sketcher program to print the title at the top of the page on which the sketch is printed.

2. Modify the printing of a sketch so that a solid black boundary line is drawn around the sketch on the page.

3. Modify Sketcher to print a single sketch laid out on four pages. The sketch should be enlarged to provide the best fit on the four pages without distorting circles—that is, the same scale should be applied to the *x* and *y* axes.

4. Use a Book object to print a cover page plus the sketch spread over four pages, as in the previous exercise.

► WHAT YOU LEARNED IN THIS CHAPTER

TOPIC	CONCEPT
Serialization	You can implement the ability to write your model object to a file and read it back by making it serializable.
The `JFileChooser` Class	The `JFileChooser` class provides a generalized way for displaying a dialog to enable a file to be chosen.
Filtering a File List	You can limit the files that are displayed in a file chooser dialog by implementing a file filter. You can define you own file filter by subclassing the `FileFilter` class.
Printing	You initiate a printing operation by creating a `PrinterJob` object. This object encapsulates the interface to your printer and is used to manage the printing process.
Printers	A `PrintService` object encapsulates a printer and its capabilities.
Page Formatting	A `PageFormat` object defines the format for a page, and methods for this object provide information on the paper size and orientation, and the printable area on the page.
Paper	An object of type `Paper` defines the physical characteristics of a sheet of paper for the printer.
Print Dialogs	You can display a print dialog by calling the `printDialog()` method for a `PrinterJob` object. The no-argument version of `printDialog()` displays the native print dialog, whereas the version accepting a single argument of type `PrintRequestAttributeSet` displays a Java print dialog.
Printing a Page	Printing a page is always done by an object of a class that implements the `Printable` interface. You print a page by calling methods for the `Graphics` object passed to the `print()` method in the `Printable` interface by the `PrinterJob` object.
Printing Multiple Pages	You can manage multipage print jobs by implementing the `Pageable` interface in a class. This enables you to use different `PageFormat` objects to print different pages.
The `Book` Class	A `Book` object can encapsulate a series of pages to be printed. Each `Printable` object that is appended to a book prints one or more pages in a given format.

22

Java and XML

WHAT YOU WILL LEARN IN THIS CHAPTER:

➤ What a well-formed XML document is

➤ What constitutes a valid XML document

➤ What the components in an XML document are and how they are used

➤ What a DTD is and how it is defined

➤ What namespaces are and why you use them

➤ What the SAX and DOM APIs are and how they differ

➤ How you read documents using SAX

The Java Development Kit (JDK) includes capabilities for processing *Extensible Markup Language (XML)* documents. The classes that support XML processing are collectively referred to as JAXP, the Java API for XML Processing. In this chapter and the next, you explore not only how you can read XML documents, but also how you can create and modify them. This chapter provides a brief outline of XML and some related topics, plus a practical introduction to reading XML documents from within your Java programs using one of the two mechanisms you have available for this. In the next chapter I discuss how you can modify XML documents and how you create new XML documents programmatically. Inevitably, I can only skim the surface in a lot of areas because XML itself is a huge topic. However, you should find enough in this chapter and the next to give you a good feel for what XML is about and how you can handle XML documents in Java.

XML

XML, or the *Extensible Markup Language*, is a system- and hardware-independent language for defining data and its structure within an XML document. An *XML document* is a Unicode text file that contains data together with *markup* that defines the structure of the data. Because an XML document is a text file, you can create XML using any plain text editor, although an editor designed for creating and editing XML obviously makes things easier. The precise definition of XML is in the hands of the World Wide Web Consortium (W3C), and if you want to consult the current XML specifications, you can find them at www.w3.org/XML.

The term *markup* derives from a time when the paper draft of a document to be printed was *marked up* by hand to indicate to the typesetter how the printed form of the document should look. Indeed, the ancestry of XML can be traced back to a system that was originally developed by IBM in the 1960s to automate and standardize markup for system reference manuals for IBM hardware and software products. XML markup looks similar to HTML in that it consists of tags and attributes added to the text in a file. However, the superficial appearance is where the similarity between XML and HTML ends. XML and HTML are profoundly different in purpose and capability.

The Purpose of XML

Although an XML document can be created, read, and understood by a person, XML is primarily for communicating data from one computer to another. XML documents are therefore more typically generated and processed by computer programs. An XML document defines the structure of the data it contains so a program that receives it can properly interpret it. Thus XML is a tool for transferring information and its structure between computer programs. HTML, on the other hand, is solely for describing how data should look when it is displayed or printed. The structuring information that appears in an HTML document relates to the presentation of the data as a visible image. The purpose of HTML is data presentation.

HTML provides you with a set of tags that is essentially fixed and geared to the presentation of data. XML is a language in which you can define new sets of tags and attributes to suit different kinds of data—indeed, to suit any kind of data including *your* particular data. Because XML is extensible, it is often described as a *meta-language*—a language for defining new languages, in other words. The first step in using XML to exchange data is to define the language that you intend to use for that purpose in XML.

Of course, if I invent a set of XML markup to describe data of a particular kind, you need to know the rules for creating XML documents of this type if you want to create, receive, or modify them. As you later see, the definition of the markup that has been used within an XML document can be included as part of the document. It also can be provided as a separate entity, in a file identified by a URI, for example, that can be referenced within any document of that type. The use of XML has already been standardized for very diverse types of data. XML languages exist for describing the structures of chemical compounds and musical scores, as well as plain old text such as in this book.

Processing XML in Java

The JAXP provides you with the means for reading, creating, and modifying XML documents from within your Java programs. To understand and use this application program interface (API) you need to be reasonably familiar with two basic topics:

➤ What an XML document is for and what it consists of

➤ What a DTD is and how it relates to an XML document

You also need to be aware of what an XML namespace is, if only because JAXP has methods relating to handling these. You can find more information on JAXP at `http://jaxp.java.net`.

In case you are new to XML, I introduce the basic characteristics of XML and DTDs before explaining how you apply some of the classes and methods provided by JAXP to process XML documents. I also briefly explore what XML namespaces are for. If you are already comfortable with these topics you can skip most of this chapter and pick up where I start talking about SAX. Let's start by looking into the general organization of an XML document.

XML DOCUMENT STRUCTURE

An XML document basically consists of two parts, a *prolog* and a *document body*:

➤ **The prolog:** Provides information necessary for the interpretation of the contents of the document body. It contains two optional components, and because you can omit both, the prolog itself is optional. The two components of the prolog, in the sequence in which they must appear, are as follows:

➤ An *XML declaration* that defines the version of XML that applies to the document and may also specify the particular Unicode character encoding used in the document and whether the document is standalone or not. Either the character encoding or the standalone specification can be omitted from the XML declaration, but if they do appear, they must be in the given sequence.

➤ A *document type declaration* specifying an external *Document Type Definition (DTD)* that identifies markup declarations for the elements used in the body of the document, or explicit markup declarations, or both.

➤ **The document body:** Contains the data. It comprises one or more *elements* where each element is defined by a begin tag and an end tag. The elements in the document body define the structure of the data. There is always a single *root element* that contains all the other elements. All of the data within the document is contained within the elements in the document body.

Processing instructions (PI) for the document may also appear at the end of the prolog and at the end of the document body. Processing instructions are instructions intended for an application that processes the document in some way. You can include comments that provide explanations or other information for human readers of the XML document as part of the prolog and as part of the document body.

Well-Formed XML Documents

When an XML document is said to be *well-formed*, it just means that it conforms to the rules for writing XML as defined by the XML specification. Essentially, an XML document is well-formed if its prolog and body are consistent with the rules for creating these. In a well-formed document there must be only one root element, and all elements must be properly nested. I summarize more specifically what is required to make a document well-formed a little later in this chapter, after you have looked into the rules for writing XML.

An *XML processor* is a software module that is used by an application to read an XML document and gain access to the data and its structure. An XML processor also determines whether an XML document is well-formed or not. Processing instructions are passed through to an application without any checking or analysis by the XML processor. The XML specification describes how an XML processor should behave when reading XML documents, including what information should be made available to an application for various types of document content.

Here's an example of a well-formed XML document:

```
<proverb>Too many cooks spoil the broth.</proverb>
```

The document just consists of a root element that defines a proverb. There is no prolog, and formally, you don't have to supply one, but it would be much better if the document did include at least the XML version that is applicable, like this:

```
<?xml version="1.0"?>
<proverb>Too many cooks spoil the broth.</proverb>
```

The first line is the prolog, and it consists of just an XML declaration, which specifies that the document is consistent with XML version 1.0. The XML declaration must start with <?xml with no spaces within this five character sequence. You could also include an encoding declaration following the version specification in the prolog that specifies the Unicode encoding used in the document. For example:

```
<?xml version="1.0" encoding="UTF-8"?>
<proverb>Too many cooks spoil the broth.</proverb>
```

The first line states that as well as being XML version 1.0, the document uses the "UTF-8" Unicode encoding. If you omit the encoding specification, "UTF-8" or "UTF-16" is assumed, and because "UTF-8" includes ASCII as a subset, you don't need to specify an encoding if all you are using is ASCII text. The version and the character encoding specifications must appear in the order shown. If you reverse them you have broken the rules, so the document is no longer well-formed.

If you want to specify that the document is not dependent on any external definitions of markup, you can add a `standalone` specification to the prolog like this:

```
<?xml version="1.0" encoding="UTF-8" standalone="yes"?>
<proverb>Too many cooks spoil the broth.</proverb>
```

Specifying the value for `standalone` as `"yes"` indicates to an XML processor that the document is self-contained; there is no external definition of the markup, such as a DTD. A value of `"no"` indicates that the document is dependent on an external definition of the markup used, possibly in an external DTD.

Valid XML Documents

A *valid* XML document is a well-formed document that has an associated DTD (you learn more about creating DTDs later in this chapter). In a valid document the DTD must be consistent with the rules for creating a DTD and the document body must be consistent with the DTD. A DTD essentially defines a markup language for a given type of document and is identified in the DOCTYPE declaration in the document prolog. It specifies how all the elements that may be used in the document can be structured, and the elements in the body of the document must be consistent with it.

The previous example is well-formed, but not valid, because it does not have an associated DTD that defines the `<proverb>` element. Note that there is nothing *wrong* with an XML document that is not valid. It may not be ideal, but it is a perfectly legal XML document. *Valid* in this context is a technical term that means only that a document has a DTD.

An XML processor may be *validating* or *non-validating*. A validating XML processor checks that an XML document has a DTD and that its contents are correctly specified. It also verifies that the document is consistent with the rules expressed in the DTD and reports any errors that it finds. A non-validating XML processor does not check that the document is consistent with the DTD. As you later see, you can usually choose whether the XML processor that you use to read a document is validating or non-validating simply by switching the validating feature on or off.

Here's a variation on the example from the previous section with a document type declaration added:

```
<?xml version="1.0" encoding="UTF-8" standalone="no"?>
<!DOCTYPE proverb SYSTEM "proverb.dtd">
<proverb>Too many cooks spoil the broth.</proverb>
```

A document type declaration always starts with `<!DOCTYPE` so it is easily recognized. The name that appears in the DOCTYPE declaration, in this case `proverb`, must always match that of the root element for the document. I have specified the value for `standalone` as `"no"`, but it would still be correct if I left it out because the default value for `standalone` is `"no"` if there are external markup declarations in the document. The DOCTYPE declaration indicates that the markup used in this document can be found in the DTD at the URI `proverb.dtd`. You read a lot more about the DOCTYPE declaration later in this chapter.

Having an external DTD for documents of a given type does not eliminate all the problems that may arise when exchanging data. Obviously, confusion may arise when several people independently create DTDs for the same type of document. My DTD for documents containing sketches created by Sketcher is unlikely to be the same as yours. Other people with sketching applications may be inventing their versions of a DTD for representing a sketch, so the potential for conflicting definitions for markup is considerable. To obviate the difficulties that this sort of thing would cause, standard markup languages are being developed in XML that can be used universally for documents of common types. For example, the Mathematical Markup Language (MathML) is a language defined in XML for mathematical documents, and the Synchronized Multimedia Integration Language (SMIL) is a language for creating documents that contain multimedia presentations. There is also the Scalable Vector Graphics (SVG) language for representing 2D graphics, such as design drawings or even sketches created by Sketcher.

Let's understand a bit more about what XML markup consists of.

Elements in an XML Document

XML markup divides the contents of a document into elements by enclosing segments of the data between tags. As I said, there is always one root element that contains all the other elements in a document. In the earlier example, the following is an element:

```
<proverb> Too many cooks spoil the broth.</proverb>
```

In this case, this is the only element and is therefore the root element. *A start tag*, `<proverb>`, indicates the beginning of an element, and an *end tag*, `</proverb>`, marks its end. The name of the element, `proverb` in this case, always appears in both the start and end tags. The text between the start and end tags for an element is referred to as *element content* and in general may consist of just data, which is referred to as *character data*; other elements, which is described as *markup*; or a combination of character data and markup; or it may be empty. An element that contains no data and no markup is referred to as an *empty element*.

When an element contains plain text, the content is described as *parsed character data* (PCDATA). This means that the XML processor parses it—it analyzes it, in other words—to see if it can be broken down further. PCDATA allows for a mixture of ordinary data and other elements, referred to as *mixed content*, so a parser looks for the characters that delimit the start and end of markup tags. Consequently, ordinary text must not contain characters that might cause it to be recognized as a tag. You can't include < or & characters explicitly as part of the text within an element, for example. It could be a little inconvenient to completely prohibit such characters within ordinary text, so you can include them when you need to by using *predefined entities*. XML recognizes the predefined entities in Table 22-1 that represent characters that are otherwise recognized as part of markup:

TABLE 22-1: XML Predefined Entities

CHARACTER	PREDEFINED ENTITY
&	&amp;
'	&apos;
"	&quot;
<	&lt;
>	&gt;

Here's an element that makes use of a predefined entity:

```
<text> This is parsed character data within a &lt;text&gt; element.</text>
```

The content of this element is the following string:

```
This is parsed character data within a <text> element.
```

Here's an example of an XML document containing several elements:

```
<?xml version="1.0"?>
<address>
  <buildingnumber>29</buildingnumber>
  <street>South LaSalle Street</street>
  <city>Chicago</city>
  <state>Illinois</state>
  <zip>60603</zip>
</address>
```

This document evidently defines an address. Each tag pair identifies and categorizes the information between the tags. The data between `<address>` and `</address>` is an address, which is a composite of five further elements that each contain character data that forms part of the address. You can easily identify what each of the components of the address is from the tags that enclose each subunit of the data.

Rules for Tags

The tags that delimit an element have a precise form. Each element start tag must begin with < and end with >, and each element end tag must start with </ and end with >. The tag name—also known as the element type name—identifies the element and differentiates it from other elements. Note that the element name must immediately follow the opening < in the case of a start tag and the </ in the case of an end tag. If you insert a space here it is incorrect and is flagged as an error by an XML processor.

Because the `<address>` element contains all of the other elements that appear in the document, this is the root element. When one element encloses another, it must always do so completely if the document is to be well-formed. Unlike HTML, where a somewhat cavalier use of the language is usually tolerated, XML elements must *never* overlap. For example, you can't have

```
<address><zip>60603</address></zip>
```

An element that is enclosed by another element is referred to as the *child* of the enclosing element, and the enclosing element is referred to as the *parent* of the child element. In the earlier example of a document that defined an address, the `<address>` element is the parent of the other four because it directly encloses each of them, and the enclosed elements are child elements of the `<address>` element. In a well-formed document, each start tag must always be matched by a corresponding end tag, and vice versa. If this isn't the case, the document is not well-formed.

Don't forget that there must be only one root element that encloses all the other elements in a document. This implies that you cannot have an element of the same type as the root element as a child of any element in the document.

Empty Elements

You already know that an element can contain nothing at all, so just a start tag immediately followed by an end tag is an *empty element*. For example:

```
<commercial></commercial>
```

You have an alternative way to represent empty elements. Instead of writing a start and an end tag with nothing between them, you can write an empty element as a single tag with a forward slash immediately following the tag name:

```
<commercial/>
```

This is equivalent to a start tag followed by an end tag. There must be no spaces between the opening < and the element name, or between the / and the > marking the end of the tag.

You may be thinking at this point that an empty element is of rather limited use, whichever way you write it. Although by definition an empty element has no content, it can and often does contain additional information that is provided within *attributes* that appear within the tag. You see how you add attributes to an element a little later in this chapter. An empty element can be used as a marker or flag to indicate something about the data within its parent. For example, you might use an empty element as part of the content for an `<address>` element to indicate that the address corresponds to a commercial property. Absence of the `<commercial/>` element indicates a private residence.

Document Comments

When you create an XML document using an editor, it is often useful to add explanatory text to the document. You can include comments in an XML document like this:

```
<!-- Prepared on 14th January 2011 -->
```

Comments can go just about anywhere in the prolog or the document body, but not inside a start tag or an end tag, or within an empty element tag. You can spread a comment over several lines if you wish, like this:

```
<!--
  Eeyore, who is a friend of mine,
  has lost his tail.
-->
```

For compatibility with SGML, from which XML is derived, the text within a comment should not contain a sequence of two or more hyphens, and it must not end with a hyphen. A comment that ends with ---> is not well-formed and is rejected by an XML processor. Although an XML processor of necessity scans comments to distinguish them from markup and document data, they are not part of the character data within a document. XML processors need not make comments available to an application, although some may do so.

Element Names

If you're going to be creating elements then you're going to have to give them names, and XML is very generous in the names you're allowed to use. For example, there aren't any reserved words to avoid in XML, as there are in most programming languages, so you do have a lot of flexibility in this regard. However, there are certain rules that you must follow. The names you choose for elements must begin with either a letter or an underscore and can include digits, periods, and hyphens. Here are some examples of valid element names:

```
net_price   Gross-Weight   _sample   clause_3.2   pastParticiple
```

In theory you can use colons within a name but because colons have a special purpose in the context of names, you should not do so. XML documents use the Unicode character set, so any of the national language alphabets defined within that set may be used for names. HTML users need to remember that tag names in XML are case-sensitive, so <Address> is not the same as <address>.

Note also that names starting with uppercase or lowercase x followed by m followed by l are reserved, so you must not define names that begin xml or XmL or any of the other six possible sequences.

Defining General Entities

There is a frequent requirement to repeat a given block of parsed character data in the body of a document. An obvious example is some kind of copyright notice that you may want to insert in various places. You can define a named block of parsed text like this:

```
<!ENTITY copyright "© 2011 Ivor Horton">
```

This is an example of declaration of a *general entity*. You can put declarations of general entities within a DOCTYPE declaration in the document prolog or within an external DTD. I describe how a little later in this chapter. The block of text that appears between the double quotes is identified by the name copyright. You could equally well use single quotes as delimiters for the string. Wherever you want to insert this text in the document, you just need to insert the name delimited by an ampersand at the beginning and a semicolon at the end, thus:

```
&copyright;
```

This is called an *entity reference*. This is exactly the same notation as the predefined entities representing markup characters that you saw earlier. It causes the equivalent text to be inserted at this point when the document is parsed. A general entity is parsed text, so you need to take care that the document is still well-formed and valid after the substitution has been made.

An entity declaration can include entity references. For example, I could declare the copyright entity like this:

```
<!ENTITY copyright "© 2011 Ivor Horton &documentDate;">
```

The text contains a reference to a documentDate entity. Entity references may appear in a document only after their corresponding entity declarations, so the declaration for the documentDate entity must precede the declaration for the copyright entity:

```
<!ENTITY documentDate "24th January 2011">
<!ENTITY copyright "© 2011 Ivor Horton &documentDate;">
```

Entity declarations can contain nested entity references to any depth, so the declaration for the documentDate entity could contain other entity references. Substitutions for entity references are made recursively by the XML processor until all references have been resolved. An entity declaration must not directly or indirectly contain a reference to itself though.

You can also use general entities that are defined externally. You use the SYSTEM keyword followed by the URL for where the text is stored in place of the text in the ENTITY declaration. For example:

```
<!ENTITY usefulstuff SYSTEM "http://www.some-server.com/inserts/stuff.txt">
```

The reference &usefulstuff; represents the contents of the file stuff.txt.

CDATA Sections

It is possible to embed *unparsed character data (CDATA)* anywhere in a document where character data can occur. You do this by placing the unparsed character data in a CDATA section, which begins with <![CDATA[and ends with]]>. The data is described as unparsed because the XML processor does not analyze it in any way but makes it available to an application. The data within a CDATA section can be anything at all—it can even be binary data. You can use a CDATA section to include markup in a document that you don't want to have parsed. For example

```
<explanation> A typical circle element is written as:
<![CDATA[
  <circle diameter="30">
    <position x="40" y="50"/>
  </circle>
]]>
</explanation>
```

The lines shown in bold are within a CDATA section, and although they look suspiciously like markup, an XML processor looking for markup does not scan them. I have used some of the reserved characters in here without escaping them, but because the data in a CDATA section is not parsed, they are not identified as markup.

Element Attributes

You can put additional information within an element in the form of one or more *attributes*. An attribute is identified by an attribute name, and the value is specified as a string between single or double quotes. For example:

```
<elementname attributename="Attribute value"> ... </elementname>
```

As I said earlier, empty elements frequently have attributes. Here's an example of an empty element with three attributes:

```
<color red="255" green="128" blue="64"></color>
```

This is normally written in the shorthand form, like this:

```
<color red="255" green="128" blue="64" />
```

You can use single quotes to delimit an attribute value if you want. The names of the three attributes here are red, green, and blue, which identify the primary components of the color. The values for these between 0 and 255 represent the contribution of each primary color to the result. Attribute names are defined using the same rule as element names. The attributes for an element follow the element name in the start tag (or the only tag in the case of an empty element) and are separated from it by at least one space. If a tag has multiple attributes, they must be separated by spaces. You can also put spaces on either side of the = sign, but it is clearer without, especially where there are several attributes. HTML fans should note that a comma separator between attributes is not allowed in XML and is reported as an error.

A string that is an attribute value must not contain a delimiting character explicitly within the string, but you can put a double quote as part of the value string if you use single quotes as delimiters, and vice versa. For example, you could write the following:

```
<textstuff answer="it's mine"   explanation='He said"It is mine"'/>
```

The value for the answer attribute uses double quotes as delimiters, so it can contain a single quote explicitly; thus the value is it's mine. Similarly, the value for the second attribute uses single quotes so the string can contain a double quote, so its value is He said "It is mine". Of course, someone is bound to want both a single quote and a double quote as part of the value string. Easy, just use an escape sequence within the value for the one that is a delimiter. For example, you could rewrite the previous example as

```
<textstuff answer='it&apos;s mine' explanation="He said&quot;It's mine&quot;"/>
```

In general it's easiest to stick to a particular choice of delimiter for strings and always escape occurrences of the delimiter within a string.

You can define a circle by a diameter and a position. You can easily define a circle in XML—in fact, there are many ways in which you could do this. Here's one example:

```
<circle diameter="30">
  <position x="40" y="50"/>
</circle>
```

The diameter attribute for the <circle> tag specifies the diameter of the circle, and its position is specified by an empty <position/> tag, with the x and y coordinates of the circle's position specified by attributes x and y. A reasonable question to ask is whether this is the best way of representing a circle. Let's explore the options in this context a little further.

Attributes versus Elements

Obviously you could define a circle without using attributes, maybe like this:

```
<circle>
  <diameter>30</diameter>
  <position>
    <x-coordinate>40</x-coordinate>
    <y-coordinate>50</y-coordinate>
  </position>
</circle>
```

This is the opposite extreme. There are no attributes here, only elements. Where the content of an element is one or more other elements—as in the case of the <circle> and <position> elements here—it is described as *element content*. A document design in which all the data is part of element content and no attributes are involved is described as *element-normal*.

Of course, it is also possible to represent the data defining a circle just using attributes within a single element:

```
<circle positionx="40" positiony="50" diameter="30"/>
```

Now you have just one element defining a circle with all the data defined by attribute values. Where all the data in a document is defined as attribute values, it is described as *attribute-normal*.

An element can also contain a mixture of text and markup—so-called *mixed content*—so you have another way in which you could define a circle in XML, like this:

```
<circle>
  <position>
    <x-coordinate>40</x-coordinate>
    <y-coordinate>50</y-coordinate>
  </position>
  30
</circle>
```

Now the value for the diameter just appears as text as part of the content of the <circle> element along with the position element. The disadvantage of this arrangement is that it's not obvious what the text is, so some information about the structure has been lost compared to the previous example.

So which is the better approach, to go for attributes or elements? Well, it can be either, or both, if you see what I mean. It depends on what the structure of the data is, how the XML is generated, and how it will be used. One overriding consideration is that an attribute is a single value. It has no inner structure, so anything that does have substructure must be expressed using elements. Where data is essentially hierarchical, representing family trees in XML, for example, you should use nested elements to reflect the structure of the data. Where the data is serial or tabular, temperature and rainfall or other weather data over time, for example, you may well use attributes within a series of elements within the root element.

If you are generating an XML document interactively using an editor, then readability is an important consideration. Poor readability encourages errors. You'll lean toward whatever makes the editing easier—and for the most part, elements are easier to find and edit than attributes. Attribute values should be short for readability, so this limits the sort of data that you can express as an attribute. You probably would not want to see the soliloquy from Shakespeare's *Hamlet* appearing as an attribute value, for example. That said, if the XML is computer-generated and is not primarily intended for human viewing, the choice is narrowed down to the most efficient way to handle the data in the computer. Attributes and their values are readily identified in a program, so documents are likely to make use of attributes wherever the structure of the data does not require otherwise. You see how this works out in practice when you get to use the Java API for processing XML.

Whitespace and Readability

The indentation shown in the examples so far has been included just to provide you with visual cues to the structure of the data. It is not required, and an XML processor ignores the whitespace between elements. When you are creating XML in an editor, you can use whitespace between elements to make it easier for a human reader to understand the document. Whitespace can consist of spaces, tabs, carriage returns, and linefeed characters. You can see that a circle expressed without whitespace, as shown below, is significantly less readable:

```
<circle><position><x-coordinate>40</x-coordinate><y-coordinate>50
</y-coordinate></position>30</circle>
```

Having said that, you don't have complete freedom in deciding where you put whitespace within a tag. The tag name must immediately follow the opening < or </ in a tag, and there can be no space within an opening </ delimiter, or a closing /> delimiter in the case of an empty element. You must also separate an attribute from the tag name or from another attribute with at least one space. Beyond that you can put additional spaces within a tag wherever you like.

DATA STRUCTURE IN XML

The ability to nest elements is fundamental to defining the structure of the data in a document. We can easily represent the structure of the data in our XML fragment defining an address, as shown in Figure 22-1.

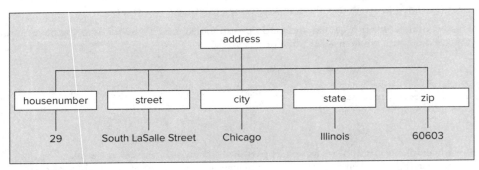

FIGURE 22-1

The structure follows directly from the nesting of the elements. The `<address>` element contains all of the others directly, so the nested elements are drawn as subsidiary or child elements of the `<address>` element. The items that appear within the tree structure—the elements and the data items—are referred to as *nodes*.

Figure 22-2 shows the structure of the first circle definition in XML that you saw in the previous section. Even though there's an extra level of elements in this diagram, there are strong similarities to the structure shown in Figure 22-1.

You can see that both structures have a single root element, <address> in the first example and <circle> in the second. You can also see that each element contains either other elements or some data that is a segment of the document content. In both diagrams all the document content lies at the bottom. Nodes at the extremities of a tree are referred to as *leaf nodes*.

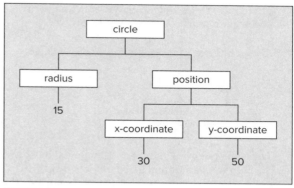

FIGURE 22-2

In fact an XML document *always* has a structure similar to this. Each element in a document can contain other elements, or text, or elements and text, or it can be empty.

DOCUMENT TYPE DEFINITIONS

You have seen several small examples of XML, and in each case it was fairly obvious what the content was meant to represent, but where are the rules that ensure such data is represented consistently and correctly in different documents? Do the <diameter> and <position> elements have to be in that sequence in a <circle> element, and could you omit either of them?

Clearly there has to be a way to determine what is correct and what is incorrect for any particular element in a document. As I mentioned earlier, a DTD defines how valid elements are constructed for a particular type of document, so the XML for purchase order documents in a company could be defined by one DTD, and sales invoice documents by another. The Document Type Definition for a document is specified in a *document type declaration*—commonly known as a DOCTYPE declaration—that appears in the document prolog following any XML declaration. A DTD essentially defines a *vocabulary* for describing data of a particular kind—the set of elements that you use to identify the data, in other words. It also defines the possible relationships between these elements—how they can be nested. The contents of a document of the type identified by a particular DTD must be defined and structured according to rules that make up the DTD. Any document of a given type can be checked for validity against its DTD.

A DTD can be an integral part of a document, but it is usually, and more usefully, defined separately. Including a DTD in an XML document makes the document self-contained, but it does increase its bulk. It also means that the DTD has to appear within every document of the same type. A separate DTD that is external to a document avoids this and provides a single reference point for all documents of a particular type. An external DTD also makes maintenance of the DTD for a document type easier, as it only needs to be changed in one place for all documents that make use of it. Let's look at how you identify the DTD for a document and then investigate some of the ways in which elements and their attributes can be defined in a DTD.

Declaring a DTD

You use a document type declaration (a DOCTYPE declaration) in the prolog of an XML document to specify the DTD for the document. An XML 1.0 document can have only one DOCTYPE declaration. You can include the markup declarations for elements used in the document explicitly within the DOCTYPE statement, in which case the declarations are referred to as the *internal subset*. You can also specify a URI that identifies the DTD for the document, usually in the form of a URL. In this case the set of declarations is referred to as the *external subset*. If you include explicit declarations as well as a URI referencing an external DTD, the document has both an internal and an external subset. Here is an example of an XML document that has an external subset:

```
<?xml version="1.0"?>
<!DOCTYPE address SYSTEM "http://docserver/dtds/AddressDoc.dtd">
<address>
  <buildingnumber> 29 </buildingnumber>
  <street> South LaSalle Street</street>
  <city>Chicago</city>
  <state>Illinois</state>
  <zip>60603</zip>
</address>
```

The name following the DOCTYPE keyword must always match the root element name in the document, so the DOCTYPE declaration here indicates that the root element in the document has the name address. The declaration also indicates that the DTD in which this and the other elements in the document are declared is an external DTD located at the URI following the SYSTEM keyword. This URI, which is invariably a URL, is called the *system ID* for the DTD.

In principle, you can also specify an external DTD by a *public ID* using the keyword PUBLIC in place of SYSTEM. A public ID is just a unique public name that identifies the DTD—a Uniform Resource Name (URN), in other words. As you probably know, the idea behind URNs is to get over the problem of changes to URLs. Public IDs are intended for DTDs that are available as public standards for documents of particular types, such as SVG. However, there is a slight snag. Because there is no mechanism defined for resolving public IDs to find the corresponding URL, if you specify a public ID, you still have to supply a system ID with a URL so the XML processor can find it, so you won't see public IDs in use much.

If the file containing the DTD is stored on the local machine, you can specify its location relative to the directory containing the XML document. For example, the following DOCTYPE declaration implies that the DTD is in the same directory as the document itself:

```
<!DOCTYPE address SYSTEM "AddressDoc.dtd">
```

The AddressDoc.dtd file includes definitions for the elements that may be included in a document containing an address. In general, a relative URL is assumed to be relative to the location of the document containing the reference.

Defining a DTD

In looking at the details of how we put a DTD together, I'll use examples in which the DTD is an internal subset, but the declarations in an external DTD are exactly the same. Here's an example of a document with an integral DTD:

```
<?xml version="1.0"?>
<!DOCTYPE proverb [  <!ELEMENT proverb (#PCDATA)>   ]>
<proverb>A little knowledge is a dangerous thing.</proverb>
```

All the internal definitions for elements used within the document appear between the square brackets in the DOCTYPE declaration. In this case just one element is declared, the root element, and the element content is PCDATA—parsed character data.

You could define an external DTD in a file with the name proverbDoc.dtd in the same directory as the document. The file would contain just a single line:

```
<!ELEMENT proverb (#PCDATA)>
```

The XML document would then be the following:

```
<?xml version="1.0"?>
<!DOCTYPE proverb SYSTEM "proverbDoc.dtd">
<proverb>A little knowledge is a dangerous thing.</proverb>
```

The DTD is referenced by a relative URI that is relative to the directory containing the document.

When you want both an internal and external subset, you just put both in the DOCTYPE declaration, with the external DTD reference appearing first. Entities from both are available for use in the document, but where there is any conflict between them, the entities defined in the internal subset take precedence over those declared in the external subset.

The syntax for defining elements and their attributes is rather different from the syntax for XML markup. It also can get quite complex, so I'm not able to go into it comprehensively here. However, you do need to have a fair idea of how a DTD is put together in order to understand the operation of the Java API for XML, so let's look at some of the ways in which you can define elements in a DTD.

Defining Elements in DTDs

The DTD defines each type of element that can appear in the document using an ELEMENT type declaration. For example, the <address> element could be defined like this:

```
<!ELEMENT address (buildingnumber, street, city, state, zip)>
```

This defines the element with the name address. The information between the parentheses specifies what can appear within an <address> element. The definition states that an <address> element contains exactly one each of the elements <buildingnumber>, <street>, <city>, <state>, and <zip>, in that sequence. This is an example of *element content* because only elements are allowed within an <address> element. Note the space that appears between the element name and the parentheses enclosing the content definition. This is required, and a parser flags the absence of at least one space here as an error. The ELEMENT identifier must be in capital letters and must immediately follow the opening "<!."

The preceding definition of the <address> element makes no provision for anything other than the five elements shown, and in that sequence. Thus, any whitespace that you put between these elements in a document is not part of the content and is ignored by a parser; therefore, it is known as *ignorable whitespace*. That said, you can still find out if there is whitespace there when the document is parsed, as you later see.

You can define the <buildingnumber> element like this:

```
<!ELEMENT buildingnumber (#PCDATA)>
```

This states that the element can contain only parsed character data, specified by #PCDATA. This is just ordinary text, and because it is parsed, it cannot contain markup. The # character preceding the word PCDATA is necessary just to ensure it cannot be confused with an element or attribute name—it has no other significance. Because element and attribute names must start with a letter or an underscore, the # prefix to PCDATA ensures that it cannot be interpreted as such.

The PCDATA specification does provide for markup—child elements—to be mixed in with ordinary text. In this case you must specify the names of the elements that can occur mixed in with the text. If you want to allow a <suite> element specifying a suite number to appear alongside the text within a <buildingnumber> element, you could express it like this:

```
<!ELEMENT buildingnumber (#PCDATA|suite)*>
```

This indicates that the content for a <buildingnumber> element is parsed character data, and the text can be combined with <suite> elements. The | operator here has the same meaning as the | operator you read about in the context of regular expressions in Chapter 15. It means one or other of the two operands, but not both. The * following the parentheses is required here and has the same meaning as the * operator that you also read about in the context of regular expressions. It means that the operand to the left can appear zero or more times.

If you want to allow several element types to be optionally mixed in with the text, you separate them by |. Note that it is not possible to control the sequence in which mixed content appears.

The other elements used to define an address are similar, so you could define the whole document with its DTD like this:

```
<?xml version="1.0"?>
<!DOCTYPE address
[
  <!ELEMENT address (buildingnumber, street, city, state, zip)>
  <!ELEMENT buildingnumber (#PCDATA)>
  <!ELEMENT street (#PCDATA)>
```

```
        <!ELEMENT city (#PCDATA)>
        <!ELEMENT state (#PCDATA)>
        <!ELEMENT zip (#PCDATA)>
  ]>
  <address>
    <buildingnumber> 29 </buildingnumber>
    <street> South LaSalle Street</street>
    <city>Chicago</city>
    <state>Illinois</state>
    <zip>60603</zip>
  </address>
```

Note that you have no way with DTDs to constrain the parsed character data in an element definition. It would be nice to be able to specify that the building number had to be numeric, for example, but the DTD grammar and syntax provide no way to do this. This is a serious limitation of DTDs and one of the driving forces behind the development of XML Schemas, which is an XML-based description language that supports data types and offers an alternative to DTDs. I introduce XML Schemas a little later in this chapter.

If you were to create the DTD for an address document as a separate file, the file contents would just consist of the element definitions:

```
  <!ELEMENT address (buildingnumber, street, city, state, zip)>
  <!ELEMENT buildingnumber (#PCDATA)>
  <!ELEMENT street (#PCDATA)>
  <!ELEMENT city (#PCDATA)>
  <!ELEMENT state (#PCDATA)>
  <!ELEMENT zip (#PCDATA)>
```

The DOCTYPE declaration identifies the DTD for a particular document, so it is not part of the DTD. If the preceding DTD were stored in the AddressDoc.dtd file in the same directory as the document, the DOCTYPE declaration in the document would be the following:

```
  <?xml version="1.0"?>
  <!DOCTYPE address SYSTEM "AddressDoc.dtd">
  <address>
    <buildingnumber> 29 </buildingnumber>
    <street> South LaSalle Street</street>
    <city>Chicago</city>
    <state>Illinois</state>
    <zip>60603</zip>
  </address>
```

Of course, the DTD file would also include definitions for element attributes, if there were any. These will be useful later, so save the DTD (as AddressDoc.dtd) and the preceding XML file (as Address.xml, perhaps) in your Beg Java Stuff directory that is in your user.home directory.

One further possibility you need to consider is that in many situations it is desirable to allow some child elements to be omitted. For example, <buildingnumber> may not be included in some cases. The <zip> element, while highly desirable, might also be left out in practice. We can indicate that an element is optional by using the *cardinality operator*, ?. This operator expresses the same idea as the equivalent regular expression operator, and it indicates that a child element may or may not appear. The DTD would then look like this:

```
  <!DOCTYPE address
  [
    <!ELEMENT address (buildingnumber?, street, city, state, zip?)>
    <!ELEMENT buildingnumber (#PCDATA)>
    <!ELEMENT street (#PCDATA)>
    <!ELEMENT city (#PCDATA)>
    <!ELEMENT state (#PCDATA)>
    <!ELEMENT zip (#PCDATA)>
  ]>
```

The ? operator following an element indicates that the element may be omitted or may appear just once. This is just one of three cardinality operators that you use to specify how many times a particular child element can appear as part of the content for the parent. The cardinality of an element is simply the number of possible occurrences for the element. The other two cardinality operators are *, which you have already seen, and +. In each case the operator follows the operand to which it applies. You now have four operators

TABLE 22-2: Operators for Element Declarations in a DTD

OPERATOR	DESCRIPTION
+	This operator indicates that there can be one or more occurrences of its operand. In other words, there *must* be at least one occurrence, but there may be more.
*	This operator indicates that there can be zero or more occurrences of its operand. In other words, there can be none or any number of occurrences of the operand to which it applies.
?	This indicates that its operand may appear once or not at all.
|	This operator indicates that there can be an occurrence of either its left operand or its right operand, but not both.

that you can use in element declarations in a DTD, and they are each similar in action to their equivalent in the regular expression context (see Table 22-2):

You might want to allow a building number or a building name in an address, in which case the DTD could be written as follows:

```
<!ELEMENT address ((buildingnumber | buildingname), street, city, state, zip?)>
<!ELEMENT buildingnumber (#PCDATA)>
<!ELEMENT buildingname (#PCDATA)>
<!ELEMENT street (#PCDATA)>
<!ELEMENT city (#PCDATA)>
<!ELEMENT state (#PCDATA)>
<!ELEMENT zip (#PCDATA)>
```

The DTD now states that either `<buildingnumber>` or `<buildingname>` must appear as the first element in `<address>`. But you might want to allow neither, in which case you would write the third line as the following:

```
<!ELEMENT address ((buildingnumber | buildingname)?, street, city, state, zip?)>
```

The ? operator applies to the parenthesized expression (`buildingnumber | buildingname`), so it now states that either `<buildingnumber>` or `<buildingname>` may or may not appear, so you allow one, or the other, or none.

Of course, you can use the | operator repeatedly to express a choice between any number of elements, or indeed, subexpressions between parentheses. For example, given that you have defined elements `Linux`, `Solaris`, and `Windows`, you might define the element `operatingsystem` as

```
<!ELEMENT operatingsystem (Linux | Solaris | Windows)>
```

If you want to allow an arbitrary operating system to be identified as a further alternative, you could write

```
<!ELEMENT operatingsystem (AnyOS | Linux | Solaris | Windows)>
<!ELEMENT AnyOS (#PCDATA)>
```

You can combine the operators you've seen to produce definitions for content of almost unlimited complexity. For example:

```
<!ELEMENT breakfast ((tea|coffee), orangejuice?,
                     ((egg+, (bacon|sausage)) | cereal) , toast)>
```

This states that `<breakfast>` content is either a `<tea>` or `<coffee>` element, followed by an optional `<orangejuice>` element, followed by either one or more `<egg>` elements and a `<bacon>` or `<sausage>` element, or a `<cereal>` element, with a mandatory `<toast>` element bringing up the rear. However, while you can produce mind-boggling productions for defining elements, it is wise to keep things as simple as possible.

After all this complexity, you mustn't forget that an element may also be empty, in which case it can be defined like this:

```
<!ELEMENT position EMPTY>
```

This states that the `<position>` element has no content. Elements can also have attributes, so let's take a quick look at how they can be defined in a DTD.

Defining Element Attributes

You use an `ATTLIST` declaration in a DTD to define the attributes for a particular element. As you know, attributes are name-value pairs associated with a particular element, and values are typically, but not exclusively, text. Where the value for an attribute is text, it is enclosed between quotation marks, so it is always unparsed character data. Attribute values that consist of text are therefore specified just as `CDATA`. No preceding # character is necessary in this context because there is no possibility of confusion.

You could declare the elements for a document containing circles as follows:

```
<?xml version="1.0"?>

<!DOCTYPE circle
[
   <!ELEMENT circle (position)>
   <!ATTLIST circle
            diameter CDATA #REQUIRED
   >

   <!ELEMENT position EMPTY>
   <!ATTLIST position
            x CDATA #REQUIRED
            y CDATA #REQUIRED
   >
]>

<circle diameter="30">
  <position x="30" y="50"/>
</circle>
```

Three items define each attribute—the attribute name, the type of value (`CDATA`), and whether or not the attribute is mandatory. This third item may also define a default value for the attribute, in which case this value is assumed if the attribute is omitted. The `#REQUIRED` specification against an attribute name indicates that it must appear in the corresponding element. You specify the attribute as `#IMPLIED` if it need not be included. In this case the XML processor does not supply a default value for the attribute. An application is expected to have a default value of its own for the attribute value that is implied by the attribute's omission.

Save this XML in your `Beg Java Stuff` directory with a suitable name such as `"circle with DTD.xml;"` it comes in handy in the next chapter.

You specify a default value for an attribute between double quotes. For example:

```
<!ATTLIST circle
        diameter CDATA "2"
>
```

This indicates that the value of `diameter` is 2 if the attribute is not specified for a `<circle>` element.

You can also insist that a value for an attribute must be one of a fixed set. For example, suppose you had a `color` attribute for your circle that could be only red, blue, or green. You could define it like this:

```
<!ATTLIST circle
        color (red|blue|green) #IMPLIED
>
```

The value for the `color` attribute in a `<circle>` element must be one of the options between the parentheses. In this case the attribute can be omitted because it is specified as `#IMPLIED`, and an application processing it supplies a default value. To make the inclusion of the attribute mandatory, you define it as

```
<!ATTLIST circle
        color (red|blue|green) #REQUIRED
>
```

An important aspect of defining possible attribute values by an enumeration like this is that an XML editor can help the author of a document by prompting with the list of possible attribute values from the DTD when the element is being created.

An attribute that you declare as `#FIXED` must always have the default value. For example:

```
<!ATTLIST circle
        color (red|blue|green)  #REQUIRED
        line_thickness medium   #FIXED
>
```

Here the XML processor supplies an application only with the value `medium` for the `thickness` attribute. If you were to specify this attribute for the `<circle>` element in the body of the document you could use only the default value; otherwise, it is an error.

Defining Parameter Entities

You often need to repeat a block of information at different places in a DTD. A *parameter entity* identifies a block of parsed text by a name that you can use to insert the text at various places within a DTD. Note that parameter entities are for use only within a DTD. You cannot use parameter entity references in the body of a document. You declare general entities in the DTD when you want to repeat text within the document body.

The form for a parameter entity is very similar to what you saw for general entities, except that a `%` character appears between `ENTITY` and the entity name, separated from both by a space. For example, it is quite likely that you would want to repeat the `x` and `y` attributes that you defined in the `<position>` element in the previous section in other elements. You could define a parameter entity for these attributes and then use that wherever these attributes appear in an element declaration. Here's the parameter entity declaration:

```
<!ENTITY % coordinates "x CDATA #REQUIRED y CDATA #REQUIRED">
```

Now you can use the entity name to insert the `x` and `y` attribute definitions in an attribute declaration:

```
<!ATTLIST position %coordinates; >
```

A parameter entity declaration must precede its use in a DTD.

The substitution string in a parameter entity declaration is parsed and can include parameter and general entity references. As with general entities, you can also define a parameter entity by a reference to a URI containing the substitution string.

Other Types of Attribute Values

There are a further eight possibilities for specifying the type of the attribute value. I'm not going into detail on these, but a brief description of each is in Table 22-3 so you can recognize them:

TABLE 22-3: Other Types of Attribute Values

VALUE	DESCRIPTION
ENTITY	An entity defined in the DTD. An entity here is a name identifying an unparsed entity defined elsewhere in the DTD by an `ENTITY` tag. The entity may or may not contain text. An entity could represent something very simple, such as `&lt;`, which refers to a single character, or it could represent something more substantial, such as an image.
ENTITIES	A list of entities defined in the DTD, separated by spaces.

continues

TABLE 22-3 *(continued)*

VALUE	DESCRIPTION
ID	An ID is a unique name identifying an element in a document. This is to enable internal references to a particular element from elsewhere in the document.
IDREF	A reference to an element elsewhere in a document via its ID.
IDREFS	A list of references to IDs, separated by spaces.
NMTOKEN	A name conforming to the XML definition of a name. This just says that the value of the attribute is consistent with the XML rules for a name.
NMTOKENS	A list of name tokens, separated by spaces.
NOTATION	A name identifying a notation—which is typically a format specification for an entity such as a JPEG or PostScript file. The notation is identified elsewhere in the DTD using a NOTATION tag that may also identify an application capable of processing an entity in the given format.

A DTD for Sketcher

With what you know of XML and DTDs, you can have a stab at putting together a DTD for storing Sketcher files as XML. As I said before, an XML language has already been defined for representing and communicating two-dimensional graphics. This is called Scalable Vector Graphics, and you can find it at www.w3.org/TR/SVG/. Although this would be the choice for transferring 2D graphics as XML documents in a real-world context, the objective here is to exercise your knowledge of XML and DTDs, so you'll reinvent your own version of this wheel, even though it has fewer spokes and may wobble a bit.

First, let's consider what the general approach is going to be. The objective is to define a DTD that enables you to exercise the Java API for XML with Sketcher, so you define the language to make it an easy fit to Sketcher rather than worrying about the niceties of the best way to represent each geometric element. Because Sketcher was a vehicle for trying out various capabilities of the Java class libraries, it evolved in a somewhat Topsy-like fashion, with the result that the classes defining geometric entities are not necessarily ideal. However, you just map these directly in XML to avoid the mathematical hocus pocus that would be necessary if you adopted a more formal representation of geometry in XML.

You want to be able to reconstruct the elements in an existing sketch from the XML, so this does not necessarily require the same data as you used to create the elements in the first place. Essentially, you want to reconstruct the fields in an Element object. For the geometric elements, this means reconstructing the object that represents a particular element, plus its position, rotation angle, bounding rectangle, and color.

The XML Element for a Sketch

A sketch is a very simple document. It's basically a sequence of lines, circles, rectangles, curves, and text. You can therefore define the root element <sketch> in the DTD as the following:

```
<!ELEMENT sketch (line|circle|rectangle|curve|text)*>
```

This says that a sketch consists of zero or more of any of the elements between the parentheses. You now need to define each of these elements.

The XML Element for a Line Element in a Sketch

A line is easy. It is defined by its location, which is its start point and a Line2D.Double object. It also has an orientation—its rotation angle—and a color. You could define a <line> element like this:

```
<!ELEMENT line (color, position, bounds, endpoint)>
  <!ATTLIST line
        angle CDATA                    #REQUIRED
  >
```

A line is fully defined by two points, its position, and its end point, which is relative to the origin. A line has a `bounds` rectangle, as all the elements do, so you define another type of element, `<bounds>`, for this rectangle.

You could define color by a `color` attribute to the `<line>` element with a set of alternative values, but to allow the flexibility for lines of any color, it would be better to define a `<color>` element with three attributes for RGB values. In this case you can define the `<color>` element as

```
<!ELEMENT color EMPTY>
  <!ATTLIST color
          R CDATA                    #REQUIRED
          G CDATA                    #REQUIRED
          B CDATA                    #REQUIRED
  >
```

You can now define the `<position>` and `<endpoint>` elements. These are both points defined by an (x, y) coordinate pair, so you would sensibly define them consistently. Empty elements with attributes are the most economical way here, and you can use a parameter entity for the attributes:

```
<!ENTITY % coordinates "x CDATA #REQUIRED y CDATA #REQUIRED">
<!ELEMENT position EMPTY>
  <!ATTLIST position %coordinates;>
<!ELEMENT endpoint EMPTY>
  <!ATTLIST endpoint %coordinates;>
```

You can define a `<bounds>` element with the coordinates of its top-left corner and the width and height as attributes:

```
<!ENTITY % dimensions "width CDATA #REQUIRED height CDATA #REQUIRED">
<!ELEMENT bounds EMPTY>
  <!ATTLIST bounds
            %coordinates;
            %dimensions;>
```

You could conceivably omit the top-left corner coordinates because they are the same as the position for the sketch element. However, including them enables you to reconstruct the bounding rectangle object with no dependency on the `position` field having been reconstructed previously.

The XML Element for a Rectangle Element in a Sketch

You can define a rectangle very similarly to a line because it is defined by its position, which corresponds to the top-left corner, plus a rectangle at the origin with a width and height. The width and height attributes are specified by a parameter entity because you are able to use this in the XML element for a rectangle. A rectangle also has a color in which it is to be drawn, a rotation angle, and a bounding rectangle. Here's how this looks in the DTD:

```
<!ELEMENT rectangle (color, position, bounds)>
  <!ATTLIST rectangle
          angle CDATA                #REQUIRED
          %dimensions;>
```

As with a line, the rotation angle is specified by an attribute, as are the width and height of the `Rectangle2D.Double` object.

The XML Element for a Circle Element in a Sketch

The `<circle>` element is no more difficult. It has a position and the `Ellipse2D.Double` object has a width and a height, but these are the same, being the diameter of the circle. Like other elements, it has a color, a rotation angle (remember, we rotate circles about the top-left corner of the enclosing rectangle in Sketcher), and a bounding rectangle. You can define it like this:

```
<!ELEMENT circle (color, position, bounds)>
  <!ATTLIST circle
          angle CDATA                #REQUIRED
          diameter CDATA             #REQUIRED
  >
```

The XML Element for a Curve Element in a Sketch

The `<curve>` element is a little more complicated because it's defined by an arbitrary number of points, but it's still quite easy:

```
<!ELEMENT curve (color, position, bounds, point+)>
  <!ATTLIST curve  angle CDATA  #REQUIRED>
<!ELEMENT point EMPTY>
  <!ATTLIST point %coordinates;>
```

The start point of the curve is defined by the `<position>` element, and the `GeneralPath` object that defines a curve includes at least one `<point>` element in addition to the origin, which is specified by the + operator. The `<point>` element just has attributes for the coordinate pair.

The XML Element for a Text Element in a Sketch

You need to allow for the font name and its style and point size, a rotation angle for the text, and a color—plus the text itself, of course, and its position. A `Text` element also has a bounding rectangle that is required to construct it. You have some options as to how you define this element. You could use mixed element content in a `<text>` element, combining the text string with `<font>` and `<position>` elements, for example.

The disadvantage of this is that you cannot limit the number of occurrences of the child elements and how they are intermixed with the text. You can make the definition more precisely controlled by enclosing the text in its own element. Then you can define the `<text>` element as having element content—like this:

```
<!ELEMENT text (color, position, bounds, font, string)>
  <!ATTLIST text
          angle    CDATA  #REQUIRED
          maxascent CDATA  #REQUIRED
  >

<!ELEMENT font EMPTY>
  <!ATTLIST font
          fontname  CDATA              #REQUIRED
          fontstyle (plain|bold|italic) #REQUIRED
          pointsize CDATA              #REQUIRED
  >

<!ELEMENT string (#PCDATA)>
```

The `text` element has a `maxascent` attribute in addition to the `angle` attribute to specify the value of the maximum ascent for the font. The `<font>` and `<string>` elements are new. The `<font>` element provides the name, style, and size of the font as attribute values, and because nothing is required beyond that, it is an empty element. You could specify the style as CDATA because its value is just an integer, but that would make the XML for a sketch rather less readable because the font style would not be obvious from the integer value. The `<string>` element content is just the text to be displayed. Other children of the `<text>` element specify the color and position of the text.

The Complete Sketcher DTD

That's all you need. The complete DTD for Sketcher documents is the following:

```
<?xml version="1.0" encoding="UTF-8"?>
<!ELEMENT sketch (line|circle|rectangle|curve|text)*>

<!ELEMENT color EMPTY>
  <!ATTLIST color
          R CDATA                   #REQUIRED
          G CDATA                   #REQUIRED
          B CDATA                   #REQUIRED
  >
```

```
<!ENTITY % coordinates "x CDATA #REQUIRED y CDATA #REQUIRED">

<!ENTITY % dimensions "width CDATA #REQUIRED height CDATA #REQUIRED">

<!ELEMENT position EMPTY>
   <!ATTLIST position %coordinates;>

<!ELEMENT endpoint EMPTY>
   <!ATTLIST endpoint %coordinates;>

<!ELEMENT bounds EMPTY>
   <!ATTLIST bounds
             %coordinates;
             %dimensions;>

<!ELEMENT string (#PCDATA)>

<!ELEMENT point EMPTY>
   <!ATTLIST point %coordinates;>

<!ELEMENT font EMPTY>
   <!ATTLIST font
             fontname  CDATA                            #REQUIRED
             fontstyle (plain|bold|italic|bold-italic)  #REQUIRED
             pointsize CDATA                            #REQUIRED
   >

<!ELEMENT line (color, position, bounds, endpoint)>
   <!ATTLIST line
             angle CDATA                   #REQUIRED
   >

<!ELEMENT rectangle (color, position, bounds)>
   <!ATTLIST rectangle
             angle CDATA                   #REQUIRED
             %dimensions;
   >

<!ELEMENT circle (color, position, bounds)>
   <!ATTLIST circle
             angle CDATA                   #REQUIRED
             diameter CDATA                #REQUIRED
   >

<!ELEMENT curve (color, position, bounds, point+)>
   <!ATTLIST curve  angle CDATA  #REQUIRED>
<!ELEMENT text (color, position, bounds, font, string)>
   <!ATTLIST text
             angle     CDATA  #REQUIRED
             maxascent CDATA  #REQUIRED
   >
```

You can use this DTD to represent any sketch in XML. Stash it away in your `Beg Java Stuff` directory as `sketcher.dtd`. You will try it out later.

RULES FOR A WELL-FORMED DOCUMENT

Now that you know a bit more about XML elements and what goes into a DTD, I can formulate what you must do to ensure your XML document is well-formed. The rules for a document to be well-formed are quite simple:

1. If the XML declaration appears in the prolog, it must include the XML version. Other specifications in the XML document must be in the prescribed sequence—character encoding followed by `standalone` specification.

2. If the document type declaration appears in the prolog, the DOCTYPE name must match that of the root element, and the markup declarations in the DTD must be according to the rules for writing markup declarations.

3. The body of the document must contain at least one element, the root element, which contains all the other elements, and an instance of the root element must not appear in the content of another element. All elements must be properly nested.

4. Elements in the body of the document must be consistent with the markup declarations identified by the DOCTYPE declaration.

The rules for writing an XML document are absolutely strict. Break one rule and your document is not well-formed and is not processed. This strict application of the rules is essential because you are communicating data and its structure. If any laxity were permitted, it would open the door to uncertainty about how the data should be interpreted. HTML used to be quite different from XML in this respect. Until recently, the rules for writing HTML were only loosely applied by HTML readers such as web browsers.

For example, even though a paragraph in HTML should be defined using a start tag, <p>, and an end tag, </p>, you can usually get away with omitting the end tag, and you can use both capital and lowercase p, and indeed close a capital P paragraph with a lowercase p, and vice versa. You can often have overlapping tags in HTML and get away with that, too. Although it is not to be recommended, a loose application of the rules for HTML is not so harmful because HTML is concerned only with data presentation. The worst that can happen is that the data does not display quite as you intended.

In 2000, the W3C released the XHTML 1.0 standard that makes HTML an XML language, so more and more HTML documents are conforming to this. The enduring problem is, of course, that the Internet has accumulated a great deal of material over many years that is still very useful but that will never be well-formed XML, so browsers may never be fully XML-compliant.

XML NAMESPACES

Even though they are very simple, XML namespaces can be very confusing. The confusion arises because it is so easy to make assumptions about what they imply when you first meet them. Let's look briefly at why you have XML namespaces in the first place, and then see what an XML namespace actually is.

You saw earlier that an XML document can have only one DOCTYPE declaration. This can identify an external DTD by a URI or include explicit markup declarations, or it may do both. What happens if you want to combine two or more XML documents that each has its own DTD into a single document? The short answer is that you can't—not easily anyway. Because the DTD for each document has been defined without regard for the other, element name collisions are a real possibility. It may be impossible to differentiate between different elements that share a common name, and in this case major revisions of the documents' contents, as well as a new DTD, are necessary to deal with this. It won't be easy.

XML namespaces are intended to help deal with this problem. They enable names used in markup to be qualified, so that you can make duplicate names that are used in different markup unique by putting them in separate namespaces. An XML namespace is just a collection of element and attribute names that is identified by a URI. Each name in an XML namespace is qualified by the URI that identifies the namespace. Thus, different XML namespaces may contain common names without causing confusion because each name is notionally qualified by the unique URI for the namespace that contains it.

I say "notionally qualified" because you don't usually qualify element and attribute names using the URI directly, although you could. Normally, in the interests of not making the markup overly verbose, you use another name called a *namespace prefix* whose value is the URI for the namespace. For example, I could have a namespace that is identified by the URI www.wrox.com/Toys and a namespace prefix, toys, that contains a declaration for the name rubber_duck. I could have a second namespace with the URI www.wrox.com/BathAccessories and the namespace prefix bathAccessories that also defines the name rubber_duck. The rubber_duck name from the first namespace is referred to as toys:rubber_duck and that from the second namespace is bathAccessories:rubber_duck, so there is no possibility of confusing them. The colon is used in the qualified name to separate the namespace prefix from the local name, which is why I said earlier in the chapter that you should avoid the use of colons in ordinary XML names.

Let's come back to the confusing aspects of namespaces for a moment. There is a temptation to imagine that the URI that identifies an XML namespace also identifies a document somewhere that specifies the names in the namespace. This is not required by the namespace specification. The URI is just a unique identifier for the namespace and a unique qualifier for a set of names. It does not necessarily have any other purpose, or even have to refer to a real document; it only needs to be unique. The definition of how names within a given namespace relate to one another and the rules for markup that uses them is an entirely separate question. This may be provided by a DTD or some other mechanism, such as an XML Schema.

Namespace Declarations

A namespace is associated with a particular element in a document, which of course can be, but does not have to be, the root element. A typical namespace declaration in an XML document looks like this:

```
<sketcher:sketch xmlns:sketcher="http://www.wrox.com/dtds/sketches">
```

A namespace declaration uses a special reserved attribute name, `xmlns`, within an element, and in this instance the namespace applies to the `<sketch>` element. The name `sketcher` that is separated from `xmlns` by a colon is the namespace prefix, and it has the value `www.wrox.com/dtds/sketches`. You can use the namespace prefix to qualify names within the namespace, and because this maps to the URI, the URI is effectively the qualifier for the name. The URL that I've given here is hypothetical—it doesn't actually exist, but it could. The sole purpose of the URI identifying the namespace is to ensure that names within the namespace are unique, so it doesn't matter whether it exists or not. You can add as many namespace declarations within an element as you want, and each namespace declared in an element is available within that element and its content.

With the namespace declared with the `sketcher` prefix, you can use the `<circle>` element that is defined in the `sketcher` namespace like this:

```
<sketcher:sketch xmlns:sketcher="http://www.wrox.com/dtds/sketches">
   <sketcher:circle angle="0" diameter="30">
     <sketcher:color R="150" G="250" B="100"/>
     <sketcher:position x="30" y="50"/>
     <sketcher:bounds x="30" y="50"
                        width="32" height="32">
     </sketcher:bounds>
   </sketcher:circle>
</sketcher:sketch>
```

Each reference to the element name is qualified by the namespace prefix `sketcher`. A reference in the same document to a `<circle>` element that is defined within another namespace can be qualified by the prefix specified in the declaration for that namespace. By qualifying each element name by its namespace prefix, you avoid any possibility of ambiguity.

A namespace has *scope*—a region of an XML document over which the namespace declaration is visible. The scope of a namespace is the content of the element within which it is declared, plus all direct or indirect child elements. The preceding namespace declaration applies to the `<sketch>` element and all the elements within it. If you declare a namespace in the root element for a document, its scope is the entire document.

You can declare a namespace without specifying a prefix. This namespace then becomes the default namespace in effect for this element, and its content and unqualified element names are assumed to belong to this namespace. Here's an example:

```
<sketch xmlns="http://www.wrox.com/dtds/sketches">
```

There is no namespace prefix specified, so the colon following `xmlns` is omitted. This namespace becomes the default, so you can use element and attribute names from this namespace without qualification and they are all implicitly within the default namespace. For example:

```
<sketch xmlns="http://www.wrox.com/dtds/sketches">
   <circle angle="0" diameter="30">
     <color R="150" G="250" B="100"/>
     <position x="30" y="50"/>
     <bounds x="30" y="50"
```

```
            width="32" height="32">
      </bounds>
    </circle>
  </sketch>
```

This markup is a lot less cluttered than the earlier version that used qualified names, which makes it much easier to read. It is therefore advantageous to declare the namespace that you use most extensively in a document as the default.

You can declare several namespaces within a single element. Here's an example of a default namespace in use with another namespace:

```
<sketch xmlns="http://www.wrox.com/dtds/sketches"
        xmlns:print="http://www.wrox.com/dtds/printed">
  <circle angle="0" diameter="30">
    <color R="150" G="250" B="100"/>
    <position x="30" y="50"/>
    <bounds   x="30" y="50"
              width="32" height="32">
    </bounds>
  </circle>
  <print:circle print:lineweight="3" print:linestyle="dashed"/>
</sketch>
```

Here the namespace with the prefix print contains names for elements relating to hardcopy presentation of sketch elements. The <circle> element in the print namespace is qualified by the namespace prefix so it is distinguished from the element with the same name in the default namespace.

XML Namespaces and DTDs

For a document to be valid, you must have a DTD, and the document must be consistent with it. The way in which a DTD is defined has no specific provision for namespaces. The DTD for a document that uses namespaces must therefore define the elements and attributes using qualified names, and must also make provision for the xmlns attribute, with or without its prefix, in the markup declaration for any element in which it can appear. Because the markup declarations in a DTD have no specific provision for accommodating namespaces, a DTD is a less than ideal vehicle for defining the rules for markup when namespaces are used. The XML Schema specification provides a much better solution, and overcomes a number of other problems associated with DTDs.

XML SCHEMAS

Because of the limitations of DTDs that I mentioned earlier, the W3C has developed the XML Schema language for defining the content and structure of sets of XML documents, and this language is now a W3C standard. You use the XML Schema Definition language to create descriptions of particular kinds of XML documents in a similar manner to the way you use DTDs, and such descriptions are referred to as XML Schemas and fulfill the same role as DTDs. The XML Schema language is itself defined in XML and is therefore implicitly extensible to support new capabilities when necessary. Because the XML Schema language enables you to specify the type and format of data within an XML document, it provides a way for you to define and create XML documents that are inherently more precise, and therefore safer than documents described by a DTD.

It's easy to get confused when you are working with XML Schemas. One primary source of confusion is the various levels of language definition you are involved with. At the top level, you have XML—everything you are working with in this context is defined in XML. At the next level you have the XML Schema Definition language—defined in XML, of course—and you use this language to define an XML Schema, which is a specification for a set of XML documents. At the lowest level you define an XML document—such as a document describing a Sketcher sketch—and this document is defined according to the rules you have defined in your XML Schema for Sketcher documents. Figure 22-3 shows the relationships between these various XML documents.

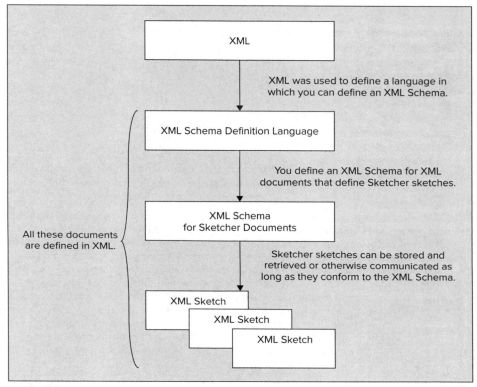

FIGURE 22-3

The XML Schema language is sometimes referred to as *XSD*, from XML Schema Definition language. The XML Schema namespace is usually associated with the prefix name xsd, and files containing a definition for a class of XML documents often have the extension .xsd. You also often see the prefix xs used for the XML Schema namespace, but in fact you can use anything you like. A detailed discussion of the XML Schema language is a substantial topic that really requires a whole book to do it justice. I'm just giving you enough of a flavor of how you define XML document schemas so that you're able to see how it differs from a DTD.

Defining a Schema

The elements in a schema that defines the structure and content of a class of XML documents are organized in a similar way to the elements in a DTD. A schema has a single root element that is unique, and all other elements must be contained within the root element and must be properly nested. Every schema consists of a schema root element with a number of nested subelements. Let's look at a simple example.

Here's a possible schema for XML documents that contain an address:

```
<?xml version="1.0" ?>
<xsd:schema xmlns:xsd="http://www.w3.org/2001/XMLSchema">

<xsd:annotation>
    <xsd:documentation>
        This schema defines documents that contain an address.
    </xsd:documentation>
</xsd:annotation>

<!--This declares document content. -->
```

```
<xsd:element name="address" type="AddressType"/>

<!--This defines an element type that is used in the declaration of content. -->
<xsd:complexType name="AddressType">
  <xsd:sequence>
   <xsd:element name="buildingnumber" type="xsd:positiveInteger"/>
   <xsd:element name="street" type="xsd:string"/>
   <xsd:element name="city"    type="xsd:string"/>
   <xsd:element name="state"   type="xsd:string"/>
   <xsd:element name="zip"     type="xsd:decimal"/>
  </xsd:sequence>
 </xsd:complexType>
</xsd:schema>
```

You might like to contrast this schema with the DTD you saw earlier that defined XML documents with similar content. This schema defines documents that consist of an `<address/>` root element that contains a sequence of child elements with the names `buildingnumber`, `street`, `city`, `state`, and `zip`.

The root element in the schema definition is the `xsd:schema` element, and that has an attribute with the name `xmlns` that identifies an XML namespace. The value you specify for the `xmlns` attribute is a URI that is the namespace name for the content document, and because the current document is a schema, the namespace is the one corresponding to elements in the XML Schema Definition language. The `xsd` that follows the colon is the prefix that is used to identify element names from the `"http://www.w3.org/2001/XMLSchema"` namespace, so `xsd` is shorthand for the full namespace name. Thus `schema`, `complexType`, `sequence`, and `element` are all names of elements in a namespace defined for the XML Schema Definition language. The root element for every XML Schema is a `schema` element. Don't lose sight of what a schema is; it's a definition of the form of XML documents of a particular type, so it declares the elements that can be used in such a document and how they may be structured. A document that conforms to a particular schema does not have to identify the schema, but it can. I come back to how you reference a schema when you are defining an XML document a little later in this chapter.

The example uses an `<annotation/>` element to include some simple documentation in the schema definition. The text that is the documentation appears within a child `<documentation/>` element. You can also use an `<appInfo/>` child element within an `<annotation/>` element to reference information located at a given URI. Of course, you can also use XML comments, `<!--comment-->`, within a schema, as the example shows.

In an XML Schema, a *declaration* specifies an element that is content for a document, whereas a *definition* defines an element type. The `xsd:element` element is a declaration that the content of a document consists of an `<address/>` element. Contrast this with the `xsd:complexType` element, which is a definition of the `AddressType` type for an element and does not declare document content. The `xsd:element` element in the schema declares that the `address` element is document content and happens to be of type `AddressType`, which is the type defined by the `xsd:complexType` element.

Now let's take a look at some of the elements that you use to define a document schema in a little more detail.

Defining Schema Elements

As I said, the `xsd:complexType` element in the sample schema defines a type of element, not an element in the document. A complex element is simply an element that contains other elements, or that has attributes, or both. Any elements that are complex elements need an `xsd:complexType` definition in the schema to define a type for the element. You place the definitions for child elements for a complex element between the `complexType` start and end tags. You also place the definitions for any attributes for a complex element between the `complexType` start and end tags. You can define a simple type using an `xsd:simpleType` definition in the schema. You would use a simple type definition to constrain attribute values or element content in some way. You see examples of this a little later in this chapter.

In the example you specify that any element of type `AddressType` contains a sequence of *simple elements* — a `buildingnumber` element, a `street` element, a `city` element, a `state` element, and a `zip` element. A simple element is an element that does not have child elements or attributes; it can contain only data, which can be of a variety of standard types or of a type that you define. The definition of each simple element that appears within an element of type `AddressType` uses an `xsd:element` element in which the `name` attribute specifies the name of the element being defined and the `type` attribute defines the type of data that can appear within the element.

You can also control the number of occurrences of an element by specifying values for two further attributes within the `xsd:element` tag, as shown in Table 22-4:

TABLE 22-4: Attributes Specifying the Number of Element Occurrences

ATTRIBUTE	DESCRIPTION
minOccurs	The value defines the minimum number of occurrences of the element and must be a positive integer (which can be 0). If this attribute is not defined, then the minimum number of occurrences of the element is 1.
maxOccurs	The value defines the maximum number of occurrences of the element and can be a positive integer or the value unbounded. If this attribute is not defined, then the maximum number of occurrences of the element is 1.

Thus, if both of these attributes are omitted, as is the case with the child element definitions in the sample schema for elements of type `AddressType`, the minimum and maximum numbers of occurrences are both one, so the element must appear exactly once. If you specify `minOccurs` as 0, then the element is optional. Note that you must not specify a value for `minOccurs` that is greater than `maxOccurs`, and the value for `maxOccurs` must not be less than `minOccurs`. You should keep in mind that both attributes have default values of 1 when you specify a value for just one attribute.

Specifying Data Types

In the example, each of the definitions for the five simple elements within an address element has a type specified for the data that it contains, and you specify the data type by a value for the `type` attribute. The data in a `buildingnumber` element is specified to be of type `positiveInteger`, and the others are all of type `string`. These two types are relatively self-explanatory, corresponding to positive integers greater than or equal to 0, and strings of characters. The XML Schema Definition language enables you to specify many different values for the `type` attribute in an `element` definition. Here are a few other examples:

DATA TYPE	EXAMPLES OF DATA
integer	25, -998, 12345, 0, -1
negativeInteger	-1, -2, -3, -12345, and so on
nonNegativeInteger	0, 1, 2, 3, and so on
hexBinary	0DE7, ADD7
long	25, 123456789, -9999999
float	2.71828, 5E5, 500.0, 0, -3E2, -300.0, NaN, INF, -INF
double	3.14159265, 1E30, -2.5, NaN, -INF, INF
boolean	true, false, 1, 0
date	2010-12-31
language	en-US, en, de

The `float` and `double` types correspond to values within the ranges for 32-bit and 64-bit floating-point values, respectively. The `date` type is of the form yyyy-mm-dd so there can be no confusion. There are many more standard types within the XML Schema Definition language, and because this is extensible, you can also define data types of your own.

You can also define a default value for a simple element by using the `default` attribute within the definition of the element. For example, within an XML representation of a sketch you undoubtedly need to have an element defining a color. You might define this as a simple element like this:

```
<xsd:element name="color" type="xsd:string" default="blue"/>
```

This defines a color element containing data that is a string and a default value for the string of `"blue."` In a similar way, you can define the content for a simple element to be a fixed value by specifying the content as the value for the `fixed` attribute within the `xsd:element` tag.

Defining Attributes for Complex Elements

You use the `xsd:attribute` tag to define an attribute for a complex element. Let's take an example to see how you do this. Suppose you decided that you would define a circle in an XML document for a sketch using a `<circle/>` element, where the coordinates of the center, the diameter, and the color are specified by attributes. Within the document schema, you might define the type for an element representing a circle like this:

```
<xsd:complexType name="CircleType">
 <xsd:attribute name="x" type="xsd:integer"/>
 <xsd:attribute name="y" type="xsd:integer"/>
 <xsd:attribute name="diameter" type="xsd:nonNegativeInteger"/>
 <xsd:attribute name="color" type="xsd:string"/>
</xsd:complexType>
```

The elements that define the attributes for the `<circle/>` element type appear within the `complexType` element, just like child element definitions. You specify the attribute name and the data type for the value in exactly the same way as for an element. The type specification is not mandatory. If you leave it out, it just means that anything goes as a value for the attribute.

You can also specify in the definition for an attribute whether it is optional or not by specifying a value for the `use` attribute within the `xsd:attribute` element. The value can be either `"optional"` or `"required."` For a circle element, none of the attributes are optional, so you might modify the complex type definition to the following:

```
<xsd:complexType name="CircleType">
 <xsd:attribute name="x" type="xsd:integer" use="required"/>
 <xsd:attribute name="y" type="xsd:integer" use="required"/>
 <xsd:attribute name="diameter" type="xsd:double" use="required"/>
 <xsd:attribute name="color" type="xsd:string" use="required"/>
</xsd:complexType>
```

Restrictions on Values

You can place restrictions on values for element content and element attributes. Such restrictions are referred to as *facets*. Quite often you want to restrict the values that can be assigned to attributes. For example, the diameter of a circle certainly cannot be zero or negative, and a color may be restricted to standard colors. You could do this by adding a simple type definition that defines the restrictions for these values. For example:

```
<xsd:complexType name="circle">
 <xsd:attribute name="x" type="xsd:integer" use="required"/>
 <xsd:attribute name="y" type="xsd:integer" use="required"/>
 <xsd:attribute name="diameter" use="required">
  <xsd:simpleType>
   <xsd:restriction base="xsd:double">
    <xsd:minExclusive value="1.0"/>
   </xsd:restriction>
  </xsd:simpleType>
 </xsd:attribute>
 <xsd:attribute name="color" use="required">
  <xsd:simpleType>
   <xsd:restriction base="xsd:string">
    <xsd:enumeration value="red"/>
```

```
        <xsd:enumeration value="blue"/>
        <xsd:enumeration value="green"/>
        <xsd:enumeration value="yellow"/>
      </xsd:restriction>
    </xsd:simpleType>
  </xsd:attribute>
</xsd:complexType>
```

The `diameter` and `color` attributes have facets that specify the values that are acceptable. The `simpleType` element that appears within the `xsd:attribute` elements specifies the constraints on the values for each attribute. You can also use the `simpleType` element with an `xsd:element` element definition to constrain the content for an element in a similar way. The `xsd:restriction` element defines the constraints, and you have a considerable range of options for specifying them, many more than I can possibly explain here. The `base` attribute in the `xsd:restriction` element defines the type for the value that is being restricted, and this attribute specification is required.

I've used an `xsd:minExclusive` specification to define an exclusive lower limit for values of the `diameter` attribute, and this specifies that the value must be greater than `"1.0."` Alternatively, you might prefer to use `xsd:minInclusive` with a value of `"2.0"` to set a sensible minimum value for the diameter. You also have the option of specifying an upper limit on numerical values by specifying either `maxInclusive` or `maxExclusive` values. For the `color` attribute definition, I've introduced a restriction that the value must be one of a fixed set of values. Each value that is allowed is specified in an `xsd:enumeration` element, and there can be any number of these. Obviously, this doesn't just apply to strings; you can restrict the values for numeric types to be one of an enumerated set of values. For the color attribute the value must be one of the four string values specified.

Defining Groups of Attributes

Sometimes several different elements have the same set of attributes. To avoid having to repeat the definitions for the elements in such a set for each element that requires them, you can define an attribute group. Here's an example of a definition for an attribute group:

```
<xsd:attributeGroup name="coords">
    <xsd:attribute name="x" type="xsd:integer" use="required"/>
    <xsd:attribute name="y" type="xsd:integer" use="required"/>
</xsd:attributeGroup>
```

This defines a group of two attributes with names x and y that specify x and y coordinates for a point. The name of this attribute group is `coords`. In general, an attribute group can contain other attribute groups. You could use the `coords` attribute group within a complex type definition like this:

```
<xsd:complexType name="PointType">
    <xsd:attributeGroup ref="coords"/>
</xsd:complexType>
```

This defines the element type `PointType` as having the attributes that are defined in the `coords` attribute group. The `ref` attribute in the `xsd:attributeGroup` element specifies that this is a reference to a named attribute group. You can now use the `PointType` element type to define elements. For example:

```
<xsd:element name="position" type="PointType"/>
```

This declares a `<point/>` element to be of type `PointType`, and thus have the required attributes x and y.

Specifying a Group of Element Choices

The `xsd:choice` element in the Schema Definition language enables you to specify that one out of a given set of elements included in the choice definition must be present. This is useful in specifying a schema for Sketcher documents because the content is essentially variable—it can be any sequence of any of the basic types of elements. Suppose that you have already defined types for the geometric and text elements that can occur in a sketch. You could use an `xsd:choice` element in the definition of a complex type for a `<sketch/>` element:

```
<xsd:complexType name="SketchType">
    <xsd:choice minOccurs="0" maxOccurs="unbounded">
        <xsd:element name="line" type="LineType"/>
        <xsd:element name="rectangle" type="RectangleType"/>
        <xsd:element name="circle" type="CircleType"/>
        <xsd:element name="curve" type="CurveType"/>
        <xsd:element name="text" type="TextType"/>
    </xsd:choice>
</xsd:complexType>
```

This defines that an element of type `SketchType` contains zero or more elements that are each one of the five types identified in the `xsd:choice` element. Thus, each element can be any of the types `LineType`, `RectangleType`, `CircleType`, `CurveType`, or `TextType`, which are types for the primitive elements in a sketch that are defined elsewhere in the schema. Given this definition for `SketchType`, you can declare the content for a sketch to be the following:

```
<xsd:element name="sketch" type="SketchType"/>
```

This declares the contents of an XML document for a sketch to be a `<sketch/>` element that has zero or more elements of any of the types that appeared in the preceding `xsd:choice` element. This is exactly what is required to accommodate any sketch, so this single declaration defines the entire contents of all possible sketches. All you need is to fill in a few details for the element types. I think you know enough about XML Schema to put together a schema for Sketcher documents.

A SCHEMA FOR SKETCHER

As I noted when I discussed a DTD for Sketcher, an XML document that defines a sketch can have a very simple structure. Essentially, it can consist of a `<sketch/>` element that contains a sequence of zero or more elements that define lines, rectangles, circles, curves, or text. These child elements may be in any sequence, and there can be any number of them. To accommodate the fact that any given child element must be one of five types of elements, you could use some of the XML fragments from earlier sections to make an initial stab at an outline of a Sketcher schema like this:

```
<?xml version="1.0" encoding="UTF-8"?>
<xsd:schema xmlns:xsd="http://www.w3.org/2001/XMLSchema">

    <!--The entire document content -->
    <xsd:element name="sketch" type="SketchType"/>

    <!--Type for a sketch root element -->
    <xsd:complexType name="SketchType">
        <xsd:choice minOccurs="0" maxOccurs="unbounded">
            <xsd:element name="line" type="LineType"/>
            <xsd:element name="rectangle" type="RectangleType"/>
            <xsd:element name="circle" type="CircleType"/>
            <xsd:element name="curve" type="CurveType"/>
            <xsd:element name="text" type="TextType"/>
        </xsd:choice>
    </xsd:complexType>

    <!--Other definitions that are needed...  -->
</xsd:schema>
```

This document references the XML Schema language namespace, so it's evidently a definition of a schema. The documents that this schema defines have no namespace specified, so elements on documents conforming to this schema do not need to be qualified. The entire content of a Sketcher document is declared to be an element with the name `sketch` that is of type `SketchType`. The `<sketch/>` element is the root element, and because it can have child elements, it must be defined as a complex type. The child elements within a `<sketch/>` element are the elements specified by the `xsd:choice` element, which represents a selection of one of the five complex elements that can occur in a sketch. The `minOccurs` and `maxOccurs` attribute values for the `xsd:choice` element determines that there may be any number of such elements, including zero. Thus, this definition accommodates XML documents describing any Sketcher sketch. All you now need to do is fill in the definitions for the possible varieties of child elements.

Defining Line Elements

Let's define the same XML elements in the schema for Sketcher as the DTD for Sketcher defines. On that basis, a line element has four child elements specifying the color, position, and end point for a line, plus an attribute that specifies the rotation angle. You could define the type for a `<line/>` element in the schema like this:

```
<!--Type for a sketch line element -->
<xsd:complexType name="LineType">
    <xsd:sequence>
        <xsd:element name="color" type="ColorType"/>
        <xsd:element name="position" type="PointType"/>
        <xsd:element name="bounds" type="BoundsType"/>
        <xsd:element name="endpoint" type="PointType"/>
    </xsd:sequence>
    <xsd:attribute name="angle" type="xsd:double" use="required"/>
</xsd:complexType>
```

This defines the type for a `<line/>` element in a sketch. An element of type `LineType` contains four child elements, `<color/>`, `<position/>`, `<bounds/>`, and `<endpoint/>`. These are enclosed within a `<sequence/>` schema definition element, so they must all be present and must appear in a sketch document in the sequence in which they are specified here. The element type definition also specifies an attribute with the name `angle` that must be included in any element of type `LineType`.

Of course, you now must define the types that you have used in the definition of the complex type, `LineType`: the `ColorType`, `PointType`, and `BoundsType` element types.

Defining a Type for Color Elements

As I discussed in the context of the DTD for Sketcher, the data for a `<color/>` element is supplied by three attributes that specify the RGB values for the color. You can therefore define the element type like this:

```
<!--Type for a sketch element color -->
<xsd:complexType name="ColorType">
    <xsd:attribute name="R" type="xsd:nonNegativeInteger" use="required"/>
    <xsd:attribute name="G" type="xsd:nonNegativeInteger" use="required"/>
    <xsd:attribute name="B" type="xsd:nonNegativeInteger" use="required"/>
</xsd:complexType>
```

This is a relatively simple complex type definition. There are just the three attributes—R, G, and B—that all have integer values that can be 0 or greater, and are all mandatory.

You could improve this. As well as being non-negative integers, the color component values must be between 0 and 255. You could express this by adding facets for the color attributes, as follows:

```
<!--Type for a sketch element color -->
<xsd:complexType name="ColorType">
    <xsd:attribute name="R" use="required">
        <xsd:simpleType>
            <xsd:restriction base="xsd:nonNegativeInteger">
                <xsd:maxInclusive value="255"/>
            </xsd:restriction>
        </xsd:simpleType>
    </xsd:attribute>
    <xsd:attribute name="G" use="required">
```

```
        <xsd:simpleType>
            <xsd:restriction base="xsd:nonNegativeInteger">
                <xsd:maxInclusive value="255"/>
            </xsd:restriction>
        </xsd:simpleType>
    </xsd:attribute>
    <xsd:attribute name="B" use="required">
        <xsd:simpleType>
            <xsd:restriction base="xsd:nonNegativeInteger">
                <xsd:maxInclusive value="255"/>
            </xsd:restriction>
        </xsd:simpleType>
    </xsd:attribute>
</xsd:complexType>
```

Now, only values from 0 to 255 are acceptable for the color components.

Defining a Type for Point Elements

You saw a definition for the `PointType` element type earlier:

```
<!--Type for elements representing points -->
<xsd:complexType name="PointType">
    <xsd:attributeGroup ref="coords"/>
</xsd:complexType>
```

This references the attribute group with the name `coords`, so this must be defined elsewhere in the schema. You've also seen this attribute group definition before:

```
<!--Attribute group for an x,y integer coordinate pair -->
<xsd:attributeGroup name="coords">
  <xsd:attribute name="x" type="xsd:integer" use="required"/>
  <xsd:attribute name="y" type="xsd:integer" use="required"/>
</xsd:attributeGroup>
```

You are able to use this attribute group in the definitions for other element types in the schema. The definition of this attribute group must appear at the top level in the schema, within the root element; otherwise, it is not possible to refer to it from within an element declaration.

Defining a Type for Bounds Elements

The `BoundsType` corresponds to the bounding rectangle for an element. You need to specify the coordinates of the top-left corner and its width and height:

```
<!--Type for a bounding rectangle for a sketch element -->
<xsd:complexType name="BoundsType">
 <xsd:attributeGroup ref="coords"/>
 <xsd:attribute name="width" use="required">
  <xsd:simpleType>
   <xsd:restriction base="xsd:nonNegativeInteger">
    <xsd:minExclusive value="2"/>
   </xsd:restriction>
  </xsd:simpleType>
 </xsd:attribute>
 <xsd:attribute name="height" use="required">
  <xsd:simpleType>
   <xsd:restriction base="xsd:nonNegativeInteger">
    <xsd:minExclusive value="2"/>
   </xsd:restriction>
  </xsd:simpleType>
 </xsd:attribute>
</xsd:complexType>
```

The width and height are identified and are both restricted to be non-negative integers with a minimum value of 2.

Defining a Rectangle Element Type

The definition of the type for a `<rectangle/>` element is somewhat similar to the `LineType` definition:

```
<!--Type for a sketch rectangle element -->
<xsd:complexType name="RectangleType">
    <xsd:sequence>
        <xsd:element name="color" type="ColorType"/>
        <xsd:element name="position" type="PointType"/>
        <xsd:element name="bounds" type="BoundsType"/>
    </xsd:sequence>
    <xsd:attribute name="width" use="required">
        <xsd:simpleType>
            <xsd:restriction base="xsd:double">
                <xsd:minInclusive value="2.0"/>
            </xsd:restriction>
        </xsd:simpleType>
    </xsd:attribute>
    <xsd:attribute name="height" use="required">
        <xsd:simpleType>
            <xsd:restriction base="xsd:double">
                <xsd:minInclusive value="2.0"/>
            </xsd:restriction>
        </xsd:simpleType>
    </xsd:attribute>
</xsd:complexType>
```

This references the schema element types `ColorType`, `PointType`, and `BoundsType`, and all of these have already been defined. The definition for the `width` and `height` attributes are slightly different from the `<bounds/>` element because they are floating-point values. This is because they relate to a `Rectangle2D.Double` object whereas a bounding rectangle is a `java.awt.Rectangle` object with integer width and height values.

Defining a Circle Element Type

There's nothing new in the definition of `CircleType`:

```
<!--Type for a sketch circle element -->
<xsd:complexType name="CircleType">
    <xsd:sequence>
        <xsd:element name="color" type="ColorType"/>
        <xsd:element name="position" type="PointType"/>
        <xsd:element name="bounds" type="BoundsType"/>
    </xsd:sequence>
    <xsd:attribute name="diameter" use="required">
        <xsd:simpleType>
            <xsd:restriction base="xsd:double">
                <xsd:minExclusive value="2.0"/>
            </xsd:restriction>
        </xsd:simpleType>
    </xsd:attribute>
    <xsd:attribute name="angle" type="xsd:double" use="required"/>
</xsd:complexType>
```

The child elements appear within a sequence element, so their sequence is fixed. You have the diameter and angle for a circle specified by attributes that both have values of type `double`, and are both mandatory. The diameter is restricted to non-negative values with a minimum of 2.0.

Defining a Curve Element Type

A type for the curve element introduces something new because the number of child elements is variable. A curve is defined by the origin plus one or more points, so the type definition must allow for an unlimited number of child elements defining points. Here's how you can accommodate that:

```xml
<!--Type for a sketch curve element -->
<xsd:complexType name="CurveType">
    <xsd:sequence>
        <xsd:element name="color" type="ColorType"/>
        <xsd:element name="position" type="PointType"/>
        <xsd:element name="bounds" type="BoundsType"/>
        <xsd:element name="point" type="PathPointType" minOccurs="1"
                                                       maxOccurs="unbounded"/>
    </xsd:sequence>
    <xsd:attribute name="angle" type="xsd:double" use="required"/>
</xsd:complexType>
```

The flexibility in the number of `point` elements is specified through the `minOccurs` and `maxOccurs` attribute values. The value of 1 for `minOccurs` ensures that there is always at least one, and the unbounded value for `maxOccurs` allows an unlimited number of `point` elements to be present. These elements are going to be points with floating-point coordinates because that's what you get from the `GeneralPath` object that defines a curve. You can define this element type like this:

```xml
<!--Type for elements representing points in a general path -->
<xsd:complexType name="PathPointType">
    <xsd:attribute name="x" type="xsd:double" use="required"/>
    <xsd:attribute name="y" type="xsd:double" use="required"/>
</xsd:complexType>
```

This is a straightforward complex element with attributes for the coordinate values, which are specified as type `double`.

Defining a Text Element Type

The type for `<text/>` elements is the odd one out, but it's not difficult. It involves four child elements for the color, the position, the font, and the text itself, plus an attribute to specify the angle. The type definition is as follows:

```xml
<!--Type for a sketch text element -->
<xsd:complexType name="TextType">
    <xsd:sequence>
        <xsd:element name="color" type="ColorType"/>
        <xsd:element name="position" type="PointType"/>
        <xsd:element name="bounds" type="BoundsType"/>
        <xsd:element name="font" type="FontType"/>
        <xsd:element name="string" type="xsd:string"/>
    </xsd:sequence>
    <xsd:attribute name="angle" type="xsd:double" use="required"/>
    <xsd:attribute name="maxascent" type="xsd:integer" use="required"/>
</xsd:complexType>
```

The text string itself is a simple `<string/>` element, but the font is a complex element that requires a type definition:

```xml
<!--Type for a font used by a sketch text element -->
<xsd:complexType name="FontType">
    <xsd:attribute name="fontname" type="xsd:string" use="required"/>
    <xsd:attribute name="fontstyle" use="required">
        <xsd:simpleType>
            <xsd:restriction base="xsd:string">
                <xsd:enumeration value="plain"/>
                <xsd:enumeration value="bold"/>
```

```
                <xsd:enumeration value="italic"/>
                <xsd:enumeration value="bold-italic"/>
            </xsd:restriction>
        </xsd:simpleType>
    </xsd:attribute>
</xsd:complexType>
```

The style attribute for the `<font/>` element can be only one of four fixed values. You impose this constraint by defining an enumeration of the four possible string values within a `simpleType` definition for the attribute value. The `xsd:simpleType` definition is implicitly associated with the `style` attribute value because the type definition is a child of the `xsd:attribute` element.

The Complete Sketcher Schema

If you assemble all the fragments into a single file, you have the following definition for the Sketcher schema that defines XML documents containing a sketch:

```xml
<?xml version="1.0" encoding="UTF-8"?>
<xsd:schema xmlns:xsd="http://www.w3.org/2001/XMLSchema">
    <xsd:element name="sketch" type="SketchType"/>

    <!--Type for a sketch root element -->
    <xsd:complexType name="SketchType">
        <xsd:choice minOccurs="0" maxOccurs="unbounded">
            <xsd:element name="line" type="LineType"/>
            <xsd:element name="rectangle" type="RectangleType"/>
            <xsd:element name="circle" type="CircleType"/>
            <xsd:element name="curve" type="CurveType"/>
            <xsd:element name="text" type="TextType"/>
        </xsd:choice>
    </xsd:complexType>

    <!--Type for a color element -->
    <xsd:complexType name="ColorType">
      <xsd:attribute name="R" use="required">
        <xsd:simpleType>
            <xsd:restriction base="xsd:nonNegativeInteger">
                <xsd:maxInclusive value="255"/>
            </xsd:restriction>
        </xsd:simpleType>
      </xsd:attribute>
      <xsd:attribute name="G" use="required">
        <xsd:simpleType>
            <xsd:restriction base="xsd:nonNegativeInteger">
                <xsd:maxInclusive value="255"/>
            </xsd:restriction>
        </xsd:simpleType>
      </xsd:attribute>
      <xsd:attribute name="B" use="required">
        <xsd:simpleType>
            <xsd:restriction base="xsd:nonNegativeInteger">
                <xsd:maxInclusive value="255"/>
            </xsd:restriction>
        </xsd:simpleType>
      </xsd:attribute>
    </xsd:complexType>

    <!--Type for a bounding rectangle for a sketch element -->
    <xsd:complexType name="BoundsType">
     <xsd:attributeGroup ref="coords"/>
     <xsd:attribute name="width" use="required">
      <xsd:simpleType>
```

```xml
        <xsd:restriction base="xsd:nonNegativeInteger">
         <xsd:minExclusive value="2"/>
        </xsd:restriction>
      </xsd:simpleType>
    </xsd:attribute>
    <xsd:attribute name="height" use="required">
     <xsd:simpleType>
      <xsd:restriction base="xsd:nonNegativeInteger">
       <xsd:minExclusive value="2"/>
      </xsd:restriction>
     </xsd:simpleType>
    </xsd:attribute>
   </xsd:complexType>

   <!--Type for a sketch line element -->
   <xsd:complexType name="LineType">
       <xsd:sequence>
           <xsd:element name="color"/>
           <xsd:element name="position"/>
           <xsd:element name="bounds"/>
           <xsd:element name="endpoint"/>
       </xsd:sequence>
       <xsd:attribute name="angle" type="xsd:double" use="required"/>
   </xsd:complexType>

   <!--Type for a sketch rectangle element -->
   <xsd:complexType name="RectangleType">
       <xsd:sequence>
           <xsd:element name="color" type="ColorType"/>
           <xsd:element name="position" type="PointType"/>
           <xsd:element name="bounds" type="BoundsType"/>
       </xsd:sequence>
   <xsd:attribute name="width" use="required">
       <xsd:simpleType>
           <xsd:restriction base="xsd:double">
               <xsd:minInclusive value="2.0"/>
           </xsd:restriction>
       </xsd:simpleType>
   </xsd:attribute>
   <xsd:attribute name="height" use="required">
       <xsd:simpleType>
           <xsd:restriction base="xsd:double">
               <xsd:minInclusive value="2.0"/>
           </xsd:restriction>
       </xsd:simpleType>
     </xsd:attribute>
     <xsd:attribute name="angle" type="xsd:double" use="required"/>
   </xsd:complexType>

   <!--Type for a sketch circle element -->
   <xsd:complexType name="CircleType">
       <xsd:sequence>
           <xsd:element name="color" type="ColorType"/>
           <xsd:element name="position" type="PointType"/>
           <xsd:element name="bounds" type="BoundsType"/>
       </xsd:sequence>
       <xsd:attribute name="diameter" use="required">
           <xsd:simpleType>
             <xsd:restriction base="xsd:double">
                 <xsd:minExclusive value="2.0"/>
             </xsd:restriction>
           </xsd:simpleType>
```

```
                </xsd:attribute>
                <xsd:attribute name="angle" type="xsd:double" use="required"/>
        </xsd:complexType>

        <!--Type for a sketch curve element -->
        <xsd:complexType name="CurveType">
            <xsd:sequence>
                <xsd:element name="color" type="ColorType"/>
                <xsd:element name="position" type="PointType"/>
                <xsd:element name="bounds" type="BoundsType"/>
                <xsd:element name="point" type="PathPointType" minOccurs="1"
                                                    maxOccurs="unbounded"/>
            </xsd:sequence>
                <xsd:attribute name="angle" type="xsd:double" use="required"/>
        </xsd:complexType>

        <!--Type for a sketch text element -->
        <xsd:complexType name="TextType">
            <xsd:sequence>
                <xsd:element name="color" type="ColorType"/>
                <xsd:element name="position" type="PointType"/>
                <xsd:element name="bounds" type="BoundsType"/>
                <xsd:element name="font" type="FontType"/>
                <xsd:element name="string" type="xsd:string"/>
            </xsd:sequence>
                <xsd:attribute name="angle" type="xsd:double" use="required"/>
                <xsd:attribute name="maxascent" type="xsd:integer" use="required"/>
        </xsd:complexType>

        <!--Type for a font element -->
        <xsd:complexType name="FontType">
            <xsd:attribute name="fontname" type="xsd:string" use="required"/>
            <xsd:attribute name="fontstyle" use="required">
                <xsd:simpleType>
                    <xsd:restriction base="xsd:string">
                        <xsd:enumeration value="plain"/>
                        <xsd:enumeration value="bold"/>
                        <xsd:enumeration value="italic"/>
                        <xsd:enumeration value="bold-italic"/>
                    </xsd:restriction>
                </xsd:simpleType>
            </xsd:attribute>
        </xsd:complexType>

        <!--Type for elements representing points -->
        <xsd:complexType name="PointType">
            <xsd:attributeGroup ref="coords"/>
        </xsd:complexType>

        <!--Type for elements representing points in a general path -->
        <xsd:complexType name="PathPointType">
            <xsd:attribute name="x" type="xsd:double" use="required"/>
            <xsd:attribute name="y" type="xsd:double" use="required"/>
        </xsd:complexType>

        <!--Type for a color element -->
        <xsd:complexType name="ColorType">
            <xsd:attribute name="R" type="xsd:nonNegativeInteger" use="required"/>
            <xsd:attribute name="G" type="xsd:nonNegativeInteger" use="required"/>
            <xsd:attribute name="B" type="xsd:nonNegativeInteger" use="required"/>
        </xsd:complexType>

<!--Attribute group for an x,y integer coordinate pair -->
```

```
<xsd:attributeGroup name="coords">
  <xsd:attribute name="x" type="xsd:integer" use="required"/>
  <xsd:attribute name="y" type="xsd:integer" use="required"/>
</xsd:attributeGroup>

</xsd:schema>
```

This is somewhat longer than the DTD for Sketcher, but it does provide several advantages. All the data in the document now has types specified so the document is more precisely defined. This schema is XML, so the documents and the schema are defined in fundamentally the same way and are equally communicable. There is no problem combining one schema with another because namespaces are supported, and every schema can be easily extended. You can save this as a file `Sketcher.xsd`.

A Document That Uses a Schema

A document that has been defined in accordance with a particular schema is called an *instance document* for that schema. An instance document has to identify the schema to which it conforms, and this is done using attribute values within the root element of the document. Here's an XML document for a sketch that identifies the location of the schema:

```
<sketch
  xmlns:xsi="http://www.w3.org/2001/XMLSchema-instance"
  xsi:noNamespaceSchemaLocation="file:/D:/Beg%20Java%20Stuff/Sketcher.xsd">
  <!-- Elements defined for the sketch... -->
</sketch>
```

The value for the `xmlns` attribute identifies the namespace name `http://www.w3.org/2001/XMLSchema-instance` and specifies `xsi` as the prefix used to represent this namespace name. In an instance document, the value for the `noNamespaceSchemaLocation` attribute in the `xsi` namespace is a hint about the location where the schema for the document can be found. Here the `noNamespaceSchemaLocation` value is a URI for a file on the local machine, and the spaces are escaped because this is required within a URI. The value you specify for the `xsi:noNamespaceSchemaLocation` attribute is always regarded as a hint, so in principle an application or parser processing this document is not obliged to take account of this. In practice, though, this usually is taken into account when the document is processed, unless there is good reason to ignore it.

You define a value for the `noNamespaceSchemaLocation` attribute because a sketch document has no namespace; if it had a namespace, you would define a value for the `schemaLocation` attribute that includes two URIs separated by whitespace within the value specification — the URI for the namespace and a URI that is a hint for the location of the namespace. Obviously, because one or more spaces separate the two URIs, the URIs cannot contain unescaped spaces.

PROGRAMMING WITH XML DOCUMENTS

Right at the beginning of this chapter I introduced the notion of an XML processor as a module that is used by an application to read XML documents. An XML processor parses a document and makes the elements, together with their attributes and content, available to the application, so it is also referred to as an *XML parser*. In case you haven't met the term before, a *parser* is just a program module that breaks down text in a given language into its component parts. A natural language processor would have a parser that identifies the grammatical segments in each sentence. A compiler has a parser that identifies variables, constants, operators, and so on in a program statement. An application accesses the content of a document through an API provided by an XML parser and the parser does the job of figuring out what the document consists of.

Java supports two complementary APIs for processing an XML document that I'm introducing at a fairly basic level:

➤ **SAX**, which is the Simple API for XML parsing

➤ **DOM**, which is the Document Object Model for XML

The support in JDK 7 is for DOM level 3 and for SAX version 2.0.2. JDK 7 also supports *XSLT 1.0*, where *XSL* is the Extensible Stylesheet Language and T is Transformations—a language for transforming one XML document into another, or into some other textual representation such as HTML. However, I'm concentrating on the basic application of DOM and SAX in this chapter and the next, with a brief excursion into using XSLT in a very simple way in the context of DOM in Chapter 23.

Before I get into detail on these APIs, let's look at the broad differences between SAX and DOM, and get an idea of the circumstances in which you might choose to use one rather than the other.

 NOTE *Java also supports a streaming API for XML processing capability that is called StAX. This provides more control of the parsing process than you get with SAX and DOM and requires a lot less memory than DOM. StAX is particularly useful when you are processing XML with limited memory available.*

SAX Processing

SAX uses an *event-based* process for reading an XML document that is implemented through a callback mechanism. This is very similar to the way in which you handle GUI events in Java. As the parser reads a document, each parsing event, such as recognizing the start or end of an element, results in a call to a particular method associated with that event. Such a method is often referred to as a *handler*. It is up to you to implement these methods to respond appropriately to the event. Each of your methods then has the opportunity to react to the event, which results in it being called in any way that you want. In Figure 22-4 you can see the events that would arise from the XML shown.

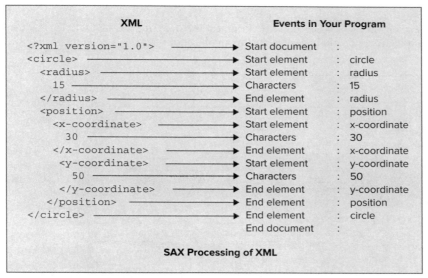

FIGURE 22-4

Each type of event results in a different method in your program being called. There are, for example, different events for registering the beginning and end of a document. You can also see that the start and end of each element results in two further kinds of events, and another type of event occurs for each segment of document data. Thus, this particular document involves five different methods in your program being called—some of them more than once, of course, so there is one method for each type of event.

Because of the way SAX works, your application inevitably receives the document a piece at a time, with no representation of the whole document. This means that if you need to have the whole document available to your program with its elements and content properly structured, you have to assemble it yourself from the information supplied piecemeal to your callback methods.

Of course, it also means that you don't have to keep the entire document in memory if you don't need it, so if you are just looking for particular information from a document—all <phonenumber> elements, for example—you can just save those as you receive them through the callback mechanism, and you can discard the rest. As a consequence, SAX is a particularly fast and memory-efficient way of selectively processing the contents of an XML document.

First of all, SAX itself is not an XML document parser; it is a public domain definition of an interface to an XML parser, where the parser is an external program. The public domain part of the SAX API is in three packages that are shipped as part of the JDK:

➤ org.xml.sax: This defines the Java interfaces specifying the SAX API and the InputSource class that encapsulates a source of an XML document to be parsed.

➤ org.xml.sax.helpers: This defines a number of helper classes for interfacing to a SAX parser.

➤ org.xml.sax.ext: This defines interfaces representing optional extensions to SAX2 to obtain information about a DTD, or to obtain information about comments and CDATA sections in a document.

In addition to these, the javax.xml.parsers package provides factory classes that you use to gain access to a parser.

In Java terms there are several interfaces involved. The XMLReader interface specifies the methods that the SAX parser calls as it recognizes elements, attributes, and other components of an XML document. You must provide a class that implements these methods and responds to the method calls in the way that you want.

DOM Processing

DOM works quite differently from SAX. When an XML document is parsed, the whole XML tree is assembled in memory and returned to your application encapsulated in an object of type org.w3c.dom.Document, as Figure 22-5 illustrates.

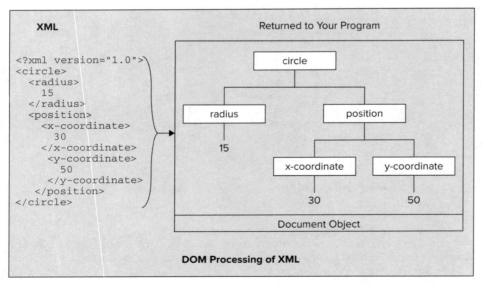

DOM Processing of XML

FIGURE 22-5

After you have the Document object available, you can call the Document object's methods to navigate through the elements in the document tree starting with the root element. With DOM, the entire document is available for you to process as often and in as many ways as you want. This is a major advantage over SAX processing. The downside to this is the amount of memory occupied by the document—there is no choice, you get it all, no matter how big it is. With some documents the amount of memory required may be prohibitively large.

DOM has one other unique advantage over SAX. It enables you to modify existing documents and create new ones. If you want to create an XML document programmatically and then transfer it to an external destination, such as a file or another computer, DOM is a better API for this than SAX because SAX has no direct provision for creating or modifying XML documents. I'll discuss how you can use a DOM parser in the next chapter.

 NOTE *StAX also has the capability for creating XML documents.*

ACCESSING PARSERS

The `javax.xml.parsers` package defines four classes supporting the processing of XML documents:

➤ `SAXParserFactory`: Enables you to create a configurable factory object that you can use to create a `SAXParser` object.

➤ `SAXParser`: Defines an object that wraps a SAX-based parser.

➤ `DocumentBuilderFactory`: Enables you to create a configurable factory object that you can use to create a `DocumentBuilder` object encapsulating a DOM-based parser.

➤ `DocumentBuilder`: Defines an object that wraps a DOM-based parser.

All four classes are abstract. This is because JAXP is designed to allow different parsers and their factory classes to be plugged in. Both DOM and SAX parsers are developed independently of the Java JDK, so it is important to be able to integrate new parsers as they come along. The Xerces parser that is currently distributed with the JDK is controlled and developed by the Apache Project, and it provides a very comprehensive range of capabilities. However, you may want to take advantage of the features provided by other parsers from other organizations, and JAXP allows for that.

These abstract classes act as wrappers for the specific factory and parser objects that you need to use for a particular parser and insulate your code from a particular parser implementation. An instance of a factory object that can create an instance of a parser is created at runtime, so your program can use a different parser without changing or even recompiling your code. Now that you have a rough idea of the general principles, let's get down to specifics and practicalities, starting with SAX.

USING SAX

To process an XML document with SAX, you first have to establish contact with the parser that you want to use. The first step toward this is to create a `SAXParserFactory` object like this:

```
SAXParserFactory spf = SAXParserFactory.newInstance();
```

The `SAXParserFactory` class is defined in the `javax.xml.parsers` package along with the `SAXParser` class that encapsulates a parser. The `SAXParserFactory` class is abstract, but the static `newInstance()` method returns a reference to an object of a class type that is a concrete implementation of `SAXParserFactory`. This is the factory object for creating an object encapsulating a SAX parser.

Before you create a parser object, you can condition the capabilities of the parser object that the `SAXParserFactory` object creates. For example, the `SAXParserFactory` object has methods for determining whether the parser that it attempts to create is namespace-aware or validates the XML as it is parsed. The `isNamespaceAware()` method returns `true` if the parser it creates is namespace-aware and returns `false` otherwise. The `isValidating()` method returns `true` if the parser it creates validates the XML during parsing and returns `false` otherwise.

You can set the factory object to produce namespace-aware parsers by calling its `setNamespaceAware()` method with an argument value of `true`. An argument value of `false` sets the factory object to produce parsers that are not namespace-aware. A parser that is namespace-aware can recognize the structure of names in a namespace—with a colon separating the namespace prefix from the name. A namespace-aware parser can report the URI and local name separately for each element and attribute. A parser that is not namespace-aware reports only an element or attribute name as a single name, even when it contains a colon. In other words, a parser that is not namespace-aware treats a colon as just another character that is part of a name.

Similarly, calling the `setValidating()` method with an argument value of `true` causes the factory object to produce parsers that can validate the XML. A validating parser can verify that the document body has a DTD or a schema, and that the document content is consistent with the DTD or schema identified within the document.

You can now use the `SAXParserFactory` object to create a `SAXParser` object as follows:

```
SAXParser parser = null;
try {
 parser = spf.newSAXParser();
}catch(SAXException | ParserConfigurationException e){
   e.printStackTrace();
   System.exit(1);
}
```

The `SAXParser` object that you create here encapsulates the parser supplied with the JDK. The `newSAXParser()` method for the factory object can throw the two exceptions you are catching here. A `ParserConfigurationException` is thrown if a parser cannot be created consistent with the configuration determined by the `SAXParserFactory` object, and a `SAXException` is thrown if any other error occurs. For example, if you call the `setValidating()` option and the parser does not have the capability for validating documents, `SAXException` will be thrown. This should not arise with the parser supplied with the JDK, though, because it supports both of these features.

The `ParserConfigurationException` class is defined in the `javax.xml.parsers` package and the `SAXException` class is in the `org.xml.sax` package. Now let's see what the default parser is by putting together the code fragments you have looked at so far.

TRY IT OUT Accessing a SAX Parser

Here's the code to create a `SAXParser` object and output some details about it to the command line:

Available for download on Wrox.com

```
import javax.xml.parsers.*;
import org.xml.sax.SAXException;

public class TrySAX {
  public static void main(String args[]) {
    // Create factory object
    SAXParserFactory spf = SAXParserFactory.newInstance();
    System.out.println(
      "Parser will " + (spf.isNamespaceAware() ? "" : "not ") + "be namespace aware");
    System.out.println(
              "Parser will " + (spf.isValidating() ? "" : "not ") + "validate XML");

    SAXParser parser = null;                   // Stores parser reference
    try {
     parser = spf.newSAXParser();             // Create parser object
    }catch(SAXException | ParserConfigurationException e){
       e.printStackTrace();
       System.exit(1);
    }

    System.out.println("Parser object is: " + parser);
  }
}
```

When I ran this I got the following output:

```
Parser will not be namespace aware
Parser will not validate XML
Parser object is: com.sun.org.apache.xerces.internal.jaxp.SAXParserImpl@4c71d2
```

How It Works

The output shows that the default configuration for the SAX parser produced by the SAXParserFactory object spf is neither namespace-aware nor validating. The parser supplied with the JDK is the Xerces parser from the XML Apache Project. This parser implements the W3C standard for XML, the de facto SAX2 standard, and the W3C DOM standard. It also provides support for the W3C standard for XML Schema. You can find detailed information on the advantages of this particular parser on the http://xml.apache.org website.

The code to create the parser works as I have already discussed. After you have an instance of the factory method, you use that to create an object encapsulating the parser. Although the reference is returned as type SAXParser, the object is of type SAXParserImpl, which is a concrete implementation of the abstract SAXParser class for a particular parser.

The Xerces parser is capable of validating XML and can be namespace-aware. All you need to do is specify which of these options you require by calling the appropriate method for the factory object. You can set the parser configuration for the factory object spf so that you get a validating and namespace-aware parser by adding two lines to the program:

```
// Create factory object
SAXParserFactory spf = SAXParserFactory.newInstance();
spf.setNamespaceAware(true);
spf.setValidating(true);
```

If you compile and run the code again, you should get output something like the following:

```
Parser will be namespace aware
Parser will validate XML
Parser object is: com.sun.org.apache.xerces.internal.jaxp.SAXParserImpl@18e18a3
```

You arrive at a SAXParser instance without tripping any exceptions, and you clearly now have a namespace-aware and validating parser. By default the Xerces parser validates an XML document with a DTD. To get it to validate a document with an XML Schema, you need to set another option for the parser, as I discuss in the next section.

Parser Features and Properties

Specific parsers, such as the Xerces parser that you get with the JDK, define their own features and properties that control and report on the processing of XML documents. A *feature* is an option in processing XML that is either on or off, so a feature is set as a boolean value, either true or false. A *property* is a parameter that you set to a particular object value, usually of type String. There are standard SAX2 features and properties that may be common to several parsers, and non-standard features and properties that are parser-specific. Note that although a feature or property may be standard for SAX2, this does not mean that a SAX2 parser necessarily supports it.

Querying and Setting Parser Features

Namespace awareness and validating capability are both features of a parser, and you already know how you tell the parser factory object that you want a parser with these features turned on. In general, each parser feature is identified by a name that is a fully qualified URI, and the standard features for SAX2 parsing have names within the namespace http://xml.org/sax/features/. For example, the feature specifying namespace awareness has the name http://xml.org/sax/features/namespaces. Here are a few of the standard features that are defined for SAX2 parsers:

➤ namespaces: When true, the parser replaces prefixes to element and attribute names with the corresponding namespace URIs. If you set this feature to true, the document must have a schema that supports the use of namespaces. All SAX parsers must support this feature.

➤ namespace-prefixes: When true, the parser reports the original prefixed names and attributes used for namespace declarations. The default value is false. All SAX parsers must support this feature.

➤ validation: When true, the parser validates the document and reports any errors. The default value is false.

➤ external-general-entities: When true, the parser includes general entities.

➤ string-interning: When true, all element and attribute names, namespace URIs, and local names use Java string interning so each of these corresponds to a unique object. This feature is always true for the Xerces parser.

➤ external-parameter-entities: When true, the parser includes external parameter entities and the external DTD subset.

➤ lexical-handler/parameter-entities: When true, the beginning and end of parameter entities will be reported.

You can find a more comprehensive list in the description for the org.xml.sax package that is in the JDK documentation. There are other non-standard features for the Xerces parser. Consult the documentation for the parser on the Apache website for more details. Apart from the namespaces and namespaces-prefixes features that all SAX2 parsers are required to implement, there is no set collection of features for a SAX2 parser, so a parser may implement any number of arbitrary features that may or may not be in the list of standard features.

You have two ways to query and set features for a parser. You can call the getFeature() and setFeature() methods for the SAXParserFactory object to do this before you create the SAXParser object. The parser that is created then has the features switched on. Alternatively, you can create a SAXParser object using the factory object and then obtain an org.sax.XMLReader object reference from it by calling the getXMLReader() method. You can then call the getFeature() and setFeature() methods for the XMLReader object. XMLReader is the interface that a concrete SAX2 parser implements to allow features and properties to be set and queried. The principle difference in use between calling the factory object methods and calling the XMLReader object methods is that the methods for a SAXParserFactory object can throw an exception of type javax.xml.parsers.ParserConfigurationException if a parser cannot be created with the feature specified.

After you have created an XMLParser object, you can obtain an XMLReader object reference from the parser like this:

```
XMLReader reader = null;
try{
  reader = parser.getXMLReader();
} catch(org.xml.sax.SAXException e) {
  System.err.println(e.getMessage());
}
```

The getFeature() method that the XMLReader interface declares for querying a feature expects an argument of type String that identifies the feature you are querying. The method returns a boolean value that indicates the state of the feature. The setFeature() method expects two arguments; the first is of type String and identifies the feature you are setting, and the second is of type boolean and specifies the state to be set. The setFeature() method can throw exceptions of type org.xml.SAXNotRecognizedException if the feature is not found, or of type org.xml.sax.SAXNotSupportedException if the feature name was recognized but cannot be set to the boolean value you specify. Both exception types have SAXException as a base, so you can use this type to catch either of them. Here's how you might set the features for the Xerces parser so that it supports namespace prefixes:

```
String nsPrefixesFeature = "http://xml.org/sax/features/namespace-prefixes";
XMLReader reader = null;
try{
  reader = parser.getXMLReader();
  reader.setFeature(nsPrefixesFeature, true);
} catch(org.xml.sax.SAXException e) {
  System.err.println(e.getMessage());
}
```

This sets the feature to make the parser report the original prefixed element and attribute names.

If you want to use the SAXParserFactory object to set the features before you create the parser object, you could do it like this:

```
String nsPrefixesFeature = "http://xml.org/sax/features/namespace-prefixes";
SAXParserFactory spf = SAXParserFactory.newInstance();
SAXParser parser = null;
try {
  spf.setFeature(nsPrefixesFeature, true);
  parser = spf.newSAXParser();
  System.out.println("Parser object is: "+ parser);
}
catch(SAXException | ParserConfigurationException e) {
  e.printStackTrace();
  System.exit(1);
}
```

You must call the setFeature() method for the SAXParserFactory object in a try block because of the exceptions it may throw.

Setting Parser Properties

As I said at the outset, a property is a parser parameter with a value that is an object, usually a String object. Some properties have values that you set to influence the parser's operation, but the values for other properties are set by the parser for you to retrieve to provide information about the parsing process.

You can set the properties for a parser by calling the setProperty() method for the SAXParser object after you have created it. The first argument to the method is the name of the property as type String, and the second argument is the value for the property. A property value can be of any class type, as the parameter type is Object, but it is usually of type String. The setProperty() method throws a SAXNotRecognizedException if the property name is not recognized or a SAXNotSupportedException if the property name is recognized but not supported. Both of these exception classes are defined in the org.xml.sax package. Alternatively, you can get and set properties using the XMLReader object reference that you used to set features. The XMLReader interface declares the getProperty() and setProperty() methods with the same signatures as those for the SAXParser object.

You can also retrieve the values for some properties during parsing to obtain additional information about the most recent parsing event. You use the parser's getProperty() method in this case. The argument to the method is the name of the property, and the method returns a reference to the property's value.

As with features, there is no defined set of parser properties, so you need to consult the parser documentation for information on these. There are four standard properties for a SAX parser, none of which are required to be supported by a SAX parser. Because these properties involve the more advanced features of SAX parser operation, they are beyond the scope of this book, but if you are interested, they are documented in the description for the org.xml.sax package that you can find in the JDK documentation.

Parsing Documents with SAX

To parse a document using the SAXParser object you simply call its parse() method. You have to supply two arguments: the first identifies the XML document, and the second is a reference of type org.xml.sax.helpers.DefaultHandler to a handler object that you have created to process the contents of the document. The DefaultHandler object must contain a specific set of public methods that the SAXParser object expects to be able to call for each event, where each type of event corresponds to a particular syntactic element it finds in the document.

The DefaultHandler class already contains do-nothing definitions for subsets of all the callback methods that a SAXParser object supporting SAX2.0 expects to be able to call. Thus, all you have to do is define a class that extends the DefaultHandler class and override the methods in the base class for the events that you are interested in. There is the org.xml.sax.ext.DefaultHandler2 class that extends the DefaultHandler class. This adds methods to support extensions to SAX2, but I won't be going into these.

Let's not gallop too far ahead, though. You need to look into the versions of the parse() method that you have available before you can get into handling parsing events. The SAXParser class defines ten overloaded versions of the parse() method, but you are interested in only five of them. The other five use a deprecated handler type HandlerBase that was applicable to SAX1, so you can ignore those and just look at the versions that relate to SAX2. All versions of the method have a return type of void, and the five varieties of the parse() method that you consider are as follows:

➤ parse(File file, DefaultHandler handler): Parses the document in the file specified by file using handler as the object containing the callback methods called by the parser. This throws an IOException if an I/O error occurs and an IllegalArgumentException if file is null.

➤ parse(String uri, DefaultHandler dh): Parses the document specified by uri using dh as the object defining the callback methods. This throws an exception of type SAXException if uri is null, and an exception of type IOException if an I/O error occurs.

➤ parse(InputStream in, DefaultHandler dh): Parses in as the source of the XML with dh as the event handler. This throws an IOException if an I/O error occurs and an IllegalArgumentException if input is null.

➤ parse(InputStream in, DefaultHandler dh, String systemID): Parses input as the previous method, but uses systemID to resolve any relative URIs.

➤ parse(InputSource srce, DefaultHandler dh): Parses the document specified by srce using dh as the object providing the callback methods to be called by the parser.

The InputSource class is defined in the org.xml.sax package. It defines an object that wraps a variety of sources for an XML document that you can use to pass a document reference to a parser. You can create an InputSource object from a java.io.InputStream object, a java.io.Reader object encapsulating a character stream, or a String specifying a URI—either a public name or a URL. If you specify the document source as a URL, it must be fully qualified.

Implementing a SAX Handler

As I said, the DefaultHandler class in the org.xml.sax.helpers package provides a default do-nothing implementation of each of the callback methods a SAX parser may call. These methods are declared in four interfaces that are all implemented by the DefaultHandler class:

➤ The ContentHandler interface declares methods that are called to identify the content of a document to an application. You should usually implement all the methods defined in this interface in your subclass of DefaultHandler.

➤ The EntityResolver interface declares one method, resolveEntity(), that is called by a parser to pass a public and/or system ID to your application to allow external entities in the document to be resolved.

➤ The DTDHandler interface declares two methods that are called to notify your application of DTD-related events.

➤ The ErrorHandler interface defines three methods that are called when the parser has identified an error of some kind in the document.

All four interfaces are defined in the org.xml.sax package. Of course, the parse() method for the SAXParser object expects you to supply a reference of type DefaultHandler as an argument, so you have no choice but to extend the DefaultHandler class in your handler class. This accommodates just about anything you want to do because you decide which base class methods you want to override.

The methods that you must implement to deal with parsing events that relate to document content are those declared by the ContentHandler interface, so let's concentrate on those first:

➤   void startDocument(): Called when the start of a document is recognized.

➤   void endDocument(): Called when the end of a document is recognized.

➤   void startElement(String uri, String localName, String qName, Attributes attr): Called when the start of an element is recognized. Up to three names may be provided for the element:

>   ➤   uri: The namespace URI for the element name. This is an empty string if there is no URI or if namespace processing is not being done.

>   ➤   localName: The unqualified local name for the element. This is an empty string if namespace processing is not being done. In this case the element name is reported via the qName parameter.

>   ➤   qName: The qualified name for the element. This is just the name if the parser is not namespace-aware. (A colon, if it appears, is then just an ordinary character.)

>   ➤   attr: Encapsulates the attributes for the element that have explicit values.

➤   void endElement(String uri, String localName, String qName): Called when the end of an element is recognized. The parameters are as described for the startElement() method.

➤   void characters(char[] ch, int start, int length): Called for each segment of character data that is recognized. Note that a contiguous segment of text within an element can be returned as several chunks by the parser via several calls to this method. The characters that are available are from ch[start] to ch[start+length-1], and you must not try to access the array outside these limits.

➤   void ignorableWhitespace(char[] ch, int start, int length): Called for each segment of ignorable whitespace that is recognized within the content of an element. Note that a contiguous segment of ignorable whitespace within an element can be returned as several chunks by the parser via several calls to this method. The whitespace characters that are available are from ch[start] to ch[start+length-1], and you must not try to access the array outside these limits.

➤   void startPrefixMapping(String prefix, String uri): Called when the start of a prefix URI namespace mapping is identified. Most of the time you can disregard this method, as a parser automatically replaces prefixes for elements and attribute names by default.

➤   void endPrefixMapping(String prefix): Called when the end of a prefix URI namespace mapping is identified. Most of the time you can disregard this method for the reason noted in the preceding method.

➤   void processingInstruction(String target, String data): Called for each processing instruction that is recognized.

➤   void skippedEntity(String name): Called for each entity that the parser skips.

➤   void setDocumentLocator(Locator locator): Called by the parser to pass a Locator object to your code that you can use to determine the location in the document of any SAX document event. The Locator object can provide the public identifier, the system ID, the line number, and the column number in the document for any event. Just implement this method if you want to receive this information for each event.

Your implementations of these methods can throw an exception of type SAXException if an error occurs.

When the startElement() method is called, it receives a reference to an object of type org.xml.sax. Attributes as the last argument. This object encapsulates information about all the attributes for the element. The Attributes interface declares methods you can call for the object to obtain details of each attribute name, its type, and its value. These methods use either an index value to select a particular attribute or an attribute name—either a prefix qualified name or a name qualified by a namespace name. I just describe the methods relating to using an index because that's what the code examples use. Index values start from 0. The methods that the `Attributes` interface declares for accessing attribute information using an index are as follows:

➤ `int getLength()`: Returns a count of the number of attributes encapsulated in the `Attributes` object.

➤ `String getLocalName(int index)`: Returns a string containing the local name of the attribute for the `index` value passed as the argument.

➤ `String getQName(int index)`: Returns a string containing the XML 1.0 qualified name of the attribute for the `index` value passed as the argument.

➤ `String getType(int index)`: Returns a string containing the type of the attribute for the `index` value passed as the argument. The type is returned as one of the following:
`"CDATA"`, `"ID"`, `"IDREF"`, `"IDREFS"`, `"NMTOKEN"`, `"NMTOKENS"`, `"ENTITY"`, `"ENTITIES"`, `"NOTATION"`

➤ `String getValue(int index)`: Returns a string containing the value of the attribute for the `index` value passed as the argument.

➤ `String getURI(int index)`: Returns a string containing the attribute's namespace URI, or an empty string if no URI is available.

If the index value that you supply to any of these `getXXX()` methods here is out of range, then the method returns `null`.

Given a reference, `attr`, of type `Attributes`, you can retrieve information about all the attributes with the following code:

```
int attrCount = attr.getLength();
if(attrCount>0) {
  System.out.println("Attributes:");
  for(int i = 0 ; i < attrCount ; ++i ) {
    System.out.println("  Name : " + attr.getQName(i));
    System.out.println("  Type : " + attr.getType(i));
    System.out.println("  Value: " + attr.getValue(i));
  }
}
```

This is very straightforward. You look for data on attributes only if the value returned by the `getLength()` method is greater than zero. You then retrieve information about each attribute in the `for` loop.

The `DefaultHandler` class is just like the adapter classes you have used for defining GUI event handlers. To implement your own handler class you just extend the `DefaultHandler` class and define your own implementations for the methods that you are interested in. The same caveat applies here that applied with adapter classes—you must be sure that the signatures of your methods are correct. The best way to do this is to use the `@Override` annotation. Let's try implementing a handler class.

TRY IT OUT Handling Parsing Events

Let's first define a handler class to deal with document parsing events. You just implement a few of the methods from the `ContentHandler` interface in this—only those that apply to a very simple document—and you don't need to worry about errors for the moment. Here's the code:

Available for download on Wrox.com

```
import org.xml.sax.helpers.DefaultHandler;
import org.xml.sax.Attributes;

public class MySAXHandler extends DefaultHandler {
  @Override
  public void startDocument() {
    System.out.println("Start document: ");
  }

  @Override
  public void endDocument()  {
    System.out.println("End document");
```

```
    }

    @Override
    public void startElement(String uri, String localName, String qname,
                                                     Attributes attr) {
      System.out.println("Start element: local name: " + localName +
                              " qname: " + qname + " uri: " + uri);
      int attrCount = attr.getLength();
      if(attrCount > 0) {
        System.out.println("Attributes:");
        for(int i = 0 ; i < attrCount ; ++i ) {
          System.out.println("  Name : " + attr.getQName(i));
          System.out.println("  Type : " + attr.getType(i));
          System.out.println("  Value: " + attr.getValue(i));
        }
      }
    }

    @Override
    public void endElement(String uri, String localName, String qname) {
      System.out.println("End element: local name: " + localName +
                              " qname: " + qname + " uri: " + uri);
    }

    @Override
    public void characters(char[] ch, int start, int length) {
      System.out.println("Characters: " + new String(ch, start, length));
    }

    @Override
    public void ignorableWhitespace(char[] ch, int start, int length) {
      System.out.println("Ignorable whitespace: " + length + " characters.");
    }
  }
```

Directory "TrySAXHandler 1"

Each handler method just outputs information about the event to the command line.

Now you can define a program to use a handler of this class type to parse an XML document. You can make the example read the name of the XML file to be processed from the command line. Here's the code:

```
import javax.xml.parsers.*;
import org.xml.sax.SAXException;
import java.io.*;

public class TrySAXHandler {
  public static void main(String args[]) {
    if(args.length == 0) {
      System.out.println("No file to process. Usage is:" +
                                      "\njava TrySax \"filename\" ");
      return;
    }
    File xmlFile = new File(args[0]);
    if(xmlFile.exists()) {
      process(xmlFile);
    } else {
      System.out.println(xmlFile + " does not exist.");
    }
  }

  private static void process(File file) {
    SAXParserFactory spf = SAXParserFactory.newInstance();
    SAXParser parser = null;
    spf.setNamespaceAware(true);
```

```
        spf.setValidating(true);
        System.out.println("Parser will " +
                    (spf.isNamespaceAware() ? "" : "not ") + "be namespace aware");
        System.out.println("Parser will " + (spf.isValidating() ? "" : "not ")
                                                        + "validate XML");

        try {
         parser = spf.newSAXParser();
         System.out.println("Parser object is: " + parser);

        } catch(SAXException | ParserConfigurationException e) {
          e.printStackTrace();
          System.exit(1);

        }

        System.out.println("\nStarting parsing of "+file+"\n");
        MySAXHandler handler = new MySAXHandler();
        try {
           parser.parse(file, handler);
        }  catch(IOException | SAXException e) {
          e.printStackTrace();
        }
     }
   }
}
```

Directory "TrySAXHandler 1"

I created the `circle.xml` file with the following content:

```
<?xml version="1.0"?>
<circle diameter="40" angle="0">
  <color R="255" G="0" B="0"/>
  <position x="10" y="15"/>
  <bounds x="10" y="15"
          width="42" height="42"/>
</circle>
```

Directory "TrySAXHandler 1"

I saved this in my `Beg Java Stuff` directory, but you can put it wherever you want and adjust the command-line argument accordingly.

On my computer the program produced the following output:

```
Parser will be namespace aware
Parser will validate XML
Parser object is: com.sun.org.apache.xerces.internal.jaxp.SAXParserImpl@159d510

Starting parsing of D:\Beg Java Stuff\circle.xml

Start document:
Start element: local name: circle qname: circle uri:
Attributes:
  Name : diameter
  Type : CDATA
  Value: 40
  Name : angle
  Type : CDATA
  Value: 0
Characters:

Length: 3
Start element: local name: color qname: color uri:
Attributes:
```

```
          Name : R
          Type : CDATA
          Value: 255
          Name : G
          Type : CDATA
          Value: 0
          Name : B
          Type : CDATA
          Value: 0
       End element: local name: color qname: color uri:
       Characters:

       Length: 3
       Start element: local name: position qname: position uri:
       Attributes:
          Name : x
          Type : CDATA
          Value: 10
          Name : y
          Type : CDATA
          Value: 15
       End element: local name: position qname: position uri:
       Characters:

       Length: 3
       Start element: local name: bounds qname: bounds uri:
       Attributes:
          Name : x
          Type : CDATA
          Value: 10
          Name : y
          Type : CDATA
          Value: 15
          Name : width
          Type : CDATA
          Value: 42
          Name : height
          Type : CDATA
          Value: 42
       End element: local name: bounds qname: bounds uri:
       Characters:

       Length: 1
       End element: local name: circle qname: circle uri:
       End document
```

How It Works

Much of the code in the `TrySAXHandler` class is the same as in the previous example. The `main()` method first checks for a command-line argument. If there isn't one, you output a message and end the program. The code following the creation of the `java.io.File` object calls `exists()` for the object to make sure the file does exist.

Next you call the static `process()` method with a reference to the `File` object for the XML document as the argument. This method creates the `XMLParser` object in the way you've seen previously and then creates a handler object of type `MySAXHandler` for use by the parser. The parsing process is started by calling the `parse()` method for the parser object, `parser`, with the `file` reference as the first argument and the `handler` reference as the second argument. This identifies the object whose methods are called for parsing events.

You have overridden six of the do-nothing methods that are inherited from `DefaultHandler` in the `MySAXHandler` class and the output indicates which ones are called. Your method implementations just output a message along with the information that is passed as arguments. You can see from the output that there is no URI for a namespace in the document, so the value for `qname` is identical to `localname`.

The output shows that the `characters()` method is called with just whitespace in the `ch` array. You could see how much whitespace by adding another output statement for the value of `length`. This whitespace is ignorable whitespace that appears between the elements, but the parser is not recognizing it as such. This is because there is no DTD to define how elements are to be constructed in this document, so the parser has no way to know what can be ignored.

You can see that the output shows string values for both a `local name` and a `qname`. This is because you have the namespace awareness feature switched on. If you comment out the statement that calls `setNamespaceAware()` and recompile and re-execute the example, you see that only a `qname` is reported. Both the `local name` and URI outputs are empty.

You get all the information about the attributes, too, so the processing of attributes works without a DTD or a schema.

Processing a Document with a DTD

You can run the example again with the `Address.xml` file that you saved earlier in the `Beg Java Stuff` directory to see how using a DTD affects processing. This should have the following contents:

```xml
<?xml version="1.0"?>
<!DOCTYPE address SYSTEM "AddressDoc.dtd">
<address>
  <buildingnumber> 29 </buildingnumber>
  <street> South Lasalle Street</street>
  <city>Chicago</city>
  <state>Illinois</state>
  <zip>60603</zip>
</address>
```

Directory "TrySAXHandler 1"

The `AddressDoc.dtd` file in the same directory as `Address.xml` should contain the following:

```
<!ELEMENT address (buildingnumber, street, city, state, zip)>
    <!ELEMENT buildingnumber (#PCDATA)>
    <!ELEMENT street (#PCDATA)>
    <!ELEMENT city (#PCDATA)>
    <!ELEMENT state (#PCDATA)>
    <!ELEMENT zip (#PCDATA)>
```

Directory "TrySAXHandler 1"

If the path to the file contains spaces, you need to specify the path between double quotes in the command-line argument. I got the following output:

```
Parser will be namespace aware
Parser will validate XML
Parser object is: com.sun.org.apache.xerces.internal.jaxp.SAXParserImpl@2515

Starting parsing of D:\Beg Java Stuff\Address.xml

Start document:
Start element: local name: address qname: address uri:
Ignorable whitespace: 3 characters.
Start element: local name: buildingnumber qname: buildingnumber uri:
Characters:  29
End element: local name: buildingnumber qname: buildingnumber uri:
Ignorable whitespace: 3 characters.
Start element: local name: street qname: street uri:
Characters:  South Lasalle Street
End element: local name: street qname: street uri:
Ignorable whitespace: 3 characters.
```

```
Start element: local name: city qname: city uri:
Characters: Chicago
End element: local name: city qname: city uri:
Ignorable whitespace: 3 characters.
Start element: local name: state qname: state uri:
Characters: Illinois
End element: local name: state qname: state uri:
Ignorable whitespace: 3 characters.
Start element: local name: zip qname: zip uri:
Characters: 60603
End element: local name: zip qname: zip uri:
Ignorable whitespace: 1 characters.
End element: local name: address qname: address uri:
End document
```

You can see that with a DTD, the ignorable whitespace is recognized as such, and is passed to your `ignorableWhitespace()` method. A validating parser must call this method to report whitespace in element content. Although the parser is validating the XML, you still can't be sure that the document is valid based on the output you are getting. If any errors are found, the default do-nothing error-handling methods that are inherited from the `DefaultHandler` class are called, so there's no indication of when errors are found. You can fix this quite easily by modifying the `MySAXHandler` class, but let's first look at processing some other XML document flavors.

Processing a Document with Namespaces

You can convert the `Address.xml` file to use a namespace by modifying the root element like this:

```
<address xmlns="http://www.wrox.com/AddressNamespace">
```

With this change to the XML file, the URI for the default namespace is `http://www.wrox.com/AddressNamespace`. This doesn't really exist, but it doesn't need to. It's just a unique qualifier for the names within the namespace.

You also need to use a different DTD that takes into account the use of a namespace, so you must modify the `DOCTYPE` declaration in the document:

```
<!DOCTYPE address SYSTEM "AddressNamespaceDoc.dtd">
```

You can now save the revised XML document with the name `AddressNamespace.xml`.

You must also create the new DTD. This is the same as `AddressDoc.dtd` with the addition of a declaration for the `xmlns` attribute for the `<address>` element:

```
<!ATTLIST address xmlns CDATA #IMPLIED>
```

If you run the previous example with this version of the XML document, you should see the URI in the output. Because the namespace is the default, there is no prefix name, so the values for the `localname` and `qname` parameters to the `startElement()` and `endElement()` methods are the same.

Using Qualified Names

You can change the document to make explicit use of the namespace prefix like this:

Available for
download on
Wrox.com

```
<?xml version="1.0"?>
<!DOCTYPE addresses:address SYSTEM "AddressNamespaceDoc.dtd">
<addresses:address  xmlns:addresses=" http://www.wrox.com/AddressNamespace">
  <addresses:buildingnumber> 29 </addresses:buildingnumber>
  <addresses:street> South Lasalle Street</addresses:street>
  <addresses:city>Chicago</addresses:city>
  <addresses:state>Illinois</addresses:state>
  <addresses:zip>60603</addresses:zip>
</addresses:address>
```

Directory "TrySAXHandler 2 with extra callback methods"

I saved this as `AddressNamespace1.xml`. Unfortunately, you also have to update the DTD. Otherwise, if the qualified names are not declared in the DTD, they are regarded as errors. You need to change the DTD to the following:

```
<!ELEMENT addresses:address (addresses:buildingnumber, addresses:street,
                             addresses:city, addresses:state, addresses:zip)>
<!ATTLIST addresses:address xmlns:addresses CDATA #IMPLIED>
<!ELEMENT addresses:buildingnumber (#PCDATA)>
<!ELEMENT addresses:street (#PCDATA)>
<!ELEMENT addresses:city (#PCDATA)>
<!ELEMENT addresses:state (#PCDATA)>
<!ELEMENT addresses:zip (#PCDATA)>
```

Directory "TrySAXHandler 2 with extra callback methods"

I saved this as `AddressNamespaceDoc1.dtd`. The namespace prefix is `addresses`, and each element name is qualified by the namespace prefix. You can usefully add implementations for two further callback methods in the `MySAXHandler` class:

```
@Override
public void startPrefixMapping(String prefix, String uri) {
    System.out.println(
                    "Start \"" + prefix + "\" namespace scope. URI: " + uri);
}

@Override
public void endPrefixMapping(String prefix) {
    System.out.println("End \"" + prefix + "\" namespace scope.");
}
```

Directory "TrySAXHandler 2 with extra callback methods"

The parser doesn't call these methods by default. You have to switch the `http://xml.org/sax/features/namespace-prefixes` feature on to get this to happen. You can add a call to the `setFeature()` method for the parser factory object to do this in the `process()` method that you defined in the `TrySAXHandler` class, immediately before you create the parser object in the `try` block:

```
spf.setFeature("http://xml.org/sax/features/namespace-prefixes",true);
parser = spf.newSAXParser();
```

You place the statement here rather than after the call to the `setValidating()` method because the `setFeature()` method can throw an exception of type `ParserConfigurationException` and it needs to be in a `try` block. Now the parser calls the `startPrefixMapping()` method at the beginning of each namespace scope, and the `endPrefixMapping()` method at the end. If you parse this document, you see that each of the `qname` values is the local name qualified by the namespace prefix. You should also see that the start and end of the namespace scope are recorded in the output.

Handling Other Parsing Events

I have considered only events arising from the recognition of document content, those declared in the `ContentHandler` interface. In fact, the `DefaultHandler` class defines do-nothing methods declared in the other three interfaces that you saw earlier. For example, when a parsing error occurs, the parser calls a method to report the error. Three methods for error reporting are declared in the `ErrorHandler` interface and are implemented by the `DefaultHandler` class:

➤ `void warning(SAXParseException spe)`: Called to notify conditions that are not errors or fatal errors. The exception object, `spe`, contains information to enable you to locate the error in the original document.

➤ `void error(SAXParseException spe)`: Called when an error has been identified. An error is anything in a document that violates the XML specification but is recoverable and allows the parser to continue processing the document normally.

➤   void fatalError(SAXParseException spe): Called when a fatal error has been identified. A fatal error is a non-recoverable error. After a fatal error the parser does not continue normal processing of the document.

Each of these methods is declared to throw an exception of type SAXException, but you don't have to implement them so that they do this. With the warning() and error() methods you probably want to output an error message and return to the parser so it can continue processing. Of course, if your fatalError() method is called, processing of the document does not continue anyway, so it would be appropriate to throw an exception in this case.

Obviously your implementation of any of these methods wants to make use of the information from the SAXParseException object that is passed to the method. This object has four methods that you can call to obtain additional information that help you locate the error:

➤   int getLineNumber(): Returns the line number of the end of the document text where the error occurred. If this is not available, −1 is returned.

➤   int getColumnNumber(): Returns the column number within the document that contains the end of the text where the error occurred. If this is not available, −1 is returned. The first column in a line is column 1.

➤   String getPublicID(): Returns the public identifier of the entity where the error occurred, or null if no public identifier is available.

➤   String getSystemID(): Returns the system identifier of the entity where the error occurred, or null if no system identifier is available.

A simple implementation of the warning() method could be like this:

```
@Override
public void warning(SAXParseException spe) {
    System.out.println("Warning at line " + spe.getLineNumber());
    System.out.println(spe.getMessage());
}
```

Directory "TrySAXHandler 3 with error reporting"

This outputs a message indicating the document line number where the error occurred. It also outputs the string returned by the getMessage() method inherited from the base class, SAXException. This usually indicates the nature of the error that was detected.

You could implement the error() callback method similarly, but you might want to implement fatalError() so that it throws an exception. For example:

```
@Override
public void fatalError(SAXParseException spe) throws SAXException {
    System.out.println("Fatal error at line " + spe.getLineNumber());
    System.out.println(spe.getMessage());
    throw spe;
}
```

Directory "TrySAXHandler 3 with error reporting"

Here you just rethrow the SAXParseException after outputting an error message indicating the line number that caused the error. The SAXParseException class is a subclass of SAXException, so you can rethrow spe as the superclass type. Don't forget the import statements in the MySAXHandler source file for the SAXException and SAXParseException class names from the org.xml.sax package.

You could try these out with the previous example by adding them to the MySAXHandler class. You could introduce a few errors into the XML file to get these methods called. Try deleting the DOCTYPE declaration or deleting the forward slash on an element end tag, or even just deleting one character in an element name.

Parsing a Schema Instance Document

You can create a simple instance of a document that uses the `Sketcher.xsd` schema you developed earlier. Here's the definition of the XML document contents:

```xml
<?xml version="1.0" encoding="UTF-8"?>
<sketch xmlns:xsi="http://www.w3.org/2001/XMLSchema-instance"

          xsi:noNamespaceSchemaLocation="file:/D:/Beg%20Java%20Stuff/Sketcher.xsd">
    <circle diameter="40" angle="0.0">
        <color R="255" G="0" B="0"/>
        <position x="10" y="10"/>
        <bounds   x="10" y="10"
                  width="42" height="42"/>
    </circle>
    <line angle="0.0">
        <color R="0" G="0" B="255"/>
        <position x="10" y="10"/>
        <bounds   x="10" y="10"
                  width="22" height="32"/>
        <endpoint x="30" y="40"/>
    </line>
    <rectangle width="30.0" height="20.0" angle="0.0">
        <color R="255" G="0" B="0"/>
        <position x="30" y="40"/>
        <bounds   x="30" y="40"
                  width="32" height="22"/>
    </rectangle>
</sketch>
```

Directory "TryParsingSchemaInstance"

This defines a sketch that consists of three elements: a circle, a line, and a rectangle. The location of the schema is specified by the value for the `noNamespaceSchemaLocation` attribute, which here corresponds to the `Sketcher` `.xsd` file in the `Beg Java Stuff` directory. You can save the document as `sketch1.xml` in the same directory.

An XML document may have the applicable schema identified by the value for the `noNamespaceSchemaLocation` attribute, or the schema may not be identified explicitly in the document. You have the means for dealing with both of these situations in Java.

A `javax.xml.validation.Schema` object encapsulates a schema. You create a `Schema` object by calling methods for a `javax.xml.validation.SchemaFactory` object that you generate by calling the static `newInstance()` method for the `SchemaFactory` class. It works like this:

```java
SchemaFactory sf =
          SchemaFactory.newInstance("http://www.w3.org/2001/XMLSchema");
```

A `SchemaFactory` object compiles a schema from an external source in a given Schema Definition Language into a `Schema` object that can subsequently be used by a parser. The argument to the static `newInstance()` method in the `SchemaFactory` class identifies the schema language that the schema factory can process. The only alternative to the argument used in the example to specify the XML Schema language is `"http://relaxng.org/ns/structure/1.0,"` which is another schema language for XML. At the time of writing, `Schema` objects encapsulating DTDs are not supported.

The `javax.xml.XMLConstants` class defines `String` constants for basic values required when you are processing XML. The class defines a constant with the name `W3C_XML_NS_URI` that corresponds to the URI for the Schema Definition Language, so you could use this as the argument to the `newInstance()` method in the `SchemaFactory` class, like this:

```java
SchemaFactory sf = SchemaFactory.newInstance(W3C_XML_NS_URI);
```

This statement assumes you have statically imported the names from the `XMLConstants` class.

After you have identified the Schema Definition Language to be used, you can create a `Schema` object from a schema definition. Here's an example of how you might do this:

```
File schemaFile = Paths.get(System.getProperty("user.home")).
        resolve("Beginning Java Stuff").resolve("sketcher.xsd").toFile();
try {
  Schema schema = sf.newSchema(schemaFile);
}catch(SAXException e) {
 e.printStackTrace();
  System.exit(1);
}
```

The `newSchema()` method for the `SchemaFactory` object creates and returns a `Schema` object from the file specified by the `File` object you pass as the argument. There are versions of the `newSchema()` method with parameters of type `java.net.URL` and `java.xml.transform.Source`. An object that implements the `Source` interface represents an XML source. There's also a version of `newSchema()` that accepts an argument that is an array of `Source` object references and generates a `Schema` object from the input from all of the array elements.

Now that you have a `Schema` object, you can pass it to the `SAXParserFactory` object before you create your `SAXParser` object to process XML documents:

```
SAXParserFactory spf = SAXParserFactory.newInstance();
spf.setSchema(schema);
```

The parser you create by calling the `newSAXParser()` method for this `SAXParserFactory` object validates documents using the schema you have specified. XML documents are validated in this instance, even when the `isValidating()` method returns `false`, so it's not essential that you configure the parser to validate documents.

In many situations the document itself identifies the schema to be used. In this case you call the `newSchema()` method for the `SchemaFactory` object with no argument specified:

```
try {
  Schema schema = sf.newSchema();
}catch(SAXException e) {
 e.printStackTrace();
  System.exit(1);
}
```

A special `Schema` object is created by the `newSchema()` method that assumes the schema for the document is identified by hints within the document. Note that you still need to call `newSchema()` within a `try` block here because the method throws an exception of type `SAXException` if the operation fails for some reason. If the operation is not supported, an exception of type `UnsupportedOperationException` is thrown, but because this is a subclass of `RuntimeException`, you are not obliged to catch it.

TRY IT OUT Parsing a Schema Instance Document

Here's a variation on the `TrySAXHandler` class that parses a schema instance document:

```
import javax.xml.parsers.*;
import java.io.*;
import javax.xml.validation.SchemaFactory;
import org.xml.sax.SAXException;
import static javax.xml.XMLConstants.*;

public class TryParsingSchemaInstance {
  public static void main(String args[]) {
    if(args.length == 0) {
      System.out.println("No file to process. Usage is:" +
            "\n  java TrySax \"xmlFilename\" " +
            "\nor:\n  java TrySaxHandler \"xmlFilename\" \"schemaFileName\" ");
      return;
    }
```

```
      File xmlFile = new File(args[0]);
      File schemaFile = args.length > 1 ? new File(args[1]) : null;
      process(xmlFile, schemaFile);
    }

    private static void process(File file, File schemaFile) {
      SAXParserFactory spf = SAXParserFactory.newInstance();
      SAXParser parser = null;
      spf.setNamespaceAware(true);
      try {
        SchemaFactory sf = SchemaFactory.newInstance(W3C_XML_SCHEMA_NS_URI);
        spf.setSchema(
                schemaFile == null ? sf.newSchema() : sf.newSchema(schemaFile));
        parser = spf.newSAXParser();
      } catch(SAXException | ParserConfigurationException e) {
        e.printStackTrace();
        System.exit(1);
      }

      System.out.println("\nStarting parsing of " + file + "\n");
      MySAXHandler handler = new MySAXHandler();
      try {
        parser.parse(file, handler);
      } catch(IOException | SAXException e) {
        e.printStackTrace();
      }
    }
  }
}
```

Directory "TryParsingSchemaInstance"

You need to copy the MySAXHandler.java source file from the previous example to the folder you are using for this example. You have the option of supplying an additional command-line argument when you run the program. The first argument is the name of the XML file to be parsed, as in the TrySAXHandler example; the second argument is the path to the schema that is to be used to parse the file. When the second argument is present, the program processes the XML file using the specified schema. If the second argument is absent, the XML file is processed using the schema specified by hints in the document.

Processing the sketch1.xml file that I defined in the previous section resulted in the following output:

```
Starting parsing of D:\Beg Java Stuff\sketch1.xml

Start document:
Start "xsi" namespace scope. URI: http://www.w3.org/2001/XMLSchema-instance
Start element: local name: sketch qname: sketch uri:
Attributes:
  Name : xsi:noNamespaceSchemaLocation
  Type : CDATA
  Value: file:/D:/Beg%20Java%20Stuff/Sketcher.xsd
Ignorable whitespace: 5 characters.
Start element: local name: circle qname: circle uri:
Attributes:
  Name : diameter
  Type : CDATA
  Value: 40
  Name : angle
  Type : CDATA
  Value: 0.0
Ignorable whitespace: 9 characters.
```

This is followed by a lot more output that ends:

```
Start element: local name: rectangle qname: rectangle uri:
Attributes:
```

```
    Name : width
    Type : CDATA
    Value: 30.0
    Name : height
    Type : CDATA
    Value: 20.0
    Name : angle
    Type : CDATA
    Value: 0.0
Ignorable whitespace: 9 characters.
Start element: local name: color qname: color uri:
Attributes:
    Name : R
    Type : CDATA
    Value: 255
    Name : G
    Type : CDATA
    Value: 0
    Name : B
    Type : CDATA
    Value: 0
End element: local name: color qname: color uri:
Ignorable whitespace: 9 characters.
Start element: local name: position qname: position uri:
Attributes:
    Name : x
    Type : CDATA
    Value: 30
    Name : y
    Type : CDATA
    Value: 40
End element: local name: position qname: position uri:
Ignorable whitespace: 9 characters.
Start element: local name: bounds qname: bounds uri:
Attributes:
    Name : x
    Type : CDATA
    Value: 30
    Name : y
    Type : CDATA
    Value: 40
    Name : width
    Type : CDATA
    Value: 32
    Name : height
    Type : CDATA
    Value: 22
End element: local name: bounds qname: bounds uri:
Ignorable whitespace: 5 characters.
End element: local name: rectangle qname: rectangle uri:
Ignorable whitespace: 1 characters.
End element: local name: sketch qname: sketch uri:
End "xsi" namespace scope.
End document
```

Of course, you can also try the example specifying the schema location by the second argument on the command line.

How It Works

The only significant difference from what you had in the previous example that processed a document with a DTD is the creation of the Schema object to identify the schema to be used. When you supply a second command-line argument, a File object encapsulating the schema file path is created and a reference to this is passed as the second argument to the process() method. The process() method uses the second argument that you pass to it to determine how to create the `Schema` object that is passed to the `setSchema()` method for the `SAXParserFactory` object:

```
SchemaFactory sf = SchemaFactory.newInstance(W3C_XML_SCHEMA_NS_URI);
spf.setSchema(schemaFile == null ? sf.newSchema() : sf.newSchema(schemaFile));
```

The argument to the `newInstance()` method is the constant from the `XMLConstants` class that defines the URI for the Schema Definition Language. There's a static `import` statement for the static names in this class, so you don't need to qualify the name of the constant. The `Schema` object is created either by passing the non-null `File` reference `schemaFile` to the `newSchema()` method or by calling the `newSchema()` method with no argument. In both cases the `Schema` object that is created is passed to the `setSchema()` method for the parser factory object. The parser that is subsequently created by the `SAXParserFactory` object uses the schema encapsulated by the `Schema` object to validate documents. In this way the program is able to process documents for which the schema is specified by hints in the document, as well as documents for which the schema is specified independently through the second command-line argument.

SUMMARY

In this chapter I discussed the fundamental characteristics of XML and how Java supports the analysis and synthesis of XML documents. This is very much an introductory chapter on XML and only covers enough of the topic for you to understand the basic facilities that you have in Java for processing XML documents. In the next chapter you see how you can synthesize an XML document programmatically so you can write it to a file. You also find out how you can read an XML document and use it to reconstitute Java class objects.

EXERCISES

You can download the source code for the examples in the book and the solutions to the following exercises from www.wrox.com.

1. Write a program using SAX that counts the number of occurrences of each element type in an XML document and displays them. The document file to be processed should be identified by the first command-line argument.

2. Modify the program resulting from the previous exercise so that it accepts optional additional command-line arguments that are the names of elements. When there are two or more command-line arguments, the program should count and report only on the elements identified by the second and subsequent command-line arguments.

▶ WHAT YOU LEARNED IN THIS CHAPTER

TOPIC	CONCEPT
XML	XML is a language for describing data that is to be communicated from one computer to another. Data is described in the form of text that contains the data, plus markup that defines the structure of the data. XML is also a meta-language because you can use XML to create new languages for defining and structuring data.
XML Document Structure	An XML document consists of a prolog and a document body. The document body contains the data and the prolog provides the information necessary for interpreting the document body.
Markup	Markup consists of XML elements that may also include attributes, where an attribute is a name-value pair.
Well-Formed XML	A well-formed XML document conforms to a strict set of rules for document definition, as defined by the XML language specification.
DTDs	The structure and meaning of a particular type of XML document can be defined within a Document Type Definition (DTD). A DTD can be defined in an external file or it can be part of a document.
Valid XML Documents	A valid XML document is a well-formed document that has a DTD.
DOCTYPE Declarations	A DTD is identified by a DOCTYPE declaration in a document.
XML Elements	XML markup divides the contents of a document into elements by enclosing segments of the data between tags.
Element Attributes	Attributes provide a way for you to embed additional data within an XML element.
CDATA Sections	A CDATA section in an XML document contains unparsed character data that is not analyzed by an XML processor.
Schemas	Using the Schema Definition language to define a schema for XML documents provides a more flexible alternative to DTDs.
The SAX API	The SAX API defines a simple event-driven mechanism for analyzing XML documents.
SAX Parsers	A SAX parser is a program that parses an XML document and identifies each element in a document by calling a particular method in your program. The methods that are called by a parser to identify elements are those defined by the SAX API.
SAX Parsing Events	You can create a class that has methods to handle SAX2 parsing events by extending the DefaultHandler class that defines do-nothing implementations of the methods. The DefaultHandler2 class extends DefaultHandler to provide methods for extensions to SAX2.
DOM Parsers	A DOM parser makes an entire XML document available encapsulated in an object of type Document. You can call methods for the Document object to extract the contents of the document.

23

Creating and Modifying XML Documents

WHAT YOU WILL LEARN IN THIS CHAPTER:

- ➤ What the Document Object Model is
- ➤ How you create a DOM parser
- ➤ How you access the contents of a document using DOM
- ➤ How you can create and update a new XML document
- ➤ What the Extensible Stylesheet Language (XSL) is
- ➤ How the Extensible Stylesheet Language Transformation (XSLT) language relates to XSL
- ➤ How you can use a `Transformer` object to read and write XML files
- ➤ How to modify Sketcher to store and retrieve sketches as XML documents

In this chapter you explore what you can do with the Document Object Model (DOM) application program interface (API). As I outlined in the previous chapter, DOM uses a mechanism that is completely different from Simple API for XML (SAX). As well as providing an alternative mechanism for parsing XML documents, DOM also adds the capability for you to modify them and create new ones. You also make a short excursion into XSLT and apply it with DOM in Sketcher. By the end of this chapter you have a version of Sketcher that can store and retrieve sketches as XML files.

THE DOCUMENT OBJECT MODEL

As you saw in the previous chapter, a DOM parser presents you with a `Document` object that encapsulates an entire XML structure. You can call methods for this object to navigate through the document tree and process the elements and attributes in whatever way you want. This is quite different from SAX, but there is still quite a close relationship between DOM and SAX.

The mechanism for getting access to a DOM parser is very similar to what you used to obtain a SAX parser. You start with a factory object that you obtain like this:

```
DocumentBuilderFactory builderFactory = DocumentBuilderFactory.newInstance();
```

The `newInstance()` method is a static method in the `javax.xml.parsers.DocumentBuilderFactory` class for creating factory objects. As with SAX, this approach of dynamically creating a factory object that you then use to create a parser allows you to change the parser you are using without modifying or recompiling your code. The factory object creates a `javax.xml.parsers.DocumentBuilder` object that encapsulates a DOM parser:

```
DocumentBuilder builder = null;
try {
  builder = builderFactory.newDocumentBuilder();
} catch(ParserConfigurationException e) {
  e.printStackTrace();
}
```

When a DOM parser reads an XML document, it makes it available in its entirety as an `org.w3c.dom.Document` object. The name of the class that encapsulates a DOM parser has obviously been chosen to indicate that it can also build new `Document` objects. A DOM parser can throw exceptions of type `SAXException`, and parsing errors in DOM are handled in essentially the same way as in SAX2. The `DocumentBuilderFactory`, `DocumentBuilder`, and `ParserConfigurationException` classes are all defined in the `javax.xml.parsers` package. Let's jump straight in and try this out for real.

TRY IT OUT Creating an XML Document Builder

Here's the code to create a document builder object:

```
import javax.xml.parsers.*;
import javax.xml.parsers.ParserConfigurationException;

public class TryDOM {
  public static void main(String args[]) {
    DocumentBuilderFactory builderFactory = DocumentBuilderFactory.newInstance();
    DocumentBuilder builder = null;
    try {
      builder = builderFactory.newDocumentBuilder();
    }
    catch(ParserConfigurationException e) {
      e.printStackTrace();
      System.exit(1);
    }
    System.out.println(
            "Builder Factory = " + builderFactory + "\nBuilder = " + builder);
  }
}
```

Directory "TryDOM 1"

I got the following output:

```
Builder Factory = com.sun.org.apache.xerces.internal.jaxp.DocumentBuilderFactoryImpl@3f4ebd
Builder = com.sun.org.apache.xerces.internal.jaxp.DocumentBuilderImpl@4a5c78
```

How It Works

The static `newInstance()` method in the `DocumentBuilderFactory` class returns a reference to a factory object. You call the `newDocumentBuilder()` method for the factory object to obtain a reference to a `DocumentBuilder` object that encapsulates a DOM parser. This is the default parser. If you want the parser to validate the XML or provide other capabilities, you can set the parser features before you create the `DocumentBuilder` object by calling methods for the `DocumentBuilderFactory` object.

You can see that you get a version of the Xerces parser as a DOM parser. Many DOM parsers are built on top of SAX parsers, and this is the case with the Xerces parser.

SETTING DOM PARSER FEATURES

The idea of a feature for a DOM parser is the same as with SAX—a parser option that can be either on or off. The following methods are provided by the `DocumentBuilderFactory` object for setting DOM parser features:

➤   `void setNamespaceAware(boolean aware)`: Calling this method with a `true` argument sets the parser to be namespace-aware. The default setting is `false`.

➤   `void setValidating(boolean validating)`: Calling this method with a `true` argument sets the parser to validate the XML in a document as it is parsed. The default setting is `false`.

➤   `void setIgnoringElementContentWhitespace(boolean ignore)`: Calling this method with a `true` argument sets the parser to remove ignorable whitespace so the `Document` object produced by the parser does not contain ignorable whitespace. The default setting is `false`.

➤   `void setIgnoringComments(boolean ignore)`: Calling this method with a `true` argument sets the parser to remove comments as the document is parsed. The default setting is `false`.

➤   `void setExpandEntityReferences(boolean expand)`: Calling this method with a `true` argument sets the parser to expand entity references into the referenced text. The default setting is `true`.

➤   `void setCoalescing(boolean coalesce)`: Calling this method with a `true` argument sets the parser to convert `CDATA` sections to text and append it to any adjacent text. The default setting is `false`.

By default the parser that is produced is neither namespace-aware nor validating. You should at least set these two features before creating the parser. This is quite simple:

```
DocumentBuilderFactory builderFactory = DocumentBuilderFactory.newInstance();
builderFactory.setNamespaceAware(true);
builderFactory.setValidating(true);
```

If you add the bolded statements to the example, the `newDocumentBuilder()` method for the factory object should now return a validating and namespace-aware parser. With a validating parser, you should define an `ErrorHandler` object that deals with parsing errors. You identify the `ErrorHandler` object to the parser by calling the `setErrorHandler()` method for the `DocumentBuilder` object:

```
builder.setErrorHandler(handler);
```

Here `handler` refers to an object that implements the three methods declared in the `org.xml.sax.ErrorHandler` interface. I discussed these in the previous chapter in the context of SAX parser error handling, and the same applies here. If you do create a validating parser, you should always implement and register an `ErrorHandler` object. Otherwise, the parser may not work properly.

The factory object has methods corresponding to each of the `getXXX()` methods in the preceding table to check the status of parser features. The checking methods all have corresponding names of the form `isXXX()`, so to check whether a parser is namespace-aware, you call the `isNamespaceAware()` method. Each method returns `true` if the parser to be created has the feature set, and `false` otherwise.

You can identify a schema to be used by a DOM parser when validating documents. You pass a reference to a `Schema` object to the `setSchema()` method for the `DocumentBuilderFactory` object. The parser that you create then uses the specified schema when validating a document.

PARSING A DOCUMENT

After you have created a `DocumentBuilder` object, you just call its `parse()` method with a document source as an argument to parse a document. The `parse()` method returns a reference of type `Document` to an object that encapsulates the entire XML document. The `Document` interface is defined in the `org.w3c.dom` package.

There are five overloaded versions of the `parse()` method that provide various options for you to identify the source of the XML document to be parsed. They all return a reference to a `Document` object encapsulating the XML document:

➤ `parse(File file)`: Parses the document in the file identified by `file`.

➤ `parse(String uri)`: Parses the document at the URI `uri`.

➤ `parse(InputSource srce)`: Parses the document read from `srce`.

➤ `parse(InputStream in)`: Parses the document read from the stream `in`.

➤ `parse(InputStream in, String systemID)`: Parses the document read from the stream `in`. The `systemID` argument is used as the base to resolve relative URIs in the document.

All five versions of the `parse()` method can throw three types of exception. An `IllegalArgumentException` is thrown if you pass `null` to the method for the parameter that identifies the document source. The method throws an `IOException` if any I/O error occurs and a `SAXException` in the event of a parsing error. The last two exceptions must be caught. Note that it is a `SAXException` that can be thrown here. Exceptions of type `DOMException` arise only when you are navigating the element tree for a `Document` object.

The `org.xml.sax.InputSource` class defines objects that encapsulate a source of an XML document. The `InputSource` class defines constructors that enable you to create an object from a `java.io.InputStream` object, a `java.io.Reader` object, or a `String` object specifying a URI for the document source. If the URI is a URL, it must not be a relative URL.

You could `parse()` a document that is stored in a file using the `DocumentBuilder` object `builder` like this:

```
Path xmlFile = Paths.get(System.getProperty("user.home")).
                         resolve("Beginning Java Stuff").resolve("circlewithDTD.bin");
Document xmlDoc = null;
try (BufferedInputStream in = new BufferedInputStream(Files.newInputStream(xmlFile))){
  xmlDoc = builder.parse(in);
} catch(SAXException | IOException e) {
  e.printStackTrace();
  System.exit(1);
}
```

This creates a `Path` object for the file and creates an input stream for the file in the `try` block. Calling `parse()` for the `builder` object with the input stream as the argument parses the XML file and returns it as a `Document` object. Note that the entire XML file contents are encapsulated by the `Document` object, so in practice this can require a lot of memory.

To compile this code you need `import` statements for the `BufferedInputStream` and `IOException` names in the `java.io` package, and `Paths`, `Path`, and `Files` names in the `java.nio.file` package, as well as the `org.w3c.dom.Document` class name. After this code executes, you can call methods for the `xmlDoc` object to navigate through the elements in the document tree structure. Let's look at what the possibilities are.

NAVIGATING A DOCUMENT OBJECT TREE

The `org.w3c.dom.Node` interface is fundamental to all objects that encapsulate components of an XML document, and this includes the `Document` object itself. It represents a type that encapsulates a node in the document tree. `Node` is also a super-interface of a number of other interfaces that declare methods for accessing document components. The subinterfaces of `Node` that identify components of a document are the following:

➤ `Element`: Represents an XML element.

➤ `Text`: Represents text that is part of element content. This is a subinterface of `CharacterData`, which is a subinterface of `Node`. `Text` references, therefore, have methods from all three interfaces.

➤ CDATASection : Represents a CDATA section—unparsed character data. This extends Text.

➤ Comment: Represents a document comment. This interface extends the CharacterData interface.

➤ DocumentType: Represents the type of a document.

➤ Document: Represents the entire XML document.

➤ DocumentFragment: Represents a lightweight document object that encapsulates a subtree of a document.

➤ Entity : Represents an entity that may be parsed or unparsed.

➤ EntityReference : Represents a reference to an entity.

➤ Notation: Represents a notation declared in the DTD for a document. A notation is a definition of an unparsed entity type.

➤ ProcessingInstruction: Represents a processing instruction for an application.

Each of these interfaces declares its own set of methods and inherits the fields and methods declared in the Node interface. Every XML document is modeled as a hierarchy of nodes that are accessible as one or another of the interface types in the list. At the top of the node hierarchy for a document is the Document node that is returned by the parse() method. Each type of node may or may not have child nodes in the hierarchy, and those that do can have only certain types of child nodes. The types of nodes in a document that can have children are shown in Table 23-1:

TABLE 23-1: Nodes that Can Have Children

NODE TYPE	POSSIBLE CHILDREN
Document	Element (only 1), DocumentType (only 1), Comment, ProcessingInstruction
Element	Element, Text, Comment, CDATASection, EntityReference, ProcessingInstruction
Attr	Text, EntityReference
Entity	Element, Text, Comment, CDATASection, EntityReference, ProcessingInstruction
EntityReference	Element, Text, Comment, CDATASection, EntityReference, ProcessingInstruction

Of course, what each node may have as children follows from the XML specification, not just the DOM specification. There is one other type of node that extends the Node interface—DocumentFragment. This is not formally part of a document in the sense that a node of this type is a programming convenience. It is used to house a fragment of a document—a subtree of elements—for use when moving fragments of a document around, for example, so it provides a similar function to a Document node but with less overhead. A DocumentFragment node can have the same range of child nodes as an Element node.

The starting point for exploring the entire document tree is the root element for the document. You can obtain a reference to an object that encapsulates the root element by calling the getDocumentElement() method for the Document object:

```
Element root = xmlDoc.getDocumentElement();
```

This method returns the root element for the document as type Element. You can also get the node corresponding to the DOCTYPE declaration as type DocumentType like this:

```
DocumentType doctype = xmlDoc.getDoctype();
```

If there is no DOCTYPE declaration, or the parser cannot find the DTD for the document, the getDocType() method returns null. If the value returned is not null, you can obtain the contents of the DTD as a string by calling the getInternalSubset() method for the DocumentType object:

```
System.out.println("Document type:\n" + doctype.getInternalSubset());
```

This statement outputs the contents of the DTD for the document.

After you have an object encapsulating the root element for a document, the next step is to obtain its child nodes. You can use the getChildNodes() method that is defined in the Node interface for this. This method returns a org.w3c.dom.NodeList reference that encapsulates all the child elements for that element. You can call this method for any node that has children, including the Document node, if you wish. You can therefore obtain the child elements for the root element with the following statement:

```
NodeList children = root.getChildNodes();
```

A NodeList reference encapsulates an ordered collection of Node references, each of which will be one of the possible node types for the current node. So with an Element node, any of the Node references in the list that is returned can be of type Element, Text, Comment, CDATASection, EntityReference, or ProcessingInstruction. Note that if there are no child nodes, the getChildNodes() method returns a NodeList reference that is empty, not null. You call the getChildNodes() method to obtain a list of child nodes for any node type that can have them.

The NodeList interface declares just two methods: The getLength() method returns the number of nodes in the list as type int, and the item() method returns a Node reference to the object at index position in the list specified by the argument of type int.

You can use these methods to iterate through the child elements of the root element, perhaps like this:

```
Node[] nodes = new Node[children.getLength()];
for(int i = 0 ; i < nodes.getLength() ; ++i) {
  nodes[i] = children.item(i);
}
```

You allocate sufficient elements in the nodes array to accommodate the number of child nodes and then populate the array in the for loop.

Node Types

Of course, you will normally be interested in the specific types of nodes that are returned, so you will want to extract them as specific types, or at least determine what they are before processing them. This is not difficult. One possibility is to test the type of any node using the instanceof operator. Here's one way you could extract just the child nodes that are of type Element and store them in a vector container:

```
Vector<Element> elements = new Vector<>();
Node node = null;
for(int i = 0 ; i < nodes.getLength() ; ++i) {
  node = children.item(i);
  if(node instanceof Element) {
    elements.add(node);
  }
}
```

Another possibility is provided by the getNodeType() method that is declared in the Node interface. This method returns a value of type short that is one of the following constants that are defined in the Node interface:

- ➤ DOCUMENT_NODE
- ➤ DOCUMENT_TYPE_NODE
- ➤ DOCUMENT_FRAGMENT_NODE
- ➤ DOCUMENT_POSITION_IMPLEMENTATION_SPECIFIC
- ➤ DOCUMENT_POSITION_PRECEDING
- ➤ DOCUMENT_POSITION_FOLLOWING
- ➤ DOCUMENT_POSITION_CONTAINED_BY
- ➤ DOCUMENT_POSITION_CONTAINS

- DOCUMENT_POSITION_DISCONNECTED
- CDATA_SECTION_NODE
- ENTITY_REFERENCE_NODE
- ENTITY_NODE
- TEXT_NODE
- COMMENT_NODE
- NOTATION_NODE
- ELEMENT_NODE
- ATTRIBUTE_NODE
- PROCESSING_INSTRUCTION_NODE

The advantage of using the `getNodeType()` method is that you can test for the node type using a `switch` statement with the constants as case values. This makes it easy to farm out processing for nodes of various types to separate methods.

A simple loop like the one in the previous code fragment is not a very practical approach to navigating a document. In general, you have no idea of the level to which elements are nested in the document, and this loop examines only one level. You need an approach that allows any level of nesting. This is a job for recursion. Let's put together a working example to illustrate how you can do this.

TRY IT OUT Listing a Document

You can extend the previous example to list the nodes in a document. You add a `static` method to the `TryDOM` class to list child elements recursively. You also add a helper method that identifies what each node is. The program outputs details of each node followed by its children. Here's the code:

Available for download on Wrox.com

```java
import javax.xml.parsers.*;
import org.xml.sax.*;
import org.w3c.dom.*;
import java.io.*;
import java.nio.file.*;
import static org.w3c.dom.Node.*;                          // For node type constants

public class TryDOM implements ErrorHandler {
  public static void main(String args[]) {
    if(args.length == 0) {
      System.out.println("No file to process." + "Usage is:\njava TryDOM \"filename\"");

      System.exit(1);
    }
    DocumentBuilderFactory builderFactory = DocumentBuilderFactory.newInstance();
    builderFactory.setNamespaceAware(true);                // Set namespace aware
    builderFactory.setValidating(true);                    // & validating parser

    DocumentBuilder builder = null;
    try {
      builder = builderFactory.newDocumentBuilder();       // Create the parser
      builder.setErrorHandler(new TryDOM());               // Error handler is TryDOM instance
    } catch(ParserConfigurationException e) {
      e.printStackTrace();
      System.exit(1);
    }

    Path xmlFile = Paths.get(args[0]);
    Document xmlDoc = null;
```

```java
    try (BufferedInputStream in = new BufferedInputStream(
                                      Files.newInputStream(xmlFile))){

    xmlDoc = builder.parse(in);
  } catch(SAXException | IOException e) {
    e.printStackTrace();
    System.exit(1);
  }
  DocumentType doctype = xmlDoc.getDoctype();      // Get the DOCTYPE node
  if(doctype == null) {                            // If it's not null...
    System.out.println("DOCTYPE is null");
  } else {                                         // ...output it
    System.out.println("DOCTYPE node:\n" + doctype.getInternalSubset());
  }

  System.out.println("\nDocument body contents are:");
  listNodes(xmlDoc.getDocumentElement(), " ");     // Root element & children
}

// output a node and all its child nodes
static void listNodes(Node node, String indent) {
  // List the current node
  String nodeName = node.getNodeName();
  System.out.println(indent + " Node: " + nodeName);
  System.out.println(indent + " Node Type: " + nodeType(node.getNodeType()));

  NodeList list = node.getChildNodes();            // Get the list of child nodes
  if(list.getLength() > 0) {                       // If there are some...
    //...list them & their children...
    // ...by calling listNodes() for each
    System.out.println(indent+" Child Nodes of " + nodeName + " are:");
    for(int i = 0 ; i < list.getLength() ; ++i) {
      listNodes(list.item(i),indent + "  ");
    }
  }
}

// Method to identify the node type
static String nodeType(short type) {
  switch(type) {
    case ELEMENT_NODE:                  return "Element";
    case DOCUMENT_TYPE_NODE:            return "Document type";
    case ENTITY_NODE:                   return "Entity";
    case ENTITY_REFERENCE_NODE:         return "Entity reference";
    case NOTATION_NODE:                 return "Notation";
    case TEXT_NODE:                     return "Text";
    case COMMENT_NODE:                  return "Comment";
    case CDATA_SECTION_NODE:            return "CDATA Section";
    case ATTRIBUTE_NODE:                return "Attribute";
    case PROCESSING_INSTRUCTION_NODE:   return "Attribute";
  }
  return "Unidentified";
}

public void fatalError(SAXParseException spe) throws SAXException {
  System.out.println("Fatal error at line " + spe.getLineNumber());
  System.out.println(spe.getMessage());
  throw spe;
}

public void warning(SAXParseException spe) {
  System.out.println("Warning at line " + spe.getLineNumber());
  System.out.println(spe.getMessage());
}
```

```
    public void error(SAXParseException spe) {
      System.out.println("Error at line " + spe.getLineNumber());
      System.out.println(spe.getMessage());
    }
  }
```

Directory "TryDOM 2 with node details output"

I have removed the statement that outputs details of the parser from the previous version of the TryDOM class to reduce the output a little. Run this with a document file AddressWithDTD.xml that contains the following:

```
<?xml version="1.0"?>
<!DOCTYPE address
[
    <!ELEMENT address (buildingnumber, street, city, state, zip)>
    <!ATTLIST address xmlns CDATA #IMPLIED>
    <!ELEMENT buildingnumber (#PCDATA)>
    <!ELEMENT street (#PCDATA)>
    <!ELEMENT city (#PCDATA)>
    <!ELEMENT state (#PCDATA)>
    <!ELEMENT zip (#PCDATA)>
]>

<address>
  <buildingnumber> 29 </buildingnumber>
  <street> South Lasalle Street</street>
  <city>Chicago</city>
  <state>Illinois</state>
  <zip>60603</zip>
</address>
```

Directory "TryDOM 2 with node details output"

This is the Address.xml document from the previous chapter with the DTD included in the document. If you store this file in the same directory as the source file, you can just put the file name as the command-line argument, like this:

```
java TryDOM AddressWithDTD.xml
```

The program produces quite a lot of output starting with:

```
DOCTYPE node:
<!ELEMENT address (buildingnumber,street,city,state,zip)>
<!ATTLIST address xmlns CDATA #IMPLIED>
<!ELEMENT buildingnumber (#PCDATA)>
<!ELEMENT street (#PCDATA)>
<!ELEMENT city (#PCDATA)>
<!ELEMENT state (#PCDATA)>
<!ELEMENT zip (#PCDATA)>


Document body contents are:
Node: address
 Node Type: Element
 Child Nodes of address are:
   Node: #text
   Node Type: Text
   Node: buildingnumber
   Node Type: Element
   Child Nodes of buildingnumber are:
     Node: #text
     Node Type: Text
```

and so on down to the last few lines:

```
Node: zip
Node Type: Element
Child Nodes of zip are:
   Node: #text
   Node Type: Text
Node: #text
Node Type: Text
```

How It Works

Because you have set the parser configuration in the factory object to include validating the XML, you have to provide an org.xml.sax.ErrorHandler object for the parser. The TryDOM class implements the warning(), error(), and fatalError() methods declared by the ErrorHandler interface, so an instance of this class takes care of it.

You call the getDoctype() method for the Document object to obtain the node corresponding to the DOCTYPE declaration:

```
DocumentType doctype = xmlDoc.getDoctype();        // Get the DOCTYPE node
if(doctype == null) {                              // If it's not null...
  System.out.println("DOCTYPE is null");
} else {                                           // ...output it
  System.out.println("DOCTYPE node:\n" + doctype.getInternalSubset());
}
```

You can see from the output that you get the complete text of the DTD from the document.

After outputting a header line showing where the document body starts, you output the contents, starting with the root element. The listNodes() method does all the work. You pass a reference to the root element that you obtain from the Document object with the following statement:

```
listNodes(xmlDoc.getDocumentElement(), " ");        // Root element & children
```

The first argument to listNodes() is the node to be listed, and the second argument is the current indent for output. On each recursive call of the method, you append a couple of spaces. This results in each nested level of nodes being indented in the output by two spaces relative to the parent node output.

The first step in the listNodes() method is to get the name of the current node by calling its getNodeName() method:

```
String nodeName = node.getNodeName();               // Get name of this node
```

The next statement outputs the node itself:

```
System.out.println(indent + " " + nodeName);
```

You then output the type of the current node with the following statement:

```
System.out.println(indent + " Node Type: " + nodeType(node.getNodeType()));
```

The indent parameter defines the indentation for the current node. Calling getNodeType() for the node object returns a value of type short that identifies the node type. You then pass this value to the nodeType() helper method that you've added to the TryDOM class. The code for the helper method is just a switch statement with the constants from the Node interface that identify the types of nodes as case values. I just included a representative set in the code, but you can add case labels for all 18 constants if you want.

The remainder of the listNodes() code iterates through the child nodes of the current node if it has any:

```
NodeList list = node.getChildNodes();               // Get the list of child nodes
if(list.getLength() > 0) {                           // As long as there are some...
  System.out.println(indent+"Child Nodes of " + nodeName + " are:");
    //...list them & their children...
    // ...by calling listNodes() for each
    for(int i = 0 ; i < list.getLength() ; ++i) {
      listNodes(list.item(i),indent + "  ");
    }
```

The `for` loop simply iterates through the list of child nodes obtained by calling the `getChildNodes()` method. Each child is passed as an argument to the `listNodes()` method, which lists the node and iterates through its children. In this way the method works through all the nodes in the document. You can see that you append an extra couple of spaces to `indent` in the second argument to the `listNodes()` call for a child node. The `indent` parameter in the next level down references a string that is two spaces longer. This ensures that the output for the next level of nodes is indented relative to the current node.

Ignorable Whitespace and Element Content

Some of the elements have multiple `#text` elements recorded in the output. The `#text` elements arise from two things: text that represents element content and ignorable whitespace that is there to present the markup in a readable fashion. If you don't want to see the ignorable whitespace, you can get rid of it quite easily. You just need to set another parser feature in the factory object:

```
builderFactory.setNamespaceAware(true);          // Set namespace aware
builderFactory.setValidating(true);              // and validating parser
builderFactory.setIgnoringElementContentWhitespace(true);
```

Calling this method results in a parser that does not report ignorable whitespace as a node, so you don't see it in the Document object. If you run the example again with this change, the `#text` nodes arising from ignorable whitespace are no longer there.

That still leaves some other `#text` elements that represent element content, and you really do want to access that and display it. In this case you can use the `getWholeText()` method for a node of type `Text` to obtain all of the content as a single string. You could modify the code in the `listNodes()` method in the example to do this:

Available for
download on
Wrox.com

```
static void listNodes(Node node, String indent) {
    // List the current node
    String nodeName = node.getNodeName();
    System.out.println(indent + " Node: " + nodeName);
    short type =node.getNodeType();
    System.out.println(indent+" Node Type: " + nodeType(type));
    if(type == TEXT_NODE){
      System.out.println(indent + " Content is: " + ((Text)node).getWholeText());
    }

    // Now list the child nodes
    NodeList list = node.getChildNodes();          // Get the list of child nodes
    if(list.getLength() > 0) {                      // As long as there are some...
      //...list them & their children...
      // ...by calling listNodes() for each
      System.out.println(indent + " Child Nodes of " + nodeName + " are:");
      for(int i = 0 ; i < list.getLength() ; ++i) {
        listNodes(list.item(i),indent + "  ");
      }
    }
}
```

Directory "TryDOM 3 with node content"

Here you store the integer that identifies the node type in a variable, `type`, that you test to see if it is a text node. If it is, you get the contents by calling the `getWholeText()` method for the node. You have to cast the node reference to type `Text`; otherwise, you would not be able to call the `getWholeText()` method because it is declared in the `Text` interface, which is a subinterface of `Node`. If you run the example again with this further addition, you get the contents of the nodes displayed, too.

Even though you have set the parser feature to ignore ignorable whitespace, you could still get `#text` elements that contained just whitespace. The `Text` interface declares the `isElementContentWhitespace()` method that you can use to check for this—when you don't want to display an empty line, for example.

Accessing Attributes

You usually want to access the attributes for an element, but only if it has some. You can test whether an element has attributes by calling its `hasAttributes()` method. This returns `true` if the element has attributes and `false` otherwise, so you might use it like this:

```
short type = node.getNodeType();
if(type == ELEMENT_NODE && node.hasAttributes()) {
    // Process the element with its attributes

} else {
    // Process the element without attributes
}
```

The `getAttributes()` method returns a `NamedNodeMap` reference that contains the attributes, the `NamedNodeMap` interface being defined in the `org.w3c.dom` package. In general, a `NamedNodeMap` object is a collection of `Node` references that can be accessed by name, or serially by iterating through the collection. Because the nodes are attributes in this instance, the nodes are actually of type `Attr`. In fact, you can call the `getAttributes()` method for any node type, and it returns `null` if an element has no attributes. Thus, you could omit the test for the element type in the `if` condition, and the code works just as well.

The `NamedNodeMap` interface declares the following methods for retrieving nodes from the collection:

➤   `Node item(int index)`: Returns the node at position `index`.

➤   `int getLength()`: Returns the number of `Node` references in the collection.

➤   `Node getNamedItem(String name)`: Returns the node with the node name `name`.

➤   `Node getNamedItemNS(String uri, String localName)`: Returns the node with the name `localName` in the namespace at `uri`.

Obviously the last two methods apply when you know what attributes to expect. You can apply the first two methods to iterate through the collection of attributes in a `NamedNodeMap`:

```
if(node.hasAttributes()) {
  NamedNodeMap attrs = node.getAttributes();
  for(int i = 0 ; i < attrs.getLength() ; ++i) {
    Attr attribute = (Attr)attrs.item(i);
    // Process the attribute...
  }
}
```

You now are in a position to obtain each of the attributes for an element as a reference of type `Attr`. To get at the attribute name and value you call the `getName()` and `getValue()` methods declared in the `Attr` interface, respectively, both of which return a value of type `String`. You can put that into practice in another example.

You can modify the `listNodes()` method in the previous example to include attributes with the elements. Here's the revised version:

```
static void listNodes(Node node) {
    System.out.println(indent + " Node: " + nodeName);
    short type =node.getNodeType();
    System.out.println(indent + " Node Type: " + nodeType(type));
    if(type == TEXT_NODE){
      System.out.println(indent + " Content is: " + ((Text)node).getWholeText());
    } else if(node.hasAttributes()) {
      System.out.println(indent+" Element Attributes are:");
      NamedNodeMap attrs = node.getAttributes();        //...get the attributes
      for(int i = 0 ; i < attrs.getLength() ; ++i) {
```

```
                 Attr attribute = (Attr)attrs.item(i);           // Get an attribute
                 System.out.println(indent + " " + attribute.getName() +
                                           " = " + attribute.getValue());
              }
           }

         NodeList list = node.getChildNodes();          // Get the list of child nodes
         if(list.getLength() > 0) {                     // If there are some...
           //...list them & their children...
           // ...by calling listNodes() for each
           System.out.println(indent + "Child Nodes of " + nodeName + " are:");
           for(int i = 0 ; i < list.getLength() ; ++i){
             listNodes(list.item(i), indent + "  ");
           }
         }
      }
```

Directory "TryDOM 4 listing elements with attributes"

You can recompile the code with these changes and run the example with the `circle with DTD.xml` file that you created when I was discussing DTDs. The content of this file is the following:

```
<?xml version="1.0"?>
<!DOCTYPE circle
[
    <!ELEMENT circle (position)>
    <!ATTLIST circle
            diameter CDATA #REQUIRED
    >

    <!ELEMENT position EMPTY>
    <!ATTLIST position
            x CDATA #REQUIRED
            y CDATA #REQUIRED
    >
]>

<circle diameter="30">
  <position x="30" y="50"/>
</circle>
```

Directory "TryDOM 4 listing elements with attributes"

The output from the example processing this file should be

```
DOCTYPE node:
<!ELEMENT circle (position)>
<!ATTLIST circle diameter CDATA #REQUIRED>
<!ELEMENT position EMPTY>
<!ATTLIST position x CDATA #REQUIRED>
<!ATTLIST position y CDATA #REQUIRED>


Document body contents are:
 Node: circle
 Node Type: Element
 Element Attributes are:
 diameter = 30
 Child Nodes of circle are:
   Node: position
   Node Type: Element
   Element Attributes are:
   x = 30
   y = 50
```

How It Works

All the new code to handle attributes is in the `listNodes()` method. After verifying that the current node does have attributes, you get the collection of attributes as a `NamedNodeMap` object. You then iterate through the collection extracting each node in turn. Nodes are indexed from zero, and you obtain the number of nodes in the collection by calling its `getLength()` method. Because an attribute node is returned by the `item()` method as type `Node`, you have to cast the return value to type `Attr` to call the methods in this interface. You output the attribute and its value, making use of the `getName()` and `getValue()` methods for the `Attr` object in the process of assembling the output string.

It isn't used in the example, but the `Attr` interface also declares a `getSpecified()` method that returns `true` if the attribute value was explicitly set in the document rather than being a default value from the DTD. The `Attr` interface also declares a `getOwnerElement()` method that returns an `Element` reference to the element to which this attribute applies.

TRANSFORMING XML

The Extensible Stylesheet Language (XSL) is a standard language for describing how an XML document should be transformed and/or displayed. XSL has three parts to it, referred to as the XSL family:

➤ XSL-FO is a standard language for formatting XML documents.

➤ XSLT is a standard language for transforming an XML document into another XML document, so you could transform an XML document into HTML or XHTML, for example.

➤ XPath is a language for describing how you navigate through an XML document.

XSL is a huge topic that is generally far beyond the scope of this book. Indeed, you can find whole books dedicated to the topic, so it is impossible for me to discuss it at length here. Nonetheless, the JAXP XSLT capability provided by `javax.xml.transform.Transformer` objects can be very helpful when you want to transfer an XML document to or from an external file, so I'm just explaining how you can use the Java support for XSLT to do that.

Transformer Objects

The `Transformer` class is the basis for applying Extensible Style Sheet Language Transformations (XSLT) in Java. A `Transformer` object transforms an XML document, the *source tree*, into another XML document, the *result tree*. What happens to the XML during the transformation depends on the XSL style sheet associated with the source tree and how you set the parameters and properties for the `Transformer` object. I am going to sidestep most of the details of that and just use a transformer that does nothing. Surprisingly, a transformer that does nothing can do quite a lot. First I'll explain how you create a `Transformer` object and then I'll describe how you might use it.

Creating Transformer Objects

There are no public constructors defined in the `Transformer` class, so you must call a method for a `TransformerFactory` object to create one; this type is defined in the `javax.xml.transform` package. The `TransformerFactory` class does not have any public constructors either, so you must call the static `newInstance()` method to get a factory object for creating transformers. After you have a factory object, you can call its `newTransformer()` method with no parameters to create a `Transformer` object that is an identity transform; in other words, it does nothing in transferring the source XML to the result XML. This is the method I use in examples.

Here's how you create a `Transformer` object that does nothing:

```
TransformerFactory factory = TransformerFactory.newInstance();
Transformer transformer = factory.newTransformer();
```

Both methods can throw exceptions, so you should call them from within a `try` block. The `newInstance()` method can throw `TransformerFactoryConfigurationError` if the factory object cannot be created. The `newTransformer()` method throws `TransformerConfigurationException` if the `Transformer` object cannot be created.

There is a `newTranformer()` method overload that requires an argument of type `Source` that encapsulates an XSLT document that defines the transformation to be applied by the `Transformer` object .

Using Transformer Objects

You apply a transformation to a source document by calling the `transform()` method for a `Transformer` object with the XML source and destination objects as arguments, in that order. You specify the source as a reference of type `javax.xml.transform.Source` and the destination as a reference of type `javax.xml.transform.Result`. Both `Source` and `Result` are interface types, so what you can use as a source or destination for a transformation is determined by the classes that implement these interfaces.

There are five classes that implement the `Source` interface, but I use only the `DOMSource` class that is defined in the `javax.xml.transform.dom` package and the `StreamSource` class that is defined in the `javax.xml.transform.stream` package. The `DOMSource` object encapsulates a `Document` object containing an XML document, so a `Document` object can be a source for a transformation. You could create a `DOMSource` object from a `Document` object, `xmlDoc`, like this:

```
DOMSource source = new DOMSource(xmlDoc.getDocumentNode());
```

A `DOMSource` object accesses the contents of a `Document` object through its XML root node. This constructor creates a `DOMSource` object from the document node for the `Document` object. Another constructor accepts a `String` reference as a second argument that specifies the base URI associated with the root node. You can construct a `DOMSource` object using the no-arg constructor and then call `setNode()` for the object to identify the document's root node. If no root node is set, then a transform operation creates an empty `Document` object for use as the source.

A `StreamSource` object encapsulates an input stream that is a source of XML markup. This implies that a file containing XML can be a source for a transformation. There are `StreamSource` constructors that create objects from a `File` object, an `InputStream` object, a `Reader` object, or a `String` specifying a URL that identifies the input stream. Here's how you could create a `StreamSource` object from an `InputStream` object:

```
Path file = Paths.get(System.getProperty("user.home")).
                            resolve("Beginning Java Stuff").resolve("Address.xml");
try(BufferedInputStream xmlIn = new BufferedInputStream(Files.newInputStream(file))) {
  StreamSource source = new StreamSource(xmlIn);
  // Code to use the source...

} catch (IOException e) {
  e.printStackTrace();
}
```

You just pass the `xmlIn` stream object to the `StreamSource` constructor to make the file the source for a transform operation. You create `xmlIn` from the `Path` object, `file`, in the way you have seen several times before. The `try` block is necessary for the stream operations, not for the `StreamSource` constructor.

The `Result` interface is implemented by six classes, but I'm only introducing `javax.xml.transform.dom.DOMResult` and `StreamResult` from the `javax.xml.transform.stream` package. A `DOMResult` object encapsulates a `Document` object that results from a transformation of a `Source` object. A `StreamResult` object encapsulates an output stream, which could be a file or just the command line, and the markup that results from a transformation is written to the stream. Creating `DOMResult` and `StreamResult` objects is similar to creating source objects.

Both the source and destination for a `transform()` operation can be either a `Document` object or a stream, so you can use a transform to transfer the XML contained in a `Document` object to a file or to create a

Document object from a file that contains XML markup. Suppose that you have a `Document` object, `xmlDoc`, that you want to write to a file. Here's how you could use a `Transformer` object to do it:

```
Path file = Paths.get(System.getProperty("user.home")).
                 resolve("Beginning Java Stuff").resolve("MyXMLDoc.xml");
try(BufferedOutputStream xmlOut = new BufferedOutputStream(Files.newOutputStream(file))) {
   // Create a factory object for XML transformers
   TransformerFactory factory = TransformerFactory.newInstance();
   Transformer transformer = factory.newTransformer();

   // Make the transformer indent the output
   transformer.setOutputProperty(OutputKeys.INDENT, "yes");

   // Create the source and result objects for the transform
   DOMSource source = new DOMSource(xmlDoc.getDocumentNode());
   StreamResult xmlFile = new StreamResult(xmlOut);

   transformer.transform(source, xmlFile);    // Execute transform
} catch (TransformerConfigurationException tce) {
   System.err.println("Transformer Factory error: " + tce.getMessage());
} catch (TransformerException te) {
   System.out.println("Transformation error: " + te.getMessage());
} catch (IOException e) {
   e.printStackTrace();
}
```

The process is very simple. You use the `TransformerFactory` object you have created to create the `Transformer` object. You set the property value for the transformer that corresponds to the `INDENT` key constant in the `javax.xml.transform.OutputKeys` class. This class defines constants that identify property keys for `Transformer` objects. Setting the value for `INDENT` to "yes" makes the transformer insert additional whitespace in the output so that elements appear on separate lines. With the default "no" value for the property, the output would not contain any newline characters between elements and so would be difficult to read. Instead of using the `OutputKeys` constant, you could use the `String` that is the key, "indent," but using the constant is the preferred approach. With the `Transformer` object set up, you create the `Source` object from the root node in the `xmlDoc` object. You create the `Result` object from the output stream, `xmlOut`, that encapsulates the file.

Transformer Properties

The `OutputKeys` class defines the following static fields that identify property keys for a `Transformer` object (see Table 23-2):

TABLE 23-2: OutputKeys Constants that Identify Transformer Properties

FIELD NAME	VALUE FOR KEY
INDENT	"yes" causes the processor to insert whitespace in the output. Default is "no."
DOCTYPE_SYSTEM	The system identifier to be used in the DOCTYPE declaration as a string.
DOCTYPE_PUBLIC	The public identifier to be used in the DOCTYPE declaration as a string.
ENCODING	The encoding to be used for the output.
MEDIA_TYPE	The MIME content type for the result tree.
CDATA_SECTION_ELEMENTS	A list of element names whose text child nodes should be output as CDATA.
OMIT_XML_DECLARATION	"yes" causes the processor to omit the XML declaration in the output. The default is "no."
STANDALONE	"yes" causes the processor to output a standalone document declaration.
METHOD	Specifies the method to be used for the result tree, for example, "xml," "html," or "text."
VERSION	The version of the output method.

I'm only using the first two OutputKeys fields from the table. The DOCTYPE_SYSTEM property value is required for a DOCTYPE declaration to be included in the output, and you use this in Sketcher.

Dealing with Transformer Errors

A Transformer object can report errors by calling methods declared by the javax.xml.transform. ErrorListener interface. You can specify an object that is an error listener for a Transformer object like this:

```
transformer.setErrorListener(errorListener);
```

The errorListener object that is the argument must be of a class type that implements the ErrorListener interface.

ErrorListener declares three methods, all with a void return type, and all can throw a TransformerException:

➤ error(TransformerException te) is called when a recoverable error occurs. The transformer continues to process the document after this error. You can implement the method to throw a TransformerException if you want to terminate processing of the document.

➤ fatalError(TransformerException te) is called when a non-recoverable error occurs. Processing the document may continue after this error but usually it won't. Your implementation of this method should handle the error or throw a TransformerException if that is not possible, or if you want to terminate document processing.

➤ void warning(TransformerException te) is called to report conditions that are not errors or fatal errors. After this method returns, processing always continues. You can terminate processing of the document by throwing a TransformerException from this method.

You are not obliged to implement an ErrorListener for a transformer to receive notification of errors. If you don't, the default behavior is to report all errors to System.err and not to throw any exceptions. In general you should implement an ErrorListener for a transformer to deal with errors appropriately. Throwing a TransformerException from within the error handler is optional, but if the method does throw an exception, the implementation must declare that it does.

CREATING DOCUMENT OBJECTS

The simplest way to create a Document object programmatically is to call the newDocument() method for a DocumentBuilder object, and it returns a reference to a new empty Document object:

```
Document newDoc = builder.newDocument();
```

This is rather limited, especially because there's no way to modify the DocumentType node to reflect a suitable DOCTYPE declaration because the DocumentType interface does not declare any.

There's an alternative approach that provides a bit more flexibility, but it is not quite so direct. You first call the getDOMImplementation() method for the DocumentBuilder object:

```
DOMImplementation domImpl = builder.getDOMImplementation();
```

This returns an org.w3c.dom.DOMImplementation reference to an object that encapsulates the underlying DOM implementation.

There are three methods you can call for a DOMImplementation object:

➤ Document createDocument(
                    String namespaceURI,
                    String qualifiedName,
                    DocumentType doctype):
Creates a Document object with the root element having the name qualifiedName in the namespace specified by namespaceURI. The third argument specifies the DOCTYPE node to be added to the

document. If you don't want to declare a DOCTYPE then doctype can be null. The method throws a DOMException if the second argument is incorrect in some way.

➤ `DocumentType createDocumentType(`
                    `String qualifiedName,`
                    `String publicID,`
                    `String systemID):`
Creates a `DocumentType` node that represents a DOCTYPE declaration. The first argument is the qualified name of the root element, the second is the public ID of the external subset of the DTD, and the third is its system ID. The method also throws a DOMException if the first argument contains an illegal character or is not of the correct form.

➤ `boolean hasFeature(String feature, String version):`
Returns true if the DOM implementation has the feature with the name feature. The second argument specifies the DOM version number for the feature and can be either `"1.0"` or `"2.0"` with DOM Level 2.

You can see from the first two methods here that there is a big advantage to using a DOMImplementation object to create a document. First of all, you can create a `DocumentType` object by calling the `createDocumentType()` method:

```
DocumentType doctype = null;
Path dtdFile = Paths.get(System.getProperty("user.home")).
                        resolve("Beginning Java Stuff").resolve("sketcher.dtd");

try {
  doctype = domImpl.createDocumentType("sketch", null, dtdFile.toString());

} catch(DOMException e) {
  // Handle the exception...
}
```

This creates a `DocumentType` node for an external DOCTYPE declaration. The first argument is the name of the document type, sketch, and the third argument is the system ID—the path to the DTD as a string, which identifies the DTD for documents of this type. There is no public ID in this case because the second argument is null.

You can now use the `DocumentType` object in the creation of a `Document` object:

```
Document newDoc = null;
try {
  doctype = domImpl.createDocumentType("sketch", null, "sketcher.dtd");
  newDoc = domImpl.createDocument(null, "sketch", doctype);
} catch(DOMException e) {
  // Handle the exception...
}
```

If you were creating a document without a DTD, you would just specify the third argument to the `createDocument()` method as null.

The DOMException that may be thrown by either the `createDocumentType()` or the `createDocument()` method has a public field of type int that has the name code. This field stores an error code that identifies the type of error that caused the exception, so you can check its value to determine the cause of the error. This exception can be thrown by a number of different methods that create nodes in a document, so the values that code can have are not limited to the two methods you have just used. There are 17 possible values for code that are defined in the DOMException class, but obviously you would check only for those that apply to the code in the try block where the exception may arise.

The possible values for code in a DOMException object are:

➤ INVALID_CHARACTER_ERR: An invalid character has been specified. In the previous code fragment this would mean the second argument to `createDocument()` specifying the root element name contains an invalid character.

➤ DOMSTRING_SIZE_ERR: The specified range of text does not fit into a DOMString value. A DOMString value is defined in the DOM Level 3 specification and is equivalent to a Java String type.

➤ HIERARCHY_REQUEST_ERR: You tried to insert a node where it doesn't belong.

➤ WRONG_DOCUMENT_ERR: You tried to use a node in a different document from the one that created it.

➤ NO_DATA_ALLOWED_ERR: You specified data for a node that does not support data.

➤ NO_MODIFICATION_ALLOWED_ERR: You attempted to modify an object where modifications are prohibited.

➤ NOT_FOUND_ERR: You tried to reference a node that does not exist.

➤ NOT_SUPPORTED_ERR: The object type or operation that you requested is not supported.

➤ INUSE_ATTRIBUTE_ERR: You tried to add an attribute that is in use elsewhere.

➤ INVALID_STATE_ERR: You tried to use an object that is not usable.

➤ SYNTAX_ERR: You specified an invalid or illegal string.

➤ INVALID_MODIFICATION_ERR: You tried to modify the type of the underlying object.

➤ NAMESPACE_ERR: You tried to create or modify an object such that it would be inconsistent with namespaces in the document.

➤ INVALID_ACCESS_ERR: A parameter or operation is not supported by the underlying object.

➤ VALIDATION_ERR: An operation to remove or insert a node relative to an existing node would make the node invalid.

➤ TYPE_MISMATCH_ERR: The type of an object is not compatible with the expected type of the parameter associated with the object.

➤ WRONG_DOCUMENT_ERR: The document does not support the DocumentType node specified.

The createDocument() method can throw a DOMException with code set to INVALID_CHARACTER_ERR, NAMESPACE_ERR, NOT_SUPPORTED_ERR, or WRONG_DOCUMENT_ERR. The createDocumentType() method can also throw a DOMException with code set to any of the first three values for createDocument().

You therefore might code the catch block in the previous fragment like this:

```
catch(DOMException e) {
  switch(e.code) {
    case DOMException.INVALID_CHARACTER_ERR:
      System.err.println("Qualified name contains an invalid character.");
      break;
    case DOMException.NAMESPACE_ERR:
      System.err.println("Qualified name is malformed or invalid.");
      break;
    case DOMException.WRONG_DOCUMENT_ERR:
      System.err.println("Document does not support this doctype");
      break;
    case DOMException.NOT_SUPPORTED_ERR:
      System.err.println("Implementation does not support XML.");
      break;
    default:
      System.err.println("Code not recognized: " + e.code);
      break;
  }
  System.err.println(e.getMessage());
}
```

Of course, you can also output the stack trace, return from the method, or even end the program here if you want.

Adding to a Document

The `org.w3c.Document` interface declares methods for adding nodes to a `Document` object. You can create nodes encapsulating elements, attributes, text, entity references, comments, CDATA sections, and processing instructions, so you can assemble a `Document` object representing a complete XML document. The methods declared by the `Document` interface are the following:

➤ `Element createElement(String name)`: Returns a reference to an object encapsulating an element with name as the tag name. The method throws a DOMException with INVALID_CHARACTER_ERR set if name contains an invalid character.

➤ `Element createElementNS(String nsURI, String qualifiedName)`: Returns a reference to an object encapsulating an element with qualifiedName as the tag name in the namespace nsURI. The method throws a DOMException with INVALID_CHARACTER_ERR set if qualifiedName contains an invalid character or NAMESPACE_ERR if it has a prefix "xml" and nsURI is not http://www.w3.org/XML/1998/namespace.

➤ `Attr createAttribute(String name)`: Returns a reference to an Attr object with name as the attribute name and its value as "". The method throws a DOMException with INVALID_CHARACTER_ERR set if name contains an invalid character.

➤ `Attr createAttribute(String nsURI, String qualifiedName)`: Returns a reference to an Attr object with qualifiedName as the attribute name in the namespace nsURI and its value as "". The method throws a DOMException with INVALID_CHARACTER_ERR set if the name contains an invalid character or NAMESPACE_ERR if the name conflicts with the namespace.

➤ `Text createTextNode(String text)`: Returns a reference to a node containing the string text.

➤ `Comment createComment(String comment)`: Returns a reference to a node containing the string comment.

➤ `CDATASection createCDATASection(String data)`: Returns a reference to a node with the value data. Throws a DOMException if you try to create this node when the Document object encapsulates an HTML document.

➤ `EntityReference createEntityReference(String name)`: Returns a reference to an node with the name specified. Throws a DOMException with the code INVALID_CHARACTER_ERR if name contains invalid characters and NOT_SUPPORTED_ERR if the Document object is an HTML document.

➤ `ProcessingInstruction createProcessingInstruction(String target, String name)`: Returns a reference to a node with the specified name and target. Throws a DOMException with the code INVALID_CHARACTER_ERR if target contains illegal characters and NOT_SUPPORTED_ERR if the Document object is an HTML document.

➤ `DocumentFragment createDocumentFragment()`: Creates an empty object. You can insert a DocumentFragment object into a Document object using methods that the Document and DocumentFragment interfaces inherit from the Node interface. You can use the same methods to insert nodes into a DocumentFragment object.

The return types are defined in the `org.w3c.dom` package. The references to HTML in the preceding list arise because a `Document` object can be used to encapsulate an HTML document. Our interest is purely XML so I'm not discussing this aspect further.

Of course, having a collection of nodes within a document does not define any structure. To establish the structure of a document you have to associate each attribute node that you have created with the appropriate element, and you must also make sure that each element other than the root is a child of some element. Along with all the other types of node, the `org.w3c.dom.Element` interface inherits two methods from the `Node` interface that enable you to make one node a child of another:

➤ `Node appendChild(Node child)`: Appends `child` to the end of the list of existing child nodes and returns `child`. The method throws a `DOMException` with the code `HIERARCHY_REQUEST_ERR` if the current node does not allow children, `WRONG_DOCUMENT_ERR` if `child` belongs to a document other than the one that created this node, or `NO_MODIFICATION_ALLOWED_ERR` if the current node is read-only.

➤ `Node insertBefore(Node child,Node existing)`: Inserts `child` as a child node immediately before `existing` in the current list of child nodes and returns `child`. This method throws `DOMException` with the same error codes as the preceding method, plus the error code `NOT_FOUND_ERR` if `existing` is not a child of the current node.

The `Element` interface also declares four methods that you use for adding attributes:

➤ `Attr setAttributeNode(Attr attr)`: Adds `attr` to the element. If an attribute node with the same name already exists, `attr` replaces it. The method returns either a reference to an existing `Attr` node that has been replaced or `null`. The method can throw a `DOMException` with the following codes:

  ➤ `WRONG_DOCUMENT_ERR` if `attr` belongs to another document.

  ➤ `NO_MODIFICATION_ALLOWED_ERR` if the element is read-only.

  ➤ `INUSE_ATTRIBUTE_ERR` if `attr` already belongs to another element.

➤ `Attr setAttributeNodeNS(Attr attr)`: Same as the previous method, but applies to an element defined within a namespace.

➤ `void setAttribute(String name,String value)`: Adds a new attribute node with the specified `name` and `value`. If the attribute has already been added, its value is changed to `value`. The method can throw `DOMException` with the following codes:

  ➤ `INVALID_CHARACTER_ERR` if `name` contains an illegal character.

  ➤ `NO_MODIFICATION_ALLOWED_ERR` if the element is read-only.

➤ `void setAttributeNS(String nsURI,String qualifiedName,String value)`
Same as the previous method, but with the attribute within the namespace `nsURI`. In addition, this method throws a `DOMException` with the code `NAMESPACE_ERR` if `qualifiedName` is invalid or not within the namespace.

You know enough about constructing a `Document` object to have a stab at putting together an object encapsulating a real XML document, so let's try it in the context of the Sketcher application.

STORING A SKETCH AS XML

You have already defined a DTD in the previous chapter that is suitable for defining a sketch. The code to store a sketch as an XML document instead of as a serialized object simply maps sketch elements to the corresponding XML elements. These elements are child nodes for a document node representing the entire sketch. You can create a `Document` object with a `DocumentType` node specifying `sketcher.dtd` as the DTD via a `DOMImplementation` object from a `DocumentBuilder` object. You can do this with statements in a `try` block:

```
Document doc = null;
try {
        DocumentBuilderFactory builderFactory = DocumentBuilderFactory.newInstance();
        builderFactory.setNamespaceAware(true);
        builderFactory.setValidating(true);
```

```
        builderFactory.setIgnoringElementContentWhitespace(true);
        Path dtdFile = Paths.get(System.getProperty("user.home")).
                    resolve("Beginning Java Stuff").resolve("sketcher.dtd");
        DOMImplementation domImpl = builderFactory.newDocumentBuilder().getDOMImplementation();
        doc = domImpl.createDocument(null, "sketch", domImpl.createDocumentType(
                                                "sketch", null, dtdFile.toString())));
    } catch(ParserConfigurationException e) {
      e.printStackTrace();
      // Display the error and terminate the current activity...

    } catch(DOMException e) {
      // Determine the kind of error from the error code,
      // display the error, and terminate the current activity...
    }
```

The first statement creates a `DocumentBuilderFactory` object. The factory object is set to be namespace-aware and validating, so any document builder object you create validates the document against the DTD. A `DOMImplementation` object is obtained and stored in `domImpl`. This is used in the next statement to create the `Document` object for a sketch and its `DocumentType` object defining the `DOCTYPE` declaration for `sketcher.dtd`. Eventually you add code like this to the `SketcherFrame` class, but I'm leaving that to one side for the moment and looking at how you can fill out the detail of the `Document` object from the objects representing elements in a sketch.

A sketch in XML is a simple two-level structure. The root node in an XML representation of a sketch is a `<sketch>` element, and the child elements are XML elements defining sketch elements. To define the complete XML structure you need only to add an `org.w3c.dom.Element` node as a child of the root node for each element in the sketch. A good way to implement this would be to add a method to each of the sketch `Element` inner classes that creates its own `org.w3c.dom.Element` node and adds it to the root node for a `Document` object. This makes each object that encapsulates a sketch element able to create its own XML representation.

You have to modify the `Element` class as well as its inner classes that define concrete Sketcher class elements. The inner classes are `Element.Line`, `Element.Rectangle`, `Element.Circle`, `Element.Curve`, and `Element.Text`. The nodes that you must add for each kind of geometric element derive directly from the declaration in the DTD, so it helps if you have this handy while you go through these classes. If you have it as a file from when I discussed it in the last chapter, maybe you can print a copy.

Adding Element Nodes

Polymorphism is going to be a big help in generating the XML for a sketch, so let's first define an abstract method in the `Element` base class to add an element node to a document. You can add the declaration immediately after the declaration for the other abstract methods, like this:

```
public abstract void draw(Graphics2D g2D);
public abstract void modify(Point start, Point last);
public abstract void addElementNode(Document document);
```

The parameter for this method is a reference to a `Document` object that encapsulates the XML for a sketch. An implementation adds a child node and adds it to the document. Each of the inner classes to `Element` implement this method.

You need a couple of `import` statements at the beginning of the `Element.java` file in Sketcher:

```
import org.w3c.dom.Document;
import org.w3c.dom.Attr;
```

Note that you need to use `org.w3c.dom.Element` to reference the XML element class type to avoid a potential clash with your sketch `Element` type.

The XML elements that you create from sketch elements all need `<position>`, `<color>`, and `<bounds>` elements as children. If you define methods to create these in the `Element` class, they are inherited in each of the subclasses of `Element`. Here's how you can define a method in the `Element` class to create a `<color>` element:

```
// Create an XML element for color
protected org.w3c.dom.Element createColorElement(Document doc) {
   org.w3c.dom.Element colorElement = doc.createElement("color");

   Attr attr = doc.createAttribute("R");
   attr.setValue(String.valueOf(color.getRed()));
   colorElement.setAttributeNode(attr);

   attr = doc.createAttribute("G");
   attr.setValue(String.valueOf(color.getGreen()));
   colorElement.setAttributeNode(attr);

   attr = doc.createAttribute("B");
   attr.setValue(String.valueOf(color.getBlue()));
   colorElement.setAttributeNode(attr);
   return colorElement;
}
```

Directory "Sketcher reading and writing XML"

The method for creating the node for a `<position>` element uses essentially the same process, but you have several nodes representing points that are the same apart from their names. You can share the code by putting it into a method in the `Element` class that you call with the appropriate XML element name as an argument:

```
protected org.w3c.dom.Element createPointTypeElement(Document doc,
                                                  String name,
                                                  String xValue,
                                                  String yValue) {
   org.w3c.dom.Element element = doc.createElement(name);

   Attr attr = doc.createAttribute("x");       // Create attribute x
   attr.setValue(xValue);                       // and set its value
   element.setAttributeNode(attr);              // Insert the x attribute

   attr = doc.createAttribute("y");            // Create attribute y
   attr.setValue(yValue);                       // and set its value
   element.setAttributeNode(attr);              // Insert the y attribute
   return element;
}
```

Directory "Sketcher reading and writing XML"

This creates an element with the name specified by the second argument, so you can use this in another method in the `Element` class to create a node for a `<position>` element:

```
// Create the XML element for the position of a sketch element
protected org.w3c.dom.Element createPositionElement(Document doc) {
   return createPointTypeElement(doc, "position",
                             String.valueOf(position.x),
                             String.valueOf(position.y));
}
```

Directory "Sketcher reading and writing XML"

You are able to create `<endpoint>` or `<point>` nodes in the same way in methods that you implement in the subclasses of `Element`.

You can create a `<bounds>` element like this:

```java
protected org.w3c.dom.Element createBoundsElement(Document doc) {
  org.w3c.dom.Element boundsElement = doc.createElement("bounds");

  Attr attr = doc.createAttribute("x");
  attr.setValue(String.valueOf(bounds.x));
  boundsElement.setAttributeNode(attr);

  attr = doc.createAttribute("y");
  attr.setValue(String.valueOf(bounds.y));
  boundsElement.setAttributeNode(attr);

  attr = doc.createAttribute("width");
  attr.setValue(String.valueOf(bounds.width));
  boundsElement.setAttributeNode(attr);

  attr = doc.createAttribute("height");
  attr.setValue(String.valueOf(bounds.height));
  boundsElement.setAttributeNode(attr);
  return boundsElement;
}
```

Directory "Sketcher reading and writing XML"

This method extracts the x and y coordinates of the top-left corner and the values of the `width` and `height` for the `bounds` member of the Sketcher `Element` class and sets these as attribute values for the `<bounds>` XML element.

Adding a Line Node

The method to add a `<line>` node to the `Document` object creates an XML `<line>` element with an `angle` attribute and then adds four child elements: `<color>`, `<position>`, `<endpoint>`, and `<bounds>`. You can add the following implementation of the `addElementNode()` method to the `Element.Line` class:

```java
// Create XML element for a line
public void addElementNode(Document doc) {
  org.w3c.dom.Element lineElement = doc.createElement("line");

  // Create the angle attribute and attach it to the <line> node
  Attr attr = doc.createAttribute("angle");
  attr.setValue(String.valueOf(angle));
  lineElement.setAttributeNode(attr);

  // Append the <color>, <position>, and <endpoint> nodes as children
  lineElement.appendChild(createColorElement(doc));
  lineElement.appendChild(createPositionElement(doc));
  lineElement.appendChild(createBoundsElement(doc));
  lineElement.appendChild(createEndpointElement(doc));

  // Append the <line> node to the document root node
  doc.getDocumentElement().appendChild(lineElement);
}
```

Directory "Sketcher reading and writing XML"

Calling this method with a reference to the `Document` object that represents the sketch as an argument adds a `<line>` child node corresponding to the `Element.Line` object. To complete this you must add the `createEndpointElement()` method to the `Element.Line` class:

```java
// Create XML element for the end point of a line
private org.w3c.dom.Element createEndpointElement(Document doc) {
  return createPointTypeElement(doc, "endpoint",
                     String.valueOf(line.x2), String.valueOf(line.y2));
}
```

Directory "Sketcher reading and writing XML"

This method creates an XML `<endpoint>` element by calling the `createPointTypeElement()` method that `Line` inherits from the base class.

Adding a Rectangle Node

Next you can add the method to the `Rectangle` class that creates a `<rectangle>` child element in the `Document` object:

Available for download on Wrox.com

```
// Create an XML element for a rectangle
public void addElementNode(Document doc) {
  org.w3c.dom.Element rectElement = doc.createElement("rectangle");

  // Create the width & height attributes and attach them to the node
  Attr attr = doc.createAttribute("width");
  attr.setValue(String.valueOf(rectangle.width));
  rectElement.setAttributeNode(attr);
  attr = doc.createAttribute("height");
  attr.setValue(String.valueOf(rectangle.height));
  rectElement.setAttributeNode(attr);

  // Create the angle attribute and attach it to the <rectangle> node
  attr = doc.createAttribute("angle");
  attr.setValue(String.valueOf(angle));
  rectElement.setAttributeNode(attr);

  // Append the <color>, <position>, and <bounds> nodes as children
  rectElement.appendChild(createColorElement(doc));
  rectElement.appendChild(createPositionElement(doc));
  rectElement.appendChild(createBoundsElement(doc));

  doc.getDocumentElement().appendChild(rectElement);
}
```

Directory "Sketcher reading and writing XML"

After creating the node for the `Rectangle` object, you set the width, height, and angle as attributes. You then append the child elements for the element color, position, and bounding rectangle. Finally you append the `<rectangle>` element as a child for the document root node.

Adding a Circle Node

Creating the node for a `<circle>` element in the `Element.Circle` class is not very different:

Available for download on Wrox.com

```
// Create an XML element for a circle
public void addElementNode(Document doc) {
  org.w3c.dom.Element circleElement = doc.createElement("circle");

  // Create the diameter attribute and attach it to the <circle> node
  Attr attr = doc.createAttribute("diameter");
  attr.setValue(String.valueOf(circle.width));
  circleElement.setAttributeNode(attr);

  // Create the angle attribute and attach it to the <circle> node
  attr = doc.createAttribute("angle");
  attr.setValue(String.valueOf(angle));
  circleElement.setAttributeNode(attr);

  // Append the <color> and <position> nodes as children
  circleElement.appendChild(createColorElement(doc));
  circleElement.appendChild(createPositionElement(doc));
  circleElement.appendChild(createBoundsElement(doc));

  doc.getDocumentElement().appendChild(circleElement);
}
```

Directory "Sketcher reading and writing XML"

There's nothing new here. You can use either the `width` or the `height` member of the `Ellipse2D.Double` class object as the diameter of the circle because they have the same value.

Adding a Curve Node

Creating an XML `<curve>` node for an `Element.Curve` object is a bit more long-winded. A curve is represented by a `GeneralPath` object, and you have to add all the defining points after the first as child elements to the `<curve>` element. You can obtain a special iterator object of type `java.awt.geom.PathIterator` for a `GeneralPath` object by calling its `getPathIterator()` method. The `PathIterator` object provides access to all the information you need to re-create the `GeneralPath` object.

`PathIterator` is an interface that declares methods for retrieving details of the segments that make up a `GeneralPath` object, so a reference to an object of type `PathIterator` encapsulates all the data defining that path.

The argument to `getPathIterator()` is an `AffineTransform` object that is applied to the path. This provides for the possibility that a single `GeneralPath` object may be used to create a number of different appearances on the screen simply by applying different transformations to the same object. You might have a `GeneralPath` object that defines a complicated object, a boat, for example. You could draw several boats on the screen from the one object simply by applying a transform before you draw each boat to set its position and orientation.

In Sketcher you want an iterator for the unmodified path, so you pass a default `AffineTransform` object that does nothing to the `getPathIterator()` method.

The `PathIterator` interface declares five methods:

➤ `int currentSegment(double[] coords)`: coords is used to store data relating to the current segment as `double` values and must have six elements to record the coordinate pairs. This is to record coordinates for one, two, or three points, depending on the current segment type. Our case only uses line segments so coordinates for one point are always returned. The method returns one of the following constants defined in the `PathIterator` interface:

➤ `SEG_MOVETO` if the segment corresponds to a `moveTo()` operation. The coordinates of the point moved to are returned as the first two elements of the array coords.

➤ `SEG_LINETO` if the segment corresponds to a `lineTo()` operation. The coordinates of the end point are returned as the first two elements of the array coords.

➤ `SEG_QUADTO` if the segment corresponds to a `quadTo()` operation. The coordinates of the control point for the quadratic segment are returned as the first two elements of the coords array, and the end point coordinates are returned in the third and fourth elements.

➤ `SEG_CUBICTO` if the segment corresponds to a `curveTo()` operation. The coords array contains coordinates of the first control point, the second control point, and the end point of the cubic curve segment.

➤ `SEG_CLOSE` if the segment corresponds to a `closePath()` operation. No values are returned in the coords array.

➤ `int currentSegment(float[] coords)`: Stores data for the current segment as `float` values. The value returned is the same as it is in the previous method.

➤ `int getWindingRule()`: Returns a value identifying the winding rule in effect. The value can be `WIND_EVEN_ODD` or `WIND_NON_ZERO`.

➤ `void next()`: Moves the iterator to the next segment as long as there is another segment.

➤ `boolean isDone()`: Returns `true` if the iteration is complete and returns `false` otherwise.

You have all the tools you need to get the data on every segment in the path. You just need to get a `PathIterator` reference and use the `next()` method to go through the segments in the path. The case for an `Element.Curve` object is simple: You have only a single `moveTo()` segment that is always to (0, 0) followed by one or more `lineTo()` segments. Even though this is a fixed pattern, you still test the return value from the `currentSegment()` method to show how it's done and in case there are errors.

The first segment is a special case. It is always a move to (0, 0), whereas all the others are lines. Thus the procedure is to get the first segment and discard it after verifying it is a move, and then get the remaining segments in a loop. Here's the code to create the XML:

```
// Create an XML element for a curve
public void addElementNode(Document doc) {
    org.w3c.dom.Element curveElement = doc.createElement("curve");

    // Create the angle attribute and attach it to the <curve> node
    Attr attr = doc.createAttribute("angle");
    attr.setValue(String.valueOf(angle));
    curveElement.setAttributeNode(attr);

    // Append the <color> and <position> nodes as children
    curveElement.appendChild(createColorElement(doc));
    curveElement.appendChild(createPositionElement(doc));
    curveElement.appendChild(createBoundsElement(doc));

    // Get the defining points via a path iterator
    PathIterator iterator = curve.getPathIterator(new AffineTransform());
    int maxCoordCount = 6;                       // Maximum coordinates for a segment
    float[] temp = new float[maxCoordCount];     // Stores segment data

    int result = iterator.currentSegment(temp);  // Get first segment
    assert result == PathIterator.SEG_MOVETO;    // ... should be move to

    iterator.next();                             // Next segment
    while(!iterator.isDone())    {               // While you have segments
      result = iterator.currentSegment(temp);    // Get the segment data
      assert result == PathIterator.SEG_LINETO;  // Should all be lines

      // Create a <point> node and add it to the list of children
      curveElement.appendChild(createPointTypeElement(doc, "point",
                                     String.valueOf(temp[0]),
                                     String.valueOf(temp[1])));
      iterator.next();                           // Go to next segment
    }
    doc.getDocumentElement().appendChild(curveElement);
}
```

Directory "Sketcher reading and writing XML"

The angle attribute and the position, color, and bounds elements are added in the same way as for other elements. You use a `PathIterator` object to go through all the points in the path that defines the curve. You add one `<point>` node as a child of the `Element` node for a curve for each defining point after the first. The assertion in the loop verifies that each segment is a line segment.

Adding a Node for a Text Element

A node for an `Element.Text` object is a little different and also involves quite a lot of code. As well as the usual `<color>`, `<position>`, and `<bounds>` child nodes, you also have to append a `<font>` node to define the font and a `<string>` node containing the text. The `<font>` node has three attributes that define the font name, the font style, and the point size. There is also an attribute to record the `maxAscent` value. Here's the code:

```
// Create an XML element for a sketch Text element
public void addElementNode(Document doc) {
    org.w3c.dom.Element textElement = doc.createElement("text");
```

```
// Create the angle attribute and attach it to the <text> node
Attr attr = doc.createAttribute("angle");
attr.setValue(String.valueOf(angle));
textElement.setAttributeNode(attr);

// Create the maxascent attribute and attach it to the <text> node
attr = doc.createAttribute("maxascent");
attr.setValue(String.valueOf(maxAscent));
textElement.setAttributeNode(attr);

// Append the <color> and <position> nodes as children
textElement.appendChild(createColorElement(doc));
textElement.appendChild(createPositionElement(doc));
textElement.appendChild(createBoundsElement(doc));

// Create and apppend the <font> node
org.w3c.dom.Element fontElement = doc.createElement("font");
attr = doc.createAttribute("fontname");
attr.setValue(font.getName());
fontElement.setAttributeNode(attr);

attr = doc.createAttribute("fontstyle");
String style = null;
int styleCode = font.getStyle();
if(styleCode == Font.PLAIN) {
  style = "plain";
} else if(styleCode == Font.BOLD) {
  style = "bold";
} else if(styleCode == Font.ITALIC) {
  style = "italic";
} else if(styleCode == Font.ITALIC + Font.BOLD) {
    style = "bold-italic";
}
assert style != null;
attr.setValue(style);
fontElement.setAttributeNode(attr);

attr = doc.createAttribute("pointsize");
attr.setValue(String.valueOf(font.getSize()));
fontElement.setAttributeNode(attr);
textElement.appendChild(fontElement);

// Create the <string> node
org.w3c.dom.Element string = doc.createElement("string");
string.setTextContent(text);
textElement.appendChild(string);

doc.getDocumentElement().appendChild(textElement);
}
```

Directory "Sketcher reading and writing XML"

Most of this code is what you have seen for other types of sketch element. Because the font style attribute value can be `"plain,"` `"bold,"` `"bold-italic,"` or just `"italic,"` you have a series of `if` statements to determine the attribute value. A `Font` object stores the style as an integer with different values for plain, bold, and italic. The values for bold and italic may be combined, in which case the attribute value is `"bold-italic."`

All the element objects in a sketch can now add their own XML element nodes to a `Document` object. You should now be able to use this capability to create a document that encapsulates the entire sketch.

Creating a Document Object for a Complete Sketch

You can add a `createDocument()` method to the `SketcherFrame` class to create a `Document` object and populate it with the nodes for the elements in the current sketch model. Creating the `Document` object uses the code fragment you saw earlier. You need to add some `import` statements at the beginning of the `SketcherFrame.java` source file for the new interfaces and classes you are using:

```
import javax.xml.parsers.*;
import org.w3c.dom.*;
```

Here's the method definition you can add to the class:

Available for download on Wrox.com

```
// Creates a DOM Document object encapsulating the current sketch
public Document createDocument() {
  Document doc = null;
  try {
    DocumentBuilderFactory builderFactory = DocumentBuilderFactory.newInstance();
    builderFactory.setNamespaceAware(true);
    builderFactory.setValidating(true);
    builderFactory.setIgnoringElementContentWhitespace(true);
    DocumentBuilder builder = builderFactory.newDocumentBuilder();
    builder.setErrorHandler(this);
    DOMImplementation domImpl = builder.getDOMImplementation();
    Path dtdFile = Paths.get(System.getProperty("user.home")).
                            resolve("Beginning Java Stuff").resolve("sketcher.dtd");
    doc = domImpl.createDocument(null, "sketch", domImpl.createDocumentType(
                                        "sketch", null, dtdFile.toString()));
  } catch(ParserConfigurationException pce) {
    JOptionPane.showMessageDialog(this,
                              "Parser configuration error while creating document",
                              "DOM Parser Error",
                              JOptionPane.ERROR_MESSAGE);
    System.err.println(pce.getMessage());
    pce.printStackTrace();
    return null;
  } catch(DOMException de) {
    JOptionPane.showInternalMessageDialog(null,
                              "DOM exception thrown while creating document",
                              "DOM Error",
                              JOptionPane.ERROR_MESSAGE);
    System.err.println(de.getMessage());
    de.printStackTrace();
    return null;
  }

  // Each element in the sketch can create its own node in the document
  SketcherModel elements = theApp.getModel();  // Get the sketch
  for(Element element : elements) {            // For each element...
    element.addElementNode(doc);               // ...add its node.
  }
  return doc;
}
```

Directory "Sketcher reading and writing XML"

Notice that this assumes that the DTD file for Sketcher should be in your `Beg Java Stuff` folder. If it isn't, amend the code accordingly. You call `setErrorHandler()` for the `DocumentBuilder` object to make the `SketcherFrame` object the handler for parsing errors. This implies that you must make the `SketcherFrame` class implement the `ErrorHandler` interface.

You pop up a dialog and return `null` if something goes wrong when you are creating the `Document` object. In case of a `DOMException` being thrown, you could add a `switch` statement to analyze the value in the `code` member of the exception and provide a more specific message in the dialog.

To implement the `ErrorHandler` interface, first amend the first line of the `SketcherFrame` class definition:

```
public class SketcherFrame extends JFrame
                implements ActionListener, Observer, Printable, ErrorHandler {
```

Now you can add the following three method definitions that are required:

```
// Handles recoverable errors from parsing XML
public void error(SAXParseException spe) {
    JOptionPane.showMessageDialog(SketcherFrame.this,
                    "Error at line " + spe.getLineNumber() + "\n" + spe.getMessage(),
                    "DOM Parser Error",
                    JOptionPane.ERROR_MESSAGE);
}

// Handles fatal errors from parsing XML
public void fatalError(SAXParseException spe) throws SAXParseException {
    JOptionPane.showMessageDialog(SketcherFrame.this,
                    "Fatal error at line " + spe.getLineNumber() + "\n" + spe.getMessage(),
                    "DOM Parser Error",
                    JOptionPane.ERROR_MESSAGE);
    throw spe;
}

// Handles warnings from parsing XML
public void warning(SAXParseException spe) {
    JOptionPane.showMessageDialog(SketcherFrame.this,
                    Warning at line " + spe.getLineNumber() + "\n" + spe.getMessage(),
                    "DOM Parser Error",
                    JOptionPane.ERROR_MESSAGE);
}
```

Directory "Sketcher reading and writing XML"

In each case you display a dialog providing information about the error. For a fatal error, you throw `SAXParseException`, which terminates parsing. There should not be any errors occurring because you are processing XML that was created by the code in Sketcher. You need another import statement in `SketcherFrame.java`:

```
import org.xml.sax.*;
```

The `SketcherFrame` object can now create a DOM `Document` object encapsulating the entire sketch. All you now need is some code to provide the GUI for exporting sketches as XML, and code to use the `Document` object to write an XML file.

Saving a Sketch as XML

Of course, you could modify Sketcher so that you could set an option to save sketches either as objects or as XML documents. However, to keep things simple you will add menu items to the File menu to export or import a sketch as XML. In this way, you keep the code for reading and writing XML files separate from the code for reading and writing .ske files.

In broad terms, here's what you have to do to the `SketcherFrame` class to save a sketch as an XML file:

> ➤ Add Import XML and Export XML menu items.
> ➤ Implement the process of creating an XML document from the `Document` object that the `createDocument()` method creates in response to an Export XML menu item event.
> ➤ Implement writing the XML document that is generated from a sketch to a file.

You can add new `FileAction` objects for the two new menu items. Clearly, a lot of the work is in the implementation of the new functionality in the `actionPerformed()` method in the `FileAction` class, so let's start with the easy bit—adding the new menu items to the File menu. First, you can add two new fields for the menu items by changing the existing definition in the `SketcherFrame` class:

```
private FileAction newAction,    openAction,   closeAction,
                   saveAction,   saveAsAction, printAction,
                   exportAction, importAction, exitAction;
```

You can create the `Action` objects for the two new menu items in the `createFileMenuActions()` method, following the creation of the `Action` item for the Print menu item:

```
printAction = new FileAction("Print", 'P', CTRL_DOWN_MASK);
exportAction = new FileAction("Export XML", 'E', CTRL_DOWN_MASK);
importAction = new FileAction("Import XML", 'I', CTRL_DOWN_MASK);
exitAction = new FileAction("Exit", 'X', CTRL_DOWN_MASK);
```

The new fields store references to the `Action` objects for the new menu items. You don't need to add these to the `actions` array definition because you use the array to create toolbars for corresponding menu items and you won't be adding toolbar buttons for the XML I/O operations.

You can add the `SHORT_DESCRIPTION` property values for the new `Action` objects in the `createFileMenuActions()` method, where it does this for the other `Action` objects:

```
exportAction.putValue(SHORT_DESCRIPTION, "Export sketch as an XML file");
importAction.putValue(SHORT_DESCRIPTION, "Import sketch from an XML file");
```

You can add the menu items to the File menu in the `createFileMenu()` method, immediately before the statement adding the separator that precedes the `exitAction`:

```
fileMenu.addSeparator();                            // Add separator
fileMenu.add(exportAction);                         // Export XML menu item
fileMenu.add(importAction);                         // Import XML menu item
fileMenu.addSeparator();                            // Add separator
fileMenu.add(exitAction);                           // Print sketch menu item
menuBar.add(fileMenu);                              // Add the file menu
```

Next you can add an extra `else if` block in the `actionPerformed()` method in the `FileAction` class to respond to events from the new menu items:

```
public void actionPerformed(ActionEvent e) {
  // Code for if statement as before...
  } else if(this == exitAction) {
    // Code to handle exitAction event as before...
  } else if(this == exportAction) {
    exportXMLOperation();                           // Export sketch as XML

  } else if(this == importAction) {
    importXMLOperation();                           // Import an XML sketch
  }
}
```

The `exportXMLOperation()` method you add to the `SketcherFrame` class takes care of handling events for the Export XML menu item, and the `importXMLOperation()` method deals with events for the Import XML menu item.

Exporting a Sketch as XML

To export a sketch as XML, you can use the `showDialog()` method that creates a file chooser dialog to identify the file for the XML markup output. The dialog uses a new file filter that you can define as a field in the `SketcherFrame` class:

```
private ExtensionFilter xmlFileFilter = new ExtensionFilter(
                                ".xml", "XML Sketch files (*.xml)");
```

This defines a filter for files with the extension .xml. The `showDialog()` method should ensure that a selected file path ends in XML when the `xmlFileFilter` is in effect because this is an indicator that the dialog is used for an XML file operation. You can implement this by adding a statement to the `showDialog()` method:

```
Path selectedFile = null;
if(file == null) {
  selectedFile = Paths.get(
            fileChooser.getCurrentDirectory().toString(), DEFAULT_FILENAME);
} else {
  selectedFile = file;
}
selectedFile = setFileExtension(
                    selectedFile, filter == xmlFileFilter ? ".xml" : ".ske");
fileChooser.setSelectedFile(new File(selectedFile.toString()));
```

The second argument to the `setFileExtension()` method call is `".xml"` when the XML file filter is in effect and `".ske"` otherwise. Note that this only guarantees that the file that is initially selected has the extension .xml. The path that is returned may not.

You can implement the method to export a sketch as XML in the `SketcherFrame` class like this:

```
// Export a sketch as XML
private void exportXMLOperation() {
  Path selectedFile = null;
  if(currentSketchFile == null) {
    selectedFile = Paths.get(
              fileChooser.getCurrentDirectory().toString(), DEFAULT_FILENAME);
  } else {
    selectedFile = currentSketchFile;
  }
  // Make extension .xml
  selectedFile = setFileExtension(selectedFile, ".xml");

  Path file = showDialog("Export Sketch as XML", "Export",
                    "Export sketch as XML", xmlFileFilter, selectedFile);
  if(file == null) {                         // No file selected...
    return;                                  // ... so we are done.
  }

  if(Files.exists(file) &&                   // If the path exists and...
      JOptionPane.NO_OPTION ==               // .. NO selected in dialog...
        JOptionPane.showConfirmDialog(
                    this,
                    file.getFileName() + " exists. Overwrite?",
                    "Confirm Save As",
                    JOptionPane.YES_NO_OPTION,
                    JOptionPane.WARNING_MESSAGE)) {
        return;                              // ...do nothing
  }
  saveXMLSketch(file);
}
```

Directory "Sketcher reading and writing XML"

The `exportXMLOperation()` method uses the `showDialog()` method that you create for use when you are saving the sketch normally. The dialog has a filter for XML files in effect, so the user should only see those in the file list. If the dialog returns a non-null path, you first ensure the extension is .xml. Then you check whether the file exists and provide the user with the option to overwrite it if it does. Finally you call `saveXMLSketch()` to write the file, so you had better implement that next.

Writing the XML File

The chosen file is passed to a new `saveXMLSketch()` method in `SketcherFrame` that writes the XML document to the file. You can create a `Document` object encapsulating the XML markup for the current sketch and then use a `Transformer` object to write the file in the way that you saw earlier in this chapter. Here's the code:

```java
// Write XML sketch to file
private void saveXMLSketch(Path file) {
  Document document = createDocument();          // XML representation of the sketch
  Node node = document.getDocumentElement();     // Document tree base
  try(BufferedOutputStream xmlOut =
                   new BufferedOutputStream(Files.newOutputStream(file))) {
    TransformerFactory factory = TransformerFactory.newInstance();

    // Create transformer
    Transformer transformer = factory.newTransformer();
    transformer.setErrorListener(this);

    // Set properties - add whitespace for readability
    //                 - include DOCTYPE declaration in output
    transformer.setOutputProperty(OutputKeys.INDENT, "yes");
    transformer.setOutputProperty(
            OutputKeys.DOCTYPE_SYSTEM, "D:/Beg Java Stuff/sketcher.dtd");

    // Source is the document object - result is the file
    DOMSource source = new DOMSource(node);
    StreamResult xmlFile = new StreamResult(xmlOut);
    transformer.transform(source, xmlFile);        // Write XML to file
  } catch (TransformerConfigurationException tce) {
      System.err.println("Transformer Factory error: " + tce.getMessage());
  } catch (TransformerException te) {
      System.err.println("Transformation error: " + te.getMessage());
  } catch (IOException e) {
      System.err.println("I/O error writing XML file: " + e.getMessage());
  }
}
```

Directory "Sketcher reading and writing XML"

You first create a `Document` object for the sketch by calling the `createDocument()` method that you added to `SketcherFrame` earlier in this chapter. You create an output stream corresponding to the `Path` object that is passed to the method in the `try` block. To create a `Transformer` object that writes the file, you first create a `TransformerFactory` object by calling the static `newInstance()` method. Calling the `newTransformer()` method with no arguments for the factory object creates a `Transformer` object that represents an identity transform. You set the `SketcherFrame` object to be the error listener for the `Transformer` object so `SketcherFrame` needs to implement the `ErrorListener` interface.

You set the values for two properties for the transformer. You set the value for `INDENT` key to "yes" so whitespace is inserted between elements in the output and the value for `DOCTYPE_SYSTEM` key to the file path for the DTD.

To write the file, you define the `Document` object as the source for the transform and the `xmlFile` output stream object as the result. Calling `transform()` for the `transformer` object with these as arguments writes the file.

To implement the `ErrorListener` interface in the `SketcherFrame` class, first amend the first line of the class definition:

```java
public class SketcherFrame extends JFrame
    implements ActionListener, Observer, Printable, ErrorHandler, ErrorListener {
```

Next add definitions for the methods declared in the interface:

```java
// Handles recoverable errors from transforming XML
public void error(TransformerException te) {
  System.err.println("Error transforming XML: " + te.getMessage());
}
```

```
// Handles fatal errors from transforming XML
public void fatalError(TransformerException te) {
  System.err.println("Fatal error transforming XML: " + te.getMessage());
  System.exit(1);
}

// Handles warnings from transforming XML
public void warning(TransformerException te) {
  System.err.println("Warning transforming XML: " + te.getMessage());
}
```

Directory "Sketcher reading and writing XML"

Each method just outputs an error message. With a fatal error, you abort the program. You could throw `TransformerException` if you want to simply stop the transformer. Some more import statements are needed in `SketcherFrame.java`:

```
import javax.xml.transform.*;
import javax.xml.transform.stream.*;
import javax.xml.transform.dom.*;
import javax.xml.validation.*;
```

You should be able to recompile Sketcher at this point if you want to try out writing a sketch as XML. The file that is produced should be quite readable, and you can view it using any plain text editor, such as Notepad.

READING AN XML REPRESENTATION OF A SKETCH

Reading a sketch from an XML file is the reverse of writing it. You can use a `Transformer` object to create a `Document` object from the XML markup in the file. You can then iterate through the child nodes in the `Document` object and create sketch `Element` objects from them. You need a way to create sketch elements from the XML elements, and the obvious way to tackle this is to add constructors to the classes derived from the `Element` class that create an object from the `Node` object that encapsulates the XML for the element. These new instructors must be able to call a base class constructor as the first statement. However, the existing `Element` class constructors are not suitable because they require arguments that are not available when one of the new constructors starts executing. Let's see how you can accommodate this and provide for initializing the base class fields.

Creating the Base Class Object from XML

You can add a no-arg constructor to the Sketcher `Element` class to solve the problem:

```
protected Element() {}
```

This constructor creates the object but does not initialize the base class fields. That is down to the derived class constructors.

If the `Element` class has methods to initialize its fields from an XML node object, these can be used by all of the derived classes when an object is to be created from XML. Here's the method to initialize the `angle` field:

```
// Set angle field value from a node
protected void setAngleFromXML(Node node) {
  angle = Double.valueOf(((Attr)(node.getAttributes().getNamedItem("angle"))).
getValue());
}
```

Directory "Sketcher reading and writing XML"

The `Node` object that is passed to the method contains the value for `angle` as an attribute. Calling `getAttributes()` for `node` returns all the attributes as a `NamedNodeMap` object. Calling `getNamedItem()`

for this object returns the attribute, with the name you pass as the argument, as a `Node` object. The `getValue()` method for a `Node` object returns its value as a `String` object, so passing this to the static `valueOf()` method in the `Double` class returns the `angle` value as type `double`.

This pattern for obtaining the value of an attribute from a `Node` object appears frequently. Here's how you can initialize the `position` field with another method in the `Element` class:

```
// Set position field from a node
protected void setPositionFromXML(Node node) {
  NamedNodeMap attrs = node.getAttributes();
  position = new Point(
            Integer.valueOf(((Attr)(attrs.getNamedItem("x"))).getValue()),
            Integer.valueOf(((Attr)(attrs.getNamedItem("y"))).getValue()));
}
```

Directory "Sketcher reading and writing XML"

This method closely parallels the previous method. You extract the values for the coordinates of the point from the attributes as integers. You then pass these to a `Point` class constructor.

The code to initialize the `color` field is very similar:

```
// Set color field from a node
protected void setColorFromXML(Node node) {
  NamedNodeMap attrs = node.getAttributes();
  color = new Color(
            Integer.valueOf(((Attr)(attrs.getNamedItem("R"))).getValue()),
            Integer.valueOf(((Attr)(attrs.getNamedItem("G"))).getValue()),
            Integer.valueOf(((Attr)(attrs.getNamedItem("B"))).getValue()));
}
```

Directory "Sketcher reading and writing XML"

This works essentially the same way as the previous method. You extract each of the color component values as integers from the corresponding attributes and pass them to the `Color` class constructor.

Creating the `java.awt.Rectangle` object that you need to initialize the `bounds` field is virtually the same:

```
// Set bounds field from a node
protected void setBoundsFromXML(Node node) {
  NamedNodeMap attrs = node.getAttributes();
  bounds = new java.awt.Rectangle(
        Integer.valueOf(((Attr)(attrs.getNamedItem("x"))).getValue()),
        Integer.valueOf(((Attr)(attrs.getNamedItem("y"))).getValue()),
        Integer.valueOf(((Attr)(attrs.getNamedItem("width"))).getValue()),
        Integer.valueOf(((Attr)(attrs.getNamedItem("height"))).getValue()));
}
```

Directory "Sketcher reading and writing XML"

You obtain the four attribute values in exactly the same way as in the other methods.

Creating Elements from XML Nodes

You add a constructor to each of the inner classes of `Element` that has a parameter of type `Node`. The `Node` object passed to each constructor encapsulates the XML child element that was created from an object of the inner class type. The subclasses of `Element` inherit the methods you have added that initialize the base class fields, so they can be called from the new constructor. A call to the no-arg `Element` class constructor is inserted automatically as the first statement in each of the new inner class constructors. Let's start with the `Element.Line` class constructor.

Creating a Line Object from an XML Node

A `Node` object that defines a line has the angle as an attribute, and four child nodes specifying the position, color, bounds, and the line end point. Here's the constructor to decode that lot:

```java
// Create Line object from XML node
public Line(Node node) {
  setAngleFromXML(node);
  NodeList childNodes = node.getChildNodes();
  Node aNode = null;
  for(int i = 0 ; i < childNodes.getLength() ; ++i) {
    aNode = childNodes.item(i);
    switch(aNode.getNodeName()) {
      case "position":
        setPositionFromXML(aNode);
        break;
      case "color":
        setColorFromXML(aNode);
        break;
      case "bounds":
        setBoundsFromXML(aNode);
        break;
      case "endpoint":
        NamedNodeMap coords = aNode.getAttributes();
        line = new Line2D.Double();
        line.x2 = Double.valueOf(((Attr)(coords.getNamedItem("x"))).getValue());
        line.y2 = Double.valueOf(((Attr)(coords.getNamedItem("y"))).getValue());
        break;
      default:
        System.err.println("Invalid node in <line>: " + aNode);
        break;
    }
  }
}
```

Directory "Sketcher reading and writing XML"

You set the angle for the line by calling the method that you added to the base class for this purpose. The `getChildNode()` method returns the child nodes in a `NodeList` object. You iterate over all the nodes in the `childNodes` list in the `for` loop. Calling `getItem()` for `childNodes` returns the `Node` object at the index position you pass to the method. You then process the node in the `switch` statement, selecting on the basis of the node name, which is a `String`. Each of the base class fields are set by calling one or other of the methods you have defined. For the `<endpoint>` node, you reconstruct the `Line2D.Double` object from the attributes for the node. Calling the no-arg constructor for `Line2D.Double` creates an object with the start and end points as (0,0), so you just have to set the end point coordinates, which are stored in `line.x2` and `line.y2`.

Creating a Rectangle Object from an XML Node

Most of the code to reconstruct an `Element.Rectangle` object is the same as for a line:

```java
// Create Rectangle object from XML node
public Rectangle(Node node) {
  setAngleFromXML(node);
  NodeList childNodes = node.getChildNodes();
  Node aNode = null;
  for(int i = 0 ; i < childNodes.getLength() ; ++i) {
    aNode = childNodes.item(i);
    switch(aNode.getNodeName()) {
      case "position":
        setPositionFromXML(aNode);
```

```
          break;
        case "color":
          setColorFromXML(aNode);
          break;
        case "bounds":
          setBoundsFromXML(aNode);
          break;
        default:
          System.err.println("Invalid node in <rectangle>: " + aNode);
          break;
      }
    }
    NamedNodeMap attrs = node.getAttributes();
    rectangle = new Rectangle2D.Double();
    rectangle.width = Double.valueOf(((Attr)(attrs.getNamedItem("width"))).getValue());
    rectangle.height =
          Double.valueOf(((Attr)(attrs.getNamedItem("height"))).getValue());
  }
```

Directory "Sketcher reading and writing XML"

The no-arg constructor for a `Rectangle2D.Double` object creates an object at (0,0) with a width and height of zero. The width and height of the rectangle are recorded as XML attributes, so you retrieve these and set the width and height of the object that you have created.

Creating a Circle Object from an XML Node

This constructor is almost identical to the previous constructor:

```
// Create Circle object from XML node
public Circle(Node node) {
  setAngleFromXML(node);
  NodeList childNodes = node.getChildNodes();
  Node aNode = null;
  for(int i = 0 ; i < childNodes.getLength() ; ++i) {
    aNode = childNodes.item(i);
    switch(aNode.getNodeName()) {
      case "position":
        setPositionFromXML(aNode);
        break;
      case "color":
        setColorFromXML(aNode);
        break;
      case "bounds":
        setBoundsFromXML(aNode);
        break;
      default:
        System.err.println("Invalid node in <circle>: " + aNode);
        break;
    }
  }
  NamedNodeMap attrs = node.getAttributes();
  circle = new Ellipse2D.Double();
  circle.width = circle.height =
        Double.valueOf(((Attr)(attrs.getNamedItem("diameter"))).getValue());
}
```

Directory "Sketcher reading and writing XML"

There's not a lot to say about this that is new. You reconstruct the `Ellipse2D.Double` object using the no-arg constructor and set its width and height to be the value you extract for the `"diameter"` attribute from the `<circle>` element.

Creating a Curve Object from an XML Node

Creating an `Element.Curve` object is inevitably different from previous object types, but not substantially different. The initial `MOVE_TO` segment for the general path is to the origin, so that requires no information from the `Node` object. The remaining `LINE_TO` segments are specified by `<point>` child nodes, so you just need to add a segment to the `GeneralPath` object corresponding to each `<point>` child node that is present. Here's the code:

Available for download on Wrox.com

```java
// Create Curve object from XML node
public Curve(Node node) {
  curve = new GeneralPath();
  curve.moveTo(origin.x, origin.y);          // Set current position as origin
  setAngleFromXML(node);
  NodeList childNodes = node.getChildNodes();
  Node aNode = null;
  for(int i = 0 ; i < childNodes.getLength() ; ++i) {
    aNode = childNodes.item(i);
    switch(aNode.getNodeName()) {
      case "position":
        setPositionFromXML(aNode);
        break;
      case "color":
        setColorFromXML(aNode);
        break;
      case "bounds":
        setBoundsFromXML(aNode);
        break;
      case "point":
        NamedNodeMap attrs = aNode.getAttributes();
        curve.lineTo(
            Double.valueOf(((Attr)(attrs.getNamedItem("x"))).getValue()),
            Double.valueOf(((Attr)(attrs.getNamedItem("y"))).getValue()));
      break;
      default:
        System.err.println("Invalid node in <curve>: " + aNode);
        break;
    }
  }
}
```

Directory "Sketcher reading and writing XML"

The base class fields are set in the same way as for other objects. You create an empty `GeneralPath` object before the loop that iterates over the child nodes and set the first segment as a move to the origin. For each child node with the name `"point"` you add a `LINE_TO` segment using the values stored as attributes for the `<point>` node. This re-creates the original curve representation.

Creating a Text Object from an XML Node

A `<text>` XML node has the `angle` and the `maxAscent` field values as attributes, and you extract those first. Here's the code for the constructor:

Available for download on Wrox.com

```java
// Create Text object from XML node
public Text(Node node) {
  NamedNodeMap attrs = node.getAttributes();
  angle = Double.valueOf(((Attr)(attrs.getNamedItem("angle"))).getValue());
  maxAscent =
      Integer.valueOf(((Attr)(attrs.getNamedItem("maxascent"))).getValue());

  NodeList childNodes = node.getChildNodes();
  Node aNode = null;
  for(int i = 0 ; i < childNodes.getLength() ; ++i) {
```

```
      aNode = childNodes.item(i);
      switch(aNode.getNodeName()) {
        case "position":
          setPositionFromXML(aNode);
          break;
        case "color":
          setColorFromXML(aNode);
          break;
        case "bounds":
          setBoundsFromXML(aNode);
          break;
        case "font":
          setFontFromXML(aNode);
        break;
        case "string":
          text = aNode.getTextContent();
          break;
        default:
          System.err.println("Invalid node in <text>: " + aNode);
          break;
      }
    }
  }
```

Directory "Sketcher reading and writing XML"

The process for extracting child nodes from the `Node` object passed to the constructor is as you have seen for the other constructors. For the `<string>` child node, you call its `getTextContent()` method to obtain the text for the object. You call a new method that creates the font field from a node corresponding to a `<font>` child element. You can add the `setFontFromXML()` method to the `Element.Text` class like this:

Available for download on Wrox.com

```
// Set the font field from an XML node
private void setFontFromXML(Node node) {
  NamedNodeMap attrs = node.getAttributes();
  String fontName = ((Attr)(attrs.getNamedItem("fontname"))).getValue();
  String style = ((Attr)(attrs.getNamedItem("fontstyle"))).getValue();
  int fontStyle = 0;
  switch(style){
    case "plain":
      fontStyle = Font.PLAIN;
      break;
    case "bold":
      fontStyle = Font.BOLD;
      break;
    case "italic":
      fontStyle = Font.ITALIC;
      break;
    case "bold-italic":
      fontStyle = Font.ITALIC|Font.BOLD;
      break;
    default:
      System.err.println("Invalid font style code: " + style);
      break;
  }
  int pointSize =
      Integer.valueOf(((Attr)(attrs.getNamedItem("pointsize"))).getValue());
  font = new Font(fontName, fontStyle, pointSize);
}
```

Directory "Sketcher reading and writing XML"

The font name, style, and point size are all recorded as attributes for the `<font>` XML node. The font style is recorded as one of four possible strings, so for each of these you set the value of the `fontStyle` variable to the corresponding integer constant from the Font class. Because you need to extract the node attributes directly here, you extract the angle value along with the other attributes, rather than calling the base class method.

That completes creating sketch elements from XML nodes. The final piece is to handle the Import XML menu item event.

Handling Import XML Events

You can define the ImportXMLOperation() method in SketcherFrame like this:

Available for
download on
Wrox.com

```
// Handle Import XML menu item events
private void importXMLOperation() {
  checkForSave();

  // Now get the destination file path
  Path file = showDialog(
                  "Open XML Sketch File",           // Dialog window title
                  "Open",                           // Button label
                  "Read a sketch from an XML file", // Button tooltip text
                  xmlFileFilter,                    // File filter
                  null);                            // No file selected
  if(file != null) {
    openXMLSketch(file);
  }
}
```

Directory "Sketcher reading and writing XML"

Reading an XML file containing a sketch replaces the current sketch, so you call checkForSave() in case the current sketch has not been saved. If the showDialog() method returns a non-null Path object, you pass it to the openXMLFile() method that reads the sketch from the file at the specified path.

Reading the XML File

You read the XML file and create a Document object from it using a Transformer object.

Available for
download on
Wrox.com

```
// Read an XML sketch from a file
private void openXMLSketch(Path file) {
  try (BufferedInputStream xmlIn =
                    new BufferedInputStream(Files.newInputStream(file))){
    StreamSource source = new StreamSource(xmlIn);
    DocumentBuilderFactory builderFactory =
                                  DocumentBuilderFactory.newInstance();
    builderFactory.setNamespaceAware(true);
    builderFactory.setValidating(true);
    DocumentBuilder builder = builderFactory.newDocumentBuilder();
    builder.setErrorHandler(this);
    Document xmlDoc = builder.newDocument();
    DOMResult result = new DOMResult(xmlDoc);

    // Create a factory object for XML transformers
    TransformerFactory factory = TransformerFactory.newInstance();
    Transformer transformer = factory.newTransformer();  // Create transformer
    transformer.setErrorListener(this);
    transformer.transform(source, result);               // Read the XML file
    theApp.insertModel(createModelFromXML(xmlDoc));       // Create the sketch

    // Change file extension to .ske
    currentSketchFile = setFileExtension(file, ".ske");
    setTitle(frameTitle+currentSketchFile);              // Update the window title
    sketchChanged = false;                              // Status is unchanged
  } catch(ParserConfigurationException e) {
    e.printStackTrace();
    System.exit(1);
```

```
        } catch(Exception e) {
        System.err.println(e);
        JOptionPane.showMessageDialog(this,
                            "Error reading a sketch file.",
                            "File Input Error",
                            JOptionPane.ERROR_MESSAGE);
        }
    }
```

Directory "Sketcher reading and writing XML"

The `DocumentBuilder` object sets the `SketcherFrame` object to be the error handler, so the methods that you have already added to Sketcher report any parsing errors. The same applies to the `Transformer` object. The `SketcherFrame` object is the error listener, so the methods in `SketcherFrame` that implement `ErrorListener` are invoked if transformer errors occur. The `createModel()` method creates a `SketcherModel` object from the `Document` object that is created from the contents of the file. You just need to implement this in `SketcherFrame` to complete reading a sketch from an XML file.

Creating the Model

You know that a sketch in XML is a two-level structure. There is a root element, `<sketch>`, that contains one XML child element for each of the elements in the original sketch. Therefore, to re-create the sketch, you just need to extract the children of the root node in the `Document` object and then figure out what kind of sketch element each child represents. Whatever it is, you want to create a sketch element object of that type and add it to a model. You have already added a constructor to each of the classes that define sketch elements to create an object from an XML node. Here's the code for the `SketcherFrame` method that uses them to create a sketch model:

Available for
download on
Wrox.com

```java
private SketcherModel createModelFromXML(Document xmlDoc) {
    SketcherModel model = new SketcherModel();
    NodeList nodes = xmlDoc.getDocumentElement().getChildNodes();
    // The child nodes should be elements representing sketch elements
    if(nodes.getLength() > 0) {                    // If there are some...
        Node elementNode = null;
        for(int i = 0 ; i<nodes.getLength() ; ++i){    // ...process them
            elementNode = nodes.item(i);
            switch(elementNode.getNodeName()) {
                case "line":
                    model.add(new Element.Line(elementNode));
                    break;
                case "rectangle":
                    model.add(new Element.Rectangle(elementNode));
                    break;
                case "circle":
                    model.add(new Element.Circle(elementNode));
                    break;
                case "curve":
                    model.add(new Element.Curve(elementNode));
                    break;
                case "text":
                    model.add(new Element.Text(elementNode));
                    break;
                default:
                    System.err.println("Invalid XML node: " + elementNode);
                    break;
            }
        }
    }
    return model;
}
```

Directory "Sketcher reading and writing XML"

This method works in a straightforward fashion. You get the child nodes of the root node as a
NodeList object by calling getChildNodes() for the object returned by getDocumentElement().
You determine what kind of element each child node is by checking its name in the switch statement. You
call a sketch Element constructor corresponding to the node name to create the sketch element to be added
to the model. Each of these constructors creates an object from the Node object reference that is passed as
the argument. If the child node name does not correspond to any of the sketch elements, you output an
error message.

That's all the code you need. If everything compiles, you are ready to try exporting and importing sketches.
If it doesn't compile, chances are good there's an import statement missing. The import statements that I
have in SketcherFrame.java now are:

```
import javax.swing.*;
import javax.swing.border.*;
import java.awt.event.*;
import java.awt.*;
import java.nio.file.*;
import java.io.*;
import java.util.*;
import java.awt.image.BufferedImage;
import java.awt.font.TextLayout;
import java.awt.geom.Rectangle2D;
import javax.print.PrintService;
import javax.print.attribute.HashPrintRequestAttributeSet;
import java.awt.print.*;
import javax.xml.parsers.*;
import org.w3c.dom.*;
import javax.xml.transform.*;
import javax.xml.transform.stream.*;
import javax.xml.transform.dom.*;
import org.xml.sax.*;
import javax.xml.validation.*;

import static java.awt.event.InputEvent.*;
import static java.awt.AWTEvent.*;
import static java.awt.Color.*;
import static Constants.SketcherConstants.*;
import static javax.swing.Action.*;
```

I have the following set of imports in Element.java:

```
import java.awt.*;
import java.io.Serializable;
import static Constants.SketcherConstants.*;
import java.awt.geom.*;
import org.w3c.dom.Document;
import org.w3c.dom.Attr;
import org.w3c.dom.Node;
import org.w3c.dom.NodeList;
import org.w3c.dom.NamedNodeMap;
```

Check your version of the code to make sure you have them all. It's easy to miss one or two!

TRY IT OUT   Sketches in XML

You can try various combinations of elements to see how they look in XML. Make sure that the sketcher.
dtd file is in the directory that you identified in the code. If you don't, you aren't able to import XML sketches
because the DTD will not be found. Don't forget you can look at the XML using any text editor and in most
browsers. I created the sketch shown in Figure 23-1.

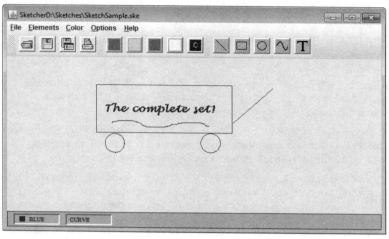

FIGURE 23-1

When I exported this sketch I got an XML file with the following contents:

```
<?xml version="1.0" encoding="UTF-8"?>
<?xml version="1.0" encoding="UTF-8"?>
<!DOCTYPE sketch SYSTEM "D:/Beg Java Stuff/sketcher.dtd">
<sketch>
<line angle="0.0">
<color B="255" G="0" R="0"/>
<position x="147" y="67"/>
<bounds height="54" width="108" x="147" y="67"/>
<endpoint x="107.0" y="53.0"/>
</line>
<rectangle angle="0.0" height="72.0" width="110.0">
<color B="255" G="0" R="0"/>
<position x="339" y="73"/>
<bounds height="73" width="111" x="339" y="73"/>
</rectangle>
<circle angle="0.0" diameter="90.0">
<color B="255" G="0" R="0"/>
<position x="136" y="124"/>
<bounds height="91" width="91" x="136" y="124"/>
</circle>
<curve angle="0.0">
<color B="255" G="0" R="0"/>
<position x="310" y="202"/>
<bounds height="24" width="94" x="310" y="182"/>
<point x="1.0" y="-1.0"/>
<point x="2.0" y="-3.0"/>
                        <!-- points cut here for the sake of brevity -->
<point x="93.0" y="-12.0"/>
<point x="93.0" y="-13.0"/>
<point x="92.0" y="-13.0"/>
</curve>
<text angle="0.0" maxascent="21">
<color B="255" G="0" R="0"/>
<position x="201" y="259"/>
<bounds height="30" width="163" x="201" y="259"/>
<font fontname="Serif" fontstyle="bold" pointsize="20"/>
<string>The Complete Set!</string>
</text>
</sketch>
```

This file is also available as `Sample Sketch.xml` in the code download for this book from the Wrox Press website, `www.wrox.com`. You could try importing it into Sketcher and see if you get the same sketch.

SUMMARY

In this chapter I discussed how you can use a DOM parser to analyze XML and how JAXP supports the synthesis and modification of XML documents using DOM. You have also seen how you can use a XSLT `Transformer` object to create an XML file from a `Document` object and vice versa.

If you managed to get to the end of this chapter having built your own working version of Sketcher, you are to be congratulated, especially if you started out as a newcomer to programming. I'm sure I don't need to tell you that it's quite a challenge to acquire the knowledge and understanding necessary to do this.

An important point I want to emphasize is that the Sketcher program is just a demonstration and test vehicle. It is an environment in which you have been able to try out various Java programming techniques and work with reasonably large chunks of code, but it is not a good example of how the application should be built. Because its development has been Topsy-like, without much regard for where it would finally end up, Sketcher contains many inconsistencies and inefficiencies that would not be there if the application had been designed from the ground up.

At this point you have a good knowledge of the Java language and experience with some of the basic facilities provided by the Java class libraries. I have only been able to introduce you to a small proportion of the total available in the support libraries. There are vast tracts of capability still to explore. There are packages that provide a sound API, support for cryptography, drag-and-drop capability, networking application support, and many more. It is well worth browsing the Java documentation.

Enjoy your Java programming!

EXERCISES

You can download the source code for the examples in the book and the solutions to the following exercises from `www.wrox.com`.

1. Write a program using DOM that counts the number of occurrences of each element type in an XML document and displays them. The document file should be identified by the first command-line argument. The program should also accept optional, additional command-line arguments that are the names of elements. When there are two or more command-line arguments, the program should count and report only on the elements identified by the second and subsequent command-line arguments.

2. Implement the XML Import capability in Sketcher using SAX, rather than DOM.

CONFER PROGRAMMER TO PROGRAMMER ABOUT THIS TOPIC.
Visit p2p.wrox.com

▶ **WHAT YOU LEARNED IN THIS CHAPTER**

TOPIC	CONCEPT
DOM Parsers	An object of type `DocumentBuilder` encapsulates a DOM parser.
Creating a DOM Parser	You create an object encapsulating a DOM parser by using a `DocumentBuilderFactory` object that you obtain by calling the static `newInstance()` method that is defined in the `DocumentFactoryBuilder` class.
Parsing XML	You can parse an XML document by passing the document as an argument to the `parse()` method for a `DocumentBuilder` object.
Document Objects	A DOM parser creates a `Document` object that encapsulates an entire XML document as a tree of `Node` objects.
Analyzing XML Documents	The DOM API includes the `Document` class methods that enable you to analyze an XML document by navigating through the nodes in a `Document` object.
Creating XML Documents	The DOM API includes `Document` class methods for creating an XML document programmatically encapsulated by a `Document` object.
Creating XML with a DTD	When you want to create a new XML document that includes a DTD, you use the `createDocument()` method for a `DOMImplementation` object, rather than the `newDocument()` method for a `DocumentBuilder` object.
Creating a DOCTYPE Element	You can create a `DOCTYPE` element by calling the `createDocumentType()` method for a `DOMImplementation` object. You can then pass the `DocumentType` object to the `createDocument()` method for the `DOMImplementation` object to create a `Document` object that include the `DOCTYPE` element..
XSLT	A `Transformer` object encapsulates an XSLT transform. You create a `Transformer` object by first creating a `TransformerFactory` object and calling its `newTransformer()` method. The argument to the method is a `Source` object encapsulating the transform. The version with no argument creates a transformer that is the identity transform that does nothing.
Reading and Writing XML Files	You can use a `Transformer` object that encapsulates the identity transform to write a `Document` object as an XML file, or to read an XML file and create a `Document` object from it.

Keywords

The following keywords are reserved in Java, so you must not use them as names in your programs:

abstract	assert	boolean	break
byte	case	catch	char
class	const	continue	default
do	double	else	enum
extends	final	finally	float
for	goto	if	implements
import	instanceof	int	interface
long	native	new	package
private	protected	public	return
short	static	strictfp	super
switch	synchronized	this	throw
throws	transient	try	void
volatile	while		

Although they are not keywords, you should not use the boolean values true and false or the value null as names in your programs.

Note that const and goto have not been used in the Java language up to now, but they are still reserved words and you must not use them as names.

B

Computer Arithmetic

In the chapters of this book, I have deliberately kept discussion of binary arithmetic to a minimum. However, it is important overall, and fundamental to understanding how some operators work, so I'm including a summary of the subject in this appendix. If you feel confident about your math knowledge, this is all old hat to you and you need read no farther. If you find the math parts tough, then this appendix should show you how easy it really is.

BINARY NUMBERS

First let's consider what you mean when you write a common everyday number such as 321 or 747. Put more precisely you mean

321 is:

$$3 \times (10 \times 10) + 2 \times (10) + 1$$

and 747 is:

$$7 \times (10 \times 10) + 4 \times (10) + 7$$

Because it is built around powers of ten, you call this the decimal system (derived from the Latin *decimalis*, meaning *of tithes*, which was a tax of 10 percent—ah, those were the days . . .).

Representing numbers in this way is very handy for people with ten fingers and ten toes, or creatures with ten of any kind of appendage for that matter. However, your PC is quite unhandy in this context, being built mainly of switches that are either on or off. This is okay for counting up to two, but not spectacular at counting to ten. For this reason your computer represents numbers to base 2 rather than base 10. This is called the *binary* system of counting, analogous to the *bi*cycle (two wheels), but nothing whatever to do with bibacity, which means an inclination to drink a lot. With the decimal system, to base 10, the digits used can be from 0 to 9. In the binary system, to base 2, the digits can only be 0 or 1, ideal when you have only on/off switches to represent them; off is usually 0, and on is 1—simple. Each digit in the binary system is called a *bit*, which is a contraction of binary digit. In an exact analogy to the usual base 10 counting, the binary number 1101 is therefore:

$$1 \times (2 \times 2 \times 2) + 1 \times (2 \times 2) + 0 \times (2) + 1$$

which, if you work it out, amounts to 13 in the decimal system. In Table B-1, you can see the decimal equivalents of 8-bit binary numbers illustrated.

TABLE B-1: Decimal Equivalents of 8-bit Binary Numbers

BINARY	DECIMAL	BINARY	DECIMAL
0000 0000	0	1000 0000	128
0000 0001	1	1000 0001	129
0000 0010	2	1000 0010	130
. . .	. . .	. . .	. . .
0001 0000	16	1001 0000	144
0001 0001	17	1001 0001	145
. . .	. . .	. . .	. . .
0111 1100	124	1111 1100	252
0111 1101	125	1111 1101	253
0111 1110	126	1111 1110	254
0111 1111	127	1111 1111	255

Note that by using just 7 bits, you can represent all the decimal numbers from 0 to 127, which is a total of 2^7, or 128 numbers; and using all 8 bits you get 256, which corresponds to 2^8 numbers. In general, if you have n bits available, you can represent 2^n positive integers with values from 0 to 2^{n-1}. Of course, I am only talking in the context positive numbers so far. If you also need the same number of negative numbers, you need more bits. I get to negative numbers in a moment.

Hexadecimal Numbers

When you get to work with larger binary numbers—for example, numbers with 24 bits:

```
1111 0101 1011 1001 1110 0001
```

the notation starts to be a little cumbersome, particularly when you consider that if you apply the method you saw in the previous section to work out what this is in decimal notation, it's only 16,103,905, a miserable 8 decimal digits. You can sit more angels on a pinhead than that. Well, as it happens, you have an excellent alternative.

Arithmetic to base 16 is a very convenient option. Numbers to base 16 are *hexadecimal* numbers. Each digit can have values from 0 to 15 (the digits from 10 to 15 being represented by the letters A to F as shown in Table B-2, or by a to f if you're averse to capitalization) and values from 0 to 15 correspond quite nicely with the range of values that four binary digits can represent.

TABLE B-2: Base 16 Conversion Table

HEXADECIMAL	DECIMAL	BINARY
0	0	0000
1	1	0001
2	2	0010
3	4	0011
4	4	0100
5	5	0101
6	6	0110
7	7	0111

HEXADECIMAL	DECIMAL	BINARY
8	8	1000
9	9	1001
A	10	1010
B	11	1011
C	12	1100
D	13	1101
E	14	1110
F	15	1111

Because a hexadecimal digit corresponds exactly to four binary bits, you can represent a binary number as a hexadecimal number just by taking successive groups of four binary digits starting from the right, and writing the equivalent base 16 digit for each group. Look as this binary number:

```
1111 0101 1011 1001 1110 0001
```

If you replace each group of four bits with the equivalent hexadecimal digit, you get:

F5B9E1

You have six hexadecimal digits corresponding to the six groups of four binary digits. Just to show it all really works out with no cheating, you can convert this number directly from hexadecimal to decimal, by again using the analogy with the meaning of a decimal number, as follows:

F5B9E1 is:

$$15 \times (16 \times 16 \times 16 \times 16 \times 16) +$$

$$5 \times (16 \times 16 \times 16 \times 16) +$$

$$11 \times (16 \times 16 \times 16) +$$

$$9 \times (16 \times 16) + 14 \times (16) + 1$$

This in turn turns out to be:

$$15{,}728{,}640 + 327{,}680 + 45{,}056 + 2304 + 224 + 1$$

which fortunately totals to the same number that you got when you converted the original binary number to a decimal value.

Octal Numbers

In Chapter 2 you read that you can define octal integer literals, which are integers to base 8. These were invented by Charles XII of Sweden in 1717, along with the idea of representing numbers to base 64, but this is not the reason they appear in Java. The octal representation is there because historically computers stored binary integers in units that were multiples of 3 bits, the early-1960's vintage IBM 7090 with 36-bit words to store integers being just one example where 12 octal digits could be used to specify a 36-bit binary value. Some of the programming languages of the time offered the economy of writing binary values as octal. As programming languages evolved, the octal representation was carried along down through the years from one language to the next bigger, better, and more powerful language, right up to today. There they are, octal numbers, still lurking in C, C++, and now Java, even though they have very little purpose.

Octal digits can have the values from 0 to 7 and computation is exactly analogous to hexadecimal arithmetic, with 8 instead of 16 as the base. Octal literals are easily confused with decimal integers. The only differentiation is the leading 0 (zero) in the representation of octal literals in Java. Unless you have discovered a situation where they are essential, or you enjoy a perverse approach to programming, octal literals are best avoided.

Negative Binary Numbers

Another aspect to binary arithmetic that you need to understand is how negative numbers are represented. So far you have assumed everything is positive—the optimist's view, if you will— that your glass is still half full. But you can't avoid the negative side of life forever—the pessimist's perspective that your glass is already half empty. How do you indicate a negative number? Well, you have only binary digits at your disposal, so they must contain the solution.

For numbers where you want to allow the possibility of negative values (referred to as *signed* numbers) you must first decide on a fixed length (in other words, fix the number of binary digits in a number) and then designate the leftmost binary digit as a sign bit. You have to fix the length to avoid any confusion about which bit is the sign bit as opposed to other bits that are digits. A single bit is quite capable of representing the sign of a number because a number can be either positive—corresponding to a sign bit being 0, or negative—indicated by the sign bit being 1.

Of course, you can have some numbers with 8 bits, and some with 16 bits, or whatever number of bits you like, as long as you know what the length is in each case. If the sign bit is 0 the number is positive, and if it is 1, the number is negative. This would seem to solve the problem, but not quite. If you add −8 in binary to +12 you would really like to get the answer +4. If you carry out that operation simplistically, just putting the sign bit of the positive value to 1 to make it negative, and then doing the arithmetic with conventional carries from one bit position to the next on the left, it doesn't quite work:

12 in binary is	0000 1100
−8 in binary you suppose is	1000 1000

Because +8 is 0000 1000, the binary representation for −8 is the same, but with the leftmost bit set to 1. If we now add these together we get:

12 + (−8) is	1001 0100

The value 1001 0100 seems to be −20 according to the rules, which is not what you wanted at all. It's definitely not +4, which you know is 0000 0100. "Ah," I hear you say, "you can't treat a sign just like another digit." But that is just what you *do* have to do when dealing with computers because, dumb things that they are, they have trouble coping with anything else. So you really need a different representation for negative numbers if the same process for addition is to work regardless of the sign of the operands. Well, because the same process for arithmetic operations should work regardless of the signs of the operands, you could try subtracting +12 from +4 and see what you get. Whatever the result is should be −8:

+4 is	0000 0100
Take away +12	0000 1100
and you get	1111 1000

For each digit from the fourth from the right onward you had to borrow 1 to do the sum, analogously to our usual decimal method for subtraction. This supposedly is +8, and even though it doesn't look much like it, it really is. Just try adding it to +12 or +15 in binary and you see that it works. So what is it? It turns out that the answer is what is called the *2's complement* representation of negative binary numbers.

Now here I am going to demand a little faith on your part and avoid getting into explanations of why it works. I'm just showing you how the 2's complement form of a negative number can be constructed from a positive value and that it does work, so you can prove it to yourself. Let's return to the previous example where you need the 2's complement representation of −8. We start with +8 in binary:

0000 1000

You now flip each binary digit—if it is one make it zero, and vice versa:

1111 0111

This is called the *1's complement form*, and if you now add 1 to this, you get the 2's complement form:

	1111 0111
Add one to this	0000 0001
and we get:	1111 1000

Now this looks pretty similar to the representation of −8 you got from subtracting +12 from +4. So just to be sure, let's try the original sum of adding −8 to +12:

+12 is	0000 1100
Our version of −8 is	1111 1000
and you get:	0000 0100

So the answer is 4—magic! It works! The carry propagates through all the leftmost 1's, setting them back to zero. One fell off the end, but you shouldn't worry about that. It's probably the one you borrowed from off the end in the subtraction sum you did earlier to get −8. In fact, you are making the implicit assumption that the sign bit, 1 or 0, repeats forever to the left. If you try a few examples of your own, you'll find it always works quite automatically. The really great thing is, it makes arithmetic very easy (and fast) for your computer.

FLOATING-POINT NUMBERS

You often have to deal with very large numbers: the number of protons in the universe, for example, which needs around 79 decimal digits. Clearly there are lots of situations where you need more than the 10 decimal digits you get from a 4-byte binary number. Equally, there are lots of very small numbers: the amount of time in minutes, for example, that it takes the typical car salesman to accept your cash offer on his lightly used 1999 Honda Accord (only 387,604 miles, and keyless entry because the key got lost along the way. . .). A mechanism for handling both these kinds of numbers is—as you might have guessed from the title of this section—*floating-point* numbers.

A floating-point representation of a number is a decimal point followed by a fixed number of digits, multiplied by a power of 10 to get the number you want. It's easier to demonstrate than explain, so let's take some examples. The number 365 in normal decimal notation would be written in floating-point form as the following:

0.365E03

Here, the E stands for *exponent* and is the power of ten that the 0.365 bit (the mantissa) is multiplied by, to get the required value. That is:

$$0.365 \times (10 \times 10 \times 10)$$

which is clearly 365.

Now let's look at a smallish number:

.365E−04

This is evaluated as $.365 \times 10^{-4}$, which is .0000365—exactly the time in minutes required by the car salesman to accept your money and put up the "Closed" sign.

The number of digits in the mantissa of a floating-point number is called the *precision*, and depends on the type of the floating-point number that you are using. The Java type float provides the equivalent of approximately 7 decimal digits, and the type double provides around 17 decimal digits. The number of decimal digits is approximate because the mantissa is binary, not decimal, and there's not an exact mapping between binary and decimal digits.

Suppose you have a large number such as 2,134,311,179. How does this look as a floating-point number? Well, as a decimal representation of a number of type float it looks like:

$$0.2134311E10$$

It's not quite the same. You have lost three low-order digits, so you have approximated our original value as 2,134,311,000. This is a small price to pay for being able to handle such a vast range of numbers, typically from 10^{-38} to 10^{+38} either positive or negative, as well as having an extended representation that goes from a minute 10^{-308} to a mighty 10^{+308}. As you can see, they are called floating-point numbers for the fairly obvious reason that the decimal point "floats," depending on the exponent value.

Aside from the fixed precision limitation in terms of accuracy, there is another aspect you may need to be conscious of. You need to take great care when adding or subtracting numbers of significantly different magnitudes. A simple example demonstrates the kind of problem that can arise. You can first consider adding .365E−3 to .365E+7. You can write this as a decimal sum:

$$.000365 + 3,650,000$$

This produces the result:

$$3,650,000.000365$$

which when converted back to floating-point with seven-digit accuracy becomes

$$.3650000E+7$$

So you might as well not have bothered. The problem lies directly with the fact that you carry only seven-digit precision. The seven digits of the larger number are not affected by any of the digits of the smaller number because they are all farther to the right. Oddly enough, you must also take care when the numbers are very nearly equal. If you compute the difference between such numbers you may end up with a result that has only one or two digits' precision. It is quite easy in such circumstances to end up computing with numbers that are total garbage.

One final point about using floating-point values—many values that have an exact representation as a decimal value cannot be represented exactly in binary floating-point form. For example, 0.2 as a decimal value cannot be represented exactly as a binary floating-point value. This means that when you are working with such values, you have tiny errors in your values right from the start. One effect of this is that accumulating the sum of 100 values that are all 0.2 will not produce 20 as the result. If you try this out in Java, the result is 20.000004, slightly more than you bargained for. (Unfortunately the banks do not use floating-point values for your deposits—it could have been a sure-fire way to make money without working.)

You can conclude from this that although floating-point numbers are a powerful way of representing a very wide range of values in your programs, you must always keep in mind their limitations. If you are conscious of the range of values that you are likely to be working with, you can usually adopt an approach to performing the calculations that you need that avoids the sorts of problems I have described. In other words, if you keep the pitfalls in mind when working with floating-point values, you have a reasonable chance of stepping around or over them.

INDEX

J

S

T

Y

Try Safari Books Online FREE
for 15 days + 15% off for up to 12 Months*

Read this book for free online—along with thousands of others—with this 15-day trial offer.

With Safari Books Online, you can experience searchable, unlimited access to thousands of technology, digital media and professional development books and videos from dozens of leading publishers. With one low monthly or yearly subscription price, you get:

- Access to hundreds of expert-led instructional videos on today's hottest topics.

- Sample code to help accelerate a wide variety of software projects

- Robust organizing features including favorites, highlights, tags, notes, mash-ups and more

- Mobile access using any device with a browser

- Rough Cuts pre-published manuscripts

START YOUR FREE TRIAL TODAY!
Visit **www.safaribooksonline.com/wrox14** to get started.

*Available to new subscribers only. Discount applies to the Safari Library and is valid for first 12 consecutive monthly billing cycles. Safari Library is not available in all countries.

An Imprint of WILE
Now you know.